Lecture Notes in Artificial Intelligence   4005

Edited by J. G. Carbonell and J. Siekmann

Subseries of Lecture Notes in Computer Science

Gabor Lugosi   Hans Ulrich Simon (Eds.)

Learning
Theory

19th Annual Conference on Learning Theory, COLT 2006
Pittsburgh, PA, USA, June 22-25, 2006
Proceedings

 Springer

Series Editors

Jaime G. Carbonell, Carnegie Mellon University, Pittsburgh, PA, USA
Jörg Siekmann, University of Saarland, Saarbrücken, Germany

Volume Editors

Gabor Lugosi
Pompeu Fabra University
Ramon Trias Fargas 25-27, 08005, Barcelona, Spain
E-mail: lugosi@upf.es

Hans Ulrich Simon
Ruhr University Bochum, Department of Mathematics
Building NA 1/73, 44780 Bochum, Germany
E-mail: simon@lmi.rub.de

Library of Congress Control Number: 2006927286

CR Subject Classification (1998): I.2.6, I.2.3, I.2, F.4.1, F.2, F.1.1

LNCS Sublibrary: SL 7 – Artificial Intelligence

ISSN   0302-9743
ISBN-10   3-540-35294-5 Springer Berlin Heidelberg New York
ISBN-13   978-3-540-35294-5 Springer Berlin Heidelberg New York

Springer is a part of Springer Science+Business Media

springer.com

© Springer-Verlag Berlin Heidelberg 2006
Printed in Germany

Typesetting: Camera-ready by author, data conversion by Scientific Publishing Services, Chennai, India
Printed on acid-free paper   SPIN: 11776420   06/3142   5 4 3 2 1 0

Preface

This volume contains papers presented at the 19th Annual Conference on Learning Theory (previously known as the Conference on Computational Learning Theory) held at the Carnegie Mellon University in Pittsburgh, USA, June 22–25, 2006.

The technical program contained 43 papers selected from 102 submissions, 2 open problems selected from among 4 contributed, and 3 invited lectures. The invited lectures were given by Luc Devroye on "Random Multivariate Search Trees," by György Turán on "Learning and Logic," and by Vladimir Vovk on "Predictions as Statements and Decisions." The abstracts of these papers are included in this volume.

The Mark Fulk Award is presented annually for the best paper co-authored by a student. This year the Mark Fulk award was supplemented with three further awards funded by the *Machine Learning Journal*. We were therefore able to select four student papers for prizes. The students selected were Guillaume Lecué for the single-author paper "Optimal Oracle Inequality for Aggregation of Classifiers Under Low Noise Condition," Homin K. Lee and Andrew Wan for the paper "DNF are Teachable in the Average Case" (co-authored by Rocco A. Servedio), Alexander A. Sherstov for the paper "Improved Lower Bounds for Learning the Intersections of Halfspaces" (co-authored by Adam R. Klivans), and Dávid Pál for the paper "A Sober Look at Clustering Stability" (co-authored by Ulrike von Luxburg and Shai Ben-David).

The trend of the previous two years of receiving more than 100 submissions continued. The selected papers cover a wide range of topics (including clustering, un- and semisupervised learning, statistical learning theory, regularized learning and kernel methods, query learning and teaching, inductive inference, learning algorithms and limitations on learning, online aggregation, online prediction and reinforcement learning). Online Prediction with 11 selected papers is particularly well represented. The large number of quality submissions placed a heavy burden on the Program Committee of the conference: Peter Auer (University of Leoben), Peter Bartlett (UC Berkeley), Léon Bottou (NEC Laboratories America), Nicolò Cesa-Bianchi (Università degli Studi di Milano), Koby Crammer (University of Pennsylvania), Yoav Freund (UC, San Diego), Claudio Gentile (Universitá dell'Insubria, Varese), Lisa Hellerstein (Polytechnic University, Brooklyn, NY), Ralf Herbrich (Microsoft Research Cambridge), Sham M. Kakade (Toyota Technology Institute), Ravi Kannan (Yale University), Jyrki Kivinen (University of Helsinki), Shie Mannor (McGill University), Shahar Mendelson (The Australian National University and Technion, I.I.T.), Massimiliano Pontil (University College London), Dan Roth (University of Illinois at Urbana-Champaign), Alex Smola (National ICT Australia), Ingo Steinwart (Los Alamos National Laboratory), Christino Tamon (Clarkson University), Santosh Vempala (MIT),

Ulrike von Luxburg (Fraunhofer IPSI), Vladimir Vovk (Royal Holloway), Thomas Zeugmann (Hokkaido University), and Tong Zhang (Yahoo). We are extremely grateful for their careful and thorough reviewing and for the detailed discussions that ensured the very high quality of the final program. We would like to have mentioned the sub-reviewers who assisted the Program Committee, but unfortunately space constraints do not permit us to include this long list of names and we must simply ask them to accept our thanks anonymously.

We are particularly grateful to Avrim Blum, the conference Local Chair, and his administrative assistant Nicole Stenger. They handled the conference publicity and all the local arrangements to ensure a successful event. We would also like to thank Microsoft for providing the software used in the Program Committee deliberations, Niko List for creating the conference website, and Sanjoy Dasgupta for maintaining the learningtheory.org website. Jyrki Kivinen assisted the organization of the conference in his role as head of the COLT Steering Committee. We would also like to thank the ICML organizers for ensuring a smooth co-location of the two conferences including an "overlap day," June 25.

Finally, we would like to thank Google, IBM, the *Machine Learning Journal*, and National ICT Australia (Statistical Machine Learning Program) for their sponsorship of the conference.

April 2006

Gábor Lugosi
Hans Ulrich Simon
Program Co-chairs
COLT 2006

Sponsored by:

Table of Contents

Regularized Learning and Kernel Methods

Query Learning and Teaching

Inductive Inference

Learning Algorithms and Limitations on Learning

Online Aggregation

Online Prediction and Reinforcement Learning I

Open Problems

Random Multivariate Search Trees

Luc Devroye

School of Computer Science, McGill Univeristy
Montreal, Canada
luc@cs.mcgill.ca

Trees are commonly used to store data so that they can be efficiently retrieved and used in applications. For multidimensional data, one could consider kd-trees, quadtrees, BSP trees, simplex trees, grid trees, epsilon nets, and many other structures. The height of these trees is logarithmic in the data size for random input. Some search operations such as range search and nearest neighbor search have surprising complexities. So, we will give a brief survey of the known results on random multivariate trees and point out the challenges ahead of us.

G. Lugosi and H.U. Simon (Eds.): COLT 2006, LNAI 4005, p. 1, 2006.
© Springer-Verlag Berlin Heidelberg 2006

On Learning and Logic*

György Turán

University of Illinois at Chicago, Chicago, USA,
Hungarian Academy of Sciences and University of Szeged,
Research Group on Artificial Intelligence, Szeged, Hungary
gyt@uic.edu

A brief survey is given of learning theory in a logic framework, concluding with some topics for further research. The idea of learning using logic is traced back to Turing's 1951 radio address [15]. An early seminal result is that clauses have a least general generalization [18]. Another important concept is inverse resolution [16]. As the most common formalism is logic programs, the area is often referred to as inductive logic programming, with yearly ILP conferences since 1991.

Positive learnability results include an equivalence and membership query algorithm for CLASSIC, a version of description logic [4], a PAC algorithm obtained with the product homomorphism method [10], and an algorithm for first-order Horn formulas [12], which also uses queries but has an efficient implementation using examples only [2]. Each algorithm is based on some kind of product of structures. Positive and negative PAC-learnability results for ILP are surveyed in [3]. The notion of a certificate of exclusion from a concept class, characterizing query complexity [8, 9], could be of interest outside of learning theory as well. A certificate size upper bound for monadic second order logic over trees, implying a theoretically efficient, though not practical, learning algorithm, is given in [7].

The integration of both learning and reasoning, and of logical and probabilistic approaches is important for the development of intelligent systems [13, 5, 19]. Another related objective is to provide agents with commonsense reasoning capability. It stands to reason that such agents should be able to learn. A point of entry into this many-faceted problem area is belief revision, the study of how to revise a knowledge base if new information is received that may be inconsistent with what is known. Here one usually begins with postulates required of a rational revision process, such as the AGM postulates [1], aimed at formalizing the requirement of minimal change. There are representation results, constructions (akin to learning algorithms) and connections to probabilistic reasoning. It seems to be a challenging general question whether successful learning and rational revision can be combined. Sofar, this has been considered mostly in inductive inference [11, 14], but it is also discussed in machine learning ([20] and recently [17]). The efficient revision of theories with queries is studied in [6].

* This material is based upon work supported by the National Science Foundation under Grant No. CCF-0431059.

G. Lugosi and H.U. Simon (Eds.): COLT 2006, LNAI 4005, pp. 2–3, 2006.

References

1. C. E. Alchourrón, P. Gärdenfors, D. Makinson: On the logic of theory change: partial meet functions for contraction and revision, *J. Symbolic Logic* **50** (1985), 510-530.
2. M. Arias, R. Khardon, J. Maloberti: Learning Horn expressions with LOGAN-H, Tufts University Computer Science Technical Report 2005-4.
3. W. W. Cohen, C. D. Page: Polynomial learnability and inductive logic programming: methods and results, *New Generation Computing* **13** (1995), 369-409.
4. M. Frazier, L. Pitt: CLASSIC learning, *Machine Learning* **25** (1996), 151-193.
5. L. Getoor, N. Friedman, D. Koller, A. Pfeffer: Learning probabilistic relational models, in: *Relational Data Mining*, S. Džeroski, N. Lavrač, eds., 307-335. Kluwer, 2001.
6. J. Goldsmith, R. H. Sloan, B. Szörényi, Gy. Turán: Theory revision with queries: Horn, read-once and parity formulas, *Artificial Intelligence* **156** (2004), 139-176.
7. M. Grohe, Gy. Turán: Learnability and definability in trees and similar structures, *Theory of Computing Systems* **37** (2004), 193-220.
8. T. Hegedűs: Generalized teaching dimensions and the query complexity of learning, *8th Annual Conference on Computational Learning Theory* (1995), 108-117.
9. L. Hellerstein, K. Pillaipakkamnatt, V. Raghavan, D. Wilkins: How many queries are needed?, *J. of the ACM* **43** (1996), 840-862.
10. T. Horváth, Gy. Turán: Learning logic programs with structured background knowledge, *Artificial Intelligence* **128** (2001), 31-97.
11. K. T. Kelly, O. Schulte, V. Hendricks: Reliable belief revision, in: *Logic and Scientific Methods*, M. L. Dalla Chiara et al. eds. Kluwer, 1997.
12. R. Khardon: Learning function-free Horn expressions, *Machine Learning* **37** (1999), 241-275.
13. R. Khardon, D. Roth: Learning to reason, *J. of the ACM* **44** (1997), 697-725.
14. E. Martin, D. Osherson: Scientific discovery based on belief revision, *J. of Symbolic Logic* **62** (1997), 1352-1370.
15. S. Muggleton: Logic and learning: Turing's legacy, in: *Machine Intelligence*, K. Furukawa, D. Michie, S. Muggleton, eds. **13** (1994), 37-56.
16. S. Muggleton, W. Buntine: Machine invention of first-order predicates by inverting resolution, *5. International Machine Learning Conference* (1988), 339-352.
17. M. Pagnucco, D. Rajaratnam: Inverse resolution as belief change, *19. International Joint Conference on Artificial Intelligence* (2005), 540-545.
18. G. D. Plotkin: A note on inductive generalization, in: *Machine Intelligence*, B. Meltzer, D. Michie, eds. **5** (1970), 153-163.
19. M. Richardson, P. Domingos: Markov logic networks, *Machine Learning* **62** (2006), 107-136.
20. S. Wrobel: *Concept Formation and Knowledge Revision*. Kluwer, 1994.

Predictions as Statements and Decisions

Vladimir Vovk

Computer Learning Research Centre, Department of Computer Science
Royal Holloway, University of London, Egham, Surrey TW20 0EX, UK
vovk@cs.rhul.ac.uk

Prediction is a complex notion, and different predictors (such as people, computer programs, and probabilistic theories) can pursue very different goals. In this talk I will review some popular kinds of prediction and argue that the theory of competitive on-line learning can benefit from the kinds of prediction that are now foreign to it.

The standard goal for predictor in learning theory is to incur a small loss for a given loss function measuring the discrepancy between the predictions and the actual outcomes. Competitive on-line learning concentrates on a "relative" version of this goal: the predictor is to perform almost as well as the best strategies in a given benchmark class of prediction strategies. Such predictions can be interpreted as decisions made by a "small" decision maker (i.e., one whose decisions do not affect the future outcomes).

Predictions, or *probability forecasts*, considered in the foundations of probability are statements rather than decisions; the loss function is replaced by a procedure for testing the forecasts. The two main approaches to the foundations of probability are measure-theoretic (as formulated by Kolmogorov) and game-theoretic (as developed by von Mises and Ville); the former is now dominant in mathematical probability theory, but the latter appears to be better adapted for uses in learning theory discussed in this talk.

An important achievement of Kolmogorov's school of the foundations of probability was construction of a universal testing procedure and realization (Levin, 1976) that there exists a forecasting strategy that produces ideal forecasts. Levin's ideal forecasting strategy, however, is not computable. Its more practical versions can be obtained from the results of game-theoretic probability theory. For a wide class of forecasting protocols, it can be shown that for any computable game-theoretic law of probability there exists a computable forecasting strategy that produces ideal forecasts, as far as this law of probability is concerned. Choosing suitable laws of probability we can ensure that the forecasts agree with reality in requisite ways.

Probability forecasts that are known to agree with reality can be used for making good decisions: the most straightforward procedure is to select decisions that are optimal under the forecasts (the principle of minimum expected loss). This gives, *inter alia*, a powerful tool for competitive on-line learning; I will describe its use for designing prediction algorithms that satisfy the property of universal consistency and its more practical versions.

In conclusion of the talk I will discuss some limitations of competitive on-line learning and possible directions of further research.

G. Lugosi and H.U. Simon (Eds.): COLT 2006, LNAI 4005, p. 4, 2006.
© Springer-Verlag Berlin Heidelberg 2006

A Sober Look at Clustering Stability

Shai Ben-David[1], Ulrike von Luxburg[2], and Dávid Pál[1]

[1] David R. Cheriton School of Computer Science,
University of Waterloo,
Waterloo, Ontario, Canada
{shai, dpal}@cs.uwaterloo.ca
[2] Fraunhofer IPSI, Darmstadt, Germany
ulrike.luxburg@ipsi.fraunhofer.de

Abstract. Stability is a common tool to verify the validity of sample based algorithms. In clustering it is widely used to tune the parameters of the algorithm, such as the number k of clusters. In spite of the popularity of stability in practical applications, there has been very little theoretical analysis of this notion. In this paper we provide a formal definition of stability and analyze some of its basic properties. Quite surprisingly, the conclusion of our analysis is that for large sample size, stability is fully determined by the behavior of the objective function which the clustering algorithm is aiming to minimize. If the objective function has a unique global minimizer, the algorithm is stable, otherwise it is unstable. In particular we conclude that stability is not a well-suited tool to determine the number of clusters - it is determined by the symmetries of the data which may be unrelated to clustering parameters. We prove our results for center-based clusterings and for spectral clustering, and support our conclusions by many examples in which the behavior of stability is counter-intuitive.

1 Introduction

Clustering is one of the most widely used techniques for exploratory data analysis. Across all disciplines, from social sciences over biology to computer science, people try to get a first intuition about their data by identifying meaningful groups among the data points. Despite this popularity of clustering, distressingly little is known about theoretical properties of clustering (von Luxburg and Ben-David, 2005). In particular, the problem of choosing parameters such as the number k of clusters is still more or less unsolved.

One popular method for model selection in clustering has been the notion of stability, see for instance Ben-Hur et al. (2002), Lange et al. (2004). The intuitive idea behind that method is that if we repeatedly sample data points and apply the clustering algorithm, then a "good" algorithm should produce clusterings that do not vary much from one sample to another. In other words, the algorithm is stable with respect to input randomization. As an example, stability measurements are often employed in practice for choosing the number, k, of clusters. The rational behind this heuristics is that in a situation where k is too large,

G. Lugosi and H.U. Simon (Eds.): COLT 2006, LNAI 4005, pp. 5–19, 2006.

the algorithm "randomly" has to split true clusters, and the choice of the cluster it splits might change with the randomness of the sample at hand, resulting in instability. Alternatively, if we choose k too small, then we "randomly" have to merge several true clusters, the choice of which might similarly change with each particular random sample, in which case, once again, instability occurs. For an illustration see Figure 1.

The natural framework for a discussion of stability is that of sample-based algorithms. Much like statistical learning, this framework assumes that there exist some fixed but unknown probability distribution of the data, and the algorithm gets an i.i.d. random sample as input and aims to approximate a solution that is optimal w.r.t. that data distribution. In this paper we focus on clustering algorithms which choose their clustering based on some objective function which they minimize or maximize. The advantage of such cost-based clusterings is that they enjoy an explicit notion of the quality of a clustering. Popular examples in this class are center based and algorithms and spectral clustering.

For such algorithms there are two different sources of instability. The first one is based on the structure of the underlying space and has nothing to do with the sampling process. If there exist several different clusterings which minimize the objective function on the whole data space, then the clustering algorithm cannot decide which one to choose. The clustering algorithm cannot resolve this ambiguity which lies in the structure of the space. This is the kind of instability that is usually expected to occur when stability is applied to detect the correct number of clusters. However, in this article we argue that this intuition is not justified and that stability rarely does what we want in this respect. The reason is that for many clustering algorithms, this kind of ambiguity usually happens only if the data space has some symmetry structure. As soon the space is not perfectly symmetric, the objective function has a unique minimizer (see Figure 1) and stability prevails. Since we believe that most real world data sets are not perfectly symmetric, this leads to the conclusion that for this purpose, stability is not the correct tool to use.

A completely different notion of instability is the one based on the sampling process. As we can only evaluate the objective function on the given sample points, the variance in the sampling process leads to variance in the values of the empirically computed objective function, which in turn results in variance in the choice of the clusterings. This is the kind of stability that has been studied extensively in supervised learning (Bousquet and Elisseeff, 2002, Kutin and Niyogi, 2002, Rakhlin and Caponnetto, 2005). A similar effect happens if we do not have the computational power to exactly compute the global minimum of the objective function, as it for example is the case for the highly non-convex k-means objective function. This type of instability typically diminishes as sample sizes grow. Alternatively, one can reduce this type of instability to the previous case by considering the set of ε-minimizers of the objective function (Rakhlin and Caponnetto, 2005). The set of ε-minimizers of a function is the set of all clusterings for which the quality function is at most ε from the minimal value. If we now know that we only have enough sample points to estimate

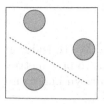 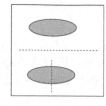 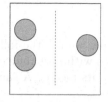 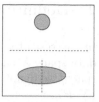

Fig. 1. The left two panels show situations where the constructed clustering (depicted by the dashed line) is highly instable, either because the chosen number of clusters is too small or too large. Note that both figures depict very symmetric situations. The right two panels show situations where clustering algorithms return stable results even though they construct a wrong number of clusters. Note that those two figures are not symmetric.

the objective function up to precision ε, then the instability in the algorithm consists in "randomly" picking one of the clusterings in the set of ε-minimizers. In this paper we mainly focus on the first kind of stability. Therefore, we mainly consider the asymptotic behavior of stability as sample sizes grow to infinity.

In this work we analyze the behavior of stability of a large abstract family of clustering algorithms - algorithms that are driven by an objective function (or 'risk') that they aim to minimize. We postulate some basic abstract requirements on such algorithms (such as convergence in probability to a minimum risk solutions as cluster sizes grow to infinity), and show that for algorithms satisfying these requirements, stability is fully determined by the symmetry structure of the underlying data distribution. Specifically, if the risk has a unique minimizer the algorithm is stable, and if there exist a non-trivial symmetry of the set of risk-minimizing solutions, stability fails. Since these symmetry parameters are independent of the number of clusters, we can easily prove that in many cases stability fails to indicate the correct (or even a reasonable) number of clusterings. Our results apply in particular to two large families of clustering algorithms, center based clustering and spectral clustering.

We would like to stress that our findings do not contradict the stability results for supervised learning. The main difference between classification and clustering is that in classification we are only interested in some function which minimizes the risk, but we never explicitly look at this function. In clustering however, we do distinguish between functions even though they have the same risk. It is exactly this fundamental difference which makes clustering so difficult to analyze.

After formulating our basic definitions in Section 2, we formulate an intuitive notion of risk minimizing clustering in Section 3. Section 4 presents our first central result, namely that existence of a unique risk-minimizer implies stability, and Section 5 present the complementary, instability result, for symmetric data structures. We end in section 6 by showing that two popular versions of spectral clustering display similar characterizations of stability in terms of basic data symmetry structure. Throughout the paper, we demonstrate the impact of our results by describing simple examples of data structures for which stability fails to meet 'common knowledge' expectations.

2 Definitions

In the rest of the paper we use the following standard notation. We consider a data space X endowed with probability measure P. If X happens to be a metric space, we denote by ℓ its metric. A sample $S = \{x_1, ..., x_m\}$ is drawn i.i.d from (X, P).

Definition 1 (Clustering). *A clustering $\mathcal{C}$ of a set X is a finite partition $\mathcal{C} : X \to \mathbb{N}$. The sets $C_i := \{x \in X; \mathcal{C}(x) = i\}$ are called clusters. We introduce the notation $x \sim_\mathcal{C} y$ if $C(x) = C(y)$ and $x \not\sim_\mathcal{C} y$ otherwise. In case the clustering is clear from context we drop the subscript and simply write $x \sim y$ or $x \not\sim y$.*

Definition 2 (Clustering algorithm). *Any function A, that for any given finite sample $S \subset X$ computes a clustering of X, is called a clustering algorithm.*

Note that by default, the clustering constructed by an algorithm is only defined on the sample points. However, many algorithms such as center-based clusterings or spectral clustering have natural extensions of the clustering constructed on the sample to the whole data space X. For details see section 6.

Notation 1. *For a finite sample (a multiset), S, let P_S be the uniform probability distribution over S.*

Definition 3 (Clustering distance). *Let $\mathcal{P}$ be family of probability distributions over some domain X. Let $\mathcal{S}$ be a family of clusterings of X. A clustering distance is function $d : \mathcal{P} \times \mathcal{S} \times \mathcal{S} \to [0, 1]$ satisfying for any $P \in \mathcal{P}$ and any $\mathcal{C}_1, \mathcal{C}_2, \mathcal{C}_3 \in \mathcal{S}$*

1. $d_P(\mathcal{C}_1, \mathcal{C}_1) = 0$
2. $d_P(\mathcal{C}_1, \mathcal{C}_2) = d_P(\mathcal{C}_2, \mathcal{C}_1)$ *(symmetry)*
3. $d_P(\mathcal{C}_1, \mathcal{C}_3) \le d_P(\mathcal{C}_1, \mathcal{C}_2) + d_P(\mathcal{C}_2, \mathcal{C}_3)$ *(triangle inequality)*

We do not require that a clustering distance satisfies that if $d_P(\mathcal{C}_1, \mathcal{C}_2) = 0$ then $\mathcal{C}_1 = \mathcal{C}_2$. As a prototypic example we consider the Hamming distance (or pair-counting distance):

Definition 4 (Hamming distance). *For two clusterings $\mathcal{C}_1, \mathcal{C}_2$ of (X, P), the Hamming distance is defined as*

$$d_P(\mathcal{C}_1, \mathcal{C}_2) = \Pr_{\substack{x \sim P \\ y \sim P}} [(x \sim_{\mathcal{C}_1} y) \oplus (x \sim_{\mathcal{C}_2} y)],$$

where $\oplus$ denotes the logical XOR operation.

It can easily be checked that d_P indeed is a clustering distance. The first two properties trivially hold, and the triangle inequality follows from

$$d_P(\mathcal{C}_1, \mathcal{C}_3) = \Pr_{\substack{x \sim P \\ y \sim P}} [(x \sim_{\mathcal{C}_1} y) \oplus (x \sim_{\mathcal{C}_3} y)]$$

$$= \Pr_{\substack{x \sim P \\ y \sim P}} [((x \sim_{\mathcal{C}_1} y) \oplus (x \sim_{\mathcal{C}_2} y)) \oplus ((x \sim_{\mathcal{C}_2} y) \oplus (x \sim_{\mathcal{C}_3} y))]$$

$$\leq \Pr_{\substack{x \sim P \\ y \sim P}} [(x \sim_{\mathcal{C}_1} y) \oplus (x \sim_{\mathcal{C}_2} y)] + \Pr_{\substack{x \sim P \\ y \sim P}} [(x \sim_{\mathcal{C}_2} y) \oplus (x \sim_{\mathcal{C}_3} y)]$$

$$= d_P(\mathcal{C}_1, \mathcal{C}_2) + d_P(\mathcal{C}_2, \mathcal{C}_3).$$

Proposition 5. *The Hamming distance d_P satisfies*

$$d_P(\mathcal{C}, \mathcal{D}) \leq 1 - \sum_i \sum_j (\Pr[C_i \cap D_j])^2$$

Proof. This follows by straight forward transformations:

$$d_P(\mathcal{C}, \mathcal{D}) = 1 - \Pr_{\substack{x \sim P \\ y \sim P}} [(x \sim_{\mathcal{C}} y) \wedge (x \sim_{\mathcal{D}} y)] - \Pr_{\substack{x \sim P \\ y \sim P}} [(x \nsim_{\mathcal{C}} y) \wedge (x \nsim_{\mathcal{D}} y)]$$

$$\leq 1 - \Pr_{\substack{x \sim P \\ y \sim P}} [(x \sim_{\mathcal{C}} y) \wedge (x \sim_{\mathcal{D}} y)]$$

$$= 1 - \sum_i \sum_j \Pr_{\substack{x \sim P \\ y \sim P}} [(x, y \in C_i) \wedge (x, y \in D_j)]$$

$$= 1 - \sum_i \sum_j (\Pr[C_i \cap D_j])^2 \qquad \square$$

Now we define the fundamental notion of this paper:

Definition 6. *Let P be probability distribution over X. Let d be a clustering distance. Let A be clustering algorithm. The stability of the algorithm A for the sample size m with respect to the probability distribution P is*

$$stab(A, P, m) = \mathop{\mathbb{E}}_{\substack{S_1 \sim P^m \\ S_2 \sim P^m}} d_P(A(S_1), A(S_2)).$$

The stability of the algorithm A with respect to the probability distribution P is

$$stab(A, P) = \limsup_{m \to \infty} stab(A, P, m).$$

We say that algorithm A is stable for P, if $stab(A, P) = 0$.

Note that the algorithm A which for any input only produces the clustering consisting of one cluster X, is stable on any probability distribution P. More generally, any A which is a constant function is stable.

3 Risk Optimizing Clustering Algorithms

A large class of clustering algorithms choose the clustering by optimizing some risk function. The large class of center based algorithms falls into this category, and spectral clustering can also be interpreted in this way.

Definition 7 (Risk optimization scheme). *A risk optimization scheme is defined by a quadruple* $(X, \mathcal{S}, \mathcal{P}, R)$, *where* X *is some domain set,* $\mathcal{S}$ *is a set of legal clusterings of* X, *and* $\mathcal{P}$ *is a set of probability distributions over* X, *and* $R : \mathcal{P} \times \mathcal{S} \to \mathbb{R}_0^+$ *is an objective function (or risk) that the clustering algorithm aims to minimize.*

Denote $opt(P) := \inf_{\mathcal{C} \in \mathcal{S}} R(P, \mathcal{C})$. *For a sample* $S \subseteq X$, *we call* $R(P_S, \mathcal{C})$ *the* empirical risk *of* $\mathcal{C}$. *A clustering algorithm* A *is called* R-minimizing, *if* $R(P_S, A(S)) = opt(P_S)$, *for any sample* S.

Generic examples are *center based algorithms* such as k-means and k-medians. Those clusterings pick a set of k center points $c_1, ..., c_k$ and then assign each point in the metric space to the closest center point. Such a clustering is a k-cell Voronoi diagram over (X, ℓ). To choose the centers, k-means minimizes the risk function

$$R(P, \mathcal{C}) = \underset{x \sim P}{\mathbb{E}} \min_{1 \leq i \leq k} (\ell(x, c_i))^2 \mid \mathrm{Vor}(c_1, c_2, \ldots, c_k) = \mathcal{C}$$

while k-medians algorithm minimizes

$$R(P, \mathcal{C}) = \underset{x \sim P}{\mathbb{E}} \min_{1 \leq i \leq k} \ell(x, c_i) \mid \mathrm{Vor}(c_1, c_2, \ldots, c_k) = \mathcal{C}$$

Usually, risk based algorithms are meant to converge to the true risk as sample sizes grow to infinity.

Definition 8 (Risk convergence). *Let* A *be an* R-*minimizing clustering algorithm. We say that* A *is* risk converging, *if for every* $\epsilon > 0$ *and every* $\delta \in (0, 1)$ *there is* m_0 *such that for all* $m > m_0$

$$\underset{S \sim P^m}{\mathrm{Pr}} [R(P, A(S)) < opt(P) + \epsilon] > 1 - \delta$$

for any probability distribution $P \in \mathcal{P}$.

For example, in the case of k-mean and k-medians on bounded subset of $\mathbb{R}^d$ with Euclidean metric, Ben-David (2004) has shown that they both minimize risk from samples.

4   Stability of Risk Minimizing Algorithms

In this section we investigate the stability of risk optimizing clustering algorithms. We will see that their stability solely depends on the existence of a unique minimizer of the risk function. In this section we fix a risk minimization scheme $(X, \mathcal{S}, \mathcal{P}, R)$.

Definition 9. *Let* d *be a clustering distance. We say that a probability distribution* P *has* unique minimizer $\mathcal{C}^*$ *if*

$$(\forall \eta > 0) \ (\exists \epsilon > 0) \ (R(P, \mathcal{C}) < opt(P) + \epsilon \implies d_P(\mathcal{C}^*, \mathcal{C}) < \eta).$$

More generally, we say a probability distribution P has n distinct minimizers, if there exists $\mathcal{C}_1^*, \mathcal{C}_2^*, \ldots, \mathcal{C}_n^*$ such that $d_P(\mathcal{C}_i^*, \mathcal{C}_j^*) > 0$ for all $i \neq j$, and

$$(\forall \eta > 0) \ (\exists \epsilon > 0) \ (R(P, \mathcal{C}) < opt(P) + \epsilon \implies (\exists \ 1 \leq i \leq n) \ d_P(\mathcal{C}_i^*, \mathcal{C}) < \eta).$$

Note that there is a technical subtlety here; the definition does not require that there is only a single clustering with the minimal cost, but rather that for any two optima $\mathcal{C}_1^*, \mathcal{C}_2^*$, $d_P(\mathcal{C}_1^*, \mathcal{C}_2^*) = 0$. Technically, we can overcome this difference by forming equivalence classes of clusterings, saying that two clusterings are equivalent if their clustering distance is zero. Similarly, n distinct optima correspond n such equivalence classes of optimal clusterings.

Theorem 10 (Stability theorem). *If P has unique minimizer $\mathcal{C}^*$, then any R-minimizing clustering algorithm which is risk converging is stable on P.*

Proof. Let A be a risk converging R-minimizing clustering algorithm. Suppose we are given $\zeta > 0$ and want to show that for large enough m is $stab(A, P, m) < \zeta$. Let us pick $\delta \in (0, 1)$ and $\eta > 0$, both small enough so that

$$2(\eta + \delta) < \zeta. \tag{1}$$

Let $\mathcal{C}^*$ be the unique minimizer, then for η there is some $\epsilon > 0$ such that

$$R(P, \mathcal{C}) < opt(P) + \epsilon \implies d_P(\mathcal{C}, \mathcal{C}^*) < \eta. \tag{2}$$

Since A is risk converging, there is m_0 such that for all $m > m_0$

$$\Pr_{S \sim P^m} [R(P, A(S)) \geq opt(P) + \epsilon] < \delta. \tag{3}$$

Combining (2) and (3), for $m > m_0$ we have

$$\Pr_{S \sim P^m} [d_P(A(S), \mathcal{C}^*) \geq \eta] \leq \Pr_{S \sim P^m} [R(P, A(S)) \geq opt(P) + \epsilon] < \delta. \tag{4}$$

Finally, for $m > m_0$ we bound the stability as

$$stab(A, P, m) = \mathop{\mathbb{E}}_{\substack{S_1 \sim P^m \\ S_2 \sim P^m}} d_P(A(S_1), A(S_2))$$

$$\leq \mathop{\mathbb{E}}_{\substack{S_1 \sim P^m \\ S_2 \sim P^m}} [d_P(A(S_1), \mathcal{C}^*) + d_P(\mathcal{C}^*, A(S_2))]$$

$$= 2 \mathop{\mathbb{E}}_{S \sim P^m} d_P(A(S), \mathcal{C}^*)$$

$$\leq 2 \left(\eta \cdot \Pr_{S \sim P^m} [d_P(A(S), \mathcal{C}^*) < \eta] + 1 \cdot \Pr_{S \sim P^m} [d_P(A(S), \mathcal{C}^*) \geq \eta] \right)$$

$$\leq 2 \left(\eta + \Pr_{S \sim P^m} [R(P, A(S)) \geq opt(P) + \epsilon] \right)$$

$$\leq 2(\eta + \delta)$$

$$< \zeta.$$

$\square$

Note that this result applies in particular to the k-means and the k-median clustering paradigms (namely, to clustering algorithms that minimize any of these common risk functions).

4.1   Unexpected Behaviors of Stability

As a first example to the surprising consequences of Theorem 10, consider the uniform distribution over the unit interval $[0, 1]$. It is not hard to figure out that, for any number of clusters, k, both k-medians and k-means have exactly one risk minimizer—the clustering

$$C(x) = i, \qquad x \in \left[\frac{i-1}{k}, \frac{i}{k} \right).$$

Therefore, from the stability theorem, it follows that both k-medians and k-means clustering are stable on the interval uniform distribution *for any value of* k. Similarly consider the stability of k-means and k-medians on the two rightmost examples on the Figure 1. The rightmost example on the picture has for $k = 3$ unique minimizer as shown and therefore is stable, although the correct choice of k should be 2. The second from right example has, for $k = 2$, a unique minimizer as shown, and therefore is again stable, although the correct choice of k should be 3 in that case. Note also that in both cases, the uniqueness of minimizer is implied by the asymmetry of the data distributions. It seems that the number of optimal solutions is the key to instability. For the important case of Euclidean space $\mathbb{R}^d$ we are not aware of any example such that the existence of two optimal sets of centers does not lead to instability. We therefore conjecture:

Conjecture 11 (Instability). If P has multiple minimizers then any R-minimizing algorithm which is risk converging is unstable on P.

While we cannot, at this stage, prove the above conjecture in the generality, we can prove that a stronger condition, *symmetry*, does imply instability for center based algorithms and spectral clustering algorithms.

5   Symmetry and Instability

In this subsection we define a formal notion of symmetry for metric spaces with a probability distribution. We prove that if there are several risk minimizers which are "symmetric" to each other, then risk minimizing algorithms are bound to be unstable on this distribution. Before we can formulate claim precisely we need introduce some further notation and definitions.

Definition 12 (Measure-preserving symmetry). *Let P be a probability distribution over (X, ℓ). A function $g : X \rightarrow X$, is called P-preserving symmetry of (X, ℓ) if,*

1. *For any P-measurable set $A \subseteq X$, $\Pr[A] = \Pr[g(A)]$.*
2. $\Pr_{\substack{x \sim P \\ y \sim P}} [\ell(x, y) = \ell(g(x), g(y))] = 1.$

Note 1: For any finite sample S (a multi-set), if g is an isometry on S then g is also an $\hat{S}$-preserving symmetry, where $\hat{S}$ is any discrete distribution on S. In what follows we adopt the following notation: If $g : X \to X$, then for set $A \subset X$ by $g[A] = \{g(x) \mid x \in A\}$. For a probability distribution P let P_g be defined by $P_g[A] = P[g^{-1}(A)]$ for every set A whose pre-image is measurable. If g is one-to-one then for a clustering $\mathcal{C} : X \to \mathbb{N}$ we define $g[\mathcal{C}]$ by $(g[\mathcal{C}])(x) = \mathcal{C}(g^{-1}(x))$, or in other words that the clusters of $g[\mathcal{C}]$ are images of clusters of $\mathcal{C}$ under g.[1]

Definition 13 (Distance-Distribution dependent risk). *We say that a risk function R is ODD if it depends only on distances and distribution. Formally, R is ODD if for every probability distribution P, every P-preserving symmetry g, and every clustering $\mathcal{C}$*

$$R(P, \mathcal{C}) = R(P, g(\mathcal{C})).$$

Note 2: For any finite sample S, if g is an isometry on S and R is ODD, then for every clustering $\mathcal{C}$, $R(P_S, \mathcal{C}) = R(P_S, g(\mathcal{C})) = R(g(P_S), g(\mathcal{C}))$. This follows from Note 1 and the definition of R being ODD.

Definition 14 (Distance-Distribution dependent clustering distance). *We say that a clustering distance d is ODD if it depends only on distances and distribution. Formally, d is ODD if for every probability distribution P, every P-preserving symmetry g, and any two clusterings $\mathcal{C}_1, \mathcal{C}_2$*

$$d_P(\mathcal{C}_1, \mathcal{C}_2) = d_P(g(\mathcal{C}_1), g(\mathcal{C}_2)).$$

Note that every natural notion of distance (in particular the Hamming distance and information based distances) is ODD.

Theorem 15 (Instability from symmetry). *Let R be an ODD risk function, and d an ODD clustering distance. Let P be probability distribution so that for some n, P has n distinct minimizers, and let g be a P-symmetry such that for every R-minimizer $\mathcal{C}^*$, $d_P(\mathcal{C}^*, g(\mathcal{C}^*)) > 0$, then any R-minimizing clustering algorithm which is risk convergent is unstable on P.*

Proof. Let the optimal solutions minimizing the risk be $\{\mathcal{C}_1^*, \mathcal{C}_2^*, \ldots, \mathcal{C}_n^*\}$. Let $r = \min_{1 \leq i \leq n} d_P(\mathcal{C}_i^*, g(\mathcal{C}_i^*))$. Let $\epsilon > 0$ be such that

$$R(P, \mathcal{C}) < opt(P) + \epsilon \implies (\exists\, 1 \leq i \leq n)\, d_P(\mathcal{C}_i^*, \mathcal{C}) < r/4$$

(the existence of such an ϵ is implied by having n distinct minimizers for P). Let $T = \{S \in X^m \mid R(P, A(S)) < opt(P) + \epsilon\}$. By the risk-convergence of A, there exist some m_0 such that for all $m > m_0$, $P(T) > 0.9$.

For $1 \leq i \leq n$, let $T_i = \{S \in T \mid d_p(\mathcal{C}_i^*, A(S)) \leq r/4\}$. Clearly, there exist some i_0 for which $P(T_{i_0}) \geq 0.9/n$. Since g is a symmetry, and R is ODD, $g(S) \in T$ for every sample $S \in T$.

Since $d_P(\mathcal{C}_{i_0}^*, g(\mathcal{C}_{i_0}^*)) \geq r$, and, for all $S \in T_{i_0}$, $d_P(\mathcal{C}_{i_0}^*, A(S)) \leq r/4$, and d_P is ODD, we get that for all $S \in T_{i_0}$, $d_P(g(\mathcal{C}_{i_0}^*), A(g(S))) \leq r/4$. The triangle

---

[1] We can also handle the case where g fails to be one-to-one on a set of probability of zero. For the sake of clarity we omit this technicality.

inequality for d_P implies now that for every $S \in T_{i_0}$ and every $S' \in g[T_{i_0}]$, $d_P(A(S), A(S')) \geq r/2$. Finally, since g is a P-symmetry, one gets $P(g[T_{i_0}]) \geq 0.9/n$.

We are now in a position to lower-bound the stability for all $m \geq m_0$:

$$
\begin{aligned}
stab(A, P, m) &= \mathop{\mathbb{E}}_{\substack{S \sim P^m \\ S' \sim P^m}} d_P(A(S), A(S')) \\
&\geq \frac{r}{2} \mathop{\Pr}_{\substack{S \sim P^m \\ S' \sim P^m}} \left[d_P(A(S), A(S')) \geq \frac{r}{2} \right] \\
&\geq \frac{r}{2} \mathop{\Pr}_{\substack{S \sim P^m \\ S' \sim P^m}} [S \in T_{i_0} \wedge S' \in g[T_{i_0}]] \\
&= \frac{r}{2} \mathop{\Pr}_{S \sim P^m} [S \in T_{i_0}] \mathop{\Pr}_{S' \sim P^m} [S' \in g[T_{i_0}]] \\
&\geq \frac{r(0.9)^2}{2n^2}
\end{aligned}
$$

Therefore the stability at infinity, $stab(A, P)$, is positive as well, and hence A is unstable on P. $\qquad \square$

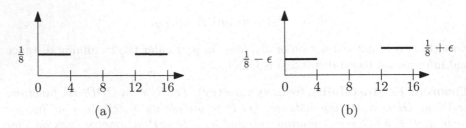

Fig. 2. The densities of two "almost the same" probability distributions over $\mathbb{R}$ are shown. (a) For $k = 3$, are the k-means and k-medians unstable. (b) For $k = 3$, are the k-means and k-medians stable.

For example, if X is the real line $\mathbb{R}$ with the standard metric $\ell(x, y) = |x - y|$ and P is the uniform distribution over $[0, 4] \cup [12, 16]$ (see Figure 2a), then $g(x) = 16 - x$ is a P-preserving symmetry. For $k = 3$, both k-means and k-median have exactly two optimal triples of centers $(2, 13, 15)$ and $(1, 3, 14)$. Hence, for $k = 3$, both k-means and k-medians are unstable on P.

However, if we change the distribution slightly, such that the weight of the first interval is little bit less than $1/2$ and the weight of the second interval is accordingly a little bit above $1/2$, while retaining uniformity on each individual interval (see Figure 2b), there will be only one optimal triple of centers, namely, $(2, 13, 15)$. Hence, for the same value, $k = 3$, k-means and k-medians become stable. This illustrates again how unreliable is stability as an indicator of a meaningful number of clusters.

6 Stability of Spectral Clustering

In this section we show similar stability results for spectral clustering. Namely, we show that the existence of a unique minimizer for the associated risk implies stability, and that the existence of non-trivial symmetries implies instability. We consider two variants of spectral clustering, the standard one, and a less standard version related to kernel k-means.

Assume we are given n data points $x_1, ..., x_m$ and their pairwise similarities $s(x_i, x_j)$. Let W denote the similarity matrix, D the corresponding degree matrix, and L the normalized graph Laplacian $L = D^{-1}(D - W)$. One of the standard derivations of normalized spectral clustering is by the normalized cut criterion (Shi and Malik, 2000). The ultimate goal is to construct k indicator vectors $v_i = (v_i^1, ..., v_i^m)^t$ with $v_i^j \in \{0, 1\}$ such that the normalized cut $Ncut = \text{tr}(V^t LV)$ is minimized. Here V denotes the $m \times k$ matrix containing the indicator vectors v_i as columns. As it is NP hard to solve this discrete optimization problem exactly, we have to resort to relaxations. In the next two subsections we investigate the stability of two different spectral clustering algorithms based on two different relaxations.

6.1 Stability of the Standard Spectral Clustering Algorithm

The "standard relaxation" as used in Shi and Malik (2000) is to relax the integer condition $v_i^j \in \{0, 1\}$ to $v_i^j \in \mathbb{R}$. It can be seen that the solution of the relaxed problem is then given by the first k eigenvectors $v_1, ..., v_k$ of the matrix L. To construct a clustering from those eigenvectors we then embed the data points x_i into the k-dimensional Euclidean space by $T_v : x_i \mapsto z_i := (v_1^{(i)}, ..., v_k^{(i)})$. Then we apply the standard k-means clustering algorithm to the embedded points $z_1, ..., z_m$ to obtain the final clustering $\mathcal{C}$ into k clusters. This algorithm cannot easily be cast into a problem where we minimize one single cost function. Instead we proceed in two stages. In the first one we minimize the eigenvector cost function $\text{tr}(V^t LV)$, and in the second one the standard k-means objective function on the embedded points z_i.

To discuss the distance between spectral clusterings based on different samples, we first have to extend a clustering constructed on each sample to the whole data space X. For spectral clustering there exists a natural extension operator as follows (see von Luxburg et al. (2004) for details). We extend an eigenvector v_i of eigenvalue λ_i to a function $\hat{f}_i : X \to \mathbb{R}$ by defining $\hat{f}_i(x) = (\sum_{j=1}^m s(x, x_j) v_i^{(j)})/(m(1-\lambda_i))$. Next we extend the embedding $T_v : \{x_1, .., x_m\} \to \mathbb{R}^k$ to an embedding $T_{\hat{f}} : X \to \mathbb{R}^k$ by $T_{\hat{f}} : x \mapsto z := (\hat{f}_1^{(i)}, ..., \hat{f}_k^{(i)})$. Note that $T_{\hat{f}}(x_i) = T_v(x_i)$. Now we perform k-means clustering on the images of the sample points z_i in $\mathbb{R}^k$. Finally, this clustering is extended by the standard extension operator for k-means, that is we assign all points z to the closest center c_i, where $c_1, ..., c_k \in \mathbb{R}^k$ are the centers constructed by k-means on the embedded data points $z_1, ..., z_m$. Then we define the exended clustering on X by setting $x \sim_{\mathcal{C}} y$ if the images of x and y are in the same cluster in $\mathbb{R}^k$.

Theorem 16 (Stability of normalized spectral clustering). *Let the data space X be compact, and the similarity function s be non-negative, symmetric, continuous, and bounded away from 0. Assume that the limit clustering based on $\mathcal{L}$ is unique (that is, the first k eigenfunctions $f_1, ..., f_k$ of the limit operator $\mathcal{L}$ are unique and the k-means objective function applied to $T_f(X)$ has a unique minimizer). Let $\mathcal{C}$ and $\mathcal{D}$ be the extensions of the spectral clusterings computed from two independent samples $x_1, ..., x_m$ and $x'_1, ..., x'_m$. Then $\lim_{m \to \infty} d_P(\mathcal{C}, \mathcal{D}) = 0$ in probability.*

Proof. (Sketch) The proof is based on techniques developed in von Luxburg et al. (2004), to where we refer for all details. The uniqueness of the first eigenfunctions implies that for large enough m, the first k eigenvalues of $\mathcal{L}$ have multiplicity one. Denote the eigenfunctions of $\mathcal{L}$ by f_i, the eigenvectors based on the first sample by v_i, and the ones based on the second sample by w_i. Let $\hat{f}_i$ and $\hat{g}_i$ the extensions of those eigenvectors. In von Luxburg et al. (2004) it has been proved that $\|\hat{f}_i - f_i\|_\infty \to 0$ and $\|\hat{g}_i - f_i\|_\infty \to 0$ almost surely. Now denote by $T_{\hat{f}}$ the embedding of X to $\mathbb{R}^k$ based on the functions $(\hat{f}_i)_{i=1,...,k}$, by $T_{\hat{g}}$ the one based on $(\hat{g}_i)_{i=1,...,k}$, and by T_f the one based on $(f_i)_{i=1,...,k}$. Assume that we are given a fixed set of centers $c_1, ..., c_k \in \mathbb{R}^k$. By the convergence of the eigenfunctions we can conclude that $\sup_{s=1,...,k} \big| \|T_{\hat{f}}(x) - c_s\| - \|(T_f(x) - c_s\| \big| \to 0$ a.s.. In particular, this implies that if we fix a set of centers $c_1, ..., c_k$ and cluster the space X based on the embeddings $T_{\hat{f}}$ and T_f, then the two resulting clusterings $\mathcal{C}$ and $\mathcal{D}$ of X will be very similar if the sample size m is large. In particular, $\sup_{i=1,...,k} P(C_i \triangle D_i) \to 0$ a.s., where $\triangle$ denotes the symmetric difference between sets. Together with Proposition 5, for a fixed set of centers this implies $d_P(\mathcal{C}, \mathcal{D}) \to 0$ almost surely. Finally we have to deal with the fact that the centers used by spectral clustering are not fixed, but are the ones computed by minimizing the k-means objective function on the embedded sample. Note that the convergence of the eigenvectors also implies that the k-means objective functions based $\hat{z}_i$ and z_i, respectively, are uniformly close to each other. As a consequence, the minimizers of both functions are uniformly close to each other, which by the stability results proved above leads to the desired result.   □

6.2   Stability of the Kernel-k-Means Version of Spectral Clustering

In this subsection we would like to consider another spectral relaxation. It can be seen that minimizing Ncut is equivalent to solving a weighted kernel-k-means problem with weight matrix $1/nD$ and the kernel matrix $D^{-1}WD^{-1}$ (cf. I. Dhillon, 2005). The solution of this problem can also be interpreted as a relaxation of the original problem, as we can only compute a local instead of the global minimum of the kernel-k-means objective function. This approximate solution usually does not coincide with the solution of the standard relaxation presented in the last section.

Theorem 17 (Stability of kernel-k-means spectral clustering). *Let the data space X be compact, and the similarity function s be non-negative, symmetric, continuous, and bounded away from 0. If there exists a unique optimizer* *of the kernel-k-means objective function, then the kernel-k-means relaxation of spectral clustering is stable.*

Proof. First we need to show that the sample based objective function converges to the true objective function. This is a combination of the results of von Luxburg et al. (2004) and those above. In von Luxburg et al. (2004) it has been proved that the sample based degree function converges to a continuous function d on the space X. This implies that the weights used in the weight matrix $W = D$ converge. Then we can apply the same techniques as in the standard k-means setting to show the convergence of the weighted kernel-k-means objective function and the stability of the algorithm. $\square$

6.3 Symmetry Leads to Instability of Spectral Clustering

As it is the case for center based clustering, symmetry is one of the main reasons why standard spectral clustering can be instable. In this section we would like to briefly sketch how this can be seen. Symmetry of graphs is usually described in terms of their automorphism groups (see Chan and Godsil (1997) for an overview). An automorphism of an undirected graph G with vertices $x_1, ..., x_m$ and edge weights $w(x_i, x_j)$ is a surjective mapping $\phi : \{1, ..., m\} \to \{1, ..., m\}$ such that $w(x_{\phi(i)}, x_{\phi(j)}) = w(x_i, x_j)$ for all i, j. The set of all automorphisms of a graph forms a group, the automorphism group $Aut(G)$. It is a subgroup of the symmetric group S_m. It is easy to see that if $v = (v_1, ..., v_m)^t$ is an eigenvector of L with eigenvalue λ, and ϕ a graph automorphism, then $\phi(v) := (v_{\phi(1)}, ..., v_{\phi(m)})$ is also an eigenvector of L with eigenvalue λ. If v and $\phi(v)$ are linearly independent, then the eigenvalue λ will have geometric multiplicity larger than 1. This immediately leads to ambiguity: from the point of view of spectral clustering, all vectors in the eigenspace of λ are equally suitable, as all of them have the same Rayleigh coefficient. But different eigenvectors can lead to different clusterings. As a very simple example consider the graph with 4 vertices connected as a square. The Laplacian L of this graph has the eigenvalues $0, 1, 1, 2$ and the eigenvectors $v_1 = (1, 1, 1, 1)$, $v_2 = (1, 0, -1, 0)$, $v_3 = (0, 1, 0, -1)$, and $v_4 = (-1, 1, -1, 1)$. The eigenspace of the second eigenvalue thus consists of all vectors of the form $(a, b, -a, -b)$. The spectral embedding based on this eigenvector maps the data points to $\mathbb{R}$ by $x_1 \mapsto a$, $x_2 \mapsto b$, $x_3 \mapsto -a$, and $x_4 \mapsto -b$. The centers construcuted by k-means are then either $\pm(a + b)/2$ or $\pm(a - b)/2$, depending on whether a and b have the same sign or not. In the first case, the resulting clustering is $\{x_1, x_2\}, \{x_3, x_4\}$, in the second case it is $\{x_1, x_3\}, \{x_2, x_4\}$. Thus we obtain the two completely symmetric solutions of spectral clustering which we would expect from the square symmetry of the data points.

Now let us consider the underlying data space X. The role of automorphisms is now played by measure preserving symmetries as defined above. Assume that (X, P) possesses such a symmetry. Of course, even if X is symmetric, the similarity graph based on a finite sample drawn from X usually will not be perfectly symmetric. However, if the sample size is large enough, it will be "nearly symmetric". It can be seen by perturbation theory that the resulting eigenvalues and eigenvectors will be "nearly" the same ones as resulting from a perfectly symmetric graph. In particular, which eigenvectors exactly will be used by the spectral embedding will only depend on small perturbations in the sample. This will exactly lead to the unstable situation sketched above.

7   Conclusions

Stability is being widely used in practical applications as a heuristics for tuning parameters of clustering algorithms, like the number of clusters, or various stopping criteria. In this work, we have set forward formal definitions for stability and some related clustering notions and used this framework to provide theoretical analysis of stability. Our results show that stability is determined by the structure of the set of optimal solutions to the risk minimization objective. Namely, the existence of a unique minimizer implies stability, and the existence of a symmetry permuting such minimizers implies instability. These results indicate that, contrary to common belief (and practice), stability does NOT reflect the validity or meaningfulness of the choice of the number of clusters. Instead, the parameters it measures are rather independent of clustering parameters. Furthermore, our results reduce the problem of stability estimation to concrete geometric and optimization properties of the data distribution. In this paper we prove these results for a wide class of center based and spectral clustering algorithms.

It would be interesting to investigate similar questions with respect to other popular clustering paradigms. Another intriguing issue is to try to figure out what features of real life data make stability successful as a clustering validation tool in practice. As shown in this paper, by our results and examples, stability is not the right tool for such purposes. The success of stability in choosing number of clusters should be viewed as an exception rather than the rule.

Bibliography

S. Ben-David. A framework for statistical clustering with constant time approximation algorithms for k-median clustering. In J. Shawe-Taylor and Y. Singer, editors, *Proceedings of the 17th Annual Conference on Learning Theory (COLT)*, pages 415–426. Springer, 2004.

A. Ben-Hur, A. Elisseeff, and I. Guyon. A stability based method for discovering structure in clustered data. In *Pacific Symposium on Biocomputing*, 2002.

O. Bousquet and A. Elisseeff. Stability and generalization. *JMLR*, 2(3):499–526, 2002.

A. Chan and C. Godsil. Symmetry and eigenvectors. In G. Hahn and G. Sabidussi, editors, *Graph Symmetry, Algebraic Methods and Applications.* Kluwer, 1997.

B. Kulis I. Dhillon, Y. Guan. A unified view of kernel k-means, spectral clustering, and graph partitioning. Technical Report TR-04-25, UTCS Technical Report, 2005.

S. Kutin and P. Niyogi. Almost-everywhere algorithmic stability and generalization error. Technical report, TR-2002-03, University of of Chicago, 2002.

T. Lange, V. Roth, M. Braun, and J.Buhmann. Stability-based validation of clustering solutions. *Neural Computation*, 2004.

A. Rakhlin and A. Caponnetto. Stability properties of empirical risk minimization over donsker classes. Technical report, MIT AI Memo 2005-018, 2005.

J. Shi and J. Malik. Normalized cuts and image segmentation. *IEEE Transactions on Pattern Analysis and Machine Intelligence*, 22(8):888–905, 2000.

U. von Luxburg, M. Belkin, and O. Bousquet. Consistency of spectral clustering. Technical Report 134, Max Planck Institute for Biological Cybernetics, 2004.

U. von Luxburg and S. Ben-David. Towards a statistical theory of clustering. In *PASCAL workshop on Statistics and Optimization of Clustering*, 2005.

PAC Learning Axis-Aligned Mixtures of Gaussians with No Separation Assumption

Jon Feldman[1,*], Rocco A. Servedio[2,**], and Ryan O'Donnell[3,***]

[1] Google
jonfeld@google.com
[2] Columbia University
rocco@cs.columbia.edu
[3] Microsoft Research
odonnell@microsoft.com

Abstract. We propose and analyze a new vantage point for the learning of mixtures of Gaussians: namely, the PAC-style model of learning probability distributions introduced by Kearns et al. [13]. Here the task is to construct a hypothesis mixture of Gaussians that is statistically indistinguishable from the actual mixture generating the data; specifically, the KL divergence should be at most ϵ.

In this scenario, we give a poly(n/ϵ) time algorithm that learns the class of mixtures of any constant number of axis-aligned Gaussians in $\mathbf{R}^n$. Our algorithm makes *no* assumptions about the separation between the means of the Gaussians, nor does it have any dependence on the minimum mixing weight. This is in contrast to learning results known in the "clustering" model, where such assumptions are unavoidable.

Our algorithm relies on the method of moments, and a subalgorithm developed in [9] for a discrete mixture-learning problem.

1 Introduction

In [13] Kearns et al. introduced an elegant and natural model of learning unknown probability distributions. In this framework we are given a class $\mathcal{C}$ of probability distributions over $\mathbf{R}^n$ and access to random data sampled from an unknown distribution $\mathbf{Z}$ that belongs to $\mathcal{C}$. The goal is to output a hypothesis distribution $\mathbf{Z}'$ which with high confidence is ϵ-close to $\mathbf{Z}$ as measured by the the Kullback-Leibler (KL) divergence, a standard measure of the distance between probability distributions (see Section 2 for details on this distance measure). The learning algorithm should run in time poly(n/ϵ). This model is well-motivated by its close analogy to Valiant's classical Probably Approximately Correct (PAC) framework for learning Boolean functions [17].

---

* Some of this work was done while supported by an NSF Mathematical Sciences Postdoctoral Research Fellowship at Columbia University.
** Supported in part by NSF award CCF-0347282, by NSF award CCF-0523664, and by a Sloan Foundation Fellowship.
*** Some of this work was done while at the Institute for Advanced Study.

G. Lugosi and H.U. Simon (Eds.): COLT 2006, LNAI 4005, pp. 20–34, 2006.

Several notable results, both positive and negative, have been obtained for learning in the Kearns et al. framework of [13], see, e.g., [10, 15]. Here we briefly survey some of the positive results that have been obtained for learning various types of *mixture distributions*. (Recall that given distributions $\mathbf{X}^1, \ldots, \mathbf{X}^k$ and mixing weights $\pi^1, \ldots, \pi^k$ that sum to 1, a draw from the corresponding mixture distribution is obtained by first selecting i with probability π^i and then making a draw from $\mathbf{X}^i$.) Kearns et al. gave an efficient algorithm for learning certain mixtures of *Hamming balls*; these are product distributions over $\{0,1\}^n$ in which each coordinate mean is either p or $1 - p$ for some p fixed over all mixture components. Subsequently Freund and Mansour [11] and independently Cryan et al. [4] gave efficient algorithms for learning a mixture of two arbitrary product distributions over $\{0,1\}^n$. Recently, Feldman et al. [9] gave a poly(n)-time algorithm that learns a mixture of any $k = O(1)$ many arbitrary product distributions over the discrete domain $\{0, 1, \ldots, b - 1\}^n$ for any $b = O(1)$.

1.1 Results

As described above, research on learning mixture distributions in the PAC-style model of Kearns et al. has focused on distributions over discrete domains. In this paper we consider the natural problem of learning mixtures of Gaussians in the PAC-style framework of [13]. Our main result is the following theorem:

Theorem 1. (Informal version) *Fix any $k = O(1)$, and let $\mathbf{Z}$ be any unknown mixture of axis-aligned Gaussians over $\mathbf{R}^n$. There is an algorithm that, given samples from $\mathbf{Z}$ and any ϵ, $\delta > 0$ as inputs, runs in time* $\mathrm{poly}(n/\epsilon) \cdot \log(1/\delta)$ *and with probability $1 - \delta$ outputs a mixture $\mathbf{Z}'$ of k axis-aligned Gaussians over $\mathbf{R}^n$ satisfying $KL(\mathbf{Z}\|\mathbf{Z}') \leq \epsilon$.*

A signal feature of this result is that it requires no assumptions about the Gaussians being "separated" in space. It also has no dependence on the minimum mixing weight. We compare our result with other works on learning mixtures of Gaussians in the next section.

Our proof of Theorem 1 works by extending the basic approach for learning mixtures of product distributions over discrete domains from [9]. The main technical tool introduced in [9] is the WAM (Weights And Means) algorithm; the correctness proof of WAM is based on an intricate error analysis using ideas from the singular value theory of matrices. In this paper, we use this algorithm in a continuous domain to estimate the parameters of the Gaussian mixture. Dealing with this more complex class of distributions requires tackling a whole new set of issues around sampling error that did not exist in the discrete case.

Our results strongly suggest that the techniques introduced in [9] (and extended here) extend to PAC learning mixtures of other classes of product distributions, both discrete and continuous, such as exponential distributions or Poisson distributions. Though we have not explicitly worked out those extensions in this paper, we briefly discuss general conditions under which our techniques are applicable in Section 7.

1.2 Comparison with Other Frameworks for Learning Mixtures of Gaussians

There is a vast literature in statistics on modeling with mixture distributions, and on estimating the parameters of unknown such distributions from data. The case of mixtures of Gaussians is by far the most studied case; see, e.g., [14, 16] for surveys. Statistical work on mixtures of Gaussians has mainly focused on finding the distribution parameters (mixing weights, means, and variances) of *maximum likelihood*, given a set of data. Although one can write down equations whose solutions give these maximum likelihood values, solving the equations appears to be a computationally intractable problem. In particular, the most popular algorithm used for solving the equations, the *EM Algorithm* of Dempster et al. [7], has no efficiency guarantees and may run slowly or converge only to local optima on some instances.

A change in perspective led to the first provably efficient algorithm for learning: In 1999, Dasgupta [5] suggested learning in the *clustering* framework. In this scenario, the learner's goal is to group all the sample points according to which Gaussian in the mixture they came from. This is the strongest possible criterion for success one could demand; when the learner succeeds, it can easily recover accurate approximations of all parameters of the mixture distribution. However, a strong assumption is required to get such a strong outcome: it is clear that the learner cannot possibly succeed unless the Gaussians are guaranteed to be sufficiently "separated" in space. Informally, it must at least be the case that, with high probability, no sample point "looks like" it might have come from a different Gaussian in the mixture other than the one that actually generated it.

Dasgupta gave a polynomial time algorithm that could cluster a mixture of *spherical* Gaussians of *equal radius*. His algorithm required separation on the order of $n^{1/2}$ times the standard deviation. This was improved to $n^{1/4}$ by Dasgupta and Schulman [6], and this in turn was significantly generalized to the case of completely general (i.e., elliptical) Gaussians by Arora and Kannan [2]. Another breakthrough came from Vempala and Wang [18] who showed how the separation could be reduced, in the case of mixtures of k spherical Gaussians (of different radii), to the order of $k^{1/4}$ times the standard deviation, times factors logarithmic in n. This result was extended to mixtures of general Gaussians (indeed, log-concave distributions) in works by Kannan et al. [12] and Achlioptas and McSherry [1], with some slightly worse separation requirements. It should also be mentioned that these results all have a running time dependence that is polynomial in $1/\pi_{min}$, where π_{min} denotes the minimum mixing weight.

Our work gives another learning perspective that allows us to deal with mixtures of Gaussians that satisfy *no* separation assumption. In this case clustering is simply not possible; for any data set, there may be many different mixtures of Gaussians under which the data are plausible. This possibility also leads to the seeming intractability of finding the *maximum* likelihood mixture of Gaussians. Nevertheless, we feel that this case is both interesting and important, and that under these circumstances identifying *some* mixture of Gaussians which is statistically indistinguishable from the true mixture is a worthy task. This is precisely what the PAC-style learning scenario we work in requires, and what our main algorithm efficiently achieves.

Reminding the reader that they work in significantly different scenarios, we end this section with a comparison between other aspects of our algorithm and algorithms in the clustering model. Our algorithm works for mixtures of axis-aligned Gaussians. This is stronger than the case of spherical Gaussians considered in [5, 6, 18], but weaker than the case of general Gaussians handled in [2, 12, 1]. On the other hand, in Section 7 we discuss the fact that our methods should be readily adaptable to mixtures of a wide variety of discrete and continuous distributions — essentially, any distribution where the "method of moments" from statistics succeeds. The clustering algorithms discussed have polynomial running time dependence on k, the number of mixture components, whereas our algorithm's running time is polynomial in n only if k is a constant. We note that in [9], strong evidence was given that (for the PAC-style learning problem that we consider) such a dependence is unavoidable at least in the case of learning mixtures of product distributions on the Boolean cube. Finally, unlike the clustering algorithms mentioned, our algorithm has no running time dependence on $1/\pi_{\min}$.

1.3 Overview of the Approach and the Paper

An important ingredient of our approach is a slight extension of the WAM algorithm, the main technical tool introduced in [9]. The algorithm takes as input a parameter $\epsilon > 0$ and samples from an unknown mixture $\mathbf{Z}$ of k product distributions $\mathbf{X}^1, \dots, \mathbf{X}^k$ over $\mathbf{R}^n$. The output of the algorithm is a list of candidate descriptions of the k mixing weights and kn coordinate means of the distributions $\mathbf{X}^1, \dots, \mathbf{X}^k$. Roughly speaking, the guarantee for the algorithm proved in [9] is that with high probability at least one of the candidate descriptions that the algorithm outputs is "good" in the following sense: it is an additive ϵ-accurate approximation to each of the k true mixing weights $\pi^1, \dots, \pi^k$ and to each of the true coordinate means $\mu_j^i = \mathbf{E}[\mathbf{X}_j^i]$ for which the corresponding mixing weight π^i is not too small. We give a precise specification in Section 3.

As described above, when WAM is run on a mixture distribution it generates candidate estimates of mixing weights and means. However, to describe a Gaussian we need not only its mean but also its variance. To achieve this we run WAM *twice*, once on $\mathbf{Z}$ and once on what might be called "$\mathbf{Z}^2$" — i.e., for the second run, each time a draw $(z_1, \dots, z_n)$ is obtained from $\mathbf{Z}$ we convert it to $(z_1^2, \dots, z_n^2)$ and use that instead. It is easy to see that $\mathbf{Z}^2$ corresponds to a mixture of the distributions $(\mathbf{X}^1)^2, \dots, (\mathbf{X}^k)^2$, and thus this second run gives us estimates of the mixing weights (again) and also of the coordinate *second moments* $\mathbf{E}[(\mathbf{X}_j^i)^2]$. Having thus run WAM twice, we essentially take the "cross-product" of the two output lists to obtain a list of candidate descriptions, each of which specifies mixing weights, means, and second moments of the component Gaussians. In Section 4 we give a detailed description of this process and prove that with high probability at least one of the resulting candidates is a "good" description (in the sense of the preceding paragraph) of the mixing weights, coordinate means, and coordinate variances of the Gaussians $\mathbf{X}^1, \dots, \mathbf{X}^k$.

To actually PAC learn the distribution $\mathbf{Z}$, we must find this good description among the candidates in the list. A natural idea is to apply some sort of

maximum likelihood procedure. However, to make this work, we need to guarantee that the list contains a distribution that is close to the target in the sense
of KL divergence. Thus, in Section 5, we show how to convert each "parametric"
candidate description into a mixture of Gaussians such that any additively accurate description indeed becomes a mixture distribution with close KL divergence
to the unknown target. (This procedure also guarantees that the candidate distributions satisfy some other technical conditions that are needed by the maximum
likelihood procedure.) Finally, in Section 6 we put the pieces together and show
how a maximum likelihood procedure can be used to identify a hypothesis mixture
of Gaussians that has small KL divergence relative to the target mixture.

2 Preliminaries

The PAC learning framework for probability distributions. We work
in the Probably Approximately Correct model of learning probability distributions which was proposed by Kearns et al. [13]. In this framework the learning
algorithm is given access to samples drawn from the target distribution $\mathbf{Z}$ to
be learned, and the learning algorithm must (with high probability) output an
accurate approximation $\mathbf{Z}'$ of the target distribution $\mathbf{Z}$. Following [13], we use
the *Kullback-Leibler (KL) divergence* (also known as the *relative entropy*) as our
notion of distance. The KL divergence between distributions $\mathbf{Z}$ and $\mathbf{Z}'$ is

$$\mathrm{KL}(\mathbf{Z}\|\mathbf{Z}') := \int \mathbf{Z}(x) \ln(\mathbf{Z}(x)/\mathbf{Z}'(x)) \, dx$$

where here we have identified the distributions with their pdfs. The reader is
reminded that KL divergence is not symmetric and is thus not a metric. KL
divergence is a stringent measure of the distance between probability distances.
In particular, it holds [3] that $0 \leq \|\mathbf{Z} - \mathbf{Z}'\|_2 \leq (2\ln 2)\sqrt{\mathrm{KL}(\mathbf{Z}\|\mathbf{Z}')}$, where $\|\cdot\|_1$
denotes total variation distance; hence if the KL divergence is small then so is
the total variation distance.

We make the following formal definition:

Definition 1. *Let $\mathcal{D}$ be a class of probability distributions over $\mathbf{R}^n$. An efficient
(proper) learning algorithm for $\mathcal{D}$ is an algorithm which, given ϵ, $\delta > 0$ and
samples drawn from any distribution $\mathbf{Z} \in \mathcal{D}$, runs in $\mathrm{poly}(n, 1/\epsilon, 1/\delta)$ time and,
with probability at least $1 - \delta$, outputs a representation of a distribution $\mathbf{Z}' \in \mathcal{D}$
such that $\mathrm{KL}(\mathbf{Z}\|\mathbf{Z}') \leq \epsilon$.*

Mixtures of axis-aligned Gaussians. Here we recall some basic definitions
and establish useful notational conventions for later.

A Gaussian distribution over $\mathbf{R}$ with mean μ and variance σ has probability
density function $f(x) = (1/\sqrt{2\pi}\sigma) \exp\left(-\frac{(x-\mu)^2}{2\sigma^2}\right)$. An *axis-aligned* Gaussian
over $\mathbf{R}^n$ is a product distribution over n univariate Gaussians.

If we expect to learn a mixture of Gaussians, we need each Gaussian to have
reasonable parameters in each of its coordinates. Indeed, consider just the problem of learning the parameters of a single one-dimensional Gaussian: If the variance is enormous, we could not expect to estimate the mean efficiently; or, if

the variance was extremely close to 0, any slight error in the hypothesis would lead to a severe penalty in KL divergence. These issues motivate the following definition:

Definition 2. *We say that* $\mathbf{X}$ *is a* d-dimensional $(\mu_{\max}, \sigma_{\min}^2, \sigma_{\max}^2)$-bounded Gaussian *if* $\mathbf{X}$ *is a* d-dimensional axis-aligned Gaussian with the property that each of its one-dimensional coordinate Gaussians $\mathbf{X}_j$ has mean $\mu_j \in [-\mu_{\max}, \mu_{\max}]$ and variance $(\sigma_j)^2 \in [\sigma_{\min}^2, \sigma_{\max}^2]$.

Notational convention: *Throughout the rest of the paper all Gaussians we consider are* $(\mu_{\max}, \sigma_{\min}^2, \sigma_{\max}^2)$-bounded, *where for notational convenience we assume that the numbers* $\mu_{\max}$, $\sigma_{\max}^2$ *are at least 1 and that the number* $\sigma_{\min}^2$ *is at most 1. We will denote by* L *the quantity* $\mu_{\max}\sigma_{\max}/\sigma_{\min}$, *which in some sense measures the bit-complexity of the problem. Given distributions* $\mathbf{X}^1, \ldots, \mathbf{X}^k$ *over* $\mathbf{R}^n$, *we write* μ_j^i *to denote* $\mathbf{E}[\mathbf{X}_j^i]$, *the* j-th coordinate mean of the i-th component distribution, and we write $(\sigma_j^i)^2$ *to denote* $\mathrm{Var}[\mathbf{X}_j^i]$, *the variance in coordinate* j *of the* i-th distribution.

A mixture of k axis-aligned Gaussians $\mathbf{Z} = \pi_1 \mathbf{X}^1 + \cdots + \pi_k \mathbf{X}^k$ is completely specified by the parameters π^i, μ_j^i, and $(\sigma_j^i)^2$. Our learning algorithm for Gaussians will have a running time that depends polynomially on L; thus the algorithm is not strongly polynomial.

3 Listing Candidate Weights and Means with WAM

We first recall the basic features of the WAM algorithm from [9] and then explain the extension we require. The algorithm described in [9] takes as input a parameter $\epsilon > 0$ and samples from an unknown mixture $\mathbf{Z}$ of k distributions $\mathbf{X}^1, \ldots, \mathbf{X}^k$ where each $\mathbf{X}^i = (\mathbf{X}_1^i, \ldots, \mathbf{X}_n^i)$ is assumed to be a product distribution over the bounded domain $[-1, 1]^n$. The goal of WAM is to output accurate estimates for the mixing weights π^i and coordinate means μ_j^i; what the algorithm actually outputs is a list of candidate "parametric descriptions" of the means and mixing weights, where each candidate description is of the form $(\{\hat{\pi}^1, \ldots, \hat{\pi}^k\}, \{\hat{\mu}_1^1, \hat{\mu}_2^1, \ldots, \hat{\mu}_n^k\})$.

We now explain the notion of a "good" estimate of parameters from Section 1.3 in more detail. As motivation, note that if a mixing weight π^i is very low then the WAM algorithm (or indeed any algorithm that only draws a limited number of samples from $\mathbf{Z}$) may not receive any samples from $\mathbf{X}^i$, and thus we would not expect WAM to construct an accurate estimate for the coordinate means $\mu_1^i, \ldots, \mu_n^i$. We thus have the following definition from [9]:

Definition 3. *A candidate* $(\{\hat{\pi}^1, \ldots, \hat{\pi}^k\}, \{\hat{\mu}_1^1, \hat{\mu}_2^1, \ldots, \hat{\mu}_n^k\})$ *is said to be* parametrically ϵ-accurate *if:*

1. $|\hat{\pi}^i - \pi^i| \le \epsilon$ *for all* $1 \le i \le k$;
2. $|\hat{\mu}_j^i - \mu_j^i| \le \epsilon$ *for all* $1 \le i \le k$ *and* $1 \le j \le n$ *such that* $\pi^i \ge \epsilon$.

Very roughly speaking, the WAM algorithm in [9] works by exhaustively "guessing" (to a certain prescribed granularity that depends on ϵ) values for the mixing weights and for k^2 of the kn coordinate means. Given a guess, the algorithm tries to approximately solve for the remaining $k(n - k)$ coordinate means using the guessed values and the sample data; in the course of doing this the algorithm uses estimates of the expectations $\mathbf{E}[\mathbf{Z}_j\mathbf{Z}_{j'}]$ that are obtained from the sample data. From each guess the algorithm thus obtains one of the candidates in the list that it ultimately outputs.

The assumption [9] that each distribution $\mathbf{X}^i$ in the mixture is over $[-1, 1]^n$ has two nice consequences: each coordinate mean need only be guessed within a bounded domain $[-1, 1]$, and estimating $\mathbf{E}[\mathbf{Z}_j\mathbf{Z}_{j'}]$ is easy for a mixture $\mathbf{Z}$ of such distributions. Inspection of the proof of correctness of the WAM algorithm shows that these two conditions are all that is really required. We thus introduce the following:

Definition 4. *Let* $\mathbf{X}$ *be a distribution over* $\mathbf{R}$. *We say that* $\mathbf{X}$ *is* $\lambda(\epsilon, \delta)$-*samplable if there is an algorithm* $\mathcal{A}$ *which, given access to draws from* $\mathbf{X}$, *runs for* $\lambda(\epsilon, \delta)$ *steps and outputs (with probability at least* $1 - \delta$ *over the draws from* $\mathbf{X}$) *a quantity* $\hat{\mu}$ *satisfying* $|\hat{\mu} - \mathbf{E}[\mathbf{X}]| \leq \epsilon$.

With this definition in hand an obvious (slight) generalization of WAM, which we denote WAM$'$, suggests itself. The main result about WAM$'$ that we need is the following (the proof is essentially identical to the proof in [9] so we omit it):

Theorem 2. *Let* $\mathbf{Z}$ *be a mixture of product distributions* $\mathbf{X}^1, \ldots, \mathbf{X}^k$ *with mixing weights* $\pi^1, \ldots, \pi^k$ *where each* $\mu_j^i = \mathbf{E}[\mathbf{X}_j^i]$ *satisfies* $|\mu_j^i| \leq U$ *and* $\mathbf{Z}_j\mathbf{Z}_{j'}$ *is* $\mathrm{poly}(U/\epsilon) \cdot \log(1/\delta)$-*samplable for all* $j \neq j'$. *Given* U *and any* $\epsilon, \delta > 0$, WAM$'$ *runs in time* $(nU/\epsilon)^{O(k^3)} \cdot \log(1/\delta)$ *and outputs a list of* $(nU/\epsilon)^{O(k^3)}$ *many candidates descriptions, at least one of which (with probability at least* $1 - \delta$) *is parametrically* ϵ-*accurate.*

4   Listing Candidate Weights, Means, and Variances

Through the rest of the paper we assume that $\mathbf{Z}$ is a k-wise mixture of independent $(\mu_{\max}, \sigma_{\min}^2, \sigma_{\max}^2)$-bounded Gaussians $\mathbf{X}^1, \ldots, \mathbf{X}^k$, as discussed in Section 2. Recall also the notation L from that section.

As described in Section 1.3, we will run WAM$'$ twice, once on the original mixture of Gaussians $\mathbf{Z}$ and once on the squared mixture $\mathbf{Z}^2$. In order to do this, we must show that both $\mathbf{Z} = \pi_1\mathbf{X}^1 + \cdots + \pi_k\mathbf{X}^k$ and $\mathbf{Z}^2 = \pi_1(\mathbf{X}^1)^2 + \cdots + \pi_k(\mathbf{X}^k)^2$ satisfy the conditions of Theorem 2. The bound $|\mu_j^i| \leq \mu_{\max}$ on coordinate means is satisfied by assumption for $\mathbf{Z}$, and for $\mathbf{Z}^2$ we have that each $\mathbf{E}[(\mathbf{X}_j^i)^2]$ is at most $\sigma_{\max}^2 + \mu_{\max}^2$. It remains to verify the required samplability condition on products of two coordinates for both $\mathbf{Z}$ and $\mathbf{Z}^2$; i.e. we must show that both the random variables $\mathbf{Z}_j\mathbf{Z}_{j'}$ are samplable and that the random variables $\mathbf{Z}_j^2\mathbf{Z}_{j'}^2$ are samplable. We do this in the following proposition, whose straightforward but technical proof is deferred to the full version of this paper [8]:

Proposition 1. *Suppose* $\mathbf{Z} = (\mathbf{Z}_1, \mathbf{Z}_2)$ *is the mixture of* k *two-dimensional* $(\mu_{\max}, \sigma^2_{\min}, \sigma^2_{\max})$*-bounded Gaussians. Then both the random variable* $\mathbf{W} :=$ $\mathbf{Z}_1\mathbf{Z}_2$ *and the random variable* $\mathbf{W}^2$ *are* $\mathrm{poly}(L/\epsilon) \cdot \log(1/\delta)$*-samplable.*

The proof of the following theorem explains precisely how we can run WAM′ twice and how we can combine the two resulting lists (one containing candidate descriptions consisting of mixing weights and coordinate means, the other containing candidate descriptions consisting of mixing weights and coordinate second moments) to obtain a single list of candidate descriptions consisting of mixing weights, coordinate means, and coordinate variances.

Theorem 3. *Let* $\mathbf{Z}$ *be a mixture of* $k = O(1)$ *axis-aligned Gaussians* $\mathbf{X}^1, \ldots, \mathbf{X}^k$ *over* $\mathbf{R}^n$, *described by parameters* $(\{\pi^i\}, \{\mu^i_j\}, \{\sigma^i_j\})$. *There is an algorithm with the following property: For any* $\epsilon, \delta > 0$, *given samples from* $\mathbf{Z}$ *the algorithm runs in* $\mathrm{poly}(nL/\epsilon) \cdot \log(1/\delta)$ *time and with probability* $1 - \delta$ *outputs a list of* $\mathrm{poly}(nL/\epsilon)$ *many candidates* $(\{\hat{\pi}^i\}, \{\hat{\mu}^i_j\}, \{\hat{\sigma}^i_j\})$ *such that for at least one candidate in the list, the following holds:*

1. $|\hat{\pi}^i - \pi^i| \leq \epsilon$ *for all* $i \in [k]$; *and*
2. $|\hat{\mu}^i_j - \mu^i_j| \leq \epsilon$ *and* $|(\hat{\sigma}^i_j)^2 - (\sigma^i_j)^2| \leq \epsilon$ *for all* i, j *such that* $\pi^i \geq \epsilon$.

Proof. First run the algorithm WAM′ with the random variable $\mathbf{Z}$, taking the parameter "U" in WAM′ to be L, taking "δ" to be $\delta/2$, and taking "ϵ" to be $\epsilon/(6\mu_{\max})$. By Proposition 1 and Theorem 2, this takes at most the claimed running time. WAM′ outputs a list List1 of candidate descriptions for the mixing weights and expectations, List1 $= [\ldots, (\hat{\pi}^i, \hat{\mu}^i), \ldots]$, which with probability at least $1 - \delta/2$ contains at least one candidate description which is parametrically $\epsilon/(6\mu_{\max})$-accurate.

Define $(s^i_j)^2 = \mathbf{E}[(\mathbf{X}^i_j)^2] = (\sigma^i_j)^2 + (\mu^i_j)^2$. Run the algorithm WAM′ again on the squared random variable $\mathbf{Z}^2$, with "U" $= \sigma^2_{\max} + \mu^2_{\max}$, "$\delta$" $= \delta/2$, and "ϵ" $= \epsilon/2$. By Proposition 1, this again takes at most the claimed running time. This time WAM′ outputs a list List2 of candidates for the mixing weights (again) and second moments, List2 $= [\ldots, (\hat{\hat{\pi}}^i, (\hat{s}^i_j)^2) \ldots]$, which with probability at least $1 - \delta/2$ has a "good" entry which satisfies

1. $|\hat{\hat{\pi}}^i - \pi^i| \leq \epsilon/2$ *for all* $i = 1 \ldots k$; *and*
2. $|(\hat{s}^i_j)^2 - (s^i_j)^2| \leq \epsilon/2$ *for all* i, j *such that* $\pi^i \geq \epsilon/2$.

We now form the "cross product" of the two lists. (Again, this can be done in the claimed running time.) Specifically, for each pair consisting of a candidate $(\hat{\pi}^i, \hat{\mu}^i_j)$ in List1 and a candidate $(\hat{\hat{\pi}}^i, (\hat{s}^i_j)^2)$ in List2, we form a new candidate consisting of mixing weights, means, and variances, namely $(\hat{\pi}^i, \hat{\mu}^i_j, (\hat{\sigma}^i_j)^2)$ where $(\hat{\sigma}^i_j)^2 = (\hat{s}^i_j)^2 - (\hat{\mu}^i_j)^2$. (Note that we simply discard $\hat{\hat{\pi}}^i$.)

When the "good" candidate from List1 is matched with the "good" candidate from List2, the resulting candidate's mixing weights and means satisfy the desired bounds. For the variances, we have that $|(\hat{\sigma}^i_j)^2 - (\sigma^i_j)^2|$ is at most

$$|(\hat{s}^i_j)^2 - (s^i_j)^2| + |(\hat{\mu}^i_j)^2 - (\mu^i_j)^2| \leq \frac{\epsilon}{2} + |\hat{\mu}^i_j - \mu^i_j| \cdot |\hat{\mu}^i_j + \mu^i_j| \leq \frac{\epsilon}{2} + \frac{\epsilon}{6\mu_{\max}} \cdot 3\mu_{\max} = \epsilon.$$

This proves the theorem.

5   From Parametric Estimates to Bona Fide Distributions

At this point we have a list of candidate "parametric" descriptions $(\{\hat{\pi}^i\}, \{\hat{\mu}_j^i\}, \{(\hat{\sigma}_j^i)^2\})$ of mixtures of Gaussians, at least one of which is parametrically accurate in the sense of Theorem 3. In Section 5.1 we describe an efficient way to convert any parametric description into a true mixture of Gaussians such that:

(i) any parametrically accurate description becomes a distribution with close KL divergence to the target distribution; and
(ii) every mixture distribution that results from the conversion has a pdf that satisfies certain upper and lower bounds (that will be required for the maximum likelihood procedure).

The conversion procedure is conceptually straightforward — it essentially just truncates any extreme parameters to put them in a "reasonable" range — but the details establishing correctness are fairly technical. By applying this conversion to each of the parametric descriptions in our list from Section 4, we obtain a list of mixture distribution hypotheses all of which have bounded pdfs and at least one of which is close to the target $\mathbf{Z}$ in KL divergence (see Section 5.2). With such a list in hand, we will be able to use maximum likelihood (in Section 6) to identify a single hypothesis which is close in KL divergence.

5.1   The Conversion Procedure

In this section we prove:

Theorem 4. *There is a simple efficient procedure $\mathcal{A}$ which takes values $(\{\hat{\pi}^i\}, \{\hat{\mu}_j^i\}, \{(\hat{\sigma}_j^i)^2\})$ and a value $M > \mu_{\max}$ as inputs and outputs a true mixture $\dot{\mathbf{Z}}$ of k many n-dimensional $(\mu_{\max}, \sigma_{\min}^2, \sigma_{\max}^2)$-bounded Gaussians with mixing weights $\dot{\pi}^1, \ldots, \dot{\pi}^k$ satisfying*

(a) $\sum_{i=1}^k \dot{\pi}^i = 1$, and
(b) $\alpha_0 \leq \dot{\mathbf{Z}}(x) \leq \beta_0$ for all $x \in [-M, M]^n$,

where $\alpha_0 := \left[\frac{1}{\sqrt{2\pi}\sigma_{\max}} \cdot \exp\left(\frac{-2M^2}{\sigma_{\min}^2} \right) \right]^n$ and $\beta_0 := 1/(\sqrt{2\pi}\sigma_{\min})^n$.
Furthermore, suppose $\mathbf{Z}$ is a mixture of Gaussians $\mathbf{X}^1, \ldots, \mathbf{X}^k$ with mixing weights π^i, means μ_j^i, and variances $(\sigma_j^i)^2$ and that the following are satisfied:

(c) for $i = 1 \ldots k$ we have $|\pi^i - \hat{\pi}^i| \leq \epsilon_{\text{wts}}$ where $\epsilon_{\text{wts}} \leq 1/(12k)^3$; and
(d) for all i, j such that $\pi^i \geq \epsilon_{\text{minwt}}$ we have $|\mu_j^i - \hat{\mu}_j^i| \leq \epsilon_{\text{means}}$ and $|(\sigma_j^i)^2 - (\hat{\sigma}_j^i)^2| \leq \epsilon_{\text{vars}}$.

Then $\dot{\mathbf{Z}}$ will satisfy $\text{KL}(\mathbf{Z}||\dot{\mathbf{Z}}) \leq \eta(\epsilon_{\text{means}}, \epsilon_{\text{vars}}, \epsilon_{\text{wts}}, \epsilon_{\text{minwt}})$, where

$$\eta(\epsilon_{\text{means}}, \epsilon_{\text{vars}}, \epsilon_{\text{wts}}, \epsilon_{\text{minwt}}) := n \cdot \left(\frac{\epsilon_{\text{vars}}}{2\sigma_{\min}^2} + \frac{\epsilon_{\text{means}}^2 + \epsilon_{\text{vars}}}{2(\sigma_{\min}^2 - \epsilon_{\text{vars}})} \right)$$
$$+ k\epsilon_{\text{minwt}} \cdot n \cdot \left(\frac{\sigma_{\max}^2 + 2\mu_{\max}^2}{\sigma_{\min}^2} \right) + 13k\epsilon_{\text{wts}}^{1/3}.$$

Proof. We construct a mixture $\dot{\mathbf{Z}}$ of product distributions $\dot{\mathbf{X}}^1, \dots, \dot{\mathbf{X}}^k$ by defining new mixing weights $\dot{\pi}^i$, expectations $\dot{\mu}^i_j$, and variances $(\dot{\sigma}^i_j)^2$. The procedure $\mathcal{A}$ is defined as follows:

1. For all i, j, set

$$\dot{\mu}^i_j = \begin{cases} -\mu_{\max} & \text{if } \hat{\mu}^i_j < -\mu_{\max} \\ \mu_{\max} & \text{if } \hat{\mu}^i_j > \mu_{\max} \\ \hat{\mu}^i_j & \text{o.w.} \end{cases} \quad \text{and} \quad \dot{\sigma}^i_j = \begin{cases} \sigma_{\min} & \text{if } \hat{\sigma}^i_j < \sigma_{\min} \\ \sigma_{\max} & \text{if } \hat{\sigma}^i_j > \sigma_{\max} \\ \hat{\sigma}^i_j & \text{o.w.} \end{cases}$$

2. For all $i = 1, \dots, k$ let $\ddot{\pi}^i = \begin{cases} \hat{\pi}^i & \text{if } \hat{\pi}^i \geq \epsilon_{\text{wts}} \\ \epsilon_{\text{wts}} & \text{if } \hat{\pi}^i < \epsilon_{\text{wts}}. \end{cases}$

   Let s be such that $s \sum_{i=1}^k \ddot{\pi}^i = 1$. Take $\dot{\pi}^i = s\ddot{\pi}^i$. (This is just a normalization so the mixing weights sum to precisely 1.)

It is clear from this construction that condition (a) is satisfied. For (b), the bounds on $\dot{\sigma}^i_j$ are easily seen to imply that $\dot{\mathbf{X}}^i(x) \leq 1/(\sqrt{2\pi}\sigma_{\min})^n =: \beta_0$ for all $x \in \mathbf{R}^n$, and hence the same upper bound holds for the mixture $\dot{\mathbf{Z}}(x)$, being a convex combination of the values $\dot{\mathbf{X}}^i(x)$. Similarly, using the fact that $M \geq \mu_{\max}$ together with the bounds on $\dot{\mu}^i_j$ and $\dot{\sigma}^i_j$, we have that $\dot{\mathbf{X}}^i(x) \geq \left[\frac{1}{\sqrt{2\pi}\sigma_{\max}} \cdot \exp\left(\frac{-2M^2}{\sigma_{\min}^2} \right) \right]^n =: \alpha_0$, for all $x \in [-M, M]^n$, and this lower bound holds for $\dot{\mathbf{Z}}(x)$ as well.

We now prove the second half of the theorem; so suppose that conditions (c) and (d) hold. Our goal is to apply the following proposition (proved in [9]) to bound $\text{KL}(\mathbf{Z}||\dot{\mathbf{Z}})$:

Proposition 2. *Let* $\pi^1, \dots, \pi^k$, $\gamma^1, \dots, \gamma^k \geq 0$ *be mixing weights satisfying* $\sum \pi^i = \sum \gamma^i = 1$. *Let* $\mathcal{I} = \{i : \pi^i \geq \epsilon_3\}$. *Let* $\mathbf{P}^1, \dots, \mathbf{P}^k$ *and* $\mathbf{Q}^1, \dots, \mathbf{Q}^k$ *be distributions. Suppose that*

1. $|\pi^i - \gamma^i| \leq \epsilon_1$ *for all* $i \in [k]$;
2. $\gamma^i \geq \epsilon_2$ *for all* $i \in [k]$;
3. $\text{KL}(\mathbf{P}^i||\mathbf{Q}^i) \leq \epsilon_{\mathcal{I}}$ *for all* $i \in \mathcal{I}$;
4. $\text{KL}(\mathbf{P}^i||\mathbf{Q}^i) \leq \epsilon_{\text{all}}$ *for all* $i \in [k]$.

Then, letting $\mathbf{P}$ *denote the* π*-mixture of the* $\mathbf{P}^i$*'s and* $\mathbf{Q}$ *the* γ*-mixture of the* $\mathbf{Q}^i$*'s, for any* $\epsilon_4 > \epsilon_1$ *we have* $\text{KL}(\mathbf{P}||\mathbf{Q}) \leq \epsilon_{\mathcal{I}} + k\epsilon_3\epsilon_{\text{all}} + k\epsilon_4 \ln \frac{\epsilon_4}{\epsilon_2} + \frac{\epsilon_1}{\epsilon_4 - \epsilon_1}$.

More precisely, our goal is to apply this proposition with parameters

$$\epsilon_1 = 3k\epsilon_{\text{wts}}; \quad \epsilon_2 = \epsilon_{\text{wts}}/2; \quad \epsilon_3 = \epsilon_{\text{minwt}}; \quad \epsilon_{\mathcal{I}} = n \cdot \left(\frac{\epsilon_{\text{vars}}}{2\sigma_{\min}^2} + \frac{\epsilon_{\text{means}}^2 + \epsilon_{\text{vars}}}{2(\sigma_{\min}^2 - \epsilon_{\text{vars}})} \right);$$

$$\epsilon_{\text{all}} = n \cdot \left(\frac{\sigma_{\max}^2 + 2\mu_{\max}^2}{\sigma_{\min}^2} \right); \quad \epsilon_4 = \epsilon_{\text{wts}}^{2/3}/2.$$

To satisfy the conditions of the proposition, we must (1) upper bound $|\pi^i - \dot{\pi}^i|$ for all i; (2) lower bound $\dot{\pi}^i$ for all i; (3) upper bound $\text{KL}(\mathbf{X}^i||\dot{\mathbf{X}}^i)$ for all i such that $\pi^i \geq \epsilon_{\text{minwt}}$; and (4) upper bound $\text{KL}(\mathbf{X}^i||\dot{\mathbf{X}}^i)$ for all i. We now do this.

(1) **Upper bounding** $|\pi^i - \dot{\pi}^i|$. A straightforward argument given in [9] shows that assuming $\epsilon_{\text{wts}} \leq 1/(2k)$, we get $|\pi^i - \dot{\pi}^i| \leq 3k\epsilon_{\text{wts}}$.

(2) **Lower bounding** $\dot{\pi}^i$. In [9] it is also shown that $\dot{\pi}^i \geq \frac{\epsilon_{\text{wts}}}{2}$ assuming that $\epsilon_{\text{wts}} \leq 1/k$.

(3) **Upper bounding** $\text{KL}(\mathbf{X}^i||\dot{\mathbf{X}}^i)$ **for all** i **such that** $\pi^i \geq \epsilon_{\text{minwt}}$. Fix an i such that $\pi^i \geq \epsilon_{\text{minwt}}$ and fix any $j \in [n]$. Consider some particular μ_j^i and $\dot{\mu}_j^i$ and σ_j^i and $\dot{\sigma}_j^i$, so we have $|\mu_j^i - \hat{\mu}_j^i| \leq \epsilon_{\text{means}}$ and $|(\sigma_j^i)^2 - (\hat{\sigma}_j^i)^2| \leq \epsilon_{\text{vars}}$. Since $|\mu_j^i| \leq \mu_{\text{max}}$, by the definition of $\dot{\mu}_j^i$ we have that $|\mu_j^i - \dot{\mu}_j^i| \leq \epsilon_{\text{means}}$, and likewise we have $|(\sigma_j^i)^2 - (\dot{\sigma}_j^i)^2| \leq \epsilon_{\text{vars}}$. Let $\mathbf{P}$ and $\mathbf{Q}$ be the one-dimensional Gaussians with means μ_j^i and $\dot{\mu}_j^i$ and variances σ_j^i and $\dot{\sigma}_j^i$ respectively. Using standard properties of the KL-divergence of one-dimensional Gaussians (see Appendix C of [8]), it can be shown that $\text{KL}(\mathbf{P}||\mathbf{Q}) \leq \frac{\epsilon_{\text{vars}}}{2\sigma_{\text{min}}^2} + \frac{\epsilon_{\text{means}}^2 + \epsilon_{\text{vars}}}{2(\sigma_{\text{min}}^2 - \epsilon_{\text{vars}})}$. Each $\dot{\mathbf{X}}^i$ is the product of n such Gaussians. Since KL divergence is additive for product distributions (again see Appendix C of [8]) we have the following bound for each i such that $\pi^i \geq \epsilon_{\text{minwt}}$:

$$\text{KL}(\mathbf{X}^i||\dot{\mathbf{X}}^i) \leq n \cdot \left(\frac{\epsilon_{\text{vars}}}{2\sigma_{\text{min}}^2} + \frac{\epsilon_{\text{means}}^2 + \epsilon_{\text{vars}}}{2(\sigma_{\text{min}}^2 - \epsilon_{\text{vars}})} \right).$$

(4) **Upper bounding** $\text{KL}(\mathbf{X}^i||\dot{\mathbf{X}}^i)$ **for all** $i \in [k]$. Using the fact that both $\mathbf{X}^i$ and $\dot{\mathbf{X}}^i$ are $(\mu_{\text{max}}, \sigma_{\text{min}}^2, \sigma_{\text{max}}^2)$-bounded, it can be shown (see [8]) that we have

$$\text{KL}(\mathbf{X}^i||\dot{\mathbf{X}}^i) \leq n \left(\frac{\sigma_{\text{max}}^2 + 2\mu_{\text{max}}^2}{\sigma_{\text{min}}^2} \right).$$

Proposition 2 now gives us

$$\text{KL}(\mathbf{Z}||\dot{\mathbf{Z}}) \leq n \cdot \left(\frac{\epsilon_{\text{vars}}}{2\sigma_{\text{min}}^2} + \frac{\epsilon_{\text{means}}^2 + \epsilon_{\text{vars}}}{2(\sigma_{\text{min}}^2 - \epsilon_{\text{vars}})} \right) + k\epsilon_{\text{minwt}} \cdot n \cdot \left(\frac{\sigma_{\text{max}}^2 + 2\mu_{\text{max}}^2}{\sigma_{\text{min}}^2} \right) + R,$$

where $R = k\epsilon_4 \ln \frac{\epsilon_4}{\epsilon_2} + \frac{\epsilon_1}{\epsilon_4 - \epsilon_1} = \frac{k}{2}\epsilon_{\text{wts}}^{2/3} \ln(\epsilon_{\text{wts}}^{-1/3}) + \frac{3k\epsilon_{\text{wts}}}{\epsilon_{\text{wts}}^{2/3}/2 - 3k\epsilon_{\text{wts}}}$. Using the fact that $\ln x \leq x^{1/2}$ for $x > 1$, the first of these two terms is at most $\frac{k}{2}\epsilon_{\text{wts}}^{1/2}$. Using the fact that $\epsilon_{\text{wts}} < 1/(12k)^3$, the second of these terms is at most $12k\epsilon_{\text{wts}}^{1/3}$. So R is at most $13k\epsilon_{\text{wts}}^{1/3}$ and the theorem is proved.

5.2   Getting a List of Distributions One of Which Is KL-Close to the Target

In this section we show that combining the conversion procedure from the previous subsection with the results of Section 4 lets us obtain the following:

Theorem 5. *Let* $\mathbf{Z}$ *be any unknown mixture of* $k = O(1)$ *axis-aligned Gaussians over* $\mathbf{R}^n$. *There is an algorithm with the following property: for any* $\epsilon, \delta > 0$, *given samples from* $\mathbf{Z}$ *the algorithm runs in* $\text{poly}(nL/\epsilon) \cdot \log(1/\delta)$ *time and with probability* $1 - \delta$ *outputs a list of* $\text{poly}(nL/\epsilon)$ *many mixtures of Gaussians with the following properties:*

1. *For any $M > \mu_{\max}$ such that $M = \mathrm{poly}(nL/\epsilon)$, every distribution $\mathbf{Z}'$ in the list satisfies $\exp(-\mathrm{poly}(nL/\epsilon)) \le \mathbf{Z}'(x) \le \mathrm{poly}(L)^n$ for all $x \in [-M, M]^n$.*
2. *Some distribution $\mathbf{Z}^{\star}$ in the list satisfies $\mathrm{KL}(\mathbf{Z}\|\mathbf{Z}^{\star}) \le \epsilon$.*

Note that Theorem 5 guarantees that $\mathbf{Z}'(x)$ has bounded mass only on the range $[-M, M]^n$, whereas the support of $\mathbf{Z}$ goes beyond this range. This issue is addressed in the proof of Theorem 7, where we put together Theorem 5 and the maximum likelihood procedure.

Proof of Theorem 5: We will use a specialization of Theorem 3 in which we have different parameters for the different roles that ϵ plays:

Theorem 3' *Let $\mathbf{Z}$ be a mixture of $k = O(1)$ axis-aligned Gaussians $\mathbf{X}^1, \ldots, \mathbf{X}^k$ over $\mathbf{R}^n$, described by parameters $(\{\pi^i\}, \{\mu^i_j\}, \{\sigma^i_j\})$. There is an algorithm with the following property: for any $\epsilon_{\mathrm{means}}, \epsilon_{\mathrm{vars}}, \epsilon_{\mathrm{wts}}, \epsilon_{\mathrm{minwt}}, \delta > 0$, given samples from $\mathbf{Z}$, with probability $1 - \delta$ it outputs a list of candidates $(\{\hat{\pi}^i\}, \{\hat{\mu}^i_j\}, \{\hat{\sigma}^i_j\})$ such that for at least one candidate in the list, the following holds:*

1. *$|\hat{\pi}^i - \pi^i| \le \epsilon_{\mathrm{wts}}$ for all $i \in [k]$; and*
2. *$|\hat{\mu}^i_j - \mu^i_j| \le \epsilon_{\mathrm{means}}$ and $|(\hat{\sigma}^i_j)^2 - (\sigma^i_j)^2| \le \epsilon_{\mathrm{vars}}$ for all i, j such that $\pi^i \ge \epsilon_{\mathrm{minwt}}$.*

The runtime is $\mathrm{poly}(nL/\epsilon') \cdot \log(1/\delta)$ where $\epsilon' = \min\{\epsilon_{\mathrm{wts}}, \epsilon_{\mathrm{means}}, \epsilon_{\mathrm{vars}}, \epsilon_{\mathrm{minwt}}\}$.

Let $\epsilon, \delta > 0$ be given. We run the algorithm of Theorem 3' with parameters $\epsilon_{\mathrm{means}} = \frac{\epsilon \sigma^2_{\min}}{12n}$, $\epsilon_{\mathrm{vars}} = 2\epsilon_{\mathrm{means}}$, $\epsilon_{\mathrm{minwt}} = \frac{\epsilon \sigma^2_{\min}}{3kn(\sigma^2_{\max} + 2\mu^2_{\max})}$ and $\epsilon_{\mathrm{wts}} = \frac{\epsilon^3}{(39k)^3}$. With these parameters the algorithm runs in time $\mathrm{poly}(nL/\epsilon) \cdot \log(1/\delta)$. By Theorem 3', we get as output a list of $\mathrm{poly}(nL/\epsilon)$ many candidate parameter settings $(\{\hat{\pi}^i\}, \{\hat{\mu}^i_j\}, \{\hat{\sigma}^i_j\})$ with the guarantee that with probability $1 - \delta$ at least one of the settings satisfies

- $|\pi^i - \hat{\pi}^i| \le \epsilon_{\mathrm{wts}}$ for all $i \in [k]$, and
- $|\hat{\mu}^i_j - \mu^i_j| \le \epsilon_{\mathrm{means}}$ and $|(\hat{\sigma}^i_j)^2 - (\sigma^i_j)^2| \le \epsilon_{\mathrm{vars}}$ for all i, j such that $\pi^i \ge \epsilon_{\mathrm{minwt}}$.

We now pass each of these candidate parameter settings through Theorem 4. (Note that $\epsilon_{\mathrm{wts}} < 1/(12k^3)$ as required by Theorem 4.) By Theorem 4, for any $M = \mathrm{poly}(nL/\epsilon)$ all the resulting distributions will satisfy $\exp(-\mathrm{poly}(nL/\epsilon)) \le \mathbf{Z}'(x) \le \mathrm{poly}(L)^n$ for all $x \in [-M, M]^n$. It is easy to check that under our parameter settings, each of the three component terms of η (i.e. $n \cdot \left(\frac{\epsilon_{\mathrm{vars}}}{2\sigma^2_{\min}} + \frac{\epsilon^2_{\mathrm{means}} + \epsilon_{\mathrm{vars}}}{2(\sigma^2_{\min} - \epsilon_{\mathrm{vars}})} \right)$, $k\epsilon_{\mathrm{minwt}} \cdot n \left(\frac{\sigma^2_{\max} + 2\mu^2_{\max}}{\sigma^2_{\min}} \right)$, and $13k\epsilon^{1/3}_{\mathrm{wts}}$) is at most $\epsilon/3$. Thus $\eta(\epsilon_{\mathrm{means}}, \epsilon_{\mathrm{vars}}, \epsilon_{\mathrm{wts}}, \epsilon_{\mathrm{minwt}}) \le \epsilon$, so one of the resulting distributions $\mathbf{Z}^{\star}$ must satisfy $\mathrm{KL}(\mathbf{Z}\|\mathbf{Z}^{\star}) \le \epsilon$.

6   Putting It All Together

6.1   Identifying a Good Distribution Using Maximum Likelihood

Theorem 5 gives us a list of distributions at least one of which is close to the target distribution we are trying to learn. Now we must *identify* some distribution in the list which is close to the target. We use a natural maximum likelihood algorithm described in [9] to help us accomplish this:

Theorem 6. *[9] Let β, α, $\epsilon > 0$ be such that $\alpha < \beta$. Let $\mathcal{Q}$ be a set of hypothesis distributions for some distribution $\mathbf{P}$ over the space X such that at least one $\mathbf{Q}^* \in \mathcal{Q}$ has $\mathrm{KL}(\mathbf{P}||\mathbf{Q}^*) \leq \epsilon$. Suppose also that $\alpha \leq \mathbf{Q}(x) \leq \beta$ for all $\mathbf{Q} \in \mathcal{Q}$ and all x such that $\mathbf{P}(x) > 0$.*

Run the ML algorithm on $\mathcal{Q}$ using a set $\mathcal{S}$ of independent samples from $\mathbf{P}$, where $\mathcal{S} = m$. Then, with probability $1 - \delta$, where $\delta \leq (|\mathcal{Q}| + 1) \cdot \exp\left(-2m\frac{\epsilon^2}{\log^2(\beta/\alpha)}\right)$, the algorithm outputs some distribution $\mathbf{Q}^{\mathrm{ML}} \in \mathcal{Q}$ which has $\mathrm{KL}(\mathbf{P}||\mathbf{Q}^{\mathrm{ML}}) \leq 4\epsilon$.

6.2   The Main Result

Here we put the pieces together and give our main learning result for mixtures of Gaussians.

Theorem 7. *Let $\mathbf{Z}$ be any unknown mixture of k n-dimensional Gaussians. There is a $(nL/\epsilon)^{O(k^3)} \cdot \log(1/\delta)$ time algorithm which, given samples from $\mathbf{Z}$ and any $\epsilon, \delta > 0$ as inputs, outputs a mixture $\mathbf{Z}'$ of k Gaussians which with probability at least $1 - \delta$ satisfies $\mathrm{KL}(\mathbf{Z}||\mathbf{Z}') \leq \epsilon$.*

Proof. Run the algorithm given by Theorem 5. With probability $1 - \delta$ this produces a list of $T = (nL/\epsilon)^{O(k^3)} \cdot \log(1/\delta)$ hypothesis distributions, one of which, $\mathbf{Z}^*$, has KL divergence at most ϵ from $\mathbf{Z}$ and all of which have their pdfs bounded between $\exp(-\mathrm{poly}(nL/\epsilon))$ and $\mathrm{poly}(L)^n$ for all $x \in [-M, M]^n$, where $M > \mu_{\max}$ is any $\mathrm{poly}(nL/\epsilon)$.

We now consider $\mathbf{Z}_M$, the M-truncated version of $\mathbf{Z}$; this is simply the distribution obtained by restricting the support of $\mathbf{Z}$ to be $[-M, M]^n$ and scaling so that $\mathbf{Z}_M$ is a distribution. The proof of the following proposition appears in the full version of this paper [8], with $\mathbf{Z}_M$ being formally defined there as well:

Proposition 3. *Let $\mathbf{P}$ and $\mathbf{Q}$ be any mixtures of n-dimensional Gaussians. Let $\mathbf{P}_M$ denote the M-truncated version of $\mathbf{P}$. For some $M = \mathrm{poly}(nL/\epsilon)$ we have $|\mathrm{KL}(\mathbf{P}_M||\mathbf{Q}) - \mathrm{KL}(\mathbf{P}||\mathbf{Q})| \leq 4\epsilon + 2\epsilon \cdot \mathrm{KL}(\mathbf{P}||\mathbf{Q})$.*

This proposition implies that $\mathrm{KL}(\mathbf{Z}_M||\mathbf{Z}^*) \leq 7\epsilon$.

Now run the ML algorithm with $m = \mathrm{poly}(nL/\epsilon)\log(M/\delta)$ on this list of hypothesis distributions *using $\mathbf{Z}_M$ as the target distribution*. (We can obtain draws from $\mathbf{Z}_M$ using rejection sampling from $\mathbf{Z}$; with probability $1 - \delta$ this incurs only a negligible increase in the time required to obtain m draws.) Note that running the algorithm with $\mathbf{Z}_M$ as the target distribution lets us assert that all hypothesis distributions have pdfs bounded above and below on the support of the target distribution, as is required by Theorem 6. (In contrast, since the support of $\mathbf{Z}$ is all of $\mathbf{R}^n$, we cannot guarantee that our hypothesis distributions have pdf bounds on the support of $\mathbf{Z}$.) By Theorem 6, with probability at least $1-\delta$ the ML algorithm outputs a hypothesis $\mathbf{Z}^{\mathrm{ML}}$ such that $\mathrm{KL}(\mathbf{Z}_M||\mathbf{Z}^{\mathrm{ML}}) \leq 28\epsilon$.

It remains only to bound $\mathrm{KL}(\mathbf{Z}||\mathbf{Z}^{\mathrm{ML}})$. By Proposition 3 we have

$$\mathrm{KL}(\mathbf{Z}||\mathbf{Z}^{\mathrm{ML}}) \leq 28\epsilon + 4\epsilon + 2\epsilon \cdot \mathrm{KL}(\mathbf{Z}||\mathbf{Z}^{\mathrm{ML}})$$

which implies that $\mathrm{KL}(\mathbf{Z}||\mathbf{Z}^{\mathrm{ML}}) \leq 33\epsilon$. The running time of the overall algorithm is $(nL/\epsilon)^{O(k^3)} \cdot \log(1/\delta)$ and the theorem is proved.

7   Extensions to Other Distributions

In this paper we have shown how to PAC learn mixtures of any constant number of distributions, each of which is an n-dimensional Gaussian product distribution. This expands upon the work by Feldman et al. [9] which worked for discrete distributions in place of Gaussians. It should be clear from our work that in fact many "nice" univariate distributions can be handled similarly. Also, it should be noted that the n coordinates need not come from the same family of distributions; for example, our methods would handle mixtures where some attributes had discrete distributions and the remainder had Gaussian distributions.

What level of "niceness" do our methods require for a parameterized family of univariate distributions on $\mathbf{R}$? First and foremost, it should be amenable to the "method of moments" from statistics. By this it is meant that it should be possible to solve for the parameters of the distribution given a constant number of the moments. Distributions in this category include gamma distributions, chi-square distributions, beta distributions, exponential — more generally, Weibull — distributions, and more. As a trivial example, the unknown parameter of an exponential distribution is simply its mean. As a slightly more involved example, given a beta distribution with unknown parameters α and β (the pdf for which is proportional to $x^{\alpha-1}(1-x)^{\beta-1}$ on $[0,1]$), these parameters can be determined from mean and variance estimates via

$$\alpha = \mathbf{E}[\mathbf{X}] \left(\frac{\mathbf{E}[\mathbf{X}](1 - \mathbf{E}[\mathbf{X}])}{\mathrm{Var}[\mathbf{X}]} - 1 \right), \qquad \beta = (1 - \mathbf{E}[\mathbf{X}]) \left(\frac{\mathbf{E}[\mathbf{X}](1 - \mathbf{E}[\mathbf{X}])}{\mathrm{Var}[\mathbf{X}]} - 1 \right).$$

So long as the univariate distribution family can be determined by a constant number of moments, our basic strategy of running WAM multiple times to determine moment estimates and then taking the cross-products of these lists can be employed.

There are only two more concerns that need to be addressed for a given parameterized family of distributions. First, one needs an analogue of Proposition 1, showing that products of independent random variables from the distribution family are efficiently samplable. (In fact, this should hold for *mixtures* of such, but this is very likely to be implied in any reasonable case.) This immediately holds for any distribution with bounded support; it will also typically hold for "reasonable" probability distributions that have pdfs with rapidly decaying tails.

Second, one needs an analogue of Theorem 4. This requires that it should be possible to convert accurate candidate parameter values into a KL-close actual distribution. It seems that this will typically be possible so long as the distributions in the family are not highly concentrated at any particular point. The conversion procedure should also have the property that the distributions it output have pdfs that are bounded below/above by at most exponentially small/large values, at least on polynomially-sized domains. This again seems to be a mild constraint, satisfiable for reasonable distributions with rapidly decaying tails.

In summary, we believe that for most parameterized distribution families "D" of interest, performing a small amount of technical work should be sufficient to show that our methods can learn "mixtures of products of D's". We leave the problem of checking these conditions for distribution families of interest as an avenue for future research.

References

[1] D. Achlioptas and F. McSherry. On spectral learning of mixtures of distributions. In *Proceedings of the 18th Annual COLT*, pages 458–469, 2005.

[2] S. Arora and R. Kannan. Learning mixtures of arbitrary Gaussians. In *Proceedings of the 33rd Symposium on Theory of Computing*, pages 247–257, 2001.

[3] T. Cover and J. Thomas. *Elements of Information Theory*. Wiley, 1991.

[4] M. Cryan, L. Goldberg, and P. Goldberg. Evolutionary trees can be learned in polynomial time in the two state general Markov model. *SIAM Journal on Computing*, 31(2):375–397, 2002.

[5] S. Dasgupta. Learning mixtures of gaussians. In *Proceedings of the 40th Annual Symposium on Foundations of Computer Science*, pages 634–644, 1999.

[6] S. Dasgupta and L. Schulman. A Two-round Variant of EM for Gaussian Mixtures. In *Proceedings of the 16th Conf. on UAI*, pages 143–151, 2000.

[7] A. P. Dempster, N. M. Laird, and D. B. Rubin. Maximum likelihood from incomplete data via the EM algorithm. *J. Royal Stat. Soc. Ser. B*, 39:1–38, 1977.

[8] J. Feldman, R. O'Donnell, and R. Servedio. PAC learning mixtures of Gaussians with no separation assumption. Available at http://research.microsoft.com/~odonnell.

[9] J. Feldman, R. O'Donnell, and R. Servedio. Learning mixtures of product distributions over discrete domains. In *Proc. 46th IEEE FOCS*, pages 501–510, 2005.

[10] Y. Freund, M. Kearns, D. Ron, R. Rubinfeld, R. Schapire, and L. Sellie. Efficient learning of typical finite automata from random walks. *Information and Computation*, 138(1):23–48, 1997.

[11] Y. Freund and Y. Mansour. Estimating a mixture of two product distributions. In *Proceedings of the 12th Annual COLT*, pages 183–192, 1999.

[12] R. Kannan, H. Salmasian, and S. Vempala. The spectral method for general mixture models. In *Proceedings of the 18th Annual COLT*, pages 444–457, 2005.

[13] M. Kearns, Y. Mansour, D. Ron, R. Rubinfeld, R. Schapire, and L. Sellie. On the learnability of discrete distributions. In *Proc. 26th STOC*, pages 273–282, 1994.

[14] B. Lindsay. *Mixture models: theory, geometry and applications*. Institute for Mathematical Statistics, 1995.

[15] M. Naor. Evaluation may be easier than generation. In *Proceedings of the 28th Symposium on Theory of Computing (STOC)*, pages 74–83, 1996.

[16] D.M. Titterington, A.F.M. Smith, and U.E. Makov. *Statistical analysis of finite mixture distributions*. Wiley & Sons, 1985.

[17] L. Valiant. A theory of the learnable. *Communications of the ACM*, 27(11):1134–1142, 1984.

[18] S. Vempala and G. Wang. A spectral algorithm for learning mixtures of distributions. In *Proceedings of the 43rd IEEE FOCS*, pages 113–122, 2002.

Stable Transductive Learning

Ran El-Yaniv and Dmitry Pechyony*

Computer Science Department
Technion - Israel Institute of Technology
{rani,pechyony}@cs.technion.ac.il

Abstract. We develop a new error bound for transductive learning algorithms. The slack term in the new bound is a function of a relaxed notion of *transductive stability*, which measures the sensitivity of the algorithm to most pairwise exchanges of training and test set points. Our bound is based on a novel concentration inequality for symmetric functions of permutations. We also present a simple sampling technique that can estimate, with high probability, the weak stability of transductive learning algorithms with respect to a given dataset. We demonstrate the usefulness of our estimation technique on a well known transductive learning algorithm.

1 Introduction

Unlike supervised or semi-supervised *inductive* learning models, in *transduction* the learning algorithm is not required to generate a general hypothesis that can predict the label of any unobserved point. It is only required to predict the labels of a given test set of points, provided to the learner before training. At the outset, it may appear that this learning framework should be "easier" in some sense than induction. Since its introduction by Vapnik more than 20 years ago [18], the theory of transductive learning has not advanced much despite the growing attention it has been receiving in the past few years.

We consider Vapnik's *distribution-free* transductive setting where the learner is given an "individual sample" of $m+u$ unlabeled points in some space and then receives the labels of points in an m-subset that is chosen uniformly at random from the $m + u$ points. The goal of the learner is to label the remaining *test set* of u unlabeled points as accurately as possible. *Our* goal is to identify learning principles and algorithms that will guarantee small as possible error in this game. As shown in [19], error bounds for learning algorithms in this distribution-free setting apply to a more popular *distributional* transductive setting where both the labeled sample of m points and the test set of u points are sampled i.i.d. from some unknown distribution.

Here we present novel transductive error bounds that are based on new notions of *transductive stability*. The *uniform stability* of a transductive algorithm is its worst case sensitivity for an exchange of two points, one from the labeled

---

* Supported in part by the IST Programme of the European Community, under the PASCAL Network of Excellence, IST-2002-506778.

G. Lugosi and H.U. Simon (Eds.): COLT 2006, LNAI 4005, pp. 35–49, 2006.

training set and one from the test set. Our uniform stability result is a rather straightforward adaptation of the results of Bousquet and Elisseeff [4] for inductive learning. Unfortunately, our empirical evaluation of this new bound (that will be presented elsewhere) indicates that it is of little practical merit because the required stability rates, which enable a non-vacuous bound, are not met by useful transductive algorithms.

We, therefore, follow the approach taken by Kutin and Niyogi [12] in induction and define a notion of *weak transductive stability* that requires overall stability 'almost everywhere' but still allows the algorithm to be sensitive to some fraction of the possible input exchanges. To utilize this weak transductive stability we develop a novel concentration inequality for symmetric functions of permutations based on Azuma's martingale bound. We show that for sufficiently stable algorithms, their empirical error is concentrated near their transductive error and the slack term is a function of their weak stability parameters. The resulting error bound is potentially applicable to any transductive algorithm.

To apply our transductive error bound to a specific algorithm, it is necessary to know a bound on the weak stability of the algorithm. To this end, we develop a data-dependent estimation technique based on sampling that provides high probability estimates of the algorithm's weak stability parameters. We apply this routine on the algorithm of [20].

2   Related Work

The transductive learning framework was proposed by Vapnik [18, 19]. Two transductive settings, distribution-free and distributional, are considered and it is shown that error bounds for the distribution-free setting imply the same bounds in the distributional case. Vapnik also presented general bounds for transductive algorithms in the distribution-free setting. Observing that any hypothesis space is effectively finite in transduction, the Vapnik bounds are similar to VC bounds for finite hypothesis spaces but they are implicit in the sense that tail probabilities are not estimated but are specified in the bound as the outcome of some computational routine. Vapnik bounds can be refined to include prior "beliefs" as noted in [5]. Similar implicit but somewhat tighter bounds were developed in [3]. Explicit general bounds of a similar form as well as PAC-Bayesian bounds for transduction were presented in [5].

Exponential concentration bounds in terms of *uniform stability* were first considered by Bousquet and Elisseeff [4] in the context of induction. Quite a few variations of the inductive stability concept were defined and studied in [4, 12, 15]. It is not clear, however, what is the precise relation between these definitions and the associated error bounds. It is noted in [9, 15] that many important learning algorithms (e.g., SVM) are not stable under any of the stability definitions, including the significantly relaxed notion of weak stability introduced by Kutin and Niyogi [11, 12]. Hush et al. [9] attempted to remedy this by considering 'graphical algorithms' and a new geometrical stability definition, which captures a modified SVM (see also [4]).

Stability was first considered in the context of transductive learning by Belkin et al. [2]. There the authors applied uniform inductive stability notions and results of [4] to a specific graph-based transductive learning algorithm.[1] However, the algorithm considered has the deficiency that it always labels half of the points by '-1' and the other half by '+1'.

We present general bounds for transduction based on particularly designed definitions of transductive stability, which we believe are better suited for capturing practical algorithms. Our weak stability bounds have relatively "standard" form of empirical error plus a slack term (unlike most weak stability bounds for induction [12, 15, 16]). Kearns and Ron [10] were the first to develop standard risk bounds based on weak stability. Their bounds are "polynomial", depending on $1/\delta$, unlike the "exponential" bounds we develop here (depending on $\ln 1/\delta$).

3   Problem Setup and Preliminaries

We consider the following transductive setting [18]. A *full sample* $X_{m+u} = \{x_i\}_{i=1}^{m+u}$ consisting of $m + u$ unlabeled examples in some space $\mathcal{X}$ is given. For each point $x_j \in X_{m+u}$, let $y_j \in \{\pm 1\}$ be its unknown deterministic label. A *training set* S_m consisting of m labeled points is generated as follows. Sample a subset of m points $X_m \subset X_{m+u}$ uniformly at random from all m-subsets of the full sample. For each point $x_i \in X_m$, obtain its uniquely determined label y_i from the teacher. Then, $S_m = (X_m, Y_m) = (z_i = \langle x_i, y_i \rangle)_{i=1}^m$. The set of remaining u (unlabeled) points $X_u = X_{m+u} \setminus X_m$ is called the *test set*. We use the notation I_r^s for the set of (indices) $\{r, \ldots, s\}$ (for integers $r < s$). For simplicity we abuse notation, and unless otherwise stated, the indices I_1^m are reserved for training set points and the indices I_{m+1}^{m+u} for test set points.

The goal of the transductive learning algorithm $\mathcal{A}$ is to utilize both the labeled training points S_m and the unlabeled test points X_u and generate a *soft classification* $\mathcal{A}_{S_m, X_u}(x_i) \in [-1, 1]$ for each (test) point x_i so as to minimize its *transductive error* with respect to some loss function ℓ, $R_u(\mathcal{A}) \overset{\Delta}{=} R_u(\mathcal{A}_{S_m, X_u}) \overset{\Delta}{=} \frac{1}{u} \sum_{i=m+1}^{m+u} \ell(\mathcal{A}_{S_m, X_u}(x_i), y_i)$. We consider the standard 0/1-loss and margin-loss functions denoted by ℓ and ℓ_γ, respectively.[2] In applications of the 0/1 loss function we always apply the sign function on the soft classification $\mathcal{A}_{S_m, X_u}(x)$. The *empirical error* of $\mathcal{A}$ is $\hat{R}_m(\mathcal{A}) \overset{\Delta}{=} \hat{R}_m(\mathcal{A}_{S_m, X_u}) \overset{\Delta}{=} \frac{1}{m} \sum_{i=1}^m \ell(\mathcal{A}_{S_m, X_u}(x_i), y_i)$. When using the margin loss function we denote the training and transductive errors of $\mathcal{A}$ by $\hat{R}_m^\gamma(\mathcal{A})$ and $R_u^\gamma(\mathcal{A})$, respectively.

---

[1] There is still some disagreement between authors about the definitions of 'semi-supervised' and 'transductive' learning. The authors of [2] study a transductive setting (according to the terminology presented here) but call it 'semi-supervised'.

[2] For a positive real γ, $\ell_\gamma(y_1, y_2) = 0$ if $y_1 y_2 \geq \gamma$ and $\ell_\gamma(y_1, y_2) = \min\{1, \ 1 - y_1 y_2/\gamma\}$ otherwise.

Note that in this transductive setting there is no underlying distribution as in (semi-supervised) inductive models.[3] Also, training examples are *dependent* due to the sampling without replacement of the training set from the full sample.

We require the following standard definitions and facts about martingales.[4] Let $\mathbf{B}_1^n \stackrel{\Delta}{=} (B_1, \ldots, B_n)$ be a sequence of random variables. The sequence $\mathbf{W}_0^n \stackrel{\Delta}{=} (W_0, W_1, \ldots, W_n)$ is called a *martingale* w.r.t. the *underlying* sequence $\mathbf{B}_1^n$ if for any $1 \le i \le n$, W_i is a function of $\mathbf{B}_1^i$ and $\mathbf{E}_{B_i} \{ W_i | \mathbf{B}_1^{i-1} \} = W_{i-1}$. The sequence of random variables $\mathbf{d}_1^n = (d_1, d_2, \ldots, d_n)$, where $d_i \stackrel{\Delta}{=} W_i - W_{i-1}$, is called the *martingale difference sequence* of $\mathbf{W}_n$. An elementary fact is that $\mathbf{E}_{B_i} \{ d_i | \mathbf{B}_1^{i-1} \} = 0$.

Let $f(\mathbf{Z}_1^n) \stackrel{\Delta}{=} f(Z_1, \ldots, Z_n)$ be an arbitrary function of n (possibly dependent) random variables. Let $W_0 \stackrel{\Delta}{=} \mathbf{E}_{\mathbf{Z}_1^n} \{ f(\mathbf{Z}_1^n) \}$ and $W_i \stackrel{\Delta}{=} \mathbf{E}_{\mathbf{Z}_1^n} \{ f(\mathbf{Z}_1^n) | \mathbf{Z}_1^i \}$ for any $1 \le i \le n$. An elementary fact is that $\mathbf{W}_0^n$ is a martingale w.r.t. the underlying sequence $\mathbf{Z}_n$. Thus we can obtain a martingale from any function of (possibly dependent) random variables. This routine of obtaining a martingale from an arbitrary function is called *Doob's martingale process*. Let $\mathbf{d}_1^n$ be the martingale difference sequence of $\mathbf{W}_0^n$. Then $\sum_{i=1}^n d_i = W_n - W_0 = f(\mathbf{Z}) - \mathbf{E}_{\mathbf{Z}_1^n} \{ f(\mathbf{Z}_1^n) \}$. Consequently, to bound the deviation of $f(\mathbf{Z})$ from its mean it is sufficient to bound the martingale difference sum. A fundamental inequality, providing such a bound, is the Azuma inequality.

Lemma 1 (Azuma,[1]). *Let $\mathbf{W}_0^n$ be a martingale w.r.t. $\mathbf{B}_1^n$ and $\mathbf{d}_1^n$ be its difference sequences. Suppose that for all $i \in I_1^n$, $|d_i| \le b_i$. Then*

$$\mathbf{P}_{\mathbf{B}_1^n} \{ W_n - W_0 > \epsilon \} < \exp \left(-\frac{\epsilon^2}{2 \sum_{i=1}^n b_i^2} \right) . \tag{1}$$

4   Uniform Stability Bound

Given a training set S_m and a test set X_u and two indices $i \in I_1^m$ and $j \in I_{m+1}^{m+u}$, let $S_m^{ij} \stackrel{\Delta}{=} S_m \setminus \{ z_i \} \cup \{ z_j = \langle x_j, y_j \rangle \}$ and $X_u^{ij} \stackrel{\Delta}{=} X_u \setminus \{ x_j \} \cup \{ x_i \}$ (e.g., S_m^{ij} is S_m with the ith example (from the training set) and jth example (from the test set) exchanged). The following definition of stability is a straightforward adaptation of the uniform stability definition from [4] to our transductive setting.

Definition 1 (Uniform Transductive Stability). *A transductive learning algorithm $\mathcal{A}$ has* uniform transductive stability β *if for all choices of $S_m \subset S_{m+u}$, for all $i \in I_1^m$, $j \in I_{m+1}^{m+u}$,*

$$\max_{1 \le k \le m+u} \left| \mathcal{A}_{S_m, X_u}(x_k) - \mathcal{A}_{S_m^{ij}, X_u^{ij}}(x_k) \right| \le \beta . \tag{2}$$

---

[3] As discussed earlier, Vapnik also considers a second transductive setting where examples are drawn from some unknown distribution; see Chapter 8 in [19]. Results in the model we study here apply to the other model (Theorem 8.1 in [19]).

[4] See, e.g., [7], Chapt. 12 and [6] Sec. 9.1 for more details.

Let $\mathbf{Z} \triangleq \mathbf{Z}_1^{m+u} \triangleq (Z_1, \ldots, Z_{m+u})$ be a *random permutation vector* where the variable Z_k, $k \in I_1^{m+u}$, is the kth component of a permutation of I_1^{m+u}, chosen uniformly at random. Let $\mathbf{Z}^{ij}$ be a perturbed permutation vector obtained by exchanging Z_i and Z_j in $\mathbf{Z}$. A function f on permutations of I_1^{m+u} is called (m, u)-*symmetric* permutation function if $f(\mathbf{Z}) = f(Z_1, \ldots, Z_{m+u})$ is symmetric on $Z_1, \ldots, Z_m$ as well as on $Z_{m+1}, \ldots, Z_{m+u}$.

Let $H_2(n) \triangleq \sum_{i=1}^{n} \frac{1}{i^2}$ and $K(m, u) \triangleq u^2(H_2(m+u) - H_2(u))$. It can be verified that $K(m, u) < m$. The following lemma is obtained[5] by a straightforward application of the Azuma inequality to a martingale obtained from $f(\mathbf{Z})$ by Doob's process.

Lemma 2. *Let $\mathbf{Z}$ be a random permutation vector. Let $f(\mathbf{Z})$ be an (m, u)-symmetric permutation function satisfying $\left| f(\mathbf{Z}) - f(\mathbf{Z}^{ij}) \right| \leq \beta$ for all $i \in I_1^m$, $j \in I_{m+1}^{m+u}$. Then*

$$\mathbf{P}_{\mathbf{Z}} \left\{ f(\mathbf{Z}) - \mathbf{E}_{\mathbf{Z}} \left\{ f(\mathbf{Z}) \right\} \geq \epsilon \right\} \leq \exp\left(-\frac{\epsilon^2}{2\beta^2 K(m, u)} \right) . \tag{3}$$

Our first transductive error bound is obtained by applying Lemma 2 to the function $R_u^\gamma(\mathcal{A}) - \hat{R}_m^\gamma(\mathcal{A})$ and bounding $\mathbf{E}\{R_u^\gamma(\mathcal{A}) - \hat{R}_m^\gamma(\mathcal{A})\}$ using an adaptation of Lemma 7 from [4] to our setting.

Theorem 1. *Let $\mathcal{A}$ be a transductive learning algorithm with transductive uniform stability β. Let $\tilde{\beta} \triangleq \frac{(u-1)\beta}{u\gamma} + \frac{(m-1)\beta}{m\gamma} + \frac{1}{m} + \frac{1}{u}$. Then, for all $\gamma > 0$ and $\delta \in (0, 1)$, with probability at least $1 - \delta$ over the draw of the training/test sets (S_m, X_u),*

$$R_u(\mathcal{A}) \leq \hat{R}_m^\gamma(\mathcal{A}) + \beta/\gamma + \tilde{\beta}\sqrt{2K(m, u)\ln(1/\delta)} . \tag{4}$$

The tightness of the bound (4) depends on the transductive uniform stability β of algorithm $\mathcal{A}$. If $\beta = O(1/m)$ and $u = \Omega(m)$, then the slack terms in (4) amount to $O(\sqrt{\ln(1/\delta)/m}/\gamma)$. However, in our experience this stability rate is never met by useful transductive algorithms.

5   Weak Stability Bound

The impractical requirement of the uniform stability concept motivates a weaker notion of stability that we develop here. The following definition is inspired by a definition of Kutin for inductive learning (see Definition 1.7 in [11]).

Definition 2 (Weak Permutation Stability). *Let $\mathbf{Z}$ be a random permutation vector. A function $f(\mathbf{Z})$ has weak permutation stability $(\beta, \beta_1, \delta_1)$ if f has uniform stability β and*

$$\mathbf{P}_{\mathbf{Z}, i \sim I_1^m, j \sim I_{m+1}^{m+u}} \left\{ \left| f(\mathbf{Z}) - f(\mathbf{Z}^{ij}) \right| \leq \beta_1 \right\} \geq 1 - \delta_1 , \tag{5}$$

where $i \sim I$ denotes a choice of $i \in I$ uniformly at random.

---

[5] All omitted proofs will appear in the full version of the paper.

This weaker notion of stability only requires that $|f(\mathbf{Z}) - f(\mathbf{Z}^{ij})|$ be bounded with respect to most exchanges, allowing for a δ_1-fraction of outliers. To utilize Definition 2 we develop in Lemma 3 a new concentration inequality for symmetric permutation functions that satisfy the new weak stability property.

Lemma 3. *Let $\mathbf{Z}$ be a random permutation vector and $f(\mathbf{Z})$ be an (m, u)-symmetric permutation function. Suppose that $f(\mathbf{Z})$ has weak permutation stability $(\beta, \beta_1, \delta_1)$. Let $\delta \in (0, 1)$ be given, and for $i \in I_1^m$, let $\theta_i \in (0, 1)$, $\Psi \triangleq \delta_1 \sum_{i=1}^{m} 1/\theta_i$ and $b_i \triangleq \frac{((1-\theta_i)\beta_1 + \theta_i \beta)}{(m+u-i+1)(1-\Psi)}$. If $\Psi < 1$, then with probability at least $(1 - \delta) \cdot (1 - \Psi)$ over the choices of $\mathbf{Z}$,*

$$f(\mathbf{Z}) \leq \mathbf{E_Z} \{f(\mathbf{Z})\} + u \sqrt{2 \sum_{i=1}^{m} b_i^2 \ln \frac{1}{\delta}} \ . \tag{6}$$

Note that the confidence level can be made arbitrarily small by selecting appropriate θ_i and δ_1 (thus trading-off β_1).

Proof. Let $\mathbf{W}_0^{m+u}$ be a martingale generated from $f(\mathbf{Z})$ by Doob's process. We derive bounds on the martingale differences d_i, $i \in I_1^{m+u}$, and apply Lemma 1.

Let $\boldsymbol{\pi}_1^{m+u} = \pi_1, \ldots, \pi_{m+u}$ be a specific permutation of I_1^{m+u}. In the proof we use the following shortcut: $\mathbf{Z}_1^r = \boldsymbol{\pi}_1^r$ abbreviates the r equalities $Z_1 = \pi_1, \ldots, Z_r = \pi_r$. Let θ_i be given. For $r \in I_1^m$, we say that the prefix $\boldsymbol{\pi}_1^r$ of a permutation $\boldsymbol{\pi}_1^{m+u}$ is (r, θ_r)-*admissible* (w.r.t. a fixed β_1) if it guarantees that

$$\mathbf{P}_{\mathbf{Z}, j \sim I_{m+1}^{m+u}} \left\{ |f(\mathbf{Z}) - f(\mathbf{Z}^{rj})| \leq \beta_1 \mid \mathbf{Z}_1^r = \boldsymbol{\pi}_1^r \right\} \geq 1 - \theta_r \ . \tag{7}$$

If the prefix $\boldsymbol{\pi}_1^r$ does not satisfy (7), we say that it is not (r, θ_r)-admissible. Let $\zeta(r, \theta_r)$ be the probability that $\mathbf{Z}_1^r$ is not (r, θ_r)-admissible. Our goal is to bound $\zeta(r, \theta_r)$. For any fixed $1 \leq r \leq m$ we have,

$$t(r) \triangleq \mathbf{P}_{\mathbf{Z}, j \sim I_{m+1}^{m+u}} \left\{ |f(\mathbf{Z}) - f(\mathbf{Z}^{rj})| > \beta_1 \right\}$$

$$= \sum_{\substack{\text{all possible} \\ \text{prefixes } \boldsymbol{\pi}_1^r}} \left(\mathbf{P}_{\mathbf{Z}, j \sim I_{m+1}^{m+u}} \left\{ |f(\mathbf{Z}) - f(\mathbf{Z}^{rj})| > \beta_1 \mid \mathbf{Z}_1^r = \boldsymbol{\pi}_1^r \right\} \cdot \mathbf{P_Z} \left\{ \mathbf{Z}_1^r = \boldsymbol{\pi}_1^r \right\} \right)$$

$$\geq \sum_{\substack{\text{non-} \\ \text{admissible} \\ \text{prefixes } \boldsymbol{\pi}_1^r}} \left(\mathbf{P}_{\mathbf{Z}, j \sim I_{m+1}^{m+u}} \left\{ |f(\mathbf{Z}) - f(\mathbf{Z}^{rj})| > \beta_1 \mid \mathbf{Z}_1^r = \boldsymbol{\pi}_1^r \right\} \cdot \mathbf{P_Z} \left\{ \mathbf{Z}_1^r = \boldsymbol{\pi}_1^r \right\} \right)$$

$$\geq \theta_r \cdot \sum_{\substack{\text{non-admissible} \\ \text{prefixes } \boldsymbol{\pi}_1^r}} \mathbf{P_Z} \left\{ \mathbf{Z}_1^r = \boldsymbol{\pi}_1^r \right\} = \theta_r \zeta(r, \theta_r) \ . \tag{8}$$

Since $f(\mathbf{Z})$ is (m, u)-permutation symmetric, $t(r) = t$ is constant. Since $f(\mathbf{Z})$ has weak permutation stability $(\beta, \beta_1, \delta_1)$,

$$\delta_1 \geq \mathbf{P}_{\mathbf{Z}, i \sim I_1^m, j \sim I_{m+1}^{m+u}} \left\{ |f(\mathbf{Z}) - f(\mathbf{Z}^{ij})| > \beta_1 \right\} = \sum_{r=1}^{m} \frac{1}{m} \cdot t(r) = t \geq \theta_r \zeta(r, \theta_r) \ . \tag{9}$$

Consequently, $\zeta(r, \theta_r) \leq \delta_1/\theta_r$. Or next goal is to bound d_r for (r, θ_r)-admissible prefixes. Let $l(k)$ be an index l such that $Z_l = k$. If $\boldsymbol{\pi}_1^r = (\boldsymbol{\pi}_1^{r-1}, \pi_r = k)$ is (r, θ_r)-admissible, then

$$
\begin{aligned}
|d_r| &= |W_r - W_{r-1}| = \left| \mathbf{E_Z} \left\{ f(\mathbf{Z}) \mid \mathbf{Z}_1^r = \boldsymbol{\pi}_1^r \right\} - \mathbf{E_Z} \left\{ f(\mathbf{Z}) \mid \mathbf{Z}_1^{r-1} = \boldsymbol{\pi}_1^{r-1} \right\} \right| \\
&= \left| \mathbf{E_Z} \left\{ f(\mathbf{Z}^{rl(k)}) - f(\mathbf{Z}) \mid \mathbf{Z}_1^{r-1} = \boldsymbol{\pi}_1^{r-1} \right\} \right| \\
&= \left| \mathbf{E}_{\mathbf{Z}, j \sim I_r^{m+u}} \left\{ f(\mathbf{Z}) - f(\mathbf{Z}^{rj}) \mid \mathbf{Z}_1^r = \boldsymbol{\pi}_1^r \right\} \right| \quad (10) \\
&\leq \mathbf{E}_{\mathbf{Z}, j \sim I_r^{m+u}} \left\{ \left| f(\mathbf{Z}^{rj}) - f(\mathbf{Z}) \right| \mid \mathbf{Z}_1^r = \boldsymbol{\pi}_1^r \right\} \\
&= \mathbf{P}_{j \sim I_r^{m+u}} \{ j \in I_r^m \} \cdot \mathbf{E}_{\mathbf{Z}, j \sim I_r^m} \left\{ \left| f(\mathbf{Z}^{rj}) - f(\mathbf{Z}) \right| \mid \mathbf{Z}_1^r = \boldsymbol{\pi}_1^r \right\} \quad (11) \\
&\quad + \mathbf{P}_{j \sim I_r^{m+u}} \{ j \in I_{m+1}^{m+u} \} \cdot \mathbf{E}_{\mathbf{Z}, j \sim I_{m+1}^{m+u}} \left\{ \left| f(\mathbf{Z}^{rj}) - f(\mathbf{Z}) \right| \mid \mathbf{Z}_1^r = \boldsymbol{\pi}_1^r \right\} \quad (12) \\
&\leq \frac{u\left((1-\theta_r)\beta_1 + \theta_r \beta\right)}{m + u - r + 1} \triangleq b_r \; . \quad (13)
\end{aligned}
$$

The inequality (13) follows because (i) the expectation in (11) is zero since f is (m, u)-permutation symmetric; and (ii) $\boldsymbol{\pi}_1^r$ is (r, θ_r)-admissible, implying that the expectation in (12) is bounded by $(1 - \theta_r)\beta_1 + \theta_r \beta$.

A permutation $\boldsymbol{\pi}_1^{m+u}$ is *good* if for all $r \in I_1^m$ its r-prefixes, $\boldsymbol{\pi}_1^r$, are admissible (w.r.t. the corresponding θ_r). Since $\zeta(r, \theta_r) \leq \delta_1/\theta_r$, we have

$$
\mathbf{P_Z} \{ \mathbf{Z} \text{ not good} \} \leq \sum_{r=1}^m \mathbf{P_Z} \{ \mathbf{Z}_1^r \text{ not admissible} \} = \sum_{r=1}^m \zeta(r, \theta_r) \leq \sum_{r=1}^m \frac{\delta_1}{\theta_r} = \Psi \; .
\tag{14}
$$

Thus, with probability at least $1 - \Psi$, the random permutation $\mathbf{Z}$ is good, in which case we have $|d_r| \leq b_r$ for all $r \in I_1^m$.

Consider the space $\mathcal{G}$ of all good permutations. Let $\mathbf{V}_0^{m+u}$ be a martingale obtained by Doob's process operated on f and $\mathcal{G}$. Then, using (13) we bound the martingale difference sequence $\mathbf{d'}_1^{m+u}$ of $\mathbf{V}_0^{m+u}$ as follows.

$$
\begin{aligned}
|d_i'| &\leq \mathbf{P}_{j \sim I_r^{m+u}} \{ j \in I_{m+1}^{m+u} \} \times \\
&\quad \mathbf{E}_{\mathbf{Z} \in \mathcal{G}, j \sim I_{m+1}^{m+u}} \left\{ \left| f(\mathbf{Z}^{rj}) - f(\mathbf{Z}) \right| \mid \mathbf{Z}_1^r = \boldsymbol{\pi}_1^r, \; \boldsymbol{\pi}_1^r \text{ is admissible} \right\} \quad (15) \\
&\leq \mathbf{P}_{j \sim I_r^{m+u}} \{ j \in I_{m+1}^{m+u} \} \times \\
&\quad \frac{\mathbf{E}_{\mathbf{Z}, j \sim I_{m+1}^{m+u}} \left\{ \left| f(\mathbf{Z}^{rj}) - f(\mathbf{Z}) \right| \mid \mathbf{Z}_1^r = \boldsymbol{\pi}_1^r, \; \boldsymbol{\pi}_1^r \text{ is admissible} \right\}}{\mathbf{P_Z} \{ \mathbf{Z} \in \mathcal{G} \}} \\
&\leq \frac{u\left((1-\theta_r)\beta_1 + \theta_r \beta\right)}{(m + u - r + 1)(1 - \Psi)} \triangleq b_r \; . \quad (16)
\end{aligned}
$$

Since $f(\mathbf{Z})$ is (m, u)-permutation symmetric, it follows from (10) that for any $r \in I_{m+1}^{m+u}$, $d_r' = 0$. Therefore, we can apply Lemma 1 to the martingale $\mathbf{V}_0^{m+u}$. We obtain a bound on the deviation of $V_{m+u} - V_0 = f(\mathbf{Z}) - \mathbf{E_Z} \{ f(\mathbf{Z}) \}$. Our result (6) is completed by equating the resulting bound to δ and isolating ϵ. $\quad \square$

It follows from Definition 2 that β_1 depends on δ_1. Hence, the bound (6) depends on the following parameters: $\delta_1, \theta_i, i \in I_1^m$. It can be shown that if $\beta_1 = O(1/m)$,

$\delta_1 = O(1/m^2)$ and $\theta_i = O(1/m)$ for all $i \in I_1^m$, then the slack term in (6) is $O(\sqrt{\ln(1/\delta)/m})$ and the bound's confidence can be made arbitrarily close to 1.

Our goal now is to derive an error bound for transductive algorithms by utilizing the weak stability notion. To this end, we now define weak transductive stability for algorithms. The following definition, which contains three conditions and six parameters, is somewhat cumbersome but we believe it facilitates tighter bounds than can possibly be achieved using a simpler definition (that only includes condition (18) below); see also the discussion that follows this definition. For a fixed full sample, we abbreviate $\mathcal{A}^{ij}(x, (S_m, X_u)) \triangleq |\mathcal{A}_{S_m, X_u}(x) - \mathcal{A}_{S_m^{ij}, X_u^{ij}}(x)|$.

Definition 3 (Weak Transductive Stability). *A transductive learning algorithm $\mathcal{A}$ has* weak transductive stability $(\beta, \beta_1, \beta_2, \delta_1^a, \delta_1^b, \delta_2)$ *if it has uniform transductive stability β and the following conditions (17) and (18) hold.*

$$\mathbf{P}_{(S_m, X_u), i \sim I_1^m, j \sim I_{m+1}^{m+u}} \left\{ \mathbf{P}_{x \sim X_{m+u}} \left\{ \mathcal{A}^{ij}(x, (S_m, X_u)) \leq \beta_1 \right\} \geq 1 - \delta_1^a \right\} \geq 1 - \delta_1^b \ . \tag{17}$$

$$\mathbf{P}_{(S_m, X_u), i \sim I_1^m, j \sim I_{m+1}^{m+u}} \left\{ \mathcal{A}^{ij}(x_i, (S_m, X_u)) \leq \beta_2 \right\} \geq 1 - \delta_2 \ . \tag{18}$$

While in (17) we quantify the sensitivity of the algorithm w.r.t. all examples in X_{m+u}, in (18) only the exchanged examples are considered. A number of weak stability definitions for induction is given in [10, 12, 15]. Ignoring the differences between induction and transduction, our condition (17) poses a qualitatively weaker constraint than the 'weak hypothesis stability' (Definition 3.5 in [12]), and a stronger constraint than the 'weak error stability' (Definition 3.8 in [12]). Our condition (18) is a straightforward adaptation of the 'cross-validation stability' (Definition 3.12 in [12]) to our transductive setting.

It should be possible to show, using a technique similar to the one used in the proof of Theorem 3.16 in [12], that (18) implies (17). In this case a simpler weak stability definition may suffice but, using our techniques, the resulting error bound would be looser.

Let $\Delta(i, j, s, t) \triangleq \ell_\gamma(\mathcal{A}_{S_m^{ij}, X_u^{ij}}(x_t), y_t) - \ell_\gamma(\mathcal{A}_{S_m, X_u}(x_s), y_s)$. For the proof of the forthcoming error bound we need the following technical lemma.

Lemma 4. $\mathbf{E}_{(S_m, X_u)} \left\{ R_u^\gamma(\mathcal{A}) - \hat{R}_m^\gamma(\mathcal{A}) \right\} = \mathbf{E}_{(S_m, X_u), i \sim I_1^m, j \sim I_{m+1}^{m+u}} \left\{ \Delta(i, j, i, i) \right\}.$

Theorem 2. *Let $\mathcal{A}$ be an algorithm with weak transductive classification stability $(\beta, \beta_1, \beta_2, \delta_1^a, \delta_1^b, \delta_2)$. Suppose that $u \geq m$ and $\delta_1^a < \frac{m}{m+u}$.[6] Let $\gamma > 0$, $\delta \in (0, 1)$ be given and set*

$$\tilde{\beta}_1 \triangleq \frac{u-1}{u} \cdot \frac{\beta_1}{\gamma} + \frac{\delta_1^a(m+u)\beta + [m - 1 - \delta_1^a(m+u)]\beta_1}{m\gamma} + \frac{1}{m} + \frac{1}{u} \ , \tag{19}$$

$$\tilde{\beta} \triangleq \frac{u-1}{u} \cdot \frac{\beta}{\gamma} + \frac{m-1}{m} \cdot \frac{\beta}{\gamma} + \frac{1}{m} + \frac{1}{u} \ . \tag{20}$$

---

[6] The proof for the cases $\delta_1^a > \frac{m}{m+u}$ and $m > u$ is very similar to the proof given below and is omitted.

For any $\theta_i \in (0,1)$, $i \in I_1^m$, set $\Psi \triangleq \sum_{i=1}^m \frac{\delta_i^b}{\theta_i}$ and $b_i \triangleq \frac{u\left((1-\theta_i)\tilde{\beta}_1 + \theta_i \tilde{\beta}\right)}{(m+u-i+1)(1-\Psi)}$. If $\Psi < 1$, then with probability at least $(1-\delta) \cdot (1-\Psi)$ over the draw of the training/test sets (S_m, X_u),

$$R_u(\mathcal{A}) \leq \hat{R}_m^\gamma(\mathcal{A}) + \left[(1-\delta_2)\frac{\beta_2}{\gamma} + \delta_2\frac{\beta}{\gamma}\right] + \sqrt{2\sum_{i=1}^m b_i^2 \ln\frac{1}{\delta}} . \qquad (21)$$

Proof. We derive bounds on the weak permutation stability of the function $f(S_m, X_u) \triangleq R_u^\gamma(\mathcal{A}) - \hat{R}_m^\gamma(\mathcal{A})$ and its expected value. Then we apply Lemma 3. For $i \in I_1^m$, $j \in I_{m+1}^{m+u}$, we have (by expanding the risk expressions),

$$\left| R_u^\gamma(\mathcal{A}) - \hat{R}_m^\gamma(\mathcal{A}) - \left(R_u^\gamma(\mathcal{A}_{S_m^{ij}, X_u^{ij}}) - \hat{R}_m^\gamma(\mathcal{A}_{S_m^{ij}, X_u^{ij}}) \right) \right| \leq$$

$$\frac{1}{u}\sum_{\substack{k=m+1, \\ k\neq j}}^{m+u} |\Delta(i,j,k,k)| + \frac{1}{u}|\Delta(i,j,j,i)| + \frac{1}{m}\sum_{\substack{k=1, \\ k\neq i}}^m |\Delta(i,j,k,k)| + \frac{1}{m}|\Delta(i,j,i,j)| .$$

$$(22)$$

Since ℓ_γ has Lipschitz constant γ, it follows from (17) that

$$\mathbf{P}_{(S_m, X_u), i \sim I_1^m, j \sim I_{m+1}^{m+u}} \left\{ \mathbf{P}_{k \sim I_1^{m+u}} \left\{ |\Delta(i,j,k,k)| \leq \beta_1/\gamma \right\} \geq 1 - \delta_1^a \right\} \geq 1 - \delta_1^b .$$

$$(23)$$

We say that the example x_k is *bad* if $|\Delta(i,j,k,k)| > \beta_1/\gamma$. According to (23), with probability at least $1 - \delta_1^b$ over the choices of $((S_m, X_u), i, j)$, there are at most $(1-\delta_1^a)(m+u)$ bad examples. If $u \geq m$, the terms in the second summation in (22) have greater weight (which is $1/m$) than the terms in the first summation (weighted by $1/u$). In the worst case all bad examples appear in the second summation in which case (22) is bounded by (19) with probability at least $1 - \delta_1^b$ over the choices of $((S_m, X_u), i, j)$.

The right hand side of (22) is always bounded by $\tilde{\beta}$. Therefore, the function $f(S_m, X_u)$ has weak permutation stability $(\tilde{\beta}, \tilde{\beta}_1, \delta_1^b)$. By applying Lemma 3 to $f(S_m, X_u)$, we obtain that with probability at least $(1-\delta)(1-\Psi)$,

$$R_u^\gamma(\mathcal{A}) \leq \hat{R}_m^\gamma(\mathcal{A}) + \mathbf{E}_{(S_m, X_u)}\left\{ R_u^\gamma(\mathcal{A}) - \hat{R}_m^\gamma(\mathcal{A}) \right\} + \sqrt{2\sum_{i=1}^m b_i^2 \ln\frac{1}{\delta}} . \qquad (24)$$

Since ℓ_γ has Lipschitz constant γ, it follows from (18) that

$$\mathbf{P}_{(S_m, X_u), i \sim I_1^m, j \sim I_{m+1}^{m+u}} \left\{ |\Delta(i,j,i,i)| \leq \beta_2/\gamma \right\} \geq 1 - \delta_2 . \qquad (25)$$

Therefore, the right hand side of the equality in Lemma 4 is bounded from above by $\beta_2(1-\delta_2)/\gamma + \beta\delta_2/\gamma$. By substituting this bound to (24) and using the inequality $R_u^\gamma(\mathcal{A}) \geq R_u(\mathcal{A})$, we obtain (21). $\qquad \square$

It follows from Definition 3 that β_1 depends on δ_1^a and δ_1^b, and that β_2 depends on δ_2. Hence the bound (21) depends on the following parameters: $\delta_1^a, \delta_1^b, \delta_2, \theta_i,$ $i \in I_1^m$. It is possible to show that if $u = \Omega(m)$, $\delta_1^b = O(1/m^2)$ and $\beta_1, \beta_2, \delta_1^a, \delta_2,$ θ_i are each $O(1/m)$, then the slack term in (21) is $O(\sqrt{\ln(1/\delta)/m}/\gamma)$ and the bound's confidence can be made arbitrarily close to 1.

6   High Confidence Stability Estimation

In this section we describe a routine that can generate useful upper bounds on the weak stability parameters (Definition 3) of transductive algorithms. The routine generates these estimates with arbitrarily high probability and is based on a sampling-based quantile estimation technique. Given a particular learning algorithm, our stability estimation routine relies on an "oracle" that bounds the sensitivity of the transductive algorithm with respect to a small change in the input. We present such an oracle for a familiar practical algorithm. In Sec. 6.1 we describe the quantile estimation method, which is similar to the one presented in [14]; in Sec. 6.2 we present the bounding algorithm, and in Sec. 6.3 we consider a known transductive algorithm and present a few numerical examples of the application of these methods.

6.1   Quantile Estimation

Consider a very large set Ω of N numbers. Define the q-*quantile* of Ω to be the $\lceil qN \rceil$-th smallest element of Ω (i.e., it is the $\lceil qN \rceil$-th element in an increasing order sorted list of all elements in Ω). Our goal is to bound the q-quantile x_q from above as tightly as possible, with high confidence, by sampling a "small" number $k \ll N$ of elements. For any $\epsilon \in (0,1)$ we generate a bound β such that $\mathbf{P}\{x_q \leq \beta\} \geq 1 - \epsilon$. The idea is to sample $k = k(q, \epsilon)$ elements from Ω uniformly at random, compute their exact $(\bar{q} \stackrel{\Delta}{=} q + \frac{1-q}{2})$-quantile $x_{\bar{q}}$, and output $\beta \stackrel{\Delta}{=} x_{\bar{q}}$. Denote by $\texttt{quantile}(q, \epsilon, \Omega)$ the resulting routine whose output is $\beta = x_{\bar{q}}$.

Lemma 5. *For any* $q, \epsilon \in (0,1)$. *If* $k = k(q, \epsilon) = \frac{2\ln(1/\epsilon)}{(1-q)^2}$, *then*

$$\mathbf{P}\left\{x_q \leq \texttt{quantile}(q, \epsilon, \Omega)\right\} \geq 1 - \epsilon . \tag{26}$$

Proof. For $i \in I_1^k$ let X_i be the indicator random variable obtaining 1 if the ith drawn element (from Ω) is smaller than x_q, and 0 otherwise. Set $Q = \frac{1}{k}\sum_{i=1}^k X_i$. Clearly, $\mathbf{E}Q \leq q$. By Hoeffding's inequality and using the definition of $\bar{q}$, we get

$$\mathbf{P}\{Q > \bar{q}\} = \mathbf{P}\left\{Q - q > \frac{1-q}{2}\right\}$$

$$\leq \mathbf{P}\left\{Q - \mathbf{E}Q > \frac{1-q}{2}\right\} \leq \exp\left(-\frac{k(1-q)^2}{2}\right) . \tag{27}$$

Therefore, with "high probability" the number kQ of sample points that are smaller than x_q is smaller than $k\bar{q}$. Hence, at least $(1 - \bar{q})k$ points in the sample are larger than x_q. $\texttt{quantile}$ returns the smallest of them. Equating the right hand side of (27) to ϵ and solving for k yields the stated sample size. $\qquad\square$

6.2   Stability Estimation Algorithm

Let $\mathcal{A}$ be a transductive learning algorithm. We assume that some (rough) bound on $\mathcal{A}$'s uniform stability β is known. If no tight bound is known, we take the maximal default value, which is 2, as can be seen in Definition 1. Our goal is to find useful bounds for the weak stability parameters of Definition 3. Let the values of δ_1^a, δ_1^b and δ_2 be given. We aim at finding upper bounds on β_1 and β_2.

Definition 4 (The diff Oracle). *Consider a fixed labeled training set $S_m = (X_m, Y_m)$ given to the learning algorithm. Let $\mathtt{diff}(\tilde{X}_m, \tilde{X}_u, i, j, r|S_m)$ be an "oracle" function defined for any possible partition $(\tilde{X}_m, \tilde{X}_u)$ of the full sample and indices $i \in I_1^m$, $j \in I_{m+1}^{m+u}$ and $r \in I_1^{m+u}$. diff provides an upper bound on*

$$\left| \mathcal{A}_{\tilde{S}_m, \tilde{X}_u}(x_r) - \mathcal{A}_{\tilde{S}_m^{ij}, \tilde{X}_u^{ij}}(x_r) \right| , \tag{28}$$

where $\tilde{S}_m$ is any possible labeling of $\tilde{X}_m$ that "agrees" with S_m on points in $X_m \cap \tilde{X}_m$. Note that here we assume that I_1^m is the set indices of points in $\tilde{X}_m$ (and indices in X_m are not specified and can be arbitrary indices in I_1^{m+u}).

We assume that we have an accesses to a useful $\mathtt{diff}(\tilde{X}_m, \tilde{X}_u, i, j, r|S_m)$ function that provides a tight upper bound on (28). We now describe our stability estimation algorithm that applies diff.

Let K be the set of all possible quadruples $(\tilde{X}_m, \tilde{X}_u, i, j)$ as in Definition 4. Define $\Omega_1 = \{\omega(t) : t \in K\}$, $\omega(t) = \omega(\tilde{X}_m, \tilde{X}_u, i, j)$ is a $(1 - \delta_1^a)$-quantile of the set $\Phi = \left\{ \mathtt{diff}(\tilde{X}_m, \tilde{X}_u, i, j, r|S_m), r = 1, \ldots, m + u \right\}$. It is not hard to see that for any $\epsilon \in (0, 1)$, with probability at least $1 - \epsilon$ (over random choices made by the quantile routine), $\mathtt{quantile}(1 - \delta_1^b, \epsilon, \Omega_1)$ is an upper bound on the weak stability parameter β_1 of Definition 3. Likewise, let $\Omega_2 = \{\omega(t) : t \in K\}$, but now $\omega(t) = \omega(\tilde{X}_m, \tilde{X}_u, i, j) = \mathtt{diff}(\tilde{X}_m, \tilde{X}_u, i, j, i)$. It is not hard to see that for any ϵ, with probability at least $1 - \epsilon$, $\mathtt{quantile}(1 - \delta_2, \epsilon, \Omega_2)$ is an upper bound on the weak stability parameter β_2 of Definition 3.

Thus, our weak stability estimation algorithm simply applies quantile twice with appropriate parameters. To actually draw the samples, quantile utilizes the diff function. Let v be the time complexity of computing diff oracle. By Lemma 5 the number of samples that should be drawn, in order to obtain with probability at least $1 - \epsilon$ the bound on q-quantile, is $O(\ln(1/\epsilon)/(1 - q)^2)$. It can be verified that the complexity of our stability estimation algorithm is $O(\ln(1/\epsilon)(m + u)v/\min\{(\delta_1^b)^2, (\delta_2)^2\})$. As discussed after Theorem 2, δ_1^b should be $O(1/m^2)$ to ensure that the bound (21) has arbitrarily high confidence. This constraint entails a time complexity of $\Omega(m^4(m+u))$. Hence currently our ability to use the stability estimation routine in conjunction with the transductive error bound is limited to very small values of m.

6.3   Stability Estimation Examples

In this section we consider the transductive learning algorithm of Zhou et al. [20] and demonstrate a data-dependent estimation of its weak stability parameters using our method. While currently there is no comprehensive empirical comparison between all available transductive algorithms, this algorithm appears to be among the more promising ones [8]. We chose this algorithm, denoted by CM (stands for 'Consistency Method'; see [8]), because we could easily develop a useful diff "oracle" for it. We were also able to efficiently implement diff "oracle" for the algorithm of Zhu et al. [21], which will be presented elsewhere.

We start with the brief description of the CM algorithm. Let W be a symmetric $(m + u) \times (m + u)$ affinity matrix of the full sample X_{m+u}. We assume that $W_{ii} = 0$. In this paper we use RBF kernels, parameterized by σ, to construct W. Let D be a diagonal matrix, whose (i, i)-element is the sum of the ith row in W. A normalized Laplacian of W is $L = D^{-1/2}WD^{-1/2}$. Let α be a parameter in $(0, 1)$. Let Y be an $(m + u) \times 1$ vector of available full sample labels, where the entries corresponding to training examples are ± 1 and entries of unlabeled examples are 0. We assume w.l.o.g. that the first m entries in Y correspond to the m labeled training examples. Let $P = (I - \alpha L)^{-1}$. The CM algorithm produces soft-classification $F = P \cdot Y$. In other words, if p_{ij} is the (i, j)th entry of P and f_i is the ith entry of F, the point x_i receives the soft-classification

$$f_i = \sum_{j=1}^{m} p_{ij}y_j .$$ (29)

To obtain useful bounds on the (weak) stability of CM we require the following benign technical modifications of CM that would not change the *hard* classification it generates over test set examples.

1. We prevent over-fitting to the training set by setting $p_{ii} = 0$.
2. To enable a comparison between stability values corresponding to different settings of the parameters α and σ, we ensure that the dynamic range of f_i is normalized w.r.t. different values of α and σ. That is, instead of using (29) for prediction we use

$$f_i = \frac{\sum_{j=1}^{m} p_{ij}y_j}{\sum_{j=1}^{m} p_{ij}} .$$ (30)

The first modification prevents possible over-fitting to the training set since for any $i \in I_1^{m+u}$, in the original CM the value of p_{ii} is much larger than any of the other p_{ij}, $j \neq i$, and therefore, the soft classification of the training example x_i is almost completely determined by its given label y_i. Hence by (29), when x_i is exchanged with some test set example x_j, the soft classification change of x_i will probably be large. Therefore, the stability condition (18) cannot be satisfied with small values of β_2. By setting $p_{ii} = 0$ we prevent this problem and only affect the soft and hard classification of training examples (and keep the soft classifications of test points intact). The second modification clearly changes the dynamic range of all soft classifications but does not alter any hard classification.

To use our stability estimation algorithm one should provide an implementation of diff. We show that for the CM algorithm diff($\tilde{X}_m, \tilde{X}_u, i, j, r | S_m$) can be effectively implemented as follows. For notational convenience we assume here (and also in Definition 4) that examples in $\tilde{X}_m$ have indices in I_1^m. Let $\tau(r) = \sum_{k=1, k \neq i}^{m} p_{rk}$ and $\tau_y(r) = \sum_{k=1, k \neq i}^{m} p_{rk} y_k$. It follows from (30) that

$$\left| A_{\tilde{S}_m, \tilde{X}_u}(x_r) - A_{\tilde{S}_m^{ij}, \tilde{X}_u^{ij}}(x_r) \right| == \left| \frac{(p_{rj} - p_{ri}) \cdot \sum_{k=1, k \neq i, x_k \notin X_m}^{m} p_{rk} y_k + T}{(\tau(r) + p_{ri})(\tau(r) + p_{rj})} \right|, \tag{31}$$

where $T \overset{\Delta}{=} (p_{rj} - p_{ri}) \cdot \sum_{k=1, k \neq i, x_k \in X_m}^{m} p_{rk} y_k + \tau(r) \cdot (p_{ri} y_i - p_{rj} y_j) + p_{ri} p_{rj} (y_i - y_j)$.

To implement $\texttt{diff}(\tilde{X}_m, \tilde{X}_u, i, j, r | S_m)$ we should upper bound (31). Suppose first that the values of y_i and y_j are known. Then, T is constant and the only unknowns in (31) are the y_k's in the first summation. Observe that (31) is maximal when all values of these y_k's are -1 or all of them are $+1$. Hence by taking the maximum over these possibilities we obtain an upper bound on (31). If y_i (or y_j) is unknown then, similarly, for each of its possible assignments we compute (31) and take the maximum. In the worst case, when both y_i and y_j are unknown, we compute the maximum of (31) over the eight possible assignments for these two variables and the y_k's in the first summation. it can be verified that the time complexity of the above $\texttt{diff}$ oracle is $O(m)$.

We now show two numerical examples of stability estimations for the CM algorithm with respect to two UCI datasets. These results were obtained by implementing the modified CM algorithm and the stability estimation routine applied with the above implementation of $\texttt{diff}$. For each "experiment" we ran the modified CM algorithm with 21 different hyper-parameter settings for α and σ, each resulting in a different application of the algorithm.[7]

We considered two UCI datasets, musk and mush. From each dataset we generated 30 random full samples X_{m+u} each consisting of 400 points. We divided each full sample instance to equally sized training and test sets uniformly at random. The high confidence (95%) estimation of stability parameter β_1 (see Definition 3) w.r.t. $\delta_1^a = \delta_1^b = 0.1$, and the corresponding empirical and true risks are shown in Fig. 1. The graphs for the β_2 parameter are qualitatively similar and are omitted here. Indices in the x-axis correspond to the 21 applications of CM and are sorted in increasing order of true risk. Each stability and error value depicted is an average over the 30 random full samples. We also depict a high confidence (95%) true stability estimates, obtained *in hindsight* by using the unknown labels in the computation of $\texttt{diff}$. The uniform stability graphs correspond to *lower bounds* obtained by taking the maximal soft classification change encountered while estimating the true weak stability.

It is evident that the (true) weak stability is often significantly lower than the (lower bound on) the uniform stability. In cases where the weak and uniform stabilities are similar, the CM algorithm performs poorly. The estimated weak stability behaves qualitatively the same as the true weak stability. When the uniform stability obtains lower values the algorithm performs very poorly. This may indicate that a good uniform stability is correlated with degenerated behavior (similar phenomenon was observed in [2]). In contrast, we see that very

---

[7] We naively took $\alpha \in \{0.01, 0.5, 0.99\}$ and $\sigma \in \{0.1, 0.2, 0.3, 0.4, 0.5, 1, 2\}$ and these were our first and only choices.

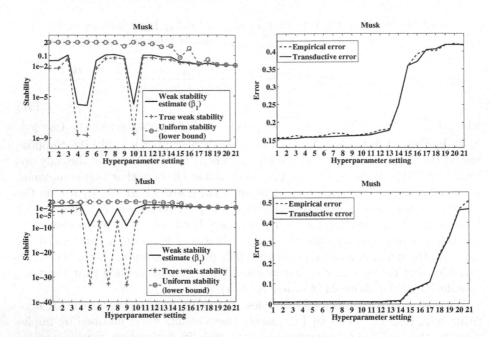

Fig. 1. Stability estimates (left) and the corresponding empirical/true errors (right) for musk and mush datasets

good weak stability can coincide with very high performance. Finally, we note that these graphs do not demonstrate that good weak stability is proportional to low discrepancy between the empirical end true errors.

7 Concluding Remarks

This paper has presented new error bounds for transductive learning. The bounds are based on novel definitions of uniform and weak transductive stability. We have also shown that weak transductive stability can be bounded with high confidence in a data-dependent manner and demonstrated the application of this estimation routine on a known transductive algorithm. As far as we know this is the first attempt to generate truly data-dependent high confidence stability estimates based on all available information including the labeled samples.

We note that similar risk bounds based on weak stability can be obtained for induction. However, the adaptation of Definition 3 to induction (see also inductive definitions of weak stability in [10, 12, 15]) depends on the probability space of training sets, which is unknown in general. This prevents the estimation of weak stability using our method.

As discussed, to derive stability bounds with sufficient confidence our stability estimation routine is required to run in $\Omega(m^4(m+u))$ time, which precluded, at this stage, an empirical evaluation of our bounds. In future work we will attempt to overcome this obstacle by tightening our bound, perhaps using the techniques from [13, 17]. A second direction would be to develop a more suitable weak stability definition. We also plan to consider other known transductive algorithms and develop for them a suitable implementation of the diff oracle.

References

1. K. Azuma. Weighted sums of certain dependent random variables. *Tohoku Mathematical Journal*, 19:357–367, 1967.
2. M. Belkin, I. Matveeva, and P. Niyogi. Regularization and semi-supervised learning on large graphs. In *COLT*, pages 624–638, 2004.
3. A. Blum and J. Langford. PAC-MDL Bounds. In *COLT*, pages 344–357, 2003.
4. O. Bousquet and A. Elisseeff. Stability and generalization. *Journal of Machine Learning Research*, 2:499–526, 2002.
5. P. Derbeko, R. El-Yaniv, and R. Meir. Explicit learning curves for transduction and application to clustering and compression algorithms. *Journal of Artificial Intelligence Research*, 22:117–142, 2004.
6. L. Devroye, L. Györfi, and G. Lugosi. *A Probabilistic Theory of Pattern Recognition*. Springer Verlag, New York, 1996.
7. G.R. Grimmett and D.R. Stirzaker. *Probability and Random Processes*. Oxford Science Publications, 1995. Second edition.
8. T.M. Huang and V. Kecman. Performance comparisons of semi-supervised learning algorithms. In *ICML Workshop "Learning with Partially Classified Training Data"*, pages 45–49, 2005.
9. D. Hush, C. Scovel, and I. Steinwart. Stability of unstable learning algorithms. Technical Report LA-UR-03-4845, Los Alamos National Laboratory, 2003.
10. M. Kearns and D. Ron. Algorithmic stability and sanity-check bounds for leave-one-out cross-validation. *Neural Computation*, 11(6):1427–1453, 1999.
11. S. Kutin. Extensions to McDiarmid's inequality when differences are bounded with high probability. Technical Report TR-2002-04, University of Chicago, 2002.
12. S. Kutin and P. Niyogi. Almost-everywhere algorithmic stability and generalization error. In *UAI*, pages 275–282, 2002.
13. M. Ledoux. *The concentration of measure phenomenon*. Number 89 in Mathematical Surveys and Monographs. American Mathematical Society, 2001.
14. G.S. Manku, S. Rajagopalan, and B.G. Lindsay. Approximate medians and other quantiles in one pass and with limited memory. In *SIGMOD*, volume 28, pages 426–435, 1998.
15. S. Mukherjee, P. Niyogi, T. Poggio, and R. Rifkin. Statistical learning: Stability is sufficient for generalization and necessary and sufficient for consistency of empirical risk minimization. Technical Report AI Memo 2002–024, MIT, 2004.
16. A. Rakhlin, S. Mukherjee, and T. Poggio. Stability results in learning theory. *Analysis and Applications*, 3(4):397–419, 2005.
17. M. Talagrand. *Majorizing measures: the generic chaining*. Springer Verlag, 2005.
18. V. N. Vapnik. *Estimation of Dependences Based on Empirical Data*. Springer Verlag, New York, 1982.
19. V. N. Vapnik. *Statistical Learning Theory*. Wiley Interscience, New York, 1998.
20. D. Zhou, O. Bousquet, T.N. Lal, J. Weston, and B. Scholkopf. Learning with local and global consistency. In *NIPS*, pages 321–328, 2003.
21. X. Zhu, Z. Ghahramani, and J.D. Lafferty. Semi-supervised learning using gaussian fields and harmonic functions. In *ICML*, pages 912–919, 2003.

Uniform Convergence of Adaptive Graph-Based Regularization

Matthias Hein

Max Planck Institute for Biological Cybernetics, Tübingen, Germany

Abstract. The regularization functional induced by the graph Laplacian of a random neighborhood graph based on the data is adaptive in two ways. First it adapts to an underlying manifold structure and second to the density of the data-generating probability measure. We identify in this paper the limit of the regularizer and show uniform convergence over the space of Hölder functions. As an intermediate step we derive upper bounds on the covering numbers of Hölder functions on compact Riemannian manifolds, which are of independent interest for the theoretical analysis of manifold-based learning methods.

1 Introduction

Naturally graphs are inherently discrete objects. However if there exists an underlying continuous structure certain neighborhood graphs can be seen as approximations of the underlying continuous structure. The main goal of this paper is to show how that the smoothness functional $S(f)$ induced by the graph Laplacian of a neighborhood graph built from random samples can be defined in such a way that its continuum limit approximates a desired continuous quantity.

In principle such considerations have been the motivation to build algorithms based on the graph Laplacian for dimensionality reduction, clustering and semi-supervised learning, see e.g. [2, 1, 15, 6]. However the theoretical study of this motivation in particular when the data in $\mathbb{R}^d$ lies on a Euclidean submanifold has been only started quite recently. In [9], see also [3], it was shown that the pointwise limit of the normalized graph Laplacian is the weighted Laplace Beltrami operator. The first work where the limit of $S(f)$ has been studied was [4]. There the limit of $S(f)$ for a single function in the case when the data generating probability measure P has full support in $\mathbb{R}^d$ was derived in a two step process, first $n \to \infty$, then letting the neighborhood size $h \to 0$. In this paper we extend this result in several ways. First we extend it to the setting where the data lies on a submanifold[1] M of $\mathbb{R}^d$, second we introduce data-dependent weights for the graph which are used to control the influence of the density p of P on the limit functional, third we do the limit process $n \to \infty$ and $h \to 0$ simultaneously, so that we actually get rates for $h(n)$ and finally we perform this limit uniformly over the function space of Hölder functions.

---

[1] All the results apply also in the case where P has full d-dimensional support in $\mathbb{R}^d$.

G. Lugosi and H.U. Simon (Eds.): COLT 2006, LNAI 4005, pp. 50–64, 2006.
© Springer-Verlag Berlin Heidelberg 2006

We include also an extensive discussion of the properties of the limit smoothness functional and why and how it can be interesting in different learning algorithms such as regression, semi-supervised learning and clustering. In particular the adaptation to the two independent structures inherent to the data, the geometry of the data manifold M and the density p of P, are discussed.

2 Regularization with the Graph Laplacian and Its Continuous Limit

The first part of this section introduces the smoothness functional induced by the graph Laplacian for an undirected graph, in particular the neighborhood graph studied in this paper. In the second part we will sketch our main result, the uniform convergence of the smoothness functional induced by the graph Laplacian over the space of α-Hoelder functions. In particular we study the adaptation of the continuous limit functional to the geometry of the data manifold and the density of the data generating measure and possible applications thereof in semi-supervised learning, regression and clustering.

2.1 The Graph Laplacian and Its Induced Smoothness Functional

Let (V, E) be a undirected graph, where V is the set of vertices with $|V| = n$ and E the set of edges. Since the graph is undirected we have a symmetric adjacency matrix W. Moreover we define the degree function as $d_i = \sum_{j=1}^{n} w_{ij}$. Then it can be shown, see [9], that once one has fixed Hilbert spaces $\mathcal{H}_V, \mathcal{H}_E$ of functions on V and E and a discrete differential operator $\nabla : \mathcal{H}_V \to \mathcal{H}_E$, the graph Laplacian[2] $\Delta : \mathcal{H}_V \to \mathcal{H}_V$ is defined as $\Delta = \nabla^*\nabla$, where ∇^* is the adjoint of d. In the literature one mainly finds two types of graph Laplacian, the normalized one $\Delta_{\text{norm}} = \mathbb{1} - D^{-1}W$ and the unnormalized one $\Delta_{\text{unnorm}} = D - W$, where $D_{ij} = d_i\delta_{ij}$. The smoothness functional $S(f) : \mathcal{H}_V \to \mathbb{R}_+$ induced by the graph Laplacian is defined as

$$S(f) = \langle \nabla f, \nabla f \rangle_{\mathcal{H}_E} = \langle f, \Delta f \rangle_{\mathcal{H}_V}.$$

Note that $S(f)$ defines a semi-norm on $\mathcal{H}_V$. It is can be shown that Δ_{norm} and Δ_{unnorm} induce the same $S(f)$ explicitly given as:

$$S(f) = \frac{1}{2\,n(n-1)} \sum_{i \neq j}^{n} w_{ij}\big(f(i) - f(j)\big)^2.$$

$S(f)$ coincides for the two graph Laplacians since $S(f)$ is independent of the choice of the inner product in $\mathcal{H}_V$, see [8, sec. 2.1.5]. Note that the smoothness functional $S(f)$ penalizes a discrete version of the first derivative of f.

In this paper we study certain neighborhood graphs that is the weights depend on the Euclidean distance. The vertex set is an i.i.d. sample $\{X_i\}_{i=1}^{n}$ of the data

---

[2] This holds also for directed graphs, see [8, sec. 2.1].

generating probability measure P. Of special interest is the case where P has support on a m-dimensional submanifold M in $\mathbb{R}^d$. Similar to Coifman and Lafon in [6] for the continuous case we define the weights of the graph as follows:

$$w_{\lambda,h,n}(X_i, X_j) = \frac{1}{h^m} \frac{k(\|i(X_i) - i(X_j)\|^2 / h^2)}{(d_{h,n}(X_i) d_{h,n}(X_j))^{\lambda}}, \quad \lambda \in \mathbb{R}.$$

where $d_{h,n}(X_i) = \frac{1}{nh^m} \sum_{j=1}^{n} k(\|X_i - X_j\|^2 / h^2)$ is the degree function corresponding to the weights k. Note that since k is assumed to have compact support, the parameter h determines the neighborhood of a point. We will denote by $S_{\lambda,h,n}(f)$ the smoothness functional with respect to the weights $w_{\lambda,h,n}$,

$$S_{\lambda,h,n}(f) = \frac{1}{2\,n(n-1)h^2} \sum_{i,j=1}^{n} (f(X_j) - f(X_i))^2 w_{\lambda,h,n}(X_i, X_j).$$

2.2   The Continuous Regularizer Induced by the Weighted Laplacian

The weighted Laplacian is the natural extension of the Laplace-Beltrami operator[3] on a Riemannian manifold, when the manifold is equipped with a measure P which is in our case the probability measure generating the data.

Definition 1 (Weighted Laplacian). *Let (M, g_{ab}) be a Riemannian manifold with measure P where P has a differentiable density p with respect to the natural volume element $dV = \sqrt{\det g}\, dx$, and let Δ_M be the Laplace-Beltrami operator on M. Then we define the s-th weighted Laplacian Δ_s as*

$$\Delta_s := \Delta_M + \frac{s}{p} g^{ab}(\nabla_a p)\nabla_b = \frac{1}{p^s} g^{ab}\nabla_a(p^s\nabla_b) = \frac{1}{p^s} \operatorname{div}(p^s \operatorname{grad}). \tag{1}$$

The weighted Laplacian induces a smoothness functional $S_{\Delta_s} : C_c^{\infty}(M) \to \mathbb{R}_+$,

$$S_{\Delta_s}(f) := -\int_M f(\Delta_s f)\, p^s\, dV = \int_M \langle \nabla f, \nabla f \rangle\, p^s\, dV,$$

The following sketch of our main Theorem 6 shows that one can choose a function $h(n)$ such that $S_{\lambda,h,n}(f)$ approximates $S_{\Delta_\gamma}(f)$ uniformly for $\gamma = 2 - 2\lambda$.

Sketch of main result. *Let $\mathcal{F}_\alpha(s)$ be the ball of radius s in the space of Hölder functions on M. Define $\gamma = 2 - 2\lambda$, then there exists a constant c depending only on k such that for $\alpha \geq 3$ and $h(n) = O(n^{-\frac{\alpha}{2\alpha+2m+m^2+m\alpha}})$,*

$$\sup_{f \in \mathcal{F}_\alpha(s)} \left| S_{\lambda,h,n}(f) - c\,S_{\Delta_\gamma}(f) \right| = O\left(n^{-\frac{\alpha}{2\alpha+2m+m^2+m\alpha}} \right) \quad a.s.$$

---

[3] The Laplace-Beltrami operator on a manifold M is the natural equivalent of the Laplacian in $\mathbb{R}^d$, defined as

$$\Delta_M f = \operatorname{div}(\operatorname{grad} f) = \nabla^a \nabla_a f$$

We refer to Section 4 for a more detailed account of the results. Let us analyze now the properties of the limit smoothness functional S_{Δ_γ}

$$S_{\Delta_\gamma}(f) = \int_M \|\nabla f\|_{T_x M}^2 \, p(x)^{2-2\lambda} \sqrt{\det g}\, dx$$

Note first that $\|\nabla f\|_{T_x M}$ is the norm of the gradient of f on M. The meaning becomes clearer when we express $\|f\|_{T_x M}$ as a local Lipschitz constant[4] $L_x^M(f)$,

$$\|\nabla f\|_{T_x M} = L_x^M(f) = \sup_{y \in M} \frac{|f(x) - f(y)|}{d_M(x,y)} \neq \sup_{y \in M} \frac{|f(x) - f(y)|}{\|x - y\|} = L_x^{\mathbb{R}^d}(f)$$

Most important the smoothness of f is measured with respect to the metric of M or in other words with respect to the intrinsic parameterization. That is a small $\|f\|_{T_x M}$ implies that $f(x) \simeq f(y)$ if x and y are close in the metric of M but not in the metric[5] of $\mathbb{R}^d$. Therefore as desired the graph Laplacian based smoothness functional adapts to the intrinsic geometry of the data.

Next we motivate how the adaptation to the density p controlled by λ can be used in learning algorithms. For $\gamma > 0$ the functional S_{Δ_γ} prefers functions f which are smooth in high-density regions whereas changes are less penalized in low-density regions. This is a desired property for semi-supervised learning where one assumes especially if one has only a few labeled points that the classifier should be almost constant in high-density regions whereas changes of the classifier are allowed in low-density regions, see e.g [4]. However also the case $\gamma < 0$ is interesting. Then minimizing $S_{\Delta_\gamma}(f)$ implies the opposite: smoothness of the function f is enforced where one has little data, and more variation of f is allowed where more data points are sampled. Such a penalization seems appropriate for regression and has been considered by Canu and Elisseeff in [5]. Another application is spectral clustering. The eigenfunctions of Δ_γ can be seen as the limit partioning of spectral clustering for the normalized graph Laplacian (however a rigorous proof has not been given yet). We show now that for $\gamma > 0$ the eigenfunction correponding to the first non-zero eigenvalue is likely to change its sign in a low-density region. Let us assume for a moment that M is compact without boundary and that $p(x) > 0, \forall x \in M$, then the eigenspace for the first eigenvalue $\lambda_0 = 0$ is given by the constant functions. The next eigenvalue λ_1 can be determined by the Rayleigh-Ritz variational principle

$$\lambda_1 = \inf_{u \in C^\infty(M)} \left\{ \frac{\int_M \|\nabla u\|^2 p(x)^\gamma dV(x)}{\int_M u^2(x) p(x)^\gamma dV(x)} \, \Big| \, \int_M u(x) p(x)^\gamma dV(x) = 0 \right\}.$$

Since the first eigenfunction has to be orthogonal to the constant functions, it has to change its sign. However since $\|\nabla u\|^2$ is weighted by p^γ it is obvious that for $\gamma > 0$ the function changes its sign in a region of low density.

---

[4] f is continuously differentiable so both terms coincide.

[5] Note that small $\|x - y\|$ does not imply that $d_M(x,y)$ is small e.g. imagine a spiral.

3   Covering Numbers for α-Hölder Functions on Compact Riemannian Manifolds with Boundary

In this section we derive bounds on the covering numbers of α-Hölder functions on compact Riemannian manifolds with boundary. This generalizes the classical bounds for Euclidean space derived by Kolmogorov and Tihomirov [12, 14]. We use in this section the following short notation: For any vector $k = (k_1, \ldots, k_d)$ of d integers, $D^k = \frac{\partial^k}{\partial x_1^{k_1} \ldots \partial x_d^{k_d}}$ with $k = \sum_{i=1}^{d} k_i$.

3.1   Technicalities on Compact Riemannian Manifolds with Boundary

We briefly introduce the framework of manifolds with boundary of bounded geometry developed by Schick in [13] for non-compact Riemannian manifolds, which we will use frequently in the following. It makes explicit several geometric properties which are usually implicitly assumed due to compactness of the manifold. Note that the boundary ∂M is an isometric submanifold of M. It has a second fundamental form $\overline{II}$ which should not be mixed up with the second fundamental form II of M with respect to the ambient space $\mathbb{R}^d$. We denote by $\overline{\nabla}$ the connection and by $\overline{R}$ the curvature of ∂M. Moreover let ν be the normal inward vector field at ∂M and let K be the normal geodesic flow defined as $K : \partial M \times [0, \infty) \to M : (x', t) \to \exp_{x'}^M(t\nu_{x'})$. Then the collar set $N(s)$ is defined as $N(s) := K(\partial M \times [0, s])$ for $s \geq 0$.

Definition 2 (Manifold with boundary of bounded geometry). *Let M be a manifold with boundary ∂M (possibly empty). It has bounded geometry if the following holds:*

- *(N) Normal Collar: there exists $r_C > 0$ so that the geodesic collar*

$$\partial M \times [0, r_C) \to M : (t, x) \to \exp_x(t\nu_x)$$

  is a diffeomorphism onto its image (ν_x is the inward normal vector).
- *(IC) The injectivity radius[6] $r_{\mathrm{inj}}(\partial M)$ of ∂M is positive.*
- *(I) Injectivity radius of M: There is $r_i > 0$ so that if $r \leq r_i$ then for $x \in M \backslash N(r)$ the exponential map is a diffeomorphism on $B_M(0, r) \subset T_x M$ so that normal coordinates are defined on every ball $B_M(x, r)$ for $x \in M \backslash N(r)$.*
- *(B) Curvature bounds: For every $k \in \mathbb{N}$ there is C_k so that $|\nabla^i R| \leq C_k$ and $\overline{\nabla}^i \overline{II} \leq C_k$ for $0 \leq i \leq k$.*

The injectivity radius makes no sense at the boundary since $\mathrm{inj}(x) \to 0$ as $d(x, \partial M) \to 0$. Therefore we replace next to the boundary normal coordinates with normal collar coordinates. In our proofs we divide M into the set $N(r)$[7] and $M \backslash N(r)$. On $M \backslash N(r)$ we work like on a manifold without boundary and on $N(r)$ we use normal collar coordinates defined below.

---

[6] The injectivity radius $\mathrm{inj}(x)$ at a point x is the largest r such that the exponential map $\exp_x$ is defined on $B_{\mathbb{R}^m}(0, r)$ and injective. In general we refer the reader to Section 2.2. of [8] for basic notions of differential geometry needed in this paper.

[7] Note that for sufficiently small r, $N(r) = \{x \in M \mid d(x, \partial M) \leq r\}$.

Definition 3 (normal collar coordinates). *Let M be a Riemannian manifold with boundary ∂M. Fix $x' \in \partial M$ and an orthonormal basis of $T_{x'}\partial M$ to identify $T_{x'}\partial M$ with $\mathbb{R}^{m-1}$. For $r_1, r_2 > 0$ sufficiently small (such that the following map is injective) define normal collar coordinates,*

$$n_{x'} : B_{\mathbb{R}^{m-1}}(0, r_1) \times [0, r_2] \to M : (v, t) \to \exp^M_{\exp^{\partial M}_{x'}(v)}(t\nu).$$

The tuple (r_1, r_2) is called the width of the normal collar chart $n_{x'}$ and we denote by $n(x', r_1, r_2)$ the set $n_{x'}(B_{\mathbb{R}^{m-1}}(0, r_1) \times [0, r_2])$.

We denote further by $n(x, r)$ the set $\exp_x(B_{\mathbb{R}^m}(0, r))$. The next lemma is often used in the following.

Lemma 1 ([13]). *Let (M, g) be a m-dimensional Riemannian manifold with boundary of bounded geometry. Then there exists $R_0 > 0$ and constants $S_1 > 0$ and S_2 such that for all $x \in M$ and $r \leq R_0$ one has*

$$S_1 r^m \leq \mathrm{vol}(B_M(x, r)) \leq S_2 r^m, \quad \forall x \in M$$
$$S_1 r^m \leq \mathrm{vol}(n(x', r, r)) \leq S_2 r^m, \quad \forall x' \in \partial M$$

Definition 4 (radius of curvature). *The radius of curvature of M is defined as $\rho = \frac{1}{\Pi_{\max} + \overline{\Pi}_{\max}}$, where $\Pi_{\max} = \sup_{x \in M} \|\Pi\|_x$ and $\overline{\Pi}_{\max} = \sup_{x \in \partial M} \|\overline{\Pi}\|_x$.*

The radius of curvature tells us how much the manifold M and its boundary ∂M are curved with respect to the ambient space $\mathbb{R}^d$. It is used in the next lemma to compare distances in $\mathbb{R}^d$ with distances in M.

Lemma 2 ([8]). *Let M have a finite radius of curvature $\rho > 0$. We further assume that $\kappa := \inf_{x \in M} \inf_{y \in M \setminus B_M(x, \pi\rho)} \|x - y\| > 0$. Then $B_{\mathbb{R}^d}(x, \kappa/2) \cap M \subset B_M(x, \kappa) \subset B_M(x, \pi\rho)$. Particularly, if $x, y \in M$ and $\|x - y\| \leq \kappa/2$,*

$$\frac{1}{2} d_M(x, y) \leq \|x - y\|_{\mathbb{R}^d} \leq d_M(x, y) \leq \kappa.$$

Note that for a compact manifold (with boundary) one has $\rho > 0$ and $\kappa > 0$.

3.2 Covering Numbers for α-Hölder Functions

Definition 5 (α-Hölder functions). *For $\alpha > 0$ denote by $\underline{\alpha}$ the greatest integer smaller than α. Let M be a compact Riemannian manifold and let $(U_i, \phi_i)_{i \in I}$ be an atlas of normal coordinate charts, $\phi_i : U_i \subset \mathbb{R}^m \to M$, such that $M \subset \cup_i \phi_i(U_i)$. Then for a $C^{\underline{\alpha}}$-function $f : M \to \mathbb{R}$, let*

$$\|f\|_\alpha = \max_{k \leq \underline{\alpha}} \sup_{i \in I} \sup_{x \in U_i} \left| D^k(f \circ \phi_i)(x) \right|$$

$$+ \max_{k = \underline{\alpha}} \sup_{i \in I} \sup_{x, y \in U_i} \frac{\left| D^k(f \circ \phi_i)(x) - D^k(f \circ \phi_i)(y) \right|}{d(x, y)^{\alpha - \underline{\alpha}}}$$

The function space $\mathcal{F}_\alpha = \{f \in C^{\underline{\alpha}} \mid \|f\|_\alpha < \infty\}$ is the Banach space of Hölder functions. $\mathcal{F}_\alpha(s)$ denotes a ball of radius s in $\mathcal{F}_\alpha$. We define further

$$\|f\|_{C^k(M)} = \max_{k \leq \underline{\alpha}} \sup_{i \in I} \sup_{x \in U_i} \left| D^k(f \circ \phi_i)(x) \right|.$$

Note that since all transition maps between normal charts and their derivatives are uniformly bounded the above definition of $\|f\|_{C^k(M)}$ could be equivalently replaced[8] with the invariant (coordinate independent) norm of the k-th derivatives defined by Hebey in [7] as, $\left\|\nabla^k f\right\|^2 = g^{i_1 j_1} \ldots g^{i_k j_k} \nabla_{i_1} \ldots \nabla_{i_k} f \nabla_{j_1} \ldots \nabla_{j_k} f$. For the Lipschitz type condition it is unclear if there exists an equivalent invariant definition. However the following results for $\mathcal{F}_\alpha$ remain true if we assume that the $\underline{\alpha} + 1$-first derivatives are uniformly bounded. This small change leads for sure to a norm which is equivalent to a coordinate independent norm on M.

In order to construct a convering of $\mathcal{F}_\alpha$ we first need a covering of M with normal and normal collar charts.

Theorem 1. *Let M be a compact m-dimensional Riemannian manifold and let $\epsilon \leq \min\{R_0, \text{inj}(\partial M), r_i\}$. Then there exists a maximal ϵ-separated subset $T_1 := \{x'_{i_1}\}_{i \in I_1}$ of ∂M and a maximal ϵ-separated subset $T_2 := \{x_{i_2}\}_{i \in I_2}$ of $M \backslash N(\epsilon)$ such that*

- $N(\epsilon) \subset \bigcup_{i \in I_1} n(x'_i, \epsilon, \epsilon)$ *and* $M \backslash N(\epsilon) \subset \bigcup_{i \in I_2} n(x_i, \epsilon)$,
- $|I_1| \leq 2\frac{S_2 \, \text{vol}(\partial M)}{S_1} \left(\frac{2}{\epsilon}\right)^{m-1}$, *and* $|I_2| \leq \frac{\text{vol}(M)}{S_1} \left(\frac{2}{\epsilon}\right)^m$.

Theorem 2. *Let M be a compact m-dimensional manifold and let $s > 0$ and $\epsilon \leq (3se^{2m})(\min\{R_0, \text{inj}(\partial M), r_i\})^\alpha$. Then there exists a constant K depending only on α, m and M such that*

$$\log \mathcal{N}(\epsilon, \mathcal{F}_\alpha(s), \|\cdot\|_\infty) \leq K \left(\frac{s}{\epsilon}\right)^{\frac{m}{\alpha}}$$

The proof of these theorems can be found in the appendix. The main differences of the proof of Theorem 2 to the classical one in [12, 14] are that the function and its derivatives are discretized in different normal charts so that one has to check that coordinate changes between these normal charts do not destroy the usual argument and an explicit treatment of the boundary.

4 Uniform Convergence of the Smoothness Functional Induced by the Graph Laplacian

4.1 Assumptions

We ignore in this paper measurability problems, see [14] for a discussion. All results in this section are formulated under the following assumptions on the submanifold M, the density p and the kernel k:

Assumption 1. – $i : M \to \mathbb{R}^d$ *is a smooth, isometric embedding,*
- M *is a smooth compact manifold with boundary (∂M can be empty),*
- P *has a density p with respect to the natural volume element dV on M,*
- $p \in C^3(M)$ *and $p(x) > 0, \forall\, x \in M$,*

---

[8] In the sense that the resulting norms are equivalent.

- the sample $X_i, i = 1, \ldots, n$ is drawn i.i.d. from P.
- $k : \mathbb{R}_+^* \to \mathbb{R}$ is measurable, non-negative and non-increasing,
- $k \in C^2(\mathbb{R}_+^*)$, that is in particular k, $\frac{\partial k}{\partial x}$ and $\frac{\partial^2 k}{\partial x^2}$ are bounded,
- k has compact support on $[0, R_k^2]$,
- $k(0) = 0$, and $\exists r_k > 0$ such that $k(x) \geq \frac{\|k\|_\infty}{2}$ for $x \in]0, r_k]$.

Since M is compact, M is automatically a manifold of bounded geometry. In particular all curvatures (intrinsic as well as extrinsic) are bounded. In order to emphasize the distinction between extrinsic and intrinsic properties of the manifold we always use the slightly cumbersome notations $x \in M$ (intrinsic) and $i(x) \in \mathbb{R}^d$ (extrinsic). The kernel functions k which are used to define the weights of the graph are always functions of the squared norm in $\mathbb{R}^d$. The condition $k(0) = 0$ implies that the graph has no loops[9]. In particular the kernel is not continuous at the origin. All statements could also be proved without this condition. The advantage of this condition is that some estimators become thereby unbiased. Finally let us introduce the notation , $k_h(t) = \frac{1}{h^m} k \left(\frac{t}{h^2} \right)$. and the following two constants related to the kernel function k,

$$C_1 = \int_{\mathbb{R}^m} k(\|y\|^2) dy < \infty, \quad C_2 = \int_{\mathbb{R}^m} k(\|y\|^2) y_1^2 dy < \infty. \tag{2}$$

4.2 Results and Proofs

The smoothness functional $S_{\lambda,h,n}(f)$ has been defined in Section 2 as

$$S_{\lambda,h,n}(f) = \frac{1}{2\,n(n-1)h^2} \sum_{i,j=1}^{n} (f(X_j) - f(X_i))^2 \frac{1}{h^m} \frac{k(\|i(X_i) - i(X_j)\|^2 / h^2)}{(d_{h,n}(X_i) d_{h,n}(X_j))^\lambda}.$$

Note that this sum is a U-statistic of order 2. We define further p_h as the convolution of the density with the kernel

$$p_h(x) = \int_M k_h(\|i(x) - i(y)\|^2) p(y) \sqrt{\det g}\, dy. \tag{3}$$

and $\tilde{S}_{\lambda,h,n}(f)$ as $S_{\lambda,h,n}(f)$ with $d_{h,n}(x)$ replaced by $p_h(x)$. The following proposition will be often used.

Proposition 1 ([9]). *For any $x \in M \backslash \partial M$, there exists an $h_0(x) > 0$ such that for all $h < h_0(x)$ and any $f \in C^3(M)$,*

$$\int_M k_h \left(\|i(x) - i(y)\|_{\mathbb{R}^d}^2 \right) f(y) p(y) \sqrt{\det g}\, dy$$

$$= C_1 p(x) f(x) + \frac{h^2}{2} C_2 \Big(p(x) f(x) S(x) + (\Delta_M (pf))(x) \Big) + O(h^3),$$

where $S(x) = \frac{1}{2} \Big[- R\big|_x + \frac{1}{2} \|\sum_a \Pi(\partial_a, \partial_a)\|_{T_{i(x)} \mathbb{R}^d}^2 \Big]$ and $O(h^3)$ is a function depending on x, $\|f\|_{C^3}$ and $\|p\|_{C^3}$.

---

[9] An edge from a vertex to itself is called a loop.

Furthermore we use the following result which basically identifies the extended degree-function of the graph defined as $d_{h,n}(x) = \frac{1}{n}\sum_{i=1}^{n} k_h(\|x - X_i\|)$, as a kernel density estimator on the submanifold M.

Proposition 2 (Pointwise consistency of $d_{h,n}(x)$ [8]). *Let $x \in M/\partial M$, then there exist constants b_1, b_2 such that*

$$\mathrm{P}(|d_{h,n}(x) - p_h(x)| > \epsilon) \leq 2\exp\left(-\frac{nh^m\,\epsilon^2}{2b_2 + 2/3b_1\,\epsilon}\right)$$

In particular if $h \to 0$ and $nh^m/\log n \to \infty$, $\lim_{n\to\infty} d_{h,n}(x) = C_1\,p(x)$ a.s..

We refer to [8] for a comparison with a similar result of Hendricks et al. in [10]. In [8] the limit of the smoothness functional $S_{\lambda,h,n}$ was shown for a single function using a Bernstein-type inequality of Hoeffding [11] for U-statistics.

Theorem 3 (Strong consistency of the smoothness functional $S_{\lambda,h,n}$). *Let $f \in C^3(M)$. If $h \to 0$ and $nh^m/\log n \to \infty$,*

$$\lim_{n\to\infty} S_{\lambda,h,n}(f) = \frac{C_2}{2C_1^\lambda}\int_M \|\nabla f\|_{T_x M}^2\, p(x)^{2-2\lambda}\sqrt{\det g}\, dx, \quad \text{almost surely.}$$

We extend now this theorem to uniform convergence over balls in the function space of α-Hölder functions. As a first step we prove an abstract uniform convergence result without specifying the function class $\mathcal{F}$.

Theorem 4. *Let $\mathcal{F}$ be a function class with $\sup_{f\in\mathcal{F}}\sup_{x\in M}\|\nabla_x f\| \leq s$. Then there exist constants $C', C > 0$ such that for all $\frac{C's^2}{nh^m} < \epsilon < 1/C$ and $0 < h < h_{\max}$, with probability greater than $1 - 2\left(C\,n + \mathcal{N}\left(\frac{\epsilon h^{m+1}}{2C\,s}, \mathcal{F}, \|\cdot\|_\infty\right)\right)e^{-\frac{nh^m\,(1/s)^4\,\epsilon^2}{4C}}$,*

$$\sup_{f\in\mathcal{F}}\left|S_{\lambda,h,n}(f) - \mathbb{E}\,\tilde{S}_{\lambda,h,n}(f)\right| \leq \epsilon$$

Proof. First we decompose the term as follows:

$$\sup_{f\in\mathcal{F}}|S_{\lambda,h,n}(f) - \mathbb{E}\,\tilde{S}_{\lambda,h,n}(f)|$$

$$\leq \sup_{f\in\mathcal{F}}|S_{\lambda,h,n}(f) - \tilde{S}_{\lambda,h,n}(f)| + \sup_{f\in\mathcal{F}}|\tilde{S}_{\lambda,h,n}(f) - \mathbb{E}\,\tilde{S}_{\lambda,h,n}(f)| =: I + II$$

We start with the term I. Define $U_{n,h}(f) = \frac{2R_k^2\,s^2}{n(n-1)}\sum_{i,j=1}^{n} k_h(\|i(X_i) - i(X_j)\|)$ and let us work in the following on the event $\mathcal{E}_1$ where

$$\max_{1\leq i\leq n}|d_{h,n}(X_i) - p_h(X_i)| \leq \tau, \quad \text{and} \quad |U_{n,h}(f) - \mathbb{E}\,U_{n,h}(f)| \leq \tau$$

From Proposition 2 and the proof of Theorem 3 we know that there exists a constant C such that $\mathcal{E}_1$ holds with probability greater than $1 - Cne^{-\frac{nh^m\tau^2}{C}}$ for $\tau \geq \frac{C}{nh^m}$. Since M is compact, we have $\forall x \in M, 0 < D_1 \leq p_h(x) \leq D_2$. Using a Taylor expansion of $x \to x^{-\lambda}$ with

$$\beta = \min\{d_{h,n}(X_i)d_{h,n}(X_j), p_h(X_i)p_h(X_j)\}^{-\lambda-1} \leq (D_1 - \tau)^{-2(\lambda+1)},$$

we get for $\tau < D_1/2$,

$$\left| \frac{1}{(d_{h,n}(X_i)d_{h,n}(X_j))^\lambda} - \frac{1}{(p_h(X_i)p_h(X_j))^\lambda} \right| \leq \lambda \beta \left[(D_2 + \tau)\tau + D_2\tau \right] \leq C'\tau,$$

where C' is independent of X_i and X_j. By Lemma 1 and 2 we get for $hR_k \leq \min\{\kappa/2, R_0/2\}$, $\mathbb{E}\, U_{n,h}(f) \leq 2^{m+1} S_2\, R_k^{m+2}\, s^2\, D_2\, \|k\|_\infty$ so that for $\tau \leq \mathbb{E}\, U_{n,h}(f)$ we get on $\mathcal{E}_1$

$$\sup_{f \in \mathcal{F}} |S_{\lambda,h,n}(f) - \tilde{S}_{\lambda,h,n}(f)| \leq \frac{2R_k^2\, s^2\, C'\, \tau}{n(n-1)} \sum_{i,j=1}^n k_h(\|i(X_i) - i(X_j)\|)$$

$$\leq \left(2^{m+1} S_2\, R_k^{m+2}\, s^2\, D_2\, \|k\|_\infty + \tau \right) C'\tau \leq \frac{\epsilon}{4},$$

where we have set $\tau = \frac{\epsilon}{C'\, 2^{m+2} S_2\, R_k^{m+2}\, s^2\, D_2\, \|k\|_\infty}$. Now let us deal with II. By assumption we have a δ-covering of $\mathcal{F}$ in the $\|\cdot\|_\infty$-norm. We rewrite the U-statistic $\tilde{S}_{\lambda,h,n}(f) = \frac{1}{n(n-1)} \sum_{i,j} h_f(X_i, X_j)$ with kernels h_f indexed by $f \in \mathcal{F}$, where

$$h_f(x, y) = \frac{1}{h^{m+2}} \frac{k(\|i(x) - i(y)\|)}{(p_h(x)p_h(y))^\lambda} \left[f(x) - f(y) \right]^2$$

The δ-covering $C_\delta(\mathcal{F})$ of $\mathcal{F}$ induces a covering of $\mathcal{H}_\mathcal{F} = \{h_f \mid f \in \mathcal{F}\}$.

$$|h_f(x, y) - h_g(x, y)| \leq \frac{8\,\|k\|_\infty}{h^{1+m} D_1^{2\lambda}}\, s\, R_k\, \|f - g\|_\infty \leq \frac{C}{2}\, s\, \frac{\|f - g\|_\infty}{h^{m+1}},$$

where we have used Lemmas 1,2 and have set $C = \frac{16\|k\|_\infty\, R_k}{D_1^{2\lambda}}$. We conclude that a δ-covering of $\mathcal{F}$ induces a $\frac{Cs}{h^{m+1}}\delta$-covering of $\mathcal{H}_\mathcal{F}$. This implies that for any $f \in \mathcal{F}$ there exists a $g \in C_\delta(\mathcal{F})$ such that,

$$|\tilde{S}_{\lambda,h,n}(f) - \mathbb{E}\,\tilde{S}_{\lambda,h,n}(f)| \leq C\frac{s\delta}{h^{m+1}} + |\tilde{S}_{\lambda,h,n}(g) - \mathbb{E}\,\tilde{S}_{\lambda,h,n}(g)|$$

We denote by $\mathcal{E}_2$ the event where $\sup_{g \in C_\delta(\mathcal{F})} |\tilde{S}_{\lambda,h,n}(g) - \mathbb{E}\,\tilde{S}_{\lambda,h,n}(g)| \leq \epsilon/4$ and choose $\delta \leq \frac{h^{m+1}}{Cs}\frac{\epsilon}{2}$. In the proof of Theorem 3 it is shown that for one function g there exist constants K_1 and K_2 independent of h, s and the function class $\mathcal{F}$ such that the following Bernstein-type inequality holds

$$\mathbb{P}\left(|\tilde{S}_{\lambda,h,n}(g) - \mathbb{E}\,\tilde{S}_{\lambda,h,n}(g)| \geq \frac{\epsilon}{4} \right) \leq 2e^{-\frac{[n/2]h^m\,(1/s)^4\,\epsilon^2}{32K_1 + 32/3\frac{\epsilon}{s^2}K_2}}.$$

Taking the union bound over the covering $C_\delta(\mathcal{F})$ yields

$$\mathbb{P}\left(\sup_{g \in C_\delta(F)} |\tilde{S}_{\lambda,h,n}(g) - \mathbb{E}\,\tilde{S}_{\lambda,h,n}(g)| \geq \frac{\epsilon}{4} \right) \leq 2\mathcal{N}\left(\delta, \mathcal{F}, \|\cdot\|_\infty \right) e^{-\frac{[n/2]h^m\,(1/s)^4\,\epsilon^2}{32K_1 + 32/3\frac{\epsilon}{s^2}K_2}}$$

In total we have on the event $\mathcal{E}_1$ and $\mathcal{E}_2$

$$\sup_{g\in\mathcal{F}} |S_{\lambda,h,n}(g) - \mathbb{E}\,\tilde{S}_{\lambda,h,n}(g)| \leq I + II \leq \frac{\epsilon}{4} + \frac{\epsilon}{2} + \frac{\epsilon}{4} \leq \epsilon$$

Putting the results for $\mathcal{E}_1$ and $\mathcal{E}_2$ together we are done. $\qquad\square$

Note that despite $\mathcal{F}$ is not required to be uniformly bounded in the previous theorem, one gets only finite covering numbers in the $\|\cdot\|_\infty$ norm under this condition. In order to get finite sample bounds, we need to know how far $\mathbb{E}\,\tilde{S}_{\lambda,h,n}$ is away from its limit for finite h uniformly over a certain function class $\mathcal{F}$.

Theorem 5. *Let $\mathcal{F}$ be a function class such that $\sup_{f\in\mathcal{F}} \|f\|_{C^3(M)} \leq s$. Then there exist constants $C', C'' > 0$ depending only on M, p and the kernel k such that for all $h < C' \min\{\frac{\pi\rho}{3}, \frac{r_i}{3}, \frac{\kappa}{2R_k}, \frac{R_0}{R_k}\}$,*

$$\sup_{f\in\mathcal{F}} \left| \mathbb{E}\,\tilde{S}_{\lambda,h,n} - \frac{C_2}{2C_1^\lambda} \int_M \langle \nabla f, \nabla f \rangle_{T_x M}\, p(x)^{2-2\lambda} \sqrt{\det g}\, dx \right| \leq C'' s^2 h$$

Proof. Let us first define

$$B_{\lambda,h}(x) := \frac{1}{2h^2} \int_M (f(x) - f(y))^2 k_h(\|i(x) - i(y)\|) \frac{p(y)}{(p_h(x)p_h(y))^\lambda} dV(y).$$

so that $\mathbb{E}\,\tilde{S}_{\lambda,h,n} = \int_M B_{\lambda,h}(x)\,p(x)\,dV(x)$. Now we decompose M as $M = M\backslash N(r) \cup N(r)$, where $r \leq r_i$ (see Definition 2), which implies that for all $x \in M\backslash N(r)$ there exist normal coordinates on the ball $B_M(x,r)$, that is $\mathrm{inj}(M\backslash N(r)) = r$. The expansion of Proposition 1 holds pointwise for $h_0 \leq \frac{C'}{3}\min\{\pi\rho, \mathrm{inj}(x)\}$[10]. Since ρ is lower-bounded due to compactness of M and $\mathrm{inj}(M\backslash N(r)) = r$ we can use Proposition 1 uniformly over $M\backslash N(r)$, which yields

$$\sup_{x\in M\backslash N(r)} \left| B_{\lambda,h}(x) - \frac{C_2}{2C_1^\lambda} \langle \nabla f, \nabla f \rangle_{T_x M}\, p(x)^{1-2\lambda} \right| \leq C'' s^2 h,$$

where C'' is independent of $\mathcal{F}$. Therefore the bound holds uniformly over the function class $\mathcal{F}$. Next we have two error terms I and II:

$$I := \int_{N(r)} B_{\lambda,h}(x)p(x)dV(x), \quad II := \frac{C_2}{2C_1^\lambda} \int_{N(r)} \|\nabla f\|^2 p^{2-2\lambda}(x)dV(x)$$

Let us first deal with I. By Lemma 2 we have for $hR_k \leq \frac{\kappa}{2}$, $d_M(x,y) \leq 2\|x - y\| \leq 2hR_k$ (due to compact support of k). Together with the volume bound from Lemma 1 we get for $hR_k \leq \min\{\kappa/2, R_0/2\}$:

$$|B_{\lambda,h}(x)| \leq \frac{2s^2 R_k^2 \|k\|_\infty \|p\|_\infty}{D_1^{2\lambda}} S_2 2^m R_k^m$$

---

[10] The factor $1/3$ arises since we have to take care that also for all points $y \in B_M(x,r/3)$ we can do the expansion for $p_h(y)$.

Again using the volume bound from Proposition 1 for $r \leq R_0$ yields:

$$I \leq \frac{2s^2 R_k^2 \|k\|_\infty \|p\|_\infty^2}{D_1^{2\lambda}} S_2 2^m R_k^m S_2\, r\, \text{vol}(\partial M) := C''' s^2\, r$$

By the volume bound and $\|\nabla f\|_\infty \leq s$ we get $II \leq C'''' s^2 r$. For $r \leq \pi\rho$ we choose $h = C\, r$ for some constant C so that all error terms are of order $s^2\, h$. $\square$

Theorems 4 and 5 together provide a finite sample result for the convergence of $S_{\lambda,h,n}$ over a sufficiently smooth function class $\mathcal{F}$. We use now the upper bounds on the covering numbers of a ball of α-Hölder functions in order to get an explicit finite sample bound and rates for $h(n)$. Moreover we let $s(n) \to \infty$ so that in the limit we get uniform convergence for all α-Hölder functions.

Theorem 6. *Let $\mathcal{F}_\alpha(s)$ be the ball of radius s in the space of Hölder functions $\mathcal{F}_\alpha$ on M. Define $\gamma = 2 - 2\lambda$ and $c = \frac{C_2}{2C_1^\lambda}$, then for $\alpha \geq 3$ and $h \to 0$ and $nh^{\frac{m^2+m+\alpha m}{\alpha}} \to \infty$,*

$$\sup_{f \in \mathcal{F}_\alpha(s)} \left| S_{\lambda,h,n}(f) - c\, S_{\Delta_\gamma}(f) \right| = O\left(\frac{s^2}{(nh^{\frac{m^2+m+\alpha m}{\alpha}})^{\frac{\alpha}{2\alpha+m}}} \right) + O(s^2\, h) \quad \text{a.s.}$$

The optimal rate for h is $h = O(n^{-\frac{\alpha}{2\alpha+2m+m^2+m\alpha}})$.
Let $s = log(n)$, then if $h \to 0$ and $nh^{\frac{m^2+m+\alpha m}{\alpha}}/log(n)^{\frac{4\alpha+2m}{\alpha}} \to \infty$ one has,

$$\forall f \in \mathcal{F}_\alpha, \quad \lim_{n \to \infty} S_{\lambda,h,n}(f) = \frac{C_2}{2C_1^\lambda} \int_M \|\nabla f\|_{T_x M}^2\, p(x)^{2-2\lambda} \sqrt{\det g}\, dx, \quad \text{a.s..}$$

Proof. For $\alpha > 3$, we have $\mathcal{F}_\alpha \subset C^3(M)$ and $\|f\|_{C^3(M)} \leq \|f\|_{\mathcal{F}_\alpha}, \forall f \in \mathcal{F}_\alpha$, so that we can apply Theorems 4 and 5. The first statement follows for sufficiently small h and by plugging the bound on the covering numbers of $\mathcal{F}_\alpha(s)$ from Theorem 2 into Theorem 4 and putting Theorem 4 and 5 together. The dominating terms of $log\, \text{P}(\sup_{f \in \mathcal{F}_\alpha(s)} |S_{\lambda,h,n}(f) - \mathbb{E}\, S_{\lambda,h,n}(f)| > \epsilon)$ are

$$\left(\frac{2C\, s^2}{\epsilon\, h^{m+1}} \right)^{\frac{m}{\alpha}} - \frac{nh^m\, (1/s)^4\, \epsilon^2}{4C} = \left(\frac{2C\, s^2}{\epsilon\, h^{m+1}} \right)^{\frac{m}{\alpha}} \left[1 - \frac{nh^{\frac{m^2+m+\alpha m}{\alpha}}\, (1/s)^{4+2\frac{m}{\alpha}}\, \epsilon^{2+\frac{m}{\alpha}}}{C'} \right]$$

so that for the given rate the term in the bracket can be made negative and and the whole term is summable so that almost sure convergence follows by the Borel-Cantelli Lemma. The optimal rate for $h(n)$ can be computed by equating the two order-terms. For the second statement we simply choose $s = log(n)$. $\square$

This theorem provides uniform convergence of the adaptive regularization functional $S_{\lambda,h,n}(f)$ over the large class of α-Hölder functions. We think that this theorem will be helpful to prove consistency results for algorithms which use $S_{\lambda,h,n}(f)$ as a regularizer. As expected the rate depends only on the intrinsic dimension m and not on the extrinsic dimension d. At least for low-dimensional submanifolds we can therefore get a good approximation of the continuous regularization functional even if we work in a high-dimensional space.

References

[1] M. Belkin and P. Niyogi. Laplacian eigenmaps for dimensionality reduction and data representation. *Neural Comp.*, 15(6):1373–1396, 2003.

[2] M. Belkin and P. Niyogi. Semi-supervised learning on manifolds. *Machine Learning*, 56:209–239, 2004.

[3] M. Belkin and P. Niyogi. Towards a theoretical foundation for Laplacian-based manifold methods. In P. Auer and R. Meir, editors, *Proc. of the 18th Conf. on Learning Theory (COLT)*, Berlin, 2005. Springer.

[4] O. Bousquet, O. Chapelle, and M. Hein. Measure based regularization. In S. Thrun, L. Saul, and B. Schölkopf, editors, *Adv. in Neur. Inf. Proc. Syst. (NIPS)*, volume 16. MIT Press, 2004.

[5] S. Canu and A. Elisseeff. Regularization, kernels and sigmoid net. unpublished, 1999.

[6] S. Coifman and S. Lafon. Diffusion maps. Preprint, Jan. 2005, to appear in Appl. and Comp. Harm. Anal., 2005.

[7] E. Hebey. *Nonlinear analysis on manifolds: Sobolev spaces and inequalities.* Courant Institute of Mathematical Sciences, New York, 1998.

[8] M. Hein. *Geometrical aspects of statistical learning theory.* PhD thesis, MPI für biologische Kybernetik/Technische Universität Darmstadt, 2005. http://www.kyb.mpg.de/publication.html?user=mh.

[9] M. Hein, J.-Y. Audibert, and U. von Luxburg. From graphs to manifolds - weak and strong pointwise consistency of graph Laplacians. In P. Auer and R. Meir, editors, *Proc. of the 18th Conf. on Learning Theory (COLT)*, Berlin, 2005. Springer.

[10] H. Hendriks, J.H.M. Janssen, and F.H. Ruymgaart. Strong uniform convergence of density estimators on compact Euclidean manifolds. *Statist. Prob. Lett.*, 16:305–311, 1993.

[11] W. Hoeffding. Probability inequalities for sums of bounded random variables. *J. Amer. Statist. Assoc.*, 58:13–30, 1963.

[12] A. N. Kolmogorov and V. M. Tihomirov. ε-entropy and ε-capacity of sets in functional spaces. *Amer. Math. Soc. Transl.*, 17:277–364, 1961.

[13] T. Schick. Manifolds with boundary of bounded geometry. *Math. Nachr.*, 223:103–120, 2001.

[14] A. W. van der Vaart and J. A. Wellner. *Weak convergence and empirical processes.* Springer, New-York, second edition, 2001.

[15] D. Zhou, O. Bousquet, T. N. Lal, J. Weston, and B. Schölkopf. Learning with local and global consistency. In S. Thrun, L. Saul, and B. Schölkopf, editors, *Adv. in Neur. Inf. Proc. Syst. (NIPS)*, volume 16. MIT Press, 2004.

Appendix. Covering Numbers for α-Hölder Functions on Compact Riemannian Manifolds (with Boundary)

Proof. [Proof of Theorem 1] The first property follows by the maximality of the separated subsets. It remains to prove the upper bounds on the cardinality of I_1 and I_2. The sets $\{n(x'_i, \frac{\epsilon}{2}, \frac{\epsilon}{2})\}_{i \in I_1}$ and $\{n(x_i, \frac{\epsilon}{2})\}_{i \in I_2}$ are disjoint. Therefore

$$\sum_{i \in I_1} \text{vol}\left(n(x'_{i_1}, \frac{\epsilon}{2}, \frac{\epsilon}{2})\right) \le \text{vol}\left(N(\epsilon)\right), \qquad \sum_{i \in I_2} \text{vol}\left(n(x_{i_2}, \frac{\epsilon}{2})\right) \le \text{vol}\left(M\right).$$

Then use $\mathrm{vol}\left(N(\epsilon)\right) \leq S_2\epsilon\,\mathrm{vol}\left(\partial M\right)$ and the volume bounds in Lemma 1.   □

Now we are ready to prove the result on covering numbers for $\mathcal{F}_\alpha(s)$.

Proof. [Proof of Theorem 2] Let $\delta = \left(\frac{\epsilon}{3s\,e^{2m}}\right)^{1/\alpha}$ and let $T_1 = \{z_i'\}_{i\in I_1}$ and $T_2 = \{z_i\}_{i\in I_2}$ describe a maximal δ-separated set of ∂M and $M\backslash N(\delta)$ as in Theorem 1. For each vector $k = (k_1,\ldots,k_d)$ with $k \leq \underline{\alpha}$ we form for each $f \in \mathcal{F}_\alpha(s)$ the two vectors

$$A_k f = \left(\left[\frac{D^k(f\circ\phi_{z_1'})(0)}{s\,\delta^{\alpha-k}}\right],\ldots,\left[\frac{D^k(f\circ\phi_{z_{|I_1|}'})(0)}{s\,\delta^{\alpha-k}}\right]\right)$$

$$B_k f = \left(\left[\frac{D^k(f\circ\phi_{z_1})(0)}{s\,\delta^{\alpha-k}}\right],\ldots,\left[\frac{D^k(f\circ\phi_{z_{|I_2|}})(0)}{s\,\delta^{\alpha-k}}\right]\right),$$

where $[\cdot]$ denotes rounding to the closest integer and ϕ denotes the normal charts corresponding to the points in T_1 and T_2. Note that the vector $A_k f$ is well-defined since all derivatives of f are uniformly bounded. Now let f_1 and f_2 be two functions such that $A_k f_1 = A_k f_2$ and $B_k f_1 = B_k f_2$ for each $k \leq \underline{\alpha}$. Define $g = f_1 - f_2$, then one has for every $z \in T_1 \cup T_2$

$$|D^k g(z)| = |D^k f_1(z) - D^k f_2(z)| \leq s\,\delta^{\alpha-k} \tag{4}$$

Moreover for every $x \in M\backslash N(\delta)$ there exists an $z_i \in T_2$ such that $d(x,z_i) \leq \delta$ and for every $x \in N(\delta)$ there exists an $z_i' \in T_1$ such that $d(x,z_i') \leq 2\delta$ (this follows from the definition of normal collar charts and the triangle inequality[11]). Since $M \subset M\backslash N(\delta) \cup N(\delta)$ there exists for each $x \in M$ a corresponding normal chart ϕ_z based on $z \in N_1 \cup N_2$ such that for each coordinate $x_i = (\phi_z^{-1}(x))_i$, $i = 1,\ldots,m$ of x one has $x_i \leq \max\{\delta, 2\delta\} = 2\delta$. Now we do a Taylor expansion of g around $z = \phi_z(0)$ in the normal chart ϕ_z and get for $x = \phi_z((x_1,\ldots,x_m))$:

$$g(x)=\sum_{k\leq\underline{\alpha}} D^k(g\circ\phi_z)(0)\prod_{i=1}^{m}\frac{x_i^{k_i}}{k_i!}+\sum_{k=\underline{\alpha}}\left(D^k(g\circ\phi_z)(\lambda x_i) - D^k(g\circ\phi_z)(0)\right)\prod_{i=1}^{m}\frac{x_i^{k_i}}{k_i!}$$

with $\lambda \in [0,1]$. By (4) and the Lipschitz property of functions in $\mathcal{F}_\alpha(s)$ we get

$$|g(x)| \leq \sum_{k\leq\underline{\alpha}} s\delta^{\alpha-k}\frac{(2\delta)^k}{k!} + 2s\frac{m^\alpha}{\underline{\alpha}!}2^\alpha\delta^\alpha \leq \delta^\alpha e^{2m}(s + 2s) \leq 3se^{2m}\delta^\alpha = \epsilon,$$

so that the covering numbers of an ϵ-covering of $\mathcal{F}_\alpha(s)$ are upper bounded by the number of possible matrices Af and Bf for $f \in \mathcal{F}_\alpha(s)$. The number of possible derivatives $\leq \underline{\alpha}$ is upper bounded by $\sum_{i=0}^{\alpha} m^i = \frac{m^\alpha-1}{m-1}$ for $m > 1$ and α for $m = 1$. Since in $\mathcal{F}_\alpha(s)$ the derivatives fulfill $|D^k f(x)| \leq s$ for each k, $A_k f$ contains $\frac{2}{\delta^{\alpha-k}} + 2$ values which is upper bounded by $\frac{2}{\delta^\alpha} + 2$. Thus for one

---

[11] One follows the geodesic along the boundary which is shorter than δ and then the geodesic along the inward normal vector which has also length shorter than δ.

point in the covering the number of different values in Af is upper bounded by $\left(\frac{2}{\delta^\alpha}+2\right)^{2m^\alpha}$ for $m \geq 2$ and $\left(\frac{2}{\delta^\alpha}+2\right)^\alpha$ for $m = 1$. The same holds for $B_k f$.

Assume now we reorder the set N_1 in such a way that for each $j > 1$ there is an index $i < j$ such that $d(z_i', z_j') \leq 2\delta$. We compute now the range over which values of $A_k f(z_j')$ vary given the values of $A_k f(z_i')$. The problem is that the derivatives of f at z_j' and z_i' are given with respect to different normal charts $\phi_{z_j'}$ and $\phi_{z_i'}$. In order to compare $A_k f(z_j')$ with $A_k f(z_i')$ we therefore have to change coordinates. Let x^μ be the coordinates with respect to $\phi_{z_j'}$ and y^μ with respect to $\phi_{z_i'}$. Then one has e.g. for the second derivative,

$$\frac{\partial^2 f}{\partial x_\mu \partial x_\nu} = \frac{\partial^2 f}{\partial y_\beta \partial y_\gamma}\frac{\partial y_\beta}{\partial x_\mu}\frac{\partial y_\gamma}{\partial x_\nu} + \frac{\partial f}{\partial y_\alpha}\frac{\partial^2 y_\alpha}{\partial x_\mu \partial x_\nu} =: C_y^2 f,$$

with the obvious generalization to higher orders. By Taylor's theorem one gets

$$D_x^k f(x_j) = D_x^k(f \circ \phi_{z_j'})(0) = \sum_{k+l \leq \alpha} D_x^{k+l}(f \circ \phi_{z_j'})(x^i)\frac{x^l}{l!} + R = \sum_{k+l \leq \alpha} C_y^{k+l}(0)\frac{x^l}{l!} + R$$

Define $B_y^{k+l}(0)$ as $C_y^{k+l}(0)$ with derivatives replaced by their discretized values,

$$\frac{\partial^k f}{\partial y_{i_1} \ldots \partial y_{i_k}}(0) \longrightarrow s\,\delta^{\alpha-k}\left[\frac{\partial^k f}{\partial y_{i_1} \ldots \partial y_{i_k}}(0)\frac{1}{s\,\delta^{\alpha-k}}\right]$$

Given now all the discretized values $Af(z_i')$ we arrive at

$$\left|D_x^k(f \circ \phi_{z_j'})(0) - \sum_{k+l \leq \alpha} B_y^{k+l}(0)\frac{x^l}{l!}\right| \leq \sum_{k+l \leq \alpha} \left|C_y^{k+l}(0) - B_y^{k+l}(0)\right|\frac{x^l}{l!} + |R|$$

The leading term of the summands can be upper bounded as follows

$$\left|C_y^{k+l}(0) - B_y^{k+l}(0)\right| \leq s\,(\Gamma\,m)^k \delta^{\alpha-k-l}$$

where $\Gamma = \max_{i,j} \max_{k \leq \alpha} \sup_{x \in M} D^k(\phi_{z_i'}^{-1} \circ \phi_{z_j'})$. It can be shown that the remainder term $|R|$ is of order $s\,\delta^{\alpha-k}$, so that in total we get that there exists a constant C depending on Γ, m and α such that

$$\left|D_x^k(f \circ \phi_{z_j'})(0) - \sum_{k+l \leq \alpha} B_y^{k+l}(0)\frac{x^l}{l!}\right| \leq C\,s\,\delta^{\alpha-k}$$

That implies that given the values of Af at x_i the values of Af at x_j vary over an interval of size $C\,s\,\frac{\delta^{\alpha-k}}{\delta^{\alpha-k}} = C\,s$. Using our previous bound on the number of possible values of Af for one point we get that the total number of values of Af is upper bounded as follows:

$$|Af| \leq \left(\frac{2}{\delta^\alpha}+2\right)^{2m^\alpha}((C\,s)^{2m^\alpha})^{|I_1|}$$

The same can be done for $|Bf|$. Replacing $|I_1|$ resp. $|I_2|$ with the numbers from Theorem 1 and upper bounding $\log(1/\epsilon)$ by $(1/\epsilon)^{m/\alpha}$ finishes the proof. $\qquad\square$

The Rademacher Complexity of Linear Transformation Classes

Andreas Maurer

Adalbertstr. 55
D-80799 München
andreasmaurer@compuserve.com

Abstract. Bounds are given for the empirical and expected Rademacher
complexity of classes of linear transformations from a Hilbert space H to
a finite dimensional space. The results imply generalization guarantees
for graph regularization and multi-task subspace learning.

1 Introduction

Rademacher averages have been introduced to learning theory as an efficient
complexity measure for function classes, motivated by tight, sample or distribution dependent generalization bounds ([10], [2]). Both the definition of
Rademacher complexity and the generalization bounds extend easily from real-
valued function classes to function classes with values in $\mathbb{R}^m$, as they are relevant
to multi-task learning ([1], [12]).

There has been an increasing interest in multi-task learning which has shown
to be very effective in experiments ([7], [1]), and there have been some general
studies of its generalisation performance ([4], [5]). For a large collection of tasks
there are usually more data available than for a single task and these data may be
put to a coherent use by some constraint of 'relatedness'. A practically interesting
case is linear multi-task learning, extending linear large margin classifiers to
vector valued large-margin classifiers. Different types of constraints have been
proposed: Evgeniou et al ([8], [9]) propose graph regularization, where the vectors
defining the classifiers of related tasks have to be near each other. They also show
that their scheme can be implemented in the framework of kernel machines.
Ando and Zhang [1] on the other hand require the classifiers to be members
of a common low dimensional subspace. They also give generalization bounds
using Rademacher complexity, but these bounds increase with the dimension of
the input space. This paper gives dimension free bounds which apply to both
approaches.

1.1 Multi-task Generalization and Rademacher Complexity

Suppose we have m classification tasks, represented by m independent random
variables (X^l, Y^l) taking values in $\mathcal{X} \times \{-1, 1\}$, where X^l models the random
occurrence of input data in some input space $\mathcal{X}$, and Y^l models the corresponding
binary output for learning task $l \in \{1, ..., m\}$. The draw of an iid sample for the

G. Lugosi and H.U. Simon (Eds.): COLT 2006, LNAI 4005, pp. 65–78, 2006.
© Springer-Verlag Berlin Heidelberg 2006

l-th task is described by a sequence $\left(X_i^l, Y_i^l\right)_{i=1}^n$ of independent random variables, each identically distributed to $\left(X^l, Y^l\right)$. Write $(\mathbf{X}, \mathbf{Y})$ for the combined random variable taking values in $\mathcal{X}^{mn} \times \{-1, 1\}^{mn}$.

One now seeks a function $\mathbf{f} = \left(f^1, ..., f^m\right) : \mathcal{X} \to \mathbb{R}^m$ such that predicting Y^l to be $sgn\left(f^l\right)$ is correct with high average probability. To this end one searches a function class $\mathcal{F}$ of functions $\mathbf{f} : \mathcal{X} \to \mathbb{R}^m$ for a member with a small average empirical error estimate. The choice of the function class $\mathcal{F}$ expresses the constraints of 'relatedness' which we want to impose. This procedure is justified by the following result. ([1], [12]):

Theorem 1. *Let ϕ be the function on $\mathbb{R}$ defined by*

$$\phi(t) = \begin{cases} 1 & if \quad t \leq 0 \\ 1 - t & if \ 0 \leq t \leq 1 \\ 0 & if \quad 1 \leq t \end{cases}.$$

Let $\mathcal{F}$ be a class of functions $\mathbf{f} = \left(f^1, ..., f^m\right) : \mathcal{X} \to \mathbb{R}^m$ and fix $\delta > 0$. Then with probability greater than $1 - \delta$ we have for all $\mathbf{f} \in \mathcal{F}$

$$\frac{1}{m} \sum_{l=1}^m \Pr\left\{ sgn\left(f^l\left(X^l\right)\right) \neq Y^l \right\}$$

$$\leq \frac{1}{mn} \sum_{l=1}^m \sum_{i=1}^n \phi\left(Y^l f^l\left(X_i^l\right)\right) + \hat{\mathcal{R}}_n^m\left(\mathcal{F}\right)(\mathbf{X}) + \sqrt{\frac{9 \ln(2/\delta)}{2mn}}.$$

The first term on the right hand side is an empirical large-margin error estimate. Selecting a function class $\mathcal{F}$ means that we make a bet that we will be able to find within $\mathcal{F}$ a solution with a reasonably low value for this term. The other two terms bound the estimation error. The last term decays quickly with the product mn and depends only logarithmically on the confidence parameter δ and will not concern us very much. The remaining term is a complexity measure of the class $\mathcal{F}$ when acting on the data set $\mathbf{X}$.

Definition 1. *For $l \in \{1, ..., m\}$ and $i \in \{1, ..., n\}$ let σ_i^l be independent random variables, distributed uniformly in $\{-1, 1\}$. The empirical Rademacher complexity of a class $\mathcal{F}$ of functions $\mathbf{f} : \mathcal{X} \to \mathbb{R}^m$ is the function $\hat{\mathcal{R}}_n^m\left(\mathcal{F}\right)$ defined on $\mathcal{X}^{nm}$ by*

$$\hat{\mathcal{R}}_n^m\left(\mathcal{F}\right)(\mathbf{x}) = E_\sigma \left[\sup_{\mathbf{f} = (f^1, ..., f^m) \in \mathcal{F}} \frac{2}{mn} \sum_{l=1}^m \sum_{i=1}^n \sigma_i^l f^l\left(x_i^l\right) \right].$$

Theorem 1 above explains the value of bounds on this function, the principal subject of this paper. There is also a version of Theorem 1 involving the expectation $E_{\mathbf{X}} \left[\hat{\mathcal{R}}_n^m\left(\mathcal{F}\right)(\mathbf{X}) \right]$ with a slightly better final term. We have restricted ourselves to classification for definiteness. Substitution of our results in other generalization bounds using Rademacher complexities should make them applicable to multi-task regression.

1.2   Bounds on the Rademacher Complexity

This paper assumes that the input space $\mathcal{X}$ is contained in the closed unit ball of a real separable Hilbert space H (fixed from now on) and that $\mathcal{F}$ is a class of bounded linear transformations $V : H \to \mathbb{R}^m$. Such transformations correspond to m-tuples $(v^1, ..., v^m) \in H^m$ of vectors in H such that the l-th component of V is given by $V(x)_l = \langle v^l, x \rangle$ (we denote this by $V \leftrightarrow (v^1, ..., v^m)$). Thresholding the functional $x \to \langle v^l, x \rangle$ gives the classifier for the l-th task. The assumption $\|X^l\| \leq 1$ is also a notational convenience, but we would always need $E\left[\|X^l\|^2\right] < \infty$ for part (I) and $E\left[\|X^l\|^4\right] < \infty$ for part (II) of the following theorem, which is the main contribution of this work.

Theorem 2. *Let $\mathcal{F}$ be a set of linear transformations $V : H \to \mathbb{R}^m$ and $\mathbf{x} \in H^{mn}$ with $\|\mathbf{x}_i^l\|^2 \leq 1$.*

(I) Then for every positive definite operator A on $\mathbb{R}^m$

$$\hat{\mathcal{R}}_n^m(\mathcal{F})(\mathbf{x}) \leq \frac{2}{\sqrt{n}} \sup_{V \in \mathcal{F}} \left(\frac{\|A^{1/2}V\|_2}{\sqrt{m}} \right) \sqrt{\frac{tr(A^{-1})}{m}}.$$

(II) Let $p \in [4, \infty]$ and let q be the conjugate exponent, that is $p^{-1} + q^{-1} = 1$. Then

$$\hat{\mathcal{R}}_n^m(\mathcal{F})(\mathbf{x}) \leq \frac{2}{\sqrt{n}} \sup_{V \in \mathcal{F}} \left(\frac{\|V\|_q}{\sqrt{m}} \right) \sqrt{\left\|\hat{C}(\mathbf{x})\right\|_{p/2} + \sqrt{\frac{2}{m}}}$$

and

$$E\left[\hat{\mathcal{R}}_n^m(\mathcal{F})(\mathbf{X})\right] \leq \frac{2}{\sqrt{n}} \sup_{V \in \mathcal{F}} \left(\frac{\|V\|_q}{\sqrt{m}} \right) \sqrt{\|C_m\|_{p/2} + \sqrt{\frac{3}{m}}}$$

Here $\hat{C}(\mathbf{x})$ is the empirical covariance operator of the data set $\mathbf{x}$, that is the covariance operator corresponding to the empirical distribution $1/(mn) \sum_{l,i} \delta_{x_i^l}$ on H, while C_m is the covariance operator corresponding to the mixture of data-distributions[1]. $C_m = (1/m) C^l$, where C^l is the covariance operator for the data-distribution of the l-th task. The Schatten-norms $\|...\|_p$ are defined for compact operators T by

$$\|T\|_p = \left(\sum_i \mu_i^p \right)^{1/p},$$

where the μ_i are the singular values of T. The norms $\|T\|_p$ are a decreasing function in p. See section 2 for more detailed definitions. For $V \leftrightarrow (v^1, ..., v^m) : H \to \mathbb{R}^m$ we have

$$\|V\|_2 = \left(\sum_l \|v^l\|^2 \right)^{1/2}.$$

---

[1] Here δ_x is the unit mass concentrated at x.

1.3   Interpretation of the Bounds

Each of the bounds in Theorem 2 has been grouped in three factors: The factor $2/\sqrt{n}$ is important, because it insures learnability as long as the other two factors remain bounded or increase slowly enough with the sample size n.

Next comes a regularization factor depending on $\mathcal{F}$ and a norm, which encodes the relatedness-constraint. Equating the supremum to some chosen constant B defines a maximal function class $\mathcal{F}$ which is necessarily convex. The first bound for example gives rise to the function class $\mathcal{F} = \{V : m^{-1/2} \left\| A^{1/2}V \right\|_2 < B\}$. For such classes the constant B can of course be substituted for the supremum, giving the bounds a simpler appearance. The $m^{-1/2}$ will typically be cancelled by allowing the individual functional components v^i of $V \leftrightarrow (v^1, ..., v^m) \in \mathcal{F}$ to have norm of unit order on average, that is $\|V\|_2^2 = \sum_l \left\| v^l \right\|^2 = O(m)$ or $\left\| A^{1/2}V \right\|_2^2 = O(m)$.

The third factor gives the bound proper and depends on the situation studied. It will typically decrease to some limiting positive value, as the number of tasks m increases.

If we set $A = I$ then part (I) above can be recognized as a trival extension of existing bounds ([2]) for single task linear large margin classifiers. It corresponds to the noninteracting case, essentially equivalent to single task learning. If we set $A = L + \eta I$, where L is the Laplacian on a graph with m vertices, and $\eta > 0$ a small regularization constant, then we obtain bounds to justify the graph regularization schemes in [9], concisely relating generalization to the spectrum of the Laplacian. This will be explained in some detail in section 3.

Part (II) of the theorem can be applied to subspace learning. The norms $\|T\|_p$ can be viewed as combined measures of amplitude and dimensionality (or rank if T has finite dimensional range), and imposing a bound on $\|V\|_q$ is a combined form of amplitude and dimensional regularization. The conceptually simplest way to do this is to consider the class $\mathcal{F}_{B,d}$ of transformations $V \leftrightarrow (v^1, ..., v^m)$ such that $\|V\|_2^2 = \sum_l \left\| v^l \right\|^2 \le B^2 m$ and $rank(V) \le d$ (a notation which extends to the case $d = \infty$). Then all the individual linear classifiers v^l are constrained to lie in some d-dimensional subspace of H. This subspace can be freely chosen after seeing the data, so the above bounds become generalisation guarantees for subspace selection through multitask learning. This corresponds to the regularization in [1]. In this case the regularization factor can be shown to be equal to

$$\sup_{V \in \mathcal{F}_{B,d}} \left(\frac{\|V\|_q}{\sqrt{m}} \right) = Bd^{\frac{2-q}{2q}} = Bd^{\frac{p-2}{2p}}.$$

If $p = q = 2$ then this is just B and there will be no penalty on dimension. Correspondingly the bound will exhibit no benefit from constraining d. If $p = 4$ and $q = 4/3$ then we obtain $Bd^{1/4}$ and for $p = \infty$ and $q = 1$ it is $Bd^{1/2}$, corresponding to increasing penalties on the dimensionality. The class $\mathcal{F}_{B,d}$ is practical and corresponds to the scheme in [1], but it is not convex, while setting

$\mathcal{F} = \left\{ V : \|V\|_q \leq B \right\}$ and replacing ϕ by the hinge loss always results in a convex optimization problem.

The data- or distribution dependent third factor in (II) contains two terms. The decrease in m with essentially the fourth root may be an artifact of our proof. As the number of tasks increases the norm of the covariances becomes dominant. Since we restricted ourselves to data in the unit ball, we will have $\left\| \hat{C}(\mathbf{x}) \right\|_1 \leq 1$ and $\|C_m\|_1 \leq 1$, so the amplitude is essentially normalized. Let us assume that the mixture of data-distributions is uniform on a k-dimensional unit sphere in H. Then C_m has k eigenvalues, all equal to $1/k$, so $\|C_m\|_{p/2} = k^{\frac{2-p}{p}}$. If we combine this with the $\mathcal{F}_{B,d}$ regularization considered above we obtain the bound

$$ E\left[\hat{\mathcal{R}}_n^m \left(\mathcal{F}_{B,d} \right) \mathbf{X} \right] \leq \frac{2B}{\sqrt{n}} \left(\left(\frac{d}{k} \right)^{\frac{p-2}{p}} + d^{\frac{p-2}{p}} \sqrt{\frac{3}{m}} \right)^{1/2}. $$

The limiting value as the number m of tasks increases depends only on the fraction $\rho = d/k$, which might be viewed as the ratio of utilized information to totally present information k. If $\rho < 1$ multi-task learning will always be an improvement over single task learning for sufficiently large m (modulo the important requirement that the tasks are sufficiently related to arrive at a small empirical error despite the regularisation). In the limit $m \to \infty$ the best exponent is $p = \infty$ leading to the bound

$$ \limsup_{m \to \infty} E\left[\hat{\mathcal{R}}_n^m \left(\mathcal{F}_{B,d} \right) (\mathbf{X}) \right] \leq \frac{2B}{\sqrt{n}} \rho^{1/2}. $$

For small values of m and large d smaller values of p will give a better bound.

If $\rho \geq 1$ constraining to $\mathcal{F}_{B,d}$ will bring no improvement over $\mathcal{F}_{B,\infty}$. This is understandable because constraining to at most d-dimensional subspaces has little effect when the data-distribution is already less than d-dimensional. Normally we expect that there exist low-dimensional subspaces expressing the relevant information in a chaos of data, which is the same as assuming $\rho \ll 1$.

A precursor of this paper is [12], where a result like part (II) of Theorem 2 is given for the case $p = 4$. It does not extend to larger values of p however, nor is it directly applicable to graph regularization.

The next section gives missing definitions and some important preliminary result. Section 3 gives a proof of part (I) of Theorem 2 and applies it to graph regularization. Section 4 is dedicated to the proof of part (II) of Theorem 2.

2 Definitions, Schatten-Norms and Hoelders Inequality

Throughout this paper we will use superscripts $l, r \in \{1, ..., m\}$ to index one of m learning tasks and we fix a real, separable Hilbert space H with inner product $\langle ., . \rangle$ and norm $\|.\|$, and assume the random variables X_i^l to be as described in the introduction. For a bounded operator T on H we generally use T^* to denote the adjoint and write $|T|^2 = T^*T$.

Let T be a compact operator from H to a Hilbert space H' and $\mu_i = \mu_i(T)$ its sequence of singular values in descending order, counting multiplicities. The μ_i are just the necessarily nonnegative eigenvalues of $(T^*T)^{1/2} = |T|$ (see [14] for background). For such operators T and $p \geq 1$ define

$$\|T\|_p = \left(\sum_i \mu_i^p \right)^{1/p} \quad \text{and} \quad \mathcal{I}_p = \left\{ T : \|T\|_p < \infty \right\}.$$

We also define $\|T\|_\infty = \sup_i \mu_i = \mu_0$ and $\mathcal{I}_\infty$ as the set of all compact operators from H to another Hilbert space H'. As the notation indicates, $\|.\|_p$ does indeed define a norm making $\mathcal{I}_p$ into a Banach space. For $1 \leq p_1 \leq p_2 \leq \infty$ we have $\|T\|_{p_2} \leq \|T\|_{p_1}$. For $T \in \mathcal{I}_1$ the trace $tr(T)$ is defined by

$$tr(T) = \sum_i \langle Te_i, e_i \rangle,$$

where (e_i) is an orthonormal basis of H. This series converges absolutely and its limit is independent of the choice of basis. If A and B are in $\mathcal{I}_2$ then A^*B is in $\mathcal{I}_1$ and the inner product

$$\langle A, B \rangle_2 = tr(A^*B)$$

makes $\mathcal{I}_2$ into a Hilbert space, the space of Hilbert-Schmidt operators. This work will rely on Hoelder's inequality for compact operators, a beautiful classical theorem (see e.g. Reed-Simon [13]).

Theorem 3. Let $1 \leq p \leq \infty$ and $q^{-1} + p^{-1} = 1$. If $A \in \mathcal{I}_p$ and $B \in \mathcal{I}_q$ then $AB \in \mathcal{I}_1$ and $|\langle A, B \rangle_2| = |tr(A^*B)| \leq \|A\|_p \|B\|_q$.

Let V be a bounded operator $V : H \to \mathbb{R}^m$. Let $\left(e^l \right)_{l=1}^m$ be the canonical basis for $\mathbb{R}^m$. By the Riesz theorem there is an m-tuples $\left(v^1, ..., v^m \right) \in H^m$ of vectors in H such that

$$\langle Vx, e^l \rangle = \langle v^l, x \rangle \tag{1}$$

holds for all l. Conversely, if $\left(v^1, ..., v^m \right) \in H^m$ then the formula

$$Vx = \sum_{l=1}^m \langle v^l, x \rangle e^l$$

defines a bounded linear transformation V such that (1) holds. We will just write $V \leftrightarrow \left(v^1, ..., v^m \right)$ for this bijection. Observe that if $V, W : H \to \mathbb{R}^m$ with $V \leftrightarrow \left(v^1, ..., v^m \right)$ and $W \leftrightarrow \left(w^1, ..., w^m \right)$, then

$$tr(W^*V) = \sum_{l=1}^m \langle v^l, w^l \rangle. \tag{2}$$

Definition 2. *For a configuration* $\boldsymbol{\sigma} = \left(\sigma_i^l\right)_{(l,i)=1}^{(m,n)} \in \{-1,1\}^{nm}$ *of the Radema-cher variables and* $\mathbf{x} = \left(x_i^l\right)_{(l,i)=1}^{(m,n)} \in H^{nm}$ *with* $\left\|x_i^l\right\| \leq 1$ *define a linear transfor-mation* $W(\boldsymbol{\sigma}, \mathbf{x}) : H \to \mathbb{R}^m$ *by* $W(\boldsymbol{\sigma}, \mathbf{x}) \leftrightarrow \left(w^1(\boldsymbol{\sigma}, \mathbf{x}), ..., w^m(\boldsymbol{\sigma}, \mathbf{x})\right)$ *and*

$$w^l(\boldsymbol{\sigma}, \mathbf{x}) = \sum_{i=1}^n \sigma_i^l x_i^l.$$

When there is no ambiguity we drop the explicit dependance on either $\boldsymbol{\sigma}$ or $\mathbf{x}$ or both. W is thus an operator-valued random variable and its components $w^l = \sum_{i=1}^n \sigma_i^l x_i^l$ are vector valued random variables.

In our context the beauty of Hoelder's inequality is that it immediately splits the Rademacher complexity into a regularizing factor, depending on the function class $\mathcal{F}$ used for learning, and a data dependent factor:

Lemma 1. *For conjugate exponents* $p, q \geq 1$ *with* $1/p + 1/q = 1$ *and* $\mathbf{x} = \left(x_i^l\right)_{(l,i)=1}^{(m,n)} \in H^{nm}$ *and a class* $\mathcal{F}$ *of bounded linear transformations* $V : H \to \mathbb{R}^m$, *we have*

$$\hat{\mathcal{R}}_n^m(\mathcal{F})(\mathbf{x}) \leq \frac{2}{\sqrt{n}} \left(\sup_{V \in \mathcal{F}} \frac{\|V\|_q}{\sqrt{m}} \right) \left(\frac{E_\sigma \left[\|W(\boldsymbol{\sigma}, \mathbf{x})\|_p \right]}{\sqrt{mn}} \right).$$

Proof. Using the trace formula (2) and Hoelder's inequality (Theorem 3) we obtain

$$\hat{\mathcal{R}}_n^m(\mathcal{F})(\mathbf{x}) = E_\sigma \left[\sup_{V \in \mathcal{F}} \frac{2}{mn} \sum_{l=1}^m \sum_{i=1}^n \sigma_i^l \left\langle x_i^l, v^l \right\rangle \right]$$

$$= E_\sigma \left[\sup_{V \in \mathcal{F}} \frac{2}{mn} \sum_{l=1}^m \left\langle w^l, v^l \right\rangle \right]$$

$$= E_\sigma \left[\sup_{V \in \mathcal{F}} \frac{2}{mn} \operatorname{tr}(W^* V) \right]$$

$$\leq \frac{2}{mn} E_\sigma \left[\sup_{V \in \mathcal{F}} \|V\|_q \|W\|_p \right].$$

$\square$

For every $x \in H$ we define an operator Q_x by $Q_x y = \langle y, x \rangle x$ for $y \in H$. The following facts are easily verified:

Lemma 2. *Let* $x, y \in H$ *and* $p \in [1, \infty]$. *Then*
(i) $Q_x \in \mathcal{I}_p$ *and* $\|Q_x\|_p = \|x\|^2$.
(ii) $\langle Q_x, Q_y \rangle_2 = \langle x, y \rangle^2$.
(iii) *If* $V \leftrightarrow \left(v^1, ..., v^m\right) : H \to \mathbb{R}^m$ *then* $|V|^2 = \sum_{l=1}^m Q_{v^l}$.

Let X be a random variable with values in H, such that $E\left[\|\|X\|\|\right] \leq \infty$. The linear functional $y \in H \mapsto E\left[\langle X, y \rangle\right]$ is bounded by $E\left[\|\|X\|\|\right]$ and thus defines (by the Riesz Lemma) a unique vector $E\left[X\right] \in H$ such that $E\left[\langle X, y \rangle\right] = \langle E\left[X\right], y \rangle, \forall y \in H$, with $\|E\left[X\right]\| \leq E\left[\|\|X\|\|\right]$.

If we also have $E\left[\|X\|^2\right] \leq \infty$ then we can apply the same construction to the random variable Q_X with values in the Hilbert space $\mathcal{I}_2$: By Lemma 2 (i) $E\left[\|Q_X\|_2\right] = E\left[\|X\|^2\right] \leq \infty$, so there is a unique operator $E\left[Q_X\right] \in \mathcal{I}_2$ such that $E\left[\langle Q_X, T \rangle_2\right] = \langle E\left[Q_X\right], T \rangle_2, \forall T \in \mathcal{I}_2$.

Definition 3. *The operator $E\left[Q_X\right]$ is called the covariance operator of X.*

We summarize some of its properties in the following lemma (see e.g. [12]). Property (ii) is sometimes taken as the defining property of the covariance operator.

Lemma 3. *The covariance operator $E\left[Q_X\right] \in \mathcal{I}_2$ has the following properties.*
(i) $\|E\left[Q_X\right]\|_2 \leq E\left[\|Q_X\|_2\right]$.
(ii) $\langle E\left[Q_X\right] y, z \rangle = E\left[\langle y, X \rangle \langle z, X \rangle\right], \forall y, z \in H$.
(iii) $tr\left(E\left[Q_X\right]\right) = E\left[\|X\|^2\right]$.

If $\mathbf{x} \in H^{mn}$ with $\mathbf{x} = \left(x_i^l : l \in \{1, ..., m\}, i \in \{1, ..., n\}\right)$ is a data-set, $\hat{E}$ be the expectation corresponding to the empirical distribution $1/\left(mn\right) \sum_{l,i=1}^{m,n} \delta_{x_i^l}$. The corresponding empirical covariance $\hat{C}\left(\mathbf{x}\right)$ is the operator

$$\hat{C}\left(\mathbf{x}\right) = \hat{E}\left[Q_X\right] = \frac{1}{mn} \sum_{l=1}^{m} \sum_{i=1}^{n} Q_{x_i^l}.$$

3   Graph Regularization

We give a proof of part (I) of Theorem 2 and sketch how it applies to graph regularization as described in [8] and [9].

Proof (of Theorem 2, part (I)). Beginning as in the proof of Lemma 1 we obtain from Hoelder's inequality in the simplest (Schwarz-) case $p = q = 2$

$$\hat{\mathcal{R}}_n^m\left(\mathcal{F}\right)\left(\mathbf{x}\right) = E_\sigma\left[\sup_{V \in \mathcal{F}} \frac{2}{mn} tr\left(W^* V\right)\right]$$

$$= E_\sigma\left[\sup_{V \in \mathcal{F}} \frac{2}{mn} tr\left(W^* A^{-1/2} A^{1/2} V\right)\right]$$

$$\leq \frac{2}{\sqrt{n}} \sup_{V \in \mathcal{F}} \left(\frac{\|A^{1/2} V\|_2}{\sqrt{m}}\right) \frac{E_\sigma\left[\|W^* A^{-1/2}\|_2\right]}{\sqrt{mn}}.$$

To prove part (I) it therefore suffices to show that $E_\sigma\left[\|W^* A^{-1/2}\|_2\right] \leq \left(n \, tr\left(A^{-1}\right)\right)^{1/2}$. Using Jensen's inequality, independence and symmetry of the Rademacher variables, we obtain

$$E_\sigma \left[\left\| W^* A^{-1/2} \right\|_2 \right]^2 \leq E \left[\left\| W^* A^{-1/2} \right\|_2^2 \right] = E \left[tr \left(W^* A^{-1} W \right) \right]$$

$$= \sum_{l=1}^{m} \sum_{r=1}^{m} A_{lr}^{-1} \sum_{i=1}^{n} \sum_{j=1}^{n} E \left[\sigma_i^l \sigma_j^r \right] \langle x_i^l, x_j^r \rangle$$

$$= \sum_{l=1}^{m} A_{ll}^{-1} \sum_{i=1}^{n} \left\| x_i^l \right\|^2$$

$$\leq n \, tr \left(A^{-1} \right),$$

as required.   □

Suppose that we have some way to quantify the 'relatedness' ω_{lr} of any pair (l, r) of distinct learning tasks, where we require symmetry $\omega_{lr} = \omega_{rl}$ and nonnegativity $\omega_{lr} \geq 0$. For simplicity we will assume connectivity in the sense that for all pairs (l, r), there is a sequence of indices $(l_i)_{i=0}^{K}$ such that $l = l_0$ and $r = l_K$ and $\omega_{l_{k-1} l_k} > 0$ for all $1 \leq k \leq K$.

The idea of graph regularization ([8], [9]) is to use a regularizer $J(V) = J(v^1, ..., v^m)$, which forces the classifiers of related tasks to be near each other, penalizing the squared distance $\left\| v^l - v^r \right\|^2$ proportional to ω_{lr}. Such a regularizer is

$$J(V) = \frac{1}{2m} \sum_{l,r} \omega_{lr} \left\| v^l - v^r \right\|^2 + \frac{\eta}{m} \sum_{l=1}^{m} \left\| v^l \right\|^2$$

$$= \frac{1}{m} \sum_{l,r} (L + \eta I)_{lr} \langle v^l, v^r \rangle,$$

where L is the Laplacian of the graph with m vertices and edge-weights ω, and I is the identity in $\mathbb{R}^m$. We have slightly departed from the form given in [9] by adding the term in η. We will however see, that a large number m of tasks allows η to be chosen small.

Fix $B > 0$. We will bound the Rademacher complexity of the function class $\mathcal{F} = \{ V : J(V) \leq B^2 \}$. Substitution of our bound in Theorem 1 will then lead to generalisation guarantees for graph regularisation.

To bound $\hat{\mathcal{R}}_n^m (\mathcal{F})$ note that a transformation $V \leftrightarrow (v^1, ..., v^m)$ belongs to $\mathcal{F}$ if and only if

$$\sum_{l,r} (L + \eta I)_{lr} \langle v^l, v^r \rangle \leq mB^2 \iff tr \left(V^* (L + \eta I) V \right) \leq mB^2$$

$$\iff m^{-1/2} \left\| (L + \eta I)^{1/2} V \right\|_2 \leq B.$$

Using Theorem 2 (I) with $A = L + \eta I$ therefore gives

$$\hat{\mathcal{R}}_n^m(\mathcal{F}) \le \frac{2B}{\sqrt{n}} \sqrt{\frac{tr\left((L+\eta I)^{-1}\right)}{m}}$$

$$= \frac{2B}{\sqrt{n}} \sqrt{\frac{1}{m}\sum_{i=2}^m \frac{1}{\lambda_i + \eta} + \frac{1}{m\eta}} \tag{3}$$

$$\le \frac{2B}{\sqrt{n}} \sqrt{\frac{1}{\lambda_2} + \frac{1}{m\eta}}, \tag{4}$$

where $\lambda_2, ..., \lambda_m$ are the nonzero eigenvalues of the Laplacian in (now) ascending order (with $\lambda_1 = 0$ having multiplicity 1 - it is here that we used connectivity). For a large number of tasks m we can choose η small, say $\eta = O\left(1/\sqrt{m}\right)$, and the contribution of the Laplacian becomes dominant. Which of the bounds (3) or (4) is preferable depends on the nature of the Laplacian, which in turn depends on the coupling constants ω_{lr}.

For a particularly simple example consider $\omega_{lr} = c/m$ for all distinct tasks l and r, where c is some positive constant. The regularizer then becomes

$$J(V) = \frac{1}{2m}\sum_{l,r} \frac{c}{m}\left\|v^l - v^r\right\|^2 + \frac{\eta}{m}\sum_{l=1}^m \left\|v^l\right\|^2$$

$$= \frac{c}{m}\sum_l \left\|v^l - \frac{1}{m}\sum_r v^r\right\|^2 + \frac{\eta}{m}\sum_{l=1}^m \left\|v^l\right\|^2,$$

and can be recognized as the regularizer in section 3.1.1 in [9]. The corresponding Laplacian is $L_{lr} = c\left(\delta_{lr} - 1/m\right)$, and the nonzero eigenvalues are all equal to c. Substitution in the bound (4) then gives

$$\hat{\mathcal{R}}_n^m(\mathcal{F}) \le \frac{2B}{\sqrt{n}} \sqrt{\frac{1}{c} + \frac{1}{m\eta}},$$

exhibiting both the benefit of assuming a large 'relatedness' c of the tasks, and the increasing irrelevance of the general regularization parameter η for a large number m of tasks.

4   Bounding the Expected Norm of $W(\sigma, \mathbf{x})$

Now we prove part (II) of Theorem 2. Hoelders inequality essentially reduces the problem of the proof to the analysis of the expected norm of $W = W(\sigma, \mathbf{x})$, $W \leftrightarrow (w^1, ..., w^m)$. Our idea of proof is to instead study $|W|^2$, which is easier to deal with. We compute the expectation and bound the variance of this random variable

Lemma 4. We have the two identities

(i) $E_\sigma\left[|W(\sigma, \mathbf{x})|^2\right] = mn\hat{C}(\mathbf{x})$

(ii) $E_\mathbf{x} E_\sigma\left[|W(\sigma, \mathbf{X})|^2\right] = mnC_m$

Proof. For a fixed configuration $\mathbf{x}$ and any $y, z \in H$ we have, by independence and symmetry of the Rademacher variables,

$$
\langle E_\sigma \left[W^* W \right] y, z \rangle = E_\sigma \left[\langle Wy, Wz \rangle \right] = \sum_{l=1}^{m} E_\sigma \left[\langle w^l, y \rangle \langle w^l, z \rangle \right]
$$

$$
= \sum_{l=1}^{m} \sum_{i=1}^{n} \sum_{j=1}^{n} E_\sigma \left[\sigma_i^l \sigma_j^l \right] \langle x_i^l, y \rangle \langle x_j^l, z \rangle
$$

$$
= \sum_{l=1}^{m} \sum_{i=1}^{n} \langle x_i^l, y \rangle \langle x_i^l, z \rangle = \left\langle \sum_{l=1}^{m} \sum_{i=1}^{n} Q_{x_i^l} y, z \right\rangle
$$

$$
= mn \left\langle \hat{C} \left(\mathbf{x} \right) y, z \right\rangle.
$$

The second equation follows from replacing $\mathbf{x}$ by $\mathbf{X}$ in the first one and applying $E_{\mathbf{X}}$. $\qquad\square$

Lemma 5. *For fixed* $\mathbf{x} \in H^{mn}$ *with* $\left\| x_i^l \right\| \leq 1$ *we have*

$$
E_\sigma \left[\left\| \left| W \left(\sigma, \mathbf{x} \right) \right|^2 - E_\sigma \left[\left| W \left(\sigma, \mathbf{x} \right) \right|^2 \right] \right\|_2 \right] \leq n\sqrt{2m}.
$$

Also

$$
E_{\mathbf{X}} E_\sigma \left[\left\| \left| W \left(\sigma, \mathbf{X} \right) \right|^2 - E_{\mathbf{X}} E_\sigma \left[\left| W \left(\sigma, \mathbf{X} \right) \right|^2 \right] \right\|_2 \right] \leq n\sqrt{3m}
$$

Proof. We use the representation $\left| W \right|^2 = \left| W \left(\sigma, \mathbf{x} \right) \right|^2 = \sum_{l=1}^{m} Q_{w^l}$ as introduced in section 2, Lemma 2, with

$$
w^l = w^l \left(\sigma, \mathbf{x} \right) = \sum_{i=1}^{n} \sigma_i^l x_i^l.
$$

To prove the first inequality we keep $\mathbf{x}$ fixed. Let the η_i^l be iid copies of σ_i^l and write $\hat{W} = W \left(\eta, \mathbf{x} \right)$ and $\hat{w}^l = w^l \left(\eta, \mathbf{x} \right)$. Then

$$
E_\sigma \left[\left\| \left| W \right|^2 - E_\sigma \left[\left| W \right|^2 \right] \right\|_2^2 \right] = E_{\sigma, \eta} \left[\left\langle \left| W \right|^2, \left| W \right|^2 \right\rangle_2 - \left\langle \left| W \right|^2, \left| \hat{W} \right|^2 \right\rangle_2 \right]
$$

$$
= \sum_{l=1}^{m} \sum_{r=1}^{m} E_{\sigma, \eta} \left[\langle Q_{w^l}, Q_{w^r} \rangle_2 - \langle Q_{w^l}, Q_{\hat{w}^r} \rangle_2 \right]
$$

$$
= \sum_{l=1}^{m} E_{\sigma, \eta} \left[\langle Q_{w^l}, Q_{w^l} \rangle_2 - \langle Q_{w^l}, Q_{\hat{w}^l} \rangle_2 \right],
$$

because of the independence of w^l and w^r for $l \neq r$. The l-th term in the last expression is equal to

$$
E_{\sigma, \eta} \left[\left\| w^l \right\|^4 - \langle w^l, \hat{w}^l \rangle^2 \right] = \sum_{i, j, i', j'} E_{\sigma, \eta} \left[\sigma_i^l \sigma_j^l \sigma_{i'}^l \sigma_{j'}^l - \sigma_i^l \eta_j^l \sigma_{i'}^l \eta_{j'}^l \right] \langle x_i^l, x_j^l \rangle \langle x_{i'}^l, x_{j'}^l \rangle.
$$

By independence and symmetry of the σ variables the expectation on the right will have the value one if $i = j$ and $i' = j'$ or if $i = j'$ and $i' = j$. If $i = i'$ and $j = j'$ a cancellation will occur, so the expectation will be zero. In all other cases it vanishes because there will be some factor of the σ_k^l occurring only once. We conclude that

$$E_{\sigma,\eta}\left[\left\|w^l\right\|^4 - \left\langle w^l, \hat{w}^l\right\rangle^2\right] = \sum_{i,j}\left(\left\|x_i^l\right\|^2\left\|x_j^l\right\|^2 + \left\langle x_i^l, x_j^l\right\rangle^2\right) \le 2n^2.$$

Summing over l we get with Jensen's inequality,

$$E_\sigma\left[\left\|\left|W\right|^2 - E_\sigma\left[\left|W\right|^2\right]\right\|_2\right] \le \left(E_\sigma\left[\left\|\left|W\right|^2 - E_\sigma\left[\left|W\right|^2\right]\right\|_2^2\right]\right)^{1/2} \le \left(2mn^2\right)^{1/2},$$

which is the first inequality.

To prove the second inequality we also introduce iid copies $\hat{X}_i^l$ of X_i^l and write $W = W\left(\sigma, \mathbf{X}\right)$ and $\hat{W} = W\left(\eta, \hat{\mathbf{X}}\right)$. Proceeding as before we obtain

$$E_{\sigma,\mathbf{X}}\left[\left\|\left|W\right|^2 - E_{\sigma,\mathbf{X}}\left[\left|W\right|^2\right]\right\|_2^2\right] = \sum_{l=1}^{m}E_{\sigma,\eta,\mathbf{X},\hat{\mathbf{X}}}\left[\left\|w^l\right\|^4 - \left\langle w^l, \hat{w}^l\right\rangle^2\right].$$

Now we have

$$E_{\sigma,\eta,\mathbf{X},\hat{\mathbf{X}}}\left[\left\|w^l\right\|^4 - \left\langle w^l, \hat{w}^l\right\rangle^2\right] \le E_{\sigma,\mathbf{X}}\left[\left\|w^l\right\|^4\right]$$

$$= \sum_{i,j,i',j'}E_\sigma\left[\sigma_i^l\sigma_j^l\sigma_{i'}^l\sigma_{j'}^l\right]E_\mathbf{X}\left[\left\langle x_i^l, x_j^l\right\rangle\left\langle x_{i'}^l, x_{j'}^l\right\rangle\right].$$

Now $E_\sigma\left[\sigma_i^l\sigma_j^l\sigma_{i'}^l\sigma_{j'}^l\right]$ will be nonzero and equal to one if either $i = j$ and $i' = j'$ or $i = i'$ and $j = j'$ or $i = j'$ and $j = i'$, which gives a bound of $3n^2$ on the above expectation. Summing over l we obtain

$$E_{\sigma,\mathbf{X}}\left[\left\|W^*W - E\left[W^*W\right]\right\|_2^2\right] \le 3mn^2$$

and the conclusion follows from Jensen's inequality. $\square$

Proof (of Theorem 2, part (II)). We have from Lemma 4, the triangle inequality, the nonincreasing nature of spectral norms $\|.\|_q$ and Lemma 5 for any $q \ge 2$

$$E_\sigma\left[\left\|\left|W\right|^2\right\|_q\right] - mn\left\|\hat{C}\left(\mathbf{x}\right)\right\|_q = E_\sigma\left[\left\|\left|W\right|^2\right\|_q - \left\|E_\sigma\left[\left|W\right|^2\right]\right\|_q\right]$$

$$\le E_\sigma\left[\left\|\left|W\right|^2 - E_\sigma\left[\left|W\right|^2\right]\right\|_q\right]$$

$$\le E_\sigma\left[\left\|\left|W\right|^2 - E_\sigma\left[\left|W\right|^2\right]\right\|_2\right]$$

$$\le n\sqrt{2m}.$$

Similarly we obtain $E_\mathbf{X}E_\sigma\left[\left\|\left|W\right|^2\right\|_q\right] - mn\left\|C_m\right\|_q \le n\sqrt{3m}$. It follows from Jensen's inequality that for $p \ge 4$

$$(mn)^{-1/2} E_\sigma \left[\|W\|_p \right] = (mn)^{-1/2} E_\sigma \left[\left\| |W|^2 \right\|_{p/2}^{1/2} \right]$$

$$\leq (mn)^{-1/2} \left(E_\sigma \left[\left\| |W|^2 \right\|_{p/2} \right] \right)^{1/2}$$

$$\leq (mn)^{-1/2} \left(mn \left\| \hat{C} (\mathbf{x}) \right\|_{p/2} + n\sqrt{2m} \right)^{1/2}$$

$$= \left(\left\| \hat{C} (\mathbf{x}) \right\|_{p/2} + \sqrt{\frac{2}{m}} \right)^{1/2} .$$

In the same way we obtain

$$(mn)^{-1/2} E_{\mathbf{X}} E_\sigma \left[\|W\|_p \right] \leq \left(\|C_m\|_{p/2} + \sqrt{\frac{3}{m}} \right)^{1/2} .$$

Substitution in Lemma 1 completes the proof.   □

5   Conclusion

We showed that an application of Hoelder's inequality to bound the Rademacher complexity of linear transformation classes leads to generalization bounds for various regularization schemes of multi-task learning. Two major defects of the results presented are the following:

- The decrease in the r.h.s of the bound in part II of Theorem 2 with $O \left(m^{-1/4} \right)$. Is this a necessary feature or an artifact of a clumsy proof? In [12] there is a similar bound with $O \left(m^{-1/2} \right)$, but it requires that the transformations can be factored $V = ST$ where $S : H \to \mathbb{R}^m$ has the property $\|S^* e^l\| \leq 1$ for the canonical basis $\left(e^l \right)$ of $\mathbb{R}^m$. Also the result in [12] is worse in the limit $m \to \infty$, diverging for constant ρ and $d \to \infty$ (in context and notation of section 1.3).
- Part II of Theorem 2 might well be valid for all $p \in [2, \infty]$, instead of just $p \in \{2\} \cup [4, \infty]$ (the case $p = 2$ follows trivially from part I). This would follow if something like Lemma 5 was true also for the 1-norm instead of the 2-norm.

References

1. R. K. Ando, T. Zhang, A framework for learning predictive structures from multiple tasks and unlabeled data, *Journal of Machine Learning Research*, 6: 1817-1853, 2005.
2. P. L. Bartlett and S. Mendelson. Rademacher and Gaussian Complexities: Risk Bounds and Structural Results. *Journal of Machine Learning Research*, 3: 463-482, 2002.
3. P.Bartlett, O.Bousquet and S.Mendelson. Local Rademacher complexities. Available online: http://www.stat.berkeley.edu/~bartlett/papers/bbm-lrc-02b.pdf.

4. J.Baxter, Theoretical Models of Learning to Learn, in *Learning to Learn*, S.Thrun, L.Pratt Eds. Springer 1998
5. J.Baxter, A Model of Inductive Bias Learning, *Journal of Artificial Intelligence Research* 12: 149-198, 2000
6. S. Ben-David and R. Schuller. Exploiting task relatedness for multiple task learning. In *COLT 03*, 2003.
7. R.Caruana, Multitask Learning, in *Learning to Learn*, S.Thrun, L.Pratt Eds. Springer 1998.
8. T. Evgeniou and M. Pontil, Regularized multi-task learning. *Proc. Conference on Knowledge Discovery and Data Mining*, 2004.
9. T. Evgeniou, C. Micchelli and M. Pontil, Learning multiple tasks with kernel methods. *JMLR*, 6: 615-637, 2005.
10. V. Koltchinskii and D. Panchenko, Empirical margin distributions and bounding the generalization error of combined classifiers, *The Annals of Statistics*, Vol. 30, No 1, 1-50.
11. M. Ledoux and M. Talagrand, *Probability in Banach Spaces: isoperimetry and processes*. Springer, 1991.
12. A. Maurer, Bounds for linear multi-task learning. *Journal of Machine Learning Research*, 7:117–139, 2006.
13. Michael Reed and Barry Simon. *Fourier Analysis, Self-Adjointness*, part II of *Methods of Mathematical Physics, Academic Press*, 1980.
14. Michael Reed and Barry Simon. *Functional Analysis*, part I of *Methods of Mathematical Physics, Academic Press*, 1980.
15. S.Thrun, Lifelong Learning Algorithms, in *Learning to Learn*, S.Thrun, L.Pratt Eds. Springer 1998

Function Classes That Approximate the Bayes Risk

Ingo Steinwart, Don Hush, and Clint Scovel

CCS-3, Los Alamos National Laboratory, Los Alamos NM 87545, USA
{ingo, dhush, jcs}@lanl.gov

Abstract. Many learning algorithms approximately minimize a risk functional over a predefined function class. In order to establish consistency for such algorithms it is therefore necessary to know whether this function class approximates the Bayes risk. In this work we present necessary and sufficient conditions for the latter. We then apply these results to reproducing kernel Hilbert spaces used in support vector machines (SVMs). Finally, we briefly discuss universal consistency of SVMs for non-compact input domains.

1 Introduction

Many learning problems such as classification and regression are characterized by a loss function $L : X \times Y \times \mathbb{R} \to [0, \infty]$ and an unknown distribution P on $X \times Y$. Having a sample set $T \in (X \times Y)^n$ drawn in an i.i.d. fashion from P the learning goal is then to find a measurable function $f : X \to \mathbb{R}$ whose *L-risk*

$$\mathcal{R}_{L,\mathrm{P}}(f) := \int_{X \times Y} L(x, y, f(x)) \, d\mathrm{P}(x, y)$$

is close to the *Bayes L-risk*, i.e. the smallest possible risk

$$\mathcal{R}_{L,\mathrm{P}}^* := \inf \{ \mathcal{R}_{L,\mathrm{P}}(f) \mid f : X \to \mathbb{R} \text{ measurable} \}.$$

In order to find such a function many learning methods minimize a (modified) empirical risk over a predefined function class F. Examples of such learning methods include empirical risk minimization, SVMs, (regularized) boosting, some neural networks, and certain decision trees.

In a first step of the consistency analysis of such a learning method one typically shows that the algorithm produces with high probability a function f_T whose risk $\mathcal{R}_{L,\mathrm{P}}(f_T)$ is close to the F-optimal L-risk $\mathcal{R}_{L,\mathrm{P},F}^* := \inf_{f \in F} \mathcal{R}_{L,\mathrm{P}}(f)$. In order to show that $\mathcal{R}_{L,\mathrm{P}}(f_T)$ is close to the Bayes risk $\mathcal{R}_{L,\mathrm{P}}^*$ it thus remains to prove that the function class F is (L, P)-*rich*, i.e. that it satisfies

$$\mathcal{R}_{L,\mathrm{P},F}^* = \mathcal{R}_{L,\mathrm{P}}^*. \tag{1}$$

In this work we provide both necessary and sufficient conditions for (1) for a variety of loss functions and distributions. Moreover, we apply these general conditions to reproducing kernel Hilbert spaces (RKHSs) used in SVMs. In particular,

G. Lugosi and H.U. Simon (Eds.): COLT 2006, LNAI 4005, pp. 79–93, 2006.

for universal kernels introduced in [1] we establish (L, P)-richness for essentially all reasonable continuous loss functions. Furthermore, for kernels acting on discrete spaces X we establish the first sufficient conditions for (L, P)-richness, and we also show that the Gaussian RBF kernels are rich for $X := \mathbb{R}^d$. Finally, we use these results to discuss consistency of SVMs over non-compact input domains.

The rest of this work is organized as follows. In Section 2 we introduce basic notions for loss functions and provide various examples of losses satisfying these notions. In Section 3 we then present our main results on richness and apply them to RKHSs. Finally, the proofs of all results are gathered in Section 4.

2   Preliminaries: Losses and Their Risks

In the following X is always a measurable space if not mentioned otherwise and $Y \subset \mathbb{R}$ is always a closed subset. Moreover, $\mathcal{L}_0(X)$ denotes the set of all measurable functions $f : X \to \mathbb{R}$, and $L_p(\mu)$ stands for the standard space of p-integrable functions with respect to the measure μ on X.

Let us now introduce the fundamental definitions of this work:

Definition 1. *A function* $L : X \times Y \times \mathbb{R} \to [0, \infty]$ *is called a* loss function *if it is measurable. In this case* L *is called:*

i) convex *if* $L(x, y, .) : \mathbb{R} \to [0, \infty]$ *is convex for all* $x \in X$, $y \in Y$.
ii) continuous *if* $L(x, y, .) : \mathbb{R} \to [0, \infty]$ *is continuous for all* $x \in X$, $y \in Y$.

It is obvious that the risk of a convex loss is convex on $\mathcal{L}_0(X)$. However, in general the risk of a continuous loss is not continuous. In order to ensure this continuity (cf. Lemma 2) we need the following definition:

Definition 2. *We call a loss function* $L : X \times Y \times \mathbb{R} \to [0, \infty]$ *a* Nemitski loss function *if there exist a measurable function* $b : X \times Y \to [0, \infty)$ *and an increasing function* $h : [0, \infty) \to [0, \infty)$ *with*

$$L(x, y, t) \leq b(x, y) + h(|t|), \qquad (x, y, t) \in X \times Y \times \mathbb{R}. \qquad (2)$$

Furthermore, we say that L *is a* Nemitski loss of order $p \in (0, \infty)$, *if there exists a constant* $c > 0$ *with* $h(t) = c\, t^p$ *for all* $t \geq 0$. *Finally, if* P *is a distribution on* $X \times Y$ *with* $b \in L_1(\mathrm{P})$ *we say that* L *is a* P-integrable Nemitski loss.

Note that P-integrable Nemitski loss functions L satisfy $\mathcal{R}_{L,\mathrm{P}}(f) < \infty$ for all $f \in L_\infty(\mathrm{P}_X)$, and consequently we also have $\mathcal{R}_{L,\mathrm{P}}(0) < \infty$ and $\mathcal{R}_{L,\mathrm{P}}^* < \infty$.

Let us now present some examples of loss functions that satisfy the above definitions. We begin with the class of locally Lipschitz continuous loss functions:

Example 1. A loss $L : X \times Y \times \mathbb{R} \to [0, \infty)$ is called *locally Lipschitz continuous* if

$$|L|_{a,1} := \sup_{\substack{t,t' \in [-a,a] \\ t \neq t'}} \sup_{\substack{x \in X \\ y \in Y}} \frac{|L(x, y, t) - L(x, y, t')|}{|t - t'|} < \infty, \qquad a > 0. \qquad (3)$$

Moreover, L is called *Lipschitz continuous* if $|L|_1 := \sup_{a>0} |L|_{a,1} < \infty$.

Note that if $Y \subset \mathbb{R}$ is a *finite* subset and $L : Y \times \mathbb{R} \to [0, \infty)$ is a convex loss function then L is a locally Lipschitz continuous loss function. Moreover, a locally Lipschitz continuous loss function L is a Nemitski loss since (3) yields

$$L(x, y, t) \leq L(x, y, 0) + |L|_{|t|,1} |t|, \qquad (x, y, t) \in X \times Y \times \mathbb{R}. \qquad (4)$$

In particular, a locally Lipschitz continuous loss L is a P-integrable Nemitski loss if and only if $\mathcal{R}_{L,\mathrm{P}}(0) < \infty$. Moreover, if L is Lipschitz continuous then L is a Nemitski loss of order 1.   ◁

The following two examples present some commonly used types of loss functions that satisfy the above definitions:

Example 2. A loss $L : Y \times \mathbb{R} \to [0, \infty)$ of the form $L(y, t) = \varphi(yt)$ for a suitable function $\varphi : \mathbb{R} \to \mathbb{R}$ and all $y \in Y := \{-1, 1\}$ and $t \in \mathbb{R}$, is called *margin-based*. Recall that margin-based losses such as the (squared) hinge loss, the AdaBoost loss, the logistic loss and the least squares loss are used in many classification algorithms. Obviously, L is convex, continuous, or (locally) Lipschitz continuous if and only if φ is. In addition, convexity of L implies local Lipschitz continuity of L. Moreover, L is always a P-integrable Nemitski loss since we have

$$L(y, t) \leq \max\{\varphi(-t), \varphi(t)\}$$

for all $y \in Y$ and all $t \in \mathbb{R}$. From this we can also easily derive a characterization for L being a P-integrable Nemitski loss of order p.   ◁

Example 3. A loss $L : Y \times \mathbb{R} \to [0, \infty)$ of the form $L(y, t) = \psi(y - t)$ for a suitable function $\psi : \mathbb{R} \to \mathbb{R}$ and all $y \in Y := \mathbb{R}$ and $t \in \mathbb{R}$, is called *distance-based*. Distance-based losses such as the least squares loss, Huber's insensitive loss, the logistic loss, or the ϵ-insensitive loss are usually used for regression. It is easy to see that L is convex, continuous, or Lipschitz continuous if and only if ψ is. Let us say that L is of *upper growth* $p \in [1, \infty)$ if there is a $c > 0$ with

$$\psi(r) \leq c \left(|r|^p + 1 \right), \qquad r \in \mathbb{R}.$$

Then it is obvious that L is of upper growth type 1 if it is Lipschitz continuous, and if L is convex the converse implication also holds. In addition, a distance-based loss function of upper growth type $p \in [1, \infty)$ is a Nemitski loss of order p, and if the distribution P satisfies $\mathbb{E}_{(x,y) \sim \mathrm{P}} |y|^p < \infty$ it is also P-integrable.   ◁

3   Main Results

In this section we present our main results establishing (L, P)-richness, i.e. Equation (1). Let us begin with some *sufficient* conditions:

Theorem 1. *Let $L : X \times Y \times \mathbb{R} \to [0, \infty]$ be a continuous loss function, P be a distribution on $X \times Y$ such that L is a P-integrable Nemitski loss, and*

$F \subset L_\infty(\mathrm{P}_X)$. *Furthermore, assume that for all* $g \in L_\infty(\mathrm{P}_X)$ *there exists a sequence* $(f_n) \subset F$ *with* $\sup_{n \geq 1} \|f_n\|_\infty < \infty$ *and*

$$\lim_{n \to \infty} f_n(x) = g(x) \tag{5}$$

for P_X*-almost all* $x \in X$. *Then* F *is* (L, P)*-rich.*

Note that the assumptions on F in Theorem 1 are satisfied if and only if for all $g \in L_\infty(\mathrm{P}_X)$ there exists a sequence $(f_n) \subset F$ with $\sup_{n \geq 1} \|f_n\|_\infty < \infty$ and $f_n \to g$ in probability P_X.

   Let us now provide an interesting example of a set F satisfying the assumption of Theorem 1. To this end let X be a compact topological Hausdorff space, $k : X \times X \to \mathbb{R}$ be a continuous kernel and H be its associated RKHS. Following [1] we say that H (or k) is universal if H is dense in the space $C(X)$ of continuous functions $f : X \to \mathbb{R}$, equipped with the $\|.\|_\infty$-norm. For examples of such kernels we refer to [1]. Now the following result applies Theorem 1 to universal kernels:

Corollary 1. *Let* X *be a compact metric space,* $L : X \times Y \times \mathbb{R} \to [0, \infty]$ *be a continuous loss function, and* P *be a distribution on* $X \times Y$ *such that* L *is a* P*-integrable Nemitski loss. Then every universal RKHS over* X *is* (L, P)*-rich.*

At first glance it seems disappointing that Corollary 1 only holds for compact *metric* spaces. However, the following theorem shows that these spaces are the only ones which permit universal kernels:

Theorem 2. *For a compact topological Hausdorff space* X *the following statements are equivalent:*

   i) There exists a universal kernel k *on* X.
   ii) X *is metrizable, i.e. there exists a metric generating the topology.*

Most common losses are of some order $p \in [1, \infty)$. For such losses we now present a weaker sufficient condition for richness than that of Theorem 1:

Theorem 3. *Let* $L : X \times Y \times \mathbb{R} \to [0, \infty]$ *be a continuous loss function and* P *be a distribution on* $X \times Y$ *such* L *is a* P*-integrable Nemitski loss of order* $p \in [1, \infty)$. *Then every dense subset* $F \subset L_p(\mathrm{P}_X)$ *is* (L, P)*-rich.*

Note that if F is a dense subset of $L_p(\mathrm{P}_X)$ for some $p \in [1, \infty)$ then it is also a dense subset of $L_q(\mathrm{P}_X)$ for all q with $1 \leq q \leq p$. Consequently, the denseness assumption in Theorem 3 becomes stronger for loss functions of higher order.

   The condition that F is dense in $L_p(\mu)$ can often be guaranteed by means from functional analysis. In the following we will illustrate this for RKHSs. To this end let $k : X \times X \to \mathbb{R}$ be a measurable kernel and H be its associated RKHS. Given a measure μ on X and a real number $p \in [1, \infty)$ we define

$$\|k\|_{L_p(\mu)} := \left(\int_X k^{\frac{p}{2}}(x, x) d\mu(x) \right)^{\frac{1}{p}}.$$

It is elementary to check that the inclusion $I : H \to L_p(\mu)$ is well-defined and continuous if $\|k\|_{L_p(\mu)} < \infty$. Furthermore, its adjoint operator I' is the integral operator $T_k : L_{p'}(\mu) \to H$ defined by

$$T_k g(x) := \int_X k(x, x') g(x') d\mu(x'), \qquad g \in L_{p'}(\mu),\ x \in X, \qquad (6)$$

where p' is defined by $\frac{1}{p} + \frac{1}{p'} = 1$. With these preparations we can now characterize when H is dense in $L_p(\mu)$:

Proposition 1. *Let X be a measurable space, μ be a measure on X, k be a measurable kernel on X with RKHS H such that $\|k\|_{L_p(\mu)} < \infty$ for some $p \in [1, \infty)$. Then the following statements are equivalent:*

i) H is dense in $L_p(\mu)$.
ii) The integral operator $T_k : L_{p'}(\mu) \to H$ defined by (6) is injective.

The next result provides injectivity for the integral operators of the Gaussian RBF kernels k_σ defined by $k_\sigma(x, x') := \exp(-\|x - x'\|_2^2/\sigma^2)$, $x, x' \in \mathbb{R}^d$, $\sigma > 0$.

Theorem 4. *Let μ be a finite measure on $\mathbb{R}^d$ and H_σ be the RKHS of k_σ. Then $T_{k_\sigma} : L_{p'}(\mu) \to H_\sigma$ is injective for all $p \in (1, \infty)$ and all $\sigma > 0$.*

Combining Theorem 4 with a stability argument in the sense of [2], it is not hard to show that an SVM with e.g. the hinge loss and a Gaussian RBF kernel is classification consistent for all distributions P on $\mathbb{R}^d \times \{-1, 1\}$. This extends the known consistency result [3, 4] from bounded to unbounded input domains.

If P_X is absolutely continuous with respect to some measure μ then Proposition 1 yields the following sufficient condition for H being dense in $L_p(P_X)$:

Corollary 2. *Let X be a measurable space, μ be a measure on X, and k be a measurable kernel on X with RKHS H and $\|k\|_{L_p(\mu)} < \infty$ for some $p \in [1, \infty)$. Assume that $T_k : L_{p'}(\mu) \to H$ is injective. Then H is dense in $L_q(h\mu)$ for all $q \in [1, p]$ and all measurable $h : X \to [0, \infty)$ with $h \in L_s(\mu)$, where $s := \frac{p}{p-q}$.*

Let us now investigate denseness properties of RKHSs over discrete spaces X. To this end let us write $\ell_p(X) := L_p(\nu)$, where $p \in [1, \infty]$ and ν is the counting measure on X. Note that these spaces obviously satisfy $\ell_p(X) \subset \ell_q(X)$ for $p \leq q$ which is used in the proof of the following corollary:

Corollary 3. *Let X be a countable set and k be a kernel on X with $\|k\|_{\ell_p(X)} < \infty$ for some $p \in [1, \infty)$. If k satisfies*

$$\sum_{x, x' \in X} k(x, x') f(x) f(x') > 0 \qquad (7)$$

for all $f \in \ell_{p'}(X)$ with $f \neq 0$ then the RKHS of k is dense in $L_q(\mu)$ for all $q \in [1, \infty)$ and all distributions μ on X.

Note that the sharpest case $p = q = \infty$ is excluded in the above corollary. The reason for this is that the dual of $\ell_\infty(X)$ is *not* $\ell_1(X)$. However, if instead we consider the *pre*-dual of $\ell_1(X)$, namely the Banach space

$$c_0(X) := \{f : X \to \mathbb{R} \,|\, \forall \varepsilon > 0 \,\exists \text{ finite } A \subset X \text{ such that } \forall x \in X \backslash A : |f(x)| \leq \varepsilon\}$$

which is equipped with the usual $\|.\|_\infty$-norm, then we obtain:

Theorem 5. *Let X be a countable set and k be a bounded kernel on X that satisfies $k(.,x) \in c_0(X)$ for all $x \in X$, and (7) for all $f \in \ell_1(X)$ with $f \neq 0$. Then the RKHS of k is (L, P)-rich for all distribution P on $X \times Y$ and all continuous, P-integrable Nemitski losses $L : X \times Y \times \mathbb{R} \to [0, \infty)$.*

It is not hard to see that there exist non-trivial kernels satisfying the assumptions of Theorem 3 and Theorem 5. Using a stability argument we hence see that for all countable X there exist non-trivial, universally consistent SVMs.

Let us now present some *necessary* conditions for (L, P)-richness. To this end we first recall some concepts from [5]: let $L : Y \times \mathbb{R} \to [0, \infty]$ be a loss function and Q be a distribution on Y. We define the *inner L-risk* of Q by

$$\mathcal{C}_{L,\mathrm{Q}}(t) := \int_Y L(y,t)\,d\mathrm{Q}(y), \qquad\qquad t \in \mathbb{R}.$$

Furthermore, the *minimal inner L-risk* is denoted by $\mathcal{C}^*_{L,\mathrm{Q}} := \inf_{t \in \mathbb{R}} \mathcal{C}_{L,\mathrm{Q}}(t)$, and the corresponding set of (non-trivial) minimizers is defined by

$$\mathcal{M}_{L,\mathrm{Q}}(0^+) := \{t \in \mathbb{R} : \mathcal{C}_{L,\mathrm{Q}}(t) = \mathcal{C}^*_{L,\mathrm{Q}}\}$$

if $\mathcal{C}^*_{L,\mathrm{Q}} < \infty$, and by $\mathcal{M}_{L,\mathrm{Q}}(0^+) := \emptyset$ otherwise. Finally, we need the *self-calibration function* which is defined by

$$\delta_{\max,L}(\varepsilon,\mathrm{Q}) := \inf\{\mathcal{C}_{L,\mathrm{Q}}(t) - \mathcal{C}^*_{L,\mathrm{Q}} : t \in \mathbb{R} \text{ with } |t - t'| \geq \varepsilon \text{ for all } t' \in \mathcal{M}_{L,\mathrm{Q}}(0^+)\}$$

for $\varepsilon \in [0, \infty)$ and Q with $\mathcal{C}^*_{L,\mathrm{Q}} < \infty$. Note that in [5] this function is denoted by $\delta_{\max,\check{L},L}(\varepsilon,\mathrm{Q})$. Moreover, in [5] it was shown that $\mathcal{M}_{L,\mathrm{Q}}(0^+) = \{t^*_\mathrm{Q}\}$ implies

$$\delta_{\max,L}(|t - t^*_{L,\mathrm{Q}}|, \mathrm{Q}) \leq \mathcal{C}_{L,\mathrm{Q}}(t) - \mathcal{C}^*_{L,\mathrm{Q}}, \qquad\qquad t \in \mathbb{R},$$

i.e. the self-calibration function quantifies how well an approximate minimizer of $\mathcal{C}_{L,\mathrm{Q}}(.)$ approximates the exact minimizer t^*_Q. Finally, given a set of distributions $\mathcal{Q}$ on Y we say that a distribution P on $X \times Y$ is of type $\mathcal{Q}$ if its conditional probabilities satisfy $\mathrm{P}(.|x) \in \mathcal{Q}$ for P_X-almost all $x \in X$.

Now we can formulate our first necessary condition for (L, P)-richness:

Theorem 6. *Let $L : Y \times \mathbb{R} \to [0, \infty)$ be a convex loss function such that there exists two distributions Q_1, Q_2 on Y, and two real numbers $t^*_1 \neq t^*_2$ with $\mathcal{M}_{L,\mathrm{Q}_1}(0^+) = \{t^*_1\}$ and $\mathcal{M}_{L,\mathrm{Q}_2}(0^+) = \{t^*_2\}$. Furthermore, let X be a measurable space and μ be a distribution on X. Assume that $F \subset L_\infty(\mu)$ is a (L, P)-rich linear subspace for all $\{\mathrm{Q}_1, \mathrm{Q}_2\}$-type distributions P on $X \times Y$ with $\mathrm{P}_X = \mu$. Then for all $g \in L_\infty(\mu)$ there exists a sequence $(f_n) \subset F$ with*

$$\lim_{n \to \infty} f_n(x) = g(x) \qquad\qquad \text{for } \mu\text{-almost all } x \in X.$$

Corollary 4. *Let X, L and Q_1, Q_2 be as in Theorem 6. Furthermore, let k be a measurable kernel on X whose RKHS H is (L, P)-rich for all $\{Q_1, Q_2\}$-type distributions P on $X \times Y$. Then k is strictly positive definite.*

There is an gap between the sufficient condition of Theorem 1 and the necessary condition of Theorem 6. Our next goal is to close this gap for certain Nemitski losses of order p. To this end we first present the following necessary condition which uses an additional assumption on the self-calibration function:

Theorem 7. *Let $L : Y \times \mathbb{R} \to [0, \infty)$ be a convex loss function such that there exists two distributions Q_1, Q_2 on Y, and two real numbers $t_1^* \neq t_2^*$ with $\mathcal{M}_{L,Q_1}(0^+) = \{t_1^*\}$ and $\mathcal{M}_{L,Q_2}(0^+) = \{t_2^*\}$. In addition assume that there exist constants $B > 0$ and $p > 0$ with*

$$\delta_{\max,L}(\varepsilon, Q_i) \geq B\, \varepsilon^p, \qquad \varepsilon > 0,\ i = 1, 2.$$

Furthermore, let X be a measurable space, μ be a distribution on X, and $F \subset L_p(\mu)$ be a (L, P)-rich linear subspace for all $\{Q_1, Q_2\}$-type distributions P on $X \times Y$ with $P_X = \mu$. Then F is dense in $L_p(\mu)$.

By combining Theorem 3 with Theorem 7 we now obtain the following characterization of (L, P)-richness:

Theorem 8. *Let $L : Y \times \mathbb{R} \to [0, \infty)$ be a convex Nemitski loss of order $p \in [1, \infty)$, i.e. we have (2) with $b : Y \to [0, \infty)$. Furthermore, let Q_1, Q_2 be distributions on Y with $b \in L_1(Q_1) \cap L_1(Q_2)$, and $t_1^*, t_2^* \in \mathbb{R}$ be real numbers with $\mathcal{M}_{L,Q_1}(0^+) = \{t_1^*\}$, $\mathcal{M}_{L,Q_2}(0^+) = \{t_2^*\}$, and $t_1^* \neq t_2^*$. In addition, assume that there exists a constant $B > 0$ such that their self-calibration functions satisfy*

$$\delta_{\max,L}(\varepsilon, Q_i) \geq B\, \varepsilon^p, \qquad \varepsilon > 0,\ i = 1, 2.$$

Furthermore, let X be a measurable space, μ be a distribution on X, and $F \subset L_p(\mu)$ be a subspace. Then the following statements are equivalent:

i) F is (L, P)-rich for all distributions P on $X \times Y$ with $P_X = \mu$ for which L is a P-integrable Nemitski loss of order p.

ii) F is (L, P)-rich for all $\{Q_1, Q_2\}$-type distributions P on $X \times Y$ with $P_X = \mu$.

iii) F is dense in $L_p(\mu)$.

The following examples illustrate that many important loss functions satisfy the assumptions of Theorem 8:

Example 4. For $p \geq 1$ let L be the loss defined by $L(y, t) := |y - t|^p$, $y, t \in \mathbb{R}$. Furthermore, let $Q_1 := \delta_{\{y_1\}}$, $Q_1 := \delta_{\{y_2\}}$ be two Dirac distributions on $\mathbb{R}$ with $y_1 \neq y_2$. Then L, Q_1, and Q_2 satisfy the assumptions of Theorem 8 for p.

In order to see this, we first observe with Example 3 that L is a Nemitski loss of order p. Furthermore, for the Dirac measure $Q := \delta_{\{y_0\}}$ at some $y_0 \in \mathbb{R}$ we have $\mathcal{C}_{L,Q}(t) = |t - y_0|^p$, $t \in \mathbb{R}$. Consequently, we have $\mathcal{C}_{L,Q}^* = 0$ and $\mathcal{M}_{L,Q}(0^+) = \{y_0\}$. With these equalities it is easy to check that the self-calibration function of L is

$$\delta_{\max,L}(\varepsilon, Q) = \varepsilon^p, \qquad \varepsilon \geq 0. \qquad \triangleleft$$

The above example shows that F being a dense subspace of $L_p(\mathrm{P}_X)$ characterizes the (L, P)-richness. Moreover, it also shows that restricting the class of distributions to noise-free distributions P, i.e. to distributions with $\mathrm{P}(.|x) = \delta_{\{f(x)\}}$ for measurable functions $f : X \to \mathbb{R}$, does not change this characterization. In other words, if we do not want to impose further assumptions on P then F being dense in $L_p(\mathrm{P}_X)$ is the condition we should look for.

The following example provides a similar characterization for the ϵ-insensitive loss function used in the standard SVM formulation for regression:

Example 5. Let $\epsilon > 0$ and L be the ϵ-insensitive loss defined by $L(y, t) := \max\{0, |y - t| - \epsilon\}$, $y, t \in \mathbb{R}$. Furthermore, for $y_1, y_2 \in \mathbb{R}$ with $y_1 \neq y_2$ we define $Q_i := \frac{1}{2}\delta_{\{y_i - \epsilon\}} + \frac{1}{2}\delta_{\{y_i + \epsilon\}}$, $i = 1, 2$. Then L, Q_1, and Q_2 satisfy the assumptions of Theorem 8 for $p = 1$.

In order to see this, we first observe that L is a Nemitski loss of order 1. Let us define $\psi(r) := \max\{0, |r| - \epsilon\}$, $r \in \mathbb{R}$. For Q_i, $i = 1, 2$ we then have

$$2\mathcal{C}_{L,Q_i}(t) = \psi(y_i - \epsilon - t) + \psi(y_i + \epsilon - t), \qquad t \in \mathbb{R},$$

and thus we have $\mathcal{C}_{L,Q_i}(y_i) = 0 \leq \mathcal{C}_{L,Q_i}(t)$ for all $t \in \mathbb{R}$. For $t \geq 0$ this yields

$$\mathcal{C}_{L,Q_i}(y_i \pm t) - \mathcal{C}_{L,Q_i}^* = \frac{1}{2}\psi(\epsilon + t) + \frac{1}{2}\psi(\epsilon - t) \geq \frac{1}{2}\psi(\epsilon + t) = \frac{t}{2},$$

and hence we find both $\mathcal{M}_{L,Q_i}(0^+) = \{y_i\}$ and $\delta_{\max,L}(\varepsilon, Q) = \frac{\varepsilon}{2}$ for $\varepsilon \geq 0$.   ◁

Our last example provides a characterization of richness for the hinge loss used in the standard SVM formulation for classification:

Example 6. Let L be the hinge loss defined by $L(y, t) := \max\{0, 1 - yt\}$, $y \in Y := \{-1, 1\}$, $t \in \mathbb{R}$. Furthermore, let Q_1, Q_2 be distributions on Y with $\eta_1 := Q_1(\{1\}) \in (0, 1/2)$ and $\eta_2 := Q_2(\{1\}) \in (1/2, 1)$. Then L, Q_1, and Q_2 satisfy the assumptions of Theorem 8 for $p = 1$.

In order to see this we first observe that L is Lipschitz continuous and hence a Nemitski loss of order 1. Moreover, it is well-known that $\mathcal{M}_{L,\eta}(0^+) = \{\mathrm{sign}(2\eta - 1)\}$ for $\eta \neq 0, \frac{1}{2}, 1$, and in addition, for such η an elementary calculation shows

$$\delta_{\max,L}(\varepsilon, \eta) = \varepsilon \min\{\eta, 1 - \eta, 2\eta - 1\}, \qquad \varepsilon \geq 0.   ◁$$

Note that unlike the distributions in Example 4 the distributions in Example 6 are noisy. This is due to the fact that only noise makes the hinge loss minimizer unique. Moreover, note that using e.g. the least squares loss for a classification problem requires $L_2(\mu)$-denseness which in general is a strictly stronger condition than the $L_1(\mu)$-denseness required for the hinge loss or the logistic loss. This is remarkable since the target functions for the former two losses are bounded, whereas in general the target function for the logistic loss is not even integrable.

Obviously, Condition (7) implies that k is strictly positive definite, and we have already seen in Corollary 1 that this property is *necessary* for richness. Our last result now shows that in general it is *not sufficient*:

Theorem 9. *There exists a bounded strictly positive definite kernel k on $X := \mathbb{N}_0$ with $k(., x) \in c_0(X)$ for all $x \in X$, such that for all measures μ on X with $\mu(\{x\}) > 0$, $x \in X$, the RKHS H of k is not dense in $L_1(\mu)$.*

4   Proofs

Lemma 1. *Let* $L : X \times Y \times \mathbb{R} \to [0, \infty]$ *be a continuous loss,* P *be a distribution on* $X \times Y$, *and* $(f_n) \subset \mathcal{L}_0(X)$ *be a sequence that converges to an* $f \in \mathcal{L}_0(X)$ *in probability* P_X. *Then we have* $\mathcal{R}_{L,P}(f) \leq \liminf_{n \to \infty} \mathcal{R}_{L,P}(f_n)$.

Proof. Since (f_n) converges in probability, there exists a subsequence (f_{n_k}) of (f_n) with

$$\lim_{k \to \infty} \mathcal{R}_{L,P}(f_{n_k}) = \liminf_{n \to \infty} \mathcal{R}_{L,P}(f_n)$$

and $f_{n_k}(x) \to f(x)$ for P_X-almost all $x \in X$. By the continuity of L we then have $L(x, y, f_{n_k}(x)) \to L(x, y, f(x))$ almost surely and hence Fatou's lemma gives

$$\mathcal{R}_{L,P}(f) = \int_{X \times Y} \lim_{k \to \infty} L\big(x, y, f_{n_k}(x)\big)\, d\mathrm{P}(x,y) \leq \liminf_{k \to \infty} \int_{X \times Y} L\big(x, y, f_{n_k}(x)\big)\, d\mathrm{P}(x,y)$$

$$= \liminf_{n \to \infty} \mathcal{R}_{L,P}(f_n)\,. \qquad \square$$

Lemma 2. *Let* P *be a distribution on* $X \times Y$ *and* $L : X \times Y \times \mathbb{R} \to [0, \infty]$ *be a continuous,* P*-integrable Nemitski loss function. Then we have:*

i) *Let* $f_n \in \mathcal{L}_0(X)$, $n \geq 1$, *be functions with* $B := \sup_{n \geq 1} \|f_n\|_\infty < \infty$. *If the sequence* (f_n) *converges* P_X-almost surely to an $f \in \mathcal{L}_0(X)$ then we have

$$\lim_{n \to \infty} \mathcal{R}_{L,P}(f_n) = \mathcal{R}_{L,P}(f)\,.$$

ii) *The map* $\mathcal{R}_{L,P} : L_\infty(P_X) \to [0, \infty)$ *is continuous.*
iii) *If* L *is of order* $p \in [1, \infty)$ *then* $\mathcal{R}_{L,P} : L_p(P_X) \to [0, \infty)$ *is continuous.*

Proof. i). Obviously, f is a bounded and measurable function with $\|f\|_\infty \leq B$. Furthermore, the continuity of L shows $L(x, y, f_{n_k}(x)) \to L(x, y, f(x))$ almost surely. In addition, for P-almost all $(x, y) \in X \times Y$ and all $n \geq 1$ we have

$$\big|L\big(x, y, f_n(x)\big) - L\big(x, y, f(x)\big)\big| \leq 2b(x, y) + 2h(B)\,.$$

Since the function on the right hand side is P-integrable, we then obtain the assertion from Lebesgue's convergence theorem and

$$\big|\mathcal{R}_{L,P}(f_n) - \mathcal{R}_{L,P}(f)\big| \leq \int_X \big|L\big(x, y, f_n(x)\big) - L\big(x, y, f(x)\big)\big|\, d\mathrm{P}(x,y)\,.$$

ii). This is a direct consequence of Condition (2) and i).
iii). Since L is a P-integrable Nemitski loss of order p we find $\mathcal{R}_{L,P}(f) < \infty$ for all $f \in L_p(P_X)$. Now let $(f_n) \subset L_p(P_X)$ be a sequence converging to some $f \in L_p(P_X)$. Lemma 1 then yields $\mathcal{R}_{L,P}(f) \leq \liminf_{n \to \infty} \mathcal{R}_{L,P}(f_n)$. Moreover, $\tilde{L}(x, y, t) := b(x, y) + c|t|^p - L(x, y, t)$ is also a continuous loss, and hence we have

$$\|b\|_{L_1(\mathrm{P})} + c\|f\|_p^p - \mathcal{R}_{L,P}(f) = \mathcal{R}_{\tilde{L},P}(f) \leq \liminf_{n \to \infty} \mathcal{R}_{\tilde{L},P}(f_n)$$

$$= \|b\|_{L_1(\mathrm{P})} + \liminf_{n \to \infty} c\|f_n\|_p^p - \mathcal{R}_{L,P}(f_n)$$

by Lemma 1. Using the fact that $\|.\|_p^p$ is a continuous function on $L_p(P_X)$, we thus obtain $\limsup_{n \to \infty} \mathcal{R}_{L,P}(f_n) \leq \mathcal{R}_{L,P}(f)$. $\qquad \square$

Lemma 3. *Let* $L : X \times Y \times \mathbb{R} \to [0, \infty]$ *be a loss, and* P *be a distribution on* $X \times Y$ *such that* L *is a* P*-integrable Nemitski loss. Then* $L_\infty(\mathrm{P}_X)$ *is* (L, P)*-rich.*

Proof. Let us fix a measurable function $f : X \to \mathbb{R}$ with $\mathcal{R}_{L,\mathrm{P}}(f) < \infty$. Then the functions $f_n := \mathbf{1}_{\{|f| \leq n\}} f$, $n \geq 1$, are bounded, and an easy calculation shows

$$\left| \mathcal{R}_{L,\mathrm{P}}(f_n) - \mathcal{R}_{L,\mathrm{P}}(f) \right| \leq \int_{\{|f| > n\} \times Y} \left| L(x, y, 0) - L(x, y, f(x)) \right| d\mathrm{P}(x, y)$$

$$\leq \int_{\{|f| > n\} \times Y} b(x, y) + h(0) + L\big(x, y, f(x)\big) \, d\mathrm{P}(x, y)$$

for all $n \geq 1$. In addition, the integrand in the last integral is integrable since $\mathcal{R}_{L,\mathrm{P}}(f) < \infty$ and $b \in L_1(\mathrm{P})$, and consequently Lebesgue's theorem yields $\mathcal{R}_{L,\mathrm{P}}(f_n) \to \mathcal{R}_{L,\mathrm{P}}(f)$ for $n \to \infty$. From this we easily get the assertion. $\square$

Proof (of Theorem 1). By Lemma 3 we know $\mathcal{R}^*_{L,\mathrm{P},L_\infty(\mathrm{P}_X)} = \mathcal{R}^*_{L,\mathrm{P}}$, and since $F \subset L_\infty(\mathrm{P}_X)$ we also have $\mathcal{R}^*_{L,\mathrm{P},F} \geq \mathcal{R}^*_{L,\mathrm{P},L_\infty(\mathrm{P}_X)}$. In order to show the converse inequality we fix a $g \in L_\infty(\mathrm{P}_X)$. Let $(f_n) \subset F$ be a sequence of functions according to the assumptions of the theorem. Lemma 2 then yields $\mathcal{R}_{L,\mathrm{P}}(f_n) \to \mathcal{R}_{L,\mathrm{P}}(g)$, and hence we easily find $\mathcal{R}^*_{L,\mathrm{P},F} \leq \mathcal{R}^*_{L,\mathrm{P},L_\infty(\mathrm{P}_X)}$. $\square$

Proof (of Corollary 1). Let us fix a $g \in L_\infty(\mathrm{P}_X)$. Then there exists a sequence $(g_n) \subset C(X)$ with $\|g_n\|_\infty \leq \|g\|_\infty$ for all $n \geq 1$ and $g_n(x) \to g(x)$ for P_X-almost all $x \in X$. Moreover, the universality of H gives functions $f_n \in H$ with $\|f_n - g_n\|_\infty \leq 1/n$ for all $n \geq 1$. Since this yields both $\|f_n\|_\infty \leq 1 + \|g\|_\infty$, $n \geq 1$, and $f_n(x) \to g(x)$ almost surely, we obtain the assertion by Theorem 1. $\square$

Proof (of Theorem 2). By [6, Thm. 3.2.11 and Cor. 3.3.2] we know that X is completely regular and hence [7, Thm. V.6.6.] shows that X is metrizable if and only if $C(X)$ is separable.

$i) \Rightarrow ii)$. Let H be the RKHS of k and $\Phi : X \to H$ be the canonical feature map. Then Φ is continuous and thus $\Phi(X)$ is compact. Since H is obviously a metric space we hence see that $\Phi(X)$ is separable, and consequently so is $H = \overline{\mathrm{span}\, \Phi(X)}$. Since H is dense in $C(X)$ we then obtain that $C(X)$ is separable.

$ii) \Rightarrow i)$. Since our preliminary consideration shows that $C(X)$ is separable there exists a dense subset $\{f_n : n \in \mathbb{N}\}$ of $C(X)$. For $n \in \mathbb{N}$ we define $\Phi_n := 2^{-n} \|f_n\|_\infty^{-1} f_n$ if $f_n \neq 0$ and $\Phi_n := 0$ otherwise. Then it is easy to see that $\Phi(x) := (\Phi_n(x))_n$ satisfies $\Phi(x) \in \ell_2$ for all $x \in X$ and hence

$$k(x, x') := \langle \Phi(x), \Phi(x') \rangle_{\ell_2}, \qquad x, x' \in X,$$

defines a kernel on X with feature map $\Phi : X \to \ell_2$. Let us now fix an $f \in C(X)$ and an $\varepsilon > 0$. Then there exists an integer n with $\|f_n - f\|_\infty \leq \varepsilon$. We define $w := 2^n \|f_n\|_\infty e_n$, where (e_n) is the canonical orthonormal basis (ONB) of ℓ_2. This gives $\langle w, \Phi(x) \rangle = f_n(x)$ for all $x \in X$, and since $H := \{\langle v, \Phi(.) \rangle : v \in \ell_2\}$ is the RKHS of k we obtain the universality of k. $\square$

Proof (of Theorem 3). Since $L_\infty(P_X) \subset L_p(P_X)$ we have $\mathcal{R}^*_{L,P,L_p(P_X)} = \mathcal{R}^*_{L,P}$ by Lemma 3. Now the assertion easily follows from the denseness of F in $L_p(P_X)$ and the continuity of $\mathcal{R}_{L,P} : L_p(P_X) \to [0, \infty)$ established in Lemma 2.   □

Proof (of Proposition 1). It is easy to check that T_k is the adjoint operator of the inclusion map $I : H \to L_p(\mu)$. Recalling that I has dense image if and only if its adjoint is injective (see e.g. [8, Satz III.4.5]) we then obtain the assertion.   □

Proof (of Theorem 4). Let us fix an $f \in L_{p'}(\mu)$ with $T_{k_\sigma} f = 0$. For $t > 0$ we write $g_t(x, x') := (4\pi t)^{-d/2} k_{2\sqrt{t}}(x, x')$, and define

$$u(x,t) := \int_{\mathbb{R}^d} g_t(x, x') f(x') d\mu(x'), \qquad x \in \mathbb{R}^d, t > 0.$$

Differentiation then shows that u satisfies the heat equation $\partial_t u = \partial_{xx} u$ and since $T_{k_\sigma} f = 0$ implies $u(x, \frac{\sigma^2}{4}) = 0$ for all $x \in \mathbb{R}^d$ the unique continuation theorem of Itô and Yamabe [9] implies that $u(x, t) = 0$ for all $x \in \mathbb{R}^d$ and $t > 0$. Now let $h : \mathbb{R}^d \to \mathbb{R}$ be a continuous function with compact support. Then we obviously have $\|h\|_\infty < \infty$, $h \in L_p(\mu)$, and

$$0 = \int_{\mathbb{R}^d} h(x) u(x,t) dx = \int_{\mathbb{R}^d} h(x) \left(\int_{\mathbb{R}^d} g_t(x, x') f(x') d\mu(x') \right) dx, \quad t > 0. \quad (8)$$

Since μ is finite it follows that $f \in L_1(\mu)$ and that $h(x) g_t(x, x') f(x')$ is integrable with respect to the product of μ and the Lebesgue measure on $\mathbb{R}^d$. Let us define

$$h_t(x') := \int_{\mathbb{R}^d} g_t(x, x') h(x) dx, \qquad x' \in \mathbb{R}^d.$$

For $t > 0$ Fubini's theorem and (8) then yields

$$0 = \int_{\mathbb{R}^d} f(x') \left(\int_{\mathbb{R}^d} g_t(x, x') h(x) dx \right) d\mu(x') = \int_{\mathbb{R}^d} f(x') h_t(x') d\mu(x'). \quad (9)$$

Now fix an $x \in \mathbb{R}^d$ and an $\varepsilon > 0$. Then there exists a $\delta > 0$ such that for all $x' \in \mathbb{R}^d$ with $|x' - x| \le \delta$ we have $|h(x') - h(x)| \le \epsilon$. Since $\int_{\mathbb{R}^d} g_t(x, x') dx = 1$, $x' \in \mathbb{R}^d$ we hence obtain

$$h_t(x) - h(x) = \int_{|x'-x| \le \delta} (h(x') - h(x)) g_t(x, x') dx' + \int_{|x'-x| > \delta} (h(x') - h(x)) g_t(x, x') dx'.$$

The absolute value of the first term is bounded by ϵ and the absolute value of the second term can be made less than ϵ by choosing t small enough. Therefore we conclude that $\lim_{t \to 0} h_t(x) = h(x)$, $x \in \mathbb{R}^d$. Moreover, we have $|h_t(x)| \le \|h\|_\infty < \infty$, and hence the dominated convergence theorem and (9) yield

$$0 = \int_{\mathbb{R}^d} f(x') h(x') d\mu(x') = \langle f, h \rangle_{L_{p'}(\mu), L_p(\mu)}.$$

Since it follows from [10, Thm. 29.12] and [10, Thm. 29.14] that the continuous functions with compact support are dense in $L_p(\mu)$, we conclude $f = 0$.   □

Proof (of Corollary 2). Let us fix an $f \in L_{q'}(h\mu)$. Then we have $f|h|^{\frac{1}{q'}} \in L_{q'}(\mu)$ and for r defined by $\frac{1}{q'} + \frac{1}{r} = \frac{1}{p'}$ Hölder's inequality and $\frac{r}{q} = s$ thus yield

$$\|fh\|_{L_{p'}(\mu)} = \big\| f|h|^{\frac{1}{q'}} |h|^{\frac{1}{q}} \big\|_{L_{p'}(\mu)} \leq \big\| f|h|^{\frac{1}{q'}} \big\|_{L_{q'}(\mu)} \big\| |h|^{\frac{1}{q}} \big\|_{L_r(\mu)} < \infty.$$

Moreover, if $f \neq 0$ in $L_{q'}(h\mu)$ we have $\mu\{fh \neq 0\} > 0$ and hence we obtain

$$0 \neq T_k(fh) = \int_X f(x)h(x)k(.,x)\,d\mu(x) = \int_X f(x)k(.,x)\,d(h\mu)(x).$$

Since the latter integral describes the integral operator $L_{q'}(h\mu) \to H$ we then obtain the assertion by Proposition 1.   □

Proof (of Corollary 3). Let us fix an $f \in \ell_{p'}(X)$ with $f \neq 0$. Then we have $T_k f \in H \subset \ell_p(X)$ and hence we obtain

$$\langle T_k f, f \rangle_{\ell_p(X), \ell_{p'}(X)} = \sum_{x,x' \in X} k(x,x')f(x)f(x') > 0.$$

This shows that $T_k : \ell_{p'}(X) \to H$ is injective. Now let μ be a distribution on X and ν be the counting measure on X. Then there exists a function $h \in \ell_1(X)$ with $\mu = h\nu$. Since for $q \in [1,p]$ we have $s := \frac{p}{p-q} \geq 1$ we then find $h \in \ell_s(X)$ and hence we obtain the assertion by applying Corollary 2. In addition, for $q > p$ we have $\|k\|_{\ell_q(X)} \leq \|k\|_{\ell_p(X)} < \infty$ and $\ell_{q'}(X) \subset \ell_{p'}(X)$, and consequently, this case follows from the already shown case $q = p$.   □

Proof (of Theorem 5). The completeness of $c_0(X)$ and $k(.,x) \in c_0(X)$, $x \in X$, implies that the inclusion $I : H \to c_0(X)$ is well-defined. In addition, k is bounded and thus I is continuous. Moreover, a simple calculation shows that its adjoint operator is the integral operator $T_k : \ell_1(X) \to H$ which is injective by (7). Consequently, H is dense in $c_0(X)$, and by Lemma 2 we hence find $\mathcal{R}_{L,P,H}^* = \mathcal{R}_{L,P,c_0(X)}^*$. Therefore it remains to show that $c_0(X)$ is (L,P)-rich. To this end let ν be the counting measure on X and $h : X \to [0,1]$ be the map that satisfies $P_X = h\nu$. In addition recall that we have $\mathcal{R}_{L,P}(0) < \infty$ since L is a P-integrable Nemitski loss. Given an $\varepsilon > 0$ there hence exists a finite set $A \subset X$ with

$$\sum_{x \in X \setminus A} h(x) \int_Y L(x,y,0)d\text{P}(y|x) \leq \varepsilon.$$

In addition, there exists a $g : X \to \mathbb{R}$ with $\mathcal{R}_{L,P}(g) \leq \mathcal{R}_{L,P}^* + \varepsilon$. Let us define $f := \mathbf{1}_A g$. Then we have $f \in c_0(X)$ and

$$\mathcal{R}_{L,P}(f) = \sum_{x \in A} h(x) \int_Y L(x,y,g(x))d\text{P}(y|x) + \sum_{x \in X \setminus A} h(x) \int_Y L(x,y,0)d\text{P}(y|x)$$

$$\leq \mathcal{R}_{L,P}(g) + \varepsilon.$$ □

Lemma 4. *Let μ be a distribution on X. Assume that we have a subspace $F \subset L_\infty(\mu)$ such that for all measurable $A \subset X$ there exists a sequence $(f_n) \subset F$ with $\lim_{n \to \infty} f_n(x) = \mathbf{1}_A(x)$ for μ-almost all $x \in X$. Then for all $g \in L_\infty(\mu)$ there exists a sequence $(f_n) \subset F$ with $\lim_{n \to \infty} f_n(x) = g(x)$ for μ-almost all $x \in X$.*

Proof. We first observe that for step functions $g \in L_\infty(\mu)$ the assertion immediately follows from the fact that F is a vector space. Let us now fix an arbitrary $g \in L_\infty(\mu)$. For $n \geq 1$ there then exists a step function $g_n \in L_\infty(\mu)$ with $\|g_n - g\|_\infty \leq 1/n$. Moreover, for this g_n there exists a sequence $(f_{m,n})_{m \geq 1} \subset F$ with $\lim_{m \to \infty} f_{m,n}(x) = g_n(x)$ for μ-almost all $x \in X$. By Egoroff's theorem we then find a measurable subset $A_n \subset X$ with $\mu(X \setminus A_n) \leq 1/n$ and

$$\lim_{m \to \infty} \|(f_{m,n} - g_n)_{|A_n}\|_\infty = 0.$$

Consequently, there is an index $m_n \geq 1$ with $\|(f_{m_n,n} - g_n)_{|A_n}\|_\infty \leq 1/n$. By putting all estimates together we now obtain

$$\mu(\{x \in X : |f_{m_n,n}(x) - g(x)| \leq 2/n\}) \geq 1 - 1/n, \qquad n \geq 1.$$

This shows that $(f_{m_n,n})_{n \geq 1}$ converges to g in probability μ, and consequently there exists a subsequence of it that converges to g almost surely. $\square$

Proof (of Theorem 6). Let $\mathcal{A}$ be the σ-algebra of X. We fix an $A_1 \in \mathcal{A}$, and write $A_2 := \emptyset$. Let us define two distributions P_1 and P_2 on $X \times Y$ by

$$P_i(\,.\,|x) := \begin{cases} Q_1 & \text{if } x \in A_i \\ Q_2 & \text{if } x \in X \setminus A_i \end{cases}$$

and $(P_i)_X := \mu$ for $i = 1, 2$. Our assumptions on Q_1 and Q_2 guarantee $\mathcal{C}^*_{L,Q_1} < \infty$ and $\mathcal{C}^*_{L,Q_2} < \infty$, and hence we find $\mathcal{R}^*_{L,P_i} < \infty$ for $i = 1, 2$. Moreover, every function minimizing $\mathcal{R}_{L,P_i}$ has μ-almost surely the form

$$f^*_{L,P_i} := t^*_1 \mathbf{1}_{A_i} + t^*_2 \mathbf{1}_{X \setminus A_i}, \qquad i = 1, 2.$$

Now, our assumptions yield $\mathcal{R}^*_{L,P_i,F} = \mathcal{R}^*_{L,P_i}$, $i = 1, 2$, and hence there are sequences $(f^{(1)}_n) \subset F$ and $(f^{(2)}_n) \subset F$ with $\lim_{n \to \infty} \mathcal{R}_{L,P_i}(f^{(i)}_n) = \mathcal{R}^*_{L,P_i}$ for $i = 1, 2$. By Remark 2.39 in [5] we then have

$$\lim_{n \to \infty} f^{(i)}_n = f^*_{L,P_i}, \qquad i = 1, 2, \tag{10}$$

in probability $\hat{\mu}$, where $\hat{\mu}$ is the extension of μ to the μ-completed σ-algebra of $\mathcal{A}$. Now observe that all functions in (10) are $\mathcal{A}$-measurable, and hence (10) actually holds in probability μ. Consequently, there exist subsequences $(f^{(1)}_{n_j})$ and $(f^{(2)}_{n_j})$ for which (10) holds μ-almost surely. For

$$f_j := \frac{1}{t^*_1 - t^*_2}\left(f^{(1)}_{n_j} - f^{(2)}_{n_j}\right), \qquad j \geq 1,$$

we then have $f_j \in F$, and in addition our construction yields

$$\lim_{j \to \infty} f_j = \frac{1}{t_1^* - t_2^*}(f_{L,P_1}^* - f_{L,P_2}^*) = \frac{1}{t_1^* - t_2^*}(t_1^* 1_{A_1} + t_2^* 1_{X \setminus A_1} - t_2^* 1_X) = 1_{A_1}$$

μ-almost surely. By Lemma 4 we thus obtain the assertion.   □

Proof (of Corollary 4). Let $x_1, \ldots, x_n \in X$ be mutually different points and μ be the associated empirical distribution. Obviously, it suffices to show that the kernel matrix $K := (k(x_i, x_j))$ has full rank. Let us assume the converse, i.e. that there exists an $y \in \mathbb{R}^n$ with $K\alpha \neq y$ for all $\alpha \in \mathbb{R}^n$. Since $K\mathbb{R}^n$ is closed there exists an $\varepsilon > 0$ with $\|K\alpha - y\|_\infty \geq \varepsilon$ for all $\alpha \in \mathbb{R}^n$. Moreover, by decomposing H into $\text{span}\{k(., x_i) : i = 1, \ldots, n\}$ and its orthogonal complement we see that for every $f \in H$ there is an $\alpha \in \mathbb{R}^n$ with

$$f(x_j) = \sum_{i=1}^n \alpha_i k(x_j, x_i), \qquad j = 1, \ldots, n,$$

and hence for all $f \in H$ there is an index $j \in \{1, \ldots, n\}$ with $|f(x_j) - y_j| > \varepsilon$. On the other hand, Theorem 6 gives a sequence $(f_n) \subset H$ with $f_n(x_i) \to y_i$ for all $i \in \{1, \ldots, n\}$. Since $\{1, \ldots, n\}$ is finite we then easily find a contradiction.   □

Lemma 5. *Let μ be a distribution on X and $p > 0$. Assume that $F \subset L_p(\mu)$ is a linear subspace such that for all measurable $A \subset X$ there exists a sequence $(f_n) \subset F$ with $\lim_{n \to \infty} \|f_n - 1_A\|_{L_p(\mu)} = 0$. Then F is dense in $L_p(\mu)$.*

Proof. If $g \in L_p(\mu)$ is a measurable step function there obviously exists a sequence $(f_n) \subset F$ with $\lim_{n \to \infty} \|f_n - g\|_p = 0$. Moreover, if $g \in L_p(\mu)$ is bounded and n is an integer there exists a measurable step function g_n with $\|g_n - g\|_\infty \leq 1/n$. In addition, we have just see that there exists an $f_n \in F$ with $\|f_n - g_n\|_p \leq 1/n$, and hence we find $\lim_{n \to \infty} \|f_n - g\|_p = 0$. Finally, for general $g \in L_p(\mu)$ we then find an approximating sequence by first approximating g with the bounded measurable functions $g_n := 1_{|g| \leq n} g$, $n \geq 1$, and then approximating these g_n with suitable functions $f_n \in F$.   □

Proof (of Theorem 7). Following the argument used in the proof of Theorem 6 we may assume without loss of generality that X is a complete measurable space. Let us now fix a measurable $A_1 \subset X$, and write $A_2 := \emptyset$. Furthermore, we define the distributions P_i, the functions f_{L,P_i}^*, and the approximating sequences $(f_n^{(i)}) \subset F$, $i = 1, 2$, as in the proof of Theorem 6. Then $\lim_{n \to \infty} \mathcal{R}_{L,P_i}(f_n^{(i)}) = \mathcal{R}_{L,P_i}^*$, $i = 1, 2$, together with Remark 2.41 in [5] yields

$$\lim_{n \to \infty} \|f_n^{(i)} - f_{L,P_i}^*\|_{L_p(\mu)} = 0.$$

For $f_n := \frac{1}{t_1^* - t_2^*}(f_n^{(1)} - f_n^{(2)})$, $n \geq 1$, we then obtain $\lim_{n \to \infty} \|f_n - 1_{A_1}\|_{L_p(\mu)} = 0$, and hence we obtain the assertion by Lemma 5.   □

Proof (of Theorem 9). Let us write $p_n := \mu(\{n\})$, $n \in \mathbb{N}_0$. Moreover, let $(b_i)_{i\geq 1}$ be a strictly positive sequence with $\|(b_i)\|_2 = 1$ and $(b_i) \in \ell_1$. Furthermore, let (e_n) be the canonical ONB of ℓ_2. We write $\Phi(0) := (b_i)$ and $\Phi(n) := e_n$, $n \geq 1$. Then we have $\Phi(n) \in \ell_2$ for all $n \in \mathbb{N}_0$ and hence

$$k(n,m) := \langle \Phi(n), \Phi(m) \rangle_{\ell_2}, \qquad n, m \geq 0,$$

defines a kernel. Obviously, $\{\Phi(n) : n \geq 1\}$ is (algebraically) linearly independent and from this it is easy to conclude that k is strictly positive definite. Moreover, an easy calculation shows $k(0,0) = 1$, $k(n,m) = \delta_{n,m}$, and $k(n,0) = b_n$ for $n, m \geq 1$. Since $b_n \to 0$ we hence find $k(.,n) \in c_0(X)$ for all $n \in \mathbb{N}_0$. Let us define $f : \mathbb{N}_0 \to \mathbb{R}$ by $f(0) := 1$ and $f(n) := -\frac{b_n}{p_n}p_0$ for $n \geq 1$. Then we have $\|f\|_{L_1(\mu)} = p_0 + p_0\|(b_i)\|_{\ell_1} < \infty$, and a simple calculation shows

$$T_k f(0) = k(0,0)f(0)p_0 + \sum_{n=1}^{\infty} k(0,n)f(n)p_n = p_0 - p_0 \sum_{n=1}^{\infty} b_n^2 = 0.$$

Moreover, for $m \geq 1$ our construction yields

$$T_k f(m) = k(m,0)f(0)p_0 + \sum_{n=1}^{\infty} k(m,n)f(n)p_n = b_m f(0)p_0 - f(m)p_m = 0. \quad \square$$

References

1. Steinwart, I.: On the influence of the kernel on the consistency of support vector machines. J. Mach. Learn. Res. **2** (2001) 67–93
2. Bousquet, O., Elisseeff, A.: Stability and generalization. J. Mach. Learn. Res. **2** (2002) 499–526
3. Steinwart, I.: Consistency of support vector machines and other regularized kernel machines. IEEE Trans. Inform. Theory **51** (2005) 128–142
4. Zhang, T.: Statistical behaviour and consistency of classification methods based on convex risk minimization. Ann. Statist. **32** (2004) 56–134
5. Steinwart, I.: How to compare loss functions and their risks. Technical Report (2005) http://www.c3.lanl.gov/~ingo/pubs.shtml.
6. Schurle, A.: Topics in Topology. Elsevier North Holland (1979)
7. Conway, J.B.: A Course in Functional Analysis. 2nd edn. Springer (1990)
8. Werner, D.: Funktionalanalysis. Springer, Berlin (1995)
9. Itô, S., Yamabe, H.: A unique continuation theorem for solutions of a parabolic differential equation. J. Math. Soc. Japan **10** (1958) 314–321
10. Bauer, H.: Measure and Integration Theory. De Gruyter, Berlin (2001)

Functional Classification with Margin Conditions

Magalie Fromont[1] and Christine Tuleau[2]

[1] Université Rennes 2
Place du Recteur Henri Le Moal - CS 24307
35043 Rennes Cedex, France
magalie.fromont@uhb.fr
[2] Université Paris-Sud, Bâtiment 425
91405 Orsay Cedex, France
Université Paris X - Nanterre. MODAL'X.
christine.tuleau@math.u-psud.fr

Abstract. Let (X, Y) be a $\mathcal{X} \times \{0, 1\}$-valued random pair and consider a sample $(X_1, Y_1), \ldots, (X_n, Y_n)$ drawn from the distribution of (X, Y). We aim at constructing from this sample a classifier that is a function which would predict the value of Y from the observation of X. The special case where $\mathcal{X}$ is a functional space is of particular interest due to the so called *curse of dimensionality*. In a recent paper, Biau *et al.* [1] propose to filter the X_i's in the Fourier basis and to apply the classical $k-$Nearest Neighbor rule to the first d coefficients of the expansion. The selection of both k and d is made automatically via a penalized criterion. We extend this study, and note here the penalty used by Biau *et al.* is too heavy when we consider the minimax point of view under some margin type assumptions. We prove that using a penalty of smaller order or equal to zero is preferable both in theory and practice. Our experimental study furthermore shows that the introduction of a small-order penalty stabilizes the selection process, while preserving rather good performances.

1 Introduction

Let (X, Y) be a random pair of variables such that X takes its values in a measurable space $\mathcal{X}$ and Y in $\{0, 1\}$, with unknown distribution denoted by P. Given n independent copies $(X_1, Y_1), \ldots, (X_n, Y_n)$ of (X, Y), the purpose of classification is to construct a function, called a *classifier*, $\phi_n : \mathcal{X} \to \{0, 1\}$ based on $(X_1, Y_1), \ldots, (X_n, Y_n)$, which allows to predict the value of Y from the observation of X. When the value of Y is not fully determined by X and $(X_1, Y_1), \ldots, (X_n, Y_n)$, the prediction suffers from the classification error defined by $L(\phi_n) = \mathbb{P}[\phi_n(X) \neq Y | (X_i, Y_i), i = 1 \ldots n]$. Introducing the regression function $\eta : x \mapsto \mathbb{P}[Y = 1 | X = x]$, the function ϕ^* minimizing the classification error $L(\phi) = \mathbb{P}[\phi(X) \neq Y]$ over all the measurable functions $\phi : \mathcal{X} \to \{0, 1\}$ is defined by $\phi^*(x) = \mathbb{I}_{\eta(x) > 1/2}$. In statistical terms, classification deals with the estimation of this function ϕ^* called the *Bayes classifier* from the sample $(X_1, Y_1), \ldots, (X_n, Y_n)$, and the theoretical performance of any estimator ϕ_n can

G. Lugosi and H.U. Simon (Eds.): COLT 2006, LNAI 4005, pp. 94–108, 2006.

be evaluated by comparing $\mathbb{E}[L(\phi_n)]$ with $L(\phi^*)$. In particular, ϕ_n is said to be universally consistent if $\mathbb{E}[L(\phi_n)]$ tends to $L(\phi^*)$ as n tends to ∞ for every P.

The case where $\mathcal{X} = \mathbb{R}^d$ has been widely studied and many references are devoted to it (see [2] and [3] for a review).

In many real-world applications, coming from food processing industry or speech recognition for example, the data are more accurately represented by discretized functions than by standard vectors. In this paper, we focus on such applications, and hence we assume that $\mathcal{X}$ is a functional space, for example $\mathbb{L}_2(\mathbb{R})$.

The most simple and popular classifiers are probably the kernel and k-Nearest Neighbor rules. From a theoretical point of view, these rules are known to be universally consistent when $\mathcal{X} = \mathbb{R}^d$ since Stone's [4] and Devroye and Krzyżak's [5] striking results. But the issue is not so clear when $\mathcal{X}$ is an infinite dimensional space, and authors investigate it only since a few years. Dabo-Niang and Rhomari [6], and Abraham et al. [7] deal with kernel rules. Kulkarni and Posner [8] give convergence rates of the k-Nearest Neighbor regression estimator under some regularity conditions on η. Cerou and Guyader [9] establish a universal consistency result for the k-Nearest Neighbor rule in a separable space under a less restrictive regularity condition termed the Besicovich condition.

However, such direct approaches suffer from the phenomenon commonly referred to as the *curse of dimensionality*. Thus, they are not expected to achieve good rates of convergence. To overcome this difficulty, most of the traditional effective methods for $\mathbb{R}^d$-valued data analysis have been adapted to handle functional data under the general name of Functional Data Analysis. A key reference for this growing research field is the series of books by Ramsay and Silverman ([10] and [11]). Both linear and nonlinear classification schemes have thus been exploited (see [12], [13], [14], [15]).

In a recent paper, Biau et al. [1] propose to filter the functional data X_i in the Fourier basis and to apply the k-Nearest Neighbor rule to the first d coefficients of the expansion. The choice of both the dimension d and number of neighbors k is made automatically by a minimization of a penalized empirical classification error performed after some data-splitting device. The resulting classifier is proved to satisfy an oracle type inequality, and hence to be universally consistent. As noted by the authors, similar results could be obtained for other universally consistent classification procedures in finite dimension. In this spirit, the Support Vector Machines procedures are investigated by Rossi and Villa [16].

The approach of Biau et al. [1] is central to our paper. After a careful study of this work, two main issues remain unsolved. The authors underline their preferring to implement the procedure based on the minimization of the empirical classification error without any penalization. However, the theoretical properties presented do not explain why this choice is expected to give good results. Furthermore, as pointed out in the beginning of the simulation study and previously by Hengartner et al. [17] for the question of bandwidth selection in local linear regression smoothers, the data-splitting device can be unstable. Such an instability has particularly notable effects on the selected d and k, as investigated in Section 4 of the paper by Biau et al. [1]. To overcome this problem,

Biau *et al.* suggest to consider many random splits of the data, and to take the classifier corresponding to the medians of the selected d's and k's, or to take a combination of the different classifiers. Whereas such techniques are commonly used in practice, they have no theoretical foundation in the present classification context. In this paper, we address to both issues.

In Section 2, we prove that the penalty of order $n^{-1/2}$ considered by Biau *et al.* [1] is too large when some margin-type assumptions hold. From a recent result of Boucheron, Bousquet and Massart, we obtain a new oracle type inequality that justifies the use of a penalty equal to zero or of order smaller than $n^{-1/2}$. In Section 3, we illustrate this theoretical advance with an experimental study. We deal with realistic data coming from speech recognition or food industry contexts and with simple simulated data. Section 4 is then devoted to the problem of the instability of the data-splitting device. Our intention is not to give a justification for the combination techniques used by Biau *et al.* [1], since we are not able to. In fact, we show that the introduction of a small-order penalization, such as the one allowed by the theoretical result can be viewed as a stabilization tool for the selection process.

2   Functional Classification Via (Non)Penalized Criteria

We present here Biau *et al.*'s [1] classification scheme that we consider all along the paper. After describing the procedure and the theoretical properties obtained in [1] in a general context, we investigate them under some margin assumptions.

2.1   Functional Classification in a General Context

By using the same framework and notation as in the introduction, we assume that $\mathcal{X}$ is an infinite dimensional separable space. We consider a complete system of $\mathcal{X}$ that we denote by $\{\psi_j, \ j \in \mathbb{N}\setminus\{0\}\}$. For every i in $\{1, \ldots, n\}$, X_i can thus be expressed as a series expansion $X_i = \sum_{j=1}^{\infty} X_{i,j}\psi_j$ and for d in $\mathbb{N}\setminus\{0\}$, we set $\mathbf{X}_i^d = (X_{i,1}, \ldots, X_{i,d})$. In the same way, $\mathbf{x}^d$ denotes the first d coefficients in the expansion of any new element x in $\mathcal{X}$. The procedure developed by Biau *et al.* [1] is described as follows.

- The data are split into a training set $\mathbb{D}_{\mathcal{T}_l} = \{(X_i, Y_i), i \in \mathcal{T}_l\}$ of length l and a validation set $\mathbb{D}_{\mathcal{V}_m} = \{(X_i, Y_i), i \in \mathcal{V}_m\}$ of length m such that $n = l + m$ with $1 \leq l \leq n - 1$. A usual choice for l will be $\lceil n/2 \rceil$.
- For each k in $\{1, \ldots, l\}$, d in a subset $\mathcal{D}$ of $\mathbb{N}\setminus\{0\}$, let $\hat{p}_{l,k,d}$ be the k-Nearest Neighbor rule on $\mathbb{R}^d$ constructed from the set $\{(\mathbf{X}_i^d, Y_i), i \in \mathcal{T}_l\}$. Let $\mathbf{x}$ be an element of $\mathbb{R}^d$. The set $\{(\mathbf{X}_i^d, Y_i), i \in \mathcal{T}_l\}$ is reordered according to increasing Euclidean distances $\|\mathbf{X}_i^d - \mathbf{x}\|$, and the reordered variables are denoted by $(\mathbf{X}_{(1)}^d(\mathbf{x}), Y_{(1)}(\mathbf{x})), \ldots, (\mathbf{X}_{(l)}^d(\mathbf{x}), Y_{(l)}(\mathbf{x}))$. Thus $\mathbf{X}_{(k)}^d(\mathbf{x})$ is the k-th nearest neighbor of $\mathbf{x}$ amongst $\{\mathbf{X}_i^d, \ i \in \mathcal{T}_l\}$. When $\|\mathbf{X}_{i_1}^d - \mathbf{x}\| = \|\mathbf{X}_{i_2}^d - \mathbf{x}\|$, $\mathbf{X}_{i_1}^d$ is declared closer to $\mathbf{x}$ if $i_1 < i_2$. Then $\hat{p}_{l,k,d}(\mathbf{x})$ is defined by

$$\hat{p}_{l,k,d}(\mathbf{x}) = \begin{cases} 0 & \text{if } \sum_{i=1}^{k} \mathbb{I}_{Y_{(i)}(\mathbf{x})=0} \geq \sum_{i=1}^{k} \mathbb{I}_{Y_{(i)}(\mathbf{x})=1} \\ 1 & \text{otherwise.} \end{cases}$$

We introduce the corresponding functional classifier defined by

$$\hat{\phi}_{l,k,d}(x) = \hat{p}_{l,k,d}(\mathbf{x}^d) \text{ for all } x \text{ in } \mathcal{X}.$$

– The appropriate k and d are simultaneously selected from the validation set by minimizing a penalized empirical classification error:

$$(\hat{k}, \hat{d}) = \underset{k \in \{1,\ldots,l\},\ d \in \mathcal{D}}{\mathrm{argmin}} \left(\frac{1}{m} \sum_{i \in \mathcal{V}_m} \mathbb{I}_{\{\hat{\phi}_{l,k,d}(X_i) \neq Y_i\}} + \mathrm{pen}(d) \right), \qquad (1)$$

where $\mathrm{pen}(d)$ is a positive penalty term that can be equal to zero.
– The final classifier is defined by

$$\hat{\phi}_n(x) = \hat{\phi}_{l,\hat{k},\hat{d}}(x) \text{ for all } x \text{ in } \mathcal{X}. \qquad (2)$$

Let us recall the central result of the paper by Biau *et al.* [1].

Proposition 1 (Biau, Bunea, Wegkamp). *Introduce $(\lambda_d, d \in \mathbb{N} \backslash \{0\})$ such that $\Delta = \sum_{d \in \mathbb{N} \backslash \{0\}} e^{-2\lambda_d^2} < +\infty$. Let $l > 1/\Delta$, m with $l + m = n$, and $\hat{\phi}_n$ be the classification rule defined by (2) with $\mathcal{D} = \mathbb{N} \backslash \{0\}$ and $\mathrm{pen}(d) = \lambda_d/\sqrt{m}$ (penalized case). Then there exists a constant $c(\Delta) > 0$ such that*

$$\mathbb{E}[L(\hat{\phi}_n)] - L(\phi^*) \leq$$
$$\inf_{d \in \mathbb{N} \backslash \{0\}} \left\{ L_d^* - L(\phi^*) + \inf_{1 \leq k \leq l} \left\{ \mathbb{E}[L(\hat{\phi}_{l,k,d})] - L_d^* \right\} + \mathrm{pen}(d) \right\} + c(\Delta) \sqrt{\frac{\log l}{m}},$$
$$\tag{3}$$

where L_d^* is the minimal classification error when the feature space is $\mathbb{R}^d$. The same result holds when $\hat{\phi}_n$ is the classification rule defined by (2) with $\mathcal{D} = \{1, \ldots, d_n\}$ and $\mathrm{pen}(d) = 0$ (nonpenalized case), but at the price that the last term $c(\Delta) \sqrt{\log l/m}$ is replaced by $c(\Delta) \sqrt{\log l d_n/m}$.

The quantity $L_d^* - L(\phi^*)$ can be viewed as an approximation term. By using some classical martingale arguments, one proves that it tends to 0 as d tends to ∞. Moreover, from Stone's [18] consistency result in $\mathbb{R}^d$, one deduces that for d in $\mathbb{N} \backslash \{0\}$, $\mathbb{E}[L(\hat{\phi}_{l,k,d})]$ tends to L_d^* as $l \to \infty$, $k \to \infty$, $k/l \to 0$ whatever the distribution P. The classifier $\hat{\phi}_n$ is thus universally consistent. A universal strong consistency result can also be obtained under a mild condition on the distribution of X. Of course, such results are fully satisfactory from an asymptotic point of view. In the following section, we consider the proposed classifier from a nonasymptotic point of view. In particular, in order to evaluate the accuracy of the rates achieved in (3), a brief overview of the present knowledge on the minimax bounds in the general classification framework is given.

2.2 Minimax Bounds

Classical Bounds for Vapnik-Chervonenkis Classes. We consider here a class of classifiers $S = \{\mathbb{I}_C, C \in \mathcal{C}\}$, where $\mathcal{C}$ is a class of subsets of $\mathcal{X}$, with Vapnik-Chervonenkis dimension $V(\mathcal{C}) < \infty$.

A first risk bound was given by Vapnik and Chervonenkis [19] for the Empirical Risk Minimizer $\hat{\varphi}_n$. For any distribution P such that $\phi^* \in S$, one has $\mathbb{E}[L(\hat{\varphi}_n)] - L(\phi^*) \leq \kappa_1 \sqrt{V(\mathcal{C}) \log n / n}$. As pointed out by Lugosi [20], the factor $\log n$ in the upper bound can be removed by using a chaining argument, and the bound becomes optimal in a minimax sense. Vapnik and Chervonenkis [21] actually proved that for any classifier φ_n,

$$\sup_{P,\ \phi^* \in S} \mathbb{E}[L(\varphi_n)] - L(\phi^*) \geq \kappa_2 \sqrt{V(\mathcal{C})/n} \ \text{ if } n \geq \kappa_3 V(\mathcal{C}).$$

In the following, we call this case the *global case*, since the risk bounds are obtained without any restriction on the class S except it is based on a VC class. Considering the over-optimistic situation called the *zero-error case* where the Bayes classification error is assumed to be equal to zero, Devroye and Wagner [22], Vapnik [23], and Blumer *et al.* [24] obtained various forms of the following result: if $L(\phi^*) = 0$, then the ERM $\hat{\varphi}_n$ has a mean classification error not larger than $\kappa_4 V(\mathcal{C}) \log n / n$. Up to a logarithmic factor, this upper bound is known to be optimal in a minimax sense since Vapnik and Chervonenkis [21] and Haussler *et al.* [25] established that for any classifier φ_n,

$$\sup_{P,\ \phi^* \in S,\ L(\phi^*)=0} \mathbb{E}[L(\varphi_n)] \geq \kappa_5 V(\mathcal{C})/n \ \text{ if } n \geq \kappa_6 V(\mathcal{C}).$$

The main point here is that the minimax risk in the zero-error case is of smaller order of magnitude than in the global case, and that the difference is really significant ($V(\mathcal{C}) \log n / n$ instead of $\sqrt{V(\mathcal{C})/n}$). This leads to the intuition that if the Bayes classification error is not exactly equal to zero but very small, the bounds in the global case can be refined.

Lugosi [20] and Devroye and Lugosi [26] give such refined bounds as a kind of interpolation between the global case and the zero-error one. By carefully studying their proofs, the behavior of the regression function η around $1/2$ turns out to be crucial. Mammen and Tsybakov [27] first analyzed the influence of this behaviour by introducing some *margin* assumptions.

Risk Bounds Under Margin Assumptions. Let P_X be the marginal distribution of X, and $\mathbb{E}_X$ be the expectation w.r.t. P_X. For $\theta \geq 1$, we denote by $\mathrm{GMA}(\theta)$ the following general margin assumption introduced by Mammen and Tsybakov [27] and Tsybakov [28]:

$$\mathrm{GMA}(\theta): \quad \exists h > 0, \ L(\phi) - L(\phi^*) \geq h \mathbb{E}_X[|\phi(X) - \phi^*(X)|]^\theta, \ \forall \phi : \mathcal{X} \to \{0,1\}.$$

We also introduce some versions of this general margin assumption that can be more easily interpreted with

$$\mathrm{MA}(\alpha): \ \mathbb{P}[|\eta(X) - 1/2| \leq u] \leq C_1 u^\alpha, \ \forall u > 0,$$
$$\mathrm{MA}(\infty): \ \exists h > 0, \ |2\eta(x) - 1| \geq h, \ \forall x \in \mathcal{X}.$$

The limit case MA(∞) is studied in details by Massart and Nédélec [29].
It is easy to see that MA(α) implies GMA($(1+\alpha)/\alpha$) (See Proposition 1 from
Tsybakov [28] for instance), and that MA(∞) implies GMA(1).
The risk bounds are now given under two kinds of complexity assumptions.
CA1: $\phi^* \in \mathcal{S} = \{\mathbb{I}_C, C \in \mathcal{C}\}$, $\mathcal{C}$ being a class of subsets of $\mathcal{X}$, with VC dimension
$V(\mathcal{C}) < \infty$, and there exists some countable subset S of $\mathcal{S}$ such that for every ϕ
in $\mathcal{S}$, there exists a sequence $(\phi_k)_{k \geq 1}$ of elements of S such that for all (x, y) in
$\mathcal{X} \times \{0, 1\}$, $\mathbb{I}_{y \neq \phi_k(x)}$ tends to $\mathbb{I}_{y \neq \phi(x)}$ as k tends to ∞.
CA2: $\phi^* \in \mathcal{S}$, $H(\varepsilon, \mathcal{S}, \mathbb{L}_1(P_X)) \leq C_2 \varepsilon^{-\rho}$ for any $\varepsilon > 0$, where $H(\varepsilon, \mathcal{S}, \mathbb{L}_1(P_X))$ is
the ε-entropy with bracketing of the set $\mathcal{S}$ with respect to the $\mathbb{L}_1(P_X)$ norm.
Massart and Nédélec [29] establish that if the assumption CA1 is satisfied, and
GMA(θ) holds with $\theta \geq 1$ and $h \geq (V(\mathcal{C})/n)^{1/(2\theta)}$, then the ERM $\hat{\varphi}_n$ satisfies:

$$\mathbb{E}[L(\hat{\varphi}_n)] - L(\phi^*) \leq \kappa_7 \left(V(\mathcal{C})(1 + \log(nh^{2\theta}/V(\mathcal{C})))/(nh)\right)^{\frac{\theta}{2\theta-1}}. \tag{4}$$

They also discuss the optimality of this upper bound in a minimax sense for the
case MA(∞). They prove in particular that for any classifier φ_n, if $2 \leq V(\mathcal{C}) \leq n$,

$$\sup\nolimits_{P, \text{ MA}(\infty), \text{ CA1}} \mathbb{E}[L(\varphi_n)] - L(\phi^*) \geq \kappa_8 \left\{(V(\mathcal{C})/(nh)) \wedge \sqrt{V(\mathcal{C})/(nh)}\right\}.$$

As for the assumption CA2, Tsybakov [28] obtains the following upper bound
for the ERM $\hat{\varphi}_n$ computed on an ε-net on $\mathcal{S}$ with respect to the $\mathbb{L}_1(P_X)$ norm.
For $\varepsilon = cn^{-1/(1+\rho)}$, if GMA($\theta$) and CA2 are satisfied, then

$$\mathbb{E}[L(\hat{\varphi}_n)] - L(\phi^*) \leq \kappa_9 \left\{n^{-\frac{\theta}{2\theta+\rho-1}} \wedge n^{-1/2}\right\}.$$

Massart and Nédélec [29] refine this result by exhibiting the dependency of the
risk bound with respect to the margin parameter h in GMA(θ). This upper
bound is then proved to be optimal in a minimax sense by Tsybakov [28] when
$\mathcal{X} = [0, 1]^d$, and by Massart and Nédélec [29] in the special case MA(∞).
It has been proved recently that such fast rates of convergence are not only
achieved by ERM type classifiers. Bartlett *et al.* [30] thus obtained striking
results for the minimizer of the empirical risk based on convex loss functions.
Audibert and Tsybakov [31] also proved that when $\mathcal{X} = \mathbb{R}^d$, under another
type of margin assumption (expressed in terms of smoothness for the regression
function η), fast rates of convergence can be achieved by some plug-in classifiers.
In view of these results, Proposition 1 gives some rates of convergence that
fit the minimax risk bounds in the global case. However, under some margin
assumption, the rates of convergence will not be satisfactory any more. Indeed,
on the one hand, one can see that the order of magnitude of the penalty term
$(\lambda_d/\sqrt{m})$ in the penalized case is too large as compared to the rates faster than
$1/\sqrt{m}$ that are expected. On the other hand, in the nonpenalized case, the right
hand side of the inequality (3) makes a term of order $\sqrt{\log l d_n/m}$ appear. This
term can not be seen as a residual term when considering any margin assumption
any more, and hence the oracle type inequality (3) has to be refined.

2.3   Functional Classification with Margin Conditions

The key point in the proof of Proposition 1 is a general inequality which is at the root of many model selection results. This inequality follows from the definition of $\hat{\phi}_n$. Setting $L_m(\phi) = m^{-1}\sum_{i \in V_m} \mathbb{I}_{\{\phi(X_i) \neq Y_i\}}$ for all $\phi : \mathcal{X} \to \{0,1\}$, one has

$$L(\hat{\phi}_n) - L(\phi^*) \leq L(\hat{\phi}_{l,k,d}) - L(\phi^*) + \mathrm{pen}(d) - \mathrm{pen}(\hat{d})$$
$$+ L(\hat{\phi}_{l,\hat{k},\hat{d}}) - L_m(\hat{\phi}_{l,\hat{k},\hat{d}}) - L(\hat{\phi}_{l,k,d}) + L_m(\hat{\phi}_{l,k,d}). \quad (5)$$

Since $L(\hat{\phi}_{l,k,d}) - L_m(\hat{\phi}_{l,k,d})$ is centered, the inequality (3) is obtained by choosing a penalty such that $\mathrm{pen}(\hat{d})$ is large enough to compensate for $L(\hat{\phi}_{l,\hat{k},\hat{d}}) - L_m(\hat{\phi}_{l,\hat{k},\hat{d}})$, but such that $\mathrm{pen}(d)$ is small enough (of order at most $1/\sqrt{m}$) to fit the minimax risk bounds in the global case. The main issue is then to evaluate the fluctuations of $L(\hat{\phi}_{l,\hat{k},\hat{d}}) - L_m(\hat{\phi}_{l,\hat{k},\hat{d}})$. Biau *et al.* use Hoeffding's inequality. Their inequality is thus essentially based on the fact that the functions are bounded. The following result is obtained via Bernstein's inequality which allows to control the fluctuations of the quantity $L(\hat{\phi}_{l,\hat{k},\hat{d}}) - L_m(\hat{\phi}_{l,\hat{k},\hat{d}}) - L(\hat{\phi}_{l,k,d}) + L_m(\hat{\phi}_{l,k,d})$ by taking its variance into account. Its proof follows the same lines as the proof of a general result of Boucheron, Bousquet and Massart (see [32]).

Proposition 2. *Assume that $n \geq 2$ and let $\hat{\phi}_n$ be the classifier defined by (2) with a finite subset $\mathcal{D}$ of $\mathbb{N}\backslash\{0\}$ and with penalty terms $\mathrm{pen}(d)$ that can be equal to zero. For any $\beta > 0$, if $GMA(\theta)$ holds with $\theta \geq 1$ and $h \leq 1$, then*

$$(1 - \beta)\mathbb{E}[L(\hat{\phi}_n) - L(\phi^*)|\mathbb{D}_{T_l}]$$
$$\leq (1 + \beta) \inf_{k \in \{1,\ldots,l\},\; d \in \mathcal{D}} \left\{ \left(L(\hat{\phi}_{l,k,d}) - L(\phi^*)\right) + \mathrm{pen}(d) \right\}$$
$$+ \frac{\beta^{-1}\left(1 + \log(l|\mathcal{D}|)\right) + 4\beta}{2(mh)^{\frac{\theta}{2\theta-1}}} + \frac{1 + \log(l|\mathcal{D}|)}{3m}. \quad (6)$$

Comments. With the same arguments as Biau *et al.* [1], the oracle type inequality (6) directly leads to a consistency result. Now, from a nonasymptotic point of view, the terms $((2\beta)^{-1}\left(1 + \log(l|\mathcal{D}|)\right) + 2\beta)(mh)^{-\theta/(2\theta-1)}$ and $(1+\log(l|\mathcal{D}|))/3m$ are at most of the same order as the minimax risk given by (4). This guarantees that they can actually be viewed as residual terms in the final risk bound.

Furthermore, as soon as the penalty terms $\mathrm{pen}(d)$ are small enough, that is with a smaller order of magnitude than the residual terms or than $\inf_{1 \leq k \leq l}\{\mathbb{E}[L(\hat{\phi}_{l,k,d})] - L_d^*\}$, they will not alterate the rate of convergence. In a recent work, Györfi [33] proved that under some local Lipschitz condition on the regression function η, assuming that the margin condition $MA(\alpha)$ is satisfied, then $\inf_{1 \leq k \leq l}\{\mathbb{E}[L(\hat{\phi}_{l,k,d})] - L_d^*\}$ is at most of order $(\log m)^{(1+\alpha)/2}m^{-(1+\alpha)/(2+d)}$. This allows us to consider in practice penalties such that $\mathrm{pen}(d) = 0$, $\mathrm{pen}(d) = \log d/m$, $\mathrm{pen}(d) = d^{1/\gamma}/m$ with $\gamma \in \mathbb{N}\backslash\{0\}$ or $\mathrm{pen}(d) = d/m^2$ for instance. Some experimental results are presented in Section 3 in order to compare the performances of the classification procedure with these various penalties.

Proof. Starting from the general inequality (5), we need to evaluate the fluctuations of $L(\hat{\phi}_{l,\hat{k},\hat{d}}) - L_m(\hat{\phi}_{l,\hat{k},\hat{d}}) - L(\hat{\phi}_{l,k,d}) + L_m(\hat{\phi}_{l,k,d})$. The pair $(\hat{k},\hat{d})$ being randomly selected, it is therefore a matter of controlling $L(\hat{\phi}_{l,k',d'}) - L_m(\hat{\phi}_{l,k',d'}) - L(\hat{\phi}_{l,k,d}) + L_m(\hat{\phi}_{l,k,d})$ uniformly for (k',d') in $\{1,\ldots,l\} \times \mathcal{D}$. We use here the following version of Bernstein's inequality due to Birgé and Massart.

Lemma 1 (Birgé, Massart [34]). *Let $\xi_1,\ldots,\xi_n$ be independent random variables such that $\mathbb{E}\left[\sum_{i=1}^{n} |\xi_i|^q/n\right] \le (q!/2)vc^{q-2}$ for all $q \ge 2$, for some positive constants v and c. Then, for any positive x,*

$$\mathbb{P}\left(\frac{1}{n}\sum_{i=1}^{n}(\xi_i - \mathbb{E}[\xi_i]) \ge \sqrt{\frac{2vx}{n}} + \frac{cx}{n}\right) \le e^{-x}.$$

Since

$$L(\hat{\phi}_{l,k',d'}) - L_m(\hat{\phi}_{l,k',d'}) - L(\hat{\phi}_{l,k,d}) + L_m(\hat{\phi}_{l,k,d})$$
$$= \frac{1}{m}\sum_{i\in\mathcal{V}_m}\left(\mathbb{I}_{\{\hat{\phi}_{l,k,d}(X_i)\neq Y_i\}} - \mathbb{I}_{\{\hat{\phi}_{l,k',d'}(X_i)\neq Y_i\}}\right.$$
$$\left. - \mathbb{E}\left[\mathbb{I}_{\{\hat{\phi}_{l,k,d}(X_i)\neq Y_i\}} - \mathbb{I}_{\{\hat{\phi}_{l,k',d'}(X_i)\neq Y_i\}}\Big|\mathbb{D}_{\mathcal{T}_l}\right]\right),$$

we have to find an upper bound for $\mathbb{E}\left[\left|\mathbb{I}_{\{\hat{\phi}_{l,k,d}(X_i)\neq Y_i\}} - \mathbb{I}_{\{\hat{\phi}_{l,k',d'}(X_i)\neq Y_i\}}\right|^q\Big|\mathbb{D}_{\mathcal{T}_l}\right]$ for every i in $\mathcal{V}_m$, $q \ge 2$. For any integer $q \ge 2$,

$$\mathbb{E}\left[\left|\mathbb{I}_{\{\hat{\phi}_{l,k,d}(X_i)\neq Y_i\}} - \mathbb{I}_{\{\hat{\phi}_{l,k',d'}(X_i)\neq Y_i\}}\right|^q\Big|\mathbb{D}_{\mathcal{T}_l}\right]$$
$$\le \mathbb{E}_X\left[\left|\hat{\phi}_{l,k,d}(X) - \phi^*(X)\right|\right] + \mathbb{E}_X\left[\left|\hat{\phi}_{l,k',d'}(X) - \phi^*(X)\right|\right].$$

Under the assumption $GMA(\theta)$, we then have

$$\mathbb{E}\left[\left|\mathbb{I}_{\{\hat{\phi}_{l,k,d}(X_i)\neq Y_i\}} - \mathbb{I}_{\{\hat{\phi}_{l,k',d'}(X_i)\neq Y_i\}}\right|^q\Big|\mathbb{D}_{\mathcal{T}_l}\right]$$
$$\le \left(\frac{L(\hat{\phi}_{l,k,d}) - L(\phi^*)}{h}\right)^{\frac{1}{\theta}} + \left(\frac{L(\hat{\phi}_{l,k',d'}) - L(\phi^*)}{h}\right)^{\frac{1}{\theta}}$$
$$\le \frac{q!}{2}\left(\frac{1}{3}\right)^{q-2}\left(\left(\frac{L(\hat{\phi}_{l,k,d}) - L(\phi^*)}{h}\right)^{\frac{1}{\theta}} + \left(\frac{L(\hat{\phi}_{l,k',d'}) - L(\phi^*)}{h}\right)^{\frac{1}{\theta}}\right).$$

Introduce now a collection of positive numbers $\{x_{(k',d')}, k' \in \{1,\ldots,l\}, d' \in \mathcal{D}\}$ such that $\Sigma = \sum_{k'\in\{1,\ldots,l\},d'\in\mathcal{D}} e^{-x_{(k',d')}} < \infty$. From Lemma 1, we deduce that for any $x > 0$, $k' \in \{1,\ldots,l\}$, $d' \in \mathcal{D}$, conditionally given $\mathbb{D}_{\mathcal{T}_l}$, with probability at least $\left(1 - e^{-\left(x+x_{(k',d')}\right)}\right)$,

$$L(\hat{\phi}_{l,k',d'}) - L_m(\hat{\phi}_{l,k',d'}) - L(\hat{\phi}_{l,k,d}) + L_m(\hat{\phi}_{l,k,d})$$
$$\le \sqrt{\frac{2(x+x_{(k',d')})}{m}}\sqrt{\left(\frac{L(\hat{\phi}_{l,k,d}) - L(\phi^*)}{h}\right)^{\frac{1}{\theta}} + \left(\frac{L(\hat{\phi}_{l,k',d'}) - L(\phi^*)}{h}\right)^{\frac{1}{\theta}}} + \frac{1}{3}\frac{x+x_{(k',d')}}{m}.$$

From the general inequality (5), we obtain that conditionally given $\mathbb{D}_{\mathcal{T}_l}$, with probability at least $(1 - \Sigma e^{-x})$,

$$L(\hat{\phi}_n) - L(\phi^*) \leq L(\hat{\phi}_{l,k,d}) - L(\phi^*) + \text{pen}(d) - \text{pen}(\hat{d}) + \frac{1}{3}\frac{x + x_{(\hat{k},\hat{d})}}{m}$$

$$+ \sqrt{\frac{2(x + x_{(\hat{k},\hat{d})})}{m}}\sqrt{\left(\frac{L(\hat{\phi}_{l,k,d}) - L(\phi^*)}{h}\right)^{\frac{1}{\theta}} + \left(\frac{L(\hat{\phi}_n) - L(\phi^*)}{h}\right)^{\frac{1}{\theta}}}. \quad (7)$$

Since h is assumed to be smaller than 1, and $\theta \geq 1$, we have

$$\sqrt{\frac{2(x + x_{(\hat{k},\hat{d})})}{m}}\sqrt{\left(\frac{L(\hat{\phi}_{l,k,d}) - L(\phi^*)}{h}\right)^{\frac{1}{\theta}} + \left(\frac{L(\hat{\phi}_n) - L(\phi^*)}{h}\right)^{\frac{1}{\theta}}}$$

$$\leq \sqrt{\frac{2(x + x_{(\hat{k},\hat{d})})}{(mh)^{\frac{\theta}{2\theta-1}}}}\sqrt{\left(\left(L(\hat{\phi}_{l,k,d}) - L(\phi^*)\right)^{\frac{1}{\theta}} + \left(L(\hat{\phi}_n) - L(\phi^*)\right)^{\frac{1}{\theta}}\right)\left((mh)^{-\frac{\theta}{2\theta-1}}\right)^{1-\frac{1}{\theta}}}.$$

By successively using the elementary inequalities $a^{\frac{1}{\theta}}b^{1-\frac{1}{\theta}} \leq a + b$ and $\sqrt{ab} \leq \beta^{-1}a/4 + \beta b$ for $a \geq 0$, $b \geq 0$, $\beta > 0$, we establish that

$$\sqrt{\frac{2(x + x_{(\hat{k},\hat{d})})}{m}}\sqrt{\left(\frac{L(\hat{\phi}_{l,k,d}) - L(\phi^*)}{h}\right)^{\frac{1}{\theta}} + \left(\frac{L(\hat{\phi}_n) - L(\phi^*)}{h}\right)^{\frac{1}{\theta}}}$$

$$\leq \frac{\beta^{-1}(x + x_{(\hat{k},\hat{d})})}{2(mh)^{\frac{\theta}{2\theta-1}}} + \beta\left(L(\hat{\phi}_{l,k,d}) - L(\phi^*) + L(\hat{\phi}_n) - L(\phi^*) + \frac{2}{(mh)^{\frac{\theta}{2\theta-1}}}\right).$$

It follows from (7) that conditionally given $\mathbb{D}_{\mathcal{T}_l}$, with probability at least $(1 - \Sigma e^{-x})$,

$$L(\hat{\phi}_n) - L(\phi^*) \leq L(\hat{\phi}_{l,k,d}) - L(\phi^*) + \text{pen}(d) - \text{pen}(\hat{d}) + \frac{1}{3}\frac{x + x_{(\hat{k},\hat{d})}}{m}$$

$$+\beta\left(L(\hat{\phi}_{l,k,d}) - L(\phi^*) + L(\hat{\phi}_n) - L(\phi^*) + \frac{2}{(mh)^{\frac{\theta}{2\theta-1}}}\right) + \frac{\beta^{-1}\left(x + x_{(\hat{k},\hat{d})}\right)}{2(mh)^{\frac{\theta}{2\theta-1}}}.$$

By taking $x_{(k',d')} = \log(l|\mathcal{D}|)$ for every $k' \in \{1,\ldots,l\}$, $d' \in \mathcal{D}$, we have that conditionally given $\mathbb{D}_{\mathcal{T}_l}$, with probability at least $(1 - e^{-x})$,

$$(1 - \beta)(L(\hat{\phi}_n) - L(\phi^*)) \leq (1 + \beta)(L(\hat{\phi}_{l,k,d}) - L(\phi^*)) + \text{pen}(d) + \frac{2\beta}{(mh)^{\frac{\theta}{2\theta-1}}}$$

$$+ \frac{\beta^{-1}(x + \log(l|\mathcal{D}|))}{2(mh)^{\frac{\theta}{2\theta-1}}} + \frac{1}{3}\frac{x + \log(l|\mathcal{D}|)}{m}.$$

Integrating the inequality

$$\mathbb{P}\left(\left[(1-\beta)(L(\hat{\phi}_n)-L(\phi^*))-(1+\beta)(L(\hat{\phi}_{l,k,d})-L(\phi^*))-\text{pen}(d)\right.\right.$$

$$\left.\left.-\frac{2\beta}{(mh)^{\frac{\theta}{2\theta-1}}}-\frac{\beta^{-1}\log(l|\mathcal{D}|)}{2(mh)^{\frac{\theta}{2\theta-1}}}-\frac{1}{3}\frac{\log(l|\mathcal{D}|)}{m}\right]_+ \geq \left(\frac{\beta^{-1}}{2(mh)^{\frac{\theta}{2\theta-1}}}+\frac{1}{3m}\right)x\bigg|\mathbb{D}_{\mathcal{T}_l}\right)\leq e^{-x},$$

with respect to x finally leads to

$$(1-\beta)\mathbb{E}[L(\hat{\phi}_n)-L(\phi^*)|\mathbb{D}_{\mathcal{T}_l}] \leq (1+\beta)\left(L(\hat{\phi}_{l,k,d})-L(\phi^*)\right)+\text{pen}(d)$$

$$+\frac{\beta^{-1}\left(1+\log(l|\mathcal{D}|)\right)+4\beta}{2(mh)^{\frac{\theta}{2\theta-1}}}+\frac{1+\log(l|\mathcal{D}|)}{3m}.$$

Since (k,d) can be arbitrarily chosen, this concludes the proof of Proposition 2.

3   Experimental Study

In this section, we study from a practical point of view the performance of the classifier $\hat{\phi}_n$ defined by (2) with various penalty functions defined as follows: $\text{pen}_0(d) = 0$, $\text{pen}_B(d) = \log(d)/\sqrt{n}$, $\text{pen}_1(d) = \log(d)/n$, $\text{pen}_2(d) = \sqrt{d}/n$, $\text{pen}_3(d) = \log(d)/n^2$, $\text{pen}_4(d) = \sqrt{d}/n^2$. In particular, we aim at showing that the penalty pen_B proposed by Biau et al. [1] is too heavy and that lower penalization schemes can have a significant impact on the performance of the procedure.

To quantify this impact, we investigate the test error as defined below. The available data are randomly split into two parts of size $n = 3p/4$ and $t = p/4$ respectively. The first part is then split into a training set $\mathbb{D}_{\mathcal{T}_l}$ of length $l = p/4$ and a validation set $\mathbb{D}_{\mathcal{V}_m}$ of length $m = p/2$, and the classifier $\hat{\phi}_n$ is constructed as described in Section 2.1. Precisely, the training set is used to build the collection of estimators $\{\hat{\phi}_{l,k,d},\ k \in \{1,\ldots,l\},\ d \in \mathcal{D}\}$, whereas the validation set is used to select the parameters $\hat{k}$ and $\hat{d}$, and thus to select the estimator $\hat{\phi}_n = \hat{\phi}_{l,\hat{k},\hat{d}}$ in the collection. The responses of the second part of the data can hence be predicted thanks to this estimator, and compared to the "true" labels. Finally, the test error that we consider is the mean of the differences between the predictions and the "true" responses. In addition to the test error, we evaluate the performance of the procedure in terms of dimension selection. More precisely, we study the order and stability of the selected dimension $\hat{d}$, as investigated in [1].

We actually recall that our main purpose consists in constructing a classifier that satisfies an oracle type inequality such as (6). This means that we want to select a classifier that mimicks the oracle which is defined here as the element $\hat{\phi}_{l,\bar{k},\bar{d}}$ minimizing the risk $\mathbb{E}[L(\hat{\phi}_{l,k,d})] - L(\phi^*)$. Our classifier $\hat{\phi}_n = \hat{\phi}_{l,\hat{k},\hat{d}}$ will then mimick this oracle only if the selected dimension $\hat{d}$ is close to the one of the oracle $\bar{d}$, that achieves the best trade-off between the bias and variance terms (or the best trade-off between efficiency and consistency). We refer to a recent paper by Yang [35] for further details about this question in a regression model. For our experiments, we use both realistic data coming from speech recognition and food industry problems and simple simulated data.

3.1   A Speech Recognition Problem

In this section, we study data coming from the speech recognition problem considered by Biau *et al.* [1]. These data, created by Biau and available at http://www.math.univ-montp2fr/~biau/bbwdata.tgz, consist of three sets, each containing $p = 100$ recordings of two words. The first set deals with the words *"boat"* and *"goat"* whose labels are respectively 1 and 0. The second set corresponds to the phonemes *"sh"* and *"ao"* with labels 1 and 0 respectively, and the third to the words *"yes"* (label 1) and *"no"* (label 0). Each recording is the discretization of the corresponding signal and it contains 8192 points.

Assuming that the original speech signals belong to $\mathbb{L}_2(\mathbb{R})$, we choose, for the complete system $\{\psi_j,\ j \in \mathbb{N}\backslash\{0\}\}$ involved in the procedure, the Fourier basis:

$$\psi_1(t) = 1, \quad \psi_{2q}(t) = \sqrt{2}cos(2\pi qt), \quad \psi_{2q+1}(t) = \sqrt{2}sin(2\pi qt), \quad q = 1, 2, \ldots.$$

The coefficients of the Fourier series expansion of each data are evaluated using a Fast Fourier Transform. We compute the mean of the test error for the classifier $\hat{\phi}_n$ over $N = 100$ iterations of the splitting device of the data (into two parts of size $n = l + m$, with $l = 25$ and $m = 50$, and $t = 25$ respectively).

Table 1 summarizes the results obtained for each of the three data sets.

Table 1. For each penalty, on the first row, the mean of test error is given. On the second row, the first number is the median of the selected dimension d and the number in parentheses is the standard deviation.

words *goat boat*	pen_0	pen_B	pen_1	pen_2	pen_3, pen_4
mean test error	0.162	0.3128	0.2428	0.2526	0.2192
selected d	16(13.3)	1(0.3)	7(9.2)	5(5.3)	9(11.6)
phonemes *ao sh*	pen_0	pen_B	pen_1	pen_2	pen_3, pen_4
mean test error	0.1528	0.3948	0.1744	0.176	0.1688
selected d	5(6.1)	1(1)	5(4.5)	5(3.1)	5(5.9)
words *yes no*	pen_0	pen_B	pen_1	pen_2	pen_3, pen_4
mean test error	0.0976	0.4384	0.1372	0.134	0.1356
selected d	10(6.3)	1(0.7)	9(4.2)	9(2.3)	9(5.7)

Comments:
(i) We can notice that the penalty pen_B first proposed by Biau, Bunea and Wegkamp from a theoretical point of view is not relevant since the corresponding mean of test error is the largest one observed. For example, for the third set, the mean of test error with pen_B is more than twice the one with pen_0. This phenomenon has already been pointed out by Biau, Bunea and Wegkamp, as they chose to study in practice the nonpenalized procedure. Furthermore, the fact that the selected dimension $\hat{d}$ with pen_B is always very small ($\hat{d} = 1$ for more than 90% of the experiments) corroborates the idea that this penalty is too heavy, and that the nonpenalized procedure will be more appropriate. However, a refined study of the other penalization schemes shows that it can be interesting

to consider procedures with some penalties of small order. For the penalties pen_1 and pen_2, we obtain larger mean test errors than the ones obtained with the nonpenalized procedure. Nevertheless, the difference between these mean tests errors and the best one is not so great for at least one set of data, whereas we can see that they allow to select lower dimensions $\hat{d}$ with smaller standard deviations. This stabilization of the dimension selection process does not occur with the penalties pen_3 and pen_4, which are too small to have a real impact. In view of these results, it is clear that the use of a penalized procedure, but with an appropriate penalty, could be of particular relevance.

(*ii*) We should here notice that the Fourier basis may not be the most appropriate one for the decomposition of the data in the present case. Indeed, a recent work by Berlinet, Biau and Rouvière [36] proves that the above mean test errors can be improved by considering wavelet expansions. However, it appears that the instability in the selection of the dimension $\hat{d}$ by the nonpenalized procedure still holds, and that slightly penalizing the criteria could overcome this difficulty.

(*iii*) We have to take into account the fact that the number of observations is small ($p = 100$), and that this could entail some difficulties in the interpretation of the results.

3.2   A Food Industry Problem

We focus here on a classification problem which comes from the food industry. The data available on statlib are recorded on a Tecator Infratec Food and Feed Analyzer working in the wavelet range 850-1050 nm by the Near Infrared Transmission principle. They contain $p = 215$ observations of the neared infrared absorbance spectrum of finely chopped pure meat, with different fat contents. Each observation is composed of a 100 channel spectrum of absorbances and the corresponding fat content. The absorbance is $-\log_{10}$ of the transmittance measured by the spectrometer, and the fat content, measured in percent, is determined by analytic chemistry. The classification problem consists in separating meat samples with a high fat content (more than 20%) from samples with a low fat content (less than 20%).

We use here the same procedure as in the previous section, with a number of iterations N equal to 100. The splitting device is made with $n = l + m$, $l = 53$, $m = 108$, and $t = 54$. The obtained results are summarized in Table 2.

The same behavior as in the previous application to the speech recognition problem can be observed here. Hence, our conclusions remain valid, all the more as the number of observations is more important here.

Table 2. For each penalty, on the first row, the mean of test error is given. On the second row, the first number is the median of the selected dimension d and the number in parentheses is the standard deviation.

	pen_0	pen_B	pen_1	pen_2	pen_3, pen_4
mean test error	0.2698	0.3509	0.2988	0.3016	0.2928
selected d	9(9.6)	1(0.1)	5(4)	5(3.6)	6(6.8)

We performed the same procedure on simple simulated data with a great number of observations. The results detailed in Tuleau [37] confirm our previous conclusions, in the sense that they show that using a penalized procedure with a well-chosen penalty term (of order $\log(d)/n$ or $\sqrt{d}/n$) may improve the stability of the dimension selection process, whereas it does not alterate the mean test error too much. Such procedures may hence be a good compromise between the requirement of efficiency in terms of mean test error and stability of the dimension selection process.

The question of the stabilization process however requires more attention. In the above experimental study, we have to take into account that the observed instability of the nonpenalized procedure may come not only from the procedure used to construct the estimator $\hat{\phi}_n$ itself, but also from the split of the original data set into two parts, the second one being used for the computation of the test error. In the following section, we address the question of the stabilization of the procedure used to construct the estimator $\hat{\phi}_n$ only.

4   Stabilizing the Data-Splitting Device

As explained in Section 2, the classification scheme proposed by Biau *et al.* requires a data-splitting device, which can lead to some instability. We aim here at confirming the intuition, emerged from the previous section, that penalizing the procedure with a well-chosen penalty may overcome this difficulty, without altering too much the performance of the procedure in terms of test error.

Since we exclusively focus on the data-splitting device involved in the procedure itself, we first split the original data into two *fixed* parts of size $n = 2p/3$ and $t = p/3$ respectively. Then, on the first part, we perform, N times, the procedure described in Section 2.1 involving for each repetition a *random* splitting. The test error is finally computed through the second part of the data. The results obtained for Biau's data are given in Table 3.

Table 3. For each penalty, on the first row, the mean of test error is given. On the second row, the first number is the median of the selected dimension d and the number in parentheses is the standard deviation.

words *goat boat*	pen_0	pen_B	pen_1	pen_2	pen_3, pen_4
mean test error	0.1684	0.272	0.18	0.168	0.1932
selected d	15(15.5)	1(0.2)	6(10.3)	5(3.5)	14(14.7)
phonemes *ao sh*	pen_0	pen_B	pen_1	pen_2	pen_3, pen_4
mean test error	0.1684	0.4088	0.2064	0.2112	0.208
selected d	7(5.4)	1(0.8)	5(3.3)	5(2.6)	6(5.3)
words *yes no*	pen_0	pen_B	pen_1	pen_2	pen_3, pen_4
mean test error	0.0604	0.378	0.1016	0.1012	0.1036
selected d	10(5.9)	1(1.5)	9(4.3)	9(2.3)	9(5.7)

The analysis of the results of Table 3 shows that a real stabilization occurs for well-adapted penalties (pen_1 and pen_2). The results for the other data sets (food industry and simple simulated data) are similar. For sake of shortness, we do not include them.

At this stage, we can reasonably say that we have an idea of the good order of the appropriate penalization, which is $\log(d)/m$ or $\sqrt{d}/m$. It is clear that the precise determination of the appropriate penalty to use (that is of the possible multiplicative factor in the penalty) is still a question of interest. We hope that a future theoretical work will lead to the calibration of such a precise penalty that would achieve the best trade-off between the mean test error and the stability of the selection process.

Acknowledgements

The authors wish to express their thanks to Pascal Massart for many fruitful discussions, and Gérard Biau and Laurent Rouvière for making available the data used here and some programs to allow fair comparisons with variants of their method.

References

1. Biau, G., Bunea, F., Wegkamp, M.: Functional classification in Hilbert spaces. IEEE Trans. Inf. Theory **51** (2005) 2163–2172
2. Devroye, L., Györfi, L., Lugosi, G.: A probabilistic theory of pattern recognition. Applications of Mathematics. Springer, New York (1996)
3. Boucheron, S., Bousquet, O., Lugosi, G.: Theory of classification: some recent advances. ESAIM Probability and Statistics **9** (2005) 323–375
4. Stone, C.: Consistent nonparametric regression. Ann. Statist. **5** (1977) 595–645
5. Devroye, L., Krzyzak, A.: An equivalence theorem for L^1 convergence of the kernel regression estimate. Journal of the Statistical Planning and Inference **23** (1989) 71–82
6. Dabo-Niang, S., Rhomari, N.: Nonparametric regression estimation when the regressor takes its values in a metric space. Technical report, Université Paris VI (2001) http://www.ccr.jussieu.fr/lsta.
7. Abraham, C., Biau, G., Cadre, B.: On the kernel rule for function classification. Technical report (2003) Université de Montpellier, http://www.math.univ-montp2.fr/~biau/publications.html.
8. Kulkarni, S., Posner, S.: Rates of convergence of nearest neighbor estimation under arbitrary sampling. IEEE Trans. Inf. Theory **41** (1995) 1028–1039
9. Cerou, F., Guyader, A.: Nearest neighbor classification in infinite dimension. Technical report, IRISA, Rennes, France (2005)
10. Ramsay, J., Silverman, B.: Functional data analysis. Springer Series in Statistics. Springer-Verlag, New York (1997)
11. Ramsay, J., Silverman, B.: Applied functional data analysis. Springer Series in Statistics. Springer-Verlag, New York (2002) Methods and case studies.
12. Hastie, T., Buja, A., Tibshirani, R.: Penalized discriminant analysis. Ann. Statist. **23** (1995) 73–102

13. Hall, P., Poskitt, D., Presnell, B.: A functional data-analytic approach to signal discrimination. Technometrics **43** (2001) 1–9
14. Ferraty, F., Vieu, P.: Curves discrimination: a nonparametric functional approach. Comput. Statist. Data Anal. **44** (2003) 161–173
15. Hastie, T., Tibshirani, R.: Discriminant adaptive nearest neighbor classification. IEEE Trans. Pattern Anal. Mach. Intell. **18** (1996) 607–616
16. Rossi, F., Villa, N.: Classification in Hilbert spaces with support vector machines. In: Proceedings of ASMDA 2005, Brest, France (2005) 635–642
17. Hengartner, N., Matzner-Lober, E., Wegkamp, M.: Bandwidth selection for local linear regression. Journal of the Royal Statistical Society, Series B **64** (2002) 1–14
18. Stone, C.: Consistent nonparametric regression. Ann. Statist. **5** (1977) 595–645
19. Vapnik, V., Chervonenkis, A.: On the uniform convergence of relative frequencies of events to their probabilities. Theory Probab. Appl. **16** (1971) 264–280
20. Lugosi, G.: Pattern classification and learning theory. In Györfi, L., ed.: Principles of Nonparametric Learning. Springer, Wien, New York (2002) 1–56
21. Vapnik, V., Chervonenkis, A.: Teoriya raspoznavaniya obrazov. Statisticheskie problemy obucheniya (Theory of pattern recognition. Statistical problems of learning). Nauka, Moscow (1974)
22. Devroye, L., Wagner, T.: Nonparametric discrimination and density estimation. Technical Report 183, Electronics Research Center, University of Texas (1976)
23. Vapnik, V.: Estimation of dependences based on empirical data. Springer-Verlag, New York (1982)
24. Blumer, A., Ehrenfeucht, A., Haussler, D., Warmuth, M.: Learnability and the Vapnik-Chervonenkis dimension. J. Assoc. Comput. Mach. **36** (1989) 929–965
25. Haussler, D., Littlestone, N., Warmuth, M.: Predicting $\{0, 1\}$-functions on randomly drawn points. Inf. Comput. **115** (1994) 248–292
26. Devroye, L., Lugosi, G.: Lower bounds in pattern recognition and learning. Pattern Recognition **28** (1995) 1011–1018
27. Mammen, E., Tsybakov, A.: Smooth discrimination analysis. Ann. Statist. **27** (1999) 1808–1829
28. Tsybakov, A.: Optimal aggregation of classifiers in statistical learning. Ann. Statist. **32** (2004) 135–166
29. Massart, P., Nédélec, E.: Risk bounds for statistical learning. Ann. Statist. (2005) To appear.
30. Bartlett, P., Jordan, M., McAuliffe, J.: Convexity, classification, and risk bounds. Journal of the American Statistical Association **101** (2006) 138–156
31. Audibert, J.Y., Tsybakov, A.: Fast learning rates for plug-in estimators under margin condition. Preprint (2005)
32. Massart, P.: Concentration inequalities and model selection. Lectures given at the Saint-Flour summer school of probability theory. To appear in *Lect. Notes Math.* (2003)
33. Györfi, L.: On the rate of convergence of k-nearest-neighbor classification rule. Preprint (2005)
34. Birgé, L., Massart, P.: Minimum contrast estimators on sieves: exponential bounds and rates of convergence. Bernoulli **4** (1998) 329–375
35. Yang, Y.: Can the strengths of AIC and BIC be shared? a conflict between model identification and regression estimation. Biometrika **92** (2005) 937–950
36. Berlinet, A., Biau, G., Rouvière, L.: Functional learning with wavelets. To appear in IEEE Trans. Inf. Theory (2005)
37. Tuleau, C.: Sélection de variables pour la discrimination en grande dimension et classification de données fonctionnelles. PhD thesis, Université Paris Sud (2005)

Significance and Recovery of Block Structures in Binary Matrices with Noise

Xing Sun[1] and Andrew Nobel[1,2]

[1] Department of Statistics and Operation Research
[2] Department of Computer Science
University of North Carolina at Chapel Hill
Chapel Hill, NC 27599, USA
{xingsun, nobel}@email.unc.edu

Abstract. Frequent itemset mining (FIM) is one of the core problems in the field of Data Mining and occupies a central place in its literature. One equivalent form of FIM can be stated as follows: given a rectangular data matrix with binary entries, find every submatrix of 1s having a minimum number of columns. This paper presents a theoretical analysis of several statistical questions related to this problem when noise is present. We begin by establishing several results concerning the extremal behavior of submatrices of ones in a binary matrix with random entries. These results provide simple significance bounds for the output of FIM algorithms. We then consider the noise sensitivity of FIM algorithms under a simple binary additive noise model, and show that, even at small noise levels, large blocks of 1s leave behind fragments of only logarithmic size. Thus such blocks cannot be directly recovered by FIM algorithms, which search for submatrices of all 1s. On the positive side, we show how, in the presence of noise, an error-tolerant criterion can recover a square submatrix of 1s against a background of 0s, even when the size of the target submatrix is very small.

1   Introduction

Frequent itemset mining (FIM) [1, 2], also known as market basket analysis, is a central and well-studied problem in the field of Data Mining, and occupies a central place in its literature. It is closely related to a variety of related, more general problems, such as bi-clustering and subspace clustering [28, 7, 3, 10] that are of active interest to the Data Mining community. A variety of applications using FIM and other related bi-clustering algorithms can be found in [21, 14]. In the FIM problem the available data is described by a list $S = \{s_1, \ldots, s_n\}$ of items and a set $T = \{t_1, \ldots, t_m\}$ of transactions. Each transaction t_i consists of a subset of the items in S. (If S contains the items available for purchase at a store, then each t_i represents a record of items purchased during one transaction, without multiplicity.) The goal of FIM is to identify sets of items that appear together in more than k transactions, where $k \geq 1$ is a threshold for "frequent". The data for the FIM problem can readily be represented by an $m \times n$ binary matrix $\mathbf{X}$, with $x_{i,j} = 1$ if transaction t_i contains item s_j, and $x_{i,j} = 0$ otherwise.

G. Lugosi and H.U. Simon (Eds.): COLT 2006, LNAI 4005, pp. 109–122, 2006.

In this form the FIM problem can be stated as follows: given $\mathbf{X}$ and $k \geq 1$, find every submatrix of 1s in $\mathbf{X}$ having at least k columns. Frequent itemset algorithms perform an exhaustive search for such submatrices.

The application of FIM to large data sets for the purposes of exploratory analysis raises a number of natural statistical questions. In this paper we present (preliminary) answers to three such questions. The first question considers significance. In particular, how significant is the the discovery of a moderately sized submatrix of 1s in a large data matrix? To address this question, we establish probability bounds on the size of the largest submatrix of 1s in a random binary matrix. These bounds improve upon existing inequalities in the literature, and yield approximate p-values for discovered submatrices under the null hypothesis that the data consists of independent Bernoulli random variables.

Much of the data to which data mining methods are applied are obtained by high-throughput technologies or the automated collection of data from diverse sources with varying levels of reliability. The resulting data sets are often subject to moderate levels of error and noise. Our second question involves the behavior and performance of FIM in the presence of noise. Standard frequent itemset algorithms do not account for noise or errors in their search for submatrices of 1s. We consider the noise sensitivity of FIM under a simple binary additive noise model and show that, even at small noise levels, blocks of 1s is broken into fragments of logarithmic size. Thus such blocks cannot be directly recovered by standard frequent itemset algorithms.

Lastly, we consider the problem of recovering a block of 1s in the presence of additive noise using an error-tolerant criterion (approximate frequent itemsets) that allows submatrices containing a limited fraction of zeros. We show how the AFI criterion can recover a square submatrix of 1s against a background of 0s, even when the size of the target submatrix is very small.

1.1 Overview

The next section contains several results on the size of maximal submatrices of ones in a random matrix with independent Bernoulli entries. In addition, we present a small simulation study that explores the applicability of the asymptotic theory to small samples. Section 2 is devoted to the description of the additive noise model and the noise sensitivity of standard FIM. In Section 3 we consider the recoverability of block structures in the presence of noise using the approximate frequent itemset criterion.

2 Frequent Itemsets in Random Matrices

There is a large literature on ordinary (full-space) clustering that spans 50 years. While there has been recent attention and progress on the problem of cluster validation [30], [17], [11], there is no general and systematic treatment of signifiance for full-space clustering. FIM is more amenable to significance analysis than full-space clustering, as attention shifts from high-dimensional objects (the rows or columns of the data matrix) to the entries of the data matrix itself, which are organized into a simple two-dimensional array. Here we consider several questions related to the size and statistical significance of frequent itemsets in a random matrix. The focus is on the size of the largest submatrix of 1s, or a specified fraction of 1s, in a binary matrix with Bernoulli entries. For simplicity of exposition, we emphasize the case of square matrices and square submatrices. Some extensions to the non-square case are described in Section 2.3 below.

2.1   Square Submatrices of 1s

Let $\mathbf{X}$ be an $m \times n$ binary matrix. A submatrix of $\mathbf{X}$ is a collection $\mathbf{U} = \{x_{i,j} : i \in A, j \in B\}$ where $A \subseteq \{1, \ldots, m\}$ and $B \subseteq \{1, \ldots, n\}$. The Cartesian product $C = A \times B$ will be called the index set of $\mathbf{U}$. Given $C = A \times B$, define $\mathbf{X}[C]$ to be the submatrix of $\mathbf{X}$ with index set C. When no ambiguity will arise, C will also be referred to as a submatrix of $\mathbf{X}$. Note that $\mathbf{X}$ can be viewed as the adjacency matrix of a bi-partite graph $G(\mathbf{X})$. The graph $G(\mathbf{X})$ has vertex set V equal to the disjoint union $V = V_r \cup V_c$, where V_r corresponds to the rows of $\mathbf{X}$, V_c corresponds to its columns, and there is an edge between $i \in V_r$ and $j \in V_c$ if and only if $x_{i,j} = 1$. With this association, submatrices of ones in $\mathbf{X}$ are in one-to-one correspondence with bi-cliques in $G(\mathbf{W})$. This connection is the basis for the SAMBA bi-cluster algorithm of Tanay *et al.* [29].

Definition. Given any binary matrix $\mathbf{X}$, let $M(\mathbf{X})$ be the largest value of k such that $\mathbf{X}$ contains a $k \times k$ submatrix of 1s.

Definition. Let $\mathbf{Z}_n$ denote an $n \times n$ binary matrix whose entries are independent Bernoulli(p) random variables, with $p \in (0, 1)$. We will write $\mathbf{Z}_n \sim \text{Bern}(p)$.

A natural starting point for studying the significance of FIM is $M(\mathbf{Z}_n)$, the size of the largest submatrix of 1s in a binary matrix with independent Bernoulli entries. To obtain bounds on $M(\mathbf{Z}_n)$, let $U_k(n)$ be the number of $k \times k$ submatrices of 1s in $\mathbf{Z}_n$. Then, using Stirling's approximation, it is easy to show that $EU_k(n) = \binom{n}{k}^2 p^{k^2} \approx (2\pi)^{-1} n^{2n+1} k^{-2k-1} (n-k)^{-2(n-k)-1} p^{k^2}$. The first moment method from combinatorial probability suggests that $M(\mathbf{Z}_n)$ will be close to the value of k for which $EU_k(n) = 1$. Accordingly, define $s(n)$ to be any positive solution of the equation

$$1 = \phi_n(s) = (2\pi)^{-\frac{1}{2}} n^{n+\frac{1}{2}} s^{-s-\frac{1}{2}} (n-s)^{-(n-s)-\frac{1}{2}} p^{\frac{s^2}{2}}. \tag{1}$$

A routine but involved analysis shows that any solution $s(n)$ of (1) must satisfy the relation

$$s(n) = 2 \log_b n - 2 \log_b \log_b n + C + o(1), \tag{2}$$

where $b = p^{-1}$ and C is a positive constant. Moreover, by standard calculus, it can be shown that $\phi_n(\cdot)$ is monotone decreasing when $\log_b n < s < 2 \log_b n$. Thus when n is sufficiently large, there is only one solution of (1) in the interval $(\log_b n, 2 \log_b n)$, and therefore $s(n)$ is uniquely defined. Define $k(n) = \lceil s(n) \rceil$. A simple application of the first moment method yields a bound on the probability that $M(\mathbf{Z}_n)$ is larger than $k(n)$, which can be used to assess the statistical significance of submatrices of ones identified by bi-clustering algorithms.

Proposition 1. *Fix $0 < \gamma < 1$. When n is sufficiently large, for every integer $1 \le r \le \gamma n$ we have $P\{M(\mathbf{Z}_n) \ge k(n) + r\} \le 2\,n^{-2r}\,(\log_b n)^{3r}$, where $b = p^{-1}$.*

Proof. To establish the bound with n independent of r, it suffices to consider a sequence $r = r_n$ that changes with n in such a way that $1 \le r_n \le \gamma n$. Fix n for the moment, let $l = k(n) + r_n$, and let $U_l(n)$ be be the number of $l \times l$ submatrices of 1s in $\mathbf{Z}_n$. Then by Markov's inequality and Stirling's approximation,

$$P(M(\mathbf{Z}_n) \ge r) = P(U_l \ge 1) \le E(U_l) = \binom{n}{l}^2 p^{l^2} \le 2\phi_n(l)^2. \qquad (3)$$

A straightforward calculation using the definition of $\phi_n(\cdot)$ shows that

$$2\phi_n(l)^2 = 2\,\phi_n^2(k(n))\,p^{r\cdot k(n)}\,[\,A_n(r)\,B_n(r)\,C_n(r)\,D_n(r)\,]^2, \qquad (4)$$

where

$$A_n(r) = \left(\frac{n - r - k(n)}{n - k(n)}\right)^{-n+r+k(n)+\frac{1}{2}} \qquad B_n(r) = \left(\frac{r + k(n)}{k(n)}\right)^{-k(n)-\frac{1}{2}}$$

$$C_n(r) = \left(\frac{n - k(n)}{r + k(n)}\,p^{\frac{k(n)}{2}}\right)^r \qquad D_n(r) = p^{\frac{r^2}{2}}$$

Note that $p^{r\cdot k(n)} = o(n^{-2r}(\log_b n)^{3r})$, and that $\phi_n^2(k(n)) \le 1$ by the monotonicity of $\phi_n(\cdot)$ and the definition of $k(n)$. Thus it suffices to show that $A_n(r) \cdot B_n(r) \cdot C_n(r) \cdot D_n(r) \le 1$ when n is sufficiently large. To begin, note that for any fixed $\delta \in (0, 1/2)$, when n is sufficiently large,

$$C_n(r)^{\frac{1}{r}} = \frac{n - k(n)}{r + k(n)}\,p^{\frac{k(n)}{2}} \le \frac{n}{k(n)}\,p^{\frac{k(n)}{2}} \le \frac{n}{(2-\delta)\log_b n}\,\frac{\frac{2+\delta}{2}\log_b n}{n}$$

which is less than one. In order to show $A_n(r) \cdot B_n(r) \cdot D_n(r) \le 1$, we consider two possibilities for the asymptotic behavior of $r = r_n$.

Case 1. Suppose $r/k(n) \to 0$ as $n \to \infty$. In this case, $B_n(r)^{\frac{1}{r}} = (1 + o(1))\,e^{-1}$. Moreover, $r/n \to 0$, which implies that $A_n(r)^{\frac{1}{r}} = (1 + o(1))\,e$. Thus

$$A_n(r) \cdot B_n(r) \cdot D_n(r) = ((1 + o(1))^2 p^{\frac{r}{2}})^r \le 1$$

when n is sufficiently large.

Case 2. Suppose $\liminf_n r/k(n) > 0$. In this case a routine calculation shows that $B_n(r) \le 1$ for any $r \ge 1$, so it suffices to show that

$$A_n(r) \cdot D_n(r) \le 1. \qquad (5)$$

Note that $D_n(r) = (p^{\frac{r}{2}})^r$ and $A_n(r)^{\frac{1}{r}} = (1 + o(1))\,e$ when $r = o(n - k(n))$. Thus (5) holds when $r = o(n - k(n))$.

It remains to consider the case $o(n-k(n)) < r < \gamma n$. As $\sqrt{(2 + \frac{2}{1-\gamma})n/\log b} = o(n - k(n))$, it suffices to assume that $\sqrt{(2 + \frac{2}{1-\gamma})n/\log b} < r < \gamma n$. In this case,

$$
\log_b A_n(r) \cdot D_n(r) = \log_b \left[\left(1 + \frac{r}{n - k(n) - r} \right)^{n-r-k(n)-\frac{1}{2}} p^{\frac{r^2}{2}} \right]
$$

$$
\leq n \log_b \left(1 + \frac{r}{n - r - k(n)} \right) - \frac{(2 + \frac{2}{1-\gamma})n}{2 \log b} \leq 0,
$$

where the last inequality comes from the fact that $\log_b(1 + x) \leq x/\log b$ for $x \geq 0$.   ∎

An inspection of the proof shows that the inequality of Proposition 1 is obtained via a standard union (Bonferroni) type bound on the probability of finding a $k \times k$ submatrix of 1s in $\mathbf{Z}_n$. In general, union bounds are rather loose, and indeed, with additional calculation, one can improve the upper bound in Proposition 1 to $n^{-(4-\delta)r}(\log_b n)^{3r}$ for any $\delta > 0$. Nevertheless, a more refined second moment argument (see Theorem 1 below) shows that the threshold $k(n)$ can not be improved.

Bollobás [5] and Grimmett and McDiarmid [12] established analogous bounds for the size of a maximal clique in a random graph, with the larger threshold $k(n) = 2 \log_b n$. Koyutürk and Szpankowski [16] studied the problem of finding dense patterns in binary data matrices. They used a Chernoff type bound for the binomial distribution to assess whether an individual submatrix has an enriched fraction of ones, and employed the resulting test as the basis for a heuristic search for significant bi-clusters. Tanay et al. [28] assessed the significance of bi-clusters in a real-valued matrix using likelihood-based weights, a normal approximation and a standard Bonferroni bound to account for the multiplicity of submatrices.

As noted above, $M(\mathbf{Z}_n)$ is the size of the largest bi-clique in a random $n \times n$ bi-partite graph. Bollobás and Erdős [4] and Matula [20] studied the size of the largest clique in a standard random graph with n vertices, where each edge is included with probability p, independent of the other edges. In particular, they obtained strong almost sure results on the asymptotic size of maximal cliques. Bollobás [5] gives a good account of these results. By extending the arguments in [4, 20] to bi-cliques one may establish the following analogous result; the proof is rather technical and is omitted. Assume that for each n the matrix $\mathbf{Z}_n$ is the upper left corner of an infinite array $\{z_{i,j} : i, j \geq 1\}$ of Bernoulli(p) random variables with $0 < p < 1$.

Theorem 1. *With probability one, $|M(\mathbf{Z}_n) - s(n)| < \frac{3}{2}$ when n is sufficiently large. Thus $M(\mathbf{Z}_n)$ eventually concentrates on one of the (at most three) integers within distance 3/2 of the real number $s(n)$.*

Dawande et al. [8] used first and second moment arguments to show (in our terminology) that $P(\log_b n \leq M(\mathbf{Z}_n) \leq 2 \log_b n) \rightarrow 1$ as n tends to infinity. Extending this work, Park and Szpankowski [25] showed that if $\tilde{M}$ is the side-length of the largest square submatrix of 1s in an $m \times n$ Bernoulli matrix, then

$P(|\tilde{M} - \log_b(mn)| > \epsilon \log(mn)) \leq O((mn)^{-1}(\log(mn))^6)$. When $m = n$ their result implies that $(2 - \epsilon)\log_b n \leq M(\mathbf{Z}_n) \leq (2 + \epsilon)\log_b n$ eventually almost surely.

2.2   Submatrices with Large Fraction of Ones

In situations where noise is present, one may wish to look for submatrices having a large fraction of 1s, rather than requiring the stronger condition that every entry be equal to 1. Let $\mathbf{X}$ be a binary matrix, and let $\mathbf{U}$ be a submatrix of $\mathbf{X}$ with index set C. Let

$$F(\mathbf{U}) = |C|^{-1}\sum_{(i,j)\in C} x_{i,j}$$

be the fraction of ones in $\mathbf{U}$. Fix $\tau \in (0,1)$ and define $M_\tau(\mathbf{X})$ to be the largest k such that $\mathbf{X}$ contains a $k \times k$ submatrix $\mathbf{U}$ with $F(\mathbf{U}) \geq \tau$.

Proposition 2. *Fix* $0 < \gamma < 1$ *and suppose that* $0 < p < \tau < 1$. *When* n *is sufficiently large,* $P(M_\tau(\mathbf{Z}_n) \geq 2\log_{b^*} n + r) \leq 2n^{-2r}(\log_{b^*} n)^{3r}$ *for each* $1 \leq r \leq \gamma n$. *Here* $b^* = \exp\{3(\tau - p)^2/8p\}$.

Proof. For $l \geq 1$ let $V_l(n)$ be the number of $l \times l$ submatrices $\mathbf{U}$ of $\mathbf{Z}_n$ with $F(\mathbf{U}) \geq \tau$. Note that $E(V_l(n)) = \binom{n}{l}^2 P(F(\mathbf{Z}_l) \geq \tau)$. The random variable $l^2 \cdot F(\mathbf{Z}_l)$ has a Binomial(l^2, p) distribution. Using a standard inequality for the tails of the binomial distribution, (*c.f.* Problem 8.3 of [9]), we find that $P(F(\mathbf{Z}_l) \geq \tau) \leq q^{l^2}$ where $q = 1/b^*$. It then follows from Stirling's approximation that $EV_l(n) \leq 2$ when $l = l(n) = 2\log_{b^*} n$. For $l = r + l(n)$, $P(M_\tau(\mathbf{Z}_n) \geq l) \leq E(V_l(n))$ and the stated inequality then follows from arguments analogous to those in the proof of Proposition 1.   ∎

Note that the base $b^* = \exp\{3(\tau - p)^2/8p\}$ may not always yield the best upper bound. When $p \geq \frac{1}{2}$, b^* can be replaced by $\exp\{(\tau - p)^2/2p(1-p)\}$ (*cf.* [22]). When $\tau \to 1$, $b^* = \exp\{3(\tau - p)^2/8p\}$ fails to converge to p^{-1}, so that the probability bound above does not coincide with that of Proposition 1. In this case, the disparity may be remedied by using an alternative bound for the tails of the binomial (*e.g.* [15]) and a corresponding base for the logarithm.

2.3   Non-square Matrices

The restriction to square matrices above can readily be relaxed, yielding bounds for data sets with more transactions than items, or vice versa. Suppose that $\mathbf{Z}_{m,n} \sim \text{Bern}(p)$ is an $m \times n$ random matrix with $\frac{m}{n} = \alpha$ for some $\alpha > 0$. For any $\rho \geq 1$, let $M_\alpha^\rho(\mathbf{Z})$ be the largest k such that there exists at least one $\lceil \rho k \rceil \times k$ submatrix of 1s in $\mathbf{Z}$. One may extend Proposition 1 as follows.

Proposition 3. *Fix* $0 < \gamma < 1$. *When* n *is sufficiently large,*

$$P\{M_\alpha^\rho(\mathbf{Z}) \geq k(\alpha, \rho, n) + r\} \leq n^{-(\rho+1)r} 2(\log_b n)^{(\rho+2)r} \qquad (6)$$

for each $1 \leq r \leq \gamma n$. *Here* $k(\alpha, \rho, n) = \frac{\rho+1}{\rho}\log_b n + \log_b \frac{\alpha}{\rho}$.

One may generalize Proposition 3 to submatrices with large fractions of 1s by replacing b with the base b^* of Proposition 2.

Park and Szpankowski [25] established probability bounds on the maximum area of non-square submatrices and showed that such submatrices have aspect ratio close to zero. In addition they established probability bounds for square submatrices (discussed above) that provide weaker inequalities like those in Proposition 3 when $\rho = 1$.

Propositions 1, 2 and 3 can provide bounds on the statistical significance of submatrices discovered by frequent itemset mining algorithms, under the null hypothesis that the observed data is purely random. Suppose for example that an FIM algorithm is applied to a $4{,}000 \times 100$ binary matrix $\mathbf{Y}$, 65% of whose entries are equal to 1. Suppose that the algorithm finds a 44×25 submatrix $\mathbf{U}$ of ones in $\mathbf{Y}$. Applying Proposition 3 with $p = 0.65$, $\alpha = 40$ and $\rho = 1.76$ we find that $k(\alpha, \rho, n) = 24$ and that the probability of finding such a matrix $\mathbf{U}$ in a purely random matrix is at most

$$2\, n^{-(1.76+1)\,\times\,(25-24)} \left(\log_b n\right)^{(1.76+2)\times(25-24)} \approx 0.04467.$$

Thus $\mathbf{U}$ may be assigned a p-value $p(\mathbf{U}) \le 0.04467$. On the other hand, consider the case that an error tolerant FIM algorithm finds an 73×25 submatrix $\mathbf{U}'$ in Y with 95% 1s. Since in this case $p > \frac{1}{2}$, the discussion immediately after Proposition 2 suggests using $b^* = \exp\{(0.95 - p)^2/2p(1 - p)\} = 1.2187$ for a better bound. By plugging each corresponding term into (6), one obtains a nominal p-value $p(\mathbf{U}') \le 0.04802$.

2.4 Simulations

The results of the previous section hold for n sufficiently large. To test their validity for moderate values of n, we carried out a simple simulation study on Z_n with $n = 40$ and 80, and $p = .2$. In each case, we generated 400 such matrices and applied the FP-growth algorithm [13] to identify all maximal submatrices of ones. For each maximal submatrix of ones we recorded the length of its shorter side. The maximum of these values is $M(\mathbf{Z}_n)$. We recorded $M(\mathbf{Z}_n)$ in each of the 400 simulations and compared its value to the corresponding bounds $s(40) \approx 3.553$ and $s(80) \approx 4.582$. Table 1 summarizes the results. In each case $|M(\mathbf{Z}_n) - s(n)| \le 1$.

Table 1. Simulation results on $\hat{M}(Z_n)$ based on 400 replications for each n

n	$s(n)$	k	Proportion of $M(\mathbf{Z}_n) = k$
40	3.553	3	85.75%
		4	14.25%
80	4.582	4	97%
		5	3%

3 Noise Sensitivity of FIM

3.1 Statistical Noise Model

In order to account for and study the potential effects of noise on FIM, we consider a simple noise model. Under the model the observed data matrix $\mathbf{Y}$ is equal to the component-wise modulo 2 sum of a "true" unobserved data matrix $\mathbf{X}$ and a noise matrix $\mathbf{Z}$ whose entries are independent Bernoulli(p) random variables. Formally,

$$\mathbf{Y} = \mathbf{X} \oplus \mathbf{Z} \tag{7}$$

so that $y_{i,j} = x_{i,j}$ if $z_{i,j} = 0$ and $y_{i,j} = 1 - x_{i,j}$ if $z_{i,j} = 1$. The model (7) is the binary version of the standard additive noise model in statistical inference. It is equivalent to the simple communication model, widely studied in information theory, in which the values of $\mathbf{X}$ are observed after being passed through a memoryless binary symmetric channel.

3.2 Noise Sensitivity

If the matrix $\mathbf{X}$ in (7) contains interesting structure, for example a large submatrix of ones, there is reason to hope that this structure would be readily apparent in the observed matrix $\mathbf{Y}$ and could be recovered by standard frequent itemset algorithms without much effort. Unfortunately this is not necessarily the case, as the next result shows.

Let $\mathbf{X}$ be an $n \times n$ binary matrix, and let $\mathbf{Y} = \mathbf{X} \oplus \mathbf{Z}$ with $\mathbf{Z} \sim \text{Bern}(p)$ and $0 < p < \frac{1}{2}$. We are interested in how $M(\mathbf{Y})$ depends on $\mathbf{X}$, and in particular how the value of $M(\mathbf{Y})$ reflects block structures (submatrices of 1s) in $\mathbf{X}$. If $\mathbf{X} = \mathbf{0}$ then $\mathbf{Y} \sim \text{Bern}(p)$. In this case, Proposition 1 and Theorem 1 ensure that $M(\mathbf{Y})$ is roughly $2 \log_b n$ with $b = p^{-1}$. At the other extreme, if $\mathbf{X} = \mathbf{1}$ then it is easy to see that $\mathbf{Y} \sim \text{Bern}(1 - p)$, and in this case $M(\mathbf{Y})$ is roughly $2 \log_{b'} n$ with $b' = (1 - p)^{-1}$. The latter case represents the best possible situation in regards to maximizing $M(\mathbf{Y})$.

Proposition 4. *Let $b' = (1 - p)^{-1}$ and fix $0 < \gamma < 1$. When n is sufficiently large, $P\{M(\mathbf{Y}) \geq 2 \log_{b'} n + r\} \leq 2 \, n^{-2r} \, (\log_{b'} n)^{3r}$ for every matrix X and for every integer $1 \leq r \leq \gamma n$.*

Proof. Fix n and let $\mathbf{W}_n = \{w_{i,j}\}$ be an $n \times n$ binary matrix with independent entries, defined on the same probability space as $\{z_{i,j}\}$, such that

$$w_{i,j} = \begin{cases} \text{Bern}\left(\frac{1-2p}{1-p}\right) & \text{if } x_{ij} = y_{ij} = 0 \\ 1 & \text{if } x_{ij} = 0, y_{ij} = 1 \\ y_{i,j} & \text{if } x_{ij} = 1 \end{cases} \tag{8}$$

Note that the above definition is valid since we assume $p < \frac{1}{2}$ here. Define $\tilde{\mathbf{Y}}_n = \mathbf{Y}_n \vee \mathbf{W}_n$ to be the entrywise maximum of $\mathbf{Y}_n$ and $\mathbf{W}_n$. Clearly $M(\mathbf{Y}_n) \leq M(\tilde{\mathbf{Y}}_n)$, as any submatrix of ones in $\mathbf{Y}_n$ must also be present in $\tilde{\mathbf{Y}}_n$. Moreover, it is easy to check that $P(\tilde{y}_{i,j} = 1) = 1 - p$ for each $1 \leq i, j \leq n$, so that $\tilde{\mathbf{Y}}_n \sim \mathrm{Bern}(1 - p)$. The result now follows from Proposition 1. ∎

Proposition 4 has the following consequence. No matter what type of block structures might exist in $\mathbf{X}$, in the presence of random noise these structures leave behind only logarithmic sized fragments in the observed data matrix. In particular, under the additive noise model (7) block structures in $\mathbf{X}$ cannot be recovered, even approximately, by standard frequent itemset algorithms that look for submatrices of ones without errors.

4   Recovery

Here we consider the simple problem of recovering, in the presence of noise, a submatrix of ones against a background of zeros. Proposition 4 shows that standard FIM algorithms are sensitive to noise, and are not readily applicable to the recovery problem. This shortcoming can be remedied by algorithms that look instead for submatrices having a large *fraction* of ones. Several recent papers [24, 18, 19, 27, 23, 6, 31] in the data mining literature have addressed this question, each using a criterion that weakens the all 1s model of FIM. Below we show how one such criterion, introduced in [18], can be used to recover block structures in noise.

Let $\mathbf{X}$ be an $n \times n$ binary matrix that consists of an $l \times l$ submatrix of ones, with index set C^*, and all other entries equal to 0. (The rows and columns of C^* need not be contiguous.) Given an observation $\mathbf{Y} = \mathbf{X} \oplus \mathbf{Z}$ of $\mathbf{X}$ with $\mathbf{Z} \sim \mathrm{Bern}(p)$ and $0 < p < 1/2$, we wish to recover the submatrix C^*.

Let p_0 be any number such that $p < p_0 < 1/2$, and let $\tau = 1 - p_0$ be an associated error threshold. If U is an $a \times b$ submatrix of $\mathbf{Y}$, denote its rows and columns by $u_{1*}, \ldots, u_{a*}$ and $u_{*1}, \ldots, u_{*b}$, respectively. The following definition of error-tolerant itemsets was introduced in [18]. An algorithm for finding such itemsets is given in [19].

Definition. An $a \times b$ submatrix C of $\mathbf{Y}$ is a τ-*approximate frequent itemset* (AFI) if $F(u_{i*}) \geq \tau$ and $F(u_{*j}) \geq \tau$ for each $i = 1, \ldots, a$ and $j = 1, \ldots, b$. Let $\mathrm{AFI}_\tau(\mathbf{Y})$ be the collection of all τ-AFIs in $\mathbf{Y}$.

We estimate C^* by the index of the largest square AFI in the observed matrix $\mathbf{Y}$. More precisely, let $\mathcal{C}$ be the family of index sets of square submatrices $C \in \mathrm{AFI}_\tau(\mathbf{Y})$, and define

$$\hat{C} = \mathrm{argmax}_{C \in \mathcal{C}} |C|$$

to be any maximal sized submatrix in $\mathcal{C}$. Note that $\mathcal{C}$ and $\hat{C}$ depend only on the observed matrix $\mathbf{Y}$. Let the ratio

$$\Lambda = |\hat{C} \cap C^*| / |\hat{C} \cup C^*|$$

measure the overlap between the estimated index set $\hat{C}$ and the true index set C^*. Thus $0 \leq \Lambda \leq 1$, and values of Λ close to one indicate better overlap.

Theorem 2. *Let $0 < p < p_0 < 1/2$ and $\tau = 1 - p_0$. When n is sufficiently large, for any $0 < \alpha < 1$ such that $12\alpha^{-1}(\log_b n + 2) \le l$ we have*

$$P\left(\Lambda \le \frac{1-\alpha}{1+\alpha}\right) \le \Delta_1(l) + \Delta_2(\alpha, l).$$

Here $\Delta_1(l) = 2e^{-\frac{l(p-p_0)^2}{3p}}$, $\Delta_2(\alpha, l) = 2n^{-\frac{1}{6}\alpha l + 2\log_b n}$, and $b = \exp\{3(1-2p_0)^2/8p\}$.

The conditions of Theorem 2 require that the noise level $p < 1/2$ and that the user-specified parameter p_0 satisfies $p < p_0 < 1/2$. Thus, in advance, one only needs to know an upper bound on the noise level p. Theorem 2 can readily be applied to the asymptotic recovery of structure in a sequential framework. Suppose that $\{\mathbf{X}_n : n \ge 1\}$ is a sequence of square binary matrices, where $\mathbf{X}_n$ is $n \times n$ and consists of an $l_n \times l_n$ submatrix C_n^* of 1s with all other entries equal to 0. For each n we observe $\mathbf{Y}_n = \mathbf{X}_n \oplus \mathbf{Z}_n$, where $\mathbf{Z}_n \sim \text{Bern}(p)$. Let Λ_n measure the overlap between C_n^* and the estimate $\hat{C}_n$ produced by the AFI recovery method above. The following result follows from Theorem 2 and the Borel Cantelli lemma.

Corollary 1. *If $l_n \ge 12\psi(n)(\log_b n + 2)$ where $\psi(n) \to \infty$ as $n \to \infty$, then eventually almost surely*

$$\Lambda_n \le \frac{1 - \psi(n)^{-1}}{1 + \psi(n)^{-1}}.$$

Reuning-Scherer studied several recovery problems in [26]. In the case considered above, he calculated the fraction of 1s in every row and every column of $\mathbf{Y}$, and then selected those rows and columns with a large fraction of 1s. His algorithm is consistent when $l \ge n^\alpha$ for $\alpha > 1/2$. However, a simple calculation using the central limit theorem demonstrates that individual row and column sums alone are not sufficient to recover C^* when $l \le n^\alpha$ for $\alpha < 1/2$. In this case, one gains considerable power by directly considering submatrices and, as the result above demonstrates, one can consistently recover C_n^* if $l_n / \log n \to \infty$.

The following two lemmas will be used in the proof of Theorem 2. Lemma 1 implies that $|\hat{C}|$ is greater than or equal to $|C^*|$ with high probability. Lemma 2 shows that $\hat{C}$ can only contain a small proportion of entries outside C^*. The proofs of Lemma 1, and a sketch of the proof of Lemma 2, can be found in the Appendix.

Lemma 1. *Under the conditions of Theorem 2, $P\left(|\hat{C}| < l^2\right) \le \Delta_1(l)$.*

Lemma 2. *Let $\mathcal{A}$ be the collection of $C \in \mathcal{C}$ such that $|C| > \frac{l^2}{2}$ and $\frac{|C \cap C^{*c}|}{|C|} \ge \alpha$. Let A be the event that $\mathcal{A} \ne \emptyset$. If n is sufficiently large, then $l \ge 12\alpha^{-1}(\log_b n + 2)$ implies*

$$P(A) \le \Delta_2(\alpha, l)$$

Proof of Theorem 2. Let E be the event that $\{\Lambda \le \frac{1-\alpha}{1+\alpha}\}$. It is clear that E can be expressed as the union of two disjoint events E_1 and E_2, where

$$E_1 = \{|\hat{C}| < |C^*|\} \cap E \qquad (9)$$

and

$$E_2 = \{|\hat{C}| \geq |C^*|\} \cap E \tag{10}$$

One can bound $P(E_1)$ by $\Delta_1(l)$ via Lemma 1.

It remains to bound $P(E_2)$. By the definition of Λ, the inequality $\Lambda \leq \frac{1-\alpha}{1+\alpha}$ can be rewritten equivalently as

$$1 + \frac{|\hat{C} \cap C^{*c}|}{|\hat{C} \cap C^*|} + \frac{|\hat{C}^c \cap C^*|}{|\hat{C} \cap C^*|} \geq \frac{1+\alpha}{1-\alpha}.$$

When $|\hat{C}| \geq |C^*|$, one can verify that $|\hat{C} \cap C^{*c}| \geq |\hat{C}^c \cap C^*|$, which implies that

$$1 + \frac{|\hat{C} \cap C^{*c}|}{|\hat{C} \cap C^*|} + \frac{|\hat{C}^c \cap C^*|}{|\hat{C} \cap C|} \leq 1 + 2\frac{|\hat{C} \cap C^{*c}|}{|\hat{C} \cap C^*|}.$$

Therefore, $E_2 \subset E_2^*$, where

$$E_2^* = \{|\hat{C}| \geq |C^*|\} \cap \left\{ 1 + 2\frac{|\hat{C} \cap C^{*c}|}{|\hat{C} \cap C^*|} \geq \frac{1+\alpha}{1-\alpha} \right\}$$

$$\subset \{|\hat{C}| > \frac{l^2}{2}\} \cap \left\{ 1 + 2\frac{|\hat{C} \cap C^{*c}|}{|\hat{C} \cap C^*|} \geq \frac{1+\alpha}{1-\alpha} \right\}.$$

Notice that $1 + 2\frac{|\hat{C} \cap C^{*c}|}{|\hat{C} \cap C^*|} \geq \frac{1+\alpha}{1-\alpha}$ implies $\frac{|\hat{C} \cap C^{*c}|}{|\hat{C}|} \geq \alpha$. Therefore, by Lemma 2, $P(E_2^*) \leq \Delta_2(\alpha, l)$. ∎

5   Conclusion

The problem of data mining has commonly been approached from the point of view of data structures and algorithms, in a setting that is primarily deterministic. This paper addresses several statistical questions related to the basic problem of frequent itemset mining, namely significance, noise-tolerance and recovery. The probabilistic bounds given here provide a preliminary basis for assessing the significance of discovered itemsets, with or without errors, and give one objective criterion for sifting through the (potentially large) number of frequent itemsets in a data matrix. The results on the noise sensitivity of standard FIM provide some justification for the current efforts on error-tolerant algorithms. Further justification is provided by the use of one such method for recovery of block structures.

Acknowledgements

The research presented here was supported part by NSF grant DMS 040636.

References

[1] R. Agrawal, T. Imielinski, and A. Swami. Mining association rules between sets of items in large databases. *Proceedings of ACM SIGMOD'93*, 207 - 216, 1993.

[2] R. Agrawal, H. Mannila, R. Srikant, H. Toivonen, and A Verkamo. Fast discovery of association rules. *Advances in Knowledge Discovery and Data Mining*, 307 - 328, AAAI/MITPress, 1996.

[3] R. Agrawal, J. Gehrke, D. Gunopulos and P.Raghavan. Automatic subspace clustering of high dimensional data for data mining applications. *Proceedings of ACM SIGMOD'98*, 94 - 105, 1998.

[4] B. Bollobás and P. Erdős. Cliques in random graphs. *Math. Proc. Cam. Phil. Soc.*, 80: p 419 - 427, 1976.

[5] B. Bollobás. *Random Graphs* second edition. Cambridge Studies in Advanced Mathematics, 2001.

[6] D. Chakrabarti, S. Papadimitriou, D. Modha and C. Faloutsos. Fully Automatic Cross-Associations. *Proceedings of ACM SIGKDD'04*, 79 - 88, 2004.

[7] Y. Cheng and G.M. Church. Biclustering of expression data. *Proceedings of ISMB'00*, 93- 103, 2000.

[8] M. Dawande, P. Keskinocak, J. Swaminathan, and S. Tayur. On bipartite and multipartite clique problems. *J. Algorithms* 41(2): 388 - 403, 2001.

[9] L. Devroye, L. Györfi, and G, Lugosi. *A Probabilistic Theory of Pattern Recognition*. Springer, New York 1996.

[10] I. Dhillon, S. Mallela, and D. Modha. Information-Theoretic Co-clustering. *Proceedings of ACM SIGKDD'03*, 89 - 98, 2003

[11] S.Dudoit and J. Fridlyand. Bagging to improve the accuracy of a clustering procedure. *Bioinformatics*, 19(9): 1090 - 1099, 2003.

[12] G.R. Grimmett and C.J.H. McDiarmid. On colouring random graphs. *Math. Proc. Cam. Phil. Soc.*, 77: 313 - 324, 1975.

[13] J. Han, J. Pei, and Y. Yin. Mining Frequent Patterns without Candidate Generation. *Proceedings of ACM SIGMOD'00*, 1 - 12, 2000.

[14] D. J. Hand, H. Mannila and P. Smyth. *Principles of Data Mining*. MIT Press 2001

[15] R. Karp. *Probabilistic Analysis of Algorithms*. Class Notes, UC-Berkeley 1988.

[16] M. Koyutürk, W. Szpankowski,and A. Grama. Biclustering Gene-Feature Matrices for Statistically Significant Dense Patterns. *IEEE Computer Society Bioinformatics Conference*, 480 - 483, Stanford, 2004.

[17] T. Lange, V. Roth, M. Braun, and J. Buhmann. Stability-Based Validation of Clustering Solution. *Neural Computation*, 16(6): 1299 - 1323, 2004.

[18] J. Liu, S. Paulsen, W. Wang, A. B. Nobel, and J. Prins. Mining Approximate Frequent Itemsets from Noisy Data. *Proceedings of ICDM'05*, 721 - 724, 2005.

[19] J. Liu, S. Paulsen, X. Sun, W. Wang, A.B. Nobel, and J. Prins. Mining approximate frequent itemsets in the presence of noise: algorithm and analysis. To appear in *Proceedings of SDM* 2006.

[20] D. Matula. The largest clique size in a random graph. Southern Methodist University, *Tech. Report*, CS 7608, 1976.

[21] S. Madeira and A. Oliveira. Biclustering algorithms for biological data analysis: A survey. *IEEE/ACM Transactions on Computational Biology and Bioinformatics* 1(1): 24 - 45, 2004

[22] M. Okamoto. Some inequalities relating to the partial sum of binomial probabilities. *Annals of the Institute of Statistical Mathematics*, 10: 29 - 35, 1958

[23] J. Pei, A.K. Tung, and J. Han. Fault-tolerant frequent pattern mining: Problems and challenges. *Proceedings of DMKD'01*, 2001.

[24] J. Pei, G. Dong, W. Zou, and J. Han. Mining Condensed Frequent-Pattern Bases. *Knowledge and Information Systems*, 6(5): 570 - 594, 2002.

[25] G. Park and W. Szpankowshi. Analysis of biclusters with applications to gene expression data. *Proceeding of AoA'05*, 2005.

[26] J. D. Reuning-Scherer. Mixture Models for Block Clustering. Phd Thesis, Yale university 1997.

[27] J. K. Seppänen, and H. Mannila. Dense Itemsets. *Proceedings of ACM SIGKDD'04*, 683 - 688, 2004.

[28] A. Tanay, R. Sharan, and R. Shamir. Discovering statistically significant biclusters in gene expression data. *Bioinformatics*, 18(1): 136 - 144, 2002.

[29] A. Tanay, R. Sharan and R. Shamir. Biclustering Algorithms: A Survey. In *Handbook of Computational Molecular Biology*, Chapman & Hall/CRC, Computer and Information Science Series, 2005. In press.

[30] R. Tibshirani, G. Walther and T. Hastie. Estimating the number of clusters in a dataset via gap statistic. *Technical Report 208*, Dept of Statistics, Stanford University, 2000.

[31] C. Yang, U. Fayyad, and P. S. Bradley. Efficient discovery of error-tolerant frequent itemsets in high dimensions. *Proceedings of ACM SIGKDD'01*, 194 - 203, 2001.

Appendix

Proof of Lemma 1. Let $u_{1*}, ..., u_{l*}$ be corresponding rows of C^* in $\mathbf{Y}$ and let V be the number of rows satisfying $F(u_{i*}) < 1 - p_0$, where $F(\cdot)$ is the function measuring the fraction of ones. By Markov's inequality,

$$P(V \geq 1) \leq E(V) = \sum_{i=1}^{l} P(F(u_{i*}) < 1 - p_0). \tag{11}$$

Using standard bounds on the tails of the binomial distribution, when l_n is sufficiently large,

$$P(V \geq 1) \leq l \cdot e^{-\frac{3l(p-p_0)^2}{8p}} \leq e^{-\frac{1}{3p}l(p-p_0)^2}, \tag{12}$$

when l is sufficiently large.

Let $u_{*1}, ..., u_{*l}$ be corresponding columns of C^* in $\mathbf{Y}$ and let V' be the number of columns satisfying $F(u_{*i}) < 1 - p_0$. A similar calculation as above shows that

$$P(V' \geq 1) \leq E(V') \leq l \cdot e^{-3\frac{l(p-p_0)^2}{8p}}$$
$$\leq e^{-\frac{1}{3p}l(p-p_0)^2}.$$

Since $\{|\hat{C}| < l^2 = |C^*|\} \subset \{C^* \notin AFI_\tau(\mathbf{Y})\} \subset \{V \geq 1\} \cup \{V' \geq 1\}$,

$$P\{|\hat{C}| < l^2\} \leq P(V \geq 1) + P(V' \geq 1)$$
$$\leq 2e^{-\frac{1}{3p}l_n(p-p_0)^2} = \Delta_1(l). \qquad \blacksquare$$

The proof of Lemma 2, relies on two basic facts below. The proof of Fact 2 is technical and is omitted.

Fact 1. Given $0 < \tau_0 < 1$, if there exists a $k \times r$ binary matrix M satisfying $F(M) \geq \tau_0$, then for $v = \min\{k, r\}$, there exists a $v \times v$ submatrix D of M such that $F(D) \geq \tau_0$.

Proof. Without loss of generality, we assume $v = k \leq r$. Then we rank each column according to its fraction of ones, and reorder the columns in descending order. Let the reordered matrix be M^1. Let $D = M^1[(1,...,v) \times (1,...,v)]$. One can verify that $F(D) \geq \tau_0$. $\qquad \blacksquare$

Fact 2. Let $1 < \gamma < 2$ be a constant, and let W be an $n \times n$ binary matrix. Let R_1 and R_2 be two square submatrices of W satisfying (i) $|R_2| = k^2$, (ii) $|R_1 \backslash R_2| > k^\gamma$ and (iii) $R_1 \in AFI_\tau(W)$. Then there exists a square submatrix $D \subset R_1 \backslash R_2$ such that $|D| \geq k^{2\gamma-2}/9$ and $F(D) \geq \tau$.

Proof of Lemma 2. If $C \in \mathcal{A}$ then
(i) $|C^*| = l^2$,
(ii) $|C \backslash C^*| = |C| \cdot \frac{|C \cap C^{*c}|}{|C|} \geq \frac{l^2 \cdot \alpha}{2} = l^\gamma$, where $\gamma = 2 + \log_l \frac{\alpha}{2}$,
(iii) $C \in AFI_{1-p_0}(\mathbf{Y})$.
Thus, by Fact 2, there exists a $v \times v$ submatrix D of $C \backslash C^*$ such that $F(D) \geq 1 - p_0$ and $v \geq \frac{\alpha l}{6}$, which implies that

$$\max_{c \in C} M^\tau(C \cap C^{*c}) \geq v \geq \frac{\alpha l}{6},$$

where $\tau = 1 - p_0$.

Let $\mathbf{W}(\mathbf{Y}, C^*)$ be a $n \times n$ binary random matrix, where $w_{ij} = y_{ij}$ if $(i,j) \notin C^*$, and $w_{ij} \sim Bern(p)$ otherwise. It is clear that

$$M^\tau(\mathbf{W}) \geq \max_{c \in C} M^\tau(C \cap C^{*c}) \geq \frac{\alpha l}{6}.$$

By Proposition 2, when n is sufficiently large and $l \geq 12\alpha^{-1}(\log_b n + 2)$, we can bound $P(A)$ with

$$P(A) \leq P(\max_{c \in C} M^\tau(C \cap C^{*c}) \geq \frac{\alpha l}{6})$$
$$\leq P(M^\tau(\mathbf{W}) \geq \frac{\alpha l}{6}) \leq 2n^{-(\alpha l/6 - 2\log_{b'} n)}, \qquad (13)$$

where $b' = e^{\frac{3(1-p_0-p)^2}{8p}}$. As $p_0 > p$, it is trivial to verify that $b < b'$. Consequently, one can bound the RHS of inequality (13) by $\Delta_2(\alpha, l)$. $\qquad \blacksquare$

Maximum Entropy Distribution Estimation with Generalized Regularization

Miroslav Dudík and Robert E. Schapire

Princeton University, Department of Computer Science,
35 Olden Street, Princeton, NJ 08540
{mdudik, schapire}@cs.princeton.edu

Abstract. We present a unified and complete account of maximum entropy distribution estimation subject to constraints represented by convex potential functions or, alternatively, by convex regularization. We provide fully general performance guarantees and an algorithm with a complete convergence proof. As special cases, we can easily derive performance guarantees for many known regularization types, including ℓ_1, ℓ_2, ℓ_2^2 and $\ell_1 + \ell_2^2$ style regularization. Furthermore, our general approach enables us to use information about the structure of the feature space or about sample selection bias to derive entirely new regularization functions with superior guarantees. We propose an algorithm solving a large and general subclass of generalized maxent problems, including all discussed in the paper, and prove its convergence. Our approach generalizes techniques based on information geometry and Bregman divergences as well as those based more directly on compactness.

1 Introduction

The maximum entropy (maxent) approach to probability distribution estimation was first proposed by Jaynes [1], and has since been used in many areas of computer science and statistical learning, especially natural language processing [2, 3], and more recently in species habitat modeling [4]. In maxent, one is given a set of samples from a target distribution over some space, and a set of known constraints on the distribution. The distribution is then estimated by a distribution of maximum entropy satisfying the given constraints. The constraints are often represented using a set of *features* (real-valued functions) on the space, with the expectation of every feature required to match its empirical average. By convex duality, this turns out to be the unique Gibbs distribution maximizing the likelihood of the samples.

While intuitively appealing, this approach fails to produce good estimates when the number of features is large compared with the number of samples. Conceptually, constraining maxent to match a large number of feature averages exactly forces the algorithm to approximate the empirical distribution too closely. From the dual perspective, the family of Gibbs distributions is too expressive and the algorithm overfits. Common approaches to counter overfitting are regularization [5, 6, 7, 8], introduction of a prior [9], feature selection [2, 3], discounting [5, 6] and constraint relaxation [10, 11]. Thus, there are many ways to control overfitting in maxent calling for a general treatment.

In this work, we study a generalized form of maxent. Although mentioned by other authors as *fuzzy maxent* [5, 6, 7], we give the first complete theoretical treatment of this

G. Lugosi and H.U. Simon (Eds.): COLT 2006, LNAI 4005, pp. 123–138, 2006.

very general framework, including fully general performance guarantees, algorithms and convergence proofs. Independently, Altun and Smola [12] derive a different theoretical treatment (see discussion below). As special cases, our results allow us to easily derive performance guarantees for many known regularized formulations, including ℓ_1, ℓ_2, ℓ_2^2 and $\ell_1 + \ell_2^2$ regularizations.

A crucial insight of our general analysis is that maxent relaxations corresponding to tighter constraints on the feature expectations yield better performance guarantees. Applying our analysis to the special case in which such a confidence region is polyhedral allows us to derive novel regularization functions and a corresponding analysis for two cases of particular interest. The first case is when some information about structure of the feature space is available, for example, when some features are known to be squares or products of other "base" features, corresponding to constraints on variances or covariances of the base features. The second case is when the sample selection process is known to be biased. Both of these cases were studied previously [4, 13]. Here, we apply our general framework to derive improved generalization bounds using an entirely new form of regularization. These results improve on bounds for previous forms of regularization by up to a factor of eight — an improvement that would otherwise require a 64-fold increase in the number of training examples.

In the second part, we propose an algorithm solving a large and general subclass of generalized maxent problems. We show convergence of our algorithm using techniques that unify previous approaches and extend them to a more general setting. Specifically, our unified approach generalizes techniques based on information geometry and Bregman divergences [3, 14] as well as those based more directly on compactness [11]. The main novel ingredient is a modified definition of an auxiliary function, a customary measure of progress, which we view as a surrogate for the difference between the primal and dual objective rather than a bound on the change in the dual objective.

There are many standard maxent algorithms, such as iterative scaling [3, 15], gradient descent, Newton and quasi-Newton methods [16] and their regularized versions [5, 6, 9, 10, 17]. In this paper, we focus on an algorithm that performs sequential updates of feature weights similarly to boosting and sequential algorithms considered in [11, 14]. Sequential updates are especially desirable when the number of features is very large or when they are produced by a weak learner. When the number of features is small, techniques developed here can be directly applied to derive a parallel update algorithm analogous to the one proposed in [11] for ℓ_1-regularized maxent (details omitted).

Previous Work. There have been many studies of maxent and logistic regression, which is a conditional version of maxent, with ℓ_1-style regularization [9, 10, 11, 17, 18], ℓ_2^2-style regularization [5, 6, 7, 8] as well as some other types of regularization such as $\ell_1 + \ell_2^2$-style [10] and ℓ_2-style regularization [19]. In a recent work, Altun and Smola [12] explore regularized formulations (with duality and performance guarantees) where the entropy is replaced by an arbitrary Bregman or Csiszár divergence and regularization equals a norm raised to a power greater than one. With the exception of [8, 11, 12], previous work does not include guarantees applicable to our case, albeit Krishnapuram et al. [17] and Ng [18] give guarantees for ℓ_1-regularized logistic regression.

2   Preliminaries

The goal is to estimate an unknown *target distribution* π over a *sample space* $\mathcal{X}$ based on *samples* $x_1, \ldots, x_m \in \mathcal{X}$. We assume that samples are independently distributed according to π and denote the *empirical distribution* by $\tilde{\pi}(x) = |\{1 \le i \le m : x_i = x\}|/m$. The structure of the problem is specified by real valued functions $f_1, \ldots, f_n$ on the sample space, called *features* and by a distribution q_0 representing a *default estimate*. The vector of all n features is denoted by $\boldsymbol{f}$ and the image of $\mathcal{X}$ under $\boldsymbol{f}$, the *feature space*, is denoted by $\boldsymbol{f}(\mathcal{X})$. We assume that features capture all the relevant information available for the problem at hand and q_0 is the distribution we would choose if we were given no samples. The distribution q_0 is most often assumed uniform.

Let $p[f]$ denote the expectation of a function $f(x)$ when x is chosen randomly according to distribution p. For a limited number of samples, we expect that $\tilde{\pi}$ will be a poor estimate of π under any reasonable distance measure. On the other hand, for a given function f, we do expect $\tilde{\pi}[f]$, the empirical average of f, to be rather close to its true expectation $\pi[f]$. It is quite natural, therefore, to seek an approximation p under which f_j's expectation is equal to $\tilde{\pi}[f_j]$ for every f_j.

There will typically be many distributions satisfying these constraints. The *maximum entropy principle* suggests that, from among all distributions that satisfy them, we choose the distribution that minimizes entropy relative to the default estimate q_0. When q_0 is uniform this is the same as maximizing the entropy. Here, as usual, the entropy of a distribution p is defined as $\mathrm{H}(p) = p[\ln(1/p)]$ and the relative entropy, or Kullback-Leibler divergence, as $\mathrm{D}(p \parallel q) = p[\ln(p/q)]$. Thus, the maximum entropy principle chooses the distribution that satisfies the constraints, but imposes as little additional information as possible when compared with q_0.

Instead of minimizing entropy relative to q_0, we can consider all *Gibbs distributions*

$$q_\lambda(x) = q_0(x)e^{\lambda \cdot \boldsymbol{f}(x)}/Z_\lambda$$

where $Z_\lambda = \sum_{x \in \mathcal{X}} q_0(x)e^{\lambda \cdot \boldsymbol{f}(x)}$ is a normalizing constant and $\lambda \in \mathbb{R}^n$. It can be proved [3] that the maxent distribution is the maximum likelihood distribution from the closure of the set of Gibbs distributions. Equivalently, it is the distribution that achieves the infimum over all values of λ of the empirical log loss $\mathrm{L}_{\tilde{\pi}}(\lambda) = -\frac{1}{m}\sum_{i=1}^{m} \ln q_\lambda(x_i)$.

The convex programs corresponding to the two optimization problems are

$$\mathcal{P}_{\text{basic}} : \quad \min_{p \in \Delta} \mathrm{D}(p \parallel q_0) \text{ subject to } p[\boldsymbol{f}] = \tilde{\pi}[\boldsymbol{f}]$$

$$\mathcal{Q}_{\text{basic}} : \quad \inf_{\lambda \in \mathbb{R}^n} \mathrm{L}_{\tilde{\pi}}(\lambda)$$

where Δ is the simplex of probability distributions over $\mathcal{X}$.

In general, we use $\mathrm{L}_p(\lambda) = -p[\ln q_\lambda]$ to denote the log loss of q_λ relative to the distribution p. It differs from relative entropy $\mathrm{D}(p \parallel q_\lambda)$ only by the constant $\mathrm{H}(p)$. We will use the two interchangeably as objective functions.

3   Convex Analysis Background

Throughout this paper we make use of convex analysis. The most relevant concepts are convex conjugacy and Fenchel's duality which we introduce here (see also [20, 21]).

Consider a function $\psi : \mathbb{R}^n \to (-\infty, \infty]$. The *effective domain* of ψ is the set $\mathrm{dom}\,\psi = \{u \in \mathbb{R}^n \mid \psi(u) < \infty\}$. A point u where $\psi(u) < \infty$ is called *feasible*. The *epigraph* of ψ is the set of points above its graph $\{(u, t) \in \mathbb{R}^n \times \mathbb{R} \mid t \geq \psi(u)\}$. We say that ψ is *convex* if its epigraph is a convex set. A convex function is called *proper* if it is not uniformly equal to ∞. It is called *closed* if its epigraph is closed. For a proper convex function, closedness is equivalent to lower semi-continuity (ψ is lower semi-continuous if $\liminf_{u' \to u} \psi(u') \geq \psi(u)$ for all u).

If ψ is a closed proper convex function then its *conjugate* is defined by

$$\psi^*(\lambda) = \sup_{u \in \mathbb{R}^n} [\lambda \cdot u - \psi(u)].$$

The conjugate provides an alternative description of ψ in terms of tangents to ψ's epigraph. It turns out that ψ^* is also a closed proper convex function and $\psi^{**} = \psi$ (for a proof see Corollary 12.2.1 of [20]). From the definition of conjugate, we obtain *Fenchel's inequality*

$$\forall \lambda, u : \ \lambda \cdot u \leq \psi^*(\lambda) + \psi(u).$$

In this work we use several examples of closed proper convex functions. The first of them is relative entropy, with the second argument fixed, viewed as a function of its first argument and extended to $\mathbb{R}^{\mathcal{X}}$ in the following manner: $\psi(p) = D(p \parallel q_0)$ if $p \in \Delta$ and equals infinity otherwise. The conjugate of relative entropy is the log partition function $\psi^*(r) = \ln\left(\sum_{x \in \mathcal{X}} q_0(x) e^{r(x)}\right)$.

Relative entropy is also an example of a Bregman divergence which generalizes some common distance measures including the squared Euclidean distance. We use two properties satisfied by any Bregman divergence $B(\cdot \parallel \cdot)$:

(B1) $B(a \parallel b) \geq 0$

(B2) if $B(a_t \parallel b_t) \to 0$ and $b_t \to b^*$ then $a_t \to b^*$.

Another example of a closed proper convex function is an *indicator function* of a closed convex set $C \subseteq \mathbb{R}^n$, denoted by I_C, which equals 0 when its argument lies in C and infinity otherwise. The conjugate of an indicator function is a *support function*. For $C = \{v\}$, we obtain $I_{\{v\}}^*(\lambda) = \lambda \cdot v$. For a box $R = [-\beta, \beta]^n$, we obtain a scaled ℓ_1 norm $I_R^*(\lambda) = \beta \|\lambda\|_1$, and for a Euclidean ball $B = \{u \mid \|u\|_2 \leq \beta\}$, a scaled ℓ_2 norm, $I_B^*(\lambda) = \beta \|\lambda\|_2$. If C is a convex hull of closed convex sets C_1, C_2 then

$$I_C^*(\lambda) = \max\{I_{C_1}^*(\lambda), I_{C_2}^*(\lambda)\}. \tag{1}$$

The following identities can be proved from the definition of the conjugate function:

$$\text{if } \varphi(u) = \psi(\gamma u + c) \qquad \text{then } \varphi^*(\lambda) = \psi^*(\lambda/\gamma) - \lambda \cdot c/\gamma \tag{2}$$
$$\text{if } \varphi(u) = \sum_j \varphi_j(u_j) \qquad \text{then } \varphi^*(\lambda) = \sum_j \varphi_j^*(\lambda_j) \tag{3}$$

where $\gamma \in \mathbb{R} \setminus \{0\}$ and $c \in \mathbb{R}^n$ are constants and u_j, λ_j refer to components of u, λ.

We conclude with a version of *Fenchel's Duality Theorem* which relates a convex minimization problem to a concave maximization problem using conjugates. The following result is essentially Corollary 31.2.1 of [20] under a stronger set of assumptions.

Theorem 1 (Fenchel's Duality). *Let* $\psi : \mathbb{R}^n \to (-\infty, \infty]$ *and* $\varphi : \mathbb{R}^m \to (-\infty, \infty]$ *be closed proper convex functions and* A *a real-valued* $m \times n$ *matrix. Assume that* $\operatorname{dom} \psi^* = \mathbb{R}^n$ *or* $\operatorname{dom} \varphi = \mathbb{R}^m$. *Then*

$$\inf_{u} \left[\psi(u) + \varphi(Au) \right] = \sup_{\lambda} \left[-\psi^*(A^{\mathsf{T}}\lambda) - \varphi^*(-\lambda) \right].$$

We refer to the minimization over u as the primal problem and the maximization over λ as the dual problem. When no ambiguity arises, we also refer to the minimization over λ of the negative objective as the dual problem. We call u a primal feasible point if the primal objective is finite at u and analogously define a dual feasible point.

4   Generalized Maximum Entropy

In this paper we study a generalized maxent problem

$$\mathcal{P}: \quad \min_{p \in \Delta} \left[\mathrm{D}(p \parallel q_0) + \mathrm{U}(p[f]) \right]$$

where $\mathrm{U} : \mathbb{R}^n \to (-\infty, \infty]$ is an arbitrary closed proper convex function. It is viewed as a *potential* for the maxent problem. We further assume that q_0 is positive on $\mathcal{X}$, i.e. $\mathrm{D}(p \parallel q_0)$ is finite for all $p \in \Delta$, and $p_0[f]$ is a feasible point of U for at least one distribution p_0. The latter will typically be satisfied by the empirical distribution.

The definition of generalized maxent captures many cases of interest including the basic maxent, ℓ_1-regularized maxent and ℓ_2^2-regularized maxent. The basic maxent is obtained by using a point indicator potential $\mathrm{U}^{(0)}(u) = \mathrm{I}_{\{\tilde{\pi}[f]\}}(u)$, whereas, as shown in [11], ℓ_1-regularized maxent corresponds to box constraints $|\tilde{\pi}[f_j] - p[f_j]| \leq \beta$, which can be represented by $\mathrm{U}^{(1)}(u) = \mathrm{I}_C(u)$ where $C = \tilde{\pi}[f] + [-\beta, \beta]^n$. Finally, as pointed out in [6, 7], ℓ_2^2-regularized maxent is obtained using the potential $\mathrm{U}^{(2)}(u) = \|\tilde{\pi}[f] - u\|_2^2/(2\alpha)$ which incurs an ℓ_2^2-style penalty for deviating from empirical averages.

To simplify the exposition, we use the notation $\mathrm{U}_{p_0}(u) = \mathrm{U}(p_0[f] - u)$ for a potential centered at p_0. Thus the basic maxent potential $\mathrm{U}^{(0)}(u) = \mathrm{I}_{\{\tilde{\pi}[f]\}}(u)$ could have been specified by defining $\mathrm{U}_{\tilde{\pi}}^{(0)}(u) = \mathrm{I}_{\{0\}}(u)$ and similarly the box potential by defining $\mathrm{U}_{\tilde{\pi}}^{(1)}(u) = \mathrm{I}_{[-\beta, \beta]^n}(u)$ and the ℓ_2^2 penalty by defining $\mathrm{U}_{\tilde{\pi}}^{(2)}(u) = \|u\|_2^2/(2\alpha)$.

The primal objective of generalized maxent will be referred to as P:

$$P(p) = \mathrm{D}(p \parallel q_0) + \mathrm{U}(p[f]).$$

Note that P attains its minimum over Δ, because Δ is compact and P is lower semi-continuous. The minimizer of P is unique by strict convexity of $\mathrm{D}(p \parallel q_0)$.

To derive the dual of $\mathcal{P}$, define the matrix $F_{jx} = f_j(x)$ and use Fenchel's duality:

$$\min_{p \in \Delta} \left[\mathrm{D}(p \parallel q_0) + \mathrm{U}(p[f]) \right] = \min_{p \in \Delta} \left[\mathrm{D}(p \parallel q_0) + \mathrm{U}(Fp) \right]$$

$$= \sup_{\lambda \in \mathbb{R}^n} \left[-\ln \left(\sum_{x \in \mathcal{X}} q_0(x) \exp\{(F^{\mathsf{T}}\lambda)_x\} \right) - \mathrm{U}^*(-\lambda) \right] \quad (4)$$

$$= \sup_{\lambda \in \mathbb{R}^n} \left[-\ln Z_\lambda - \mathrm{U}^*(-\lambda) \right]. \quad (5)$$

In Eq. (4), we apply Theorem 1. We use $(F^\top \lambda)_x$ to denote the entry of $F^\top \lambda$ indexed by x. In Eq. (5), we note that $(F^\top \lambda)_x = \lambda \cdot f(x)$ and thus the expression inside the logarithm equals the normalization constant of q_λ. The dual objective will be referred to as Q:

$$Q(\lambda) = -\ln Z_\lambda - U^*(-\lambda).$$

We could rewrite Q in terms of the conjugate of a centered potential. By Eq. (2)

$$U^*_{p_0}(\lambda) = U^*(-\lambda) + \lambda \cdot p_0[f], \tag{6}$$

hence the dual objective can be rewritten as

$$Q(\lambda) = -D(p_0 \parallel q_\lambda) + D(p_0 \parallel q_0) - U^*_{p_0}(\lambda).$$

For any fixed distribution p_0, $D(p_0 \parallel q_0)$ is a finite constant, so maximizing $Q(\lambda)$ is equivalent to minimizing $D(p_0 \parallel q_\lambda) + U^*_{p_0}(\lambda)$, or $L_{p_0}(\lambda) + U^*_{p_0}(\lambda)$. Using $p_0 = \tilde{\pi}$ we obtain a dual analogous to $\mathcal{Q}_{\text{basic}}$:

$$\mathcal{Q}: \quad \inf_{\lambda \in \mathbb{R}^n} \left[L_{\tilde{\pi}}(\lambda) + U^*_{\tilde{\pi}}(\lambda) \right].$$

Note that a minimizing λ does not depend on a particular choice of p_0. In particular, a minimizer of $\mathcal{Q}$ is also a minimizer of $L_\pi(\lambda) + U^*_\pi(\lambda)$. This observation will be used in Section 5 to prove performance guarantees.

The objective of $\mathcal{Q}$ has two terms. The first of them is the empirical log loss and the second one can be viewed as a regularization term penalizing "complex" solutions. From a Bayesian perspective, $U^*_{\tilde{\pi}}$ corresponds to negative log of the prior. Thus, minimizing $L_{\tilde{\pi}}(\lambda) + U^*_{\tilde{\pi}}(\lambda)$ is equivalent to maximizing the posterior.

In case of the basic maxent, we obtain $U^{(0)*}_{\tilde{\pi}}(\lambda) = I^*_{\{0\}}(\lambda) = 0$ and thus recover the basic dual. For the box potential, we obtain $U^{(1)*}_{\tilde{\pi}}(\lambda) = I^*_{[-\beta,\beta]^n}(\lambda) = \beta \|\lambda\|_1$ which corresponds to an ℓ_1-style regularization and a Laplace prior. For the ℓ_2^2 potential, we obtain $U^{(2)*}_{\tilde{\pi}}(\lambda) = \alpha \|\lambda\|_2^2 / 2$ which corresponds to an ℓ_2^2-style regularization and a Gaussian prior.

Results of this section are summarized in the following theorem:

Theorem 2 (Maxent Duality). *Let* q_0, U, P, Q *be as above. Then*

$$\min_{p \in \Delta} P(p) = \sup_{\lambda \in \mathbb{R}^n} Q(\lambda). \tag{i}$$

Moreover, if $\lim_{t \to \infty} Q(\lambda_t) = \sup_{\lambda \in \mathbb{R}^n} Q(\lambda)$ *then the sequence of* $q_t = q_{\lambda_t}$ *has a limit and*

$$P\left(\lim_{t \to \infty} q_t \right) = \min_{p \in \Delta} P(p). \tag{ii}$$

Sketch of proof. Eq. (i) is a consequence of Fenchel's duality as was shown earlier. It remains to prove Eq. (ii). Let p_0 be the minimizer of P. Centering primal and dual objectives at p_0, we obtain by Eq. (i) and the assumption

$$D(p_0 \parallel q_0) + U_{p_0}(0) = \lim_{t \to \infty} \left[-D(p_0 \parallel q_t) + D(p_0 \parallel q_0) - U^*_{p_0}(\lambda_t) \right].$$

Denoting terms with the limit 0 by $o(1)$ and rearranging yields

$$U_{p_0}(0) + U_{p_0}^*(\lambda_t) = -D(p_0 \parallel q_t) + o(1).$$

The left-hand side is by Fenchel's inequality nonnegative, so $D(p_0 \parallel q_t) \to 0$ by property (B1). Therefore, by property (B2), every convergent subsequence of $q_1, q_2, \ldots$ has the limit p_0. Since the q_t's come from the compact set Δ, we obtain $q_t \to p_0$.   □

Thus, in order to solve the primal, it suffices to find a sequence of λ's maximizing the dual. This will be the goal of the algorithm in Section 6.

5   Bounding the Loss on the Target Distribution

In this section, we derive bounds on the performance of generalized maxent relative to the true distribution π. That is, we are able to bound $L_\pi(\hat{\lambda})$ in terms of $L_\pi(\lambda^*)$ when $q_{\hat{\lambda}}$ maximizes the dual objective Q and q_{λ^*} is any Gibbs distribution. In particular, bounds hold for the Gibbs distribution minimizing the true loss. Note that $D(\pi \parallel q_\lambda)$ differs from $L_\pi(\lambda)$ only by the constant term $H(\pi)$, so identical bounds also hold for $D(\pi \parallel q_{\hat{\lambda}})$ in terms of $D(\pi \parallel q_{\lambda^*})$.

The crux of our method is the lemma below. Even though its proof is remarkably simple, it is sufficiently general to cover all cases of interest.

Lemma 1. *Let $\hat{\lambda}$ maximize Q. Then for an arbitrary Gibbs distribution q_{λ^*}*

$$L_\pi(\hat{\lambda}) \le L_\pi(\lambda^*) + 2U(\pi[f]) + U^*(\lambda^*) + U^*(-\lambda^*) \tag{i}$$

$$L_\pi(\hat{\lambda}) \le L_\pi(\lambda^*) + (\lambda^* - \hat{\lambda}) \cdot (\pi[f] - \tilde{\pi}[f]) + U_{\tilde{\pi}}^*(\lambda^*) - U_{\tilde{\pi}}^*(\hat{\lambda}). \tag{ii}$$

Proof. Optimality of $\hat{\lambda}$ with respect to $L_\pi(\lambda) + U_\pi(\lambda) = -Q(\lambda) + const.$ yields

$$L_\pi(\hat{\lambda}) \le L_\pi(\lambda^*) + U_\pi^*(\lambda^*) - U_\pi^*(\hat{\lambda})$$

$$\le L_\pi(\lambda^*) + (\lambda^* - \hat{\lambda}) \cdot \pi[f] + U^*(-\lambda^*) - U^*(-\hat{\lambda}). \tag{7}$$

Eq. (7) follows from Eq. (6). Now Eq. (i) can be obtained by applying Fenchel's inequality to the second term of Eq. (7):

$$(\lambda^* - \hat{\lambda}) \cdot \pi[f] \le U^*(\lambda^*) + U(\pi[f]) + U^*(-\hat{\lambda}) + U(\pi[f]).$$

Eq. (ii) also follows from (7) by centering the conjugate potential at $\tilde{\pi}$.   □

A special case which we discuss in more detail is when U is an indicator of a closed convex set C, such as $U^{(0)}$ and $U^{(1)}$ of the previous section. In this case, the right hand side of Lemma 1.i will be infinite unless $\pi[f]$ lies in C. In order to apply Lemma 1.i, we ensure that $\pi[f] \in C$ with high probability. Therefore, we choose C as a confidence region for $\pi[f]$. If $\pi[f] \in C$ then for any Gibbs distribution q_{λ^*}

$$L_\pi(\hat{\lambda}) \le L_\pi(\lambda^*) + I_C^*(\lambda^*) + I_C^*(-\lambda^*). \tag{8}$$

For a fixed $\boldsymbol{\lambda}^*$ and non-empty C, $I_C^*(\boldsymbol{\lambda}^*) + I_C^*(-\boldsymbol{\lambda}^*)$ is always nonnegative and proportional to the size of C's projection onto a line parallel with $\boldsymbol{\lambda}^*$. Thus, smaller confidence regions yield better performance guarantees.

A common method of obtaining confidence regions is to bound the difference between empirical averages and true expectations. There exists a huge array of techniques to achieve this. Before moving to specific examples, we state a general result which follows directly from Eq. (8). We assume that confidence regions are obtained by scaling some symmetric prototype C_0 and shifting it to empirical averages.

Theorem 3. *Assume that $\tilde{\pi}[\boldsymbol{f}] - \pi[\boldsymbol{f}] \in \beta C_0$ where C_0 is a closed convex set symmetric around the origin, $\beta > 0$ and βC_0 denotes $\{\beta u \mid u \in C_0\}$. Let $\hat{\boldsymbol{\lambda}}$ minimize the regularized log loss $L_{\tilde{\pi}}(\boldsymbol{\lambda}) + \beta I_{C_0}^*(\boldsymbol{\lambda})$. Then for an arbitrary Gibbs distribution $q_{\boldsymbol{\lambda}^*}$*

$$L_\pi(\hat{\boldsymbol{\lambda}}) \leq L_\pi(\boldsymbol{\lambda}^*) + 2\beta I_{C_0}^*(\boldsymbol{\lambda}^*).$$

5.1 Maxent with Polyhedral Regularization

We now apply the foregoing general results to some specific cases of interest. To begin, we consider potentials which are indicator functions of polytopes. The simplest case is the box indicator $U^{(1)}$, for which Dudík, Phillips and Schapire [11] give generalization bounds. However, when additional knowledge about structure of the feature space is available or when samples are biased, other polytopes yield tighter confidence regions and hence better performance guarantees, as we now show.

Feature Space Derived Potential. When values of $\boldsymbol{f}(x)$ lie inside a polytope with a possibly very large number of facets then a symmetrized version of this polytope can be used as a prototype for the confidence region. For example, suppose that values $\boldsymbol{f}(x)$ lie inside the polytope $\{u \mid a_{\bar{j}} \leq \boldsymbol{\mu}_{\bar{j}} \cdot u \leq b_{\bar{j}}$ for $\bar{j} = 1, \ldots, \bar{n}\}$ where $\boldsymbol{\mu}_{\bar{j}} \in \mathbb{R}^n, a_{\bar{j}}, b_{\bar{j}} \in \mathbb{R}$ are constants. Then the following holds:

Theorem 4. *Let $\boldsymbol{\mu}_{\bar{j}}, a_{\bar{j}}, b_{\bar{j}}$ be as above. Let $\delta > 0$ and let $\hat{\boldsymbol{\lambda}}$ minimize $L_{\tilde{\pi}}(\boldsymbol{\lambda}) + \beta I_{C_0}^*(\boldsymbol{\lambda})$ with $\beta = \sqrt{\ln(2\bar{n}/\delta)/(2m)}$ and $C_0 = \{u \mid |\boldsymbol{\mu}_{\bar{j}} \cdot u| \leq b_{\bar{j}} - a_{\bar{j}}$ for all $\bar{j}\}$. Then with probability at least $1 - \delta$, for every Gibbs distribution $q_{\boldsymbol{\lambda}^*}$,*

$$L_\pi(\hat{\boldsymbol{\lambda}}) \leq L_\pi(\boldsymbol{\lambda}^*) + I_{C_0}^*(\boldsymbol{\lambda}) \sqrt{2 \ln(2\bar{n}/\delta)/m}.$$

Proof. By Hoeffding's inequality, for a fixed $\bar{j}$, the probability that $|\boldsymbol{\mu}_{\bar{j}} \cdot (\tilde{\pi}[\boldsymbol{f}] - \pi[\boldsymbol{f}])|$ exceeds $\beta(b_{\bar{j}} - a_{\bar{j}})$ is at most $2e^{-2\beta^2 m} = \delta/\bar{n}$. By the union bound, the probability of this happening for any $\bar{j}$ is at most δ. Thus, $\tilde{\pi}[\boldsymbol{f}] - \pi[\boldsymbol{f}] \in \beta C_0$ with probability at least $1 - \delta$ and the claim follows from Theorem 3. $\qquad\square$

This performance bound decreases as $1/\sqrt{m}$ with an increasing number of samples and grows only logarithmically with the number of facets of the bounding polytope. Thus, bounding polytopes can have a very large number of facets and still yield good bounds for moderate sample sizes. When deciding between several polytopes based on this bound, the increase in the number of facets should be weighed against the decrease in the regularization $I_{C_0}^*$ as will be demonstrated in examples below.

Means and Variances. As a specific application, consider a set of $n = 2K$ features indexed as $f_k, f_{kk}, 1 \le k \le K$, such that $0 \le f_k(x) \le 1$ and $f_{kk}(x) = f_k^2(x)$. Note that the best Gibbs distribution is the one that matches f_k's true means and variances. These types of features were successfully used with box constraints in habitat modeling [4]. Box constraints yield the guarantee

$$L_\pi(\hat{\boldsymbol{\lambda}}) \le L_\pi(\boldsymbol{\lambda}^*) + \|\boldsymbol{\lambda}^*\|_1 \sqrt{2\ln(4K/\delta)/m}.$$

Noting that $t - 1/4 \le t^2 \le t$ for $t \in [0, 1]$, it is possible to obtain a tighter polytope

$$C_0 = \{u \mid |u_k| \le 1, |u_{kk}| \le 1, |u_k - u_{kk}| \le 1/4 \text{ for all } k\}$$

and the guarantee

$$L_\pi(\hat{\boldsymbol{\lambda}}) \le L_\pi(\boldsymbol{\lambda}^*) + I_{C_0}^*(\boldsymbol{\lambda}^*) \sqrt{2\ln(6K/\delta)/m}.$$

In this case, it is possible to derive $I_{C_0}^*$ explicitly:

$$I_{C_0}^*(\boldsymbol{\lambda}) = \sum_k (7|\lambda_k + \lambda_{kk}| + |\lambda_k| + |\lambda_{kk}|)/8.$$

Note that $I_{C_0}^*(\boldsymbol{\lambda})$ may be up to eight times smaller than $\|\boldsymbol{\lambda}\|_1$ while the relative increase of the bound due to an increase in $\bar{n}$ is close to 1 for moderate sizes of K. Thus, the bound may decrease up to eight times for moderate K. Such improvement would require a 64-fold increase in the number of training samples using ℓ_1-regularization.

Means, Variances and Covariances. In this example, we expand the feature set to include also covariance terms $f_{kl}(x) = f_k(x)f_l(x)$ where $1 \le k < l \le K$. In this case the box can be restricted to a much tighter set

$$C_0 = \{u \mid |u_k| \le 1, |u_{kk}| \le 1, |u_k - u_{kk}| \le 1/4 \text{ for all } k,$$
$$|u_{kl}| \le 1, |u_k - u_{kl}| \le 1, |u_l - u_{kl}| \le 1,$$
$$|u_k + u_l - 2u_{kl}| \le 1, |u_{kk} + u_{ll} - 2u_{kl}| \le 1 \text{ for all } k < l\}.$$

Note that $\bar{n}$ increases approximately fivefold from $K(K+3)/2$ to $5K(K+1/5)/2$ resulting in only slight relative increase of the bound for moderate K. This is outweighed by the decrease of the bound due to a tighter confidence region.

Debiased Potential. In previous work [13], we considered the problem of using maxent when the data was sampled in a biased manner. Here we show how superior bounds can be obtained using our generalized maxent framework.

In previous examples, confidence regions were symmetric sets centered at empirical averages of features. Here, however, asymmetric regions are more appropriate. We assume now that samples do not come from the target distribution π, but from the *biased distribution* πs, where $s \in \Delta$ is the *sampling distribution* and $\pi s(x) = \pi(x)s(x)/\sum_{x' \in \mathcal{X}} \pi(x')s(x')$ corresponds to the probability of observing x given that it is sampled by both π and s. We assume that s is known and strictly positive. Further, let $s_{\min} = \min_x s(x)$ and $s_{\max} = \max_x s(x)$. We use the following theorem to derive confidence intervals of true feature expectations from biased samples.

Theorem 5 (Theorem 2 of [13]). $\pi s[f/s]/\pi s[1/s] = \pi[f]$.

Earlier [13] we derived, for example by Hoeffding's inequality, confidence intervals $[c_j, d_j]$ for $\pi s[f_j/s]$ and an interval $[c_0, d_0]$ for $\pi s[1/s]$. We converted these into box constraints for $\pi[f]$ by Theorem 5. However, Theorem 5 can also be used to obtain a tighter confidence region:

$$C = \bigcup_{c_0 \leq t \leq d_0} \{u \mid c_j/t \leq u_j \leq d_j/t \text{ for all } j\}$$
$$= \underset{t=c_0, d_0}{\text{convex hull}} \{u \mid c_j/t \leq u_j \leq d_j/t \text{ for all } j\}. \tag{9}$$

Eq. (1) can be used to obtain an explicit form of I_C^*. Working out Hoeffding's bounds, applying Lemma 1.i and converting $I_C^*(\lambda) + I_C^*(-\lambda)$ into a sample independent form under the assumption that terms on the left-hand side of Theorem 5 lie in their confidence intervals, we obtain the following guarantee (the proof is omitted):

Theorem 6. *Assume that features $f_1, \ldots, f_n$ are bounded in $[0, 1]$. Let s be as above and let $\widetilde{\pi s}$ denote the empirical distribution of samples drawn from πs. Let $\delta > 0$ and let $\hat{\lambda}$ minimize $\ln Z_\lambda + I_C^*(-\lambda)$ where*

$$I_C^*(-\lambda) = \max_{t=c_0, d_0} \left[\frac{-\lambda \cdot \widetilde{\pi s}[f/s] + \beta \|\lambda\|_1}{t} \right]$$

with $\beta = \sqrt{\ln(2(n+1)/\delta)/(2m)}/s_{\min}$, $c_0 = \max\{1/s_{\max}, \widetilde{\pi s}[1/s] - \beta\}$, $d_0 = \widetilde{\pi s}[1/s] + \beta$. Then with probability at least $1 - \delta$, for every Gibbs distribution q_{λ^*},

$$L_\pi(\hat{\lambda}) \leq L_\pi(\lambda^*) + \frac{\|\lambda^*\|_1 + |\lambda^* \cdot \pi[f]|}{\sqrt{m}} \cdot \frac{\pi[s]}{s_{\min}} \cdot \left(\alpha + \alpha^2 \frac{s_{\max}}{s_{\min}\sqrt{m}} \right) \tag{10}$$

where $\alpha = \sqrt{2 \ln(2(n+1)/\delta)}$.

This bound shares many of the favorable properties of the bound of Theorem 4. In particular, it decreases as the square root of the number of samples and grows only logarithmically with the number of features. It also increases with the level of correlation between the sampling and target distributions as measured by the ratio $\pi[s]/s_{\min}$. Intuitively, this dependence should not be surprising, because high values of $\pi[s]/s_{\min}$ mean that π puts more weight on points with larger bias. As a result, it is more difficult to disambiguate effects of s and π on the sampling process.

When using box constraints, as in [13], we obtain an analogous bound with the term $|\lambda^* \cdot \pi[f]|$ in Eq. (10) replaced by a larger term $\sum_j |\lambda_j^*| |\pi[f_j]|$. Improvement in the guarantee due to the new regularization will be the most significant when λ^* and $\pi[f]$ are close to orthogonal. This is true for almost all directions of λ^* as the dimension of the feature space increases.

5.2   Maxent with ℓ_2-Regularization

In some cases, tighter performance guarantees can be obtained by using non-polyhedral confidence regions. In this section we consider confidence regions which take the shape of a Euclidean ball. We use an ℓ_2 version of Hoeffding's inequality and apply Theorem 3 to obtain performance guarantees (the proof is omitted).

Theorem 7. *Let $D_2 = \sup_{x,x' \in \mathcal{X}} \|f(x) - f(x')\|_2$ be the ℓ_2 diameter of $f(\mathcal{X})$. Let $\delta > 0$ and let $\hat{\lambda}$ minimize $L_{\tilde{\pi}}(\lambda) + \beta\|\lambda\|_2$ with $\beta = D_2\left[1 + (2 + \sqrt{2})\sqrt{\ln(1/\delta)}\right]/\sqrt{2m}$. Then with probability at least $1 - \delta$, for every Gibbs distribution q_{λ^*},*

$$L_\pi(\hat{\lambda}) \leq L_\pi(\lambda^*) + \|\lambda^*\|_2 D_2\left[\sqrt{2} + 2(1 + \sqrt{2})\sqrt{\ln(1/\delta)}\right]/\sqrt{m}.$$

Unlike results of the previous section, this bound does not explicitly depend on the number of features and only grows with the ℓ_2 diameter of the feature space. The ℓ_2 diameter is small for example when the feature space consists of sparse binary vectors.

An analogous bound can also be obtained for ℓ_1-regularized maxent by Theorem 4:

$$L_\pi(\hat{\lambda}) \leq L_\pi(\lambda^*) + \|\lambda^*\|_1 D_\infty \sqrt{2\ln(2n/\delta)/m}.$$

This bound increases with the ℓ_∞ diameter of the feature space and also grows slowly with the number of features. It provides some insight for when we expect ℓ_1-regularization to perform better than ℓ_2-regularization. For example, consider a scenario when the total number of features is large, but the best approximation of π can be derived from a small number of relevant features. Increasing the number of irrelevant features, we may keep $\|\lambda^*\|_1$, $\|\lambda^*\|_2$ and D_∞ fixed while D_2 may increase as $\Omega(\sqrt{n})$. Thus the guarantee for ℓ_2-regularized maxent grows as $\Omega(\sqrt{n})$ while the guarantee for ℓ_1-regularized maxent grows only as $\Omega(\sqrt{\ln n})$. Note, however, that in practice the distribution returned by ℓ_2-regularized maxent may perform better than indicated by this guarantee. For a comparison of ℓ_1 and ℓ_2^2 regularization in the context of logistic regression see [18].

5.3 Maxent with ℓ_2^2-Regularization

So far we have considered potentials that take the form of an indicator function. In this section we present a result for the ℓ_2^2 potential $U_{\tilde{\pi}}^{(2)}(u) = \|u\|_2^2/(2\alpha)$ which grows continuously with increasing distance from empirical averages. In addition to probabilistic guarantees (which we do not discuss in this section), it is possible to derive guarantees on the expected performance. However, these guarantees require an *a priori* bound on $\|\lambda^*\|_2$ and thus are not entirely uniform.

Expectation guarantees can be simply obtained by taking an expectation in Lemma 1.i and bounding the trace of the feature covariance matrix by $D_2^2/2$. Instead, we use a stability bound on $\|\lambda^* - \hat{\lambda}\|_2$ along the lines of [8], then apply Lemma 1.ii and only then bound the trace. This results in tighter guarantees (also tighter than those in [8]). Optimizing α under the condition $\|\lambda^*\|_2 \leq L_2$ then yields the following:

Theorem 8. *Let D_2 be the ℓ_2 diameter of $f(\mathcal{X})$ and let $L_2 > 0$. Let $\hat{\lambda}$ minimize $L_{\tilde{\pi}}(\lambda) + \alpha\|\lambda\|_2^2/2$ with $\alpha = D_2/(L_2\sqrt{m})$. Then for all λ^* such that $\|\lambda^*\| \leq L_2$*

$$E\left[L_\pi(\hat{\lambda})\right] \leq L_\pi(\lambda^*) + L_2 D_2/\sqrt{m}.$$

Expectation guarantees can also be obtained for regularization types of the form $U_{\tilde{\pi}}^*(\lambda) = \beta I_{C_0}^*(\lambda) + \alpha\|\lambda\|_2^2/2$. Using that $U_{\tilde{\pi}}(u) \leq \min\{I_{\beta C_0}(u), \|u\|_2^2/(2\alpha)\}$, the expectation is derived by distinguishing whether $\tilde{\pi}[f] - \pi[f]$ lies in βC_0 or not (with a small probability δ). The resulting guarantee contains one term proportional to $I_{C_0}^*(\lambda^*)/\sqrt{m}$ and another proportional to $L_2 D_2/\sqrt{m}$ with δ controlling the tradeoff.

6 A Sequential-Update Algorithm and Convergence Proof

In this section, we present an algorithm for the generalized maxent and proof of convergence. The algorithm covers a wide class of potentials including the basic, box and ℓ_2^2 potential. Polyhedral and ℓ_2-ball potentials do not fall in this class, but the corresponding maxent problems can be transformed and our algorithm can still be applied.

As explained in Section 4, the goal of the algorithm is to produce a sequence $\lambda_1, \lambda_2, \ldots$ maximizing the objective function Q in the limit. We assume that the potential U is *decomposable* in the sense that it can be written as a sum of coordinate potentials $U(\boldsymbol{u}) = \sum_j U_j(u_j)$, each of which is a closed proper convex functions bounded from below. The conjugate potential U^* then equals the sum of conjugate coordinate potentials U_j^* (see Eq. (3)) and $U_j^*(0) = \sup_{u_j} [-U_j(u_j)]$ is finite for all j.

Throughout this section we assume that values of features f_j lie in the interval $[0, 1]$ and that features and coordinate potentials are non-degenerate in the sense that ranges $f_j(\mathcal{X})$ and intersections dom $U_j \cap [0, 1]$ differ from $\{0\}$ and $\{1\}$.

Our algorithm works by iteratively adjusting the single weight λ_j that maximizes (an approximation of) the change in Q. To be more precise, suppose we add δ to λ_j. Let λ' be the resulting vector of weights. By decomposability and convexity, we can bound the change in the objective (analogously to [11]):

$$Q(\lambda') - Q(\lambda) \geq -\ln\big(1 + (e^\delta - 1)q_\lambda[f_j]\big) - U_j^*(-\lambda_j - \delta) + U_j^*(-\lambda_j). \quad (11)$$

Our algorithm starts with $\lambda_1 = 0$ and then, on each iteration, maximizes this lower bound over all choices of (j, δ). For the maximizing j, it adds the corresponding δ to λ_j. This is repeated until convergence. We assume that for each j the maximizing δ is finite. This will be the case if the potential and features are non-degenerate.

For maxent with box constraints, the minimizing δ can be derived explicitly yielding the algorithm of [11]. For a general potential note that (11) is strictly concave in δ so we can use any of a number of search methods to find the optimal δ.

Reductions from Non-decomposable Potentials. Polyhedral and ℓ_2-ball potentials are not decomposable. When a polyhedral potential is represented as an intersection of halfspaces $\boldsymbol{\mu}_{\bar{\jmath}} \cdot \boldsymbol{u} \geq a_{\bar{\jmath}}$, it suffices to use transformed features $\bar{f}_{\bar{\jmath}}(x) = \boldsymbol{\mu}_{\bar{\jmath}} \cdot \boldsymbol{f}(x)$ with coordinate potentials corresponding to inequality constraints. Note that the debiased potential polytope (9) is not described in this form. However, it is not too difficult to obtain such a representation. It turns out that this representation uses $O(n^2)$ halfspaces and is thus polynomial in the original problem size.

In case of an ℓ_2-ball potential, we replace the constraint $\|\tilde{\pi}[\boldsymbol{f}] - p[\boldsymbol{f}]\|_2 \leq \beta$ by $\|\tilde{\pi}[\boldsymbol{f}] - p[\boldsymbol{f}]\|_2^2 \leq \beta^2$ which yields an equivalent primal $\mathcal{P}'$. If $\beta > 0$ then, by the Lagrange duality and Slater's conditions [21], we know there exists $\mu \geq 0$ such that the solution of $\mathcal{P}'$ is the same as the solution of

$$\mathcal{P}'' : \quad \min_{p \in \Delta} \big[\mathrm{D}(p \parallel q_0) + \mu \left(\|\tilde{\pi}[\boldsymbol{f}] - p[\boldsymbol{f}]\|_2^2 - \beta^2 \right) \big].$$

The sought-after μ is the one which maximizes the value of $\mathcal{P}''$. Since the value of $\mathcal{P}''$ is concave in μ, we can employ a range of search techniques to find the optimal μ, using our algorithm to solve an instance of ℓ_2^2-regularized maxent in each iteration.

Convergence. In order to prove convergence of our algorithm, we will measure its progress towards solving the primal and dual. One measure of progress is the difference between the primal evaluated at q_λ and the dual at λ:

$$P(q_\lambda) - Q(\lambda) = U(q_\lambda[f]) + U^*(-\lambda) + \lambda \cdot q_\lambda[f].$$

By Theorem 1, this difference is non-negative and equals zero exactly when q_λ solves primal and λ solves the dual.

However, for many potentials of interest, including equality and inequality constraints, the difference between primal and dual may remain infinite throughout the computation. Therefore, we introduce an *auxiliary function*, defined, somewhat non-standardly, as a surrogate for this difference.

Definition 1. *A function* $A : \mathbb{R}^n \times \mathbb{R}^n \to (-\infty, \infty]$ *is called an* auxiliary function *if*

$$A(\lambda, a) = U(a) + U^*(-\lambda) + \lambda \cdot a + B(a \parallel q_\lambda[f]) \tag{12}$$

where $B(\cdot \parallel \cdot) : \mathbb{R}^n \times \mathbb{R}^n \to (-\infty, \infty]$ *satisfies conditions* (B1) *and* (B2).

Unlike the previous applications of auxiliary functions [3, 14], we do not assume that $A(\lambda, a)$ bounds a change in the dual objective and we also make no continuity assumptions. However, an auxiliary function is always non-negative since by Fenchel's inequality $U(a) + U^*(-\lambda) \geq -\lambda \cdot a$ and hence $A(\lambda, a) \geq B(a \parallel q_\lambda[f]) \geq 0$. Moreover, if $A(\lambda, a) = 0$ then $q_\lambda[f] = a$ and $A(\lambda, a) = P(q_\lambda) - Q(\lambda) = 0$, i.e. by maxent duality, q_λ solves the primal and λ solves the dual.

It turns out, as we show in Lemma 3 below, that the optimality property generalizes to the case when $A(\lambda_t, a_t) \to 0$ provided that $Q(\lambda_t)$ has a finite limit. In particular, it suffices to find a suitable sequence of a_t's for λ_t's produced by our algorithm to show its convergence. Note that the optimality in the limit trivially holds when λ_t's and a_t's come from a compact set, because $A(\hat\lambda, \hat a) = 0$ at a cluster point of $\{(\lambda_t, a_t)\}$ by the lower semi-continuity of U and U*.

In the general case, we follow the technique used by [3] for the basic maxent: we consider a cluster point $\hat q$ of $\{q_{\lambda_t}\}$ and show that (i) $\hat q$ is primal feasible and (ii) the difference $P(\hat q) - Q(\lambda_t)$ approaches zero. In case of the basic maxent, $A(\lambda, a) = B(\tilde\pi[f] \parallel q_\lambda[f])$ whenever finite. Thus, (i) is obtained by (B2), and noting that $P(\hat q) - Q(\lambda) = D(\hat q \parallel q_\lambda)$ yields (ii). For a general potential, however, claims (i) and (ii) seem to require a novel approach. In both steps, we use decomposability and the technical Lemma 2 (the proof is omitted).

Lemma 2. *Let* U_{p_0} *be a decomposable potential centered at a feasible point* p_0. *Let* $S = \operatorname{dom} U_{p_0} = \{u \in \mathbb{R}^n \mid U_{p_0}(u) < \infty\}$ *and* $T_c = \{\lambda \in \mathbb{R}^n \mid U^*_{p_0}(\lambda) \leq c\}$. *Then there exists* $\alpha_c \geq 0$ *such that* $\lambda \cdot u \leq \alpha_c \|u\|_1$ *for all* $u \in S, \lambda \in T_c$.

Lemma 3. *Let* $\lambda_1, \lambda_2, \ldots \in \mathbb{R}^n$, $a_1, a_2, \ldots \in \mathbb{R}^n$ *be sequences such that* $Q(\lambda_t)$ *has a finite limit and* $A(\lambda_t, a_t) \to 0$ *as* $t \to \infty$. *Then* $\lim_{t \to \infty} Q(\lambda_t) = \sup_\lambda Q(\lambda)$.

Sketch of proof. Let q_t denote q_{λ_t}. Consider a convergent subsequence of q_t's, index it by τ and denote its limit by $\hat q$. As noted earlier, $A(\lambda, a) \geq B(a \parallel q_\lambda[f])$. Since

$A(\lambda_\tau, a_\tau) \rightarrow 0$, we obtain that $B(a_\tau \parallel q_\tau[f]) \rightarrow 0$ and thus $a_\tau \rightarrow \hat{q}[f]$. Rewrite Eq. (12) in terms of potentials and conjugate potentials centered at an arbitrary feasible point p_0 (which must exist by assumption), denoting terms with zero limits by $o(1)$:

$$U_{p_0}(p_0[f] - a_\tau) = -U_{p_0}^*(\lambda_\tau) + \lambda_\tau \cdot (p_0[f] - a_\tau) + o(1). \tag{13}$$

We use Eq. (13) to show first the feasibility and then the optimality of $\hat{q}$.

Feasibility. We bound the right hand side of Eq. (13). The first term $-U_{p_0}^*(\lambda_\tau)$ is, by Fenchel's inequality, bounded above by $U_{p_0}(0)$. The second term $\lambda_\tau \cdot (p_0[f] - a_\tau)$ can be bounded above by Lemma 2. Taking limits yields feasibility.

Optimality. Since $\hat{q}$ is feasible, we can set p_0 equal to $\hat{q}$ in Eq. (13). Using Lemma 2 and taking limits we obtain that $U_{\hat{q}}(0) \leq \lim_{\tau \to \infty}[-U_{\hat{q}}^*(\lambda_\tau)]$. Adding $D(\hat{q} \parallel q_0)$ to both sides yields $P(\hat{q}) \leq \lim_{\tau \to \infty} Q(\lambda_\tau)$ which by the maxent duality implies the optimality of $\hat{q}$. □

Theorem 9. *The sequential-update algorithm produces a sequence $\lambda_1, \lambda_2, \ldots$ for which $\lim_{t \to \infty} Q(\lambda_t) = \sup_\lambda Q(\lambda)$.*

Sketch of proof. It suffices to show that $Q(\lambda_t)$ has a finite limit and present an auxiliary function A and a sequence $a_1, a_2, \ldots$ for which $A(\lambda_t, a_t) \rightarrow 0$.

Note that $Q(\lambda_1) = Q(0) = -U^*(0)$ is finite by decomposability and Q is bounded above by feasibility of the primal. For each j let $F_{t,j}$ denote the maximum over δ of the lower bound (11) in step t. Note that $F_{t,j}$ is nonnegative since the bound is zero when $\delta = 0$. Thus $Q(\lambda_t)$ is nondecreasing and hence has a finite limit.

In each step, $Q(\lambda_{t+1}) - Q(\lambda_t) \geq F_{t,j} \geq 0$. Since $Q(\lambda_t)$ has a finite limit, we obtain $F_{t,j} \rightarrow 0$. We will use $F_{t,j}$ to construct A. Rewrite $F_{t,j}$ using Fenchel's duality:

$$F_{t,j} = \max_\delta \left[-\ln(1 + (e^\delta - 1)q_t[f_j]) - U_j^*(-\lambda_{t,j} - \delta) + U_j^*(-\lambda_{t,j}) \right]$$

$$= \max_\delta \left[-\ln\left\{ (1 - q_t[f_j])e^{0 \cdot \delta} + q_t[f_j]e^{1 \cdot \delta} \right\} - U_j'^*(-\delta) \right] + U_j^*(-\lambda_{t,j}) \tag{14}$$

$$= \min_{\bar{a}, a} \left[D((\bar{a}, a) \parallel (1 - q_t[f_j], q_t[f_j])) + U_j'(0 \cdot \bar{a} + 1 \cdot a) \right] + U_j^*(-\lambda_{t,j}) \tag{15}$$

$$= \min_{0 \leq a \leq 1} \left[D(a \parallel q_t[f_j]) + U_j(a) + a \cdot \lambda_{t,j} \right] + U_j^*(-\lambda_{t,j}). \tag{16}$$

In Eq. (14), we write $U_j'^*(u)$ for $U_j^*(u - \lambda_{t,j})$. In Eq. (15), we applied Theorem 1, noting that the conjugate of the log partition function is the relative entropy. The value of relative entropy $D((\bar{a}, a) \parallel (1 - q_t[f_j], q_t[f_j]))$ is infinite whenever $(\bar{a}, a)$ is not a probability distribution, so it suffices to consider pairs where $0 \leq a \leq 1$ and $\bar{a} = 1 - a$. In Eq. (16), we use $D(a \parallel q_t[f_j])$ as a shorthand for $D((1 - a, a) \parallel (1 - q_t[f_j], q_t[f_j]))$ and use Eq. (2) to convert U_j' into U_j.

The minimum in Eq. (16) is always attained because a comes from a compact set. Let $a_{t,j}$ denote a value attaining this minimum. We define the auxiliary function $A(\lambda, a)$ as the sum over j of Eq. (16) (evaluated at $a = a_j$ and with $\lambda_{t,j}$ replaced by λ_j). Now $A(\lambda_t, a_t) = \sum_j F_{t,j} \rightarrow 0$ and the result follows by Lemma 3. □

7 Conclusion and Future Work

In this work, we have explored one direction of generalizing maxent: replacing equality constraints in the primal by an arbitrary convex potential or, equivalently, adding a convex regularization term to the maximum likelihood estimation in the dual. In our unified approach, we derived performance guarantees for many existing and novel regularization types and presented an algorithm covering a wide range of potentials.

As the next step, we would like to explore whether theoretical superiority of the new regularization types results in improved performance on real-world data. If this turns out to be the case, we would like to investigate strategies for obtaining tighter confidence regions and hence better performing regularizations using sample-derived statistics or properties of the feature space.

An alternative line of generalizations arises by replacing relative entropy in the primal objective by an arbitrary Bregman or Csiszár divergence along the lines of [12, 14]. Analogous duality results as well as a modified algorithm apply in the new setting, but performance guarantees do not directly translate to the case when divergences are derived from samples. Divergences of this kind are used in many cases of interest such as logistic regression (a conditional version of maxent), boosting or linear regression. In the future, we would like to generalize performance guarantees to this setting.

Finally, the convergence rate of the present algorithm and a possible tradeoff between statistical guarantees and computational efficiency of different regularizations is open for future research.

Acknowledgements. We would like to thank Steven Phillips for many helpful discussions. Authors received support through NSF grant CCR-0325463.

References

1. Jaynes, E.T.: Information theory and statistical mechanics. Phys. Rev. **106** (1957) 620–630
2. Berger, A.L., Della Pietra, S.A., Della Pietra, V.J.: A maximum entropy approach to natural language processing. Computational Linguistics **22**(1) (1996) 39–71
3. Della Pietra, S., Della Pietra, V., Lafferty, J.: Inducing features of random fields. IEEE Transactions on Pattern Analysis and Machine Intelligence **19**(4) (1997) 1–13
4. Phillips, S.J., Dudík, M., Schapire, R.E.: A ME approach to species distribution modeling. In: Proceedings of the Twenty-First International Conference on Machine Learning. (2004)
5. Lau, R.: Adaptive statistical language modeling. Master's thesis, MIT Department of Electrical Engineering and Computer Science (1994)
6. Chen, S.F., Rosenfeld, R.: A survey of smoothing techniques for ME models. IEEE Transactions on Speech and Audio Processing **8**(1) (2000) 37–50
7. Lebanon, G., Lafferty, J.: Boosting and maximum likelihood for exponential models. Technical Report CMU-CS-01-144, CMU School of Computer Science (2001)
8. Zhang, T.: Class-size independent generalization analysis of some discriminative multicategory classification. In: Advances in Neural Information Processing Systems 17. (2005)
9. Goodman, J.: Exponential priors for maximum entropy models. In: Conference of the North American Chapter of the Association for Computational Linguistics. (2004)
10. Kazama, J., Tsujii, J.: Evaluation and extension of ME models with inequality constraints. In: Conference on Empirical Methods in Natural Language Processing. (2003) 137–144

11. Dudík, M., Phillips, S.J., Schapire, R.E.: Performance guarantees for regularized maximum entropy density estimation. In: COLT 2004. (2004) 472–486
12. Altun, Y., Smola, A.: Unifying divergence minimization and statistical inference via convex duality. In: COLT 2006. (2006)
13. Dudík, M., Schapire, R.E., Phillips, S.J.: Correcting sample selection bias in ME density estimation. In: Advances in Neural Information Processing Systems 18. (2006)
14. Collins, M., Schapire, R.E., Singer, Y.: Logistic regression, AdaBoost and Bregman distances. Machine Learning **48**(1) (2002) 253–285
15. Darroch, J.N., Ratcliff, D.: Generalized iterative scaling for log-linear models. The Annals of Mathematical Statistics **43**(5) (1972) 1470–1480
16. Malouf, R.: A comparison of algorithms for maximum entropy parameter estimation. In: Proceedings of the Sixth Conference on Natural Language Learning. (2002) 49–55
17. Krishnapuram, B., Carin, L., Figueiredo, M.A.T., Hartemink, A.J.: Sparse multinomial logistic regression: Fast algorithms and generalization bounds. IEEE Transactions on Pattern Analysis and Machine Intelligence **27**(6) (2005) 957–968
18. Ng, A.Y.: Feature selection, L_1 vs. L_2 regularization, and rotational invariance. In: Proceedings of the Twenty-First International Conference on Machine Learning. (2004)
19. Newman, W.: Extension to the ME method. IEEE Trans. on Inf. Th. **IT-23**(1) (1977) 89–93
20. Rockafellar, R.T.: Convex Analysis. Princeton University Press (1970)
21. Boyd, S., Vandenberghe, L.: Convex Optimization. Cambridge University Press (2004)

Unifying Divergence Minimization and Statistical Inference Via Convex Duality

Yasemin Altun[1] and Alex Smola[2]

[1] Toyota Technological Institute at Chicago, Chicago, IL 60637, USA*
altun@tti-c.org
[2] National ICT Australia, North Road, Canberra 0200 ACT, Australia
alex.smola@nicta.com.au

Abstract. In this paper we unify divergence minimization and statistical inference by means of convex duality. In the process of doing so, we prove that the dual of approximate maximum entropy estimation is maximum a posteriori estimation as a special case. Moreover, our treatment leads to stability and convergence bounds for many statistical learning problems. Finally, we show how an algorithm by Zhang can be used to solve this class of optimization problems efficiently.

1 Introduction

It is quite well-known that maximum likelihood optimization is the convex dual of maximum entropy estimation. An immediate question one can raise is whether maximum a posteriori (MAP) estimates have similar counterparts. In this paper, we are interested in a general form of this question, that is which statistical inference methods can be cast as duals of various maximum entropy optimization and whether such estimates can be obtained efficiently. To this extent, we develop a theory of regularized divergence minimization that unifies a collection of related approaches. By means of convex duality, we are able to give a common treatment to methods such as the following.

- In the regularized LMS minimization methods of Arsenin and Tikhonov [24], and of Morozov [16], the problem of minimizing

$$\|x\|_2^2 \text{ subject to } \|Ax - b\|_2^2 \leq \epsilon$$

  is studied as a means of improving the stability of the problem $Ax = b$.
- Ruderman and Bialek [21] study a related problem where instead of a quadratic penalty on x, the negative Shannon entropy function is minimized

$$-H(x) \text{ subject to } \|Ax - b\|_2^2 \leq \epsilon$$

  In other words, the problem of solving $Ax = b$ is stabilized by finding the maximum entropy distribution which satisfies the constraint.

---

* Parts of this work were done when the author was visiting National ICT Australia.

G. Lugosi and H.U. Simon (Eds.): COLT 2006, LNAI 4005, pp. 139–153, 2006.
© Springer-Verlag Berlin Heidelberg 2006

- Dudik et al. [10] study a density estimation problem that can be viewed as one of solving a variant of the above, namely that of minimizing

$$-H(x) \text{ subject to } \|Ax - b\|_\infty \leq \epsilon$$

where the constraint encode deviations of the measured values of some *moments* or *features* and their expected values.
- When x is the conditional probability of the outputs given observations, the above optimization corresponds to conditional maximum entropy methods.

The problem we study is abstractly the regularized inverse problem

$$\underset{x \in \mathcal{X}}{\text{minimize}} f(x) \text{ subject to } \|Ax - b\|_\mathcal{B} \leq \epsilon,$$

where $\mathcal{X}$ and $\mathcal{B}$ are Banach spaces. By defining $\mathcal{X}$, $\mathcal{B}$ and f appropriately, the above methods become examples of this general problem. Using the convex duality framework, Fenchel's duality in particular, the regularized inverse problem can be solved by optimizing the unconstraint dual problem.

There are many studies that investigate specific forms of this duality. Most of these focus on analyzing various loss functions on exponential families as the convex dual of entropy maximization via equality constraints, i. e. $Ax = b$. For example, Lafferty [14] analyze logistic regression and exponential loss as a special case of Bregman divergence minimization and propose a family of sequential update algorithms. Similar treatments are given in [13, 8]. Previous work on approximate divergence minimization ($\epsilon > 0$) focused on minimizing KL divergence such that its convex dual is penalized by ℓ_1 or ℓ_2 norm terms, eg. [7]. In [10], which is the starting point of our work, Dudik et al. show that if f is KL divergence and $\mathcal{B}$ is ℓ_∞, the convex dual is ℓ_1 norm regularized maximum likelihood. Recently, [12] and [11] generalized these results to ℓ_p and $\ell_2, \ell_1 + \ell_2$ norm regularizations respectively.

In this paper, we improve over previous work by providing a unified framework of relating various statistical inference methods to a large family of divergence functions with inequality constraints in Banach spaces. In particular, we investigate two important classes of divergences, namely Csiszár and Bregman divergences as the minimization function f. These divergences, parameterized by a function h, include many important special cases, such as KL divergence. Once the dual counterparts of h, $\mathcal{X}$ and $\mathcal{B}$ are determined, the dual optimization problems, which correspond to various statistical inference methods, are derived immediately. This allows us to produce the cited work as special cases and can establish other inference methods. For example, we prove that the MAP estimate is the convex dual of approximate maximum entropy optimization. This general framework also points at directions to develop new learning methods by using different combinations of entropy functions and regularization methods.

By relating a class of methods through our framework, we unify previous results in terms of stability and convergence bounds with simpler proofs and provide bounds for some techniques with no such results. We also derive risk bounds for arbitrary linear classes and divergences. Finally, we show that a single algorithm can efficiently optimize this large class of optimization problems with good convergence rates.

One important advantage of working in Banach spaces, apart from its unifying property, is its ability to allow sophisticated regularization schemes via norm definitions. For example, we can perform different regularizations on subsets of basis functions which is particularly useful when there are several distinctly different sets of basis functions. Eg. in structured output prediction, the basis functions capturing inter-label dependencies have very different properties than the basis functions capturing observation-label dependencies.

From a regularization point of view, our approach provides a natural interpretation to the regularization coefficient ϵ, which corresponds to the approximation parameter in the primal problem. Studying the concentration of empirical means, we show that a good value of ϵ is proportional to $O(1/\sqrt{m})$ where m is the sample size. Noting that the regularization parameter is generally chosen by cross validation techniques in practice, our framework gives an enhanced interpretation of regularized optimization problems.

2   Fenchel Duality

We now give a formal definition of the class of inverse problems we solve. Denote by $\mathcal{X}$ and $\mathcal{B}$ Banach spaces and let $A : \mathcal{X} \to \mathcal{B}$ be a bounded linear operator between those two spaces. Here A corresponds to an "observation operator", e.g. mapping distributions into a set of moments, marginals, etc. Moreover, let $b \in \mathcal{B}$ be the target of the estimation problem. Finally, denote by $f : \mathcal{X} \to \mathbb{R}$ and $g : \mathcal{B} \to \mathbb{R}$ convex functions and let $\epsilon \geq 0$.

Problem 1 (Regularized inverse). *Our goal is to find $x \in \mathcal{X}$ which solves the following convex optimization problem:*

$$\underset{x \in \mathcal{X}}{\text{minimize}} \, f(x) \text{ subject to } \|Ax - b\|_{\mathcal{B}} \leq \epsilon.$$

Example 2 (Density estimation). *Assume that x is a density, f is the negative Shannon-Boltzmann entropy, b contains the observed values of some moments or features, A is the expectation operator of those features wrt. the density x and the Banach space $\mathcal{B}$ is ℓ_p.*

We show in Section 3.2 that the dual to Example 2 is a MAP estimation problem.

In cases where $\mathcal{B}$ and $\mathcal{X}$ are finite dimensional the problem is easily solved by calculating the corresponding Lagrangian, setting its derivative to 0 and solving for x. In the infinite dimensional case, more careful analysis is required to ensure continuity and differentiability. We use Fenchel's conjugate duality theorem to study this problem by formulating the primal-dual space relations of convex optimization problems in our general setting. We need the following definition:

Definition 3. *Denote by* dom f *the domain of* f, cont f *the set of points where* f *if finite and continuous. Define* core(S) *such that* $s \in$ core(S) *if* $\bigcup_{\lambda > 0} \lambda(S - s) \subseteq \mathcal{X}$ *where* $\mathcal{X}$ *is a Banach space and* $S \subseteq \mathcal{X}$.

Definition 4 (Convex conjugate). *Denote by* $\mathcal{X}$ *a Banach space and let* $\mathcal{X}^*$ *be its dual. The convex conjugate of a function* $f : \mathcal{X} \to \mathbb{R}$ *is*

$$f^*(x^*) = \sup_{x \in \mathcal{X}} \{\langle x, x^* \rangle - f(x)\}.$$

We present Fenchel's theorem[1] where the primal problem is of the form $f(x) + g(Ax)$. Problem 1 becomes an instance of the latter for suitably defined g.

Theorem 5 (Fenchel Duality [3, Th. 4.4.3]). *Let* $g : \mathcal{B} \to \mathbb{R}$ *be a convex function on* $\mathcal{B}$ *and other variables as above. Define* t *and* d *as follows:*

$$t = \inf_{x \in \mathcal{X}} \{f(x) + g(Ax)\} \ and \ d = \sup_{x^* \in \mathcal{B}^*} \{-f^*(A^*x^*) - g^*(-x^*)\}.$$

Assume that f, g *and* A *satisfy one of the following constraint qualifications:*
a) $0 \in \mathrm{core}(\mathrm{dom}\, g - A\,\mathrm{dom}\, f)$ *and* f *and* g *are lower semi continuous (lsc)*
b) $A\,\mathrm{dom}\, f \cap \mathrm{cont}\, g \neq \emptyset$
In this case $t = d$, *where the dual solution* d *is attainable if it is finite.*

We now apply Fenchel's duality theorem to convex constraint optimization problems, such as Problem 1, since the dual problem is easier to solve in certain cases.

Lemma 6 (Fenchel duality with constraints). *In addition to the assumptions of Theorem 5, let* $b \in \mathcal{B}$ *and* $\epsilon \geq 0$. *Define* t *and* d *as follows:*

$$t = \inf_{x \in \mathcal{X}} \{f(x) \ subject \ to \ \|Ax - b\|_{\mathcal{B}} \leq \epsilon\}$$
$$and \ d = \sup_{x^* \in \mathcal{B}^*} \{-f^*(A^*x^*) + \langle b, x^* \rangle - \epsilon \|x^*\|_{\mathcal{B}*}\}$$

$t = d$ *with dual attainment, if* f *is lsc and for* $B := \{\bar{b} \in \mathcal{B} \ with \ \|\bar{b}\| \leq 1\}$ *the following constraint qualification holds:*

$$\mathrm{core}(A\,\mathrm{dom}\, f) \cap (b + \epsilon\,\mathrm{int}(B)) \neq \emptyset. \qquad (CQ)$$

Proof. Define g in Theorem 5 as the characteristic function on $\epsilon B + b$, i.e.

$$g(\bar{b}) = \chi_{\epsilon B + b}(\bar{b}) = \{0 \text{ if } \bar{b} \in \epsilon B + b \text{ ; } \infty \text{ otherwise }\} \qquad (1)$$

The convex conjugate of g is given by

$$g^*(x^*) = \sup_{\bar{b}} \{\langle \bar{b}, x^* \rangle \ subject \ to \ \bar{b} - b \in \epsilon B\}$$
$$= -\langle x^*, b \rangle + \epsilon \sup_{\bar{b}} \{\langle \bar{b}, x^* \rangle \ subject \ to \ \bar{b} \in B\} = \epsilon \|x^*\|_{\mathcal{B}*} - \langle x^*, b \rangle$$

Theorem 5 and the relation $\mathrm{core}(B) = \mathrm{int}(B)$ prove the lemma. This result can trivially be extend to other convex sets, with the unit ball as an instance. ∎

---

[1] For a comprehensive presentation of Fenchel's duality, we refer the reader to [3, 20].

The constraint qualification (CQ) ensures the non-emptiness of the sub-differential. $\epsilon = 0$ leads to equality constraints $Ax = b$, for which CQ requires b to be an element of core$(A \operatorname{dom} f)$. If the equality constraints are not feasible $b \notin \operatorname{core}(A \operatorname{dom} f)$, which can be the case in real problems, the solution diverges.

Such problems may be rendered feasible by relaxing the constraints ($\epsilon > 0$), which corresponds to expanding the search space by defining an ϵ ball around b and searching for a point in the intersection of this ball and core$(A \operatorname{dom} f)$. In the convex dual problem, this relaxation is penalized with the norm of the dual parameters scaling linearly with the relaxation parameter ϵ.

In practice it is difficult to check whether (CQ) holds. One solution is to solve the dual optimization problem and infer that the condition holds if the solution does not diverge. To assure a finite solution, we restrict the function class such that f^* is Lipschitz and perturb the regularization slightly by taking its kth power, resulting in a Lipschitz continuous optimization. For instance Support Vector Machines perform this type of adjustment to ensure feasibility [9].

Lemma 7. *Denote by $\mathfrak{X}$ a Banach space, let $b \in \mathfrak{X}^*$ and let $k > 1$. Assume that $f(Ax)$ is convex and Lipschitz continuous in x with Lipschitz constant C. Then*

$$\inf_{x \in \mathfrak{X}} \left\{ f(Ax) - \langle b, x \rangle + \epsilon \, \|x\|^k \right\} \tag{2}$$

does not diverge and the norm of x is bounded by $\|x\|_{\mathfrak{X}} \leq \left[(\|b\|_{\mathfrak{X}^*} + C) / k\epsilon \right]^{\frac{1}{k-1}}$.

Proof [sketch]. Note that the overall Lipschitz constant of the objective function (except for the norm) is bounded by $\|b\|_{\mathfrak{X}^*} + C$. The objective function cannot increase further if the slope due to the norm is larger than what the Lipschitz constant admits. Solving for $\epsilon k \|x\|_{\mathfrak{X}}^{k-1} = \|b\|_{\mathfrak{X}^*} + C$ proves the claim. ∎

3 Divergence Minimization and Convex Duality

Given this general framework of duality for regularized inverse problems, we consider applications to problems in statistics. For the remainder of the section x is either a density or a conditional density over the domain $\mathfrak{T}$. For this reason we use p instead of x to denote the variable of the optimization problem.

Denote by $\psi : \mathfrak{T} \to \mathcal{B}$ feature functions and let $A : \mathfrak{X} \to \mathcal{B}$ be the expectation operator of the feature map with respect to p. In other words, $Ap := \mathbf{E}_{t \sim p} [\psi(t)]$. With some abuse of notation we will use the shorthand $\mathbf{E}_p[\psi]$ whenever convenient. Finally denote by $\tilde{\psi} = b$ the observed value of the features $\psi(t)$, which are derived, e.g. via $b = m^{-1} \sum_{i=1}^{m} \psi(t_i)$ for $t_i \in S$, the sample of size m.

This setting allows us to study various statistical learning methods within convex duality framework. One of the corollaries which follows immediately from the more general result in Lemma 12 is the well-known duality of maximum (Shannon) entropy is maximum likelihood (ML) estimation. Another is that the dual of *approximate* maximum entropy is MAP estimation.

Theorem 8. *Assume that f is the negative Shannon entropy, that is $f(p) :=$*
$-H(p) = \int_{\mathfrak{T}} \log p(t) dp(t)$. *Under the above conditions we have*

$$\min_p - H(p) \text{ subject to } \left\| \mathbf{E}_p[\psi] - \tilde{\psi} \right\| \leq \epsilon \text{ and } \int_{\mathfrak{T}} dp(t) = 1 \quad (3)$$

$$= \max_\phi \left\langle \phi, \tilde{\psi} \right\rangle - \log \int_{\mathfrak{T}} \exp(\langle \phi, \psi(t) \rangle) dt - \epsilon \|\phi\| + e^{-1}$$

Equivalently ϕ maximizes $\Pr(S|\phi)\Pr(\phi)$ and $\Pr(\phi) \propto \exp(-\epsilon \|\phi\|)$.

In order to provide a common treatment to various statistical inference techniques, as well as give insight into the development of new ones, we study two important classes of divergence functions, Csiszár's divergences and Bregman divergences. Csiszár divergence, which includes Amari's α divergences as special cases, gives an asymmetric distance between two infinite-dimensional density functions induced by a manifold. Bregman divergences are commonly defined over distributions over a finite domain. The two classes of divergences intersect at the KL divergence. To avoid technical problems we assume that the constraint qualifications are satisfied (e.g. via Lemma 7).

3.1 Csiszár Divergences

Definition 9. *Denote by $h : \mathbb{R} \to \mathbb{R}$ a convex lsc function and let p, q be two distributions on $\mathfrak{T}$. Then the Csiszár divergence is given by*

$$f_h(q, p) = \int q(t) h\left(\frac{p(t)}{q(t)}\right) dt. \quad (4)$$

Different choices for h lead to different divergence measures. For instance $h(\xi) = \xi \log \xi$ yields the Kullback-Leibler divergence. Commonly, q is fixed and optimization is performed with respect to p, which we denote by $f_{h,q}(p)$. Since $f_{h,q}(p)$ is convex and expectation is a linear operator, we can apply Lemma 6 to obtain the convex conjugate of Csiszár's divergence optimization:

Lemma 10 (Duality of Csiszár Divergence). *Assume that the conditions of Lemma 6 hold. Moreover let f be defined as a Csiszár divergence. Then*

$$\min_p \left\{ f_{h,q}(p) | \|E_p[\psi] - \tilde{\psi}\|_{\mathcal{B}} \leq \epsilon \right\} = \max_\phi \left\{ -f_{h,q}^*(\langle \phi, \psi(.) \rangle) + \left\langle \phi, \tilde{\psi} \right\rangle - \epsilon \|\phi\|_{\mathcal{B}^*} \right\}.$$

Moreover the solutions $\hat{p}$ and $\hat{\phi}$ are connected by $\hat{p}(t) = q(t)(h^*)' \left(\left\langle \psi(t), \hat{\phi} \right\rangle \right)$.

Proof. The adjoint of the linear operator A is given by $\langle Ax, \phi \rangle = \langle A^*\phi, x \rangle$. Letting A be the expectation wrt p, we have $\left\langle \int_{\mathfrak{T}} p(t)\psi(t), \phi \right\rangle = \int_{\mathfrak{T}} p(t) \left\langle \psi(t), \phi \right\rangle dt = (A^*\phi)(p)$ for $A^*\phi = \langle \phi, \psi(.) \rangle$. Next note that $f^*(\langle \phi, \psi(\cdot) \rangle) = \int_{\mathfrak{T}} q(t) h^*(\langle \phi, \psi(t) \rangle) dt$. Plugging this into Lemma 6, we obtain the first claim.

Using attainability of the solution it follows that there exist $\hat{p}$ and $\hat{\phi}$ which solve the corresponding optimization problems. Equating both sides we have

$$\int_{\mathfrak{T}} q(t) h\left(\frac{\hat{p}(t)}{q(t)}\right) dt = -f^*(\langle \phi, \psi(.) \rangle) + \left\langle \tilde{\psi}, \hat{\phi} \right\rangle - \epsilon \|\hat{\phi}\|_{B^*} = -f^*(\langle \phi, \psi(.) \rangle) + \left\langle \hat{\phi}, E_{\hat{p}}[\psi] \right\rangle.$$

Here the last equality follows from the definition of the constraints (see the proof of Lemma 6). Taking the derivative at the solution $\hat{p}$ (due to constraint qualification) and noticing the derivative of the first term on RHS vanishes, we get $h'\left(\frac{\hat{p}}{q}\right) = \left\langle \hat{\phi}, \psi \right\rangle$. Using the relation $(h')^{-1} = (h^*)'$ completes the proof. ∎

Since we are dealing with probability distributions, it is convenient to add the constraint $\int_{\mathcal{J}} dp(t) = 1$. We have the following corollary.

Corollary 11 (Csiszár divergence and probability constraints). *Define all variables as in Lemma 10. We have*

$$\min_p \left\{ f_{h,q}(p) \text{ subject to } \left\| \mathbf{E}_p\left[\psi\right] - \tilde{\psi} \right\|_{\mathcal{B}} \le \epsilon \text{ and } \int_{\mathcal{J}} dp(t) = 1 \right\}$$

$$= \max_\phi \left\{ -f_{h,q}^* \left(\langle \phi, \psi(.) \rangle - \Lambda \right) + \left\langle \phi, \tilde{\psi} \right\rangle - \Lambda - \epsilon \left\| \phi \right\|_{\mathcal{B}^*} \right\} =: -\mathcal{L}_{\tilde{\psi}}^C(\phi). \quad (5)$$

Here the solution is given by $\hat{p}(t) = q(t)(h^*)'(\langle \psi(t), \hat{\phi} \rangle - \Lambda(\hat{\phi}))$ where $\Lambda(\hat{\phi})$ is the log-partition function which ensures that p be a probability distribution ($\Lambda(\hat{\phi})$ is the minimizer of (5) with respect to Λ).

Proof [sketch]. Define $\mathcal{P} = \{p | \int_{\mathcal{J}} dp(t) = 1\}$ and f in Lemma 6 as $f(p) = f_{h,q}(p) + \chi_{\mathcal{P}}(p)$. Then, for $\Lambda_p = \infty$ if $p \notin \mathcal{P}$, the convex conjugate of f is $f^*(p^*) = \sup_p\{\langle p, p^* \rangle - f_{h,q}(p) - \Lambda_p(\int_{\mathcal{J}} dp(t) - 1)\} = \Lambda_{p^*} + (f_{h,q})^*(p^* - \Lambda_{p^*})$. Performing the steps in the proof of Lemma 10 gives the result. ∎

A special case of this duality is the minimization of KL divergence as we investigate in the next section. Note that new inference techniques can be derived using other h functions, eg. Tsallis' entropy, which is preferable over Shannon's entropy in fields as statistical mechanics, as it does not diverge for $p(t) = 0$.

3.2 MAP and Maximum Likelihood Via KL Divergence

Defining h in (4) as $h(\xi) := \xi \ln(\xi)$ we have $h^*(\xi^*) = \exp(\xi^* - 1)$. Then Csiszár's divergence becomes the KL divergence. Applying Corollary 11 we have:

Lemma 12 (KL divergence with probability constraints). *Define all variables as in Lemma 11. We have*

$$\min_p \left\{ KL(p\|q) \text{ subject to } \left\| \mathbf{E}_p\left[\psi\right] - \tilde{\psi} \right\|_{\mathcal{B}} \le \epsilon \text{ and } \int_{\mathcal{J}} dp(t) = 1 \right\}$$

$$= \max_\phi \left\{ \left\langle \phi, \tilde{\psi} \right\rangle - \log \int_{\mathcal{J}} q(t) \exp(\langle \phi, \psi(t) \rangle) dt - \epsilon \|\phi\|_{\mathcal{B}^*} + e^{-1} \right\} \quad (6)$$

where the unique solution is given by $\hat{p}_{\hat{\phi}}(t) = q(t) \exp \left(\left\langle \hat{\phi}, \psi(t) \right\rangle - \Lambda_{\hat{\phi}} \right)$.

Proof. The dual of f is $f_{h,q}^*(x^*) = \int_{\mathcal{J}} q(t) \exp(x^*(t) - 1) dt$. Hence we have

$$\int_{\mathcal{J}} q(t) \exp \left(\langle \phi, \psi(t) \rangle - \Lambda_\phi - 1 \right) dt + \left\langle \phi, \tilde{\psi} \right\rangle - \Lambda_\phi - \epsilon \left\| \phi \right\|_{\mathcal{B}^*}$$

We can solve for optimality in Λ_ϕ which yields $\Lambda_\phi = \log \int_{\mathcal{T}} q(t) \exp\left(\langle \phi, \psi(t) \rangle\right) dt$. Substituting this into the objective function proves the claim. ∎

Thus, optimizing approximate KL divergence leads to exponential families. Many well known statistical inference methods can be viewed as special cases. Let $\mathcal{P} = \{p | p \in \mathcal{X}, \int_{\mathcal{T}} dp(t) = 1\}$ and $q(t) = 1, \forall t \in \mathcal{T}$.

Example 13. *For $\epsilon = 0$, we get the well known duality between Maximum Entropy and Maximum Likelihood estimation.*

$$\min_{p \in \mathcal{P}} \left\{ -H(p) \text{ subject to } \mathbf{E}_p\left[\psi\right] = \tilde{\psi} \right\} = \max_\phi \left\langle \phi, \tilde{\psi} \right\rangle - \log \int_{\mathcal{T}} \exp(\langle \phi, \psi(t) \rangle) dt + e^{-1}$$

Example 14. *For $\mathcal{B} = \ell_\infty$ we get the density estimation problem of [10]*

$$\min_{p \in \mathcal{P}} \left\{ -H(p) \text{ subject to } \left\| \mathbf{E}_p\left[\psi\right] - \tilde{\psi} \right\|_\infty \le \epsilon \right\}$$

$$= \max_\phi \left\langle \phi, \tilde{\psi} \right\rangle - \log \int_{\mathcal{T}} \exp(\langle \phi, \psi \rangle (t)) dt - \epsilon \|\phi\|_1 + e^{-1}$$

If $\mathcal{B}$ is a reproducing kernel Hilbert space of spline functions we obtain the density estimator of [18], who use an RKHS penalty on ϕ.

The well-known overfitting behavior of ML can be explained by the constraint qualification (CQ) of Section 2. While it can be shown that in exponential families the constraint qualifications are satisfied [25] if we consider the closure of the marginal polytope, the solution may be on (or close to) a vertex of the marginal polytope. This can lead to large (or possibly diverging) values of ϕ. Hence, regularization by approximate moment matching is useful to ensure that such divergence does not occur.

Regularizing ML with ℓ_2 and ℓ_1 norm terms is a common practice [7], where the regularization coefficient ϵ is determined by cross validation techniques. The analysis above provides a unified treatment of the regularization methods. More importantly, it leads to a principled way of determining ϵ as in Section 4.

Note that if $t \in \mathcal{T}$ is an input-output pair $t = (x, y)$ we could maximize the entropy of either the *joint* probability density $p(x, y)$ or the *conditional* model $p(y|x)$, which is what we really need to estimate $y|x$. If we maximize the entropy of $p(y|x)$ and $\mathcal{B}$ is a RKHS with kernel $k(t, t') := \langle \psi(t), \psi(t') \rangle$ we obtain a range of conditional estimation methods:

- $\psi(t) = y\psi_x(x)$ and $y \in \{\pm 1\}$ gives binary Gaussian Process classification [17].
- $\psi(t) = (y, y^2)\psi_x(x)$ gives the heteroscedastic GP regression estimates of [15].
- Decomposing $\psi(t)$ gives various graphical models and conditional random fields as described in [1].
- $\psi(t) = y\psi_x(x)$ and ℓ_∞ space gives as its dual ℓ_1 regularization typically used in sparse classification methods.

One advantage of using convex duality in Banach spaces is that it provides a *unified* approach (including bounds) for different regularization/relaxation schemes as above. It also provides flexibility for complex choices of regularization, eg. defining different regularizations for features with different characteristics.

3.3 Bregman Divergence

The Bregman divergence between two distributions p and q for a convex function h acting on the space of probabilities is given by

$$\triangle_h(p,q) = h(p) - h(q) - \langle (p-q), \nabla_q h(q) \rangle. \tag{7}$$

Note $\triangle_h(p,q)$ is convex in p. Applying Fenchel's duality theory, we have

Corollary 15 (Duality of Bregman Divergence). *Assume that the conditions of Lemma 6 hold. Moreover let f be defined as a Bregman divergence. Then*

$$\min_p \left\{ \triangle_h(p,q) \text{ subject to } \left\| \mathbf{E}_p\left[\psi\right] - \tilde{\psi} \right\|_{\mathcal{B}} \leq \epsilon \right\}$$
$$= \max_\phi \left\{ -h^* \left(\langle \phi - \phi_q, \psi \rangle \right) + \left\langle \phi, \tilde{\psi} \right\rangle - \epsilon \|\phi\|_{\mathcal{B}^*} \right\} =: -\mathcal{L}_{\tilde{\psi}}^{\mathcal{B}}(\phi). \tag{8}$$

Proof. Defining $H_q(p) = h(p) - \langle p, h'(q) \rangle$, $\triangle_h(p,q) = H_q(p) - h^*(\phi_q)$. The convex conjugate of H_q is $H_q^*(\phi) = \sup_p \langle p, \phi + h'(q) \rangle - h(p) = h^*(\phi - \phi_q)$, since $h'(q) = \phi_q$. Since q is constant, we get the equality (up to a constant) by plugging H_q^* into Lemma 6. ∎

As in Csiszár's divergence, the KL divergence becomes a special case of Bregman divergence by defining h as $h(p) := \int_{\mathcal{T}} p(t) \ln(p(t)) dt$. Thus, we can achieve the same results in Section 3.2 using Bregman divergences as well. Also, it has been shown in various studies that Boosting which minimizes exponential loss can be cast as a special case of Bregman divergence problem with linear equality constraints [8, 13]. An immediate result of Corollary 15, then, is to generalize these approaches by relaxing the equality constraints wrt. various norms and achieve regularized exp-loss optimization problems leading to different regularized boosting approaches. Due to space limitations, we omit the details.

4 Bounds on the Dual Problem and Uniform Stability

Generalization performances of estimators achieved by optimizing various convex functions in Reproducing Kernel Hilbert Spaces have been studied extensively. See e.g. [22, 5] and references therein. Producing similar results in the general form of convex analysis allows us to unify previous results via simpler proofs and tight bounds.

4.1 Concentration of Empirical Means

One of the key tools in the analysis of divergence estimates is the fact that deviations of the random variable $\tilde{\psi} = \frac{1}{m} \sum_i \psi(t_i)$ are well controlled.

Theorem 16. *Denote by $T := \{t_1, \ldots, t_m\} \subseteq \mathcal{T}$ a set of random variables drawn from p. Let $\psi : \mathcal{T} \to \mathcal{B}$ be a feature map into a Banach space $\mathcal{B}$ which is uniformly bounded by R. Then the following bound holds*

$$\left\| \frac{1}{m} \tilde{\psi} - \mathbf{E}_p\left[\psi(t)\right] \right\|_{\mathcal{B}} \leq 2R_m(\mathcal{F}, p) + \epsilon \tag{9}$$

with probability at least $1 - \exp\left(-\frac{\epsilon^2 m}{R^2}\right)$. *Here* $R_m(\mathcal{F}, p)$ *denotes the Rademacher average wrt the function class* $\mathcal{F} := \{\phi_p(\cdot) = \langle \psi(t), \phi_p \rangle$ *where* $\|\phi\|_{\mathcal{B}^*} \leq 1\}$.

Moreover, if $\mathcal{B}$ *is a RKHS with kernel* $k(t, t')$ *the RHS of (9) can be tightened to* $\sqrt{m^{-1} \mathbf{E}_p [k(t, t) - k(t, t')]} + \epsilon$. *The same bound for* ϵ *as above applies.*

See [2] for more details and [23] for earlier results on Hilbert Spaces.

Proof. The first claim follows immediately from [2, Theorem 9 and 10]. The second part is due to an improved calculation of the expected value of the LHS of (9). We have by convexity

$$
\mathbf{E}_p \left[\left\| \frac{1}{m} \sum_{i=1}^{m} \psi(t_i) - \mathbf{E}_p [\psi(t)] \right\|_{\mathcal{B}} \right] \leq \mathbf{E}_p \left[\left\| \frac{1}{m} \sum_{i=1}^{m} \psi(t_i) - \mathbf{E}_p [\psi(t)] \right\|_{\mathcal{B}}^2 \right]^{\frac{1}{2}}
$$

$$
= \quad m^{-\frac{1}{2}} \sqrt{\mathbf{E}_p \left[\|\psi(t) - \mathbf{E}_p [\psi(t)]\|^2 \right]} = m^{-\frac{1}{2}} \sqrt{\mathbf{E}_p [k(t, t) - k(t, t')]}
$$

The concentration inequality for bounding large deviations remains unchanged wrt. the Banach space case, where the same tail bound holds. ∎

The usefulness of Theorem 16 arises from the fact that it allows us to determine ϵ in the inverse problem. If m is small, it is sensible to choose a large value of ϵ and with increasing m our precision should improve with $O(\frac{1}{\sqrt{m}})$. [2] This gives us a *principled* way of determining ϵ based on statistical principles.

4.2   Stability with Respect to Changes in *b*

Next we study the stability of constrained optimization problems when changing the empirical mean parameter b. To denote the generality, we use A, b notation rather than $E, \tilde{\psi}$. Consider the convex dual problem of Lemma 6 and the objective function of its special case (7). Both can be summarized as

$$
L(\phi, b) := f(A\phi) - \langle b, \phi \rangle + \epsilon \|\phi\|_{\mathcal{B}^*}^k \tag{10}
$$

where $\epsilon > 0$ and $f(A\phi)$ is a convex function. We first show that for any b', the difference between the value of $L(\phi, b')$ obtained by minimizing $L(\phi, b)$ with respect to ϕ and vice versa is bounded.

Theorem 17. *Denote by* ϕ, ϕ' *the minimizers of* $L(\cdot, b)$ *and* $L(\cdot, b')$ *respectively. Then the following chain of inequalities holds:*

$$
L(\phi, b') - L(\phi', b') \leq \langle b' - b, \phi' - \phi \rangle \leq \|b' - b\|_{\mathcal{B}} \|\phi' - \phi\|_{\mathcal{B}^*} \tag{11}
$$
$$
and \; L(\phi, b) - L(\phi', b') \leq \langle \phi, b' - b \rangle \leq \|b' - b\|_{\mathcal{B}} \|\phi'\|_{\mathcal{B}^*} \tag{12}
$$

---

[2] Rademacher averages typically scale as $O(\frac{1}{\sqrt{m}})$. Setting ϵ larger than that loosens the bound. If ϵ is set for a smaller value, then the constraints become stricter than necessary, since the bound is going to be dominated by the Rademacher term.

Proof. To show (11) we only need to prove the first inequality. The second one follows by Hölder's theorem:

$$L(\phi, b') - L(\phi', b') = L(\phi, b') - L(\phi, b) + L(\phi, b) - L(\phi', b) + L(\phi', b) - L(\phi', b')$$
$$\leq \langle b - b', \phi \rangle + \langle \phi', b' - b \rangle$$

We used the fact that by construction $L(\phi', b) \geq L(\phi, b)$. To show (12) we use almost the same chain of inequalities, bar the first two terms.   ∎

In general, $\|\phi - \phi'\|$ can be bounded using Lemma 7,

$$\|\phi' - \phi\|_{\mathcal{B}^*} \leq \|\phi\|_{\mathcal{B}^*} + \|\phi'\|_{\mathcal{B}^*} \leq 2 \left(C/k\epsilon\right)^{\frac{1}{k-1}}. \tag{13}$$

For the special case of $\mathcal{B}$ being a RKHS, however, one can obtain considerably tighter bounds directly on $\|\phi' - \phi\|$ in terms of the deviations in b' and b:

Lemma 18. *Assume that $\mathcal{B}$ is a Hilbert space and let $k = 2, \epsilon > 0$ in (10). Let ϕ and ϕ' be the minimizers of $L(\cdot, b)$ and $L(\cdot, b')$ respectively, where L is defined as in (10). The the following bound holds:*

$$\|\phi - \phi'\| \leq \tfrac{1}{\epsilon} \|b - b'\| \tag{14}$$

Proof. The proof idea is similar to that of [6, 22]. We construct an auxiliary function $R : \mathcal{B} \to \mathbb{R}$ via

$$R(z) = \langle A^*[f'(A\phi) - f'(A\phi')] + b' - b, z - \phi' \rangle + \epsilon \|z - \phi'\|^2.$$

Clearly $R(\phi') = 0$ and R is a *convex* function in z. Taking derivatives of $R(z)$ one can check that its minimum is attained at ϕ:

$$\partial_z R(z) = A^* f'(A\phi) - b - A^* f'(A\phi') + b' + 2\epsilon(z - \phi')$$

For $z = \phi$, this equals $\partial_\phi L(\phi, b) - \partial_{\phi'} L(\phi', b')$ which vanishes due to optimality in L. From this, we have

$$0 \geq \langle A^*[f'(A\phi) - f'(A\phi')] + b' - b, \phi - \phi' \rangle + \epsilon \|\phi - \phi'\|^2.$$
$$\geq \langle b' - b, \phi - \phi' \rangle + \epsilon \|\phi - \phi'\|^2 \geq -\|b - b'\| \|\phi - \phi'\| + \epsilon \|\phi - \phi'\|^2$$

Here the first inequality follows from $R(\phi') > R(\phi)$, the second follows from the fact that for convex functions $\langle g'(a) - g'(b), a - b \rangle \geq 0$, and the third inequality is an application of Cauchy-Schwartz. Solving for $\|\phi - \phi'\|$ proves the claim.   ∎

4.3   Risk Bounds

We are now in a position to combine concentration and stability results derived in the previous two sections into risk bounds for the values of divergences.

Theorem 19. *Assume that $b = \frac{1}{m} \sum_{i=1}^{m} \psi(t)$ and let $b^* := \mathbf{E}_p [\psi(t)]$. Moreover, denote by ϕ, ϕ^* the minimizers of $L(\cdot, b)$ and $L(\cdot, b^*)$ respectively. Finally assume that $\|\psi(t)\| \leq R$ for all $t \in \mathcal{T}$. Then*

$$\|\phi\| [2R_m(\mathcal{F}, p) + \epsilon] \leq L(\phi^*, b^*) - L(\phi, b) \leq \|\phi^*\| [2R_m(\mathcal{F}, p) + \epsilon] \tag{15}$$

where each inequality holds with probability $1 - \exp\left(-\frac{\epsilon^2 m}{R^2}\right)$.

Proof. Combination of Theorem 16 and (12) of Theorem 17. ∎

Note that this is considerably stronger than a corresponding result of [10], as it applies to arbitrary linear classes and divergences as opposed to ℓ_∞ spaces and Shannon entropy. A stronger version of the above bounds can be obtained easily for RKHSs, where the Rademacher average is replaced by a variance bound.

If we want to bound the performance of estimate x with respect to the actual loss $L(\cdot, b^*)$ rather than $L(\cdot, b)$ we need to invoke (11). In other words, we show that on the true statistics the loss of the estimated parameter cannot be much larger than the loss of true parameter.

Theorem 20. *With the same assumptions as Theorem 19 we have with probability at least $1 - \exp\left(-\frac{\epsilon^2 m}{R^2}\right)$*

$$L(\phi, b^*) - L(\phi^*, b^*) \leq 2 \left(\frac{C}{k\epsilon}\right)^{\frac{1}{k-1}} (2\mathcal{R}_n(\mathcal{F}_{\mathcal{B}}) + \epsilon). \tag{16}$$

Here C is the Lipschitz constant of $f(A\cdot)$. If $\mathcal{B}$ is an RKHS we have with probability at least $1 - \exp\left(-\frac{\epsilon^2 m}{50R^4}\right)$ for $m \geq 2$

$$L(\phi, b^*) - L(\phi^*, b^*) \leq \frac{1}{\epsilon} \left[\frac{1}{m} \mathbf{E}_p [k(t,t) - k(t,t')] + \epsilon\right]. \tag{17}$$

Proof. To prove (16) we use (11) which bounds

$$L(\phi, b^*) - L(\phi^*, b^*) \leq \|b^* - b\|_{\mathcal{B}} (\|\phi\|_{\mathcal{B}^*} + \|\phi^*\|_{\mathcal{B}^*}).$$

The first factor is bounded by (9) of Theorem 16. The second term is bounded via Lemma 7. A much tighter bound is available for RKHS. Using (11) in conjunction with (14) of Lemma (18) yields

$$L(\phi, b^*) - L(\phi^*, b^*) \leq \frac{1}{\epsilon} \|b - b^*\|^2$$

We establish a bound for $\|b - b^*\|^2$ by a standard approach, i.e. by computing the mean and then bounding the tail of the random variable. By construction

$$\mathbf{E}\left[\|b - b^*\|^2\right] = \mathbf{E}\left[\left\|\frac{1}{m} \sum_{i=1}^{m} \psi(t_i) - \mathbf{E}[\psi(t)]\right\|^2\right] = \frac{1}{m} \mathbf{E}\left[\|\psi(t) - \mathbf{E}[\psi(t')]\|^2\right]$$

Using $k(t, t') = \langle \psi(t), \psi(t') \rangle$ yields the mean term. To bound the tail we use McDiarmid's bound. For this, we need to check by how much $\|b - b^*\|^2$ changes if we replace one term $\psi(t_i)$ by an arbitrary $\psi(t'_i)$ for some $t'_i \in \mathcal{T}$. We have

$$\left\| b + \tfrac{1}{m}(\psi(t'_i) - \psi(t_i)) - b^* \right\|^2 - \left\| b - b^* \right\|^2$$
$$\leq \tfrac{1}{m} \left\| \psi(t'_i) - \psi(t_i) \right\| \left\| 2(b + b^*) + \tfrac{1}{m}(\psi(t'_i) - \psi(t_i)) \right\| \leq 10R^2/m$$

for $m \geq 2$. Plugging this into McDiarmid's bound yields that $\|b - b^*\|^2$ deviates from its expectation by more than ϵ with probability less than $\exp\left(-\frac{m\epsilon^2}{50R^4}\right)$. ∎

Theorem 20 also holds for $\mathcal{L}^B_\psi$. Since the KL divergence is an example of Csiszár's divergence, using this bound allows us to achieve stability results for MAP estimates immediately.

5 Optimization Algorithm and Convergence Properties

In the most general form, our primal, $f(x)$ subject to $\|Ax - b\|_B \leq \epsilon$, is an abstract program, where both the constraint space $\mathcal{B}$ and the domain $\mathcal{X}$ may be infinite, i.e. both the primal and the dual are infinite programs. Thus, except for special cases finding an optimal solution in polynomial time may be impossible. A sparse greedy approximation algorithm proposed by Zhang [26] is an efficient way of solving this class of problems efficiently, providing good rates of convergence (in contrast, the question of a convergence *rate* remains open in [10]).

Algorithm 1. Sequential greedy approximation [26]

1: **input:** sample of size m, statistics b, base function class $\mathcal{B}^*_{\text{base}}$, approximation ϵ, number of iterations K, and radius of the space of solutions R
2: Set $\phi = 0$.
3: **for** $k = 1, \ldots, K$ **do**
4:     Find $(\hat{\imath}, \hat{\lambda})$ such that for $e_i \in \mathcal{B}^*_{\text{base}}$ and $\lambda \in [0, 1]$ the following is approximately minimized:

$$L((1 - \lambda)\phi + \lambda R e_i, b)$$

5:     Update $\phi \leftarrow (1 - \hat{\lambda})\phi + \hat{\lambda} R e_{\hat{\imath}}$
6: **end for**

Algorithm 1 requires that we have an efficient way of updating ϕ by drawing from a base class of parameters $\mathcal{B}^*_{\text{base}}$ which "generates" the space of parameters $\mathcal{B}^*$. In other words, we require that $\text{span}\mathcal{B}^*_{\text{base}} = \mathcal{B}^*$. For instance we could pick $\mathcal{B}^*_{\text{base}}$ to be the set of vertices of the unit ball in $\mathcal{B}^*$.

Since Step 4 in Algorithm 1 only needs to be approximate. In other words, we only need to find $(\hat{\imath}, \hat{\lambda})$ such that the so-found solution is within δ_k of the optimal solution, as long as $\delta_k \to 0$ for $k \to \infty$.

Note the dependency on R: one needs to modify the setting of [26] to make it applicable to arbitrary convex sets. As long as R is chosen sufficiently large such as to include the optimal solution the conditions of [26] apply.

Theorem 21 ([26, Theorem II.1]). *Let M_β be an upper bound on $L''(\phi)$. If the optimization is performed exactly at each step (i.e. $\delta_k = 0$ for all k) we have*

$$L(\phi^k, b) - L(\hat{\phi}, b) \le 2M/(k+2) \tag{18}$$

where $\hat{\phi}$ is the true minimizer of $L(\phi, b)$.

This has an interesting implication when considering the fact that deviations between the optimal solution of $L(\phi^*, b^*)$ for the true parameter b^* and the solution achieved via $L(\phi, b)$ are $O(1/\sqrt{m})$, as discussed in Section 4.3. It is essentially pointless to find a better solution than within $O(1/\sqrt{m})$ for a sample of size m. Hence we have the following corollary:

Corollary 22. *Zhang's algorithm only needs $O(\sqrt{m})$ steps for a set of observations of size m to obtain almost optimal performance.*

When the dual is a finite program, it is possible to achieve linear convergence rates (where the difference in (18) goes to 0 exponentially fast in k) [19]. The obvious special case when the dual is a finite dimensional optimization problem is when the index set I over the statistics is finite.

Let us now consider $\mathcal{X}$ itself is a finite dimensional problem, for example, when we want to estimate the conditional density $p(y|x)$ of a classification task wrt inequality constraints in a Banach space. In that case, our primal is a semi-infinite program (SIP), i.e. optimization over a finite dimensional vector space wrt infinite number of constraints. Then, using a Helly-type theorem [4], one can show that the SIP can be reduced to a finite program (i.e. with finite number of constraints) and we immediately get a finite dual program. This is a generalization of a family of results commonly referred to as Representer Theorems.

6   Conclusion

We presented a generalized framework of convex duality that allows us to unify a large class of existing inference algorithms via divergence minimization, to provide statistical bounds for the estimates, and to provide a practical algorithm.

We expect the following set of problems to be a fertile ground for future research. Alternative divergence measures, such as Tsallis or Sharma-Mittal entropy and combining these with various constraint relaxation schemes can lead to new statistical inference techniques. The generality of Banach spaces allow us to define useful regularization schemes. An interesting question is what becomes of structured estimation methods when applied in conjunction with Zhang's algorithm. Likewise, the connection between Boosting and an approximate solution of inverse problems has not been explored yet. Finally, it may be possible to minimize the divergence directly in transductive settings.

Acknowlegements. We thank Tim Sears, Thomas Gaertner and Vishy Vishwanathan. National ICT Australia is funded through the Australian Government's *Baking Australia's Ability* initiative, in part through the Australian Research Council. This work was supported by the PASCAL Network of Excellence.

References

1. Y. Altun, T. Hofmann, and A. J. Smola. Exponential families for conditional random fields. In *Uncertainty in Artificial Intelligence UAI*, pages 2–9, 2004.
2. K. Borgwardt, A. Gretton, and A.J. Smola. Kernel discrepancy estimation. Technical report, NICTA, Canberra, 2006.
3. J. Borwein and Q.J. Zhu. *Techniques of Variational Analysis*. Springer, 2005.
4. J. M. Borwein. Semi-infinite programming: How special is it? In *A. V. Fiacco and K.O. Kortanek, ed., Semi-Infinite Programming and Applications*. Springer, 1983.
5. O. Bousquet, S. Boucheron, and G. Lugosi. Theory of classification: a survey of recent advances. *ESAIM: Probability and Statistics*, 2004. submitted.
6. O. Bousquet and A. Elisseeff. Stability and generalization. *JMLR*, 2:499–526, 2002.
7. S. Chen and R. Rosenfeld. A Gaussian prior for smoothing maximum entropy models. Technical Report CMUCS-99-108, Carnegie Mellon University, 1999.
8. M. Collins, R. E. Schapire, and Y. Singer. Logistic regression, adaboost and bregman distances. In *COLT'00*, pages 158–169, 2000.
9. C. Cortes and V. Vapnik. Support vector networks. *Machine Learning*, 20:273–297, 1995.
10. M. Dudik, S. Phillips, and R. E. Schapire. Performance guarantees for regularized maximum entropy density estimation. In *Proceedings of COLT'04*, 2004.
11. M. Dudik and R.E. Schapire. Maximum entropy distribution estimation with generalized regularization. In *COLT*, 2006.
12. M. P. Friedlander and M. R. Gupta. On minimizing distortion and relative entropy. *IEEE Transactions on Information Theory*, 52(1), 2006.
13. J. Kivinen and M. Warmuth. Boosting as entropy projection. In *COLT'99*, 1999.
14. J. Lafferty. Additive models, boosting, and inference for generalized divergences. In *COLT '99*, pages 125–133, New York, NY, USA, 1999. ACM Press.
15. Q. V. Le, A. J. Smola, and S. Canu. Heteroscedastic gaussian process regression. In *International Conference on Machine Learning ICML 2005*, 2005.
16. V.A. Morozov. *Methods for solving incorrectly posed problems*. Springer, 1984.
17. R. Neal. Priors for infinite networks. Technical report, U. Toronto, 1994.
18. I. Nemenman and W. Bialek. Occam factors and model independent bayesian learning of continuous distributions. *Physical Review E*, 65(2):6137, 2002.
19. G. Rätsch, S. Mika, and M.K. Warmuth. On the convergence of leveraging. In *Advances in Neural Information Processing Systems (NIPS)*, 2002.
20. R.T. Rockafellar. *Convex Analysis*. Princeton University Press, 1970.
21. D. L. Ruderman and W. Bialek. Statistics of natural images: Scaling in the woods. *Phys Rev. Letters*, 1994.
22. B. Schölkopf and A. Smola. *Learning with Kernels*. MIT Press, 2002.
23. J. Shawe-Taylor and N. Cristianini. *Kernel Methods for Pattern Analysis*. Cambridge University Press, 2004.
24. A. N. Thikhonov and V. Y. Arsenin. *Solutions of Ill-Posed Problems*. Wiley, 1977.
25. M. J. Wainwright and M. I. Jordan. Graphical models, exponential families, and variational inference. Technical Report 649, UC Berkeley, September 2003.
26. T. Zhang. Sequential greedy approximation for certain convex optimization problems. *IEEE Transactions on Information Theory*, 49(3):682–691, March 2003.

Mercer's Theorem, Feature Maps, and Smoothing

Ha Quang Minh[1], Partha Niyogi[1], and Yuan Yao[2]

[1] Department of Computer Science, University of Chicago
1100 East 58th St, Chicago, IL 60637, USA
[2] Department of Mathematics, University of California, Berkeley
970 Evans Hall, Berkeley, CA 94720, USA
minh,niyogi@cs.uchicago.edu, yao@math.berkeley.edu

Abstract. We study Mercer's theorem and feature maps for several positive definite kernels that are widely used in practice. The smoothing properties of these kernels will also be explored.

1 Introduction

Kernel-based methods have become increasingly popular and important in machine learning. The central idea behind the so-called "kernel trick" is that a closed form Mercer kernel allows one to efficiently solve a variety of non-linear optimization problems that arise in regression, classification, inverse problems, and the like. It is well known in the machine learning community that kernels are associated with "feature maps" and a kernel based procedure may be interpreted as mapping the data from the original input space into a potentially higher dimensional "feature space" where linear methods may then be used. One finds many accounts of this idea where the input space X is mapped by a feature map $\Phi : X \to \mathcal{H}$ (where $\mathcal{H}$ is a Hilbert space) so that for any two points $x, y \in X$, we have $K(x, y) = \langle \phi(x), \phi(y) \rangle_{\mathcal{H}}$.

Yet, while much has been written about kernels and many different kinds of kernels have been discussed in the literature, much less has been explicitly written about their associated feature maps. In general, we do not have a clear and concrete understanding of what exactly these feature maps are. Our goal in this paper is to take steps toward a better understanding of feature maps by explicitly computing them for a number of popular kernels for a variety of domains. By doing so, we hope to clarify the precise nature of feature maps in very concrete terms so that machine learning researchers may have a better feel for them.

Following are the main points and new results of our paper:

1. As we will illustrate, feature maps and feature spaces are not unique. For a given domain X and a fixed kernel K on $X \times X$, there exist in fact infinitely many feature maps associated with K. Although these maps are essentially equivalent, in a sense to be made precise in Section 4.3, there are subtleties that we wish to emphasize. For a given kernel K, the feature maps of K

G. Lugosi and H.U. Simon (Eds.): COLT 2006, LNAI 4005, pp. 154–168, 2006.

induced by Mercer's theorem depend fundamentally on the domain X, as
will be seen in the examples of Section 2. Moreover, feature maps do not
necessarily arise from Mercer's theorem, examples of which will be given in
Section 4.2. The importance of Mercer's theorem, however, goes far beyond
the feature maps that it induces: the eigenvalues and eigenfunctions associated with K play a central role in obtaining error estimates in learning
theory, see for example [8], [4]. For this reason, the determination of the
spectrum of K, which is highly nontrivial in general, is crucially important
in its own right. Theorems 2 and 3 in Section 2 give the complete spectrum
of the polynomial and Gaussian kernels on S^{n-1}, including sharp rates of
decay of their eigenvalues. Theorem 4 gives the eigenfunctions and a recursive formula for the computation of eigenvalues of the polynomial kernel on
the hypercube $\{-1, 1\}^n$.

2. One domain that we particularly focus on is the unit sphere S^{n-1} in $\mathbb{R}^n$,
for several reasons. First, it is a special example of a compact Riemannian
manifold and the problem of learning on manifolds has attracted attention
recently, see for example [2], [3]. Second, its symmetric and homogeneous
nature allows us to obtain complete and explicit results in many cases. We
believe that S^{n-1} together with kernels defined on it is a fruitful source
of examples and counterexamples for theoretical analysis of kernel-based
learning. We will point out that intuitions based on low dimensions such as
$n = 2$ in general do not carry over to higher dimensions - Theorem 5 in
Section 3 gives an important example along this line. We will also consider
the unit ball B^n, the hypercube $\{-1, 1\}^n$, and $\mathbb{R}^n$ itself.

3. We will also try to understand the smoothness property of kernels on S^{n-1}.
In particular, we will show that the polynomial and Gaussian kernels define
Hilbert spaces of functions whose norms may be interpreted as smoothness
functionals, similar to those of splines on S^{n-1}. We will obtain precise and
sharp results on this question in the paper. This is the content of Section 5.
The smoothness implications allow us to better understand the applicability
of such kernels in solving smoothing problems.

Notation. For $X \subset \mathbb{R}^n$ and μ a Borel measure on X, $L^2_\mu(X) = \{f : X \to \mathbb{C} : \int_X |f(x)|^2 d\mu(x) < \infty\}$. We will also use $L^2(X)$ for $L^2_\mu(X)$ and dx for $d\mu(x)$ if
μ is the Lebesgue measure on X. The surface area of the unit sphere S^{n-1} is
denoted by $|S^{n-1}| = \frac{2\pi^{\frac{n}{2}}}{\Gamma(\frac{n}{2})}$.

2 Mercer's Theorem

One of the fundamental mathematical results underlying learning theory with
kernels is Mercer's theorem. Let X be a closed subset of $\mathbb{R}^n$, $n \in \mathbb{N}$, μ a Borel
measure on X, and $K : X \times X \to \mathbb{R}$ a symmetric function satisfying: for any
finite set of points $\{x_i\}_{i=1}^N$ in X and real numbers $\{a_i\}_{i=1}^N$

$$\sum_{i,j=1}^N a_i a_j K(x_i, x_j) \geq 0 \tag{1}$$

K is said to be a positive definite kernel on X. Assume further that

$$\int_X \int_X K(x,t)^2 d\mu(x) d\mu(t) < \infty \qquad (2)$$

Consider the induced integral operator $L_K : L^2_\mu(X) \to L^2_\mu(X)$ defined by

$$L_K f(x) = \int_X K(x,t) f(t) d\mu(t) \qquad (3)$$

This is a self-adjoint, positive, compact operator with a countable system of non-negative eigenvalues $\{\lambda_k\}_{k=1}^\infty$ satisfying $\sum_{k=1}^\infty \lambda_k^2 < \infty$. L_K is said to be Hilbert-Schmidt and the corresponding $L^2_\mu(X)$-normalized eigenfunctions $\{\phi_k\}_{k=1}^\infty$ form an orthonormal basis of $L^2_\mu(X)$. We recall that a Borel measure μ on X is said to be strictly positive if the measure of every nonempty open subset in X is positive, an example being the Lebesgue measure in $\mathbb{R}^n$.

Theorem 1 (Mercer). *Let $X \subset \mathbb{R}^n$ be closed, μ a strictly positive Borel measure on X, K a continuous function on $X \times X$ satisfying (1) and (2). Then*

$$K(x,t) = \sum_{k=1}^\infty \lambda_k \phi_k(x) \phi_k(t) \qquad (4)$$

where the series converges absolutely for each pair $(x,t) \in X \times X$ and uniformly on each compact subset of X.

Mercer's theorem still holds if X is a finite set $\{x_i\}$, such as $X = \{-1,1\}^n$, K is pointwise-defined positive definite and $\mu(x_i) > 0$ for each i.

2.1   Examples on the Sphere S^{n-1}

We will give explicit examples of the eigenvalues and eigenfunctions in Mercer's theorem on the unit sphere S^{n-1} for the polynomial and Gaussian kernels. We need the concept of spherical harmonics, a modern and authoritative account of which is [6]. Some of the material below was first reported in the kernel learning literature in [9], where the eigenvalues for the polynomial kernels with $n = 3$, were computed. In this section, we will carry out computations for a general $n \in \mathbb{N}$, $n \geq 2$.

Definition 1 (Spherical Harmonics). *Let $\Delta_n = -\left[\frac{\partial^2}{\partial x_1^2} + \ldots + \frac{\partial^2}{\partial x_n^2} \right]$ denote the Laplacian operator on $\mathbb{R}^n$. A homogeneous polynomial of degree k in $\mathbb{R}^n$ whose Laplacian vanishes is called a homogeneous harmonic of order k. Let $\mathcal{Y}_k(n)$ denote the subspace of all homogeneous harmonics of order k on the unit sphere S^{n-1} in $\mathbb{R}^n$. The functions in $\mathcal{Y}_k(n)$ are called spherical harmonics of order k. We will denote by $\{Y_{k,j}(n;x)\}_{j=1}^{N(n,k)}$ any fixed orthonormal basis for $\mathcal{Y}_k(n)$ where $N(n,k) = \dim \mathcal{Y}_k(n) = \frac{(2k+n-2)(k+n-3)!}{k!(n-2)!}$, $k \geq 0$.*

Theorem 2. *Let* $X = S^{n-1}$, $n \in \mathbb{N}$, $n \geq 2$. *Let* μ *be the uniform probability distribution on* S^{n-1}. *For* $K(x,t) = \exp(-\frac{\|x-t\|^2}{\sigma^2})$, $\sigma > 0$

$$\lambda_k = e^{-2/\sigma^2}\sigma^{n-2}I_{k+n/2-1}(\frac{2}{\sigma^2})\Gamma(\frac{n}{2}) \tag{5}$$

for all $k \in \mathbb{N} \cup \{0\}$, *where* I *denotes the modified Bessel function of the first kind, defined below. Each* λ_k *occurs with multiplicity* $N(n,k)$ *with the corresponding eigenfunctions being spherical harmonics of order* k *on* S^{n-1}. *The* λ_k's *are decreasing if* $\sigma \geq (\frac{2}{n})^{1/2}$. *Furthermore*

$$(\frac{2e}{\sigma^2})^k \frac{A_1}{(2k+n-2)^{k+\frac{n-1}{2}}} < \lambda_k < (\frac{2e}{\sigma^2})^k \frac{A_2}{(2k+n-2)^{k+\frac{n-1}{2}}} \tag{6}$$

for A_1, A_2 *depending on* σ *and* n *given below.*

Remark 1. $A_1 = e^{-2/\sigma^2-1/12}\frac{1}{\sqrt{\pi}}(2e)^{\frac{n}{2}-1}\Gamma(\frac{n}{2})$, $A_2 = e^{-2/\sigma^2+1/\sigma^4}\frac{1}{\sqrt{\pi}}(2e)^{\frac{n}{2}-1}\Gamma(\frac{n}{2})$. *For* $\nu, z \in \mathbb{C}$, $I_\nu(z) = \sum_{j=0}^{\infty}\frac{1}{j!\Gamma(\nu+j+1)}(\frac{z}{2})^{\nu+2j}$.

Theorem 3. *Let* $X = S^{n-1}$, $n \in \mathbb{N}$, $n \geq 2$, *and* $d \in \mathbb{N}$. *Let* μ *be the uniform probability distribution on* S^{n-1}. *For* $K(x,t) = (1 + \langle x,t \rangle)^d$, *the nonzero eigenvalues of* $L_K : L^2_\mu(X) \to L^2_\mu(X)$ *are*

$$\lambda_k = 2^{d+n-2}\frac{d!}{(d-k)!}\frac{\Gamma(d+\frac{n-1}{2})\Gamma(\frac{n}{2})}{\sqrt{\pi}\Gamma(d+k+n-1)} \tag{7}$$

for $0 \leq k \leq d$. *Each* λ_k *occurs with multiplicity* $N(n,k)$, *with the corresponding eigenfunctions being spherical harmonics of order* k *on* S^{n-1}. *Furthermore, the* λ_k's *form a decreasing sequence and*

$$\frac{B_1}{(k+d+n-2)^{2d+n-\frac{3}{2}}} < \lambda_k < \frac{B_2}{(k+d+n-2)^{d+n-\frac{3}{2}}} \tag{8}$$

where $0 \leq k \leq d$, *for* B_1, B_2 *depending on* d, n *given below.*

Remark 2. $B_1 = e^d(2e)^{d+n-2}d!\frac{\Gamma(d+\frac{n-1}{2})\Gamma(\frac{n}{2})}{2\pi\sqrt{\pi}e^{1/6}d^{d+\frac{1}{2}}}$, $B_2 = e^d(2e)^{d+n-2}d!\frac{\Gamma(d+\frac{n-1}{2})\Gamma(\frac{n}{2})}{\sqrt{2\pi}}$.

2.2   Example on the Hypercube $\{-1,1\}^n$

We will now give an example with the hypercube $\{-1,1\}^n$. Let $\mathcal{M}_k = \{\alpha = (\alpha_i)_{i=1}^n, \alpha_i \in \{0,1\}, |\alpha| = \alpha_1 + \cdots + \alpha_n = k\}$, then the set $\{x^\alpha\}_{\alpha \in \mathcal{M}_k, 0 \leq k \leq n}$, consists of multilinear monomials $\{1, x_1, x_1x_2, \ldots, x_1 \ldots x_n\}$.

Theorem 4. *Let* $X = \{-1,1\}^n$. *Let* $d \in \mathbb{N}$, $d \leq n$ *be fixed. Let* $K(x,t) = (1 + \langle x,t \rangle)^d$ *on* $X \times X$. *Let* μ *be the uniform distribution on* X, *then the nonzero eigenvalues* λ_k^d's *of* $L_K : L^2_\mu(X) \to L^2_\mu(X)$ *satisfy*

$$\lambda_k^{d+1} = k\lambda_{k-1}^d + \lambda_k^d + (n-k)\lambda_{k+1}^d \tag{9}$$

$$\lambda_0^d \geq \lambda_1^d \geq \ldots \geq \lambda_{d-1}^d = \lambda_d^d = d! \tag{10}$$

and $\lambda_k^d = 0$ for $k > d$. The corresponding $L_\mu^2(X)$-normalized eigenfunctions for each λ_k are $\{x^\alpha\}_{\alpha \in M_k}$.

Example 1 (d = 2). The recurrence relation (9) is nonlinear in two indexes and hence a closed analytic expression for λ_k^d is hard to find for large d. It is straightforward, however, to write a computer program for computing λ_k^d. For $d = 2$

$$\lambda_0^2 = n+1 \quad \lambda_1^2 = 2 \quad \lambda_2^2 = 2$$

with corresponding eigenfunctions $1, \{x_1, \ldots, x_n\}$, and $\{x_1 x_2, x_1 x_3, \ldots, x_{n-1} x_n\}$, respectively.

2.3   Example on the Unit Ball B^n

Except for the homogeneous polynomial kernel $K(x,t) = \langle x,t \rangle^d$, the computation of the spectrum of L_K on the unit ball B^n is much more difficult analytically than that on S^{n-1}. For $K(x,t) = (1 + \langle x,t \rangle)^d$ and small values of d, it is still possible, however, to obtain explicit answers.

Example 2 ($X = B^n$, $K(x,t) = (1 + \langle x,t \rangle)^2$). Let μ be the uniform measure on B^n. The eigenspace spanned by $\{x_1, \ldots, x_n\}$ corresponds to the eigenvalue $\lambda_1 = \frac{2}{(n+2)}$. The eigenspace spanned by $\{\|x\|^2 Y_{2,j}(n; \frac{x}{\|x\|})\}_{j=1}^{N(n,2)}$ corresponds to the eigenvalue $\lambda_2 = \frac{2}{(n+2)(n+4)}$. The eigenvalues that correspond to $span\{1, \|x\|^2\}$ are

$$\lambda_{0,1} = \frac{(n+2)(n+5) + \sqrt{D}}{2(n+2)(n+4)} \quad \lambda_{0,2} = \frac{(n+2)(n+5) - \sqrt{D}}{2(n+2)(n+4)}$$

where $D = (n+2)^2(n+5)^2 - 16(n+4)$.

3   Unboundedness of Normalized Eigenfunctions

It is known that the L_μ^2-normalized eigenfunctions $\{\phi_k\}$ are generally unbounded, that is in general

$$\sup_{k \in \mathbb{N}} \|\phi_k\|_\infty = \infty$$

This was first pointed out by Smale, with the first counterexample given in [14]. This phenomenon is very common, however, as the following result shows.

Theorem 5. *Let $X = S^{n-1}$, $n \geq 3$. Let μ be the Lebesgue measure on S^{n-1}. Let $f : [-1,1] \to \mathbb{R}$ be a continuous function, giving rise to a Mercer kernel $K(x,t) = f(\langle x,t \rangle)$ on $S^{n-1} \times S^{n-1}$. If infinitely many of the eigenvalues of $L_K : L_\mu^2(S^{n-1}) \to L_\mu^2(S^{n-1})$ are nonzero, then for the set of corresponding L_μ^2-normalized eigenfunctions $\{\phi_k\}_{k=1}^\infty$*

$$\sup_{k \in \mathbb{N}} \|\phi_k\|_\infty = \infty \tag{11}$$

Remark 3. This is in sharp contrast with the case $n = 2$, where we will show that

$$\sup_k ||\phi_k||_\infty \leq \frac{1}{\sqrt{\pi}}$$

with the supremum attained on the functions $\{\frac{\cos k\theta}{\sqrt{\pi}}, \frac{\sin k\theta}{\sqrt{\pi}}\}_{k \in \mathbb{N}}$. Theorem 5 applies in particular to the Gaussian kernel $K(x,t) = \exp(-\frac{||x-t||^2}{\sigma^2})$. Hence care needs to be taken in applying analysis that requires $C_K = \sup_k ||\phi_k||_\infty < \infty$, for example [5].

4   Feature Maps

4.1   Examples of Feature Maps Via Mercer's Theorem

A natural feature map that arises immediately from Mercer's theorem is

$$\Phi_\mu : X \to \ell^2 \quad \Phi_\mu(x) = (\sqrt{\lambda_k}\phi_k(x))_{k=1}^\infty \tag{12}$$

where if only $N < \infty$ of the eigenvalues are strictly positive, then $\Phi_\mu : X \to \mathbb{R}^N$. This is the map that is often covered in the machine learning literature.

Example 3 ($n = d = 2, X = S^{n-1}$). Theorem 3 gives the eigenvalues $(3\pi, 2\pi, \frac{\pi}{2})$, with eigenfunctions $(\frac{1}{\sqrt{2\pi}}, \frac{x_1}{\sqrt{\pi}}, \frac{x_2}{\sqrt{\pi}}, \frac{2x_1x_2}{\sqrt{\pi}}, \frac{x_1^2-x_2^2}{\sqrt{\pi}}) = (\frac{1}{\sqrt{2\pi}}, \frac{\cos\theta}{\sqrt{\pi}}, \frac{\sin\theta}{\sqrt{\pi}}, \frac{\sin 2\theta}{\sqrt{\pi}}, \frac{\cos 2\theta}{\sqrt{\pi}})$, where $x_1 = \cos\theta$, $x_2 = \sin\theta$, giving rise to the feature map

$$\Phi_\mu(x) = (\sqrt{\frac{3}{2}}, \sqrt{2}x_1, \sqrt{2}x_2, \sqrt{2}x_1x_2, \frac{x_1^2 - x_2^2}{\sqrt{2}})$$

Example 4 ($n = d = 2$, $X = \{-1,1\}^2$). Theorem 4 gives

$$\Phi_\mu(x) = (\sqrt{3}, \sqrt{2}x_1, \sqrt{2}x_2, \sqrt{2}x_1x_2)$$

Observation 1. *(i) As our notation suggests, Φ_μ depends on the particular measure μ that is in the definition of the operator L_K and thus is not unique. Each measure μ gives rise to a different system of eigenvalues and eigenfunctions $(\lambda_k, \phi_k)_{k=1}^\infty$ and therefore a different Φ_μ.*
(ii) In Theorem 3 and 2, the multiplicity of the λ_k's means that for each choice of orthonormal bases of the space $\mathcal{Y}_k(n)$ of spherical harmonics of order k, there is a different feature map. Thus are infinitely many feature maps arising from the uniform probability distribution on S^{n-1} alone.

4.2   Examples of Feature Maps Not Via Mercer's Theorem

Feature maps do not necessarily arise from Mercer's theorem. Consider any set X and any pointwise-defined, positive definite kernel K on $X \times X$. For each $x \in X$, let $K_x : X \to \mathbb{R}$ be defined by $K_x(t) = K(x,t)$ and

$$\mathcal{H}_K = \overline{\text{span}}\{K_x : x \in X\} \tag{13}$$

be the Reproducing Kernel Hilbert Space (RKHS) induced by K, with the inner product $\langle K_x, K_t \rangle_K = K(x, t)$, see [1]. The following feature map is then immediate:

$$\Phi_K : X \to \mathcal{H}_K \quad \Phi_K(x) = K_x \tag{14}$$

In this section we discuss, via examples, two other methods for obtaining feature maps. Let $X \subset \mathbb{R}^n$ be any subset. Consider the Gaussian kernel $K(x, t) = \exp(-\frac{||x-t||^2}{\sigma^2})$ on $X \times X$, which admits the following expansion

$$K(x, t) = \exp(-\frac{||x - t||^2}{\sigma^2}) = e^{-\frac{||x||^2}{\sigma^2}} e^{-\frac{||t||^2}{\sigma^2}} \sum_{k=0}^{\infty} \frac{(2/\sigma^2)^k}{k!} \sum_{|\alpha|=k} C_\alpha^k x^\alpha t^\alpha \tag{15}$$

where $C_\alpha^k = \frac{k!}{(\alpha_1)!\dots(\alpha_n)!}$, which implies the feature map: $\Phi_g : X \to \ell^2$ where

$$\Phi_g(x) = e^{-\frac{||x||^2}{\sigma^2}} (\sqrt{\frac{(2/\sigma^2)^k C_\alpha^k}{k!}} x^\alpha)_{|\alpha|=k, k=0}^{\infty}$$

Remark 4. The standard polynomial feature maps in machine learning, see for example ([7], page 28), are obtained exactly in the same way.

Consider next a special class of kernels that is widely used in practice, called **convolution kernels**. We recall that for a function $f \in L^1(\mathbb{R}^n)$, its Fourier transform is defined to be

$$\hat{f}(\xi) = \int_{\mathbb{R}^n} f(x) e^{-i\langle \xi, x \rangle} dx$$

By Fourier transform computation, it may be shown that if $\mu : \mathbb{R}^n \to \mathbb{R}$ is even, nonnegative, such that $\mu, \sqrt{\mu} \in L^1(\mathbb{R}^n)$, then the kernel $K : \mathbb{R}^n \times \mathbb{R}^n \to \mathbb{R}$ defined by

$$K(x, t) = \int_{\mathbb{R}^n} \mu(u) e^{-i\langle x-t, u \rangle} du \tag{16}$$

is continuous, symmetric, positive definite. Further more, for any $x, t \in \mathbb{R}^n$

$$K(x, t) = \frac{1}{(2\pi)^n} \int_{\mathbb{R}^n} \widehat{\sqrt{\mu}}(x - u) \widehat{\sqrt{\mu}}(t - u) du \tag{17}$$

The following then is a feature map of K on $X \times X$

$$\Phi_{conv} : X \to L^2(\mathbb{R}^n) \tag{18}$$

$$\Phi_{conv}(x)(u) = \frac{1}{(2\pi)^{\frac{n}{2}}} \widehat{\sqrt{\mu}}(x - u)$$

For the Gaussian kernel $e^{-\frac{||x-t||^2}{\sigma^2}} = (\frac{\sigma}{2\sqrt{\pi}})^n \int_{\mathbb{R}^n} e^{-\frac{\sigma^2||u||^2}{4}} e^{-i\langle x-t, u \rangle} du$ and

$$(\Phi_{conv}(x))(u) = (\frac{2}{\sigma\sqrt{\pi}})^{\frac{n}{2}} e^{-\frac{2||x-u||^2}{\sigma^2}}$$

One can similarly obtain feature maps for the inverse multiquadric, exponential, or B-spline kernels. The identity $e^{-\frac{||x-t||^2}{\sigma^2}} = (\frac{4}{\pi\sigma^2})^{\frac{n}{2}} \int_{\mathbb{R}^n} e^{-\frac{2||x-u||^2}{\sigma^2}} e^{-\frac{2||t-u||^2}{\sigma^2}} du$ can also be verified directly, as done in [10], where implications of the Gaussian feature map $\Phi_{conv}(x)$ above are also discussed.

4.3   Equivalence of Feature Maps

It is known ([7], page 39) that, given a set X and a pointwise-defined, symmetric, positive definite kernel K on $X \times X$, all feature maps from X into Hilbert spaces are essentially equivalent. In this section, we will make this statement precise. Let $\mathcal{H}$ be a Hilbert space and $\Phi : X \to \mathcal{H}$ be such that $\langle \Phi_x, \Phi_t \rangle_{\mathcal{H}} = K(x, t)$ for all $x, t \in X$, where $\Phi_x = \Phi(x)$. The evaluation functional $L_x : \mathcal{H} \to \mathbb{R}$ given by $L_x v = \langle v, \Phi_x \rangle_{\mathcal{H}}$, where x varies over X, defines an inclusion map

$$L_\Phi : \mathcal{H} \to \mathbb{R}^X \quad (L_\Phi v)(x) = \langle v, \Phi_x \rangle_{\mathcal{H}}$$

where $\mathbb{R}^X$ denotes the vector space of pointwise-defined, real-valued functions on X. Observe that as a vector space of functions, $\mathcal{H}_K \subset \mathbb{R}^X$.

Proposition 1. *Let $\mathcal{H}_\Phi = \overline{\mathrm{span}\{\Phi_x : x \in X\}}$, a subspace of $\mathcal{H}$. The restriction of L_Φ on $\mathcal{H}_\Phi$ is an isometric isomorphism between $\mathcal{H}_\Phi$ and $\mathcal{H}_K$.*

Proof. First, L_Φ is bijective from $\mathcal{H}_\Phi$ to the image $L_\Phi(\mathcal{H}_\Phi)$, since $\ker L_\Phi = \mathcal{H}_\Phi^\perp$. Under the map L_Φ, for each $x, t \in X$, $(L_\Phi \Phi_x)(t) = \langle \Phi_x, \Phi_t \rangle = K_x(t)$, thus $K_x \equiv L_\Phi \Phi_x$ as functions on X. This implies that $\mathrm{span}\{K_x : x \in X\}$ is isomorphic to $\mathrm{span}\{\Phi_x : x \in X\}$ as vector spaces. The isometric isomorphism of $\mathcal{H}_\Phi = \overline{\mathrm{span}\{\Phi_x : x \in X\}}$ and $\mathcal{H}_K = \overline{\mathrm{span}\{K_x : x \in X\}}$ then follows from $\langle \Phi_x, \Phi_t \rangle_{\mathcal{H}} = K(x, t) = \langle K_x, K_t \rangle_K$. This completes the proof.

Remark 5. Each choice of Φ is thus equivalent to a factorization of the map $\Phi_K : x \to K_x \in \mathcal{H}_K$, that is the following diagram is commutative

$$
\begin{array}{ccc}
x \in X & \xrightarrow{\quad \Phi_K \quad} & K_x \in \mathcal{H}_K \\
& \searrow{\scriptstyle \Phi} \qquad \nearrow{\scriptstyle L_\Phi} & \\
& \Phi_x \in \mathcal{H}_\Phi &
\end{array}
\tag{19}
$$

We will call $\Phi_K : x \to K_x \in \mathcal{H}_K$ the *canonical feature map* associated with K.

5   Smoothing Properties of Kernels on the Sphere

Having discussed feature maps, we will in this section analyze the smoothing properties of the polynomial and Gaussian kernels and compare them with those of spline kernels on the sphere S^{n-1}. In the spline smoothing problem on S^1 as described in [11], one solves the minimization problem

$$\frac{1}{m} \sum_{i=1}^m (f(x_i) - y_i)^2 + \lambda \int_0^{2\pi} (f^{(m)}(t))^2 dt \tag{20}$$

for $x_i \in [0, 2\pi]$ and $f \in W_m$, where $J_m(f) = \int_0^{2\pi} (f^{(m)}(t))^2 dt$ is the square norm of the RKHS

$$W_m^0 = \{f : f, f', \dots, f^{(m-1)} \text{ absolutely continuous}, f^{(m)} \in L^2[0, 2\pi],$$
$$f^{(j)}(0) = f^{(j)}(2\pi), j = 0, 1, \dots, m - 1\}$$

The space W_m is then the RKHS defined by

$$W_m = \{1\} \oplus W_m^0 = \{f : \|f\|_K^2 = \tfrac{1}{4\pi^2}\left(\int_0^{2\pi} f(t)dt\right)^2 + \int_0^{2\pi} (f^{(m)}(t))^2 dt < \infty\}$$

induced by a kernel K. *One particular feature of spline smoothing, on S^1, S^2, or $\mathbb{R}^n$, is that in general the RKHS W_m does not have a closed form kernel K that is efficiently computable.* This is in contrast with the RKHS that are used in kernel machine learning, all of which correspond to closed-form kernels that can be evaluated efficiently. It is not clear, however, whether the norms in these RKHS correspond to smoothness functionals. In this section, we will show that for the polynomial and Gaussian kernels on S^{n-1}, they do.

5.1   The Iterated Laplacian and Splines on the Sphere S^{n-1}

Splines on S^{n-1} for $n = 2$ and $n = 3$, as treated by Wahba [11], [12], can be generalized to any $n \geq 2$, $n \in \mathbb{N}$, via the iterated Laplacian (also called the Laplace-Beltrami operator) on S^{n-1}. The RKHS corresponding to W_m in (20) is a subspace of $L^2(S^{n-1})$ described by

$$\mathcal{H}_K = \{f : \|f\|_K^2 = \frac{1}{|S^{n-1}|^2}\left(\int_{S^{n-1}} f(x)dx\right)^2 + \int_{S^{n-1}} f(x)\Delta^m f(x)dx < \infty\}$$

The Laplacian Δ on S^{n-1} has eigenvalues $\lambda_k = k(k + n - 2)$, $k \geq 0$, with corresponding eigenfunctions $\{Y_{k,j}(n; x)\}_{j=1}^{N(n,k)}$, which form an orthonormal basis in the space $\mathcal{Y}_k(n)$ of spherical harmonics of order k. For $f \in L^2(S^{n-1})$, if we use the expansion $f = \frac{a_0}{\sqrt{|S^{n-1}|}} + \sum_{k=1}^{\infty}\sum_{j=1}^{N(n,k)} a_{k,j}Y_{k,j}(n; x)$ then the space $\mathcal{H}_K$ takes the form

$$\mathcal{H}_K = \{f \in L^2(S^{n-1}) : \|f\|_K^2 = \frac{a_0^2}{|S^{n-1}|} + \sum_{k=1}^{\infty}[k(k + n - 2)]^m \sum_{j=1}^{N(n,k)} a_{k,j}^2 < \infty\}$$

and thus the corresponding kernel is

$$K(x, t) = 1 + \sum_{k=1}^{\infty} \frac{1}{[k(k + n - 2)]^m} \sum_{j=1}^{N(n,k)} Y_{k,j}(n; x)Y_{k,j}(n; t) \qquad (21)$$

which is well-defined iff $m > \frac{n-1}{2}$. Let $P_k(n; t)$ denote the Legendre polynomial of degree k in dimension n, then (21) takes the form

$$K(x, t) = 1 + \frac{1}{|S^{n-1}|} \sum_{k=1}^{\infty} \frac{N(n, k)}{[k(k + n - 2)]^m} P_k(n; \langle x, t\rangle) \qquad (22)$$

which does not have a closed form in general - for the case $n = 3$, see [11].

Remark 6. Clearly m can be replaced by any real number $s > \frac{n-1}{2}$.

5.2   Smoothing Properties of Polynomial and Gaussian Kernels

Let ∇_{n-1}^* denote the gradient operator on S^{n-1} (also called the first-order Bel-trami operator, see [6] page 79 for a definition). Let $Y_k \in \mathcal{Y}_k(n)$, $k \geq 0$, then

$$||\nabla_{n-1}^* Y_k||_{L^2(S^{n-1})}^2 = \int_{S^{n-1}} |\nabla_{n-1}^* Y_k(x)|^2 dS^{n-1}(x) = k(k+n-2) \qquad (23)$$

This shows that spherical harmonics of higher-order are less smooth. This is particularly straightforward in the case $n = 2$ with the Fourier basis functions $\{1, \cos k\theta, \sin k\theta\}_{k \in \mathbb{N}}$ - as k increases, the functions oscillate more rapidly.

It follows that any regularization term $||f||_K^2$ in problems such as (20), where K possesses a decreasing spectrum λ_k - k corresponds to the order of the spherical harmonics - will have a smoothing effect. That is, the higher-order spherical harmonics, which are less smooth, will be penalized more. The decreasing spectrum property is true for the spline kernels, the polynomial kernel $(1 + \langle x, t \rangle)^d$, and the Gaussian kernel for $\sigma \geq (\frac{2}{n})^{1/2}$, as we showed in Theorems 2 and 3. Hence all these kernels possess smoothing properties on S^{n-1}.

Furthermore, Theorem 2 shows that for the Gaussian kernel, for all $k \geq 1$

$$(\frac{2e}{\sigma^2})^k \frac{A_1}{(2k+n-2)^{k+\frac{n-1}{2}}} < \lambda_k < (\frac{2e}{\sigma^2})^k \frac{A_2}{(2k+n-2)^{k+\frac{n-1}{2}}}$$

and Theorem 3 shows that for the polynomial kernel $(1 + \langle x, t \rangle)^d$

$$\frac{B_1}{(k+d+n-2)^{2d+n-\frac{3}{2}}} < \lambda_k < \frac{B_2}{(k+d+n-2)^{d+n-\frac{3}{2}}}$$

for $0 \leq k \leq d$. Compare these with the eigenvalues of the spline kernels

$$\lambda_k = \frac{1}{[k(k+n-2)]^m}$$

for $k \geq 1$, we see that the Gaussian kernel has the sharpest smoothing property, as can be seen from the exponential decay of the eigenvalues.

For $K(x, t) = (1 + \langle x, t \rangle)^d$, if $d > 2m - n + \frac{3}{2}$, then K has sharper smoothing property than a spline kernel of order m. Moreover, all spherical harmonics of order greater than d are filtered out, hence choosing K amounts to choosing a hypothesis space of bandlimited functions on S^{n-1}.

References

1. N. Aronszajn. Theory of Reproducing Kernels. *Transactions of the American Mathematical Society*, vol. 68, pages 337-404, 1950.
2. M. Belkin, P. Niyogi, and V. Sindwani. Manifold Regularization: a Geometric Framework for Learning from Examples. University of Chicago Computer Science Technical Report TR-2004-06, 2004, accepted for publication.

3. M. Belkin and P. Niyogi. Semi-supervised Learning on Riemannian Manifolds. *Machine Learning*, Special Issue on Clustering, vol. 56, pages 209-239, 2004.
4. E. De Vito, A. Caponnetto, and L. Rosasco. Model Selection for Regularized Least-Squares Algorithm in Learning Theory. *Foundations of Computational Mathematics*, vol. 5, no. 1, pages 59-85, 2005.
5. J. Lafferty and G. Lebanon. Diffusion Kernels on Statistical Manifolds. *Journal of Machine Learning Research*, vol. 6, pages 129-163, 2005.
6. C. Müller. *Analysis of Spherical Symmetries in Euclidean Spaces*. Applied Mathematical Sciences 129, Springer, New York, 1997.
7. B. Schölkopf and A.J. Smola. *Learning with Kernels*. The MIT Press, Cambridge, Massachusetts, 2002.
8. S. Smale and D.X. Zhou. Learning Theory Estimates via Integral Operators and Their Approximations, 2005, to appear.
9. A.J. Smola, Z.L. Ovari and R.C. Williamson. Regularization with Dot-Product Kernels. *Advances in Information Processing Systems*, 2000.
10. I. Steinwart, D. Hush, and C. Scovel. An Explicit Description of the Reproducing Kernel Hilbert Spaces of Gaussian RBF Kernels Kernels. Los Alamos National Laboratory Technical Report LA-UR-04-8274, December 2005.
11. G. Wahba. Spline Interpolation and Smoothing on the Sphere. *SIAM Journal of Scientific and Statistical Computing*, vol. 2, pages 5-16, 1981.
12. G. Wahba. *Spline Models for Observational Data*. CBMS-NSF Regional Conference Series in Applied Mathematics 59, Society for Industrial and Applied Mathematics, Philadelphia, 1990.
13. G.N. Watson. *A Treatise on the Theory of Bessel Functions*, 2nd edition, Cambridge University Press, Cambridge, England, 1944.
14. D.X. Zhou. The Covering Number in Learning Theory. *Journal of Complexity*, vol. 18, pages 739-767, 2002.

A   Proofs of Results

The proofs for results on S^{n-1} all make use of properties of spherical harmonics on S^{n-1}, which can be found in [6]. We will prove Theorem 2 (Theorem 3 is similar) and Theorem 5.

A.1   Proof of Theorem 2

Let $f : [-1, 1] \to \mathbb{R}$ be a continuous function. Let $Y_k \in \mathcal{Y}_k(n)$ for $k \geq 0$. Then the Funk-Hecke formula ([6], page 30) states that for any $x \in S^{n-1}$:

$$\int_{S^{n-1}} f(\langle x, t \rangle) Y_k(t) dS^{n-1}(t) = \lambda_k Y_k(x) \tag{24}$$

where

$$\lambda_k = |S^{n-2}| \int_{-1}^{1} f(t) P_k(n; t)(1 - t^2)^{\frac{n-3}{2}} dt \tag{25}$$

and $P_k(n; t)$ denotes the Legendre polynomial of degree k in dimension n. Since the spherical harmonics $\{\{Y_{k,j}(n; x)\}_{j=1}^{N(n,k)}\}_{k=0}^{\infty}$ form an orthonormal basis for $L^2(S^{n-1})$, an immediate consequence of the Funk-Hecke formula is that if K on

$S^{n-1} \times S^{n-1}$ is defined by $K(x,t) = f(\langle x,t \rangle)$, and μ is the Lebesgue measure on S^{n-1}, then the eigenvalues of $L_K : L^2_\mu(S^{n-1}) \to L^2_\mu(S^{n-1})$ are given precisely by (25), with the corresponding orthonormal eigenfunctions of λ_k being $\{Y_{k,j}(n;x)\}_{j=1}^{N(n,k)}$. The multiplicity of λ_k is therefore $N(n,k) = \dim(\mathcal{Y}_k(n))$.

On S^{n-1} $e^{-\frac{\|x-t\|^2}{\sigma^2}} = e^{-\frac{2}{\sigma^2}} e^{\frac{2\langle x,t \rangle}{\sigma^2}}$. Thus

$$\lambda_k = e^{-\frac{2}{\sigma^2}} |S^{n-2}| \int_{-1}^{1} e^{\frac{2t}{\sigma^2}} P_k(n;t)(1-t^2)^{\frac{n-3}{2}} dt$$

$$= e^{-\frac{2}{\sigma^2}} |S^{n-2}| \sqrt{\pi} \Gamma(\tfrac{n-1}{2})(\sigma^2)^{n/2-1} I_{k+n/2-1}(\tfrac{2}{\sigma^2}) \text{ by Lemma 1}$$

$$= e^{-2/\sigma^2} \sigma^{n-2} I_{k+n/2-1}(\tfrac{2}{\sigma^2}) \Gamma(\tfrac{n}{2}) |S^{n-1}|$$

Normalizing by setting $|S^{n-1}| = 1$ gives the required expression for λ_k as in (5).

Lemma 1. *Let* $f(t) = e^{rt}$, *then*

$$\int_{-1}^{1} f(t) P_k(n;t)(1-t^2)^{\frac{n-3}{2}} dt = \sqrt{\pi} \Gamma\left(\frac{n-1}{2}\right) \left(\frac{2}{r}\right)^{n/2-1} I_{k+n/2-1}(r) \qquad (26)$$

Proof. We apply the following which follows from ([13], page 79, formula 9)

$$\int_{-1}^{1} e^{rt}(1-t^2)^{\nu-1} dt = \sqrt{\pi} \left(\frac{2}{r}\right)^{\nu-1/2} \Gamma(\nu) I_{\nu-1/2}(r) \qquad (27)$$

and Rodrigues' rule ([6], page 23), which states that for $f \in C^k([-1,1])$

$$\int_{-1}^{1} f(t) P_k(n;t)(1-t^2)^{\frac{n-3}{2}} dt = R_k(n) \int_{-1}^{1} f^{(k)}(t)(1-t^2)^{k+\frac{n-3}{2}} dt \qquad (28)$$

where $R_k(n) = \frac{1}{2^k} \frac{\Gamma(\frac{n-1}{2})}{\Gamma(k+\frac{n-1}{2})}$. For $f(t) = e^{rt}$, we have

$$\int_{-1}^{1} e^{rt} P_k(n;t)(1-t^2)^{\frac{n-3}{2}} dt = R_k(n) r^k \int_{-1}^{1} e^{rt}(1-t^2)^{k+\frac{n-3}{2}}$$

$$= R_k(n) r^k \sqrt{\pi} \left(\tfrac{2}{r}\right)^{k+n/2-1} \Gamma(k+\tfrac{n-1}{2}) I_{k+n/2-1}(r)$$

Substituting in the values of $R_k(n)$ gives the desired answer. $\square$

Lemma 2. *The sequence* $\{\lambda_k\}_{k=0}^{\infty}$ *is decreasing if* $\sigma \geq \left(\frac{2}{n}\right)^{1/2}$.

Proof. We will first prove that $\frac{\lambda_k}{\lambda_{k+1}} > (k+n/2)\sigma^2$. We have

$$I_{k+n/2}(\tfrac{2}{\sigma^2}) = (\tfrac{1}{\sigma^2})^{k+n/2} \sum_{j=0}^{\infty} \frac{(\frac{1}{\sigma^2})^{2j}}{j! \Gamma(j+k+n/2+1)}$$

$$= (\tfrac{1}{\sigma^2})^{k+n/2} \sum_{j=0}^{\infty} \frac{(\frac{1}{\sigma^2})^{2j}}{j!(j+k+n/2)\Gamma(j+k+n/2)}$$

$$< (\tfrac{1}{\sigma^2})^{k+n/2} \frac{1}{k+n/2} \sum_{j=0}^{\infty} \frac{(\frac{1}{\sigma^2})^{2j}}{j! \Gamma(j+k+n/2)} = \frac{1}{\sigma^2(k+n/2)} I_{k+n/2-1}(\tfrac{2}{\sigma^2})$$

which implies $\frac{\lambda_k}{\lambda_{k+1}} > (k + n/2)\sigma^2$. The inequality $\frac{\lambda_k}{\lambda_{k+1}} \geq 1$ thus is satisfied if $\sigma^2(k + n/2) \geq 1$ for all $k \geq 0$. It suffices to require that it holds for $k = 0$, that is $\sigma^2 n/2 \geq 1 \iff \sigma \geq \left(\frac{2}{n}\right)^{1/2}$. $\qquad\square$

Proof (of (6)). By definition of $I_\nu(z)$, we have for $z > 0$

$$I_\nu(z) < \frac{(\frac{z}{2})^\nu}{\Gamma(\nu+1)} \sum_{j=0}^\infty \frac{(\frac{z}{2})^{2j}}{j!} = \frac{(\frac{z}{2})^\nu}{\Gamma(\nu+1)} e^{z^2/4}$$

Then for $\nu = k + \frac{n}{2} - 1$ and $z = \frac{2}{\sigma^2}$: $I_{k+\frac{n}{2}-1}(\frac{2}{\sigma^2}) < \frac{1}{\Gamma(k+\frac{n}{2})}(\frac{1}{\sigma})^{2k+n-2}e^{1/\sigma^4}$. Consider Stirling's series for $a > 0$

$$\Gamma(a+1) = \sqrt{2\pi a}\left(\frac{a}{e}\right)^a\left[1 + \frac{1}{12a} + \frac{1}{288a^2} - \frac{139}{51840a^3} + \cdots\right] \qquad (29)$$

Thus for all $a > 0$ we can write $\Gamma(a+1) = e^{A(a)}\sqrt{2\pi e}\left(\frac{a}{e}\right)^{a+\frac{1}{2}}$ where $0 < A(a) < \frac{1}{12a}$. Hence for all $k \geq 1$

$$\Gamma(k + \frac{n}{2}) = e^{A(k,n)}\sqrt{2\pi e}(\frac{k+\frac{n}{2}-1}{e})^{k+\frac{n-1}{2}} = e^{A(k,n)}\sqrt{2\pi e}(\frac{2k+n-2}{2e})^{k+\frac{n-1}{2}}$$

where $0 < A(k,n) < \frac{1}{12(k+\frac{n}{2}-1)} \leq \frac{1}{12}$. Then

$$I_{k+\frac{n}{2}-1}(\frac{2}{\sigma^2}) < \frac{1}{\sqrt{\pi}}\frac{(2e)^{k+\frac{n}{2}-1}}{(2k+n-2)^{k+\frac{n-1}{2}}}(\frac{1}{\sigma})^{2k+n-2}e^{1/\sigma^4} \text{ implying (6).}$$

The other direction is obtained similarly. $\qquad\square$

A.2   Proof of Theorem 5

We will first show an upper bound for $\|Y_k\|_\infty$, where Y_k is any $L^2(S^{n-1})$-normalized function in $\mathcal{Y}_k(n)$, then exhibit a one-dimensional subspace of functions in $\mathcal{Y}_k(n)$ that attain this upper bound. Observe that Y_k belongs to an orthonormal basis $\{Y_{k,j}(n;x)\}_{j=1}^{N(n,k)}$ of $\mathcal{Y}_k(n)$. The following highlights the crucial difference between the case $n = 2$ and $n \geq 3$.

Lemma 3. *For any $n \geq 2$, $k \geq 0$, for all $j \in \mathbb{N}$, $1 \leq j \leq N(n,k)$*

$$\|Y_{k,j}(n;.)\|_\infty \leq \sqrt{\frac{N(n,k)}{|S^{n-1}|}} \qquad (30)$$

In particular, for $n = 2$ and all $k \geq 0$: $\|Y_{k,j}(n;.)\|_\infty \leq \frac{1}{\sqrt{\pi}}$.

Proof. The Addition Theorem for spherical harmonics ([6], page 18) states that for any $x, \alpha \in S^{n-1}$

$$\sum_{j=1}^{N(n,k)} Y_{k,j}(n;x)\overline{Y_{k,j}(n;\alpha)} = \frac{N(n,k)}{|S^{n-1}|}P_k(n; \langle x, \alpha \rangle)$$

which implies that for any $x \in S^{n-1}$

$$|Y_{k,j}(n;x)|^2 \leq \frac{N(n,k)}{|S^{n-1}|}P_k(n;\langle x,x\rangle) = \frac{N(n,k)}{|S^{n-1}|}P_k(n;1) = \frac{N(n,k)}{|S^{n-1}|}$$

giving us the first result. For $n = 2$, we have $N(n,k) = 1$ for $k = 0$, $N(n,k) = 2$ for $k \geq 1$, and $|S^1| = 2\pi$, giving us the second result. $\qquad\square$

Definition 2. *Consider the group $O(n)$ of all orthogonal transformations in $\mathbb{R}^n$, that is $O(n) = \{A \in \mathbb{R}^{n\times n} : A^T A = AA^T = I\}$. A function $f : S^{n-1} \to \mathbb{R}$ is said to be **invariant** under a transformation $A \in O(n)$ if $f_A(x) = f(Ax) = f(x)$ for all $x \in S^{n-1}$. Let $\alpha \in S^{n-1}$. The **isotropy** group $J_{n,\alpha}$ is defined by $J_{n,\alpha} = \{A \in O(n) : A\alpha = \alpha\}$.*

Lemma 4. *Assume that $Y_k \in \mathcal{Y}_k(n)$ is invariant with respect to $J_{n,\alpha}$ and satisfies $\int_{S^{n-1}} |Y_k(x)|^2 dS^{n-1}(x) = 1$. Then Y_k is unique up to a multiplicative constant $C_{\alpha,n,k}$ with $|C_{\alpha,n,k}| = 1$ and*

$$||Y_k||_\infty = |Y_k(\alpha)| = \sqrt{\frac{N(n,k)}{|S^{n-1}|}} \tag{31}$$

Proof. If Y_k is invariant with respect to $J_{n,\alpha}$, then by ([6], Lemma 3, page 17), it must satisfy $Y_k(x) = Y_k(\alpha)P_k(n;\langle x,\alpha\rangle)$, showing that the subspace of $\mathcal{Y}_k(n)$ invariant with respect to $J_{n,\alpha}$ is one-dimensional. The Addition Theorem implies that for any $\alpha \in S^{n-1}$

$$\int_{S^{n-1}} |P_k(n;\langle x,\alpha\rangle)|^2 dS^{n-1}(x) = \frac{|S^{n-1}|}{N(n,k)}$$

By assumption, we then have

$$1 = \int_{S^{n-1}} |Y_k(x)|^2 dS^{n-1}(x) = |Y_k(\alpha)|^2 \int_{S^{n-1}} |P_k(n;\langle x,\alpha\rangle)|^2 dS^{n-1}(x)$$

$$= |Y_k(\alpha)|^2 \frac{|S^{n-1}|}{N(n,k)}, \text{ giving us } |Y_k(\alpha)| = \sqrt{\frac{N(n,k)}{|S^{n-1}|}}. \text{ Thus we for all } x \in S^{n-1}$$

$$|Y_k(x)| = \sqrt{\frac{N(n,k)}{|S^{n-1}|}}|P_k(n;\langle x,\alpha\rangle)| \leq \sqrt{\frac{N(n,k)}{|S^{n-1}|}}$$

by the property $|P_k(n;t)| \leq 1$ for $|t| \leq 1$. Thus $||Y_k||_\infty = \sqrt{\frac{N(n,k)}{|S^{n-1}|}}$ as desired. $\quad\square$

Proposition 2 (Orthonormal basis of $\mathcal{Y}_k(n)$ [6]). *Let $n \geq 3$. Let $e_1,\ldots,e_n$ be the canonical basis of $\mathbb{R}^n$. Let $x \in S^{n-1}$. We write $x = te_n + \sqrt{1-t^2}\begin{pmatrix} x_{(n-1)} \\ 0 \end{pmatrix}$ where $t \in [-1,1]$ and $x_{(n-1)} \in S^{n-2}$, $(x_{(n-1)},0)^T \in \text{span}\{e_1,\ldots,e_{n-1}\}$. Suppose that for $m = 0,1,\ldots,k$, the orthonormal bases $Y_{m,j}$, $j = 1,\ldots,N(n-1,m)$ of $\mathcal{Y}_m(n-1)$ are given, then an orthonormal basis for $\mathcal{Y}_k(n)$ is*

$$Y_{k,m,j}(n;x) = A_k^m(n;t)Y_{m,j}(n-1;x_{(n-1)}) : j = 1,2\ldots,N(n-1,m) \tag{32}$$

starting with the Fourier basis for $n = 2$, where

$$A_k^m(n;t) = \frac{\sqrt{2^{2-n}(2k+n-2)(k-m)!(k+n+m-3)!}}{k!\Gamma(\frac{n-1}{2})}P_k^m(n;t) \tag{33}$$

168   H.Q. Minh, P. Niyogi, and Y. Yao

Proposition 3. *Let $n \in \mathbb{N}$, $n \geq 3$. Let μ be the Lebesgue measure on S^{n-1}. For each $k \geq 0$, any orthonormal basis of the space $\mathcal{Y}_k(n)$ of spherical harmonics of order k contains an L_μ^2-normalized spherical harmonic Y_k such that*

$$||Y_k||_\infty = \sqrt{\frac{N(n,k)}{|S^{n-1}|}} = \sqrt{\frac{(2k+n-2)(k+n-3)!}{k!(n-2)!|S^{n-1}|}} \to \infty \qquad (34)$$

as $k \to \infty$, where $|S^{n-1}| = \frac{2\pi^{\frac{n}{2}}}{\Gamma(\frac{n}{2})}$ is the surface area of S^{n-1}.

Proof. Let $x = te_n + \sqrt{1-t^2}\begin{pmatrix} x_{(n-1)} \\ 0 \end{pmatrix}$, $-1 \leq t \leq 1$. For each $k \geq 0$, the orthonormal basis for $\mathcal{Y}_k(n)$ in Proposition 2 contains the function

$$Y_{k,0,1}(n;x) = A_k^0(t)Y_{0,1}(n-1;x_{(n-1)}) = A_k^0(t)\frac{1}{\sqrt{|S^{n-2}|}} \qquad (35)$$

$$Y_{k,0,1}(n;x) = \frac{1}{\Gamma(\frac{n-1}{2})}\sqrt{\frac{(2k+n-2)(k+n-3)!}{2^{n-2}k!|S^{n-2}|}}P_k(n;t) = \sqrt{\frac{N(n,k)}{|S^{n-1}|}}P_k(n;t)$$

Then $Y_{k,0,1}(n;x)$ is invariant with respect to $J_{n,\alpha}$ where $\alpha = (0,\ldots,0,1)$. Thus $Y_k = Y_{k,0,1}$ is the desired function for the current orthonormal basis. For any orthonormal basis of $\mathcal{Y}_k(n)$, the result follows by Lemma 4 and rotational symmetry on the sphere. $\qquad \square$

Proof (of Theorem 5). By the Funk-Hecke formula, all spherical harmonics of order k are eigenfunctions corresponding to the eigenvalue λ_k as given by (25). If infinitely many of the λ_k's are nonzero, then the corresponding set of $L^2(S^{n-1})$-orthonormal eigenfunctions $\{\phi_k\}$, being an orthonormal basis of $L^2(S^{n-1})$, contains a spherical harmonic Y_k satisfying (34), for infinitely many k. It follows from Proposition 3 then that $\sup_k ||\phi_k||_\infty = \infty$. $\qquad \square$

Learning Bounds for Support Vector Machines with Learned Kernels

Nathan Srebro[1] and Shai Ben-David[2]

[1] University of Toronto Department of Computer Science, Toronto ON, Canada
[2] University of Waterloo School of Computer Science, Waterloo ON, Canada
nati@cs.toronto.edu, shai@cs.uwaterloo.ca

Abstract. Consider the problem of learning a kernel for use in SVM classification. We bound the estimation error of a large margin classifier when the kernel, relative to which this margin is defined, is chosen from a family of kernels based on the training sample. For a kernel family with *pseudodimension* d_ϕ, we present a bound of $\sqrt{\tilde{\mathcal{O}}(d_\phi + 1/\gamma^2)/n}$ on the estimation error for SVMs with margin γ. This is the first bound in which the relation between the margin term and the family-of-kernels term is **additive** rather then multiplicative. The pseudodimension of families of linear combinations of base kernels is the number of base kernels. Unlike in previous (multiplicative) bounds, there is no non-negativity requirement on the coefficients of the linear combinations. We also give simple bounds on the pseudodimension for families of Gaussian kernels.

1 Introduction

In support vector machines (SVMs), as well as other similar methods, prior knowledge is represented through a *kernel function* specifying the inner products between an implicit representation of input points in some Hilbert space. A large margin linear classifier is then sought in this implicit Hilbert space. Using a "good" kernel function, appropriate for the problem, is crucial for successful learning: The kernel function essentially specifies the permitted hypothesis class, or at least which hypotheses are preferred.

In the standard SVM framework, one commits to a fixed kernel function apriori, and then searches for a large margin classifier with respect to this kernel. If it turns out that this fixed kernel in inappropriate for the data, it might be impossible to find a good large margin classifier. Instead, one can search for a data-appropriate kernel function, from some class of allowed kernels, permitting large margin classification. That is, search for both a kernel *and* a large margin classifier with respect to the kernel. In this paper we develop bounds for the sample complexity cost of allowing such kernel adaptation.

1.1 Learning the Kernel

As in standard hypothesis learning, the process of learning a kernel is guided by some family of potential kernels. A popular type of kernel family consists of

G. Lugosi and H.U. Simon (Eds.): COLT 2006, LNAI 4005, pp. 169–183, 2006.

kernels that are a linear, or convex, combinations of several base kernels [1, 2, 3][1]:

$$\mathcal{K}_{\text{linear}}(K_1, \ldots, K_k) \stackrel{\text{def}}{=} \left\{ K_{\boldsymbol{\lambda}} = \sum_{i=1}^k \lambda_i K_i \mid K_{\boldsymbol{\lambda}} \succcurlyeq 0 \text{ and } \sum_{i=1}^k \lambda_i = 1 \right\} \quad (1)$$

$$\mathcal{K}_{\text{convex}}(K_1, \ldots, K_k) \stackrel{\text{def}}{=} \left\{ K_{\boldsymbol{\lambda}} = \sum_{i=1}^k \lambda_i K_i \mid \lambda_i \geq 0 \text{ and } \sum_{i=1}^k \lambda_i = 1 \right\} \quad (2)$$

Such kernel families are useful for integrating several sources of information, each encoded in a different kernel, and are especially popular in bioninformatics applications [4, 5, 6, and others].

Another common approach is learning (or "tuning") parameters of a para-meterized kernel, such as the covariance matrix of a Gaussian kernel, based on training data [7, 8, 9, 10, and others]. This amounts to learning a kernel from a parametric family, such as the family of Gaussian kernels:

$$\mathcal{K}_{\text{Gaussian}}^{\ell} \stackrel{\text{def}}{=} \left\{ K_A : (x_1, x_2) \mapsto e^{-(x_1-x_2)'A(x_1-x_2)} \mid A \in \mathbb{R}^{\ell \times \ell}, \ A \succcurlyeq 0 \right\} \quad (3)$$

Infinite-dimensional kernel families have also been considered, either through *hyperkernels* [11] or as convex combinations of a continuum of base kernels (e.g. convex combinations of Gaussian kernels) [12, 13]. In this paper we focus on finite-dimensional kernel families, such as those defined by equations (1)–(3).

Learning the kernel matrix allows for greater flexibility in matching the target function, but this of course comes at the cost of higher estimation error, i.e. a looser bound on the expected error of the learned classifier in terms of its empirical error. Bounding this estimation gap is essential for building theoretical support for kernel learning, and this is the focus of this paper.

1.2 Learning Bounds with Learned Kernels—Previous Work

For standard SVM learning, with a fixed kernel, one can show that, with high probability, the estimation error (gap between the expected error and empirical error) of a learned classifier with margin γ is bounded by $\sqrt{\tilde{\mathcal{O}}(1/\gamma^2)/n}$ where n is the sample size and the $\tilde{\mathcal{O}}()$ notation hides logarithmic factors in its argu-ment, the sample size and the allowed failure probability. That is, the number of samples needed for learning is $\tilde{\mathcal{O}}(1/\gamma^2)$.

Lanckriet *et al.* [1] showed that when a kernel is chosen from a convex combi-nation of k base kernels, the estimation error of the learned classifier is bounded by $\sqrt{\tilde{\mathcal{O}}(k/\gamma^2)/n}$ where γ is the margin of the learned classifier under the learned kernel. Note the multiplicative interaction between the margin complexity term $1/\gamma^2$ and the number of base kernels k. Recently, Micchelli *et al.* [14] derived bounds for the family of Gaussian kernels of equation (3). The dependence of

---

[1] Lanckriet *et al.* [1] impose a bound on the trace of the Gram matrix of $K_{\boldsymbol{\lambda}}$—this is equivalent to bounding $\sum \lambda_i$ when the base kernels are normalized.

these bounds on the margin and the complexity of the kernel family is also multiplicative—the estimation error is bounded by $\sqrt{\tilde{\mathcal{O}}(C_\ell/\gamma^2)/n}$, where C_ℓ is a constant that depends on the input dimensionality ℓ.

The multiplicative interaction between the margin and the complexity measure of the kernel class is disappointing. It suggests that learning even a few kernel parameters (e.g. the coefficients λ) leads to a multiplicative increase in the required sample size. It is important to understand whether such a multiplicative increase in the number of training samples is in fact necessary.

Bousquet and Herrmann [2, Theorem 2] and Lanckriet *et al.* [1] also discuss bounds for families of convex and linear combinations of kernels that appear to be independent of the number of base kernels. However, we show in the Appendix that these bounds are meaningless: The bound on the expected error is never less than one. We are not aware of any previous work describing meaningful explicit bounds for the family of linear combinations of kernels given in equation (1).

1.3 New, Additive, Learning Bounds

In this paper, we bound the estimation error, when the kernel is chosen from a kernel family $\mathcal{K}$, by $\sqrt{\tilde{\mathcal{O}}(d_\phi + 1/\gamma^2)/n}$, where d_ϕ is the *pseudodimension* of the family $\mathcal{K}$ (Theorem 2; the pseudodimension is defined in Definition 5). This establishes that the bound on the required sample size, $\tilde{\mathcal{O}}(d_\phi + 1/\gamma^2)$ grows only **additively** with the dimensionality of the allowed kernel family (up to logarithmic factors). This is a much more reasonable price to pay for not committing to a single kernel apriori.

The pseudodimension of most kernel families matches our intuitive notion of the dimensionality of the family, and in particular:

- The pseudodimension of a family of linear, or convex, combinations of k base kernels (equations 1,2) is at most k (Lemma 7).
- The pseudodimension of the family $\mathcal{K}_{\text{Gaussian}}^\ell$ of Gaussian kernels (equation 3) for inputs $x \in \mathbb{R}^\ell$, is at most $\ell(\ell + 1)/2$ (Lemma 9). If only diagonal covariances are allowed, the pseudodimension is ℓ (Lemma 10). If the covariances (and therefore A) are constrained to be of rank at most k, the pseudodimension is at most $k\ell \log_2(22k\ell)$ (Lemma 11).

1.4 Plan of Attack

For a fixed kernel, it is well known that, with probability at least $1 - \delta$, the estimation error of all margin-γ classifiers is at most $\sqrt{\mathcal{O}(1/\gamma^2 - \log \delta)/n}$ [15]. To obtain a bound that holds for all margin-γ classifiers with respect to *any* kernel K in some *finite* kernel family $\mathcal{K}$, consider a union bound over the $|\mathcal{K}|$ events "the estimation error is large for some margin-γ classifier with respect to K" for each $K \in \mathcal{K}$. Using the above bound with δ scaled by the cardinality $|\mathcal{K}|$, the union bound ensures us that with probability at least $1 - \delta$, the estimation error will be bounded by $\sqrt{\mathcal{O}(\log |\mathcal{K}| + 1/\gamma^2 - \log \delta)/n}$ for all margin-γ classifiers with respect to any kernel in the family.

In order to extend this type of result also to infinite-cardinality families, we employ the standard notion of ϵ-nets: Roughly speaking, even though a continuous family $\mathcal{K}$ might be infinite, many kernels in it will be very similar and it will not matter which one we use. Instead of taking a union bound over all kernels in $\mathcal{K}$, we only take a union bound over "essentially different" kernels. In Section 4 we use standard results to show that the number of "essentially different" kernels in a family grows exponentially only with the dimensionality of the family, yielding an additive term (almost) proportional to the dimensionality.

As is standard in obtaining such bounds, our notion of "essentially different" refers to a specific sample and so symmetrization arguments are required in order to make the above conceptual arguments concrete. To do so cleanly and cheaply, we use an ϵ-net of *kernels* to construct an ϵ-net of *classifiers* with respect to the kernels, noting that the size of the ϵ-net increases only multiplicatively relative to the size of an ϵ-net for any one kernel (Section 3). An important component of this construction is the observation that kernels that are close as real-valued functions also yield similar classes of classifiers (Lemma 2). Using our constructed ϵ-net, we can apply standard results bounding the estimation error in terms of the log-size of ϵ-nets, without needing to invoke symmetrization arguments directly.

For the sake of simplicity and conciseness of presentation, the results in this paper are stated for binary classification using a homogeneous large-margin classifier, i.e. not allowing a bias term, and refer to zero-one error. The results can be easily extended to other loss functions and to allow a bias term.

2   Preliminaries

Notation: We use $\|v\|$ to denote the norm of a vector in an abstract Hilbert space. For a vector $v \in \mathbb{R}^n$, $\|v\|$ is the Euclidean norm of v. For a matrix $A \in \mathbb{R}^{n \times n}$, $\|A\|_2 = \max_{\|v\|=1} \|Av\|$ is the L_2 operator norm of A, $|A|_\infty = \max_{ij} |A_{ij}|$ is the l_∞ norm of A and $A \succcurlyeq 0$ indicates that A is positive semi-definite (p.s.d.) and symmetric. We use boldface $\mathbf{x}$ for samples (multisets, though we refer to them simply as sets) of points, where $|\mathbf{x}|$ is the number of points in a sample.

2.1   Support Vector Machines

Let $(x_1, y_1), \ldots, (x_n, y_n)$ be a training set of n pairs of input points $x_i \in \mathcal{X}$ and target labels $y_i \in \{\pm 1\}$. Let $\phi : \mathcal{X} \to \mathcal{H}$ be a mapping of input points into a Hilbert space $\mathcal{H}$ with inner product $\langle \cdot, \cdot \rangle$. A vector $w \in \mathcal{H}$ can be used as a predictor for points in $\mathcal{X}$, predicting the label $\text{sign}(\langle w, \phi(x) \rangle)$ for input x. Consider learning by seeking a unit-norm predictor w achieving low empirical hinge loss $\hat{h}^\gamma(w) = \frac{1}{n} \sum_{i=1}^n \max(\gamma - y_i \langle w, \phi(x_i) \rangle, 0)$, relative to a margin $\gamma > 0$.

The Representer Theorem [16, Theorem 4.2] guarantees that the predictor w minimizing $\hat{h}^\gamma(w)$ can be written as $w = \sum_{i=1}^n \alpha_i \phi(x_i)$. For such w, predictions $\langle w, \phi(x) \rangle = \sum_i \alpha_i \langle \phi(x_i), \phi(x) \rangle$ and the norm $\|w\|^2 = \sum_{ij} \alpha_i \alpha_j \langle \phi(x_i), \phi(x_j) \rangle$ depend only on inner products between mappings of input points. The Hilbert space $\mathcal{H}$ and mapping ϕ can therefore be represented implicitly by a *kernel function* $K : \mathcal{X} \times \mathcal{X} \to \mathbb{R}$ specifying these inner products: $K(\tilde{x}, x^{\bullet}) = \langle \phi(\tilde{x}), \phi(x^{\bullet}) \rangle$.

Definition 1. *A function* $K : \mathcal{X} \times \mathcal{X} \to \mathbb{R}$ *is a* **kernel function** *if for some Hilbert space* $\mathcal{H}$ *and mapping* $\phi : \mathcal{X} \to \mathcal{H}$, $K(\overset{\circ}{x}, \overset{\bullet}{x}) = \langle \phi(\overset{\circ}{x}), \phi(\overset{\bullet}{x}) \rangle$ *for all* $\overset{\circ}{x}, \overset{\bullet}{x}$.

For a set $\mathbf{x} = \{x_1, \dots, x_n\} \subset \mathcal{X}$ of points, it will be useful to consider their Gram matrix $K_{\mathbf{x}} \in \mathbb{R}^{n \times n}$, $K_{\mathbf{x}}[i,j] = K(x_i, x_j)$. A function $K : \mathcal{X} \times \mathcal{X} \to \mathbb{R}$ is a kernel function iff for any finite $\mathbf{x} \subset \mathcal{X}$, the Gram matrix $K_{\mathbf{x}}$ is p.s.d [16].

When specifying the mapping ϕ implicitly through a kernel function, it is useful to think about a predictor as a function $f : \mathcal{X} \to \mathbb{R}$ instead of considering w explicitly. Given a kernel K, learning can then be phrased as choosing a predictor from the class

$$\mathcal{F}_K \overset{\text{def}}{=} \{x \mapsto \langle w, \phi(x) \rangle \mid \|w\| \leq 1, \ K(\overset{\circ}{x}, \overset{\bullet}{x}) = \langle \phi(\overset{\circ}{x}), \phi(\overset{\bullet}{x}) \rangle \} \tag{4}$$

minimizing

$$\hat{h}^{\gamma}(f) \overset{\text{def}}{=} \frac{1}{n} \sum_{i=1}^{n} \max(\gamma - y_i f(x_i), 0). \tag{5}$$

For a set of points $\mathbf{x} = \{x_1, \dots, x_n\}$, let $f(\mathbf{x}) \in \mathbb{R}^n$ be the vector whose entries are $f(x_i)$. The following restricted variant of the Representer Theorem characterizes the possible prediction vectors $f(\mathbf{x})$ by suggesting the matrix square root of the Gram matrix ($K_{\mathbf{x}}^{1/2} \succ 0$ such that $K_{\mathbf{x}} = K_{\mathbf{x}}^{1/2} K_{\mathbf{x}}^{1/2}$) as a possible "feature mapping" for points in $\mathbf{x}$:

Lemma 1. *For any kernel function* K *and set* $\mathbf{x} = \{x_1, \dots, x_n\}$ *of* n *points:*

$$\{f(\mathbf{x}) \mid f \in \mathcal{F}_K\} = \{K_{\mathbf{x}}^{1/2} \tilde{w} \mid \tilde{w} \in \mathbb{R}^n, \|\tilde{w}\| \leq 1\},$$

Proof. For any $f \in \mathcal{F}_K$ we can write $f(x) = \langle w, \phi(x) \rangle$ with $\|w\| \leq 1$ (equation 4). Consider the projection $w_{\|} = \sum_i \alpha_i \phi(x_i)$ of w onto $\text{span}(\phi(x_1), \dots, \phi(x_n))$. We have $f(x_i) = \langle w, \phi(x_i) \rangle = \langle w_{\|}, \phi(x_i) \rangle = \sum_j \alpha_j K(x_j, x_i)$ and $1 \geq \|w\|^2 \geq \|w_{\|}\|^2 = \sum_{ij} \alpha_i \alpha_j K(x_i, x_j)$. In matrix form: $f(\mathbf{x}) = K_{\mathbf{x}} \alpha$ and $\alpha' K_{\mathbf{x}} \alpha \leq 1$. Setting $\tilde{w} = K_{\mathbf{x}}^{1/2} \alpha$ we have $f(\mathbf{x}) = K_{\mathbf{x}} \alpha = K_{\mathbf{x}}^{1/2} K_{\mathbf{x}}^{1/2} \alpha = K_{\mathbf{x}}^{1/2} \tilde{w}$ while $\|\tilde{w}\|^2 = \alpha' K_{\mathbf{x}}^{1/2} K_{\mathbf{x}}^{1/2} \alpha = \alpha K_{\mathbf{x}} \alpha \leq 1$. This establishes that the left-hand side is a subset of the right-hand side.

For any $\tilde{w} \in \mathbb{R}^n$ with $\|\tilde{w}\| \leq 1$ we would like to define $w = \sum_i \alpha_i \phi(x_i)$ with $\alpha = K_{\mathbf{x}}^{-1/2} \tilde{w}$ and get $\langle w, \phi(x_i) \rangle = \sum_j \alpha_j \langle \phi(x_j), \phi(x_i) \rangle = K_{\mathbf{x}} \alpha = K_{\mathbf{x}} K_{\mathbf{x}}^{-1/2} \tilde{w} = K_{\mathbf{x}}^{1/2} \tilde{w}$. However, $K_{\mathbf{x}}$ might be singular. Instead, consider the singular value decomposition $K_{\mathbf{x}} = USU'$, with $U'U = I$, where zero singular values have been removed, i.e. S is an all-positive diagonal matrix and U might be rectangular. Set $\alpha = US^{-1/2}U'\tilde{w}$ and consider $w = \sum_i \alpha_i \phi(x_i)$. We can now calculate:

$$\langle w, \phi(x_i) \rangle = \sum_j \alpha_j \langle \phi(x_j), \phi(x_i) \rangle = K_{\mathbf{x}} \alpha$$

$$= USU' \cdot US^{-1/2}U'\tilde{w} = US^{1/2}U'\tilde{w} = K_{\mathbf{x}}^{1/2}\tilde{w} \tag{6}$$

while $\|w\|^2 = \alpha' K \alpha = \tilde{w}'US^{-1/2}U' \cdot USU' \cdot US^{-1/2}U'\tilde{w} = \tilde{w}'UU'\tilde{w} \leq \|\tilde{w}\|^2 \leq 1$ $\square$

To remove confusion we note some differences between the presentation here and other common, and equivalent, presentations of SVMs. Instead of fixing the margin γ and minimizing the empirical hinge loss, it is common to try to maximize γ while minimizing the loss. The most common combined objective, in our notation, is to minimize $\frac{1}{\gamma^2} + C \cdot \frac{1}{\gamma}\hat{h}^\gamma(w)$ for some trade-off parameter C. This is usually done with a change of variable to $\tilde{w} = w/\gamma$, which results in an equivalent problem where the margin is fixed to one, and the norm of $\tilde{w}$ varies. Expressed in terms of $\tilde{w}$ the objective is $\|\tilde{w}\|^2 + C \cdot \hat{h}^1(\tilde{w})$. Varying the trade-off parameter C is equivalent to varying the margin and minimizing the loss. The variant of the Representer Theorem given in Lemma 1 applies to *any* predictor in $\mathcal{F}_K$, but only describes the behavior of the predictor on the set $\mathbf{x}$. This will be sufficient for our purposes.

2.2   Learning Bounds and Covering Numbers

We derive generalization error bounds in the standard agnostic learning setting. That is, we assume data is generated by some unknown joint distribution $P(X, Y)$ over input points in $\mathcal{X}$ and labels in ± 1. The training set consists of n i.i.d. samples (x_i, y_i) from this joint distribution. We would like to bound the difference $\text{est}^\gamma(f) = \text{err}(f) - \widehat{\text{err}}^\gamma(f)$ (the *estimation error*) between the expected error rate

$$\text{err}(f) = \Pr_{X,Y}(Yf(X) \le 0), \tag{7}$$

and the empirical *margin* error rate

$$\widehat{\text{err}}^\gamma(f) = \frac{|\{i \mid y_i f(x_i) < \gamma\}|}{n}. \tag{8}$$

The main challenge of deriving such bounds is bounding the estimation error *uniformly* over all predictors in a class. The technique we employ in this paper to obtain such uniform bounds is bounding the covering numbers of classes.

Definition 2. *A subset $\tilde{A} \subset A$ is an ϵ-net of A under the metric d if for any $a \in A$ there exists $\tilde{a} \in \tilde{A}$ with $d(a, \tilde{a}) \le \epsilon$. The covering number $\mathcal{N}_d(A, \epsilon)$ is the size of the smallest ϵ-net of A.*

We will study coverings of classes of predictors under the sample-based l_∞ metric, which depends on a sample $\mathbf{x} = \{x_1, \ldots, x_n\}$:

$$d_\infty^{\mathbf{x}}(f_1, f_2) = \max_{i=1}^{n} |f_1(x_i) - f_2(x_i)| \tag{9}$$

Definition 3. *The uniform l_∞ covering number $\mathcal{N}_n(\mathcal{F}, \epsilon)$ of a predictor class $\mathcal{F}$ is given by considering all possible samples $\mathbf{x}$ of size n:*

$$\mathcal{N}_n(\mathcal{F}, \epsilon) = \sup_{|\mathbf{x}|=n} \mathcal{N}_{d_\infty^{\mathbf{x}}}(\mathcal{F}, \epsilon)$$

The uniform l_∞ covering number can be used to bound the estimation error uniformly. For a predictor class $\mathcal{F}$ and fixed $\gamma > 0$, with probability at least $1 - \delta$ over the choice of a training set of size n [17, Theorem 10.1]:

$$\sup_{f \in \mathcal{F}} \text{est}^\gamma(f) \leq \sqrt{8 \frac{1 + \log \mathcal{N}_{2n}(\mathcal{F}, \gamma/2) - \log \delta}{n}} \qquad (10)$$

The uniform covering number of the class $\mathcal{F}_K$ (unit-norm predictors corresponding to a kernel function K; recall eq. (4)), with $K(x,x) \leq B$ for all x, can be bounded by applying Theorems 14.21 and 12.8 of Anthony and Bartlett [17]:

$$\mathcal{N}_n(\mathcal{F}, \epsilon) \leq 2 \left(\frac{4nB}{\epsilon^2} \right)^{\frac{16B}{\epsilon^2} \log_2 \left(\frac{\epsilon e n}{4\sqrt{B}} \right)} \qquad (11)$$

yielding $\sup_{f \in \mathcal{F}_K} \text{est}^\gamma(f) = \sqrt{\tilde{\mathcal{O}}(B/\gamma^2)/n}$ and implying that $\tilde{\mathcal{O}}(B/\gamma^2)$ training examples are enough to guarantee that the estimation error diminishes.

2.3 Learning the Kernel

Instead of committing to a fixed kernel, we consider a family $\mathcal{K} \subseteq \{K : \mathcal{X} \times \mathcal{X} \to \mathbb{R}\}$ of allowed kernels and the corresponding predictor class:

$$\mathcal{F}_\mathcal{K} = \cup_{K \in \mathcal{K}} \mathcal{F}_K \qquad (12)$$

The learning problem is now one of minimizing $\hat{h}^\gamma(f)$ for $f \in \mathcal{F}_\mathcal{K}$. We are interested in bounding the estimation error uniformly for the class $\mathcal{F}_\mathcal{K}$ and will do so by bounding the covering numbers of the class. The bounds will depend on the "dimensionality" of $\mathcal{K}$, which we will define later, the margin γ, and a bound B such that $K(x,x) \leq B$ for all $K \in \mathcal{K}$ and all x. We will say that such a kernel family is *bounded by* B. Note that $\sqrt{B}$ is the radius of a ball (around the origin) containing $\phi(x)$ in the implied Hilbert space, and scaling ϕ scales both $\sqrt{B}$ and γ linearly. Our bounds will therefore depend on the *relative margin* $\gamma/\sqrt{B}$.

3 Covering Numbers with Multiple Kernels

In this section, we will show how to use bounds on covering numbers of a family $\mathcal{K}$ of kernels to obtain bounds on the covering number of the class $\mathcal{F}_\mathcal{K}$ of predictors that are low-norm linear predictors under some kernel $K \in \mathcal{K}$. We will show how to combine an ϵ-net of $\mathcal{K}$ with ϵ-nets for the classes $\mathcal{F}_K$ to obtain an ϵ-net for the class $\mathcal{F}_\mathcal{K}$. In the next section, we will see how to bound the covering numbers of a kernel family $\mathcal{K}$ and will then be able to apply the main result of this section to get a bound on the covering number of $\mathcal{F}_\mathcal{K}$.

In order to state the main result of this section, we will need to consider covering numbers of kernel families. We will use the following sample-based metric between kernels. For a sample $\mathbf{x} = \{x_1, \ldots, x_n\}$:

$$D_\infty^\mathbf{x}(K, \tilde{K}) \stackrel{\text{def}}{=} \max_{i,j=1}^n |K(x_i, x_j) - \tilde{K}(x_i, x_j)| = \left| K_\mathbf{x} - \tilde{K}_\mathbf{x} \right|_\infty \qquad (13)$$

Definition 4. *The* **uniform l_∞ kernel covering number** $\mathcal{N}_n^D(\mathcal{K}, \epsilon)$ *of a kernel class $\mathcal{K}$ is given by considering all possible samples* **x** *of size n:*

$$\mathcal{N}_n^D(\mathcal{K}, \epsilon) = \sup_{|\mathbf{x}|=n} \mathcal{N}_{D_\infty^{\mathbf{x}}}(\mathcal{K}, \epsilon)$$

Theorem 1. *For a family $\mathcal{K}$ of kernels bounded by B and any $\epsilon < 1$:*

$$\mathcal{N}_n(\mathcal{F}_\mathcal{K}, \epsilon) \leq 2 \cdot \mathcal{N}_n^D(\mathcal{K}, \tfrac{\epsilon^2}{4n}) \cdot \left(\tfrac{16nB}{\epsilon^2}\right)^{\frac{64B}{\epsilon^2} \log\left(\frac{\epsilon en}{8\sqrt{B}}\right)}$$

In order to prove Theorem 1, we will first show how all the predictors of one kernel can be approximated by predictors of a nearby kernel. Roughly speaking, we do so by showing that the possible "feature mapping" $K_\mathbf{x}^{1/2}$ of Lemma 1 does not change too much:

Lemma 2. *Let $K, \tilde{K}$ be two kernel functions. Then for any predictor $f \in \mathcal{F}_K$ there exists a predictor $\tilde{f} \in \mathcal{F}_{\tilde{K}}$ with $d_\infty^{\mathbf{x}}(f, \tilde{f}) \leq \sqrt{nD_\infty^{\mathbf{x}}(K, \tilde{K})}$.*

Proof. Let $w \in \mathbb{R}^n$, $\|w\| = 1$ such that $f(\mathbf{x}) = K_\mathbf{x}^{1/2} w$, as guaranteed by Lemma 1. Consider the predictor $\tilde{f} \in \mathcal{F}_{\tilde{K}}$ such that $\tilde{f}(\mathbf{x}) = \tilde{K}_\mathbf{x}^{1/2} w$, guaranteed by the reverse direction of Lemma 1:

$$d_\infty^{\mathbf{x}}(f, \tilde{f}) = \max_i \left| f(x_i) - \tilde{f}(x_i) \right| \leq \left\| f(\mathbf{x}) - \tilde{f}(\mathbf{x}) \right\| \tag{14}$$

$$= \left\| K_\mathbf{x}^{1/2} w - \tilde{K}_\mathbf{x}^{1/2} w \right\| \leq \left\| K_\mathbf{x}^{1/2} - \tilde{K}_\mathbf{x}^{1/2} \right\|_2 \|w\| \leq \sqrt{\left\| K_\mathbf{x} - \tilde{K}_\mathbf{x} \right\|_2} \cdot 1 \tag{15}$$

$$\leq \sqrt{n \left| K_\mathbf{x} - \tilde{K}_\mathbf{x} \right|_\infty} = \sqrt{n D_\infty^{\mathbf{x}}(K, \tilde{K})} \tag{16}$$

See, e.g., Theorem X.1.1 of Bhatia [18] for the third inequality in (15). □

Proof of Theorem 1: Set $\epsilon_\mathrm{K} = \frac{\epsilon^2}{4n}$ and $\epsilon_\mathrm{F} = \epsilon/2$. Let $\tilde{\mathcal{K}}$ be an ϵ_K-net of $\mathcal{K}$. For each $\tilde{K} \in \tilde{\mathcal{K}}$, let $\tilde{\mathcal{F}}_{\tilde{K}}$ be an ϵ_F-net of $\mathcal{F}_{\tilde{K}}$. We will show that

$$\widetilde{\mathcal{F}_\mathcal{K}} \stackrel{\text{def}}{=} \cup_{\tilde{K} \in \tilde{\mathcal{K}}} \tilde{\mathcal{F}}_{\tilde{K}} \tag{17}$$

is an ϵ-net of $\mathcal{F}_\mathcal{K}$. For any $f \in \mathcal{F}_\mathcal{K}$ we have $f \in \mathcal{F}_K$ for some $K \in \mathcal{K}$. The kernel K is covered by some $\tilde{K} \in \tilde{\mathcal{K}}$ with $D_\infty^{\mathbf{x}}(K, \tilde{K}) \leq \epsilon_\mathrm{K}$. Let $\tilde{f} \in \mathcal{F}_{\tilde{K}}$ be a predictor with $d_\infty^{\mathbf{x}}(f, \tilde{f}) \leq \sqrt{nD_\infty^{\mathbf{x}}(K, \tilde{K})} \leq \sqrt{n\epsilon_\mathrm{K}}$ guaranteed by Lemma 2, and $\tilde{\tilde{f}} \in \tilde{\mathcal{F}}_{\tilde{K}}$ such that $d_\infty^{\mathbf{x}}(\tilde{f}, \tilde{\tilde{f}}) \leq \epsilon_\mathrm{F}$. Then $\tilde{\tilde{f}} \in \widetilde{\mathcal{F}_\mathcal{K}}$ is a predictor with:

$$d_\infty^{\mathbf{x}}(f, \tilde{\tilde{f}}) \leq d_\infty^{\mathbf{x}}(f, \tilde{f}) + d_\infty^{\mathbf{x}}(\tilde{f}, \tilde{\tilde{f}}) \leq \sqrt{n\epsilon_\mathrm{K}} + \epsilon_\mathrm{F} = \epsilon \tag{18}$$

This establishes that $\widetilde{\mathcal{F}_\mathcal{K}}$ is indeed an ϵ-net. Its size is bounded by

$$\left| \widetilde{\mathcal{F}_\mathcal{K}} \right| \leq \sum_{\tilde{K} \in \tilde{\mathcal{K}}} \left| \tilde{\mathcal{F}}_{\tilde{K}} \right| \leq \left| \tilde{\mathcal{K}} \right| \cdot \max_K \left| \tilde{\mathcal{F}}_{\tilde{K}} \right| \leq \mathcal{N}_n^D(\mathcal{K}, \tfrac{\epsilon^2}{4n}) \cdot \max_K \mathcal{N}_n(\mathcal{F}_K, \epsilon/2). \tag{19}$$

Substituting in (11) yields the desired bound. □

4 Learning Bounds in Terms of the Pseudodimension

We saw that if we could bound the covering numbers of a kernel family $\mathcal{K}$, we could use Theorem 1 to obtain a bound on the covering numbers of the class $\mathcal{F}_{\mathcal{K}}$ of predictors that are low-norm linear predictors under some kernel $K \in \mathcal{K}$. We could then use (10) to establish a learning bound. In this section, we will see how to bound the covering numbers of a kernel family by its *pseudodimension*, and use this to state learning bounds in terms of this measure. To do so, we will use well-known results bounding covering numbers in terms of the pseudodimension, paying a bit of attention to the subtleties of the differences between Definition 4 of uniform *kernel* covering numbers, and the standard Definition 3 of uniform covering numbers.

To define the pseudodimension of a kernel family we will treat kernels as functions from pairs of points to the reals:

Definition 5. *Let $\mathcal{K} = \{K : \mathcal{X} \times \mathcal{X} \to \mathbb{R}\}$ be a kernel family. The class $\mathcal{K}$ **pseudo-shatters** a set of n pairs of points $(x_1^\heartsuit, x_1^\spadesuit), \ldots, (x_n^\heartsuit, x_n^\spadesuit)$ if there exist thresholds $t_1, \ldots, t_n \in \mathbb{R}$ such that for any $b_1, \ldots, b_n \in \{\pm 1\}$ there exists $K \in \mathcal{K}$ with $\mathrm{sign}(K(x_i^\heartsuit, x_i^\spadesuit) - t_i) = b_i$. The **pseudodimension** $d_\phi(\mathcal{K})$ is the largest n such that there exists a set of n pairs of points that are pseudo-shattered by $\mathcal{K}$.*

The uniform l_∞ covering numbers of a class G of real-valued functions taking values in $[-B, B]$ can be bounded in terms of its pseudodimension. Let d_ϕ be the pseudodimension of G; then for any $n > d_\phi$ and $\epsilon > 0$ [17, Theorem 12.2]:

$$\mathcal{N}_n(G, \epsilon) \leq \left(\frac{enB}{\epsilon d_\phi}\right)^{d_\phi} \tag{20}$$

We should be careful here, since the covering numbers $\mathcal{N}_n(\mathcal{K}, \epsilon)$ are in relation to the metrics:

$$d_\infty^{\heartsuit\spadesuit}(K, \tilde{K}) = \max_{i=1}^n |K(x_i^\heartsuit, x_i^\spadesuit) - \tilde{K}(x_i^\heartsuit, x_i^\spadesuit)| \tag{21}$$

defined for a sample $\mathbf{x}^{\heartsuit\spadesuit} \subset \mathcal{X} \times \mathcal{X}$ of *pairs* of points $(x_i^\heartsuit, x_i^\spadesuit)$. The supremum in Definition 3 of $\mathcal{N}_n(\mathcal{K}, \epsilon)$ should then be taken over all samples of n *pairs* of points. Compare with (13) where the kernels are evaluated over the n^2 pairs of points (x_i, x_j) arising from a sample of n points.

However, for any sample of n points $\mathbf{x} = \{x_1, \ldots, x_n\} \subset \mathcal{X}$, we can always consider the n^2 point pairs $\mathbf{x}^2 = \{(x_i, x_j)|i, j = 1..n\}$ and observe that $D_\infty^{\mathbf{x}}(K, \tilde{K}) = d_\infty^{\mathbf{x}^2}(K, \tilde{K})$ and so $\mathcal{N}_{D_\infty^{\mathbf{x}}}(\mathcal{K}, \epsilon) = \mathcal{N}_{d_\infty^{\mathbf{x}^2}}(\mathcal{K}, \epsilon)$. Although such sets of point pairs do not account for all sets of n^2 point pairs in the supremum of Definition 3, we can still conclude that for any $\mathcal{K}, n, \epsilon > 0$:

$$\mathcal{N}_n^D(\mathcal{K}, \epsilon) \leq \mathcal{N}_{n^2}(\mathcal{K}, \epsilon) \tag{22}$$

Combining (22) and (20):

Lemma 3. *For any kernel family $\mathcal{K}$ bounded by B with pseudodimension d_ϕ:*

$$\mathcal{N}_n^D(\mathcal{K}, \epsilon) \leq \left(\frac{en^2 B}{\epsilon d_\phi}\right)^{d_\phi}$$

Using Lemma 3 and relying on (10) and Theorem 1 we have:

Theorem 2. *For any kernel family* $\mathcal{K}$*, bounded by* B *and with pseudodimension* d_ϕ*, and any fixed* $\gamma > 0$*, with probability at least* $1 - \delta$ *over the choice of a training set of size* n*:*

$$\sup_{f \in \mathcal{F}_\mathcal{K}} est^\gamma(f) \leq \sqrt{8 \frac{2 + d_\phi \log \frac{128en^3B}{\gamma^2 d_\phi} + 256 \frac{B}{\gamma^2} \log \frac{\gamma en}{8\sqrt{B}} \log \frac{128nB}{\gamma^2} - \log \delta}{n}}$$

Theorem 2 is stated for a fixed margin but it can also be stated uniformly over all margins, at the price of an additional $|\log \gamma|$ term (e.g. [15]). Also, instead of bounding $K(x, x)$ for all x, it is enough to bound it only on average, i.e. require $\mathbf{E}[K(X, X)] \leq B$. This corresponds to bounding the trace of the Gram matrix as was done by Lanckriet *et al.*. In any case, we can set $B = 1$ without loss of generality and scale the kernel and margin appropriately. The learning setting investigated here differs slightly from that of Lanckriet *et al.*, who studied transduction, but learning bounds can easily be translated between the two settings.

5   The Pseudodimension of Common Kernel Families

In this section, we analyze the pseudodimension of several kernel families in common use. Most pseudodimension bounds we present follow easily from well-known properties of the pseudodimension of function families, which we review at the beginning of the section. The analyses in this section serve also as examples of how the pseudodimension of other kernel families can be bounded.

5.1   Preliminaries

We review some basic properties of the pseudodimension of a class of functions:

Fact 4. *If* $G' \subseteq G$ *then* $d_\phi(G') \leq d_\phi(G)$*.*

Fact 5 ([17, Theorem 11.3]). *Let* G *be a class of real-valued functions and* $\sigma : \mathbb{R} \mapsto \mathbb{R}$ *a monotone function. Then* $d_\phi(\{\sigma \circ g \mid g \in G\}) \leq d_\phi(G)$*.*

Fact 6 ([17, Theorem 11.4]). *The pseudodimension of a* k*-dimensional vector space of real-valued functions is* k*.*

We will also use a classic result of Warren that is useful, among other things, for bounding the pseudodimension of classes involving low-rank matrices. We say that the real-valued functions $(g_1, g_2, \ldots, g_m)$ *realize* a sign vector $b \in \{\pm 1\}^m$ iff there exists an input x for which $b_i = \text{sign}\, g_i(x)$ for all i. The number of sign vectors realizable by m polynomials of degree at most d over $\mathbb{R}^n$, where $m \geq n$, is at most $(4edm/n)^n$ [19].

5.2   Combination of Base Kernels

Since families of linear or convex combinations of k base kernels are subsets of k-dimensional vector spaces of functions, we can easily bound their pseudodimension by k. Note that the pseudodimension depends only on the *number* of base kernels, but does not depend on the particular choice of base kernels.

Lemma 7. *For any finite set of kernels* $S = \{K_1, \ldots K_k\}$,

$$d_\phi(\mathcal{K}_{convex}(S)) \le d_\phi(\mathcal{K}_{linear}(S)) \le k$$

Proof. We have $\mathcal{K}_{\text{convex}} \subseteq \mathcal{K}_{\text{linear}} \subseteq \text{span } S$ where $\text{span } S = \{\sum_i \lambda_i K_i | \lambda_i \in \mathbb{R}\}$ is a vector space of dimensionality $\le k$. The bounds follow from Facts 4 and 6.   □

5.3   Gaussian Kernels with a Learned Covariance Matrix

Before considering the family $\mathcal{K}_{\text{Gaussian}}$ of Gaussian kernels, let us consider a single-parameter family that generalizes tuning a single scale parameter (i.e. variance) of a Gaussian kernel. For a function $d : \mathcal{X} \times \mathcal{X} \to \mathbb{R}^+$, consider the class

$$\mathcal{K}_{\text{scale}}(d) \overset{\text{def}}{=} \left\{ K_\lambda^d : (x_1, x_2) \mapsto e^{-\lambda d(x_1, x_2)} \mid \lambda \in \mathbb{R}^+ \right\}. \tag{23}$$

The family of spherical Gaussian kernels is obtained with $d(x_1, x_2) = \|x_1 - x_2\|^2$.

Lemma 8. *For any function* d, $d_\phi(\mathcal{K}_{scale}(d)) \le 1$.

Proof. The set $\{-\lambda d \mid \lambda \in \mathbb{R}^+\}$ of functions over $\mathcal{X} \times \mathcal{X}$ is a subset of a one-dimensional vector space and so has pseudodimension at most one. Composing them with the monotone exponentiation function and using Fact 5 yields the desired bound.   □

In order to analyze the pseudodimension of more general families of Gaussian kernels, we will use the same technique of analyzing the functions in the exponent and then composing them with the exponentiation function. Recall that class $\mathcal{K}_{\text{Gaussian}}^\ell$ of Gaussian kernels over $\mathbb{R}^\ell$ defined in (3).

Lemma 9. $d_\phi(\mathcal{K}_{Gaussian}^\ell) \le \ell(\ell+1)/2$

Proof. Consider the functions at the exponent: $\{(x_1, x_2) \mapsto -(x_1 - x_2)A(x_1 - x_2) \mid A \in \mathbb{R}^{\ell \times \ell}, A \succcurlyeq 0\} \subset \text{span}\{(x_1, x_2) \mapsto (x_1 - x_2)[i] \cdot (x_1 - x_2)[j] \mid i \le j \le \ell\}$ where $v[i]$ denotes the ith coordinate of a vector in $\mathbb{R}^\ell$. This is a vector space of dimensionality $\ell(\ell + 1)$ and the result follows by composition with the exponentiation function.   □

We next analyze the pseudodimension of the family of Gaussian kernels with a diagonal covariance matrix, i.e. when we apply an arbitrary scaling to input coordinates:

$$\mathcal{K}_{\text{Gaussian}}^{(\ell-\text{diag})} = \left\{ K_{\bar{\lambda}} : (x_1, x_2) \mapsto e^{-(\bar{\lambda}'(x_1 - x_2))^2} \mid \bar{\lambda} \in \mathbb{R}^\ell \right\} \tag{24}$$

Lemma 10. $d_\phi(\mathcal{K}_{Gaussian}^{(\ell-diag)}) \leq \ell$

Proof. We use the same arguments. The exponents are spanned by the ℓ functions $(x_1, x_2) \mapsto ((x_1 - x_2)[i])^2$. $\square$

As a final example, we analyze the pseudodimension of the family of Gaussian kernels with a low-rank covariance matrix, corresponding to a low-rank A in our notation:

$$\mathcal{K}_{Gaussian}^{\ell,k} = \left\{ (x_1, x_2) \mapsto e^{-(x_1-x_2)'A(x_1-x_2)} \mid A \in \mathbb{R}^{\ell \times \ell}, \; A \succeq 0, \; \text{rank}\, A \leq k \right\}$$

This family corresponds to learning a dimensionality reducing linear transformation of the inputs that is applied before calculating the Gaussian kernel.

Lemma 11. $d_\phi(\mathcal{K}_{Gaussian}^{\ell,k}) \leq kl \log_2(8ek\ell)$

Proof. Any $A \succeq 0$ of rank at most k can be written as $A = U'U$ with $U \in \mathbb{R}^{k \times \ell}$. Consider the set $G = \{(x^\heartsuit, x^\spadesuit) \mapsto -(x^\heartsuit - x^\spadesuit)'U'U(x^\heartsuit - x^\spadesuit) \mid U \in \mathbb{R}^{k \times \ell}\}$ of functions at the exponent. Assume G pseudo-shatters a set of m point pairs $S = \{(x_1^\heartsuit, x_1^\spadesuit) \dots, (x_m^\heartsuit, x_m^\spadesuit)\}$. By the definition of pseudo-shattering, we get that there exist $t_1, \dots, t_m \in \mathbb{R}$ so that for every $b \in \{\pm 1\}^m$ there exist $U_b \in \mathbb{R}^{k \times \ell}$ with $b_i = \text{sign}\left(-(x_i^\heartsuit - x_i^\spadesuit)'U'U(x_i^\heartsuit - x_i^\spadesuit) - t_i\right)$ for all $i \leq m$. Viewing each $p_i(U) \stackrel{\text{def}}{=} -(x_i^\heartsuit - x_i^\spadesuit)'U'U(x_i^\heartsuit - x_i^\spadesuit) - t_i$ as a quadratic polynomial in the $k\ell$ entries of U, where $x_i^\heartsuit - x_i^\spadesuit$ and t_i determine the coefficients of p_i, we get a set of m quadratic polynomials over $k\ell$ variables which realize all 2^m sign vectors. Applying Warren's bound [19] discussed above we get $2^m \leq (8em/k\ell)^{k\ell}$ which implies $m \leq kl \log_2(8ek\ell)$. This is a bound on the number of points that can be pseudo-shattered by G, and hence on the pseudodimension of G, and by composition with exponentiation we get the desired bound. $\square$

6   Conclusion and Discussion

Learning with a *family* of allowed kernel matrices has been a topic of significant interest and the focus of considerable body of research in recent years, and several attempts have been made to establish learning bounds for this setting. In this paper we establish the first generalization error bounds for kernel-learning SVMs where the margin complexity term and the dimensionality of the kernel family interact *additively* rather then *multiplicatively* (up to log factors). The additive interaction yields stronger bounds. We believe that the implied additive bounds on the sample complexity represent its correct behavior (up to log factors), although this remains to be proved.

The results we present significantly improve on previous results for convex combinations of base kernels, for which the only previously known bound had a multiplicative interaction [1], and for Gaussian kernels with a learned covariance matrix, for which only a bound with a multiplicative interaction and an unspecified dependence on the input dimensionality was previously shown [14]. We also provide the first explicit non-trivial bound for linear combinations of base kernels—a bound that depends only on the (relative) margin and the number of base kernels. The techniques we introduce for obtaining bounds based on the pseudodimension of the class of kernels should readily apply to straightforward derivation of bounds for many other classes.

We note that previous attempts at establishing bounds for this setting [1, 2, 14] relied on bounding the Rademacher complexity [15] of the class $\mathcal{F}_\mathcal{K}$. However, generalization error bounds derived solely from the Rademacher complexity $\mathcal{R}[\mathcal{F}_\mathcal{K}]$ of the class $\mathcal{F}_\mathcal{K}$ *must* have a multiplicative dependence on $\sqrt{B}/\gamma$: The Rademacher complexity $\mathcal{R}[\mathcal{F}_\mathcal{K}]$ scales linearly with the scale $\sqrt{B}$ of functions in $\mathcal{F}_\mathcal{K}$, and to obtain an estimation error bound it is multiplied by the Lipschitz constant $1/\gamma$ [15]. This might be avoidable by clipping predictors in $\mathcal{F}_\mathcal{K}$ to the range $[-\gamma, \gamma]$:

$$\mathcal{F}_\mathcal{K}^\gamma \stackrel{\text{def}}{=} \{f_{[\pm\gamma]} \mid f \in \mathcal{F}_\mathcal{K}\}, \quad f_{[\pm\gamma]}(x) = \begin{cases} \gamma & \text{if } f(x) \geq \gamma \\ f(x) & \text{if } \gamma \geq f(x) \geq -\gamma \\ -\gamma & \text{if } -\gamma \geq f(x) \end{cases} \tag{25}$$

When using the Rademacher complexity $\mathcal{R}[\mathcal{F}_\mathcal{K}]$ to obtain generalization error bounds in terms of the margin error, the class is implicitly clipped and only the Rademacher complexity of $\mathcal{F}_\mathcal{K}^\gamma$ is actually relevant. This Rademacher complexity $\mathcal{R}[\mathcal{F}_\mathcal{K}^\gamma]$ is bounded by $\mathcal{R}[\mathcal{F}_\mathcal{K}]$. In our case, it seems that this last bound is loose. It is possible though, that covering numbers of $\mathcal{K}$ can be used to bound $\mathcal{R}[\mathcal{F}_\mathcal{K}^\gamma]$ by $\mathcal{O}\left(\gamma \log \mathcal{N}_{2n}^D(\mathcal{K}, 4B/n^2) + \sqrt{B}\right)/\sqrt{n}$, yielding a generalization error bound with an additive interaction, and perhaps avoiding the log factors of the margin complexity term $\tilde{\mathcal{O}}(B/\gamma^2)$ of Theorem 2.

References

1. Lanckriet, G.R., Cristianini, N., Bartlett, P., Ghaoui, L.E., Jordan, M.I.: Learning the kernel matrix with semidefinite programming. J Mach Learn Res **5** (2004) 27–72

2. Bousquet, O., Herrmann, D.J.L.: On the complexity of learning the kernel matrix. In: Adv. in Neural Information Processing Systems 15. (2003)

3. Crammer, K., Keshet, J., Singer, Y.: Kernel design using boosting. In: Advances in Neural Information Processing Systems 15. (2003)

4. Lanckriet, G.R.G., De Bie, T., Cristianini, N., Jordan, M.I., Noble, W.S.: A statistical framework for genomic data fusion. Bioinformatics **20** (2004)

5. Sonnenburg, S., Rätsch, G., Schafer, C.: Learning interpretable SVMs for biological sequence classification. In: Research in Computational Molecular Biology. (2005)

6. Ben-Hur, A., Noble, W.S.: Kernel methods for predicting protein-protein interactions. Bioinformatics **21** (2005)

7. Cristianini, N., Campbell, C., Shawe-Taylor, J.: Dynamically adapting kernels in support vector machines. In: Adv. in Neural Information Proceedings Systems 11. (1999)

8. Chapelle, O., Vapnik, V., Bousquet, O., Makhuerjee, S.: Choosing multiple parameters for support vector machines. Machine Learning **46** (2002) 131–159

9. Keerthi, S.S.: Efficient tuning of SVM hyperparameters using radius/margin bound and iterative algorithms. IEEE Tran. on Neural Networks **13** (2002) 1225–1229
10. Glasmachers, T., Igel, C.: Gradient-based adaptation of general gaussian kernels. Neural Comput. **17** (2005) 2099–2105
11. Ong, C.S., Smola, A.J., Williamson, R.C.: Learning the kernel with hyperkernels. J. Mach. Learn. Res. **6** (2005)
12. Micchelli, C.A., Pontil, M.: Learning the kernel function via regularization. J. Mach. Learn. Res. **6** (2005)
13. Argyriou, A., Micchelli, C.A., Pontil, M.: Learning convex combinations of continuously parameterized basic kernels. In: 18th Annual Conf. on Learning Theory. (2005)
14. Micchelli, C.A., Pontil, M., Wu, Q., Zhou, D.X.: Error bounds for learning the kernel. Research Note RN/05/09, University College London Dept. of Computer Science (2005)
15. Koltchinskii, V., Panchenko, D.: Empirical margin distributions and bounding the generalization error of combined classifiers. Ann. Statist. **30** (2002)
16. Smola, A.J., Schölkopf, B.: Learning with Kernels. MIT Press (2002)
17. Anthony, M., Bartlett, P.L.: Neural Networks Learning: Theoretical Foundations. Cambridge University Press (1999)
18. Bhatia, R.: Matrix Analysis. Springer (1997)
19. Warren, H.E.: Lower bounds for approximation by nonlinear manifolds. T. Am. Math. Soc. **133** (1968) 167–178

A   Analysis of Previous Bounds

We show that some of the previously suggested bounds for SVM kernel learning can never lead to meaningful bounds on the expected error.

Lanckriet *et al.* [1, Theorem 24] show that for any class $\mathcal{K}$ and margin γ, with probability at least $1 - \delta$, every $f \in \mathcal{F}_{\mathcal{K}}$ satisfies:

$$\text{err}(f) \leq \widehat{\text{err}}^{\gamma}(f) + \tfrac{1}{\sqrt{n}}\left(4 + \sqrt{2\log(1/\delta)} + \sqrt{\tfrac{\mathcal{C}(\mathcal{K})}{n\gamma^2}}\right) \qquad (26)$$

Where $\mathcal{C}(\mathcal{K}) = \mathbf{E}_{\sigma}[\max_{K \in \mathcal{K}} \sigma' K_{\mathbf{x}} \sigma]$, with σ chosen uniformly from $\{\pm 1\}^{2n}$ and $\mathbf{x}$ being a set of n training and n test points. The bound is for a transductive setting and the Gram matrix of both training and test data is considered. We continue denoting the empirical margin error, on the n training points, by $\widehat{\text{err}}^{\gamma}(f)$, but now $\text{err}(f)$ is the test error on the specific n test points.

The expectation $\mathcal{C}(\mathcal{K})$ is not easy to compute in general, and Lanckriet *et al.* provide specific bounds for families of linear, and convex, combinations of base kernels.

A.1   Bound for Linear Combinations of Base Kernels

For the family $\mathcal{K} = \mathcal{K}_{\text{linear}}$ of linear combinations of base kernels (equation (1)), Lanckriet *et al.* note that $\mathcal{C}(\mathcal{K}) \leq c \cdot n$, where $c = \max_{K \in \mathcal{K}} \text{tr} K_{\mathbf{x}}$ is an upper bound on the trace of the possible Gram matrices. Substituting this explicit bound on $\mathcal{C}(\mathcal{K})$ in (26) results in:

$$\text{err}(f) \le \widehat{\text{err}}^{\gamma}(f) + \tfrac{1}{\sqrt{n}}\left(4 + \sqrt{2\log(1/\delta)} + \sqrt{\tfrac{c}{\gamma^2}}\right) \qquad (27)$$

However, the following lemma shows that if a kernel allows classifying much of the training points within a large margin, then the trace of its Gram matrix cannot be too small:

Lemma 12. *For all $f \in \mathcal{F}_K$: $\operatorname{tr} K_\mathbf{x} \ge \gamma^2(1 - \widehat{\text{err}}^{\gamma}(f))n$*

Proof. Let $f(x) = \langle w, \phi(x)\rangle$, $\|w\| = 1$. Then for any i for which $y_i f(x_i) = y_i \langle w, \phi(x_i)\rangle \ge \gamma$ we must have $\sqrt{K(x_i, x_i)} = \|\phi(x_i)\| \ge \gamma$. Hence $\operatorname{tr} K_\mathbf{x} \ge \sum_{i|y_i f(x_i) \ge \gamma} K(x_i, x_i) \ge |\{i|y_i f(x_i) \ge \gamma\}| \cdot \gamma^2 = (1 - \widehat{\text{err}}^{\gamma}(f))n \cdot \gamma^2$. □

Using Lemma 12 we get that the right-hand side of (27) is at least:

$$\widehat{\text{err}}^{\gamma}(f) + \tfrac{4 + \sqrt{2\log(1/\delta)}}{\sqrt{n}} + \sqrt{\tfrac{\gamma^2(1 - \widehat{\text{err}}^{\gamma}(f))n}{n\gamma^2}} > \widehat{\text{err}}^{\gamma}(f) + \sqrt{1 - \widehat{\text{err}}^{\gamma}(f)} \ge 1 \quad (28)$$

A.2 Bound for Convex Combinations of Base Kernels

For the family $\mathcal{K} = \mathcal{K}_{\text{convex}}$ of convex combinations of base kernels (equation (2)), Lanckriet *et al.* bound $\mathcal{C}(\mathcal{K}) \le c \cdot \min\left(m, n\max_{K_i} \tfrac{\|(K_i)_\mathbf{x}\|_2}{\operatorname{tr}((K_i)_\mathbf{x})}\right)$, where m is the number of base kernels, $c = \max_{K \in \mathcal{K}} \operatorname{tr}(K_\mathbf{x})$ as before, and the maximum is over the base kernels K_i. The first minimization argument yields a non-trivial generalization bound that is multiplicative in the number of base kernels, and is discussed in Section 1.2. The second argument yields the following bound, which was also obtained by Bousquet and Herrmann [2]:

$$\text{err}(f) \le \widehat{\text{err}}^{\gamma}(f) + \tfrac{1}{\sqrt{n}}\left(4 + \sqrt{2\log(1/\delta)} + \sqrt{\tfrac{c \cdot b}{\gamma^2}}\right) \qquad (29)$$

where $b = \max_{K_i} \|(K_i)_\mathbf{x}\|_2 / \operatorname{tr}((K_i)_\mathbf{x})$. This implies $\|K_\mathbf{x}\|_2 \le b \cdot \operatorname{tr} K_\mathbf{x} \le b \cdot c$ for all base kernels and so (by convexity) also for all $K \in \mathcal{K}$. However, similar to the bound on the trace of Gram matrices in Lemma 12, we can also bound the L_2 operator norm required for classification of most points with a margin:

Lemma 13. *For all $f \in \mathcal{F}_K$: $\|K_\mathbf{x}\|_2 \ge \gamma^2(1 - \widehat{\text{err}}^{\gamma}(f))n$*

Proof. From Lemma 1 we have $f(\mathbf{x}) = K_\mathbf{x}^{1/2} w$ for some w such that $\|w\| \le 1$, and so $\|K_\mathbf{x}\|_2 = \|K_\mathbf{x}^{1/2}\|_2^2 \ge \|K_\mathbf{x}^{1/2} w\|^2 = \|f(\mathbf{x})\|^2$. To bound the right-hand side, consider that for $(1 - \widehat{\text{err}}^{\gamma}(f))n$ of the points in $\mathbf{x}$ we have $|f(x_i)| = |y_i f(x_i)| \ge \gamma$, and so $\|f(\mathbf{x})\|^2 = \sum_i f(x_i)^2 \ge (1 - \widehat{\text{err}}^{\gamma}(f))n \cdot \gamma^2$. □

Lemma 13 implies $bc \ge \gamma^2(1 - \widehat{\text{err}}^{\gamma}(f))n$ and a calculation similar to (28) reveals that the right-hand side of (29) is always greater than one.

On Optimal Learning Algorithms for Multiplicity Automata

Laurence Bisht, Nader H. Bshouty, and Hanna Mazzawi

Department of Computer Science
Technion, Haifa 32000, Israel
{bisht, bshouty, hanna}@cs.technion.ac.il

Abstract. We study polynomial time learning algorithms for Multiplicity Automata (MA) and Multiplicity Automata Function (MAF) that minimize the access to one or more of the following resources: Equivalence queries, Membership queries or Arithmetic operations in the field $\mathcal{F}$. This is in particular interesting when access to one or more of the above resources is significantly more expensive than the others.

We apply new algebraic approach based on Matrix Theory to simplify the algorithms and the proofs of their correctness. We improve the arithmetic complexity of the problem and argue that it is almost optimal. Then we prove tight bound for the minimal number of equivalence queries and almost (up to log factor) tight bound for the number of membership queries.

1 Introduction

In computational learning theory, one of the interesting problems studied in the literature is learning the classes of Multiplicity Automata (MA) and Multiplicity Automata Function (MAF) over any field from membership (substitution) and equivalence queries [20, 12, 6, 13, 7, 4, 5, 11, 10]. This class includes many interesting classes such as: decision trees, disjoint DNF, $O(\log n)$-term DNF, multivariate polynomials, DFA, boxes and more. In all the algorithms in the literature, it is assumed that the cost of all the resources are the same. In practice, one resource may be more expensive than the others. For example, if the field is the reals then arithmetic operation is not one unit step.

In this paper we study polynomial time learning algorithms for Multiplicity Automata that minimize the access to one or more of the following resources: Equivalence queries, Membership queries or Arithmetic operations in the field $\mathcal{F}$. First, we improve the arithmetic complexity of the problem and argue that it is optimal. Then prove tight bound for the minimal number of equivalence queries and almost (up to log factor) tight bound for the number of membership queries.

We summarize the contributions of the paper in the following:

1. **Matrix Approach:** Representing MA in algebraic structure enables using the theory of matrices. We show that the representation of any MA is unique up to similarity of matrices. This gives simple algorithms and analysis.
2. **Arithmetic Complexity:** With this new algebraic approach we use techniques from algebraic complexity to improve the arithmetic complexity of

G. Lugosi and H.U. Simon (Eds.): COLT 2006, LNAI 4005, pp. 184–198, 2006.

the problem. We also introduce a new hypothesis class called the Extended Multiplicity Automata class (EMA) and learn MA from this class with arithmetic complexity that is *independent* of the alphabet size. We show that the arithmetic complexity in this algorithm is optimal in the sense that it is equal to the arithmetic complexity of computing the target function in all the counterexamples received by the algorithm.

3. **Equivalence Query Complexity**: We prove a lower bound for the number of equivalence queries. Then we give a polynomial time learning algorithm for MA that is optimal in the equivalence query complexity.

4. **Membership Query Complexity**: We give a lower bound for the number of queries which is almost tight (up to *log* factor). This gives an almost tight lower bound for the number of membership queries.

5. **Results for MAF:** In the full paper, we also obtain results similar to the above for MAF. We introduce a new representation of a MAF called the compressed MAF and use it to show learnability that obtains optimal number of equivalence queries and almost optimal number of membership queries and arithmetic operations for MAF.

2   Preliminaries

2.1   Concept Classes

Let $\Sigma = \{\sigma_1, \ldots, \sigma_t\}$ be a finite alphabet of size t and $\mathcal{F}$ be a field. A *Multiplicity Automaton Function* (MAF) with an alphabet Σ over a field $\mathcal{F}$ with n variables is a function $f : \Sigma^n \to \mathcal{F}$ of the form $f(w_1 w_2 \cdots w_n) = \Lambda_1^{(w_1)} \cdots \Lambda_n^{(w_n)}$ where for every $\sigma \in \Sigma$ and every i, $\Lambda_i^{(\sigma)}$ is $s_i \times s_{i+1}$ matrix with entries from $\mathcal{F}$ and $s_1 = s_{n+1} = 1$. We define the *size of f at level i* as $\text{size}_i(f) = s_i$, the *width* of f is $\text{size}_{\max}(f) = \max_i s_i$ and the *size* of f, $\text{size}(f)$, is $\sum_i s_i$. See full paper for a graph representation of MAF.

A *Multiplicity Automaton* (MA) with an alphabet Σ over a field $\mathcal{F}$ is a function $f : \Sigma^* \to \mathcal{F}$ of the form $f(w_1 w_2 \cdots w_m) = \beta \Lambda^{(w_1)} \Lambda^{(w_2)} \cdots \Lambda^{(w_m)} \gamma^T$ where for each $\sigma \in \Sigma$, $\Lambda^{(\sigma)}$ is $s \times s$ matrix and β, γ are s vectors over $\mathcal{F}$. We define $\Lambda^{(\varepsilon)} = I$ the identity matrix and $\Lambda^{(\sigma w)} = \Lambda^{(\sigma)} \Lambda^{(w)}$ for every $\sigma \in \Sigma$ and string w. Then we can write $f(w) = \beta \Lambda^{(w)} \gamma^T$ for any string w. We call s the *size* of the MA f. See full paper for a graph representation of MA.

An *Extended Multiplicity Automaton* (EMA) with an alphabet Σ over a field $\mathcal{F}$ is a function $f : \Sigma^* \to \mathcal{F}$ of the form $f(w_1 w_2 \cdots w_m) = \beta \Lambda^{(w_1)} \hat{\Lambda} \Lambda^{(w_2)} \hat{\Lambda} \cdots \Lambda^{(w_m)} \hat{\Lambda} \gamma^T$, where $\Lambda^{(\sigma)}$, $\hat{\Lambda}$ are $s \times s$ matrices and β, γ are s vectors over $\mathcal{F}$. Obviously, an EMA is an MA with $\tilde{\Lambda}^{(\sigma)} = \Lambda^{(\sigma)} \hat{\Lambda}$. See full paper for a graph representation of EMA.

2.2   Properties of MA

In this section we give some properties of MA

The next Theorem shows that if we have $2s$ strings $x_1, \ldots, x_s, y_1, \ldots, y_s$ such that the matrix $[f(x_i \cdot y_j)]_{i,j}$ (the i, jth entry is $f(x_i \cdot y_j)$) is non-singular, then we can construct the MA for f.

Theorem 1. *Let $f(x) = \beta \Lambda^{(x)} \gamma^T$ be an MA of size s. Let $x_1, \ldots, x_s, y_1, \ldots, y_s$ be strings in Σ^* such that $[f(x_i \cdot y_j)]_{i,j}$ is non-singular. Then $f(x) = \beta_0 \Lambda_0^{(x)} \gamma_0^T$ where*

$$\Lambda_0^{(\sigma)} = M^{(\sigma)} N^{-1}, \quad \gamma_0 = (f(x_1), \ldots, f(x_s)), \quad \beta_0 = (f(y_1), \ldots, f(y_s)) N^{-1}$$

and $M^{(\sigma)} = [f(x_i \cdot \sigma \cdot y_j)]_{i,j}$ and $N = [f(x_i \cdot y_j)]_{i,j}$.

Proof. Let

$$K = \begin{pmatrix} \beta \Lambda^{(x_1)} \\ \beta \Lambda^{(x_2)} \\ \vdots \\ \beta \Lambda^{(x_s)} \end{pmatrix} \quad \text{and} \quad L = (\Lambda^{(y_1)} \gamma^T | \cdots | \Lambda^{(y_s)} \gamma^T).$$

Now we have $N = KL$, $M^{(\sigma)} = K \Lambda^{(\sigma)} L$, $(f(x_1), \ldots, f(x_s))^T = K\gamma^T$ and $(f(y_1), \ldots, f(y_s)) = \beta L$. Since $N = KL$ is non-singular, K and L are non-singular. Now it straightforward to show that for any word w we have $\beta_0 \Lambda_0^{(w)} \gamma_0^T = \beta \Lambda^{(w)} \gamma^T = f(w)$. ∎

Now, we show that the MA representation is unique up to similarity

Lemma 1. *Let $f(x) = \beta_1 \Lambda_1^{(x)} \gamma_1^T$ and $g(x) = \beta_2 \Lambda_2^{(x)} \gamma_2^T$ be two MAs of size s. We have $f(x) \equiv g(x)$ if and only if there is a non-singular matrix J such that $\beta_2 = \beta_1 J^{-1}$, $\gamma_2^T = J\gamma_1^T$ and $\Lambda_2^{(\sigma)} = J\Lambda_1^{(\sigma)} J^{-1}$ for every $\sigma \in \Sigma$.*

Proof. The "If" part of the Lemma is straightforward. For the "only if" part, define K_1, L_1 and K_2, L_2, as defined in the proof of Theorem 1, for $\beta_1 \Lambda_1^{(x)} \gamma_1^T$ and $\beta_2 \Lambda_2^{(x)} \gamma_2^T$, respectively. Then $N = K_1 L_1 = K_2 L_2$ and $M^{(\sigma)} = K_1 \Lambda_1^{(\sigma)} L_1 = K_2 \Lambda_2^{(\sigma)} L_2$. Now for $J = K_2^{-1} K_1$ we have $J = L_2 L_1^{-1}$ and $\Lambda_2^{(\sigma)} = J\Lambda_1^{(\sigma)} J^{-1}$. ∎

A similar result is proved for MAF in the full paper.

2.3 The Learning Model

Our learning model is the *exact* learning model [2, 17]. In this model a *teacher* has a *target function* f that the *learner* (*learning algorithm*) wants to learn from queries. In the *equivalence query*, the learner gives the teacher a hypothesis h. The teacher returns either *yes*, signifying that h is equivalent to f, or *no* with a *counterexample*, which is an assignment $(b, f(b))$ such that $h(b) \neq f(b)$. In the *membership query*, the learner gives the teacher an assignment a. The teacher returns $f(a)$.

We say that the learner *learns* a class of functions C, if for every function $f \in C$, the learner outputs a hypothesis h that is equivalent to f. The goal of the learner is to learn in polynomial time where "polynomial time" means polynomial in the *size* of the shortest representation of f and the longest counterexample returned by the teacher.

3   The Algorithm and Its Analysis

In this section we introduce a simple algorithm similar to the one in [4] with the theory of matrices. Then we give a simple proof for its correctness. We will assume $|\Sigma| > 1$. See the full paper for unary alphabet.

3.1   The Learning Algorithm for MA

The algorithm initially asks $EQ(0)$ and receives a counterexample x_1. Then it defines $X = \{x_1\}$ and $Y = \{y_1 = \varepsilon\}$. At stage ℓ it uses two sets of strings $X = \{x_1, x_2, \ldots, x_\ell\}$ and $Y = \{y_1 = \varepsilon, y_2, \ldots, y_\ell\}$ where $N(X, Y) = N = [f(x_i \cdot y_j)]_{i,j}$ is a non-singular matrix. Then the algorithm defines the hypothesis defined in Theorem 1. That is, $h(x) = \beta_0 \Lambda_0^{(x)} \gamma_0^T$ where

$$\Lambda_0^{(\sigma)} = M^{(\sigma)} N^{-1}, \quad \gamma_0 = (f(x_1), \ldots, f(x_\ell)), \quad \beta_0 = (f(y_1), \ldots, f(y_\ell)) N^{-1}$$

and

$$M^{(\sigma)} = [f(x_i \cdot \sigma \cdot y_j)]_{i,j}$$

for every $\sigma \in \Sigma$. Notice that $\gamma_0^T = N e_1^T$ where e_i is the ith unit vector.

Now the algorithm asks equivalence query with $h(x)$ and receives a counterexample $z \in \Sigma^*$ where $f(z) \neq h(z)$. The algorithm then finds a prefix $w \cdot \sigma$ of z, where $\sigma \in \Sigma$, such that (see Fact 1 in the next subsection)

$$(f(w \cdot y_1), \ldots, f(w \cdot y_\ell)) = \beta_0 \Lambda_0^{(w)} N \tag{1}$$

and

$$(f(w \cdot \sigma \cdot y_1), \ldots, f(w \cdot \sigma \cdot y_\ell)) \neq \beta_0 \Lambda_0^{(w \cdot \sigma)} N, \tag{2}$$

and adds $x_{\ell+1} = w$ to X and $y_{\ell+1} = \sigma \cdot y_{i_0}$ to Y where i_0 is any entry that satisfies $f(w \cdot \sigma \cdot y_{i_0}) \neq \beta_0 \Lambda_0^{(w \cdot \sigma)} N e_{i_0}^T$. Such entry exists because of (2). Then it goes to stage $\ell + 1$.

3.2   Correctness of the Algorithm

We first show that such $w \cdot \sigma$, that satisfies (2), exists and then show that the new matrix $N(\hat{X}, \hat{Y})$, where $\hat{X} = \{x_1, \ldots, x_\ell, x_{\ell+1}\}$ and $\hat{Y} = \{y_1, \ldots, y_\ell, y_{\ell+1}\}$, is non-singular.

Fact 1. *If $f(z) \neq h(z)$ then there is a prefix $w \cdot \sigma$ for z that satisfies (1).*

Proof. It is enough to show that the first equality in (1) is true for $w = \varepsilon$ and the second inequality in (2) is true for $w = z$. For the prefix $w = \varepsilon$ we have $(f(y_1), \ldots, f(y_\ell)) = \beta_0 N = \beta_0 \Lambda_0^{(\varepsilon)} N$. Now for $w = z$, $f(z \cdot y_1) = f(z) \neq h(z) = \beta_0 \Lambda_0^{(z)} \gamma_0^T = \beta_0 \Lambda_0^{(z)} N e_1^T$. ∎

Now we show

Fact 2. *The new matrix $\hat{N} = N(\hat{X}, \hat{Y})$ is non-singular.*

Proof. We have $\hat{X} = X \cup \{w\}$ and $\hat{Y} = Y \cup \{\sigma \cdot y_{i_0}\}$. Therefore

$$\hat{N} = \begin{pmatrix} N & M^{(\sigma)} e_{i_0}^T \\ \beta_0 \Lambda_0^{(w)} N & f(w \cdot \sigma \cdot y_{i_0}) \end{pmatrix}.$$

Now since $M^{(\sigma)} = \Lambda_0^{(\sigma)} N$,

$$\begin{pmatrix} I & 0 \\ \beta_0 \Lambda_0^{(w)} & -1 \end{pmatrix} \hat{N} = \begin{pmatrix} N & M^{(\sigma)} e_{i_0}^T \\ 0 & \beta_0 \Lambda_0^{(w \cdot \sigma)} N e_{i_0}^T - f(w \cdot \sigma \cdot y_{i_0}) \end{pmatrix},$$

and $\beta_0 \Lambda_0^{(w \cdot \sigma)} N e_{i_0}^T - f(w \cdot \sigma \cdot y_{i_0}) \neq 0$, the rank of $\hat{N}$ is $\ell + 1$. ∎

3.3   The Complexity of the Algorithm

In all the results, m is the longest counterexample received by the learner and the time complexity is linear in the number of queries and arithmetic operations.

A straightforward algebraic computation gives the same query and arithmetic complexity as in [4]. In [4], Beimel et. al. proved the following.

Theorem 2. *Let $\mathcal{F}$ be a field, and $f : \Sigma^* \to \mathcal{F}$ be an MA of size s. Then f is learnable as MA from $s + 1$ equivalence queries and $O((|\Sigma| + \log m)s^2)$ membership queries in*

$$O(|\Sigma| s M(s) + m s^3) = O(|\Sigma| s^{3.37} + m s^3)$$

arithmetic operations. Here, $M(s)$ is the complexity of $s \times s$ matrix multiplication.

In the next section we improve the arithmetic complexity to $O(|\Sigma| s^3 + m s^3)$ using MA hypothesis and then to $O(m s^3)$ using EMA hypothesis.

4   Almost Optimal Arithmetic Complexity

In this section we prove the following

Theorem 3. *Let $\mathcal{F}$ be a field, and $f : \Sigma^* \to \mathcal{F}$ be an MA of size s. Then f is learnable as EMA from $s + 1$ equivalence queries and $O((|\Sigma| + \log m)s^2)$ membership queries with*

$$O(m s^3)$$

arithmetic operations.

Notice that the arithmetic complexity in the Theorem is independent of how large is the alphabet. The arithmetic complexity is almost optimal in the following sense: It is known, [9], that the equivalence query complexity of any polynomial time learning algorithm for MA is at least $\tilde{\Omega}(s)$. Computing the target hypothesis in $\tilde{\Omega}(s)$ strings of length m takes $\tilde{\Omega}(ms^3)$ arithmetic operations in the field. So the optimality is in the sense that the arithmetic complexity of the algorithm is within logarithmic factor of the arithmetic complexity for computing the target hypothesis in all the counterexamples received in the algorithm.

Proof of Theorem 3. At stage ℓ the algorithm asks equivalence query with a hypothesis $h(x)$ and receives a counterexample $z \in \Sigma^*$. Then for every prefix w of z it computes $\beta_0 \Lambda_0^{(w)}$ and $\beta_0 \Lambda_0^{(w)} N$. This can be done in $O(m\ell^2)$ arithmetic operations. Then the algorithm does a binary search to find a prefix that satisfies (1). This takes $\ell \log m$ membership queries. Then it builds $\hat{N}$. Notice that all the entries of $\hat{N}$ are already known from previous computations. To build $\hat{M}^{(\sigma)}$ for all $\sigma \in \Sigma$ it needs to ask membership queries to find $f(x_{\ell+1} \cdot \sigma \cdot y_i)$, $f(x_i \cdot \sigma \cdot y_{\ell+1})$ and $f(x_{\ell+1} \cdot \sigma \cdot y_{\ell+1})$. This takes $(2\ell+1)|\Sigma|$ membership queries. By Lemma 2 below $\hat{N}^{-1}$ and each $\hat{\Lambda}_0^{(\sigma)}$ can be computed with $O(\ell^2)$ arithmetic operations. Therefore it needs $O(|\Sigma|\ell^2)$ arithmetic operations to compute all $\hat{\Lambda}_0^{(\sigma)}$. Finally, to compute $\hat{\beta}_0$ it needs $O(\ell^2)$ arithmetic operations.

This gives arithmetic complexity $O(|\Sigma|s^3 + ms^3)$ and the algorithm outputs MA. In the case where the output can be EMA, we can omit the step that computes $\Lambda_0^{(\sigma)}$ for every σ and output the EMA

$$f(w) = \hat{\beta}_0 M^{(w_1)} N^{-1} M^{(w_2)} N^{-1} \cdots M^{(w_{|w|})} N^{-1} \hat{\gamma}_0^T .$$

This gives the result.   ∎

The results for MAF are in the full paper.

Lemma 2. *Let N and M be two $\ell \times \ell$ matrices with entries from $\mathcal{F}$ and $\Lambda = MN^{-1}$. Let $u, \lambda \in \mathcal{F}^\ell$ be such that $u = \lambda N$. Let*

$$\hat{N} = \begin{pmatrix} N & v^T \\ u & \xi \end{pmatrix}, \hat{M} = \begin{pmatrix} M & p^T \\ q & \eta \end{pmatrix}$$

where $\hat{N}$ is nonsingular matrix where $v, q, p \in \mathcal{F}^\ell$ and $\xi, \eta \in \mathcal{F}$. Then

$$\hat{N}^{-1} = \frac{1}{\omega} \begin{pmatrix} \omega N^{-1} - (N^{-1}v^T)\lambda & N^{-1}v^T \\ \lambda & -1 \end{pmatrix}$$

where $\omega = \lambda v^T - \xi$ and

$$\hat{M}\hat{N}^{-1} = \frac{1}{\omega} \begin{pmatrix} \omega\Lambda - (\Lambda v^T)\lambda + p^T\lambda & \Lambda v^T - p^T \\ \omega(qN^{-1}) - ((qN^{-1})v^T)\lambda + \eta\lambda & (qN^{-1})v^T - \eta \end{pmatrix} .$$

From the definitions of MA and EMA we have

Fact 3. *1. For an MA f of size s and a string $a \in \Sigma^*$, $f(a)$ can be computed in $|a|s^2$ arithmetic operations.*
2. For an EMA f of size s and a string $a \in \Sigma^*$, $f(a)$ can be computed in $2|a|s^2$ arithmetic operations.

Can we compute $f(a)$ faster? Proving lower bounds for the number of arithmetic complexity of problems is one of the hardest tasks in algebraic complexity. Techniques used today give only lower bounds that are linear in the number of distinct variables of the problem. For example, the best lower bound for matrix multiplication is $2.5s^2$ for any field, [3] and $3s^2$ for the binary field, [21]. In the problem of computing $f(a)$ for any MA f and any $a \in \Sigma^*$, the number of distinct variables is $\min(|\Sigma|, |a|)s^2 + 2s$, which is the number of the entries of $\Lambda^{(\sigma)}$, β and γ. To the best of our knowledge, no better lower bound is known for this problem. This bound does not match the upper bound in Fact 3, which we believe is optimal up to some log factor.

In the full paper, the following slightly better upper bound is proved

Fact 4. *We have*
For an MA or EMA f of size s and t strings $a_1, \ldots, a_t$, $a_i \in \Sigma^*$ and $|a_i| \le m$ for every i, $f(a_i)$ can be computed in

$$O\left(\frac{ts^2 m \log |\Sigma|}{\log(ts^2 m / M(s))}\right)$$

arithmetic operations when $(ts^2 m)/M(s) > 2$ and $O(ts^2 m)$ arithmetic operations otherwise.

5 An Optimal Arithmetic Complexity

In this section we define a compressed MA that, with the results of the previous section, will further improve the arithmetic complexity of the algorithm. The bound we achieve here matches the arithmetic complexity of computing the target in all the s counterexamples received in the algorithm.

We first add a new symbol $\flat$ to the alphabet Σ and call it *blank*. For this symbol $\Lambda_0^{(\flat)} = I$ the identity matrix. This means that for any $w \in (\Sigma \cup \{\flat\})^*$, $f(w)$ is equal to $f(\hat{w})$ where $\hat{w}$ is w without the blanks.

Let $\hat{f}$ be a function $\hat{f} : \Sigma^* \to \mathcal{F}$. Define a function $f : (\Sigma \cup \{\flat\})^* \to \mathcal{F}$ where $f(w) = \hat{f}(\hat{w})$. It is clear that the size of $\hat{f}$ is equal to the MA size of f.

For an alphabet Σ we define the alphabet $\Sigma^{[\ell]} = \{[w_1 w_2 \cdots w_\ell] \mid w_i \in \Sigma\}$. Define an operator $\phi : \Sigma^{[\ell]} \to \Sigma^\ell$ where $\phi([w_1 w_2 \cdots w_\ell]) = w_1 w_2 \cdots w_\ell$. For a function $f : \Sigma^* \to \mathcal{F}$ we define the *ℓ-compressed function* $f^{[\ell]} : (\Sigma^{[\ell]})^* \to \mathcal{F}$ as follows: $f^{[\ell]}(u_1 u_2 \cdots u_t) = f(\phi(u_1)\phi(u_2)\cdots\phi(u_t))$.

It is easy to see that the MA size of $f^{[\ell]}$ is at most the MA size of f. Just define $\Lambda_0^{([w_1 w_2 \cdots w_\ell])} = \Lambda_0^{(w_1)} \Lambda_0^{(w_2)} \cdots \Lambda_0^{(w_\ell)}$. It is also easy to see that membership queries and equivalence queries to $f^{[\ell]}$ can be simulated using membership queries and equivalence queries to f and if we learn $f^{[\ell]}$ we can construct f in linear time.

Using the above representation with $\ell = (\epsilon(\log m + \log s))/(\log |\Sigma|)$ we have

Lemma 3. *Let $\mathcal{F}$ be a field, and $f : \Sigma^* \to \mathcal{F}$ be an MA of size s. Then for any constant ϵ, f is learnable as EMA from $s + 1$ equivalence queries and $m^\epsilon s^{2+\epsilon}$ membership queries with*

$$O\left(\frac{ms^3 \log|\Sigma|}{\log m + \log s}\right)$$

arithmetic operations.

In the full paper we show that this bound is true even if the learner does not know m and s.

6   Almost Optimal Query Complexity

In this section we prove a lower bound for the number of queries and show that the main algorithm is optimal up to $(\log m)/|\Sigma|$.

We first prove the following

Theorem 4. *Any learning algorithm that learns MA of size at most s over any field must ask at least $|\Sigma|s^2 - s^2$ queries.*

Proof. Let $\mathcal{F}$ be any field and $\Sigma = \{\sigma_1, \ldots, \sigma_{|\Sigma|}\}$. Define the field extension $\mathcal{K} = \mathcal{F}(\{z_{i,j,k}\})$ of $\mathcal{F}$ with $s^2|\Sigma|$ algebraically independent elements $\{z_{i,j,k}| i,j = 1, \ldots, s$, $k = 1, \ldots, |\Sigma|\}$. Denote by z the vector $((z_{i,j,k})_{i,j,k})$ (that contains $z_{i,j,k}$ in some order). Consider any algorithm A that learns MA over any field. Then A, in particular, learns MA over $\mathcal{K}$.

Consider $\Lambda^{(\sigma_k)} = [z_{i,j,k}]_{i,j}$, $\gamma = \beta = e_1$ and the MA $f(x) = \beta \Lambda^{(x)} \gamma^T$. We run the algorithm A on the target f. Let $f(w_1), \ldots, f(w_t)$ be the queries asked to the membership query or received by the equivalence query in A. Notice that for all $r = 1, \ldots, t$, $f(w_r) = \beta \Lambda^{(w_r)} \gamma^T = p_r(z)$ for some multivariate polynomial p_r. The algorithm finds $\beta_0, \Lambda_0^{(\sigma)}$ and γ_0 where $f(x) = \beta_0 \Lambda_0^{(x)} \gamma_0^T$. By Lemma 1 there is a non-singular matrix K with entries from $\mathcal{K}$ such that $\Lambda^{(\sigma_k)} = K^{-1} \Lambda_0^{(\sigma_k)} K$ for every k. Since the entries of $\Lambda^{(\sigma_k)}$, $k = 1, \ldots, |\Sigma|$ are algebraically independent and are generated from the entries of K and $p_r(z)$ we must have: The number of entries of K, plus, the number of the polynomials p_r is at least the number of entries of $\Lambda^{(\sigma_k)}$, $k = 1, \ldots, |\Sigma|$. This gives $t + s^2 \geq |\Sigma|s^2$ which implies the result. ∎

Notice that the lower bound in Theorem 4 is true for learning algorithms that are independent of the ground field $\mathcal{F}$, i.e., learning algorithms that learn MA for any field. We now show that any algorithm that learns MA in some specific field $\mathcal{F}$ requires the same number of queries (up to constant factor).

Theorem 5. *Let $\mathcal{F}$ be any field. Any algorithm that learns MA of size at most s over $\mathcal{F}$ must ask at least $(|\Sigma|s^2 - s^2 - O(s))/4 = \Omega(|\Sigma|s^2)$ queries.*

Proof. Assume w.l.o.g that s is even and $r = s/2$. Let $\Sigma = \{\sigma_0, \sigma_1, \ldots, \sigma_{t-1}\}$. Let A be an algorithm that learns MA of size at most s over $\mathcal{F}$. Notice here that A may not learn MA over larger fields, so the technique used in the previous Theorem cannot be applied here. We will show an adversarial strategy that forces A to ask at least $|\Sigma|r^2 - r^2$ queries. Consider the $r \times r$ matrix

$$\Lambda_0 = \begin{pmatrix} 0\,1\,0\,0\,\cdots\,0 \\ 0\,0\,1\,0\,\cdots\,0 \\ 0\,0\,0\,1\,\cdots\,0 \\ \vdots\ \vdots\ \vdots\ \vdots\ \ddots\ \vdots \\ 0\,0\,0\,0\,\cdots\,1 \\ 1\,0\,0\,0\,\cdots\,0 \end{pmatrix}.$$

Define the subset $C \subset MA$ where for each $f \in C$ we have

$$\Lambda^{(\sigma_0)} = \begin{pmatrix} \Lambda_0 & 0 \\ 0 & \Lambda_0 \end{pmatrix} \text{ and } \Lambda^{(\sigma_i)} = \begin{pmatrix} \Lambda_i & \Lambda_i \\ -\Lambda_i & -\Lambda_i \end{pmatrix}$$

for $i > 0$. where each Λ_i is $r \times r$ 0-1 matrix, and $\beta = e_r$ and $\gamma = e_1$ are $(2r)$-vectors.

We now show the following properties of the functions in C

Claim. We have: for every $f \in C$

1. $f(x \cdot \sigma_0^i \cdot y) = f(x \cdot \sigma_0^{i \bmod r} \cdot y)$ for any two strings x and y.
2. $f(\sigma_0^i \cdot \sigma_k \cdot \sigma_0^{r-j+1}) = \Lambda_k[i,j]$ for $1 \le i, j \le r$.
3. $f(x) = 0$ for every x that contains more than one symbol from $\{\sigma_1, \ldots, \sigma_{t-1}\}$.

Proof of Claim. (1) follows from the fact that $\Lambda_0^r = I$, the identity matrix.

To prove (2), let $1 \le i, j \le r$. Notice that $\beta(\Lambda^{(\sigma_0)})^i = e_i$ and $(\Lambda^{(\sigma_0)})^j \gamma^T = e_{r-j+1}^T$. Also, for any $s \times s$ matrix Z we have $\beta(\Lambda^{(\sigma_0)})^i Z (\Lambda^{(\sigma_0)})^{r-j+1} \gamma^T = Z_{i,j}$. Then

$$f(\sigma_0^i \cdot \sigma_k \cdot \sigma_0^{r-j+1}) = \beta \Lambda^{(\sigma_0^i \cdot \sigma_k \cdot \sigma_0^{r-j+1})} \gamma^T = \beta(\Lambda^{(\sigma_0)})^i \Lambda^{(\sigma_k)} (\Lambda^{(\sigma_0)})^{r-j+1} \gamma^T = \Lambda_k[i,j].$$

Now $(\Lambda^{(\sigma_0)})^i \Lambda^{(\sigma_k)} (\Lambda^{(\sigma_0)})^j$ is of the form $\begin{pmatrix} \Delta & \Delta \\ -\Delta & -\Delta \end{pmatrix}$ and multiplying two matrices of such form gives the zero matrix. This implies (3). ∎

Now when the algorithm asks membership query with a string x. If x contains two symbols from $\{\sigma_1, \ldots, \sigma_{t-1}\}$ then the adversary returns 0 and if $x = \sigma_0^i$ then the algorithm returns 1 if $i \bmod r = 1$ and 0 otherwise. In those cases the learner does not gain any information about the function. When the algorithm asks membership query with $x = \sigma_0^i \cdot \sigma_k \cdot \sigma_0^j$ then the adversary answers with arbitrary value from $\{0,1\}$. The learner then knows one of the entries of $\Lambda^{(\sigma_k)}$. If the learner asks again a membership query with $x = \sigma_0^i \cdot \sigma_k \cdot \sigma_0^j$ the adversary returns the same answer.

If the algorithm asks equivalence query with any hypothesis h, the adversary finds some entry $\Lambda_k[i,j]$ that the learner doesn't know from previous query and returns the string $\sigma_0^i \cdot \sigma_k \cdot \sigma_0^{r-j+1}$ as a counterexample.

Notice that each query determines exactly one entry in $\Lambda_k[i,j]$. Since we have $|\Sigma|r^2 - r^2$ entries the algorithm will ask at least $|\Sigma|r^2 - r^2$ queries. ∎

The lower bound for the MAF is in the full paper.

7 Optimal Equivalence Query Complexity

In this section we prove a tight bound for the number of equivalence queries of any polynomial time algorithm for MA.

It is known from [16] that under certain cryptographic assumptions DFA (and therefore MA) is not learnable from equivalence queries only in polynomial time. Similar to the technique used in [8, 9] one can prove the following:

Theorem 6. *Any polynomial time learning algorithm for MA must ask at least*

$$\Omega\left(\frac{s\log|\Sigma|}{\log s}\right)$$

equivalence queries.

This proves that the main algorithm in this paper in almost optimal. We now show that this lower bound is tight.

7.1 The Algorithm

Let $f(x) = \beta \Lambda^{(x)} \gamma^T$ be the target MA. The algorithm begins by asking $MQ(\varepsilon)$, we assume, without loss of generality, that $f(\varepsilon) \neq 0$, [4]. The algorithm then defines $X = \{x_1 = \varepsilon\}$ and $Y = \{y_1 = \varepsilon\}$. As in the main algorithm, the algorithm maintains two sets of strings $X = \{x_1, x_2, \ldots, x_\ell\}$ and $Y = \{y_1, y_2, \ldots, y_\ell\}$. Also, $N(X, Y) = N = [f(x_i \cdot y_j)]_{i,j}$ is non-singular matrix. For some fixed integer $k \geq 3$ the algorithm defines $h(x) = \beta_0 \Lambda_0^{(x)} \gamma_0^T$, where $\Lambda_0^{(\sigma)} = M^{(\sigma)} N^{-1}$,

$$\gamma_0 = (f(x_1), f(x_2), \ldots, f(x_\ell)), \quad \beta_0 = (f(y_1), f(y_2), \ldots, f(y_\ell)) N^{-1}$$

and $M^{(\tau)} = [f(x_i \cdot \tau \cdot y_j)]_{i,j}$ for $\tau \in \Sigma^{\leq k} \stackrel{\text{def}}{=} \cup_{i \leq k} \Sigma^i$. Note that $\gamma_0 = N e_1^T$ and $\beta_0 = e_1$.

Now instead of asking an equivalence query, the algorithm performs an internal checking step. It tries to find a counterexample using membership queries. The algorithm checks for all i, j and $\tau \in \Sigma^{\leq k}$ whether $f(x_i \cdot \tau \cdot y_j) = h(x_i \cdot \tau \cdot y_j)$ by asking membership queries. If for some i, j and $\tau \in \Sigma^{\leq k}$, $f(x_i \cdot \tau \cdot y_j) \neq h(x_i \cdot \tau \cdot y_j)$ then the algorithm has found a counterexample and it proceeds as in the main algorithm. Otherwise, the algorithm asks an equivalence query and receives a counterexample $z = z_1 z_2 \cdots z_{|z|}$.

Our goal is to show that the algorithm uses z to generate k additional independent rows and columns in N. For $k = (\log s)/\log|\Sigma|$ we obtain a polynomial time learning algorithm that asks at most

$$\frac{s}{k} = O\left(\frac{s\log|\Sigma|}{\log s}\right)$$

equivalence queries.

Fact 5. *Before the algorithm asks an equivalence query $M^{(\tau)} = \Lambda_0^{(\tau)} N$ for every $\tau \in \Sigma^{\leq k}$.*

Proof. Let

$$K = \begin{pmatrix} \beta_0 \Lambda_0^{(x_1)} \\ \beta_0 \Lambda_0^{(x_2)} \\ \vdots \\ \beta_0 \Lambda_0^{(x_\ell)} \end{pmatrix} \quad \text{and} \quad L = (\Lambda_0^{(y_1)} \gamma_0^T | \cdots | \Lambda_0^{(y_\ell)} \gamma_0^T).$$

For every $\sigma \in \Sigma$ we have

$$M^{(\sigma)} = K\Lambda_0^{(\sigma)} L \quad \text{and} \quad N = KL.$$

Thus,

$$\Lambda_0^{(\sigma)} = M^{(\sigma)} N^{-1} = K\Lambda_0^{(\sigma)} K^{-1}.$$

Now, for every $\tau = \tau_1 \tau_2 \cdots \tau_{|\tau|} \in \Sigma^{\leq k}$, we have

$$M^{(\tau)} = [f(x_i \cdot \tau \cdot y_j)]_{i,j} = [h(x_i \cdot \tau \cdot y_j)]_{i,j} = K\Lambda_0^{(\tau)} L = K\Lambda_0^{(\tau_1)} \Lambda_0^{(\tau_2)} \cdots \Lambda_0^{(\tau_{|\tau|})} L$$
$$= K\Lambda_0^{(\tau_1)} K^{-1} \cdot K\Lambda_0^{(\tau_2)} K^{-1} \cdots \cdot K\Lambda_0^{(\tau_{|\tau|})} K^{-1} \cdot KL = \Lambda_0^{(\tau)} N. \quad \blacksquare$$

Next, the algorithm searches for the minimal length prefix w_1 of z, such that for some $\sigma_1 \in \Sigma$

$$(f(w_1 \cdot \sigma_1 \cdot y_1), f(w_1 \cdot \sigma_1 \cdot y_2), \ldots, f(w_1 \cdot \sigma_1 \cdot y_\ell)) \neq \beta_0 \Lambda_0^{(w_1 \cdot \sigma_1)} N.$$

Such prefix exists since $f(z \cdot y_1) = f(z) \neq h(z) = \beta_0 \Lambda_0^{(z)} \gamma_0^T = \beta_0 \Lambda_0^{(z)} N e_1^T$. Since w_1 is minimal, we get that $(f(w_1 \cdot y_1), f(w_1 \cdot y_2), \ldots, f(w_1 \cdot y_\ell)) = \beta_0 \Lambda_0^{(w_1)} N$. By Fact 5 for all $\tau \in \Sigma^{\leq 2}$, $M^{(\tau)} = \Lambda_0^{(\tau)} N$ and thus,

$$(f(\tau \cdot y_1), f(\tau \cdot y_2), \ldots, f(\tau \cdot y_\ell)) = e_1 M^{(\tau)} = e_1 \Lambda_0^{(\tau)} N = \beta_0 \Lambda_0^{(\tau)} N, \quad (3)$$

and therefore we have $|w_1| > 1$.

Now the algorithm searches for minimal length prefix w_2 of w_1, such that for some $\sigma_2 \in \Sigma$

$$(f(w_2 \cdot \sigma_2 \sigma_1 \cdot y_1), f(w_2 \cdot \sigma_2 \sigma_1 \cdot y_2), \ldots, f(w_2 \cdot \sigma_2 \sigma_1 \cdot y_\ell)) \neq \beta_0 \Lambda_0^{(w_2 \cdot \sigma_2 \sigma_1)} N.$$

Again by Fact 5 for all $\tau \in \Sigma^{\leq 3}$ it follows that $M^{(\tau)} = \Lambda_0^{(\tau)} N$ and, as in (3) we conclude that $|w_2| > 1$.

The algorithm repeats the above construction k times. Denote by $\sigma^{(i)} = \sigma_i \sigma_{i-1} \cdots \sigma_1$. In the jth iteration it searches for a minimal length prefix w_j of w_{j-1} such that for some $\sigma_j \in \Sigma$

$$(f(w_j \cdot \sigma_j \cdot \sigma^{(j-1)} \cdot y_1), \ldots, f(w_j \cdot \sigma_j \cdot \sigma^{(j-1)} \cdot y_\ell)) \neq \beta_0 \Lambda_0^{(w_j \cdot \sigma_j \cdot \sigma^{(j-1)})} N.$$

After k iterations, the algorithm has a set of strings $W = \{w_1, w_2, \ldots, w_k\}$ and strings $\sigma^{(i)}$ for $1 \leq i \leq k$.

Lemma 4. *For every $1 \leq i \leq k$ and $i > j$ it follows that*

$$(f(w_i \cdot \sigma^{(j)} \cdot y_1), f(w_i \cdot \sigma^{(j)} \cdot y_2), \ldots, f(w_i \cdot \sigma^{(j)} \cdot y_\ell)) = \beta_0 \Lambda_0^{(w_i \cdot \sigma^{(j)})} N$$

Proof. Suppose on the contrary that there exists i and j, such that, $i > j$ and

$$(f(w_i \cdot \sigma^{(j)} \cdot y_1), f(w_i \cdot \sigma^{(j)} \cdot y_2), \ldots, f(w_i \cdot \sigma^{(j)} \cdot y_\ell)) \neq \beta_0 \Lambda_0^{(w_i \cdot \sigma^{(j)})} N,$$

since $i > j$ then w_i is a prefix of w_j, contradiction to the minimality of w_j. ∎

To conclude, we found a set of strings $W = \{w_1, w_2, \ldots, w_k\}$ and strings $\sigma^{(i)}$ that satisfy the following properties for every $1 \leq i \leq k$ and $i > j$:

$$(f(w_i \cdot \sigma^{(j)} \cdot y_1), f(w_i \cdot \sigma^{(j)} \cdot y_2), \ldots, f(w_i \cdot \sigma^{(j)} \cdot y_\ell)) = \beta_0 \Lambda_0^{(w_i \cdot \sigma^{(j)})} N \qquad (4)$$

and

$$(f(w_i \cdot \sigma^{(i)} \cdot y_1), f(w_i \cdot \sigma^{(i)} \cdot y_2), \ldots, f(w_i \cdot \sigma^{(i)} \cdot y_\ell)) \neq \beta_0 \Lambda_0^{(w_i \cdot \sigma^{(i)})} N. \qquad (5)$$

Now the algorithm adds W to X, that is, $\hat{X} = X \bigcup W$, and $\sigma^{(j)} \cdot y_{i_j}$ to Y where i_j is any entry that satisfies

$$f(w_j \cdot \sigma^{(j)} \cdot y_{i_j}) \neq \beta_0 \Lambda_0^{(w_j \cdot \sigma^{(j)})} N e_{i_j}^T, \qquad (6)$$

that is, $\hat{Y} = Y \bigcup \{\sigma^{(1)} \cdot y_{i_1}, \sigma^{(2)} \cdot y_{i_2}, \ldots, \sigma^{(k)} \cdot y_{i_k}\}$.

We now prove that the new matrix $\hat{N} = \hat{N}(\hat{X}, \hat{Y})$

$$\hat{N} = \begin{pmatrix} N & M^{(\sigma^{(1)})} e_{i_1}^T & M^{(\sigma^{(2)})} e_{i_2}^T & \cdots & M^{(\sigma^{(k)})} e_{i_k}^T \\ \beta_0 \Lambda_0^{(w_1)} N & f(w_1 \cdot \sigma^{(1)} \cdot y_{i_1}) & f(w_1 \cdot \sigma^{(2)} \cdot y_{i_2}) & \cdots & f(w_1 \cdot \sigma^{(k)} \cdot y_{i_k}) \\ \beta_0 \Lambda_0^{(w_2)} N & f(w_2 \cdot \sigma^{(1)} \cdot y_{i_1}) & f(w_2 \cdot \sigma^{(2)} \cdot y_{i_2}) & \cdots & f(w_2 \cdot \sigma^{(k)} \cdot y_{i_k}) \\ \beta_0 \Lambda_0^{(w_3)} N & f(w_3 \cdot \sigma^{(1)} \cdot y_{i_1}) & f(w_3 \cdot \sigma^{(2)} \cdot y_{i_2}) & \cdots & f(w_3 \cdot \sigma^{(k)} \cdot y_{i_k}) \\ \vdots & \vdots & \vdots & \ddots & \vdots \\ \beta_0 \Lambda_0^{(w_k)} N & f(w_k \cdot \sigma^{(1)} \cdot y_{i_1}) & f(w_k \cdot \sigma^{(2)} \cdot y_{i_2}) & \cdots & f(w_k \cdot \sigma^{(k)} \cdot y_{i_k}) \end{pmatrix}$$

is non-singular.

By Fact 5 above, $M^{(\tau)} = \Lambda_0^{(\tau)} N$ for all $\tau \in \Sigma^{\leq k}$ and by (5) and (6) for all j:

$$\beta_0 \Lambda^{(w_j \cdot \sigma^{(j)})} N e_{i_j}^T - f(w_j \cdot \sigma^{(j)} \cdot y_{i_j}) \neq 0,$$

we get that:

$$\begin{pmatrix} I & 0 & 0 & 0 & \cdots & 0 \\ \beta_0 \Lambda_0^{(w_1)} & -1 & 0 & 0 & \cdots & 0 \\ \beta_0 \Lambda_0^{(w_2)} & 0 & -1 & 0 & \cdots & 0 \\ \beta_0 \Lambda_0^{(w_3)} & 0 & 0 & -1 & \cdots & 0 \\ \vdots & \vdots & \vdots & \vdots & \ddots & \vdots \\ \beta_0 \Lambda_0^{(w_k)} & 0 & 0 & 0 & \cdots & -1 \end{pmatrix} \hat{N} =$$

$$\begin{pmatrix} N & M^{(\sigma^{(1)})}e_{i_1}^T & M^{(\sigma^{(2)})}e_{i_2}^T & \cdots & M^{(\sigma^{(k)})}e_{i_k}^T \\ 0 & \zeta_1 - f(w_1 \cdot \sigma^{(1)} \cdot y_{i_1}) & \cdots & \cdots & \cdots \\ 0 & 0 & \zeta_2 - f(w_2 \cdot \sigma^{(2)} \cdot y_{i_2}) \cdots & & \cdots \\ \vdots & \vdots & \vdots & \ddots & \vdots \\ 0 & 0 & 0 & \cdots \zeta_k - f(w_k \cdot \sigma^{(k)} \cdot y_{i_k}) \end{pmatrix},$$

where

$$\zeta_j = \beta_0 \Lambda_0^{(w_j \cdot \sigma^{(j)})} N e_{i_j}.$$

Therefore the result follows.   ∎

7.2   The Complexity

In this subsection we analyze the complexity of the algorithm above. We will show that this algorithm achieves the lower bound of equivalence queries complexity for learning MA.

We show

Theorem 7. *Let $\mathcal{F}$ be a field, and $f : \Sigma^* \to \mathcal{F}$ be an MA of size s. Then f is learnable as MA from $r \leq \lceil s/k \rceil$ equivalence queries and $O(r|\Sigma| \cdot msk + |\Sigma|^k s^2)$ membership queries in $O(r \cdot |\Sigma|ms^2k + (s - r \cdot (k-1))|\Sigma|^k M(s))$ arithmetic operations, for some fixed integer k.*

Proof. We already proved that each time a counterexample is received we add k rows and columns to N. As a result, when the size of the target MA is s, r is bounded by $\lceil s/k \rceil$.

When the algorithm asks an equivalence query and gets a counterexample z, it finds the sets W and $\{\sigma^{(i)} | 1 \leq i \leq k\}$. Denote by $w_0 = z$, the algorithm finds a minimal length prefix w' of w_0 for which

$$(f(w' \cdot \sigma' \cdot y_1), f(w' \cdot \sigma' \cdot y_2), \ldots, f(w' \cdot \sigma' \cdot y_\ell)) \neq \beta_0 \Lambda_0^{(w' \cdot \sigma')} N$$

for some $\sigma' \in \Sigma$.

Then it assigns $W \leftarrow \{w_1 = w'\}$ and $\sigma^{(1)} = \sigma'$. In the jth iteration, it finds a minimal prefix w' of w_{j-1} such that

$$(f(w'\cdot\sigma'\cdot\sigma^{(j-1)}\cdot y_1), f(w'\cdot\sigma'\cdot\sigma^{(j-1)}\cdot y_2), ..., f(w'\cdot\sigma'\cdot\sigma^{(j-1)}\cdot y_\ell)) \neq \beta_0 \Lambda_0^{(w'\cdot\sigma'\cdot\sigma^{(j-1)})} N$$

for some $\sigma' \in \Sigma$.

Then $W \leftarrow W \cup \{w_j = w'\}$ and $\sigma^{(j)} = \sigma' \cdot \sigma^{(j-1)}$. The algorithm runs k iterations, each iteration j takes at most $|\Sigma|ms$ membership queries and computes $\beta_0 \Lambda_0^{(w'\cdot\sigma'\cdot\sigma^{(j-1)})} N$ for every prefix w' of w_{j-1} which takes $O(|\Sigma|ms^2)$ arithmetic operations. Thus after each counterexample, the total number of membership queries asked is $O(|\Sigma|msk)$ and the total number of arithmetic operations is $O(|\Sigma|ms^2k)$. Notice that, we already computed $\Lambda_0^{\sigma^{(j-1)}} N$ since $|\sigma^{(j-1)}| \leq k$.

Now, we have $\hat{X} = W \bigcup X$ and $\hat{Y} = Y \bigcup \{\sigma^{(j)} \cdot y_{i_j} | j = 1 \ldots, k\}$ and i_j is any entry that satisfies (6).

All entries of $\hat{N}$ are known. To update the matrices $\hat{M}^{(\tau)}$ for all $\tau \in \Sigma^{\leq k}$, the algorithm asks $O(s^2 \cdot |\Sigma|^k)$ membership queries during its run.

By Lemma 5 below we can find N^{-1} and $\Lambda_0^{(\sigma)}$, for every $\sigma \in \Sigma$, in $O(s^2 \log(s)|\Sigma|)$ arithmetic operations.

Finally our algorithm performs the internal checking step, it needs to compute $\Lambda_0^{(\tau)} N$ for every $\tau \in \Sigma^{\leq k}$. For this, the algorithm multiplies $\sum_{i=1}^{k} |\Sigma|^i = O(|\Sigma|^k)$ matrices each of size at most $s \times s$. Since multiplying two matrices of size $s \times s$ takes $M(s)$ arithmetic operations, to perform internal checking the algorithm needs $O(|\Sigma|^k M(s))$ arithmetic operations.

When finding a counterexample z during the internal checking, z will be of the form $x_i \cdot \tau' \cdot y_j$ for some $x_i \in X$, $y_j \in Y$ and $\tau' \in \Sigma^{\leq k}$. For minimal length $\tau' = \tau_1' \tau_2' \cdots \tau_{|\tau'|}'$, such that z remains a counterexample, the algorithm adds $x_i \cdot \tau_1' \tau_2' \ldots \tau_{|\tau'|-1}'$ to X and $\tau_{|\tau'|}' \cdot y_j$ to Y.

In this case, updating N and $\Lambda^{(\sigma)}$, for every $\sigma \in \Sigma$, will be as in the proof of Theorem 3 and it will cost $O(|\Sigma|s^2)$ arithmetic operations at most.

To conclude, if the algorithm asks r equivalence queries, each time it asks $O(|\Sigma|msk)$ membership queries and needs $O(|\Sigma|ms^2k)$ arithmetic operations. Consequently, the algorithm will find $s - r \cdot k$ counterexamples, by asking membership queries in the internal check, each time it needs $O(|\Sigma|s^2)$ arithmetic operations. Moreover, each time the algorithm performs an internal checking it takes $O(|\Sigma|^k M(s))$ arithmetic operations.

Summing all the above, when learning a target MA function of size s, we need $O(r \cdot |\Sigma|msk + |\Sigma|^k s^2)$ membership queries and $O(r \cdot |\Sigma|ms^2k + (s - r \cdot (k - 1))|\Sigma|^k M(s))$ arithmetic operations. ∎

Lemma 5. *Let N and M be two $\ell \times \ell$ matrices with entries from $\mathcal{F}$ and $\Lambda = MN^{-1}$. Let $u, \Delta \in \mathcal{F}^{\log \ell \times \ell}$ be such that $u = \Delta N$.*

$$\hat{N} = \begin{pmatrix} N & v^T \\ u & \xi \end{pmatrix}, \hat{M} = \begin{pmatrix} M & p^T \\ q & \eta \end{pmatrix}$$

where $\hat{N}$ is nonsingular matrix where $v, q, p \in \mathcal{F}^{\log \ell \times \ell}$ and $\xi, \eta \in \mathcal{F}^{\log \ell \times \ell}$. Then

$$\hat{N}^{-1} = \begin{pmatrix} N^{-1} - (N^{-1}v^T \omega^{-1})\Delta & N^{-1}v^T \omega^{-1} \\ \omega^{-1}\Delta & -\omega^{-1} \end{pmatrix}$$

where $\omega = \lambda v^T - \xi$ and

$$\hat{M}\hat{N}^{-1} = \begin{pmatrix} \Lambda - (\Lambda v^T \omega^{-1})\Delta + p^T \omega^{-1}\Delta & \Lambda v^T \omega^{-1} - p^T \omega^{-1} \\ (qN^{-1}) - ((qN^{-1})v^T \omega^{-1})\Delta + \eta\omega^{-1}\Delta & (qN^{-1})v^T \omega^{-1} - \eta\omega^{-1} \end{pmatrix}.$$

See the full paper for the MAF results.

Acknowledgement. We would like to thank Lawrance Khoury for his contribution to the preliminary version of the paper.

198   L. Bisht, N.H. Bshouty, and H. Mazzawi

References

1. D. Angluin. Learning regular sets from queries and counterexamples. *Information and Computation*, 75(2), 87-106, 1987.
2. D. Angluin. Queries and concept learning. *Machine Learning*, 2, 319–342, 1987.
3. M. Bläser. Lower bounds for the multiplicative complexity of matrix multiplication. *Comput. Complexity*, 8(3), 203–226, 1999.
4. A. Beimel, F. Bergadano, N. H. Bshouty, E. Kushilevitz, S. Varricchio. Learning functions represented as multiplicity automata. *J. ACM*, 47(3), 506–530, 2000.
5. F. Bergadano, N. H. Bshouty, C. Tamon, S. Varricchio. On Learning Programs and Small Depth Circuits. *EuroCOLT.* 150–161, 1997.
6. F. Bergadano, N. H. Bshouty, S. Varricchio. Learning Multivariate Polynomials from Substitution and Equivalence Queries. http://www.eccc.uni-trier.de/eccc , 1996.
7. F. Bergadano, D. Catalano, S. Varricchio. Learning Sat-k-DNF Formulas from Membership Queries.*STOC 96*, 126–130, 1996.
8. J. L. Balcázar, J. Díaz, R. Gavaldá, O. Watanabe. A note on the query complexity of learning DFA. *ALT 92.* 53–62. 1992.
9. N. H. Bshouty, S. A. Goldman, T. R. Hancock, S. Matar. Asking Questions to Minimize Errors. *J. Comput. Syst. Sci.* 52(2), 268–286, 1996.
10. A. Beimel, E. Kushilevitz: Learning Boxes in High Dimension. *Algorithmica*, 22(1/2), 76–90, 1998.
11. N. H. Bshouty, C. Tamon, D. K. Wilson. Learning matrix functions over rings. *Algorithmica* 22(1/2), 91–111, 1998.
12. F. Bergadano, S. Varricchio. Learning Behaviors of Automata from Multiplicity and Equivalence Queries. *SIAM J. Comput.* 25(6), 1268–1280, 1996.
13. F. Bergadano and S. Varricchio. Learning behaviors of automata from shortest counterexamples. *EuroCOLT 95*, 380-391, 1996.
14. D. Coppersmith and S. Winograd. Matrix multiplication via arithmetic progressions. *Journal of Symbolic Computation*, 9, 251-280, 1990.
15. N. Elkies. On finite sequences satisfying linear recursions. Available at http://xxx.lanl.gov/abs/math.CO/0105007.
16. M. J. Kearns, L. G. Valiant. Cryptographic Limitations on Learning Boolean Formulae and Finite Automata. *J. ACM*, 41(1), 67–95, 1994.
17. N. Littlestone. Learning quickly when irrelevant attributes abound: A new linear-threshold algorithm. *Machine Learning*, 2, 285–318, 1987.
18. N. Littlestone and M. K. Warmuth. The weighted majority algorithm. *Information and Computation*, 108(2), 212–261, 1994.
19. W. Maass and G. Turán. Lower bound methods and seperation results for on-line learning models. *Machine Learning* , 9, 107–145, 1992.
20. H. Ohnishi, H. Seki, and T. Kasami. A polynomial time learning algorithm for recognizable series.*IEICE Transactions on Information and Systems*, E77-D(5), 1077–1085, 1994.
21. A. Shpilka. Lower Bounds for Matrix Product. *SIAM J. Comput.* 32(5), 1185–1200, 2003.

Exact Learning Composed Classes
with a Small Number of Mistakes

Nader H. Bshouty and Hanna Mazzawi

Department of Computer Science
Technion, Haifa, 32000, Israel
{bshouty, hanna}@cs.technion.ac.il

Abstract. The Composition Lemma is one of the strongest tools for learning complex classes. It shows that if a class is learnable then composing the class with a class of polynomial number of concepts gives a learnable class. In this paper we extend the Composition Lemma as follows: we show that composing an attribute efficient learnable class with a learnable class with polynomial shatter coefficient gives a learnable class.

This result extends many results in the literature and gives polynomial learning algorithms for new classes.

1 Introduction

The Composition Lemma is one of the strongest tools for learning complex classes. It shows that if a class C is learnable then composing C with polynomial number of concepts G gives a learnable class $C(G)$. This Lemma is used for learning k-CNF of size s (CNF with s terms where each term is of size at most k) in time $O(n^k)$ and $O(sk \log n)$ equivalence queries, k-DL (decision list with terms in the nodes of size at most k) in time $O(n^{3k})$ and $O(n^{2k})$ equivalence queries. Those results was later applied to learning decision tree and CDNF (boolean functions with polynomial size CNF and DNF) in quasi-polynomial time [6,3], and DNF in sub-exponential time [4,8,13].

In this paper we extend the Composition Lemma as follows: We show that composing an attribute efficient learnable class with a learnable class with polynomial shatter coefficient gives a learnable class. Since classes of constant VC dimension has polynomial shatter coefficient, we can apply our result for any class of constant VC dimension.

The following subsections give some results and compare them with the results known from the literature.

1.1 Conjunction of Concepts

Let C be a class with constant VC-dimension, d, that is learnable in polynomial time with q equivalence queries. It is known from [5] that $\bigwedge_k C = \{g_1 \wedge \cdots \wedge g_k \mid g_i \in C\}$ is learnable in $(2kq)^{dd^\perp}$ time and equivalence queries where $d^\perp$ is the VC-dimension of the dual class[1] of C. In most applications $d^\perp \geq d$ (for

---

[1] The dual class $C^\perp$ of C is the set of functions $g_x : C \to \{0,1\}$ where $g_x(f) = f(x)$.

G. Lugosi and H.U. Simon (Eds.): COLT 2006, LNAI 4005, pp. 199–213, 2006.
© Springer-Verlag Berlin Heidelberg 2006

example halfspaces), which gives at least $(2kq)^{d^2}$ time and query complexity. Our algorithm in this paper runs in time $O((k^2q)^{d+2})$ and asks

$$O(k^2 q \log(kq))$$

equivalence queries. This significantly improves the query complexity of the algorithm.

Our algorithm also runs in polynomial time for classes with polynomial shatter coefficient. This cannot be handled by the previous technique developed in [5]. In particular, if $C_1, C_2, \ldots, C_\ell$ are learnable classes with polynomial shatter coefficient then

$$C_1 \wedge C_2 \wedge \cdots \wedge C_\ell = \{f_1 \wedge f_2 \wedge \cdots \wedge f_\ell \mid f_i \in C_i\}$$

is learnable.

1.2 Halfspace of Functions and Other Classes

Let C be a class with polynomial shatter coefficient that is learnable in polynomial time. Then the class $\mathrm{HS}(C) = \{a_1 f_1 + a_2 f_2 + \cdots + a_\ell f_\ell \geq 0 \mid f_1, \ldots, f_\ell \in C\}$ and $k\text{-CNF}(C) = \{H(f_1, \ldots, f_\ell) \mid H \text{ is } k\text{-CNF }\}$ are learnable in polynomial time. Those classes includes many interesting classes. For example, let $X = \{1, 2, \ldots, n\}^d$ and let C be the set of all halfspaces over X that depends on a constant number of variables. Then $\mathrm{HS}(C)$ is the class of depth two Neural Networks with constant fan-in at the hidden nodes [2]. Also the class $k\text{-CNF}(C)$ is interesting because it includes the geometric class of union of $k = O(1)$ n-dimensional polytopes with facets that depends on $j = O(1)$ variables. In particular, it includes the class of union of $O(1)$ boxes in the n-dimensional space. In the constant dimensional space it includes the classes: union of any number of polytopes with constant number of facets, a polytope (with any number of facets) and union of constant number of polytopes. In particular, it contains the union of any number of boxes in the constant dimensional space.

In [2], Auer et. al. already showed that $\mathrm{HS}(C)$ and $k\text{-CNF}(C)$ are learnable in polynomial time for C that is halfspaces that depends on a constant number of variables. Our result in this paper shows that $\mathrm{HS}(C)$ and $k\text{-CNF}(C)$ are learnable in polynomial time for *any* learnable class C with polynomial shatter coefficient.

Another example is the class of boolean functions on strings that is a threshold of weighted substrings. For $w \in \{0, 1\}^{\leq n}$ let $f_w : \{0, 1\}^n \to \{0, 1\}$ be the function $f_w(x) = 1$ if and only if w is a substring of x, i.e., there is i such that $w = x_i x_{i+1} \cdots x_{i+|w|-1}$. Consider the class C of all f_w where w is a string over $\{0, 1\}$. Then the class of threshold of weighted substrings is $\mathrm{HS}(C)$. We show that C has a polynomial shatter coefficient and therefore the class $\mathrm{HS}(C)$ is learnable in polynomial time.

2 Preliminaries

Let X be a set of instances. We call X the *instance space*. A *concept over* X is a boolean function $f : X \to \{0, 1\}$. A *concept class* C *over* X is a set of concepts over X.

We say that f is *positive* (respectively, *negative*) on $x \in X$ if $f(x) = 1$ (respectively, $f(x) = 0$). We say that f is *positive* (respectively, *negative*) on $X' \subset X$ if for every $x \in X'$ we have $f(x) = 1$ (respectively, $f(x) = 0$).

For a concept f over X and $X' \subseteq X$ we define the *projection* $f|_{X'} : X' \to \{0,1\}$ where $f|_{X'}(x) = f(x)$ for every $x \in X'$. For a concept class C over X, the *projection of C* over X' is $C|_{X'} = \{f|_{X'} : f \in C\}$. We say that f_1 *agrees with* f_2 on X' if $f_1|_{X'} \equiv f_2|_{X'}$, i.e., for every $x \in X'$ we have $f_1(x) = f_2(x)$.

Let $Q \subseteq X$. We say that the concept class F over X is *complete* (concept class) for Q (with respect to C) if $C|_Q \subseteq F|_Q$. In other words, for every $f \in C$ there is $h \in F$ that agrees with f on Q. We say that Q is *shattered* by C if $C|_Q = 2^Q$. The Vapnik-Chervonenkis VC-dimension of C, $\mathrm{VCdim}(C)$, is the size of the largest set shattered by C. We define the *shatter coefficient* $\mathcal{S}(C, m)$ to be the maximal size of $C|_Q$ where $|Q| = m$.

The following is proved by Sauer, [12], and independently by Perles and Shelah.

Lemma 1. *Let C be a concept class over X. For a finite set $Q \subseteq X$ and $C' = C|_Q$ we have*

$$|C'| \leq g(|Q|, d) \triangleq \sum_{i=0}^{d} \binom{|Q|}{i} \leq \left(\frac{e|Q|}{d} \right)^d$$

where $d = \mathrm{VCdim}(C)$.

In particular, there is a complete concept class for Q with respect to C of size at most $g(|Q|, d)$.

Sauer Lemma does not always give the best bound. Consider the following example

Example. Let $X = \Re^n$ where $\Re$ is the set of the real numbers and suppose $n = 2^\ell$. Consider the function $f_{i,a} : X \to \{0,1\}$ where $f_{i,a}(x_1, \ldots, x_n) = 1$ if and only if $x_i > a$. Consider the concept class $C = \{f_{i,a} \mid i = 1, \ldots, n \text{ and } a \in \Re\}$. The VC-dimension of C is at least $\ell = \log n$ because the set $\{q_1, \ldots, q_\ell\}$ where $\{(q_{1,i}, q_{2,i}, \ldots, q_{\ell,i}) \mid i = 1, \ldots, \ell\} = \{0,1\}^\ell$ is shattered by the set of functions $\{f_{i,0} \mid i = 1, \ldots, n\} \subset C$. Now Sauer bound for $C|_Q$ gives at least $(|Q|/\log n)^{\log n}$ where it is easy to see that the size of $C|_Q$ is at most $n(|Q| + 1)$.

Therefore, we will sometimes use the following properties to find upper bounds on the shatter coefficient

Lemma 2. *Let C, C_1 and C_2 be concept classes over X and $\sigma : \{0,1\}^2 \to \{0,1\}$. Define $\sigma(C_1, C_2) = \{\sigma(f_1, f_2) \mid f_1 \in C_1, f_2 \in C_2\}$ and $C_1 \otimes_\sigma C_2 = \{f : X \times X \to \{0,1\};\ f(x,y) = \sigma(f_1(x), f_2(y)) \mid f_1 \in C_1, f_2 \in C_2\}$. We have*

1. $\mathcal{S}(C, m) \leq g(m, \mathrm{VCdim}(C))$.
2. $\mathcal{S}(C_1 \cup C_2, m) \leq \mathcal{S}(C_1, m) + \mathcal{S}(C_2, m)$.
3. $\mathcal{S}(\sigma(C_1, C_2), m) \leq \mathcal{S}(C_1, m)\mathcal{S}(C_2, m)$.
4. $\mathcal{S}(C, m_1 + m_2) \leq \mathcal{S}(C, m_1)\mathcal{S}(C, m_2)$.
5. $\mathcal{S}(C_1 \otimes_\sigma C_2, m) \leq \mathcal{S}(C_1, m)\mathcal{S}(C_2, m)$.

We will also consider a family of concept classes $\mathcal{C} = \{C^{(n)}\}$, $n = 1, 2, \cdots$ where $C^{(n)}$ is a concept class over an instance space $X^{(n)}$. When it is clear from the context, we will just call $\mathcal{C}$ a concept class.

For the instance space $X^{(n)} = \{0,1\}^n$ and a concept class $\mathcal{C}$, we say that $\mathcal{C}$ is *closed under combinations* (with repetition) if for every $x_{i_1}, \ldots, x_{i_k} \in \{x_1, \ldots, x_\ell\}$ and a concept $\hat{f} \in C^{(k)}$ there is a concept $f \in C^{(\ell)}$ such that

$$\hat{f}(x_{i_1}, \ldots, x_{i_k}) \equiv f(x_1, \ldots, x_\ell).$$

Let $\mathcal{C}_1 = \{C_1^{(n)}\}$ be a concept class over $\{0,1\}^n$ and let $\mathcal{C}_2$ be a concept class over X. The *composition* of the two concept classes is a concept class over X defined as

$$\mathcal{C}_1(\mathcal{C}_2) = \{f(p_1, \ldots, p_k) \mid f \in C_1^{(k)}, p_1, \ldots, p_k \in \mathcal{C}_2, k = 1, 2, \cdots\}.$$

2.1 The Learning Model

In the *exact learning* model, [1, 9], a *teacher* has a boolean function f, called the *target function*, which is a member of a concept class C over an instance space X. The goal of the *learner* is to find a hypothesis h that is logically equivalent to f. The learner can ask the teacher *equivalence queries*. In each equivalence query the learner sends the teacher a *hypothesis* $h : X \to \{0,1\}$ from some *class of hypothesis H*. The teacher answers "YES" if h is logically equivalent to f, and provides a *counterexample*, x_0 such that $f(x_0) \neq h(x_0)$, otherwise. We will regard the learner as a *learning algorithm*, the teacher as an oracle EQ, and the equivalence query as a call to this oracle, EQ(h).

We say that a learning algorithm $\mathcal{A}$ *learns* C from H in time $t(\mathcal{A})$ and $q(\mathcal{A})$ equivalence queries if for every target function $f \in C$, $\mathcal{A}$ runs in time at most $t(\mathcal{A})$, asks at most $q(\mathcal{A})$ equivalence queries with hypothesis from H and output a hypothesis from H that is logically equivalent to the target function f. If such algorithm exists, then we say that C is *learnable* from H in time $t(\mathcal{A})$ and $q(\mathcal{A})$ equivalence queries.

Throughout the paper we will assume that H is decidable in polynomial time. That is, given a boolean formula h, the learner can decide in polynomial time whether $h \in H$.

For a concept class $\mathcal{C} = \{C^{(n)}\}$ over $\{0,1\}^n$. We say that algorithm $\mathcal{A}$ learns $\mathcal{C}$ from $\mathcal{H} = \{H^{(n)}\}$ in time $t(\mathcal{A}(n))$ and $q(\mathcal{A}(n))$ equivalence queries if for every n, $\mathcal{A}(n)$ learns $C^{(n)}$ from $H^{(n)}$ in time $t(\mathcal{A}(n))$ and $q(\mathcal{A}(n))$ equivalence queries.

3 The Composition Lemma

In this section we prove (for completeness) the following well known composition Lemma [7, 11].

Lemma 3. **(Composition Lemma)** *Let $\mathcal{C} = \{C^{(n)}\}$ be a concept class over $\{0,1\}^n$ that is closed under combinations. Suppose $\mathcal{C}$ is learnable from $\mathcal{H}$ in time*

$t(\mathcal{A}(n))$ and $q(\mathcal{A}(n))$ equivalence queries. Let $G = \{g_1, \ldots, g_\ell\}$ be a concept class over X where each g_i is computable in time $Com(G)$. Then, the algorithm $\mathcal{A}(G)$ in Figure 1 learns $\mathcal{C}(G)$ from $\mathcal{H}(G)$ in time $O(\ell \cdot q(\mathcal{A}(\ell)) \cdot Com(G) + t(\mathcal{A}(\ell)))$ and asks $q(\mathcal{A}(\ell))$ equivalence queries.

Algorithm $\mathcal{A}(G = \{g_1, \ldots, g_\ell\})$.

1. $\ell \leftarrow |G|$;
2. **Run** $\mathcal{A}(\ell)$ with the following changes in each step
3.   **If** $\mathcal{A}(\ell)$ asks $EQ(h(x_1, \ldots, x_\ell))$
4.   **then** Ask $EQ(h(g_1, \ldots, g_\ell))$.
5.   **If** the oracle answers "YES" **then** return($h(g_1, \ldots, g_\ell)$)
6.   **If** the oracle answers $q \in X$
7.   **then** give $(g_1(q), \ldots, g_\ell(q))$ to $\mathcal{A}(\ell)$
8.   **If** $\mathcal{A}(\ell)$ outputs h **then** return($h(g_1, \ldots, g_\ell)$)

Fig. 1. An algorithm that learns $\mathcal{C}(G)$

Proof. Let $\hat{f}(g_{i_1}, \ldots, g_{i_k}) \in \mathcal{C}(G)$ be the target function where $\hat{f} \in C^{(k)}$ and $g_{i_1}, \ldots, g_{i_k} \in G$. Since the concept class is close under combinations, there is a function $f \in C^{(\ell)}$ such that $\hat{f}(g_{i_1}, \ldots, g_{i_k}) \equiv f(g_1, \ldots, g_\ell)$.

Now since each counterexample q for $h(g_1, \ldots, g_\ell)$ satisfies

$$h(g_1(q), \ldots, g_\ell(q)) \neq \hat{f}(g_{i_1}(q), \ldots, g_{i_k}(q)) = f(g_1(q), \ldots, g_\ell(q)),$$

the assignment $(g_1(q), \ldots, g_\ell(q))$ is a counterexample for h with respect to the function f. Since $\mathcal{A}$ learns $\mathcal{C}$ from $\mathcal{H}$, it will learn some $h \in H^{(\ell)}$ that is logically equivalent to the function $f \in C^{(\ell)}$. Then

$$\hat{f}(g_{i_1}, \ldots, g_{i_k}) \equiv f(g_1, \ldots, g_\ell) \equiv h(g_1, \ldots, g_\ell).$$

The algorithm runs in time at most $O(\ell \cdot q(\mathcal{A}(\ell)) \cdot Com(G) + t(\mathcal{A}(\ell)))$ and asks $q(\mathcal{A}(\ell))$ equivalence queries. $\blacksquare$

Notice that when $|G|$ is exponentially large then the complexity is exponential. In the next section we show that, with some constraints on $\mathcal{C}$ and G, a modified version of the composition lemma gives an algorithm with small time and query complexity even when G is exponentially large.

4 The Algorithm

In this section we give our main algorithm. The main idea of our algorithm is the following: The learner wants to learn $\mathcal{C}_1(\mathcal{C}_2)$ for a large concept class

C_2 using learning algorithms $\mathcal{A}_1$ and $\mathcal{A}_2$ for $\mathcal{C}_1$ and $\mathcal{C}_2$, respectively. Since the complexity in the composition lemma (Lemma 3) depends on $|C_2|$, which may be exponentially large, the learner cannot use the composition lemma. Instead it does the following: Let $f(p_1, \ldots, p_k)$ be the target function that the learner is trying to learn. At some stage of the learning process the learner has a set of examples Q. It uses this set with the algorithm $\mathcal{A}_2$ to learn a complete concept for Q, $G = \{g_1, \ldots, g_\ell\} \subset C_2$ with respect to C_2. This set may not contain $p_1, \ldots, p_k$ but for each p_i there is g_{r_i} that is "close" to p_i. By "close" we mean that g_{r_i} is a hypothesis of some equivalence query in $\mathcal{A}_2$ when $\mathcal{A}_2$ runs with the target p_i over the instance space Q. Then the learner assumes that $p_1, \ldots, p_k \in G$ and runs the algorithm $\mathcal{A}_1(G)$. When $\mathcal{A}_1(G)$ runs more than it should or gets stuck then the learner knows that the assumption was wrong. But fortunately, we are able to prove that one of the new counterexamples the learner obtains from running $\mathcal{A}_1(G)$ provides a counterexample for one of the g_{r_i}. The learner then adds all the counterexamples to Q and runs the algorithm again. Eventually, the set G will contain $p_1, \ldots, p_k$ and $\mathcal{A}_1(G)$ will learn the target function.

We show that if $C_2|_Q$ is small and $\mathcal{A}_1$ has small complexity then $\mathcal{C}_1(C_2)$ is learnable.

In subsection 4.1 we show how to build G and then in subsection 4.2 we give our main algorithm followed by a proof of correctness and complexity analysis.

4.1   Find All Consistent Hypotheses

Let C be a concept class and H be a hypothesis class. Let $\mathcal{A}$ be a learning algorithm that learns C from H in time $t(\mathcal{A})$ and $q(\mathcal{A})$ equivalence queries. In this subsection we give an algorithm that, for a set of points $Q = \{q_1, q_2, \ldots, q_\ell\}$, outputs a set of hypothesis $F \subset H$ such that $C|_Q \subseteq F|_Q$. That is, the algorithm generates $F \subseteq H$ that is complete for Q with respect to C.

The first algorithm in this subsection is **Find_Hypothesis**$(\mathcal{A}, P, Q\backslash P)$ in Figure 2. It searches for a hypothesis $h \in H$ that is positive on P and negative on $Q\backslash P$ for some $P \subseteq Q$. For such hypothesis h we say that h is *consistent with* $(P, Q\backslash P)$. The algorithm is very similar to the algorithm in [5].

We now prove

Fact 1. *Let C be a concept class over X. Let $\mathcal{A}$ be a learning algorithm that learns C from H in time $t(\mathcal{A})$ and $q(\mathcal{A})$ equivalence queries. Let Q be a set of ℓ instances from X and $P \subseteq Q$. **Find_Hypothesis***$(\mathcal{A}, P, Q\backslash P)$ in Figure 2 runs in time $O(t(\mathcal{A}) + \ell \cdot q(\mathcal{A}))$ and outputs $h \in H$ that satisfies the following:*

1. *If there is $f \in C$ that is consistent with $(P, Q\backslash P)$ then h is consistent with $(P, Q\backslash P)$.*
2. *If there in no $f \in H$ that is consistent with $(P, Q\backslash P)$ then h is "NULL".*
3. *If there is $f \in C$ that is consistent with $(P, Q\backslash P)$ and $\mathcal{A}$ halts then $h \equiv f$.*

Proof. The algorithm runs the learning algorithm $\mathcal{A}$ (line 2), counts the number of its steps (lines 1 and 3) and the number of times it asks equivalence queries (lines 1 and 5). If $\mathcal{A}$ runs more than $t(\mathcal{A})$ steps, asks more than $q(\mathcal{A})$ equivalence queries or gets stuck (this also includes the cases where the algorithm asks $EQ(h)$ or outputs h where $h \notin H$), then it returns "NULL" (lines 3,5 and 13). This indicates that there exists no consistent hypothesis in C for $(P, Q\backslash P)$.

For each equivalence query $EQ(h)$ that $\mathcal{A}$ asks, the algorithm returns to $\mathcal{A}$ a counterexample from P or $Q\backslash P$, i.e., some point $q \in P$ where $h(q) = 0$ or $q \in Q\backslash P$ where $h(q) = 1$ (lines 4-8). Obviously, if the algorithm cannot find such point then the hypothesis h is consistent with $(P, Q\backslash P)$ (line 6-7).

Algorithm **Find_Hypothesis**$(\mathcal{A}, P, Q\backslash P)$.

1. $time \leftarrow 0$; $query \leftarrow 0$;
2. **Run** $\mathcal{A}$ with the following changes in each step
3. $time \leftarrow time + 1$;
4.   **If** $\mathcal{A}$ asks $EQ(h)$ where $h \in H$
5.   **then** $query \leftarrow query + 1$;
6.   **If** h consistent with $(P, Q\backslash P)$
7.   **then** return(h);
8.   **else** give $\mathcal{A}$ a counterexample from P or $Q\backslash P$.
9.   **If** $\mathcal{A}$ outputs h
10.   **then If** h consistent with $(P, Q\backslash P)$
11.   **then** return(h);
12.   **else** return$(NULL)$;
13.   **If** $\mathcal{A}$ cannot execute this step **or** $time > t(\mathcal{A})$ **or** $query > q(\mathcal{A})$
14.   **then** return$(NULL)$;

Fig. 2. An algorithm that finds a hypothesis that is consistent with $(P, Q\backslash P)$

Now if there is $f \in C$ that is consistent with $(P, Q\backslash P)$ then either one of the hypothesis $h \in H$ in the equivalence queries is consistent with $(P, Q\backslash P)$ or, since the learning algorithm $\mathcal{A}$ learns C, the algorithm $\mathcal{A}$ halts and outputs $h \in H$ that is equivalent to f. In both cases, the output hypothesis is in H and consistent with $(P, Q\backslash P)$.

If there is no $f \in C$ that is consistent with $(P, Q\backslash P)$ then either $\mathcal{A}$ outputs an $h \in H$ that is consistent with $(P, Q\backslash P)$, gets stuck, goes into an infinite loop or outputs a hypothesis that is not consistent with $(P, Q\backslash P)$. In the latter three cases the algorithm outputs "NULL". ∎

The second algorithm, **Find_Complete_Concept** in Figure 3, finds $F \subseteq H$ that is complete for Q with respect to C. It starts with a hypothesis h_0 that is consistent with $(\emptyset, \emptyset)$ (line 1). At stage i in the **For** command (line 2) the set (of hypothesis h in) $\mathcal{F}_{i-1}$ is complete for $Q_{i-1} = \{q_1, \ldots, q_{i-1}\}$ with respect to C. For each hypothesis g that is consistent with $(P, Q_{i-1}\backslash P)$ (line 4) it runs **Find_Hypothesis** to try to find a hypothesis $g_1 \in H$ that is consistent with $(P \cup \{q_i\}, Q_{i-1}\backslash P)$ (line 5) and a hypothesis $g_2 \in H$ that is consistent with

Algorithm **Find_Complete_Concept**$(\mathcal{A}, Q = \{q_1, \ldots, q_\ell\})$.

1. $h_0 \leftarrow$ **Find_Hypothesis**$(\mathcal{A}, \emptyset, \emptyset)$; $\mathcal{F}_0 \leftarrow \{((\emptyset, \emptyset), h_0)\}$;
2. **For** $i = 1$ to ℓ **do**
3. $\mathcal{F}_i \leftarrow \emptyset$; $Q_{i-1} \leftarrow \{q_1, \ldots, q_{i-1}\}$;
4.   **For all** $((P, Q_{i-1}\backslash P), g) \in \mathcal{F}_{i-1}$ **do**
5. $g_1 \leftarrow$ **Find_Hypothesis**$(\mathcal{A}, P \cup \{q_i\}, Q_{i-1}\backslash P)$.
6. $g_2 \leftarrow$ **Find_Hypothesis**$(\mathcal{A}, P, (Q_{i-1}\backslash P) \cup \{q_i\})$.
7.   **If** $g_1 \neq$ "NULL" **then** $\mathcal{F}_i \leftarrow \mathcal{F}_i \cup \{((P \cup \{q_i\}, Q_{i-1}\backslash P), g_1)\}$
8.   **If** $g_2 \neq$ "NULL" **then** $\mathcal{F}_i \leftarrow \mathcal{F}_i \cup \{((P, (Q_{i-1}\backslash P) \cup \{q_i\}), g_2)\}$
9. $F \leftarrow \{h \mid ((P, Q\backslash P), h) \in \mathcal{F}_\ell\}$
10. output(F).

Fig. 3. An algorithm that outputs a complete concept for Q with respect to C

$(P, (Q_{i-1}\backslash P) \cup \{q_i\})$ (line 6). That is, it assumes that q_i is positive and then tries to find a consistent hypothesis $g_1 \in H$ and then assumes that it is negative and again tries to find a consistent hypothesis $g_2 \in H$. If such hypothesis exists then it puts it in $\mathcal{F}_i$ (lines 7 and 8).

We now show

Fact 2. *Let C be a concept class over X. Let $\mathcal{A}$ be a learning algorithm that learns C from H in time $t(\mathcal{A})$ and $q(\mathcal{A})$ equivalence queries. Let Q be a subset of X.* **Find_Complete_Concept***$(\mathcal{A}, Q)$ runs in time at most*

$$O\left(|Q|(t(\mathcal{A}) + |Q| \cdot q(\mathcal{A})) \cdot \mathcal{S}(H, |Q|)\right)$$

and outputs $F \subseteq H$ that is complete for Q with respect to C of size at most $\mathcal{S}(H, |Q|)$.

Proof. Obviously, $\mathcal{S}(H, i-1) \leq \mathcal{S}(H, i)$ and therefore, $|\mathcal{F}_i| \leq |\mathcal{F}_{|Q|}| \leq \mathcal{S}(H, |Q|)$. Therefore, the algorithm **Find_Complete_Concept**$(\mathcal{A}, Q)$ runs **Find_Hypothesis** at most $2|Q|\mathcal{S}(H, |Q|)$ times. By Fact 1 the result follows.   ∎

We will further improve the complexity of **Find_Complete_Concept** and prove some new properties of the algorithm that will be used in the sequel.

First, we will assume that in **Find_Hypothesis** when $\mathcal{A}$ asks equivalence query, the algorithm always chooses the counterexample in Q with the smallest index and sends it to $\mathcal{A}$. See the algorithm in Figure 2 line 8. This requirement is not necessary but it simplifies the analysis. Second, if **Find_Hypothesis** stops in step 7, i.e., the hypothesis in the equivalence query h (in step 4) is consistent with $(P, Q\backslash P)$, then the next time we call **Find_Hypothesis** $(\mathcal{A}, P \cup \{q\}, Q\backslash P)$ and **Find_Hypothesis** $(\mathcal{A}, P, (Q\backslash P) \cup \{q\})$ the following facts are true:

1. The hypothesis h is consistent either with $(P \cup \{q\}, Q\backslash P)$ or $(P, (Q\backslash P) \cup \{q\})$ and therefore for one of them the algorithm **Find_Complete_Concept** does not need to call **Find_Hypothesis**.

2. For the other one, **Find_Hypothesis** does not need to start running $\mathcal{A}$ from the beginning. It can just continue running it from step 4, i.e., returns the counterexample q to $\mathcal{A}$ and continue running $\mathcal{A}$ until either a new consistent hypothesis is found or it returns "NULL".

Third, if **Find_Hypothesis** stops in step 11, then the algorithm can stop calling **Find_Hypothesis** for the descendants of $(P, Q \backslash P)$ and add h to F.

We will call this new algorithm **Find_Complete**. Now we have

Fact 3. *Let C be a concept class over X. Let $\mathcal{A}$ be a learning algorithm that learns C from H in time $t(\mathcal{A})$ and $q(\mathcal{A})$ equivalence queries. Let Q be a subset of X.* **Find_Complete***$(\mathcal{A}, Q)$ runs in time at most*

$$O\left(\left(t(\mathcal{A}) + |Q| \cdot q(\mathcal{A})\right) \cdot \mathcal{S}(H, |Q|)\right)$$

and outputs $F \subseteq H$ of size at most $\mathcal{S}(H, |Q|)$ that is complete for Q with respect to C.

Proof. This follows from the fact that the algorithm runs only one time for every hypothesis in $\mathcal{F}_{|Q|}$. ∎

4.2 The Main Algorithm

In this section we give our main algorithm.

Let $\mathcal{C}_1 = \{C_1^{(n)}\}$ be a concept class over $\{0, 1\}^n$ and $\mathcal{A}_1$ be a learning algorithm for $\mathcal{C}_1$. Let $\mathcal{C}_2$ be a concept class over X and $\mathcal{A}_2$ be a learning algorithm for $\mathcal{C}_2$. Consider the algorithm $\mathcal{A}_1(\mathcal{A}_2)$ in Figure 4. At some stage of the algorithm it has some set of examples Q. It generates a set $G \subseteq H$ that is complete for Q with respect to $\mathcal{C}_2$ (line 2). The algorithm then learns $\mathcal{A}_1(G)$ using the composition Lemma (see lines 4-19). If the algorithm fails (see lines 3, 5, 12-18 and 19) then it reruns the algorithm with the examples in Q and all the counterexamples received from $\mathcal{A}_1(G)$ (see steps 11 and 17).

We prove

Theorem 1. *Let $\mathcal{C}_1 = \{C_1^{(n)}\}$ be a concept class over $\{0, 1\}^n$ that is closed under combinations and $\mathcal{A}_1$ be a learning algorithm that learns $\mathcal{C}_1$ from $\mathcal{H}_1$ in time $t(\mathcal{A}_1(n))$ and $q(\mathcal{A}_1(n))$ equivalence queries. Let $\mathcal{C}_2$ be a concept class over X and $\mathcal{A}_2$ be a learning algorithm that learns $\mathcal{C}_2$ from H_2 in time $t(\mathcal{A}_2)$ and $q(\mathcal{A}_2)$ equivalence queries. Then $\mathcal{A}_1(\mathcal{A}_2)$ learns $\mathcal{C}_1(\mathcal{C}_2)$ from $\mathcal{H}_1(H_2)$ in time*

$$O\left(\mathcal{S}(H_2, \rho_\tau)(t(\mathcal{A}_2) + \rho_\tau \cdot q(\mathcal{A}_2)) + \tau \cdot t(\mathcal{A}_1(\mathcal{S}(H_2, \rho_\tau)))\right)$$

and ρ_τ equivalence queries where $\tau = q(\mathcal{A}_2) \cdot k$, $\rho_0 = 0$,

$$\rho_{i+1} = \rho_i + q(\mathcal{A}_1(\mathcal{S}(H_2, \rho_i))),$$

and the target function is $f(p_1, p_2, \ldots, p_k)$.

Algorithm $\mathcal{A}_1(\mathcal{A}_2)$.

1. $Q \leftarrow \emptyset;\ s \leftarrow 0;$
2. $G \leftarrow$ **Find_Complete**$(\mathcal{A}_2, Q);$
3. $time \leftarrow 0;\ query \leftarrow 0;\ \ell \leftarrow |G|;$
4. **Run** $\mathcal{A}_1(\ell)$ with the following changes in each step
5. $time \leftarrow time + 1;$
6.   **If** $\mathcal{A}_1(\ell)$ asks EQ$(h(x_1, \ldots, x_\ell))$
7.   **then** Ask EQ$(h(g_1, \ldots, g_\ell))$ where $G = \{g_1, \ldots, g_\ell\}.$
8.   **If** the oracle answers "YES" **then** return$(h(g_1, \ldots, g_\ell))$
9.   **If** the oracle answers $q \in X$
10.   **then** give $(g_1(q), \ldots, g_\ell(q))$ to $\mathcal{A}_1(\ell)$
11. $s \leftarrow s + 1;\ q_s \leftarrow q;\ Q \leftarrow Q \cup \{q_s\};$
12. $query \leftarrow query + 1;$
13.   **If** $\mathcal{A}_1(\ell)$ outputs h
14.   **then** Ask EQ$(h(g_1, \ldots, g_\ell))$ where $G = \{g_1, \ldots, g_\ell\}.$
15.   **If** the oracle answer "YES" **then** return$(h(g_1, \ldots, g_\ell))$
16.   **If** the oracle answer $q \in X$
17.   **then** $s \leftarrow s + 1;\ q_s \leftarrow q;\ Q \leftarrow Q \cup \{q_s\};$
18.   **goto** 2.
19.   **If** $\mathcal{A}_1(\ell)$ cannot execute this step **or**
       $time > t(\mathcal{A}_1(\ell))$ **or** $query > q(\mathcal{A}_1(\ell)) + 1$
20.   **then goto** 2.;

Fig. 4. An algorithm that learns $\mathcal{C}_1(\mathcal{C}_2)$

Proof. Let $f(p_1, \ldots, p_k)$ be the target function where $f \in C_1^{(k)}$ and $p_1, \ldots, p_k \in C_2$. At stage i the algorithm has a set of instances Q collected from the equivalence queries. Since $G \leftarrow$ **Find_Complete**$(\mathcal{A}_2, Q)$, for every $P \subseteq Q$, if there is a concept in C_2 that is consistent with $(P, Q \backslash P)$ then there is $g \in G$ that is consistent with $(P, Q \backslash P)$. Therefore, for every $j = 1, \ldots, k$ there is $g_{r_j} \in G$ that is consistent with $(P_j, Q \backslash P_j)$ where $P_j = \{q \in Q \mid p_j(q) = 1\}$. That is, $p_j|_Q = g_{r_j}|_Q$. Each g_{r_j} was obtained by running $\mathcal{A}_2$ with $(P_j, Q \backslash P_j)$ in **Find_Hypothesis**$(\mathcal{A}_2, P_j, Q \backslash P_j)$. We denote by $m(\mathcal{A}_2, P_j, Q \backslash P_j)$ the number of equivalence queries that $\mathcal{A}_2$ asks in **Find_Hypothesis**$(\mathcal{A}_2, P_j, Q \backslash P_j)$ before it outputs g_{r_j}. By Fact 1, if $\mathcal{A}_2$ halts then $p_j \equiv g_{r_j}$ and therefore $m(\mathcal{A}_2, P_j, Q \backslash P_j) \le q(\mathcal{A}_2)$ for every j.

Now we will show that if the algorithm goes to step 2 (from step 18 or 20), i.e., $\mathcal{A}_1$ fails to find the target, the new set Q' which is Q with the new counterexamples from $\mathcal{A}_1(G)$, satisfies $m(\mathcal{A}_2, P_j', Q' \backslash P_j') > m(\mathcal{A}_2, P_j, Q \backslash P_j)$ for at least one j where $P_j' = \{q \in Q' \mid p_j(q) = 1\}$. In other words, one of the new points in Q' is a counterexample for one of the hypothesis g_{r_j}. This will show that after at most $q(\mathcal{A}_2) \cdot k$ stages the set G contains $p_1, \ldots, p_k$. When $p_1, \ldots, p_k$ are in G then the algorithm $\mathcal{A}_1(G)$ (steps 4-20) will learn the target.

We will now show that either one of the new points is a counterexample for one of the g_{r_j} or the learner has learned the target. Suppose none of the points in $Q'\backslash Q$ is a counterexample for $g_{r_1}, \ldots, g_{r_k}$. That is, for every $j \leq k$ and every $q \in Q'\backslash Q$ we have $g_{r_j}(q) = p_j(q)$. Then, for every $q \in Q'\backslash Q$ we have

$$f(p_1(q), \ldots, p_k(q)) = f(g_{r_1}(q), \ldots, g_{r_k}(q)).$$

Since the algorithm runs $\mathcal{A}_1(G)$ and each counterexample for the target $f(p_1, \ldots, p_k)$ is also a counterexample for $f(g_{r_1}, \ldots, g_{r_k})$, the algorithm $\mathcal{A}_1(G)$ will learn h that is equivalent to $f(g_{r_1}, \ldots, g_{r_k})$. Then, when the algorithm asks equivalence queries with $h \equiv f(g_{r_1}, \ldots, g_{r_k})$ it either receives a counterexample q and then for this $q \in Q'\backslash Q$ we have $f(p_1(q), \ldots, p_k(q)) \neq h(q) = f(g_{r_1}(q), \ldots, g_{r_k}(q))$ which is a contradiction, or, it receives "YES" and then we have $f(g_{r_1}, \ldots, g_{r_k}) \equiv h \equiv f(p_1, \ldots, p_k)$. This completes the correctness of the algorithm.

We now prove its complexity. Let ρ_i be the size of $|Q|$ at stage i. Then $\rho_0 = 0$ and at stage $i + 1$ we have $|G| = \mathcal{S}(H_2, \rho_i)$ and therefore $\mathcal{A}_1(G)$ generates $q(\mathcal{A}_1(\mathcal{S}(H_2, \rho_i)))$ more counterexamples. Therefore, $\rho_{i+1} = q(\mathcal{A}_1(\mathcal{S}(H_2, \rho_i))) + \rho_i$. Since the algorithm runs at most $\tau = q(\mathcal{A}_2) \cdot k$ stages, the number of equivalence queries in the algorithm is at most ρ_τ.

The time complexity is the time for **Find_Complete** with ρ_τ examples, which is equal to $O\left(\mathcal{S}(H_2, \rho_\tau)(t(\mathcal{A}_2) + \rho_\tau \cdot q(\mathcal{A}_2))\right)$ plus the time for running $\mathcal{A}_1$ at each stage, which is equal to $\sum_{i=1}^{\tau} t(\mathcal{A}_1(\mathcal{S}(H_2, \rho_i))) \leq \tau \cdot t(\mathcal{A}_1(\mathcal{S}(H_2, \rho_\tau)))$.   ∎

In the following section we give some applications of the main Theorem

5   Applications

In this section we first prove

Theorem 2. *Let $\bigwedge$ be the set of monotone conjunctions (monomials) over $V = \{x_1, x_2, \cdots\}$. Let C be a concept class that is learnable from H in time t and q equivalence queries. Suppose $\mathcal{S}(H, m) \leq \gamma m^d$ for some d and $\gamma \geq 2$ that are independent of m. Then $\bigwedge_k C = \{g_1 \wedge \cdots \wedge g_k \mid g_i \in C\}$ is learnable in time $O(\gamma \rho^d(t + \rho q))$ and*

$$\rho = O(k^2 q d \log(kqd\gamma^{1/d} \log \gamma))$$

equivalence queries.

In particular, when H has polynomial size shatter coefficient then $\bigwedge_k C$ is learnable in time $O(\gamma \rho_0^d(t + \rho_0 q))$ and

$$\rho_0 = O(k^2 q \log(kq\gamma))$$

equivalence queries.

Proof. We use WINNOW1 for learning $\bigwedge$, [9]. For a conjunction over $\{0, 1\}^n$ with k relevant variables, WINNOW1 runs in time $O(nk \log n)$ and asks $ck \log n$ equivalent queries for some constants c. By Theorem 1 the number of equivalence queries ρ satisfies $\rho \leq \rho_\tau$ where $\tau = qk$, $\rho_0 = 0$ and

$$\rho_{i+1} = \rho_i + ck \log(\mathcal{S}(H, \rho_i)) \leq \rho_i + cdk \log \rho_i + ck \log \gamma.$$

Then

$$\rho_\tau = \sum_{i=0}^{\tau-1} (\rho_{i+1} - \rho_i)$$

$$\leq \sum_{i=1}^{\tau-1} cdk \log \rho_i + ck \log \gamma$$

$$\leq cdk\tau \log \rho_\tau + ck\tau \log \gamma.$$

Now, using Fact 4 below, we have

$$\rho \leq \rho_\tau \leq 2cdk\tau \log(c^2 dk^2 \tau^2 \log \gamma) + ck\tau \log \gamma = O(k^2 qd \log(kqd\gamma^{1/d} \log \gamma)).$$

By Theorem 1 the time complexity follows. ∎

Fact 4. *Let* $\alpha, \beta > 2$ *be constants and* $\rho \geq 1$ *that satisfies*

$$\rho \leq \alpha \log \rho + \beta.$$

Then

$$\rho \leq 2\alpha \log(\alpha\beta) + \beta.$$

Proof. Consider the two increasing monotone functions $f(x) = x$ and $g(x) = \alpha \log x + \beta$ for $x \geq 1$. Both functions intersect at one point ρ_0 that satisfies $\rho_0 = \alpha \log \rho_0 + \beta$. For $x > \rho_0$ we have $f(x) > g(x)$ and for $1 < x < \rho_0$ we have $f(x) < g(x)$. Therefore, it is enough to show that for $\rho_1 = 2\alpha \log(\alpha\beta) + \beta$ we have $g(\rho_1) < f(\rho_1)$.

Now since $\alpha, \beta > 2$ we have

$$g(\rho_1) = \alpha \log(2\alpha \log(\alpha\beta) + \beta) + \beta$$
$$< \alpha \log(2\alpha\beta \log(\alpha\beta)) + \beta$$
$$< \alpha \log((\alpha\beta)^2) + \beta = \rho_1 = f(\rho_1). \quad ∎$$

Let C be a concept class with constant VC-dimension, d, that is learnable in polynomial time with q equivalence queries. It is known from [5] that $\bigwedge_k C = \{g_1 \wedge \cdots \wedge g_k \mid g_i \in C\}$ is learnable in $(2kq)^{dd^\perp}$ time and equivalence queries where $d^\perp$ is the VC-dimension of the dual concept class of C. In most applications $d^\perp \geq d$ (for example halfspaces), which gives at least $(2kq)^{d^2}$ time and equivalence queries. Theorem 2 shows that this concept class is learnable in time $O((k^2 q)^{d+2})$ and

$$O(k^2 q \log(kq))$$

equivalence queries. This significantly improves the query complexity in [5].

Our algorithm also runs in polynomial time for concept classes with polynomial shatter coefficient. This cannot be handled by the previous technique developed in [5].

We now show

Corollary 1. *Let C_i be a concept class that is learnable from H_i in time t_i and q_i equivalence queries for $i = 1, \ldots, k$. Suppose $S(H_i, m) \leq \gamma_i m^{d_i}$ for $i = 1, \ldots, k$ where each d_i and $\gamma_i > 2$ are independent of m. Then the concept class*

$$C_1 \wedge C_2 \wedge \cdots \wedge C_k = \{f_1 \wedge f_2 \wedge \cdots \wedge f_k \mid f_i \in C_i\}$$

is learnable in time $O(\gamma k \rho^d (t + \rho q))$ and

$$\rho = O(k^2 q d \log(k q d \gamma^{1/d} \log \gamma))$$

equivalence queries where $q = \sum_i q_i$, $t = \sum_i t_i$, $\gamma = \max_i \gamma_i$ and $d = \max_i d_i$.

In particular, when each H_i has polynomial size shatter coefficient then $C_1 \wedge C_2 \wedge \cdots \wedge C_k$ is learnable in time $O(\gamma k \rho_0^d (t + \rho_0 q))$ and

$$\rho = O(k^2 q \log(k q \gamma))$$

equivalence queries.

Proof Sketch. Consider $C = \cup_i C_i$ and $H = \cup_i H_i$. Then C is learnable in time t and q equivalence queries. Now since

$$S(H_1 \cup \cdots \cup H_k, m) \leq \sum_{i=1}^{k} \gamma_i m^{d_i} \leq k \gamma m^d,$$

by Theorem 2 the result follows.   ∎

We now show the above results with WINNOW2, [9].

For any halfspace $f(x) = [a_1 x_1 + \cdots + a_n x_n \geq b]$ let $\alpha(f)$ be the minimal $\sum_{i=1}^{n} \mu_i / \delta^2$ such that for all $(x_1, \ldots, x_n) \in \{0, 1\}^n$ we have

$$\sum_{i=1}^{n} \mu_i x_i \geq 1 \quad \text{if} \quad f(x_1, \ldots, x_n) = 1$$

and

$$\sum_{i=1}^{n} \mu_i x_i \leq 1 - \delta \quad \text{if} \quad f(x_1, \ldots, x_n) = 0.$$

Then we have

Theorem 3. *Let HS_α be the set of halfspaces f over $V = \{x_1, x_2, \cdots\}$ with $\alpha(f) \leq \alpha$. Let C be a concept class that is learnable from H in time t and q equivalence queries. Suppose $S(H, m) \leq \gamma m^d$ for some d and $\gamma \geq 2$ that are independent of m. Then $HS_\alpha(C)$ is learnable in time $O(\gamma \rho^d (t + \rho q))$ and*

$$\rho = O(\alpha k q d \log(\alpha k q d \gamma^{1/d} \log \gamma))$$

equivalence queries.

In particular, when H has polynomial size shatter coefficient then $HS_\alpha(C)$ is learnable in time $O(\gamma \rho_0^d (t + \rho_0 q))$ and

$$\rho_0 = O(\alpha k q \log(\alpha k q \gamma))$$

equivalence queries.

As an application of Theorem 3 consider the concept class of boolean functions on strings that is a threshold of weighted substrings. For $w \in \{0,1\}^{\leq n}$ let $f_w :$ $\{0,1\}^n \to \{0,1\}$ be the function $f_w(x) = 1$ if and only if x contains w as a substring, i.e., there is i such that $w = x_i x_{i+1} \cdots x_{i+|w|-1}$. Consider the concept class W of all f_w for all strings w over $\{0,1\}$. Then the concept class of threshold of weighted substrings is $\mathrm{HS}_\alpha(W)$.

We show

Theorem 4. *Let HS_α be the set of halfspaces f over $V = \{x_1, x_2, \cdots\}$ with $\alpha(f) \leq \alpha$. Then $\mathrm{HS}_\alpha(W)$ is learnable in time $O(\gamma \rho_0^d(t + \rho_0 q))$ and asks*

$$\rho_0 = O(\alpha k n^2 \log(\alpha k n))$$

equivalence queries.

Proof. Since m strings can have at most $n^2 m$ different substrings, we have $\mathcal{S}(W, m) \leq n^2 m$. Now it is easy to see that W is learnable from W with $q \leq n^2$ equivalence queries. Then with Theorem 3 the result follows. ∎

In the full paper we give more results on learning k-$\mathrm{CNF}(C)$ and show how to handle errors in the answers to the equivalence queries.

Acknowledgement. We would like to thank Adam Klivans for pointing to us some of the work done in the area.

References

1. D. Angluin. Queries and Concept Learning. *Machine Learning*, 2, 319–342, 1988.
2. P. Auer, S. Kwek, W. Maass, M. K. Warmuth. Learning of Depth Two Neural Networks with Constant Fan-in at the Hidden Nodes. *Electronic Colloquium on Computational Complexity (ECCC)*, 7(55), 2000.
3. A. Blum. Rank-r Decision Trees are a Subclass of r-Decision Lists. *Inf. Process. Lett.* 42(4), 183–185, 1992.
4. N. H. Bshouty. A Subexponential Exact Learning Algorithm for DNF Using Equivalence Queries. *Inf. Process. Lett.* 59(1), 37–39 1996.
5. N. H. Bshouty. A new Composition Theorem for Learning Algorithms. In *Proceedings of the 30th annual ACM Symposium on Theory of Computing (STOC)*, 583–589, 1998.
6. A. Ehrenfeucht, D. Haussler. Learning Decision Trees from Random Examples. *Inf. Comput.* 82(3), 231–246, 1989.
7. M. Kearns, M. Li, L. Pitt and L. Valiant. On the learnability of boolean formulae. *In Proceeding of the 19th ACM Symposium on the Theory of Computing*, 285–294, 1987.
8. A. R. Klivans, R. A. Servedio. Learning DNF in time $2^{\tilde{O}(n^{1/3})}$. *J. Comput. Syst. Sci.* 68(2), 303–318, 2004.
9. N. Littlestone. Learning when irrelevant attributes abound. A new linear-threshold algorithm. *Machine Learning*, 2, 285–318, 1988.
10. W. Maass and M. K. Warmuth. Efficienct Learning with Virtual Threshold Gates. *Information and Computation*, 141, 66–83, 1998.

11. L. Pitt and M. K. Warmuth. Prediction-preserving reducibility. *Journal of Computer and System Science*, 41(3), 430–467, 1990.
12. N. Sauer. On the dencity of families of sets. *J. Combinatorial Theory*, Ser. A 13, 145–147, 1972.
13. J. Tarui, T. Tsukiji. Learning DNF by Approximating Inclusion-Exclusion Formulae.*IEEE Conference on Computational Complexity*, 215–220, 1999.
14. L. G. Valiant. A theory of the learnable. *Communication of the ACM*, 27(11), 1984.

DNF Are Teachable in the Average Case

Homin K. Lee, Rocco A. Servedio*, and Andrew Wan

Columbia University, New York, NY 10027, USA

Abstract. We study the average number of well-chosen labeled examples that are required for a helpful teacher to uniquely specify a target function within a concept class. This "average teaching dimension" has been studied in learning theory and combinatorics and is an attractive alternative to the "worst-case" teaching dimension of Goldman and Kearns [7] which is exponential for many interesting concept classes. Recently Balbach [3] showed that the classes of 1-decision lists and 2-term DNF each have linear average teaching dimension.

As our main result, we extend Balbach's teaching result for 2-term DNF by showing that for any $1 \leq s \leq 2^{\Theta(n)}$, the well-studied concept classes of at-most-s-term DNF and at-most-s-term monotone DNF each have average teaching dimension $O(ns)$. The proofs use detailed analyses of the combinatorial structure of "most" DNF formulas and monotone DNF formulas. We also establish asymptotic separations between the worst-case and average teaching dimension for various other interesting Boolean concept classes such as juntas and sparse GF_2 polynomials.

1 Introduction

Many results in computational learning theory consider learners that have some form of access to an oracle that provides labeled examples. Viewed as teachers, these oracles tend to be unhelpful as they typically either provide random examples selected according to some distribution, or they put the onus on the learner to select the examples herself. In noisy learning models, oracles are even allowed to lie from time to time.

In this paper we study a learning model in which the oracle acts as a helpful teacher [7,8]. Given a target concept c (this is simply a Boolean function over some domain X) that belongs to a concept class $\mathcal{C}$, the teacher provides the learner with a carefully chosen set of examples that are labeled according to c. This set of labeled examples is called a *teaching set* and must have the property that no other concept $c' \neq c$ in $\mathcal{C}$ is consistent with the teaching set; thus every learner that outputs a consistent hypothesis will correctly identify c as the target concept. The minimum number of examples in any teaching set for c is called the *teaching dimension of c with respect to $\mathcal{C}$*, and the maximum value of the teaching dimension over all concepts in $\mathcal{C}$ is the *teaching dimension of $\mathcal{C}$*.

Some concept classes that are easy to learn can be very difficult to teach in the worst case in this framework. As one example, let the concept class $\mathcal{C}$ over

---

* Supported in part by NSF award CCF-0347282, by NSF award CCF-0523664, and by a Sloan Foundation Fellowship.

G. Lugosi and H.U. Simon (Eds.): COLT 2006, LNAI 4005, pp. 214–228, 2006.
© Springer-Verlag Berlin Heidelberg 2006

finite domain X contain $|X| + 1$ concepts which are the $|X|$ singletons and the empty set. Any teaching set for the empty set must contain every example in X, since if $x \in X$ is missing from the set then the singleton concept $\{x\}$ is not ruled out by the set. Thus the teaching dimension for this concept class is $|X|$.

Many interesting concept classes include the empty set and all singletons, and thus have teaching dimension $|X|$. Consequently for many concept classes the (worst-case) teaching dimension is not a very interesting measure. With this motivation, researchers have considered the *average teaching dimension*, namely the average value of the teaching dimension of c as c ranges over all of $\mathcal{C}$.

Anthony *et al.* [2] showed that the average teaching dimension of the class of linearly separable Boolean functions over $\{0,1\}^n$ is $O(n^2)$. Kuhlmann [9] showed that concept classes with VC dimension 1 over finite domains have constant average teaching dimension and also gave a bound on the average teaching dimension of concept classes $\mathcal{B}^d(c)$ (balls of center c and size $\leq d$). Kushilevitz *et al.* [10] constructed a concept class $\mathcal{C}$ that has an average teaching dimension of $\Omega(\sqrt{|\mathcal{C}|})$ (this lower bound was also proved in [6]) and also showed that every concept class has average teaching dimension at most $O(\sqrt{|\mathcal{C}|})$. More recently, Balbach [3] showed that the classes of 2-term DNF and 1-decision lists each have average teaching dimension linear in n.

Our Results. Our main results are the following theorems, proved in Sections 3 and 4, which show that the well-studied concept classes of monotone DNF formulas and DNF formulas are efficiently teachable in the average case:

Theorem 1. *Fix any* $1 \leq s \leq 2^{\Theta(n)}$ *and let* $\mathcal{C}$ *be the concept class of all Boolean functions over* $\{0,1\}^n$ *representable as a monotone DNF with at most s terms. Then the average teaching dimension of* $\mathcal{C}$ *is* $O(ns)$.

Theorem 2. *Fix any* $1 \leq s \leq 2^{\Theta(n)}$ *and let* $\mathcal{C}$ *be the concept class of all Boolean functions over* $\{0,1\}^n$ *representable as a DNF with at most s terms. Then the average teaching dimension of* $\mathcal{C}$ *is* $O(ns)$.

Theorem 2 is a broad generalization of Balbach's result on the average teaching dimension of the concept class of DNF with at most two terms. It is easy to see that even the class of at-most-2-term DNFs has exponential worst-case teaching dimension; as we show in Section 3, the worst-case teaching dimension of at-most-s-term monotone DNFs is exponential as well. Thus our results show that there is a dramatic difference between the worst-case and average teaching dimensions for these concept classes.

We also consider some other well-studied concept classes, namely juntas and sparse GF_2 polynomials. For the class of k-juntas, we show in Section 5 that while the worst-case teaching dimension has a logarithmic dependence on n (the number of irrelevant variables), the average teaching dimension has no dependence on n. For a certain class of sparse GF_2 polynomials (roughly, the class of GF_2 polynomials with fewer than $\log n$ terms; see Section 6), we show that while the worst-case teaching dimension is $n^{\Theta(\log \log n)}$, the average teaching dimension is $O(n \log n)$. Thus in each case we establish an asymptotic separation between the worst-case teaching dimension and the average teaching dimension. Our results suggest that rich and interesting concept classes that are difficult to learn in many models may in fact be easy to teach in the average case.

Due to space constraints some proofs are omitted; see [11] for these proofs.

2   Preliminaries

Our domain is $X = \{0,1\}^n$, and we refer to Boolean functions $c : \{0,1\}^n \rightarrow \{0,1\}$ as *concepts*. A collection of concepts $\mathcal{C} \subseteq 2^{\{0,1\}^n}$ is a *concept class*. For a given instance $x \in X$, the value of $c(x)$ is referred to as a *label*, and for $y \in \{0,1\}$, the pair (x,y), is referred to as a *labeled example*. If $y = 0$ ($y = 1$) then the pair is called a *negative (positive) example*. A concept class $\mathcal{C}$ is *consistent* with a set of labeled examples if $c(x) = y$ for all the examples in the set.

A set S of labeled examples is a *teaching set for c with respect to $\mathcal{C}$* if c is the only concept in $\mathcal{C}$ that is consistent with S; thus every learner that outputs a consistent hypothesis from $\mathcal{C}$ will correctly identify c as the target concept. The minimum number of examples in any teaching set for c is called the *teaching dimension of c with respect to $\mathcal{C}$* (sometimes written $TD(c)$ when $\mathcal{C}$ is understood), and the maximum value of the teaching dimension over all concepts in $\mathcal{C}$ is the (worst-case) *teaching dimension of $\mathcal{C}$*. The *average teaching dimension* of $\mathcal{C}$ is the average value of the teaching dimension of c with respect to $\mathcal{C}$ for all c, i.e., $\frac{1}{|\mathcal{C}|} \sum_{c \in \mathcal{C}} TD(c)$.

We use Boolean variables $x_1, \ldots, x_n$ and write $\bar{x}_i$ to denote the negated literal on variable x_i. We will often refer to a logical assignment of the variables as a string and vice-versa; thus, a string $y \in \{0,1\}^n$ corresponds to a truth-value assignment to the variables $x_1, \ldots, x_n$. Given a set S of variables, we write $\mathbf{0}|_{S=1}$ to denote the truth assignment that sets each variable in S to 1 and sets all other variables to 0. The truth assignment $\mathbf{1}|_{S=0}$ is defined similarly.

Two strings $y, z \in \{0,1\}^n$ are *neighbors* if they differ in exactly one bit position. Given $x, y \in \{0,1\}^n$ we write $x \leq y$ if $x_i \leq y_i$ for all $i = 1, \ldots, n$, and we write $x < y$ if we have $x \leq y$ and $x \neq y$.

DNF Formulas. A *term* is a conjunction of Boolean literals. A term over n variables is represented by a string $T \in \{0,1,*\}^n$, where the k-th character of T is denoted $T[k]$. The value of $T[k]$ is 0, 1, or $*$ depending on whether x_k occurs negated, unnegated, or not at all in the term. If $x \in \{0,1\}^n$ is an assignment that satisfies T, we sometimes say that T *covers* x. Note that the satisfying assignments of a term T form a subcube of dimension $n - |T|$ within $\{0,1\}^n$, where $|T|$ denotes the number of non-$*$ entries in T.

An *s-term DNF formula* ϕ is an OR of s terms $\phi = T_1 \vee \cdots \vee T_s$. A satisfying assignment to the DNF is sometimes referred to as a *positive point* and an unsatisfying assignment as a *negative point*.

A term T_i is said to be *compatible* with a set of labeled examples S if T_i does not cover any negative example in S. A term T_i is said to *imply* another term T_j if every positive point of T_i is also a positive point of T_j. We similarly say that a term T implies a DNF formula ϕ, or that a DNF formula ϕ_1 implies another DNF formula ϕ_2. Two different DNF formulas ϕ_1 and ϕ_2 are said to be *logically equivalent* if each implies the other, *i.e.*, if they are different syntactic representations of the same Boolean function. Throughout the paper we will use Greek letters $\phi, \varphi, \ldots$ to denote formulas (which are syntactic objects) and Roman letters $f, g, \ldots$ to denote Boolean functions (which are abstract mappings from $\{0,1\}^n$ to $\{0,1\}$).

We write $\mathcal{D}_s$ to denote the class of "exactly-s-term" DNFs; this is the class of all Boolean functions $f \colon \{0,1\}^n \to \{0,1\}$ that have some s-term DNF representation and have no s'-term DNF representation for any $s' < s$. Similarly, we write $\mathcal{D}_{\leq s}$ to denote the class of "at-most-s-term" DNFs, which is $\mathcal{D}_{\leq s} = \cup_{s' \leq s} \mathcal{D}_{s'}$. Note that the elements of $\mathcal{D}_s$ and $\mathcal{D}_{\leq s}$ are "semantic" functions, not syntactic formulas. The class $\mathcal{D}_{\leq s}$ corresponds to the standard notion of "s-term DNF" which is a well studied concept class in computational learning theory.

A *monotone DNF formula*, or mDNF, is a DNF formula that contains no negated literals. The classes of exactly-s-term mDNFs and at-most-s-term mDNFs are denoted $\mathcal{M}_s$ and $\mathcal{M}_{\leq s}$ and are defined in analogy with $\mathcal{D}_s$ and $\mathcal{D}_{\leq s}$ above. The following fact is well known:

Fact 1. *If $f \in \mathcal{M}_s$ then there is a unique (up to ordering of the terms) s-term mDNF representation $\phi = T_1 \vee \cdots \vee T_s$ for f.*

3   Monotone DNFs

Worst-case teaching dimension of at-most-s-term mDNFs. Here we state upper and lower bounds on the worst-case teaching dimension of $\mathcal{M}_{\leq s}$. See [11] for proofs of these statements.

Theorem 3. *The teaching dimension of $\mathcal{M}_{\leq s}$ is at most $n^s + s$.*

Theorem 4. *Given s, let $s' \leq s$ be any value such that $(s'-1)$ divides n. Then the teaching dimension of $\mathcal{M}_{\leq s}$ is at least $(\frac{n}{s'-1})^{s'-1}$.*

Average-case teaching dimension of at-most-s-term mDNFs. We now prove Theorem 1. The idea is to show that almost every at-most-s-term monotone DNF in fact has exactly s terms; as we will see, these exactly-s-term monotone DNFs can be taught very efficiently with $O(ns)$ examples. The remaining concepts are so few that they can be handled with a brute-force approach and the overall average teaching dimension will still be $O(ns)$.

We start with a simple lemma from [7]:

Lemma 1 ([7]). *Let c be any concept in $\mathcal{M}_s$. Then the teaching dimension of c with respect to $\mathcal{M}_{\leq s}$ is at most $(n+1)s$.*

Lemma 2. *For $1 \leq i < \frac{1}{4} e^{\frac{n}{72}}$, we have $\frac{2^{ni-1}}{i!} \leq |\mathcal{M}_i| \leq \frac{2^{ni}}{i!}$.*

Proof. The upper bound is easy: the number of i-term mDNFs is at most the number of ways to choose i terms from the set of all 2^n many monotone terms over variables $x_1, \ldots, x_n$. The latter quantity is $\binom{2^n}{i} \leq \frac{2^{ni}}{i!}$.

For the lower bound we consider all 2^{ni} ways to select a sequence of i terms (with replacement) from the set of all 2^n possible monotone terms. We show that at least half of these 2^{ni} ways result in a sequence $T_1, \ldots, T_i$ of terms which are pairwise incomparable, *i.e.*, no T_i implies any other T_j. Each such sequence yields an i-term mDNF, and each such mDNF occurs $i!$ times because of different orderings of the terms in a sequence. This gives the lower bound.

Note that a collection of i monotone terms $T_1, \ldots, T_i$ will be pairwise incomparable if the following two conditions hold: (1) Each of the i terms contains between $5n/12$ and $7n/12$ many variables, and (2) Viewing each term T_i as a set of variables, for any $j \neq k$ the symmetric difference $|T_j \Delta T_k|$ is of size at least $n/4$. (This is because if $|T_j|, |T_k| \in [5n/12, 7n/12]$ and $T_j \subseteq T_k$, then the symmetric difference must be of size at most $n/6$.)

For condition (1), Hoeffding's bound implies that a uniformly selected monotone term T will contain fewer than $5n/12$ or more than $7n/12$ many variables with probability at most $2e^{-n/72}$, so a union bound gives that condition (1) fails with probability at most $2ie^{-n/72}$. For condition 2, observe that given two uniform random terms T_j, T_k, each variable x_ℓ is independently in their symmetric difference with probability $1/2$. Thus Hoeffding's bound implies that $|T_j \Delta T_k| < n/4$ with probability at most $e^{-n/8}$. By a union bound, the probability that condition (2) fails is at most $\binom{i}{2}e^{-n/8}$. Thus for $i < \frac{1}{4}e^{\frac{n}{72}}$, the probability that conditions (1) and (2) both hold is at least $1/2$. $\qquad\square$

Fix $1 \leq s \leq \frac{1}{4}e^{\frac{n}{72}}$. It is easy to check that by Lemma 2, for any $k < s$ we have $|\mathcal{M}_k| < \frac{1}{2}|\mathcal{M}_{k+1}|$. Thus (again by Lemma 2) we have $|\mathcal{M}_{\leq s-1}| \leq \frac{2^{ns-n+1}}{(s-1)!}$ while $|\mathcal{M}_s| \geq \frac{2^{ns-1}}{s!}$. Combining these bounds gives that $\frac{|\mathcal{M}_s|}{|\mathcal{M}_{\leq s-1}|} \geq \frac{2^n}{4s}$. By Lemma 1, each concept $c \in \mathcal{M}_{\leq s}$ which is in $\mathcal{M}_s$ can be taught using $n(s+1)$ examples. Each of the remaining concepts can surely be taught using at most 2^n examples. We thus have that the average teaching dimension of $\mathcal{M}_{\leq s}$ is at most

$$\frac{(n+1)s|\mathcal{M}_s| + 2^n|\mathcal{M}_{\leq s-1}|}{|\mathcal{M}_s| + |\mathcal{M}_{\leq s-1}|} \leq (n+1)s + \frac{2^n}{1 + 2^n/4s} \leq (n+1)s + 4s,$$

giving us the following result which is a slightly sharper version of Theorem 1:

Theorem 5. *Let s be any value $1 \leq s \leq \frac{1}{4}e^{\frac{n}{72}}$. The class $\mathcal{M}_{\leq s}$ of at-most-s-term monotone DNF has average teaching dimension at most $s(n+5)$.*

Note that if $s > \frac{1}{4}e^{\frac{n}{72}}$, then 2^n is bounded by some fixed polynomial in s, and thus the worst-case teaching number 2^n is actually $\text{poly}(n, s)$ for such a large s. This gives the following corollary which says that the class of at-most-s-term monotone DNF is efficiently teachable on average for all possible values of s:

Corollary 1. *Let s be any value $1 \leq s \leq 2^n$. The class $\mathcal{M}_{\leq s}$ of at-most-s-term monotone DNF has average teaching dimension $\text{poly}(n, s)$.*

4 DNFs

Now we will tackle the teaching dimension of the unrestricted class of size-at-most-s DNFs. The high-level approach is similar to the monotone case, but the details are more complicated. The idea is to identify a subset $\mathcal{S}$ of $\mathcal{D}_{\leq s}$ and show that (i) any function $f \in \mathcal{S}$ can be uniquely specified within all of $\mathcal{D}_{\leq s}$ using only $O(ns)$ examples; and (ii) at most a $\frac{O(s)}{2^n}$ fraction of all functions in $\mathcal{D}_{\leq s}$ do not belong to $\mathcal{S}$. Given (i) and (ii) it is easy to conclude that the average teaching number of $\mathcal{D}_{\leq s}$ is $O(ns)$.

The challenge is to devise a set $\mathcal{S}$ that satisfies both conditions (i) and (ii). In the monotone case using Fact 1 it was easy to show that $\mathcal{M}_s$ is an easy-to-teach subset, but non-monotone DNF are much more complicated (no analogue of Fact 1 holds for non-monotone DNF) and it is not at all clear that all functions in $\mathcal{D}_s$ are easy to teach. Thus we must use a more complicated set $\mathcal{S}$ of easy-to-teach functions; we define this set and prove that it is indeed easy to teach in Section 4.2. (This argument uses Balbach's results for exactly-2-term DNFs.) The argument that (ii) holds for $\mathcal{S}$ is correspondingly more complex than the counting argument for mDNFs because of $\mathcal{S}$'s more involved structure; we give this in Section 4.3.

4.1 Preliminaries

We will borrow some terminology from Balbach [3]. Two terms T_i and T_j have a *strong difference* at k if $T_i[k], T_j[k] \in \{0, 1\}$ and $T_i[k] \neq T_j[k]$ (*e.g.*, $x_1 \bar{x}_5 x_6$ and $\bar{x}_5 \bar{x}_6 x_{12} x_{23}$ have a strong difference at position 6). Two terms have a *weak difference* at k if $T_i[k] \in \{0, 1\}$ and $T_j[k] = *$ or vice-versa. Two weak differences at positions k and ℓ are *of the same kind* if $T_i[k], T_i[\ell] \in \{0, 1\}$ and $T_j[k] = T_j[\ell] = *$ or vice-versa, that is both $*$'s occur in the same term (*e.g.*, $\bar{x}_5 x_6$ and $\bar{x}_5 \bar{x}_6 x_{12} x_{23}$ have two weak differences of the same kind at positions 12 and 23). Two weak differences at positions k and ℓ are *of different kinds* if $T_i[k], T_j[\ell] \in \{0, 1\}$ and $T_j[k] = T_i[\ell] = *$ or vice-versa (*e.g.*, $\bar{x}_5 x_6$ and $\bar{x}_5 x_{12}$ have two weak differences of different kinds at positions 6 and 12).

Now we introduce some new terminology. Given $y \in \{0, 1\}^n$ which satisfies a term T, we denote by $N_T(y)$ the set consisting of y and all its neighbors that do *not* satisfy T. A satisfying assignment $y \in \{0, 1\}^n$ of a term T in ϕ is called a *cogent corner point of* T if all the neighbors of y that satisfy ϕ satisfy T, and all the neighbors that do not satisfy T do not satisfy ϕ. Note that if y is a cogent corner point of T, then each of the neighbors of y in $N_T(y)$ does not satisfy ϕ. A pair of points $y, z \in \{0, 1\}^n$ that satisfy a term T are said to be *antipodal around* T if $y_k = \bar{z}_k$ for all k such that $T[k] = *$. A pair of points are *cogent antipodal points around* T if they are both cogent corner points of T and antipodal around T. This leads us to our first preliminary lemma:

Lemma 3. *Let* $\phi = T_1 \vee \cdots \vee T_s$ *be any DNF. Let* y *be a cogent corner point of* T_i. *Any* $\widehat{T}$ *that covers* y *and is compatible with* $N_{T_i}(y)$ *must imply* T_i.

Proof. Let $\widehat{T}$ be any term that covers y. Observe that for each literal ℓ in T_i, if $\widehat{T}$ did not contain ℓ then $\widehat{T}$ would not be compatible with $N_{T_i}(y)$ since the corresponding negative neighbor of y is contained in $N_{T_i}(y)$ but would be covered by $\widehat{T}$. It follows that every literal in T_i is also present in $\widehat{T}$, and consequently $\widehat{T}$ implies T_i. □

Two terms are said to be *close* if they have at most one strong difference. Note that there is no strong difference between two terms if and only if they have some satisfying assignment in common, and there is one strong difference between two terms if and only if they have neighboring satisfying assignments.

Given a Boolean function $f \colon \{0,1\}^n \to \{0,1\}$, we let G_f denote the undirected graph whose vertices are the satisfying assignments of f and whose edges are pairs of neighboring satisfying assignments. A *cluster* C of f is a set of satisfying assignments that form a connected component in G_f. We sometimes abuse notation and write C to refer to the Boolean function whose satisfying assignments are precisely the points in C. We say that a DNF ϕ computes cluster C if the set of satisfying assignments for ϕ is precisely C. The *DNF-size* of a cluster C is the minimum number of terms in any DNF that computes C. For intuition, we can view a cluster as being a connected set of positive points that have a "buffer" of negative points separating them from all other positive points. The following lemma is immediate:

Lemma 4. *Let f be an element of $\mathcal{D}_s$, i.e. f is an exactly-s-term DNF. Let $C_1, \ldots, C_r$ be the clusters of f. Then $DNF\text{-}size(C_1) + \cdots + DNF\text{-}size(C_r) = s$.*

4.2 Teaching $\mathcal{S}$

We are now ready to define our "nice" (easy to teach) subset $\mathcal{S} \subseteq \mathcal{D}_{\leq s}$ of size-at-most-s DNFs. (We emphasize that $\mathcal{S}$ is a set of functions, not of DNF expressions.) $\mathcal{S}$ consists of those exactly-s-term DNFs (so in fact $\mathcal{S} \subseteq \mathcal{D}_s$) all of whose clusters either: (1) have DNF-size 1; (2) have DNF-size 2; or (3) have DNF-size k, for some k, and are computed by a DNF $\phi = T_1 \vee \cdots \vee T_k$ in which each T_i has a pair of cogent antipodal points around it.

Note that if a cluster has DNF-size 1, then it clearly satisfies condition (3) above (in fact every pair of antipodal points for the term is cogent). Thus we can simplify the description of $\mathcal{S}$: it is the set of all exactly s-term DNFs all of whose clusters either: (i) have DNF-size k and are computed by a DNF $\phi = T_1 \vee \cdots \vee T_k$ in which each T_i has a pair of cogent antipodal points around it, or (ii) have DNF-size exactly 2. (Note that there do in fact exist Boolean functions of DNF-size 2 for which any two-term representation $T_1 \vee T_2$ has some term T_i with no pair of cogent antipodal points around it, e.g., $\overline{x}_1 \overline{x}_3 \vee x_2 x_3$, and thus condition (ii) is non-redundant.)

The teaching set for functions in $\mathcal{S}$. We will use the following theorem due to Balbach [3]:

Theorem 6. *Let c be any element of $\mathcal{D}_2$ (i.e., an exactly-2-term DNF). The teaching dimension of c with respect to $\mathcal{D}_{\leq 2}$ is at most $2n + 4$.*

The teaching set specified in [3] to prove Theorem 6 consists of at most 5 positive points along with some negative points. Given $f \in \mathcal{D}_2$, we define $BTS(f)$ to be the union of the teaching set specified in [3] together with all negative neighbors of the (at most five) positive points described above (the set specified in [3] already contains some of these points). With this definition a straightforward consequence of the analysis of [3] is the following:

Lemma 5. *Let $\phi = T_1 \vee \cdots \vee T_s$ be a DNF that has a cluster C with DNF-size 2. Let $BTS(C)$ be as described above. Let y be a satisfying assignment for ϕ that is contained in C. Then any term $\widehat{T}$ that covers y and is consistent with $BTS(C)$ must imply C.*

Given any function $f \in \mathcal{S}$, our teaching set $TS(f)$ for f will be as follows. For each cluster C of f, if C:

- **satisfies condition (i):** then for each term T_i described in condition (i), the set $TS(f)$ contains a pair y, z of cogent antipodal points for T_i (these are positive examples) and contains all negative neighbors of these two positive examples (*i.e.*, $TS(f)$ contains $N_{T_i}(y)$ and $N_{T_i}(z)$). Thus $TS(f)$ includes at most $k(2 + 2n)$ many points from such a cluster.
- **does not satisfy condition (i) but satisfies (ii):** then we will give the set $BTS(C)$ described above. By Theorem 6 and the definition of $BTS(C)$, we have that $BTS(C)$ contains at most $7n + 4$ points.

Lemma 4 now implies that $TS(f)$ contains at most $O(ns)$ points.

Correctness of the teaching set construction. We now prove that the set $TS(f)$ is indeed a teaching set that uniquely specifies f within all of $\mathcal{D}_{\leq s}$.

We first observe that any term compatible with $TS(f)$ can only cover positive examples from one cluster of ϕ.

Lemma 6. *Let y be any positive example in $TS(f)$ and let T be any term that covers y and is compatible with $TS(f)$. Let C be the cluster of ϕ that covers y. Then if z is any positive example in $TS(f)$ that is not covered by C, T does not cover z.*

Proof. If C satisfies condition (i) then y must be a cogent corner point and Lemma 3 gives the desired conclusion. If C does not satisfy (i) but satisfies (ii), then the conclusion follows from Lemma 5. $\qquad\square$

The next two lemmas show that any set of terms that covers the positive examples of a given cluster must precisely compute the entire cluster and only the cluster of the original function:

Lemma 7. *Let C be any case (i) cluster of DNF-size k. Let P_C be the intersection of the positive examples in $TS(f)$ with C. Let $\widehat{T}_1, \ldots, \widehat{T}_j$ be any set of $j \leq k$ terms such that the DNF $\widehat{T}_1 \vee \cdots \vee \widehat{T}_j$ both: (a) is compatible with $TS(f)$, and (b) covers every point in P_C. Then it must be the case that $j = k$ and $\widehat{T}_1 \vee \cdots \vee \widehat{T}_j$ exactly computes C (in fact each term $\widehat{T}_i$ is equivalent to T_i up to reordering).*

Proof. By Lemma 3, a term $\widehat{T}$ that covers a cogent antipodal point from term T_i cannot cover any of the other $2k - 2$ cogent antipodal points from other terms, and thus we must have $j = k$ since fewer than k terms cannot cover all of P_C. Moreover, any term $\widehat{T}_i$ must cover a pair of antipodal points corresponding to a single term (which wlog we call T_i). For each antipodal pair corresponding to a term T_i, the covering term $\widehat{T}_i$ must be of size at least $|T_i|$, and since they are cogent antipodal points, the covering term cannot be any longer than $|T_i|$, so in fact we have that $\widehat{T}_i$ and T_i are identical. This proves the lemma. □

Lemma 8. *Let C be any case (ii) cluster. Let P_C be the intersection of the positive examples in $TS(f)$ with C. Let $\widehat{T}_1, \ldots, \widehat{T}_j$ be any set of $j \leq 2$ terms such that the DNF $\widehat{T}_1 \vee \cdots \vee \widehat{T}_j$ both: (a) is compatible with $TS(f)$, and (b) covers every point in P_C. Then it must be the case that $j = 2$ and $\widehat{T}_1 \vee \widehat{T}_2$ exactly computes C.*

Proof. The fact that $BTS(C)$ is a teaching set (for the exactly-2-term DNF corresponding to C, relative to $\mathcal{D}_{\leq 2}$) implies the desired result, since no single term or 2-term DNF not equivalent to C can be consistent with $BTS(C)$, and any DNF $\widehat{T}_1 \vee \cdots \vee \widehat{T}_j$ as in the lemma must be consistent with $BTS(C)$. □

The pieces are in place for us to prove our theorem:

Theorem 7. *For any $f \in \mathcal{S}$, the set $TS(f)$ uniquely specifies f within $\mathcal{D}_{\leq s}$.*

Proof. By Lemma 6, positive points from each cluster can only be covered by terms that do not include any positive points from other clusters. By Lemmas 7 and 8, for each cluster C, the minimum number of terms required to cover all positive points in the cluster (and still be compatible with $TS(f)$) is precisely the DNF-size of C. Since f is an exactly-s-term DNF, Lemma 4 implies that using more than DNF-size(C) many terms to cover all the positive points in any cluster C will "short-change" some other cluster and cause some positive point to be uncovered. Thus any at-most-s-term DNF ϕ that is consistent with $TS(f)$ must have the property that for each cluster C, at most DNF-size(C) of its terms cover the points in P_C; so by Lemmas 7 and 8, these terms exactly compute C, and thus ϕ must exactly compute f. □

4.3 Average-Case Teaching Dimension of DNFs

Now we will show that all but at most a $\frac{O(s)}{2^n}$ fraction of functions in $\mathcal{D}_{\leq s}$ are in fact in $\mathcal{S}$. We do this by showing that at least a $1 - \frac{O(s)}{2^n}$ fraction of functions in $\mathcal{D}_{\leq s}$ are in the easy-to-teach set $\mathcal{S}$, i.e. they belong to $\mathcal{D}_s$ and are such that each cluster satisfies either condition (i) or (ii) from Section 4.2. Since we have shown that each $f \in \mathcal{S}$ can be uniquely specified within $\mathcal{D}_{\leq s}$ using $O(ns)$ examples, this will easily yield that the average teaching number over all of $\mathcal{D}_{\leq s}$ is $O(ns)$.

First we show that most functions in $\mathcal{D}_{\leq s}$ are in fact in $\mathcal{D}_s$. We can bound $|\mathcal{D}_i|$ using the same approach as we did for monotone DNFs.

Lemma 9. *For $i < (9/7)^{n/3}$, we have $\frac{1}{2} \cdot \frac{3^{ni}}{i!} \leq |\mathcal{D}_i| \leq \frac{3^{ni}}{i!}$.*

Proof. As in Lemma 2, the upper bound is easy; we may bound the number of functions in $\mathcal{D}_i$ by the number of ways to choose i terms from the set of all 3^n possible terms over variables $x_1, \ldots, x_n$. This is $\binom{3^n}{i} \leq \frac{3^{ni}}{i!}$.

For the lower bound, we first note that a DNF formula consisting of i terms that are all pairwise far from each other cannot be logically equivalent to any other DNF over a different set of i terms. We will show that at least half of all 3^{ni} possible sequences of i terms have the property that all i terms in the sequence are pairwise far from each other; this gives the lower bound (since each such set of i terms can be ordered in $i!$ different ways).

So consider a uniform random draw of i terms $T_1, \ldots, T_i$ from the set of all 3^n possible terms. The probability that T_1 and T_2 are close is the probability that they have no strong differences plus the probability that they have exactly one strong difference. This is $(7/9)^n + n(7/9)^{n-1}(2/9) < (n+1)(7/9)^n$. By a union bound over all pairs of terms, the probability that any pair of terms is close at most $\binom{i}{2}(n+1)(7/9)^n$ which is less than $1/2$ for $i < (9/7)^{n/3}$. $\qquad\square$

As in Section 3, as a corollary we have that $\frac{|\mathcal{D}_s|}{|\mathcal{D}_{\leq s-1}|} \geq \frac{3^n}{4s}$ for $s \leq (9/7)^{n/3}$.

We now bound the number of DNFs in $\mathcal{D}_s$ that are not in $\mathcal{S}$. To do this, we consider choosing s terms at random with replacement from all 3^n terms:

Lemma 10. *Fix any $s \leq (9/8)^{n/25}$. Let $f = T_1, \ldots, T_s$ be a sequence of exactly s terms selected by independently choosing each T_i uniformly from the set of all 3^n possible terms. Let $A(T_i)$ denote the event that term T_i in f has no cogent antipodal pairs, and $B(T_i)$ denote the event that there is more than one other term close to T_i in f. Then $\Pr[\exists T_i \in f : A(T_i)\&B(T_i)] \leq \frac{O(s)}{2^n}$, where the probability is taken over the choice of f.*

Using Lemma 10 we can bound the number of functions $f \in \mathcal{D}_s$ that are not in $\mathcal{S}$. If $f \in \mathcal{D}_s \setminus \mathcal{S}$, then f must have a DNF formula representation $\phi = T_1 \vee \cdots \vee T_s$ in which some term T_i (1) has no cogent antipodal pairs, and (2) has at least two other terms T_j, T_k that are close to it. (If there were no such term, then for any representation $\phi = T_1 \vee \cdots \vee T_s$ for the function f, every T_i is contained in either a cluster of DNF-size 1 or 2, or a cluster of DNF-size k with a pair of good antipodal points around it. But then ϕ would be in $\mathcal{S}$.) We will call such a syntactic DNF formula "bad." Lemma 10 tells us that the number of bad syntactic formulas is at most $\frac{3^{ns}O(s)}{2^n}$, since there are 3^{ns} syntactic formulas. Notice that any bad formula ϕ must have s distinct terms (since the function it computes belongs to $\mathcal{D}_s$), and since these terms can be ordered in $s!$ different ways, there are at least $s!$ bad formulas that compute the same function as ϕ. Consequently the number of bad functions in $\mathcal{D}_s$, $|\mathcal{D}_s \setminus \mathcal{S}|$, is at most $\frac{O(s)}{2^n} \frac{3^{ns}}{s!}$. By Lemma 9, $|\mathcal{D}_s|$ is at at least $\frac{3^{ns}}{2s!}$. This gives the following:

Corollary 2. $\frac{|\mathcal{D}_s \setminus \mathcal{S}|}{|\mathcal{D}_s|} \leq \frac{O(s)}{2^n}$.

We now proceed to prove Lemma 10.

Proof. The bulk of the argument is in showing that $\Pr[A(T_1) \& B(T_1)]$ is at most $O(1) \cdot 2^{-n}$; once this is shown a union bound gives the final result.

We condition on the outcome of T_1. Using the fact that each variable occurs independently in T_1 (either positive or negated) with probability $2/3$, a Chernoff bound gives that $\Pr[|T_1| < .08n] \leq 2^{-n}$, so we have that

$$\Pr[A(T_1) \ \& \ B(T_1)] \leq 2^{-n} + \sum_{\mathcal{T}:|\mathcal{T}| \geq .08n} \Pr[A(T_1) \ \& \ B(T_1) \mid (T_1 = \mathcal{T})] \cdot \Pr[T_1 = \mathcal{T}].$$

Next we show that $\Pr[A(T_1) \ \& \ B(T_1) \mid (T_1 = \mathcal{T})] \leq O(1) \cdot 2^{-n}$ for every $\mathcal{T}$ satisfying $|\mathcal{T}| \geq .08n$; this implies an $O(1) \cdot 2^{-n}$ bound on $\Pr[A(T_1) \ \& \ B(T_1)]$. To do this we consider a third event which we denote by $C(T_1)$; this is the event that T_1 is close to at most 25 of the terms $T_2, \ldots, T_s$. Clearly we have that

$$\begin{aligned} \Pr[A(T_1) \ \& \ B(T_1) \mid (T_1 = \mathcal{T})] &= \Pr[A(T_1) \ \& \ B(T_1) \ \& \ \neg C(T_1) \mid (T_1 = \mathcal{T})] \\ &\quad + \Pr[A(T_1) \ \& \ B(T_1) \ \& \ C(T_1) \mid (T_1 = \mathcal{T})] \ (1) \end{aligned}$$

and we proceed by bounding each of the terms in (1).

The first term is at most $\Pr[\neg C(T_1) \mid (T_1 = \mathcal{T})]$. Fix any $\alpha \in [.08, 1]$ and any term $\mathcal{T}$ of length αn, and fix $T_1 = \mathcal{T}$. Then the probability (over a random draw of T_2 as in the statement of the lemma) that T_2 is close to T_1 is the probability that T_1 and T_2 have one strong difference plus the probability that T_1 and T_2 have no strong difference, which is exactly $\alpha n \frac{1}{3} \left(\frac{2}{3}\right)^{\alpha n - 1} + \left(\frac{2}{3}\right)^{\alpha n} \leq 2\alpha n \left(\frac{2}{3}\right)^{\alpha n}$. Using the independence of the terms $T_2, \ldots, T_s$ and a union bound, it follows that the probability that there exists any set of K terms in f which are all close to T_1 is at most $\binom{s}{K} (2\alpha n)^K \left(\frac{2}{3}\right)^{K\alpha n}$. It is not hard to verify that for any $1 \leq s \leq (9/8)^{n/25}$, any $K \geq 26$, and any $\alpha \in [.08, 1]$, this quantity is asymptotically less than 2^{-n}.

It remains to bound the second term of (1) by $O(1) \cdot 2^{-n}$. We do this using the following observation:

Proposition 1. *Let $f = T_1, \ldots, T_s$ be any sequence of s terms. If T_1 has no cogent antipodal pairs with respect to f and is close to at most K of the terms $T_2, \ldots, T_s$, then there must be some term among $T_2, \ldots, T_s$ that is close to T_1 and contains at most $k = \lceil \log K \rceil + 1$ variables not already in T_1.*

Proof. We show that if every term in f close to T_1 contains more than k variables, there must remain some cogent antipodal pair for T_1. Let r be the number of variables in T_1 and let $\ell = n - r$. For any $z \in \{0,1\}^\ell$ let $Q_{T_1}(z)$ denote the set of points in $\{0,1\}^n$ consisting of the antipodal pair induced by z on T_1 (these two points each satisfy T_1) and the $2r$ neighbors of these points that do not satisfy T_1. Thus $Q_{T_1}(z) = Q_{T_1}(\bar{z})$, and there are $2^{\ell - 1}$ distinct $Q_{T_1}(z)$, each representing a possible cogent antipodal pair.

Consider a term T_i that is close to T_1, and partition its satisfying assignments according to the 2^ℓ assignments on the ℓ variables not contained in T_1. Since T_i will only eliminate the cogent antipodal pair represented by the neighborhood $Q_{T_1}(z)$ if it covers some point in $Q_{T_1}(z)$, T_i can only eliminate as many cogent antipodal pairs as it has partitions. But if T_i contains more than k of the ℓ variables not already in T_1, then there are fewer than $2^{\ell - k}$ different ways to set the ℓ bits outside of T_1 to construct a satisfying assignment for T_i, and T_i has fewer than $2^{\ell - k}$ different partitions. Since by assumption there are at most $K \leq 2^{k-1}$ terms close to T_1, there are fewer than $2^{k-1} \cdot 2^{\ell - k} = 2^{\ell - 1}$ different $Q_{\mathcal{T}}(z)$ eliminated, and $\mathcal{T}$ must have a cogent antipodal pair left. $\qquad\square$

By Proposition 1, we know that if $A(T_1)$ occurs (T_1 has no cogent antipodal pairs) and $C(T_1)$ occurs (T_1 is close to no more than $K = 25$ other terms), then there must be some term close to T_1 that has at most $k = 6$ variables not in T_1. Thus we have that $\Pr[A(T_1) \ \& \ B(T_1) \ \& \ C(T_1) \mid (T_1 = T)]$ is at most the probability there exist two terms close to T_1, one of which contains at most $k = 6$ variables not in T_1. We saw earlier that the probability that a randomly chosen term is close to T_1 is at most $2\alpha n (2/3)^{\alpha n}$. However, the probability that a randomly chosen term is close to T_1 *and* contains at most 6 variables not in T_1 is much lower (because almost all of the $(1-\alpha)n$ variables not in T_1 are constrained to be absent from the term); more precisely this probability is at most $2\alpha n \binom{(1-\alpha)n}{6} \left(\frac{2}{3}\right)^{\alpha n} \left(\frac{1}{3}\right)^{(1-\alpha)n-6}$. A union bound over all possible pairs of terms gives us that the second term of (1) is at most $2\alpha n \binom{s}{2} \binom{(1-\alpha)n}{6} 3^6 \left(\frac{2}{3}\right)^{2\alpha n} \left(\frac{1}{3}\right)^{(1-\alpha)n}$. It is straightforward to check that this is at most $O(1) \cdot 2^{-n}$ for all $1 \le s \le (9/8)^{n/25}$ and all $\alpha \in [0,1]$.

Thus, we have bounded $\Pr[A(T_1) \ \& \ B(T_1)]$ by $O(1) \cdot 2^{-n}$. A union bound over the s terms gives that $\Pr[\exists T_i \in f : A(T_i) \ \& \ B(T_i)]$ is at most $O(s)2^{-n}$, and the lemma is proved. □

Theorem 8. *Let $s \le (9/8)^{n/25}$. The average teaching dimension of $\mathcal{D}_{\le s}$, the class of DNFs over n variables with at most s terms, is $O(ns)$.*

Proof. Theorem 7 gives us that the teaching number of any concept in $\mathcal{S} \subset \mathcal{D}_s$ is $O(ns)$. By Lemma 9, we have that $|\mathcal{D}_{\le s-1}| \le \frac{4s}{3^n}|\mathcal{D}_s|$. This leaves us with $\mathcal{D}_s \setminus \mathcal{S}$, whose size we bounded by $\frac{O(s)}{2^n}|\mathcal{D}_s|$ in Corollary 2. Combining these bounds, we are ready to bound the average teaching number of $|\mathcal{D}_{\le s}|$. Since we can teach any bad concept with at most 2^n examples, the average teaching number is at most

$$\frac{O(ns)|\mathcal{S}| + 2^n(|\mathcal{D}_{\le s-1}| + |\mathcal{D}_s \setminus \mathcal{S}|)}{|\mathcal{D}_s| + |\mathcal{D}_{\le s-1}|} \le \frac{O(ns)|\mathcal{D}_s| + 2^n(\frac{4s}{3^n}|\mathcal{D}_s| + \frac{O(s)}{2^n}|\mathcal{D}_s|)}{|\mathcal{D}_s| + |\mathcal{D}_{\le s-1}|}$$
$$\le O(ns) + (2/3)^n \cdot 4s + O(s) = O(ns)$$

and the theorem is proved. □

As in Corollary 1, we have $2^n \le \text{poly}(s)$ if $s > (9/8)^{n/25}$, and thus the worst-case teaching number 2^n is actually $\text{poly}(n, s)$ for such large s. This gives the following corollary:

Corollary 3. *Let s be any value $1 \le s \le 2^n$. The class $\mathcal{D}_{\le s}$ of at-most-s-term DNF has average teaching number $\text{poly}(n, s)$.*

5   Teaching Dimension of k-Juntas

A Boolean function f over n variables depends on its i-th variable if there are two inputs $x, x' \in \{0,1\}^n$ that differ only in the i-th coordinate and that have $f(x) \neq f(x')$. A k-*junta* is a Boolean function which depends on at most k of its n input variables. The class of k-juntas (or equivalently NC_k^0 functions) is well studied in computational learning theory, see *e.g.*, [4, 12, 1]. We write $\mathcal{J}_k$ to denote the class of Boolean functions $f\colon \{0,1\}^n \to \{0,1\}$ that depend on exactly k variables, and we write $\mathcal{J}_{\leq k}$ to denote the class $\mathcal{J}_{\leq k} = \cup_{k' \leq k} \mathcal{J}_{k'}$ of Boolean functions over $\{0,1\}^n$ that depend on at most k variables, *i.e.*, $\mathcal{J}_{\leq k}$ is the class of all k-juntas.

We analyze the worst-case and average-case teaching dimensions of the class of k-juntas, and show that while the worst-case teaching dimension has a logarithmic dependence on n, the average-case dimension has no dependence on n. Thus k-juntas are another natural concept class where there is a substantial asymptotic difference between the worst-case and average teaching dimensions.

Worst-Case teaching dimension of k-juntas. We recall the following:

Definition 1. *Let $k \leq n$. A set $S \subseteq \{0,1\}^n$ is said to be an (n,k)-universal set if for any $1 \leq i_1 < i_2 \ldots < i_k \leq n$, it holds that $\forall y \in \{0,1\}^k, \exists x \in S$ satisfying $(x_{i_1}, \ldots, x_{i_k}) = (y_1, \ldots, y_k)$*

Nearly matching upper and lower bounds are known for the size of (n,k)-universal sets:

Theorem 9 ([15]). *Let $k \leq n$. Any (n,k)-universal set is of size $\Omega(2^k \log n)$, and there exists an (n,k)-universal set of size $O(k2^k \log n)$.*

This straightforwardly yields the following theorem (see [11] for proof):

Theorem 10. *The teaching dimension of $\mathcal{J}_{\leq k}$ is at least $\Omega(2^k \log n)$ and at most $O(k2^k \log n)$.*

Average-case teaching dimension of k-juntas. The idea is similar to the case of monotone DNF: we show that k-juntas with exactly k relevant variables can be taught with 2^k examples (independent of n), and then use the fact that the overwhelming majority of k-juntas have exactly k relevant variables. (See [11] for full proofs.) Using this approach it is possible to prove:

Theorem 11. *The average teaching dimension of the class $\mathcal{J}_{\leq k}$ of k-juntas is at most $2^k + o(1)$.*

6   Sparse GF_2 Polynomials

A GF_2 *polynomial* is a multilinear polynomial with $0/1$ coefficients that maps $\{0,1\}^n$ to $\{0,1\}$ where all arithmetic is done modulo 2. Since addition mod 2 corresponds to parity and multiplication corresponds to AND, a GF_2 polynomial can be viewed as a parity of monotone conjunctions. It is well known, and not hard to show, that every Boolean function $f\colon \{0,1\}^n \to \{0,1\}$ has a unique GF_2 polynomial representation.

A natural measure of the size of a GF_2 polynomial is the number of monomials that it contains. In keeping with our usual notation, let $\mathcal{G}_s$ denote the class of all Boolean functions $f\colon \{0,1\}^n \to \{0,1\}$ that have GF_2 polynomial representations with exactly s monomials and let $\mathcal{G}_{\leq s}$ denote $\cup_{s' \leq s} \mathcal{G}_{s'}$. We sometimes refer to functions in $\mathcal{G}_{\leq s}$ as being s-*sparse* GF_2 *polynomials*. The class of s-sparse GF_2 polynomials has been studied by several researchers in learning theory and complexity theory, see *e.g.*, [13,5,14].

Roth and Benedek [13] showed that any $f \in \mathcal{G}_{\leq s}$ is uniquely determined by the values it assumes on those $x \in \{0,1\}^n$ that contain at least $n - (1 + \lfloor \log_2 s \rfloor)$ many 1s. They also showed that it is in fact necessary to specify the value of f on every such point even in order to uniquely determine the parity (even or odd) of $|f^{-1}(1)|$ where f ranges over all of $\mathcal{G}_{\leq s}$. We thus have:

Theorem 12 ([13]). *Fix any $1 \leq s \leq 2^n$. The (worst-case) teaching dimension of $\mathcal{G}_{\leq s}$ is $\sum_{i=0}^{1 + \lfloor \log_2 s \rfloor} \binom{n}{i}$ (which is $n^{\Theta(\log s)}$ for s subexponential in n).*

In contrast, we show in the next subsection that if s is sufficiently small, the average-case teaching dimension of $\mathcal{G}_{\leq s}$ is $O(ns)$:

Theorem 13. *Fix $1 \leq s \leq (1 - \epsilon) \log_2 n$, where $\epsilon > 0$ is any constant. Then the average-case teaching dimension of $\mathcal{G}_{\leq s}$ is at most $ns + 2s$.*

For $s = \omega(1)$, $s < (1 - \epsilon) \log_2 n$, this gives a superpolynomial separation between worst-case and average-case teaching dimension of s-sparse GF_2 polynomials.

Proof of Theorem 13. We now define the "nice" (easy-to-teach) subset of $\mathcal{G}_{\leq s}$, in analogy with $\mathcal{S}$ in Section 4. We say that a function $f = M_1 \oplus \cdots \oplus M_s \in \mathcal{G}_s$ is *individuated* if for each $i = 1, \ldots, s$ there is some $j \in \{1, \ldots, n\}$ such that the variable x_j occurs in monomial M_i and does not occur in any of the other $s - 1$ monomials. Let $\mathcal{I} \subseteq \mathcal{G}_s$ denote the set of all functions in $\mathcal{G}_s$ that are individuated.

Any function in $\mathcal{I}$ can be specified using few examples (see [11] for proof):

Lemma 11. *For any $f \in \mathcal{I}$, the teaching dimension of f with respect to $\mathcal{G}_{\leq s}$ is at most $ns + 2s - 1$.*

Now observe that $|\mathcal{G}_s| = \binom{2^n}{s} < \frac{2^{ns}}{s!}$, and thus $(\frac{2^n}{s})^s \leq |\mathcal{G}_{\leq s}| = |\mathcal{G}_s| + |\mathcal{G}_{\leq s-1}| < \frac{2^{ns}}{s!} + (s-1)\frac{2^{ns-n}}{(s-1)!} = \frac{2^{ns}}{s!} + \frac{2^{ns-n}}{(s-2)!}$. Our next lemma shows that almost every function in $\mathcal{G}_s$ (and thus almost every function in $\mathcal{G}_{\leq s}$) is in fact individuated (see [11] for proof):

Lemma 12. *We have $|\mathcal{I}| \geq \frac{2^{ns}}{s!}(1 - s \cdot e^{-n^\epsilon})$, and thus there are at most $s \cdot e^{-n^\epsilon} \cdot \frac{2^{ns}}{s!} + \frac{2^{ns-n}}{(s-2)!}$ many functions in $\mathcal{G}_{\leq s} \setminus \mathcal{I}$.*

By Lemma 11 we can specify any function in $\mathcal{I}$ with at most N examples, and by Theorem 12 we can specify any of the other functions in $\mathcal{G}_{\leq s}$ with at most $n^{O(\log s)}$ many examples. It follows from Lemma 12 that the average teaching dimension of $\mathcal{G}_{\leq s}$ is at most

$$\frac{N|\mathcal{I}| + n^{O(\log s)} \cdot |\mathcal{G}_{\leq s} \setminus \mathcal{I}|}{|\mathcal{G}_{\leq s}|} \leq N + \frac{n^{O(\log s)} \cdot (s \cdot e^{-n^\epsilon} \cdot \frac{2^{ns}}{s!} + \frac{2^{ns-n}}{(s-2)!})}{(\frac{2^n}{s})^s}.$$

The second term on the right simplifies to $s^s \cdot n^{O(\log s)} \cdot (s \cdot e^{-n^\epsilon}/s! + 2^{-n}/(s-2)!)$, which is easily seen to be $o(1)$ since ϵ is a constant greater than 0 and $s \leq (1-\epsilon)\log n$. This proves Theorem 13. $\Box$

While our proof technique does not extend to s that are larger than $\log n$, it is possible that different methods could establish a $\text{poly}(n, s)$ upper bound on average teaching dimension for the class $\mathcal{G}_{\leq s}$ of s-sparse GF_2 polynomials for a much larger range of values of s. This is an interesting goal for future work.

References

1. M. Alekhnovich, M. Braverman, V. Feldman, A. Klivans, and T. Pitassi. Learnability and automatizability. In *Proceedings of the 45th IEEE Symposium on Foundations of Computer Science*, pages 621–630, 2004.
2. M. Anthony, G. Brightwell, and J. Shawe-Taylor. On specifying Boolean functions by labelled examples. *Discrete Applied Math.*, 61(1):1–25, 1995.
3. F. Balbach. Teaching classes with high teaching dimension using few examples. In *Proc. 18th Annual COLT*, pages 637–651, 2005.
4. A. Blum. Learning a function of r relevant variables (open problem). In *Proc. 16th Annual COLT*, pages 731–733, 2003.
5. N. Bshouty and Y. Mansour. Simple Learning Algorithms for Decision Trees and Multivariate Polynomials. *SIAM J. Comput.*, 31(6):1909–1925, 2002.
6. J. Cherniavsky and R. Statman. Testing: An abstract approach. In *Proceedings of the 2nd Workshop on Software Testing*, 1988.
7. S. Goldman and M. Kearns. On the complexity of teaching. *Journal of Computer and System Sciences*, 50(1):20–31, February 1992.
8. S. Goldman, R. Rivest, and R. Schapire. Learning binary relations and total orders. *SIAM Journal on Computing*, 22(5):1006–1034, October 1993.
9. Christian Kuhlmann. On teaching and learning intersection-closed concept classes. In *Proc. 4th EUROCOLT*, pages 168–182, 1999.
10. E. Kushilevitz, N. Linial, Y. Rabinovich, and M. Saks. Witness sets for families of binary vectors. *J. Combinatorial Theory*, 73(2):376–380, 1996.
11. H. Lee, R. Servedio, and A. Wan. DNF are Teachable in the Average Case (full version). Available at http://www.cs.columbia.edu/~rocco/papers/dnfteach.html.
12. E. Mossel, R. O'Donnell, and R. Servedio. Learning functions of k relevant variables. *J. Comput. & Syst. Sci.*, 69(3):421–434, 2004.
13. R. Roth and G. Benedek. Interpolation and approximation of sparse multivariate polynomials over $GF(2)$. *SIAM J. Comput.*, 20(2):291–314, 1991.
14. R. Schapire and L. Sellie. Learning sparse multivariate polynomials over a field with queries and counterexamples. *J. Comput. & Syst. Sci.*, 52(2):201–213, 1996.
15. Gadiel Seroussi and Nader Bshouty. Vector sets for exhaustive testing of logic circuits. *IEEE Trans. on Information Theory*, 34(3):513–522, 1988.

Teaching Randomized Learners

Frank J. Balbach[1] and Thomas Zeugmann[2]

[1] Institut für Theoretische Informatik, Universität zu Lübeck
Ratzeburger Allee 160, 23538 Lübeck, Germany
balbach@tcs.uni-luebeck.de
[2] Division of Computer Science
Hokkaido University, Sapporo 060-0814, Japan
thomas@ist.hokudai.ac.jp

Abstract. The present paper introduces a new model for teaching *randomized learners*. Our new model, though based on the classical teaching dimension model, allows to study the influence of various parameters such as the learner's memory size, its ability to provide or to not provide feedback, and the influence of the order in which examples are presented. Furthermore, within the new model it is possible to investigate new aspects of teaching like teaching from positive data only or teaching with inconsistent teachers.

Furthermore, we provide characterization theorems for teachability from positive data for both ordinary teachers and inconsistent teachers with and without feedback.

1 Introduction

A natural teaching model consists of a teacher giving examples to a set of students with the goal that all students eventually hypothesize a certain target concept. Typically the admissible students are deterministic learning algorithms and the teaching performance is measured with respect to the worst case student. In the present paper we modify this model by assuming a partly randomized student and by measuring teaching performance in an average case fashion.

Our model is based on the teaching model introduced independently, and in different forms, by Shinohara and Miyano [19], Goldman *et al.* [11], Goldman and Kearns [9] as well as Anthony *et al.* [5]. Here, a teacher has to give enough examples to uniquely identify the target concept among all concepts in a given class. Thus, the students are all deterministic consistent learning algorithms.

By varying the set of admissible learners, the influence of different properties of the learners on the teaching process can be studied. For example, learners with limited memory should be harder to teach, whereas learners that show their current hypothesis to the teacher should ease the teaching process.

Let us consider the concept class of all Boolean functions over $\{0,1\}^n$. To teach a concept to all consistent learning algorithms, the teacher must present all 2^n examples. Teaching a concept to all consistent learners that can memorize less

G. Lugosi and H.U. Simon (Eds.): COLT 2006, LNAI 4005, pp. 229–243, 2006.

than 2^n examples is impossible; there is always a learner with a consistent, but wrong hypothesis. So teaching gets indeed harder, but in a rather abrupt way. Moreover, it does not matter whether or not the teacher knows the learner's hypothesis, since there are deterministic learners choosing their next hypothesis independently of their current one.

It seems that the worst case analysis style makes it impossible to investigate the influence of memory limitations or learner's feedback. A common remedy for this is to perform an average case analysis instead. In the present paper, we propose a rather radical approach, i.e., we replace the set of learners by a single one that is intended to represent an "average learner."

We achieve this goal by substituting the set of deterministic learners by a single randomized one. Basically, such a learner picks a hypothesis at random from all hypotheses consistent with the known examples. Teaching is successful as soon as the learner hypothesizes the target concept. For ensuring that the learner maintains this correct hypothesis, we additionally require the learner to be *conservative*, i.e., it can change its hypotheses only on examples that are inconsistent with its current hypothesis. The complexity of teaching is measured by the *expected* teaching time (cf. Section 2).

Next, we explain why this model should work. Intuitively, since at every round there is a chance to reach the target, the target will eventually be reached even if, for instance, the randomized learner can only memorize few examples. Moreover, the ability of the teacher to observe the learner's current hypothesis should be advantageous, since it enables the teacher to teach an inconsistent example in every round. Recall that only these examples can cause a hypothesis change. In Section 3, we show these intuitions to be valid.

Randomized learners show another phenomenon, too: The complexity of the teaching process now does not only depend on the examples, but also on the order in which they are given.

The randomized teaching model can be regarded as a *Markov Decision Process*. Such processes have been studied for several decades and we will make use of some results from this theory (cf. Subsection 2.3).

Sections 4 and 5 study teaching with and without feedback, respectively. Here, we focus on computing the optimal teaching times. In Sections 6 to 8 we study variations of our model: teaching from positive data, inconsistent teachers and another restriction on teachers. Theorems characterizing teachability within these model are shown.

Note that there are also other approaches to teaching. They differ from the one discussed here, since the learner is not given, but constructed to fit to the teacher. One such model is learning from good examples (cf. Freivalds et al. [8] and Jain et al. [13]). Jackson and Tomkins [12] as well as Goldman and Mathias [10] and Mathias [15] defined models of teacher/learner pairs. In their models, a kind of adversary disturbing the teaching process is necessary to avoid collusion between the teacher and the learner. Angluin and Kriķis' [3, 4] model prevents collusion by giving incompatible hypothesis spaces to teacher and learner.

2   Preliminaries

2.1   Notations

Set inclusion and proper set inclusion is denoted by "$\subseteq$" and "$\subset$," respectively. For numbers a, b with $a < b$ we write $[a, b]$ to denote the set $\{a, a + 1, \ldots, b\}$ or $\{a, a + 1, \ldots\}$ if $b = \infty$.

Let X be a finite *instance space* and $\mathcal{X} = X \times \{0, 1\}$ the corresponding set of *examples*. A *concept class* is a set $\mathcal{C} \subseteq 2^X$ of *concepts* $c \subseteq X$. An example (x, v) is *positive* if $v = 1$ and *negative* if $v = 0$. We denote the set of all examples for a concept c by $\mathcal{X}(c) = \{(x, v) \mid v = 1 \iff x \in c\} \subset \mathcal{X}$. An example (x, v) is called *consistent* with c iff $(x, v) \in \mathcal{X}(c)$.

A *teaching set* for a concept $c \in \mathcal{C}$ with respect to $\mathcal{C}$ is a set S of examples such that c is the only concept in $\mathcal{C}$ consistent with S. The *teaching dimension* $TD(c)$ is the size of the smallest teaching set. We set $TD(\mathcal{C}) := \max\{TD(c) \mid c \in \mathcal{C}\}$.

For any set S, we denote by S^* the set of all finite lists of elements from S, by S^m and $S^{\leq m}$ the set of all lists with length m and at most length m, respectively. The operator $\circ_\mu$ concatenates a list of length at most μ with a single element resulting in a list of length at most μ: $\langle x_1, \ldots, x_\ell \rangle \circ_\mu \langle y \rangle$ equals $\langle x_1, \ldots, x_\ell, y \rangle$ if $\ell < \mu$ and $\langle x_2, \ldots, x_\ell, y \rangle$ if $\ell = \mu$. We regard $\circ_\infty$ as the usual list concatenation. For a list $\boldsymbol{x}$ of examples, we set $\mathcal{C}(\boldsymbol{x}) = \{c \in \mathcal{C} \mid \boldsymbol{x} \text{ is consistent with } c\}$.

We denote by $\mathcal{M}_n$ the concept class of monomials over $\{0, 1\}^n$. We exclude the empty concept from $\mathcal{M}_n$ and can thus identify each monomial with a string from $\{0, 1, *\}^n$ and vice versa. $\mathcal{D}_n$ is the set of all 2^n concepts over $[1, n]$. The singleton classes are defined as $\mathcal{S}_n = \{\{x\} \mid x \in [1, n]\}$.

2.2   The Teaching Model

The teaching process is divided into rounds. In each round the teacher gives the learner an example of a target concept. The learner memorizes this example and computes a new hypothesis based on its last hypothesis and the known examples.

The Learner. In a sense, consistency is a minimum requirement for a learner. We thus require our learners to be consistent with all examples they know. However, the hypothesis is chosen at *random* from all consistent ones.

The memory of our learners may be limited to $\mu \geq 1$ examples. If the memory is full and a new example arrives, the oldest example is erased. In other words, the memory works like a queue. Setting $\mu = \infty$ models unlimited memory.

The goal of teaching is making the learner to hypothesize the target *and to maintain it*. Consistency alone cannot guarantee this behavior if the memory is too small. In this case, there is more than one consistent hypothesis at every round and the learner would oscillate between them rather than maintaining a single one. To avoid this, *conservativeness* is required, i.e., the learner can change its hypothesis only when taught an example inconsistent with its current one.

To study the influence of the learners' feedback to the teacher, we distinguish between private and public output of the learner. The private output is the result of the calculation during a round (i.e., new memory content and hypothesis), the public output is that part of the private one observable by the teacher. So, if the learner gives feedback, the teacher can observe in every round the complete hypothesis computed by the learner. If the learner does not give feedback, the teacher can observe nothing.

The following algorithm describes the behavior of the μ-memory learner with/ without feedback (short: L_μ^+ / L_μ^-) during one round of the teaching process.

> *Input*: memory $\boldsymbol{x} \in \mathcal{X}^{\leq \mu}$, hypothesis $h \in \mathcal{C}$, example $z \in \mathcal{X}$.
> *Private Output*: memory $\boldsymbol{x}'$, hypothesis h'.
> *Public Output*: hypothesis h' / nothing.
> 1 $\boldsymbol{x}' := \boldsymbol{x} \circ_\mu \langle z \rangle$;
> 2 **if** $z \notin \mathcal{X}(h)$ **then** pick h' uniformly at random from $\mathcal{C}(\boldsymbol{x}')$;
> 3   **else** $h' := h$;

For making our results dependent on $\mathcal{C}$ alone, rather than on an arbitrary initial state of the learner, we stipulate a special initial hypothesis, called *init*. We assume every example inconsistent with *init*. Thus, *init* is left after the first example and cannot be reached again. Moreover, the initial memory is empty.

The Teacher. A teacher is an algorithm taking initially a given target concept c^* as input. Then, in each round, it receives the public output of the learner (if any) and outputs an example for c^*.

Definition 1. *Let $\mathcal{C}$ be a concept class and $c^* \in \mathcal{C}$. Let L_μ^σ be a learner ($\sigma \in \{+,-\}$) and T be a teacher and $(h_i)_{i \in \mathbb{N}}$ be the series of random variables for the hypothesis at round i. The event "teaching success in round t," denoted by G_t, is defined as*

$$h_{t-1} \neq c^* \quad \wedge \quad \forall t' \geq t \colon h_{t'} = c^* \, .$$

The success probability of T is $\Pr \left[\bigcup_{t \geq 1} G_t \right]$. *A teaching process is successful iff the success probability equals 1. A successful teaching process is called finite iff there is a t' such that* $\Pr \left[\bigcup_{1 \leq t \leq t'} G_t \right] = 1$, *otherwise it is called infinite. For a successful teaching process we define the expected teaching time as* $\mathbb{E}[T, L_\mu^\sigma, c^*, \mathcal{C}] := \sum_{t \geq 1} t \cdot \Pr[G_t]$.

Definition 2. *Let $\mathcal{C}$ be a concept class, $c^* \in \mathcal{C}$ and L_μ^σ a learner. We call c^* teachable to L_μ^σ iff there is a successful teacher T. The optimal teaching time for c^* is*

$$E_\mu^\sigma(c^*) := \inf_T \mathbb{E}[T, L_\mu^\sigma, c^*, \mathcal{C}]$$

and the optimal teaching time for $\mathcal{C}$ is denoted by $E_\mu^\sigma(\mathcal{C}) := \max_{c \in \mathcal{C}} E_\mu^\sigma(c)$.

2.3   Markov Decision Processes

For an extensive treatment of this topic see Puterman [17] and Bertsekas [6]. A Markov Decision Process (MDP) is a probabilistic system whose state transitions can be influenced during the process by actions which incur costs. Formally, an MDP consists of a finite set S of states, an initial state $s_0 \in S$, a finite set A

of actions, a function $cost\colon S \times A \to \mathbb{R}$, and a function $p\colon S \times A \times S \to [0,1]$; $cost(s,a)$ is the cost incurred by action a in state s; $p(s,a,s')$ is the probability for the MDP to change from state s to s' under action a.

In the *total cost infinite horizon* setting, the goal is to choose actions such that the expected total cost, when the MDP runs forever, is minimal. This makes sense only if there is a costless absorbing state $s^* \in S$. In the *finite horizon* setting the MDP is only run for finitely many rounds.

The actions chosen at each point in time are described by a *policy*. This is a function depending on the observed history of the MDP and the current state. A basic result says that there is a minimum-cost policy that is *stationary*, i.e., that depends only on the current state. A stationary policy $\pi\colon S \to A$ defines a Markov chain over S and for all $s \in S$ an expected time $H(s)$ to reach s^* from s. Such a policy is optimal iff for all $s \in S$:

$$\pi(s) \in \operatorname*{argmin}_{a \in A} \left(cost(s,a) + \sum_{s' \in S} p(s,a,s') \cdot H(s') \right).$$

Finding optimal policies can be phrased as a linear programming problem and can thus be done in polynomial time in the representation size of the MDP.

3 Varying Memory Size and Feedback

As a simple example, we calculate the optimal teaching times for $\mathcal{D}_n$. To the learner L_μ^+ ($1 \le \mu \le n$) the teacher can give an example inconsistent with the current hypothesis in each round. For all such examples, there are $2^{n-\mu}$ hypotheses consistent with the μ examples in the learner's memory and learner chooses one of them. Therefore the probability of choosing the target concept is $2^{-(n-\mu)}$. Thus, considering that in the first $\mu - 1$ rounds the memory contains less then μ examples, $E_\mu^+(\mathcal{D}_n)$ is, for constant μ, asymptotically equal to $2^{n-\mu}$.

Clearly, teaching becomes faster with growing μ. Moreover the teaching speed increases continuously with μ and not abruptly as in the classical deterministic model. In particular, teaching is possible even with the smallest memory size ($\mu = 1$), although it takes very long (2^{n-1} rounds).

Teaching is more difficult when feedback is unavailable. In this situation the teacher can merely guess examples hoping that they are inconsistent with the current hypothesis. Roughly speaking, when teaching $\mathcal{D}_n$, the teacher needs two guesses on average to find such an example. Hence, the expected teaching time E_μ^- is about two times E_μ^+. Thus feedback doubles the teaching speed for $\mathcal{D}_n$.

Fact 3. *For all C and $\mu \in [1, \infty]$ all $c^* \in C$ and $\sigma \in \{+, -\}$:*
    (1) $E_\mu^+(c^*) \le E_\mu^-(c^*),$ (2) $E_\infty^\sigma(c^*) \le E_{\mu+1}^\sigma(c^*) \le E_\mu^\sigma(c^*).$
Proper inequality holds for the concepts in $\mathcal{D}_n$.

Next, we relate the deterministic model (in terms of the teaching dimension) to the randomized model (in terms of the expected teaching time). Essentially, the teaching dimension can be used to lower bound the teaching time.

Lemma 4. *Let $\mathcal{C}$ be a class and let $c^* \in \mathcal{C}$ be a target. For all $\mu \in [1, TD(c^*)]$,*

$$E_\mu^-(c^*) \geq E_\mu^+(c^*) \geq \frac{\mu(\mu-1)}{2\,TD(c^*)} + TD(c^*) + 1 - \mu,$$

and for all $\mu > TD(c^*)$, $E_\mu^-(c^*) \geq E_\mu^+(c^*) \geq TD(c^*)/2$.

Proof. Let $k = TD(c^*)$ and $\mu \in [1, TD(c^*)]$. We show the statement for E_μ^+.

Claim: For i examples $z_0, \ldots, z_{i-1} \in \mathcal{X}(c^*)$: $|\mathcal{C}(z_0, \ldots, z_{i-1})| \geq k + 1 - i$.

Proof: Suppose $|\mathcal{C}(z_0, \ldots, z_{i-1})| \leq k - i$. Then c^* can be specified with $k - i - 1$ examples with respect to $\mathcal{C}(z_0, \ldots, z_{i-1})$ (each example rules out at least one concept). Thus, c^* can be specified with $z_0, \ldots, z_{i-1}$ plus $k - i - 1$ other examples, which amounts to $k - 1$ examples. This contradicts $TD(c^*) = k$. □ Claim

Using the claim we upper bound the probabilities for reaching the target in round $i = 0, \ldots, \mu - 2$. After round i the learner knows $i + 1$ examples and therefore can choose between at least $k - i$ consistent hypotheses (see Claim). Thus, the probability for reaching c^* in round i is at most $p_i := \frac{1}{k-i}$. Beginning with round $\mu - 1$, the learner knows μ examples and has in each following round $i \geq \mu - 1$ a probability of at most $p_i = p_{\mu-1} = 1/(k+1-\mu)$ of reaching c^*.

No teaching process can be faster than one with the probabilities p_i described above. The expectation of such a process is

$$\sum_{i=0}^{\mu-2}(i+1) \cdot p_i \cdot \prod_{j=0}^{i-1}(1-p_j) \;+\; \sum_{i=\mu-1}^{\infty}(i+1) \cdot p_i \cdot \prod_{j=0}^{i-1}(1-p_j). \tag{1}$$

We start with the second sum in (1). Since $\prod_{j=0}^{\mu-2}(1-p_j) = \frac{k-\mu+1}{k}$ the product $\prod_{j=0}^{i-1}(1-p_j)$ in the this sum equals $\frac{k-\mu+1}{k} \cdot (1-p_{\mu-1})^{i-\mu+1}$. So, this sum is

$$\sum_{i=\mu-1}^{\infty}(i+1) \cdot p_{\mu-1} \cdot \frac{k-\mu+1}{k} \cdot (1-p_{\mu-1})^{i-\mu+1}$$

$$= \frac{k-\mu+1}{k} \cdot \sum_{i=0}^{\infty}(\mu+i) \cdot p_{\mu-1} \cdot (1-p_{\mu-1})^i$$

$$= \frac{k-\mu+1}{k} \cdot \left(\mu - 1 + \sum_{i=0}^{\infty}(i+1) \cdot p_{\mu-1} \cdot (1-p_{\mu-1})^i\right).$$

The sum appearing in the last line is the expectation of the first success in a Bernoulli experiment with probability $p_{\mu-1}$ and thus equals $1/p_{\mu-1} = k - \mu + 1$. For the second sum in (1) we therefore get $\frac{k-\mu+1}{k} \cdot (\mu - 1 + k - \mu + 1) = k - \mu + 1$.

Calculating the first sum in (1) yields

$$\sum_{i=0}^{\mu-2}(i+1) \cdot \frac{1}{k-i} \cdot \prod_{j=0}^{i-1}\frac{k-j-1}{k-j} = \sum_{i=0}^{\mu-2}(i+1) \cdot \frac{1}{k-i} \cdot \frac{k-i}{k} = \frac{\mu(\mu-1)}{2k}.$$

Putting it together we obtain $\frac{\mu(\mu-1)}{2k} + k + 1 - \mu$ as the value of (1).

For $\mu > TD(c^*)$ the teaching process described above takes at most $TD(c^*)$ rounds. The lower bound is therefore the same as for $\mu = TD(c^*)$. □

Input: Target $c^* \in \mathcal{M}_n$ represented by $\gamma_1 \ldots \gamma_n \in \{0, 1, *\}^n$;
 Hypothesis $h \in \mathcal{M}_n$ represented by $\eta_1 \ldots \eta_n \in \{0, 1, *\}^n$.
Output: Example $z \in \mathcal{X}(c^*)$.

1 **if** $h \supset c^*$ **output** $(\chi_1 \ldots \chi_n, 0)$ with $\chi_i = \begin{cases} \gamma_i & \text{if } \eta_i = \gamma_i \neq *, \\ 1 - \gamma_i & \text{if } i = \min\{j \mid \eta_j = * \neq \gamma_j\}, \\ 0 & \text{otherwise;} \end{cases}$

2 **else output** $(x, 1)$ with arbitrary $x \in c^*$.

Fig. 1. Optimal teacher for monomials and the learner L_1^+

4 Learners with Feedback

4.1 Learners with 1-Memory

A teaching process involving L_1^+ can be modeled as an MDP with $S = \mathcal{C} \cup \{init\}$, $A = \mathcal{X}(c^*)$, $cost(h, z) = 1$ for $h \neq c^*$ and $cost(c^*, z) = 0$. Furthermore, for $h \neq c^*$, $p(h, z, h') = 1/|\mathcal{C}(z)|$ if $z \in \mathcal{X}(h') \setminus \mathcal{X}(h)$ and $p(h, z, h') = 0$ otherwise; finally $p(c^*, z, c^*) = 1$. The initial state is $init$ and the state c^* is costless and absorbing. The memory does not need to be part of the state, since the next hypothesis only depends on the newly given example which is modeled as an action.

An example $z \in \mathcal{X}(h)$ does not change the learner's state h and is therefore useless. An optimal teacher refrains from teaching such examples and thus we can derive the following criterion by using the results from Subsection 2.3.

Lemma 5. *Let $\mathcal{C}$ be a class over X and c^* be a target. A teacher $T: \mathcal{C} \cup \{init\} \to \mathcal{X}(c^*)$ with expectations $H: \mathcal{C} \cup \{init\} \to \mathbb{R}$ is optimal iff for all $h \in \mathcal{C} \cup \{init\}$:*

$$T(h) \in \operatorname*{argmin}_{\substack{z \in \mathcal{X}(c^*) \\ z \notin \mathcal{X}(h)}} \left(1 + \frac{1}{|\mathcal{C}(z)|} \sum_{h' \in \mathcal{C}(z)} H(h') \right).$$

This criterion can be used to prove optimality for teaching algorithms.

Fact 6. *The teacher in Fig. 1 is an optimal teacher for $\mathcal{M}_n$ and the learner L_1^+.*

Proof. We define $H: \mathcal{C} \cup \{init\} \to \mathbb{R}$ as $H(h) = \frac{(3^n - 2^n)(2^n + 2^k) - 2^{n+k-1}}{3^n - 2^n + 2^{k-1}}$ for $h \supset c^*$ and $H(h) = \frac{(3^n - 2^n)(2^n + 2^k) - 2^{n+k-1} + 2^{n+1} - 3^n}{3^n - 2^n + 2^{k-1}}$ for all other h, including $init$.

It is possible (though tedious) to show that H describes the teaching times for T and that T and H satisfy the criterion of Lemma 5.   □

The teacher from Fig. 1 can be computed in linear time. It outputs a positive example whenever possible (i.e., when $h \not\supset c^*$). Since there are 2^n hypotheses consistent with a positive example and $3^n - 2^n$ consistent with a negative one, this means following a greedy strategy minimizing the number of consistent hypotheses for the learner to choose from, thus maximizing the probability for reaching c^* in the next step.

Such a greedy strategy seems sensible and is provably optimal in the case of $\mathcal{M}_n$. However, there are classes where no greedy teacher is optimal.

Definition 7. *Let C be a class over X and $c^* \in C$. A stationary teacher $T: C \cup \{init\} \to X$ for c^* is called* greedy *iff for all $h \in C: T(h) \in \mathrm{argmin}_{\substack{z \in X(c^*) \\ z \notin C(h)}} |C(z)|$.*

Fact 8. *There is a class C and target c_0 such that no greedy teacher is optimal.*

Proof. Figure 2 displays such a concept class C and target c_0. T^* with teaching times H^* is an optimal teacher and T^g with H^g is the only greedy teacher. $\quad\square$

h	x_1	x_2	x_3	x_4	x_5	$T^*(h)$	$H^*(h)$	$T^g(h)$	$H^g(h)$
$init$	–	–	–	–	–	x_1	$176/35 = 5.0285\ldots$	x_1	$2536/504 = 5.0317\ldots$
c_0	1	1	1	1	1	–	0	–	0
c_1	0	0	0	0	1	x_1	$176/35$	x_1	$2536/504$
c_2	0	0	0	1	1	x_1	$176/35$	x_1	$2536/504$
c_3	0	0	1	0	1	x_1	$176/35$	x_1	$2536/504$
c_4	0	0	1	1	1	x_1	$176/35$	x_1	$2536/504$
c_5	0	1	0	1	1	x_1	$176/35$	x_1	$2536/504$
c_6	0	1	1	0	1	x_1	$176/35$	x_1	$2536/504$
c_7	0	1	1	1	1	x_1	$176/35$	x_1	$2536/504$
c_8	1	0	0	1	0	x_2	$186/35$	x_2	$2680/504$
c_9	1	1	1	0	0	x_5	$189/35$	x_4	$2725/504$
c_{10}	1	1	1	1	0	x_5	$189/35$	x_5	$2723/504$

Fig. 2. Class with an optimal teacher T^* and a greedy teacher T^g that is not optimal. Both teachers teach c_0 to the learner L_1^+.

We now compare E_1^+ with other dimensions. The comparison of E_1^+ with the number MQ of membership queries (see Angulin [1]) is interesting because MQ and E_1^+ are both lower bounded by the teaching dimension.

Fact 9. (1) *For all C and $c^* \in C: E_1^+(c^*) \geq TD(c^*)$.*
(2) *There is no function of TD upper bounding $E_1^+(c)$.*
(3) *There is no function of E_1^+ upper bounding MQ.*
(4) *There is a concept class C with $E_1^+(C) > MQ(C)$.*
(5) *For all concept classes C, $E_1^+(C) \leq 2^{MQ(C)}$.*

Proof. (1) This follows from Lemma 4. (2) Let $C_n = \{c \subseteq [1,n] \mid |c| = 2\}$. Then $TD(C_n) = 2$, but $E_1^+(C_n) = n - 1$ because the optimal teacher gives positive examples all the time and there are $n - 1$ hypotheses consistent to such an example. (3) $E_1^+(c) = 1$ for all $c \in S_n$, but $MQ(S_n) = n-1$. (4) $MQ(D_n) = n$ and $E_1^+(D) = 2^{n-1}$. (5) It is known (see e.g., Angulin [2]) that $\log |C| \leq MQ(C)$ for all classes C. Also, $E_1^+(C) \leq |C|$ because in every step the learner cannot choose from more than $|C|$ hypotheses. Combining both inequalities yields the fact. $\quad\square$

Roughly speaking, teaching L_1^+ can take arbitrarily longer than teaching in the classical model, but is still incomparable with membership query learning.

4.2   Learners with ∞-Memory

A straightforward MDP for teaching c^* to L_∞^+ has states $S = (\mathcal{C} \cup \{init\}) \times \mathcal{X}(c^*)^{\leq |X|}$. The number of states can be reduced because two states (h, m) and (h, m') with $\mathcal{C}(m) = \mathcal{C}(m')$ are equivalent from a teacher's perspective, but in general the size of the resulting MDP will not be polynomial in the size of the matrix representation of $\mathcal{C}$. Therefore, optimal teachers cannot be computed efficiently by the known general MDP algorithms.

A similar criterion as Lemma 5 can be stated for the L_∞^+ learner, too, and used to prove optimality of algorithms. We mention, without the technical proof, that a slight modification of the algorithm in Fig. 1 is optimal for L_∞^+ and $\mathcal{M}_n$.

That computing E_∞^+ is already a hard problem can be seen as follows. First, there is always a teacher that needs at most $TD(c^*)$ rounds by giving a minimal teaching set, hence $E_\infty^+(c^*) \leq TD(c^*)$. Second, it follows from Lemma 4 that $E_\infty^+(c^*) \geq TD(c^*)/2$. This means that every algorithm computing $E_\infty^+(c^*)$ also computes a factor 2 approximation of the teaching dimension.

As it has often been noted [19, 5, 9], the problem of computing the teaching dimension is essentially equivalent to the SET-COVER (or HITTING-SET) problem which is a difficult approximation problem. Raz and Safra [18] have shown that there is no polynomial time constant-factor approximation (unless $\mathcal{P} = \mathcal{NP}$). Moreover, Feige [7] proved that SET-COVER cannot be approximated better than within a logarithmic factor (unless $\mathcal{NP} \subseteq DTime(n^{\log \log n})$).

Corollary 10. *Unless $\mathcal{NP} \subseteq DTime(n^{\log \log n})$, computing E_∞^+ is $\mathcal{NP}$-hard and cannot be approximated with a factor of $(1 - \epsilon) \log |\mathcal{C}|$ for any $\epsilon > 0$.*

Fact 11. *Let $\mathcal{C}$ be a concept class and $c^* \in \mathcal{C}$ a target. Then there is a successful teacher for the learner L_∞^+ halting after at most $|X|$ rounds that is also optimal.*

Proof. Every given example is memorized forever. Hence, an optimal teacher never presents the same example twice and after at most $|X|$ rounds there is only one consistent hypothesis for the learner to choose from, namely c^*.   □

As there is always a successful teacher giving at most $TD(c^*)$ examples, one could conjecture that there is also an optimal teacher teaching finitely within at most $TD(c^*)$ rounds. But this not the case.

Fact 12. *There is a concept class $\mathcal{C}$ and a concept $c^* \in \mathcal{C}$ such that all teachers teaching c^* to the learner L_∞^+ finitely within $TD(c^*)$ rounds are suboptimal.*

Proof. (Sketch) The concept class $\mathcal{C}$ and the concept c^* are defined by Figure 3. The teaching dimension of c^* is three and the only smallest teaching set $S := \{(x_1, 1), (x_2, 1), (x_3, 1)\}$. The only teachers finite after 3 rounds are those always giving an inconsistent example from S. Their expected teaching time is 2.6.

A teacher starting with $(x_4, 1)$ and then giving examples from S is not finite after three rounds, but has an expected teaching time of only 2.5 rounds.   □

$$
\begin{array}{cccccc}
 & x_1 & x_2 & x_3 & x_4 & x_5 & x_6 \\
init: & - & - & - & - & - & - \\
c^*: & 1 & 1 & 1 & 1 & 1 & 1 \\
 & 1 & 1 & 0 & 1 & 1 & 1 \\
 & 1 & 0 & 1 & 1 & 1 & 1 \\
 & 0 & 1 & 1 & 1 & 1 & 1 \\
 & 1 & 1 & 0 & 0 & 1 & 0 \\
 & 1 & 0 & 1 & 0 & 1 & 0 \\
 & 0 & 1 & 1 & 0 & 1 & 0 \\
 & 1 & 1 & 0 & 0 & 0 & 1 \\
 & 1 & 0 & 1 & 0 & 0 & 1 \\
 & 0 & 1 & 1 & 0 & 0 & 1 \\
 & 1 & 1 & 0 & 0 & 0 & 0 \\
 & 1 & 0 & 1 & 0 & 0 & 0 \\
 & 0 & 1 & 1 & 0 & 0 & 0 \\
\end{array}
$$

Fig. 3. Concept class and target whose optimal L_∞^+-teacher is not finite after $TD(c^*) = 3$ rounds. The optimal teacher starts with x_4 and is finite after 4 rounds (see Fact 12).

5   Learners Without Feedback

The problem of finding the optimal cost in an MDP whose states cannot be observed is much harder than in an observable MDP. In general, it is not even decidable whether the optimal cost is below a given threshold (see Madani, Hanks, and Condon [14]). We know of no obvious algorithm to decide this problem in the special case of teaching 1-memory learners.

Teaching ∞-memory learners can be seen as a finite horizon unobservable MDP since any reasonable teacher presents a different example in every round and thus can stop after at most $|X|$ rounds. The decision problem for finite horizon unobservable MDPs is $\mathcal{NP}$-complete (Mundhenk *et. al.* [16]) and the inapproximability result of Corollary 10 holds for the feedbackless case as well, since $TD(c^*)/2 \le E_\infty^-(c^*) \le TD(c^*)$.

6   Teaching Positive Examples Only

The learnability of classes from positive data is a typical question in learning theory. Similar restrictions on the data can be posed in teaching models, too. In contrast to teaching with positive *and* negative data, where all classes are teachable, we now get classes that are not teachable. More precisely we have the following characterization for teachability with positive data.

Theorem 13. *Let $\mathcal{C}$ be a concept class and $c^* \in \mathcal{C}$ a target concept. Then for all learners L_μ^σ with $\mu \in [1, \infty]$, $\sigma \in \{+, -\}$: The concept c^* is teachable from positive data iff there is no $c \in \mathcal{C}$ with $c \supset c^*$.*

Proof. For the if part, assume there is no proper superset of c^* in the class. Then the set S^+ of all positive examples for c^* is a teaching set for c^*. Learners with ∞-memory can be taught by presenting S^+, since they remember all examples and are always consistent. Learners with smaller memory can be taught by infinitely repeating S^+ in any order.

For the only-if part, assume there is a $c \in \mathcal{C}$ with $c \supset c^*$. Let $z = (x, 1) \in \mathcal{X}(c^*)$ be the first example taught. Then $c \in \mathcal{C}(z)$ and therefore there is a positive probability that the randomized learner picks c as first hypothesis. In this case, it is impossible to trigger any further mind changes by giving positive examples. Thus, with positive probability the number of examples is infinite, leading to an infinite expected number of examples. $\qquad\qquad\qquad\qquad\qquad\qquad\qquad\qquad\qquad\qquad$ $\square$

Theorem 13 also characterizes teaching with positive data in the classical teaching dimension model. If there is no $c \supset c^*$, the set of all positive examples of c^* is a teaching set, but if there is a $c \supset c^*$, then every set of positive examples for c^* is also consistent with c.

We have seen that teachability with positive data has a simple characterization. Things become a little more complicated when combined with inconsistent teachers discussed in the next section.

7   Inconsistent Teachers

Until now, teachers were required to always tell the truth, i.e., to provide examples $z \in \mathcal{X}(c^*)$. In reality it might sometimes be worthwhile to teach something which is, strictly speaking, not fully correct, but nevertheless helpful for the students. For example, human teachers sometimes oversimplify to give a clearer, yet slightly incorrect, view on the subject matter.

To model this we allow the teacher to present any example from $\mathcal{X} \times \{0, 1\}$, even inconsistent ones. One can see this as an analog to inconsistent learners in learning theory, as these learners also contradict something they actually know.

Clearly, teaching learners with ∞-memory becomes difficult after giving an inconsistent example because the target is not consistent with the memory contents any more. Even worse, there might be no consistent hypothesis available. However, the model can be adapted to this, e.g., by stipulating that a memorized example (x, v) can be "erased" by the example $(x, 1 - v)$, but here we will not pursue this further. We restrict ourselves to consider only the 1-memory learner.

We first look at inconsistent teachers in combination with teaching from positive data. In this case, for a target concept c, the only inconsistent examples allowed are of the form $(x, 1)$, where $x \notin c$. The class $\mathcal{C}_1$ in Figure 4 shows that, when only positive data are allowed, inconsistent teachers can teach concepts to L_1^+ that consistent teachers cannot. First, the teacher gives $(x_1, 1)$. If the learner guesses c^*, we are done. Otherwise, the learner must return c_1 and the teacher gives $(x_3, 1)$ which is *inconsistent* with c^*. Now, the learner has to guess c_2. Next, $(x_1, 1)$ is again given and the process is iterated until the learner returns c^*.

However, consistent teachers with both positive and negative data are more powerful as we show next.

Fact 14. *There is a class that cannot be taught to L_1^+ by an inconsistent teacher from positive data.*

$\mathcal{C}_1$:

	x_1	x_2	x_3	T
init:	–	–	–	x_1
c^*:	1	0	0	–
c_1:	1	1	0	x_3
c_2:	0	0	1	x_1

$\mathcal{C}_2$:

	x_1	x_2	x_3
init:	–	–	–
c^*:	0	1	0
c_1:	1	1	0
c_2:	0	1	1

Fig. 4. The class $\mathcal{C}_1$ can be taught to L_1^+ by the inconsistent positive-data teacher T, but cannot be taught by a consistent positive-data teacher (Theorem 13). The class $\mathcal{C}_2$ cannot be taught by an inconsistent positive-data teacher (Fact 14).

Proof. We show that $\mathcal{C}_2$ from Figure 4 is such a class. Let T be a teacher for L_1^+ mapping $\mathcal{C}_2 \cup \{init\}$ to $\{x_1, x_2, x_3\} \times \{1\}$. No matter what $T(init)$ is, the probability that the learner switches to c_1 or c_2 is positive. If the learner guesses c_1 (the c_2 case is analog), the teacher must teach $(x_3, 1)$, since all other examples are consistent with the current hypothesis c_1. But the only hypothesis consistent with $(x_3, 1)$ is c_2. Analogously, T must give $(x_1, 1)$ when the learner is in c_2, leading again to c_1. So, the probability that L_1^+ never reaches c^* is positive. □

Classes teachable by inconsistent teachers from positive data can be characterized. We associate a directed graph with the class $\mathcal{C}$. Define the graph $G(\mathcal{C}) = (V, A)$ by $V = \mathcal{C}$ and $A = \{(c, d) \mid d \setminus c \neq \emptyset\}$, i.e., there is an arc from c to d iff there is a positive example inconsistent with c but consistent with d.

Theorem 15. *Let $\mathcal{C}$ be a concept class and $G(\mathcal{C}) = (V, A)$ its associated graph. For the learner L_1^+ a concept $c^* \in \mathcal{C}$ is teachable by an inconsistent teacher from positive data iff for all $c \in V$ there is a path to c^* in $G(\mathcal{C})$.*

Proof. For the if part we have to describe a teacher. For each c let c' be a neighbor of c on a shortest path to c^*. Let T be such that for all c, $T(c)$ is consistent with c', but not with c. There is always such an example due to the definition of $G(\mathcal{C})$ and the reachability assumption.

Denote by $n = |\mathcal{C}|$ and by $p = 1/n$ the minimum probability for reaching c' when the learner receives $T(c)$ in state c. If the learner is in any state c, there is a probability of at least $p^n > 0$ for reaching c^* within the next n rounds by traversing the shortest path from c to c^*. Therefore, no matter in which state the learner is, the expected number of n-round blocks until reaching the target is at most $1/p^n$. Thus, the expected time to reach the target from any state, in particular from $init$, is at most $n/p^n < \infty$.

For the only-if part, let T be a teacher for $c^* \in \mathcal{C}$. Suppose there is a state c with no path to c^*. Then $c \supset c^*$ (otherwise $c^* \setminus c \neq \emptyset$ and $(c, c^*) \in A$). At some time, T must teach an example consistent with c^*, which is then also consistent with c. Hence, the probability for reaching c during the teaching process is positive. The graph $G(\mathcal{C})$ contains all transitions that are possible between the hypotheses by positive examples. Since c^* is not reachable from c in $G(\mathcal{C})$ there is no sequence of positive examples that can trigger hypothesis changes from c to c^*. Thus, the expected teaching time from c is infinite and hence the expected teaching time altogether. A contradiction to c^* being teachable by T. □

The criterion in Theorem 15 requires to check the reachability of a certain node from all other nodes in a directed graph. This problem is related to the REACHABILITY problem and also complete for the complexity class $\mathcal{NL}$.

While inconsistent teachers can teach classes to 1-memory learners with feedback from positive data that consistent teachers cannot teach to L_1^+ (cf. Figure 4), the situation changes if no feedback is available. That is, 1-memory learners without feedback can be taught the same classes by inconsistent teachers as by consistent teachers (cf. Theorem 13 and Theorem 16 below).

Theorem 16. *For the learner L_1^- a concept $c^* \in \mathcal{C}$ is teachable by an inconsistent teacher from positive data iff there is no $c \in \mathcal{C}$ with $c \supset c^*$.*

Proof. The if-direction follows from Theorem 13.

For the only-if part suppose that c^* is teachable by a teacher T and there is a c with $c \supset c^*$. Let $(z_i)_{i \in \mathbb{N}}$ be the series of examples taught.

Claim: T teaches inconsistent examples only finitely often.

Proof: Suppose T teaches an example $(x, 1) \notin \mathcal{X}(c^*)$ infinitely often. Without loss of generality we assume that there is a concept containing x (otherwise $(x, 1)$ would be useless and a teacher T' never giving this example would be successful, too). Whenever $(x, 1)$ is taught, the learner will not be in state c^* afterwards, i.e., there are infinitely many t such that $\Pr[h_t \neq c^*] = 1$. It follows that $\Pr[G_t] = \Pr[h_{t-1} \neq c^* \wedge \forall t' \geq t : h_t = c^*] = 0$ for all $t \geq 1$. This means that the success probability is zero, a contradiction. This proves the claim. $\square$ Claim

From the claim it follows that there is a t' such that $z_t \in \mathcal{X}(c^*)$ for all $t \geq t'$. We now show that $\Pr[h_{t'} = c^*] < 1$, i.e., it is uncertain whether the learner is in the target state. Suppose that $\Pr[h_{t'} = c^*] = 1$. Let $t \leq t'$ be minimal with $\Pr[h_t = c^*] = 1$. If $z_t \in \mathcal{X}(c^*)$ then z_t is consistent with c, too, and thus $\Pr[h_t = c^*] \leq 1/2$. If $z_t \notin \mathcal{X}(c^*)$, then $\Pr[h_t = c^*] = 0$, a contradiction.

Hence, the probability that the learner is not in the target state at time t' is positive. After t' only consistent examples are given. So there is a probability of at least $1/|\mathcal{C}|$ that the learner switches to c on the next example. As $c \supset c^*$ the target cannot be reached by positive examples any more. Thus, the success probability is less than one, a contradiction. This proves the only-if part. $\square$

8   Mind Change Forcing Teachers

In this section we deal again with consistent teachers. When teaching L_1^+ it is useless to provide an example consistent with the current hypothesis, since it does not change the state of L_1^+. In this situation the optimal teacher is necessarily "mind change forcing." But if we look at L_μ^+ ($\mu > 1$), it is not obvious that an optimal teacher has to force the learner to change its mind in every round until successful learning. While we could prove that for L_∞^+ an optimal teacher can be made "mind change forcing," it remains open whether a similar statement is true for L_μ^+ with $1 < \mu < \infty$.

Theorem 17. *Let $\mathcal{C}$ be a class and c^* be a target. Then there is an optimal teacher for L_∞^+ never giving an example consistent with the current hypothesis.*

Proof. Let T be a successful teacher that teaches a consistent example z_1 in a state (h, m) that is reached with positive probability and is not a target state. Then $z_1 \in \mathcal{X}(h) \cap \mathcal{X}(c^*)$ and $h \neq c^*$. We show that T is not optimal for this state and hence for the initial state. We do this by showing that there is another teacher T' giving an inconsistent example and being not worse than T.

After receiving z_1, the learner reaches $(h, m \cup \{z_1\})$ due to the conservativeness property. Then T teaches $z_1 = T(h, m \cup \{z_1\})$ leading to $(h, m \cup \{z_1, z_2\})$ and so on. Since $h \neq c^*$, T must eventually teach an example $z_k \notin \mathcal{C}(h)$. After teaching $z_1, \ldots, z_k$ the learner has either reached the target or assumes one of the hypotheses in $\mathcal{C}(m \cup \{z_1, \ldots, z_k\}) \setminus \{c^*\}$ with equal probability $p := 1/|\mathcal{C}(m \cup \{z_1, \ldots, z_k\})| - 1$. For the expected teaching time we have

$$H(h, m) = k + \sum_{h' \in \mathcal{C}(m \cup \{z_1, \ldots, z_k\})} p \cdot H(h', m \cup \{z_1, \ldots, z_k\})$$

The teacher T' teaches the same examples $z_1, \ldots, z_k$, but in different order, namely $z_k, z_1, \ldots, z_{k-1}$, that is with the inconsistent example first. Formally: $T'(h, m) = z_k$ and furthermore for all $i = 0, \ldots, k - 1$ and for all $h' \in \mathcal{C}(m \cup \{z_k, z_1, \ldots, z_i\})$: $T'(h', m \cup \{z_k, z_1, \ldots, z_i\}) = z_{i+1}$.

Beginning in (h, m) and being taught by T' for k rounds, the learner has either arrived at the target or assumes one of the hypotheses in $\mathcal{C}(m \cup \{z_1, \ldots, z_k\}) \setminus \{c^*\}$. Furthermore all these hypotheses are equally likely. This follows inductively from the fact that whenever a hypothesis change is triggered, say after $z_k, z_1 \ldots, z_i$, all hypotheses from $\mathcal{C}(m \cup \{z_k, z_1, \ldots, z_i\})$, and in particular all hypotheses from the subset $\mathcal{C}(m \cup \{z_1, \ldots, z_k\})$, are equally likely; no hypothesis is preferred. The probability p' for each of these hypotheses is at most $1/(|\mathcal{C}(m \cup \{z_1, \ldots, z_k\})| - 1) = p$. The expected teaching time under T' is

$$H'(h, m) \leq k + \sum_{h' \in \mathcal{C}(m \cup \{z_1, \ldots, z_k\})} p' \cdot H'(h', m \cup \{z_1, \ldots, z_k\})$$

$$= k + \sum_{h' \in \mathcal{C}(m \cup \{z_1, \ldots, z_k\})} p' \cdot H(h', m \cup \{z_1, \ldots, z_k\}) \leq H(h, m)$$

where the equality in the second line holds because T and T' are identical in the states $(h', m \cup \{z_1, \ldots, z_k\})$.

We have shown that T' is not worse than T and gives an inconsistent example in (h, m). By repeating the above argument the states in which T gives consistent examples can be moved to the "end" where they finally disappear.   □

9   Conclusions and Future Work

We have presented a model for teaching randomized learners based on the classical teaching dimension model. In our model, teachability depends, in a qualitatively plausible way, on the learner's memory size, on its ability to give feedback, and on the order of the examples taught. The model also allows to study learning theory like questions such as teaching from positive data only or teaching by inconsistent teachers. Randomization also gives more flexibility in defining the learner's behavior by using certain *a priori* probability distributions over the hypotheses. So, one can define and study learners preferring simple hypotheses.

References

[1] D. Angluin. Queries and concept learning. *Machine Learning*, 2(4):319–342, 1988.

[2] D. Angluin. Queries revisited. *Theoret. Comput. Sci.*, 313(2):175–194, 2004.

[3] D. Angluin and M. Kriķis. Teachers, learners and black boxes. In *Proc. of the 10th Annual Conference on Computational Learning Theory*, pages 285–297. ACM Press, New York, NY, 1997.

[4] D. Angluin and M. Kriķis. Learning from different teachers. *Machine Learning*, 51(2):137–163, 2003.

[5] M. Anthony, G. Brightwell, D. Cohen, and J. Shawe-Taylor. On exact specification by examples. In *Proc. of the 5th Annual ACM Workshop on Computational Learning Theory*, pages 311–318. ACM Press, New York, NY, 1992.

[6] D. P. Bertsekas. *Dynamic Programming and Optimal Control*. Athena Scientific.

[7] U. Feige. A threshold of ln n for approximating set cover. *J. of the ACM*, 45(4):634–652, 1998.

[8] R. Freivalds, E. B. Kinber, and R. Wiehagen. On the power of inductive inference from good examples. *Theoret. Comput. Sci.*, 110(1):131–144, 1993.

[9] S. A. Goldman and M. J. Kearns. On the complexity of teaching. *J. Comput. Syst. Sci.*, 50(1):20–31, 1995.

[10] S. A. Goldman and H. D. Mathias. Teaching a smarter learner. *J. Comput. Syst. Sci.*, 52(2):255–267, 1996.

[11] S. A. Goldman, R. L. Rivest, and R. E. Schapire. Learning binary relations and total orders. *SIAM J. on Computing*, 22(5):1006–1034, Oct. 1993.

[12] J. Jackson and A. Tomkins. A computational model of teaching. In *Proc. of the 5th Annual ACM Workshop on Computational Learning Theory* pages 319–326. ACM Press, New York, NY, 1992.

[13] S. Jain, S. Lange, and J. Nessel. Learning of r.e. languages from good examples. In *Algorithmic Learning Theory, 8th International Workshop, ALT '97, Sendai, Japan, October 1997, Proceedings*, Lecture Notes in Artificial Intelligence Vol. 1316, pages 32–47, Springer, 1997.

[14] O. Madani, S. Hanks, and A. Condon. On the undecidability of probabilistic planning and infinite-horizon partially observable Markov decision problems. In *Proc. of the 16th National Conference on Artificial Intelligence and 11th Conference on Innovative Applications of Artificial Intelligence*, pages 541–548, AAAI Press/The MIT Press, 1999.

[15] H. D. Mathias. A model of interactive teaching. *J. Comput. Syst. Sci.*, 54(3):487–501, 1997.

[16] M. Mundhenk, J. Goldsmith, C. Lusena, and E. Allender. Complexity of finite-horizon Markov decision process problems. *J. of the ACM*, 47(4):681–720, 2000.

[17] M. L. Puterman. *Markov Decision Processes: Discrete Stochastic Dynamic Programming*. John Wiley & Sons, 1994.

[18] R. Raz and S. Safra. A sub-constant error-probability low-degree test, and a sub-constant error-probability PCP characterization of NP. In *Proc. of the 29th ACM Symposium on Theory of Computing*, pages 475–484, 1997.

[19] A. Shinohara and S. Miyano. Teachability in computational learning. *New Generation Computing*, 8(4):337–348, 1991.

Memory-Limited U-Shaped Learning

Lorenzo Carlucci[1,*], John Case[2,**], Sanjay Jain[3,***], and Frank Stephan[4,†]

[1] Department of Computer and Information Sciences, University of Delaware,
Newark, DE 19716-2586, USA and Dipartimento di Matematica, Università di Siena,
Pian dei Mantellini 44, Siena, Italy, EU
carlucci5@unisi.it

[2] Department of Computer and Information Sciences, University of Delaware,
Newark, DE 19716-2586, USA
case@cis.udel.edu

[3] School of Computing, 3 Science Drive 2, National University of Singapore,
Singapore 117543, Republic of Singapore
sanjay@comp.nus.edu.sg

[4] School of Computing and Department of Mathematics, National University of
Singapore, 3 Science Drive 2, Singapore 117543, Republic of Singapore
fstephan@comp.nus.edu.sg

Abstract. U-shaped learning is a learning behaviour in which the learner first *learns* something, then *unlearns* it and finally *relearns* it. Such a behaviour, observed by psychologists, for example, in the learning of past-tenses of English verbs, has been widely discussed among psychologists and cognitive scientists as a fundamental example of the non-monotonicity of learning. Previous theory literature has studied whether or not U-shaped learning, in the context of Gold's formal model of learning languages from positive data, is *necessary* for learning some tasks.

It is clear that human learning involves memory limitations. In the present paper we consider, then, this question of the necessity of U-shaped learning for some learning models featuring *memory limitations*. Our results show that the question of the necessity of U-shaped learning in this memory-limited setting depends on delicate tradeoffs between the learner's ability to remember its own previous conjecture, to store some values in its long-term memory, to make queries about whether or not items occur in previously seen data *and* on the learner's choice of hypothesis space.

1 Introduction and Motivation

U-Shaped learning. *U-shaped learning* occurs when the learner first learns a correct behaviour, then abandons that correct behaviour and finally returns to it once again. This pattern of learning has been observed by cognitive and developmental psychologists in a variety of child development phenomena, such as lan-

---

* Supported in part by NSF grant number NSF CCR-0208616.
** Supported in part by NSF grant number NSF CCR-0208616.
*** Supported in part by NUS grant number R252–000–127–112.
† Supported in part by NUS grant number R252–000–212–112.

guage learning [6, 19, 24], understanding of temperature [24, 25], understanding of weight conservation [5, 24], object permanence [5, 24] and face recognition [7].

The case of language acquisition is paradigmatic. In the case of the past tense of English verbs, it has been observed that children learn correct syntactic forms (call/called, go/went), then undergo a period of overregularization in which they attach regular verb endings such as 'ed' to the present tense forms even in the case of irregular verbs (break/breaked, speak/speaked) and finally reach a final phase in which they correctly handle both regular and irregular verbs. This example of U-shaped learning behaviour has figured so prominently in the so-called "Past Tense Debate" in cognitive science that competing models of human learning are often judged on their capacity for modeling the U-shaped learning phenomenon [19, 22, 26].

Recent interest in U-shaped learning is witnessed by the fact that the *Journal of Cognition and Development* dedicated its first issue in the year 2004 to this phenomenon.

While the prior cognitive science literature on U-shaped learning was typically concerned with modeling *how* humans achieve U-shaped behaviour, [2, 8] are motivated by the question of *why* humans exhibit this seemingly inefficient behaviour. Is it a mere harmless evolutionary inefficiency or is it *necessary* for full human learning power? A technically answerable version of this question is: are there some formal learning tasks for which U-shaped behaviour is logically necessary? The answer to this latter question requires that we first describe some formal criteria of successful learning.

A learning machine **M** reads an infinite sequence consisting of the elements of any language L in arbitrary order with possibly some pause symbols # in between elements. During this process the machine outputs a corresponding sequence $e_0 e_1 \ldots$ of hypotheses (grammars) which may generate the language L to be learned. Sometimes, especially when numerically coded, we also call these hypotheses *indices*. A fundamental criterion of successful learning of a language is called *explanatory learning* (**Ex***-learning*) and was introduced by Gold in [13]. Explanatory learning requires that the learner's output conjectures stabilize in the limit to a *single* conjecture (grammar/program, description/explanation) that generates the input language.

For each such criterion, a *non U-shaped learner* is naturally modeled as a learner that never *semantically* returns to a previously abandoned correct conjecture on languages it learns according to that criterion. It is shown in [2] that every **Ex**-learnable class of languages is **Ex**-learnable by a non U-shaped learner, that is, for **Ex**-learnability, U-shaped learning is *not* necessary. In [2], it is also noted that, by contrast, for behaviourally correct learning, U-shaped learning *is* necessary for full learning power. In [8] it is shown that, for non-trivial vacillatory learning, U-shaped learning is again necessary for full learning power.

Memory-Limited Learning. It is clear that human learning involves memory limitations. In the present paper we consider the necessity of U-shaped learning in formal *memory-limited* versions of language learning. In the prior literature at least the following three types of memory-limited learning have been studied.

A most basic concept of memory-limited learning is *iterative learning* [18, 28], according to which the learner reacts to its current data item, can remember its own last conjecture but cannot store *any* of the strictly previously seen data items.

Iterative learning admits of learning non-trivial classes. For example, the class of finite sets is iteratively learnable as is a class of self-describing sets, for example, the class of languages with the least element coding a grammar for the language. Furthermore, for each $m \geq 1$, the class of unions of m of Angluin's [1] pattern languages is iteratively learnable [11].

The criterion of *n-feedback learning* is a variant of iterative learning where, in addition, the learner can make n simultaneous queries asking whether some datum has been seen in the past [11, 18]. Finally, a learner is called an *n-bounded example memory* learner [11, 18, 21] if, besides reacting to its currently seen data item and remembering its own last conjecture, it is allowed to store in "long term memory" at most n strictly previously seen data items.

For the present paper, our first intention was to study the impact of forbidding U-shaped learning in each of the above three models of memory-limited learning. So far we have had success for these problems only for some more restricted variants of the three models. Hence, we now describe these variants.

Our variants of iterative learning are motivated by two aspects of Gold's model.

The first aspect is the absolute freedom allowed regarding the *semantic* relations between successive conjectures, and between the conjectures and the input. Many forms of semantic constraints on the learner's sequence of hypotheses have been studied in the previous literature (for example, conservativity [1], consistency [1, 3], monotonicity [15, 29], set-drivenness [27]) and it is reasonable to explore their interplay with U-shaped learning in the memory-bounded setting of iterative learning.

Secondly, it is well-known that the choice of the hypothesis space from which the learner can pick its conjectures has an impact on the learning power [17, 18]. We accordingly also consider herein U-shaped iterative learning with restrictions on the hypothesis space.

For the case of feedback learning, we introduce and consider a model called *n-memoryless feedback learning* which restricts n-feedback learning so that the learner does *not* remember its last conjecture. These criteria form a hierarchy of more and more powerful learning criteria increasing in n and, for $n > 0$, are incomparable to iterative learning. The criterion of 0-memoryless feedback learning is properly contained in the criterion of iterative learning.

Finally, we introduce a more limited variant of bounded example memory, *c-bounded memory states learning* for which the learner does not remember its previous conjecture *but* can store any one out of c different *values* in its long term memory [12, 16]. For example, when $c = 2^k$, the memory is equivalent to k bits of memory. By Theorem 16, these criteria form a hierarchy of more and more powerful learning criteria increasing in c. Furthermore, the comparisons between bounded memory states learning, iterative learning and memoryless feedback learning are presented in Remark 17.

Non U-Shaped Learning. Our main objective is to investigate the relations of above discussed notions of memory limited learning with respect to non U-shapedness. In Section 3 we investigate this question first with respect to *iterative learning* and state the major open problem whether non U-shapedness is restrictive for iterative learning. In this regard, Theorem 5 shows that U-shaped learning is necessary for the full learning power of class-preserving iterative learning [18].

In Section 4 we study, in the context of iterative learning, the relation of the non U-shapedness constraint to other well studied constraints on the *semantic* behaviour of the learner's conjectures. We consider *class-consistent learning* [1, 3], according to which the learner's conjectures, on the languages it learns, must generate all the data on which they are based. *Monotonic learning* by a machine **M** [29] requires that, on any input language L that **M Ex**-learns, a new hypothesis cannot reject an element $x \in L$ that a previous hypothesis already included. Theorem 9 shows that class-consistent iterative learners can be turned into iterative non U-shaped *and* monotonic learners.

In Section 5, we consider the impact of forbidding U-shaped learning for n-memoryless feedback learning. Theorem 12 shows that U-shaped learning *is necessary* for the full learning power of n-memoryless feedback learners.

In Section 6, Theorem 18 shows that U-shaped behaviour does *not* enhance the learning power of 2-bounded memory states learners, that is, learners having 1 bit of memory.

Note. Our results herein on memory-limited models are presented only for **Ex**-*learning*. Furthermore, because of space limitations, many proofs and some results have been omitted. We refer the reader to [9] for details.

2   Notation and Preliminaries

For general background on Recursion Theory and any unexplained recursion theoretic notation, we refer the reader to [20]. The symbol $\mathbb{N}$ denotes the set of natural numbers, $\{0, 1, 2, 3, \ldots\}$. Cardinality of a set S is denoted by $\text{card}(S)$. $\text{card}(S) \leq *$ denotes that S is finite. We let $\langle \cdot, \cdot \rangle$ stand for Cantor's computable, bijective mapping $\langle x, y \rangle = \frac{1}{2}(x + y)(x + y + 1) + x$ from $\mathbb{N} \times \mathbb{N}$ onto $\mathbb{N}$. Note that $\langle \cdot, \cdot \rangle$ is monotonically increasing in both of its arguments.

By φ we denote a fixed *acceptable numbering* (programming system) for the partial-recursive functions mapping $\mathbb{N}$ to $\mathbb{N}$. By φ_i we denote the partial-recursive function computed by the program with number i in the φ-system. By Φ we denote an arbitrary fixed Blum complexity measure [4] for the φ-system. By W_i we denote the domain of φ_i. That is, W_i is then the recursively enumerable (r.e.) subset of $\mathbb{N}$ accepted by the φ-program i. The symbol $\mathcal{L}$ ranges over classes of r.e. sets and L, H range over r.e. sets. By $\overline{L}$, we denote the complement of L, that is $\mathbb{N} - L$. By $W_{i,s}$ we denote the set $\{x \leq s : \Phi_i(x) \leq s\}$.

Quite frequently used in this paper is the existence of a one-one recursive function $\text{pad}(e, X)$ with $W_{\text{pad}(e,X)} = W_e$, where — according to the context — X

might be a number, a finite set or a finite sequence. In particular, pad is chosen such that e, X can be computed from $\text{pad}(e, X)$ by a recursive function.

We now present concepts from language learning theory [13, 14]. A *sequence* σ is a mapping from an initial segment of $\mathbb{N}$ into $(\mathbb{N} \cup \{\#\})$. The empty sequence is denoted by λ. The *content* of a sequence σ, denoted $\text{content}(\sigma)$, is the set of natural numbers in the range of σ. The *length* of σ, denoted by $|\sigma|$, is the number of elements in σ. So, $|\lambda| = 0$. For $n \leq |\sigma|$, the initial sequence of σ of length n is denoted by $\sigma[n]$. So, $\sigma[0]$ is λ.

Intuitively, the pause-symbol $\#$ represents a pause in the presentation of data. We let σ, τ and γ range over finite sequences. We denote the sequence formed by the concatenation of τ at the end of σ by $\sigma\tau$. $(\mathbb{N} \cup \{\#\})^*$ denotes the set of all finite sequences.

A *text* T for a language L is a mapping from $\mathbb{N}$ into $(\mathbb{N} \cup \{\#\})$ such that L is the set of natural numbers in the range of T. $T(i)$ represents the $(i + 1)$-th element in the text. The *content* of a text T, denoted by $\text{content}(T)$, is the set of natural numbers in the range of T; that is, the language which T is a text for. $T[n]$ denotes the finite initial sequence of T with length n. We now define the basic paradigm of learning in the limit, explanatory learning.

Definition 1. A learner $\mathbf{M} : (\mathbb{N} \cup \{\#\})^* \to (\mathbb{N} \cup \{?\})$ is a (possibly partial) recursive function which assigns hypotheses to finite strings of data. $\mathbf{M}$ **Ex**-learns a class $\mathcal{L}$ (equivalently $\mathbf{M}$ is an **Ex**-learner for $\mathcal{L}$) iff, for every $L \in \mathcal{L}$ and every text T for L, $\mathbf{M}$ is defined on all initial segments of T, and there is an index n such that $\mathbf{M}(T[n]) \neq ?$, $W_{\mathbf{M}(T[n])} = L$ and $\mathbf{M}(T[m]) \in \{\mathbf{M}(T[n]), ?\}$ for all $m \geq n$. **Ex** denotes the collection of all classes of languages that can be **Ex**-learned from text.

For **Ex**-learnability one may assume without loss of generality that the learner is total. However, for some of the criteria below, such as class consistency and iterative learning, this cannot be assumed without loss of generality. The requirement for $\mathbf{M}$ to be defined on each initial segment of each text for a language in $\mathcal{L}$ is also assumed for learners with other criteria considered below.

Now we define non U-shaped learning. A non U-shaped learner never makes the sequence correct–incorrect–correct while learning a language that it actually learns. Thus, since such a learner has eventually to be correct, one can make the definition a bit simpler than the idea behind the notion suggests.

Definition 2. [2] (a) We say that $\mathbf{M}$ is *non U-shaped* on text T, if $\mathbf{M}$ never makes a mind change from a conjecture for $\text{content}(T)$ to a conjecture for a different set.

(b) We say that $\mathbf{M}$ is non U-shaped on L if $\mathbf{M}$ is non U-shaped on each text for L. We say that $\mathbf{M}$ is non U-shaped on $\mathcal{L}$ if $\mathbf{M}$ is non U-shaped on each $L \in \mathcal{L}$.

(c) Let $\mathbf{I}$ be a learning criterion. Then $\mathbf{NUI}$ denotes the collection of all classes $\mathcal{L}$ such that there exists a machine $\mathbf{M}$ that learns $\mathcal{L}$ according to $\mathbf{I}$ and is non U-shaped on $\mathcal{L}$.

3 Iterative Learning

The **Ex**-model makes the assumption that the learner has access to the full history of previous data. On the other hand it is reasonable to think that humans have more or less severe memory limitations. This observation motivates, among other criteria discussed in the present paper, the concept of *iterative learning*. An iterative learner features a severe memory limitation: it can remember its own previous conjecture but not its *past* data items. Moreover, each conjecture of an iterative learner is determined as an algorithmic function of the previous conjecture *and* of the current input data item.

Definition 3. [27] An iterative learner is a (possibly partial) function $\mathbf{M} : (\mathbb{N} \cup \{?\}) \times (\mathbb{N} \cup \{\#\}) \to (\mathbb{N} \cup \{?\})$ together with an initial hypothesis $e_0 \in \mathbb{N} \cup \{?\}$. $\mathbf{M}$ **It**-learns a class $\mathcal{L}$ iff, for every $L \in \mathcal{L}$ and every text T for L, the sequence $e_0, e_1, \ldots$ defined inductively by the rule $e_{n+1} = \mathbf{M}(e_n, T(n))$ satisfies: there exists an m such that e_m is an index for L and for all $n \geq m$, $e_n \in \{e_m, ?\}$. **It** denotes the collection of all iteratively learnable classes.

For iterative learners (without other constraints), one may assume without loss of generality that they never output ?.

It is well-known that $\mathbf{It} \subset \mathbf{Ex}$ [28]. On the other hand, iterative learning is not restrictive for behaviourally correct learning. Thus, all our notions regarding iterative learning will be modifications of the basic **Ex**-learning paradigm.

In [2] the main question regarding the necessity of U-shaped behaviour in the context of **Ex**-learning was answered in the negative. It was shown that $\mathbf{Ex} = \mathbf{NUEx}$, meaning that every **Ex**-learnable class can be learned by a non U-shaped **Ex**-learner. However, non U-shaped learning is restrictive for behaviourally correct learning and vacillatory learning [8]. Similarly, non U-shaped learning *may* become restrictive when we put memory limitations on **Ex**-learning. Our main motivation for the results presented in this section is the following problem, which remains open.

Problem 4. *Is* $\mathbf{It} = \mathbf{NUIt}$?

Many results in the present work were obtained in order to approximate an answer to this open problem.

We now briefly recall some basic relations of iterative learning with two criteria of learning that feature, like non U-shaped learning, a semantic constraint on the learner's sequence of hypotheses.

The first such notion is *set-driven learning* [27], where the hypotheses of a learner on inputs σ, τ are the same whenever content(σ) = content(τ). We denote by **SD** the collection of all classes learnable by a set-driven learner. It is shown in [16, Theorem 7.7] that $\mathbf{It} \subset \mathbf{SD}$.

A criterion that implies non U-shapedness is *conservative learning* [1]. A learner is conservative iff whenever it make a mind change from a hypothesis i to j then it has already seen some datum $x \notin W_i$. **Consv** denotes the collection of all classes having a conservative learner.

It is shown in [16] that **SD** $\subseteq$ **Consv**, thus, **It** $\subset$ **Consv**. By definition, every hypothesis abandoned by a conservative learner is incorrect and thus **Consv** $\subseteq$ **NUEx** follows. It is well known that the latter inclusion is proper. The easiest way to establish it is to use Angluin's proper inclusion **Consv** $\subset$ **Ex** [1] and the equality from **Ex** = **NUEx** [2].

Normally, in Gold-style language learning, a learner outputs as hypotheses just indices from a fixed acceptable enumeration of all r.e. languages, since all types of output (programs, grammars and so on) can be translated into these indices. There have also been investigations [1, 17, 18] where the hypothesis space is fixed in the sense that the learner has to choose its hypotheses either from this fixed space (exact learning) or from a space containing exactly the same languages (class-preserving learning).

We introduce a bit of terminology (from [1]) to explain the notion. An infinite sequence $L_0, L_1, L_2, \ldots$ of recursive languages is called *uniformly recursive* if the set $\{\langle i, x \rangle : x \in L_i\}$ is recursive. A class $\mathcal{L}$ of recursive languages is said to be an *indexed family* of recursive languages if $\mathcal{L} = \{L_i : i \in \mathbb{N}\}$ for some uniformly recursive sequence $L_0, L_1, L_2, \ldots$; the latter is called a *recursive indexing* of $\mathcal{L}$. As indexed families are quite well-behaved, Angluin found a nice characterization for when an indexed family is explanatorily learnable and they became a frequent topic for the study of more restrictive notions of learnability as, for example, in [12, 17, 18].

Let $\mathcal{L}$ be an indexed family of recursive sets. We say that a machine **M** explanatorily identifies $\mathcal{L}$ using a hypothesis space $L_0, L_1, L_2, \ldots$ iff **M**, for every $L \in \mathcal{L}$ and for every text for L, **M** converges to some j such that $L = L_j$. The hypothesis space $L_0, L_1, L_2, \ldots$ is class preserving for $\mathcal{L}$ iff it contains all and only the languages in $\mathcal{L}$. In what follows, for a learning criterion **I**, **I**^{cp} stands for class-preserving **I**-learning, the collection of all classes of languages that can be **I**-learned by some learner using a class-preserving hypothesis space.

Theorem 5. *There exists an indexed family in* **It**^{cp} − **NUEx**^{cp}.

The positive side can be done using an indexed (recursive) family as hypothesis space, whereas the diagonalization against negative side can be done for any r.e. class preserving hypothesis space.

4   Consistent and Monotonic Iterative Learning

Forbidding U-shapes is a *semantic* constraint on a learner's sequence of conjectures. In this section we study the interplay of this constraint with other well-studied semantic constraints, but in the memory-limited setting of iterative learning.

We now describe and then formally define the relevant variants of semantic constraints on the sequence of conjectures. *Consistent learning* was introduced in [3] (in the context of function learning) and essentially requires that the learner's conjectures do not contradict known data, *strong monotonic learning* was introduced in [15] and requires that semantically the learner's conjectures on every text for any language (even the ones that the learner does *not* learn) are set-theoretically nondecreasing. *Monotonic learning*, as introduced in [29], relaxes the condition of strong-monotonicity by requiring that, for each language L that the learner actually learns, the intersection of L with the language generated by a learner's conjecture is a superset of the intersection of L with the language generated by any of the learner's previous conjectures.

Definition 6. [3, 15, 29] A learner $\mathbf{M}$ is *consistent* on a class $\mathcal{L}$ iff for all $L \in \mathcal{L}$ and all σ with content$(\sigma) \subseteq L$, $\mathbf{M}(\sigma)$ it defined and an index of a set containing content(σ). **Cons** denotes the collection of all classes which have a **Ex**-learner which is consistent on the class of all sets. **ClassCons** denotes the collection of all classes $\mathcal{L}$ which have a **Ex**-learner which is consistent on $\mathcal{L}$.

A learner $\mathbf{M}$ is *strong monotonic* iff $W_i \subseteq W_j$ whenever $\mathbf{M}$ outputs on any text for any language at some time i and later j. **SMon** denotes the collection of all classes having a strong monotonic **Ex**-learner.

A learner $\mathbf{M}$ for $\mathcal{L}$ is *monotonic* iff $L \cap W_i \subseteq L \cap W_j$ whenever $\mathbf{M}$ outputs on a text for some language $L \in \mathcal{L}$ at some time i and later j. **Mon** denotes the criterion of all classes having a monotonic **Ex**-learner.

Note that there are classes $\mathcal{L} \in$ **ClassCons** such that only partial learners witness this fact. Criteria can be combined. For example, **ItCons** is the criterion consisting of all classes which have an iterative and consistent learner. The indication of an oracle as in the criterion **ItConsSMon**$[K]$ below denotes that a learner for the given class must on the one hand be iterative, consistent and strong-monotonic while on the other hand the constraint of being recursive is weakened to the permission to access a halting-problem oracle for the inference process. The next result gives some basic connections between iterative, strongly monotonic and consistent learning.

Theorem 7. (a) **ItCons** $\subseteq$ **ItConsSMon**.
(b) **ConsSMon** $\subseteq$ **ItConsSMon**.
(c) **ItSMon** $\subseteq$ **NUIt**.
(d) **SMon** $\subseteq$ **ItConsSMon**$[K]$.

Proof. (a) Given an iterative consistent learner $\mathbf{M}$ for $\mathcal{L}$, let — as in the case of normal learners — $\mathbf{M}(\sigma)$ denote the hypothesis which $\mathbf{M}$ makes after having seen the sequence σ. Now define a recursive one-one function f such that, for every index e, $W_{f(e)} = \bigcup_{\sigma \in \{\sigma' : \mathbf{M}(\sigma') = e\}} \text{content}(\sigma)$. Since $\mathbf{M}$ is consistent, content$(\sigma) \subseteq W_{\mathbf{M}(\sigma)}$ for all σ and so $W_{f(e)} \subseteq W_e$. The new learner $\mathbf{N}$ is the modification of $\mathbf{M}$ which outputs $f(e)$ instead of e; $\mathbf{N}$ is consistent since whenever one can reach a hypothesis e through a string containing a datum x then $x \in W_{f(e)}$. Since f is one-one, $\mathbf{N}$ is also iterative and follows the update rule $\mathbf{N}(f(e), x) = f(\mathbf{M}(e, x))$.

It is easy to see that $\mathbf{N}$ is strongly monotonic: Assume that $\mathbf{M}(e, y) = e'$ and x is any element of $W_{f(e)}$. Then there is a σ with $\mathbf{M}(\sigma) = e$ and $x \in \text{content}(\sigma)$. It follows that $\mathbf{M}(\sigma y) = e'$, $x \in \text{content}(\sigma y)$ and $x \in W_{f(e')}$. So $W_{f(e)} \subseteq W_{f(e')}$ and the transitiveness of the inclusion gives the strong monotonicity of $\mathbf{N}$.

It remains to show that $\mathbf{N}$ learns $\mathcal{L}$. Let $L \in \mathcal{L}$ and T be a text for L and e be the index to which $\mathbf{M}$ converges on T. The learner $\mathbf{N}$ converges on T to $f(e)$. Since $W_e = L$ it holds that $W_{f(e)} \subseteq L$. Furthermore, for every n there is $m > n$ with $\mathbf{M}(T[m]) = e$, thus $T(n) \in W_{f(e)}$ and $L \subseteq W_{f(e)}$. This completes the proof of part (a).

(b) A consistent learner never outputs ?. Now, given a strong monotonic and consistent learner $\mathbf{M}$ for some class $\mathcal{L}$, one defines a recursive one-one function $f : (\mathbb{N} \cup \{\#\})^* \to \mathbb{N}$ such that

$$W_{f(\sigma)} = W_{\mathbf{M}(\sigma)} \cup \text{content}(\sigma)$$

and initializes a new iterative learner $\mathbf{N}$ with the hypothesis $f(\lambda)$ and the following update rule for the hypothesis $f(\sigma)$ and observed datum x:

- If $\mathbf{M}(\sigma x) = \mathbf{M}(\sigma)$ then $\mathbf{N}(f(\sigma), x) = f(\sigma)$;
- If $\mathbf{M}(\sigma x) \neq \mathbf{M}(\sigma)$ then one takes the length-lexicographic first extension τ of σx such that $W_{\mathbf{M}(\eta), |\sigma|} \subseteq \text{content}(\tau)$, for all $\eta \preceq \sigma$, and defines $\mathbf{N}(f(\sigma), x) = f(\tau)$.

Note that in the second case, $\text{content}(\tau) = \text{content}(\sigma x) \cup (\bigcup_{\eta \preceq \sigma} W_{\mathbf{M}(\eta), |\sigma|})$ and that the length-lexicographic ordering is just taken to single out the first string with this property with respect to some ordering. The new iterative learner is strongly monotonic since whenever it changes the hypothesis then it does so from $f(\sigma)$ to $f(\tau)$, for some τ extending σ, and thus $W_{f(\sigma)} = \text{content}(\sigma) \cup W_{\mathbf{M}(\sigma)} \subseteq \text{content}(\tau) \cup W_{\mathbf{M}(\tau)} = W_{f(\tau)}$ as $\mathbf{M}$ is strong monotonic. Furthermore, $\mathbf{N}$ is also consistent: whenever it sees a number x outside $W_{f(\sigma)}$ then x is also outside $W_{\mathbf{M}(\sigma)}$ and $\mathbf{M}(\sigma x) \neq \mathbf{M}(\sigma)$ by the consistency of $\mathbf{M}$. Then the new τ constructed contains x explicitly and therefore $x \in W_{\mathbf{N}(f(\sigma), x)}$. By the strong monotonicity of $\mathbf{N}$, an element once incorporated into a hypothesis is also contained in all future hypotheses. So it remains to show that $\mathbf{N}$ actually learns $\mathcal{L}$.

Given $L \in \mathcal{L}$ and a text T for L, there is a sequence of strings $\sigma_0, \sigma_1, \dots$ such that $\sigma_0 = \lambda$ and $\mathbf{N}(f(\sigma_n), T(n)) = f(\sigma_{n+1})$. By induction one can show that $\sigma_n \in (L \cup \{\#\})^*$ and $W_{\mathbf{M}(\sigma_n)} \subseteq L$ for all n. There are two cases.

First, there is an n such that $\sigma_m = \sigma_n$ for all $m \geq n$. Then $L \subseteq W_{f(\sigma_n)}$ since $\mathbf{N}$ is a consistent learner and eventually converges to this hypothesis on the text L. Furthermore, $W_{f(\sigma_n)} \subseteq L$ as mentioned above, so $\mathbf{N}$ learns L.

Second, for every n there is an $m > n$ such that σ_m is a proper extension of σ_n. Let T' be the limit of all σ_n. One can easily see that T' contains data from two sources, some items taken over from T and some elements taken from sets $W_{\mathbf{M}(\eta)}$ with $\eta \preceq \sigma_n$ for some n; since $\mathbf{M}$ is strong monotonic these elements are all contained in L and so $\text{content}(T') \subseteq L$. Furthermore, for every n the element $T(n)$ is contained in $W_{f(\sigma_{n+1})}$ and thus there is an extension σ_k of σ_{n+1} which is so long that $T(n) \in W_{\mathbf{M}(\sigma_{n+1}), |\sigma_k|} \cup \text{content}(\sigma_{n+1})$. If then for some $m \geq k$ the string σ_{m+1} is a proper extension of σ_m, then $T(n) \in \text{content}(\sigma_{m+1})$. As a consequence, T' is a text for L on which $\mathbf{M}$ converges to a hypothesis e. Then, one has that for all sufficiently large m, where σ_{m+1} is a proper extension of σ_m, σ_{m+1} is actually an extension of $\sigma_m T(m)$ and $\mathbf{M}(\sigma_m T(m)) = \mathbf{M}(\sigma_m)$, which would by construction enforce that $\mathbf{N}$ does not update its hypothesis and $\sigma_{m+1} = \sigma_m$. By this contradiction, the second case does not hold and the first applies, thus $\mathbf{M}$ learns $\mathcal{L}$. This completes the proof of part (b).

(c) follows from the definition and (d) can be proved using techniques similar to part (b). □

Thus, **ItCons** and **ConsSMon** are contained in **NUIt**. Regarding part (d) above, it can be shown that one can replace K only by oracles $A \geq_T K$. Thus K is the optimal oracle in part (d).

Note that the proof of Theorem 7 (a) needs that the learner is an **ItCons**-learner and not just an **ItClassCons**-learner. In the latter case, the inference process cannot be enforced to be strong-monotonic as the following example shows.

Example 8. *The class $\mathcal{L}$ containing the set $\{0, 2, 4, 6, 8, \ldots\}$ of even numbers and all sets $\{0, 2, 4, \ldots, 2n\} \cup \{2n+1\}$ with $n \in \mathbb{N}$ is in* **ItClassCons − SMon**.

So class-consistent, iterative learners cannot be made strong monotonic, even with an oracle. However, the next result shows that they can still be made monotonic, *and*, simultaneously, non U-shaped.

Theorem 9. ItClassCons $\subseteq$ NUItMon.

5 Memoryless Feedback Learning

An iterative learner has a severe memory limitation: it can store no previously seen data. On the other hand, crucially, an iterative learner remembers its previous conjecture. In this section we introduce a model of learning in which the learner does *not* remember its last conjecture *and* can store no previous input data. The learner is instead allowed to make, at each stage of its learning process, n feedback queries asking whether some n data items have been previously seen. We call such learners n-*memoryless feedback learners*. Theorem 12 shows that U-shaped behaviour is necessary for the full learning power of n-memoryless feedback learning.

Definition 10. Suppose $n \geq 0$. An n-*memoryless feedback learner* $\mathbf{M}$ has as input one datum from a text. It then can make n-queries which are calculated from its input datum. These queries are as to whether some n data items were already seen previously in the text. From its input and the answers to these queries, it either outputs a conjecture or the ? symbol. That is, given a language L and a text T for L, $\mathbf{M}(T(k))$ is determined as follows: First, n-values $q_i(T(k))$, $i = 1, \ldots, n$, are computed. Second, n bits $b_i, i = 1, \ldots, n$ are determined and passed on to $\mathbf{M}$, where each b_i is 1 if $q_i(T(k)) \in \text{content}(T[k])$ and 0 otherwise. Third, an hypothesis e_k is computed from $T(k)$ and the b_i's. $\mathbf{M}$ **MLF**$_n$-learns L if, for all T for L, for $\mathbf{M}$ on T, there is an k such that $W_{e_k} = L$ and $e_m \in \{?, e_k\}$ for all $m > k$. **MLF**$_n$ denotes the class of all classes learnable by a n-memoryless feedback learner.

Theorem 11. *For all $n > 0$,* $\mathbf{NUMLF}_{n+1} \not\subseteq \mathbf{MLF}_n$.

It can be shown that **It** and $\mathbf{MLF}_n$ are incomparable for all $n > 0$. The next result shows that non U-shaped n-memoryless feedback learners are strictly less powerful than unrestricted n-memoryless feedback learners.

Theorem 12. *For $n > 0$,* $\mathbf{NUMLF}_n \subset \mathbf{MLF}_n$.

Proof Sketch. Let $F(e) = \max(\{1 + \varphi_i(e) : i \leq e \text{ and } \varphi_i(e)\downarrow\} \cup \{0\})$. Note that F grows faster than any partial or total recursive function. Based on this function F one now defines the family $\mathcal{L} = \{L_0, L_1, L_2, \ldots\} \cup \{H_0, H_1, H_2, \ldots\}$ where

$$L_e = \{\langle e, x\rangle : x < F(e) \text{ or } x \text{ is even}\};$$
$$H_e = \{\langle e, x\rangle : x < F(e) \text{ or } x \text{ is odd}\}.$$

We first show that $\mathcal{L} \in \mathbf{MLF}_1$. Note that the learning algorithm cannot store the last guess due to its memory limitation but might output a '?' in order to repeat that hypothesis. The parameter e is visible from each current input except '#'. The algorithm is the following:

If the new input is # or if the input is $\langle e, x\rangle$ and the Feedback says that $\langle e, x + 1\rangle$ has already appeared in the input earlier, then output ?. Otherwise, if input is $\langle e, x\rangle$ and $\langle e, x + 1\rangle$ has not yet appeared in input, then output a canonical grammar for L_e (H_e) if x is even (odd).

Consider any text T for L_e. Let n be such that $\text{content}(T[n]) \supseteq L_e \cap \{\langle e, x\rangle : x \leq F(e) + 1\}$. Then, it is easy to verify that, the learner will either output ? or a conjecture for L_e beyond $T[n]$. On the other hand, for any even $x > F(e)$, if $T(m) = \langle e, x\rangle$, then the learner outputs a conjecture for L_e after having seen $T[m + 1]$ (this happens infinitely often, by definition of L_e). Thus, the learner $\mathbf{MLF}_1$-identifies L_e. Similar argument applies for H_e. A detailed case analysis shows that $\mathcal{L} \notin \mathbf{NUMLF}_1$, see [9]. □

Proposition 13. $\mathbf{NUIt} \not\subseteq \mathbf{NUMLF}_1$.

Finally, an iterative *total* learner that can store one selected previous datum is called a $\mathbf{Bem}_1$-learner (1-bounded example memory learner) in [11, 21]. One can also consider a "memoryless" version of this concept, where a learner does not memorize its previous hypothesis, but, instead, memorizes one selected previous datum.

Proposition 14. $\mathbf{NUBem}_1 \not\subseteq \mathbf{NUMLF}_1$.

6   Bounded Memory States Learning

Memoryless feedback learners store no information about the past. Bounded memory states learners, introduced in this section, have no memory of previous conjectures but can store a bounded number of values in their long term memory.

This model allows one to separate the issue of a learner's ability to remember its previous conjecture from the issue of a learner's ability to store information about the previously seen input. Similar models of machines with bounded long term memory are studied in [16]. We now proceed with the formal definition.

Definition 15. [16] For $c > 0$, a c-bounded memory states learner is a (possibly partial) function

$$\mathbf{M} : \{0, 1, \ldots, c-1\} \times (\mathbb{N} \cup \#) \to (\mathbb{N} \cup \{?\}) \times \{0, 1, \ldots, c-1\}$$

which maps the old long term memory content plus a datum to the current hypothesis plus the new long term memory content. The long term memory has the initial value 0. There is no initial hypothesis.

$\mathbf{M}$ learns a class $\mathcal{L}$ iff, for every $L \in \mathcal{L}$ and every text T for L, there is a sequence $a_0, a_1, \ldots$ of long term memory contents and $e_0, e_1, \ldots$ of hypotheses and a number n such that, for all m, $a_0 = 0$, $W_{e_n} = L$, $\mathbf{M}(a_m, T(m)) = (e_m, a_{m+1})$ and $m \geq n \Rightarrow e_m \in \{?, e_n\}$. We denote by $\mathbf{BMS}_c$ the collection of classes learnable by a c-bounded memory states learner.

Theorem 16. *For all $c > 1$, $\mathbf{BMS}_{c-1} \subset \mathbf{BMS}_c$.*

Remark 17. One can generalize $\mathbf{BMS}_c$ to $\mathbf{ClassBMS}$ and $\mathbf{BMS}$. The learners for these criteria use natural numbers as long term memory. For $\mathbf{ClassBMS}$ we have the additional constraint that for every text of a language inside the *learnt* class, there is a constant c depending on the text such that the value of the long term memory is never a number larger than c. For $\mathbf{BMS}$ the corresponding constraint applies to all texts for all sets, even those outside the class.

One can show that $\mathbf{ClassBMS} = \mathbf{It}$. Furthermore, a class is in $\mathbf{BMS}$ iff it has a confident iterative learner, that is, an iterative learner which converges on every text, whether this text is for a language in the class to be learned or not.

It is easy to see that $\bigcup_c \mathbf{BMS}_c \subset \mathbf{BMS} \subset \mathbf{ClassBMS}$. Furthermore, $\mathbf{MLF}_0 = \mathbf{BMS}_1 = \mathbf{NUMLF}_0 = \mathbf{NUBMS}_1$, which are nontrivial. One can also show that $\mathbf{MLF}_m$ and $\mathbf{BMS}_n$ are incomparable for all $m > 0$ and $n > 1$.

We now give the main result of the present section, showing that every 2-bounded memory states learner *can* be simulated by a non U-shaped one.

Theorem 18. $\mathbf{BMS}_2 \subseteq \mathbf{NUBMS}_2$.

Proof Sketch. Suppose $\mathbf{M}$ witnesses $\mathcal{L} \in \mathbf{BMS}_2$. We assume without loss of generality that $\mathbf{M}$ does not change its memory on input $\#$, as otherwise we could easily modify $\mathbf{M}$ to work without any memory.

In the following, "$*$" stands for the case that the value does not matter and in all (legal) cases the same is done.

Define a function P such that $P(?) = ?$ and, for $e \in \mathbb{N}$, $P(e)$ is an index of the set $W_{P(e)} = \bigcup_{s \in S(e)} W_{e,s}$ where $S(e)$ is the set of all s satisfying either (a) or ((b) and (c) and (d)) below:

(a) There exists an $x \in W_{e,s}$, $\mathbf{M}(1, x) = (*, 0)$;
(b) For all $x \in W_{e,s}$, $[\mathbf{M}(0, x) = (*, 1) \Rightarrow \mathbf{M}(1, x) = (?, 1)]$;

(c) There exists an $x \in W_{e,s}$, $\mathbf{M}(0,x) = (?,1)$ or for all $x \in W_{e,s}$, $\mathbf{M}(0,x) = (*,0)$;

(d) For all $x \in W_{e,s} \cup \{\#\}$, $[\mathbf{M}(0,x) = (j,*) \Rightarrow W_{e,s} \subseteq W_j \wedge W_{j,s} \subseteq W_e]$.

Now we define for all $m \in \{0,1\}$, $j \in \mathbb{N} \cup \{?\}$ and $x \in \mathbb{N} \cup \{\#\}$,

$$\mathbf{N}(m,x) = \begin{cases} (P(j),0), & \text{if } m = 0 \text{ and } \mathbf{M}(0,x) = (j,0); \\ (j,1), & \text{if } m = 0 \text{ and } ((\mathbf{M}(0,x) = (j,1) \text{ and } \mathbf{M}(1,x) = (?,*)) \\ & \text{or } (\mathbf{M}(0,x) = (*,1) \text{ and } \mathbf{M}(1,x) = (j,*) \text{ and } j \neq ?)); \\ (j,1), & \text{if } m = 1 \text{ and } \mathbf{M}(1,x) = (j,*). \end{cases}$$

A detailed case analysis shows that $\mathbf{N}$ $\mathbf{NUBMS}_2$-identifies $\mathcal{L}$, see [9]. $\qquad\square$

7 Conclusions and Open Problems

Numerous results related to non U-shaped learning for machines with severe memory limitations were obtained. In particular, it was shown that

- there are class-preservingly iteratively learnable classes that cannot be learned without U-shapes by any iterative class-preserving learner (Theorem 5),
- class-consistent iterative learners for a class can be turned into iterative non U-shaped *and* monotonic learners for that class (Theorem 9),
- for all $n > 0$, there are n-memoryless feedback learnable classes that cannot be learned without U-shapes by any n-memoryless feedback learner (Theorem 12) and, by contrast,
- every class learnable by a 2-bounded memory states learner can be learned by a 2-bounded memory states learner without U-shapes (Theorem 18).

The above results are, in our opinion, interesting in that they show how the impact of forbidding U-shaped learning in the context of severely memory-limited models of learning is far from trivial. In particular, the tradeoffs that our results reveal between remembering one's previous conjecture, having a long-term memory, and being able to make feedback queries are delicate and perhaps surprising. The following are some of the main open problems.

- Is $\mathbf{NUIt} \subset \mathbf{It}$?
- Is $\mathbf{MLF}_1 \subseteq \mathbf{NUMLF}_n$, for $n > 1$?
- Is $\mathbf{BMS}_c \subseteq \mathbf{NUBMS}_c$, for $c > 2$?

Also, the question of the necessity of U-shaped behaviour with respect to the stronger memory-limited variants of **Ex**-learning (bounded example memory and feedback learning) from the previous literature [11, 18] remains wide open. Humans can remember *much* more than one bit and likely retain something of their prior hypotheses; furthermore, they have some access to knowledge of whether they've seen something before. Hence, the open problems of this section may prove interesting for cognitive science.

References

1. Dana Angluin. Inductive inference of formal languages from positive data. *Information and Control*, 45:117–135, 1980.
2. Ganesh Baliga, John Case, Wolfgang Merkle, Frank Stephan and Rolf Wiehagen. *When unlearning helps*. Manuscript, 2005. Preliminary version of the paper appeared at ICALP, Lecture Notes in Computer Science, 1853:844–855, 2000.
3. Janis Bārzdiņš. Inductive Inference of automata, functions and programs. *International Mathematical Congress, Vancouver*, pages 771–776, 1974.
4. Manuel Blum. A machine independent theory of the complexity of the recursive functions. *Journal of the Association for Computing Machinery* 14:322–336, 1967.
5. T. G. R. Bower. Concepts of development. In *Proceedings of the 21st International Congress of Psychology*. Presses Universitaires de France, pages 79–97, 1978.
6. Melissa Bowerman. Starting to talk worse: Clues to language acquisition from children's late speech errors. In S. Strauss and R. Stavy, editors, *U-Shaped Behavioral Growth*. Academic Press, New York, 1982.
7. Susan Carey. Face perception: Anomalies of development. In S. Strauss and R. Stavy, editors, *U-Shaped Behavioral Growth*, Developmental Psychology Series. Academic Press, pages 169–190, 1982.
8. Lorenzo Carlucci, John Case, Sanjay Jain and Frank Stephan. Non U-Shaped Vacillatory and Team Learning. *Algorithmic Learning Theory* 16th International Conference, ALT 2005, Singapore, October 2005, Proceedings. Lecture Notes in Artificial Intelligence, 3734:241–255, 2005.
9. Lorenzo Carlucci, John Case, Sanjay Jain and Frank Stephan. Memory-limited U-shaped learning (Long version of the present paper). TR51/05, School of Computing, National University of Singapore, 2005.
10. Lorenzo Carlucci, Sanjay Jain, Efim Kinber and Frank Stephan. Variations on U-shaped learning. *Eighteenth Annual Conference on Learning Theory*, Colt 2005, Bertinoro, Italy, June 2005, Proceedings. Lecture Notes in Arificial Intelligence, 3559:382–397, 2005.
11. John Case, Sanjay Jain, Steffen Lange and Thomas Zeugmann. Incremental Concept Learning for Bounded Data Mining. *Information and Computation*, 152(1):74–110, 1999.
12. Rusins Freivalds, Efim B. Kinber and Carl H. Smith. On the impact of forgetting on learning machines. *Journal of the ACM*, 42:1146–1168, 1995.
13. E. Mark Gold. Language identification in the limit. *Information and Control*, 10:447–474, 1967.
14. Sanjay Jain, Daniel Osherson, James Royer and Arun Sharma. *Systems that Learn: An Introduction to Learning Theory*. MIT Press, Cambridge, Mass., second edition, 1999.
15. Klaus-Peter Jantke. Monotonic and non-monotonic Inductive Inference, *New Generation Computing*, 8:349–360, 1991.
16. Efim Kinber and Frank Stephan. Language learning from texts: mind changes, limited memory and monotonicity. *Information and Computation*, 123:224–241, 1995.
17. Steffen Lange and Thomas Zeugmann. The learnability of recursive languages in dependence on the space of hypotheses. *GOSLER-Report*, 20/93. Fachbereich Mathematik und Informatik, TH Leipzig, 1993.
18. Steffen Lange and Thomas Zeugmann. Incremental Learning from Positive Data. *Journal of Computer and System Sciences*, 53:88–103, 1996.

19. Gary Marcus, Steven Pinker, Michael Ullman, Michelle Hollander, T. John Rosen and Fei Xu. *Overregularization in Language Acquisition*. Monographs of the Society for Research in Child Development, volume 57, no. 4. University of Chicago Press, 1992. Includes commentary by Harold Clahsen.
20. Piergiorgio Odifreddi. *Classical Recursion Theory*. North Holland, Amsterdam, 1989.
21. Daniel Osherson, Michael Stob and Scott Weinstein. *Systems that Learn: An Introduction to Learning Theory for Cognitive and Computer Scientists*. MIT Press, 1986.
22. Kim Plunkett and Virginia Marchman. U-shaped learning and frequency effects in a multi-layered perceptron: implications for child language acquisition. *Cognition*, 38(1):43–102, 1991.
23. James Royer. *A Connotational Theory of Program Structure*. Lecture Notes in Computer Science, 273. Springer, 1987.
24. Sidney Strauss and Ruth Stavy, editors. *U-Shaped Behavioral Growth*. Developmental Psychology Series. Academic Press, 1982.
25. Sidney Strauss, Ruth Stavy and N. Orpaz. The child's development of the concept of temperature. Manuscript, Tel-Aviv University. 1977.
26. Niels A. Taatgen and John R. Anderson. Why do children learn to say broke? A model of learning the past tense without feedback. *Cognition*, 86(2):123–155, 2002.
27. Kenneth Wexler and Peter W. Culicover. *Formal Principles of Language Acquisition*. MIT Press, 1980.
28. Rolf Wiehagen. Limes-Erkennung rekursiver Funktionen durch spezielle Strategien. *Journal of Information Processing and Cybernetics*, 12:93–99, 1976.
29. Rolf Wiehagen. A thesis in Inductive Inference. *Nonmonotonic and Inductive Logic, First International Workshop*, Lecture Notes in Artificial Intelligence, 543:184–207, 1990.

On Learning Languages from Positive Data and a Limited Number of Short Counterexamples

Sanjay Jain[1,*] and Efim Kinber[2]

[1] School of Computing, National University of Singapore, Singapore 117543
sanjay@comp.nus.edu.sg
[2] Department of Computer Science, Sacred Heart University, Fairfield,
CT 06432-1000, USA
kinbere@sacredheart.edu

Abstract. We consider two variants of a model for learning languages in the limit from positive data and a limited number of short negative counterexamples (counterexamples are considered to be short if they are smaller that the largest element of input seen so far). Negative counterexamples to a conjecture are examples which belong to the conjectured language but do not belong to the input language. Within this framework, we explore how/when learners using n short (arbitrary) negative counterexamples can be simulated (or simulate) using least short counterexamples or just 'no' answers from a teacher. We also study how a limited number of short counterexamples fairs against unconstrained counterexamples. A surprising result is that just one short counterexample (if present) can sometimes be more useful than any bounded number of counterexamples of least size. Most of results exhibit salient examples of languages learnable or not learnable within corresponding variants of our models.

1 Introduction

Our goal in this paper is to explore how limited amount of negative data, relatively easily available from a teacher, can help learning languages in the limit. There is a long tradition of using two popular different paradigms for exploring learning languages in the limit. One paradigm, learning languages from full positive data (all correct statements of the language), was introduced by Gold in his classical paper [Gol67]. In this model, **TxtEx**, the learner stabilizes in the limit to a grammar generating the target language. In another popular variant of this model, **TxtBc**, defined in [CL82] and [OW82] (see also [Bār74] and [CS83]) almost all conjectures outputted by the learner are correct grammars describing the target language. The second popular paradigm, learning using queries to a teacher (oracle) was introduced by D. Angluin in [Ang88]. In particular, D. Angluin considered three types of queries: subset, superset, and equivalence queries — when a learner asks if a current hypothesis generates a subset or a superset of the target language, or, respectively, generates exactly the target

---

* Supported in part by NUS grant number R252-000-127-112.

G. Lugosi and H.U. Simon (Eds.): COLT 2006, LNAI 4005, pp. 259–273, 2006.
© Springer-Verlag Berlin Heidelberg 2006

language. If the answer is negative, the teacher may provide a *counterexample* showing where the current hypothesis errs. This model has been used for exploring language learning primarily in the situation when no data was available in advance (see, for example, [LZ04b], [LZ04a]). In [JK06b], the two models were combined together: a learner gets full positive data and can query the teacher if the current conjecture is correct. On one hand, this model reflects the fact that a learner, during a process of acquisition of a new language, potentially gets access to all correct statements. On the other hand, this model adds another important tool, typically available, say, to a child learning a new language: a possibility to communicate with a teacher. Sometimes, this possibility may be really vital for successful learning. For example, if a learner of English past tense, having received on the input "call – called", "fall – fell", infers the rule implying that both past tense forms "called, cell" and "falled, fell" are possible, then this rule can be refuted only by counterexamples from a teacher.

In this context, subset queries are of primary interest, as they provide *negative counterexamples* if the learner errs, while other types of queries may provide positive 'counterexamples' eventually available on the input anyway (still, as it was shown in [JK06a], the sequel paper to [JK06b], superset and equivalence queries can make some difference even in presense of full positive data). Consequently, one can consider the learner for **NCEx** model as defined in [JK06b] (and its variant **NCBc** corresponding to **TxtBc** — **NC** here stands for 'negative counterexamples'), as making a subset query for each of its conjectures. When a learner tests every conjecture, potentially he/she can get indefinite number of counterexamples (still this number is, of course, finite if the learner learns the target language in the limit correctly). In [JK06a] the authors explored learning from positive data and *bounded* amount of additional negative data. In this context, one can consider three different scenarios of how subset queries and corresponding negative counterexamples (if any) can be used:

— only a bounded number (up to n) of subset queries is allowed during the learning process; this model was considered in [JK06a] under the name $\mathbf{SubQ}^n$;

— the learner makes subset query for every conjecture until n negative answers have been received; that is, the learner can ask potentially indefinite number of questions (however, still finite if the learning process eventually gives a correct grammar), but he is *charged* only when receiving a negative answer; this model was considered in [JK06a] under the name $\mathbf{NC}^n$;

— the learner makes subset queries for conjectures, when deemed necessary, until n negative answers have been received; in the sequel, we will refer to this model as $\mathbf{GNC}^n$, where **GNC** denotes 'generalized model of learning via negative counterexamples'.

Note that the $\mathbf{GNC}^n$ model combines the features of the first two (we have also demonstrated that it is stronger than each of the first two). All three models $\mathbf{SubQ}^n$, $\mathbf{NC}^n$, and $\mathbf{GNC}^n$ provide certain complexity measure (in the spirit of [GM98]) for learning languages that cannot be learned from positive data alone.

Negative counterexamples provided by the teacher in all these models are of arbitrary size. Some researchers in the field considered other types of negative data available for learners from full positive data. For example, negative data provided to learners in the model considered in [BCJ95] is preselected — in this situation just a very small amount of negative data can greatly enhance learning capabilities. A similar model was considered in [Mot91].

In this paper we explore models $\mathbf{SubQ}^n$, $\mathbf{NC}^n$, and $\mathbf{GNC}^n$ when the teacher provides a negative counterexample only if there is one whose size does not exceed the size of the longest statement seen so far. While learning from full positive data and negative counterexamples of arbitrary size can be interesting and insightful on its own right, providing arbitrary examples immediately (as it is assumed in the models under consideration) may be somewhat unrealistic — in fact, it may significantly slow down learning process, if not making it impossible. On the other hand, it is quite realistic to assume that the teacher can always reasonably quickly provide a counterexample (if any), if its size is bounded by the largest statement on the input seen so far. Following notation in [JK06a], we denote corresponding variants of our three models by $\mathbf{BSubQ}^n$, $\mathbf{BNC}^n$, and $\mathbf{BGNC}^n$, respectively. Following [Ang88] and [JK06a] we also consider restricted variants of the above three models — when the teacher, responding to a query, answers just 'no' if a counterexample of the size not exceeding the size of the largest statement seen so far exists — not providing the actual example; otherwise, the teacher answers 'yes'. To reflect this variant in the name of a model, we, following [JK06a], add the prefix $\mathbf{Res}$ to its name (for example, $\mathbf{ResBNC}^n$). It must be noted that, as it is shown in [JK06a], $\mathbf{BSubQ}^n$ does not provides any advantages over learning just from positive data. Therefore, we concentrate on $\mathbf{BNC}^n$, $\mathbf{BGNC}^n$ and their $\mathbf{Res}$ variants.

Our first goal in this research was to explore relationships between these two models as well as their restricted variants. Following [JK06b] and [JK06a], we also consider $\mathbf{Res}$ variants for models $\mathbf{NC}^n$, and $\mathbf{GNC}^n$ as well as their variants when the least (rather than arbitrary) counterexample is provided — in this case we use the prefix $\mathbf{L}$ (for example, $\mathbf{LNC}^n$). Consequently, we explore relationships between $\mathbf{B}$-models and models using limited number of queries (including those getting just answers 'yes' or 'no'), or limited number of arbitrary or least counterexamples, or just answers 'no'. In this context, we, in particular, demonstrate advantages that our $\mathbf{B}$-variants of learning (even $\mathbf{ResB}$) can have over $\mathbf{GNC}^n$ in terms of the number of mind changes needed to arrive to the right conjecture.

In the full version of the paper (see [JK05]), we give also a number of results relating to comparison of $\mathbf{GNC}$-model with $\mathbf{NC}$ model and comparison of learning via limited number of short counterexamples and finite number of queries. Most of our results provide salient examples of classes learnable (or not learnable) within corresponding models.

The paper has the following structure. In Section 2 we introduce necessary notation and definitions needed for the rest of the paper. In particular, we define some variants of the classical Gold's model of learning from texts (positive data): $\mathbf{TxtEx}$ — when the learner stabilizes to a correct (or nearly correct) conjecture generating the target language, and **TxtBc** — its behaviorally correct counterpart.

In Section 3, for both major models of learnability in the limit, **TxtEx** and **TxtBc**, we define two variants of learning from positive data and a uniformly bounded number of counterexamples: $\mathbf{NC}^n$ and $\mathbf{GNC}^n$, where the learner makes subset queries and is 'charged' for every negative answer from a teacher. We then define the main models considered in this paper: $\mathbf{BNC}^n$ and $\mathbf{BGNC}^n$, as well as **ResB** variants of both. We also formally define the **L** variant for all these models.

In Section 4 we explore relationships between different bounded negative counterexample models. In particular, we study the following two problems: under which circumstances, (a) **B**-learners receiving just answers 'yes' or 'no' can simulate the learners receiving short (possibly, even least) counterexamples; (b) learners receiving arbitrary short counterexamples can simulate the ones receiving the least short counterexamples. First, we note that in all variants of the paradigms **TxtEx** and **TxtBc**, an $\mathbf{LBNC}^n$-learner can be always simulated by a $\mathbf{ResBNC}^{2n-1}$-learner: $2n-1$ 'no' answers are enough to simulate n explicit negative counterexamples (similar fact holds also for the $\mathbf{LBGNC}^n$-learners). Moreover, for the $\mathbf{Bc}^*$ type of learnability (when almost all conjectures contain any finite number of errors), the number $2n-1$ in the above result drops to n (Theorem 6; note that, for learning via limited number of arbitrary or least counterexamples, the number $2n-1$ could not be lowered even for $\mathbf{Bc}^*$-learners, as shown in [JK06a]). On the other hand, the number $2n-1$ of negative answers/counterexamples cannot be lowered for the learning types $\mathbf{Ex}^*$ (when any finite number of errors in the limiting correct conjecture) and $\mathbf{Bc}^m$ (when the number of errors in almost all conjectures is uniformly bounded by some m) for both tasks (a) and (b). Namely, there exist $\mathbf{LBNC}^n\mathbf{Ex}$-learnable classes of languages that cannot be learned by $\mathbf{BGNC}^{2n-2}\mathbf{Bc}^m$ or $\mathbf{BGNC}^{2n-2}\mathbf{Ex}^*$-learners (Theorem 4) and there exist $\mathbf{BNC}^n\mathbf{Ex}$-learnable classes that cannot be learned by $\mathbf{ResBGNC}^{2n-2}\mathbf{Bc}^m$ or $\mathbf{ResBGNC}^{2n-2}\mathbf{Ex}^*$-learners (Theorem 5). We also show that a $\mathbf{LBNCEx}^*$-learner can be always simulated by a **ResBNCBc**-learner — when the number of negative answers/counterexamples is unbounded.

In Section 5 we explore relationships between our models when the counterexamples considered are short or unconstrained. First, we demonstrate how short counterexamples can be of advantage over unconstrained ones while learning from positive data and a bounded number of counterexamples. One of our central — somewhat surprising — results is that sometimes one 'no' answer, just indicating that a short counterexample exists, can do more than any number n of arbitrary (or even least) counterexamples used by (the strongest) $\mathbf{LGNC}^n\mathbf{Bc}^*$-learners (Theorem 9). Note that the advantages of least examples/counterexamples in speeding up learning has been studied in other situations also, such as learning of non-erasing pattern languages ([WZ94]). However, in our model of **BNC**-learning versus **LNC**-learning, the **LNC**-learner does get least counterexamples, and **BNC** learner gets just a counterexample, if there exists one below the maximal positive data seen so far. This seems on the surface to hurt, as **BNC**-learner is likely to get less (negative) data. In fact, that is the case when we do not bound the number of counterexamples received. However, when we consider counting/bounding, there is a *charge* for every counterexample. Consequently, a **BNC**-learner is not being charged for (unnecessary) negative data, if it does not receive it. As a result, the possibility of getting negative data which are $\leq$ maximal positive data seen in the input so far can be turned to an advantage — in terms of cost of learning. This is what is exploited in getting this result. We also show that sometimes a **ResBNC**^{1}**Ex**-learner can use just one mind change (and one 'no' answer witnessing existence of a short counterexample) to learn classes of languages not learnable by any **GNCEx**-learner using any bounded number of mind changes and an unbounded (finite) number of arbitrary counterexamples (Theorem 10). On the other hand, least counterexamples used by **NC**-type learners make a difference: any **LBNCEx**-learner using at most m mind changes and any (unbounded) number of counterexamples can be simulated by a **LNC**^{m}-learner using at most m mind changes and at most m least counterexamples.

2   Notation and Preliminaries

Any unexplained recursion theoretic notation is from [Rog67]. The symbol N denotes the set of natural numbers, $\{0, 1, 2, 3, \ldots\}$. Symbols $\emptyset, \subseteq, \subset, \supseteq$, and $\supset$ denote empty set, subset, proper subset, superset, and proper superset, respectively. Cardinality of a set S is denoted by $\mathrm{card}(S)$. I_m denotes the set $\{x \mid x \leq m\}$. The maximum and minimum of a set are denoted by $\max(\cdot), \min(\cdot)$, respectively, where $\max(\emptyset) = 0$ and $\min(\emptyset) = \infty$. $L_1 \Delta L_2$ denotes the symmetric difference of L_1 and L_2, that is $L_1 \Delta L_2 = (L_1 - L_2) \cup (L_2 - L_1)$. For a natural number a, we say that $L_1 =^a L_2$, iff $\mathrm{card}(L_1 \Delta L_2) \leq a$. We say that $L_1 =^* L_2$, iff $\mathrm{card}(L_1 \Delta L_2) < \infty$. Thus, we take $n < * < \infty$, for all $n \in N$. If $L_1 =^a L_2$, then we say that L_1 is an a-variant of L_2.

We let $\langle \cdot, \cdot \rangle$ stand for an arbitrary, computable, bijective mapping from $N \times N$ onto N [Rog67]. We assume without loss of generality that $\langle \cdot, \cdot \rangle$ is monotonically increasing in both of its arguments. We define $\pi_1(\langle x, y \rangle) = x$ and $\pi_2(\langle x, y \rangle) = y$. We can extend pairing function to multiple arguments by using $\langle i_1, i_2, \ldots, i_k \rangle = \langle i_1, \langle i_2, \langle \ldots, \langle i_{k-1}, i_k \rangle \rangle \rangle \rangle$.

We let $\{W_i\}_{i \in N}$ denote an acceptable numbering of all r.e. sets. Symbol $\mathcal{E}$ will denote the set of all r.e. languages. Symbol L, with or without decorations, ranges over $\mathcal{E}$. By $\overline{L}$, we denote the complement of L, that is $N - L$. Symbol $\mathcal{L}$, with or without decorations, ranges over subsets of $\mathcal{E}$. By $W_{i,s}$ we denote the set W_i enumerated within s steps, in some standard computable method of enumerating W_i.

We now present concepts from language learning theory. A *sequence* σ is a mapping from an initial segment of N into $(N \cup \{\#\})$. Intuitively, $\#$'s represent pauses in the presentation of data. The empty sequence is denoted by Λ. The *content* of a sequence σ, denoted $\mathrm{content}(\sigma)$, is the set of natural numbers in the range of σ. The *length* of σ, denoted $|\sigma|$, is the number of elements in σ.

So, $|\Lambda| = 0$. For $n \le |\sigma|$, the initial sequence of σ of length n is denoted by $\sigma[n]$. So, $\sigma[0]$ is Λ. We let σ, τ, and γ, with or without decorations, range over finite sequences. We denote the sequence formed by the concatenation of τ at the end of σ by $\sigma\tau$. SEQ denotes the set of all finite sequences.

A *text* T (see [Gol67]) for a language L is a mapping from N into $(N \cup \{\#\})$ such that L is the set of natural numbers in the range of T. $T(i)$ represents the $(i+1)$-th element in the text. The *content* of a text T, denoted by content(T), is the set of natural numbers in the range of T; that is, the language which T is a text for. $T[n]$ denotes the finite initial sequence of T with length n.

A *language learning machine from texts* (see [Gol67]) is an algorithmic device which computes a mapping from SEQ into N. We let $\mathbf{M}$, with or without decorations, range over learning machines. $\mathbf{M}(T[n])$ is interpreted as the grammar (index for an accepting program) conjectured by the learning machine $\mathbf{M}$ on the initial sequence $T[n]$. We say that $\mathbf{M}$ converges on T to i, (written: $\mathbf{M}(T)\!\downarrow = i$) iff $(\forall^\infty n)[\mathbf{M}(T[n]) = i]$.

There are several criteria for a learning machine to be successful on a language. Below we define some of them. All of the criteria defined below are variants of the **Ex**-style and **Bc**-style learning described in the Introduction; in addition, they allow a finite number of errors in almost all conjectures (uniformly bounded, or arbitrary). **TxtEx**-criteria is due to [Gol67]. **TxtEx**^{a} (for $a > 0$), and **TxtBc**^{a}-criteria are due to [CL82]. Osherson and Weinstein [OW82] independently considered **TxtBc**.

Suppose $a \in N \cup \{*\}$. $\mathbf{M}$ **TxtEx**^{a}-*identifies a language* L (written: $L \in$ **TxtEx**$^a(\mathbf{M})$) just in case for all texts T for L, $(\exists i \mid W_i =^a L)$ $(\forall^\infty n)[\mathbf{M}(T[n]) = i]$. $\mathbf{M}$ **TxtEx**^{a}-*identifies a class* $\mathcal{L}$ of r.e. languages (written: $\mathcal{L} \subseteq$ **TxtEx**$^a(\mathbf{M})$) just in case $\mathbf{M}$ **TxtEx**^{a}-identifies each language from $\mathcal{L}$. **TxtEx**$^a = \{\mathcal{L} \subseteq \mathcal{E} \mid (\exists \mathbf{M})[\mathcal{L} \subseteq$ **TxtEx**$^a(\mathbf{M})]\}$.

$\mathbf{M}$ **TxtBc**^{a}-*identifies an r.e. language* L (written: $L \in$ **TxtBc**$^a(\mathbf{M})$) just in case, for each text T for L, for all but finitely many n, $W_{\mathbf{M}(T[n])} =^a L$. $\mathbf{M}$ **TxtBc**^{a}-*identifies a class* $\mathcal{L}$ of r.e. languages (written: $\mathcal{L} \subseteq$ **TxtBc**$^a(\mathbf{M})$) just in case $\mathbf{M}$ **TxtBc**^{a}-identifies each language from $\mathcal{L}$. **TxtBc**$^a = \{\mathcal{L} \subseteq \mathcal{E} \mid (\exists \mathbf{M})[\mathcal{L} \subseteq$ **TxtBc**$^a(\mathbf{M})]\}$. For $a = 0$, we often write **TxtEx** and **TxtBc**, instead of **TxtEx**^{0} and **TxtBc**^{0}, respectively.

The following proposition is useful in proving many of our results.

Proposition 1. *[Gol67] Suppose L is an infinite language, $S \subseteq L$, and $L - S$ is infinite. Let $C_0 \subseteq C_1 \subseteq \cdots$ be an infinite sequence of finite sets such that $\bigcup_{i \in N} C_i = L$. Then $\{L\} \cup \{S \cup C_i \mid i \in N\}$ is not in* **TxtBc***.

We let CYL_i denote the language $\{\langle i, x\rangle \mid x \in N\}$.

3 Learning with Negative Counterexamples to Conjectures

In this section we define two models of learning languages from positive data and negative counterexamples to conjectures. Both models are based on the general idea of learning from positive data and subset queries for the conjectures.

Intuitively, for learning with negative counterexamples to conjectures, we may consider the learner being provided a text, one element at a time, along with a negative counterexample to the latest conjecture, if any. (One may view this counterexample as a response of the teacher to the subset query when it is tested if the language generated by the conjecture is a subset of the target language). One may model the list of counterexamples as a second text for negative counterexamples being provided to the learner. Thus the learning machines get as input two texts, one for positive data, and other for negative counterexamples.

We say that $\mathbf{M}(T, T')$ converges to a grammar i, iff for all but finitely many n, $\mathbf{M}(T[n], T'[n]) = i$.

First, we define the basic model of learning from positive data and negative counterexamples to conjectures. In this model, if a conjecture contains elements not in the target language, then a counterexample is provided to the learner. **NC** in the definition below stands for 'negative counterexample'.

Definition 1. [JK06b] Suppose $a \in N \cup \{*\}$.

(a) **M NCEx^a-identifies a language** L (written: $L \in \mathbf{NCEx}^a(\mathbf{M})$) iff for all texts T for L, and for all T' satisfying the condition:

$$T'(n) \in S_n, \text{ if } S_n \neq \emptyset \text{ and } T'(n) = \#, \text{ if } S_n = \emptyset,$$
$$\text{where } S_n = \overline{L} \cap W_{\mathbf{M}(T[n], T'[n])}$$

$\mathbf{M}(T, T')$ converges to a grammar i such that $W_i =^a L$.

(b) **M NCEx^a-identifies** a class $\mathcal{L}$ of languages (written: $\mathcal{L} \subseteq \mathbf{NCEx}^a(\mathbf{M})$), iff **M NCEx^a**-identifies each language in the class.

(c) $\mathbf{NCEx}^a = \{\mathcal{L} \mid (\exists \mathbf{M})[\mathcal{L} \subseteq \mathbf{NCEx}^a(\mathbf{M})]\}$.

For **LNCEx^a** criteria of inference, we consider providing the learner with the least counterexample rather than an arbitrary one. The criteria **LNCEx^a** of learning can thus be defined similarly to **NCEx^a**, by requiring $T'(n) = \min(S_n)$, if $S_n \neq \emptyset$ and $T'(n) = \#$, if $S_n = \emptyset$ in clause (a) above (instead of $T'(n)$ being an arbitrary member of S_n).

Similarly, one can define **ResNCEx^a**, where the learner is just told that the latest conjecture is or is not a subset of the input language, but is not provided any counterexamples in the case of 'no' answer.

For **BNCEx^a** criteria of inference, we update the definition of S_n in clause (a) of the definition of **NCEx^a**-identification as follows: $S_n = \overline{L} \cap W_{\mathbf{M}(T[n], T'[n])} \cap \{x \mid x \leq \max(\text{content}(T[n]))\}$.

We can similarly define the criteria of inference **ResBNCEx^a**, and **LBNCEx^a**, **NCBc^a**, **LNCBc^a**, **ResBc^a**, **BNCBc^a**, **ResBNCBc^a** and **LBNCBc^a**. We refer the reader to [JK06b] for more details, discussion and results about the various variations of **NCI**-criteria.

For $m \in N$, one may also consider the model, **NC^{m}I**, where, for learning a language L, the **NCI** learner is provided counterexamples only for its first m conjectures which are not subsets of L. For remaining conjectures, the answer provided is always $\#$. In other words, the learner is 'charged' only for the first m negative counterexamples, and the subset queries for later conjectures are not answered. Following is the formal definition.

Definition 2. [JK06a] Suppose $a \in N \cup \{*\}$, and $m \in N$.

(a) **M** $\mathbf{NC}^m\mathbf{Ex}^a$-*identifies a language* L (written: $L \in \mathbf{NC}^m\mathbf{Ex}^a(\mathbf{M})$) iff for all texts T for L, and for all T' satisfying the condition:

$$T'(n) \in S_n, \text{ if } S_n \neq \emptyset \text{ and } \mathrm{card}(\{r \mid r < n, T'(r) \neq \#\}) < m; \ T'(n) = \#,$$
$$\text{if } S_n = \emptyset \text{ or } \mathrm{card}(\{r \mid r < n, T'(r) \neq \#\}) \geq m,$$
$$\text{where } S_n = \overline{L} \cap W_{\mathbf{M}(T[n], T'[n])}$$

$\mathbf{M}(T, T')$ converges to a grammar i such that $W_i =^a L$.

(b) **M** $\mathbf{NC}^m\mathbf{Ex}^a$-*identifies* a class $\mathcal{L}$ of languages (written: $\mathcal{L} \subseteq \mathbf{NC}^m\mathbf{Ex}^a(\mathbf{M})$), iff **M** $\mathbf{NC}^m\mathbf{Ex}^a$-identifies each language in the class.

(c) $\mathbf{NC}^m\mathbf{Ex}^a = \{\mathcal{L} \mid (\exists \mathbf{M})[\mathcal{L} \subseteq \mathbf{NC}^m\mathbf{Ex}^a(\mathbf{M})]\}$.

For $a \in N \cup \{*\}$ and $\mathbf{I} \in \{\mathbf{Ex}^a, \mathbf{Bc}^a\}$, one can similarly define $\mathbf{BNC}^m\mathbf{I}$, $\mathbf{LBNC}^m\mathbf{I}$, $\mathbf{ResBNC}^m\mathbf{I}$ and $\mathbf{LNC}^m\mathbf{I}$, $\mathbf{ResNC}^m\mathbf{I}$ and $\mathbf{NC}^m\mathbf{Bc}^a$.

GNCI-identification model is same as the model of **NCI**-identification, except that counterexamples are provided to the learner only when it explicitly requests for such via a 'is this conjecture a subset of the target language' question (which we refer to as conjecture-subset question). This clearly does not make a difference if there is no bound on the number of questions asked resulting in counterexamples. However when there is a bound on number of counterexamples, then this may make a difference, as the **GNC**-learner may avoid getting a counterexample on some conjecture by not asking the conjecture-subset question. Thus, we will only deal with **GNC** model when there is a requirement of a bounded number of counterexamples. For $a \in N \cup \{*\}$ and $\mathbf{I} \in \{\mathbf{Ex}^a, \mathbf{Bc}^a\}$, one can define $\mathbf{GNC}^m\mathbf{I}$, $\mathbf{LGNC}^m\mathbf{I}$, $\mathbf{ResGNC}^m\mathbf{I}$ and $\mathbf{BGNC}^m\mathbf{I}$, $\mathbf{LBGNC}^m\mathbf{I}$, $\mathbf{ResBGNC}^m\mathbf{I}$, similarly to **NC** variants.

Note a subtle difference between models $\mathbf{LBGNC}^n$ and $\mathbf{LGNC}^n$: in the model $\mathbf{LBGNC}^n$, the teacher provides the shortest counterexample only if it is smaller than some element of the input, whereas there is no such requirement for $\mathbf{LGNC}^n$ (the same is true also for **NC**-variant).

4   Relations Among Bounded Negative Counterexample Models

In this section we establish relationships between B-variants of **NC** and **GNC**-models when any short, or the least short counterexamples, or just the 'no' answers about existence of short counterexamples are used.

First we establish that, similarly to the known result about **NC**-model ([JK06a]), number of counterexamples matters to the extent that $n + 1$ 'no' answers used by **BNCEx**-style learners can sometimes do more that n least counterexamples obtained by **LBGNCBc***-style learners.

Theorem 1. $\mathbf{ResBNC}^{n+1}\mathbf{Ex} - \mathbf{LBGNC}^n\mathbf{Bc}^* \neq \emptyset$.

The next result gives advantages of **GNC** model.

Theorem 2. *For all* $n, m \in N$, **ResBGNC^{1}Ex** $-$ (**LBNC^{n}Bc^m** $\cup$ **LBNC^{n}Ex***) $\neq \emptyset$.

Our main results in this section deal with the following problems: if and under which conditions, (a) **B**-learners receiving just 'yes' or 'no' answers can simulate learners receiving short (or, possibly, even least short) counterexamples, and (b) learners using arbitrary short counterexamples can simulate the ones receiving the least short counterexamples. We establish that, for both tasks (a) and (b), for the **Bc^m** and **Ex*** types of learnability, $2n - 1$ is the upper and the lower bound on the number of negative answers/examples needed for such a simulation. These results are similar to the corresponding results in [JK06a] for the model **NC**, however, there is also an interesting difference: as it will be shown below, for **Bc***-learnability, the bound $2n-1$ can be lowered to just n (for **NCBc***-learners, the lower bound $2n - 1$ still holds).

First we establish the upper bound $2n - 1$ for both tasks (a) and (b).

Theorem 3. *For all* $n \geq 1$,
  (a) **LBNC^{n}I** $\subseteq$ **ResBNC^{2n-1}I**.
  (b) **LBGNC^{n}I** $\subseteq$ **ResBGNC^{2n-1}I**.

Our next result shows that, for the **Bc^m** and **Ex*** types of learnability, the bound $2n - 1$ is tight in the strongest sense for the task (b). Namely, we show that **BNC**-learners using n least short counterexamples cannot be simulated by **BGNC**-learners using $2n - 2$ (arbitrary short) counterexamples.

Theorem 4. *For all* $n \geq 1$, **LBNC^{n}Ex** $-$ (**BGNC^{2n-2}Bc^m** $\cup$ **BGNC^{2n-2}Ex***) $\neq \emptyset$.

Now we show that the bound $2n - 1$ on the number of negative answers is tight for **Bc^m** and **Ex*** types of learnability when **ResBNC**-learners try to simulate **BNC^n**-learners.

Theorem 5. *For all* $m \in N$, **BNC^{n}Ex** $-$ (**ResBGNC^{2n-2}Bc^m** $\cup$ **ResBGNC^{2n-2}Ex***) $\neq \emptyset$.

Proof. Recall that $\langle x, y, z \rangle = \langle x, \langle y, z \rangle \rangle$. Thus, $\mathrm{CYL}_j = \{\langle j, x, y \rangle \mid x, y \in N\}$, and $\langle \cdot, \cdot, \cdot \rangle$ is increasing in all its arguments. Consider $\mathcal{L}$ defined as follows. For each $L \in \mathcal{L}$, there exists a set S, $\mathrm{card}(S) \leq n$, such that the conditions (1)–(3) hold.
(1) $L \subseteq \bigcup_{j \in S} \mathrm{CYL}_j$.
(2) $L \cap \mathrm{CYL}_j \cap \{\langle j, 0, x \rangle \mid x \in N\}$ contains exactly one element for each $j \in S$. Let this element be $\langle j, 0, \langle p_j, q_j \rangle \rangle$.
(3) For each $j \in S$,

   (3.1) W_{p_j} is a grammar for $L \cap \mathrm{CYL}_j$ or
   (3.2) $W_{p_j} \not\subseteq L$ and $W_{p_j} - L$ consists only of elements of form $\langle j, 1, 2x \rangle$ or only of elements of form $\langle j, 1, 2x + 1 \rangle$. Furthermore at least one such element is smaller than $\max(L)$. If this element is of form $\langle j, 1, 2z \rangle$, then $W_{q_j} = L \cap \mathrm{CYL}_j$. Otherwise, $L \cap \mathrm{CYL}_j$ is finite.

Intuitively, L may be considered as being divided into upto n parts, each part being subset of a cylinder, where each part satisfies the properties as given in (2) and (3).

Above class of languages can be seen to be in $\mathbf{BNC}^n\mathbf{Ex}$ as follows. On input σ, for each j such that content(σ) contains an element of CYL_j, find p_j and q_j as defined in condition 2 above (if σ does not contain any element of form $\langle j, 0, \langle p_j, q_j \rangle \rangle$, then grammar for $\emptyset$ is output on σ). Then for each of these j, learner computes a grammar for:

(a) W_{p_j} (if it has not received any counterexample from CYL_j),
(b) W_{q_j} (if the negative counterexample from CYL_j is of form $\langle j, 1, 2z \rangle$), and
(c) content$(T) \cap \mathrm{CYL}_j$, otherwise.

Then, the learner outputs a grammar for the union of the languages enumerated by the grammars computed for each j above. It is easy to verify that the above learner gets at most one counterexample from each CYL_j such that CYL_j intersects with the input language, and thus $\mathbf{BNC}^n\mathbf{Ex}$-identifies $\mathcal{L}$.

Proof of $\mathcal{L} \notin \mathbf{ResBGNC}^{2n-2}\mathbf{Bc}^m \cup \mathbf{ResBGNC}^{2n-2}\mathbf{Ex}^*$ is complex and we refer the reader to [JK05] for details. ∎

Interestingly, if we consider behaviorally correct learners that are allowed to make any finite number of errors in almost all correct conjectures, then n short (even least) counterexamples can be always substituted by just n 'no' answers. (For the model $\mathbf{NC}$, the lower bound $2n - 1$ for the simulation by $\mathbf{Res}$-type learners still holds even for $\mathbf{Bc}^*$-learnability, as shown in [JK06a]).

Theorem 6. *For all* $n \in N$, $\mathbf{LBGNC}^n\mathbf{Bc}^* \subseteq \mathbf{ResBNC}^n\mathbf{Bc}^*$.

Proof. First note that one can simulate a $\mathbf{LBGNC}^n\mathbf{Bc}^*$ learner $\mathbf{M}$ by a $\mathbf{LBNC}^n\mathbf{Bc}^*$ learner $\mathbf{M}'$ as follows. If $\mathbf{M}(\sigma, \sigma')$ does not ask a conjecture-subset question, then $\mathbf{M}'(\sigma, \sigma')$ is a grammar for $W_{\mathbf{M}(\sigma,\sigma')} - \{x \mid x \leq \max(\text{content}(\sigma))\}$; otherwise $\mathbf{M}'(\sigma, \sigma') = \mathbf{M}(\sigma, \sigma')$. It is easy to verify that on any input text T, $\mathbf{M}'$ gets exactly the same counterexamples as $\mathbf{M}$ does, and all conjectures of $\mathbf{M}'$ are finite variants of corresponding conjectures of $\mathbf{M}$. Thus, any language $\mathbf{LBGNC}^n\mathbf{Bc}^*$-identified by $\mathbf{M}$ is $\mathbf{LBNC}^n\mathbf{Bc}^*$-identified by $\mathbf{M}'$.

Hence, it suffices to show that $\mathbf{LBNC}^n\mathbf{Bc}^* \subseteq \mathbf{ResBNC}^n\mathbf{Bc}^*$. Suppose $\mathbf{M}$ $\mathbf{LBNC}^n\mathbf{Bc}^*$-identifies $\mathcal{L}$. Define $\mathbf{M}'$ as follows. Suppose T is the input text.

The idea is for $\mathbf{M}'$ to output $\max(\text{content}(T[m])) + 1$ variations of grammar output by $\mathbf{M}$ on $T[m]$. These grammars would be for the languages: $W_{\mathbf{M}(T[m])} - \{x \mid x \neq i \text{ and } x \leq \max(\text{content}(T[m']))\}$, where $T[m']$ is the input seen by $\mathbf{M}'$ when generating this i-th variant (where $0 \leq i \leq \max(\text{content}(T[m]))$). These grammars would thus allow $\mathbf{M}'$ to determine the least counterexample, if any, that the grammar output by $\mathbf{M}$ on $T[m]$ would have generated.

Formally conjectures of $\mathbf{M}'$ will be of form $P(j, m, i, s)$, where $W_{P(j,m,i,s)} = W_j - \{x \mid x \neq i \text{ and } x \leq s\}$.

We assume that $\mathbf{M}$ outputs $\emptyset$ until it sees at least one element in the input. This is to avoid having any counterexamples until input contains at least one element (which in turn makes the notation easier for the following proof).

On input $T[0]$, conjecture of $\mathbf{M}'$ is $P(\mathbf{M}(\Lambda, \Lambda), 0, 0, 0)$.

The invariants we will have is: If $\mathbf{M}'(T[m], T'[m]) = P(j, r, i, s)$, then, (i) $j = \mathbf{M}(T[r], T''[r])$, where $T''[r]$ is the sequence of least counterexamples for $\mathbf{M}$ on input $T[r]$ (for the language content(T)), (ii) $s = \max(\text{content}(T[m]))$, (iii) $r \le m$, (iv) $i \le \max(\text{content}(T[r]))$, and (v) $W_j - L$ does not contain any element $< i$. Invariants are clearly satisfied for $m = 0$.

Suppose $\mathbf{M}'(T[m], T'[m]) = P(\mathbf{M}(T[r], T''[r]), r, i, s)$. Then we define $\mathbf{M}'(T[m+1], T'[m+1])$ as follows.

If $T'(m)$ is 'no' answer, then let $T''(r) = i$, and let $\mathbf{M}'(T[m+1], T'[m+1]) = P(\mathbf{M}(T[r+1], T''[r+1]), r+1, 0, \max(\text{content}(T[m+1])))$.

Else if $i = \max(\text{content}(T[r]))$, then let $T''(r) = \#$, and let $\mathbf{M}'(T[m+1], T'[m+1]) = P(\mathbf{M}(T[r+1], T''[r+1]), r+1, 0, \max(\text{content}(T[m+1])))$.

Else, $\mathbf{M}'(T[m+1], T'[m+1]) = P(\mathbf{M}(T[r], T''[r]), r, i+1, \max(\text{content}(T[m+1])))$.

Now it is easy to verify that invariant is maintained. It also follows that T'' constructed as above is correct sequence of least counterexamples for $\mathbf{M}$ on input T. Moreover, each restricted 'no' answer in T' corresponds to a least counterexample in T''. Thus, $\mathbf{M}'$ gets exactly as many counterexamples as $\mathbf{M}$ does, and $\mathbf{M}'$ conjectures are $*$-variants of the conjectures of $\mathbf{M}$ (except that each conjecture of $\mathbf{M}$ is repeated finitely many times by $\mathbf{M}'$, with finite variations). It follows that $\mathbf{M}'$ $\mathbf{ResBNC}^n\mathbf{Bc}^*$-identifies $\mathcal{L}$. ∎

Corollary 1. *For all $n \in N$, $\mathbf{LBNC}^n\mathbf{Bc}^* = \mathbf{BNC}^n\mathbf{Bc}^* = \mathbf{ResBNC}^n\mathbf{Bc}^* = \mathbf{LBGNC}^n\mathbf{Bc}^* = \mathbf{BGNC}^n\mathbf{Bc}^* = \mathbf{ResBGNC}^n\mathbf{Bc}^*$.*

Our next result in this section shows how $\mathbf{BNCBc}$-learners using just answers 'yes' or 'no' can simulate $\mathbf{LBNCEx}^*$-learners getting unbounded number of negative answers/counterexamples.

Proposition 2. $\mathbf{LBNCEx}^* \subseteq \mathbf{ResBNCBc}$.

We now consider error hierarchy for $\mathbf{BNC}^m$-learning model.

Theorem 7. *For all $m, n \in N$,*
(a) $\mathbf{TxtEx}^{2n+1} - \mathbf{LBGNC}^m\mathbf{Bc}^n \ne \emptyset$.
(b) $\mathbf{TxtEx}^{n+1} - \mathbf{LBGNC}^m\mathbf{Ex}^n \ne \emptyset$.
(c) For $\mathbf{I} \in \{\mathbf{ResBNC}^m, \mathbf{BNC}^m, \mathbf{LBNC}^m, \mathbf{ResBGNC}^m, \mathbf{BGNC}^m, \mathbf{LBGNC}^m\}$, $\mathbf{IEx}^{2n} \subseteq \mathbf{IBc}^n$.

5 Effects of Counterexamples Being Constrained/ Not-Constrained to Be Short

In this section we explore how, within the framework of our models, short counterexamples fair against arbitrary or least counterexamples (this includes also the cases when just answers 'no' are returned instead of counterexamples).

First, we use a result from [JK06a] to establish that one answer 'no' used by an $\mathbf{NCEx}$-learner can sometimes do more than unbounded number of least (short) counterexamples used by $\mathbf{Bc}^*$-learners.

Theorem 8. *(based on [JK06a])* $\mathbf{ResNC^1Ex} - \mathbf{LBGNCBc^*} \neq \emptyset$.

From [JK06b] we have that, for $a \in N \cup \{*\}$, for $\mathbf{I} \in \{\mathbf{Ex}^a, \mathbf{Bc}^a\}$, $\mathbf{LBNCI} \subset \mathbf{ResNCI}$. Thus the next result is somewhat surprising. It shows that one short counterexample can sometimes give a learner more than any bounded number of least counterexamples. The proof exploits the fact that the learner is not charged if it does not get a counterexample.

Theorem 9. *For all $n \in N$,* $\mathbf{ResBNC^1Ex} - \mathbf{LGNC^nBc^*} \neq \emptyset$.

Proof. Let $A_k^j = \{\langle k, x \rangle \mid x \leq j\}$. Let

$$
\begin{aligned}
\mathcal{L} = \{L \mid &(\exists S \mid \mathrm{card}(S) < \infty)(\exists f : S \to N)[\\
1.\ &[k, k' \in S \ \wedge \ k < k'] \Rightarrow [\langle k, f(k) \rangle < \langle k', 0 \rangle] \ \wedge \\
2.\ &[L = \mathrm{CYL}_{\max(S)} \cup \bigcup_{k \in S - \max(S)} A_k^{f(k)} \ \text{or} \\
&L = \{\langle \max(S), f(\max(S) + 2) \rangle\} \cup \bigcup_{k \in S} A_k^{f(k)}] \ ]\}.
\end{aligned}
$$

To see that $\mathcal{L} \in \mathbf{ResBNC^1Ex}$ consider the following learner. On input σ, if no 'no' answers are yet received, then the learner first computes $k = \max(\{j \mid \langle j, x \rangle \in \mathrm{content}(\sigma)\})$. Then it outputs a grammar for $L = \mathrm{CYL}_k \cup (\mathrm{content}(\sigma) - \mathrm{CYL}_k)$. If there is a 'no' answer which has been received, then the learner outputs a grammar for $\mathrm{content}(\sigma)$. It is easy to verify that the above learner $\mathbf{ResBNC^1Ex}$-identifies $\mathcal{L}$.

Now suppose by way of contradiction that some $\mathbf{M}$ $\mathbf{LGNC^nBc^*}$-identifies $\mathcal{L}$. Let $\sigma_0 = \sigma_0' = \Lambda$, $k_0 = 0$. Inductively define $\sigma_{i+1}, \sigma_{i+1}', f(k_i), k_{i+1}$ (for $i < n$) as follows.

Let σ be smallest extension of σ_i, if any, such that $\mathrm{content}(\sigma) \subseteq \mathrm{CYL}_{k_i} \cup \bigcup_{i' < i} A_{k_{i'}}^{f(k_{i'})}$ and $\mathbf{M}$ asks a conjecture-subset question on $(\sigma, \sigma_i' \#^{|\sigma| - |\sigma_i|})$ and $W_{\mathbf{M}(\sigma, \sigma_i' \#^{|\sigma| - |\sigma_i|})}$ contains an element which is not in $\mathrm{CYL}_{k_i} \cup \bigcup_{i' < i} A_{k_{i'}}^{f(k_{i'})}$ or is larger than $\max(\mathrm{content}(\sigma))$.

If there is such a σ, then let $\sigma_{i+1} = \sigma\#$, and $\sigma_{i+1}' = \sigma_i' \#^{|\sigma| - |\sigma_i|} w$ (where w is the least element in $W_{\mathbf{M}(\sigma, \sigma_i' \#^{|\sigma| - |\sigma_i|})}$ which is not in $\mathrm{CYL}_{k_i} \cup \bigcup_{i' < i} A_{k_{i'}}^{f(k_{i'})}$ or is larger than $\max(\mathrm{content}(\sigma)))$. Let $f(k_i) = \max(\{y \mid \langle k_i, y \rangle \in \mathrm{content}(\sigma)\})$. Let k_{i+1} be such that $k_{i+1} > \langle k_i, f(k_i) \rangle$ and no element from $\mathrm{CYL}_{k_{i+1}}$ is present in $\mathrm{content}(\sigma_{i+1}')$.

Let m be largest value such that σ_m, σ_m' are defined above. Now, $\mathbf{M}$ has to $\mathbf{TxtBc^*}$-identify both $\mathrm{CYL}_{k_m} \cup \bigcup_{i < m} A_{k_m}^{f(k_m)}$ and $A_{k_m}^r \cup \{\langle k_m, r + 2 \rangle\} \cup \bigcup_{i < m} A_{k_i}^{f(k_i)}$, for all possible r, without any further counterexamples. An impossible task by Proposition 1. ∎

The above is the strongest possible result, as $\mathbf{ResNCI} \supseteq \mathbf{LBNCI}$ (see [JK06b]).

We now consider the complexity (mind change) advantages of having only short counterexamples. For this purpose, we need to modify the definition of learner slightly, to avoid biasing the number of mind changes. (This modification is used only for the rest of the current section).

Definition 3. A learner is a mapping from SEQ to $N \cup \{?\}$.

A learner **M TxtEx$_n$**-identifies $\mathcal{L}$, iff it **TxtEx**-identifies $\mathcal{L}$, and for all texts T for $L \in \mathcal{L}$, $\mathrm{card}(\{m \mid ? \neq \mathbf{M}(T[m]) \neq \mathbf{M}(T[m+1])\})$ is bounded by n.

One can similarly define the criteria with mind change bounds for learners receiving counterexamples. Our next result demonstrates that there exists a **TxtEx**-learnable language (that is, learnable just from positive data — without any subset queries) that can be learned by a **BNC^{1}Ex**-learner using just one negative answer and at most one mind change and cannot be learned by **Ex**-learners using any number of arbitrary counterexamples and any bounded number of mind changes.

Theorem 10. *There exists a $\mathcal{L}$ such that*
   (a) $\mathcal{L} \in \mathbf{ResBNC^1Ex_1}$.
   (b) $\mathcal{L} \in \mathbf{TxtEx}$, and thus in $\mathbf{NCEx}$ and $\mathbf{GNCEx}$.
   (c) For all m, $\mathcal{L} \notin \mathbf{GNCEx}_m$.

Proof. Let $L_n = \{x \mid x < n \text{ or } x = n+1\}$. Let $\mathcal{L} = \{L_n \mid n \in N\}$.

Consider the following learner. Initially output a grammar for N. If and when a 'no' answer is received, output a grammar for L_n, where n is the only counterexample received. It is easy to verify that above learner **ResBNC^{1}Ex$_1$**-identifies $\mathcal{L}$. Also, it is also easy to verify that $\mathcal{L} \in \mathbf{TxtEx}$ as one could output, in the limit on text T, a grammar for L_n, for the least n such that $n \notin \mathrm{content}(T)$.

We now show that $\mathcal{L} \notin \mathbf{NCEx}_m$. As the number of counterexamples are not bounded, it follows that $\mathcal{L} \notin \mathbf{GNCEx}_m$. Suppose by way of contradiction that **M NCEx$_m$**-identifies $\mathcal{L}$. Then consider the following strategy to construct a diagonalizing language. We will construct the diagonalizing language in stages. Construction is non-effective. We will try to define l_s and u_s, and segments σ_s, σ_s' (σ_s' is the sequence of counterexamples), for $s \leq m+1$.

The following invariants will be satisfied.
   (A) $u_s - l_s = 4^{m+3-s}$.
   (B) **M** on proper prefixes of σ_s has made s different conjectures.
   (C) $\mathrm{content}(\sigma_s) \subseteq \{x \mid x < l_s\}$.
   (D) None of the conjectures made by **M** on proper prefixes of σ_s are for the language L_r, for $l_s \leq r \leq u_s$.
   (E) $|\sigma_s'| = |\sigma_s|$.
   (F) For $r < |\sigma_s|$, $\sigma_s'(r) = \#$, implies $W_{\mathbf{M}(\sigma_s[r], \sigma_s'[r])} \subseteq \{x \mid x < l_s\}$.
   (G) For $r < |\sigma_s|$, $\sigma_s'(r) \neq \#$, implies $\sigma_s'(r) \in W_{\mathbf{M}(\sigma_s[r], \sigma_s'[r])}$, and $\sigma_s'(r) > u_s + 1$.

Initially, we let $l_0 = 0$ and $u_0 = l_0 + 4^{m+3}$, and $\sigma_0 = \sigma_0' = \Lambda$. Note that invariants are satisfied.

Stage s (for $s = 0$ to $s = m$)
1.   Let T be a text for L_{l_s} which extends σ_s.
2.   Let $t \geq |\sigma_s|$, be the least value, if any, such that $\mathbf{M}(T[t], T'[t])$ is a conjecture different from any conjecture $\mathbf{M}(T[w], T'[w])$, for $w < |\sigma_s|$, where

$$T'(w) = \begin{cases} \sigma'_s(w), & \text{if } w < |\sigma_s|; \\ \#, & \text{if } w \geq |\sigma_s| \text{ and } \mathbf{M}(T[w], T'[w]) = ?; \\ T'(r), & \text{if } w \geq |\sigma_s| \text{ and } \mathbf{M}(T[w], T'[w]) = \mathbf{M}(T[r], T'[r]), \\ & \text{for some } r < |\sigma_s|. \end{cases}$$

(* Note that, in this step, we do not need the definition of $T'(w)$ when $\mathbf{M}(T[w], T'[w])$ makes a new conjecture at or beyond σ_s. For first such w (which is t found above) $T'(w)$ will be defined below. *)

If and when such a t is found, proceed to step 3.

3.   Suppose $j = \mathbf{M}(T[t], T'[t])$.

   If W_j contains an element $z \geq l_s + \frac{3(u_s - l_s)}{4}$, then

   Let $l_{s+1} = l_s + \frac{u_s - l_s}{4}$.
   Let $u_{s+1} = l_s + \frac{2(u_s - l_s)}{4}$.
   Let $\sigma_{s+1} = T[t]\#$.
   Let $\sigma'_{s+1} = T'[t]z$.
   (* Note thus that $\mathbf{M}(T[t], T'[t])$ is not a correct grammar for L_r, where $l_{s+1} \leq r \leq u_{s+1}$. *)

Else,

   Let $l_{s+1} = l_s + \frac{3(u_s - l_s)}{4}$.
   Let $u_{s+1} = u_s$.
   Let $\sigma_{s+1} = T[t]\#$.
   Let $\sigma'_{s+1} = T'[t]\#$.
   (* Note thus that $\mathbf{M}(T[t], T'[t])$ is not a correct grammar for L_r, where $l_{s+1} \leq r \leq u_{s+1}$. *)

End stage s

It is easy to verify that invariants are satisfied. (A) clearly holds by definition of l_{s+1} and u_{s+1} in step 3. (B) holds as one extra new conjecture is found at stage s, before proceeding to stage $s+1$. (C) holds, as $l_{s+1} \geq l_s + \frac{u_s - l_s}{4} > l_s + 2$, and content($T$) as defined in step 1 is a subset of L_{l_s}. (D) holds by induction, and noting that the conjecture at $T[t]$ as found in step 2 of stage s, is made explicitly wrong by appropriate choice of l_{s+1} and u_{s+1} in step 4. (E) easily holds by construction. (F) and (G) hold by the definition of σ'_{s+1} at step 3.

Now, if step 2 does not succeed at a stage $s \leq m$, then clearly $\mathbf{M}$ does not **NCEx**-identify L_{l_s}. On the other hand if stage m does complete then $\mathbf{M}$ has already made $m + 1$ different conjectures (and thus at least m mind changes) on prefixes of σ_{m+1}, which are not grammars for $L_{l_{m+1}}$. Thus, $\mathbf{M}$ cannot **NCEx**$_m$-identify $L_{l_{m+1}}$.   ∎

Let $X = \{x \mid x > 0\}$. If we consider the class $\mathcal{L} = \{L_n \mid n > 0\} \cup \{X\}$, then we can get the above result using *class preserving* learnability (that is, the learner always uses grammars from the numbering defining the target class of languages for its conjectures, see [ZL95] for formal definition) for **ResBNC^{1}Ex**.

Theorem 11. *For all $m \in N$, (a)* **LBNCEx**$_m$ $\subseteq$ **LNCEx**$_m$.
   (b) **LBGNCEx**$_m$ $\subseteq$ **LGNCEx**$_m$.

References

[Ang88]   D. Angluin. Queries and concept learning. *Machine Learning*, 2:319–342, 1988.

[Bär74]   J. Bārzdiņš. Two theorems on the limiting synthesis of functions. In *Theory of Algorithms and Programs, vol. 1*, pages 82–88. Latvian State University, 1974. In Russian.

[BCJ95]   G. Baliga, J. Case, and S. Jain. Language learning with some negative information. *Journal of Computer and System Sciences*, 51(5):273–285, 1995.

[CL82]   J. Case and C. Lynes. Machine inductive inference and language identification. In M. Nielsen and E. M. Schmidt, editors, *Proceedings of the 9th International Colloquium on Automata, Languages and Programming*, volume 140 of *Lecture Notes in Computer Science*, pages 107–115. Springer-Verlag, 1982.

[CS83]   J. Case and C. Smith. Comparison of identification criteria for machine inductive inference. *Theoretical Computer Science*, 25:193–220, 1983.

[GM98]   W. Gasarch and G. Martin. *Bounded Queries in Recursion Theory*. Birkhauser, 1998.

[Gol67]   E. M. Gold. Language identification in the limit. *Information and Control*, 10:447–474, 1967.

[JK05]   S. Jain and E. Kinber. On learning languages from positive data and a limited number of short counterexamples. Technical Report TR21/05, School of Computing, National University of Singapore, 2005.

[JK06a]   S. Jain and E. Kinber. Learning languages from positive data and a finite number of queries. *Information and Computation*, 204:123–175, 2006.

[JK06b]   S. Jain and E. Kinber. Learning languages from positive data and negative counterexamples. *Journal of Computer and System Sciences*, 2006. To appear.

[LZ04a]   S. Lange and S. Zilles. Comparison of query learning and Gold-style learning in dependence of the hypothesis space. In Shai Ben-David, John Case, and Akira Maruoka, editors, *Algorithmic Learning Theory: Fifteenth International Conference (ALT' 2004)*, volume 3244 of *Lecture Notes in Artificial Intelligence*, pages 99–113. Springer-Verlag, 2004.

[LZ04b]   S. Lange and S. Zilles. Replacing limit learners with equally powerful one-shot query learners. In John Shawe-Taylor and Yoram Singer, editors, *Proceedings of the Seventeenth Annual Conference on Learning Theory*, volume 3120 of *Lecture Notes in Artificial Intelligence*, pages 155–169. Springer-Verlag, 2004.

[Mot91]   T. Motoki. Inductive inference from all positive and some negative data. *Information Processing Letters*, 39(4):177–182, 1991.

[OW82]   D. Osherson and S. Weinstein. Criteria of language learning. *Information and Control*, 52:123–138, 1982.

[Rog67]   H. Rogers. *Theory of Recursive Functions and Effective Computability*. McGraw-Hill, 1967. Reprinted by MIT Press in 1987.

[WZ94]   R. Wiehagen and T. Zeugmann. Ignoring data may be the only way to learn efficiently. *Journal of Experimental and Theoretical Artificial Intelligence*, 6:131–144, 1994.

[ZL95]   T. Zeugmann and S. Lange. A guided tour across the boundaries of learning recursive languages. In K. Jantke and S. Lange, editors, *Algorithmic Learning for Knowledge-Based Systems*, volume 961 of *Lecture Notes in Artificial Intelligence*, pages 190–258. Springer-Verlag, 1995.

Learning Rational Stochastic Languages

François Denis, Yann Esposito, and Amaury Habrard

Laboratoire d'Informatique Fondamentale de Marseille (L.I.F.) UMR CNRS 6166
{fdenis, esposito, habrard}@cmi.univ-mrs.fr

Abstract. Given a finite set of words $w_1, \ldots, w_n$ independently drawn according to a fixed unknown distribution law P called a *stochastic language*, a usual goal in Grammatical Inference is to infer an estimate of P in some class of probabilistic models, such as *Probabilistic Automata* (PA). Here, we study the class $\mathcal{S}_{\mathbb{R}}^{rat}(\Sigma)$ of *rational stochastic languages*, which consists in stochastic languages that can be generated by *Multiplicity Automata* (MA) and which strictly includes the class of stochastic languages generated by PA. Rational stochastic languages have minimal normal representation which may be very concise, and whose parameters can be efficiently estimated from stochastic samples. We design an efficient inference algorithm DEES which aims at building a minimal normal representation of the target. Despite the fact that no recursively enumerable class of MA computes exactly $\mathcal{S}_{\mathbb{Q}}^{rat}(\Sigma)$, we show that DEES strongly identifies $\mathcal{S}_{\mathbb{Q}}^{rat}(\Sigma)$ in the limit. We study the intermediary MA output by DEES and show that they compute rational series which converge absolutely and which can be used to provide stochastic languages which closely estimate the target.

1 Introduction

In probabilistic grammatical inference, it is supposed that data arise in the form of a finite set of words $w_1, \ldots, w_n$, built on a predefined alphabet Σ, and independently drawn according to a fixed unknown distribution law on Σ^* called a *stochastic language*. Then, a usual goal is to try to infer an estimate of this distribution law in some class of probabilistic models, such as *Probabilistic Automata* (PA), which have the same expressivity as Hidden Markov Models (HMM). PA are identifiable in the limit [6]. However, to our knowledge, there exists no efficient inference algorithm able to deal with the whole class of stochastic languages that can be generated from PA. Most of the previous works use restricted subclasses of PA such as Probabilistic Deterministic Automata (PDA) [5, 13]. On the other hand, Probabilistic Automata are particular cases of *Multiplicity Automata*, and stochastic languages which can be generated by multiplicity automata are special cases of *rational languages* that we call *rational stochastic languages*. MA have been used in grammatical inference in a variant of the exact learning model of Angluin [3, 1, 2] but not in probabilistic grammatical inference. Let us design by $\mathcal{S}_K^{rat}(\Sigma)$, the class of rational stochastic languages over K, where $K \in \{\mathbb{R}, \mathbb{Q}, \mathbb{R}^+, \mathbb{Q}^+\}$. When $K = \mathbb{Q}^+$ or $K = \mathbb{R}^+$, $\mathcal{S}_K^{rat}(\Sigma)$ is exactly the class of stochastic languages generated by PA with parameters in K. But, when $K = \mathbb{Q}$ or $K = \mathbb{R}$, we obtain strictly greater classes which provide several advantages and at least one drawback: elements of $\mathcal{S}_{K^+}^{rat}(\Sigma)$ may have significantly smaller representation in $\mathcal{S}_K^{rat}(\Sigma)$ which is clearly an advantage from a learning perspective; elements of

G. Lugosi and H.U. Simon (Eds.): COLT 2006, LNAI 4005, pp. 274–288, 2006.

$\mathcal{S}_K^{rat}(\Sigma)$ have a minimal normal representation while such normal representations do not exist for PA [7]; parameters of these minimal representations are directly related to probabilities of some natural events of the form $u\Sigma^*$, which can be efficiently estimated from stochastic samples; lastly, when K is a field, rational series over K form a vector space and efficient linear algebra techniques can be used to deal with rational stochastic languages. However, the class $\mathcal{S}_{\mathbb{Q}}^{rat}(\Sigma)$ presents a serious drawback : there exists no recursively enumerable subset of MA which exactly generates it [6]. Moreover, this class of representations is unstable: arbitrarily close to an MA which generates a stochastic language, we may find MA whose associated rational series r takes negative values and is not absolutely convergent: the global weight $\sum_{w\in\Sigma^*} r(w)$ may be unbounded or not (absolutely) defined. However, we show that $\mathcal{S}_{\mathbb{Q}}^{rat}(\Sigma)$ is strongly identifiable in the limit: we design an algorithm DEES which, for any target $P \in \mathcal{S}_{\mathbb{Q}}^{rat}(\Sigma)$ and given access to an infinite sample S drawn according to P, will converge in a finite but unbounded number of steps to a minimal normal representation of P. Moreover, DEES is efficient: it runs within polynomial time in the size of the input and it computes a minimal number of parameters with classical statistical rates of convergence. However, before converging to the target, DEES output MA which are close to the target but which do not compute stochastic languages. The question is: what kind of guarantees do we have on these intermediary hypotheses and how can we use them for a probabilistic inference purpose? We show that, since the algorithm aims at building a minimal normal representation of the target, the intermediary hypotheses r output by DEES have a nice property: they converge absolutely and their limit is 1, i.e. $\sum_{w\in\Sigma^*} |r(w)| < \infty$ and $\sum_{k\geq 0} r(\Sigma^k) = 1$. As a consequence, $r(X)$ is defined without ambiguity for any $X \subseteq \Sigma^*$, and it can be shown that $N_r = \sum_{r(u)<0} |r(u)|$ tends to 0 as the learning proceeds. Given any such series r, we can efficiently compute a stochastic language p_r, which is not rational, but satisfies $\sum_{u\in\Sigma^*} |r(u) - p_r(u)| = 2N_r$. Our conclusion is that, despite the fact that no recursively enumerable class of MA represents the whole class of rational stochastic languages, MA can be used efficiently to infer them.

Classical notions on stochastic languages, rational series, and multiplicity automata are recalled in Section 2. We study an example which shows that the representation of rational stochastic languages by MA with real parameters may be very concise. We introduce our inference algorithm DEES in Section 3 and we show that $\mathcal{S}_{\mathbb{Q}}^{rat}(\Sigma)$ is strongly indentifiable in the limit. We study the properties of the MA output by DEES in Section 4 and we show that they define absolutely convergent rational series which can be used to compute stochastic languages which are estimates of the target.

2   Preliminaries

Formal power series and stochastic languages. Let Σ^* be the set of words on the finite alphabet Σ. The empty word is denoted by ε and the length of a word u is denoted by $|u|$. For any integer k, let $\Sigma^k = \{u \in \Sigma^* : |u| = k\}$ and $\Sigma^{\leq k} = \{u \in \Sigma^* : |u| \leq k\}$. We denote by $<$ the length-lexicographic order on Σ^* and by $MinU$ the minimal element of a non empty set U according to this order; $<$ is extended to 2^{Σ^*} as follows: $U < V$ iff $[U = \emptyset$ and $V \neq \emptyset$ or $MinU < MinV$ or $(MinU = MinV$ and $U\setminus\{MinU\} < V\setminus\{MinV\})]$. A subset P of Σ^* is *prefix-closed* if for any $u, v \in \Sigma^*$,

$uv \in P \Rightarrow u \in P$. For any $S \subseteq \Sigma^*$, let $pref(S) = \{u \in \Sigma^* : \exists v \in \Sigma^*, uv \in S\}$ and $fact(S) = \{v \in \Sigma^* : \exists u, w \in \Sigma^*, uvw \in S\}$.

Let Σ be a finite alphabet and $K \in \{\mathbb{R}, \mathbb{Q}, \mathbb{R}^+, \mathbb{Q}^+\}$. A *formal power series* is a mapping r of Σ^* into K. The set of all formal power series is denoted by $K\langle\langle\Sigma\rangle\rangle$. Let us denote by $supp(r)$ the *support* of r, i.e. the set $\{w \in \Sigma^* : r(w) \neq 0\}$.

A *stochastic language* is a formal series p which takes its values in $\mathbb{R}^+$ and such that $\sum_{w \in \Sigma^*} p(w) = 1$. For any language $L \subseteq \Sigma^*$, let us denote $\sum_{w \in L} p(w)$ by $p(L)$. The set of all stochastic languages over Σ is denoted by $\mathcal{S}(\Sigma)$. For any stochastic language p and any word u such that $p(u\Sigma^*) \neq 0$, we define the stochastic language $u^{-1}p$ by $u^{-1}p(w) = \frac{p(uw)}{p(u\Sigma^*)}$. $u^{-1}p$ is called the *residual language* of p wrt u. Let us denote by $res(p)$ the set $\{u \in \Sigma^* : p(u\Sigma^*) \neq 0\}$ and by $Res(p)$ the set $\{u^{-1}p : u \in res(p)\}$. We call *sample* any finite sequence of words. Let S be a sample. We denote by P_S the empirical distribution on Σ^* associated with S. An *infinite sample* of P is an infinite i.i.d. sample drawn according to P. We denote by S_n the sequence composed of the n first words of S. We shall make a frequent use of the Borel-Cantelli Lemma which states that if $(A_k)_{k \in \mathbb{N}}$ is a sequence of events such that $\sum_{k \in \mathbb{N}} Pr(A_k) < \infty$, then the probability that a finite number of A_k occurs is 1.

Automata. Let $K \in \{\mathbb{R}, \mathbb{Q}, \mathbb{R}^+, \mathbb{Q}^+\}$. A *$K$-multiplicity automaton (MA)* is a 5-tuple $\langle \Sigma, Q, \varphi, \iota, \tau \rangle$ where Q is a finite set of states, $\varphi : Q \times \Sigma \times Q \to K$ is the transition function, $\iota : Q \to K$ is the initialization function and $\tau : Q \to K$ is the termination function. Let $Q_I = \{q \in Q | \iota(q) \neq 0\}$ be the set of *initial states* and $Q_T = \{q \in Q | \tau(q) \neq 0\}$ be the set of *terminal states*. The *support* of an MA $A = \langle \Sigma, Q, \varphi, \iota, \tau \rangle$ is the NFA $supp(A) = \langle \Sigma, Q, Q_I, Q_T, \delta \rangle$ where $\delta(q, x) = \{q' \in Q | \varphi(q, x, q') \neq 0\}$. We extend the transition function φ to $Q \times \Sigma^* \times Q$ by $\varphi(q, wx, r) = \sum_{s \in Q} \varphi(q, w, s)\varphi(s, x, r)$ and $\varphi(q, \varepsilon, r) = 1$ if $q = r$ and 0 otherwise, for any $q, r \in Q$, $x \in \Sigma$ and $w \in \Sigma^*$. For any finite subset $L \subset \Sigma^*$ and any $R \subseteq Q$, define $\varphi(q, L, R) = \sum_{w \in L, r \in R} \varphi(q, w, r)$.

For any MA A, let r_A be the series defined by $r_A(w) = \sum_{q, r \in Q} \iota(q)\varphi(q, w, r)\tau(r)$. For any $q \in Q$, we define the series $r_{A,q}$ by $r_{A,q}(w) = \sum_{r \in Q} \varphi(q, w, r)\tau(r)$. A state $q \in Q$ is *accessible* (resp. *co-accessible*) if there exists $q_0 \in Q_I$ (resp. $q_t \in Q_T$) and $u \in \Sigma^*$ such that $\varphi(q_0, u, q) \neq 0$ (resp. $\varphi(q, u, q_t) \neq 0$). An MA is *trimmed* if all its states are accessible and co-accessible. From now, we only consider trimmed MA.

A *Probabilistic Automaton (PA)* is a trimmed MA $\langle \Sigma, Q, \varphi, \iota, \tau \rangle$ s.t. ι, φ and τ take their values in $[0, 1]$, such that $\sum_{q \in Q} \iota(q) = 1$ and for any state q, $\tau(q) + \varphi(q, \Sigma, Q) = 1$. Probabilistic automata generate stochastic languages. A *Probabilistic Deterministic Automaton (PDA)* is a PA whose support is deterministic.

For any class C of multiplicity automata over K, let us denote by $\mathcal{S}_K^C(\Sigma)$ the class of all stochastic languages which are recognized by an element of C.

Rational series and rational stochastic languages. Rational series have several characterization ([12, 4, 11]). Here, we shall say that a formal power series over Σ is *K-rational* iff there exists a K-multiplicity automaton A such that $r = r_A$, where $K \in \{\mathbb{R}, \mathbb{R}^+, \mathbb{Q}, \mathbb{Q}^+\}$. Let us denote by $K^{rat}\langle\langle\Sigma\rangle\rangle$ the set of K-rational series over Σ and by $\mathcal{S}_K^{rat}(\Sigma) = K^{rat}\langle\langle\Sigma\rangle\rangle \cap \mathcal{S}(\Sigma)$, the set of *rational stochastic languages* over K. Rational stochastic languages have been studied in [7] from a language theoretical

$\mathcal{S}(\Sigma)$	$\mathcal{S}(\Sigma) \cap \mathbb{Q}^+\langle\langle\Sigma\rangle\rangle$
$\mathcal{S}_{\mathbb{R}}^{rat}(\Sigma)$	$\mathcal{S}_{\mathbb{Q}}^{rat}(\Sigma) = \mathcal{S}_{\mathbb{R}}^{rat}(\Sigma) \cap \mathbb{Q}^+(\Sigma)$
$\mathcal{S}_{\mathbb{R}+}^{rat}(\Sigma) = \mathcal{S}_{\mathbb{R}+}^{PA}(\Sigma)$	$\mathcal{S}_{\mathbb{R}+}^{rat}(\Sigma) \cap \mathbb{Q}^+\langle\langle\Sigma\rangle\rangle$
	$\mathcal{S}_{\mathbb{Q}+}^{rat}(\Sigma) = \mathcal{S}_{\mathbb{Q}+}^{PA}(\Sigma)$
$\mathcal{S}_{\mathbb{R}}^{PDA}(\Sigma) = \mathcal{S}_{\mathbb{R}+}^{PDA}(\Sigma)$	$\mathcal{S}_{\mathbb{Q}}^{PDA}(\Sigma) = \mathcal{S}_{\mathbb{Q}+}^{PDA}(\Sigma) = \mathcal{S}_{\mathbb{R}}^{PDA}(\Sigma) \cap \mathbb{Q}\langle\langle\Sigma\rangle\rangle$

Fig. 1. Inclusion relations between classes of rational stochastic languages (see [7])

point of view. Inclusion relations between classes of rational stochastic languages are summarized on Fig 1. It is worth noting that $\mathcal{S}_{\mathbb{R}}^{PDA}(\Sigma) \subsetneq \mathcal{S}_{\mathbb{R}}^{PA}(\Sigma) \subsetneq \mathcal{S}_{\mathbb{R}}^{rat}(\Sigma)$.

Let P be a rational stochastic language. The MA $A = \langle \Sigma, Q, \varphi, \iota, \tau \rangle$ is a *reduced representation* of P if (i) $P = P_A$, (ii) $\forall q \in Q, P_{A,q} \in \mathcal{S}(\Sigma)$ and (iii) the set $\{P_{A,q} : q \in Q\}$ is linearly independent. It can be shown that $Res(P)$ spans a finite dimensional vector subspace $[Res(P)]$ of $\mathbb{R}\langle\langle\Sigma\rangle\rangle$. Let Q_P be the smallest subset of $res(P)$ s.t. $\{u^{-1}P : u \in Q_P\}$ spans $[Res(P)]$. It is a finite prefix-closed subset of Σ^*. Let $A = \langle \Sigma, Q_P, \varphi, \iota, \tau \rangle$ be the MA defined by:

- $\iota(\varepsilon) = 1$, $\iota(u) = 0$ otherwise; $\tau(u) = u^{-1}P(\varepsilon)$,
- $\varphi(u, x, ux) = u^{-1}P(x\Sigma^*)$ if $u, ux \in Q_P$ and $x \in \Sigma$,
- $\varphi(u, x, v) = \alpha_v u^{-1}P(x\Sigma^*)$ if $x \in \Sigma, ux \in (Q_P\Sigma \backslash Q_P) \cap res(P)$ and $(ux)^{-1}P = \sum_{v \in Q_P} \alpha_v v^{-1}P$.

It can be shown that A is a reduced representation of P; A is called the *prefix-closed reduced representation* of P. Note that the parameters of A correspond to natural components of the residual of P and can be estimated by using samples of P.

We give below an example of a rational stochastic language which cannot be generated by a PA. Moreover, for any integer N there exists a rational stochastic language which can be generated by a multiplicity automaton with 3 states and such that the smallest PA which generates it has N states. That is, considering rational stochastic language makes it possible to deal with stochastic languages which cannot be generated by PA; it also permits to significantly decrease the size of their representation.

Proposition 1. *For any $\alpha \in \mathbb{R}$, let A_α be the MA described on Fig. 2. Let $S_\alpha = \{(\lambda_0, \lambda_1, \lambda_2) \in \mathbb{R}^3 : r_{A_\alpha} \in \mathcal{S}(\Sigma)\}$. If $\alpha/(2\pi) = p/q \in \mathbb{Q}$ where p and q are relatively prime, S_α is the convex hull of a polygon with q vertices which are the residual languages of any one of them. If $\alpha/(2\pi) \notin \mathbb{Q}$, S_α is the convex hull of an ellipse, any point of which is a stochastic language that cannot be computed by a PA.*

Proof (sketch). Let r_{q_0}, r_{q_1} and r_{q_2} be the series associated with the states of A_α. We have

$$r_{q_0}(a^n) = \frac{\cos n\alpha - \sin n\alpha}{2^n}, r_{q_1}(a^n) = \frac{\cos n\alpha + \sin n\alpha}{2^n} \text{ and } r_{q_2}(a^n) = \frac{1}{2^n}.$$

The sums $\sum_{n \in \mathbb{N}} r_{q_0}(a^n)$, $\sum_{n \in \mathbb{N}} r_{q_1}(a^n)$ and $\sum_{n \in \mathbb{N}} r_{q_2}(a^n)$ converge since $|r_{q_i}(a^n)| = O(2^{-n})$ for $i = 0, 1, 2$. Let us denote $\sigma_i = \sum_{n \in \mathbb{N}} r_{q_i}(a^n)$ for $i = 0, 1, 2$. Check that

$$\sigma_0 = \frac{4 - 2\cos\alpha - 2\sin\alpha}{5 - 4\cos\alpha}, \quad \sigma_1 = \frac{4 - 2\cos\alpha + 2\sin\alpha}{5 - 4\cos\alpha} \text{ and } \sigma_2 = 2.$$

Consider the 3-dimensional vector subspace $\mathcal{V}$ of $\mathbb{R}\langle\langle\Sigma\rangle\rangle$ generated by r_{q_0}, r_{q_1} and r_{q_2} and let $r = \lambda_0 r_{q_0} + \lambda_1 r_{q_1} + \lambda_2 r_{q_2}$ be a generic element of $\mathcal{V}$. We have $\sum_{n\in\mathbb{N}} r(a^n) = \lambda_0\sigma_0 + \lambda_1\sigma_1 + \lambda_2\sigma_2$. The equation $\lambda_0\sigma_0 + \lambda_1\sigma_1 + \lambda_2\sigma_2 = 1$ defines a plane $\mathcal{H}$ in $\mathcal{V}$.

Consider the constraints $r(a^n) \geq 0$ for any $n \geq 0$. The elements r of $\mathcal{H}$ which satisfies all the constraints $r(a^n) \geq 0$ are exactly the stochastic languages in $\mathcal{H}$.

If $\alpha/(2\pi) = k/h \in \mathbb{Q}$ where k and h are relatively prime, the set of constraints $\{r(a^n) \geq 0\}$ is finite: it delimites a convex regular polygon P in the plane $\mathcal{H}$. Let p be a vertex of P. It can be shown that its residual languages are exactly the h vertices of P and any PA generating p must have at least h states.

If $\alpha/(2\pi) \notin \mathbb{Q}$, the constraints delimite an ellipse E. Let p be an element of E. It can be shown, by using techniques developed in [7], that its residual languages are dense in E and that no PA can generate p. $\qquad\square$

Matrices. We consider the Euclidan norm on $\mathbb{R}^n$: $\|(x_1, \ldots, x_n)\| = (x_1^2 + \ldots + x_n^2)^{1/2}$. For any $R \geq 0$, let us denote by $B(\overrightarrow{0}, R)$ the set $\{x \in \mathbb{R}^n : \|x\| \leq R\}$. The induced norm on the set of $n \times n$ square matrices M over $\mathbb{R}$ is defined by: $\|M\| = sup\{\|Mx\| : x \in \mathbb{R}^n \text{ with } \|x\| = 1\}$. Some properties of the induced norm: $\|Mx\| \leq \|M\| \cdot \|x\|$ for all $M \in \mathbb{R}^{n\times n}, x \in \mathbb{R}^n$; $\|MN\| \leq \|M\| \cdot \|N\|$ for all $M, N \in \mathbb{R}^{n\times n}$; $\lim_{k\to\infty} \|M^k\|^{1/k} = \rho(M)$ where $\rho(M)$ is the *spectral radius* of M, i.e. the maximum magnitude of the eigenvalues of M (Gelfand's Formula).

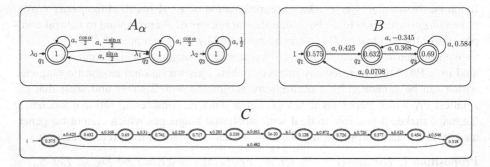

Fig. 2. When $\lambda_0 = \lambda_2 = 1$ and $\lambda_1 = 0$, the MA $A_{\pi/6}$ defines a stochastic language P whose prefixed reduced representation is the MA B (with approximate values on transitions). In fact, P can be computed by a PDA and the smallest PA computing it is C.

3   Identifying $\mathcal{S}_{\mathbb{Q}}^{rat}(\Sigma)$ in the Limit

In this section, we show that the class of rational stochastic languages is *strongly identifiable in the limit* (see [8, 6] for a definition of this learning model).

Let S be a non empty finite sample of Σ^*, let Q be a prefix-closed subset of $pref(S)$, let $v \in pref(S) \setminus Q$, and let $\epsilon > 0$. We denote by $I(Q, v, S, \epsilon)$ the following set of inequalities over the set of variables $\{x_u | u \in Q\}$:

$$I(Q, v, S, \epsilon) = \{|v^{-1}P_S(w\Sigma^*) - \sum_{u \in Q} x_u u^{-1}P_S(w\Sigma^*)| \le \epsilon | w \in fact(S)\} \cup \{\sum_{u \in Q} x_u = 1\}.$$

Let DEES be the following algorithm:

```
Input: a sample S
Output: a prefix-closed reduced MA A = ⟨Σ, Q, φ, ι, τ⟩
Q ← {ε}, ι(ε) = 1, τ(ε) = P_S(ε), F ← Σ ∩ pref(S)
while F ≠ ∅ do {
    v = ux = MinF where u ∈ Σ* and x ∈ Σ, F ← F \ {v}
    if I(Q, v, S, |S|^{-1/3}) has no solution then{
        Q ← Q ∪ {v}, ι(v) = 0, τ(v) = P_S(v)/P_S(vΣ*),
        φ(u, x, v) = P_S(vΣ*)/P_S(uΣ*), F ← F ∪ {vx ∈ res(P_S)|x ∈ Σ}}
    else{
        let (α_w)_{w∈Q} be a solution of I(Q, v, S, |S|^{-1/3})
        φ(u, x, w) = α_w P_S(vΣ*) for any w ∈ Q}}
```

Lemma 1. *Let P be a stochastic language and let $u_0, u_1, \ldots, u_n \in Res(P)$ be such that $\{u_0^{-1}P, u_1^{-1}P, \ldots, u_n^{-1}P\}$ is linearly independent. Then, with probability one, for any infinite sample S of P, there exist a positive number ϵ and an integer M such that $I(\{u_1, \ldots, u_n\}, u_0, S_m, \epsilon)$ has no solution for every $m \ge M$.*

Proof. Let S be an infinite sample of P. Suppose that for every $\epsilon > 0$ and every integer M, there exists $m \ge M$ such that $I(\{u_1, \ldots, u_n\}, u_0, S_m, \epsilon)$ has a solution. Then, for any integer k, there exists $m_k \ge k$ such that $I(\{u_1, \ldots, u_n\}, u_0, S_{m_k}, 1/k)$ has a solution $(\alpha_{1,k}, \ldots, \alpha_{n,k})$. Let $\rho_k = Max\{1, |\alpha_{1,k}|, \ldots, |\alpha_{n,k}|\}$, $\gamma_{0,k} = 1/\rho_k$ and $\gamma_{i,k} = -\alpha_{i,k}/\rho_k$ for $1 \le i \le n$. For every k, $Max\{|\gamma_{i,k}| : 0 \le i \le n\} = 1$. Check that

$$\forall k \ge 0, \left| \sum_{i=0}^{n} \gamma_{i,k} u_i^{-1} P_{S_{m_k}}(w\Sigma^*) \right| \le \frac{1}{\rho_k k} \le \frac{1}{k}.$$

There exists a subsequence $(\alpha_{1,\phi(k)}, \ldots, \alpha_{n,\phi(k)})$ of $(\alpha_{1,k}, \ldots, \alpha_{n,k})$ such that $(\gamma_{0,\phi(k)}, \ldots, \gamma_{n,\phi(k)})$ converges to $(\gamma_0, \ldots, \gamma_n)$. We show below that we should have $\sum_{i=0}^{n} \gamma_i u_i^{-1} P(w\Sigma^*) = 0$ for every word w, which is contradictory with the independence assumption since $Max\{\gamma_i : 0 \le i \le n\} = 1$.

Let $w \in fact(supp(P))$. With probability 1, there exists an integer k_0 such that $w \in fact(S_{m_k})$ for any $k \ge k_0$. For such a k, we can write

$$\gamma_i u_i^{-1} P = (\gamma_i u_i^{-1} P - \gamma_i u_i^{-1} P_{S_{m_k}}) + (\gamma_i - \gamma_{i,\phi(k)}) u_i^{-1} P_{S_{m_k}} + \gamma_{i,\phi(k)} u_i^{-1} P_{S_{m_k}}$$

and therefore

$$|\sum_{i=0}^{n} \gamma_i u_i^{-1} P(w\Sigma^*)| \le \sum_{i=0}^{n} |u_i^{-1}(P - P_{S_{m_k}})(w\Sigma^*))| + \sum_{i=0}^{n} |\gamma_i - \gamma_{i,\phi(k)}| + \frac{1}{k}$$

which converges to 0 when k tends to infinity. $\qquad \square$

Let P be a stochastic language over Σ, let $\mathcal{A} = (A_i)_{i \in I}$ be a family of subsets of Σ^*, let S be a finite sample drawn according to P, and let P_S be the empirical distribution associated with S. It can be shown [14, 10] that for any confidence parameter δ, with a probability greater than $1 - \delta$, for any $i \in I$,

$$|P_S(A_i) - P(A_i)| \le c\sqrt{\tfrac{\text{VC}(\mathcal{A}) - \log \frac{\delta}{4}}{Card(S)}} \tag{1}$$

where $\text{VC}(\mathcal{A})$ is the dimension of Vapnik-Chervonenkis of $\mathcal{A}$ and c is a universal constant. When $\mathcal{A} = (\{w\Sigma^*\})_{w \in \Sigma^*}$, $\text{VC}(\mathcal{A}) \le 2$. Indeed, let $r, s, t \in \Sigma^*$ and let $Y = \{r, s, t\}$. Let u_{rs} (resp. u_{rt}, u_{st}) be the longest prefix shared by r and s (resp. r and t, s and t). One of these 3 words is a prefix of the two other ones. Suppose that u_{rs} is a prefix of u_{rt} and u_{st}. Then, there exists no word w such that $w\Sigma^* \cap Y = \{r, s\}$. Therefore, no subset containing more than two elements can be shattered by $\mathcal{A}$.

Let $\Psi(\epsilon, \delta) = \frac{c^2}{\epsilon^2}(2 - \log \frac{\delta}{4})$.

Lemma 2. *Let $P \in \mathcal{S}(\Sigma)$ and let S be an infinite sample of P. For any precision parameter ϵ, any confidence parameter δ, any $n \ge \Psi(\epsilon, \delta)$, with a probability greater than $1 - \delta$, $|P_n(w\Sigma^*) - P(w\Sigma^*)| \le \epsilon$ for all $w \in \Sigma^*$.*

Proof. Use inequality (1). □

Check that for any α such that $-1/2 < \alpha < 0$ and any $\beta < -1$, if we define $\epsilon_k = k^\alpha$ and $\delta_k = k^\beta$, there exists K such that for all $k \ge K$, we have $k \ge \Psi(\epsilon_k, \delta_k)$. For such choices of α and β, we have $\lim_{k \to \infty} \epsilon_k = 0$ and $\sum_{k \ge 1} \delta_k < \infty$.

Lemma 3. *Let $P \in \mathcal{S}(\Sigma)$, $u_0, u_1, \ldots, u_n \in res(P)$ and $\alpha_1, \ldots, \alpha_n \in \mathbb{R}$ be such that $u_0^{-1}P = \sum_{i=1}^n \alpha_i u_i^{-1}P$. Then, with probability one, for any infinite sample S of P, there exists K s.t. $I(\{u_1, \ldots, u_n\}, u_0, S_k, k^{-1/3})$ has a solution for every $k \ge K$.*

Proof. Let S be an infinite sample of P. Let $\alpha_0 = 1$ and let $R = Max\{|\alpha_i| : 0 \le i \le n\}$. With probability one, there exists K_1 s.t. $\forall k \ge K_1, \forall i = 0, \ldots, n, |u_i^{-1}S_k| \ge \Psi([k^{1/3}(n+1)R]^{-1}, [(n+1)k^2]^{-1})$. Let $k \ge K_1$. For any $X \subseteq \Sigma^*$,

$$|u_0^{-1}P_{S_k}(X) - \sum_{i=1}^n \alpha_i u_i^{-1} P_{S_k}(X)| \le |u_0^{-1}P_{S_k}(X) - u_0^{-1}P(X)| + \sum_{i=1}^n |\alpha_i||u_i^{-1}P_{S_k}(X) - u_i^{-1}P(X)|.$$

From Lemma 2, with probability greater than $1 - 1/k^2$, for any $i = 0, \ldots, n$ and any word w, $|u_i^{-1}P_{S_k}(w\Sigma^*) - u_i^{-1}P(w\Sigma^*)| \le [k^{1/3}(n+1)R]^{-1}$ and therefore, $|u_0^{-1}P_{S_k}(w\Sigma^*) - \sum_{i=1}^n \alpha_i u_i^{-1} P_{S_k}(w\Sigma^*)| \le k^{-1/3}$.

For any integer $k \ge K_1$, let A_k be the event: $|u_0^{-1}P_{S_k}(w\Sigma^*) - \sum_{i=1}^n \alpha_i u_i^{-1} P_{S_k}(w\Sigma^*)| > k^{-1/3}$. Since $Pr(A_k) < 1/k^2$, the probability that a finite number of A_k occurs is 1.

Therefore, with probability 1, there exists an integer K such that for any $k \ge K$, $I(\{u_1, \ldots, u_n\}, u_0, S_k, k^{-1/3})$ has a solution. □

Lemma 4. *Let $P \in \mathcal{S}(\Sigma)$, let $u_0, u_1, \ldots, u_n \in res(P)$ such that $\{u_1^{-1}P, \ldots, u_n^{-1}P\}$ is linearly independent and let $\alpha_1, \ldots, \alpha_n \in \mathbb{R}$ be such that $u_0^{-1}P = \sum_{i=1}^n \alpha_i u_i^{-1}P$. Then, with probability one, for any infinite sample S of P, there exists an integer K such that $\forall k \ge K$, any solution $\widehat{\alpha_1}, \ldots, \widehat{\alpha_n}$ of $I(\{u_1, \ldots, u_n\}, u_0, S_k, k^{-1/3})$ satisfies $|\widehat{\alpha_i} - \alpha_i| < O(k^{-1/3})$ for $1 \le i \le n$.*

Proof. Let $w_1, \ldots, w_n \in \Sigma^*$ be such that the square matrix M defined by $M[i,j] = u_j^{-1}P(w_i\Sigma^*)$ for $1 \leq i,j \leq n$ is invertible. Let $A = (\alpha_1, \ldots, \alpha_n)^t$, $U_0 = (u_0^{-1}P(w_1\Sigma^*), \ldots, u_0^{-1}P(w_n\Sigma^*))^t$. We have $MA = U_0$. Let S be an infinite sample of P, let $k \in \mathbb{N}$ and let $\widehat{\alpha_1}, \ldots, \widehat{\alpha_n}$ be a solution of $I(\{u_1, \ldots, u_n\}, u_0, S_k, k^{-1/3})$. Let M_k be the square matrix defined by $M_k[i,j] = u_j^{-1}P_{S_k}(w_i\Sigma^*)$ for $1 \leq i,j \leq n$, let $A_k = (\widehat{\alpha_1}, \ldots, \widehat{\alpha_n})^t$ and $U_{0,k} = (u_0^{-1}P_{S_k}(w_1\Sigma^*), \ldots, u_0^{-1}P_{S_k}(w_n\Sigma^*))^t$. We have

$$\|M_k A_k - U_{0,k}\|^2 = \sum_{i=1}^{n}[u_0^{-1}P_{S_k}(w_i\Sigma^*) - \sum_{j=1}^{n}\widehat{\alpha_j}u_j^{-1}P_{S_k}(w_i\Sigma^*)]^2 \leq nk^{-2/3}.$$

Check that

$$A - A_k = M^{-1}(MA - U_0 + U_0 - U_{0,k} + U_{0,k} - M_k A_k + M_k A_k - M A_k)$$

and therefore, for any $1 \leq i \leq n$

$$|\alpha_i - \widehat{\alpha_i}| \leq \|A - A_k\| \leq \|M^{-1}\|(\|U_0 - U_{0,k}\| + n^{1/2}k^{-1/3} + \|M_k - M\|\|A_k\|).$$

Now, by using Lemma 2 and Borel-Cantelli Lemma as in the proof of Lemma 3, with probability 1, there exists K such that for all $k \geq K$, $\|U_0 - U_{0,k}\| < O(k^{-1/3})$ and $\|M_k - M\| < O(k^{-1/3})$. Therefore, for all $k \geq K$, any solution $\widehat{\alpha_1}, \ldots, \widehat{\alpha_n}$ of $I(\{u_1, \ldots, u_n\}, u_0, S_k, k^{-1/3})$ satisfies $|\widehat{\alpha_i} - \alpha_i| < O(k^{-1/3})$ for $1 \leq i \leq n$. $\quad\square$

Theorem 1. *Let $P \in S_{\mathbb{R}}^{rat}(\Sigma)$ and A be the prefix-closed reduced representation of P. Then, with probability one, for any infinite sample S of P, there exists an integer K such that for any $k \geq K$, $DEES(S_k)$ returns a multiplicity automaton A_k whose support is the same as A's. Moreover, there exists a constant C such that for any parameter α of A, the corresponding parameter α_k in A_k satisfies $|\alpha - \alpha_k| \leq Ck^{-1/3}$.*

Proof. Let Q_P be the set of states of A, i.e. the smallest prefix-closed subset of $res(P)$ such that $\{u^{-1}P : u \in Q_P\}$ spans the same vector space as $Res(P)$. Let $u \in Q_P$, let $Q_u = \{v \in Q_P | v < u\}$ and let $x \in \Sigma$.

- If $\{v^{-1}P | v \in Q_u \cup \{ux\}\}$ is linearly independent, from Lemma 1, with probability 1, there exists ϵ_{ux} and K_{ux} such that for any $k \geq K_{ux}$, $I(Q_u, ux, S_k, \epsilon_{ux})$ has no solution.
- If there exists $(\alpha_v)_{v \in Q_u}$ such that $(ux)^{-1}P = \sum_{v \in Q_u} \alpha_v v^{-1}P$, from Lemma 3, with probability 1, there exists an integer K_{ux} such that for any $k \geq K_{ux}$, $I(Q_u, ux, S_k, k^{-1/3})$ has a solution.

Therefore, with probability one, there exists an integer K such that for any $k \geq K$, $DEES(S_k)$ returns a multiplicity automaton A_k whose set of states is equal to Q_P. Use Lemmas 2 and 4 to check the last part of the proposition. $\quad\square$

When the target is in $S_{\mathbb{Q}}^{rat}(\Sigma)$, DEES can be used to exactly identify it. The proof is based on the representation of real numbers by continuous fraction. See [9] for a survey on continuous fraction and [6] for a similar application.

Let (ϵ_n) be a sequence of non negative real numbers which converges to 0, let $x \in \mathbb{Q}$, let (y_n) be a sequence of elements of $\mathbb{Q}$ such that $|x - y_n| \leq \epsilon_n$ for all but finitely many

n. It can be shown that there exists an integer N such that, for any $n \geq N$, x is the unique rational number $\frac{p}{q}$ which satisfies $\left| y_n - \frac{p}{q} \right| \leq \epsilon_n \leq \frac{1}{q^2}$. Moreover, the unique solution of these inequalities can be computed from y_n.

Let $P \in S_{\mathbb{Q}}^{rat}(\Sigma)$, let S be an infinite sample of P and let A_k the MA output by DEES on input S_k. Let $\overline{A}_k$ be the MA derived from A_k by replacing every parameter α_k with a solution $\frac{p}{q}$ of $\left| \alpha - \frac{p}{q} \right| \leq k^{-1/4} \leq \frac{1}{q^2}$.

Theorem 2. *Let $P \in S_{\mathbb{Q}}^{rat}(\Sigma)$ and A be the prefix-closed reduced representation of P. Then, with probability one, for any infinite sample S of P, there exists an integer K such that $\forall k \geq K$, $DEES(S_k)$ returns an MA A_k such that $\overline{A}_k = A$.*

Proof. From previous theorem, for every parameter α of A, the corresponding parameter α_k in A_k satisfies $|\alpha - \alpha_k| \leq Ck^{-1/3}$ for some constant C. Therefore, if k is sufficiently large, we have $|\alpha - \alpha_k| \leq k^{-1/4}$ and there exists an integer K such that $\alpha = p/q$ is the unique solution of $\left| \alpha - \frac{p}{q} \right| \leq k^{-1/4} \leq \frac{1}{q^2}$. □

4 Learning Rational Stochastic Languages

DEES runs in polynomial time within the size of the input sample and aims at computing a representation of the target which is minimal and whose parameters depends only on the target. DEES computes estimates which converge reasonably fast to these parameters. That is, DEES compute functions which tend to the target but which are not stochastic languages and it remains to study how they can be used in a grammatical inference perspective.

Any rational stochastic language P defines a vector subspace of $\mathbb{R}\langle\langle \Sigma \rangle\rangle$ in which the stochastic languages form a compact convex subset.

Proposition 2. *Let $p_1, \ldots, p_n$ be n independent stochastic languages. Then, $\Lambda = \{\overrightarrow{\alpha} = (\alpha_1, \ldots, \alpha_n) \in \mathbb{R}^n : \sum_{i=1}^n \alpha_i p_i \in S(\Sigma)\}$ is a compact convex subset of $\mathbb{R}^n$.*

Proof. Check that Λ is closed and convex.

Now, let us show that Λ is bounded. Suppose that for any integer k, there exists $\overrightarrow{\alpha}_k \in \Lambda$ such that $\|\overrightarrow{\alpha}_k\| \geq k$. Since $\overrightarrow{\alpha}_k / \|\overrightarrow{\alpha}_k\|$ belongs to the unit sphere in $\mathbb{R}^n$, which is compact, there exists a subsequence $\overrightarrow{\alpha}_{\phi(k)}$ such that $\overrightarrow{\alpha}_{\phi(k)} / \|\overrightarrow{\alpha}_{\phi(k)}\|$ converges to some $\overrightarrow{\alpha}$ satisfying $\|\overrightarrow{\alpha}\| = 1$. Let $q_k = \sum_{i=1}^n \alpha_{k,i} p_i$ and $r = \sum_{i=1}^n \alpha_i p_i$.

For any $0 < \lambda \leq \|\overrightarrow{\alpha}_k\|$, $p_1 + \lambda \frac{q_k - p_1}{\|\overrightarrow{\alpha}_k\|} = (1 - \frac{\lambda}{\|\overrightarrow{\alpha}_k\|}) p_1 + \frac{\lambda}{\|\overrightarrow{\alpha}_k\|} q_k$ is a stochastic language since $S(\Sigma)$ is convex; for every $\lambda > 0$, $p_1 + \lambda \frac{q_{\phi(k)} - p_1}{\|\overrightarrow{\alpha}_{\phi(k)}\|}$ converges to $p_1 + \lambda r$ when $k \to \infty$, since $\alpha_{\phi(k),i} / \|\overrightarrow{\alpha}_{\phi(k)}\| \to \alpha_i$ and $\|\overrightarrow{\alpha}_{\phi(k)}\| \to \infty$) and $p_1 + \lambda r$ is a stochastic language since Λ is closed. Therefore, for any $\lambda > 0$, $p_1 + \lambda r$ is a stochastic language. Since $p_1(w) + \lambda r(w) \in [0,1]$ for every word w, we must have $r = 0$, i.e. $\alpha_i = 0$ for any $1 \leq i \leq n$ since the languages $p_1, \ldots, p_n$ are independent, which is impossible since $\|\overrightarrow{\alpha}\| = 1$. Therefore, Λ is bounded. □

The MA A output by DEES generally do not compute stochastic languages. However, we wish that the series r_A they compute share some properties with them. Next proposition gives sufficient conditions which guaranty that $\sum_{k \geq 0} r_A(\Sigma^k) = 1$.

Proposition 3. *Let $A = \langle \Sigma, Q = \{q_1, \ldots, q_n\}, \varphi, \iota, \tau \rangle$ be an MA and let M be the square matrix defined by $M[i,j] = [\varphi(q_i, \Sigma, q_j)]_{1 \leq i,j \leq n}$. Suppose that the spectral radius of M satisfies $\rho(M) < 1$. Let $\overrightarrow{\iota} = (\iota(q_1), \ldots, \iota(q_n))$ and $\overrightarrow{\tau} = (\tau(q_1), \ldots, \tau(q_n))^t$.*

1. *Then, the matrix $(I - M)$ is invertible and $\sum_{k \geq 0} M^k$ converges to $(I - M)^{-1}$.*
2. *$\forall q_i \in Q, \forall K \geq 0, \sum_{k \geq K} r_{A,q_i}(\Sigma^k)$ converges to $M^K \sum_{j=1}^{n}(I - M)^{-1}[i,j]\tau(q_j)$ and $\sum_{k \geq K} r_A(\Sigma^k)$ converges to $\overrightarrow{\iota}^t M^K (I - M)^{-1} \overrightarrow{\tau}$.*
3. *If $\forall q \in Q, \tau(q) + \varphi(q, \Sigma, Q) = 1$, then $\forall q \in Q, r_{A,q}(\sum_{k \geq 0} \Sigma^k) = 1$. If moreover $\sum_{q \in Q} \iota(q) = 1$, then $r(\sum_{k \geq 0} \Sigma^k) = 1$.*

Proof. 1. Since $\rho(M) < 1$, 1 is not an eigenvalue of M and $I - M$ is invertible. From Gelfand's formula, $\lim_{k \to \infty} \|M^k\| = 0$. Since for any integer k, $(I - M)(I + M + \ldots + M^k) = I - M^{k+1}$, the sum $\sum_{k \geq 0} M^k$ converges to $(I - M)^{-1}$.

2. Since $r_{A,q_i}(\Sigma^k) = \sum_{j=1}^{n} M^k[i,j]\tau(q_j)$, $\sum_{k \geq K} r_{A,q_i}(\Sigma^k) = M^K \sum_{j=1}^{n}(1 - M)^{-1}[i,j]\tau(q_j)$ and $\sum_{k \geq K} r_A(\Sigma^k) = \sum_{i=1}^{n} \iota(q_i) r_{A,q_i}(\Sigma^{\geq K}) = \overrightarrow{\iota}^t M^K (I - M)^{-1} \overrightarrow{\tau}$.

3. Let $s_i = r_{A,q_i}(\Sigma^*)$ for $1 \leq i \leq n$ and $\overrightarrow{s} = (s_1, \ldots, s_n)^t$. We have $(I - M)\overrightarrow{s} = \overrightarrow{\tau}$. Since $I - M$ is invertible, there exists one and only one s such that $(I - M)\overrightarrow{s} = \overrightarrow{\tau}$. But since $\tau(q) + \varphi(q, \Sigma, Q) = 1$ for any state q, the vector $(1, \ldots, 1)^t$ is clearly a solution. Therefore, $s_i = 1$ for $1 \leq i \leq n$. If $\sum_{q \in Q} \iota(q) = 1$, then $r(\Sigma^*) = \sum_{q \in Q} \iota(q) r_{A,q}(\Sigma^*) = 1$. □

Proposition 4. *Let $A = \langle \Sigma, Q, \varphi, \iota, \tau \rangle$ be a reduced representation of a stochastic language P. Let $Q = \{q_1, \ldots, q_n\}$ and let M be the square matrix defined by $M[i,j] = [\varphi(q_i, \Sigma, q_j)]_{1 \leq i,j \leq n}$. Then the spectral radius of M satisfies $\rho(M) < 1$.*

Proof. From Prop. 2, let R be such that $\{\overrightarrow{\alpha} \in \mathbb{R}^n : \sum_{i=1}^{n} \alpha_i P_{A,q_i} \in \mathcal{S}(\Sigma)\} \subseteq B(\overrightarrow{0}, R)$. For every $u \in res(P_A)$ and every $1 \leq i \leq n$, we have

$$u^{-1} P_{A,q_i} = \frac{\sum_{1 \leq j \leq n} \varphi(q_i, u, q_j) P_{A,q_j}}{P_{A,q_i}(u\Sigma^*)}.$$

Therefore, for every word u and every k, we have $|\varphi(q_i, u, q_j)| \leq R \cdot P_{A,q_i}(u\Sigma^*)$ and

$$|\varphi(q_i, \Sigma^k, q_j)| \leq \sum_{u \in \Sigma^k} |\varphi(q_i, u, q_j)| \leq R \cdot P_{A,q_i}(\Sigma^{\geq k}).$$

Now, let λ be an eigenvalue of M associated with the eigenvector v and let i be an index such that $|v_i| = Max\{|v_j| : j = 1, \ldots, n\}$. For every integer k, we have

$$M^k v = \lambda^k v \text{ and } |\lambda^k v_i| = |\sum_{j=1}^{n} \varphi(q_i, \Sigma^k, q_j) v_j| \leq nR \cdot P_{A,q_i}(\Sigma^{\geq k})|v_i|$$

which implies that $|\lambda| < 1$ since $P_{A,q_i}(\Sigma^{\geq k})$ converges to 0 when $k \to \infty$. □

If the spectral radius of a matrix is < 1, the power of M decrease exponentially fast.

Lemma 5. *Let* $M \in \mathbb{R}^{n \times n}$ *be such that* $\rho(M) < 1$. *Then, there exists* $C \in \mathbb{R}$ *and* $\rho \in [0, 1[$ *such that for any integer* $k \geq 0$, $\|M^k\| \leq C\rho^k$.

Proof. Let $\rho \in]\rho(M), 1[$. From Gelfand's formula, there exists an integer K such that for any $k \geq K$, $\|M^k\|^{1/k} \leq \rho$. Let $C = Max\{\|M^h\|/\rho^h : h < K\}$. Let $k \in \mathbb{N}$ and let $a, b \in \mathbb{N}$ be such that $k = aK + b$ and $b < K$. We have

$$\|M^k\| = \|M^{aK+b}\| \leq \|M^{aK}\| \|M^b\| \leq \rho^{aK} \|M^b\| \leq \rho^k \frac{\|M^b\|}{\rho^b} \leq C\rho^k.$$

Proposition 5. *Let* $P \in \mathcal{S}_{\mathbb{R}}^{rat}(\Sigma)$. *There exists a constant* C *and* $\rho \in [0, 1[$ *such that for any integer* k, $P(\Sigma^{\geq k}) \leq C\rho^k$.

Proof. Let $A = \langle \Sigma, Q, \varphi, \iota, \tau \rangle$ be a reduced representation of P and let M be the square matrix defined by $M[i, j] = [\varphi(q_i, \Sigma, q_j)]_{1 \leq i, j \leq n}$. From Prop. 4, the spectral radius of M is <1. From Lemma 5, there exists C_1 and $\rho \in [0, 1[$ such that $\|M^k\| \leq C_1 \rho^k$ for every integer k. Let $\vec{\iota_A} = (\iota(q_1), \ldots, \iota(q_n))$ and $\vec{\tau_A} = (\tau(q_1), \ldots, \tau(q_n))^t$. We have

$$P(\Sigma^{\geq k}) \leq \|\iota_A\| \cdot \|M^k\| \cdot \|(I - M)^{-1}\| \cdot \|\vec{\tau_A}\| \leq C\rho^k$$

with $C = C_1 \|\vec{\iota_A}\| \cdot \|(1 - M)^{-1}\| \cdot \|\vec{\tau_A}\|$. □

It is not difficult to design an MA A which generates a stochastic language P and such that $\varphi(q, u, q')$ is unbounded when $u \in \Sigma^*$. However, the next proposition proves that this situation never happens when A is a reduced representation of P.

Proposition 6. *Let* $P \in \mathcal{S}_{\mathbb{R}}^{rat}(\Sigma)$ *and let* $A = \langle \Sigma, Q, \varphi, \iota, \tau \rangle$ *be a reduced representation of* P. *Then, there exists a constant* C *and* $\rho \in [0, 1[$ *such that for any integer* k *and any pair of states* q, q', $\sum_{u \in \Sigma^k} |\varphi(q, u, q')| \leq C\rho^k$.

Proof. Let k be an integer and let $q, q' \in Q$. Let $P_k = \{u \in \Sigma^k : \varphi(q, u, q') \geq 0\}$ and $N_k = \Sigma^k \setminus P_k$.

$$P_k^{-1} P_{A,q} = \sum_{u \in P_k} \frac{P_{A,q}(u\Sigma^*)}{\sum_{u \in P_k} P_{A,q}(u\Sigma^*)} u^{-1} P_{A,q} = \sum_{q'' \in Q} \frac{\sum_{u \in P_k} \varphi(q, u, q'')}{\sum_{u \in P_k} P_{A,q}(u\Sigma^*)} P_{A,q''}$$

is a stochastic language which is a linear combination of the independent stochastic languages $P_{A,q''}$. From prop. 2, there exists a constant R which depends only on A s.t.

$$\left| \sum_{u \in P_k} \varphi(q, u, q') \right| = \sum_{u \in P_k} \varphi(q, u, q') \leq R \sum_{u \in P_k} P_{A,q}(u\Sigma^*).$$

Similarly, we have $|\sum_{u \in N_k} \varphi(q, u, q')| = \sum_{u \in N_k} |\varphi(q, u, q')| \leq R \sum_{u \in N_k} P_{A,q}(u\Sigma^*)$. Let C and $\rho \in]0, 1[$ be such that $P_{A,q}(\Sigma^{\geq k}) \leq C\rho^k$ for any state q and any integer k. We have

$$\sum_{u \in \Sigma^k} |\varphi(q, u, q')| \leq R \sum_{u \in \Sigma^k} P_{A,q}(u\Sigma^*) \leq RC\rho^k.$$

□

MA representation of rational stochastic languages are unstable (see Fig. 3). Arbitrarily close to an MA A which generates a stochastic language, we can find an MA B such that the sum $\sum_{w \in \Sigma^*} r_B(w)$ converges to any real number or even diverges. However, the next theorem shows that when A is a reduced representation of a stochastic language, any MA B sufficiently close to A defines a series which is absolutely convergent. Moreover, simple syntactical conditions ensure that $r_B(\Sigma^*) = 1$.

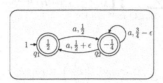

Fig. 3. These MA compute a series r_ϵ such that $\sum_{w \in \Sigma^*} r_\epsilon(w) = 1$ if $\epsilon \neq 0$ and $\sum_{w \in \Sigma^*} r_0(w) = 2/5$. Note that when $\epsilon = 0$, the series r_{0,q_1} and r_{0,q_2} are dependent.

Theorem 3. *Let $P \in \mathcal{S}^{rat}_{\mathbb{R}}(\Sigma)$ and let $A = \langle \Sigma, Q, \varphi_A, \iota_A, \tau_A \rangle$ be a reduced representation of P. Let C_A and $\rho_A \in]0, 1[$ be such that for any integer k and any pair of states q, q', $\sum_{u \in \Sigma^k} |\varphi_A(q, u, q')| \leq C_A \rho^k_A$. Then, for any $\rho > \rho_A$, there exists C and $\alpha > 0$ such that for any MA $B = \langle \Sigma, Q, \varphi_B, \iota_B, \tau_B \rangle$ satisfying*

$$\forall q, q' \in Q, \forall x \in \Sigma, |\varphi_A(q, x, q') - \varphi_B(q, x, q')| < \alpha \tag{2}$$

we have $\sum_{u \in \Sigma^k} |\varphi_B(q, u, q')| \leq C\rho^k$ for any pair of states q, q' and any integer k. As a consequence, the series r_B is absolutely convergent. Moreover, if B satisfies also

$$\forall q \in Q, \tau_B(q) + \varphi_B(q, \Sigma, Q) = 1 \text{ and } \sum_{q \in Q} \iota_B(q) = 1 \tag{3}$$

then, α can be chosen s.t. (2) implies $r_{B,q}(\Sigma^*) = 1$ for any state q and $r_B(\Sigma^*) = 1$.

Proof. Let k be such that $(2nC_A)^{1/k} \leq \rho/\rho_A$ where $n = |Q|$. There exists $\alpha > 0$ such that for any MA $B = \langle \Sigma, Q, \varphi_B, \iota_B, \tau_B \rangle$ satisfying (2), we have

$$\forall q, q' \in Q, \sum_{u \in \Sigma^k} |\varphi_B(q, u, q') - \varphi_A(q, u, q')| < C_A \rho^k_A.$$

Since $\sum_{u \in \Sigma^k} |\varphi_A(q, u, q')| \leq C_A \rho^k_A$, we must have also

$$\sum_{u \in \Sigma^k} |\varphi_B(q, u, q')| \leq 2C_A \rho^k_A \leq \frac{\rho^k}{n}.$$

Let $C_1 = Max\{\sum_{u \in \Sigma^{<k}} |\varphi_B(q, u, q')| : q, q' \in Q\}$. Let $l, a, b \in \mathbb{N}$ such that $l = ak + b$ and $b < k$. Let $u \in \Sigma^l$ and let $u = u_0 \ldots u_a$ where $|u_i| = k$ for $0 \leq i < a$ and $|u_a| = b$. For any pair of states q_0, q_{a+1}, we have

$$\varphi_B(q_0, u, q_{a+1}) = \sum_{q_1, \ldots, q_a \in Q} \prod_{i=0}^{a} \varphi_B(q_i, u_i, q_{i+1}) \text{ and}$$

$$\sum_{u\in\Sigma^l}\varphi_B(q_0,u,q_{a+1}) = \sum_{u_0,...,u_{a-1}\in\Sigma^k}\sum_{u_a\in\Sigma^b}\sum_{q_1,...,q_a\in Q}\prod_{i=0}^{a}\varphi_B(q_i,u_i,q_{i+1})$$

$$= \sum_{q_1,...,q_a\in Q}\sum_{u_0,...,u_{a-1}\in\Sigma^k}\sum_{u_a\in\Sigma^b}\prod_{i=0}^{a}\varphi_B(q_i,u_i,q_{i+1})$$

$$= \sum_{q_1,...,q_a\in Q}\prod_{i=0}^{a-1}(\sum_{u\in\Sigma^k}\varphi_B(q_i,u,q_{i+1}))(\sum_{u\in\Sigma^b}\varphi_B(q_a,u_i,q_{a+1})).$$

Hence, $\sum_{u\in\Sigma^l}|\varphi_B(q_0,u,q_{m+1})| \leq n^a \cdot \left(\frac{\rho^k}{n}\right)^a \cdot C_1 \leq C\rho^l$ where $C = \frac{C_1}{\rho^{k-1}}$.
Now, let us prove that r_B is absolutely convergent.

$$\sum_{w\in\Sigma^*}|r_B(w)| \leq \sum_{k\in\mathbb{N}}\sum_{u\in\Sigma^k}\sum_{q,q'\in Q}\iota_B(q)\varphi_B(q,u,q')\tau_B(q') \leq C'$$

where $C' = Cn^2Max\{|\iota_B(q)\tau_B(q')| : q,q' \in Q\}/(1-\rho)$.

Lastly, let M_B be the square matrix defined by $M_B[i,j] = \varphi_B(q_i,\Sigma,q_j)$. Since the spectral radius of a matrix depends continuously on its coefficients and since A is a reduced representation of a stochastic language, any MA satisfying (2) with α sufficiently small must have a spectral radius <1 (Prop. 4). Therefore, if B satisfies (3) and (2) with α sufficiently small, the Prop. 3 entails the conclusion. □

As a consequence, when the input samples are drawn according to a stochastic rational language P, with probability one, DEES computes rational series r which converge absolutely from some step and satisfy $r(\Sigma^*) = 1$. Moreover, it can easily be shown that for any $\epsilon > 0$, $\sum_{u\in\Sigma^*}|r(u) - P(u)| < \epsilon$ from some step of learning.

It remains to show how a series which converges absolutely and whose limit is 1 can be used to approximate a stochastic language.

Let r be a series over Σ such that $\sum_{w\in\Sigma^*}r(w)$ converges absolutely and whose limit is 1. Therefore, $r(X) = \sum_{u\in X}r(u)$ is defined without ambiguity for every $X \subseteq \Sigma^*$ and $r(X)$ is bounded by $\sum_{u\in\Sigma^*}|r(u)|$. Let S be the smallest subset of Σ^* such that $\varepsilon \in S$ and $\forall u \in \Sigma^*, \forall x \in \Sigma, u \in S$ and $r(ux\Sigma^*) > 0 \Rightarrow ux \in S$. S is a prefix-closed subset of Σ^* and $\forall u \in S, r(u\Sigma^*) > 0$. For every word $u \in S$, let us define $N(u) = \cup\{ux\Sigma^* : x \in \Sigma, r(ux\Sigma^*) \leq 0\} \cup \{u : \text{if } r(u) \leq 0\}$ and $N = \cup\{N(u) : u \in \Sigma^*\}$. Then, for every $u \in S$, let us define λ_u by:

$$\lambda_\varepsilon = (1 - r(N(\varepsilon)))^{-1} \text{ and } \lambda_{ux} = \lambda_u\frac{r(ux\Sigma^*)}{r(ux\Sigma^*) - r(N(ux))}.$$

Check that $r(N(u)) \leq 0$ for every $u \in S$ and therefore, $\lambda_u \leq 1$.
Let p_r be the series defined by: $p_r(u) = 0$ if $u \in N$ and $p_r(u) = \lambda_u r(u)$ otherwise. We show that p_r is a stochastic language.

Lemma 6. *1.* $p_r(\varepsilon) + \lambda_\varepsilon \sum_{x \in S \cap \Sigma} r(x\Sigma^*) = 1$.
2. For any $u \in \Sigma^*$ and any $x \in \Sigma$, if $ux \in S$ then

$$p_r(ux) + \lambda_{ux} \sum_{\{y \in \Sigma : uxy \in S\}} r(uxy\Sigma^*) = \lambda_u r(ux\Sigma^*).$$

Proof. First, check that for every $u \in S$,

$$p_r(u) + \lambda_u \sum_{x \in u^{-1}S \cap \Sigma} r(ux\Sigma^*) = \lambda_u(r(u\Sigma^*) - r(N(u))).$$

Then, $p_r(\varepsilon) + \lambda_\varepsilon \sum_{x \in S \cap \Sigma} r(x\Sigma^*) = \lambda_\varepsilon(1 - r(N(\varepsilon))) = 1$. Now, let $u \in \Sigma^*$ and $x \in \Sigma$ s.t. $ux \in S$, $p_r(ux) + \lambda_{ux} \sum_{\{y \in \Sigma : uxy \in S\}} r(uxy\Sigma^*) = \lambda_{ux}(r(ux\Sigma^*) - r(N(ux))) = \lambda_u r(ux\Sigma^*)$. □

Lemma 7. *Let Q be a prefix-closed finite subset of Σ^* and let $Q_s = (Q\Sigma \setminus Q) \cap S$. Then*

$$p_r(Q) = 1 - \sum_{ux \in Q_s, x \in \Sigma} \lambda_u r(ux\Sigma^*).$$

Proof. By induction on Q. When $Q = \{\varepsilon\}$, the relation comes directly from Lemma 6. Now, suppose that the relation is true for a prefix-closed subset Q', let $u_0 \in Q'$ and $x_0 \in \Sigma$ such that $u_0x_0 \notin Q'$ and let $Q = Q' \cup \{u_0x_0\}$. We have

$$p_r(Q) = p_r(Q') + p_r(u_0x_0) = 1 - \sum_{ux \in Q'_s, x \in \Sigma} \lambda_u r(ux\Sigma^*) + p_r(u_0x_0)$$

where $Q'_s = (Q'\Sigma \setminus Q') \cap S$, from inductive hypothesis.

If $u_0x_0 \notin S$, check that $p_r(u_0x_0) = 0$ and that $Q_s = Q'_s$. Therefore, $p_r(Q) = 1 - \sum_{ux \in Q_s, x \in \Sigma} \lambda_u r(ux\Sigma^*)$.

If $u_0x_0 \in S$, then $Q_s = Q'_s \setminus \{u_0x_0\} \cup (u_0x_0\Sigma \cap S)$. Therefore,

$$p_r(Q) = 1 - \sum_{ux \in Q_s, x \in \Sigma} \lambda_u r(ux\Sigma^*) - \lambda_{u_0} r(u_0x_0\Sigma^*)$$

$$+ \lambda_{u_0x_0} \sum_{u_0x_0x \in S, x \in \Sigma} r(u_0x_0x\Sigma^*) + p_r(u_0x_0)$$

$$= 1 - \sum_{ux \in Q_s, x \in \Sigma} \lambda_u r(ux\Sigma^*) \text{ from Lemma 6.} \qquad \square$$

Proposition 7. *Let r be a formal series over Σ such that $\sum_{w \in \Sigma^*} r(w) = 1$ the convergence being absolute. Then, p_r is a stochastic language. Moreover, $\sum_{u \in \Sigma^*} |r(u) - p_r(u)| = 2N_r$, where $N_r = \sum_{r(u) < 0} |r(u)|$.*

Proof. Clearly, $p_r(u) \in [0, 1]$ for every word u. From Lemma 7, for any integer k, $|1 - p_r(\Sigma^{\leq k})| \leq \sum_{|u| > k} |r(u)|$ which tends to 0 since r is absolutely convergent. Next, $\sum_{u \in \Sigma^*} |r(u) - p_r(u)| = \sum_{r(u) \geq 0}(r(u) - p_r(u)) - \sum_{r(u) < 0} r(u)$ since $r(u) < 0$ implies that $p_r(u) = 0$ and $r(u) \geq 0$ implies that $p_r(u) \leq r(u)$. Therefore, $\sum_{u \in \Sigma^*} |r(u) - p_r(u)| = 2N_r$ since $\sum_{u \in \Sigma^*} p_r(u) = 1$ and $\sum_{r(u) \geq 0} r(u) = 1 + N_r$. □

To sum up, given samples of a rational stochastic language p, from some steps, DEES computes MA whose structure is equal to the structure of the prefix-closed reduced representation of the target and whose parameters tend reasonably fast to the true parameters. These MA define absolutely convergent rational series r that converge to 1. Stochastic langages p_r can naturally be associated with these series, with the property that $\sum_{u \in \Sigma^*} |p(u) - p_r(u)|$ tends to 0 as the learning proceeds.

5   Conclusion

We have defined an inference algorithme DEES designed to learn rational stochastic languages which strictly contains the class of stochastic languages computable by PA (or HMM). We have shown that the class of rational stochastic languages over $\mathbb{Q}$ is strongly identifiable in the limit. Moreover, DEES is an efficient inference algorithm which can be used in practical cases of grammatical inference. The experiments we have already carried out confirm the theoretical results of this paper: the fact that DEES aims at building a natural and minimal representation of the target provides a very significant improvement of the results obtained by classical probabilistic inference algorithms.

References

1. A. Beimel, F. Bergadano, N. H. Bshouty, E. Kushilevitz, and S. Varricchio. On the applications of multiplicity automata in learning. In *IEEE Symposium on Foundations of Computer Science*, pages 349–358, 1996.
2. A. Beimel, F. Bergadano, N. H. Bshouty, E. Kushilevitz, and S. Varricchio. Learning functions represented as multiplicity automata. *Journal of the ACM*, 47(3):506–530, 2000.
3. F. Bergadano and S. Varricchio. Learning behaviors of automata from multiplicity and equivalence queries. In *Italian Conf. on Algorithms and Complexity*, 1994.
4. J. Berstel and C. Reutenauer. *Les séries rationnelles et leurs langages*. Masson, 1984.
5. R.C. Carrasco and J. Oncina. Learning stochastic regular grammars by means of a state merging method. In *ICGI*, pages 139–152, Heidelberg, September 1994. Springer-Verlag.
6. F. Denis and Y. Esposito. Learning classes of probabilistic automata. In *COLT 2004*, number 3120 in LNAI, pages 124–139, 2004.
7. F. Denis and Y. Esposito. Rational stochastic languages. Technical report, LIF - Université de Provence, http://hal.ccsd.cnrs.fr/ccsd-00019728, 2006.
8. E.M. Gold. Language identification in the limit. *Inform. Control*, 10:447–474, 1967.
9. G. H. Hardy and E. M. Wright. *An introduction to the theory of numbers*. Oxford University Press, 1979.
10. G. Lugosi. *Principles of Nonparametric Learning*, chapter Pattern classification and learning theory, pages 1–56. Springer, 2002.
11. J. Sakarovitch. *Éléments de théorie des automates*. Éditions Vuibert, 2003.
12. A. Salomaa and M. Soittola. *Automata: Theoretic Aspects of Formal Power Series*. Springer-Verlag, 1978.
13. F. Thollard, P. Dupont, and C. de la Higuera. Probabilistic DFA inference using Kullback-Leibler divergence and minimality. In *Proc. 17th ICML*. KAUFM, 975–982.
14. V. N. Vapnik. *Statistical Learning Theory*. John Wiley, 1998.

Parent Assignment Is Hard
for the MDL, AIC, and NML Costs

Mikko Koivisto

HIIT Basic Research Unit, Department of Computer Science
Gustaf Hällströmin katu 2b, FIN-00014 University of Helsinki, Finland
mikko.koivisto@cs.helsinki.fi

Abstract. Several hardness results are presented for the parent assignment problem: Given m observations of n attributes $x_1, \ldots, x_n$, find the best parents for x_n, that is, a subset of the preceding attributes so as to minimize a fixed cost function. This attribute or feature selection task plays an important role, e.g., in structure learning in Bayesian networks, yet little is known about its computational complexity. In this paper we prove that, under the commonly adopted full-multinomial likelihood model, the MDL, BIC, or AIC cost cannot be approximated in polynomial time to a ratio less than 2 unless there exists a polynomial-time algorithm for determining whether a directed graph with n nodes has a dominating set of size $\log n$, a LOGSNP-complete problem for which no polynomial-time algorithm is known; as we also show, it is unlikely that these penalized maximum likelihood costs can be approximated to within any constant ratio. For the NML (normalized maximum likelihood) cost we prove an NP-completeness result. These results both justify the application of existing methods and motivate research on heuristic and super-polynomial-time algorithms.

1   Introduction

Structure learning in Bayesian networks is often approached by minimizing a sum of costs assigned to each local structure consisting of an attribute and its parents [1, 2]. If an ordering of the attributes is given, then the subtasks of assigning optimal parents to each attribute can be solved independently of each other. Unfortunately, for many objective functions of interest, no polynomial time algorithm is known, unless one is willing to bound the number of parents above by a constant, in which case the problem can be solved in polynomial time. Consequently, researchers have proposed greedy algorithms with no performance guarantees [1] and heuristic branch-and-bound methods that find a global optimum but can be very slow in the worst case [3, 4]. However, the precise complexity of the parent assignment problem, even for the most commonly used cost functions, is unknown.

This paper focuses on the following variant of the parent assignment problem: given a data set containing m observations on n discrete attributes $x_1, \ldots, x_n$, find the parents $x_{s_1}, \ldots, x_{s_k}$ for x_n so as to minimize the Minimum Description

G. Lugosi and H.U. Simon (Eds.): COLT 2006, LNAI 4005, pp. 289–303, 2006.

Length (MDL) cost [5] under the full-multinomial model[1] [6]. This commonly adopted cost function has the important property that the optimal number of parents is always at most $\log m$ (throughout this paper we write $\log m$ for $\lceil \log_2 m \rceil$). This is because the number of parameters of the multinomial model grows exponentially in the number of parents k, whereas the error, or the negative log-likelihood, grows at most linearly in the number of observations m [7]. That said, only $O(n^{\log m})$ smallest subsets of the $n - 1$ attributes need to be evaluated, suggesting that the problem is very unlikely to be NP-hard (see, e.g., Papadimitriou and Yannakakis [8]). Still, it is important and intriguing to determine whether the problem can be solved in polynomial time.

In this paper we show that for the (two-part) MDL cost the parent assignment problem is LOGSNP-hard, in other words, at least as hard as determining whether a directed graph with n nodes has a dominating set of size $\log n$ [8]; for this LOG DOMINATING SET problem no polynomial-time algorithm is known.

Having this result, it is natural to ask whether similar results hold for other penalized maximum likelihood costs, such as Akaike's information criterion (AIC) [9] and the Normalized Maximum Likelihood (NML) criterion [10, 11]; note that the Bayesian information criterion (BIC) [12] coincides with the MDL cost. Our finding is that while MDL and AIC obey identical characterizations in terms of LOGSNP-hardness, the behavior of NML seems to be radically different: On one hand, we show that approximating the MDL or AIC cost to a ratio less than 2 is LOGSNP-hard. On the other hand, for the NML cost we can obtain an NP-completeness result; however, we currently do not know any nontrivial inapproximability result for NML.

While these results are somewhat theoretical and perhaps not very surprising, they provide evidence that the considered parent assignment problem is very unlikely to have a polynomial-time algorithm with a good quality guarantee. This justifies and motivates the application of existing search heuristics and, more importantly, research on novel super-polynomial-time algorithms.

The rest of this paper is structured as follows. In Sect. 2 we formulate some decision and optimization variants of the parent assignment problem for penalized maximum likelihood costs under the full-multinomial model. In Sect. 3 we prove the LOGSNP-hardness result for MDL by a simple reduction from LOG DOMINATING SET; this part introduces the reduction in a relatively easy and clean manner. We then use essentially the same reduction in Sect. 4 to prove the inapproximability results for MDL and AIC. We consider the case of NML in Sect. 5. In Sect. 6 we discuss some open problems and related previous work.

2 Preliminaries

For simplicity, we restrict our consideration to $\{0, 1\}$-valued attributes. Let X be an $m \times n$ data matrix, where the entry at the ith row and jth column, denoted as x_j^i, represents the ith observation of the jth attribute; submatrices are referred

---

[1] In the full-multinomial model each value configuration of the parent attributes is assigned an independent multinomial distribution of x_n.

to by indexing with subsets of row and column indexes. To distinguish between attributes and columns of the data matrix we denote x_j and x_S for the attributes, but $\mathbf{x}_j$ and $\mathbf{x}_S$ for the respective columns of X.

2.1 Penalized Maximum Likelihood Under the Full-Multinomial Model

The multinomial model of conditional probability concerns the probability distribution of a "child" variable, say x_n^i, given a set of "parents," say x_S^i where $S \subseteq \{1, \ldots, n-1\}$. In case of binary variables, this model has $2^{|S|}$ parameters $\theta_{1|u}$, one for each possible value u of x_S, specifying the probability of $x_n^i = 1$ given $x_S^i = u$, for all $i = 1, \ldots, m$; this is, in fact, a Bernoulli distribution for each value of x_S. It is convenient to also define $\theta_{0|u} = 1 - \theta_{1|u}$. The m observations are treated as independent draws, so that the total likelihood of $\mathbf{x}_n$, conditionally on $\mathbf{x}_S$, is given by

$$\prod_{i=1}^{m} \theta_{x_n^i | x_S^i} = \prod_{u \in \{0,1\}^{|S|}} \prod_{v \in \{0,1\}} \theta_{v|u}^{m_{uv}},$$

where $m_{uv} = |\{i : x_S^i = u, x_n^i = v\}|$ is the number of observations that has value u on columns S and value v on column n. It is easy to find the maximizing parameter values: $\theta_{v|u} = m_{uv}/m_u$, where $m_u = |\{i : x_S^i = u\}|$ is the number of observations that has value u on column n.

Various forms of penalized maximum likelihood can be used as a criterion for choosing between different sets of parents. These criteria operate quantitatively in the logarithmic scale. The negative of the maximum log likelihood,

$$\beta(\mathbf{x}_S, \mathbf{x}_n) = - \sum_{u \in \{0,1\}^{|S|}} \sum_{v \in \{0,1\}} m_{uv} \log \frac{m_{uv}}{m_u},$$

gets a small value when the model fits well the data; $\beta(\mathbf{x}_n, \mathbf{x}_S)$ can be viewed as the number of bits needed to describe $\mathbf{x}_n$ given $\mathbf{x}_S$ and the estimated model parameters. The MDL, AIC, and NML criteria introduce specific additive penalization terms α_{MDL}, α_{AIC}, and α_{NML}, respectively, defined by

$$\alpha_{\mathrm{MDL}}(X, S) = 2^{|S|-1} \log m,$$
$$\alpha_{\mathrm{AIC}}(X, S) = 2^{|S|},$$
$$\alpha_{\mathrm{NML}}(X, S) = \log \sum_{\mathbf{x}_n' \in \{0,1\}^m} 2^{-\beta(\mathbf{x}_S, \mathbf{x}_n')}.$$

As $\alpha_{\mathrm{MDL}}(X, S)$ and $\alpha_{\mathrm{AIC}}(X, S)$ depend on (X, S) only through the number of rows m in X and the number of elements in S, we may conveniently treat them as functions of $(m, |S|)$. If M is a label of a criterion, e.g., from {MDL, AIC, NML}, we define the corresponding penalized maximum likelihood cost as

$$\gamma_M(X, S) = \alpha_M(X, S) + \beta(\mathbf{x}_S, \mathbf{x}_n).$$

Notice that $2^{-\gamma_{\mathrm{NML}}(X,S)}$ is a conditional probability distribution of $\mathbf{x}_n$ given $\mathbf{x}_S$.

2.2 Variants of the Parent Assignment Problem

We will formally look at the parent assignment problem in the guise of one optimization problem as well as of two decision problems, which are suitable for complexity considerations. The following problems will be fixed once the penalty term α has been fixed:

MIN PARENT ASSIGNMENT (α)
Input: A 0-1 matrix X of size $m \times n$.
Output: A subset $S \subseteq \{1, \ldots, n-1\}$ such that $\gamma(X, S) = \alpha(X, S) + \beta(\mathbf{x}_S, \mathbf{x}_n)$ is minimized.

PARENT ASSIGNMENT (α)
Instance: A 0-1 matrix X of size $m \times n$ and a number t.
Question: Is there a subset $S \subseteq \{1, \ldots, n-1\}$ such that $\gamma(X, S) = \alpha(X, S) + \beta(\mathbf{x}_S, \mathbf{x}_n)$ is at most t?

SMALL PARENT ASSIGNMENT (α)
Instance: A 0-1 matrix X of size $m \times n$ and numbers t and k.
Question: Is there a subset $S \subseteq \{1, \ldots, n-1\}$ of size at most k such that $\gamma(X, S) = \alpha(X, S) + \beta(\mathbf{x}_S, \mathbf{x}_n)$ is at most t?

Of these problems, MIN PARENT ASSIGNMENT is the most natural optimization formulation of the parent assignment problem. Obviously, it is at least as hard as the corresponding decision variant, PARENT ASSIGNMENT. The second decision problem, SMALL PARENT ASSIGNMENT, involves an upper bound for the number of parents, which renders it at least as hard as PARENT ASSIGNMENT; we will not consider SMALL PARENT ASSIGNMENT until in Sect. 5.

3 MDL Parent Assignment Is Hard

In this section we show that PARENT ASSIGNMENT (α_{MDL}), or MDL-PA for short, is LOGSNP-hard. Papadimitriou and Yannakakis [8] defined the complexity class LOGSNP in order to capture computational problems that are unlikely to be NP-hard but very likely to have time complexity that scales, roughly, as $n^{\log n}$ where n is the input size.

Our proof is based on a reduction from a restricted dominating set problem defined below. As usual, for a directed graph G we call a node subset S a *dominating set* if each node i outside S is *dominated* by some node j in S, i.e., (i, j) is an arc in G.

LOG DOMINATING SET (LOG-DS)
Instance: A directed graph with $n - 1$ nodes.
Question: Does the graph have a dominating set of size $\log n$?

A couple of details are here worth noting. First, we define the problem in terms of $n - 1$ rather than n nodes, as this leads to somewhat simpler expressions in the sequel. Second, the standard problem definition (e.g., Papadimitriou and Yannakakis [8]) has $\log n$ replaced by $\log(n-1)$ (or $n-1$ by n), however, it is not difficult to show that the two problems are polynomially equivalent.

We known that LOG DOMINATING SET is an ideal representative of the class LOGSNP:

Theorem 1 ([8]). LOG DOMINATING SET *is LOGSNP-complete.*

A key observation we will exploit in our reduction is that the maximum likelihood score is highly sensitive to "collisions." We say that a subset S *has a collision* in X if there exist two rows i and i' such that

$$x_S^i = x_S^{i'} \quad \text{but} \quad x_n^i \neq x_n^{i'}.$$

Thus, a collision occurs if some value on the parents appears with both values, 0 and 1, on the child.

On one hand, if no collision occurs, then the fit is perfect.

Lemma 1. *Let X be a 0-1 matrix of size $n \times n$ and S a subset of $\{1, \ldots, n-1\}$. If S has no collision in X, then $\beta(\mathbf{x}_n, \mathbf{x}_S) = 0$.*

Proof. Suppose that S has no collision in X. Then for any u either $m_{u0} = 0$ or $m_{u1} = 0$ or both. Thus, either $m_{u0} = m_u$ or $m_{u1} = m_u$, implying $m_{u0} \log(m_{u0}/m_u) + m_{u1} \log(m_{u1}/m_u) = m_u \log 1 = 0$. As $\beta(\mathbf{x}_n, \mathbf{x}_S)$ is a sum of these terms, one for each value of u, it must equal 0. □

On the other hand, the more collisions, the larger the minimum error. We will use the following lower bound.

Lemma 2. *Let X be a 0-1 matrix of size $n \times n$ and S a subset of $\{1, \ldots, n-1\}$. If S has a collision in X, then $\beta(\mathbf{x}_n, \mathbf{x}_S) \geq 2$.*

Proof. Suppose that $x_S^i = x_S^{i'} = u$ and $0 = x_n^i \neq x_n^{i'} = 1$. Since $m_{u1}, m_{u0} \geq 1$ and $m_{u1} + m_{u0} = m_u$, we have

$$\beta(\mathbf{x}_n, \mathbf{x}_S) \geq -\left(m_{u0} \log \frac{m_{u0}}{m_u} + m_{u1} \log \frac{m_{u1}}{m_u} \right) \geq \min_{0 < p < 1} \{-\log p - \log(1-p)\} = 2.$$

□

To amplify the effect of a collision, we consider simple repetitions. We say that an $m \times n$ matrix B is obtained by stacking r copies of a $q \times n$ matrix A, or, that B is the *r-stack* of A, if $m = rq$ and the $(tq + i)$th row vector of B equals the ith row vector of A for all $t = 0, \ldots, r-1$ and $i = 1, \ldots, q$.

Lemma 3. *Let X be a 0-1 matrix of size $n \times n$ and S a subset of $\{1, \ldots, n-1\}$. Let X' be the matrix obtained by stacking r copies of X. Then $\beta(\mathbf{x}_n', \mathbf{x}_S') = r \cdot \beta(\mathbf{x}_n, \mathbf{x}_S)$.*

Proof. For X' the maximum likelihood estimate for any parameter $\theta_{v|u}$ is simply $(rm_{uv})/(rm_u) = m_{uv}/m_u$, that is, the same as for the original matrix X. □

We apply these simple observations with the following strategy. First, we map an arbitrary instance of LOG-DS, a graph G with $n - 1$ nodes, to a suitable square matrix X of size $n \times n$. Here we ensure that a set S is a dominating set in G if and only if S has no collision in X. Then, we make a matrix X' by stacking a polynomial number of copies of X. Finally, the instance of MDL-PA is defined as (X', t), where the threshold t is set to the MDL cost due to the number of model parameters. With this construction we are able to show that G has a dominating set of size $\log n$ if and only if the MDL cost is at most t for some set of parents. We next fill in the necessary details.

Let G be a directed graph on $n-1$ nodes labeled by $1, \ldots, n-1$. We define the *reflex* of G as the $n \times n$ matrix $R = \mathrm{ref}(G)$ whose entry at the ith row and jth column, R_j^i, equals 1 if (i, j) is an arc in G or $i = j$, else R_j^i equals 0. In words, $\mathrm{ref}(G)$ is made from G by adding a new node, n, with no incoming nor outgoing arcs, and then enforcing the graph be reflexive; see Fig. 1 for an example. This matrix has a desired property, as stated in the next key lemma.

Lemma 4. *Let G be a directed graph with nodes $1, \ldots, n - 1$. Then, for any subset $S \subseteq \{1, \ldots, n - 1\}$, we have*

S *is a dominating set in* G *if and only if* S *has no collision in* $\mathrm{ref}(G)$.

Proof. Let S be a subset of $\{1, \ldots, n - 1\}$. Denote $R = \mathrm{ref}(G)$ for short.

Assume first that S is a dominating set in G. Then, if S had a collision in the matrix R, we should have an index $i < n$ such that $R_S^i = R_S^n$, since only R_n^n equals 1. Accordingly, R_S^i should be a vector of 0s. But this is impossible since S is a dominating set in G, implying that G has an arc (i, j) for some $j \in S$ and, consequently, $R_j^i = 1$ by the definition of reflex.

Assume then that S is not a dominating set in G. Now it is sufficient to show that for some $i < n$ the vector R_S^i contains only 0s. Assume the contrary, that for all $i < n$ we have a $j \in S$ such that $R_j^i = 1$. But this means that every node i of G is dominated by a node $j \in S$, a contradiction. $\square$

Let us summarize the above four lemmas:

Lemma 5. *Let G be a directed graph with nodes $1, \ldots, n - 1$. Let X be the matrix obtained by stacking r copies of the reflex of G. Then, for any subset $S \subseteq \{1, \ldots, n - 1\}$, we have*

$$\beta(\mathbf{x}_S, \mathbf{x}_n) = 0, \quad \text{if } S \text{ is a dominating set in } G;$$
$$\beta(\mathbf{x}_S, \mathbf{x}_n) \geq 2r, \quad \text{if } S \text{ is not a dominating set in } G.$$

Proof. Immediate from Lemmas 1, 2, 3, and 4. $\square$

In the sequel we will use this result (Lemma 5) as a key argument. The first example of its usage is given in the proof of the next main result.

Theorem 2. MDL-PA *is LOGSNP-hard.*

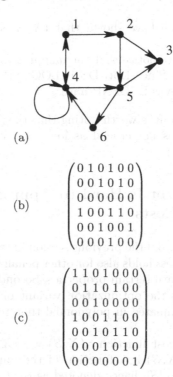

(a)

(b)
$$\begin{pmatrix} 0\,1\,0\,1\,0\,0 \\ 0\,0\,1\,0\,1\,0 \\ 0\,0\,0\,0\,0\,0 \\ 1\,0\,0\,1\,1\,0 \\ 0\,0\,1\,0\,0\,1 \\ 0\,0\,0\,1\,0\,0 \end{pmatrix}$$

(c)
$$\begin{pmatrix} 1\,1\,0\,1\,0\,0\,0 \\ 0\,1\,1\,0\,1\,0\,0 \\ 0\,0\,1\,0\,0\,0\,0 \\ 1\,0\,0\,1\,1\,0\,0 \\ 0\,0\,1\,0\,1\,1\,0 \\ 0\,0\,0\,1\,0\,1\,0 \\ 0\,0\,0\,0\,0\,0\,1 \end{pmatrix}$$

Fig. 1. The reflex of a directed graph. (a) A graph with 6 nodes, (b) the adjacency matrix of the graph, and (c) the reflex of the graph. Nodes 3 and 4 form a dominating set: every other node has an arc that points to 3 or 4.

Proof. Let G be a directed graph with nodes $1,\ldots,n-1$, an instance of LOG-DS. Let R be the reflex of G. Let X be the $rn \times n$ matrix obtained by stacking $r = n^2$ copies of R. Finally, set t to the value $\alpha_{\mathrm{MDL}}(rn, \log n)$.

Our first claim is that G is a positive instance of LOG-DS *if* (X, t) is a positive instance of MDL-PA. Assume the latter holds. Then there exists a set of parents S such that

$$\gamma_{\mathrm{MDL}}(X, S) = \alpha_{\mathrm{MDL}}(rn, |S|) + \beta(\mathbf{x}_S, \mathbf{x}_n) \le t = \alpha_{\mathrm{MDL}}(rn, \log n).$$

Clearly, S can have at most $\log n$ elements. It remains to show that S is a dominating set in G. To see this, assume the contrary: that S is not a dominating set in G. Then, by Lemma 5, $\beta(\mathbf{x}_S, \mathbf{x}_n) \ge 2r = 2n^2$ and, thereby, $\gamma_{\mathrm{MDL}}(X, S) \ge 2n^2$. But this contradicts with the earlier conclusion that $\gamma_{\mathrm{MDL}}(X, S) \le \alpha_{\mathrm{MDL}}(rn, \log n) \le (1/2)\, n \log(n^3)$.

Our second claim is that G is a positive instance of LOG-DS *only if* (X, t) is a positive instance of MDL-PA. Assume the former holds. Then there exists a dominating set S in G such that $|S| \le \log n$. Now, by Lemma 5, we have $\beta(\mathbf{x}_S, \mathbf{x}_n) = 0$. Using this we see that

$$\alpha_{\mathrm{MDL}}(rn, |S|) + \beta(\mathbf{x}_S, \mathbf{x}_n) \le t = \alpha_{\mathrm{MDL}}(rn, \log n),$$

since $|S| \leq \log n$. Thus we have shown that (X, t) is a positive instance of MDL-PA.

To complete the proof, we notice that the mapping from G to X can be computed in polynomial time. Since LOG-DS is LOGSNP-complete (Theorem 1), we conclude that MDL-PA is LOGSNP-hard.   □

Regarding the above proof, it is worth noting that the particular choice for the number of repetitions, r, is not crucial as long as r is polynomial in n and, roughly, of order $\Omega(n \log n)$.

4   Parent Assignment Is Hard to Approximate for the MDL and AIC Costs

We next extend the result from the previous section in two dimensions. First, we show that LOGSNP-hardness holds also for other penalized maximum likelihood costs, such as AIC, that have certain properties. Second, we state the hardness result in a stronger form: the optimization variant of the parent assignment problem cannot be approximated in polynomial time to a ratio smaller than 2 unless LOGSNP = P.

We consider a generic cost function $\gamma(X, S) = \alpha(X, S) + \beta(\mathbf{x}_S, \mathbf{x}_n)$, where the penalization term $\alpha(X, S)$ is a function of the number of records m and the number of parents $k = |S|$, hence denoted as $\alpha(m, k)$. In addition, we will assume that

(A1) $\alpha(m, k)$ grows at most logarithmically in m and exponentially in k,
(A2) $\alpha(m, k)$ can be evaluated in time polynomial in m and k, and
(A3) $\alpha(m, k + 1)/\alpha(m, k) \geq 2$ for all m and k.

These properties obviously hold for the MDL and AIC measures.

Proposition 1. *The functions α_{MDL} and α_{AIC} satisfy conditions (A1–A3).*

4.1   Approximating to a Ratio Less Than 2 Is Hard

We are now ready to prove the main result of this section.

Theorem 3. *Let α be a function that satisfies conditions (A1–A3). Then, for any $\epsilon > 0$, approximating* MIN PARENT ASSIGNMENT *(α) to the ratio $2 - \epsilon$ is LOGSNP-hard.*

Proof. Assume that we have a polynomial-time algorithm $\mathcal{A}$ that, given any 0-1 input matrix X of size $n \times n$, outputs a set $S \subseteq \{1, \ldots, n - 1\}$ such that

$$\gamma(X, S)/OPT(X) \leq 2 - \epsilon < 2,$$

for some $\epsilon > 0$; here $OPT(X)$ denotes the minimum of $\gamma(X, S')$ over all possible subsets S'.

We construct a reduction from LOG-DS, similar to the one in the proof of Theorem 2. First, choose constants a and b such that $\alpha(m, k) \leq a2^{bk} \log m$ for all k and m with $k \leq m$; this we can do due to condition (A1). Then, let G be a directed graph with $n - 1$ nodes, an instance of LOG-DS. Let R be the reflex of G, and let X be the $rn \times n$ matrix obtained by stacking $r = n^{n+1}$ copies of R. Let S be the set given by algorithm $\mathcal{A}$ for the input X. We claim that G has a dominating set of size at most $\log n$ if and only if

$$\gamma(X, S) < 2 \cdot \alpha(rn, \log n). \tag{1}$$

We prove the two directions separately. First, suppose G has a dominating set S^* of size $|S^*| \leq \log n$. Then

$$OPT(X) \leq \gamma(X, S^*) = \alpha(rn, |S^*|) \leq \alpha(rn, \log n);$$

the equality follows from Lemma 5, while the last inequality is due to the monotonicity of α in the second argument (implied by (A3)). Using the approximation guarantee we obtain $\gamma(X, S) < 2 \cdot OPT(X) \leq 2 \cdot \alpha(rn, \log n)$, as desired.

For the other direction, suppose G has no dominating set of size $\log n$. Then $OPT(X) \geq \alpha(rn, 1 + \log n)$, since any set S smaller than $1 + \log n$ has a cost at least $\beta(\mathbf{x}_S, \mathbf{x}_n) \geq 2r = 2n^2 \geq \alpha(rn, 1 + \log n)$; the first inequality is by Lemma 5 and the last one is due to the choice of b (for sufficiently large n). Thus, for any set S we have that $\gamma(X, S) \geq 2 \cdot \alpha(rn, \log n)$, by condition (A3). This contradicts with inequality (1), as desired.

To complete the proof, we recall that LOG-DS is LOGSNP-hard and notice that the mapping from G to X as well as the condition in inequality (1) can be computed in polynomial time.   □

We notice that the main theorem of the previous section, Theorem 2, follows as a direct corollary to the above, stronger result. Let it be also noted that an even slightly stronger result holds: we may allow the number $\epsilon > 0$ in the statement of Theorem 3 depend on the instance of the MIN PARENT ASSIGNMENT (α) problem.

By Theorem 3 and Proposition 1 we immediately have the following.

Corollary 1. *For the MDL and AIC costs, approximating* MIN PARENT AS-SIGNMENT *to a ratio less than 2 is LOGSNP-hard.*

4.2 Approximating to a Constant Ratio Looks Hard

Given the above hardness result, it is natural to ask whether MIN PARENT ASSIGNMENT (α) can be approximated to any constant ratio. As we show next, the answer is likely to be negative. Namely, the positive answer would imply a polynomial-time approximation scheme (PTAS) for the following optimization version of LOG DOMINATING SET, a problem for which no polynomial-time constant-ratio approximation algorithm is known (see Cai et al. [13]).

MIN LOG DOMINATING SET (MIN-LOG-DS)
Input: A directed graph G with $n-1$ nodes such that G has a dominating
set of size $\log n$.
Output: A minimum-cardinality dominating set of G.

The next result provides a connection between the approximation ratio of the
two problems; the result concerning constant approximation ratios follows as a
corollary, as made explicit below.

Theorem 4. *Let α be a function that satisfies conditions (A1–A3). Let $c > 0$
be constant and f an integer function with $f(n) = O(n^\mu)$ for some constant
$\mu \in [0,1)$. Then MIN PARENT ASSIGNMENT (α) on input matrix of size $m \times n$
cannot be approximated in polynomial time to the ratio $f(mn)$ unless MIN-LOG-
DS on input graph with n nodes can be approximated in polynomial time to the
ratio $1 + c \cdot \log f(n)$.*

Proof. Let us first fix some constants. Choose $\mu \in [0,1)$ such that $f(n) \le n^\mu$, for
all sufficiently large n; this we obviously can do. In addition, choose constants a
and b such that $\alpha(m, k) \le a 2^{bk} \log m$ for all k and m with $k \le m$; this we can
do due to condition (A1).

Then, assume that we have a polynomial-time algorithm $\mathcal{A}$ that, given any
0-1 input matrix X of size $n \times n$, outputs a set $S \subseteq \{1, \dots, n-1\}$ such that
$\gamma(X, S)/OPT(X) \le f(mn)$.

We now construct a reduction from the minimum dominating set problem.
We fix yet another constant $q = (b + 1 + 2\mu)/(1 - \mu)$ whose role soon becomes
clear. Let G be a directed graph with $n-1$ nodes such that G has a dominating
set of size $\log n$. We can assume that the smallest dominating set of G, denoted
by S^*, has cardinality at least $(q + 2)/c$. Namely, this restriction obviously does
not change the problem complexity (up to a polynomial factor), since one can
enumerate all node subsets up to a constant cardinality in polynomial time. Let
R be the reflex of G. Let X be the $rn \times n$ matrix obtained by stacking $r = n^q$
copies of R. Let S be the set given by algorithm $\mathcal{A}$ for the input X. We want
to show that S is approximatively minimum dominating set of G, that is, S is a
dominating set and

$$|S|/|S^*| \le 1 + c \cdot \log f(n) . \tag{2}$$

To see that S is, indeed, a dominating set of G we derive a relatively small
upper bound for $\gamma(X, S)$, as follows. For the optimal set S^* we have

$$\gamma(X, S^*) \le \alpha(m, \log n) \le a n^b \log m ,$$

which together with the assumed approximation guarantee yields

$$\begin{aligned}
\gamma(X, S) &\le f(mn) \cdot a n^b \log m \\
&\le a(rn^2)^\mu n^b \log(rn) \\
&= a(q + 1)n^{\mu(q+2)+b} \log n \\
&< n^{\mu(q+2)+b+1} \\
&= n^q ,
\end{aligned}$$

where the strict inequality holds for large enough n (as $a(q+1)\log n = o(n)$) and the last identity holds by the choice of q. This means that S must be a dominating set of G; else, by Lemma 5, we should have $\gamma(X,S) \geq 2r = 2n^q$.

It remains to show that inequality (2) holds. To this end, we first bound

$$f(mn) \geq \gamma(X,S)/OPT(X)$$
$$= \alpha(m,|S|)/\alpha(m,|S^*|)$$
$$\geq 2^{|S|-|S^*|}$$
$$= 2^{|S^*|(|S|/|S^*|-1)},$$

where the first identity holds because S and S^* are dominating sets of G, and the second inequality is due to condition (A3). Taking logs of both sides gives us, after a little rearrangement,

$$|S|/|S^*| \leq 1 + \frac{1}{|S^*|}\log f(mn)$$
$$\leq 1 + \frac{c}{q+2}\log f(n^{q+2})$$
$$\leq 1 + c \cdot \log f(n),$$

since we assumed that $|S^*| \geq (q+2)/c$ and that $f(n^{q+2}) \leq f(n)^{q+2}$ (that is, f does not grow too rapidly; a polynomial f suffices here).

To complete the proof we notice that the reduction mapping can be evaluated in polynomial time. $\square$

Corollary 2. *Let α be a function that satisfies conditions (A1–A3). Then* MIN PARENT ASSIGNMENT (α) *cannot be approximated to any constant ratio unless* MIN-LOG-DS *has a polynomial-time approximation scheme.*

Proof. Suppose that MIN PARENT ASSIGNMENT (α) can be approximated to the constant ratio $\rho > 1$ in polynomial time. Let $\epsilon > 0$ be fixed. Applying Theorem 4 with $f(n) := \rho$, for all n, and $c := \epsilon/\log \rho$ gives the approximation ratio of $1 + \epsilon$ for MIN-LOG-DS. $\square$

Cai et al. [13] discuss the computational complexity of MIN-LOG-DS. They argue that no polynomial-time algorithm can even approximate MIN-LOG-DS to *any* constant factor. However, the needed complexity theoretic assumptions are substantially stronger than the conventional P $\neq$ NP. Despite this gap, it is reasonable to assume that no PTAS exists for MIN-LOG-DS, implying the inapproximability of MIN PARENT ASSIGNMENT (α).

5   NML Parent Assignment Is NP-Complete

In this section we show that SMALL PARENT ASSIGNMENT is NP-complete for the NML cost. Recall that this formulation of the parent assignment task assumes two input numbers: an upper bound for the cost (as in PARENT ASSIGNMENT) and another upper bound for the cardinality of the parent set. The latter bound will correspond to the analogous cardinality parameter of the NP-complete DOM-INATING SET problem [14]: Given a directed graph G and a number k, does G contain a dominating set of size at most k?

We can apply the reduction scheme presented in Sect. 3. Unlike α_{MDL} and α_{AIC}, however, α_{NML} does not have any simple, data-independent expression. Therefore, we have to work a bit to show that α_{NML} grows relatively slowly in the number of parents and in the number of data records, assuming that the data set is obtained via our reduction.

Lemma 6. *Let $r \geq 1$ be an integer and X the r-stack of a 0–1 matrix of size $n \times n$. Then, for any subset $S \subseteq \{1,\ldots,n-1\}$, we have*

$$\alpha_{NML}(X,S) \leq n \log(r+1) \,.$$

Proof. Denote by $m = rn$ the number of rows in X. Write

$$2^{\alpha_{\mathrm{NML}}(X,S)} = \sum_{\mathbf{x}'_n \in \{0,1\}^m} 2^{-\beta(X',S)}$$

$$= \sum_{\mathbf{x}'_n \in \{0,1\}^m} \prod_{u \in \{0,1\}^{|S|} : m_u > 0} \left(\frac{m'_{u0}}{m_u}\right)^{m'_{u0}} \left(\frac{m'_{u1}}{m_u}\right)^{m'_{u1}},$$

where X' denotes the matrix obtained by replacing the nth column of X by the column $\mathbf{x}'_n$, and m'_{uv} is the number of rows in X' where the attributes x_S are set to u and the attribute x_n is set to v.

We can split the summation over $\mathbf{x}'_n$ into (at most) $2^{|S|}$ separate summations, one for each value $u \in \{0,1\}^{|S|}$ (that occurs in X). Within each summation it is sufficient to sum over the sufficient statistic m'_{u0}. Thus,

$$2^{\alpha_{\mathrm{NML}}(X,S)} = \prod_{u \in \{0,1\}^{|S|} : m_u > 0} \sum_{m'_{u0}=0}^{m_u} \binom{m_u}{m'_{u0}} \left(\frac{m'_{u0}}{m_u}\right)^{m'_{u0}} \left(\frac{m'_{u1}}{m_u}\right)^{m'_{u1}}. \tag{3}$$

Since $\binom{k}{j} z^j (1-z)^{k-j} \leq 1$ whenever $0 \leq z \leq 1$ and $0 \leq j \leq k$, we obtain

$$2^{\alpha_{\mathrm{NML}}(X,S)} \leq \prod_{u \in \{0,1\}^{|S|} : m_u > 0} (m_u + 1) \,.$$

Finally, we examine how large a value the expression on the right-hand side can take, subject to the constraints implied by the construction: $m_u = r \cdot t_u$ with $t_u \in \{0,1,\ldots,n\}$ and $\sum_u t_u = n$. We observe that if $t_u \geq t_w + 2$, then $(rt_u + 1)(rt_w + 1) < (r(t_u - 1) + 1)(r(t_w + 1) + 1)$. Without loss of generality we may now consider the case where u takes values from the largest possible set, $\{0,1\}^{n-1}$, in which case at least one t_u must equal 0 (for $n \geq 3$) or every t_u equals 1 (for $n \leq 2$). Consequently, the product $\prod_u (rt_u + 1)$ achieves its maximum value when each t_u is either 0 or 1. Hence,

$$2^{\alpha_{\mathrm{NML}}(X,S)} \leq (r+1)^n \,.$$

Taking logarithms on both sides gives the claimed inequality.   □

This upper bound proved above is rather tight and, actually, significantly larger bounds for $\alpha(X, S)$ would already suffice for rendering SMALL PARENT ASSIGN-MENT (α) NP-hard. Motivated by this fact, we formulate the hardness result in a relatively general terms.

Theorem 5. *Let $g(n) = O(poly(n))$ and $\alpha(X, S) < 2 \cdot g(n)$ whenever X is the $g(n)$-stack of a 0–1 matrix of size $n \times n$ and $S \subseteq \{1, \ldots, n - 1\}$. Then SMALL PARENT ASSIGNMENT (α) is NP-hard.*

Proof. Let (G, k) be an instance of DOMINATING SET, where G is a directed graph with nodes $1, \ldots, n - 1$ and k is a number between 1 and $n - 1$. Set $r = g(n)$ and let X denote the r-stack of the reflex of G.

It is sufficient to show that G has a dominating set of size at most k if and only if there exists a subset $S \subseteq \{1, \ldots, n - 1\}$ of size at most k such that the cost $\alpha(X, S) + \beta(\mathbf{x}_S, \mathbf{x}_n)$ is less than the threshold $t := 2 \cdot g(n) = 2r$.

Suppose first that S is a dominating set of G with $|S| \leq k$. Then, by Lemma 5, we have $\beta(\mathbf{x}_S, \mathbf{x}_n) = 0$. Since we assumed that $\alpha(X, S) < 2 \cdot g(n)$, the total cost is less than t.

Then suppose that $S \subseteq \{1, \ldots, n - 1\}$ is a set with at most k elements and a cost $\alpha(X, S) + \beta(\mathbf{x}_S, \mathbf{x}_n)$ less than $t = 2 \cdot g(n) = 2r$. Then, of course, $\beta(\mathbf{x}_S, \mathbf{x}_n) < 2r$, and so, by Lemma 5, the set S is a dominating set of G.   □

Now it is easy to prove the main result of this section:

Theorem 6. SMALL PARENT ASSIGNMENT (α_{NML}) *is NP-complete.*

Proof. To see NP-hardness, we use the substitution $r = g(n) = n^2$ in Lemma 6 and Theorem 5. Note that then $n \log(r + 1) < 2 \cdot g(n)$.

To see that SMALL PARENT ASSIGNMENT (α_{NML}) is in NP, it is sufficient to notice that $\alpha_{\mathrm{NML}}(X, S)$, for arbitrary X and S, can be evaluated in polynomial time with respect to the size of the matrix X, for example, by using the factorization (3) in the general case of $r = 1$.   □

6   Concluding Remarks

We showed that the parent assignment problem is computationally hard for some widely-used cost functions. According to the presented results, it is unlikely that one even finds a polynomial-time algorithm with a good approximation guarantee. Our reduction from the LOGSNP-hard log dominating set problem proved a relatively direct link between the two problems, however, we do not know whether the parent assignment problem for the MDL or AIC cost is LOGSNP-complete; we leave the precise complexity characterization for future research.

Our hardness results arise from three ingredients, each representing a restriction to the general parent assignment problem. Below we discuss each restriction in turn.

First, we assumed that the conditional probability model is the full-multinomial model. While this model has arguably been the most common choice in both theoretical and practical works on Bayesian networks, several other models have also been proposed, not excluding models for continuous data. To what extend similar hardness results can be proved for those models is an open question.

Second, we considered penalized maximum-likelihood costs, such as MDL, AIC, and NML, which separate the model complexity cost and the goodness of fit in a simple manner. Other important cost functions include the Bayesian cost, which is obtained by integrating the model parameters out [1, 2]. Characterizing the complexity of parent assignment for the Bayesian cost is a natural direction for future research. Although we cannot use the key lemma (Lemma 5) as such, similar argumentation based on a reduction from the (log) dominating set problem might work. Like the NML cost, the Bayesian cost does not imply the $O(\log m)$ bound for the size of the parent set [7], which probably renders the problem NP-hard.

Third, our reduction from the dominating set problem yields hard instances that, however, do not necessary represent typical datasets one encounters in practice. This motivates seeking of appropriate constraints that would allow efficient parent assignment; works on a related large-sample setting have produced interesting characterizations of the needed assumptions and the type of optimality one can achieve [15].

Finally, it should be noted that the parent assignment problem studied in this paper falls in the broad framework of combinatorial feature selection problems (e.g., [16, 17]). Koller and Sahami [16] and Charikar et al. [17] provide insightful results concerning some interesting problem classes. However, neither of these works provides any hardness or (in)approximability result for the parent assignment problem. For *linear* classifiers (hyperplanes, perceptrons) Amaldi and Kann [18] show that finding, or approximating the number of, the relevant attributes is hard, proving that "black-box" feature selection can be hard; this result, of course, does not imply that feature selection is hard for richer hypothesis classes, e.g., the full-multinomial model.

Acknowledgements

I wish to thank David Maxwell Chickering and Christopher Meek for discussions about a large-sample variant of the parent assignment problem, which partially inspired this work. I would also like to thank an anonymous reviewer for pointing out a minor flaw in an earlier version of the proof of Theorem 3.

References

1. Cooper, G.F., Herskovits, E.: A Bayesian method for the induction of probabilistic networks from data. Machine Learning **9** (1992) 309–347
2. Heckerman, D., Geiger, D., Chickering, D.M.: Learning Bayesian networks: The combination of knowledge and statistical data. Machine Learning **20** (1995) 197–243
3. Suzuki, J.: Learning Bayesian belief networks based on the Minimun Description Length principle: An efficient algorithm using the b & b technique. In: Proceedings of the Thirteenth International Conference on Machine Learning (ICML). (1996) 462–470

4. Tian, J.: A branch-and-bound algorithm for MDL learning Bayesian networks. In: Proceedings of the Sixteenth Conference on Uncertainty in Artificial Intelligence (UAI), Morgan Kaufmann (2000) 580–588
5. Rissanen, J.: Modeling by shortest data description. Automatica **14** (1978) 465–471
6. Bouckaert, R.R.: Probabilistic network construction using the minimum description length principle. In: Proceedings of the European Conference on Symbolic and Quantitative Approaches to Reasoning and Uncertainty (ECSQARU), Springer-Verlag (1993) 41–48
7. Bouckaert, R.R.: Properties of Bayesian belief network learning algorithms. In de Mantaras, R.L., Poole, D., eds.: Proceedings of the Tenth Conference on Uncertainty in Artificial Intelligence (UAI), Morgan Kaufmann (1994) 102–109
8. Papadimitriou, C., Yannakakis, M.: On limited nondeterminism and the complexity of the V-C dimension. Journal of Computer and System Sciences **53** (1996) 161–170
9. Akaike, H.: A new look at the statistical model identification. IEEE Transactions on Automatic Control **19** (1974) 716–722
10. Shtarkov, Y.M.: Universal sequential coding of single messages. Problems of Information Transmission **23** (1987) 3–17
11. Kontkanen, P., Buntine, W., Myllymäki, P., Rissanen, J., Tirri, H.: Efficient computation of stochastic complexity. In Bishop, C.M., Frey, B.J., eds.: Proceedings of the Ninth International Workshop on Artificial Intelligence and Statistics (AISTAT), Key West, FL (2003) 181–188
12. Schwarz, G.: Estimating the dimension of a model. Annals of Statistics **6** (1978) 461–464
13. Cai, L., Juedes, D., Kanj, I.: The inapproximability of non-NP-hard optimization problems. Theoretical Computer Science **289** (2002) 553–571
14. Garey, M., Johnson, D.: Computers and Intractability - A Guide to the Theory of NP-completeness. W. H. Freeman & Co., San Fransisco, CA (1971)
15. Chickering, D.M., Meek, C.: Finding optimal Bayesian networks. In: Proceedings of Eighteenth Conference on Uncertainty in Artificial Intelligence (UAI). Morgan Kaufmann, Edmonton (2002) 94–102
16. Koller, D., Sahami, M.: Toward optimal feature selection. In: Proceedings of the Thirteenth International Conference on Machine Learning (ICML), Morgan Kaufmann (1996) 284–292
17. Charikar, M., Guruswami, V., Kumar, R., Rajagopalan, S., Sahai, A.: Combinatorial feature selection problems. In: Proceedings of the 41st IEEE Symposium on Foundations of Computer Science (FOCS), IEEE (2000) 631–640
18. Amaldi, E., Kann, V.: On the approximability of minimizing nonzero variables or unsatisfied relations in linear systems. Theoretical Computer Science **209** (1998) 237–260

Uniform-Distribution Learnability of Noisy Linear Threshold Functions with Restricted Focus of Attention

Jeffrey C. Jackson*

Mathematics and Computer Science Dept.
Duquesne University, Pittsburgh PA 15282-1754 USA
jacksonj@duq.edu

Abstract. Recently, Kalai *et al.* [1] have shown (among other things) that linear threshold functions over the Boolean cube and unit sphere are agnostically learnable with respect to the uniform distribution using the hypothesis class of polynomial threshold functions. Their primary algorithm computes monomials of large constant degree, although they also analyze a low-degree algorithm for learning origin-centered halfspaces over the unit sphere. This paper explores noise-tolerant learnability of linear thresholds over the cube when the learner sees a very limited portion of each instance. Uniform-distribution weak learnability results are derived for the agnostic, unknown attribute noise, and malicious noise models. The noise rates that can be tolerated vary: the rate is essentially optimal for attribute noise, constant (roughly 1/8) for agnostic learning, and non-trivial ($\Omega(1/\sqrt{n})$) for malicious noise. In addition, a new model that lies between the product attribute and malicious noise models is introduced, and in this stronger model results similar to those for the standard attribute noise model are obtained for learning homogeneous linear thresholds with respect to the uniform distribution over the cube. The learning algorithms presented are simple and have small-polynomial running times.

1 Introduction

A linear threshold function over the Boolean cube $\{0,1\}^n$ is any function that can be defined by taking the sign of the sum of a constant threshold value plus the dot product of a fixed vector of weights and the vector of the function's inputs. While the class of linear threshold functions can be learned in polynomial time with respect to arbitrary distributions over the cube (by using any polynomial-time linear programming solver), many open questions remain concerning the learnability of linear thresholds in the presence of noise.

Significant progress on noise-tolerant learning of linear thresholds was made recently when Kalai *et al.* [1] showed (among other things) that linear threshold functions over the Boolean cube are agnostically learnable with respect to

---

* This material is based upon work supported by the National Science Foundation under Grant No. CCR-0209064.

G. Lugosi and H.U. Simon (Eds.): COLT 2006, LNAI 4005, pp. 304–318, 2006.

the uniform distribution $\mathcal{U}_n$. Specifically, their algorithm, given $\epsilon > 0$ and a uniform-distribution oracle for any function $f : \{0,1\}^n \to \{-1,1\}$, produces an approximator h such that $\mathrm{Pr}_{\mathcal{U}_n}[f \neq h]$ is at most ϵ greater than the minimal error of any linear threshold used as an approximator to f. As there are relatively few positive results for the agnostic learning model, it is perhaps somewhat surprising that a positive result could be obtained for such a rich class.

Kalai et al.'s *polynomial regression algorithm*, while polynomial-time for constant ϵ, produces as its hypothesis h a large-constant-degree polynomial threshold function. Furthermore, to produce this hypothesis, the algorithm uses estimates of Fourier coefficients of the target f that involve computing monomials of degree up to d over the examples, where d is a large constant. While Kalai et al. also show that a degree-1 version of their algorithm produces reasonably good agnostic results when learning over the unit sphere, there is not an obvious translation of their analysis to uniform-distribution learning over the discrete cube.

This paper considers uniform-distribution learning of noisy linear thresholds over the Boolean cube when the learner is restricted to look at only a very few bits k of each example. This Restricted Focus of Attention (k-RFA) model was introduced by Ben-David and Dichterman [2] and has been considered in several settings. One reason for considering this model is that, when positive RFA results are possible, the resulting learning algorithms may be—and are, in this paper—relatively simple and efficient, since they are using relatively little information in each example.

In addition, there are theoretical reasons to be particularly interested in RFA learnability of linear thresholds. It has long been known that the Chow parameters of a linear threshold function f over the cube—parameters which can be efficiently estimated while looking at only one input bit plus the label per example—provide a unique signature for f: no other Boolean function has exactly the same Chow parameters. Thus, noiseless linear thresholds are information-theoretically learnable in the 1-RFA model. It is therefore natural to ask how much we can learn about a *noisy* linear threshold function given a similarly limited amount of information.

Algorithms are presented for RFA-learning linear threshold functions over the cube with respect to the uniform distribution in several noise models (described later): a weak version of agnostic learning, attribute noise generated by an unknown noise process, malicious noise, and a new model called restricted context-sensitive attribute noise (RCSAN, pronounced arc-san). In this model, unlike attribute noise, the noise process is allowed to specify multiple noise rates for an attribute, with the choice of rate for an example $(x, f(x))$ based on the values of a restricted set of attributes of x as well as the label $f(x)$. This generalizes the product version of the attribute noise model, in which noise is applied to each attribute i of an example independently at rate p_i.

In each of these models, our algorithms produce approximating hypotheses that (with high probability) agree with the target function with probability at least $1/2 + \gamma$ for some γ that depends on how far the actual noise rate falls below the limits given next. For agnostic learning, any function f for which the optimal linear threshold function has error non-negligibly less than $1/8$ can be efficiently weakly learned. For unknown attribute noise applied to a linear threshold function, weak learning is achieved for any noise process for which the marginal attribute noise rates are all non-negligibly less than $1/2$. For malicious noise, a rate of $\Omega(1/\sqrt{n})$ can be tolerated. We consider several constrained versions of the RCSAN model. Our strongest RCSAN result shows, roughly speaking, that homogeneous linear threshold functions (linear thresholds that have a constant threshold value of 0) can be 2-RFA learned with respect to the uniform distribution as long as the maximum average noise rate over the attributes is less than $1/2$ and there is at least one known relevant attribute with no noise.

Our results are based on the observation of Kalai *et al.* [1] that the so-called low-degree Fourier algorithm is a weak agnostic learner. In particular, our basic learning algorithm is a combination of the low-degree algorithm with a randomized algorithm due to Blum *et al.* [4]) that improves on the error bound of the basic low-degree algorithm. The proof of the algorithm's error bound also depends critically on a Fourier property of linear threshold functions over the cube due to Gotsman and Linial [3]. This basic algorithm provides the agnostic, attribute, and malicious noise results. The RCSAN algorithm adds on top of this basic algorithm some Fourier-based machinery for eliminating certain noise elements that the basic algorithm does not handle especially well.

Finally, we show that in relation to our learning algorithm for the standard attribute-noise model, the RCSAN model produces noise effects that are similar to those that can be produced by the malicious model. Potentially, then, the RCSAN model could be an interesting intermediary between the attribute noise model and the more difficult malicious model in other contexts as well.

2 Preliminaries

2.1 Fourier Transform

Many of our results make use of Fourier notation and basic results. For any function $f : \{0,1\}^n \rightarrow \mathbf{R}$ and for all $a \in \{0,1\}^n$, we define $\hat{f}(a) \equiv E_{x \sim \mathcal{U}_n}[f(x)\chi_a(x)]$, where $\mathcal{U}_n$ denotes the uniform distribution over $\{0,1\}^n$, $\chi_a(x) \equiv (-1)^{a \cdot x}$, and $a \cdot x$ represents the dot product of the bit vectors a and x. Each $\hat{f}(a)$ is a *Fourier coefficient* of f. The *Fourier representation* (or *expansion*) of f is $\sum_a \hat{f}(a)\chi_a$ and is equivalent to f. $\hat{f}(0^n)$ (0^n denotes the n-bit vector containing only 0's) is called the *constant Fourier coefficient*. The *first-order Fourier coefficients* are those coefficients for which $|a| = 1$, that is, for which a contains a single 1 bit.

We use e_i to denote the n-bit vector that has a single 1 in position i (bit locations are assumed to be numbered 1 through n). For two n-bit vectors a and b, $a \oplus b$ denotes the bitwise exclusive OR of the vectors. In particular, if $i \neq j$ then $e_i \oplus e_j$ represents the vector with 1's only in positions i and j.

In this paper, Boolean functions map to $\{-1, 1\}$. Parseval's identity says that for any f, $E_{\mathcal{U}}[f^2] = \sum_a \hat{f}^2(a)$. This implies that if f is Boolean then $\sum_a \hat{f}^2(a) = 1$. It is easily seen that for all Boolean f and for all $a \in \{0,1\}^n$, $\hat{f}(a) = 2\Pr_{\mathcal{U}_n}[f = \chi_a] - 1 = 1 - 2\Pr_{\mathcal{U}_n}[f \neq \chi_a]$.

This paper focuses on noise-tolerant learnability of the class $\mathcal{L}$ of linearly separable functions over the Boolean cube. In Fourier terms, $\mathcal{L} = \cup_{n \geq 0} \mathcal{L}_n$, where $\mathcal{L}_n = \{\ell : \{0,1\}^n \to \{-1,1\} \mid \exists F = \sum_{|a| \leq 1} \hat{F}(a) \chi_a \text{ s.t. } \ell = \text{sign}(F)\}$.

2.2 Learning Models

The underlying learning model for this paper is PAC learning [5] with respect to the uniform distribution (or *with respect to uniform* for short); we assume that the reader is familiar with this model. We will often state that certain results hold "with high probability"; this should be understood to mean that these results hold with probability $1 - \delta$ for arbitrary PAC confidence parameter $\delta > 0$. In this paper, algorithms will be considered efficient if they run in polynomial time in the number of inputs n, in an estimation tolerance parameter τ (bounds on which will in turn depend on parameters of the noise model), and in $\log(1/\delta)$.

With one exception, each noise model considered can be thought of as defining a noisy oracle that, on each query, first draws a noiseless example from a standard PAC example oracle $EX(f, \mathcal{U}_n)$ and then applies some noise process to this example, returning the resulting (possibly noisy) example as the response to the query. A *noiseless example* of a function f consists of a pair $(x, f(x))$, where x is called an *instance* (or input) and $f(x)$ is called the *label* (or output) of the example. The bits of an instance x are sometimes called the *attributes* of the instance. The notation (x^j, f^j) is used to represent the jth example returned by an oracle (either noiseless or noisy). If the example comes from a noisy oracle then—depending on the noise model—either or both of x^j and f^j may be noisy versions of an underlying noiseless example.

The *agnostic learning* model introduced by Kearns *et al.* [6] is the one exception mentioned above. It can be thought of as a particularly strong form of noise applied to the labels of examples, that is, as a form of *classification noise*. When learning $\mathcal{L}$ with respect to the uniform distribution, the strong version of this model becomes the following: the learner has access to an oracle $EX(f, \mathcal{U}_n)$ for an arbitrary Boolean function $f : \{0,1\}^n \to \{-1,1\}$. Given $\epsilon > 0$, the goal of the learner is to output a (possibly randomized) hypothesis $h : \{0,1\}^n \to \{-1,1\}$ such that $\Pr_{x \sim \mathcal{U}_n}[f(x) \neq h(x)] \leq \text{opt} + \epsilon$, where opt is the minimum of $\Pr_{\mathcal{U}_n}[\ell \neq f(x)]$ over all $\ell \in \mathcal{L}_n$. Here and elsewhere, in addition to the probability being over the uniform choice of x, it is also implicitly over the random choices made by h, if h is randomized (as it will be for our algorithms). Kearns *et al.* also consider a weak version of agnostic learning, wherein the goal is to find a *weak approximator* h to the target f (*i.e.*, h such that $\Pr_{\mathcal{U}_n}[h \neq f] \leq 1/2 - 1/p$ for some p polynomial in the learning parameters), given that f is weakly approximable by some function in $\mathcal{L}$.

In all of the other noise models considered, our goal will be to produce a hypothesis h that weakly approximates f with respect to uniform. In particular, we will say that $\mathcal{L}$ is ϕ-*learnable* for ϕ a function of the tolerance τ mentioned above and various parameters of the noise processes if there is a learning algorithm $\mathcal{A}$ that, given a noisy oracle for any $f \in \mathcal{L}$, produces (with high probability) a hypothesis h such that $\Pr_{\mathcal{U}_n}[h \neq f] \leq \phi$.

In the *attribute noise* model introduced by Shackelford and Volper [7], a noise distribution $\mathcal{N}$ over $\{0,1\}^n$ defines the behavior of the noise oracle $EX^{\mathcal{N}}(f,\mathcal{U})$. After drawing a noiseless example $(x, f(x))$, the attribute noise oracle draws $a \sim \mathcal{N}$ and returns as its output the noisy example $(x \oplus a, f(x))$.

In the *malicious noise* model introduced by Valiant [8], we will think of the noisy oracle *marking* each noiseless example $(x, f(x))$ with probability η. If an noiseless example is not marked, then it is returned as the oracle's output. Otherwise, the oracle is allowed to return an arbitrary, maliciously-chosen noisy example. The oracle can be assumed to be computationally unbounded, to know the target f, and even to know the current state of the learning algorithm.

The primary remaining noise model considered, the *restricted context-sensitive attribute noise* (RCSAN) model, will be described in a later section.

2.3   Restricted Focus of Attention

In the *Restricted Focus of Attention* (k-RFA) learning model introduced by Ben-David and Dichterman [2], the learner is only allowed to see k bits of each instance. The learner chooses the bits to be seen. The primary learning algorithm presented in this paper uses examples only to estimate the constant and first-order Fourier coefficients (over noisy examples). It is easy to see from the definition of these coefficients that they can all be estimated to inverse-polynomial accuracy given a polynomially large set of examples in the 1-RFA model. One version of RCSAN learning also needs to compute estimates of $E[\chi_{e_i}(x)\chi_{e_j}(x)]$ over noisy examples; this can clearly be accomplished in the 2-RFA model. Thus, all of our results apply in the 1-RFA or 2-RFA models, but in the sequel we will present the algorithms as if they are operating without any restriction on focus.

3   Weak Agnostic/Adversarial Noise Learning

In this section, we will show that $\mathcal{L}$ is weakly agnostically learnable with respect to the uniform distribution by a 1-RFA learner as long as the target f is such that there is some $\ell \in \mathcal{L}$ satisfying (roughly) $\text{Pr}_{\mathcal{U}}[\ell \neq f] < 1/8$. However, we will find it convenient to first develop a learning result in a closely related noise model and return later to how this relates to weak agnostic learning. In the uniform-distribution *adversarial noise* model, after a target function $f \in \mathcal{L}$ has been selected but before learning begins, for some fixed $\eta > 0$ (the *adversarial noise rate*) an adversary is allowed to choose an arbitrary set of instances and corrupt their labels, producing a noisy Boolean function f^{η} that we will refer to as the η-*corrupted* version of f. The only limitation on f^{η} is that it must satisfy $\text{Pr}_{\mathcal{U}_n}[f^{\eta} \neq f] \leq \eta$.

Theorem 1. *For any $\eta, \tau > 0$, $\mathcal{L}$ is efficiently 1-RFA $(2\eta + \tau + 1/4)$-learnable with respect to the uniform distribution despite adversarial noise of rate η.*

Proof. Fix any η and τ, let $f \in \mathcal{L}$, and let f^{η} be any adversarially η-corrupted version of f. Also assume that the PAC confidence parameter $\delta > 0$ is specified.

Our learning algorithm $\mathcal{A}$ will begin by drawing a set of $m = 25(n+1)^2 \ln(2(n+1)/\delta)/2\tau^2$ examples (x^j, f^j) from the noisy example oracle $EX(f^\eta, \mathcal{U})$. For each $|a| \leq 1$, $\mathcal{A}$ will then calculate $\hat{g}(a) \equiv (1/m)\sum_j f^j \chi_a(x^j)$. That is, for each such a, $\hat{g}(a)$ is an estimate of the Fourier coefficient $\widehat{f^\eta}(a)$ of the noisy function. Standard Hoeffding bounds [9] show that, with probability at least $1 - \delta$ over the choice of examples, every $\hat{g}(a)$ will be within an additive factor of $\tau/2.5(n+1)$ of the corresponding $\widehat{f^\eta}(a)$. Next, from these estimated coefficients $\mathcal{A}$ constructs the (non-Boolean) function

$$g \equiv \sum_{|a| \leq 1} \hat{g}(a)\chi_a \ .$$

Finally, $\mathcal{A}$ defines the randomized Boolean function h as follows: $h(x) = -1$ with probability $p \equiv (1 - g(x))^2/2(1 + g^2(x))$ and $h(x) = 1$ with probability $1 - p$. $\mathcal{A}$ outputs h as its hypothesis.

Clearly we can convert $\mathcal{A}$ to a 1-RFA algorithm by drawing a separate sample to compute each $\hat{g}(a)$, and both this RFA algorithm and the original are efficient. What remains to be shown is that for h as given above, with high probability $\Pr[h \neq f] \leq 2\eta + \tau + 1/4$.

The algorithm's definition of randomized Boolean h in terms of deterministic non-Boolean approximator g comes from Blum et al. [4], who show (in their Lemma 3) that for such an h and for any Boolean function f, $\Pr[h \neq f] \leq E[(f-g)^2]/2$. Furthermore, by Parseval's identity and the linearity of the Fourier transform, $E_{\mathcal{U}}[(f-g)^2] = \sum_a (\hat{f}(a) - \hat{g}(a))^2$. Since by the definition of g we have that $\hat{g}(a) = 0$ for all $|a| > 1$, breaking this sum into two parts gives us

$$\Pr_{\mathcal{U}}[h \neq f] \leq \frac{1}{2}\sum_{|a| \leq 1}\left(\hat{f}(a) - \hat{g}(a)\right)^2 + \frac{1}{2}\sum_{|a| > 1}\hat{f}^2(a) \ . \tag{1}$$

Gotsman and Linial [3] have shown that for any $f \in \mathcal{L}$, $\sum_{|a|>1}\hat{f}^2(a) \leq 1/2$. Thus, what remains is to upper bound the first term of (1) by $2\eta+\tau$. The proof of this bound is similar to the proof of Observation 3 in [1] but uses an observation of Bshouty (personal communication) to achieve an improved 2η term rather than the 4η that would result from using the "almost triangle" inequality as in [1].

First, let $\alpha \equiv \tau/2.5(n+1)$ and recall that $\mathcal{A}$ chooses a sufficiently large set of examples such that, with high probability, for all $|a| \leq 1$ we have that $|\hat{g}(a) - \widehat{f^\eta}(a)| \leq \alpha$. This means that

$$\sum_{|a| \leq 1}\left(\hat{f}(a) - \hat{g}(a)\right)^2 \leq \sum_{|a| \leq 1}\left(|\hat{f}(a) - \widehat{f^\eta}(a)| + \alpha\right)^2$$

$$\leq \sum_{|a| \leq 1}\left(\hat{f}(a) - \widehat{f^\eta}(a)\right)^2 + 2\sum_{|a| \leq 1}|\hat{f}(a) - \widehat{f^\eta}(a)|\alpha + \sum_{|a| \leq 1}\alpha^2$$

$$\leq \sum_{|a| \leq 1}\left(\hat{f}(a) - \widehat{f^\eta}(a)\right)^2 + 5\sum_{|a| \leq 1}\alpha$$

since the Fourier coefficients of the Boolean functions f and f^η all fall in the range $[-1, 1]$. Thus the first term in (1) is bounded by $(1/2) \sum_{|a| \leq 1} (\hat{f}(a) - \widehat{f^\eta}(a))^2 + \tau$. Furthermore,

$$\sum_{|a| \leq 1} \left(\hat{f}(a) - \widehat{f^\eta}(a) \right)^2 \leq \sum_{a \in \{0,1\}^n} \left(\hat{f}(a) - \widehat{f^\eta}(a) \right)^2$$
$$= E\left[(f - f^\eta)^2 \right]$$
$$= 4 \Pr[f \neq f^\eta]$$
$$\leq 4\eta$$

where the first equality follows by again applying Parseval's identity and the second because f and f^η are both $\{-1, 1\}$-valued. $\square$

In agnostic learning terms, what we have shown is that if the target f is such that there exists an $\ell \in \mathcal{L}$ and a $\gamma > \tau$ satisfying $\Pr_\mathcal{U}[f \neq \ell] \leq 1/8 - \gamma/2$ then algorithm $\mathcal{A}$ above will (with high probability) output a randomized hypothesis h such that $\Pr_\mathcal{U}[h \neq f] \leq 1/2 - (\gamma - \tau)$, which for sufficiently large $\gamma - \tau$ means that h weakly approximates f. Thus, algorithm $\mathcal{A}$ in fact 1-RFA weakly agnostically learns $\mathcal{L}$ with respect to uniform.

4   Attribute Noise

Bshouty et al. [10] showed that the class AC^0 of polynomial-size constant-depth AND/OR circuits can be learned despite certain types of attribute noise. In particular, given mild constraints on ϵ and δ, if the attribute noise is defined by a known product distribution in which the noise rate for each bit is at most inverse polylogarithmic in n then AC^0 is learnable with respect to the uniform distribution despite such attribute noise. Based on their analysis and the observations above, we will next show that $\mathcal{L}$ is weakly learnable with respect to uniform despite an unknown attribute noise process, subject to only the mildest of constraints.

Specifically, we will make use of the following easily-shown observation from Bshouty et al. (part of the proof of their Theorem 8):

Lemma 1 (Bshouty et al.). *Let $\mathcal{N}$ be any noise distribution over $\{0,1\}^n$ and let $f : \{0,1\}^n \to \{-1,1\}$ be any Boolean function. Then for each $c \in \{0,1\}^n$, $E_{x \sim U_n, a \sim \mathcal{N}}[f(x)\chi_c(x \oplus a)] = \hat{f}(c) E_{a \sim \mathcal{N}}[\chi_c(a)]$.*

For the linear Fourier coefficients $\hat{f}(e_i)$, note that

$$E_{a \sim \mathcal{N}}[\chi_{e_i}(a)] = E_{a \sim \mathcal{N}}[(-1)^{a_i}] = 1 - 2 \Pr_{a \sim \mathcal{N}}[a_i = 1] \ .$$

Thus, for any attribute noise distribution $\mathcal{N}$ and Boolean function f, given a set S of examples $\{(x^j, f^j)\}$ generated by the attribute-noise oracle $EX^\mathcal{N}(f, \mathcal{U})$, the expected value of $(1/|S|) \sum_S f^j \chi_{e_i}(x^j)$ is $\hat{f}(e_i)(1 - 2\Pr_{a \sim \mathcal{N}}[a_i = 1])$. We write $\widehat{f^{\mathcal{N}}}(e_i)$ to denote this expected value.

For any given noise distribution $\mathcal{N}$ define $p_{\mathcal{N}} \equiv \max_{1 \leq i \leq n} \Pr_{a \sim \mathcal{N}}[a_i = 1]$. That is, $p_{\mathcal{N}}$ is an upper bound on the marginal error rate of each of the attributes. We will show that $\mathcal{L}$ can be weakly learned with respect to uniform despite unknown attribute noise $\mathcal{N}$, where $\mathcal{N}$ is arbitrary except for the constraint that $p_{\mathcal{N}}$ must be non-negligibly less than $1/2$ in order to achieve weak learning efficiently. Since learning is information-theoretically impossible given uniform attribute noise of rate $1/2$ (as this in effect replaces each instance with some other uniform-random instance), this is a very weak constraint on the noise process.

Theorem 2. *For any $\tau > 0$ and any unknown distribution $\mathcal{N}$ over $\{0,1\}^n$ such that $p_{\mathcal{N}} < 1/2$, $\mathcal{L}$ is efficiently 1-RFA $(p_{\mathcal{N}}^2 + \tau + 1/4)$-learnable with respect to uniform despite unknown $\mathcal{N}$-attribute noise.*

Proof. The proof is very similar to that of Theorem 1, except that the algorithm $\mathcal{A}$ described in that proof now operates on examples generated by an $EX^{\mathcal{N}}(f,\mathcal{U})$ oracle rather than by an $EX(f^\eta, \mathcal{U})$ oracle. Specifically, $\mathcal{A}$ will use the $\mathcal{N}$ oracle to estimate, for all $|a| \leq 1$, $\hat{g}(a)$'s that are approximations to the coefficients $\widehat{f^{\mathcal{N}}}(a) = \hat{f}(a)(1 - 2\Pr_{a \sim \mathcal{N}}[a_i = 1])$ to a tolerance of $\tau/2.5(n+1)$. The function g is defined in terms of these estimated coefficients as before, and h is again defined in terms of g. From the proof of Theorem 1 we have that

$$\Pr[h \neq f] \leq \frac{1}{2} \sum_{|a| \leq 1} (\hat{f}(a) - \widehat{f^{\mathcal{N}}}(a))^2 + \tau + \frac{1}{2} \sum_{|a| > 1} \hat{f}^2(a) .$$

Since we are considering attribute noise only, $\hat{f}(0^n) = \widehat{f^{\mathcal{N}}}(0^n)$. For every $|a| = 1$, by the definition of $p_{\mathcal{N}}$, $(\hat{f}(a) - \widehat{f^{\mathcal{N}}}(a))^2 \leq 4p_{\mathcal{N}}^2 \hat{f}^2(a)$. So $\sum_{|a| \leq 1} (\hat{f}(a) - \widehat{f^{\mathcal{N}}}(a))^2 \leq 4p_{\mathcal{N}}^2 \sum_{|a| \leq 1} \hat{f}^2(a) = 4p_{\mathcal{N}}^2 - 4p_{\mathcal{N}}^2 \sum_{|a| > 1} \hat{f}^2(a)$, where the equality follows from Parseval's identity. Inserting this into bound on $\Pr[h \neq f]$ above gives

$$\Pr[h \neq f] \leq 2p_{\mathcal{N}}^2 + \tau + \left(\frac{1}{2} - 2p_{\mathcal{N}}^2 \right) \sum_{|a| > 1} \hat{f}^2(a) .$$

Since our assumed constraint on $p_{\mathcal{N}}$ implies that $1/2 > 2p_{\mathcal{N}}^2$, this bound is maximized when $\sum_{|a| > 1} \hat{f}^2(a)$ is maximized. Using the fact that $\sum_{|a| > 1} \hat{f}^2(a) \leq 1/2$ completes the proof. □

5   Malicious Noise

Recall that in the malicious noise model, conceptually each example is "marked" independently with probability η, and those that are marked can be corrupted arbitrarily by a malicious adversary. In this model, the worst case for the algorithm $\mathcal{A}$ of Theorem 1—in terms of the bound we can prove on the approximation error of $\mathcal{A}$'s hypothesis h relative to the target f—is when the adversary chooses to make every marked example identical to all the other marked examples. This approach can be used to maximize the difference that can be achieved for a given set of marked examples between $\mathcal{A}$'s estimated coefficients $\{\hat{g}(a) : |a| \leq 1\}$ and the corresponding true coefficients $\hat{f}(a)$, which in turn maximally increases (weakens) the bound on $\Pr[h \neq f]$ provided by (1) over the $1/4 + \tau$ bound that would apply in the noise-free setting.

The magnitude of the error induced by this worst-case malicious noise process in the estimate of a fixed first-order coefficient $\hat{f}(e_i)$ depends on the magnitude of the coefficient. For instance, if the coefficient value is 0 (that is, the attribute i is irrelevant) then on average the adversary will only change the value of attribute i in half of the marked examples; the other half will already have the desired attribute value. On the other hand, if $|\hat{f}(e_i)| = 1$ then attribute i will be changed in every marked example, and the magnitude of the expected difference between $\mathcal{A}$'s estimate of $\hat{f}(e_i)$ and the true value will be 2η. The error induced in the estimate of $\hat{f}(0^n)$ similarly depends on the magnitude of this coefficient.

It follows that, for fixed marking rate η and estimation tolerance $\tau > 0$, applying algorithm $\mathcal{A}$ of the proof of Theorem 1 to malicious noise examples will with high probability produce Fourier estimates $\hat{g}(a)$ such that $(1/2) \sum_{|a| \leq 1} (\hat{f}^2(a) - \hat{g}^2(a)) \leq 4(n+1)\eta^2 + \tau$. Thus, the algorithm without modification will weakly learn $\mathcal{L}$ despite malicious noise of rate $\eta = \Omega(1/\sqrt{n})$.

However, it would obviously be a simple matter to modify the algorithm to detect a large number of identical examples and, once detected, to ignore them in computing the coefficients $\hat{g}(a)$. In fact, notice that a set of such examples corrupted in this way would no longer be uniformly distributed over the instance space, and in particular notice that the attributes would no longer be independent.

Comparing the attribute and malicious noise models, then, there are (at least) two key differences. First, while the attribute noise model adds an error vector to an underlying instance, the malicious noise model replaces the underlying instance in its entirety. Second, as Bshouty et al. [10] point out, uniformly distributed instances remain uniform after arbitrary attribute noise is applied, while (as we have just seen) this is not necessarily the case with malicious noise. That said, the malicious noise model does allow the adversary to consider the entire example when corrupting an individual attribute, so the adversary can potentially craft the corrupted examples so that the overall set of examples still appears to be drawn uniformly.

This comparison of models suggests that it might be worthwhile to consider noise models that lie between the attribute and malicious models. We consider this direction in the next section.

6   Context-Sensitive Attribute Noise

In the *restricted context-sensitive attribute noise* (RCSAN) model, the noise process is similar to that of attribute noise, but the process is potentially sensitive to the label and a limited number of attribute values. This is somewhat analogous to the RFA learning model, except it is the noise process that is restricted here. The specific version of the model considered here could be called 1-RCSAN, since we will allow the noise applied to an attribute i of an example to depend only on the example label and on the value of i itself. In the sequel, we will simply call this the RCSAN model.

Each instantiation of the RCSAN model defines four noise rates p_i^{++}, p_i^{+-}, p_i^{-+}, and p_i^{--} for each attribute $1 \leq i \leq n$. If a given pre-noise example $(x, f(x))$ is such that $\chi_{e_i}(x) = +1$ (that is, $x_i = 0$) and $f(x) = -1$ then the noise process will flip x_i from 0 to 1 with probability p_i^{+-}. The other three noise rates similarly define the probability of attribute i being corrupted in the remaining three attribute/label contexts.

This model generalizes the product attribute noise model, in which each attribute i is assigned a single context-free noise rate p_i that is applied to attribute i in every example, regardless of the value of the attribute or the label. As we saw earlier, when a uniform-distribution learning algorithm is based on estimates of first-order Fourier coefficients, the general attribute noise model—in which an arbitrary (possibly non-product) noise distribution $\mathcal{N}$ is allowed—effectively reduces to a form of product attribute noise. So, for algorithms based on estimating first-order Fourier coefficients, the restricted context-sensitive attribute noise model is strictly stronger than the attribute noise model considered in section 4.

Furthermore, with respect to the type of error induced in Fourier coefficients, the RCSAN model is in some ways more similar to malicious noise than to attribute noise. In particular, recall that the errors induced by the attribute noise model in the first-order Fourier coefficients of a target function are multiplicative in nature: each coefficient is reduced by a multiplicative factor as small as $1 - 2p_{\mathcal{N}}$. On the other hand, like the malicious noise model, the RCSAN model can induce additive error in the first-order Fourier coefficients. For example, consider an irrelevant attribute i, that is, an attribute for which $\hat{f}(e_i) = 0$. If this coefficient is estimated as the sample mean of $f^j \chi_{e_i}(x^j)$ over a set of noisy examples $\{(x^j, f^j)\}$ where the noise rates are $p_i^{++} = p_i^{--} = 0$ and $p_i^{+-} = p_i^{-+} = \eta > 0$, then the expected value of the estimate will be η.

In the remainder of this section, we will examine uniform-distribution RCSAN-tolerant learning of a subclass of linear threshold functions, the class $\mathcal{L}_h$ of *homogeneous linear threshold functions*. This class is the discrete analog of the origin-centered halfspaces considered by Kalai *et al.* [1] and others. Specifically, $\mathcal{L}_h$ is the set of all functions $f : \{0, 1\}^n \to \{-1, 1\}$ such that there is a function $F = \sum_{|a|=1} \hat{F}(a)\chi_a$ and $f = \text{sign}(F)$. We'll begin with several simple lemmas showing that $\mathcal{L}_h$ has a number of nice Fourier properties.

6.1 Properties of $\mathcal{L}_h$

Lemma 2. *If $f \in \mathcal{L}_h$ then f is balanced, that is, $E_{x \sim \mathcal{U}_n}[f(x)] = \hat{f}(0^n) = 0$.*

Proof. Let $\bar{x}$ represent the bitwise-complement of $x \in \{0, 1\}^n$. Since $f \in \mathcal{L}_h$, there is some F such that for every $x \in \{0, 1\}^n$, $f(x) = \text{sign}(\sum_{|a|=1} \hat{F}(a)\chi_a(x))$.

Fixing such an F we have that for all x, $f(\bar{x}) = \text{sign}(\sum_{|a|=1} \hat{F}(a)\chi_a(\bar{x})) = \text{sign}(-\sum_{|a|=1} \hat{F}(a)\chi_a(x)) = -f(x)$. It follows that $E_{x\sim\mathcal{U}_n}[f(x)] = 0$. □

Lemma 3. *If $f : \{0,1\}^n \to \{-1,1\}$ is in $\mathcal{L}_h$ and $1 \le i \le n$ then for any $b \in \{-1,1\}$, $\Pr_{x\sim\mathcal{U}_n}[f(x) = 1 \wedge \chi_{e_i}(x) = b] = \Pr_{x\sim\mathcal{U}_n}[f(x) = -1 \wedge \chi_{e_i}(x) = -b]$.*

Proof. Fix arbitrary $b \in \{-1,1\}$. By the proof of the preceding lemma, we know that for all $x \in \{0,1\}^n$, $f(\bar{x}) = -f(x)$. Thus, for every $x \in \{0,1\}^n$ such that $f(x) = 1$ and $\chi_{e_i}(x) = b$ there is a distinct $y = \bar{x}$ such that $f(y) = -1$ and $\chi_{e_i}(y) = -b$. Therefore, the set of such x's is no larger than the set of such y's. But it is similarly easy to see that the set of such y's is no larger than the set of such x's. Thus the sets are of equal size and have equal probability with respect to the uniform distribution. □

Lemma 4. *If $f : \{0,1\}^n \to \{-1,1\}$ is in $\mathcal{L}_h$ and $1 \le i \le n$ then for any $b \in \{-1,1\}$,*

$$\Pr_{x\sim\mathcal{U}_n}[f(x) = 1 \wedge \chi_{e_i}(x) = b] = \frac{1 + b\hat{f}(e_i)}{4}.$$

Proof. By the definition of Fourier coefficients and the previous lemma, $\hat{f}(e_i) = 2\Pr[f = \chi_{e_i}] - 1 = 2(\Pr[f = \chi_{e_i} = 1] + \Pr[f = \chi_{e_i} = -1]) - 1 = 4\Pr[f = \chi_{e_i} = 1] - 1$. This proves the $b = 1$ case. The $b = -1$ case can be proved similarly by starting with $\hat{f}(e_1) = 1 - 2\Pr[f \ne \chi_{e_i}]$. □

Lemma 5. *If $f : \{0,1\}^n \to \{-1,1\}$ is in $\mathcal{L}_h$ and $1 \le i \ne j \le n$ then for any $b_1, b_2 \in \{-1,1\}$, $\Pr_{x\sim\mathcal{U}_n}[f(x) = 1 \wedge \chi_{e_i}(x) = b_1 \wedge \chi_{e_j}(x) = b_2] = \Pr_{x\sim\mathcal{U}_n}[f(x) = -1 \wedge \chi_{e_i}(x) = -b_1 \wedge \chi_{e_j}(x) = -b_2]$*

Proof. The proof is essentially the same as that of Lemma 3. □

Lemma 6. *If $f : \{0,1\}^n \to \{-1,1\}$ is in $\mathcal{L}_h$ and $1 \le i \ne j \le n$ then $\hat{f}(e_i \oplus e_j) = 0$.*

Proof. Let χ_{ij} represent $\chi_{e_i \oplus e_j}$ and define χ_i and χ_j similarly in terms of e_i and e_j, respectively. Then applying the definition of Fourier coefficients and the preceding lemma, we have that

$$\hat{f}(e_i \oplus e_j) = 2\Pr_{x\sim\mathcal{U}_n}[f = \chi_{ij}] - 1$$

$$= 2(\Pr[f = 1 \wedge \chi_i = 1 \wedge \chi_j = 1] + \Pr[f = 1 \wedge \chi_i = -1 \wedge \chi_j = -1] +$$
$$\Pr[f = -1 \wedge \chi_i = 1 \wedge \chi_j = -1] + \Pr[f = -1 \wedge \chi_i = -1 \wedge \chi_j = 1]) - 1$$
$$= 2(\Pr[f = 1 \wedge \chi_i = 1 \wedge \chi_j = 1] + \Pr[f = 1 \wedge \chi_i = -1 \wedge \chi_j = -1] +$$
$$\Pr[f = 1 \wedge \chi_i = -1 \wedge \chi_j = 1] + \Pr[f = 1 \wedge \chi_i = 1 \wedge \chi_j = -1]) - 1$$
$$= 2\Pr[f = 1] - 1.$$

Since f is balanced (by Lemma 2), $\Pr[f = 1] = 1/2$. □

Lemma 7. *If* $f : \{0,1\}^n \to \{-1,1\}$ *is in* $\mathcal{L}_h$ *and* $1 \le i \ne j \le n$ *then for any* $b_1, b_2 \in \{-1,1\}$,

$$\Pr_{x \sim \mathcal{U}_n} [f(x) = 1 \wedge \chi_{e_i}(x) = b_1 \wedge \chi_{e_j} = b_2] = \frac{1 + b_1 \hat{f}(e_i) + b_2 \hat{f}(e_j)}{8}.$$

Proof. Fix b_1, b_2, i, and j and let f_{ij} represent the projection of f that ignores attributes i and j and instead treats every example x as if these attributes have constant values such that $\chi_{e_i}(x) = b_1$ and $\chi_{e_j}(x) = b_2$. It follows from the Fourier representation of f that $E[f_{ij}] = \hat{f}(0^n) + b_1 \hat{f}(e_i) + b_2 \hat{f}(e_j) + b_1 b_2 \hat{f}(e_i \oplus e_j)$. Furthermore, based on Lemma 2 and the preceding lemma, we know that this sum reduces to $b_1 \hat{f}(e_i) + b_2 \hat{f}(e_j)$. Of course, $E[f_{ij}]$ is also equal to $2 \Pr[f_{ij} = 1] - 1 = 2 \Pr[f = 1 \mid \chi_{e_i} = b_1 \wedge \chi_{e_j} = b_2] - 1$. Applying the definition of conditional probability and solving for $\Pr[f = 1 \wedge \chi_{e_i} = b_1 \wedge \chi_{e_j} = b_2]$ gives the lemma.   □

6.2   Learning $\mathcal{L}_h$

With these lemmas in hand, let us now consider the effect of context-sensitive noise on the estimate of a first-order Fourier coefficient of a homogeneous linear threshold function.

Lemma 8. *Let* $f : \{0,1\}^n \to \{-1,1\}$ *be any function in* $\mathcal{L}_h$ *and let* $1 \le i \le n$. *Then for any RCSAN process, the expected value of the sample mean of* $f^j \chi_{e_i}(x^j)$ *over a set of noisy examples* $\{(x^j, f^j)\}$ *is*

$$\frac{p_i^{+-} + p_i^{-+} - p_i^{++} - p_i^{--}}{2} + \hat{f}(e_i) \left(1 - \frac{p_i^{+-} + p_i^{-+} + p_i^{++} + p_i^{--}}{2} \right) \quad (2)$$

Proof. The expected value without noise is of course $\hat{f}(e_i)$. By Lemma 4, the probability that $f = \chi_{e_i} = 1$—which is also the probability that noise rate p_i^{++} applies—is $(1 + \hat{f}(e_i))/4$. The effect of attribute noise on these examples is to subtract 1 rather than adding 1 to $\sum_j f^j \chi_{e_i}(x^j)$. Thus, the expected effect of noise due to examples where $f = \chi_{e_i} = 1$ is to add $-p_i^{++}(1 + \hat{f}(e_i))/2$ to the true expected value $\hat{f}(e_i)$. Similarly, applying Lemma 3 as well as Lemma 4, the expected contribution of noise due to examples where $f = \chi_{e_i} = -1$ is $-p_i^{--}(1 + \hat{f}(e_i))/2$. Further applications of Lemmas 3 and 4 to the remaining cases gives that the expected value of the sample mean is

$$\hat{f}(e_i) + \frac{(p_i^{+-} + p_i^{-+})(1 - \hat{f}(e_i)) - (p_i^{++} + p_i^{--})(1 + \hat{f}(e_i))}{2}.$$

Rearranging this expression gives the lemma.   □

Thus, in general, the noise induced in a coefficient $\hat{f}(e_i)$ by an RCSAN process is a combination of additive error (of rate $(p_i^{+-} + p_i^{-+} - p_i^{++} - p_i^{--})/2$) and multiplicative error (of rate $1 - (p_i^{+-} + p_i^{-+} + p_i^{++} + p_i^{--})/2$).

Obviously, if the RCSAN process generating noisy examples is known, then this theorem can be used to recover a close approximation to the noiseless Fourier coefficient $\hat{f}(e_i)$ from the noisy estimate of this coefficient as long as the multiplicative factor in (2) is bounded away from 0, or equivalently, as long as the average noise rate $\bar{p}_i \equiv (p_i^{+-} + p_i^{-+} + p_i^{++} + p_i^{--})/4$ is bounded away from $1/2$. So it is easy to learn $\mathcal{L}_h$ in the RCSAN model if the noise process is known and does not completely obscure the target function.

The more interesting case, then, is if the noise process is unknown but perhaps constrained in some way. For instance, consider the constraint that for all i, the average noise probability when f and χ_{e_i} agree $((p_i^{++} + p_i^{--})/2)$ is equal to the average noise probability when they disagree. Then the additive term in (2) will vanish. In this situation, it can be seen that Theorem 2 applies, with the modification that we will use $\bar{p} \equiv \max_{i=1..n} \bar{p}_i$ in place of $p_\mathcal{N}$. In fact, if the additive term in (2) is nonzero but less than, say, $\tau/5(n+1)$ for all i, then we can modify $\mathcal{A}$ to use a (polynomial) sample size m' such that the $\hat{g}(a)$'s computed are all (with high probability) within $\tau/5(n+1)$ of the true mean values they estimate. The result is that (with high probability) each $\hat{g}(a)$ will be within $\tau/2.5(n+1)$ of its mean value, as needed for the remainder of the proof of Theorem 2. In short, as long as for every attribute i the average noise rate $\bar{p}_i$ is non-negligibly less than $1/2$ and the differences $(p_i^{+-} + p_i^{-+}) - (p_i^{++} + p_i^{--})$ are all sufficiently small, then Theorem 2 applies and $\mathcal{L}_h$ is weakly learnable with respect to uniform despite an unknown RCSAN process.

This is of course a very strong constraint on the RCSAN process. The main result of this section shows how to learn $\mathcal{L}_h$ with a much milder constraint on the RCSAN process.

Theorem 3. *For any $\tau > 0$ and given any RCSAN process, $\mathcal{L}_h$ is efficiently 2-RFA $(\bar{p}^2 + \tau + 1/4)$-learnable with respect to uniform. The RCSAN process is unknown and unconstrained except that $\bar{p} < 1/2$, there must be one known attribute k for which $\bar{p}_k = 0$, and there must be a known non-negligible value $\beta > 0$ such that $|\hat{f}(e_k)| > \beta$.*

Proof. (Sketch) The key is showing that, for every attribute $i \neq k$, we can obtain a good approximation to the additive error $((p_i^{+-} + p_i^{-+}) - (p_i^{++} + p_i^{--}))/2$ present in $\hat{g}(e_i)$ computed as the mean value of $f^j \chi_i(x^j)$ over a set of RCSAN examples $\{(x^j, f^j)\}$ (where as before χ_i is shorthand for χ_{e_i}). Once this additive error has been (mostly) eliminated from the $\hat{g}(e_i)$'s, the analysis above applies, and we can use a slight modification of the algorithm of Theorem 2 to obtain our result. So we will show how to estimate the additive error.

Let E_{ik} represent the expected value of $\chi_i(x^j)\chi_k(x^j)$ over random noisy examples (x^j, f^j) drawn according to some fixed RCSAN process. Note that, since attribute k is assumed to be noise free, if attribute i is also noise free then $E_{ik} = E_\mathcal{U}[\chi_i \chi_k] = 0$. Now consider how this changes if $p_i^{++} > 0$. By Lemma 7 we know that with probability $(1 + \hat{f}(e_i) + \hat{f}(e_k))/8$ a pre-noise example x is such that $f(x) = \chi_i(x) = \chi_k(x) = 1$. Since corrupting bit i of such an x changes $\chi_i(x)\chi_k(x)$ from $+1$ to -1, the net change in E_{ik} due to positive p_i^{++} over these x's is $-p_i^{++}(1 + \hat{f}(e_i) + \hat{f}(e_k))/4$. On the other hand, with probability $(1 + \hat{f}(e_i) - \hat{f}(e_k))/8$ we have $f(x) = \chi_i(x) = 1$ and $\chi_k(x) = -1$, and the net change in E_{ik} due to positive p_i^{++} over these x's is $p_i^{++}(1 + \hat{f}(e_i) - \hat{f}(e_k))/4$. Combining these effects, the overall change in E_{ik} due to positive p_i^{++} will be $-p_i^{++}\hat{f}(e_k)/2$. Applying Lemma 5 along with Lemma 7, we can similarly see that the contribution to E_{ik} due to positive p_i^{--} will be $-p_i^{--}\hat{f}(e_k)/2$. On the other hand, the total change due to positive p_i^{+-} and p_i^{-+} will be $(p_i^{+-} + p_i^{-+})\hat{f}(e_k)/2$. Overall, then, we see that $E_{ik} = \hat{f}(e_k)((p_i^{+-} + p_i^{-+}) - (p_i^{++} + p_i^{--}))/2$.

Our estimate for the additive error term in $\hat{g}(e_i)$, then, will be obtained by drawing a noisy sample, computing sample means that approximate E_{ik} and $\hat{f}(e_k)$, and dividing the approximation of E_{ik} by the approximation of $\hat{f}(e_k)$. We will use a sample size large enough so that this quotient is, with high probability, within an additive factor of $\tau/5(n + 1)$ of the expected additive error term in (2). Based on the earlier discussion, it should be clear that such an estimate will be sufficiently close to give us the learning result claimed.

Specifically, we will use a sample large enough to guarantee with high probability that the noisy estimate of E_{ik} is additively within $O(\beta\tau/n)$ of its expected value. By standard Hoeffding bounds, a polynomial number of examples will suffice. We will then estimate (with high probability) $\hat{f}(e_k)$ to within a multiplicative factor c close enough to 1 to achieve the desired bound on the additive error in the quotient of our estimates. It can be shown that $|1 - c| = O(\beta\tau/n)$ is sufficient for this purpose, and Chernoff bounds tell us that the sample size required will again be polynomial. ☐

7 Further Work

An obvious question whenever uniform-distribution weak learning results are derived is how far the results can be extended beyond uniform. The extant proofs of the results underlying Gotsman-Linial's observation seem to rely heavily on independence and other properties of the uniform distribution, so such a generalization may not be easy. However, if the results could be extended to a sufficiently general set of distributions, this might lead to noise-tolerant uniform-distribution strong learning algorithms for $\mathcal{L}$.

There may be interesting subclasses of $\mathcal{L}$ such that for any function f in the class the constant and first-order Fourier coefficients represent much more than half of the power spectrum of f. If the spectral power of the low-order coefficients of all of the functions in such a class were over $3/4$, then results of Kalai et al. [1] could be applied to give an efficient algorithm weakly agnostically learning $\mathcal{L}$ using $\mathcal{L}$ as the hypothesis class. Do such subclasses of $\mathcal{L}$ exist? The class of Majority functions is not such a subclass, as it can be shown that asymptotically the low-order coefficients for odd Majority functions represent roughly $2/\pi \approx .64$ of the power spectrum. Alternatively, can the Kalai et al. results be strengthened so that they could be applied to weaker approximators?

The fact that $\mathcal{L}$ can be weakly learned despite an essentially optimal rate of adversarial noise can be shown to imply that the constant 2 in the bound of

Theorem 1 cannot be improved unless the bound is also changed in some other way. How tight is the bound of Theorem 1?

Kalai *et al.* [1] also explore malicious noise learning and give a simple algorithm for uniformly learning halfspaces over the unit sphere that tolerates noise rate η up to roughly $\Omega(1/n^{1/4})$. It would be nice to have a comparable result over the cube (although it may require unrestricted focus of attention).

Can an RCSAN result similar to Theorem 3 be obtained without the need for a known noise-free attribute? Beyond this, it may be interesting to explore 1-RCSAN learnability of other classes as well as k-RCSAN learning of $\mathcal{L}$ and other classes for $k > 1$.

Acknowledgements

Rocco Servedio posed a question that started this work and reminded the author of the Gotsman-Linial result. Nati Linial graciously explained a part of the proof of that result. Nader Bshouty pointed out an improvement to the proof of the Kalai *et al.* [1] observation that the low-degree algorithm is a weak agnostic learner. Discussions with Rocco and Adam Klivans were also very helpful.

References

1. Kalai, A.T., Klivans, A.R., Mansour, Y., Servedio, R.A.: Agnostically learning halfspaces. In: Proceedings of the 46th Annual IEEE Symposium on Foundations of Computer Science. (2005) 11–20
2. Ben-David, S., Dichterman, E.: Learning with restricted focus of attention. In: Proceedings of the 6th Annual Conference on Computational Learning Theory. (1993) 287–296
3. Gotsman, C., Linial, N.: Spectral properties of threshold functions. Combinatorica **14** (1994) 35–50
4. Blum, A., Furst, M., Jackson, J., Kearns, M., Mansour, Y., Rudich, S.: Weakly learning DNF and characterizing statistical query learning using Fourier analysis. In: Proceedings of the 26th Annual ACM Symposium on Theory of Computing. (1994) 253–262 Preliminary version available as http://www.mathcs.duq.edu/~jackson/dnfsq.ps.
5. Valiant, L.G.: A theory of the learnable. Communications of the ACM **27** (1984) 1134–1142
6. Kearns, M.J., Schapire, R.E., Sellie, L.M.: Toward efficient agnostic learning. Machine Learning **17** (1994) 115–141
7. Shackelford, G., Volper, D.: Learning k-DNF with noise in the attributes. In: Proceedings of the 1988 Workshop on Computational Learning Theory. (1988) 97–103
8. Valiant, L.G.: Learning disjunctions of conjunctions. In: Proceedings of the Ninth International Joint Conference on Artificial Intelligence. Volume 1. (1985) 560–566
9. Hoeffding, W.: Probability inequalities for sums of bounded random variables. American Statistical Association Journal **58** (1963) 13–30
10. Bshouty, N.H., Jackson, J.C., Tamon, C.: Uniform-distribution attribute noise learnability. Inf. Comput. **187** (2003) 277–290

Discriminative Learning Can Succeed Where Generative Learning Fails

Philip M. Long[1] and Rocco A. Servedio[2],[*]

[1] Google, Mountain View, CA, USA
plong@google.com
[2] Columbia University, New York, NY, USA
rocco@cs.columbia.edu

Abstract. Generative algorithms for learning classifiers use training data to separately estimate a probability model for each class. New items are then classified by comparing their probabilities under these models. In contrast, discriminative learning algorithms try to find classifiers that perform well on all the training data.

We show that there is a learning problem that can be solved by a discriminative learning algorithm, but not by any generative learning algorithm (given minimal cryptographic assumptions). This statement is formalized using a framework inspired by previous work of Goldberg [3].

1   Introduction

If objects and their classifications are generated randomly from a joint probability distribution, then the optimal way to predict the class y of an item x to is maximize $\Pr[y|x]$. Applying Bayes' rule, this is equivalent to maximizing $\Pr[x|y] \Pr[y]$. This motivates what has become known as the *generative* approach to learning a classifier, in which the training data is used to learn $\Pr[\cdot|y]$ and $\Pr[y]$ for the different classes y, and the results are used to approximate the behavior of the optimal predictor for the source (see [1, 5]).

In the *discriminative* approach, the learning algorithm simply tries to find a classifier that performs well on the training data [12, 5, 9, 6]. Discriminative algorithms can (and usually do) process examples from several classes together at once, e.g. maximum margin algorithms use both positive and negative examples together to find a large margin hypothesis separating the two classes.

The main result of this paper is a computational separation between generative and discriminative learning. We describe a learning problem and prove that it has the following property: a discriminative algorithm can solve the problem in polynomial time, but no generative learning algorithm can (assuming that cryptographic one-way functions exist).

Our analysis demonstrates the possible cost of largely processing the examples from different classes separately, as generative methods do. Goldberg [3] was the

---

[*] Supported in part by NSF award CCF-0347282, by NSF award CCF-0523664, and by a Sloan Foundation Fellowship.

G. Lugosi and H.U. Simon (Eds.): COLT 2006, LNAI 4005, pp. 319–334, 2006.

first to study the effect of this limitation. His analyses concerned a modification of the PAC model in which

- the examples belonging to each class are analyzed separately,
- each analysis results in a scoring function for that class, and
- future class predictions are made by comparing the scores assigned by the different scoring functions.

He designed algorithms that provably solve a number of concrete learning problems despite the constraint of processing examples from different classes separately, and identified conditions that allow a discriminative PAC learner to be modified to work in the generative setting. The main open question formulated in [3] is whether there is a learning problem that can be solved by a discriminative algorithm but cannot be solved by a generative algorithm. We establish our main result in a framework closely related to the one proposed in [3]. The main difference between our formulation and Goldberg's is that we define a learning problem to be a collection of possible joint probability distributions over items and their classifications, whereas Goldberg defined a learning problem to be a concept class as in the PAC model.

Roughly, our proof works as follows. In the learning problem we consider the domain is divided into three parts, and a separate function provides 100% accuracy on each part. The third part is really hard: its function is cryptographically secure against any adversary (or learner) which does not "know" the "key" to the function. On the other hand, the first two parts are easy, and descriptions of their two functions can be combined to compute the key of the third function.

A discriminative algorithm can succeed by learning the first two parts and using the results to obtain the key to the third function. On the other hand, each of the first two parts is hard to learn from one kind of example: one part is hard to learn from positive examples only, and the other is hard to learn from negative examples only. Thus in the generative learning framework, the scoring function obtained using positive examples only contains no information about the subfunction which is hard to learn from positive examples, and thus in and of itself this positive scoring function contains no useful information about the key for the third function. An analogous statement is true for the negative scoring function. The tricky part of the analysis is to show that the overall predictor used by the generative algorithm – which incorporates information from both the positive and negative scoring functions – is similarly useless on the third part. Intuitively this is the case because the two scoring functions are combined in a very restricted way (simply by comparing the values that they output), and this makes it impossible for the final classifier to fully exploit the information contained in the two scoring functions.

Related work. Aside from Goldberg's paper, the most closely related work of which we are aware is due to Ng and Jordan [8]. They showed that Naive Bayes, a generative algorithm, can converge to the large-sample limit of its accuracy much more quickly than a corresponding discriminative method. For generative algorithms that work by performing maximum likelihood over restricted classes of models, they also showed, given minimal assumptions, that the large-sample limit of their accuracy is no better than a corresponding discriminative method. Note that these results compare a particular generative algorithm with a particular discriminative algorithm. In contrast, the analysis in this paper exposes a fundamental limitation faced by any generative learning algorithm, due to the fact that it processes the two classes separately.

Section 2 contains preliminaries including a detailed description and motivation of the learning model. In Section 3 we give our construction of a learning problem that separates the two models and give a high-level idea of the proof. Sections 4 and 5 give the proof of the separation.

Due to space constraints some proofs are omitted; see [7] for these proofs.

2 Definitions and Main Result

Given a domain X, we say that a *source* is a probability distribution P over $X \times \{-1, 1\}$, and a *learning problem* $\mathcal{P}$ is a set of sources. Throughout this paper the domain X will be $\{0, 1\}^n \times \{1, 2, 3\}$.

2.1 Discriminative Learning

The discriminative learning framework that we analyze is the *Probably Approximately Bayes* (PAB) [2] variant of the PAC [11] learning model. In the PAB model, in a learning problem $\mathcal{P}$ a learning algorithm is given a set of m labeled examples drawn from an unknown source $P \in \mathcal{P}$. The goal is to output a hypothesis function $h : X \to \{-1, 1\}$ which with probability $1 - \delta$ satisfies $\Pr_{(x,y) \in P}[h(x) \neq y] \leq \text{Bayes}(P) + \epsilon$, where $\text{Bayes}(P)$ is the least error rate that can be achieved on P, i.e. the minimum, over all functions h, of $\Pr_{(x,y) \in P}[h(x) \neq y]$. In a setting (such as ours) where the domain X is parameterized by n, an *efficient* learning algorithm for $\mathcal{P}$ is one that uses $\text{poly}(n, \frac{1}{\epsilon}, \frac{1}{\delta})$ many examples, runs in $\text{poly}(n, \frac{1}{\epsilon}, \frac{1}{\delta})$ time, and outputs a hypothesis that can be evaluated on any point in $\text{poly}(n, \frac{1}{\epsilon}, \frac{1}{\delta})$ time.

2.2 Generative Learning

Goldberg [3] defined a restricted "generative" variant of PAC learning. Our analysis will concern a natural extension of his ideas to the PAB model.

Roughly speaking, in the generative model studied in this paper, the algorithm first uses only positive examples to construct a "positive scoring function" $h_+ : X \to \mathbf{R}$ that assigns a "positiveness" score to each example in the input domain. It then uses only negative examples to construct (using the same algorithm) a "negative scoring function" $h_- : X \to \mathbf{R}$ that assigns a "negativeness" score to each example. The classifier output by the algorithm is the following: given example x, output 1 or -1 according to whether or not $h_+(x) > h_-(x)$.

We now give a precise description of our learning framework. In our model

- A sample $S = (x_1, y_1),...,(x_m, y_m)$ is drawn from the unknown source P;
- An algorithm A is given a filtered version of S in which
  - examples (x_t, y_t) for which $y_t = 1$ are replaced with x_t, and
  - examples (x_t, y_t) for which $y_t = -1$ are replaced with $\diamond$
  and A outputs $h_+ : X \to \mathbf{R}$.
- Next, the same algorithm A is given a filtered version of S in which
  - examples (x_t, y_t) for which $y_t = 1$ are replaced with $\diamond$, and
  - examples (x_t, y_t) for which $y_t = -1$ are replaced with x_t
  and A outputs $h_- : X \to \mathbf{R}$.
- Finally, let $h : X \to \{-1, 1\}$ be defined as $h(x) = \mathrm{sgn}(h_+(x) - h_-(x))$. If $h_+(x) = h_-(x)$ then we view $h(x)$ as outputing $\perp$ (undefined).

Algorithm A is said to be a *generative PAB learning algorithm* for $\mathcal{P}$ if for all $P \in \mathcal{P}$, for all $0 < \epsilon < \frac{1}{2}$, $0 < \delta < 1$, the hypothesis h obtained as above, with probability at least $1 - \delta$, satisfies $\Pr_{(x,y) \in P}[h(x) \neq y] \leq \mathrm{Bayes}(P) + \epsilon$. The notions of runtime and efficiency are the same as in the standard PAB framework. It is easy to see that any learning problem that can be efficiently PAB learned in the generative framework we have described can also be efficiently learned in the standard PAB framework.

2.3   Main Result

With these definitions in place we can state our main result:

Theorem 1. *If one-way functions exist, there is a learning problem that is efficiently learnable in the PAB model, but not in the generative PAB model.*

2.4   Two Unsupervised Learners Are Not Better Than One

Using different algorithms for the positive and negative examples cannot help a generative learning algorithm much; this can be formalized using an idea due to Goldberg [3]. This leads to the following extension of Theorem 1 (see Section 6 of [7] for a proof of this extension):

Theorem 2. *Suppose the generative PAB learning model is relaxed so that separate algorithms can be applied to the positive and negative examples. Then it remains true that if one-way functions exist, then there is a learning problem that can be solved in polynomial time in the standard PAB model, but not in the generative PAB model.*

3   The Construction and the Main Idea

Our construction uses pseudorandom functions; defined by Goldreich *et al.* in 1986 [4], these are central objects in modern cryptography.

Definition 1. *A pseudorandom function family (PRFF) is a collection of functions $\{f_s : \{0,1\}^{|s|} \to \{1,-1\}\}_{s\in\{0,1\}^*}$ with the following two properties:*

1. *(efficient evaluation) there is a deterministic algorithm which, given an n-bit seed s and an n-bit input x, runs in time poly(n) and outputs $f_s(x)$;*
2. *(pseudorandomness) for all constants $c > 0$, all probabilistic polynomial-time (p.p.t.) oracle algorithms A, and all sufficiently large n, we have that*

$$\left| \Pr_{F\in\mathcal{R}_n} \left[A^F(1^n) \text{ outputs } 1\right] - \Pr_{s\in\{0,1\}^n} \left[A^{f_s}(1^n) \text{ outputs } 1\right]\right| < 1/n^c.$$

Here " $\Pr_{F\in\mathcal{R}_n}$ " indicates that F is a truly random function chosen uniformly from the set of all 2^{2^n} Boolean functions mapping $\{0,1\}^n$ to $\{-1,1\}$, and " $\Pr_{s\in\{0,1\}^n}$ " indicates that s is chosen uniformly from $\{0,1\}^n$.

The notation "$A^g(1^n)$" indicates that A is run with black-box oracle access to g on a vacuous input of length n (so since A is a polynomial-time algorithm, it runs for at most poly(n) time steps). Intuitively, the pseudorandomess property ensures that in any probabilistic poly(n)-time computation which is executed with oracle access to a truly random function, a randomly chosen pseudorandom function may be used instead without affecting the outcome of the computation in a noticeable way. Well known results [4, 10] imply that pseudorandom function families exist if and only if any one-way function exists.

3.1   The Construction

We first define a class C of Boolean functions in which each function is specified by a triple (r, s, b) where $r, s \in \{-1, 0, 1\}^n$ and $b \in \{-1, 1\}$. We will use the functions in C to define the set of sources which constitute our learning problem.

A function $c_{r,s,b} \in C$ takes two inputs: an n-bit string $x \in \{0, 1\}^n$ and an index $i \in \{1, 2, 3\}$. We refer to examples of the form (x, i) as *type-i examples* for $i = 1, 2, 3$. The value of $c_{r,s,b}(x, i)$ is defined as follows:

$$c_{r,s,1}(x, i) = \begin{cases} AND_r(x) & \text{if } i = 1 \\ OR_s(x) & \text{if } i = 2 \\ f_{|r|\oplus|s|}(x) & \text{if } i = 3, \end{cases} \qquad c_{r,s,-1}(x, i) = \begin{cases} OR_r(x) & \text{if } i = 1 \\ AND_s(x) & \text{if } i = 2 \\ f_{|r|\oplus|s|}(x) & \text{if } i = 3. \end{cases}$$

Here AND_r is the conjunction of literals over $x_1, \ldots, x_n$ that is indexed by r; for instance if $n = 3$ and $r = (r_1, r_2, r_3) = (1, 0, -1)$ then $AND_r(x)$ is $x_1 \wedge \overline{x}_3$. OR_s is similarly the disjunction that is indexed by s. The notation "$|r|$" denotes the n-bit string $(|r_1|, \ldots, |r_n|) \in \{0, 1\}^n$, and the bitwise XOR $y \oplus z$ of two n-bit strings $y, z \in \{0, 1\}^n$ is the n-bit string $(y_1 \oplus z_1, \ldots, y_n \oplus z_n)$. The family $\{f_t\}_{t\in\{0,1\}^n}$ is a PRFF as described at the start of Section 3 above.

Now we describe the learning problem $\mathcal{P}$ that we use to prove our main result. Each source P in $\mathcal{P}$ is *realizable*, i.e. there is a function mapping X to $\{-1, 1\}$ with 100% accuracy (so the Bayes optimal error is 0). Specifically, for each $c_{r,s,b} \in C$, there is a source $P_{r,s,b}$ which is a distribution over labelled examples

$((x,i), c_{r,s,b}(x,i))$. Thus to describe $P_{r,s,b}$ it suffices to describe the marginal distributions over the domain $X = \{0,1\}^n \times \{1,2,3\}$ of inputs to $c_{r,s,b}$; i.e. we need to describe the distribution over positive examples, and the distribution over negative examples. These marginal distributions are as follows: for each $i = 1,2,3$ the distribution allocates $1/3$ of the total probability mass to type-i examples. For each $i = 1,2,3$, half of this $1/3$ mass is distributed uniformly over the positive type-i examples, and half over the negative type-i examples.

Note that the above description assumes that there are indeed both positive and negative examples of type i. If for some i all type-i examples have the same label, then the entire $1/3$ probability mass for type-i examples is uniformly distributed over all 2^n examples (x,i). Note that AND_r always has at least one positive example and OR_s always has at least one negative example, and consequently each source in $\mathcal{P}$ has at least $1/6$ probability weight on each label. Note also that it is possible that for a given $t \in \{0,1\}^n$, the member f_t of the pseudo-random function family used on the type-3 examples could be identically 1 or identically -1. However, the pseudorandomness of $\{f_t\}$ ensures that for any $c > 0$, for large enough n, at least a $1 - \frac{1}{n^c}$ fraction of functions in $\{f_t\}_{t \in \{0,1\}^n}$ have a fraction of positive (negative) examples which is bounded in $[\frac{1}{2} - \frac{1}{n^c}, \frac{1}{2} + \frac{1}{n^c}]$. (Otherwise, by drawing poly(n) many random examples and estimating the fraction of positive examples using this sample, a poly(n)-time algorithm would be able to distinguish a random function from $\{f_t\}_{t \in \{0,1\}^n}$ from a truly random function with nonnegligible advantage over random guessing.)

3.2   The Idea

In this section we sketch the high-level idea of why discriminative algorithms can efficiently solve this learning problem while generative algorithms cannot.

Discriminative learners can succeed: Let $P_{r,s,b}$ be any element of $\mathcal{P}$. A simple argument which we sketch in Section 4 shows that a discriminative learner can use the labelled type-1 examples (type-2 respectively) to efficiently exactly identify r (s, respectively). It can guess and check the value of b, and thus can w.h.p. exactly identify the unknown source in poly(n) time.

Generative learners cannot succeed: We show that no generative algorithm can construct a hypothesis that w.h.p. has high accuracy on type-3 examples.

More precisely, we define a particular probability distribution $\mathcal{D}$ over the sources in $\mathcal{P}$ and show that for a source selected from this distribution, no poly(n)-time generative learning algorithm can w.h.p. output a hypothesis h whose accuracy on type-3 examples is bounded away from $1/2$. This means that the overall accuracy of such a learner cannot be substantially greater than $5/6$.

The distribution $\mathcal{D}$ is as follows: to draw a source $P_{r,s,b}$ from $\mathcal{D}$,

- Toss a fair coin and set b to ± 1 accordingly;
- Select r and s by drawing each one from the following distribution TARGET over $\{-1,0,1\}^n$: a string x drawn from TARGET has each x_i independently set to be -1, 0 or 1 with probabilities $1/4$, $1/2$ and $1/4$ respectively.

Note that under $\mathcal{D}$ the strings $|r|$ and $|s|$ are independently and uniformly distributed over $\{0, 1\}^n$. This will be useful later since it means that even if one of the strings r, s is given, the seed $|r| \oplus |s|$ to the pseudorandom function $f_{|r| \oplus |s|}$ is uniformly distributed over $\{0, 1\}^n$ as required by Definition 1.

Let $P_{r,s,b}$ be a source drawn from $\mathcal{D}$. Let us suppose for now that $b = 1$, and let us consider the execution of A when it is run using a sample in which only positive examples drawn from $P_{r,s,1}$ (i.e. positive examples of the concept $c_{r,s,1}$) are uncovered. Recall that under the conditions of the generative model that we consider, the algorithm A does not "know" that it is being run using positive versus negative examples; it only receives a set of unlabelled examples.

(Throughout the following informal discussion we assume that both $r \neq 0^n$ and $s \neq 0^n$; note that the probability that either of these strings is 0^n is at most $2/2^n$. We further assume that $f_{|r| \oplus |s|}$ is not identically 1 or identically -1; recall from the discussion at the end of Section 3.1 that this fails to hold with probability $1/n^{\omega(1)}$. Under these assumptions a random example from $P_{r,s,1}$ has a $1/6$ chance of being a positive/negative type-1/2/3 example.)

The examples that A receives will be distributed as follows:

- **Type-1 examples** $(x, 1)$: By our assumptions, $1/3$ of the uncovered examples that A receives will be type-1 examples; these examples are uniformly distributed over all $x \in \{0, 1\}^n$ that satisfy $AND_r(x)$. As we will see in Section 4, it is easy for A to completely identify r using these examples.
- **Type-2 examples** $(x, 2)$: By our assumptions, $1/3$ of the uncovered examples A receives will be type-2 examples, each of which has x uniformly distributed over all strings that satisfy OR_s. As we will show in Section 5, for any $r \in \{-1, 0, 1\}^n$ the distribution of these type-2 examples (taken over the random choice of s from TARGET and the random draw of the examples from $P_{r,s,1}$) is statistically indistinguishable from the uniform distribution over $\{0, 1\}^n$ to any algorithm (such as A) that receives only poly(n) many draws. Thus, as far as A can tell, the type-2 examples it receives are independently and uniformly drawn from $\{0, 1\}^n$; intuitively we view this as meaning that A gets no useful information about s from the type-2 examples, so we informally view $|s|$ as uniform random and unknown to A.
- **Type-3 examples** $(x, 3)$: By our assumptions, $1/3$ of the uncovered examples A receives will be type-3 examples. Intuitively, since $|s|$ is uniform random and unknown to A, even though r is known to A, the seed $t = |r| \oplus |s|$ to the pseudorandom function is uniform random and unknown to A. It follows from the definition of pseudorandomness that the function f_t is indistinguishable to algorithm A from a truly random function, so type-3 examples give no useful information to A; as far as A can tell, the type-3 examples it receives are simply uniform random strings drawn from $\{0, 1\}^n$.

Thus we may informally view the hypothesis that A constructs, when run on positive examples drawn from $P_{r,s,1}$ where r and s were drawn from TARGET, as being determined only by the information "$(r, 1)$" (meaning that r is the string that governs the distribution of type-1 examples in the sample used for learning); the type-2 and type-3 examples that A receives are indistinguishable from uniform random strings. (The indistinguishability is statistical for the type-2 examples and computational for the type-3 examples; see Proposition 1 and Lemma 1 respectively of Section 5, where we make these arguments precise.) We thus write $h_{r,1}$ to denote the hypothesis that A constructs in this case.

An analogous argument shows that we may view the hypothesis that A constructs when run on negative examples drawn from $c_{r,s,1}$ as being determined only by the information "$(s,2)$" (meaning that s is the string that governs the distribution of type-2 examples in the sample); in this case the type-1 and type-3 examples in the sample are indistinguishable from truly random strings. We write $h_{s,2}$ to denote the hypothesis that A constructs in this case.

Now let us consider a setting in which the target source is $P_{-r,-s,-1}$ (where for $z \in \{-1,0,1\}^n$, the string $-z$ is simply $(-z_1, \ldots, -z_n)$) and r, s (or equivalently $-r, -s$) are independently drawn from TARGET. This time we will consider the execution of A when it is run using a sample in which only *negative* examples from $P_{-r,-s,-1}$ are uncovered, with the same assumptions on r, s and $f_{|r \oplus s|}$ as above. The examples that A receives will be distributed as follows:

- **Type-1 examples** $(x,1)$: By definition of $P_{-r,-s,-1}$, $1/3$ of the uncovered examples that A receives will be type-1 examples. These examples are uniformly distributed over all $x \in \{0,1\}^n$ that do *not* satisfy $OR_{-r}(x)$, i.e. over all x that satisfy AND_r. Thus the negative type-1 examples in this case are distributed identically to the positive type-1 examples for $P_{r,s,1}$.

- **Type-2 examples** $(x,2)$: $1/3$ of the uncovered examples A receives will be type-2 examples, each of which has x uniformly distributed over all strings that do not satisfy AND_{-s}, i.e over all strings that satisfy OR_s. Thus the negative type-2 examples for $P_{-r,-s,-1}$ are distributed identically to the positive type-2 examples for $P_{r,s,1}$ (and as in that case, algorithm A gets no useful information about s from the type-2 examples, so we may view s as uniform random and unknown to A).

- **Type-3 examples** $(x,3)$: The seed $|-r| \oplus |-s| \in \{0,1\}^n$ is identical to the seed $t = |r| \oplus |s|$ that arose from $P_{r,s,1}$ above. As above, since s is uniform random and unknown to A, the function f_t is indistinguishable from a truly random function to A.

Thus we have arrived at the following crucial observation: *A cannot distinguish between when it is run on positive examples from $P_{r,s,1}$ versus negative examples from $P_{-r,-s,-1}$.* (The two distributions differ only in the type-3 examples, where in the negative $c_{-r,-s,-1}$ case they are uniform over $f_t(-1)$ and in the positive $c_{r,s,-1}$ case they are uniform over $f_t(1)$. By the pseudorandomness of f_t these distributions are indistinguishable from each other, since they are each indistinguishable from the uniform distribution over $\{0,1\}^n$.) So we may informally view the hypothesis that A constructs as being $h_{r,1}$ in both cases.

Likewise, whether A is run on negative examples from $P_{r,s,1}$ or positive examples from $P_{-r,-s,-1}$, the resulting hypothesis is $h_{s,2}$ in both cases.

Now suppose that A is a successful generative learning algorithm in the PAB sense, i.e. the final hypothesis obtained from source $P_{r,s,1}$ (which we denote $h_{r,s,1}$, and which equals $\mathrm{sgn}(h_{r,1}(x,i) - h_{s,2}(x,i))$) has very high accuracy. Since the overall error rate of $h_{r,s,1}$ is at least $1/3$ of its error rate on type-3 examples, this means that $h_{r,s,1}(x,3)$ must be well-correlated with $f_{|r|\oplus|s|}(x)$. On the other hand, as argued above, the final hypothesis $h_{-r,-s,-1}$ obtained from source $P_{-r,-s,-1}$ is $\mathrm{sgn}(h_{s,2}(x,i) - h_{r,1}(x,i))$, and this must have high accuracy on type-3 examples from this source; so $h_{-r,-s,-1}(x,3)$ is well-correlated with $f_{|-r|\oplus|-s*|}(x)$. But this is impossible because $f_{|-r|\oplus|-s|}$ is identical to $f_{|r|\oplus|s|}$ whereas $h_{-r,-s,-1}(x,3)$ is easily seen to be the negation of $h_{r,s,1}(x,3)$.

This concludes our informal presentation of why learning problem $\mathcal{P}$ is hard for any generative learning algorithm. In Section 5 we give a precise cryptographic instantiation of the above intuitive argument to prove that generative algorithms cannot succeed.

4 Discriminative Algorithms Can Succeed

Theorem 3. *There is a polynomial-time discriminative learning algorithm that can solve learning problem $\mathcal{P}$.*

Proof Sketch. We use Valiant's algorithm [11], which keeps all literals that are not eliminated as possibilities by the training data, to learn r and s. The probability that any incorrect literal is not eliminated by q examples is at most $2n(1/2)^q$. So r and s can be learned exactly; it is easy to "guess and check" b, and thus learn the target $c_{r,s,b}$ exactly. (See [7] for a full proof.) ∎

5 Generative Algorithms Must Fail

We prove the following theorem, which shows that no generative learning algorithm can succeed on learning problem $\mathcal{P}$.

Theorem 4. *Let A be any $\mathrm{poly}(n)$-time algorithm that operates in the generative learning framework and has the following property: when run on examples from any source in $\mathcal{P}$, with probability at least $1 - 1/n$ A outputs a final hypothesis h whose error rate is at most ϵ. Then $\epsilon \geq \frac{1}{6} - o(1)$.*

Let us set up the framework. Let A be any $\mathrm{poly}(n)$ time generative algorithm. We can view A as a mapping from (filtered) samples to hypotheses. Given a sample S we write $A(S)$ to denote the hypothesis that A outputs on S, and we write $A(S)(x)$ to denote the real-valued output of this hypothesis on x.

5.1 Positive Examples from $P_{r,s,1}$

Fix any $r \in \{-1, 0, 1\}^n$. Consider a source $P_{r,s,1}$ where s is drawn from TARGET. We first show that for any generative algorithm A that takes as input a sample of $m = \mathrm{poly}(n)$ many examples from such a source with only the positive examples exposed, the type-2 examples in its sample are statistically indistinguishable from uniform random examples over $\{0,1\}^n$.

To make this precise, we need the following definitions.

Definition 2. *If P is a source, define P_+ to be the probability distribution over $X \cup \{\diamond\}$ obtained by (i) choosing (x, y) according to P, and (ii) emitting x if $y = 1$ and emitting $\diamond$ if $y = -1$. Define P_- analogously with the labels reversed.*

Definition 3. *Let $D_{r,1}^+$ be the distribution over sets S_+ of m examples from $(\{0,1\}^n \times \{1,2,3\}) \cup \{\diamond\}$ which is defined as follows: to draw a set S_+ from $D_{r,1}^+$ (i) first draw s from TARGET, and (ii) then draw each of the m examples in S_+ independently from $(P_{r,s,1})_+$.*

Definition 4. *Let $\widetilde{D}_{r,1}^+$ be the distribution over sets $\widetilde{S}_+$ of m examples from $(\{0,1\}^n \times \{1,2,3\}) \cup \{\diamond\}$ defined as follows: to draw a set $\widetilde{S}_+$ from $\widetilde{D}_{r,1}^+$, (i) first draw s and S_+ as described above from $D_{r,1}^+$, and (ii) then replace each type-2 example $(x, 2)$ in S_+ with a new example $(z, 2)$ where each time z is an independent and uniform string in $\{0,1\}^n$.*

A fairly direct calculation establishes the following (see [7] for full proof):

Proposition 1. *For large enough n, for any $r \in \{-1, 0, 1\}^n$, the distributions $D_{r,1}^+$ and $\widetilde{D}_{r,1}^+$ have statistical distance at most $2^{-n/8}$.*

Thus the distributions $D_{r,1}^+$ and $\widetilde{D}_{r,1}^+$ are statistically indistinguishable. We now recall the notion of *computational* indistinguishability of two distributions:

Definition 5. *Let $p(n)$ be a fixed polynomial and let $\{X_n\}_{n \geq 1}$ and $\{Y_n\}_{n \geq 1}$ be two families where for each n, both X_n and Y_n are distributions over $\{0,1\}^{p(n)}$. $\{X_n\}_{n \geq 1}$ and $\{Y_n\}_{n \geq 1}$ are said to be computationally indistinguishable if for all constants $c > 0$, all p.p.t. algorithms A, and all sufficiently large n, we have*

$$\left| \Pr_{S_X \in X_n}[A(S_X) = 1] - \Pr_{S_Y \in Y_n}[A(S_Y) = 1] \right| < 1/n^c.$$

Intuitively, two distributions are computationally indistinguishable (henceforth abbreviated c.i.) if no probabilistic polynomial-time algorithm can distinguish whether a random draw comes from one of the distributions or the other with nonnegligible advantage over a random guess. We will use the following facts:

- Computational indistinguishability is transitive: if X_n and Y_n are c.i., and Y_n and Z_n are c.i., then X_n and Z_n are c.i..
- If X_n and Y_n are c.i., and Y_n and Z_n have statistical distance $\|Y_n - Z_n\|_1 = 1/n^{\omega(1)}$, then X_n and Z_n are c.i..

We now show that for any generative algorithm A that takes as input a sample of $m = \text{poly}(n)$ many positive examples from $P_{r,s,1}$ (where $0^n \neq r$ is any fixed string and s is drawn from TARGET), the type-2 and type-3 examples in its sample are computationally indistinguishable from uniform random examples over $\{0,1\}^n$. That is, positive examples for OR_s cannot be reliably distinguished from uniform draws from $\{0,1\}^n$ in polynomial time, and neither can uniform random elements of $f_{|r| \oplus |s|}^{-1}(1)$.

Definition 6. *Let $\widehat{D}_{r,1}^+$ be the distribution over sets $\widehat{S}_+$ of m examples from $\{0,1\}^n \times \{1,2,3\}$ which is defined as follows: to draw a set $\widehat{S}_+$ from $\widehat{D}_{r,1}^+$, (i) first draw s and S_+ as described above from $D_{r,1}^+$, and (ii) for $i = 2,3$ replace each type-i example (x,i) in S_+ with an example (z,i) where each time z is an independent and uniform random string from $\{0,1\}^n$.*

Lemma 1. *For any $0^n \neq r \in \{-1,0,1\}^n$, the two distributions $D_{r,1}^+$ and $\widehat{D}_{r,1}^+$ are computationally indistinguishable.[1]*

Proof. Suppose to the contrary that $D_{r,1}^+$ and $\widehat{D}_{r,1}^+$ are not computationally indistinguishable. Let Z be a p.p.t. algorithm which is such that

$$| \Pr_{S_+ \in D_{r,1}^+} [Z(S_+) = 1] - \Pr_{\widehat{S}_+ \in \widehat{D}_{r,1}^+} [Z(\widehat{S}_+) = 1]| > 1/n^c \qquad (1)$$

for some $c > 0$ and infinitely many n. We show how such a Z can be used to obtain a distinguishing algorithm that "breaks" the PRFF, and thus obtain a contradiction.

Consider the following algorithm Z', which uses Z as a subroutine and accesses f as an oracle: Given black-box access to a function $f \colon \{0,1\}^n \to \{0,1\}$, construct an m-element sample S by performing the following m times:

- Toss a fair coin; if "heads," output ⋄. If "tails:"
  (*) Choose a uniform random index $i \in \{1,2,3\}$. If $i = 1$, output "$(x,1)$" where x is a uniformly chosen input that satisfies AND_r (i.e. $(x,1)$ is a random type-1 example). If $i = 2$, output "$(x,2)$" where x is a uniform random n-bit string. If $i = 3$, give random n-bit inputs to f until one is obtained (call it x) for which $f(x) = 1$; output "$(x,3)$." If more than n random n-bit inputs are tried without finding one which has $f(x) = 1$, abort the procedure (an arbitrary sample that is fixed ahead of time may be output in this case, say for example m copies of $(0^n, 1)$).

Now run Z on S and output whatever it outputs.

Recall that our plan is to show that Z, which can tell apart $D_{r,1}^+$ from $\widehat{D}_{r,1}^+$, can be used to tell a pseudo-random function from a truly random function. Roughly speaking, our first proposition says that $\widehat{D}_{r,1}^+$ is a faithful proxy for the result of applying a truly random function:

Proposition 2. *Suppose f is a truly random function. Let $D_{truerand}$ denote the distribution over samples S that results from performing (*) above $m = poly(n)$ times with f. Then the statistical distance between $D_{truerand}$ and $\widehat{D}_{r,1}^+$ is $\frac{1}{n^{\omega(1)}}$.*

Proof Sketch for Proposition 2 (see [7] for full proof). We first show that wlog we can assume that (*) above does not abort, that s (chosen in the definition of $\widehat{D}_{r,1}^+$) is not 0^n, and that $f_{|r|\oplus|s|}$ takes both positive and negative values.

---

[1] The lemma also holds for $r = 0^n$, but this result suffices and has a simpler proof.

Given these assumptions, the uniform random choice of an index $i \in \{1, 2, 3\}$ in the executions of (*) under $D_{truerand}$ faithfully simulates what is going on in $\widehat{D}_{r,1}^+$. It can be shown that we thus have that the distribution of type-1 and type-2 examples under the two distributions $D_{truerand}$ and $\widehat{D}_{r,1}^+$ are identical.

We now analyze the distribution of type-3 examples. Under $\widehat{D}_{r,1}^+$, each draw is with probability $1/3$ a type-3 example $(x, 3)$ where x is uniform over $\{0, 1\}^n$. Under $D_{truerand}$, each draw is with probability $1/3$ a type-3 example $(x, 3)$ where x is drawn uniformly from $f^{-1}(1)$, where f is a truly random function (chosen once and for all before the m draws are made). Thus, for any $m' \leq m$ the probability of receiving exactly m' type-3 examples is the same under each of the two distributions. An easy Chernoff bound shows that with probability at least $1 - \frac{1}{2^n}$, the fraction of positive examples for a truly random f is $\frac{1}{2} \pm 1/2^{\Theta(n)}$. Thus, with high probability, a truly random f has $f^{-1}(1)$ uniformly distributed over an exponentially large set. This implies that a polynomial-size sample is exponentially unlikely to have any repetitions among the positive examples of f. Symmetry implies that, conditioned on a fixed values of the number m' of positive type-3 examples, and conditioned on the event that they are distinct, any set of m' examples are equally likely to be chosen. This is of course also the case if we draw m' examples uniformly from $\{0, 1\}^n$. This establishes that the contribution to the statistical distance between $\widehat{D}_{r,1}^+$ and $D_{truerand}$ from type-3 examples is at most $1/2^{\Omega(n)}$, and establishes the proposition. (Proposition 2)∎

Our next proposition shows that $D_{r,1}^+$ is a faithful proxy for the result of using a pseudo-random function.

Proposition 3. *Suppose f is a pseudorandom function, i.e. $f = f_t$ where t is drawn uniformly from $\{0, 1\}^n$. Let $D_{pseudorand}$ denote the distribution over samples S in which the positive examples are obtained using (*) with this choice of f. Then the statistical distance between $D_{pseudorand}$ and $\widetilde{D}_{r,1}^+$ is at most $\frac{1}{n^{\omega(1)}}$.*

Proof Sketch for Proposition 3 (see [7] for full proof). As in the case of Proposition 2, we have that with probability $1 - 1/n^{\omega(1)}$ both (i) the string s chosen in the definition of $\widetilde{D}_{r,1}^+$ is not 0^n and (ii) the seed $|r| \oplus |s|$ is such that $f_{|r|\oplus|s|}$ assumes both $+$ and $-$ values, so we may assume that (i) and (ii) hold.

As in the earlier proof, since $r \neq 0^n$ this implies that each positive example from $\widetilde{D}_{r,1}^+$ has probability $1/3$ of being a type-1, type-2, or type-3 example, and the same is true for each example from $D_{pseudorand}$. Given this, the distribution of type-1 examples is easily seen to be the same under $\widetilde{D}_{r,1}^+$ and under $D_{pseudorand}$, and the same is true for the distribution of type-2 examples. The distribution of type-3 examples under $D_{pseudorand}$ is that each is chosen uniformly at random from $f_t^{-1}(1)$ where t is uniform random over $\{0, 1\}^n$, whereas the distribution of type-3 examples under $\widetilde{D}_{r,1}^+$ is that each is chosen uniformly at random from $f_t^{-1}(1)$ where $t = |r| \oplus |s|$; this string is uniform random conditioned on the event that (i) and (ii) both hold. Since the probability that either (i) or (ii) fails to hold is $1/n^{\omega(1)}$, the proposition follows.   (Proposition 3)∎

Propositions 3 and 1 together yield that $D_{pseudorand}$ has statistical distance $1/n^{\omega(1)}$ from $D_{r,1}^+$. Combining this with Proposition 2 and Equation (1), we have that the p.p.t. algorithm Z' satisfies

$$\left| \Pr_{s \in \{0,1\}^n} [(Z')^{f_s}(1^n) \text{ outputs } 1] - \Pr_{F \in \mathcal{R}_n} [(Z')^F(1^n) \text{ outputs } 1] \right| > 1/n^{c'}.$$

for infinitely many n, where c' is any constant larger than c. But this violates the fact that $\{f_t\}$ is a PRFF. This proves Lemma 1.   ∎

5.2   Negative Examples from $P_{-r,-s,-1}$

We now give results for negative examples from $P_{-r,-s,-1}$ that are dual to the results we gave for positive examples from $P_{r,s,1}$ in the last section. This will let us show (Corollary 1 below) that positive examples drawn from $P_{r,s,1}$ are computationally indistinguishable from negative examples drawn from $P_{-r,-s,-1}$.

Fix any $r \in \{-1, 0, 1\}^n$. We now consider a source $P_{-r,-s,-1}$ where s (or equivalently $-s$) is drawn from TARGET. In analogy with Definitions 3 and 4, let $D_{-r,-1}^-$ be the distribution over sets S_- of m examples from $(\{0,1\}^n \times \{1,2,3\}) \cup \{\diamond\}$ which is defined as follows: to draw a set S_- from $D_{-r,-1}^-$, (i) first draw s from TARGET, and (ii) then draw each of the m examples in S_- independently from $(P_{-r,-s,1})_-$. Let $\widehat{D}_{-r,-1}^-$ be the distribution over sets $\widehat{S}_-$ of m examples from $\{0,1\}^n \times \{1,2,3\}$ which is defined as follows: to draw a set $\widehat{S}_-$ from $\widehat{D}_{r,1}^-$, (i) first draw s and S_- as described above from $D_{-r,-1}^-$, and (ii) for $i = 2, 3$ replace each type-i example (x, i) in S_- with a fresh uniform example (z, i).

Dual arguments to those in Section 5.1 give the following Lemma 1 analogue:

Lemma 2. *For any $0^n \neq r \in \{-1, 0, 1\}^n$, the distributions $D_{-r,-1}^-$ and $\widehat{D}_{-r,-1}^-$ are computationally indistinguishable.*

The following proposition relates $D_{r,1}^+$ and $D_{-r,-1}^-$ (see [7] for proof):

Proposition 4. *For any $0 \neq r \in \{-1, 0, 1\}^n$, the distributions $\widehat{D}_{r,1}^+$ and $\widehat{D}_{-r,-1}^-$ have statistical distance at most $1/n^{\omega(1)}$.*

Lemma 1, Lemma 2 and Proposition 4 together give:

Corollary 1. *For any $0 \neq r \in \{-1, 0, 1\}^n$, the distributions $D_{r,1}^+$ and $D_{-r,-1}^-$ are computationally indistinguishable.*

5.3   Negative Examples from $P_{r,s,1}$ & positive examples from $P_{-r,-s,-1}$

Dual arguments to those of Sections 5.1 and 5.2 can be used to show that negative examples from $P_{r,s,1}$ and positive examples from $P_{-r,-s,-1}$ are c.i.. More precisely, fix any $s \in \{-1, 0, 1\}$. Similar to Definitions 3 and 4, let $D_{s,1}^-$ be the distribution over sets S_- of m examples from $(\{0,1\}^n \times \{1,2,3\}) \cup \{\diamond\}$ which is defined as follows: to draw a set S_- from $D_{s,1}^-$, (i) first draw r from TARGET, and

(ii) then draw each of the m examples in S_- independently from $(P_{r,s,1})_-$. Let $\widehat{D}^-_{s,1}$ be the distribution over sets $\widehat{S}_-$ of m examples from $(\{0,1\}^n \times \{1,2,3\}) \cup \{\diamond\}$ which is defined as follows: to draw $\widehat{S}_-$ from $\widehat{D}^-_{s,1}$, (i) first draw r and S_- as described above from $D^-_{s,1}$, and (ii) for $i = 1,3$ replace each type-i example (x,i) in S_- with a new uniform example (z,i). Dual arguments to Section 5.1 give:

Lemma 3. *For any* $0^n \neq s \in \{-1,0,1\}^n$, *the two distributions* $D^-_{s,1}$ *and* $\widehat{D}^-_{s,1}$ *are computationally indistinguishable.*

Fix any $s \in \{-1,0,1\}$. Let $D^+_{-s,-1}$ be the distribution over sets S_+ of m examples from $(\{0,1\}^n \times \{1,2,3\}) \cup \{\diamond\}$ which is defined as follows: to draw a set S_+ from $D^+_{-s,-1}$, (i) first draw r from TARGET, and (ii) then draw each of the m examples in S_+ independently from $(P_{-r,-s,-1})_+$. Let $\widehat{D}^+_{-s,-1}$ be the distribution over sets $\widehat{S}_+$ of m examples from $(\{0,1\}^n \times \{1,2,3\}) \cup \{\diamond\}$ which is defined as follows: to draw a set $\widehat{S}_+$ from $\widehat{D}^+_{-s,-1}$, (i) first draw r and S_+ as described above from $D^+_{-s,-1}$, and (ii) for $i = 1,3$ replace each type-i example (x,i) in S_+ with a fresh uniform example (z,i). As before, we have the following:

Lemma 4. *For any* $0^n \neq s \in \{-1,0,1\}^n$, *the two distributions* $D^+_{-s,-1}$ *and* $\widehat{D}^+_{-s,-1}$ *are computationally indistinguishable.*

Proposition 5. *For any* $0^n \neq s \in \{-1,0,1\}^n$, *the distributions* $\widehat{D}^-_{s,1}$ *and* $\widehat{D}^+_{-s,-1}$ *have statistical distance at most* $1/n^{\omega(1)}$.

Corollary 2. *For any* $0^n \neq s \in \{-1,0,1\}^n$, *the distributions* $D^-_{s,1}$ *and* $D^+_{-s,-1}$ *are computationally indistinguishable.*

5.4 Proof of Theorem 4

As in the theorem statement, let A be any poly(n)-time purported generative learning algorithm which, when run on examples from any source $P \in \mathcal{P}$, outputs a final hypothesis h whose error rate on P is at most ϵ with probability at least $1 - \delta$ where $\delta = 1/n$. We will show that $\epsilon \geq \frac{1}{6} - o(1)$.

Algorithm B will make use of oracle access to distributions D_Y and D_Z over m examples from $(\{0,1\}^n \times \{1,2,3\}) \cup \{\diamond\}$, and will output a bit. Here it is:

- Draw r,s independently from TARGET. Let $t = |r| \oplus |s|$.
- Draw S_Y from D_Y and S_Z from D_Z.
- Apply A to S_Y to get h_Y, and to S_Z to get h_Z, with parameters $\epsilon = \delta = 1/n$.
- Pick a uniform $x \in \{0,1\}^n$ and output the value $f_t(x) \cdot \text{sgn}(h_Y(x,3) - h_Z(x,3))$.

h_Y and h_Z will be functions for scoring elements for positivity or negativity. By applying B with different sources, each function will adopt each role. This will let us conclude that the final accuracy on type-3 examples must be low.

1. Suppose first that D_Y is $((P_{r,s,1})_+)^m$ and D_Z is $((P_{r,s,1})_-)^m$. Then with probability at least $1 - \delta - 3\epsilon - 1/n$, the output of B must be 1. (To see this, recall that by assumption, for any $r, s \in \{-1, 0, 1\}^n$ the final hypothesis A produces should be ϵ-accurate with probability $1 - \delta$. Also, as noted in Section 3.1, for r, s drawn from TARGET with probability at least (say) $1 - 1/n^2$ we have that both $0^n \neq r, s$ and $f_{|r|\oplus|s|}$ has a fraction of positive examples which is bounded by $[\frac{1}{2} - \frac{1}{n^2}, \frac{1}{2} + \frac{1}{n^2}]$, and consequently each type-3 example $(x, 3)$ has total probability weight in $[\frac{1}{3}(\frac{1}{2} - \frac{1}{n^2}), \frac{1}{3}(\frac{1}{2} + \frac{1}{n^2})]$. Consequently if A's final hypothesis has overall error rate at most ϵ under $P_{r,s,1}$ over all of $\{0,1\}^n \times \{1,2,3\}$, then its error rate on uniformly chosen type-3 examples must certainly be at most $3\epsilon + 1/n$.) Let p_1 denote the probability that B outputs 1 in this case.

2. Now, suppose that D_Y is the distribution $((P_{-r,-s,-1})_-)^m$ and, as in case 1 above, D_Z is $((P_{r,s,1})_-)^m$. Let p_2 denote the probability that B outputs 1 in this case. By Corollary 1, we know that for every fixed $0^n \neq r \in \{-1, 0, 1\}^n$, the distributions $D_{r,1}^+$ (where s is drawn from TARGET) and $D_{-r,-1}^-$ (where s is again drawn from TARGET) are computationally indistinguishable. It follows that the distributions $((P_{-r,-s,-1})_-)^m$ (where both r and s are drawn from TARGET) and $((P_{r,s,1})_+)^m$ (where both r and s are drawn from TARGET) are computationally indistinguishable. This gives us that $|p_1 - p_2| \leq 1/n^{\omega(1)}$, for otherwise B would be a polynomial-time algorithm that violates the computational indistinguishability of these distributions.

3. Now suppose that, as in Case 2, D_Y is the distribution $((P_{-r,-s,-1})_-)^m$, and that D_Z is $((P_{-r,-s,-1})_+)^m$. Let p_3 denote the probability that B outputs 1 in this case. As argued in case (2) above, Corollary 2 gives us that $((P_{r,s,1})_-)^m$ and $((P_{-r,-s,-1})_+)^m$ are computationally indistinguishable, where in both cases r, s are drawn from TARGET. This gives us that $|p_2 - p_3| < 1/n^{\omega(1)}$.

Putting together the pieces, we have that $p_3 \geq p_1 - \frac{1}{n^{\omega(1)}} \geq 1 - \delta - 3\epsilon - \frac{1}{n} - \frac{1}{n^{\omega(1)}} = 1 - o(1) - 3\epsilon$ (since $\delta = 1/n$). But under the assumption that A is a successful generative algorithm for $\mathcal{P}$, it must be the case in case (3) that $p_3 \leq \delta + 3\epsilon + o(1) = 3\epsilon + o(1)$. This is because in case (3) the hypothesis h_Y is the *negative* example hypothesis and h_Z is the *positive* example hypothesis, so the generative algorithm's final hypothesis on type-3 examples (which, as argued in case (1) above, has error at most $3\epsilon + 1/n$-accurate on such examples with probability at least $1 - \delta - o(1)$) is $\text{sgn}(h_Z(x, 3) - h_Y(x, 3))$. We thus have $3\epsilon + o(1) > p_3 > 1 - o(1) - 3\epsilon$ which gives $\epsilon \geq \frac{1}{6} - o(1)$.   (Theorem 4)∎

References

[1] R. O. Duda, P. E. Hart, and D. G. Stork. *Pattern Classification (2nd ed.)*. Wiley, 2000.

[2] P. Fischer, S. Pölt, and H. U. Simon. Probably almost Bayes decisions. In *Proceedings of the Fourth Annual COLT*, pages 88–94, 1991.

[3] P. Goldberg. When Can Two Unsupervised Learners Achieve PAC Separation? In *Proceedings of the 14th Annual COLT*, pages 303–319, 2001.

[4] O. Goldreich, S. Goldwasser, and S. Micali. How to construct random functions. *Journal of the Association for Computing Machinery*, 33(4):792–807, 1986.

[5] T. Jaakkola and D. Haussler. Exploiting generative models in discriminative classifiers. In *Advances in NIPS 11*, pages 487–493. Morgan Kaufmann, 1998.

[6] T. Jebara. *Machine learning: discriminative and generative*. Kluwer, 2003.

[7] P. Long and R. Servedio. Discriminative Learning can Succeed where Generative Learning Fails (full version). Available at http://www.cs.columbia.edu/~rocco/papers/discgen.html.

[8] A. Y. Ng and M. I. Jordan. On discriminative vs. generative classifiers: A comparison of logistic regression and naive bayes. *NIPS*, 2001.

[9] R. Raina, Y. Shen, A. Y. Ng, and A. McCallum. Classification with hybrid generative/discriminative models. *NIPS*, 2004.

[10] J. Håstad, R. Impagliazzo, L. Levin, and M. Luby. A pseudorandom generator from any one-way function. *SIAM Journal on Computing*, 28(4):1364–1396, 1999.

[11] L. G. Valiant. A theory of the learnable. In *Proc. 16th Annual ACM Symposium on Theory of Computing (STOC)*, pages 436–445. ACM Press, 1984.

[12] V. Vapnik. *Estimations of dependences based on statistical data*. Springer, 1982.

Improved Lower Bounds
for Learning Intersections of Halfspaces

Adam R. Klivans and Alexander A. Sherstov

The University of Texas at Austin
Department of Computer Sciences
Austin, TX 78712 USA
{klivans, sherstov}@cs.utexas.edu

Abstract. We prove new lower bounds for learning intersections of half-spaces, one of the most important concept classes in computational learning theory. Our main result is that any statistical-query algorithm for learning the intersection of $\sqrt{n}$ halfspaces in n dimensions must make $2^{\Omega(\sqrt{n})}$ queries. This is the first non-trivial lower bound on the statistical query dimension for this concept class (the previous best lower bound was $n^{\Omega(\log n)}$). Our lower bound holds even for intersections of *low-weight* halfspaces. In the latter case, it is nearly tight.

We also show that the intersection of two majorities (low-weight half-spaces) cannot be computed by a polynomial threshold function (PTF) with fewer than $n^{\Omega((\log n)/\log\log n)}$ monomials. This is the first super-polynomial lower bound on the PTF length of this concept class, and is nearly optimal. For intersections of $k = \omega(\log n)$ low-weight halfspaces, we improve our lower bound to $\min\{2^{\Omega(\sqrt{n})}, n^{\Omega(k/\log k)}\}$, which too is nearly optimal. As a consequence, intersections of even two halfspaces are not computable by polynomial-weight PTFs, the most expressive class of functions known to be efficiently learnable via Jackson's Harmonic Sieve algorithm. Finally, we report our progress on the *weak* learnability of intersections of halfspaces under the uniform distribution.

1 Introduction

Learning intersections of halfspaces is a fundamental and well-studied problem in computational learning theory. In addition to generalizing well-known concept classes such as DNF formulas, intersections of halfspaces are capable of representing arbitrary convex sets. While many efficient algorithms exist for PAC learning a *single* halfspace, the problem of learning the intersection of even two halfspaces remains a difficult challenge. A variety of efficient algorithms have been developed for learning natural restrictions of intersections of halfspaces in various learning models [18,9,10,13]. Progress on proving *hardness* results for learning intersections of halfspaces, however, has been limited: we are not aware of any representation-independent hardness results for learning intersections of halfspaces. The only hardness results known to us are for *proper* learning: if the

G. Lugosi and H.U. Simon (Eds.): COLT 2006, LNAI 4005, pp. 335–349, 2006.
© Springer-Verlag Berlin Heidelberg 2006

learner's output hypothesis must be from a restricted class of functions (e.g., intersections of halfspaces), then the learning problem is NP-hard with respect to randomized reductions [1].

A major part of this paper pertains to learning intersections of halfspaces in Kearns' *statistical query* model of learning [8], an elegant restriction of Valiant's PAC model [17]. A learner in the statistical query model is allowed queries of the form "What is $\Pr_{x \sim \mu}[\chi(x, f(x)) = 1]$, approximately?" Here μ is the underlying distribution on $\{-1, 1\}^n$, the function $\chi : \{-1, 1\}^n \times \{-1, 1\} \to \{-1, 1\}$ is a polynomial-time computable predicate, and $f : \{-1, 1\}^n \to \{-1, 1\}$ is the unknown concept. The motivation behind the statistical query model model is that efficient algorithms in this model are robust to classification noise.

Kearns showed that concept classes learnable via a polynomial number of statistical queries are efficiently PAC learnable. Perhaps surprisingly, virtually all known PAC learning algorithms can be adapted to work via statistical queries only; the one exception known to us is the algorithm of Blum, Kalai, and Wasserman [5] for learning parity functions. The *SQ dimension* of a concept class $\mathcal{C}$ under distribution μ is defined as the size of the largest subset $\mathcal{A} \subseteq \mathcal{C}$ of concepts such that the elements of $\mathcal{A}$ are "almost" orthogonal under μ (see Section 2.2 for a precise definition). Blum et al. [4] proved the SQ dimension of a concept class to be a measure of the number of statistical queries required to learn that class. It is well known that the concept class of parity functions has SQ dimension 2^n (the maximum possible) under the uniform distribution. This observation has been the basis of all known statistical query lower bounds.

1.1   Our Results

Our main contribution is a lower bound for learning intersections of halfspaces in the statistical query model. We construct distributions under which intersections of halfspaces have a large SQ dimension. Let MAJ_k denote the concept class of intersections of k majorities, a subclass of intersections of halfspaces.

Theorem 1. *There are (explicitly given) distributions on $\{-1, 1\}^n$ under which*

$$
\mathsf{SQ\text{-}dim}(\mathsf{MAJ}_k) = \begin{cases} n^{\Omega(k/\log k)} & \text{if} \quad \log n \le k \le \sqrt{n}, \\ \max\left\{ n^{\Omega(k/\log\log n)}, n^{\Omega(\log k)} \right\} & \text{if} \quad k \le \log n. \end{cases}
$$

Our result nearly matches the known upper bound of $n^{O(k \log k \log n)}$ on the SQ dimension of MAJ_k (and more generally, intersections of k polynomial-weight halfspaces) under all distributions. An illustrative instantiation of our theorem is as follows: for any constant $0 < \epsilon \le 1/2$, the intersection of n^ϵ halfspaces has SQ dimension $2^{\Omega(n^\epsilon)}$, the known upper bound being $2^{O(n^\epsilon \log^3 n)}$.

The previous best lower bound for this concept class was $n^{\Omega(\log n)}$. The $n^{\Omega(\log n)}$ bound holds even for n^ϵ-term DNF, a subclass of the intersection of n^ϵ halfspaces. The proof is as follows. A DNF formula with 2^t terms can compute any function on t variables. Thus, a polynomial-size DNF can compute parity on any subset of $\log n$ variables. Since any two distinct parity functions are orthogonal under the uniform distribution, the SQ dimension of polynomial-size DNF is at least $\binom{n}{\log n} = n^{\Omega(\log n)}$.

Our second contribution is a series of lower bounds for the representation of MAJ_k as a polynomial threshold function (PTF). Jackson gave the first polynomial-time algorithm, the celebrated *Harmonic Sieve* [7], for learning polynomial-size DNF formulas with membership queries under the uniform distribution. In addition, he showed that the concept class of polynomial-weight PTFs is learnable in polynomial time using the Harmonic Sieve. A natural question to ask is whether every intersection of k low-weight halfspaces, a straightforward generalization of k-term DNF, can be represented as a polynomial-weight PTF. We answer this question in the negative even for $k = 2$. Let MAJ denote the majority function, which can be represented as the low-weight halfspace $\sum x_i \geq 0$. We prove that the intersection of two majority functions not only requires large weight but also large length:

Theorem 2. *The function* $\mathrm{MAJ}(x_1, \ldots, x_n) \wedge \mathrm{MAJ}(y_1, \ldots, y_n)$ *requires PTF length* $n^{\Omega((\log n)/\log\log n)}$.

The lower bound of Theorem 2 nearly matches the $n^{O(\log n)}$ upper bound of Beigel et al. [3], proving that their PTF construction is essentially optimal. As a corollary to Theorem 2, we observe that intersections of even two low-weight halfspaces cannot be computed by polynomial-weight PTFs, the most expressive class of concepts known to be learnable via Jackson's Harmonic Sieve. We note here that intersections of a constant number of halfspaces are learnable with membership and equivalence queries in polynomial time via Angluin's algorithm for learning finite automata. For the case of intersections of $k = \omega(1)$ halfspaces, however, no polynomial-time algorithms are known. For this case, we prove PTF length lower bounds with an exponential dependence on k:

Theorem 3. *Let* $k \leq \sqrt{n}$. *Then there are (explicitly given) functions in* MAJ_k *that require PTF length* $n^{\Omega(k/\log k)}$.

This lower bound is almost tight: every function in MAJ_k is known [9] to have a PTF of length $n^{O(k \log k \log n)}$. Note that Theorem 3 improves on Theorem 2 for $k = \omega(\log n)$.

Finally, we consider the feasibility of learning intersections of halfspaces *weakly* in polynomial time under the uniform distribution. (Recall that strong learning refers to constructing a hypothesis with error ϵ in time $\mathsf{poly}(n, 1/\epsilon)$; weak learning refers to constructing a hypothesis with error $1/2 - 1/\mathsf{poly}(n)$ in time $\mathsf{poly}(n)$.) We report our progress on this problem in Section 5, proving negative results for generalizations of the problem and positive results for several restricted cases.

1.2   Our Techniques

Most of our results follow from a variety of new applications of *bent* functions, i.e., functions whose Fourier coefficients are as small as possible. Although the Fourier analysis of Boolean functions is usually relevant only to uniform-distribution learning, we apply an observation due to Bruck [6] that the flatness of a function's spectrum is directly related to the length of its PTF represen-tation, a quantity involved with arbitrary-distribution learning. We construct non-uniform distributions under which various intersections of low-weight half-spaces are capable of computing bent functions. This in turn yields a variety of lower bounds on their PTF length, depending on the construction we em-ploy. We then extend the construction of a single bent function to a family of bent functions and prove that this yields a large set of nearly orthogonal func-tions, the critical component of our SQ dimension lower bound. All functions and distributions we construct are explicitly defined.

For the near-optimal lower bound on the PTF length of the intersection of two majority functions, we combine results on the PTF degree of intersections of halfspaces due to O'Donnell and Servedio [15] with a translation lemma in circuit complexity due to Krause and Pudlák [11].

1.3   Organization

We first prove PTF length lower bounds on intersections of majorities in Sec-tion 3. We build on these results to prove our main SQ dimension lower bound in Section 4. Our discussion of weak learning appears in Section 5.

2   Preliminaries

A *Boolean function* is a mapping $\{-1, 1\}^n \to \{-1, 1\}$, where 1 corresponds to "true." In this representation, the parity χ_S of a set $S \subseteq [n]$ of bits is given by the product of the corresponding variables: $\chi_S \stackrel{\text{def}}{=} \bigoplus_{i \in S} x_i = \prod_{i \in S} x_i$. A *majority function* is a Boolean function of the form

$$\text{sign}(x_{j_1} + x_{j_2} + \dots),$$

where the x_{j_i} are distinct variables from among $x_1, \dots, x_n$. A generalization of majority is a *halfspace*

$$\text{sign}(a_1 x_{j_1} + a_2 x_{j_2} + \dots),$$

where the a_i are integral weights. Finally, a *polynomial threshold function* (PTF) has the form

$$\text{sign}(a_1 \chi_1 + a_2 \chi_2 + \dots),$$

where the a_i are integral coefficients and the χ_i are distinct parity functions over $x_1, \dots, x_n$, possibly including the constant function 1. Note that halfspaces and majorities are PTFs. One can assume w.l.o.g. that the polynomial $a_1 \chi_1 + a_2 \chi_2 + \dots$ sign-representing a PTF is nonzero on all inputs.

Two important characteristics of PTFs from a learning standpoint are weight and length. The *weight* of a PTF $\text{sign}(\sum_i a_i \chi_i)$ is $\sum_i |a_i|$. The *length* of a PTF is the number of monomials, i.e., distinct parity functions. Thus, a PTF's weight is never less than its length. A PTF is *light* (respectively, *short*) if its weight (respectively, length) is bounded by a polynomial in n.

In the above description, the polynomial (weighted sum of parities) computing a PTF f agrees in sign with f on every input. We refer to this type of sign-representation as *strong*: a polynomial p *strongly* represents a Boolean function f iff $p(x) \neq 0$ and $f(x) = \text{sign}(p(x))$ for all x. We will also need the following relaxed version of threshold computation [16]: a polynomial p *weakly* represents a Boolean function f iff $p(x) \neq 0$ for some x, and $f(x) = \text{sign}(p(x))$ on any such x. We say that a function has a strong/weak representation on a set of parities $\mathcal{A} \subseteq [n]$ iff there is a polynomial $\sum_{S \in \mathcal{A}} a_S \chi_S$ that strongly/weakly represents f. The following is a useful tool in analyzing PTFs:

Theorem 4. (Theorem of the Alternative) [2, 15] *Let $\mathcal{A} \subseteq [n]$ denote any set of parities on $x_1, \ldots, x_n$, and let $\mathcal{P}([n])$ denote the full set of the 2^n parities. Then exactly one of the following statements holds for any $f : \{-1, 1\}^n \to \{-1, 1\}$:*
(1) f has a strong representation on $\mathcal{A}$;
(2) f has a weak representation on $\mathcal{A}^\perp = \mathcal{P}([n]) \setminus \mathcal{A}$.

2.1 Fourier Transform

Consider the vector space of functions $\{-1, 1\}^n \to \mathbb{R}$, equipped with the inner product $\langle f, g \rangle = \mathbf{E}_{x \sim U} [f(x) \cdot g(x)]$. The parity functions $\{\chi_S\}_{S \subseteq [n]}$ form an orthonormal basis for this inner product space. As a result, every Boolean function f can be uniquely written as its *Fourier polynomial*

$$f = \sum_{S \subseteq [n]} \hat{f}(S) \chi_S,$$

where $\hat{f}(S) \stackrel{\text{def}}{=} \langle f, \chi_S \rangle$. Observe that $\hat{f}(\emptyset) = 2 \Pr_x[f(x) = 1] - 1$. The f-specific constants $\hat{f}(S)$ are called *Fourier coefficients*. The orthonormality of the parities yields *Parseval's identity* for Boolean functions:

$$\sum_{S \subseteq [n]} \hat{f}^2(S) = \langle f, f \rangle = 1.$$

As in signal processing, one can obtain an approximation to a function by identifying and estimating its large Fourier coefficients (the "dominant frequencies"). Although there are 2^n coefficients to consider, the large ones can be retrieved efficiently by the elegant algorithm of [12], which we refer to as "KM":

Theorem 5. [12] *Let f be any Boolean function and let $\delta, \theta > 0$ be parameters. With probability $\geq 1 - \delta$, KM outputs every $S \in [n]$ for which $|\hat{f}(S)| \geq \theta$, and no $S \in [n]$ for which $|\hat{f}(S)| \leq \theta/2$. KM runs in time $\text{poly}(n, \frac{1}{\theta}, \log \frac{1}{\delta})$.*

It is thus useful to recognize classes of functions that have large Fourier coefficients. We denote by $\mathbf{L}_\infty(f)$ the largest absolute value of a Fourier coefficient of f: $\mathbf{L}_\infty(f) \stackrel{\text{def}}{=} \max_S \{|\hat{f}(S)|\}$. The latter quantity lower-bounds the length of a PTF computing f:

Theorem 6. [6] *Any PTF computing f has length at least* $1/\mathbf{L}_\infty(f)$.

Theorem 6 implies that functions with short PTFs are weakly learnable under the uniform distribution:

Proposition 1. *If f has a PTF of length ℓ, then f is learnable to accuracy $\frac{1}{2} + \frac{1}{2\ell}$ under the uniform distribution in time* $\mathsf{poly}(n, \ell)$.

Proof. In time $\mathsf{poly}(n, \ell)$, KM identifies all parities that predict f with advantage $1/\ell$ or better. It thus suffices to show that for some parity χ, $|\mathbf{E}_x [\chi \cdot f]| \geq 1/\ell$. The latter is equivalent to showing that $\mathbf{L}_\infty(f) \geq 1/\ell$. But if we had $\mathbf{L}_\infty(f) < 1/\ell$, any PTF implementing f would require more than ℓ monomials (by Theorem 6). Thus, some parity χ predicts f with advantage $1/\ell$ or better.   □

Proposition 1 shows that PTF *length* is an indicator of weak learnability under the uniform distribution. Additionally, PTF *weight* is an indicator of strong learnability under the uniform distribution: Jackson [7] proves that the Harmonic Sieve strongly learns a function if it can be written as a polynomial-weight PTF.

For all $f : \{-1, 1\}^n \to \{-1, 1\}$, we have $\mathbf{L}_\infty(f) \geq 2^{-n/2}$ by Parseval's identity. For n even, f is called *bent* if all Fourier coefficients of f are $2^{n/2}$ in absolute value. It is known [6] that bent functions include *inner product mod 2*

$$\mathrm{IP}_n(x) = (x_1 \wedge x_2) \oplus (x_3 \wedge x_4) \oplus \cdots \oplus (x_{n-1} \wedge x_n)$$

and *complete quadratic*

$$\mathrm{CQ}_n(x) = \begin{cases} 1 & \text{if } (||x|| \bmod 4) \in \{0, 1\}, \\ -1 & \text{otherwise.} \end{cases}$$

Above and throughout the paper, $||x||$ stands for the number of -1 bits in x. In particular, $||x \oplus y||$ yields the number of bit positions where x and y differ.

Recall that a Boolean function is called *monotone* if flipping a bit from -1 to 1 in any input does not decrease the value of the function. For example, the majority function $\sum x_i \geq 0$ is monotone. A function $f(x_1, \ldots, x_n)$ is *unate* if $f(\sigma_1 \oplus x_1, \ldots, \sigma_n \oplus x_n)$ is monotone for some fixed $\sigma \in \{-1, 1\}^n$. Here σ is called the *orientation* of f. For example, the function $x_1 - 2x_2 + x_3 - 4x_5 \geq 3$ is unate with orientation $\sigma = (1, -1, 1, -1)$.

2.2   Statistical Query Dimension

The *statistical query* model, first defined by Kearns [8], is an elegant model of learning that can withstand classification noise. The SQ model has proven to be a useful formalism. In fact, a vast majority of today's efficient learning algorithms fit in this framework. The SQ dimension of a concept class, defined shortly, is a tight measure of the hardness of learning in this model. As a result, SQ dimension estimates are of considerable interest in learning theory.

A *concept class* $\mathcal{C}$ is a set of functions $\{-1, 1\}^n \to \{-1, 1\}$. The *statistical query dimension* of $\mathcal{C}$ under distribution μ, denoted $\mathbf{SQ\text{-}dim}_\mu(\mathcal{C})$, is the largest N for which there are N functions $f_1, \ldots, f_N \in \mathcal{C}$ with

$$|\mathbf{E}_{x\sim\mu}\left[f_i(x) \cdot f_j(x)\right]| \le \frac{1}{N}$$

for all $i \neq j$. We denote $\mathbf{SQ\text{-}dim}(\mathcal{C}) \stackrel{\text{def}}{=} \max_\mu\{\mathbf{SQ\text{-}dim}_\mu(\mathcal{C})\}$. The SQ dimension of a concept class fully characterizes its weak learnability in the statistical query model: a low SQ dimension implies an efficient weak-learning algorithm, and a high SQ dimension rules out such an algorithm [4]. The following two theorems make these statements precise.

Theorem 7. [4] (Upper Bound) *Let $\mathcal{C}$ be a concept class and μ a distribution s.t. $\mathbf{SQ\text{-}dim}_\mu(\mathcal{C}) = d$. Then there is a non-uniform learning algorithm for $\mathcal{C}$ that makes d queries, each of tolerance $1/(3d^3)$, and finds a hypothesis with error at most $1/2 - 1/(3d^3)$ under μ.*

Theorem 8. [4] (Lower Bound) *Let $\mathcal{C}$ be a concept class and μ a distribution s.t. $\mathbf{SQ\text{-}dim}_\mu(\mathcal{C}) = d \ge 16$. Then if all queries are made with tolerance at least $1/d^{1/3}$, at least $d^{1/3}/2$ queries are required to learn $\mathcal{C}$ to error $1/2 - 1/d^3$ under μ in the statistical query model.*

2.3 Notation

We adopt the notation $\mathbf{L}_\infty^+(f) \stackrel{\text{def}}{=} \max_{S\neq\emptyset}\{|\hat{f}(S)|\}$. We denote by MAJ_k the family of functions computable by the intersection of k majorities, each on some subset of the n variables. Throughout the paper, we view k as an arbitrary function of n, including a constant. $\mathsf{MAJ}(x_{i_1}, x_{i_2}, \ldots)$ stands for the majority value of $x_{i_1}, x_{i_2}, \ldots$. We denote the set $\{1, 2, \ldots, a\}$ by $[a]$. $\mathbf{I}[A]$ denotes 1 if the statement A is true, and 0 otherwise. The vector with -1 in the ith position and 1's elsewhere is e_i. In particular, $x \oplus e_i$ represents x with its ith bit flipped.

3 PTF Length Lower Bounds for MAJ_k

We begin by developing lower bounds on the PTF representation of intersections of low-weight halfspaces. In particular, this section establishes two of the results of this paper: Theorem 2 (proved independently in Section 3.3) and Theorem 3 (immediate from Theorems 2, 9 and 10 of this section). We will need these structural results to prove our main lower bound on the SQ dimension of intersections of halfspaces.

3.1 PTF Length of MAJ_k: An $n^{\Omega(\log k)}$ Bound

Unlike the lower bound for MAJ_2, the results in this section and the next require $k = \omega(1)$ for a super-polynomial lower bound. However, they rely solely on the fundamental Theorem 6 and are thus considerably simpler. Furthermore, the constructions below (Lemmas 2 and 3) will allow us to prove a lower bound on the SQ dimension of MAJ_k in Section 4. A key to these results is the following observation.

Lemma 1. *Let* $f(x_1, \ldots, x_n)$ *have a PTF of length* ℓ. *Then so does* $f(\chi_1, \ldots, \chi_n)$, *where each* χ_i *is any parity over* $x_1, \ldots, x_n$ *or the negation of a parity.*

Proof. Given a polynomial of length ℓ that strongly sign-represents f, make the replacement $x_i \to \chi_i$. This does not increase the number of monomials, while yielding a PTF for $f(\chi_1, \ldots, \chi_n)$. $\qquad\square$

By Lemma 1, it suffices to show that $f(\chi_1, \ldots, \chi_n)$ does not have a short PTF to prove that neither does $f(x_1, \ldots, x_n)$. We accomplish the former via a reduction to a known hard function.

Lemma 2. *Let* $k \leq 2^{n^{o(1)}}$. *Then there are explicitly given functions* $\chi_1, \chi_2, \ldots, \chi_n$ *(each a parity or the negation of a parity) such that for every fixed* $y \in \{-1,1\}^n$, $\mathrm{IP}(x \oplus y)$ *on* $\Omega(\log n \cdot \log k)$ *variables is computable by* $f(\chi_1, \chi_2, \ldots, \chi_n)$ *for some* $f \in \mathsf{MAJ}_k$.

Proof. Let $g_1, g_2, \ldots, g_{\log k}$ be copies of the IP function, each on a distinct set of variables V_i with $|V_i| = v$ for some $v = v(n,k)$ to be chosen later. Thus, $g = \bigoplus g_i$ is IP on $v \log k$ variables. At the same time, g is computable by the AND of $2^{\log k - 1} < k$ functions, each of the form $h_1 \wedge h_2 \wedge \cdots \wedge h_{\log k}$, where $h_i \in \{g_i, \neg g_i\}$. Each $h_1 \wedge h_2 \wedge \cdots \wedge h_{\log k}$ can be computed by the PTF

$$h_1 + \quad h_2 + \cdots + \quad h_{\log k} \geq \quad \log k,$$
$$\text{or} \quad 2^{v/2} h_1 + 2^{v/2} h_2 + \cdots + 2^{v/2} h_{\log k} \geq 2^{v/2} \log k. \tag{1}$$

Every h_i is a bent function on the v variables V_i, and thus $2^{v/2} h_i$ is simply the sum of the 2^v parities on V_i, each with a plus or a minus sign.

Create a new set of variables $U = \{\chi_1, \chi_2, \ldots\}$ as follows. U will contain a distinct variable for each parity on V_i ($i \in [\log k]$) and one for its negation. In addition, U will contain $2^{v/2} \log k$ variables, each of which corresponds to the constant -1. As a result, each of the k PTFs of the form (1) is a majority function in terms of U. Therefore, $\mathrm{IP}(x)$ on $v \log k$ variables is computable by $f(\chi_1, \chi_2, \ldots)$ for some $f \in \mathsf{MAJ}_k$. Furthermore, for every fixed $y \in \{-1,1\}^n$, $\mathrm{IP}(x \oplus y)$ is computable by $f_y(\chi_1, \chi_2, \ldots)$ for some $f_y \in \mathsf{MAJ}_k$. This is because for each parity, $U = \{\chi_1, \chi_2, \ldots\}$ additionally contains its negation.

It remains to show that $|U| \leq n$. Setting $v = \log n - \log \log k - 2$ yields $|U| = 2 \cdot 2^v \log k + 2^{v/2} \log k \leq n$. Thus, for $k \leq 2^{n^{o(1)}}$ the above construction computes IP on the claimed number of variables:

$$v \log k = (\log n - \log \log k - 2) \log k = \Omega(\log n \cdot \log k).$$

$\qquad\square$

Lemma 2 immediately yields the desired lower bound on PTF length.

Theorem 9. *Let* $k \leq 2^{n^{o(1)}}$. *Then the intersection of* k *majorities requires a PTF with* $n^{\Omega(\log k)}$ *monomials.*

Proof. Let $k \leq 2^{n^{o(1)}}$. By Lemma 2, there is a function $f \in \mathrm{MAJ}_k$ and a choice of signed parities $\chi_1, \ldots, \chi_n$ such that $f(\chi_1, \ldots, \chi_n)$ computes IP on $v = \Omega(\log n \cdot \log k)$ variables. Since $\mathbf{L}_\infty(f(\chi_1, \ldots, \chi_n)) = 2^{v/2}$, any PTF computing $f(\chi_1, \ldots, \chi_n)$ requires $2^{v/2} = n^{\Omega(\log k)}$ monomials by Theorem 6. By Lemma 1, the same holds for $f(x_1, \ldots, x_n)$. $\qquad\square$

3.2 PTF Length of MAJ_k: An $n^{\Omega(k/\max\{\log\log n, \log k\})}$ Bound

This section applies Lemma 1 with a different reduction. The resulting lower bound is better than that of Theorem 9 for some range of k.

Lemma 3. *Let $k \leq \sqrt{n}$. Then there are explicitly given functions $\chi_1, \chi_2, \ldots, \chi_n$ (each a parity or the negation of a parity) such that for every fixed $y \in \{-1,1\}^n$, $\mathrm{CQ}(x \oplus y)$ on $\min\left\{\Omega\left(\frac{k \log n}{\log\log n}\right), \Omega\left(\frac{k \log n}{\log k}\right)\right\}$ variables is computable by $f(\chi_1, \chi_2, \ldots, \chi_n)$ for some $f \in \mathrm{MAJ}_k$.*

Proof. Consider CQ on v variables, for some $v = v(n, k)$ to be chosen later. CQ is symmetric and can thus be represented by the AND of v predicates:

$$\mathrm{CQ}(x) = 1 \quad \Longleftrightarrow \quad \bigwedge_{s \in S} \left(\textstyle\sum_i x_i \neq s\right),$$

where $S \subseteq \{-v, \ldots, 0, \ldots, v\}, |S| \leq v$. A single PTF can check any number t of these predicates:

$$\left(\textstyle\sum_i x_i - s_1\right)^2 \left(\textstyle\sum_i x_i - s_2\right)^2 \ldots \left(\textstyle\sum_i x_i - s_t\right)^2 > 0, \qquad (2)$$

where $s_1, \ldots, s_t \in S$.

Consider the PTF $\left(\sum_i x_i + v\right)^{2t} > 0$. Multiplying out the l.h.s. yields the sum of exactly $(2v)^{2t}$ parities (not all distinct). Construct a new set of variables $U = \{\chi_1, \chi_2, \ldots\}$ to contain a variable for each of these $(2v)^{2t}$ parities and their negations. Over U, the PTF $\left(\sum_i x_i + v\right)^{2t} > 0$ is a majority. In fact, any PTF of the form (2) is a majority over U. $\mathrm{CQ}(x)$ on v variables is thus computable by $f(\chi_1, \chi_2, \ldots)$ for some $f \in \mathrm{MAJ}_k$. Furthermore, for every fixed $y \in \{-1,1\}^n$, $\mathrm{CQ}(x \oplus y)$ is computable by $f_y(\chi_1, \chi_2, \ldots)$ for some $f_y \in \mathrm{MAJ}_k$. This is because for each parity, $U = \{\chi_1, \chi_2, \ldots\}$ additionally contains its negation.

It remains to pick v such that $v \leq kt$ (the k PTFs must collectively check all v predicates) and $|U| \leq n$ (the new variable set can have size at most n):

$$v = \max\{v' : v' \leq kt \text{ and } 2(2v')^{2t} \leq n \text{ for some integer } t \geq 1\}$$

$$= \min\left\{\Omega(\sqrt{n}),\ \Omega\left(\frac{k \log n}{\log\log n}\right),\ \Omega\left(\frac{k \log n}{\log k}\right)\right\},$$

which is equivalent to $v = \min\{\Omega(k \log n/\log\log n), \Omega(k \log n/\log k)\}$ for $k \leq \sqrt{n}$. $\qquad\square$

Theorem 10. *Let $k \leq \sqrt{n}$. Then the intersection of k majorities requires a PTF with $\min\left\{n^{\Omega(k/\log\log n)}, n^{\Omega(k/\log k)}\right\}$ monomials.*

Proof. Let $k \le \sqrt{n}$. By Lemma 3, there is a function $f \in \mathsf{MAJ}_k$ and a choice of signed parities $\chi_1, \ldots, \chi_n$ such that $f(\chi_1, \ldots, \chi_n)$ computes CQ on $v = \min\{\Omega(k/\log\log n), \Omega(k/\log k)\}$ variables. Since $\mathbf{L}_\infty(f(\chi_1, \ldots, \chi_n)) = 2^{v/2}$, any PTF computing $f(\chi_1, \ldots, \chi_n)$ requires $2^{v/2}$ monomials by Theorem 6. By Lemma 1, the same holds for $f(x_1, \ldots, x_n)$. $\qquad\square$

3.3   PTF Length of MAJ_2: An $n^{\Omega((\log n)/\log\log n)}$ Bound

Our lower bound for the PTF length of MAJ_2 exploits two related results in the literature. The first is a lower bound on the degree of any PTF for MAJ_2, due to O'Donnell and Servedio [15]. We additionally amplify the degree requirements by replacing each variable in MAJ_2 by a parity on a separate set of $\approx \log n$ variables. Denote the resulting composition by $\mathsf{MAJ}_2 \circ \mathsf{PARITY}$. The second result we use is a general theorem of Krause and Pudlák [11] which, given the PTF degree of a function f, states a lower bound on the PTF length of a *related* function f^{op}. We obtain the result of this section by relating the PTF length of MAJ_2 to that of $(\mathsf{MAJ}_2 \circ \mathsf{PARITY})^{\mathrm{op}}$.

The *degree* of a function f, denoted $\deg(f)$, is the minimum degree of any polynomial that strongly represents it. For MAJ_2, we have:

Theorem 11. [15] *Let* $f(x, y) = \mathsf{MAJ}(x_1, \ldots, x_n) \wedge \mathsf{MAJ}(y_1, \ldots, y_n)$. *Then* f *has degree* $\Omega\left(\frac{\log n}{\log\log n}\right)$.

The key to the lower bound in this section is the following link between PTF degree and length requirements.

Definition 1. *For* $f : \{-1, 1\}^n \to \{-1, 1\}$, *define* $f^{\mathrm{op}} : \{-1, 1\}^{3n} \to \{-1, 1\}$ *as*

$$f^{\mathrm{op}}(x_1, \ldots, x_n,\ y_1, \ldots, y_n,\ z_1, \ldots, z_n) = f(u_1, \ldots, u_n),$$

where $u_i = (\overline{z_i} \wedge x_i) \vee (z_i \wedge y_i)$.

Proposition 2. [11] *For every Boolean function* f, f^{op} *requires PTF length* $2^{\deg(f)}$.

We need another observation.

Lemma 4. *Let* $g(x) = f\left(\bigoplus_{i=1}^{k} x_{1,i},\ \ldots,\ \bigoplus_{i=1}^{k} x_{n,i}\right)$. *Then* $\deg(g) = k \cdot \deg(f)$.

Proof. Our proof is inspired by Theorem 13 (the "XOR lemma") of [15]. The upper bound $k \cdot \deg(f)$ is trivial: take any polynomial of degree $\deg(f)$ that strongly represents f and replace each variable by its corresponding length-k parity on $x_{i,j}$. To prove that $k \cdot \deg(f)$ is also a lower bound on $\deg(g)$, note that f has no strong representation over parities of degree less than $\deg(f)$. By the Theorem of the Alternative, f has a weak representation p_w over parities of degree at least $\deg(f)$. Substituting corresponding parities on $x_{i,j}$ for the variables of p_w yields a weak representation of g; it is nonzero on many assignments to

$x_{i,j}$ since p_w is nonzero on at least one assignment to $x_1, \ldots, x_n$. The degree of any monomial in the resulting PTF for g is at least $k \cdot \deg(f)$. By the Theorem of the Alternative, g cannot have a strong representation over the parities of degree less than $k \cdot \deg(f)$. We conclude that $\deg(g) \geq k \cdot \deg(f)$. $\square$

Combining the above yields the desired bound:

Theorem 2. (Restated from page 337.) *The function* $\mathrm{MAJ}(x_1, \ldots, x_n) \wedge \mathrm{MAJ}(y_1, \ldots, y_n)$ *requires PTF length* $n^{\Omega((\log n)/\log \log n)}$.

Proof. Let $f = \mathrm{MAJ}(x_1, \ldots, x_t) \wedge \mathrm{MAJ}(x_{t+1}, \ldots, x_{2t})$. Define a new function $f^{\oplus} : (\{-1, 1\}^k)^{2t} \to \{-1, 1\}$ as

$$f^{\oplus}(x) = \mathrm{MAJ}\left(\bigoplus_{i=1}^{k} x_{1,i}, \ \ldots, \ \bigoplus_{i=1}^{k} x_{t,i}\right) \bigwedge \mathrm{MAJ}\left(\bigoplus_{i=1}^{k} x_{t+1,i}, \ \ldots, \ \bigoplus_{i=1}^{k} x_{2t,i}\right).$$

By Lemma 4, $\deg(f^{\oplus}) = k \cdot \deg(f)$. Consider now $f^{\oplus \mathrm{op}}$. For single bits $a, b, c \in \{-1, 1\}$, we have $(\bar{c} \wedge a) \vee (c \wedge b) = \frac{1}{2}(1+c)a + \frac{1}{2}(1-c)b$. As a result, $f^{\oplus \mathrm{op}}$ can be computed by the intersection of two PTFs:

$$f^{\oplus \mathrm{op}}(x, y, z) =$$

$$\left(\prod_{i=1}^{k} q_{1,i} + \ \cdots \ + \prod_{i=1}^{k} q_{t,i} \geq 0\right) \bigwedge \left(\prod_{i=1}^{k} q_{t+1,i} + \ \cdots \ + \prod_{i=1}^{k} q_{2t,i} \geq 0\right),$$

where $q_{i,j} = (1 + z_{i,j})x_{i,j} + (1 - z_{i,j})y_{i,j}$.

Therefore, $f^{\oplus \mathrm{op}}$ is computed by the intersection of two PTFs, each with weight at most $4^k t$. Lemma 1 implies that if the intersection of two majorities, each on a distinct set of $4^k t$ variables, has a PTF with ℓ monomials, then so does $f^{\oplus \mathrm{op}}$. But by Proposition 2, $f^{\oplus \mathrm{op}}$ requires a PTF of length $2^{\deg(f^{\oplus})} = 2^{k \cdot \deg(f)}$. Thus, the intersection of two majorities, each on $n = 4^k t$ variables, requires a PTF of length $2^{\frac{1}{2}(\log n - \log t) \cdot \deg(f)}$. Set $t = \sqrt{n}$. Then by Theorem 11, $\deg(f) = \Omega((\log n)/\log \log n)$, which yields a length lower bound of $n^{\Omega(\deg(f))} = n^{\Omega(\log n/\log \log n)}$. $\square$

Using a rational approximation to the sign function, it is possible to obtain a PTF for $\mathrm{MAJ}(x_1, \ldots, x_n) \wedge \mathrm{MAJ}(y_1, \ldots, y_n)$ with $n^{O(\log n)}$ monomials [3]. Our lower bound of $n^{\Omega((\log n)/\log \log n)}$ nearly matches that upper bound.

A key ingredient in our proof of the $n^{\Omega((\log n)/\log \log n)}$ lower bound on the PTF length of MAJ_2 was the non-trivial degree lower bound for the same function, due to O'Donnell and Servedio [15]. We could obtain an $n^{\omega(1)}$ lower bound for the PTF length of MAJ_2 by using the simpler $\omega(1)$ lower bound on the degree of MAJ_2 due to Minsky and Papert [14]. That would suffice to show that MAJ_2 does not have a short PTF; the proof would be analogous to that of Theorem 2.

4   A Lower Bound on the SQ Dimension of MAJ_k

Recall that the SQ dimension captures the hardness of a concept class. We explicitly construct distributions under which the intersection of n^{ϵ} majorities, for any constant $0 < \epsilon \leq 1/2$, has SQ dimension $2^{\Omega(n^\epsilon)}$. This is an exponential improvement on $n^{\Omega(\log k)}$, the best previous lower bound that was based on computing parity functions by intersections of halfspaces. We additionally prove (Section 4.1) that the latter construction could not give a bound better than $n^{\Theta(\log k)}$.

Let $f : \{-1, 1\}^n \to \{-1, 1\}$ be any function. For a fixed string $y \in \{-1, 1\}^n$, the y-*reflection of* f is the function $f_y(x) = f(x \oplus y)$. Any two distinct reflections of a bent function are uncorrelated under the uniform distribution:

Lemma 5. *Let* $f : \{-1, 1\}^n \to \{-1, 1\}$ *be a bent function. Then for any distinct* $y, y' \in \{-1, 1\}^n$, $\mathbf{E}_{x \sim U} [f(x \oplus y) \cdot f(x \oplus y')] = 0$.

Proof. For a fixed pair y, y' of distinct strings, we have $y \oplus y' \neq 1^n$. Thus,

$$
\mathbf{E}_{x \sim U} [f(x \oplus y)f(x \oplus y')] = \mathbf{E}_x \left[\left(\sum_S \hat{f}(S)\chi_S(x)\chi_S(y) \right) \left(\sum_T \hat{f}(T)\chi_T(x)\chi_T(y') \right) \right]
$$

$$
= \sum_S \sum_T \hat{f}(S)\hat{f}(T)\chi_S(y)\chi_T(y') \cdot \mathbf{E}_x [\chi_S(x)\chi_T(x)]
$$

$$
= \sum_S \hat{f}^2(S)\chi_S(y)\chi_S(y')
$$

$$
= \frac{1}{2^n} \sum_S \chi_S(y \oplus y')
$$

$$
= 0.
$$

The last equality holds because on every $z \in \{-1, 1\}^n \setminus 1^n$, exactly half of the parities evaluate to -1 and the other half, to 1. $\square$

The following is a simple consequence of Lemma 5:

Theorem 12. *Let* $\mathcal{C}$ *denote the concept class of bent functions on n variables. Then* $\mathbf{SQ\text{-}dim}_U(\mathcal{C}) = 2^n$.

Proof. Fix a bent function f and consider its 2^n reflections, themselves bent functions. By Lemma 5, any two of them are orthogonal. $\square$

Consider a function $h : \{-1, 1\}^n \to \{-1, 1\}^n$. The h-*induced distribution on* $\{-1, 1\}^n$, denoted by $h \circ U$, is the distribution given by

$$
(h \circ U)(z) = \Pr_{x \sim U} [h(x) = z]
$$

for any $z \in \{-1, 1\}^n$. Put differently, $h \circ U$ is the uniform distribution over the multiset $h(\{-1, 1\}^n)$.

Proposition 3. *Let* $f, g : \{-1, 1\}^n \to \{-1, 1\}$ *and* $h : \{-1, 1\}^n \to \{-1, 1\}^n$ *be arbitrary functions. Then* $\mathbf{E}_{x \sim h \circ U} [f(x) \cdot g(x)] = \mathbf{E}_{x \sim U} [f(h(x)) \cdot g(h(x))]$.

Proof. By definition of $h \circ U$, picking a random input according to $h \circ U$ is equivalent to picking $x \in \{-1, 1\}^n$ uniformly at random and returning $h(x)$. $\square$

We are ready to prove the claimed SQ lower bound for MAJ_k.

Theorem 1. (Restated from page 336.) *There are (explicitly given) distributions on $\{-1,1\}^n$ under which*

$$\textbf{SQ-dim}(\textsf{MAJ}_k) = \begin{cases} n^{\Omega(k/\log k)} & if \quad \log n \le k \le \sqrt{n}, \\ \max\left\{n^{\Omega(k/\log\log n)}, n^{\Omega(\log k)}\right\} & if \quad k \le \log n. \end{cases}$$

Proof. Let $k \le \log n$. Fix n monomials $\chi_1, \chi_2, \dots, \chi_n$ as in Lemma 2. Let $v = \Omega(\log n \cdot \log k)$. Then there are 2^v functions $\mathcal{F} = \{f_1, f_2, \dots, f_{2^v}\} \subset \textsf{MAJ}_k$, where each $f_i(\chi_1(x), \chi_2(x), \dots, \chi_n(x))$ computes $\text{IP}(x \oplus y)$ on v variables for a distinct $y \in \{-1,1\}^v$.

Define $h : \{-1,1\}^n \to \{-1,1\}^n$ by $h(x) = (\chi_1(x), \chi_2(x), \dots, \chi_n(x))$. Then for every two distinct $f_i, f_j \in \mathcal{F}$,

$$\begin{aligned} 0 &= \mathbf{E}_{x \sim U}\left[f_i(\chi_1(x), \dots, \chi_n(x)) \cdot f_j(\chi_1(x), \dots, \chi_n(x))\right] && \text{by Lemma 5} \\ &= \mathbf{E}_{x \sim h \circ U}\left[f_i(x) \cdot f_j(x)\right] && \text{by Proposition 3.} \end{aligned}$$

In words, every pair of functions in $\mathcal{F}$ are orthogonal under the distribution $h \circ U$. Therefore, $\textbf{SQ-dim}_{h \circ U}(\textsf{MAJ}_k) \ge |\mathcal{F}| = 2^v = n^{\Omega(\log k)}$ for $k \le \log n$. Moreover, the distribution $h \circ U$ has an explicit description: pick a random $x \in \{-1,1\}^n$ and return the n-bit string $(\chi_1(x), \dots, \chi_n(x))$, where $\chi_1, \dots, \chi_n$ are the explicitly given monomials from Lemma 2. Applying an analogous argument to Lemma 3 yields the alternate lower bound $\textbf{SQ-dim}(\textsf{MAJ}_k) = \min\{n^{\Omega(k/\log k)}, n^{\Omega(k/\log\log n)}\}$ for $k \le \sqrt{n}$. $\qquad\square$

4.1   On the SQ Dimension Under the Uniform Distribution

The distributions in Theorem 1 are non-uniform. Can we prove a comparable lower bound on the SQ dimension of $\textsf{MAJ}_k$ under the uniform distribution? A natural approach would be to compute different parities with functions in $\textsf{MAJ}_k$. Since the parities are mutually orthogonal under the uniform distribution, this would yield an SQ lower bound. In what follows, we show that this approach yields at best a trivial $n^{\Omega(\log k)}$ SQ lower bound, even for the much larger class of intersections of unate functions. Specifically, we show that intersections of k unate functions cannot compute PARITY on more than $1 + \log k$ bits.

Proposition 4. *Let f be a unate function with orientation σ. If f is false on some x with $\|x \oplus \sigma\| < n$, then f is false on some y with $\text{PARITY}(x) \ne \text{PARITY}(y)$.*

Proof. Suppose $\|x \oplus \sigma\| < n$. Then $x_i = \sigma_i$ for some i. Let $y = x \oplus e_i$. Then $\text{PARITY}(x) \ne \text{PARITY}(y)$. But $f(y) \le f(x) = -1$ and thus $f(y) = -1$. $\qquad\square$

Theorem 13. *To compute PARITY_n by the AND of unate functions, 2^{n-1} unate functions are necessary and sufficient.*

Proof. Sufficiency is straightforward: PARITY has a trivial CNF with 2^{n-1} clauses, each of which is a unate function. For the lower bound, consider $\bigwedge f_i = \text{PARITY}$, where each f_i is a unate function with orientation σ_i. By Proposition 4, f_i can be false only on the input x satisfying $\|x \oplus \sigma_i\| = n$: otherwise f_i would be false on two inputs of different parity. Thus, 2^{n-1} unate functions are needed to exclude the 2^{n-1} falsifying assignments to PARITY. $\qquad\square$

5   Weakly Learning Intersections of Halfspaces

For the proofs in this section, please refer to the full version of this paper on the authors' webpages.

Section 3 showed that the intersection f of even two majorities does not have a polynomial-length PTF. Thus, there is *some* distribution on $\{-1, 1\}^n$ under which the correlation of f with every parity is negligible (inversely superpolynomial). However, this leaves open the possibility of inverse-polynomial correlation (and thus weak learnability) under the *uniform* distribution. In other words, we would like to know if $\mathbf{L}_\infty(h_1 \wedge \cdots \wedge h_k) = 1/n^{O(1)}$ for a slow enough function k. Trivially, the intersection of $k = n^{\omega(1)}$ halfspaces has negligible Fourier coefficients. In fact, the same holds even for a CNF with $n^{\omega(1)}$ clauses since it can compute a bent function on $\omega(\log n)$ variables. Thus, we restrict our attention to $k = n^{O(1)}$.

First, we consider two generalizations of MAJ_k: the XOR of k majorities, and the AND of k unate functions. In both cases, we show that all Fourier coefficients can be negligible for $k = \omega(1)$.

Proposition 5. *Let $h_1, \ldots, h_k$ be majority functions, each on a separate set of n/k variables. Then $\mathbf{L}_\infty(h_1 \oplus \cdots \oplus h_k) = 1/n^{\omega(1)}$ for $k = \omega(1)$.*

Theorem 14. *There are unate functions $h_1, \ldots, h_k$ such that $\mathbf{L}_\infty(\bigwedge h_i) = 1/n^{\omega(1)}$ for $k = \omega(1)$.*

On the positive side, we prove that no combining function of $k = \sqrt{\log n}$ halfspaces can compute a bent function on $\omega(\log n)$ variables (which would have negligible Fourier coefficients).

Theorem 15. *Let $f = g(h_1, h_2, \ldots, h_k)$, where each $h_i : \{-1, 1\}^n \to \{-1, 1\}$ is a halfspace and $g : \{-1, 1\}^k \to \{-1, 1\}$ is an arbitrary Boolean function. If $k = o(\sqrt{n})$, then f is not bent.*

We now examine two special cases: *read-once* and *unate* functions.

Lemma 6. *Let $f = h_1 \wedge h_2 \wedge \cdots \wedge h_k$, where the h_i are arbitrary Boolean functions on disjoint variable sets. Then $\mathbf{L}_\infty(f) \geq \frac{1}{2} \max_i \{\mathbf{L}_\infty^+(h_i)\}$.*

Lemma 6 states that if at least one of $h_1, \ldots, h_k$ has a large *nonconstant* Fourier coefficient, then $f = h_1 \wedge \cdots \wedge h_k$ will have a large Fourier coefficient as well. Weak learnability is also guaranteed for all unate functions in MAJ_k. We derive this result from the benign Fourier properties of unate functions.

Theorem 16. *Let $f = g(h_1, \ldots, h_k)$, where $g : \{-1, 1\}^k \to \{-1, 1\}$ is a monotone function (e.g., AND or MAJ) and the functions $h_i : \{-1, 1\}^n \to \{-1, 1\}$ are unate with a common orientation (e.g., halfspaces with a common orientation or halfspaces on disjoint sets of variables). Then f is unate and $\mathbf{L}_\infty(f) \geq 1/(n+1)$.*

References

1. M. Alekhnovich, M. Braverman, V. Feldman, A. Klivans, and T. Pitassi. Learnability and automatizability. In *Proceedings of the 45th Annual Symposium on Foundations of Computer Science (FOCS)*, 2004.
2. J. Aspnes, R. Beigel, M. Furst, and S. Rudich. The expressive power of voting polynomials. In *STOC '91: Proceedings of the twenty-third annual ACM symposium on Theory of computing*, pages 402–409, New York, NY, USA, 1991. ACM Press.
3. R. Beigel, N. Reingold, and D. Spielman. PP is closed under intersection. In *STOC '91: Proceedings of the twenty-third annual ACM symposium on Theory of computing*, pages 1–9, New York, NY, USA, 1991. ACM Press.
4. A. Blum, M. Furst, J. Jackson, M. Kearns, Y. Mansour, and S. Rudich. Weakly learning DNF and characterizing statistical query learning using Fourier analysis. In *STOC '94: Proceedings of the twenty-sixth annual ACM symposium on Theory of computing*, pages 253–262, New York, NY, USA, 1994. ACM Press.
5. A. Blum, A. Kalai, and H. Wasserman. Noise-tolerant learning, the parity problem, and the statistical query model. *J. ACM*, 50(4):506–519, 2003.
6. J. Bruck. Harmonic analysis of polynomial threshold functions. *SIAM J. Discrete Math.*, 3(2):168–177, 1990.
7. J. C. Jackson. *The harmonic sieve: A novel application of Fourier analysis to machine learning theory and practice.* PhD thesis, Carnegie Mellon University, 1995.
8. M. Kearns. Efficient noise-tolerant learning from statistical queries. In *STOC '93: Proceedings of the twenty-fifth annual ACM symposium on theory of computing*, pages 392–401, New York, NY, USA, 1993. ACM Press.
9. A. Klivans, R. O'Donnell, and R. Servedio. Learning intersections and thresholds of halfspaces. In *Proceedings of the 43rd Annual Symposium on Foundations of Computer Science*, pages 177–186, 2002.
10. A. Klivans and R. Servedio. Learning intersections of halfspaces with a margin. In *Proceedings of the 17th Annual Conference on Learning Theory*, pages 348–362, 2004.
11. M. Krause and P. Pudlák. On the computational power of depth 2 circuits with threshold and modulo gates. In *STOC '94: Proceedings of the twenty-sixth annual ACM symposium on Theory of computing*, pages 48–57, New York, NY, USA, 1994. ACM Press.
12. E. Kushilevitz and Y. Mansour. Learning decision trees using the fourier spectrum. In *STOC '91: Proceedings of the twenty-third annual ACM symposium on Theory of computing*, pages 455–464, New York, NY, USA, 1991. ACM Press.
13. S. Kwek and L. Pitt. PAC learning intersections of halfspaces with membership queries. *Algorithmica*, 22(1/2):53–75, 1998.
14. M. L. Minsky and S. A. Papert. *Perceptrons: expanded edition.* MIT Press, Cambridge, MA, USA, 1988.
15. R. O'Donnell and R. A. Servedio. New degree bounds for polynomial threshold functions. In *STOC '03: Proceedings of the thirty-fifth annual ACM symposium on Theory of computing*, pages 325–334, New York, NY, USA, 2003. ACM Press.
16. M. E. Saks. Slicing the hypercube. *Surveys in combinatorics, 1993*, pages 211–255, 1993.
17. L. G. Valiant. A theory of the learnable. *Commun. ACM*, 27(11):1134–1142, 1984.
18. S. Vempala. A random sampling based algorithm for learning the intersection of halfspaces. In *Proceedings of the 38th Annual Symposium on Foundations of Computer Science*, pages 508–513, 1997.

Efficient Learning Algorithms Yield Circuit Lower Bounds

Lance Fortnow and Adam R. Klivans

U. Chicago Comp. Sci., 1100 E. 58th St., Chicago, IL 60637,
UT-Austin Comp. Sci., 1 University Station C0500, Austin, TX 78712
fortnow@cs.uchicago.edu,
klivans@cs.utexas.edu

Abstract. We describe a new approach for understanding the difficulty of designing efficient learning algorithms. We prove that the existence of an efficient learning algorithm for a circuit class C in Angluin's model of exact learning from membership and equivalence queries or in Valiant's PAC model yields a lower bound against C. More specifically, we prove that any subexponential time, determinstic exact learning algorithm for C (from membership and equivalence queries) implies the existence of a function f in $\mathsf{EXP}^{\mathsf{NP}}$ such that $f \notin C$. If C is PAC learnable with membership queries under the uniform distribution or Exact learnable in randomized polynomial time, we prove that there exists a function $f \in \mathsf{BPEXP}$ (the exponential time analog of BPP) such that $f \notin C$.

For C equal to polynomial-size, depth-two threshold circuits (i.e., neural networks with a polynomial number of hidden nodes), our result shows that efficient learning algorithms for this class would solve one of the most challenging open problems in computational complexity theory: proving the existence of a function in $\mathsf{EXP}^{\mathsf{NP}}$ or BPEXP that cannot be computed by circuits from C. We are not aware of any representation-independent hardness results for learning polynomial-size depth-2 neural networks.

Our approach uses the framework of the breakthrough result due to Kabanets and Impagliazzo showing that derandomizing BPP yields non-trivial circuit lower bounds.

1 Introduction

Discovering the limits of efficient learnability remains an important challenge in computational learning theory. Traditionally, computational learning theorists have reduced problems from computational complexity theory or cryptography to learning problems in order to better understand the difficulty of various classification tasks.

There are two lines of research in learning theory in this direction. First, several researchers have shown that *properly* PAC learning well-known concept classes (i.e. learning with the requirement that the output hypothesis be of the same form as the concept being learned) such as DNF formulas, finite automata, or intersections of halfspaces is NP-hard with respect to randomized reductions [1, 2, 3].

G. Lugosi and H.U. Simon (Eds.): COLT 2006, LNAI 4005, pp. 350–363, 2006.
© Springer-Verlag Berlin Heidelberg 2006

Secondly, in a seminal paper, Kearns and Valiant [4] initiated a line of research that applied results from cryptography to learning. They proved that learning polynomial-size circuits, regardless of the representation of the hypothesis of the learner, would imply the existence of algorithms for breaking cryptographic primitives. In fact, Kearns and Valiant [4] show that learning constant depth, poly-size neural networks would imply an efficient algorithm for breaking well-studied public-key cryptosystems. Various researchers have extended this work to other restricted classes of circuits [5, 6].

For some classes of circuits, however, we do not know how to create the cryptographic primitives needed to apply the Kearns-Valiant approach. It is a difficult open question, for example, as to whether polynomial-size depth-2 threshold circuits (polynomial-size neural networks) can compute cryptographic primitives. As such, we are unaware of any representation-independent hardness results for learning this class of circuits.

1.1   Reducing Circuit Lower Bounds to Learning Concept Classes

We give a new approach for showing the difficulty of proving that certain circuits classes admit efficient learning algorithms. We show that if a class of circuits C is efficiently learnable in either Angluin's exact model or Valiant's PAC model of learning, then we can prove a circuit lower bound against C. Hence, the existence of efficient learning algorithms (for many choices of C) would settle some important and well-studied open questions in circuit complexity.

Our first theorem states that a deterministic subexponential time exact learning algorithm for a concept class C implies a lower bound for Boolean circuits for a somewhat large complexity class:

Theorem 1. *Let C be a family of non-uniform, polynomial-size circuits. Assume that C is exactly learnable from membership and equivalence queries in time $2^{n^{o(1)}}$. Then there exists a function $f \in \mathsf{EXP^{NP}}$ such that $f \notin C$.*

If we take C to be the class of polynomial-size (depth-2) neural networks we obtain the following corollary:

Corollary 1. *If there exists an algorithm for exactly learning depth-2 neural networks (with a polynomial number of hidden nodes) in time $2^{n^{o(1)}}$ then there exists a function $f \in \mathsf{EXP^{NP}}$ such that f is not computable by any polynomial-size, depth-2 threshold circuit.*

Finding a function in a uniform class such as $\mathsf{EXP^{NP}}$ that cannot be computed by polynomial-size, depth-two threshold circuits has been a challenging open problem for over two decades in computational complexity. Additionally, we do not know of any representation independent hardness results for learning (depth-2) polynomial-size neural networks.

If we assume that our exact learning algorithm runs in polynomial-time rather than subexponential time we can show that even randomized exact learning algorithms imply circuit lower bounds against BPEXP, the exponential time version of BPP:

Theorem 2. *Let C be a family of non-uniform, polynomial-size circuits. Assume there exists a randomized polynomial-time algorithm for exactly learning C from membership and equivalence queries. Then there exists a function $f \in$ BPEXP such that $f \notin C$.*

We are unaware of any lower bounds for circuit classes such as polynomial-size depth-2 threshold circuits against BPEXP.

Theorems 1 and 2 also directly applies to arithmetic circuits. If, in addition, we restrict the output hypothesis of the learner to be an arithmetic circuit or formula (of possibly larger size and depth) we can replace the NP oracle in Theorem 1 with an RP oracle and obtain a finer separation of uniform and non-uniform circuit classes.

Theorem 3. *Let C be a family of non-uniform, polynomial-size arithmetic formulas. Assume that C is exactly learnable from membership and equivalence queries in polynomial-time and the hypothesis of the learner is an arithmetic formula. Then there exists a function $f \in$ EXP^{RP} such that $f \notin C$.*

If we allow both C and the hypothesis to be arithmetic circuits then there exists an $f \in$ ZPEXP^{RP} such that $f \notin C$.

We note here that proving lower bounds against polynomial-size arithmetic formulas and even depth-3 arithmetic circuits remains one of the most difficult challenges in algebraic complexity. Furthermore, as with polynomial-size neural networks, we are not aware of any representation independent hardness results for learning restricted models of arithmetic circuits.

These results also apply to the PAC model. Due to the inherent role of randomness in the definition of PAC learning, our lower bounds apply to the complexity class BPEXP:

Theorem 4. *Let C be a family of non-uniform, polynomial-size circuits. Assume that C is PAC learnable in polynomial time. Then there exists a function $f \in$ BPEXP such that $f \notin C$.*

The smallest uniform complexity class known to contain languages with super-polynomial Boolean circuit complexity is MA$_{\mathsf{EXP}}$, the exponential-time analog of Merlin-Arthur proofs (see Setion 2.1 for a discussion). BPEXP is easily seen to be contained in MA$_{\mathsf{EXP}}$.

1.2 Our Approach

The proof of Theorem 1 follows the outline of the work of Kabanets and Impagliazzo [7] on derandomizing algebraic circuits: we assume that EXP^{NP} is computable by some non-uniform circuit class C (otherwise there is nothing to prove). This implies, via a sequence of well-known reductions in complexity theory, that the Permanent is complete for EXP^{NP} (the analogous statements with EXP^{NP} replaced by BPEXP are not known to be true). At this point we need to use the supposed exact learning algorithm to construct an algorithm for computing the Permanent which runs in subexponential time and has access to an NP oracle. This leads to an immediate contradiction via time hierarchy theorems.

In the work of Kabanets and Impagliazzo, the assumption of a deterministic algorithm for polynomial-identity testing is used to develop a non-deterministic algorithm for computing the Permanent. In this work, we need to use the exact learning algorithm to construct the circuit $c \in C$ that computes the permanent. The main difficulty is that the exact learning algorithm needs access to a membership and equivalence query oracle, which we do not have. Using an idea from Impagliazzo and Wigderson's result on derandomizing BPP, we can simulate membership queries by inductively constructing circuits for the permanent on shorter input lengths. Simulating equivalence queries is slightly trickier and requires access to an NP oracle to find counterexamples.

To reduce the dependence on the NP oracle we can use randomness, but only in cases regarding arithmetic circuits and formulas, where output hypotheses can be suitably interpreted as low-degree polynomials. Our results on PAC learning and randomized Exact learners require a slightly different approach, as we are not aware of collapse consequences for the class BPEXP even if it is contained in P/poly. We appeal to work on derandomization due to Impagliazzo and Wigderson [8] that makes use of the random-self-reduciblity of the Permanent.

1.3   Outline

In Section 2 we define various learning models and state all the theorems from complexity theory necessary for proving our main result. In Section 3 we give a proof of our main result for exact learning in the Boolean case. Our results regarding learnability in the PAC model are in Section 4. In Section 5 we discuss applications to exact learning in the algebraic setting.

2   Preliminaries

Valiant's PAC model [9] and Angluin's model of Exact Learning from Membership and Equivalence queries [10] are two of the most well-studied learning models in computational learning theory. Recall that in Valiant's PAC model we fix a concept class C and a distribution D and a learner receives pairs of the form $(x, c(x))$ where x is chosen from D and c is some fixed concept in c. The learner's goal is to output, with probability $1 - \delta$, a hypothesis h such that h is a $1 - \epsilon$ accurate hypothesis with respect to c under D. We say that the learner is efficient if it requires at most t examples, runs in time at most t and outputs a hypothesis that can be evaluated in time t where $t = \mathsf{poly}(n, 1/\epsilon, 1/\delta, |c|)$ ($|c|$ denotes the size of the unknown concept). If the learner is allowed *membership queries* then it may query the unknown concept c at any point x of his choosing.

In Angluin's model of exact learning, the learner is trying to learn an unknown concept $c : \{0,1\}^n \to \{0,1\}$ and is allowed to make queries of the following form:

1. (*Membership Query*) What is the value of $c(x)$?
2. (*Equivalence Query*) Is h (the learner's current hypothesis) equal to c?

If the equivalence query is answered affirmatively, the learner outputs h and halts. Otherwise, the learner receives a counterexample, namely a point z such that $h(z) \neq c(z)$. We say that an algorithm A exactly learns a concept class C in time t if for every $c \in C$, A always halts and the time taken by A (including calls to the membership and equivalence query oracles) is bounded by t.

2.1   Uniform Versus Non-uniform Models of Computation

We frequently mention standard complexity classes EXP, RP, BPP, NP, MA, ZPP, EE, ZPEXP as well as relativized versions of the classes (e.g., EXP^{NP}). We refer the reader to the Complexity Zoo (http://www.complexityzoo.com) for further details on these classes .

We say a language L has polynomial-size circuits (P/poly) if there is a polynomial p and a sequence of logical (AND-OR-NOT) circuits $C_0, C_1, \ldots$ such that for all n,

1. The size of C_n is bounded by $p(n)$.
2. For all strings $x = x_1 \ldots x_n$, x is in L iff $C(x_1, \ldots, x_n) = 1$ where we use 1 for true and 0 for false.

Importantly, circuits describe nonuniform computation: the circuits for one input length may have no relation to the circuits for other lengths.

An algebraic circuit can only have addition, subtraction and multiplication gates, in particular no bit operations. All languages computed by algebraic circuits can be computed by a Boolean circuit (with a polynomial increase in size), but the converse is not known. A formula is a circuit described by a tree. It is well known that an arithmetic circuit is equivalent to a multivariate polynomial of degree at most exponential in the size of the circuit. Arithmetic formulas compute polynomials whose degree is at most a polynomial in the size of the formula.

The smallest complexity class known not to contain polynomial-size circuits is MA_{EXP} ([11], see also [12]), Merlin-Arthur games with an exponential-time verifier. Kabanets and Impagliazzo [7] use derandomization to show NEXP^{RP} does not have polynomial-size algebraic circuits. The relationship of NEXP^{RP} and MA_{EXP} is unknown.

It is a difficult open problem to improve upon MA_{EXP} as the smallest uniform class containing circuits of superpolynomial size even if we restrict ourselves to polynomial-size formulas, depth-2 threshold circuits (neural nets), or constant-depth logical circuits with Mod_m gates for any m not a prime power.

2.2   Hierarchy Theorems

Theorem 5. EXP^{NP} *is not contained in* $\text{SUBEXP}^{\text{NP}}$, *where* $\text{SUBEXP} = \text{DTIME}(2^{n^{o(1)}})$.

Proof. The seminal paper in computational complexity by Hartmanis and Stearns [13] shows that for any time-constructible functions $t_1(n)$ and $t_2(n)$ with $t_1^2(n) = o(t_2(n))$

$$\text{DTIME}(t_1(n)) \subsetneq \text{DTIME}(t_2(n))$$

and their proof relativizes. Theorem 5 follows by taking $t_1(n) = 2^n$, $t_2(n) = 2^{3n}$ and relativizing to SAT.   □

Let EE denote the class of languages computable in doubly-exponential time.

Theorem 6. EE *contains languages with super-polynomial circuit complexity.*

Proof. We follow a proof idea of Kannan [14]. We know by counting arguments there is some function that is not computed by circuits of size $2^{\sqrt{n}}$. In double exponential time we can, by brute force searching, find and evaluate the lexicographically least such function.   □

2.3   Properties of the Permanent

The Permanent of an $n \times n$ matrix A is defined by

$$Perm(A) = \sum_{\sigma \in S_n} a_{1\sigma(1)} a_{2\sigma(2)} \cdots a_{n\sigma(n)}$$

Valiant [15] showed that the Permanent is complete for the class #P, i.e., complete for functions counting the number of solutions of NP problems. The Permanent remains #P-complete if we compute the Permanent over a sufficiently large finite field. We will frequently abuse notation and write "Permanent is complete for class C," even though the Permanent (for large fields) is not a Boolean function. This problem is explicitly resolved in Kabanets and Impagliazzo [7].

Toda [16] shows that the polynomial-time hierarchy reduces to #P and thus the Permanent.

We will use the following two well known facts about the Permanent:

Fact 1. *(Downward Self Reducibility of the Permanent) Computing the permanent of an $n \times n$ matrix is polynomial-time (Turing) reducible to computing n instances of the Permanent over $n - 1 \times n - 1$ matrices.*

Fact 1 follows easily from the cofactor expansion of the Permanent.

The Permanent, when defined over a finite field, is also random-self reducible [17], i.e., there is an efficient randomized procedure that will take an $n \times n$ matrix A and produce $n \times n$ matrices $A_1, \ldots, A_{n+1}$ and a polynomial-time function that takes the Permanents of the A_i's and compute the Permanent of A. Each A_i is uniformly random over the space of all $n \times n$ matrices, though A_i and A_j are not independent variables.

We state this as follows:

Theorem 7. *(Random-self-reducibility of the Permanent) [18, 17] Assume that we have a circuit c that computes the Permanent on all but a $1/n^2$ fraction of inputs (n is the length of the instance) with respect to any field $F, |F| \geq n^2$. Then there exists a randomized, polynomial-time algorithm A that uses c as an oracle such that for every input x, A computes Permanent on x correctly with probabilty at least $1 - 1/n$.*

Finally, we make use of a lemma due to Kabanets and Impagliazzo:

Lemma 1. *[7] Given an arithmetic circuit C, the problem of determining if C computes the Permanent on all inputs is in coRP.*

2.4   Collapse Theorems

A long line of research in complexity theory is devoted to understanding the consequences of large uniform complexity classes being contained in small, non-uniform ones. Perhaps the most well known collapse is due to Karp and Lipton, stating that if $\mathsf{NP} \subseteq \mathsf{P/poly}$ then the polynomial-time hierarchy collapses ($\mathsf{PH} = \Sigma_2$). We will need the following two "collapse" theorems:

Theorem 8. *[19] If* $\mathsf{EXP^{NP}} \subseteq \mathsf{EXP/poly}$ *then* $\mathsf{EXP^{NP}} = \mathsf{EXP}$.

Theorem 9. *[20] If* $\mathsf{EXP} \subseteq \mathsf{P/poly}$ *then* $\mathsf{EXP} = \mathsf{MA}$.

Since $\mathsf{MA} \subseteq \mathsf{PH}$ and $\mathsf{PH} \subseteq \mathsf{P^{\#P}}$ [16] we conclude that $\mathsf{EXP^{NP}} \subseteq \mathsf{P/poly}$ implies $\mathsf{EXP^{NP}} = \mathsf{P^{\#P}}$. Applying Valiant's result on the complexity of the Permanent [15], we also have that $\mathsf{EXP^{NP}} \subseteq \mathsf{P/poly}$ implies Permanent is complete for $\mathsf{EXP^{NP}}$.

3   Lower Bounds from Exact Learning Algorithms

In this section we prove our main result: algorithms for exactly learning circuits classes yield lower bounds against those same circuit classes.

Theorem 10. *Let C be a non-uniform class of polynomial-size circuits. Assume that C is exactly learnable from membership and equivalence in time $t = 2^{n^{o(1)}}$. Then $\mathsf{EXP^{NP}} \not\subseteq C$.*

Proof. First assume that $\mathsf{EXP^{NP}} \subseteq C$ (since otherwise there is nothing to prove) and notice that since C is a class of polynomial-size circuits, Theorem 8 implies that $\mathsf{EXP^{NP}} = \mathsf{EXP} = \mathsf{P^{\#P}}$. As such, the Permanent function is now complete for $\mathsf{EXP^{NP}}$ and is computable by some $c \in C$. We wish to give a $\mathsf{poly}(n, t)$ time algorithm for computing the permanent that is allowed to make calls to an NP oracle. Because $\mathsf{EXP^{NP}}$ can be reduced to Permanent in polynomial-time, such an algorithm would violate a relativized version the time hierarchy theorem (Theorem 5) and complete the proof. Consider the following algorithm for computing the permanent:

Algorithm for Computing Permanent on input x:

For $i = 2$ to $n = |x|$:

1. Run the exact learning algorithm to find c_i, the circuit that computes permanent on inputs of length i.

2. Simulate required membership queries and equivalence queries using c_{i-1} and the NP oracle.

Output $c_n(x)$.

Computing c_1, the "base case," is trivial. The main difficulty is step 2, simulating the required membership and equivalence query oracles. If we can simulate membership and equivalence query oracles using an NP oracle, then the above steps for computing the permanent can be carried out in time $\text{poly}(n, t)$ with an NP oracle, as desired.

Simulating Membership Queries

Assume that our learning algorithm makes a membership query and requires the value of the permanent on input y of length i. By induction assume we have constructed a circuit c_{i-1} for computing the permanent on inputs of length $i - 1$. Then, by applying Fact 1, the permanent on input y can be computed via i calls to the circuit c'. As we have assumed that c' is exactly correct for all inputs of length $i - 1$, we are certain that we will obtain the correct value for the permanent on y (this is the same technique used by Impagliazzo and Wigderson [8] for making certain derandomization reductions more "uniform").

Simulating Equivalence Queries

Assume that we wish to determine if our current hypothesis h computes permanent correctly on all inputs of length i. We make the following query to the NP oracle: "Does there exist an input z such that $h(z)$ does not equal the value obtained by using the downward self-reducible property of the permanent and circuit c_{i-1} (by Fact 1, we can compute the true value of the permanent via i calls to circuit c_{i-1})?" I.e. does there exist an input z where the self-reduction fails? If there is no such input z then we are guaranteed that our hypothesis h is exactly correct on all inputs of length n. Otherwise, we can use the NP oracle to reconstruct the input z where h is incorrect. We first make a query of the form "Does there exist an input z where the self-reduction fails that begins with a 0?" If the answer is "no" then we know there must exist a counterexample that begins with a 1. Our next query is "Does there exist an input z beginning with 10 such that..." and so on for the remaining bits until we have obtained a counterexample.

Since we can construct a circuit for exactly computing the permanent on inputs of length n using an NP oracle and a circuit for the computing the permanent on inputs of length $n - 1$, we can find the circuit c that computes the permanent as required in step 1 of the above algorithm. Since c is from a polynomial-size circuit class we can evaluate $c(x)$ in polynomial time. This results in a time t, NP-oracle algorithm for computing the permanent and completes the proof.   □

We can make a similar statement regarding learnability in the mistake bounded model. Recall that in the mistake bounded model, the learner is required to make at most $\text{poly}(n, s)$ mistakes on any sequence of examples, where n is the length of the longest example and s is the size of the unknown concept to be learned. Assuming that the permanent function is computed by some circuit c, we can use the NP oracle as above to determine if our current hypothesis is exactly correct. If not, we can generate a counterexample in exactly the same manner as in the proof of Theorem 1. We have the following theorem:

Theorem 11. *Let C be a non-uniform class of polynomial-size circuits. Assume that C is efficiently learnable in the mistake bounded model. Then $\mathsf{EXP}^{\mathsf{NP}} \not\subseteq C$.*

Note again that Theorem 1 does not place any restrictions on the output hypothesis of the learner, or of the concept to be class to be learned, other than the requirement that evaluating $c(x)$ can be carried out in time $t = 2^{n^{o(1)}}$. Additionally, it is important to point out that the smallest known complexity class containing functions of superpolynomial-size circuit complexity is $\mathsf{MA_{EXP}}$, the exponential-time analogue of MA [11]. Proving $\mathsf{MA_{EXP}} \subseteq \mathsf{EXP}^{\mathsf{NP}}$ would be a tremendous derandomization.

4 Lower Bounds from Randomized Learning Algorithms

In this section we show that efficient PAC algorithms for learning a circuit class C or polynomial-time randomized Exact learning algorithms imply the existence of a function $f \in \mathsf{BPEXP}$ such that f is not in C. Our result holds even if the PAC algorithm is allowed to make membership queries to the unknown concept. As with the complexity class $\mathsf{EXP}^{\mathsf{NP}}$, it is a difficult open problem as to whether BPEXP can be computed by circuit classes such as polynomial-size, depth-2 threshold circuits, or polynomial-size arithmetic formulas. The smallest complexity class known to strictly contain these circuit classes is $\mathsf{MA_{EXP}}$. It is widely believed that BPEXP is strictly less powerful than $\mathsf{MA_{EXP}}$.

We require the following lemma, which states that if the Permanent has polynomial-size circuits from some class C and C is PAC learnable, then the Permanent is computable in BPP. This lemma is implicit in the work of Impagliazzo and Wigderson [8] (although it was used there to obtain new results in derandomization). We provide a proof in the language of PAC learning:

Lemma 2. *([8], restated) Assume that the Permanent is computed by a non-uniform class of polynomial-size circuits C. If C is PAC learnable with respect to the uniform distribution (with membership queries) then the Permanent is in BPP.*

Proof. To compute Permanent on input x of length n, assume by induction we have a randomized circuit c_{n-1} such that for every x, c_{n-1} computes the permanent correctly on x with probabilty at least $2/3$. Since C is PAC learnable, consider its associated learning algorithm A that learns any $c \in C$ in time $\mathrm{poly}(n, 1/\epsilon, 1/\delta, |c|)$. Set $\epsilon = 1/n^2$ and $\delta = 1/3n$. Let t equal the number of labeled examples and membership queries required by A for this setting of parameters.

For any input x of length $n-1$, we can amplify the probability that c_{n-1} computes x correctly to $1 - 1/3n^2t$ by taking a majoriy vote of multiple invocations of c_{n-1} on x (note that $t = n^{O(1)}$).

Now randomly choose the t points $z_1, \ldots, z_t$ (some of which may be membership queries) required by the learning algorithm. To find the labels of these points (recall the label of z_i is Permanent(z_i)), we apply Fact 1 and query c_{n-1} at the appropriate tn points. Applying a union bound we see that the probability some point is mislabeled is less than $1/3n$. Hence with probability at least

$1 - \delta - 1/3n$ we obtain a hypothesis h that computes Permanent correctly on all but a $1/n^2$ fraction of inputs. Applying Theorem 7 (the random self reducibility of the permanent), we obtain a randomized circuit c_n such that c_n computes Permanent correctly on each input with probability at least $1 - 1/n$.

Applying the union bound over all n iterations of this process, we see that the probability we fail to construct c_n properly is at most $n\delta + 1/3$. Since $\delta < 1/3n$, with probability at least $2/3$ we have obtained a randomized circuit for computing the permanent that is correct on every input with probability at least $1 - 1/n$. The lemma follows.   □

We can now state our main theorem showing PAC learning algorithms imply lower bounds against BPEXP. Since we do not know if BPEXP $\subseteq$ P/poly implies BPEXP = EXP, we must use the fact that doubly exponential time contains languages with superpolynomial circuit complexity:

Theorem 12. *Let C be a non-uniform class of polynomial-size circuits. Assume that C is PAC learnable (with membership queries) with respect to the uniform distribution in polynomial-time. Then BPEXP $\not\subseteq C$.*

Proof. First assume that EXP $\subseteq C$ as otherwise we have nothing to prove. Then applying Theorem 9 we have EXP = PSPACE = $P^{\#P}$. Thus Permanent is complete for EXP, and any EXP complete language L can be reduced to Permanent in polynomial-time. Applying Lemma 2 we have that Permanent is in BPP and thus EXP = BPP. This implies that EE $\subseteq$ BPEXP. From Theorem 6, we know that EE contains a language not computable by C. Hence BPEXP $\not\subseteq C$.   □

To extend these results to randomized Exact learning algorithms we require the following lemma:

Lemma 3. *Assume that the Permanent is computed by a non-uniform class of polynomial-size circuits C. If C is Exactly learnable from membership and equivalence queries in randomized polynomial-time then the Permanent is in BPP.*

Proof. Assume by induction we have a circuit c_{n-1} that computes Permanent correctly on at least a $1 - 1/n^2$ fraction of inputs. We say a circuit h on n inputs is *good* if it computes Permanent on at least a $1 - 1/n^3$ fraction of inputs of length n. In order to output, with high probability, a circuit c_n that is correct on at least a $1 - 1/n^2$ fraction of inputs, we run the exact learning algorithm and test whether the current hypothesis h is good. We can test, with high probability, if h is good by choosing sufficiently many random inputs and seeing if the answers obtained by c_{n-1} (applying both the downward self-reducible and random-self-reducible properties of the Permanent) agree with h. If h agrees with c_{n-1} on these random points then with high probabiltiy h is good so we set $h = c_n$. Otherwise, with high probability, we will have found a point where h differs Permanent, i.e. a counterexample, and we continue running the learning algorithm. We conclude that with high probability, in polynomial-time, we will have a circuit c_n computing Permanent on a $1 - 1/n^2$ fraction of inputs of length n. Applying Theorem 7 completes the proof. $\qquad\square$

Applying the same proof for Theorem 12 but using Lemma 3 we obtain

Theorem 13. *Let C be a non-uniform class of polynomial-size circuits. Assume that C is Exactly learnable in randomized polynomial-time. Then* $\mathsf{BPEXP} \nsubseteq C$.

Buhrman et al. [11] proved that $\mathsf{MA_{EXP}}$ contains languages with superpolynomial size circuits; this is still the smallest class known to contain languages of superpolynomial circuit complexity. Theorem 12 shows that PAC learnability of a circuit class such as depth-2 threshold circuits, even under the uniform distribution with membership queries, would implies a new lower bound. To contrast this with the work of Kabanets and Impagliazzo [7], they showed that under the assumption that there exists a non-deterministic subexponential time algorithm for polynomial identity-testing, NEXP contains languages with superpolynomial *arithmetic* circuit complexity.

5   Improved Lower Bounds from Learning Arithmetic Circuits

Several researchers have given deterministic, exact learning algorithms for various classes of algebraic models of computation including read-once arithmetic formulas, algebraic branching programs, and arithmetic circuits. Our main theorem applies to these models of computation as well. In fact, if we restrict the output hypothesis to be a polynomial-size arithmetic circuit or formula (or any hypothesis equal to a multivariate polynomial of degree bounded by $2^{n^{O(1)}}$), then we obtain a finer set of separations. We note that many exact learning algorithms for algebraic concepts do indeed output a hypothesis equal to polynomials of bounded degree (for example Bshouty et al. [21] or Klivans and Shpilka [22]). We require the following lemma:

Lemma 4. *Assume that polynomial-size arithmetic circuits are exactly learnable in polynomial-time and the output hypothesis is an arithmetic circuit. Then if Permanent is computed by polynomial-size arithmetic circuits, Permanent is in* $\mathsf{ZPP^{RP}}$.

Proof. We iteratively construct circuits $c_1, \ldots, c_n$ such that c_i computes the permanent on inputs of length i. At stage i, given c_{i-1}, membership queries are simulated as in the proof of Theorem 1. In order to find a counterexample, however, we cannot use an NP oracle. Instead, we use the fact that our output hypothesis is a polynomial-size arithmetic circuit. Lemma 1 shows that the problem of determining whether an arithmetic circuit computes permanent exactly is computable in polynomial-time given access to an RP oracle. If we discover that our hypothesis is correct we stop. Otherwise, we know that our hypothesis is not equal to the permanent.

At this point we need to compute a counterexample, namely a point z such that our current candidate for $h(z)$ does not equal Permanent of z where h is our current candidate for c_i. Since h is a polynomial-size arithmetic circuit it is equal to a polynomial of degree at most $2^{O(n^a)}$ for some fixed constant a (see Section 2.1). Thus a random z will be a counterexample if z is chosen from a field F of size $2^{O(n^{2a})}$. Thus, our algorithm chooses a random $z \in F$ and checks if $h(z)$ does not equal Permanent on z (the label for z can be computed by applying Lemma 1 and using c_{n-1}). With high probability we will obtain such a z. Due to the correctness of the learning algorithm, we will be assured of a correct hypothesis after at most $n^{O(1)}$ counterexamples. At each stage i the probability of failure can be amplified to be less than $1/3n$ so that the overall probability of failure (cumulative over all n stages) will be less than $1/3$. $\quad\square$

We can now show that learning arithmetic circuits (by arithmetic circuits) yields a lower bound against $\mathsf{ZPEXP}^{\mathsf{RP}}$. Since we know of no collapse theorems for complexity classes such as $\mathsf{ZPEXP}^{\mathsf{RP}}$ (or even $\mathsf{EXP}^{\mathsf{RP}}$) we need to use a different argument than in the proof of Theorem 1:

Theorem 14. *Let C be a non-uniform class of polynomial-size arithmetic circuits. Assume that C is exactly learnable from membership and equivalence queries in time* $\mathsf{poly}(n)$ *and that the output hypothesis is an arithmetic circuit. Then* $\mathsf{ZPEXP}^{\mathsf{RP}} \not\subseteq C$.

Proof. We may assume that 1) the Permanent is computable by circuits from C and 2) $\mathsf{EXP} \subseteq C$, as otherwise there is nothing to prove. Notice that if $\mathsf{EXP} \subseteq C$ then $\mathsf{EXP} = \mathsf{P}^{\#\mathsf{P}}$ by Theorem 9 and Permanent is complete for EXP via a polynomial-time reduction. By Lemma 4, Permanent (and thus EXP) is in $\mathsf{ZPP}^{\mathsf{RP}}$. This implies that $\mathsf{EE} \subseteq \mathsf{ZPEXP}^{\mathsf{RP}}$, but by Theorem 6, EE contains functions with superpolynomial circuit complexity. Hence $\mathsf{ZPEXP}^{\mathsf{RP}}$ must also. $\quad\square$

It is still an open problem is to whether polynomial-size arithmetic formulas are exactly learnable in polynmial-time; much progress has been made on restricted versions of this problem (for example [23, 24]). For the case of exactly learning arithmetic formulas (recall that no superpolynomial-lower bounds are known for this class) where the learner outputs a polynomial-size formula as its hypothesis, we can improve on Lemma 4:

Lemma 5. *Assume that polynomial-size arithmetic circuits are exactly learnable in polynomial-time and the output hypothesis is an arithmetic formula. Then if Permanent is computed by polynomial-size arithmetic formulas, Permanent is in* P^{RP}.

Proof. The proof is similar to the proof of Lemma 4, except that we can *deterministically* construct counterexamples using an oracle for RP. This is because the hypothesis is a formula rather than a circuit, and, as discussed in Section 2.1, its degree as a polynomial is polynomial is $O(n^a)$ for some constant a. We can then choose a field F of size $O(n^{2a})$ and substitute all values of F for x_1. For each substitution to x_1, query the RP oracle to determine if this restricted polynomial is non-zero. For some value $a = x_1 \in F$, the restricted polynomial must be non-zero. We can repeat this process to find an appropriate setting for $x_2, \ldots, x_n$. Since the size of F is at most $n^{O(1)}$, we will have found a polynomial-time algorithm for computing the permanent using an oracle for RP.   □

Following the same outline for the proof of Theorem 14 but using Lemma 5 instead of Lemma 4 we obtain the following theorem:

Theorem 15. *Let C be a non-uniform class of polynomial-size arithmetic formulas. Assume that C is exactly learnable from membership and equivalence in polynomial time and that the output hypothesis is a an arithmetic formula. Then* $\mathsf{EXP}^{\mathsf{RP}} \not\subseteq C$.

Kabanets and Impagliazzo [7] have proved that there exists a function $f \in \mathsf{NEXP}^{\mathsf{RP}}$ that has superpolynomial arithmetic circuit complexity. Note that $\mathsf{NEXP}^{\mathsf{RP}}$ is not known to be contained in either $\mathsf{EXP}^{\mathsf{RP}}$ or $\mathsf{ZPEXP}^{\mathsf{RP}}$.

Conclusions and Open Problems. One interpretation of our results is that we have given added motivation for trying to develop learning algorithms for very restricted concept classes, as they would settle important and difficult questions in computational complexity theory. Techniques from circuit lower bounds have figured prominently in the development of powerful learning algorithms in the past (e.g., Linial et al. [25]), yet we are unaware of applications from learning theory to circuit lower bounds. An interesting open problem is to show that randomized subexponential time Exact (and PAC) learning algorithms yield new circuit lower bounds.

References

1. Pitt, L., Valiant, L.: Computational limitations on learning from examples. Journal of the ACM **35** (1988) 965–984
2. Gold, E.A.: Complexity of automaton identification from given data. Information and Control **37** (1978) 302–320
3. Alekhnovich, Braverman, Feldman, Klivans, Pitassi: Learnability and automatizability. In: FOCS: IEEE Symposium on Foundations of Computer Science (FOCS). (2004)
4. Kearns, M., Valiant, L.: Cryptographic limitations on learning Boolean formulae and finite automata. Journal of the ACM **41** (1994) 67–95
5. Kharitonov, M.: Cryptographic hardness of distribution-specific learning. In: Proceedings of the Twenty-Fifth Annual Symposium on Theory of Computing. (1993) 372–381
6. Jackson, J., Klivans, A., Servedio, R.: Learnability beyond AC^0. In: Proceedings of the 34th ACM Symposium on Theory of Computing. (2002)
7. Kabanets, V., Impagliazzo, R.: Derandomizing polynomial identity tests means proving circuit lower bounds. In: Proceedings of the 35th ACM Symposium on the Theory of Computing, New York, ACM (2003) 355–364
8. Impagliazzo, R., Wigderson, A.: Randomness vs. time: Derandomization under a uniform assumption. Journal of Computer and System Sciences **63** (2001) 672–688

9. Valiant, L.: A theory of the learnable. Communications of the ACM **27** (1984) 1134–1142
10. Angluin, D.: Queries and concept learning. Machine Learning **2** (1988) 319–342
11. Buhrman, H., Fortnow, L., Thierauf, T.: Nonrelativizing separations. In: Proceedings of the 13th IEEE Conference on Computational Complexity. IEEE, New York (1998) 8–12
12. Miltersen, Vinodchandran, Watanabe: Super-polynomial versus half-exponential circuit size in the exponential hierarchy. In: COCOON: Annual International Conference on Computing and Combinatorics. (1999)
13. Hartmanis, J., Stearns, R.: On the computational complexity of algorithms. Transactions of the American Mathematical Society **117** (1965) 285–306
14. Kannan, R.: Circuit-size lower bounds and non-reducibility to sparse sets. Information and Control **55** (1982) 40–56
15. Valiant, L.: The complexity of computing the permanent. Theoretical Computer Science **8** (1979) 189–201
16. Toda, S.: PP is as hard as the polynomial-time hierarchy. SIAM Journal on Computing **20** (1991) 865–877
17. Lipton, R.: New directions in testing. In Feigenbaum, J., Merritt, M., eds.: Distributed Computing and Cryptography. Volume 2 of DIMACS Series in Discrete Mathematics and Theoretical Computer Science. American Mathematical Society, Providence (1991) 191 – 202
18. Beaver, D., Feigenbaum, J.: Hiding instances in multioracle queries. In: Proceedings of the 7th Symposium on Theoretical Aspects of Computer Science. Volume 415 of Lecture Notes in Computer Science. Springer, Berlin (1990) 37–48
19. Buhrman, H., Homer, S.: Superpolynomial circuits, almost sparse oracles and the exponential hierarchy. In: Proceedings of the 12th Conference on the Foundations of Software Technology and Theoretical Computer Science. Volume 652 of Lecture Notes in Computer Science. Springer, Berlin, Germany (1992) 116–127
20. Babai, L., Fortnow, L., Nisan, N., A.Wigderson: BPP has subexponential time simulations unless EXPTIME has publishable proofs. Computational Complexity **3** (1993) 307–318
21. Beimel, A., Bergadano, F., Bshouty, N., Kushilevitz, E., Varricchio, S.: On the applications of multiplicity automata in learning. In: Proceedings of the Thirty-Seventh Annual Symposium on Foundations of Computer Science. (1996) 349–358
22. Klivans, Shpilka: Learning arithmetic circuits via partial derivatives. In: COLT: Proceedings of the Workshop on Computational Learning Theory, Morgan Kaufmann Publishers. (2003)
23. Bshouty, Hancock, Hellerstein: Learning arithmetic read-once formulas. SICOMP: SIAM Journal on Computing **24** (1995)
24. Bshouty, Bshouty: On interpolating arithmetic read-once formulas with exponentiation. JCSS: Journal of Computer and System Sciences **56** (1998)
25. Linial, N., Mansour, Y., Nisan, N.: Constant depth circuits, fourier transform, and learnability. Journal of the ACM **40** (1993) 607–620

Optimal Oracle Inequality for Aggregation of Classifiers Under Low Noise Condition

Guillaume Lecué

Laboratoire de Probabilités et Modèles Aléatoires (UMR CNRS 7599)
Université Paris VI
4 pl.Jussieu, BP 188, 75252 Paris, France
lecue@ccr.jussieu.fr

Abstract. We consider the problem of optimality, in a minimax sense, and adaptivity to the margin and to regularity in binary classification. We prove an oracle inequality, under the margin assumption (low noise condition), satisfied by an aggregation procedure which uses exponential weights. This oracle inequality has an optimal residual: $(\log M/n)^{\kappa/(2\kappa-1)}$ where κ is the margin parameter, M the number of classifiers to aggregate and n the number of observations. We use this inequality first to construct minimax classifiers under margin and regularity assumptions and second to aggregate them to obtain a classifier which is adaptive both to the margin and regularity. Moreover, by aggregating plug-in classifiers (only $\log n$), we provide an easily implementable classifier adaptive both to the margin and to regularity.

1 Introduction

Let $(\mathcal{X}, \mathcal{A})$ be a measurable space. We consider a random variable (X, Y) with values in $\mathcal{X} \times \{-1, 1\}$ and denote by π the distribution of (X, Y). We denote by P^X the marginal of π on $\mathcal{X}$ and $\eta(x) = \mathbb{P}(Y = 1 | X = x)$ the conditional probability function of $Y = 1$ given that $X = x$. We denote by $D_n = (X_i, Y_i)_{i=1,\ldots,n}$, n i.i.d. observations of the couple (X, Y).

We recall some usual notions introduced for the classification framework. A *prediction rule* is a measurable function $f : \mathcal{X} \longmapsto \{-1, 1\}$. The *misclassification error* associated to f is

$$R(f) = \mathbb{P}(Y \neq f(X)).$$

It is well known (see, e.g., [12]) that $\min_f R(f) = R(f^*) \overset{\text{def}}{=} R^*$, where the prediction rule f^* is called *Bayes rule* and is defined by

$$f^*(x) = \text{sign}(2\eta(x) - 1).$$

The minimal risk R^* is called the *Bayes risk*. A *classifier* is a function, $\hat{f}_n = \hat{f}_n(X, D_n)$, measurable with respect to D_n and X with values in $\{-1, 1\}$, that assigns to the sample D_n a prediction rule $\hat{f}_n(., D_n) : \mathcal{X} \longmapsto \{-1, 1\}$. A key characteristic of $\hat{f}_n$ is the value of *generalization error* $\mathbb{E}[R(\hat{f}_n)]$. Here

$$R(\hat{f}_n) = \mathbb{P}(Y \neq \hat{f}_n(X) | D_n).$$

G. Lugosi and H.U. Simon (Eds.): COLT 2006, LNAI 4005, pp. 364–378, 2006.

The performance of a classifier $\hat{f}_n$ is measured by the value $\mathbb{E}[R(\hat{f}_n) - R^*]$ called the *excess risk* of $\hat{f}_n$. We say that the classifier $\hat{f}_n$ learns with the convergence rate $\phi(n)$, where $(\phi(n))_{n \in \mathbb{N}}$ is a decreasing sequence, if there exists an absolute constant $C > 0$ such that for any integer n, $\mathbb{E}[R(\hat{f}_n) - R^*] \leq C\phi(n)$. Theorem 7.2 of [12] shows that no classifier can learn with a given convergence rate for arbitrary underlying probability distribution π.

In this paper we focus on entropy assumptions which allow us to work with finite sieves. Hence, we first work with a finite model for f^*: it means that we take a finite class of prediction rules $\mathcal{F} = \{f_1, \ldots, f_M\}$. Our aim is to construct a classifier $\hat{f}_n$ which mimics the best one of them w.r.t. to the excess risk and with an optimal residual. Namely, we want to state an oracle inequality

$$\mathbb{E}\left[R(\hat{f}_n) - R^*\right] \leq a_0 \min_{f \in \mathcal{F}}(R(f) - R^*) + C\gamma(M, n), \tag{1}$$

where $a_0 \geq 1$ and $C > 0$ are some absolute constants and $\gamma(M, n)$ is the residual. The classical procedure, due to Vapnik and Chervonenkis (see, e.g. [12]), is to look for an ERM classifier, i.e., the one which minimizes the *empirical risk*

$$R_n(f) = \frac{1}{n} \sum_{i=1}^{n} \mathbb{I}_{\{Y_i f(X_i) \leq 0\}}, \tag{2}$$

over all prediction rules f in $\mathcal{F}$, where $\mathbb{I}_E$ denotes the indicator of the set E. This procedure leads to optimal theoretical results (see, e.g. Chapter 12 of [12]), but minimizing the empirical risk (2) is computationally intractable for sets $\mathcal{F}$ of classifiers with large cardinality (often depending on the sample size n), because this risk is neither convex nor continuous. Nevertheless, we might base a tractable estimation procedure on minimization of a convex surrogate ϕ for the loss ([16], [9], [7], [8], [22] and [23]). A wide variety of classification methods in machine learning are based on this idea, in particular, on using the convex loss associated to support vector machines ([11], [21]),

$$\phi(x) = \max(0, 1 - x),$$

called the *hinge-loss*. The risk associated to this loss is called the *hinge risk* and is defined by

$$A(f) = \mathbb{E}[\max(0, 1 - Yf(X))],$$

for all $f : \mathcal{X} \longmapsto \mathbb{R}$. The *optimal hinge risk* is defined by

$$A^* = \inf_f A(f), \tag{3}$$

where the infimum is taken over all measurable functions f. The Bayes rule f^* attains the infimum in (3) and, moreover, denoting by $R(f)$ the misclassification error of $\text{sign}(f)$ for all measurable functions f with values in $\mathbb{R}$, Zhang, cf. [29], has shown that,

$$R(f) - R^* \leq A(f) - A^*, \tag{4}$$

for any real valued measurable function f. Thus, minimization of the *excess hinge risk* $A(f) - A^*$ provides a reasonable alternative for minimization of the excess risk. In this paper we provide a procedure which does not need any minimization step. We use a convex combination of the given prediction rules, as explained in section 2.

The difficulty of classification is closely related to the behavior of the conditional probability function η near $1/2$ (the random variable $|\eta(X) - 1/2|$ is sometimes called the theoretical margin). Tsybakov has introduced, in [25], an assumption on the the margin, called *margin (or low noise) assumption*,

(MA) Margin (or low noise) assumption. *The probability distribution π on the space $\mathcal{X} \times \{-1, 1\}$ satisfies the margin assumption MA(κ) with margin parameter $1 \leq \kappa < +\infty$ if there exists $c_0 > 0$ such that,*

$$\mathbb{E}\left\{|f(X) - f^*(X)|\right\} \leq c_0 \left(R(f) - R^*\right)^{1/\kappa}, \tag{5}$$

for all measurable functions f with values in $\{-1, 1\}$.

Under this assumption, the risk of an ERM classifier over some fixed class $\mathcal{F}$ can converge to the minimum risk over the class with *fast rates*, namely faster than $n^{-1/2}$ (cf. [25]). On the other hand, with no margin assumption on the joint distribution π (but combinatorial or complexity assumption on the class $\mathcal{F}$), the convergence rate of the excess risk is not faster than $n^{-1/2}$ (cf. [12]).

In this paper we suggest an easily implementable procedure of aggregation of classifiers and prove the following results:

1. We obtain an oracle inequality for our procedure and we use it to show that our classifiers are adaptive both to the margin parameter (low noise exponent) and to a complexity parameter.
2. We generalize the lower bound inequality stated in Chapter 14 of [12], by introducing the margin assumption and deduce optimal rates of aggregation under low noise assumption in the spirit of Tsybakov [24].
3. We obtain classifiers with minimax fast rates of convergence on a Hölder class of conditional probability functions η and under the margin assumption.

The paper is organized as follows. In Section 2 we prove an oracle inequality for our convex aggregate, with an optimal residual, which will be used in Section 3 to construct minimax classifiers and to obtain adaptive classifiers by aggregation of them. Proofs are given in Section 4.

2   Oracle Inequality

We have M prediction rules $f_1, \ldots, f_M$. We want to mimic the best of them according to the excess risk under the margin assumption. Our procedure is using exponential weights. Similar constructions in other context can be found, e.g., in [3], [28], [13], [2], [17], [18], [27]. Consider the following aggregate which is a convex combination with exponential weights of M classifiers,

$$\tilde{f}_n = \sum_{j=1}^{M} w_j^{(n)} f_j, \tag{6}$$

where

$$w_j^{(n)} = \frac{\exp\left(\sum_{i=1}^n Y_i f_j(X_i)\right)}{\sum_{k=1}^M \exp\left(\sum_{i=1}^n Y_i f_k(X_i)\right)}, \quad \forall j = 1, \dots, M. \tag{7}$$

Since $f_1, \dots, f_M$ take their values in $\{-1, 1\}$, we have,

$$w_j^{(n)} = \frac{\exp\left(-n A_n(f_j)\right)}{\sum_{k=1}^M \exp\left(-n A_n(f_k)\right)}, \tag{8}$$

for all $j \in \{1, \dots, M\}$, where

$$A_n(f) = \frac{1}{n} \sum_{i=1}^n \max(0, 1 - Y_i f(X_i)) \tag{9}$$

is the empirical analog of the hinge risk. Since $A_n(f_j) = 2R_n(f_j)$ for all $j = 1, \dots, M$, these weights can be written in terms of the empirical risks of f_j's,

$$w_j^{(n)} = \frac{\exp\left(-2n R_n(f_j)\right)}{\sum_{k=1}^M \exp\left(-2n R_n(f_k)\right)}, \quad \forall j = 1, \dots, M.$$

Remark that, using the definition (8) for the weights, we can aggregate functions with values in $\mathbb{R}$ (like in theorem 1) and not only functions with values in $\{-1, 1\}$.

The aggregation procedure defined by (6) with weights (8), that we can called aggregation with exponential weights (AEW), can be compared to the ERM one. First, our AEW method does not need any minimization algorithm contrarily to the ERM procedure. Second, the AEW is less sensitive to the over fitting problem. Intuitively, if the classifier with smallest empirical risk is over fitted (it means that the classifier fits too much to the observations) then the ERM procedure will be over fitted. But, if other classifiers in $\mathcal{F}$ are good classifiers, our procedure will consider their "opinions" in the final decision procedure and these opinions can balance with the opinion of the over fitted classifier in $\mathcal{F}$ which can be false because of its over fitting property. The ERM only considers the "opinion" of the classifier with the smallest risk, whereas the AEW takes into account all the opinions of the classifiers in the set $\mathcal{F}$. The AEW is more temperate contrarily to the ERM. Understanding why aggregation procedure are often more efficient than the ERM procedure from a theoretical point of view is a deep question, on which we are still working at this time this paper is written. Finally, the following proposition shows that the AEW has similar theoretical property as the ERM procedure up to the residual $(\log M)/n$.

Proposition 1. *Let $M \geq 2$ be an integer, $f_1, \dots, f_M$ be M real valued functions on $\mathcal{X}$. For any integers n, the aggregate defined in (6) with weights (8) $\tilde{f}_n$ satisfies*

$$A_n(\tilde{f}_n) \leq \min_{i=1,\dots,M} A_n(f_i) + \frac{\log(M)}{n}.$$

The following theorem provides first an exact oracle inequality w.r.t. the hinge risk satisfied by the AEW procedure and second shows its optimality among all aggregation procedures. We deduce from it that, for a margin parameter $\kappa \geq 1$ and a set of M functions with values in $[-1,1]$, $\mathcal{F} = \{f_1, \ldots, f_M\}$,

$$\gamma(\mathcal{F}, \pi, n, \kappa) = \sqrt{\frac{\min_{f \in \mathcal{F}}(A(f) - A^*)^{\frac{1}{\kappa}} \log M}{n}} + \left(\frac{\log M}{n}\right)^{\frac{\kappa}{2\kappa - 1}}$$

is an optimal rate of convex aggregation of M functions with values in $[-1,1]$ w.r.t. the hinge risk, in the sense of [18].

Theorem 1 (Oracle inequality and Lower bound). *Let $\kappa \geq 1$. We assume that π satisfies $MA(\kappa)$. We denote by $\mathcal{C}$ the convex hull of a finite set of functions with values in $[-1,1]$, $\mathcal{F} = \{f_1, \ldots, f_M\}$. The AEW procedure, introduced in (6) with weights (8) (remark that the form of the weights in (8) allows to take real valued functions for the f_j's), satisfies for any integer $n \geq 1$ the following inequality*

$$\mathbb{E}\left[A(\tilde{f}_n) - A^*\right] \leq \min_{f \in \mathcal{C}}(A(f) - A^*) + C_0 \gamma(\mathcal{F}, \pi, n, \kappa),$$

where $C_0 > 0$ depends only on the constants κ and c_0 appearing in $MA(\kappa)$.

Moreover, there exists a set of prediction rules $\mathcal{F} = \{f_1, \ldots, f_M\}$ such that for any procedure $\bar{f}_n$ with values in $\mathbb{R}$, there exists a probability measure π satisfying $MA(\kappa)$ such that for any integers M, n with $\log M \leq n$ we have

$$\mathbb{E}\left[A(\bar{f}_n) - A^*\right] \geq \min_{f \in \mathcal{C}}(A(f) - A^*) + C_0' \gamma(\mathcal{F}, \pi, n, \kappa),$$

where $C_0' > 0$ depends only on the constants κ and c_0 appearing in $MA(\kappa)$.

The hinge loss is linear on $[-1,1]$, thus, model selection aggregation or convex aggregation are identical problems if we use the hinge risk and if we aggregate function with values in $[-1,1]$. Namely, $\min_{f \in \mathcal{F}} A(f) = \min_{f \in \mathcal{C}} A(f)$. Moreover, the result of Theorem 1 is obtained for the aggregation of functions with values in $[-1,1]$ and not only for prediction rules. In fact, only functions with values in $[-1,1]$ have to be considered when we use the hinge loss since, for any real valued function f, we have $\max(0, 1 - y\psi(f(x))) \leq \max(0, 1 - yf(x))$ for all $x \in \mathcal{X}, y \in \{-1,1\}$ where ψ is the projection on $[-1,1]$, thus, $A(\psi(f)) - A^* \leq A(f) - A^*$. Remark that, under $MA(\kappa)$, there exists $c > 0$ such that, $\mathbb{E}\left[|f(X) - f^*(X)|\right] \leq c(A(f) - A^*)^{1/\kappa}$ for all functions f on $\mathcal{X}$ with values in $[-1,1]$ (cf. [18]) . The proof of Theorem 1 is not given here by the lack of space. It can be found in [18]. Instead, we prove here the following slightly less general result that we will be further used to construct adaptive minimax classifiers.

Theorem 2. *Let $\kappa \geq 1$ and let $\mathcal{F} = \{f_1, \ldots, f_M\}$ be a finite set of prediction rules with $M \geq 3$. We denote by $\mathcal{C}$ the convex hull of $\mathcal{F}$. We assume that π satisfies $MA(\kappa)$. The aggregate defined in (6) with the exponential weights (7) (or (8)) satisfies for any integers n, M and any $a > 0$ the following inequality*

$$\mathbb{E}\left[A(\tilde{f}_n) - A^*\right] \leq (1 + a) \min_{f \in \mathcal{C}}(A(f) - A^*) + C\left(\frac{\log M}{n}\right)^{\frac{\kappa}{2\kappa - 1}},$$

where $C > 0$ is a constant depending only on a.

Corollary 1. *Let $\kappa \geq 1$, $M \geq 3$ and $\{f_1, \ldots, f_M\}$ be a finite set of prediction rules. We assume that π satisfies MA(κ). The AEW procedure satisfies for any number $a > 0$ and any integers n, M the following inequality, with $C > 0$ a constant depending only on a,*

$$\mathbb{E}\left[R(\tilde{f}_n) - R^*\right] \leq 2(1 + a) \min_{j=1,\ldots,M} (R(f_j) - R^*) + C\left(\frac{\log M}{n}\right)^{\frac{\kappa}{2\kappa-1}}.$$

We denote by $\mathcal{P}_\kappa$ the set of all probability measures on $\mathcal{X} \times \{-1, 1\}$ satisfying the margin assumption MA(κ). Combining Corollary 1 and the following theorem, we get that the residual

$$\left(\frac{\log M}{n}\right)^{\frac{\kappa}{2\kappa-1}}$$

is a near optimal rate of model selection aggregation in the sense of [18] when the underlying probability measure π belongs to $\mathcal{P}_\kappa$.

Theorem 3. *For any integers M and n satisfying $M \leq \exp(n)$, there exists M prediction rules $f_1, \ldots, f_M$ such that for any classifier $\hat{f}_n$ and any $a > 0$, we have*

$$\sup_{\pi \in \mathcal{P}_\kappa} \left[\mathbb{E}\left[R(\hat{f}_n) - R^*\right] - 2(1 + a) \min_{j=1,\ldots,M} (R(f_j) - R^*)\right] \geq C_1 \left(\frac{\log M}{n}\right)^{\frac{\kappa}{2\kappa-1}},$$

where $C_1 = c_0^\kappa / (4e2^{2\kappa(\kappa-1)/(2\kappa-1)}(\log 2)^{\kappa/(2\kappa-1)})$.

3 Adaptivity Both to the Margin and to Regularity

In this section we give two applications of the oracle inequality stated in Corollary 1. First, we construct classifiers with minimax rates of convergence and second, we obtain adaptive classifiers by aggregating the minimax ones. Following [1], we focus on the regularity model where η belongs to the Hölder class.

For any multi-index $s = (s_1, \ldots, s_d) \in \mathbb{N}^d$ and any $x = (x_1, \ldots, x_d) \in \mathbb{R}^d$, we define $|s| = \sum_{j=1}^{d} s_j$, $s! = s_1! \ldots s_d!$, $x^s = x_1^{s_1} \ldots x_d^{s_d}$ and $\|x\| = (x_1^2 + \ldots + x_d^2)^{1/2}$. We denote by D^s the differential operator $\frac{\partial^{s_1 + \ldots + s_d}}{\partial x_1^{s_1} \ldots \partial x_d^{s_d}}$.

Let $\beta > 0$. We denote by $\lfloor \beta \rfloor$ the maximal integer that is strictly less than β. For any $x \in (0, 1)^d$ and any $\lfloor \beta \rfloor$-times continuously differentiable real valued function g on $(0, 1)^d$, we denote by g_x its Taylor polynomial of degree $\lfloor \beta \rfloor$ at point x, namely,

$$g_x(y) = \sum_{|s| \leq \lfloor \beta \rfloor} \frac{(y - x)^s}{s!} D^s g(x).$$

For all $L > 0$ and $\beta > 0$. The $(\beta, L, [0, 1]^d)$–*Hölder class* of functions, denoted by $\Sigma(\beta, L, [0, 1]^d)$, is the set of all real valued functions g on $[0, 1]^d$ that are $\lfloor \beta \rfloor$-times continuously differentiable on $(0, 1)^d$ and satisfy, for any $x, y \in (0, 1)^d$, the inequality

$$|g(y) - g_x(y)| \leq L\|x - y\|^\beta.$$

A control of the complexity of Hölder classes is given by Kolmogorov and Tikhomorov (1961):

$$\mathcal{N}\left(\varSigma(\beta, L, [0,1]^d), \epsilon, L^\infty([0,1]^d)\right) \leq A(\beta, d)\epsilon^{-\frac{d}{\beta}}, \forall \epsilon > 0, \qquad (10)$$

where the LHS is the $\epsilon-$entropy of the $(\beta, L, [0,1]^d)-$Hölder class w.r.t. to the $L^\infty([0,1]^d)-$norm and $A(\beta, d)$ is a constant depending only on β and d.

If we want to use entropy assumptions on the set which η belongs to, we need to make a link between P^X and the Lebesgue measure, since the distance in (10) is the $L^\infty-$norm w.r.t. the Lebesgue measure. Therefore, introduce the following assumption:

(A1) *The marginal distribution P^X on $\mathcal{X}$ of π is absolutely continuous w.r.t. the Lebesgue measure λ_d on $[0,1]^d$, and there exists a version of its density which is upper bounded by $\mu_{max} < \infty$.*

We consider the following class of models. For all $\kappa \geq 1$ and $\beta > 0$, we denote by $\mathcal{P}_{\kappa,\beta}$, the set of all probability measures π on $\mathcal{X} \times \{-1,1\}$, such that

1. MA(κ) is satisfied.
2. The marginal P^X satisfies (A1).
3. The conditional probability function η belongs to $\varSigma(\beta, L, \mathbb{R}^d)$.

Now, we define the class of classifiers which attain the optimal rate of convergence, in a minimax sense, over the models $\mathcal{P}_{\kappa,\beta}$. Let $\kappa \geq 1$ and $\beta > 0$. For any $\epsilon > 0$, we denote by $\varSigma_\epsilon(\beta)$ an ϵ-net on $\varSigma(\beta, L, [0,1]^d)$ for the $L^\infty-$norm, such that, its cardinal satisfies $\log \mathrm{Card}\,(\varSigma_\epsilon(\beta)) \leq A(\beta, d)\epsilon^{-d/\beta}$. We consider the AEW procedure defined in (6), over the net $\varSigma_\epsilon(\beta)$:

$$\tilde{f}_n^\epsilon = \sum_{\eta \in \varSigma_\epsilon(\beta)} w^{(n)}(f_\eta)f_\eta, \text{ where } f_\eta(x) = 2\mathbb{1}_{(\eta(x) \geq 1/2)} - 1. \qquad (11)$$

Theorem 4. *Let $\kappa > 1$ and $\beta > 0$. Let $a_1 > 0$ be an absolute constant and consider $\epsilon_n = a_1 n^{-\frac{\beta(\kappa-1)}{\beta(2\kappa-1)+d(\kappa-1)}}$. The aggregate (11) with $\epsilon = \epsilon_n$, satisfies, for any $\pi \in \mathcal{P}_{\kappa,\beta}$ and any integer $n \geq 1$, the following inequality*

$$\mathbb{E}_\pi\left[R(\tilde{f}_n^{\epsilon_n}) - R^*\right] \leq C_2(\kappa, \beta, d)n^{-\frac{\beta\kappa}{\beta(2\kappa-1)+d(\kappa-1)}},$$

where $C_2(\kappa, \beta, d) = 2\max\left(4(2c_0\mu_{max})^{\kappa/(\kappa-1)}, CA(\beta, d)^{\frac{\kappa}{2\kappa-1}}\right)(a_1)^{\frac{\kappa}{\kappa-1}} \vee (a_1)^{-\frac{d\kappa}{\beta(\kappa-1)}}$ and C is the constant appearing in Corollary 1.

Audibert and Tsybakov (cf. [1]) have shown the optimality, in a minimax sense, of the rate obtained in theorem 4. Note that this rate is a fast rate because it can approach $1/n$ when κ is close to 1 and β is large.

The construction of the classifier $\tilde{f}_n^{\epsilon_n}$ needs the knowledge of κ and β which are not available in practice. Thus, we need to construct classifiers independent of these parameters and which learn with the optimal rate $n^{-\beta\kappa/(\beta(2\kappa-1)+d(\kappa-1))}$ if the underlying probability measure π belongs to $\mathcal{P}_{\kappa,\beta}$, for different values of κ and β. We now show that using the procedure (6) to aggregate the classifiers $\tilde{f}_n^\epsilon$, for different values of ϵ in a grid, the oracle inequality of Corollary 1 provides the result.

We use a split of the sample for the adaptation step. Denote by $D_m^{(1)}$ the subsample containing the first m observations and $D_l^{(2)}$ the one containing the $l(=n-m)$ last ones. Subsample $D_m^{(1)}$ is used to construct the classifiers $\tilde{f}_m^\epsilon$ for different values of ϵ in a finite grid. Subsample $D_l^{(2)}$ is used to aggregate these classifiers by the procedure (6). We take

$$l = \left\lceil \frac{n}{\log n} \right\rceil \quad \text{and} \quad m = n - l.$$

Set $\Delta = \log n$. We consider a grid of values for ϵ:

$$\mathcal{G}(n) = \left\{ \phi_{n,k} = \frac{k}{\Delta} : k \in \{1, \dots, \lfloor \Delta/2 \rfloor\} \right\}.$$

For any $\phi \in \mathcal{G}(n)$ we consider the step $\epsilon_m^{(\phi)} = m^{-\phi}$. The classifier that we propose is the sign of

$$\tilde{f}_n^{adp} = \sum_{\phi \in \mathcal{G}(n)} w^{[l]}(\tilde{F}_m^{\epsilon_m^{(\phi)}}) \tilde{F}_m^{\epsilon_m^{(\phi)}},$$

where $\tilde{F}_m^\epsilon(x) = \text{sign}(\tilde{f}_m^\epsilon(x))$ is the classifier associated to the aggregate $\tilde{f}_m^\epsilon$ for all $\epsilon > 0$ and the weights $w^{[l]}(F)$ are the ones introduced in (7) constructed with the observations $D_l^{(2)}$ for all $F \in \mathcal{F}(n) = \{\text{sign}(\tilde{f}_m^\epsilon) : \epsilon = m^{-\phi}, \phi \in \mathcal{G}(n)\}$:

$$w^{[l]}(F) = \frac{\exp\left(\sum_{i=m+1}^n Y_i F(X_i)\right)}{\sum_{G \in \mathcal{F}(n)} \exp\left(\sum_{i=m+1}^n Y_i G(X_i)\right)}.$$

The following Theorem shows that $\tilde{f}_n^{adp}$ is adaptive both to the low noise exponent κ and to the complexity (or regularity) parameter β, provided that (κ, β) belongs to a compact subset of $(1, +\infty) \times (0, +\infty)$.

Theorem 5. *Let K be a compact subset of $(1, +\infty) \times (0, +\infty)$. There exists a constant $C_3 > 0$ that depends only on K and d such that for any integer $n \geq 1$, any $(\kappa, \beta) \in K$ and any $\pi \in \mathcal{P}_{\kappa,\beta}$, we have,*

$$\mathbb{E}_\pi\left[R(\tilde{f}_n^{adp}) - R^*\right] \leq C_3 n^{-\frac{\kappa\beta}{\beta(2\kappa-1)+d(\kappa-1)}}.$$

Classifiers $\tilde{f}_n^{\epsilon_n}$ are not easily implementable since the cardinality of $\Sigma_{\epsilon_n}(\beta)$ is an exponential of n. An alternative procedure which is easily implementable is to aggregate plug-in classifiers constructed in Audibert and Tsybakov (cf. [1]).

We introduce the class of models $\mathcal{P}'_{\kappa,\beta}$ composed of all the underlying probability measures π such that:

1. π satisfies the margin assumption MA(κ).
2. The conditional probability function $\eta \in \Sigma(\beta, L, [0, 1]^d)$.

3. The marginal distribution of X is supported on $[0,1]^d$ and has a Lebesgue density lower bounded and upper bounded by two constants.

Theorem 6 (Audibert and Tsybakov (2005)). *Let* $\kappa > 1, \beta > 0$. *The excess risk of the plug-in classifier* $\hat{f}_n^{(\beta)} = 2\mathbb{1}_{\{\hat{\eta}_n^{(\beta)} \geq 1/2\}} - 1$ *satisfies*

$$\sup_{\pi \in \mathcal{P}'_{\kappa,\beta}} \mathbb{E}\left[R(\hat{f}_n^{(\beta)}) - R^*\right] \leq C_4 n^{-\frac{\beta\kappa}{(\kappa-1)(2\beta+d)}},$$

where $\hat{\eta}_n^{(\beta)}(\cdot)$ *is the locally polynomial estimator of* $\eta(\cdot)$ *of order* $\lfloor \beta \rfloor$ *with bandwidth* $h = n^{-\frac{1}{2\beta+d}}$ *and* C_4 *a positive constant.*

In [1], it is shown that the rate $n^{-\frac{\beta\kappa}{(\kappa-1)(2\beta+d)}}$ is minimax over $\mathcal{P}'_{\kappa,\beta}$, if $\beta \leq d(\kappa-1)$. Remark that the fast rate n^{-1} can be achieved.

We aggregate the classifiers $\hat{f}_n^{(\beta)}$ for different values of β lying in a finite grid. We use a split of the sample to construct our adaptive classifier: $l = \lceil n/\log n \rceil$ and $m = n - l$. The training sample $D_m^1 = ((X_1, Y_1), \ldots, (X_m, Y_m))$ is used for the construction of the class of plug-in classifiers

$$\mathcal{F} = \left\{ \hat{f}_m^{(\beta_k)} : \beta_k = \frac{kd}{\Delta - 2k}, k \in \{1, \ldots, \lfloor \Delta/2 \rfloor\} \right\}, \quad \text{where } \Delta = \log n.$$

The validation sample $D_l^2 = ((X_{m+1}, Y_{m+1}), \ldots, (X_n, Y_n))$ is used for the construction of weights

$$w^{[l]}(f) = \frac{\exp\left(\sum_{i=m+1}^n Y_i f(X_i)\right)}{\sum_{\bar{f} \in \mathcal{F}} \exp\left(\sum_{i=m+1}^n Y_i \bar{f}(X_i)\right)}, \quad \forall f \in \mathcal{F}.$$

The classifier that we propose is $\tilde{F}_n^{adp} = \text{sign}(\tilde{f}_n^{adp})$, where: $\tilde{f}_n^{adp} = \sum_{f \in \mathcal{F}} w^{[l]}(f)f$.

Theorem 7. *Let* K *be a compact subset of* $(1, +\infty) \times (0, +\infty)$. *There exists a constant* $C_5 > 0$ *depending only on* K *and* d *such that for any integer* $n \geq 1$, *any* $(\kappa, \beta) \in K$, *such that* $\beta < d(\kappa - 1)$, *and any* $\pi \in \mathcal{P}'_{\kappa,\beta}$, *we have,*

$$\mathbb{E}_\pi\left[R(\tilde{F}_n^{adp}) - R^*\right] \leq C_5 n^{-\frac{\beta\kappa}{(\kappa-1)(2\beta+d)}}.$$

Adaptive classifiers are obtained in Theorem (5) and (7) by aggregation of only $\log n$ classifiers. Other construction of adaptive classifiers can be found in [17]. In particular, adaptive SVM classifiers.

4   Proofs

Proof of Proposition 1. Using the convexity of the hinge loss, we have $A_n(\tilde{f}_n) \leq \sum_{j=1}^M w_j A_n(f_j)$. Denote by $\hat{i} = \arg\min_{i=1,\ldots,M} A_n(f_i)$, we have $A_n(f_i) = A_n(f_{\hat{i}}) + \frac{1}{n}(\log(w_{\hat{i}}) - \log(w_i))$ for all $i = 1, \ldots, M$ and by averaging over the w_i we get :

$$A_n(\tilde{f}_n) \leq \min_{i=1,\ldots,M} A_n(f_i) + \frac{\log(M)}{n}, \tag{12}$$

where we used that $\sum_{j=1}^{M} w_j \log\left(\frac{w_j}{1/M}\right) = K(w|u) \geq 0$ where $K(w|u)$ denotes the Kullback-Leiber divergence between the weights $w = (w_j)_{j=1,\ldots,M}$ and uniform weights $u = (1/M)_{j=1,\ldots,M}$.

Proof of Theorem 2. Let $a > 0$. Using Proposition 1, we have for any $f \in \mathcal{F}$ and for the Bayes rule f^*:

$$A(\tilde{f}_n) - A^* = (1+a)(A_n(\tilde{f}_n) - A_n(f^*)) + A(\tilde{f}_n) - A^* - (1+a)(A_n(\tilde{f}_n) - A_n(f^*))$$

$$\leq (1+a)(A_n(f) - A_n(f^*)) + (1+a)\frac{\log M}{n} + A(\tilde{f}_n) - A^* - (1+a)(A_n(\tilde{f}_n) - A_n(f^*)).$$

Taking the expectations, we get

$$\mathbb{E}\left[A(\tilde{f}_n) - A^*\right] \leq (1+a)\min_{f \in \mathcal{F}}(A(f) - A^*) + (1+a)(\log M)/n$$

$$+ \mathbb{E}\left[A(\tilde{f}_n) - A^* - (1+a)(A_n(\tilde{f}_n) - A_n(f^*))\right].$$

The following inequality follows from the linearity of the hinge loss on $[-1, 1]$:

$$A(\tilde{f}_n) - A^* - (1+a)(A_n(\tilde{f}_n) - A_n(f^*)) \leq \max_{f \in \mathcal{F}}\left[A(f) - A^* - (1+a)(A_n(f) - A_n(f^*))\right].$$

Thus, using Bernstein's inequality, we have for all $0 < \delta < 4 + 2a$:

$$\mathbb{P}\left[A(\tilde{f}_n) - A^* - (1+a)(A_n(\tilde{f}_n) - A_n(f^*)) \geq \delta\right]$$

$$\leq \sum_{f \in \mathcal{F}} \mathbb{P}\left[A(f) - A^* - (A_n(f) - A_n(f^*)) \geq \frac{\delta + a(A(f) - A^*)}{1+a}\right]$$

$$\leq \sum_{f \in \mathcal{F}} \exp\left(-\frac{n(\delta + a(A(f) - A^*))^2}{2(1+a)^2(A(f) - A^*)^{1/\kappa} + 2/3(1+a)(\delta + a(A(f) - A^*))}\right).$$

There exists a constant $c_1 > 0$ depending only on a such that for all $0 < \delta < 4+2a$ and all $f \in \mathcal{F}$, we have

$$\frac{(\delta + a(A(f) - A^*))^2}{2(1+a)^2(A(f) - A^*)^{1/\kappa} + 2/3(1+a)(\delta + a(A(f) - A^*))} \geq c_1 \delta^{2-1/\kappa}.$$

Thus, $\mathbb{P}\left[A(\tilde{f}_n) - A^* - (1+a)(A_n(\tilde{f}_n) - A_n(f^*)) \geq \delta\right] \leq M \exp(-nc_1 \delta^{2-1/\kappa})$.

Observe that an integration by parts leads to $\int_a^{+\infty} \exp\left(-bt^\alpha\right) dt \leq \frac{\exp(-ba^\alpha)}{\alpha b a^{\alpha-1}}$, for any $\alpha \geq 1$ and $a, b > 0$, so for all $u > 0$, we get

$$\mathbb{E}\left[A(\tilde{f}_n) - A^* - (1+a)(A_n(\tilde{f}_n) - A_n(f^*))\right] \leq 2u + M\frac{\exp(-nc_1 u^{2-1/\kappa})}{nc_1 u^{1-1/\kappa}}.$$

If we denote by $\mu(M)$ the unique solution of $X = M \exp(-X)$, we have $\log M/2 \leq \mu(M) \leq \log M$. For u such that $nc_1 u^{2-1/\kappa} = \mu(M)$, we obtain the result.

Proof of Corollary 1. We deduce Corollary 1 from Theorem 2, using that for any prediction rule f we have $A(f) - A^* = 2(R(f) - R^*)$ and applying Zhang's inequality $A(g) - A^* \geq (R(g) - R^*)$ fulfilled by all g from $\mathcal{X}$ to $\mathbb{R}$.

Proof of Theorem 3. For all prediction rules $f_1, \ldots, f_M$, we have

$$\sup_{f_1,\ldots,f_M} \inf_{\hat{f}_n} \sup_{\pi \in \mathcal{P}_\kappa} \left(\mathbb{E}\left[R(\hat{f}_n) - R^* \right] - 2(1+a) \min_{j=1,\ldots,M} (R(f_j) - R^*) \right)$$

$$\geq \inf_{\hat{f}_n} \sup_{\pi \in \mathcal{P}_\kappa : f^* \in \{f_1,\ldots,f_M\}} \left(\mathbb{E}\left[R(\hat{f}_n) - R^* \right] \right).$$

Thus, we look for a set of cardinality not greater than M, of the worst probability measures $\pi \in \mathcal{P}_\kappa$ from our classification problem point of view and choose $f_1, \ldots, f_M$ as the corresponding Bayes rules.

Let N be an integer such that $2^{N-1} \leq M$. Let $x_1, \ldots, x_N$ be N distinct points of $\mathcal{X}$. Let $0 < w < 1/N$. Denote by P^X the probability measure on $\mathcal{X}$ such that $P^X(\{x_j\}) = w$ for $j = 1, \ldots, N-1$ and $P^X(\{x_N\}) = 1 - (N-1)w$. We consider the set of binary sequences $\Omega = \{-1, 1\}^{N-1}$. Let $0 < h < 1$. For all $\sigma \in \Omega$ we consider

$$\eta_\sigma(x) = \begin{cases} (1 + \sigma_j h)/2 & \text{if } x = x_1, \ldots, x_{N-1}, \\ 1 & \text{if } x = x_N. \end{cases}$$

For all $\sigma \in \Omega$ we denote by π_σ the probability measure on $\mathcal{X} \times \{-1, 1\}$ with the marginal P^X on $\mathcal{X}$ and with the conditional probability function η_σ of $Y = 1$ knowing X.

Assume that $\kappa > 1$. We have $\mathbb{P}\left(|2\eta_\sigma(X) - 1| \leq t\right) = (N-1)w\mathbb{1}_{\{h \leq t\}}, \forall 0 \leq t < 1$. Thus, if we assume that $(N-1)w \leq h^{1/(\kappa-1)}$ then $\mathbb{P}\left(|2\eta_\sigma(X) - 1| \leq t\right) \leq t^{1/(\kappa-1)}$, for all $t \geq 0$, and according to [25], π_σ belongs to MA(κ).

We denote by ρ the Hamming distance on Ω (cf. [26] p.88). Let σ, σ' be such that $\rho(\sigma, \sigma') = 1$. We have

$$H^2\left(\pi_\sigma^{\otimes n}, \pi_{\sigma'}^{\otimes n}\right) = 2\left(1 - (1 - w(1 - \sqrt{1 - h^2}))^n\right).$$

We take w and h such that $w(1 - \sqrt{1 - h^2}) \leq 1/n$, thus, $H^2\left(\pi_\sigma^{\otimes n}, \pi_{\sigma'}^{\otimes n}\right) \leq \beta = 2(1 - e^{-1}) < 2$ for any integer n.

Let $\hat{f}_n$ be a classifier and $\sigma \in \Omega$. Using MA(κ), we have

$$\mathbb{E}_{\pi_\sigma}\left[R(\hat{f}_n) - R^* \right] \geq (c_0 w)^\kappa \mathbb{E}_{\pi_\sigma}\left[\left(\sum_{i=1}^{N-1} |\hat{f}_n(x_i) - \sigma_i| \right)^\kappa \right].$$

By Jensen's Lemma and Assouad's Lemma (cf. [26]) we obtain:

$$\inf_{\hat{f}_n} \sup_{\pi \in \mathcal{P}_\kappa : f^* \in \{f_\sigma : \sigma \in \Omega\}} \left(\mathbb{E}_{\pi_\sigma}\left[R(\hat{f}_n) - R^* \right] \right) \geq (c_0 w)^\kappa \left(\frac{N-1}{4}(1 - \beta/2)^2 \right)^\kappa.$$

We obtain the result by taking $w = (nh^2)^{-1}$, $N = \lceil \log M / \log 2 \rceil$ and $h = \left(n^{-1}\lceil \log M / \log 2 \rceil \right)^{(\kappa-1)/(2\kappa-1)}$.

For $\kappa = 1$, we take $h = 1/2$, thus $|2\eta_\sigma(X) - 1| \geq 1/2$ a.s. so $\pi_\sigma \in \mathrm{MA}(1)$ (cf.[25]). Putting $w = 4/n$ and $N = \lceil \log M / \log 2 \rceil$ we obtain the result.

Proof of Theorem 4. According to Theorem 1, where we set $a = 1$, we have, for any $\epsilon > 0$:

$$\mathbb{E}_\pi \left[R(\tilde{f}_n^\epsilon) - R^* \right] \leq 4 \min_{\bar{\eta} \in \Sigma_\epsilon(\beta)} (R(f_{\bar{\eta}}) - R^*) + C \left(\frac{\log \mathrm{Card} \Sigma_\epsilon(\beta)}{n} \right)^{\frac{\kappa}{2\kappa - 1}}.$$

Let $\bar{\eta}$ be a function with values in $[0,1]$ and denote by $\bar{f} = \mathbb{1}_{\bar{\eta} \geq 1/2}$ the plug-in classifier associated. We have $|2\eta - 1| \mathbb{1}_{\bar{f} \neq f^*} \leq 2|\bar{\eta} - \eta|$, thus:

$$R(\bar{f}) - R^* = \mathbb{E} \left[|2\eta(X) - 1| \mathbb{1}_{\bar{f} \neq f^*} \right] = \mathbb{E} \left[|2\eta(X) - 1| \mathbb{1}_{\bar{f} \neq f^*} \mathbb{1}_{\bar{f} \neq f^*} \right]$$

$$\leq \left| \left| |2\eta - 1| \mathbb{1}_{\bar{f} \neq f^*} \right| \right|_{L^\infty(P^X)} \mathbb{E} \left[\mathbb{1}_{\bar{f} \neq f^*} \right] \leq \left| \left| |2\eta - 1| \mathbb{1}_{\bar{f} \neq f^*} \right| \right|_{L^\infty(P^X)} c_0 \left(R(\bar{f}) - R^* \right)^{\frac{1}{\kappa}},$$

and assumption (A1) lead to

$$R(f_{\bar{\eta}}) - R^* \leq (2c_0 \mu_{max})^{\frac{\kappa}{\kappa - 1}} ||\bar{\eta} - \eta||_{L^\infty([0,1]^d)}^{\frac{\kappa}{\kappa - 1}}.$$

Hence, for any $\epsilon > 0$, we have

$$\mathbb{E}_\pi \left[R(\tilde{f}_n^\epsilon) - R^* \right] \leq D \left(\epsilon^{\frac{\kappa}{\kappa - 1}} + \left(\frac{\epsilon^{-d/\beta}}{n} \right)^{\frac{\kappa}{2\kappa - 1}} \right),$$

where $D = \max \left(4(2c_0 \mu_{max})^{\kappa/(\kappa - 1)}, CA(\beta, d)^{\frac{\kappa}{2\kappa - 1}} \right)$. For the value

$$\epsilon_n = a_1 n^{-\frac{\beta(\kappa - 1)}{\beta(2\kappa - 1) + d(\kappa - 1)}},$$

we have

$$\mathbb{E}_\pi \left[R(\tilde{f}_n^{\epsilon_n}) - R^* \right] \leq C_1 n^{-\frac{\beta \kappa}{\beta(2\kappa - 1) + d(\kappa - 1)}},$$

where $C_1 = 2D(a_1)^{\frac{\kappa}{\kappa - 1}} \vee (a_1)^{-\frac{d\kappa}{\beta(\kappa - 1)}}$

Proof of Theorem 5. We consider the following function on $(1, +\infty) \times (0, +\infty)$ with values in $(0, 1/2)$:

$$\phi(\kappa, \beta) = \frac{\beta(\kappa - 1)}{\beta(2\kappa - 1) + d(\kappa - 1)}.$$

For any n greater than $n_1 = n_1(K)$, we have $\Delta^{-1} \leq \phi(\kappa, \beta) \leq \lfloor \Delta/2 \rfloor \Delta^{-1}$ for all $(\kappa, \beta) \in K$.

Let $(\kappa_0, \beta_0) \in K$. For any $n \geq n_1$, there exists $k_0 \in \{1, \ldots, \lfloor \Delta/2 \rfloor - 1\}$ such that

$$\phi_{k_0} = k_0 \Delta^{-1} \leq \phi(\kappa_0, \beta_0) < (k_0 + 1)\Delta^{-1}.$$

We denote by $f_{\kappa_0}(\cdot)$ the increasing function $\phi(\kappa_0, \cdot)$ from $(0, +\infty)$ to $(0, 1/2)$. We set

$$\beta_{0,n} = (f_{\kappa_0})^{-1} (\phi_{k_0}).$$

There exists $m = m(K)$ such that $m|\beta_0 - \beta_{0,n}| \leq |f_{\kappa_0}(\beta_0) - f_{\kappa_0}(\beta_{0,n})| \leq \Delta^{-1}$.

Let $\pi \in \mathcal{P}_{\kappa_0,\beta_0}$. According to the oracle inequality of Corollary 1, we have, conditionally to the first subsample D_m^1:

$$\mathbb{E}_\pi \left[R(\tilde{f}_n^{adp}) - R^* | D_m^1 \right] \leq 4 \min_{\phi \in \mathcal{G}(n)} \left(R(\tilde{f}_m^{\epsilon(\phi)}) - R^* \right) + C \left(\frac{\log \mathrm{Card}(\mathcal{G}(n))}{l} \right)^{\frac{\kappa_0}{2\kappa_0-1}}.$$

Using the definition of l and the fact that $\mathrm{Card}(\mathcal{G}(n)) \leq \log n$ we get that there exists $\tilde{C} > 0$ independent of n such that

$$\mathbb{E}_\pi \left[R(\tilde{f}_n^{adp}) - R^* \right] \leq \tilde{C} \left(\mathbb{E}_\pi \left[R(\tilde{f}_{\epsilon m}^{(\phi_{k_0})}) - R^* \right] + \left(\frac{\log^2 n}{n} \right)^{\frac{\kappa_0}{2\kappa_0-1}} \right)$$

Moreover $\beta_{0,n} \leq \beta_0$, hence, $\mathcal{P}_{\kappa_0,\beta_0} \subseteq \mathcal{P}_{\kappa_0,\beta_{0,n}}$. Thus, according to Theorem 4, we have

$$\mathbb{E}_\pi \left[R(\tilde{f}_{\epsilon m}^{(\phi_{k_0})}) - R^* \right] \leq C_1(K,d) m^{-\psi(\kappa_0,\beta_{0,n})},$$

where $C_1(K,d) = \max \left(C_1(\kappa,\beta,d) : (\kappa,\beta) \in K \right)$ and $\psi(\kappa,\beta) = \frac{\beta\kappa}{\beta(2\kappa-1)+d(\kappa-1)}$. By construction, there exists $A_2 = A_2(K,d) > 0$ such that $|\psi(\kappa_0,\beta_{0,n}) - \psi(\kappa_0,\beta_0)| \leq A_2\Delta^{-1}$. Moreover for any integer n we have $n^{A_2/\log n} = \exp(A_2)$, which is a constant. We conclude that

$$\mathbb{E}_\pi \left[R(\tilde{f}_n^{adp}) - R^* \right] \leq C_2(K,d) \left(n^{-\psi(\kappa_0,\beta_0)} + \left(\frac{\log^2 n}{n} \right)^{\frac{\kappa_0}{2\kappa_0-1}} \right),$$

where $C_2(K,d) > 0$ is independent of n. We achieve the proof by observing that $\psi(\kappa_0,\beta_0) < \frac{\kappa_0}{2\kappa_0-1}$.

Proof of Theorem 7. We consider the following function on $(1,+\infty) \times (0,+\infty)$ with values in $(0,1/2)$:

$$\Theta(\kappa,\beta) = \frac{\beta\kappa}{(\kappa-1)(2\beta+d)}.$$

For any n greater than $n_1 = n_1(K)$, we have $\Delta^{-1} \leq \Theta(\kappa,\beta) \leq \lfloor\Delta/2\rfloor\,\Delta^{-1}$, for all $(\kappa,\beta) \in K$.

Let $(\kappa_0,\beta_0) \in K$ be such that $\beta_0 < (\kappa_0 - 1)d$. For any $n \geq n_1$, there exists $k_0 \in \{1,\ldots,\lfloor\Delta/2\rfloor - 1\}$ such that $k_0\Delta^{-1} \leq \Theta(\kappa_0,\beta_0) < (k_0+1)\Delta^{-1}$.

Let $\pi \in \mathcal{P}_{\kappa_0,\beta_0}$. According to the oracle inequality of Corollary 1, we have, conditionally to the first subsample D_m^1:

$$\mathbb{E}_\pi \left[R(\tilde{F}_n^{adp}) - R^* | D_m^1 \right] \leq 4 \min_{f \in \mathcal{F}} (R(f) - R^*) + C \left(\frac{\log \mathrm{Card}(\mathcal{F})}{l} \right)^{\frac{\kappa_0}{2\kappa_0-1}}.$$

Using the proof of Theorem 5 we get that there exists $\tilde{C} > 0$ independent of n such that

$$\mathbb{E}_\pi \left[R(\tilde{f}_n^{adp}) - R^* \right] \leq \tilde{C} \left(\mathbb{E}_\pi \left[R(\hat{f}_m^{(\beta_{k_0})}) - R^* \right] + \left(\frac{\log^2 n}{n} \right)^{\frac{\kappa_0}{2\kappa_0-1}} \right)$$

Moreover $\beta_{k_0} \leq \beta_0$, hence, $\mathcal{P}_{\kappa_0,\beta_0} \subseteq \mathcal{P}_{\kappa_0,\beta_{k_0}}$. Thus, according to Theorem 6, we have

$$\mathbb{E}_\pi \left[R(\hat{f}_m^{(\beta_{k_0})}) - R^* \right] \leq C_4(K,d) m^{-\Theta(\kappa_0,\beta_{k_0})},$$

where $C_4(K,d) = \max\left(C_4(\kappa,\beta,d) : (\kappa,\beta) \in K\right)$. We have $|\Theta(\kappa_0,\beta_{k_0}) - \Theta(\kappa_0,\beta_0)|$ $\leq \Delta^{-1}$ by construction. Moreover $n^{1/\log n} = e$ for any integer n. We conclude that

$$\mathbb{E}_\pi \left[R(\tilde{F}_n^{adp}) - R^* \right] \leq \tilde{C}_4(K,d) \left(n^{-\Theta(\kappa_0,\beta_0)} + \left(\frac{\log^2 n}{n} \right)^{\frac{\kappa_0}{2\kappa_0-1}} \right),$$

where $\tilde{C}_4(K,d) > 0$ is independent of n. We achieve the proof by observing that $\Theta(\kappa_0,\beta_0) < \frac{\kappa_0}{2\kappa_0-1}$, if $\beta_0 < (\kappa_0 - 1)d$.

References

1. Audibert, J.-Y. and Tsybakov, A.B.: Fast learning rates for plug-in classifiers under margin condition. (2005). Available at http://www.proba.jussieu.fr/mathdoc/preprints/index.html#2005 (Preprint PMA-998)
2. Barron, A. and Leung, G.: Information theory and mixing least-square regressions. (2004). Manuscript.
3. Barron, A. and Li, J.: Mixture density estimation, Biometrics, (1997), **53**, 603–618.
4. Bartlett, P., Freund, Y., Lee, W.S. and Schapire, R.E.: Boosting the margin: a new explanantion for the effectiveness of voting methods, (1998), Annals of Statistics, **26**, 1651–1686.
5. Bartlett, P. and Jordan, M. and McAuliffe, J.: Convexity, Classification and Risk Bounds, Technical Report 638, Department of Statistics, U.C. Berkeley, (2003). Available at http://stat-www.berkeley.edu/tech-reports/638.pdf.
6. Blanchard, G., Bousquet, O. and Massart, P.: Statistical Performance of Support Vector Machines, (2004), Available at http//mahery.math.u-psud.fr/~blanchard/publi/.
7. Boucheron, S., Bousquet, O. and Lugosi, G.: Theory of classification: A survey of some recent advances, (2005), ESAIM: Probability and statistics, 9:325-375.
8. Blanchard, G., Lugosi, G. and Vayatis, N.: On the rate of convergence of regularized boosting classifiers, JMLR, (2003), **4**, 861–894.
9. Bühlmann, P. and Yu, B.: Analyzing bagging, Ann. Statist., (2002), **30**, 4, 927–961.
10. Cristianini, N. and Shawe-Taylor, J.: An introduction to Support Vector Machines, Cambridge University Press, (2002).
11. Cortes, C. and Vapnik, V.: Support-Vector Networks, Machine Learning, **20**, 3, 273-297, (1995).
12. Devroye, L., Györfi, L. and Lugosi, G.: A Probabilistic Theory of Pattern Recognition, (1996), Springer, New York, Berlin, Heidelberg.
13. Catoni, O.: Statistical Learning Theory and Stochastic Optimization, (2001), Springer, N.Y., Ecole d'été de Probabilités de Saint-Flour 2001, Lecture Notes in Mathematics.
14. V. Koltchinskii and D. Panchenko: Empirical margin distributions and bounding the generalization error of combined classifiers, (2002), Ann. Statist., **30**, 1–50.

15. Koltchinskii, V.: Local Rademacher Complexities and Oracle Inequalities in Risk Minimization. To appear in Ann. Statist., (2005).
16. Lugosi, G. and Vayatis, N.: On the Bayes-risk consistency of regularized boosting methods, Ann. Statist., (2004), **32**, 1, 30–55.
17. Lecué, G.: Simultaneous adaptation to the margin and to complexity in classification, (2005), Available at http://hal.ccsd.cnrs.fr/ccsd-00009241/en/.
18. Lecué, G.: Optimal rates of aggregation in classification, (2006). Available at https://hal.ccsd.cnrs.fr/ccsd-00021233.
19. Massart, P.: Some applications of concentration inequalities to Statistics, (2000), Probability Theory. Annales de la Faculté des Sciences de Toulouse, **2**, 245–303, volume spécial dédié à Michel Talagrand.
20. Massart, P.: Concentration inequalities and Model Selection, (2004),Lectures notes of Saint Flour.
21. Schölkopf, B. and Smola, A.: Learning with kernels, MIT press, Cambridge University, (2002).
22. Steinwart, I. and Scovel, C.: Fast Rates for Support Vector Machines using Gaussian Kernels, (2004), Los Alamos National Laboratory Technical Report LA-UR 04-8796, submitted to Annals of Statistics.
23. Steinwart, I. and Scovel, C.: Fast Rates for Support Vector Machines, (2005), COLT 2005.
24. Tsybakov, A.B.: Optimal rates of aggregation, (2003), Computational Learning Theory and Kernel Machines. B.Schölkopf and M.Warmuth, eds. Lecture Notes in Artificial Intelligence, 2777, 303–313, Springer, Heidelberg.
25. Tsybakov, A.B.: Optimal aggregation of classifiers in statistical learning, (2004), Ann. Statist., **32**, 1, 135–166.
26. Tsybakov, A.B.: Introduction à l'estimation non-paramétrique, Springer, (2004).
27. Vovk, V.G.: Aggregating strategies. In Proceedings of the Third Annual Workshop on Computational Learning Theory, pages 371–383, 1990.
28. Yang, Y.: Mixing strategies for density estimation, (2000), Ann. Statist., **28**, 1,75–87.
29. Zhang, T.: Statistical behavior and consistency of classification methods based on convex risk minimization, (2004), Ann. Statist., **32**, 1, 56–85.

Aggregation and Sparsity Via ℓ_1 Penalized Least Squares

Florentina Bunea[1], Alexandre B. Tsybakov[2], and Marten H. Wegkamp[1]

[1] Florida State University, Department of Statistics, Tallahassee FL 32306, USA
{bunea, wegkamp}@stat.fsu.edu*
[2] Université Paris VI, Laboratoire de Probabilités et Modèles Aléatoires,
4, Place Jussieu, B.P. 188, 75252 PARIS Cedex 05, France
and
Institute for Information Transmission Problems, Moscow, Russia
tsybakov@ccr.jussieu.fr

Abstract. This paper shows that near optimal rates of aggregation and adaptation to unknown sparsity can be simultaneously achieved via ℓ_1 penalized least squares in a nonparametric regression setting. The main tool is a novel oracle inequality on the sum between the empirical squared loss of the penalized least squares estimate and a term reflecting the sparsity of the unknown regression function.

1 Introduction

In this paper we study aggregation in regression models via penalized least squares with data dependent ℓ_1 penalties. Let $\{(X_1, Y_1), \ldots, (X_n, Y_n)\}$ be a sample of independent random pairs (X_i, Y_i) with

$$Y_i = f(X_i) + W_i, \quad i = 1, \ldots, n, \tag{1}$$

where $f : \mathcal{X} \to \mathbb{R}$ is an unknown regression function to be estimated, $\mathcal{X}$ is a Borel subset of $\mathbb{R}^d$, the X_i's are random elements in $\mathcal{X}$ with probability measure μ, and the regression errors W_i have mean zero conditionally given $X_1, \ldots, X_n$. Let $\mathcal{F}_M = \{f_1, \ldots, f_M\}$ be a collection of functions. The functions f_j can be viewed either as "weak learners" or as estimators of f constructed from a training sample. Here we consider the ideal situation in which they are fixed; we concentrate on learning only. Assumptions **(A1)** and **(A2)** on the regression model (1) are supposed to be satisfied throughout the paper.

Assumption (A1). *The random variables $W_1, \ldots, W_n$ are independent with $\mathbb{E}\{W_i \mid X_1, \ldots, X_n\} = 0$ and $\mathbb{E}\{\exp(|W_i|) \mid X_1, \ldots, X_n\} \leq b$, for some $b > 0$ and all $i = 1, \ldots, n$. The random variables $X_1, \ldots, X_n$ are independent, identically distributed with measure μ.*

* Research of F. Bunea and M. Wegkamp is supported in part by NSF grant DMS 0406049.

G. Lugosi and H.U. Simon (Eds.): COLT 2006, LNAI 4005, pp. 379–391, 2006.
© Springer-Verlag Berlin Heidelberg 2006

Assumption (A2). *The functions $f : \mathcal{X} \to \mathbb{R}$ and $f_j : \mathcal{X} \to \mathbb{R}$, $j = 1, \ldots, M$, with $M \geq 2$, belong to the class $\mathcal{F}_0$ of uniformly bounded functions defined by*

$$\mathcal{F}_0 \overset{\text{def}}{=} \left\{ g : \mathcal{X} \to \mathbb{R} \mid \|g\|_\infty \leq L \right\}$$

where $L < \infty$ is a constant that is not necessarily known to the statistician and $\|g\|_\infty = \sup_{x \in \mathcal{X}} |g(x)|$.

Some references to aggregation of arbitrary estimators in regression models are [13], [10], [17], [18], [9], [2], [15], [16] and [7]. This paper extends the results of the paper [4], which considers regression with fixed design and Gaussian errors W_i.

We introduce first our aggregation scheme. For any $\lambda = (\lambda_1, \ldots, \lambda_M) \in \mathbb{R}^M$, define $f_\lambda(x) = \sum_{j=1}^M \lambda_j f_j(x)$ and let

$$M(\lambda) = \sum_{j=1}^M I_{\{\lambda_j \neq 0\}} = \text{Card } J(\lambda)$$

denote the number of non-zero coordinates of λ, where $I_{\{.\}}$ denotes the indicator function, and $J(\lambda) = \{j \in \{1, \ldots, M\} : \lambda_j \neq 0\}$. The value $M(\lambda)$ characterizes the *sparsity* of the vector λ: the smaller $M(\lambda)$, the "sparser" λ. Furthermore we introduce the residual sum of squares

$$\widehat{S}(\lambda) = \frac{1}{n} \sum_{i=1}^n \{Y_i - f_\lambda(X_i)\}^2,$$

for all $\lambda \in \mathbb{R}^M$. We aggregate the f_j's via penalized least squares. Given a penalty term $\text{pen}(\lambda)$, the penalized least squares estimator $\widehat{\lambda} = (\widehat{\lambda}_1, \ldots, \widehat{\lambda}_M)$ is defined by

$$\widehat{\lambda} = \arg \min_{\lambda \in \mathbb{R}^M} \left\{ \widehat{S}(\lambda) + \text{pen}(\lambda) \right\}, \tag{2}$$

which renders the aggregated estimator

$$\widetilde{f}(x) = f_{\widehat{\lambda}}(x) = \sum_{j=1}^M \widehat{\lambda}_j f_j(x). \tag{3}$$

Since the vector $\widehat{\lambda}$ can take any values in $\mathbb{R}^M$, the aggregate $\widetilde{f}$ is not a model selector in the traditional sense, nor is it necessarily a convex combination of the functions f_j. We consider the penalty

$$\text{pen}(\lambda) = 2 \sum_{j=1}^M r_{n,j} |\lambda_j| \tag{4}$$

with data-dependent weights $r_{n,j} = r_n(M) \|f_j\|_n$, and one can choose $r_n(M)$ of the form

$$r_n(M) = A \sqrt{\frac{\log(Mn)}{n}} \tag{5}$$

where $A > 0$ is a suitably large constant. We write $\|g\|_n^2 = \frac{1}{n}\sum_{i=1}^n g^2(X_i)$ for any $g : \mathcal{X} \to \mathbb{R}$. Note that our procedure is closely related to Lasso-type methods, see e.g. [14]. These methods can be reduced to (2) if $\text{pen}(\lambda) = \sum_{j=1}^M r|\lambda_j|$ with a tuning constant $r > 0$ that is independent of j and of the data. Note that our main results are stated for any positive $r_n(M) > 0$.

The goal of this paper is to show that the aggregate $\tilde{f}$ satisfies the following two properties.

P1. Optimality of aggregation. The loss $\|\tilde{f} - f\|_n^2$ is simultaneously smaller, with probability close to 1, than the model selection, convex and linear oracle bounds of the form $C_0 \inf_{\lambda \in H^M} \|f_\lambda - f\|_n^2 + \Delta_{n,M}$, where $C_0 \geq 1$ and $\Delta_{n,M} \geq 0$ is a remainder term independent of f. The set H^M is either the whole $\mathbb{R}^M$ (for linear aggregation), or the simplex Λ^M in $\mathbb{R}^M$ (for convex aggregation), or the set of vertices of Λ^M, except the vertex $(0,\dots,0) \in \mathbb{R}^M$ (for model selection aggregation). Optimal (minimax) values of $\Delta_{n,M}$, called optimal rates of aggregation, are given in [15], and they have the form

$$
\psi_{n,M} \asymp
\begin{cases}
M/n & \text{for (L) aggregation,} \\[2mm]
M/n & \text{for (C) aggregation, if } M \leq \sqrt{n}, \\[2mm]
\sqrt{\{\log(1 + M/\sqrt{n})\}/n} & \text{for (C) aggregation, if } M > \sqrt{n}, \\[2mm]
(\log M)/n & \text{for (MS) aggregation.}
\end{cases}
\tag{6}
$$

Corollary 2 in Section 3 below shows that these optimal rates are attained by our procedure within a $\log(M \vee n)$ factor.

P2. Taking advantage of the sparsity. If $\lambda^* \in \mathbb{R}^M$ is such that $f = f_{\lambda^*}$ (classical linear regression) or f can be sufficiently well approximated by f_{λ^*} then, with probability close to 1, the ℓ_1 norm of $\hat{\lambda} - \lambda^*$ is bounded, up to known constants and logarithms, by $M(\lambda^*)/\sqrt{n}$. This means that the estimator $\hat{\lambda}$ of the parameter λ^* adapts to the sparsity of the problem: its rate of convergence is faster when the "oracle" vector λ^* is sparser. Note, in contrast, that for the ordinary least squares estimator the corresponding rate is $M/\sqrt{n}$, with the overall dimension M, regardless on the sparsity of λ^*.

To show **P1** and **P2** we first establish a new type of oracle inequality in Section 2. Instead of deriving oracle bounds for the deviation of $\tilde{f}$ from f, which is usually the main object of interest in the literature, we obtain a stronger result. Namely, we prove a simultaneous oracle inequality for the sum of two deviations: that of $\tilde{f}$ from f and that of $\hat{\lambda}$ from the "oracle" value of λ. Similar developments in a different context are given by [5] and [12]. The two properties **P1** and **P2** can be then shown as consequences of this result.

2   Main Oracle Inequality

In this section we state our main oracle bounds. We define the matrices $\Psi_{n,M} = \left(\frac{1}{n}\sum_{i=1}^{n}f_j(X_i)f_{j'}(X_i)\right)_{1\leq j,j'\leq M}$ and the diagonal matrices $\operatorname{diag}(\Psi_{n,M}) = \operatorname{diag}(\|f_1\|_n^2,\dots,\|f_M\|_n^2)$. We consider the following assumption on the class $\mathcal{F}_M$.

Assumption (A3). *For any $n \geq 1$, $M \geq 2$ there exist constants $\kappa_{n,M} > 0$ and $0 \leq \pi_{n,M} < 1$ such that*

$$\mathbb{P}\left\{\Psi_{n,M} - \kappa_{n,M}\operatorname{diag}(\Psi_{n,M}) \geq 0\right\} \geq 1 - \pi_{n,M},$$

where $B \geq 0$ for a square matrix B, means that B is positive semi-definite.

Assumption (A3) is trivially fulfilled with $\kappa_{n,M} \equiv 1$ if $\Psi_{n,M}$ is a diagonal matrix, with some eigenvalues possibly equal to zero. In particular, there exist degenerate matrices $\Psi_{n,M}$ satisfying Assumption (A3). Assumption (A4) below implies (A3) for appropriate choices of $\kappa_{n,M}$ and $\pi_{n,M}$, see the proof of Theorem 2.

Denote the inner product and the norm in $L_2(\mu)$ by $<\cdot,\cdot>$ and $\|\cdot\|$ respectively. Define $c_0 = \min\{\|f_j\| : j \in \{1,\dots,M\}$ and $\|f_j\| > 0\}$.

Theorem 1. *Assume (A1), (A2) and (A3). Let $\widetilde{f}$ be the penalized least squares aggregate defined by (3) with penalty (4), where $r_n(M) > 0$ is an arbitrary positive number. Then, for any $n \geq 1$, $M \geq 2$ and $a > 1$, the inequality*

$$\|\widetilde{f} - f\|_n^2 + \frac{a}{a-1}\sum_{j=1}^{M}r_{n,j}|\widehat{\lambda}_j - \lambda_j| \tag{7}$$

$$\leq \frac{a+1}{a-1}\|f_\lambda - f\|_n^2 + \frac{4a^2}{\kappa_{n,M}(a-1)}r_n^2(M)M(\lambda), \qquad \forall \lambda \in \mathbb{R}^M,$$

is satisfied with probability $\geq 1 - p_{n,M}$ where

$$p_{n,M} = \pi_{n,M} + 2M\exp\left(-\frac{nr_n(M)c_0}{8\sqrt{2}L}\right) + 2M\exp\left(-\frac{nr_n^2(M)}{32b}\right)$$

$$+ 2M\exp\left(-\frac{nc_0^2}{2L^2}\right).$$

Proof of Theorem 1 is given in Section 5. This theorem is general but not ready to use because the probabilities $\pi_{n,M}$ and the constants $\kappa_{n,M}$ in Assumption (A3) need to be evaluated. A natural way to do this is to deal with the expected matrices $\Psi_M = \mathbb{E}(\Psi_{n,M}) = (\langle f_j, f_{j'}\rangle)_{1\leq j,j'\leq M}$ and $\operatorname{diag}(\Psi_M) = \operatorname{diag}(\|f_1\|^2,\dots,\|f_M\|^2)$. Consider the following analogue of Assumption (A3) stated in terms of these matrices.

Assumption (A4). *There exists $\kappa_M > 0$ such that the matrix $\Psi_M - \kappa_M\operatorname{diag}(\Psi_M)$ is positive semi-definite for any given $M \geq 2$.*

For discussion of this assumption, see [4] and Remark 1 below.

Theorem 2. *Assume (A1), (A2) and (A4). Let $\widetilde{f}$ be the penalized least squares aggregate defined by (3) with penalty (4), where $r_n(M) > 0$ is an arbitrary positive number. Then, for any $n \geq 1$, $M \geq 2$ and $a > 1$, the inequality*

$$\|\widetilde{f} - f\|_n^2 + \frac{a}{a-1} \sum_{j=1}^{M} r_{n,j} |\widehat{\lambda}_j - \lambda_j| \tag{8}$$

$$\leq \frac{a+1}{a-1} \|f_\lambda - f\|_n^2 + \frac{16a^2}{\kappa_M(a-1)} r_n^2(M) M(\lambda), \qquad \forall \lambda \in \mathbb{R}^M,$$

is satisfied with probability $\geq 1 - p_{n,M}$ where

$$p_{n,M} = 2M \exp\left(-\frac{nr_n(M)c_0}{8\sqrt{2}L}\right) + 2M \exp\left(-\frac{nr_n^2(M)}{32b}\right)$$

$$+ M^2 \exp\left(-\frac{n}{16L^4M^2}\right) + 2M \exp\left(-\frac{nc_0^2}{2L^2}\right). \tag{9}$$

Remark 1. The simplest case of Theorem 2 corresponds to a positive definite matrix Ψ_M. Then Assumption (A4) is satisfied with $\kappa_M = \xi_{\min}(M)/L^2$, where $\xi_{\min}(M) > 0$ is the smallest eigenvalue of Ψ_M. Furthermore, $c_0 \geq \xi_{\min}(M)$. We can therefore replace κ_M and c_0 by $\xi_{\min}(M)/L^2$ and $\xi_{\min}(M)$, respectively, in the statement of Theorem 2.

Remark 2. Theorem 2 allows us to treat asymptotics for $n \to \infty$ and fixed, but possibly large M, and for both $n \to \infty$ and $M = M_n \to \infty$. The asymptotic considerations can suggest a choice of the tuning parameter $r_n(M)$. In fact, it is determined by two antagonistic requirements. The first one is to keep $r_n(M)$ as small as possible, in order to improve the bound (8). The second one is to take $r_n(M)$ large enough to obtain the convergence of the probability $p_{n,M}$ to 0. It is easy to see that, asymptotically, as $n \to \infty$, the choice that meets the two requirements is given by (5). Note, however, that $p_{n,M}$ in (9) contains the terms independent of $r_n(M)$, and a necessary condition for their convergence to 0 is

$$n/(M^2 \log M) \to \infty. \tag{10}$$

This condition means that Theorem 2 is only meaningful for moderately large dimensions M.

3   Optimal Aggregation Property

Here we state corollaries of the results of Section 2 which imply property **P1**.

Corollary 1. *Assume (A1), (A2) and (A4). Let $\widetilde{f}$ be the penalized least squares aggregate defined by (3) with penalty (4), where $r_n(M) > 0$ is an arbitrary positive number. Then, for any $n \geq 1$, $M \geq 2$ and $a > 1$, the inequality*

$$\|\widetilde{f} - f\|_n^2 \leq \inf_{\lambda \in \mathbb{R}^M} \left\{ \frac{a+1}{a-1} \|f_\lambda - f\|_n^2 + \frac{16a^2}{\kappa_M(a-1)} r_n^2(M) M(\lambda) \right\}. \tag{11}$$

is satisfied with probability $\geq 1 - p_{n,M}$ where $p_{n,M}$ is given by (9).

This corollary is similar to a result in [4], but there the predictors X_i are assumed to be non-random and the oracle inequality is obtained for the expected risk. Applying the argument identical to the proof of Corollary 3.2 in [4], we deduce from Corollary 1 the following result.

Corollary 2. *Let assumptions of Corollary 1 be satisfied and let $r_n(M)$ be as in (5). Then, for any $\varepsilon > 0$, there exists a constant $C > 0$ such that the inequalities*

$$\|\tilde{f} - f\|_n^2 \leq (1 + \varepsilon) \inf_{1 \leq j \leq M} \|f_j - f\|_n^2 + C(1 + \varepsilon + \frac{1}{\varepsilon}) \frac{\log(M \vee n)}{n} \tag{12}$$

$$\|\tilde{f} - f\|_n^2 \leq (1 + \varepsilon) \inf_{\lambda \in \mathbb{R}^M} \|f_\lambda - f\|_n^2 + C(1 + \varepsilon + \frac{1}{\varepsilon}) \frac{M \log(M \vee n)}{n} \tag{13}$$

$$\|\tilde{f} - f\|_n^2 \leq (1 + \varepsilon) \inf_{\lambda \in \Lambda^M} \|f_\lambda - f\|_n^2 + C(1 + \varepsilon + \frac{1}{\varepsilon}) \overline{\psi}_n^C(M) \tag{14}$$

are satisfied with probability $\geq 1 - p_{n,M}$, where $p_{n,M}$ is given by (9) and

$$\overline{\psi}_n^C(M) = \begin{cases} (M \log n)/n & \text{if } M \leq \sqrt{n}, \\ \sqrt{(\log M)/n} & \text{if } M > \sqrt{n}. \end{cases}$$

This result shows that the optimal (M), (C) and (L) bounds given in (6) are nearly attained, up to logarithmic factors, if we choose the tuning parameter $r_n(M)$ as in (5).

4   Taking Advantage of the Sparsity

In this section we show that our procedure automatically adapts to the unknown sparsity of $f(x)$. We consider the following assumption to formulate our notion of sparsity.

Assumption (A5). *There exist $\lambda^* = \lambda^*(f)$ and a constant $C_* < \infty$ such that*

$$\|f_{\lambda^*} - f\|_\infty^2 \leq C_* r_n^2(M) M(\lambda^*). \tag{15}$$

Assumption (A5) is obviously satisfied in the parametric framework $f \in \{f_\lambda, \lambda \in \mathbb{R}^M\}$. It is also valid in many nonparametric settings. For example, if the functions f_j form a basis, and f is a smooth function that can be well approximated by the linear span of $M(\lambda^*)$ basis functions (cf., e.g., [1], [11]). The vector λ^* satisfying (15) will be called oracle. In fact, Assumption (A5) can be viewed as a definition of the oracle.

We establish inequalities in terms of $M(\lambda^*)$ not only for the pseudo-distance $\|\tilde{f} - f\|_n^2$, but also for the ℓ_1 distance $\sum_{j=1}^M |\hat{\lambda}_j - \lambda_j^*|$, as a consequence of Theorem 2. In fact, with probability close to one (see Lemma 1 below), if $\|f_j\| \geq c_0 > 0$, $\forall j = 1, \dots, M$, we have

$$\sum_{j=1}^M r_{n,j} |\hat{\lambda}_j - \lambda_j| \geq \frac{r_n(M) c_0}{2} \sum_{j=1}^M |\hat{\lambda}_j - \lambda_j|. \tag{16}$$

Together with (15) and Theorem 2 this yields that, with probability close to one,

$$\sum_{j=1}^{M} |\widehat{\lambda}_j - \lambda_j^*| \leq C r_n(M) M(\lambda^*),$$ (17)

where $C > 0$ is a constant. If we choose $r_n(M)$ as in (5), this achieves the aim described in **P2**.

Corollary 3. *Assume (A1), (A2), (A4), (A5) and $\min_{1 \leq j \leq M} \|f_j\| \geq c_0 > 0$. Let $\widetilde{f}$ be the penalized least squares aggregate defined by (3) with penalty (4), where $r_n(M) > 0$ is an arbitrary positive number. Then, for any $n \geq 1$, $M \geq 2$ we have*

$$\mathbb{P}\left(\|\widetilde{f} - f\|_n^2 \leq C_1 r_n^2(M) M(\lambda^*) \right) \geq 1 - p_{n,M}^*,$$ (18)

$$\mathbb{P}\left(\sum_{j=1}^{M} |\widehat{\lambda}_j - \lambda_j^*| \leq C_2 r_n(M) M(\lambda^*) \right) \geq 1 - p_{n,M}^*,$$ (19)

where $C_1, C_2 > 0$ are constants depending only on κ_M and c_0, $p_{n,M}^* = p_{n,M} + M \exp\{-nc_0^2/(2L^2)\}$ and the $p_{n,M}$ are given in Theorem 2.

Remark 3. Part (18) of Corollary 3 can be compared to [11] that deals with the same regression model with random design and obtain inequalities similar to (18) for a more specific setting where the f_j's are the basis functions of a reproducing kernel Hilbert space, the matrix Ψ_M is close to the identity matrix and the random errors of the model are uniformly bounded. Part (19) (the sparsity property) of Corollary 3 can be compared to [6] which treats the regression model with non-random design points $X_1, \ldots, X_n$ and Gaussian errors W_i and gives a control of the ℓ_2 (not ℓ_1) deviation between $\widehat{\lambda}$ and λ^*.

Remark 4. Consider the particular case of linear parametric regression models where $f = f_{\lambda^*}$. Assume for simplicity that the matrix Ψ_M is non-degenerate. Then all the components of the ordinary least squares estimate λ^{OLS} converge to the corresponding components of λ^* in probability with the rate $1/\sqrt{n}$. Thus we have

$$\sum_{j=1}^{M} |\lambda_j^{OLS} - \lambda_j^*| = O_p(M/\sqrt{n}),$$ (20)

as $n \to \infty$. Assume that $M(\lambda^*) \ll M$. If we knew exactly the set of non-zero coordinates $J(\lambda^*)$ of the oracle λ^*, we would perform the ordinary least squares on that set to obtain (20) with the rate $O_p(M(\lambda^*)/\sqrt{n})$. However, neither $J(\lambda^*)$, nor $M(\lambda^*)$ are known. If $r_n(M)$ is chosen as in (5) our estimator $\widehat{\lambda}$ achieves the same rate, up to logarithms without prior knowledge of $J(\lambda^*)$.

5   Proofs of the Theorems

Proof of Theorem 1. By definition, $\widetilde{f} = f_{\widehat{\lambda}}$ satisfies

$$\widehat{S}(\widehat{\lambda}) + \sum_{j=1}^{M} 2r_{n,j}|\widehat{\lambda}_j| \leq \widehat{S}(\lambda) + \sum_{j=1}^{M} 2r_{n,j}|\lambda_j|$$

for all $\lambda \in \mathbb{R}^M$, which we may rewrite as

$$\|\widetilde{f} - f\|_n^2 + \sum_{j=1}^{M} 2r_{n,j}|\widehat{\lambda}_j| \leq \|f_\lambda - f\|_n^2 + \sum_{j=1}^{M} 2r_{n,j}|\lambda_j| + \frac{2}{n}\sum_{i=1}^{n} W_i(\widetilde{f} - f_\lambda)(X_i).$$

We define the random variables $V_j = \frac{1}{n}\sum_{i=1}^{n} f_j(X_i)W_i$, $1 \leq j \leq M$ and the event $E_1 = \bigcap_{j=1}^{M}\{2|V_j| \leq r_{n,j}\}$. If E_1 holds we have

$$\frac{2}{n}\sum_{i=1}^{n} W_i(\widetilde{f} - f_\lambda)(X_i) = 2\sum_{j=1}^{M} V_j(\widehat{\lambda}_j - \lambda_j) \leq \sum_{j=1}^{M} r_{n,j}|\widehat{\lambda}_j - \lambda_j|$$

and therefore, still on E_1,

$$\|\widetilde{f} - f\|_n^2 \leq \|f_\lambda - f\|_n^2 + \sum_{j=1}^{M} r_{n,j}|\widehat{\lambda}_j - \lambda_j| + \sum_{j=1}^{M} 2r_{n,j}|\lambda_j| - \sum_{j=1}^{M} 2r_{n,j}|\widehat{\lambda}_j|.$$

Adding the term $\sum_{j=1}^{M} r_{n,j}|\widehat{\lambda}_j - \lambda_j|$ to both sides of this inequality yields further, on E_1,

$$\|\widetilde{f} - f\|_n^2 + \sum_{j=1}^{M} r_{n,j}|\widehat{\lambda}_j - \lambda_j|$$

$$\leq \|f_\lambda - f\|_n^2 + 2\sum_{j=1}^{M} r_{n,j}|\widehat{\lambda}_j - \lambda_j| + \sum_{j=1}^{M} 2r_{n,j}|\lambda_j| - \sum_{j=1}^{M} 2r_{n,j}|\widehat{\lambda}_j|$$

$$= \|f_\lambda - f\|_n^2 + \left(\sum_{j=1}^{M} 2r_{n,j}|\widehat{\lambda}_j - \lambda_j| - \sum_{j\notin J(\lambda)} 2r_{n,j}|\widehat{\lambda}_j|\right)$$

$$+ \left(-\sum_{j\in J(\lambda)} 2r_{n,j}|\widehat{\lambda}_j| + \sum_{j\in J(\lambda)} 2r_{n,j}|\lambda_j|\right).$$

Recall that $J(\lambda)$ denotes the set of indices of the non-zero elements of λ, and $M(\lambda) = \text{Card } J(\lambda)$. Rewriting the right-hand side of the previous display, we find that, on E_1,

$$\|\widetilde{f} - f\|_n^2 + \sum_{j=1}^{M} r_{n,j}|\widehat{\lambda}_j - \lambda_j| \leq \|f_\lambda - f\|_n^2 + 4\sum_{j\in J(\lambda)} r_{n,j}|\widehat{\lambda}_j - \lambda_j| \qquad (21)$$

by the triangle inequality and the fact that $\lambda_j = 0$ for $j \notin J(\lambda)$. Define the random event $E_0 = \{\Psi_{n,M} - \kappa_{n,M}\,\text{diag}(\Psi_{n,M}) \geq 0\}$. On $E_0 \cap E_1$ we have

$$\sum_{j \in J(\lambda)} r_{n,j}^2 |\widehat{\lambda}_j - \lambda_j|^2 \leq r_n^2 \sum_{j=1}^{M} \|f_j\|_n^2 |\widehat{\lambda}_j - \lambda_j|^2 \tag{22}$$

$$= r_n^2 (\widehat{\lambda} - \lambda)' \mathrm{diag}(\Psi_{n,M})(\widehat{\lambda} - \lambda)$$

$$\leq r_n^2 \kappa^{-1} (\widehat{\lambda} - \lambda)' \Psi_{n,M}(\widehat{\lambda} - \lambda)$$

$$= r_n^2 \kappa^{-1} \|\widetilde{f} - f_\lambda\|_n^2.$$

Here and later we set for brevity $r_n = r_n(M)$, $\kappa = \kappa_{n,M}$. Combining (21) and (22) with the Cauchy-Schwarz and triangle inequalities, respectively, we find further that, on $E_0 \cap E_1$,

$$\|\widetilde{f} - f\|_n^2 + \sum_{j=1}^{M} r_{n,j} |\widehat{\lambda}_j - \lambda_j|$$

$$\leq \|f_\lambda - f\|_n^2 + 4 \sum_{j \in J(\lambda)} r_{n,j} |\widehat{\lambda}_j - \lambda_j|$$

$$\leq \|f_\lambda - f\|_n^2 + 4\sqrt{M(\lambda)} \sqrt{\sum_{j \in J(\lambda)} r_{n,j}^2 |\widehat{\lambda}_j - \lambda_j|^2}$$

$$\leq \|f_\lambda - f\|_n^2 + 4 r_n \sqrt{M(\lambda)/\kappa} \left(\|\widetilde{f} - f\|_n + \|f_\lambda - f\|_n \right).$$

The preceding inequality is of the simple form $v^2 + d \leq c^2 + vb + cb$ with $v = \|\widetilde{f} - f\|_n$, $b = 4 r_n \sqrt{M(\lambda)/\kappa}$, $c = \|f_\lambda - f\|_n$ and $d = \sum_{j=1}^{M} r_{n,j} |\widehat{\lambda}_j - \lambda_j|$. After applying the inequality $2xy \leq x^2/\alpha + \alpha y^2$ ($x, y \in \mathbb{R}$, $\alpha > 0$) twice, to $2bc$ and $2bv$, respectively, we easily find $v^2 + d \leq v^2/(2\alpha) + \alpha b^2 + (2\alpha + 1)/(2\alpha) c^2$, whence $v^2 + d\{a/(a-1)\} \leq a/(a-1)\{b^2(a/2) + c^2(a+1)/a\}$ for $a = 2\alpha > 1$. On the random event $E_0 \cap E_1$, we now get that

$$\|\widetilde{f} - f\|_n^2 + \frac{a}{a-1} \sum_{j=1}^{M} r_{n,j} |\widehat{\lambda}_j - \lambda_j| \leq \frac{a+1}{a-1} \|f_\lambda - f\|_n^2 + \frac{4a^2}{\kappa(a-1)} r_n^2 M(\lambda),$$

for all $a > 1$. Using Lemma 2 proved below and the fact that $\mathbb{P}\{E_0\} \geq 1 - \pi_{n,M}$ we get Theorem 1. ∎

Proof of Theorem 2. Let $\mathcal{F} = \mathrm{span}(f_1, \ldots, f_M)$ be the linear space spanned by $f_1, \ldots, f_M$. Define the events $E_{0,*} = \{\Psi_{n,M} - (\kappa_M/4)\,\mathrm{diag}(\Psi_{n,M}) \geq 0\}$ and

$$E_2 = \bigcap_{j=1}^{M} \{\|f_j\|_n^2 \leq 2\|f_j\|^2\}, \qquad E_3 = \left\{ \sup_{f \in \mathcal{F}\setminus\{0\}} \frac{\|f\|^2}{\|f\|_n^2} \leq 2 \right\}.$$

Clearly, on E_2 we have $\mathrm{diag}(\Psi_{n,M}) \leq 2\,\mathrm{diag}(\Psi_M)$ and on E_3 we have the matrix inequality $\Psi_{n,M} \geq \Psi_M/2$. Therefore, using Assumption (A4), we get that the complement $E_{0,*}^C$ of $E_{0,*}$ satisfies $E_{0,*}^C \cap E_2 \cap E_3 = \emptyset$, which yields

$$\mathbb{P}\{E_{0,*}^C\} \leq \mathbb{P}\{E_2^C\} + \mathbb{P}\{E_3^C\}.$$

Thus, Assumption (A3) holds with $\kappa_{n,M} \equiv \kappa_M/4$ any $\pi_{n,M} \geq \mathbb{P}\{E_2^C\} + \mathbb{P}\{E_3^C\}$. Taking the particular value of $\pi_{n,M}$ as a sum of the upper bounds on $\mathbb{P}\{E_2^C\}$ and $\mathbb{P}\{E_3^C\}$ from Lemma 1 and from Lemma 3 (where we set $q = M$, $g_i = f_i$) and applying Theorem 1 we get the result. $\blacksquare$

Proof of Corollary 3. Let λ^* be a vector satisfying Assumption (A5). As in the proof of Theorem 2, we obtain that, on $E_1 \cap E_2 \cap E_3$,

$$\|\tilde{f} - f\|_n^2 + \frac{a}{a-1}\sum_{j=1}^{M} r_{n,j}|\widehat{\lambda}_j - \lambda_j^*| \leq \left\{\frac{a+1}{a-1}\|f_{\lambda^*} - f\|_n^2 + \frac{32a^2}{\kappa(a-1)}r_n^2 M(\lambda^*)\right\}$$

for all $a > 1$. We now note that, in view of Assumption (A5),

$$\|f_{\lambda^*} - f\|_n^2 \leq \|f_{\lambda^*} - f\|_\infty^2 \leq C_* r_n^2 M(\lambda^*).$$

This yields (18). To obtain (19) we apply the bound (16), valid on the event E_4 defined in Lemma 1 below, and therefore we include into $p_{n,M}^*$ the term $M\exp\left(-nc_0^2/(2L^2)\right)$ to account for $\mathbb{P}\{E_4^C\}$. $\blacksquare$

6   Technical Lemmas

Lemma 1. *Let Assumptions (A1) and (A2) hold. Then for the events*

$$E_2 = \{\|f_j\|_n^2 \leq 2\|f_j\|^2, \; \forall \; 1 \leq j \leq M\}$$
$$E_4 = \{\|f_j\| \leq 2\|f_j\|_n, \; \forall \; 1 \leq j \leq M\}$$

we have

$$\max(\mathbb{P}\{E_2^C\}, \mathbb{P}\{E_4^C\}) \leq M\exp\left(-nc_0^2/(2L^2)\right). \tag{23}$$

Proof. Since $\|f_j\| = 0 \Longrightarrow \|f_j\|_n = 0$ μ – a.s., it suffices to consider only the cases with $\|f_j\| > 0$. Inequality (23) then easily follows from the union bound and Hoeffding's inequality. $\blacksquare$

Lemma 2. *Let Assumptions (A1) and (A2) hold. Then*

$$\mathbb{P}\{E_1^C\} \leq 2M\exp\left(-\frac{nr_n^2(M)}{32b}\right) + 2M\exp\left(-\frac{nr_n c_0}{8\sqrt{2}L}\right)$$
$$+ 2M\exp\left(-\frac{nc_0^2}{2L^2}\right). \tag{24}$$

Proof. We use the following version of Bernstein's inequality (see, e.g., [3]): *Let $Z_1, \ldots, Z_n$ be independent random variables such that*

$$\frac{1}{n}\sum_{i=1}^{n}\mathbb{E}|Z_i|^m \leq \frac{m!}{2}w^2 d^{m-2},$$

for some positive constants w and d and for all $m \geq 2$. Then, for any $\varepsilon > 0$ we have

$$\mathbb{P}\left\{ \sum_{i=1}^{n}(Z_i - \mathbb{E}Z_i) \geq n\varepsilon \right\} \leq \exp\left(-\frac{n\varepsilon^2}{2(w^2 + d\varepsilon)}\right). \tag{25}$$

Here we apply this inequality to the variables $Z_{i,j} = f_j(X_i)W_i$, for each $j \in \{1, \ldots, M\}$, conditional on $X_1, \ldots, X_n$. By assumptions (A1) and (A2), we find

$$\frac{1}{n}\sum_{i=1}^{n}\mathbb{E}\left\{|Z_{i,j}|^m \mid X_1, \ldots, X_n\right\} \leq L^{m-2}\frac{1}{n}\sum_{i=1}^{n}|f_j(X_i)|^2 \mathbb{E}\left\{|W_i|^m \mid X_1, \ldots, X_n\right\}$$

$$\leq bm!L^{m-2}\|f_j\|_n^2$$

$$= \frac{m!}{2}L^{m-2}\left(\|f_j\|_n^2 2b\right).$$

Since $\|f_j\| = 0 \implies V_j = 0$ μ − a.s., it suffices to consider only the cases with $\|f_j\| > 0$. Using (25) and the union bound we find that

$$\mathbb{P}\{E_1^C | X_1, \ldots, X_n\} \leq 2 \sum_{j: \|f_j\| \geq c_0} \exp\left(-\frac{nr_n^2\|f_j\|_n^2/4}{2\left(2b\|f_j\|_n^2 + Lr_n\|f_j\|_n/2\right)}\right)$$

$$\leq 2M\exp\left(-\frac{nr_n^2}{32b}\right) + 2\sum_{j: \|f_j\| \geq c_0}\exp\left(-\frac{nr_n\|f_j\|_n}{8L}\right),$$

where the last inequality holds since

$$\exp(-x/(2\alpha)) + \exp(-x/(2\beta)) \geq \exp(-x/(\alpha + \beta))$$

for $x, \alpha, \beta > 0$. Combining the preceding display and the bound on $\mathbb{P}\{E_4^C\}$ in Lemma 1, we obtain the result. ∎

Lemma 3. *Let $\mathcal{F} = span(g_1, \ldots, g_q)$ be the linear space spanned by some functions $g_1, \ldots, g_q$ such that $g_i \in \mathcal{F}_0$. Then*

$$\mathbb{P}\left\{ \sup_{f \in \mathcal{F}\setminus\{0\}} \frac{\|f\|^2}{\|f\|_n^2} > 2 \right\} \leq q^2 \exp\left(-\frac{n}{16L^4q^2}\right).$$

Proof. Let $\phi_1, \ldots, \phi_N$ be an orthonormal basis of $\mathcal{F}$ in $L_2(\mu)$ with $N \leq q$. For any symmetric $N \times N$ matrix A, we define

$$\bar{\rho}(A) = \sup \sum_{j=1}^{N}\sum_{j'=1}^{N}|\lambda_j||\lambda_{j'}||A_{j,j'}|,$$

where the supremum is taken over sequences $\{\lambda_j\}_{j=1}^{N}$ with $\sum_j \lambda_j^2 = 1$. Applying Lemma 5.2 in [1] where we take $\mu = \nu$ in that paper's notation, we find that

$$\mathbb{P}\left\{ \sup_{f \in \mathcal{F}\setminus\{0\}} \frac{\|f\|^2}{\|f\|_n^2} > 2 \right\} \leq q^2 \exp(-n/16C)$$

where $C = \max\left(\bar{\rho}^2(A), \bar{\rho}(A')\right)$, and A, A' are $N \times N$ matrices with entries $\sqrt{<\phi_j^2, \phi_{j'}^2>}$ and $\|\phi_j \phi_{j'}\|_\infty$, respectively. Clearly,

$$\bar{\rho}(A) \le L^2 \sup_{j,j'} \sum_{j=1}^{N} \sum_{j'=1}^{N} |\lambda_j||\lambda_{j'}| = L^2 \sup_j \left(\sum_{j=1}^{N} |\lambda_j|\right)^2 \le L^2 q$$

where we used the Cauchy-Schwarz inequality. Similarly, $\bar{\rho}(A') \le L^2 q$.   ■

References

1. Baraud, Y.: Model selection for regression on a random design. ESAIM Probability & Statistics. **7** (2002) 127–146.
2. Birgé, L.: Model selection for Gaussian regression with random design. Prépublication n. 783, Laboratoire de Probabilités et Modèles Aléatoires, Universités Paris 6 - Paris 7 (2002).
   http://www.proba.jussieu.fr/mathdoc/preprints/ index.html#2002.
3. Birgé, L., Massart, P.: Minimum contrast estimators on sieves: Exponential bounds and rates of convergence. Bernouilli **4** (1998) 329 – 375.
4. Bunea, F., Tsybakov, A., Wegkamp, M.H.: Aggregation for Gaussian regression. Preprint (2005). http://www.stat.fsu.edu/~wegkamp.
5. Bunea, F., Wegkamp, M.: Two stage model selection procedures in partially linear regression. The Canadian Journal of Statistics **22** (2004) 1–14.
6. Candes, E., Tao,T.: The Dantzig selector: statistical estimation when p is much larger than n. Preprint (2005).
7. Catoni, O.: *Statistical Learning Theory and Stochastic Optimization*. Ecole d'Eté de Probabilités de Saint-Flour 2001, Lecture Notes in Mathematics, Springer, N.Y. (2004).
8. Donoho, D.L., Johnstone, I.M.: Ideal spatial adaptation by wavelet shrinkage. Biometrika **81** (1994) 425–455.
9. Györfi, L., Kohler, M., Krzyżak, A., Walk, H.: *A Distribution-Free Theory of Nonparametric Regression*. Springer, N.Y.(2002).
10. Juditsky, A., Nemirovski, A.: Functional aggregation for nonparametric estimation. Annals of Statistics **28** (2000) 681–712.
11. Kerkyacharian, G., Picard, D.: Tresholding in learning theory. Prépublication n.1017, Laboratoire de Probabilités et Modèles Aléatoires, Universités Paris 6 - Paris 7. http://www.proba.jussieu.fr/mathdoc/preprints/index.html#2005.
12. Koltchinskii, V.: Model selection and aggregation in sparse classification problems. Oberwolfach Reports: Meeting on Statistical and Probabilistic Methods of Model Selection, October 2005 (to appear).
13. Nemirovski, A.: *Topics in Non-parametric Statistics*. Ecole d'Eté de Probabilités de Saint-Flour XXVIII - 1998, Lecture Notes in Mathematics, v. 1738, Springer, N.Y. (2000).
14. Tibshirani, R.: Regression shrinkage and selection via the Lasso. Journal of the Royal Statistical Society, Series B. **58** (1996) 267–288.
15. Tsybakov, A.B.: Optimal rates of aggregation. Proceedings of 16th Annual Conference on Learning Theory (COLT) and 7th Annual Workshop on Kernel Machines. Lecture Notes in Artificial Intelligence **2777** 303–313. Springer-Verlag, Heidelberg (2003).

16. Wegkamp, M.H.: Model selection in nonparametric regression. Annals of Statistics **31** (2003) 252–273.
17. Yang, Y.: Combining different procedures for adaptive regression. J.of Multivariate Analysis **74** (2000) 135–161.
18. Yang, Y.: Aggregating regression procedures for a better performance. Bernoulli **10** (2004) 25–47.

A Randomized Online Learning Algorithm for Better Variance Control

Jean-Yves Audibert

CERTIS - Ecole des Ponts
19, rue Alfred Nobel - Cité Descartes
77455 Marne-la-Vallée - France
audibert@certis.enpc.fr

Abstract. We propose a sequential randomized algorithm, which at each step concentrates on functions having both low risk and low variance with respect to the previous step prediction function. It satisfies a simple risk bound, which is sharp to the extent that the standard statistical learning approach, based on supremum of empirical processes, does not lead to algorithms with such a tight guarantee on its efficiency. Our generalization error bounds complement the pioneering work of Cesa-Bianchi et al. [12] in which standard-style statistical results were recovered with tight constants using worst-case analysis.

A nice feature of our analysis of the randomized estimator is to put forward the links between the probabilistic and worst-case viewpoint. It also allows to recover recent model selection results due to Juditsky et al. [16] and to improve them in least square regression with heavy noise, i.e. when no exponential moment condition is assumed on the output.

1 Introduction

We are given a family $\mathcal{G}$ of functions and we want to learn from data a function that predicts as well as the best function in $\mathcal{G}$ up to some additive term called the rate of convergence. When the set $\mathcal{G}$ is finite, this learning task is often referred to as model selection aggregation.

This learning task has rare properties. First, in general an algorithm picking functions in the set $\mathcal{G}$ is not optimal (see e.g. [10, p.14]). This means that the estimator has to looked at an enlarged set of prediction functions. Secondly, in the statistical community, the only known optimal algorithms are all based on a Cesaro mean of Bayesian estimators (also referred to as progressive mixture rule). And thirdly, the proof of their optimality is not achieved by the most prominent tool in statistical learning theory: bounds on the supremum of empirical processes.

The idea of the proof, which comes back to Barron [5], is based on a chain rule and appeared to be successful for least square and entropy losses [9, 10, 6, 22, 7] and for general loss in [16].

In the online prediction with expert advice setting, without any probabilistic assumption on the generation of the data, appropriate weighting methods have

G. Lugosi and H.U. Simon (Eds.): COLT 2006, LNAI 4005, pp. 392–407, 2006.
© Springer-Verlag Berlin Heidelberg 2006

been showed to behave as well as the best expert up to a minimax-optimal additive remainder term (see [18] and references within). In this worst-case context, amazingly sharp constants have been found (see in particular [15, 12, 13, 23]). These results are expressed in cumulative loss and can be transposed to model selection aggregation to the extent that the expected risk of the randomized procedure based on sequential predictions is proportional to the expectation of the cumulative loss of the sequential procedure (see Lemma 3 for precise statement).

This work presents a sequential algorithm, which iteratively updates a prior distribution put on the set of prediction functions. Contrarily to previously mentioned works, these updates take into account the variance of the task. As a consequence, posterior distributions concentrate on simultaneously low risk functions and functions close to the previous prediction. This conservative law is not surprising in view of previous works on high dimensional statistical tasks, such as wavelet thresholding, shrinkage procedures, iterative compression schemes ([3]), iterative feature selection ([1]).

The paper is organized as follows. Section 2 introduces the notation and the existing algorithms. Section 3 proposes a unifying setting to combine worst-case analysis tight results and probabilistic tools. It details our randomized estimator and gives a sharp expectation bound. In Sections 4 and 5, we show how to apply our main result under assumptions coming respectively from sequential prediction and model selection aggregation. Section 6 contains an algorithm that satisfies a sharp standard-style generalization error bound. To the author's knowledge, this bound is not achievable with classical statistical learning approach based on supremum of empirical processes. Section 7 presents an improved bound for least square regression regression when the noise has just a bounded moment of order $s \geq 2$.

2   Notation and Existing Algorithms

We assume that we observe n pairs $Z_1 = (X_1, Y_1), \ldots, Z_n = (X_n, Y_n)$ of input-output and that each pair has been independently drawn from the same unknown distribution denoted $\mathbb{P}$. The input and output space are denoted respectively $\mathcal{X}$ and $\mathcal{Y}$, so that $\mathbb{P}$ is a probability distribution on the product space $\mathcal{Z} \triangleq \mathcal{X} \times \mathcal{Y}$. The target of a learning algorithm is to predict the output Y associated to an input X for pairs (X, Y) drawn from the distribution $\mathbb{P}$. The quality of a prediction function $g : \mathcal{X} \to \mathcal{Y}$ is measured by the risk

$$R(g) \triangleq \mathbb{E}_{\mathbb{P}(dZ)} L(Z, g),$$

where $L(Z, g)$ assesses the loss of considering the prediction function g on the data $Z \in \mathcal{Z}$. We use $L(Z, g)$ rather than $L[Y, g(X)]$ to underline that our results are not restricted to non-regularized losses, where we call non-regularized loss a loss that can be written as $l[Y, g(X)]$ for some function $l : \mathcal{Y} \times \mathcal{Y} \to \mathbb{R}$.

We will say that the loss function is convex when the function $g \mapsto L(z, g)$ is convex for any $z \in \mathcal{Z}$. In this work, we do not assume the loss function to be convex except when it is explicitly mentioned.

For any $i \in \{0, \ldots, n\}$, the *cumulative loss* suffered by the prediction function g on the first i pairs of input-output, denoted Z_1^i for short, is

$$\Sigma_i(g) \triangleq \sum_{j=1}^{i} L(Z_j, g),$$

where by convention we take Σ_0 identically equal to zero ($\Sigma_0 \equiv 0$). Throughout this work, without loss of generality, we assume that $\mathcal{Y}$ is convex so that convex combination of prediction functions are prediction functions. The symbol C will denote some positive constant whose value may differ from line to line.

To handle possibly continuous set $\mathcal{G}$, we consider that $\mathcal{G}$ is a measurable space and that we have some prior distribution π on it. The set of probability distributions on $\mathcal{G}$ will be denoted $\mathcal{M}$. The Kullback-Leibler divergence between a distribution $\rho \in \mathcal{M}$ and the prior distribution π is

$$K(\rho, \pi) \triangleq \begin{cases} \mathbb{E}_{\rho(dg)} \log\left(\frac{\rho}{\pi}(g)\right) & \text{if } \rho \ll \pi, \\ +\infty & \text{otherwise} \end{cases}$$

where $\frac{\rho}{\pi}$ denotes the density of ρ w.r.t. π when it exists (i.e. $\rho \ll \pi$). For any $\rho \in \mathcal{M}$, we have $K(\rho, \pi) \geq 0$ and when π is the uniform distribution on a finite set $\mathcal{G}$, we also have $K(\rho, \pi) \leq \log|\mathcal{G}|$. The Kullback-Leibler divergence satisfies the duality formula (see e.g. [11, p.10]): for any real-valued measurable function h defined on $\mathcal{G}$,

$$\inf_{\rho \in \mathcal{M}} \left\{ \mathbb{E}_{\rho(dg)} h(g) + K(\rho, \pi) \right\} = -\log \mathbb{E}_{\pi(dg)} e^{-h(g)}. \tag{1}$$

and that the infimum is reached for the Gibbs distribution

$$\pi_{-h} \triangleq \frac{e^{-h(g)}}{\mathbb{E}_{\pi(dg')} e^{-h(g')}} \cdot \pi(dg). \tag{2}$$

The algorithm used to prove optimal convergence rates for several different losses (see e.g. [9, 10, 6, 22, 7, 16]) is the following:

Algorithm A: Let $\lambda > 0$. Predict according to $\frac{1}{n+1} \sum_{i=0}^{n} \mathbb{E}_{\pi_{-\lambda \Sigma_i}(dg)} g$, where we recall that Σ_i maps a function $g \in \mathcal{G}$ to its cumulative loss up to time i.

In other words, for a new input x, the prediction of the output given by Algorithm A is $\frac{1}{n+1} \sum_{i=0}^{n} \frac{\int g(x) e^{-\lambda \Sigma_i(g)} \pi(dg)}{\int e^{-\lambda \Sigma_i(g)} \pi(dg)}$.

From Vovk, Haussler, Kivinen and Warmuth works ([20, 15, 21]) and the link between cumulative loss in online setting and expected risk in the batch setting (see later Lemma 3), an "optimal" algorithm is:

Algorithm B: Let $\lambda > 0$. For any $i \in \{0, \ldots, n\}$, let $\hat{h}_i$ be a prediction function such that

$$\forall z \in \mathcal{Z} \qquad L(z, \hat{h}_i) \leq -\frac{1}{\lambda} \log \mathbb{E}_{\pi_{-\lambda \Sigma_i}(dg)} e^{-\lambda L(z, g)}.$$

If one of the $\hat{h}_i$ does not exist, the algorithm is said to fail. Otherwise it predicts according to $\frac{1}{n+1} \sum_{i=0}^{n} \hat{h}_i$.

In particular, for appropriate $\lambda > 0$, this algorithm does not fail when the loss function is the square loss (i.e. $L(z, g) = [y - g(x)]^2$) and when the output space is bounded. Algorithm B is based on the same Gibbs distribution $\pi_{-\lambda\Sigma_i}$ as Algorithm A. Besides, in [15, Example 3.13], it is shown that Algorithm A is not in general a particular case of Algorithm B, and that Algorithm B will not generally produce a prediction function in the convex hull of $\mathcal{G}$ unlike Algorithm A. In Sections 4 and 5, we will see how both algorithms are connected to our generic algorithm.

We assume that the set, denoted $\bar{\mathcal{G}}$, of all measurable prediction functions has been equipped with a σ-algebra. Let $\mathcal{D}$ be the set of all probability distributions on $\bar{\mathcal{G}}$. By definition, a randomized algorithm produces a prediction function drawn according to a probability in $\mathcal{D}$. Let $\mathcal{P}$ be a set of probability distributions on $\mathcal{Z}$ in which we assume that the true unknown distribution generating the data is.

3   The Algorithm and Its Generalization Error Bound

The aim of this section is to build an algorithm with the best possible convergence rate regardless of computational issues. For any $\lambda > 0$, let δ_λ be a real-valued function defined on $\mathcal{Z} \times \mathcal{G} \times \bar{\mathcal{G}}$ that satisfies

$$\forall \rho \in \mathcal{M} \quad \exists \hat{\pi}(\rho) \in \mathcal{D}$$

$$\sup_{\mathbb{P} \in \mathcal{P}} \left\{ \mathbb{E}_{\hat{\pi}(\rho)(dg')} \mathbb{E}_{\mathbb{P}(dZ)} \log \mathbb{E}_{\rho(dg)} e^{\lambda \left[L(Z,g') - L(Z,g) - \delta_\lambda(Z,g,g') \right]} \right\} \leq 0. \quad (3)$$

Condition (3) is our probabilistic version of the generic algorithm condition in the online prediction setting (see [20, proof of Theorem 1] or more explicitly in [15, p.11]), in which we added the variance function δ_λ. Our results will be all the sharper as this variance function is small. To make (3) more readable, let us say for the moment that

- without any assumption on $\mathcal{P}$, for several usual strongly convex loss functions, we may take $\delta_\lambda \equiv 0$ provided that λ is a small enough constant (see Section 4).
- Inequality (3) can be seen as a "small expectation" inequality. The usual viewpoint is to control the quantity $L(Z, g)$ by its expectation with respect to (w.r.t.) Z and a variance term. Here, roughly, $L(Z, g)$ is mainly controlled by $L(Z, g')$ where g' is appropriately chosen through the choice of $\hat{\pi}(\rho)$, plus the additive term δ_λ. By definition this additive term does not depend on the particular probability distribution generating the data and leads to empirical compensation.
- in the examples we will be interested in throughout this work, $\hat{\pi}(\rho)$ will be either equal to ρ or to a Dirac distribution on some function, which is *not necessarily in $\mathcal{G}$*.
- for any loss function L, any set $\mathcal{P}$ and any $\lambda > 0$, one may choose $\delta_\lambda(Z, g, g') = \frac{\lambda}{2} \left[L(Z, g) - L(Z, g') \right]^2$ (see Section 6).

Our results concern the following algorithm, in which we recall that π is a prior distribution put on the set $\mathcal{G}$.

Generic Algorithm

1. Let $\lambda > 0$. Define $\hat{\rho}_0 \triangleq \hat{\pi}(\pi)$ in the sense of (3) and draw a function $\hat{g}_0$ according to this distribution. Let $S_0(g) = 0$ for any $g \in \mathcal{G}$.
2. For any $i \in \{1, \ldots, n\}$, iteratively define

$$S_i(g) \triangleq S_{i-1}(g) + L(Z_i, g) + \delta_\lambda(Z_i, g, \hat{g}_{i-1}) \qquad \text{for any } g \in \mathcal{G}.$$

and

$$\hat{\rho}_i \triangleq \hat{\pi}(\pi_{-\lambda S_i}) \qquad \text{(in the sense of (3))}$$

and draw a function $\hat{g}_i$ according to the distribution $\hat{\rho}_i$.
3. Predict with a function drawn according to the uniform distribution on $\{\hat{g}_0, \ldots, \hat{g}_n\}$.

Remark 1. When $\delta_\lambda(Z, g, g')$ does not depend on g, we recover a more standard-style algorithm to the extent that we then have $\pi_{-\lambda S_i} = \pi_{-\lambda \Sigma_i}$. Precisely our algorithm becomes the randomized version of Algorithm A. When $\delta_\lambda(Z, g, g')$ depends on g, the posterior distributions tend to concentrate on functions having small risk and small variance term.

For any $i \in \{0, \ldots, n\}$, the quantities S_i, $\hat{\rho}_i$ and $\hat{g}_i$ depend on the training data only through $Z_1, \ldots, Z_i$. Let Ω_i denote the joint distribution of $\hat{g}_0^i \triangleq (\hat{g}_0, \ldots, \hat{g}_i)$ conditional to Z_1^i, where we recall that Z_1^i denotes $(Z_1, \ldots, Z_i)$. Our randomized algorithm produces a prediction function which has three causes of randomness: the training data, the way $\hat{g}_i$ is obtained (step 2) and the uniform draw (step 3). So the expected risk of our iteratively randomized generic procedure is

$$\mathcal{E} \triangleq \mathbb{E}_{\mathbb{P}(dZ_1^n)} \mathbb{E}_{\Omega_n(d\hat{g}_0^n)} \tfrac{1}{n+1} \sum_{i=0}^n R(\hat{g}_i) = \tfrac{1}{n+1} \sum_{i=0}^n \mathbb{E}_{\mathbb{P}(dZ_1^i)} \mathbb{E}_{\Omega_i(d\hat{g}_0^i)} R(\hat{g}_i)$$

Our main result is

Theorem 1. *Let* $\Delta_\lambda(g, g') \triangleq \mathbb{E}_{\mathbb{P}(dZ)} \delta_\lambda(Z, g, g')$ *for* $g \in G$ *and* $g' \in \bar{G}$*. The expected risk of the generic algorithm satisfies*

$$\mathcal{E} \leq \min_{\rho \in \mathcal{M}} \left\{ \mathbb{E}_{\rho(dg)} R(g) + \mathbb{E}_{\rho(dg)} \mathbb{E}_{\mathbb{P}(dZ_1^n)} \mathbb{E}_{\Omega_n(d\hat{g}_0^n)} \frac{\sum_{i=0}^n \Delta_\lambda(g, \hat{g}_i)}{n+1} + \frac{K(\rho, \pi)}{\lambda(n+1)} \right\} \qquad (4)$$

In particular, when $\mathcal{G}$ *is finite and when the loss function* L *and the set* $\mathcal{P}$ *are such that* $\delta_\lambda \equiv 0$*, by taking* π *uniform on* $\mathcal{G}$*, we get*

$$\mathcal{E} \leq \min_{\mathcal{G}} R + \frac{\log |\mathcal{G}|}{\lambda(n+1)} \qquad (5)$$

Proof. Let $Z_{n+1} \in \mathcal{Z}$ be drawn according to $\mathbb{P}$ and independent from $Z_1, \ldots, Z_n$. To shorten formulae, let $\hat{\pi}_i \triangleq \pi_{-\lambda S_i}$ so that by definition we have $\hat{\rho}_i = \hat{\pi}(\hat{\pi}_i)$ in the sense of (3). Inequality (3) implies that

$$\mathbb{E}_{\hat{\pi}(\rho)(dg')} R(g') \leq -\tfrac{1}{\lambda} \mathbb{E}_{\hat{\pi}(\rho)(dg')} \mathbb{E}_{\mathbb{P}(dZ)} \log \mathbb{E}_{\rho(dg)} e^{-\lambda[L(Z,g) + \delta_\lambda(Z,g,g')]},$$

so by Fubini's theorem for any $i \in \{0, \ldots, n\}$,

$$
\mathbb{E}_{\mathbb{P}(dZ_1^i)} \mathbb{E}_{\Omega_i(d\hat{g}_0^i)} R(\hat{g}_i)
$$
$$
\leq -\tfrac{1}{\lambda} \mathbb{E}_{\mathbb{P}(dZ_1^{i+1})} \mathbb{E}_{\Omega_i(d\hat{g}_0^i)} \log \mathbb{E}_{\hat{\pi}_i(dg)} e^{-\lambda[L(Z_{i+1},g) + \delta_\lambda(Z_{i+1},g,\hat{g}_i)]}.
$$

Consequently, by the chain rule (i.e. cancellation in the sum of logarithmic terms; [5]) and by intensive use of Fubini's theorem, we get

$$
\begin{aligned}
\mathcal{E} &= \tfrac{1}{n+1} \sum_{i=0}^{n} \mathbb{E}_{\mathbb{P}(dZ_1^i)} \mathbb{E}_{\Omega_i(d\hat{g}_0^i)} R(\hat{g}_i) \\
&\leq -\tfrac{1}{\lambda(n+1)} \sum_{i=0}^{n} \mathbb{E}_{\mathbb{P}(dZ_1^{i+1})} \mathbb{E}_{\Omega_i(d\hat{g}_0^i)} \log \mathbb{E}_{\hat{\pi}_i(dg)} e^{-\lambda[L(Z_{i+1},g)+\delta_\lambda(Z_{i+1},g,\hat{g}_i)]} \\
&= -\tfrac{1}{\lambda(n+1)} \mathbb{E}_{\mathbb{P}(dZ_1^{n+1})} \mathbb{E}_{\Omega_n(d\hat{g}_0^n)} \sum_{i=0}^{n} \log \mathbb{E}_{\hat{\pi}_i(dg)} e^{-\lambda[L(Z_{i+1},g)+\delta_\lambda(Z_{i+1},g,\hat{g}_i)]} \\
&= -\tfrac{1}{\lambda(n+1)} \mathbb{E}_{\mathbb{P}(dZ_1^{n+1})} \mathbb{E}_{\Omega_n(d\hat{g}_0^n)} \sum_{i=0}^{n} \log \left(\frac{\mathbb{E}_{\pi(dg)} e^{-\lambda S_{i+1}(g)}}{\mathbb{E}_{\pi(dg)} e^{-\lambda S_i(g)}} \right) \\
&= -\tfrac{1}{\lambda(n+1)} \mathbb{E}_{\mathbb{P}(dZ_1^{n+1})} \mathbb{E}_{\Omega_n(d\hat{g}_0^n)} \log \left(\frac{\mathbb{E}_{\pi(dg)} e^{-\lambda S_{n+1}(g)}}{\mathbb{E}_{\pi(dg)} e^{-\lambda S_0(g)}} \right) \\
&= -\tfrac{1}{\lambda(n+1)} \mathbb{E}_{\mathbb{P}(dZ_1^{n+1})} \mathbb{E}_{\Omega_n(d\hat{g}_0^n)} \log \mathbb{E}_{\pi(dg)} e^{-\lambda S_{n+1}(g)}
\end{aligned}
$$

Now from the following lemma, we obtain

$$
\begin{aligned}
\mathcal{E} &\leq -\tfrac{1}{\lambda(n+1)} \log \mathbb{E}_{\pi(dg)} e^{-\lambda \mathbb{E}_{\mathbb{P}(dZ_1^{n+1})} \mathbb{E}_{\Omega_n(d\hat{g}_0^n)} S_{n+1}(g)} \\
&= -\tfrac{1}{\lambda(n+1)} \log \mathbb{E}_{\pi(dg)} e^{-\lambda \left[(n+1)R(g) + \mathbb{E}_{\mathbb{P}(dZ_1^n)} \mathbb{E}_{\Omega_n(d\hat{g}_0^n)} \sum_{i=0}^{n} \Delta_\lambda(g,\hat{g}_i) \right]} \\
&= \min_{\rho \in \mathcal{M}} \left\{ \mathbb{E}_{\rho(dg)} R(g) + \mathbb{E}_{\rho(dg)} \mathbb{E}_{\mathbb{P}(dZ_1^n)} \mathbb{E}_{\Omega_n(d\hat{g}_0^n)} \frac{\sum_{i=0}^{n} \Delta_\lambda(g,\hat{g}_i)}{n+1} + \frac{K(\rho,\pi)}{\lambda(n+1)} \right\}.
\end{aligned}
$$

Lemma 1. *Let $\mathcal{W}$ be a real-valued measurable function defined on a product space $\mathcal{A}_1 \times \mathcal{A}_2$ and let μ_1 and μ_2 be probability distribtutions on respectively $\mathcal{A}_1$ and $\mathcal{A}_2$ such that $\mathbb{E}_{\mu_1(da_1)} \log \mathbb{E}_{\mu_2(da_2)} e^{-\mathcal{W}(a_1,a_2)} < +\infty$. We have*

$$
-\mathbb{E}_{\mu_1(da_1)} \log \mathbb{E}_{\mu_2(da_2)} e^{-\mathcal{W}(a_1,a_2)} \leq -\log \mathbb{E}_{\mu_2(da_2)} e^{-\mathbb{E}_{\mu_1(da_1)} \mathcal{W}(a_1,a_2)}.
$$

Proof. It mainly comes from (1) (used twice) and Fubini's theorem.

Inequality (5) is a direct consequence of (4).

Theorem 1 bounds the expected risk of a randomized procedure, where the expectation is taken w.r.t. both the training set distribution and the randomizing distribution. From the following lemma, for convex loss functions, (5) implies

$$
\mathbb{E}_{\mathbb{P}(dZ_1^n)} R\left(\mathbb{E}_{\Omega_n(d\hat{g}_0^n)} \tfrac{1}{n+1} \sum_{i=0}^{n} \hat{g}_i \right) \leq \min_{\mathcal{G}} R + \frac{\log |\mathcal{G}|}{\lambda(n+1)}, \tag{6}
$$

where we recall that Ω_n is the distribution of $\hat{g}_0^n = (\hat{g}_0, \ldots, \hat{g}_n)$ and λ is a parameter whose typical value is the largest $\lambda > 0$ such that $\delta_\lambda \equiv 0$.

Lemma 2. *For convex loss functions, the doubly expected risk of a randomized algorithm is greater than the expected risk of the deterministic version of the randomized algorithm, i.e. if $\hat{\rho}$ denotes the randomizing distribution,*

$$
\mathbb{E}_{\mathbb{P}(Z_1^n)} R(\mathbb{E}_{\hat{\rho}(dg)} g) \leq \mathbb{E}_{\mathbb{P}(Z_1^n)} \mathbb{E}_{\hat{\rho}(dg)} R(g).
$$

Proof. The result is a direct consequence of Jensen's inequality.

In [12], the authors rely on worst-case analysis to recover standard-style statistical results such as Vapnik's bounds [19]. Theorem 1 can be seen as a complement to this pioneering work. Inequality (6) is the model selection bound that is well-known for least square regression and entropy loss, and that has been recently proved for general losses in [16].

Let us discuss the generalized form of the result. The r.h.s. of (4) is a classical regularized risk, which appears naturally in the PAC-Bayesian approach (see e.g. [8, 11, 4, 24]). An advantage of stating the result this way is to be able to deal with uncountable infinite $\mathcal{G}$. Even when $\mathcal{G}$ is countable, this formulation has some benefit to the extent that for any measurable function $h : \mathcal{G} \to \mathbb{R}$, $\min_{\rho \in \mathcal{M}}\{\mathbb{E}_{\rho(dg)}h(g) + K(\rho, \pi)\} \leq \min_{g \in \mathcal{G}} \{h(g) + \log \pi^{-1}(g)\}$.

Our generalization error bounds depend on two quantities λ and π which are the parameters of our algorithm. Their choice depends on the precise setting. Nevertheless, when $\mathcal{G}$ is finite and with no special structure a priori, a natural choice for π is the uniform distribution on $\mathcal{G}$.

Once the distribution π is fixed, an appropriate choice for the parameter λ is the minimizer of the r.h.s. of (4). This minimizer is unknown by the statistician, and it is an open problem to adaptively choose λ close to it.

4   Link with Sequential Prediction

This section aims at illustrating condition (3) and at clearly stating in our batch setting results coming from the online learning community. In [20, 15, 21], the loss function is assumed to satisfy: there are positive numbers η and c such that

$$\forall \rho \in \mathcal{M} \quad \exists g_\rho : \mathcal{X} \to \mathcal{Y} \quad \forall x \in \mathcal{X} \quad \forall y \in \mathcal{Y}$$
$$L[(x, y), g_\rho] \leq -\tfrac{c}{\eta} \log \mathbb{E}_{\rho(dg)} e^{-\eta L[(x,y),g]} \tag{7}$$

Then (3) holds both for $\lambda = \eta$ and $\delta_\lambda(Z, g, g') = -(1 - 1/c)L(Z, g')$ and for $\lambda = \eta/c$ and $\delta_\lambda(Z, g, g') = (c - 1)L(Z, g)$, and we may take in both cases $\hat{\pi}(\rho)$ as the Dirac distribution at g_ρ. This leads to the *same* procedure which is described in the following straightforward corollary of Theorem 1.

Corollary 1. *Let $g_{\pi_{-\eta \Sigma_i}}$ be defined in the sense of (7). Consider the algorithm which predicts by drawing a function in $\{g_{\pi_{-\eta \Sigma_0}}, \ldots, g_{\pi_{-\eta \Sigma_n}}\}$ according to the uniform distribution. Under assumption (7), the expected risk of this procedure satisfies*

$$\mathcal{E} \leq c \min_{\rho \in \mathcal{M}} \left\{ \mathbb{E}_{\rho(dg)} R(g) + \tfrac{K(\rho, \pi)}{\eta(n+1)} \right\}. \tag{8}$$

This result is not surprising in view of the following two results. The first one comes from worst case analysis in sequential prediction.

Theorem 2 (Haussler et al. [15], Theorem 3.8). *Let $\mathcal{G}$ be countable. For any $g \in \mathcal{G}$, let $\Sigma_i(g) = \sum_{j=1}^{i} L(Z_j, g)$ (still) denote the cumulative loss up to* *time i of the expert which always predict according to function g. The cumulative loss on Z_1^n of the strategy in which the prediction at time i is done according to $g_{\pi_{-\eta \Sigma_{i-1}}}$ in the sense of (7) is bounded by*

$$\inf_{g \in \mathcal{G}} \{ c\Sigma_n(g) + \tfrac{c}{\eta} \log \pi^{-1}(g) \}. \tag{9}$$

The second result shows how the previous bound can be transposed into our model selection context by the following lemma.

Lemma 3. *Let Z_{n+1} be a random variable independent from Z_1^n and with the same distribution $\mathbb{P}$. Let $\mathcal{A}$ be a learning algorithm which produces the prediction function $\mathcal{A}(Z_1^i)$ at time $i + 1$, i.e. from the data $Z_1^i = (Z_1, \ldots, Z_i)$. Let $\mathcal{L}$ be the randomized algorithm which produces a prediction function $\mathcal{L}(Z_1^n)$ drawn according to the uniform distribution on $\{\mathcal{A}(\emptyset), \mathcal{A}(Z_1), \ldots, \mathcal{A}(Z_1^n)\}$. The (doubly) expected risk of $\mathcal{L}$ is equal to $\frac{1}{n+1}$ times the expectation of the cumulative loss of $\mathcal{A}$ on the sequence Z_1^{n+1}.*

Proof. By Fubini's theorem, we have

$$
\begin{aligned}
\mathbb{E}R[\mathcal{L}(Z_1^n)] &= \tfrac{1}{n+1} \sum_{i=0}^{n} \mathbb{E}_{\mathbb{P}(dZ_1^n)} R[\mathcal{A}(Z_1^i)] \\
&= \tfrac{1}{n+1} \sum_{i=0}^{n} \mathbb{E}_{\mathbb{P}(dZ_1^{i+1})} L[Z_{i+1}, \mathcal{A}(Z_1^i)] \\
&= \tfrac{1}{n+1} \mathbb{E}_{\mathbb{P}(dZ_1^{n+1})} \sum_{i=0}^{n} L[Z_{i+1}, \mathcal{A}(Z_1^i)].
\end{aligned}
$$

For any $\eta > 0$, let $c(\eta)$ denote the infimum of the c for which (7) holds. Under weak assumptions, Vovk ([21]) proved that the infimum exists and studied the behaviour of $c(\eta)$ and $a(\eta) = c(\eta)/\eta$, which are key quantities of (8) and (9). Under weak assumptions, and in particular in the examples given in the table, the optimal constants in (9) are $c(\eta)$ and $a(\eta)$ ([21, Theorem 1]) and we have $c(\eta) \geq 1$, $\eta \mapsto c(\eta)$ nondecreasing and $\eta \mapsto a(\eta)$ nonincreasing. From these last properties, we understand the trade-off which occurs to choose the optimal η. Table 1 specifies (8) in different well-known learning tasks. For instance, for bounded least square regression (i.e. when $|Y| \leq B$ for some $B > 0$), the generalization error of the algorithm described in Corollary 1 when $\eta = 1/(2B^2)$ is bounded with $\min_{\rho \in \mathcal{M}} \{ \mathbb{E}_{\rho(dg)} R(g) + 2B^2 \frac{K(\rho, \pi)}{n+1} \}$.

Table 1. Value of $c(\eta)$ for different loss functions. Here B denotes a positive real.

	Output space	Loss L(Z,g)	$c(\eta)$
Entropy loss [15, Example 4.3]	$\mathcal{Y} = [0; 1]$	$Y \log \left(\frac{Y}{g(X)} \right)$ $+(1 - Y) \log \left(\frac{1-Y}{1-g(X)} \right)$	$c(\eta) = 1$ if $\eta \leq 1$ $c(\eta) = \infty$ if $\eta > 1$
Absolute loss game [15, Section 4.2]	$\mathcal{Y} = [0; 1]$	$\|Y - g(X)\|$	$\frac{\eta}{2 \log[2/(1+e^{-\eta})]}$ $= 1 + \eta/4 + o(\eta)$
Square loss [15, Example 4.4]	$\mathcal{Y} = [-B, B]$	$[Y - g(X)]^2$	$c(\eta) = 1$ if $\eta \leq 1/(2B^2)$ $c(\eta) = +\infty$ if $\eta > 1/(2B^2)$

5 Model Selection Aggregation Under Juditsky, Rigollet and Tsybakov Assumptions ([16])

The main result of [16] relies on the following assumption on the loss function L and the set $\mathcal{P}$ of probability distributions on $\mathcal{Z}$ in which we assume that the true distribution is. There exist $\lambda > 0$ and a real-valued function ψ defined on $\mathcal{G} \times \mathcal{G}$ such that for any $\mathbb{P} \in \mathcal{P}$

$$\begin{cases} \mathbb{E}_{\mathbb{P}(dZ)} e^{\lambda[L(Z,g')-L(Z,g)]} \leq \psi(g',g) & \text{for any } g, g' \in \mathcal{G} \\ \psi(g,g) = 1 & \text{for any } g \in \mathcal{G} \\ \text{the function } [g \mapsto \psi(g',g)] \text{ is concave for any } g' \in \mathcal{G} \end{cases} \tag{10}$$

Theorem 1 gives the following result.

Corollary 2. *Under assumption* (10), *the algorithm which draws uniformly its prediction function in the set* $\{\mathbb{E}_{\pi_{-\lambda\Sigma_0}(dg)}g, \dots, \mathbb{E}_{\pi_{-\lambda\Sigma_n}(dg)}g\}$ *satisfies*

$$\mathcal{E} \leq \min_{\rho \in \mathcal{M}} \left\{ \mathbb{E}_{\rho(dg)} R(g) + \tfrac{K(\rho,\pi)}{\lambda(n+1)} \right\}. \tag{11}$$

Besides for convex losses,

$$R\left(\tfrac{1}{n+1} \sum_{i=0}^{n} \mathbb{E}_{\pi_{-\lambda\Sigma_i}(dg)}g \right) \leq \min_{\rho \in \mathcal{M}} \left\{ \mathbb{E}_{\rho(dg)} R(g) + \tfrac{K(\rho,\pi)}{\lambda(n+1)} \right\}. \tag{12}$$

Proof. We start by proving that condition (3) holds with $\delta_\lambda \equiv 0$, and that we may take $\pi(\rho)$ as the Dirac distribution at the function $\mathbb{E}_{\rho(dg)}g$. By using Jensen's inequality and Fubini's theorem, assumption (10) implies that

$$\mathbb{E}_{\pi(\rho)(dg')}\mathbb{E}_{\mathbb{P}(dZ)} \log \mathbb{E}_{\rho(dg)} e^{\lambda[L(Z,g')-L(Z,g)]}$$
$$= \mathbb{E}_{\mathbb{P}(dZ)} \log \mathbb{E}_{\rho(dg)} e^{\lambda[L(Z,\mathbb{E}_{\rho(dg')}g')-L(Z,g)]}$$
$$\leq \log \mathbb{E}_{\rho(dg)}\mathbb{E}_{\mathbb{P}(dZ)} e^{\lambda[L(Z,\mathbb{E}_{\rho(dg')}g')-L(Z,g)]}$$
$$\leq \log \mathbb{E}_{\rho(dg)} \psi(\mathbb{E}_{\rho(dg')}g', g)$$
$$\leq \log \psi(\mathbb{E}_{\rho(dg')}g', \mathbb{E}_{\rho(dg)}g)$$
$$= 0,$$

so that we can apply Theorem 1. It remains to note that in this context our generic algorithm is the one described in the corollary.

In this context, our generic algorithm reduces to the randomized version of Algorithm A. From Lemma 2, for convex loss functions, (11) also holds for the risk of Algorithm A. Corollary 2 also shows that the risk bounds of [16, Theorem 3.2 and the examples of Section 4.2] hold with the same constants for our randomized algorithm (provided that the expected risk w.r.t. the training set distribution is replaced by the expected risk w.r.t. both training set and randomizing distributions).

On assumption (10) we should say that it does not a priori require the function L to be convex. Nevertheless, any known relevant examples deal with strongly convex loss functions and we know that in general the assumption will not hold for SVM loss function and for absolute loss function (since $1/n$ model selection rate are in general not achievable for these loss functions).

One can also recover the results in [16, Theorem 3.1 and Section 4.1] by taking $\delta_\lambda(Z, g, g') = \mathbf{1}_{Z \in S}[\sup_{g \in \mathcal{G}} L(Z, g) - \inf_{g \in \mathcal{G}} L(Z, g)]$ with appropriate set $S \subset \mathcal{Z}$. Once more the aggregation procedure is different because of the randomization step but the generalization error bounds are identical.

6   A Standard-Style Statistical Bound

This section proposes new results of a different kind. In the previous sections, under convexity assumptions, we were able to achieve fast rates. Here we have assumption neither on the loss function nor on the probability generating the data. Nevertheless we show that our generic algorithm applied for $\delta_\lambda(Z, g, g') = \lambda[L(Z, g) - L(Z, g')]^2/2$ satisfies a sharp standard-style statistical bound.

Theorem 3. *Let* $V(g, g') = \mathbb{E}_{\mathbb{P}(dZ)}\{[L(Z, g) - L(Z, g')]^2\}$. *Our generic algorithm applied with* $\delta_\lambda(Z, g, g') = \lambda[L(Z, g) - L(Z, g')]^2/2$ *and* $\hat{\pi}(\rho) = \rho$ *satisfies*

$$\mathcal{E} \leq \min_{\rho \in \mathcal{M}} \left\{ \mathbb{E}_{\rho(dg)} R(g) + \tfrac{1}{2}\mathbb{E}_{\rho(dg)}\mathbb{E}_{\mathbb{P}(dZ_1^n)}\mathbb{E}_{\Omega_n(d\hat{g}_0^n)} \frac{\sum_{i=0}^n V(g, \hat{g}_i)}{n+1} + \frac{K(\rho, \pi)}{\lambda(n+1)} \right\} \quad (13)$$

Proof. To check that (3) holds, it suffices to prove that for any $z \in \mathcal{Z}$,
$$\mathbb{E}_{\rho(dg')} \log \mathbb{E}_{\rho(dg)} e^{\lambda[L(z,g') - L(z,g)] - \frac{\lambda^2}{2}[L(z,g') - L(z,g)]^2} \leq 0.$$

To shorten formulae, let $\alpha(g', g) \triangleq \lambda[L(z, g') - L(z, g)]$ By Jensen's inequality and the following symmetrization trick, the previous expectation is bounded with

$$
\begin{aligned}
&\mathbb{E}_{\rho(dg')}\mathbb{E}_{\rho(dg)} e^{\alpha(g',g) - \frac{\alpha^2(g',g)}{2}} \\
&\leq \tfrac{1}{2}\mathbb{E}_{\rho(dg')}\mathbb{E}_{\rho(dg)} e^{\alpha(g',g) - \frac{\alpha^2(g',g)}{2}} + \tfrac{1}{2}\mathbb{E}_{\rho(dg')}\mathbb{E}_{\rho(dg)} e^{-\alpha(g',g) - \frac{\alpha^2(g',g)}{2}} \\
&\leq \mathbb{E}_{\rho(dg')}\mathbb{E}_{\rho(dg)} \cosh\left(\alpha(g,g')\right) e^{-\frac{\alpha^2(g',g)}{2}} \\
&\leq 1
\end{aligned}
\quad (14)
$$

where in the last inequality we used the inequality $\cosh(t) \leq e^{t^2/2}$ for any $t \in \mathbb{R}$. The first result then follows from Theorem 1.

To make (13) more explicit and to obtain a generalization error bound in which the randomizing distribution does not appear in the r.h.s. of the bound, the following corollary considers a widely used assumption that relates the variance term to the excess risk. Precisely, from Theorem 3, we obtain (proof omitted of this extended abstract)

Corollary 3. *Under the generalized Mammen and Tsybakov's assumption which states that there exist* $0 \leq \gamma \leq 1$ *and a prediction function* $\tilde{g}$ *(not necessarily in* $\mathcal{G}$*) such that* $V(g, \tilde{g}) \leq c[R(g) - R(\tilde{g})]^\gamma$ *for any* $g \in \mathcal{G}$*, the expected risk of the generic algorithm used in Theorem 3 satisfies*

– *When $\gamma = 1$,*

$$\mathcal{E} - R(\tilde{g}) \leq \min_{\rho \in \mathcal{M}} \left\{ \frac{1+c\lambda}{1-c\lambda} \left[\mathbb{E}_{\rho(dg)} R(g) - R(\tilde{g}) \right] + \frac{K(\rho,\pi)}{(1-c\lambda)\lambda(n+1)} \right\}$$

In particular, for $\mathcal{G}$ finite, π the uniform distribution, $\lambda = 1/2c$, when $\tilde{g}$ belongs to $\mathcal{G}$, we get $\mathcal{E} \leq \min_{g \in \mathcal{G}} R(g) + \frac{4c \log |\mathcal{G}|}{n+1}$.

– *When $\gamma < 1$, for any $0 < \beta < 1$ and for $\tilde{R}(g) \triangleq R(g) - R(\tilde{g})$,*

$$\mathcal{E} - R(\tilde{g}) \leq \left\{ \frac{1}{\beta} \left(\mathbb{E}_{\rho(dg)} [\tilde{R}(g) + c\lambda \tilde{R}^\gamma(g)] + \frac{K(\rho,\pi)}{\lambda(n+1)} \right) \right\} \vee \left(\frac{c\lambda}{1-\beta} \right)^{\frac{1}{1-\gamma}}.$$

To understand the sharpness of Theorem 3, we have to compare this result to the one coming from the traditional (PAC-Bayesian) statistical learning approach which relies on supremum of empirical processes.

Theorem 4. *We still use $V(g,g') = \mathbb{E}_{\mathbb{P}(dZ)} \{ [L(Z,g) - L(Z,g')]^2 \}$. The generalization error of the algorithm which draws its prediction function according to the Gibbs distribution $\pi_{-\lambda \Sigma_n}$ satisfies*

$$\mathbb{E}_{\mathbb{P}(dZ_1^n)} \mathbb{E}_{\pi_{-\lambda \Sigma_n}(dg')} R(g')$$
$$\leq \min_{\rho \in \mathcal{M}} \left\{ \mathbb{E}_{\rho(dg)} R(g) + \frac{K(\rho,\pi)+1}{\lambda n} + \lambda \mathbb{E}_{\rho(dg)} \mathbb{E}_{\mathbb{P}(dZ_1^n)} \mathbb{E}_{\pi_{-\lambda \Sigma_n}(dg')} V(g,g') \right. \quad (15)$$
$$\left. + \lambda \frac{1}{n} \sum_{i=1}^n \mathbb{E}_{\rho(dg)} \mathbb{E}_{\mathbb{P}(dZ_1^n)} \mathbb{E}_{\pi_{-\lambda \Sigma_n}(dg')} [L(Z_i,g) - L(Z_i,g')]^2 \right\}.$$

Let φ be the positive convex increasing function defined as $\varphi(t) \triangleq \frac{e^t - 1 - t}{t^2}$ and $\varphi(0) = \frac{1}{2}$ by continuity. When $\sup_{g \in \mathcal{G}, g' \in \mathcal{G}} |L(Z,g') - L(Z,g)| \leq B$, we also have

$$\mathbb{E}_{\mathbb{P}(dZ_1^n)} \mathbb{E}_{\pi_{-\lambda \Sigma_n}(dg')} R(g') \leq \min_{\rho \in \mathcal{M}} \left\{ \mathbb{E}_{\rho(dg)} R(g) \right.$$
$$\left. + \lambda \varphi(\lambda B) \mathbb{E}_{\rho(dg)} \mathbb{E}_{\mathbb{P}(dZ_1^n)} \mathbb{E}_{\pi_{-\lambda \Sigma_n}(dg')} V(g,g') + \frac{K(\rho,\pi)+1}{\lambda n} \right\}. \quad (16)$$

Proof. Let us prove (16). Let $r(g)$ denote the empirical risk of $g \in \mathcal{G}$, that is $r(g) = \frac{\Sigma_n(g)}{n}$. Let $\rho \in \mathcal{M}$ be some fixed distribution on $\mathcal{G}$. From [3, Section 8.1], with probability at least $1 - \epsilon$, for any $\mu \in \mathcal{M}$, we have

$$\mathbb{E}_{\mu(dg')} R(g') - \mathbb{E}_{\rho(dg)} R(g)$$
$$\leq \mathbb{E}_{\mu(dg')} r(g') - \mathbb{E}_{\rho(dg)} r(g)$$
$$+ \lambda \varphi(\lambda B) \mathbb{E}_{\mu(dg')} \mathbb{E}_{\rho(dg)} V(g,g') + \frac{K(\mu,\pi) + \log(\epsilon^{-1})}{\lambda n}.$$

Since $\pi_{-\lambda \Sigma_n}$ minimizes $\mu \mapsto \mathbb{E}_{\mu(dg')} r(g') + \frac{K(\mu,\pi)}{\lambda n}$, we have

$$\mathbb{E}_{\pi_{-\lambda \Sigma_n}(dg')} R(g')$$
$$\leq \mathbb{E}_{\rho(dg)} R(g) + \lambda \varphi(\lambda B) \mathbb{E}_{\pi_{-\lambda \Sigma_n}(dg')} \mathbb{E}_{\rho(dg)} V(g,g') + \frac{K(\rho,\pi) + \log(\epsilon^{-1})}{\lambda n}.$$

Then we apply the following inequality: for any random variable W, $\mathbb{E}W \leq \mathbb{E}(W \vee 0) = \int_0^{+\infty} \mathbb{P}(W \geq u) du = \int_0^1 \epsilon^{-1} \mathbb{P}(W \geq \log(\epsilon^{-1})) d\epsilon$. At last we may choose the distribution ρ minimizing the upper bound to obtain (16). Similarly using [3, Section 8.3], we may prove (15).

Remark 2. By comparing (16) and (13), we see that the classical approach requires the quantity $\sup_{g\in\mathcal{G},g'\in\mathcal{G}}|L(Z,g')-L(Z,g)|$ to be bounded and the unpleasing function φ appears. In fact, using technical small expectations theorems (see [2, Lemma 7.1]), exponential moments conditions on the above quantity would be sufficient.

The symmetrization trick used to prove Theorem 3 is performed in the prediction functions space. We do not call on the second virtual training set currently used in statistical learning theory (see [19]). Nevertheless both symmetrization tricks end up to the same nice property: we need no boundedness assumption on the loss functions. In our setting, symmetrization on training data leads to an unwanted expectation and to a constant four times larger (see the two variance terms of (15) and the discussion in [3, Section 8.3.3]). In particular, deducing from Theorem 4 a corollary similar to Corollary 3 is only possible through (16), because of the last variance term in (15) (since Σ_n depends on Z_i).

7 Application to Least Square Regression

This section shows that Theorem 1 used jointly with the symmetrization idea developed in the previous section allows to obtain improved convergence rates in heavy noise situation. We start with the following theorem concerning twice differentiable convex loss functions.

Theorem 5. *Let $B \geq b > 0$. Consider a loss function L which can be written as $L[(x,y),g] = l[y,g(x)]$, where the function $l : \mathcal{Y} \times \mathcal{Y} \to \mathbb{R}$ is twice differentiable and convex w.r.t. the second variable. Let l' and l'' denote respectively the first and second derivative of the function l w.r.t. the second variable. Let*
$$\Delta(y) = \sup_{|\alpha|\leq b,|\beta|\leq b} \left[l(y,\alpha)-l(y,\beta)\right]. \text{ Assume that } \lambda_0 \triangleq \inf_{|y|\leq B,|y'|\leq b} \frac{l''(y,y')}{[l'(y,y')]^2} > 0$$
and that $\sup_{g\in\mathcal{G},x\in\mathcal{X}}|g(x)| \leq b$.

For any $0 < \lambda \leq \lambda_0$, the algorithm which draws uniformly its prediction function among $\mathbb{E}_{\pi_{-\lambda\Sigma_0}(dg)}g,\dots,\mathbb{E}_{\pi_{-\lambda\Sigma_n}(dg)}g$ satisfies
$$\mathcal{E} \leq \min_{\rho\in\mathcal{M}} \left\{\mathbb{E}_{\rho(dg)}R(g) + \frac{K(\rho,\pi)}{\lambda(n+1)}\right\}$$
$$+\mathbb{E}\left\{\frac{\lambda\Delta^2(Y)}{2}\mathbf{1}_{\lambda\Delta(Y)<1;|Y|>B} + \left[\Delta(Y) - \frac{1}{2\lambda}\right]\mathbf{1}_{\lambda\Delta(Y)\geq 1;|Y|>B}\right\}.$$

Proof. According to Theorem 1, it suffices to check that condition (3) holds for $0 < \lambda \leq \lambda_0$, $\hat{\pi}(\rho)$ the Dirac distribution at $\mathbb{E}_{\rho(dg)}g$ and
$$\delta_\lambda[(x,y),g,g'] = \delta_\lambda(y) \triangleq \min_{0\leq\zeta\leq 1} \left[\zeta\Delta(y) + \frac{(1-\zeta)^2\lambda\Delta^2(y)}{2}\right]\mathbf{1}_{|y|>B}$$
$$= \frac{\lambda\Delta^2(y)}{2}\mathbf{1}_{\lambda\Delta(y)<1;|y|>B} + \left[\Delta(y) - \frac{1}{2\lambda}\right]\mathbf{1}_{\lambda\Delta(y)\geq 1;|y|>B}.$$

– For any $z = (x,y) \in \mathcal{Z}$ such that $|y| \leq B$, for any probability distribution ρ and for the above values of λ and δ_λ, we have
$$\mathbb{E}_{\rho(dg)}e^{\lambda[L(z,\mathbb{E}_{\rho(dg')}g')-L(z,g)-\delta_\lambda(z,g,g')]}$$
$$= e^{\lambda L(z,\mathbb{E}_{\rho(dg')}g')}\mathbb{E}_{\rho(dg)}e^{-\lambda l[y,g(x)]}$$
$$\leq e^{\lambda l[y,\mathbb{E}_{\rho(dg')}g'(x)]-\lambda l[y,\mathbb{E}_{\rho(dg)}g(x)]} = 1,$$

where the inequality comes from the concavity of $y' \mapsto e^{-\lambda l(y,y')}$ for $\lambda \leq \lambda_0$. This concavity argument goes back to [17, Section 4], and was also used in [7] and in some of the examples given in [16].

– For any $z = (x,y) \in \mathcal{Z}$ such that $|y| > B$, for any $0 \leq \zeta \leq 1$, by using twice Jensen's inequality and then by using the symmetrization trick presented in Section 6, we have

$$
\begin{aligned}
&\mathbb{E}_{\rho(dg)} e^{\lambda[L(z,\mathbb{E}_{\rho(dg')}g') - L(z,g) - \delta_\lambda(z,g,g')]} \\
&= e^{-\delta_\lambda(y)} \mathbb{E}_{\rho(dg)} e^{\lambda[L(z,\mathbb{E}_{\rho(dg')}g') - L(z,g)]} \\
&\leq e^{-\delta_\lambda(y)} \mathbb{E}_{\rho(dg)} e^{\lambda[\mathbb{E}_{\rho(dg')}L(z,g') - L(z,g)]} \\
&\leq e^{-\delta_\lambda(y)} \mathbb{E}_{\rho(dg)} \mathbb{E}_{\rho(dg')} e^{\lambda[L(z,g') - L(z,g)]} \\
&= e^{-\delta_\lambda(y)} \mathbb{E}_{\rho(dg)} \mathbb{E}_{\rho(dg')} \exp\Big\{ \lambda(1-\zeta)[L(z,g') - L(z,g)] \\
&\qquad -\tfrac{1}{2}\lambda^2(1-\zeta)^2[L(z,g') - L(z,g)]^2 \\
&\qquad +\lambda\zeta[L(z,g') - L(z,g)] + \tfrac{1}{2}\lambda^2(1-\zeta)^2[L(z,g') - L(z,g)]^2 \Big\} \\
&\leq e^{-\delta_\lambda(y)} \mathbb{E}_{\rho(dg)} \mathbb{E}_{\rho(dg')} \exp\Big\{ \lambda(1-\zeta)[L(z,g') - L(z,g)] \\
&\qquad -\tfrac{1}{2}\lambda^2(1-\zeta)^2[L(z,g') - L(z,g)]^2 + \lambda\zeta\Delta(y) + \tfrac{1}{2}\lambda^2(1-\zeta)^2\Delta^2(y) \Big\} \\
&\leq e^{-\delta_\lambda(y)} e^{\lambda\zeta\Delta(y) + \frac{1}{2}\lambda^2(1-\zeta)^2\Delta^2(y)}
\end{aligned}
$$

Taking $\zeta \in [0;1]$ minimizing the last r.h.s., we obtain that

$$
\mathbb{E}_{\rho(dg)} e^{\lambda[L(z,\mathbb{E}_{\rho(dg')}g') - L(z,g) - \delta_\lambda(z,g,g')]} \leq 1
$$

From the two previous computations, we obtain that for any $z \in \mathcal{Z}$,

$$
\log \mathbb{E}_{\rho(dg)} e^{\lambda[L(z,\mathbb{E}_{\rho(dg')}g') - L(z,g) - \delta_\lambda(z,g,g')]} \leq 0,
$$

so that condition (3) holds for the above values of λ, $\hat{\pi}(\rho)$ and δ_λ, and the result follows from Theorem 1.

In particular, for least square regression, Theorem 5 can be stated as:

Theorem 6. *Assume that* $\sup_{g \in \mathcal{G}, x \in \mathcal{X}} |g(x)| \leq b$ *for some* $b > 0$. *For any* $0 < \lambda \leq 1/(8b^2)$, *the algorithm which draws uniformly its prediction function among* $\mathbb{E}_{\pi-\lambda\Sigma_0}(dg)g, \ldots, \mathbb{E}_{\pi-\lambda\Sigma_n}(dg)g$ *satisfies:*

$$
\begin{aligned}
\mathcal{E} \leq \min_{\rho \in \mathcal{M}} \Big\{ \mathbb{E}_{\rho(dg)} R(g) + \tfrac{K(\rho,\pi)}{\lambda(n+1)} \Big\} &+ \mathbb{E}\Big\{ \big(4b|Y| - \tfrac{1}{2\lambda}\big) \mathbf{1}_{|Y| \geq (4b\lambda)^{-1}} \Big\} \\
&+ \mathbb{E}\Big\{ 8\lambda b^2 |Y|^2 \mathbf{1}_{(2\lambda)^{-1/2} - b < |Y| < (4b\lambda)^{-1}} \Big\}.
\end{aligned} \tag{17}
$$

Proof. The result follows from Theorem 5, computations of $\lambda_0 = \frac{1}{2(B+b)^2}$ and $\Delta(y) = 4b|y|$, and from the optimization of the parameter B.

Theorem 6 improves [16, Corollary 4.1] and [7, Theorem 1]. From it, we can deduce the following improvement of [16, Corollary 4.2].

Corollary 4. *Under the assumptions*

$$\begin{cases} \sup_{g \in \mathcal{G}, x \in \mathcal{X}} |g(x)| \leq b & \text{for some } b > 0 \\ \mathbb{E}|Y|^s \leq A & \text{for some } s \geq 2 \text{ and } A > 0 \\ \mathcal{G} \text{ finite} \end{cases}$$

for $\lambda = C_1 \left(\frac{\log |\mathcal{G}|}{n}\right)^{2/(s+2)}$ *where* $C_1 > 0$, *the algorithm which draws uniformly its prediction function among* $\mathbb{E}_{\pi_{-\lambda \Sigma_0}(dg)} g, \ldots, \mathbb{E}_{\pi_{-\lambda \Sigma_n}(dg)} g$ *satisfies*

$$\mathcal{E} \leq \min_{g \in \mathcal{G}} R(g) + C \left(\frac{\log |\mathcal{G}|}{n}\right)^{s/(s+2)} \tag{18}$$

for a quantity C *which depends only on* C_1, b, A *and* s.

Proof. The moment assumption on Y implies $\alpha^{s-q} \mathbb{E}|Y|^q \mathbf{1}_{|Y| \geq \alpha} \leq A$ for any $0 \leq q \leq s$ and $\alpha \geq 0$. As a consequence, the second and third term of the r.h.s. of (17) are respectively bounded with $4bA(4b\lambda)^{s-1}$ and $8\lambda b^2 A(2\lambda)^{(s-2)/2}$, so that (17) can be weakened into $\mathcal{E} \leq \min_{g \in \mathcal{G}} R(g) + \frac{\log |\mathcal{G}|}{\lambda n} + C'\lambda^{s-1} + C''\lambda^{s/2}$ for $C' = A(4b)^s$ and $C'' = A2^{2+s/2} b^2$. This gives the desired result.

In particular, with the minimal assumption $\mathbb{E}|Y|^2 \leq A$ (i.e. $s = 2$), the convergence rate is of order $n^{-1/2}$, and at the opposite, when s goes to infinity, we recover the n^{-1} rate we have under exponential moment condition on the output.

8   Conclusion and Open Problems

A learning task can be defined by a set of reference prediction functions and a set of probability distributions in which we assume that the distribution generating the data is. In this work, we propose to summarize this learning problem by the variance function of the key condition (3). We have proved that our generic algorithm based on this variance function leads to optimal rates of convergence on the model selection aggregation problem, and that it gives a nice unified view to results coming from different communities. Our results concern expected risks and it is an open problem to provide corresponding tight exponential inequalities.

Besides without any assumption on the learning task, we proved a Bernstein's type bound which has no known equivalent form when the loss function is not assumed to be bounded. Nevertheless much work still has to be done to propose algorithms having better generalization error bounds that the ones based on supremum of empirical processes. For instance, in several learning tasks, Dudley's chaining trick [14] is the only way to prove risk convergence with the optimal rate. So a natural question and another open problem is whether it is possible to combine the better variance control presented here with the chaining argument (or other localization argument used while exponential inequalities are available).

Acknowledgement. I would like to thank Nicolas Vayatis, Alexandre Tsybakov, Gilles Stoltz and the referees for their very helpful comments.

406   J.-Y. Audibert

References

1. P. Alquier. Iterative feature selection in least square regression estimation. 2005. Laboratoire de Probabilités et Modèles Aléatoires, Universités Paris 6 and Paris 7.
2. J.-Y. Audibert. Aggregated estimators and empirical complexity for least square regression. *Ann. Inst. Henri Poincaré, Probab. Stat.*, 40(6):685–736, 2004.
3. J.-Y. Audibert. A better variance control for PAC-Bayesian classification. Preprint n.905, http://www.proba.jussieu.fr/mathdoc/preprints/index.html, 2004. Laboratoire de Probabilités et Modèles Aléatoires, Universités Paris 6 and Paris 7.
4. J.-Y. Audibert. *PAC-Bayesian statistical learning theory*. PhD thesis, Laboratoire de Probabilités et Modèles Aléatoires, Universités Paris 6 and Paris 7, 2004.
5. A. Barron. Are bayes rules consistent in information? In T.M. Cover and B. Gopinath, editors, *Open Problems in Communication and Computation*, pages 85–91. Springer, 1987.
6. A. Barron and Y. Yang. Information-theoretic determination of minimax rates of convergence. *Ann. Stat.*, 27(5):1564–1599, 1999.
7. F. Bunea and A. Nobel. Sequential procedures for aggregating arbitrary estimators of a conditional mean, 2005. Technical report, Available from http://stat.fsu.edu/%7Eflori/ps/bnapril2005IEEE.pdf.
8. O. Catoni. *Statistical Learning Theory and Stochastic Optimization: Ecole d'été de Probabilités de Saint-Flour XXXI - 2001*. Lecture Notes in Mathematics. Springer Verlag.
9. O. Catoni. A mixture approach to universal model selection. preprint LMENS 97-30, Available from http://www.dma.ens.fr/edition/preprints/Index.97.html, 1997.
10. O. Catoni. Universal aggregation rules with exact bias bound. Preprint n.510, http://www.proba.jussieu.fr/mathdoc/preprints/index.html#1999, 1999.
11. O. Catoni. A PAC-Bayesian approach to adaptive classification. Preprint n.840, Laboratoire de Probabilités et Modèles Aléatoires, Universités Paris 6 and Paris 7, 2003.
12. N. Cesa-Bianchi, Y. Freund, D. Haussler, D.P. Helmbold, R.E. Schapire, and M.K. Warmuth. How to use expert advice. *J. ACM*, 44(3):427–485, 1997.
13. N. Cesa-Bianchi and G. Lugosi. On prediction of individual sequences. *Ann. Stat.*, 27(6):1865–1895, 1999.
14. R.M. Dudley. Central limit theorems for empirical measures. *Ann. Probab.*, 6:899–929, 1978.
15. D. Haussler, J. Kivinen, and M. K. Warmuth. Sequential prediction of individual sequences under general loss functions. *IEEE Trans. on Information Theory*, 44(5):1906–1925, 1998.
16. A. Juditsky, P. Rigollet, and A.B. Tsybakov. Learning by mirror averaging, 2005. Available from arxiv website.
17. J. Kivinen and M. K. Warmuth. Averaging expert predictions. *Lecture Notes in Computer Science*, 1572:153–167, 1999.
18. Merhav and Feder. Universal prediction. *IEEE Transactions on Information Theory*, 44, 1998.
19. V. Vapnik. *The nature of statistical learning theory*. Springer-Verlag, second edition, 1995.
20. V.G. Vovk. Aggregating strategies. In *COLT '90: Proceedings of the third annual workshop on Computational learning theory*, pages 371–386, San Francisco, CA, USA, 1990. Morgan Kaufmann Publishers Inc.

21. V.G. Vovk. A game of prediction with expert advice. *Journal of Computer and System Sciences*, pages 153–173, 1998.
22. Y. Yang. Combining different procedures for adaptive regression. *Journal of multivariate analysis*, 74:135–161, 2000.
23. R. Yaroshinsky, R. El-Yaniv, and S.S. Seiden. How to better use expert advice. *Mach. Learn.*, 55(3):271–309, 2004.
24. T. Zhang. Information theoretical upper and lower bounds for statistical estimation. *IEEE Transaction on Information Theory*, 2006. to appear.

Online Learning with Variable Stage Duration

Shie Mannor[1] and Nahum Shimkin[2]

[1] Department of Electrical and Computer Engingeering
McGill University, Québec H3A-2A7
shie@ece.mcgill.ca
[2] Department of Electrical Engineering
Technion, Israel Institute of Technology
Haifa 32000, Israel
shimkin@ee.technion.ac.il

Abstract. We consider online learning in repeated decision problems, within the framework of a repeated game against an arbitrary opponent. For repeated matrix games, well known results establish the existence of no-regret strategies; such strategies secure a long-term average payoff that comes close to the maximal payoff that could be obtained, in hindsight, by playing any fixed action against the observed actions of the opponent. In the present paper we consider the extended model where the duration of each stage of the game may depend on the actions of both players, while the performance measure of interest is the average payoff per unit time. We start the analysis of online learning in repeated games with variable stage duration by showing that no-regret strategies, in the above sense, do not exist in general. Consequently, we consider two classes of adaptive strategies, one based on Blackwell's approachability theorem and the other on calibrated forecasts, and examine their performance guarantees. In either case we show that the long-term average payoff is higher than a certain function of the empirical distribution of the opponent's actions, and in particular is strictly higher than the minimax value of the repeated game whenever that empirical distribution deviates from a minimax strategy in the stage game.

1 Introduction

Consider a repeated game from the viewpoint of a specific player, say player 1, who faces an arbitrary opponent, say player 2. The opponent is arbitrary in the sense that player 1 has no prediction, statistical or strategic, regarding the opponent's choice of actions. Such an opponent can represent the combined effect of several other players, as well as arbitrary-varying elements of Nature's state. The questions that arise naturally are how should player 1 act in this situation, and what performance guarantees can he secure against an arbitrary opponent.

This problem was considered by [12], in the context of repeated matrix games. Hannan introduced the Bayes envelope against the current (n-stage) empirical distribution of the opponent's actions as a performance goal for adaptive play. This quantity coincides with the highest average payoff that player 1 could

G. Lugosi and H.U. Simon (Eds.): COLT 2006, LNAI 4005, pp. 408–422, 2006.

achieve, in hindsight, by playing some fixed action against the observed action sequence of player 2. Player 1's *regret* can now be defined as the difference between the above Bayes utility and the actual n-stage average payoff obtained by player 1. Hannan established the existence of *no-regret strategies* for player 1, that guarantee non-positive regret in the long run. More precisely, an explicit strategy was presented for which the n-stage regret is (almost surely) bounded by an $O(n^{-1/2})$ term, without requiring any prior knowledge on player 2's strategy or the number of stages n.

Hannan's seminal work was continued in various directions. No-regret strategies in the above sense have been termed regret minimizing, Hannan consistent, and universally consistent. The original strategy proposed in [12] is essentially perturbed fictitious play, namely playing best-response to the current empirical distribution of player 2, to which a random perturbation is added. Subsequent works developed no-regret strategies that rely on Blackwell's approachability theory ([3]), smooth fictitious play ([10]), calibrated forecasts ([6]), and multiplicative weights ([9]) among others. We refer the reader to [5] for a discussion and an extensive literature review.

The model we consider in this paper extends the standard repeated matrix game model by associating with each stage of the game a temporal duration, which may depend on the actions chosen by both players at the beginning of that stage. Moreover, the performance measure of interest to player 1 is the average reward *per unit time* (rather than the per-stage average). We refer to this model as a *repeated variable-duration game*. The interest in this model is quite natural, as many basic games and related decision problems do have variable length: One can start, for example, with board games like Chess (where the game duration can be taken as the number of moves or the actual time played), and continue with gambling (where different options can take a different time per round), investment options, and choosing between projects or treatments with different durations. The proposed model is then the relevant one provided that the player's interest is indeed in the average reward per unit time, rather than the average reward per stage.

Our purpose then is to examine decision strategies and performance goals that are suitable for adaptive play against a arbitrary opponent in repeated variable-duration games. While this model may be viewed as the simplest non-trivial extension of standard repeated games, it turns out that a direct extension of Hannan's no-regret framework is impossible in general. We start by formulating a natural extension of Hannan's empirical Bayes utility to the present model, to which we refer as the empirical best-response envelope. This average payoff level is attainable when the stage duration depends only on player 2's action. However, a simple counter-example shows that it cannot be attained in general. Hence, in the rest of the paper we turn our attention to weaker performance goals that are attainable. This will be done using two of the basic tools that have previously been used for regret minimization in repeated matrix games, namely Blackwell's approachability theorem and calibrated play.

The paper is organized as follows. Our repeated game model is presented in Section 2, together with some preliminary properties. Section 3 defines the empirical Bayes envelope for this model, gives an example for a game in which this envelope is not attainable, and presents some more general conditions under which the same conclusion holds. Given this negative result, we look for strategies that offer some reasonable performance guarantees. In Section 4 we consider a strategy based on approachability. By applying a convexification procedure to the Bayes envelope, we exhibit a weaker performance goal, the convex Bayes envelope, which is indeed attainable. This strategy is reminiscent to our previously developed strategy in [15] for stochastic game and is provided here for reference; Section 4 can therefore be skipped by readers who are familiar with [15]. In Section 5 we introduce our main solution concept, calibrated play and its associated performance guarantees. Section 6 briefly offers directions for further study. Some of the proofs are omitted and appear in [16].

2   Model Formulation

We consider two players, player 1 (P1) and player 2 (P2), who repeatedly play a *variable-duration matrix game*. Let I and J denote the finite action sets of P1 and P2, respectively. The stage game is specified by a reward function $r : I \times J \to \mathbb{R}$ and a strictly positive duration function $\tau : I \times J \to (0, \infty)$. Thus, $r(i, j)$ denotes the reward corresponding to the action pair (i, j), and $\tau(i, j) > 0$ is the duration of the stage game. Let $\Gamma(r, \tau)$ denote this single-stage game model. We note that the reward function r is associated with P1 alone, while P2 is considered an arbitrary player whose utility and goals need not be specified.

The repeated game proceeds as follows. At the beginning of each stage k, where $k = 1, 2, \dots$, P1 chooses an action i_k and P2 simultaneously chooses an action j_k. Consequently P1 obtains a reward $r_k = r(i_k, j_k)$, and the current stage proceeds for $\tau_k = \tau(i_k, j_k)$ time units, after which the next stage begins. The average reward *per unit time* over the first n stages of play is thus given by

$$\rho_n = \frac{\sum_{k=1}^{n} r_k}{\sum_{k=1}^{n} \tau_k}. \tag{1}$$

We shall refer to ρ_n as the *(n-stage) reward-rate*. It will also be convenient to define the following per-stage averages:

$$\hat{r}_n = \frac{1}{n} \sum_{k=1}^{n} r_k, \qquad \hat{\tau}_n = \frac{1}{n} \sum_{k=1}^{n} \tau_k$$

so that $\rho_n = \hat{r}_n / \hat{\tau}_n$. The beginning of stage k will be called the k-th decision epoch or k-th decision point.

We will consider the game from the viewpoint of P1, who seeks to maximize his long-term reward rate. P2 is an *arbitrary player* whose goals are not specified, and whose strategy is not a-priori known to P1. We assume that both players can observe and recall all past actions, and that the game parameters (r and τ) are known to P1. Thus, a strategy σ^1 of P1 is a mapping $\sigma^1 : H \to \Delta(I)$, where H is the set of all possible history sequences of the form $h_k = (i_1, j_1, \ldots, i_k, j_k)$, $k \geq 0$ (with h_0 the empty sequence), and $\Delta(I)$ denotes the set of probability measures over I. P1's action i_k is thus chosen randomly according to the probability measure $x_k = \sigma(h_{k-1})$. A strategy of P1 is *stationary* if $\sigma^1 \equiv x \in \Delta(I)$, and is then denoted by $(x)^\infty$. A strategy σ^2 of P2 is similarly defined as a mapping from H to $\Delta(J)$. We denote this repeated game model by $\Gamma^\infty \equiv \Gamma^\infty(r, \tau)$.

We next establish some additional notations and terminology. It will be convenient to denote $\Delta(I)$ by X and $\Delta(J)$ by Y. An element $x \in X$ is a *mixed action* of P1, and similarly $y \in Y$ is a mixed action of P2. We shall use the bilinear extension of r and τ to mixed actions, namely $r(i, y) = \sum_j r(i, j) y_j$, and $r(x, y) = \sum_{i,j} x_i r(i, j) y_j$, and similarly for τ.

The *reward-rate* function $\rho : X \times Y \to \mathbb{R}$ is defined as

$$\rho(x, y) \triangleq \frac{r(x, y)}{\tau(x, y)} = \frac{\sum_{i,j} x_i r(i, j) y_j}{\sum_{i,j} x_i \tau(i, j) y_j}. \tag{2}$$

This function plays a central role in the following. It is easily seen (using the strong law of large numbers and the renewal theorem) that for any pair of stationary strategies $\sigma^1 = (x)^\infty$ and $\sigma^2 = (y)^\infty$ we have

$$\lim_{n \to \infty} \rho_n = \rho(x, y) \quad (a.s.) \tag{3}$$

$$\lim_{n \to \infty} \mathbb{E}(\rho_n) = \rho(x, y). \tag{4}$$

The *a.s.* qualifier indicates that the respective event holds with probability one under the probability measure induced by the players' respective strategies.

We further define an auxiliary (single-stage) game $\Gamma_0(r, \tau)$ as the zero-sum game with actions sets X for P1 and Y for P2, and payoff function $\rho(x, y)$ for P1. Note that ρ as defined by (2) is *not* bilinear in its arguments. We next establish that this game has a value, which we denote by $v(r, \tau)$, as well as some additional properties of the reward-rate function ρ.

Lemma 1 (Basic properties of ρ).

(i) $v(r, \tau) \triangleq \max_{x \in X} \min_{y \in Y} \rho(x, y) = \min_{y \in Y} \max_{x \in X} \rho(x, y)$.

(ii) Let X^* denote the set of optimal mixed actions for P1 in $\Gamma_0(r, \tau)$, namely the maximizing set in the max-min expression above, and similarly let Y^* be the minimizing set in the min-max expression. Then X^* and Y^* are closed convex sets.

(iii) For every fixed y, $\rho(\cdot, y)$ is maximized in pure actions, namely

$$\max_{x \in X} \rho(x, y) = \max_{i \in I} \rho(i, y).$$

(iv) The best-response payoff function $\rho^*(y) \triangleq \max_{x \in X} \rho(x, y)$ is Lipschitz continuous in y.

Proof. The stated results may be deduced from known ones for semi-Markov games; see [14]. For completeness, a proof can be found in [16]. □

3   No-Regret Strategies and the Best-Response Envelope

In this section we define the empirical best-response envelope as a natural extension of the corresponding concept for fixed duration games. P1's regret is defined as the difference between this envelope and the actual reward-rate, and no-regret strategies must ensure that this difference becomes small (or negative) in the long run. We first observe that no-regret strategies indeed exist when the duration of the stage game depends only on P2's action (but not on P1's). However, the main result of this section is a negative one – namely that no-regret strategies need not exist in general. This is first shown in a specific example, and then shown to hold more generally under certain conditions on the game parameters.

Let $\hat{y}_n \in Y$ denote the empirical distribution of P2's actions up to stage n. That is, $\hat{y}_n(j) = \frac{1}{n} \sum_{k=1}^{n} 1\{j_k = j\}$, where $1\{C\}$ denotes the indicator function for a condition C. Clearly $\hat{y}_n \in Y$. The *best-response envelope* (or Bayes envelope) of P1, $\rho^* : Y \to \mathbb{R}$, is defined by

$$\rho^*(y) \overset{\triangle}{=} \max_{i \in I} \frac{r(i,y)}{\tau(i,y)} = \max_{i \in I} \rho(i,y). \tag{5}$$

Observe that $\rho^*(y)$ maximizes $\rho(x,y)$ over mixed actions as well, namely

$$\rho^*(y) = \max_{x \in X} \frac{r(x,y)}{\tau(x,y)} = \max_{x \in X} \rho(x,y), \tag{6}$$

as per Lemma 1(iii).

We consider the difference $\rho^*(\hat{y}_n) - \rho_n$ as P1's n-stage *regret*. This may be interpreted as P1's payoff loss for not playing his best action against $\hat{y}_n$ over the first n stages. This leads us to the following definition.

Definition 1 (No-regret strategies). *A strategy σ^1 of P1 is a no-regret strategy if, for every strategy of P2,*

$$\liminf_{n \to \infty} (\rho_n - \rho^*(\hat{y}_n)) \geq 0 \quad (a.s.). \tag{7}$$

A no-regret strategy of P1 is said to *attain* the best-response envelope. If such a strategy exists we say that the best-response envelope ρ^* is *attainable* by P1.

The following observations provide the motivation for our regret definitions.

Lemma 2. *Suppose that P2 uses a fixed sequence of actions $(j_1, \ldots, j_n)$, with corresponding empirical distribution $\hat{y}_n$. Then $\rho^*(\hat{y}_n)$ is the maximal reward-rate ρ_n that P1 could obtain by playing any fixed action $i \in I$ over the first n stages.*

Proof. With $i_k \equiv i$ we obtain, by (1), $\rho_n = \frac{\sum_{k=1}^{n} r(i,j_k)}{\sum_{k=1}^{n} \tau(i,j_k)} = \frac{r(i,\hat{y}_n)}{\tau(i,\hat{y}_n)} = \rho(i,\hat{y}_n)$. The required conclusion follows by definition of ρ^*.   □

The last lemma indicates that ρ^* is indeed the natural extension of Hannan's best-response envelope. The Lemma implies that $\rho^*(\hat{y}_n)$ is the best reward-rate that P1 could achieve by using any fixed action given the empirical distribution $\hat{y}_n$ of P2's actions. Thus, the difference $\rho^*(\hat{y}_n) - \rho_n$ can be interpreted as P1's *regret* for not using that action throughout.

A particular case where the best-response envelope is attainable is when P1's actions do not affect the duration of the stage game. This includes the standard model with fixed stage durations.

Proposition 1. *Suppose that the stage duration depends on P2's actions only, namely $\tau(i,j) = \tau(j)$ for every action pair. Then the best-response envelope is attainable by P1.*

Proof. Since $\tau(i_k, j_k) = \tau(j_k)$, we obtain $\rho_n = \frac{\sum_{k=1}^{n} r(i_k, j_k)}{\sum_{k=1}^{n} \tau(j_k)} = \frac{\hat{r}_n}{\tau(\hat{y}_n)}$, where $\tau(\hat{y}_n) = \frac{1}{n} \sum_{k=1}^{n} \tau(j_k)$. Similarly, $\rho^*(\hat{y}_n) = \max_i (r(i, \hat{y}_n)/\tau(\hat{y}_n))$. By cancelling out the corresponding denominators it follows that the required inequality in the definition of a no-regret strategy reduces in this case to $\liminf_{n\to\infty} (\hat{r}_n - \max_i r(i, \hat{y}_n)) \geq 0$. This is just the standard definition for a repeated matrix game with fixed stage duration and reward function r, for which no-regret strategies are known to exist. $\square$

The situation becomes more intricate when the stage durations do depend on P1's actions, as demonstrated in the following example.

Example 1. **(A game with unattainable best-response envelope).** Consider the variable duration matrix game $\Gamma(r, \tau)$ defined by the following matrix:

$$\begin{pmatrix} (0,1) & (5,1) \\ (1,3) & (0,3) \end{pmatrix},$$

where P1 is the row player, P2 the column player, and the ij-th entry is $(r(i,j), \tau(i,j))$.

Proposition 2. *The best-response envelope is not attainable by P1 in the game $\Gamma^\infty(r, \tau)$ defined by Example 1.*

Proof. We will specify a strategy of P2 against which $\rho^*(y)$ cannot be attained by P1. Let N be some pre-specified integer. Consider first the following strategy for P2 over the first $2N$ stages:

$$j_n = \begin{cases} 1 \text{ for } 1 \leq n \leq N, \\ 2 \text{ for } N+1 \leq n \leq 2N. \end{cases} \tag{8}$$

We claim that for some $\epsilon_0 > 0$ and any strategy of P1, $\rho_k < \rho^*(\hat{y}_k) - \epsilon_0$ must hold either at $k = N$ or at $k = 2N$. To see that, let $\zeta_1 = \sum_1^N 1\{i_k = 1\}/N$ denote the empirical distribution of P1's action 1 over the first N stages. It is easily seen that $\rho_N = (1 - \zeta_1)/(3 - 2\zeta_1)$, and $\rho^*(\hat{y}_N) = 1/3$ (which is obtained by action 2 of P1). Thus, to obtain $\rho_N \geq \rho^*(\hat{y}_N) - \epsilon_0$ we need $\zeta_1 \leq (9\epsilon_0)/(2 + 3\epsilon_0) = O(\epsilon_0)$. Next, at $k = 2N$ we have $y_{2N} = (0.5, 0.5)$ and $\rho^*(\hat{y}_{2N}) = \max\{5/2, 1/6\} = 5/2$, which is now obtained by action 1 of P1. To compute ρ_{2N}, let $\zeta_2 = \sum_{N+1}^{2N} 1\{i_k = 1\}/N$

denote the empirical distribution of P1's action 1 over the second N-stage period. Then maximizing ρ_{2N} over $\zeta_2 \in [0,1]$ by $\zeta_2 = 1$ we get that $\rho_{2N} = (6 - \zeta_1)/(4 - 2\zeta_1)$. A simple calculation now shows that to obtain $\rho_{2N} \geq \rho^*(\hat{y}_{2N}) - \epsilon_0$ we need $\zeta_1 \geq (2 - 2\epsilon_0)/(3 - 2\epsilon_0)$. It is evident that the requirements are contradictory for ϵ_0 small enough.

To recapitulate, the essence of the above argument is: to obtain ρ_N close to $\rho^*(\hat{y}_N)$ P1 must use action 1 during most of the first N stages. But then the most he can get for ρ_{2N} is about $3/2$, which falls short of $\rho^*(\hat{y}_{2N}) = 5/2$.

We conclude that P2's stated strategy forces P1 to have positive regret at the end of stage N or at the end of stage $2N$. P2 can repeat the same strategy with a new N' much larger than N, so that the first N stages have a negligible effect. This can be done repeatedly, so that P1 has non-zero regret (larger than, say, $\epsilon_0/2$) infinitely often.   □

We close this section with a sufficient condition for *non-existence* of no-regret strategies. This condition essentially follows by similar reasoning to that of the last counterexample. We use $X^*(y)$ to denote the set of best response strategies against y. That is:

$$X^*(y) = \arg\max_{x \in X} \rho(x, y).$$

Proposition 3. *Suppose there exist* $y_1, y_2 \in Y$ *and* $\alpha \in (0,1)$ *such that:*

$$\rho^*(\alpha y_1 + (1 - \alpha)y_2) > \max_{x_1 \in X^*(y_1), \, x_2 \in X} \frac{\alpha r(x_1, y_1) + (1 - \alpha)r(x_2, y_2)}{\alpha \tau(x_1, y_1) + (1 - \alpha)\tau(x_2, y_2)}. \qquad (9)$$

Then the best-response envelope is not attainable by P1.

Proof. The proof of is similar to that of Proposition 2, and we only provide a brief outline. The strategy used by P2 over the first N stages (with N a large pre-specified number) is to play y_1 for αN stages (taking the integer part thereof) and play y_2 for the remaining $(1 - \alpha)N$ stages. We take N to be large enough so that stochastic fluctuations (due to possibly mixed actions) from the expected averages become insignificant. The empirical distribution of P1's actions at the end of the first period must then be close to some $x_1 \in X^*(y_1)$ to guarantee that ρ_n is close to $\rho^*(\hat{y}_n) \approx \rho^*(y_1)$ at $n = \alpha N$. However, Equation (9) implies then that at the end of stage N the reward rate ρ_N falls short of the best response $\rho^*(\hat{y}_N)$, no matter what actions P1 uses against y_2.   □

4   Approachability and Regret Minimization

The theory of approachability, introduced in [2], is one of the fundamental tools that have been used for obtaining no-regret strategies in repeated matrix games. The analysis in this section will allow us to specify a relaxed goal for adaptive play, the convex best-response envelope, which is always attainable, and provides some useful performance guarantees. This strategy can be thought of as a first attempt at deriving an adaptive strategy which will be shown to be dominated by the strategy considered in Section 5. Much of the analysis here is similar to our paper [15] and most proofs are therefore deferred to [16].

4.1   The Temporal Best-Response Envelope

Following [3, 15], we attempt to construct a vector-valued payoff vector $\boldsymbol{\rho}_n = (\rho_n, \hat{y}_n)$, so that attaining the best-response $\rho^*(y)$ is equivalent to approaching[1] the set

$$B_0 = \{(\rho, y) \in \mathbb{R} \times Y \, : \, \rho \geq \rho^*(y)\}.$$

However, two obstacles stand in the way of applying the approachability results. First, and foremost, ρ_n and $\hat{y}_n$ are normalized by different temporal factors. Second, B_0 need not be a convex set as the best-response envelope $\rho^*(y)$ is not convex in general, so that the simple condition for convex sets in Blackwell's original result which is exploited in [3, 15] cannot be used.

To address the first difficulty, we reformulate the approachability problem. Let π_n denote the vector of P2's *action rates*, namely

$$\pi_n = \frac{1}{\hat{\tau}_n} \hat{y}_n.$$

Note that $\pi_n(j)$ gives the temporal rate, in actions per unit time, in which action j was chosen over the first n stages. Obviously π_n is not a probability vector, as the sum of its elements is $1/\hat{\tau}_n$. The set of feasible action rates is given by

$$\Pi = \left\{ \frac{y}{\tau} \, : \, y \in Y, \, \tau \in T(y) \right\}, \qquad (10)$$

where $T(y)$ is the set of average stage durations τ which are feasible jointly with the empirical distribution y, that is, $T(y) = \left\{ \sum_j y(j)\tau(x^j, j) \, : \, x^j \in X \text{ for all } j \right\}$. Note that Π is a convex set; indeed, it is the image of the convex set $\{y, \tau : y \in Y, \, \tau \in T(y)\}$ under a linear-fractional function ([4]).

We proceed to formulate the set to be approached in terms of π instead of $\hat{y}$. Note first that the action rate vector π_n uniquely determines the empirical distribution vector $\hat{y}_n$ via $\hat{y}_n = \pi_n/|\pi_n|$, where $|\pi|$ is the sum of elements of π. Given P2's action-rate vector $\pi \in \Pi$, we define the best-response payoff for P1 as its best-response payoff against the empirical distribution $\hat{y} = \pi/|\pi|$ induced by π. That is, for $\pi \in \Pi$,

$$\tilde{\rho}^*(\pi) \triangleq \rho^* \left(\frac{\pi}{|\pi|} \right) = \max_{i \in I} \frac{\sum_j r(i,j)\pi(j)}{\sum_j \tau(i,j)\pi(j)}, \qquad (11)$$

where $|\pi|$ was cancelled out from the last expression. Thus, although defined on a different set, $\tilde{\rho}^*$ turns out to be identical in its functional form to ρ^*. We refer to $\tilde{\rho}^* : \Pi \to \mathbb{R}$ as the *temporal* best-response envelope.

Convexity of $\tilde{\rho}^*$ turns out to be a sufficient condition for existence of no-regret strategies. The proof is similar to [15] and is therefore omitted.

Theorem 1. *Suppose the temporal best-response envelope $\tilde{\rho}^*(\pi)$ is convex over its domain Π. Then P1 has a no-regret strategy (in the sense of Definition 1), namely, a strategy that attains the best-response envelope $\rho^*(\hat{y})$.*

---

[1] Formally, in approachability one has to define a vector-valued game and prove that the point-to-set distance between the average vector-valued reward and the target set goes to 0 almost surely. See [15] for an example of such analysis.

4.2   The Convex Best-Response Envelope

When $\tilde{\rho}^*$ is not convex, the preceding analysis provides no performance guarantees for P1. To proceed, we will need to relax the goal of attaining the best-response.

Definition 2 (Convex best-response envelope). *The convex best-response envelope $\tilde{\rho}^{co} : \Pi \to \mathbb{R}$ is defined as the lower convex hull of $\tilde{\rho}^*$ over its domain Π.*

We now have the following result. See [16] for a proof.

Theorem 2 ($\tilde{\rho}^{co}(\pi)$ is attainable). *The convex best-response envelope $\tilde{\rho}^{co}(\pi)$ is attainable by P1. Namely, there exists a strategy of P1 so that*

$$\liminf_{n \to \infty} (\rho_n - \tilde{\rho}^{co}(\pi_n)) \geq 0 \quad (a.s.) \tag{12}$$

for any strategy of P2.

It will be useful to formulate the performance guarantee of the last proposition in terms of the empirical distribution $\hat{y}_n$ rather than the action rates π_n. This is easily done by projecting $\tilde{\rho}^{co}$ from Π back to Y. For $\hat{y} \in Y$, define

$$\rho^{co}(\hat{y}) = \min\{\tilde{\rho}^{co}(\pi) \,:\, \pi \in \Pi, \frac{\pi}{|\pi|} = \hat{y}\}. \tag{13}$$

For simplicity we also refer to ρ^{co} as the convex best-response envelope (over Y). The following corollary to Theorem 2 is immediate.

Corollary 1 ($\rho^{co}(\hat{y})$ is attainable). *The convex best-response envelope $\rho^{co}(\hat{y})$ is attainable by P1. Namely, there exists a strategy of P1 so that*

$$\liminf_{n \to \infty} (\rho_n - \rho^{co}(\hat{y}_n)) \geq 0 \quad (a.s.). \tag{14}$$

In fact, any strategy of P1 that attains $\tilde{\rho}^{co}(\pi)$ also attains $\rho^{co}(\hat{y})$.

Figure 1 illustrates the resulting convex best-response envelope for the game of Example 1. As ρ^* is not attainable in this example, it is clear that ρ^{co} must be strictly smaller than ρ^* for some values of y, as is indeed the case.

The next lemma presents some general properties of ρ^{co} that will be related to its performance guarantees.

Lemma 3 (Properties of ρ^{co}). *The convex best-response envelope $\rho^{co}(y)$ satisfies the following properties. For each $y \in Y$,*

(i) $\mathrm{v}(r, \tau) \leq \rho^{co}(y) \leq \rho^*(y)$.
(ii) *If $\rho^*(y) > \mathrm{v}(r, \tau)$, then $\rho^{co}(y) > \mathrm{v}(r, \tau)$.*

Proof. (i) Fix y, and take any $\pi \in \Pi$ with $\pi/|\pi| = y$. Then $\rho^{co}(y) \leq \tilde{\rho}^{co}(\pi) \leq \tilde{\rho}^*(\pi) = \rho^*(y)$, where all inequalities follow directly from the definitions of the respective envelopes. Also, since $\rho^* \geq \mathrm{v}(r, \tau)$, the same property is inherited by $\tilde{\rho}^*$, $\tilde{\rho}^{co}$ and ρ^{co}, again by their respective definitions.

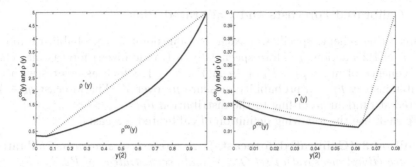

Fig. 1. $\rho^*(y)$ (dotted) and $\rho^{co}(y)$ (thick line) for the game of Example 1. The right figure zooms on the segment $[0, 0.08]$. Note that $v(r, \tau) = 5/16$ for that game.

(ii) We will show that $\rho^{co}(y) = v(r, \tau)$ implies that $\rho^{co}(y) = v(r, \tau)$. Suppose $\rho^{co}(y) = v(r, \tau)$. Then there exists some $\pi \in \Pi$ such that $\pi/|\pi| = y$ and $\tilde{\rho}^{co}(\pi) = v(r, \tau)$. By Caratheodory's Theorem there exist ℓ points $\pi_1, \ldots, \pi_\ell$ in Π (where $\ell \le 2 + |J|$) and coefficients $\alpha_1, \ldots, \alpha_\ell > 0$ with $\sum_{m=1}^{\ell} \alpha_m = 1$ such that $\pi = \sum_{m=1}^{\ell} \alpha_m \pi_m$ and $v(r, \tau) = \tilde{\rho}^{co}(\pi) = \sum_{m=1}^{\ell} \alpha_m \rho^*(\pi_m)$. Since $\rho^*(\pi) \ge v(r, \tau)$, this implies that $\rho^*(\pi_m) = v(r, \tau)$ for all m. Recall now from Lemma 1(ii) that the set Y^* of mixed actions $y \in Y$ for which $\rho^*(y) = v(r, \tau)$ is convex. The set $\Pi^* = \{\pi' \in \Pi : \pi'/|\pi'| \in Y^*\}$ is thus an image of a convex set under a linear-fractional transformation, and is therefore convex ([4]). Noting that $\pi_m \in \Pi^*$ for all m (which follows from $\rho^*(\pi_m) = v(r, \tau)$) and π is their convex combination, it follows that $\pi \in \Pi^*$ and in particular that $y = \pi/|\pi| \in Y^*$, which is equivalent to $\rho^{co}(y) = v(r, \tau)$. $\qquad\square$

Both properties that were stated in the last lemma can be observed in Fig. 1.

5   Calibrated Play

In calibrated play, P1 uses at each stage a best-response to his forecasts of the other player's action at that stage. The quality of the resulting strategy depends of course on the quality of the forecast; it is well known that using *calibrated* forecasts leads to no-regret strategies in repeated matrix games. See, for example, [6] for an overview of the relation between regret minimization and calibration. In this section we consider the consequences of calibrated play for repeated games with variable stage duration.

We start with a formal definition of calibrated forecasts and calibrated play in the next subsection. We then introduce in Subsection 5.2 the *calibration envelope* $\rho^{cal}(\hat{y})$, and show that it is attained by calibrated play in the sense that $\rho_n \ge \rho^{cal}(\hat{y}_n)$ holds asymptotically. We then proceed to compare the calibration envelope with the convex best-response envelope of the previous section, and show that $\rho^{cal} \ge \rho^{co}$.

5.1   Calibrated Forecasts and Calibrated Play

A forecasting scheme specifies at each decision point k a probabilistic forecast $q_k \in Y$ of P2's action j_k. More specifically, a (randomized) forecasting scheme is a sequence of maps $\mu_k : H_{k-1} \to \Delta(Y)$, $k \geq 1$, which associates with each possible history h_{k-1} a probability measure μ_k over Y. The forecast $q_k \in Y$ is selected at random according to the distribution μ_k.

We shall use the following definition of calibrated forecasts.

Definition 3 (Calibrated forecasts). *A forecasting scheme is* calibrated *if for every (Borel measurable) set $Q \subset Y$ and every strategy of P2,*

$$\lim_{n\to\infty} \frac{1}{n} \sum_{k=1}^{n} 1\{q_k \in Q\}(e_{j_k} - q_k) = 0 \quad a.s., \tag{15}$$

where e_j is a vector of zeros with 1 in the jth location.

This form of calibration property has been introduced into game theory by [7], and several algorithms have been devised to achieve it ([8,11,13]). These algorithms typically start with predictions that are restricted to a finite grid, gradually increasing the number of grid points (see [5] for such a construction).

In calibrated play, the active player (P1) essentially chooses a best-response action to his forecast of the other player's actions. That is: $i_k \in I^*(q_k)$, where

$$I^*(y) = \arg\max_{i \in I} \frac{r(i,y)}{\tau(i,y)}, \quad y \in Y. \tag{16}$$

To be more specific, we shall assume some fixed tie-breaking rule when $I^*(y)$ is not a singleton. Thus, we have the following definition.

Definition 4 (Calibrated Play). *A calibrated strategy for P1 in the variable-duration repeated game $\Gamma^\infty(r,\tau)$ is given by*

$$i_k = i^o(q_k) \tag{17}$$

where (q_k) is a calibrated forecast of P2's actions, and $i^0(y) \in I^*(y)$ for each $y \in Y$.

The choice of i_k as a best response to q_k in the game $\Gamma_0(r,\tau)$ with payoff $\rho(x,y)$ is motivated by the definition of the best-response envelope in (5). Note that the chosen action does *not* maximize expected one-stage reward rate, namely $\sum q_k(j)\frac{r(i,j)}{\tau(i,j)}$, which cannot be easily related to the repeated game payoff.

5.2   The Calibration Envelope

Let $Y_i^* = \{y \in Y : i \in I^*(y)\}$ denote the (closed) set of mixed actions to which $i \in I$ is a best response in $\Gamma_0(r,\tau)$. We shall assume that each Y_i^* is non-empty; actions i for which Y_i^* is empty will never be used and can be deleted from the game model.

Let $\Delta_d(Y)$ denote the set of discrete probability measures on Y, and let $m_\mu = \int y\mu(dy)$ denote the barycenter of $\mu \in \Delta_d(Y)$. The *calibration envelope* ρ^{cal} is defined as follows, for $\hat{y} \in Y$:

$$\rho^{\text{cal}}(\hat{y}) = \inf \left\{ \frac{\int r(i(y), y)\mu(dy)}{\int \tau(i(y), y)\mu(dy)} : \mu \in \Delta_d(Y), \, m_\mu = \hat{y}, \, i(y) \in I^*(y) \right\}. \quad (18)$$

The restriction to discrete measures is for technical convenience only and is of no consequence, as the infimum is already attained by a measure of finite support. This follows from the next lemma which also provides an alternative expression for ρ^{cal}, alongside a useful continuity property.

Lemma 4.

(i) Let $co(Y_i^*)$ denote the convex hull of Y_i^*. Then

$$\rho^{cal}(\hat{y}) = \min \left\{ \frac{\sum_{i \in I} \alpha_i r(i, y_i)}{\sum_{i \in I} \alpha_i \tau(i, y_i)} : \alpha \in \Delta(I), \, y_i \in co(Y_i^*), \sum_{i \in I} \alpha_i y_i = \hat{y} \right\}. \tag{19}$$

(ii) The infimum in (18) is attained by a measure μ of finite support.
(iii) $\rho^{cal}(\hat{y})$ is continuous in $\hat{y} \in Y$.

Proof. (i) Note first that the minimum in (19) is indeed attained, as we minimize a continuous function over a compact set ($co(Y_i^*)$ is closed since Y_i^* is closed). Let $\rho^1(\hat{y})$ denote the right-hand side of (19). To show that $\rho^1 \leq \rho^{\text{cal}}$, note that by Caratheodory's Theorem each $y_i \in co(Y_i^*)$ can be written as $y_i = \sum_{j \in J} \beta_{ij} y_{ij}$, with $y_{ij} \in Y_i^*$ and $\beta_i \in \Delta(J)$. It follows that for each $\hat{y}$ the argument of (19) can be written as the special case of the argument of (18), from which $\rho^1(\hat{y}) \leq \rho^{\text{cal}}(\hat{y})$ follows. Conversely, given $\mu \in \Delta_d(\hat{y})$ and the selection function $i(y) \in I^*(y)$, define $\alpha_i = \int_{y:i(y)=i} \mu(dy)$, and $y_i = \int_{y:i(y)=i} y\mu(dy)/\alpha_i$ (with y_i arbitrary if $\alpha_i = 0$). Note that $y_i \in co(Y_i^*)$, since $i(y) \in I^*(y)$ implies $y \in Y_i^*$, and y_i is defined as a convex combination of such y's. The argument of (18) is thus reduced to the form of (19), which implies that $\rho^1(\hat{y}) \leq \rho^{\text{cal}}(\hat{y})$.

(ii) Follows immediately from the indicated reduction of the argument of (19) to that of (18).

(iii) Continuity follows since the minimized function in (19) is continuous in its arguments α and (y_i), while the minimizing set is upper semi-continuous in y. $\qquad\square$

We next establish that calibrated play attains the calibration envelope.

Theorem 3 (ρ^{cal} is attainable). *Suppose P1 uses a calibrated strategy. Then, for any strategy of P2,*

$$\liminf_{n \to \infty}(\rho_n - \rho^{cal}(\hat{y}_n)) \geq 0 \quad (a.s.).$$

Proof. It will be convenient to use for this proof the shorthand notations $a_n \overset{o(n)}{=} b_n$ for $\lim_{n \to \infty}(a_n - b_n) = 0$, and $a_n \overset{o(n)}{\geq} b_n$ for $\liminf_{n \to \infty}(a_n - b_n) \geq 0$.

All relations between random variables are assumed by default to hold with probability 1. Let $Y_i = \{y \in Y : i^o(y) = i\}$, so that $q_k \in Y_i$ implies $i_k = i$; note that $Y_i \subset Y_i^*$. We thus have

$$\frac{1}{n}\sum_{k=1}^{n} r(i_k, j_k) = \frac{1}{n}\sum_{i \in I}\sum_{k=1}^{n} \mathbf{1}\{q_k \in Y_i\}r(i, j_k)$$

$$\stackrel{o(n)}{=} \frac{1}{n}\sum_{i \in I}\sum_{k=1}^{n} \mathbf{1}\{q_k \in Y_i\}r(i, q_k)$$

$$= \frac{1}{n}\sum_{i \in I}\sum_{k=1}^{n} \mathbf{1}\{q_k \in Y_i\}r(i^o(q_k), q_k)$$

$$= \frac{1}{n}\sum_{k=1}^{n} r(i^o(q_k), q_k).$$

The second ($o(n)$) equality follows from (15). Repeating the argument for τ we obtain

$$\frac{1}{n}\sum_{k=1}^{n} \tau(i_k, j_k) \stackrel{o(n)}{=} \frac{1}{n}\sum_{k=1}^{n} \tau(i^o(q_k), q_k).$$

Since $\tau(i, j)$ is bounded away from zero, it follows that

$$\rho_n \stackrel{o(n)}{=} \frac{\sum_{k=1}^{n} r(i^o(q_k), q_k)}{\sum_{k=1}^{n} \tau(i^o(q_k), q_k)}, \qquad (20)$$

while the latter expression satisfies the following inequality by definition of ρ^{cal}:

$$\frac{\sum_{k=1}^{n} r(i^o(q_k), q_k)}{\sum_{k=1}^{n} \tau(i^o(q_k), q_k)} \geq \rho^{\text{cal}}(\hat{q}_n), \qquad \text{where } \hat{q}_n = \frac{1}{n}\sum_{k=1}^{n} q_k.$$

Thus, $\rho_n \stackrel{o(n)}{\geq} \rho^{\text{cal}}(\hat{q}_n)$. Note also that from (15), with $Q = Y$, we have $\hat{y}_n \stackrel{o(n)}{=} \hat{q}_n$. The required equality now follows by continuity for $\rho^{\text{cal}}(y)$ in y, as noted in Lemma 4. $\square$

The following immediate consequence provides a sufficient condition for the best-response envelope ρ^* to be attainable, namely for the existence of no-regret strategies.

Corollary 2. *Suppose that $\rho^{cal}(y) = \rho^*(y)$ for all $y \in Y$. Then ρ^* is attainable by P1.*

The condition of the last corollary is satisfied in standard (fixed-duration) repeated matrix games. In general, however, ρ^{cal} can be strictly smaller than ρ^*. In particular, this must be the case when ρ^* is not attainable.

We proceed to establish some basic bounds on ρ^{cal}, that highlight the performance guarantees of calibrated play.

Proposition 4 (Properties of ρ^{cal}).

(a) $v(r, \tau) \le \rho^{cal}(\hat{y}) \le \rho^*(\hat{y})$ *for all* $\hat{y} \in Y$.
(b) $\rho^{cal}(\hat{y}) = \rho^*(\hat{y})$ *at the extreme points of* Y, *which correspond to the pure action set* I.
(c) For each $\hat{y} \in Y$, $\rho^*(\hat{y}) > v(r, \tau)$ *implies* $\rho^{cal}(\hat{y}) > v(r, \tau)$.

Proof. The proof is technical and appears in [16]. ∎

5.3 Comparison with the Convex Best-Response Envelope

The results obtained so far establish that both the convex best-response envelope ρ^{co} (defined in Section 4.2) and the calibration envelope ρ^{cal} are attainable, using different strategies. Here we compare these two performance envelopes, and show that the calibration envelope dominates ρ^{co}. We first show that ρ^{cal} is at least as large as ρ^{co}, and identify certain class of variable-duration games for which equality holds. We then provide an example where ρ^{cal} is strictly larger than ρ^{co}.

Proposition 5 (ρ^{cal} dominates ρ^{co}).

(i) $\rho^{cal}(\hat{y}) \ge \rho^{co}(\hat{y})$ *for all* $\hat{y} \in Y$.
(ii) If the stage durations depend on P2's actions only, namely $\tau(i, j) = \tau_0(j)$, *then* $\rho^{cal} = \rho^{co}$.

The proof is omitted; see [16].

Example 2. (ρ^{cal} **strictly dominates** ρ^{co}). Consider the variable duration matrix game $\Gamma(r, \tau)$ defined by the following matrix:

$$\begin{pmatrix} (0,1) & (2,3) \\ (2,3) & (0,1) \end{pmatrix}.$$

As before, P1 is the row player, P2 the column player, and the ij-th entry is $(r(i, j), \tau(i, j))$. A plot of $\rho^{cal} = \rho^*$ and ρ^{co} for the last example is shown in Figure 2. A detailed account of the computation can be found in [16].

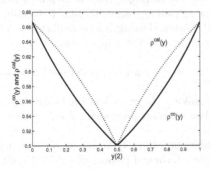

Fig. 2. $\rho^{cal}(y)$ (dotted line) and $\rho^{co}(y)$ (thick line) for the game of Example 2

6   Directions for Future Work

Several directions and issues remain for future work. First, the calibration-based scheme is quite demanding, and it should be of interest to obtain similar performance using simpler strategies. Second, a challenging question is to determine whether the performance guarantees of the calibration envelope can be improved upon, and indeed whether a sense of an *optimal* performance envelope exists in general. Finally, it would be of interest to study adaptive strategies for the variable-duration model under incomplete observation of the opponent's action, similar to the bandit problem setup in repeated matrix games ([1]).

References

1. P. Auer, N. Cesa-Bianchi, Y. Freund, and R. E. Schapire. The nonstochastic multiarmed bandit problem. *SIAM J. Comput.*, 32(1):48–77, 2002.
2. D. Blackwell. An analog of the minimax theorem for vector payoffs. *Pacific J. Math.*, 6(1):1–8, 1956.
3. D. Blackwell. Controlled random walks. In *Proc. Int. Congress of Mathematicians 1954*, volume 3, pages 336–338. North Holland, Amsterdam, 1956.
4. S. Boyd and L. Vanderberghe. *Convex Optimization.* Cambridge University Press, Cambridge, UK, 2004.
5. N. Cesa-Bianchi and G. Lugosi. *Prediction, Learning, and Games.* Cambridge University Press, New York, 2006.
6. D. P. Foster and R. Vohra. Regret in the on-line decision problem. *Games and Economic Behavior*, 29:7–35, November 1999.
7. D. P. Foster and R. V. Vohra. Calibrated learning and correlated equilibrium. *Games and Economic Behavior*, 21:40–55, 1997.
8. D. P. Foster and R. V. Vohra. Asymptotic calibration. *Biometrika*, 85:379–390, 1998.
9. Y Freund and R. E. Schapire. Adaptive game playing using multiplicative weights. *Games and Economic Behavior*, 29:79–103, 1999.
10. D. Fudenberg and D. Levine. Universal consistency and cautious fictitious play. *Journal of Economic Dynamic and Control*, 19:1065–1990, 1995.
11. D. Fudenberg and D. Levine. An easier way to calibrate. *Games and Economic Behavior*, 29:131–137, 1999.
12. J. Hannan. *Approximation to Bayes Risk in Repeated Play*, volume III of *Contribution to The Theory of Games*, pages 97–139. Princeton University Press, 1957.
13. S. Kakade and D. P. Foster. Deterministic calibration and Nash equilibrium. In *COLT*, volume 3120 of *Lecture Notes in Computer Science*, pages 33–48. Springer, 2004.
14. A. A. Lal and S. Sinha. Zero-sum two-person semi-Markov games. *J. Appl. Prob.*, 29:56–72–8, 1992.
15. S. Mannor and N. Shimkin. The empirical Bayes envelope and regret minimization in competitive Markov decision processes. *Mathematics of Operations Research*, 28(2):327–345, 2003.
16. S. Mannor and N. Shimkin. Regret minimization in repeated matrix games with variable stage duration. Technical Report EE-1524, Faculty of Electrical Engineering, Technion, February 2006.

Online Learning Meets Optimization in the Dual

Shai Shalev-Shwartz[1] and Yoram Singer[1,2]

[1] School of Computer Sci. & Eng., The Hebrew University, Jerusalem 91904, Israel
[2] Google Inc., 1600 Amphitheater Parkway, Mountain View, CA 94043, USA
{shais, singer}@cs.huji.ac.il

Abstract. We describe a novel framework for the design and analysis of online learning algorithms based on the notion of duality in constrained optimization. We cast a sub-family of universal online bounds as an optimization problem. Using the weak duality theorem we reduce the process of online learning to the task of incrementally increasing the dual objective function. The amount by which the dual increases serves as a new and natural notion of progress. We are thus able to tie the primal objective value and the number of prediction mistakes using and the increase in the dual. The end result is a general framework for designing and analyzing old and new online learning algorithms in the mistake bound model.

1   Introduction

Online learning of linear classifiers is an important and well-studied domain in machine learning with interesting theoretical properties and practical applications [3, 4, 7, 8, 9, 10, 12]. An online learning algorithm observes instances in a sequence of trials. After each observation, the algorithm predicts a yes/no ($+/-$) outcome. The prediction of the algorithm is formed by a hypothesis, which is a mapping from the instance space into $\{+1, -1\}$. This hypothesis is chosen by the online algorithm from a predefined class of hypotheses. Once the algorithm has made a prediction, it receives the correct outcome. Then, the online algorithm may choose another hypothesis from the class of hypotheses, presumably improving the chance of making an accurate prediction on subsequent trials. The quality of an online algorithm is measured by the number of prediction mistakes it makes along its run.

In this paper we introduce a general framework for the design and analysis of online learning algorithms. Our framework emerges from a new view on relative mistake bounds [10, 14], which are the common thread in the analysis of online learning algorithms. A relative mistake bound measures the performance of an online algorithm relatively to the performance of a competing hypothesis. The competing hypothesis can be chosen in hindsight from a class of hypotheses, after observing the entire sequence of examples. For example, the original mistake bound of the Perceptron algorithm [15], which was first suggested over 50 years ago, was derived by using a competitive analysis, comparing the algorithm to a linear hypothesis which achieves a large margin on the sequence of examples. Over the years, the competitive analysis technique was refined and extended to numerous prediction problems by employing complex and varied notions of progress toward a good competing hypothesis. The flurry of online learning algorithms sparked unified analyses of seemingly different online algorithms by Littlestone, Warmuth, Kivinen and colleagues [10, 13]. Most notably is the work of Grove,

G. Lugosi and H.U. Simon (Eds.): COLT 2006, LNAI 4005, pp. 423–437, 2006.

Littlestone, and Schuurmans [8] on a quasi-additive family of algorithms, which includes both the Perceptron [15] and the Winnow [13] algorithms as special cases. A similar unified view for regression was derived by Kivinen and Warmuth [10, 11]. Online algorithms for linear hypotheses and their analyses became more general and powerful by employing Bregman divergences for measuring the progress toward a good hypothesis [7, 8, 9]. In the aftermath of this paper we refer to these analyses as *primal* views.

We propose an alternative view of relative mistake bounds which is based on the notion of duality in constrained optimization. Online mistake bounds are universal in the sense that they hold for any possible predictor in a given hypothesis class. We therefore cast the universal bound as an optimization problem. Specifically, the objective function we cast is the sum of an empirical loss of a predictor and a complexity term for that predictor. The best predictor in a given class of hypotheses, which can only be determined in hindsight, is the minimizer of the optimization problem. In order to derive explicit quantitative mistake bounds we make an immediate use of the fact that dual objective lower bounds the primal objective. We therefore switch to the dual representation of the optimization problem. We then reduce the process of online learning to the task of incrementally increasing the dual objective function. The amount by which the dual increases serves as a new and natural notion of progress. By doing so we are able to tie the primal objective value, the number of prediction mistakes, and the increase in the dual. The end result is a general framework for designing online algorithms and analyzing them in the mistake bound model.

We illustrate the power of our framework by studying two schemes for increasing the dual objective. The first performs a fixed size update based solely on the last observed example. We show that this dual update is equivalent to the primal update of the quasi-additive family of algorithms [8]. In particular, our framework yields the tightest known bounds for several known quasi-additive algorithms such as the Perceptron and Balanced Winnow. The second update scheme we study moves further in the direction of optimization techniques in several accounts. In this scheme the online learning algorithm may modify its hypotheses based on *multiple* past examples. Furthermore, the update itself is constructed by maximizing or approximately maximizing the increase in the dual. While this second approach still entertains the same mistake bound of the first scheme it also serves as a vehicle for deriving new online algorithms.

2   Problem Setting

In this section we introduce the notation used throughout the paper and formally describe our problem setting. We denote scalars with lower case letters (e.g. x and ω), and vectors with bold face letters (e.g. $\mathbf{x}$ and $\boldsymbol{\omega}$). The set of non-negative real numbers is denoted by $\mathbb{R}_+$. For any $k \geq 1$, the set of integers $\{1, \ldots, k\}$ is denoted by $[k]$.

Online learning of binary classifiers is performed in a sequence of trials. At trial t the algorithm first receives an instance $\mathbf{x}_t \in \mathbb{R}^n$ and is required to predict the label associated with that instance. We denote the prediction of the algorithm on the t'th trial by $\hat{y}_t$. For simplicity and concreteness we focus on online learning of binary classifiers, namely, we assume that the labels are in $\{+1, -1\}$. After the online learning algorithm has predicted the label $\hat{y}_t$, the true label $y_t \in \{+1, -1\}$ is revealed and the algorithm pays a unit cost if its prediction is wrong, that is, if $y_t \neq \hat{y}_t$. The ultimate goal of the algorithm is to minimize the total number of prediction mistakes it makes along its run. To achieve this goal, the algorithm may update its prediction mechanism after each trial so as to be more accurate in later trials.

In this paper, we assume that the prediction of the algorithm at each trial is determined by a margin-based linear hypothesis. Namely, there exists a weight vector $\boldsymbol{w}_t \in \Omega \subset \mathbb{R}^n$ where $\hat{y}_t = \text{sign}(\langle \boldsymbol{w}_t, \mathbf{x}_t \rangle)$ is the actual binary prediction and $|\langle \boldsymbol{w}_t, \mathbf{x}_t \rangle|$ is the confidence in this prediction. The term $y_t \langle \boldsymbol{w}_t, \mathbf{x}_t \rangle$ is called the *margin* of the prediction and is positive whenever y_t and $\text{sign}(\langle \boldsymbol{w}_t, \mathbf{x}_t \rangle)$ agree. We can evaluate the performance of a weight vector $\boldsymbol{w}$ on a given example $(\mathbf{x}, y)$ in one of two ways. First, we can check whether $\boldsymbol{w}$ results in a prediction mistake which amounts to checking whether $y = \text{sign}(\langle \boldsymbol{w}, \mathbf{x} \rangle)$ or not. Throughout this paper, we use M to denote the number of prediction mistakes made by an online algorithm on a sequence of examples $(\mathbf{x}_1, y_1), \ldots, (\mathbf{x}_m, y_m)$. The second way we evaluate the predictions of an hypothesis is by using the *hinge-loss* function, defined as,

$$\ell^\gamma(\boldsymbol{w}; (\mathbf{x}, y)) = \begin{cases} 0 & \text{if } y \langle \boldsymbol{w}, \mathbf{x} \rangle \geq \gamma \\ \gamma - y \langle \boldsymbol{w}, \mathbf{x} \rangle & \text{otherwise} \end{cases} . \tag{1}$$

The hinge-loss penalizes an hypothesis for any margin less than γ. Additionally, if $y \neq \text{sign}(\langle \boldsymbol{w}, \mathbf{x} \rangle)$ then $\ell^\gamma(\boldsymbol{w}; (\mathbf{x}, y)) \geq \gamma$. Therefore, the *cumulative hinge-loss* suffered over a sequence of examples upper bounds γM. Throughout the paper, when $\gamma = 1$ we use the shorthand $\ell(\boldsymbol{w}; (\mathbf{x}, y))$.

As mentioned before, the performance of an online learning algorithm is measured by the cumulative number of prediction mistakes it makes along its run on a sequence of examples $(\mathbf{x}_1, y_1), \ldots, (\mathbf{x}_m, y_m)$. Ideally, we would like to think of the labels as if they are generated by an unknown yet *fixed* weight vector $\boldsymbol{w}^\star$ such that $y_i = \text{sign}(\langle \boldsymbol{w}^\star, \mathbf{x}_i \rangle)$ for all $i \in [m]$. Moreover, in an utopian case, the cumulative hinge-loss of $\boldsymbol{w}^\star$ on the entire sequence is zero, which means that $\boldsymbol{w}^\star$ produces the correct label with a confidence of at least γ. In this case, we would like M, the number of prediction mistakes of our online algorithm, to be independent of m, the number of examples. Usually, in such cases, M is upper bounded by $F(\boldsymbol{w}^\star)$ where $F : \Omega \to \mathbb{R}$ is a function which measures the complexity of $\boldsymbol{w}^\star$. In the more realistic case, there does not exist $\boldsymbol{w}^\star$ which perfectly predicts the data. In this case, we would like the online algorithm to be competitive with *any* fixed hypothesis $\boldsymbol{w}$. Formally, let λ and C be two positive scalars. We say that our online algorithm is (λ, C)-competitive with the set of vectors in Ω, with respect to a complexity function F and the hinge-loss ℓ^γ, if the following bound holds,

$$\forall \boldsymbol{w} \in \Omega, \quad \lambda M \leq F(\boldsymbol{w}) + C \sum_{i=1}^{m} \ell^\gamma(\boldsymbol{w}; (\mathbf{x}_i, y_i)) . \tag{2}$$

The parameter C controls the trade-off between the complexity of $\boldsymbol{w}$ (through F) and the cumulative hinge-loss of $\boldsymbol{w}$. The parameter λ is introduced for technical reasons that are provided in the next section. The main goal of this paper is to develop a general paradigm for designing online learning algorithms and analyze them in the mistake bound framework given in Eq. (2).

3   A Primal-Dual Apparatus for Online Learning

In this section we describe a methodology for designing online learning algorithms for binary classification. To motivate our construction let us first consider the special case where $\gamma = 1$, $F(\omega) = \frac{1}{2}\|\omega\|_2^2$, and $\Omega = \mathbb{R}^n$. Denote by $\mathcal{P}(\omega)$ the right hand side of Eq. (2) which in this special case amounts to,

$$\mathcal{P}(\omega) = \frac{1}{2}\|\omega\|^2 + C \sum_{i=1}^{m} \ell(\omega; (\mathbf{x}_i, y_i)) \ .$$

The bound in Eq. (2) can be rewritten as,

$$\lambda M \ \leq \ \min_{\omega \in \mathbb{R}^n} \ \mathcal{P}(\omega) \ \stackrel{\text{def}}{=} \ \mathcal{P}^\star \ . \tag{3}$$

Note that $\mathcal{P}(\omega)$ is the well-known primal objective function of the optimization problem employed by the SVM algorithm [5]. Intuitively, we view the online learning task as incrementally solving the optimization problem $\min_\omega \mathcal{P}(\omega)$. However, while $\mathcal{P}(\omega)$ depends on the entire sequence of examples $\{(\mathbf{x}_1, y_1), \ldots, (\mathbf{x}_m, y_m)\}$, the online algorithm is confined to use on trial t only the first $t - 1$ examples of the sequence. To overcome this disparity, we follow the approach that ostriches take in solving problems: we simply ignore the examples $\{(\mathbf{x}_t, y_t), \ldots, (\mathbf{x}_m, y_m)\}$ as they are not provided to the algorithm on trial t. Therefore, on trial t we use the following weight vector for predicting the label,

$$\omega_t = \underset{\omega}{\operatorname{argmin}} \ \mathcal{P}_t(\omega) \quad \text{where} \quad \mathcal{P}_t(\omega) = \frac{1}{2}\|\omega\|^2 + C \sum_{i=1}^{t-1} \ell(\omega; (\mathbf{x}_i, y_i)) \ .$$

This online algorithm is a simple (and non-efficient) adaptation of the SVM algorithm for the online setting and we therefore call it the Online-SVM algorithm (see also [12]). Since the hinge-loss $\ell(\omega; (\mathbf{x}_t, y_t))$ is non-negative we get that $\mathcal{P}_t(\omega) \leq \mathcal{P}_{t+1}(\omega)$ for any ω and therefore $\mathcal{P}_t(\omega_t) \leq \mathcal{P}_t(\omega_{t+1}) \leq \mathcal{P}_{t+1}(\omega_{t+1})$. Note that $\mathcal{P}_1(\omega_1) = 0$ and that $\mathcal{P}_{m+1}(\omega) = \mathcal{P}^\star$. Thus,

$$0 = \mathcal{P}_1(\omega_1) \leq \mathcal{P}_2(\omega_2) \leq \ \cdots \ \leq \mathcal{P}_{m+1}(\omega_{m+1}) = \mathcal{P}^\star \ .$$

Recall that our goal is to find an online algorithm which entertains the mistake bound given in Eq. (3). Suppose that we can show that for each trial t on which the online algorithm makes a prediction mistake we have that $\mathcal{P}_{t+1}(\omega_{t+1}) - \mathcal{P}_t(\omega_t) \geq \lambda > 0$. Equipped with this assumption, it follows immediately that if the online algorithm made M prediction mistakes on the entire sequence of examples then $\mathcal{P}_{m+1}(\omega_{m+1})$ should be at least λM. Since $\mathcal{P}_{m+1}(\omega_{m+1}) = \mathcal{P}^\star$ we conclude that $\lambda M \leq \mathcal{P}^\star$ which gives the desired mistake bound from Eq. (3). In summary, to prove a mistake bound one needs to show that the online algorithm constructs a sequence of lower bounds $\mathcal{P}_1(\omega_1), \ldots, \mathcal{P}_{m+1}(\omega_{m+1})$ for $\mathcal{P}^\star$. These lower bounds should become tighter and tighter with the progress of the online algorithm. Moreover, whenever the algorithm makes a prediction mistake the lower bound must increase by at least λ.

The notion of duality, commonly used in optimization theory, plays an important role in obtaining lower bounds for the minimal value of the primal objective (see for example [2]). We now take an alternative view of the Online-SVM algorithm based on the notion of duality. As we formally show later, the dual of the problem $\min_{\boldsymbol{\omega}} \mathcal{P}(\boldsymbol{\omega})$ is

$$\max_{\boldsymbol{\alpha} \in [0,C]^m} \mathcal{D}(\boldsymbol{\alpha}) \quad \text{where} \quad \mathcal{D}(\boldsymbol{\alpha}) = \sum_{i=1}^{m} \alpha_i - \frac{1}{2} \left\| \sum_{i=1}^{m} \alpha_i \, y_i \, \mathbf{x}_i \right\|^2 . \tag{4}$$

The weak duality theorem states that any value of the dual objective is upper bounded by the optimal primal objective. That is, for any $\boldsymbol{\alpha} \in [0, C]^m$ we have that $\mathcal{D}(\boldsymbol{\alpha}) \leq \mathcal{P}^\star$. If in addition strong duality holds then $\max_{\boldsymbol{\alpha} \in [0,C]^m} \mathcal{D}(\boldsymbol{\alpha}) = \mathcal{P}^\star$. As we show in the sequel, the values $\mathcal{P}_1(\boldsymbol{\omega}_1), \ldots, \mathcal{P}_{m+1}(\boldsymbol{\omega}_{m+1})$ translate to a sequence of dual objective values. Put another way, there exists a sequence of dual solutions $\boldsymbol{\alpha}_1, \ldots, \boldsymbol{\alpha}_{m+1}$ such that for all $t \in [m+1]$ we have that $\mathcal{D}(\boldsymbol{\alpha}_t) = \mathcal{P}_t(\boldsymbol{\omega}_t)$. This fact follows from a property of the dual function in Eq. (4) as we now show.

Denote by $\mathcal{D}_t$ the dual objective function of $\mathcal{P}_t$,

$$\mathcal{D}_t(\boldsymbol{\alpha}) = \sum_{i=1}^{t-1} \alpha_i - \frac{1}{2} \left\| \sum_{i=1}^{t-1} \alpha_i \, y_i \, \mathbf{x}_i \right\|^2 . \tag{5}$$

Note that $\mathcal{D}_t$ is a mapping from $[0, C]^{t-1}$ into the reals. From strong duality we know that the minimum of $\mathcal{P}_t$ equals to the maximum of $\mathcal{D}_t$. From the definition of $\mathcal{D}_t$ we get that for $(\alpha_1, \ldots, \alpha_{t-1}) \in [0, C]^{t-1}$ the following equality holds,

$$\mathcal{D}_t((\alpha_1, \ldots, \alpha_{t-1})) = \mathcal{D}((\alpha_1, \ldots, \alpha_{t-1}, 0, \ldots, 0)) .$$

Therefore, the Online-SVM algorithm can be viewed as an incremental solver of the *dual* problem, $\max_{\boldsymbol{\alpha} \in [0,C]^m} \mathcal{D}(\boldsymbol{\alpha})$, where at the end of trial t the algorithm maximizes the dual function confined to the first t variables,

$$\max_{\boldsymbol{\alpha} \in [0,C]^m} \mathcal{D}(\boldsymbol{\alpha}) \quad \text{s.t.} \quad \forall i > t, \; \alpha_i = 0 .$$

The property of the dual objective that we utilize is that it can be optimized in a sequential manner. Specifically, if on trial t we ground α_i to zero for $i \geq t$ then $\mathcal{D}(\boldsymbol{\alpha})$ does not depend on examples which have not been observed yet.

We presented two views of the Online-SVM algorithm. In the first view the algorithm constructs a sequence of *primal* solutions $\boldsymbol{\omega}_1, \ldots, \boldsymbol{\omega}_{m+1}$ while in the second the algorithm constructs a sequence of *dual* solutions which we analogously denote by $\boldsymbol{\alpha}^1, \ldots, \boldsymbol{\alpha}^{m+1}$. As we show later, the connection between $\boldsymbol{\omega}_t$ and $\boldsymbol{\alpha}^t$ is given through the equality,

$$\boldsymbol{\omega}_t = \sum_{i=1}^{m} \alpha_i^t \, y_i \, \mathbf{x}_i . \tag{6}$$

In general, any sequence of feasible dual solutions $\boldsymbol{\alpha}^1, \ldots, \boldsymbol{\alpha}^{m+1}$ can define an on-line learning algorithm by setting $\boldsymbol{\omega}_t$ according to Eq. (6). Naturally, we require that $\alpha_i^t = 0$ for all $i \geq t$ since otherwise $\boldsymbol{\omega}_t$ would depend on examples which have not been observed yet. To prove that the resulting online algorithm entertains the mistake bound given in Eq. (3) we impose two additional conditions. First, we require that $\mathcal{D}(\alpha^{t+1}) \geq \mathcal{D}(\alpha^t)$ which means that the dual objective never decreases. In addition, on trials in which the algorithm makes a prediction mistake we require that the increase of the dual objective will be strictly positive, $\mathcal{D}(\alpha^{t+1}) - \mathcal{D}(\alpha^t) \geq \lambda > 0$. To recap, any incremental solver for the dual optimization problem which satisfies the above requirements can serve as an online algorithm which meets the mistake bound given in Eq. (3).

Let us now formally generalize the above motivating discussion. Our starting point is the desired mistake bound of the form given in Eq. (2), which can be rewritten as,

$$\lambda M \leq \inf_{\boldsymbol{\omega} \in \Omega} \left(F(\boldsymbol{\omega}) + C \sum_{i=1}^{m} \ell^\gamma(\boldsymbol{\omega}; (\mathbf{x}_i, y_i)) \right) . \tag{7}$$

As in our motivating example we denote by $\mathcal{P}(\boldsymbol{\omega})$ the primal objective of the optimization problem on the right-hand side of Eq. (7). Our goal is to develop an online learning algorithm that achieves this mistake bound. First, let us derive the dual optimization problem. Using the definition of ℓ^γ we can rewrite the optimization problem as,

$$\inf_{\boldsymbol{\omega} \in \Omega, \boldsymbol{\xi} \in \mathbb{R}_+^m} F(\boldsymbol{\omega}) + C \sum_{i=1}^{m} \xi_i \tag{8}$$

$$\text{s.t. } \forall i \in [m], \ y_i\langle \boldsymbol{\omega}, \mathbf{x}_i \rangle \geq \gamma - \xi_i .$$

We further rewrite this optimization problem using the Lagrange dual function,

$$\inf_{\boldsymbol{\omega} \in \Omega, \boldsymbol{\xi} \in \mathbb{R}_+^m} \sup_{\boldsymbol{\alpha} \in \mathbb{R}_+^m} \underbrace{F(\boldsymbol{\omega}) + C \sum_{i=1}^{m} \xi_i + \sum_{i=1}^{m} \alpha_i \left(\gamma - y_i\langle \boldsymbol{\omega}, \mathbf{x}_i \rangle - \xi_i \right)}_{\overset{\text{def}}{=} \mathcal{L}(\boldsymbol{\omega}, \boldsymbol{\xi}, \boldsymbol{\alpha})} . \tag{9}$$

Eq. (9) is equivalent to Eq. (8) due to the following fact. If the constraint $y_i\langle \boldsymbol{\omega}, \mathbf{x}_i \rangle \geq \gamma - \xi_i$ holds then the optimal value of α_i in Eq. (9) is zero. If on the other hand the constraint does not hold then α_i equals ∞, which implies that $\boldsymbol{\omega}$ cannot constitute the optimal primal solution. The weak duality theorem (see for example [2]) states that,

$$\sup_{\boldsymbol{\alpha} \in \mathbb{R}_+^m} \inf_{\boldsymbol{\omega} \in \Omega, \boldsymbol{\xi} \in \mathbb{R}_+^m} \mathcal{L}(\boldsymbol{\omega}, \boldsymbol{\xi}, \boldsymbol{\alpha}) \leq \inf_{\boldsymbol{\omega} \in \Omega, \boldsymbol{\xi} \in \mathbb{R}_+^m} \sup_{\boldsymbol{\alpha} \in \mathbb{R}_+^m} \mathcal{L}(\boldsymbol{\omega}, \boldsymbol{\xi}, \boldsymbol{\alpha}) . \tag{10}$$

The dual objective function is defined to be,

$$\mathcal{D}(\boldsymbol{\alpha}) = \inf_{\boldsymbol{\omega} \in \Omega, \boldsymbol{\xi} \in \mathbb{R}_+^m} \mathcal{L}(\boldsymbol{\omega}, \boldsymbol{\xi}, \boldsymbol{\alpha}) . \tag{11}$$

Using the definition of $\mathcal{L}$, we can rewrite the dual objective as a sum of three terms,

$$\mathcal{D}(\boldsymbol{\alpha}) = \gamma \sum_{i=1}^{m} \alpha_i - \sup_{\boldsymbol{\omega} \in \Omega} \left(\langle \boldsymbol{\omega}, \sum_{i=1}^{m} \alpha_i y_i \mathbf{x}_i \rangle - F(\boldsymbol{\omega}) \right) + \inf_{\boldsymbol{\xi} \in \mathbb{R}_+^m} \sum_{i=1}^{m} \xi_i (C - \alpha_i) .$$

The last term equals to zero for $\alpha_i \in [0, C]$ and to $-\infty$ for $\alpha_i > C$. Since our goal is to maximize $\mathcal{D}(\boldsymbol{\alpha})$ we can confine ourselves to the case $\boldsymbol{\alpha} \in [0, C]^m$ and simply write,

$$\mathcal{D}(\boldsymbol{\alpha}) = \gamma \sum_{i=1}^{m} \alpha_i - \sup_{\boldsymbol{\omega} \in \Omega} \left(\langle \boldsymbol{\omega}, \sum_{i=1}^{m} \alpha_i y_i \mathbf{x}_i \rangle - F(\boldsymbol{\omega}) \right) .$$

The second term in the above presentation of $\mathcal{D}(\boldsymbol{\alpha})$ can be rewritten using the notion of conjugate functions (see for example [2]). Formally, the conjugate[1] of the function F is the function,

$$G(\boldsymbol{\theta}) = \sup_{\boldsymbol{\omega} \in \Omega} \langle \boldsymbol{\omega}, \boldsymbol{\theta} \rangle - F(\boldsymbol{\omega}) . \tag{12}$$

Using the definition of G we conclude that for $\boldsymbol{\alpha} \in [0, C]^m$ the dual objective function can be rewritten as,

$$\mathcal{D}(\boldsymbol{\alpha}) = \gamma \sum_{i=1}^{m} \alpha_i - G\left(\sum_{i=1}^{m} \alpha_i y_i \mathbf{x}_i \right) . \tag{13}$$

For instance, it is easy to verify that the conjugate of $F(\boldsymbol{\omega}) = \frac{1}{2}\|\boldsymbol{\omega}\|_2^2$ (with $\Omega = \mathbb{R}^n$) is $G(\boldsymbol{\theta}) = \frac{1}{2}\|\boldsymbol{\theta}\|^2$. Indeed, the above definition of $\mathcal{D}$ for this case coincides with the value of $\mathcal{D}$ given in Eq. (4).

We now describe a template algorithm for online classification by incrementally increasing the dual objective function. Our algorithm starts with the trivial dual solution $\boldsymbol{\alpha}^1 = \mathbf{0}$. On trial t, we use $\boldsymbol{\alpha}^t$ for defining the weight vector $\boldsymbol{\omega}_t$ which is used for predicting the label as follows. First, we define $\boldsymbol{\theta}_t = \sum_{i=1}^{t-1} \alpha_i^t y_i \mathbf{x}_i$. Throughout the paper we assume that the supremum in the definition of $G(\boldsymbol{\theta})$ is attainable and set,

$$\boldsymbol{\omega}_t = \underset{\boldsymbol{\omega} \in \Omega}{\operatorname{argmax}} \left(\langle \boldsymbol{\omega}, \boldsymbol{\theta}_t \rangle - F(\boldsymbol{\omega}) \right) . \tag{14}$$

Next, we use $\boldsymbol{\omega}_t$ for predicting the label $\hat{y}_t = \operatorname{sign}(\langle \boldsymbol{\omega}_t, \mathbf{x}_t \rangle)$. Finally, we find a new dual solution $\boldsymbol{\alpha}^{t+1}$ with the last $m - t$ elements of $\boldsymbol{\alpha}^{t+1}$ are still grounded to zero. The two requirements we imposed imply that the new value of the dual objective, $\mathcal{D}(\boldsymbol{\alpha}^{t+1})$, should be at least $\mathcal{D}(\boldsymbol{\alpha}^t)$. Moreover, if we make a prediction mistake the increase in the dual objective should be strictly positive. In general, we might not be able to guarantee a minimal increase of the dual objective. In the next section we propose sufficient conditions which guarantee a minimal increase of the dual objective whenever the algorithm makes a prediction mistake. Our template algorithm is summarized in Fig. 1.

We conclude this section with a general mistake bound for online algorithms belonging to our framework. We need first to introduce some additional notation. Let $(\mathbf{x}_1, y_1), \ldots, (\mathbf{x}_m, y_m)$ be a sequence of examples and assume that an online algorithm which is derived from the template algorithm is run on this sequence. We denote by $\mathcal{E}$ the set of trials on which the algorithm made a prediction mistake, $\mathcal{E} = \{t \in [m] : \hat{y}_t \neq y_t\}$. To remind the reader, the number of prediction mistakes of the algorithm is M and

---

[1] The function G is also called the Fenchel conjugate of F. In cases where F is differentiable with an invertible gradient, G is also called the Legendre transform of F.

INPUT: Regularization function $F(\boldsymbol{\omega})$ with domain Ω ;

            Trade-off Parameter C ; hinge-loss parameter γ

INITIALIZE: $\boldsymbol{\alpha}^1 = \mathbf{0}$

For $t = 1, 2, \ldots, m$

    define $\boldsymbol{\omega}_t = \underset{\boldsymbol{\omega} \in \Omega}{\operatorname{argmax}} \ \langle \boldsymbol{\omega}, \boldsymbol{\theta}_t \rangle - F(\boldsymbol{\omega})$ where $\boldsymbol{\theta}_t = \sum_{i=1}^{t-1} \alpha_i^t \, y_i \, \mathbf{x}_i$

    receive an instance $\mathbf{x}_t$ and predict its label: $\hat{y}_t = \operatorname{sign}(\boldsymbol{\omega}_t \cdot \mathbf{x}_t)$

    receive correct label y_t

    If $\hat{y}_t \neq y_t$

        find $\boldsymbol{\alpha}^{t+1} \in [0, C]^t \times \{0\}^{m-t}$ such that $\mathcal{D}(\boldsymbol{\alpha}^{t+1}) - \mathcal{D}(\boldsymbol{\alpha}^t) > 0$

    Else

        find $\boldsymbol{\alpha}^{t+1} \in [0, C]^t \times \{0\}^{m-t}$ such that $\mathcal{D}(\boldsymbol{\alpha}^{t+1}) - \mathcal{D}(\boldsymbol{\alpha}^t) \geq 0$

Fig. 1. The template algorithm for online classification

thus $M = |\mathcal{E}|$. Last, we denote by λ the *average* increase of the dual objective over the trials in $\mathcal{E}$,

$$\lambda = \frac{1}{|\mathcal{E}|} \sum_{t \in \mathcal{E}} \left(\mathcal{D}(\boldsymbol{\alpha}^{t+1}) - \mathcal{D}(\boldsymbol{\alpha}^t) \right) . \tag{15}$$

Recall that $F(\boldsymbol{\omega})$ is our complexity measure for the vector $\boldsymbol{\omega}$. A natural assumption on F is that $\min_{\boldsymbol{\omega} \in \Omega} F(\boldsymbol{\omega}) = 0$. The intuitive meaning of this assumption is that the complexity of the "simplest" hypothesis in Ω is zero. The following theorem provides a mistake bound for any algorithm which belongs to our framework.

Theorem 1. *Let* $(\mathbf{x}_1, y_1), \ldots, (\mathbf{x}_m, y_m)$ *be a sequence of examples. Assume that an online algorithm of the form given in Fig. 1 is run on this sequence with a function* $F : \Omega \to \mathbb{R}$ *which satisfies* $\min_{\boldsymbol{\omega} \in \Omega} F(\boldsymbol{\omega}) = 0$. *Then,*

$$\lambda M \leq \inf_{\boldsymbol{\omega} \in \Omega} \left(F(\boldsymbol{\omega}) + C \sum_{t=1}^m \ell^\gamma(\boldsymbol{\omega}; (\mathbf{x}_t, y_t)) \right) ,$$

where λ *is as defined in Eq. (15).*

Proof. We prove the claim by bounding $\mathcal{D}(\boldsymbol{\alpha}^{m+1})$ from above and below. First, let us rewrite $\mathcal{D}(\boldsymbol{\alpha}^{m+1})$ as $\mathcal{D}(\boldsymbol{\alpha}^1) + \sum_{t=1}^m \left(\mathcal{D}(\boldsymbol{\alpha}^{t+1}) - \mathcal{D}(\boldsymbol{\alpha}^t) \right)$. Recall that $\boldsymbol{\alpha}^1$ is the zero vector and therefore $\boldsymbol{\theta}_1 = \mathbf{0}$ which gives,

$$\mathcal{D}(\boldsymbol{\alpha}^1) = 0 - \max_{\boldsymbol{\omega} \in \Omega}(\langle \boldsymbol{\omega}, \mathbf{0} \rangle - F(\boldsymbol{\omega})) = \min_{\boldsymbol{\omega} \in \Omega} F(\boldsymbol{\omega}) .$$

Thus, the assumption $\min_{\boldsymbol{\omega} \in \Omega} F(\boldsymbol{\omega}) = 0$ implies that $\mathcal{D}(\boldsymbol{\alpha}^1) = 0$. Since on each round $\mathcal{D}(\boldsymbol{\alpha}^{t+1}) - \mathcal{D}(\boldsymbol{\alpha}^t) \geq 0$ we conclude that,

$$\mathcal{D}(\boldsymbol{\alpha}^{m+1}) \geq \sum_{t \in \mathcal{E}} \left(\mathcal{D}(\boldsymbol{\alpha}^{t+1}) - \mathcal{D}(\boldsymbol{\alpha}^t) \right) = |\mathcal{E}| \lambda .$$

This provides a lower bound on $\mathcal{D}(\boldsymbol{\alpha}^{m+1})$. The upper bound $\mathcal{D}(\boldsymbol{\alpha}^{m+1}) \leq \mathcal{P}^\star$ follows directly from the weak duality theorem. Comparing the upper and lower bounds concludes our proof. $\qquad \square$

The bound in Thm. 1 becomes meaningless when λ is excessively small. In the next section we analyze a few known online algorithms. We show that these algorithms tacitly impose sufficient conditions on F and on the sequence of input examples. These conditions guarantee a minimal increase of the dual objective which result in mistake bounds for each algorithm.

4   Analysis of Known Online Algorithms

In the previous section we introduced a template algorithm for online learning. In this section we analyze the family of quasi-additive online algorithms described in [8, 10, 11] using the newly introduced dual view. This family includes several known algorithms such as the Perceptron algorithm [15], Balanced-Winnow [8], and the family of p-norm algorithms [7]. Recall that we cast online learning as the problem of incrementally increasing the dual objective function given by Eq. (13). We show in this section that all quasi-additive online learning algorithms can be viewed as employing the same procedure for incrementing Eq. (13). The sole difference between the algorithms is the complexity function F which leads to different forms of the function G. We exploit this fact by providing a unified analysis and mistake bounds to all the above algorithms. The bounds we obtain are as tight as the bounds that were derived for each algorithm individually yet our proofs are simpler.

To guarantee an increase in the dual as given by Eq. (13) on erroneous trials we devise the following procedure. First, if on trial t the algorithm did not make a prediction mistake we do not change $\boldsymbol{\alpha}$ and thus set $\boldsymbol{\alpha}^{t+1} = \boldsymbol{\alpha}^t$. If on trial t there was a prediction mistake, we change only the t'th component of $\boldsymbol{\alpha}$ and set it to C. Formally, for $t \in \mathcal{E}$ the new vector $\boldsymbol{\alpha}^{t+1}$ is defined as,

$$\alpha_i^{t+1} = \begin{cases} \alpha_i^t & \text{if } i \neq t \\ C & \text{if } i = t \end{cases} \tag{16}$$

This form of update implies that the components of $\boldsymbol{\alpha}$ are either zero or C.

Before we continue with the derivation and analysis of online algorithms, let us first provide sufficient conditions for the update given by Eq. (16) which guarantee a minimal increase of the dual objective for all $t \in \mathcal{E}$. Let $t \in \mathcal{E}$ be a trial on which $\boldsymbol{\alpha}$ was updated. From the definition of $\mathcal{D}(\boldsymbol{\alpha})$ we get that the change in the dual objective due to the update is,

$$\mathcal{D}(\boldsymbol{\alpha}^{t+1}) - \mathcal{D}(\boldsymbol{\alpha}^t) = \gamma C - G(\boldsymbol{\theta}_t + C\, y_t \mathbf{x}_t) + G(\boldsymbol{\theta}_t) . \tag{17}$$

Throughout this section we assume that G is twice differentiable. (This assumption indeed holds for the algorithms we analyze.) We denote by $\boldsymbol{g}(\boldsymbol{\theta})$ the gradient of G at $\boldsymbol{\theta}$ and by $H(\boldsymbol{\theta})$ the Hessian of G, that is, the matrix of second order derivatives of G with respect to $\boldsymbol{\theta}$. We would like to note in passing that the vector function $\boldsymbol{g}(\cdot)$ is often referred to as the *link* function (see for instance [1, 7, 10, 11]).

Using Taylor expansion of G around $\boldsymbol{\theta}_t$, we get that there exists $\boldsymbol{\theta}$ for which,

$$G(\boldsymbol{\theta}_t + C\, y_t \mathbf{x}_t) \;=\; G(\boldsymbol{\theta}_t) + C\, y_t \, \langle \mathbf{x}_t, g(\boldsymbol{\theta}_t) \rangle + \frac{1}{2} C^2 \, \langle \mathbf{x}_t, H(\boldsymbol{\theta})\, \mathbf{x}_t \rangle \; . \tag{18}$$

Plugging the above equation into Eq. (17) gives that,

$$\mathcal{D}(\boldsymbol{\alpha}^{t+1}) - \mathcal{D}(\boldsymbol{\alpha}^t) \;=\; C\, (\gamma - y_t \langle \mathbf{x}_t, g(\boldsymbol{\theta}_t) \rangle) - \frac{1}{2} C^2 \, \langle \mathbf{x}_t, H(\boldsymbol{\theta})\, \mathbf{x}_t \rangle \; . \tag{19}$$

We next show that $\boldsymbol{\omega}_t = g(\boldsymbol{\theta}_t)$ and therefore the second term in the right-hand of Eq. (18) is negative. Put another way, moving $\boldsymbol{\theta}_t$ infinitesimally in the direction of $y_t \mathbf{x}_t$ decreases G. We then cap the amount by which the second order term can influence the dual value. To show that $\boldsymbol{\omega}_t = g(\boldsymbol{\theta}_t)$ note that from the definition of G and $\boldsymbol{\omega}_t$, we get that for all $\boldsymbol{\theta}$ the following holds,

$$G(\boldsymbol{\theta}_t) + \langle \boldsymbol{\omega}_t, \boldsymbol{\theta} - \boldsymbol{\theta}_t \rangle \;=\; \langle \boldsymbol{\omega}_t, \boldsymbol{\theta}_t \rangle - F(\boldsymbol{\omega}_t) + \langle \boldsymbol{\omega}_t, \boldsymbol{\theta} - \boldsymbol{\theta}_t \rangle \;=\; \langle \boldsymbol{\omega}_t, \boldsymbol{\theta} \rangle - F(\boldsymbol{\omega}_t) \; . \tag{20}$$

In addition, $G(\boldsymbol{\theta}) = \max_{\boldsymbol{\omega} \in \Omega} \langle \boldsymbol{\omega}, \boldsymbol{\theta} \rangle - F(\boldsymbol{\omega}) \geq \langle \boldsymbol{\omega}_t, \boldsymbol{\theta} \rangle - F(\boldsymbol{\omega}_t)$. Combining Eq. (20) with the last inequality gives the following,

$$G(\boldsymbol{\theta}) \geq G(\boldsymbol{\theta}_t) + \langle \boldsymbol{\omega}_t, \boldsymbol{\theta} - \boldsymbol{\theta}_t \rangle \; . \tag{21}$$

Since Eq. (21) holds for all $\boldsymbol{\theta}$ it implies that $\boldsymbol{\omega}_t$ is a sub-gradient of G. In addition, since G is differentiable its only possible sub-gradient at $\boldsymbol{\theta}_t$ is its gradient, $g(\boldsymbol{\theta}_t)$, and thus $\boldsymbol{\omega}_t = g(\boldsymbol{\theta}_t)$. The simple form of the update and the link between $\boldsymbol{\omega}_t$ and $\boldsymbol{\theta}_t$ through g can be summarized as the following simple yet general quasi-additive update:

If $\hat{y}_t = y_t$ **Set** $\boldsymbol{\theta}_{t+1} = \boldsymbol{\theta}_t$ and $\boldsymbol{\omega}_{t+1} = \boldsymbol{\omega}_t$
If $\hat{y}_t \neq y_t$ **Set** $\boldsymbol{\theta}_{t+1} = \boldsymbol{\theta}_t + C y_t \mathbf{x}_t$ and $\boldsymbol{\omega}_{t+1} = g(\boldsymbol{\theta}_{t+1})$

Getting back to Eq. (19) we get that,

$$\mathcal{D}(\boldsymbol{\alpha}^{t+1}) - \mathcal{D}(\boldsymbol{\alpha}^t) \;=\; C\, (\gamma - y_t \langle \boldsymbol{\omega}_t, \mathbf{x}_t \rangle) - \frac{1}{2} C^2 \, \langle \mathbf{x}_t, H(\boldsymbol{\theta})\, \mathbf{x}_t \rangle \; . \tag{22}$$

Recall that we assume that $t \in \mathcal{E}$ and thus $y_t \langle \mathbf{x}_t, \boldsymbol{\omega}_t \rangle \leq 0$. In addition, we later on show that $\langle \mathbf{x}, H(\boldsymbol{\theta})\mathbf{x} \rangle \leq 1$ for all $\mathbf{x} \in \Omega$ with the particular choices of G and under certain assumptions on the norm of $\mathbf{x}$. We therefore can state the following corollary.

Corollary 1. *Let G be a twice differentiable function whose domain is $\mathbb{R}^n$. Denote by H the Hessian of G and assume that for all $\boldsymbol{\theta} \in \mathbb{R}^n$ and for all $\mathbf{x}_t$ ($t \in \mathcal{E}$) we have that $\langle \mathbf{x}_t, H(\boldsymbol{\theta})\mathbf{x}_t \rangle \leq 1$. Then, under the conditions of Thm. 1 the update given by Eq. (16) ensures that, $\lambda \geq \gamma C - \frac{1}{2} C^2$.*

Example 1 (Perceptron). The Perceptron algorithm [15] is derived from Eq. (16) by setting $F(\boldsymbol{\omega}) = \frac{1}{2}\|\boldsymbol{\omega}\|^2$, $\Omega = \mathbb{R}^n$, and $\gamma = 1$. To see this, note that the conjugate function of F for this choice is, $G(\boldsymbol{\theta}) = \frac{1}{2}\|\boldsymbol{\theta}\|^2$. Therefore, the gradient of G at $\boldsymbol{\theta}_t$ is $g(\boldsymbol{\theta}_t) = \boldsymbol{\theta}_t$, which implies that $\boldsymbol{\omega}_t = \boldsymbol{\theta}_t$. We thus obtain a scaled version of the well known Perceptron update, $\boldsymbol{\omega}_{t+1} = \boldsymbol{\omega}_t + C y_t \mathbf{x}_t$. Assume that $\|\mathbf{x}_t\|_2 \leq 1$ for all $t \in [m]$.

Since the Hessian of G is the identity matrix we get that, $\langle \mathbf{x}_t, H(\boldsymbol{\theta})\, \mathbf{x}_t \rangle = \langle \mathbf{x}_t, \mathbf{x}_t \rangle \leq 1$. Therefore, we obtain the following mistake bound,

$$(C - \tfrac{1}{2}C^2)\, M \;\leq\; \min_{\boldsymbol{\omega} \in \mathbb{R}^n} \tfrac{1}{2}\|\boldsymbol{\omega}\|^2 + C \sum_{i=1}^{m} \ell(\boldsymbol{\omega}; (\mathbf{x}_i, y_i)) \; . \tag{23}$$

Note the sequence of predictions of the Perceptron algorithm does not depend on the actual value of C so long as $C > 0$. Therefore, we can choose C so as to minimize the right hand side of Eq. (23) and rewrite,

$$\forall \boldsymbol{\omega} \in \mathbb{R}^n, \;\; M \;\leq\; \min_{C \in (0,2)} \left(\frac{1}{C(1 - \tfrac{1}{2}C)} \right) \left(\frac{1}{2}\|\boldsymbol{\omega}\|^2 + C \sum_{i=1}^{m} \ell(\boldsymbol{\omega}; (\mathbf{x}_i, y_i)) \right) \, ,$$

where the domain $(0, 2)$ for C ensures that the bound will not become vacuous. Solving the right-hand side of the above equation for C yields the following mistake bound,

$$M \;\leq\; L + \frac{1}{2}\|\boldsymbol{\omega}\|^2 \left(1 + \sqrt{1 + 4L/\|\boldsymbol{\omega}\|^2} \right) \, ,$$

where $L = \sum_{i=1}^{m} \ell(\boldsymbol{\omega}; (\mathbf{x}_i, y_i))$. The proof is omitted due to the lack of space and will be presented in a long version of the paper. We would like to note that this bound is identical to the best known mistake bound for the Perceptron algorithm (see for example [7]). However, our proof technique is vastly different and enables us to derive mistake bounds for new algorithms, as we show later on in Sec. 5.

Example 2 (Balanced Winnow). We now analyze a version of the Winnow algorithm called Balanced-Winnow [8] which is also closely related to the Exponentiated-Gradient algorithm [10]. For brevity we refer to the algorithm we analyze simply as Winnow. To derive the Winnow algorithm we choose, $F(\boldsymbol{\omega}) = \sum_{i=1}^{n} \omega_i \log\left(\frac{\omega_i}{1/n} \right)$, and $\Omega = \left\{ \boldsymbol{\omega} \in \mathbb{R}_+^n : \sum_{i=1}^{n} \omega_i = 1 \right\}$. The function F is the relative entropy between the probability vector $\boldsymbol{\omega}$ and the uniform vector $(\frac{1}{n}, \ldots, \frac{1}{n})$. The relative entropy is non-negative and measures the entropic divergence between two distributions. It attains a value of zero whenever the two vectors are equal. Therefore, the minimum value of $F(\boldsymbol{\omega})$ is zero and is attained for $\boldsymbol{\omega} = (\frac{1}{n}, \ldots, \frac{1}{n})$. The conjugate of F is the logarithm of the sum of exponentials (see for example [2][pp. 93]), $G(\boldsymbol{\theta}) = \log\left(\sum_{i=1}^{n} e^{\theta_i} \right)$. The k'th element of the gradient of G is, $g_k(\boldsymbol{\theta}) = e^{\theta_k} / \left(\sum_{i=1}^{n} e^{\theta_i} \right)$. Note that $g(\boldsymbol{\theta})$ is a vector in the n-dimensional simplex and therefore $\boldsymbol{\omega}_t = g(\boldsymbol{\theta}_t) \in \Omega$. The k'th element of $\boldsymbol{\omega}_{t+1}$ can be rewritten using a multiplicative update rule,

$$\omega_{t+1,k} \;=\; \frac{1}{Z_t} e^{\theta_{t,k} + C\, y_t\, x_{t,k}} \;=\; \frac{1}{Z_t} e^{C\, y_t\, x_{t,k}}\, \omega_{t,k} \, ,$$

where Z_t is a normalization constant which ensures that $\boldsymbol{\omega}_{t+1}$ is in the simplex.

To analyze the algorithm we need to show that $\langle \mathbf{x}_t, H(\boldsymbol{\theta})\, \mathbf{x}_t \rangle \leq 1$, which indeed holds for $\|\mathbf{x}_t\|_\infty \leq 1$. The proof is omitted due to the lack of space. As a result, we obtain the following mistake bound,

$$\left(\gamma C - \frac{1}{2}C^2 \right) M \;\leq\; \min_{\boldsymbol{\omega} \in \Omega} \left(\sum_{i=1}^{n} \omega_i \log(\omega_i) + \log(n) + C \sum_{i=1}^{m} \ell'(\boldsymbol{\omega}; (\mathbf{x}_i, y_i)) \right) \, .$$

Since $\sum_{i=1}^{n} \omega_i \log(\omega_i) \leq 0$, if we set $C = \gamma$, the above bound reduces to,

$$M \leq 2 \left(\frac{\log(n)}{\gamma^2} + \min_{\omega \in \Omega} \frac{1}{\gamma} \sum_{i=1}^{m} \ell^{\gamma}(\omega; (\mathbf{x}_i, y_i)) \right) .$$

Example 3 (p-norm algorithms). We conclude this section with the analysis of the family of p-norm algorithms [7, 8]. Let $p, q \geq 1$ be two scalars such that $\frac{1}{p} + \frac{1}{q} = 1$. Define, $F(\omega) = \frac{1}{2}\|\omega\|_q^2 = \frac{1}{2} \left(\sum_{i=1}^{n} |\omega_i|^q \right)^{2/q}$, and let $\Omega = \mathbb{R}^n$. The conjugate function of F in this case is, $G(\boldsymbol{\theta}) = \frac{1}{2}\|\boldsymbol{\theta}\|_p^2$ (For a proof see [2], page 93.) and the i'th element of the gradient of G is,

$$g_i(\boldsymbol{\theta}) = \frac{\text{sign}(\theta_i) |\theta_i|^{p-1}}{\|\boldsymbol{\theta}\|_p^{p-2}} .$$

To analyze any p-norm algorithm we need again to bound for all t the quadratic form $\langle \mathbf{x}_t, H(\boldsymbol{\theta})\mathbf{x}_t \rangle$. It is possible to show (see [7, 8]) that

$$\langle \mathbf{x}, H(\boldsymbol{\theta})\mathbf{x} \rangle \leq \frac{1}{p} \left(\|\boldsymbol{\theta}\|_p^p \right)^{\frac{2}{p}-1} p(p-1) \sum_{i=1}^{n} \text{sign}(\theta_i) |\theta_i|^{p-2} x_i^2 . \qquad (24)$$

Using Holder inequality with the dual norms $\frac{p}{p-2}$ and $\frac{p}{2}$ we get that,

$$\sum_{i=1}^{n} \text{sign}(\theta_i) |\theta_i|^{p-2} x_i^2 \leq \left(\sum_{i=1}^{n} |\theta_i|^{(p-2)\frac{p}{p-2}} \right)^{\frac{p-2}{p}} \left(\sum_{i=1}^{n} x_i^{2\frac{p}{2}} \right)^{\frac{2}{p}} = \|\boldsymbol{\theta}\|_p^{p-2} \|\mathbf{x}\|_p^2 .$$

Combining the above with Eq. (24) gives, $\langle \mathbf{x}, H(\boldsymbol{\theta})\mathbf{x} \rangle \leq (p-1)\|\mathbf{x}\|_p^2$. If we further assume that $\|\mathbf{x}\|_p \leq \sqrt{1/(p-1)}$ then we can apply corollary 1 and obtain that,

$$\left(\gamma C - \frac{1}{2}C^2 \right) M \leq \min_{\omega \in \mathbb{R}^n} \left(\frac{1}{2}\|\omega\|_q^2 + C \sum_{i=1}^{m} \ell^{\gamma}(\omega; (\mathbf{x}_i, y_i)) \right) .$$

5 Deriving New Online Learning Algorithms

In the previous section we described a family of online learning algorithms. The algorithms are based on the simple procedure defined via Eq. (16) which increments the dual using a fixed-size update to a single dual variable. Intuitively, an update scheme which results in a larger increase in the dual objective on each trial is likely to yield online algorithms with refined loss bounds. In this section we outline a few new online update schemes which set α more aggressively.

The update scheme of the previous section for increasing the dual modifies α only on trials on which there was a prediction mistake ($t \in \mathcal{E}$). The update is performed by setting the t'th element of α to C and keeping the rest of the variables intact. This simple update can be enhanced in several ways. First, note that while setting α_t^{t+1} to C guarantees a sufficient increase in the dual, there might be other values α_t^{t+1} which would lead to larger increases of the dual. Furthermore, we can also update α on trials on which the prediction was correct so long as the loss is non-zero. Last, we need not restrict our update to the t'th element of $\boldsymbol{\alpha}$. We can instead update several dual variables as long as their indices are in $[t]$.

We now describe and briefly analyze a few new updates which increase the dual more aggressively. The goal here is to illustrate the power of the approach and the list of new updates we outline is by no means exhaustive. We start by describing an update which sets α_t^{t+1} adaptively, depending on the loss suffered on round t. This improved update constructs $\boldsymbol{\alpha}^{t+1}$ as follows,

$$\alpha_i^{t+1} = \begin{cases} \alpha_i^t & \text{if } i \neq t \\ \min\{\ell(\boldsymbol{\omega}_t; (\mathbf{x}_t, y_t)), C\} & \text{if } i = t \end{cases} . \tag{25}$$

As before, the above update can be used with various complexity functions for F, yielding different quasi-additive algorithms. We now provide a unified analysis for all algorithms which are based on the update given by Eq. (25). In contrast to the previous update which modified $\boldsymbol{\alpha}$ only when there was a prediction mistake, the new update modifies $\boldsymbol{\alpha}$ whenever $\ell(\boldsymbol{\omega}_t; (\mathbf{x}_t, y_t)) > 0$. This more aggressive approach leads to a more general *loss* bound while still attaining the same mistake bound of the previous section. The mistake bound still holds since whenever the algorithm makes a prediction mistake its loss is at least γ. Formally, let us define the following mitigating function,

$$\mu(x) = \frac{1}{C} \left(\min\{x, C\} \left(x - \frac{1}{2} \min\{x, C\} \right) \right) .$$

The function μ is illustrated in Fig. 2. Note that $\mu(\cdot)$ becomes very similar to the identity function for small values of C. The following theorem provides a bound on the cumulative sum of $\mu(\ell(\boldsymbol{\omega}_t, (\mathbf{x}_t, y_t)))$.

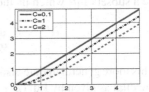

Fig. 2. The mitigating function $\mu(x)$ for different values of C

Theorem 2. *Let* $(\mathbf{x}_1, y_1), \ldots, (\mathbf{x}_m, y_m)$ *be a sequence of examples and let* $F : \Omega \to \mathbb{R}$ *be a complexity function for which* $\min_{\boldsymbol{\omega} \in \Omega} F(\boldsymbol{\omega}) = 0$. *Assume that an online algorithm is derived from Eq. (25) using* G *as the conjugate function of* F. *If* G *is twice differentiable and its Hessian satisfies,* $\langle \mathbf{x}_t, H(\boldsymbol{\theta})\mathbf{x}_t \rangle \leq 1$ *for all* $\boldsymbol{\theta} \in \mathbb{R}^n$ *and* $t \in [m]$, *then the following bound holds,*

$$\sum_{t=1}^m \mu\left(\ell(\boldsymbol{\omega}_t; (\mathbf{x}_t, y_t))\right) \leq \min_{\boldsymbol{\omega} \in \Omega} \left(\frac{1}{C} F(\boldsymbol{\omega}) + \sum_{t=1}^m \ell(\boldsymbol{\omega}; (\mathbf{x}_t, y_t)) \right) .$$

Proof. Analogously to the proof of Thm. 1, we prove this theorem by bounding $\mathcal{D}(\boldsymbol{\alpha}^{m+1})$ from above and below. The upper bound $\mathcal{D}(\boldsymbol{\alpha}^{m+1}) \leq \mathcal{P}^\star$ follows again from weak duality theorem. To derive a lower bound, note that the conditions stated in the theorem imply that $\mathcal{D}(\boldsymbol{\alpha}^1) = 0$ and thus $\mathcal{D}(\boldsymbol{\alpha}^{m+1}) = \sum_{t=1}^m \left(\mathcal{D}(\boldsymbol{\alpha}^{t+1}) - \mathcal{D}(\boldsymbol{\alpha}^t) \right)$. Define $\tau_t = \min\{\ell(\boldsymbol{\omega}_t; (\mathbf{x}_t, y_t)), C\}$ and note that the sole difference between the updates given by Eq. (25) and Eq. (16) is that τ_t replaces C. Thus, the derivation of Eq. (22) in Sec. 4 can be repeated almost verbatim with τ_t replacing C to get,

$$\mathcal{D}(\boldsymbol{\alpha}^{t+1}) - \mathcal{D}(\boldsymbol{\alpha}^t) \geq \tau_t \left(\gamma - y_t \langle \boldsymbol{\omega}_t, \mathbf{x}_t \rangle \right) - \frac{1}{2} \tau_t^2 . \tag{26}$$

Summing over $t \in [m]$ and using the definitions of $\ell(\boldsymbol{\omega}_t; (\mathbf{x}_t, y_t))$, τ_t, and μ gives that,

$$\mathcal{D}(\boldsymbol{\alpha}^{m+1}) = \sum_{t=1}^{m} \left(\mathcal{D}(\boldsymbol{\alpha}^{t+1}) - \mathcal{D}(\boldsymbol{\alpha}^t)\right) \geq C \sum_{t=1}^{m} \mu\left(\ell(\boldsymbol{\omega}_t; (\mathbf{x}_t, y_t))\right) .$$

Finally, we compare the lower and upper bounds on $\mathcal{D}(\boldsymbol{\alpha}^{m+1})$ and rearrange terms. □

Note that $\ell(\boldsymbol{\omega}_t; (\mathbf{x}_t, y_t)) \geq \gamma$ whenever the algorithm makes a prediction mistake. Since μ is a monotonically increasing function we get that the increase in the dual for $t \in \mathcal{E}$ is at least $\mu(\gamma)$. Thus, we obtain the mistake bound,

$$\lambda M \leq \mathcal{P}^{\star} \text{ where } \lambda \geq C\mu(\gamma) = \begin{cases} \gamma C - \frac{1}{2}C^2 & \text{if } C \leq \gamma \\ \frac{1}{2}\gamma^2 & \text{if } C > \gamma \end{cases} . \tag{27}$$

The new update is advantageous over the previous update since in addition to the same increase in the dual on trials with a prediction mistake it is also guaranteed to increase the dual by $\mu(\ell(\cdot))$ on the rest of the trials. Yet, both updates are confined to modifying a single dual variable on each trial. We nonetheless can increase the dual more dramatically by modifying multiple dual variables on each round. Formally, for $t \in [m]$, let I_t be a subset of $[t]$ which includes t. Given I_t, we can set $\boldsymbol{\alpha}^{t+1}$ to be,

$$\boldsymbol{\alpha}^{t+1} = \underset{\boldsymbol{\alpha} \in [0,C]^m}{\operatorname{argmax}} \mathcal{D}(\boldsymbol{\alpha}) \text{ s.t. } \forall i \notin I_t, \ \alpha_i = \alpha_i^t . \tag{28}$$

This more general update also achieves the bound of Thm. 2 and the minimal increase in the dual as given by Eq. (27). To see this, note that the requirement that $t \in I_t$ implies,

$$\mathcal{D}(\boldsymbol{\alpha}^{t+1}) \geq \max \left\{\mathcal{D}(\boldsymbol{\alpha}) : \boldsymbol{\alpha} \in [0, C]^m \text{ and } \forall i \neq t, \ \alpha_i = \alpha_i^t\right\} . \tag{29}$$

Thus the increase in the dual $\mathcal{D}(\boldsymbol{\alpha}^{t+1}) - \mathcal{D}(\boldsymbol{\alpha}^t)$ is guaranteed to be at least as large as the increase due to the previous updates. The rest of the proof of the bound is literally the same.

Let us now examine a few choices for I_t. Setting $I_t = [t]$ for all t gives the Online-SVM algorithm we mentioned in Sec. 3 by choosing $F(\boldsymbol{\omega}) = \frac{1}{2}\|\boldsymbol{\omega}\|^2$ and $\Omega = \mathbb{R}^n$. This algorithm makes use of all the examples that have been observed and thus is likely to make the largest increase in the dual objective on each trial. It does require however a full-blown quadratic programming solver. In contrast, Eq. (29) can be solved analytically when we employ the smallest possible set, $I_t = \{t\}$, with $F(\boldsymbol{\omega}) = \frac{1}{2}\|\boldsymbol{\omega}\|^2$. In this case α_t^{t+1} turns out to be the minimum between C and $\ell(\boldsymbol{\omega}_t; (\mathbf{x}_t, y_t))/\|\mathbf{x}_t\|^2$. This algorithm was described in [4] and belongs to a family of Passive Aggressive algorithms. The mistake bound that we obtain as a by product in this paper is however superior to the one in [4]. Naturally, we can interpolate between the minimal and maximal choices for I_t by setting the size of I_t to a predefined value k and choosing, say, the last k observed examples as the elements of I_t. For $k = 1$ and $k = 2$ we can solve Eq. (28) analytically while gaining modest increases in the dual. The full power of the update is unleashed for large values of k, however, Eq. (28) cannot be solved analytically and requires the usage of iterative procedures such as interior point methods.

6 Discussion

We presented a new framework for the design and analysis of online learning algorithms. Our framework yields the best known bounds for quasi-additive online classification algorithms. It also paves the way to new algorithms. There are various possible extensions of the work that we did not discuss due to the lack of space. Our framework can naturally be extended to other prediction problems such as regression, multiclass categorization, and ranking problems. Our framework is also applicable to settings where the target hypothesis is not fixed but rather drifting with the sequence of examples. In addition, the hinge-loss was used in our derivation in order to make a clear connection to the quasi-additive algorithms. The choice of the hinge-loss is rather arbitrary and it can be replaced with others such as the logistic loss. There are also numerous possible algorithmic extensions and new update schemes which manipulate multiple dual variables on each online update. Finally, our framework can be used with non-differentiable conjugate functions which might become useful in settings where there are combinatorial constraints on the number of non-zero dual variables (see [6]).

References

1. K. Azoury and M. Warmuth. Relative loss bounds for on-line density estimation with the exponential family of distributions. *Machine Learning*, 43(3):211–246, 2001.
2. S. Boyd and L. Vandenberghe. *Convex Optimization*. Cambridge University Press, 2004.
3. N. Cesa-Bianchi, A. Conconi, and C.Gentile. On the generalization ability of on-line learning algorithms. In *Advances in Neural Information Processing Systems 14*, pages 359–366, 2002.
4. K. Crammer, O. Dekel, J. Keshet, S. Shalev-Shwartz, and Y. Singer. Online passive aggressive algorithms. Technical report, The Hebrew University, 2005.
5. N. Cristianini and J. Shawe-Taylor. *An Introduction to Support Vector Machines*. Cambridge University Press, 2000.
6. O. Dekel, S. Shalev-Shwartz, and Y. Singer. The Forgetron: A kernel-based perceptron on a fixed budget. In *Advances in Neural Information Processing Systems 18*, 2005.
7. C. Gentile. The robustness of the p-norm algorithms. *Machine Learning*, 53(3), 2002.
8. A. J. Grove, N. Littlestone, and D. Schuurmans. General convergence results for linear discriminant updates. *Machine Learning*, 43(3):173–210, 2001.
9. J. Kivinen, A. J. Smola, and R. C. Williamson. Online learning with kernels. *IEEE Transactions on Signal Processing*, 52(8):2165–2176, 2002.
10. J. Kivinen and M. Warmuth. Exponentiated gradient versus gradient descent for linear predictors. *Information and Computation*, 132(1):1–64, January 1997.
11. J. Kivinen and M. Warmuth. Relative loss bounds for multidimensional regression problems. *Journal of Machine Learning*, 45(3):301–329, July 2001.
12. Y. Li and P. M. Long. The relaxed online maximum margin algorithm. *Machine Learning*, 46(1–3):361–387, 2002.
13. N. Littlestone. Learning when irrelevant attributes abound: A new linear-threshold algorithm. *Machine Learning*, 2:285–318, 1988.
14. N. Littlestone. *Mistake bounds and logarithmic linear-threshold learning algorithms*. PhD thesis, U. C. Santa Cruz, March 1989.
15. F. Rosenblatt. The perceptron: A probabilistic model for information storage and organization in the brain. *Psychological Review*, 65:386–407, 1958. (Reprinted in *Neurocomputing* (MIT Press, 1988).).

Online Tracking of Linear Subspaces

Koby Crammer

Department of Computer and Information Science, University of Pennsylvania
crammer@cis.upenn.edu

Abstract. We address the problem of online de-noising a stream of input points. We assume that the clean data is embedded in a linear subspace. We present two online algorithms for tracking subspaces and, as a consequence, de-noising. We also describe two regularization schemas which improve the resistance to noise. We analyze the algorithms in the loss bound model, and specify some of their properties. Preliminary simulations illustrate the usefulness of our algorithms.

1 Introduction and Problem Setting

Subspace analysis and subspace tracking (e.g. [1]) are important tools in various adaptive signal processing tasks, such as bearing estimation [2] and beamforming [3]. Mathematically, the algorithm receives a sequence of input vectors and returns a linear subspace that describes the data well. Assuming that the data consist of points from a low-dimensional subspace corrupted with isotropic noise which pulled it out of the original subspace [4, 5], the reconstructed subspace can be used to clear or filter the noisy data.

We present online algorithms for subspace tracking and analyze them in the loss bound model. Unlike previous analysis for these types of algorithms (e.g. [1]), we do not use any statistical assumptions over the source of the input points. The goal of the learning algorithm is to de-noise new data points by identifying this subspace. Given a data point, the algorithm is required to output the underling uncorrupted point. Specifically, we measure the performance of the algorithm relative to the *uncorrupted* version of each point, rather than the corrupted observed version. The algorithms we present can also track drifting or switching subspaces.

The tracking subspace problem shares common properties with both multivariate regression and one-class classification [6]. As in regression, the learner maintains a function (linear transformation) and outputs a vector for a given input vector. In this view, our problem is a regression from a vector space to itself that uses the class of positive semidefinite (PSD) matrices as regressors. This approach to subspace analysis [7] was used to devise sparse principal component analysis (PCA).

Similarly to one-class learning, the learner is *not* exposed to a feedback signal or to a "right" answer. The only information at hand are the input points. The goal of a one-class learner is to identify a meaningful *subset* in space, in the sense that it captures most, if not all of the points. Similarly, our primary goal is to find a meaningful *vector subspace* which contains most of the *weight* of the points. An additional similarity between one-class learning and subspace tracking is that in both cases there is a trivial solution. Given any set of points, one can always find a convex body that encloses all of

G. Lugosi and H.U. Simon (Eds.): COLT 2006, LNAI 4005, pp. 438–452, 2006.

them, and we can always find a vector subspace that contains all of their weight (using the identity matrix). In this aspect both problems are ill-defined.

We now describe the subspace tracking problem formally. Let $x_1 \ldots x_m \in \mathbb{R}^d$ be a set of column vectors. We view the problem as a filtering problem [4, 5], $x_i = y_i + \nu_i$, where y_i lies in a low dimensional linear subspace and ν_i is the unknown noise for this point. Since the goal it to track the linear subspace we assume that there exists an unknown target idempotent projection matrix Q such that $y_i = Qx_i$ and $\nu_i = (I - Q)x_i$. That is, the noise is taken to be orthogonal to the clean data, because we cannot separate noise components projected by Q onto the subspace and input points.

PCA computes an orthogonal set $A \in \mathbb{R}^{d \times n}$ of n vectors, which is the n eigenvectors corresponding to the top n eigenvalues of the covariance matrix, $\sum_i x_i x_i^\top$. This basis is often used for compression since each point $x \in \mathbb{R}^d$ is represented using n values $A^T x$. In addition, PCA can be used for de-noising with the matrix $Q = AA^T$. Since A is composed of orthonormal vectors, Q is a *projection*, that is, it is symmetric, positive semidefinite (PSD) and idempotent (its eigenvalues are either zero or one). In this paper we adopt this view of PCA, and focus on learning matrices P of this form. Unlike PCA, we do not reduce explicitly the number of components of a vector (by using the matrix A). In other words, we seek a low-dimensional subspace, but represent data in the original vector space of dimension d. Since the restriction that the eigenvalues will be *either* zero or one is algorithmically challenging because it involves integer programming, we relax the idempotency assumption. Our learning algorithms seek linear transformations which are symmetric and positive semidefinite. We refer to these transformations (P or P_i) as projections. When the projections are also idempotent (i.e. all eigenvalues are either zero or one), we will refer to them as *idempotent projections* (Q). One of the algorithms described below always maintains a linear transformation with eigenvalues *between* zero and one. This is often considered the natural relaxation of idempotency.

We present and analyze two *online* learning algorithms for filtering through subspace tracking. Both algorithms can also be used to track *non-stationary* sequences. The first algorithm is motivated by a *gradient descent* approach and the second by an *Euclidean projection*[1]. We use the loss-bound model of online learning to analyze the algorithms. The algorithms we consider work in rounds. On round i an online learning algorithm chooses a linear subspace represented by a PSD matrix P_i. It then receives a point x_i, outputs the projection of x_i onto the chosen subspace and suffers loss which is a function of the discrepancy between the projection $P_i x_i$ and the clean point Qx_i, i.e. $\ell(P_i x_i, Qx_i)$. Finally, the subspace representation is updated and the next round follows. Note that Q or Qx_i are *unrevealed* to the learner algorithm, which makes the learning task more involved. We use the matrix Q only for analysis.

Previous work on learning PSD matrices falls into two kinds. The first kind of algorithm builds a general symmetric matrix which is either restricted to be PSD (e.g. [8]) or in a second step projected back on the PSD cone [9]. The second kind of algorithm [10], employ the costly operation of matrix exponentiation which automatically yields PSD matrices. The former approaches employ loss functions which are often linear in

---

[1] We use the term projection in two ways. First, throughout the paper it refers to a symmetric PSD linear transformation. Second, we use the projection operation to derive the second of the two online algorithms.

the matrix, while the latter uses a loss which is quadratic in the matrix. In this work, we have the benefit of both approaches. Our algorithms are both very simple, involve only addition operations and maintain matrices which are guaranteed to be PSD with no additional operations, even though the quadratic loss is used.

Notation: For a matrix P, the property of being a positive semi-definite matrix is denoted by $P \succeq 0$. Given a vector $\boldsymbol{x}$, we denote by $X = \boldsymbol{x}\boldsymbol{x}^\top$ the outer-product of $\boldsymbol{x}$ with itself. A unit vector is denoted by $\hat{\boldsymbol{x}} = \boldsymbol{x}/\|\boldsymbol{x}\|$, and $\hat{X} = \hat{\boldsymbol{x}}\hat{\boldsymbol{x}}^\top$ is a rank-one symmetric matrix with eigenvalue 1. Finally, $\|P\|_p$ is ℓ_p norm of the vector generated by concatenating the columns of matrix P.

2   Gradient Algorithm

We start with the description of an online algorithm based on gradient descent. After an input point $\boldsymbol{x}_i$ has been observed we wish to update our current subspace (represented by P_i) based on this point. Since there is no corresponding feedback signal, we have no choice but to use the point itself as a guide, so we seek to decrease the loss $\ell(\boldsymbol{x}_i, P\boldsymbol{x}_i)$. This only approximates our true loss, but as we shall see in the sequel, it is enough. However, we do not want to make big changes from our current subspace, as it captures our knowledge of previous examples. Therefore, we define the following update,

$$P_{i+1} = \arg\min_P \frac{1}{2} \|P - P_i\|^2 + \alpha \ell(\boldsymbol{x}_i, P\boldsymbol{x}_i) \quad \text{s.t.} \quad P = P^\top, \; P \succeq 0 . \quad (1)$$

where $\alpha > 0$ is a trade-off parameter. In this section we focus in the squared loss,

$$\ell(\boldsymbol{x}_i, P_i \boldsymbol{x}_i) = \frac{1}{2} \|\boldsymbol{x}_i - P_i \boldsymbol{x}_i\|^2 . \quad (2)$$

The two constraints ensure that the eigenvalues of P_{i+1} are positive real numbers. Thus, similarly to PCA we will be able to reduce the dimension by performing eigendecomposition. We derive the update rule for the algorithm by solving the optimization problem. For now we omit the PSD constraint in Eq. (1). We show below that the solution of the optimization problem is in fact PSD with bounded eigenvalues.

The Lagrangian of the optimization problem defined by Eq. (1) is,

$$\mathcal{L}(P; Z) = \frac{1}{2} \|P - P_i\|^2 + \alpha \frac{1}{2} \|\boldsymbol{x}_i - P\boldsymbol{x}_i\|^2 - \text{Tr}\left[Z(P - P^T)\right] . \quad (3)$$

To solve the problem we first differentiate $\mathcal{L}$ with respect to P and set the result to zero,

$$P_{i+1} - P_i - \alpha X_i + \alpha P_{i+1} X_i - Z^T + Z = 0 . \quad (4)$$

As we shall see in Sec. 3 we can solve Eq. (4) analytically, but it involves non-linear terms arising from matrix inversion. Instead, we use the fact that, for reasonable small values of α, the matrices $P_{i+1}X_i$ and P_iX_i are close to each other. We thus approximate Eq. (4) by,

$$P_{i+1} = P_i + \alpha (X_i - P_i X_i) + \tilde{Z} , \quad (5)$$

where we define the anti-symmetric matrix $\tilde{Z} = Z^T - Z$. We eliminate $\tilde{Z}$ from the solution by enforcing the symmetry constraint $P_{i+1} = P_{i+1}^T$. Using the facts that both P_i and X_i are symmetric and that $\tilde{Z}$ is anti-symmetric we get, $P_{i+1}^T = P_i + \alpha(X_i - X_iP_i) - \tilde{Z}$. By solving the equation $P_{i+1} = P_{i+1}^T$ we extract the value of $\tilde{Z} = \frac{1}{2}\alpha(P_iX_i - X_iP_i)$. We finally get the update rule of the algorithm,

$$P_{i+1} = P_i + \alpha\left[X_i - \frac{1}{2}(P_iX_i + X_iP_i)\right]. \tag{6}$$

For the analysis of the algorithm we find it convenient to change variables,

$$P_{i+1} = P_i + \gamma_i\left[\hat{X}_i - \frac{1}{2}\left(P_i\hat{X}_i + \hat{X}_iP_i\right)\right] \quad , \quad \gamma_i = \alpha\|\boldsymbol{x}_i\|^2. \tag{7}$$

The algorithm can be viewed as performing a (stochastic) gradient descent, since the right term of Eq. (7) equal to the *symmetric* part of the gradient $\nabla_P\ell(\boldsymbol{x}, P\boldsymbol{x}_i)|_{P=P_i}$. The algorithm is summarized in Fig. 1. The description of the Regularize procedure is deferred to Sec. 4 and for now we ignore it. We refer to this algorithm as the GST algorithm, for Gradient-decent-based Subspace Tracker.

To conclude this section we show that our algorithm can be combined with Mercer kernels. We show that P_i can be written as a linear combination of outer product of the input points with coefficients $\Gamma_{p,q}$, that is, $P_i = \sum_{p,q=1}^{i-1}\Gamma_{p,q}\hat{\boldsymbol{x}}_p\hat{\boldsymbol{x}}_q^\top$. The proof proceeds by induction. The initial matrix $P_1 = 0$ clearly can be written in the required form. For the induction step we substitute $\hat{X} = \hat{\boldsymbol{x}}\hat{\boldsymbol{x}}^\top$ in Eq. (7) and use the induction assumption,

$$P_{i+1} =$$
$$P_i + \gamma_i\left[\hat{\boldsymbol{x}}_i\hat{\boldsymbol{x}}_i^\top - \frac{1}{2}\sum_{p=1}^{i-1}\hat{\boldsymbol{x}}_p\left(\sum_{q=1}^{i-1}\Gamma_{p,q}\hat{\boldsymbol{x}}_q^\top\hat{\boldsymbol{x}}_i\right)\hat{\boldsymbol{x}}_i^\top - \frac{1}{2}\sum_{q=1}^{i-1}\hat{\boldsymbol{x}}_i\left(\sum_{p=1}^{i-1}\Gamma_{p,q}\hat{\boldsymbol{x}}_i^\top\hat{\boldsymbol{x}}_p\right)\hat{\boldsymbol{x}}_q^\top\right].$$

The terms in the brackets are of the desired form and furthermore the matrix P_i is of the desired form due to the induction assumption. From the last equation we can recursively set the values of the matrix Γ : $\Gamma_{i,i} = \gamma_i$, $\Gamma_{q,i} = \Gamma_{i,q} = \sum_{p=1}^{i-1}\Gamma_{p,q}\hat{\boldsymbol{x}}_i^\top\hat{\boldsymbol{x}}_p$ for $q = 1\ldots i-1$. We have shown that all the steps of the online algorithm depends in the input data through inner product operations and thus can replace the standard inner product with any Mercer kernel.

2.1 Analysis

Before we prove a loss bound on the performance of the algorithm, we first fulfill our promise and show that indeed the algorithm maintains a positive semidefinite linear transformation P_i. This property is somewhat surprising in light of the following observation. Standard linear algebra computation shows that the rank of the matrix $\hat{X}_i - \frac{1}{2}(P_i\hat{X}_i + \hat{X}_iP_i)$ is either one or two. In the latter case, the eigenvalues of this matrix are, $\lambda_\pm = \frac{1}{2}\left(1 \pm \sqrt{1 + \hat{\boldsymbol{x}}_i^\top P_iP_i\hat{\boldsymbol{x}}_i - (\hat{\boldsymbol{x}}_i^\top P_i\hat{\boldsymbol{x}}_i)^2}\right)$. The smaller eigenvalue

λ_- is negative since $\hat{\boldsymbol{x}}_i^\top P_i P_i \hat{\boldsymbol{x}}_i - (\hat{\boldsymbol{x}}_i^\top P_i \hat{\boldsymbol{x}}_i)^2 \geq 0$. Thus on each iteration some of the eigenvalues of P_{i+1} are potentially smaller than those of P_i. If some of the eigenvalues of P_i are zero then some of the eigenvalues of P_{i+1} can be negative [11].

Specifically, we show by induction that for any linear transformation that can be derived along the run of the algorithm $P_1 \ldots P_{m+1}$ we have that $0 \preceq P_{i+1} \preceq bI$ assuming $\gamma_i \in [0, a]$, where $b = 4/(4-a)$. This requirement is easily fulfilled by setting the tradeoff parameter to be in the range $\alpha \in [0, a/R^2]$ where $R^2 = \max_i \|\boldsymbol{x}_i\|^2$. Since the initialization of the linear transformation is such that $0 \preceq P_1 \preceq bI$, then it suffices to show that the claim holds inductively. Finally, although the lemma is general we assume below that the learning rate is set to $\alpha = 1 = a$ and thus the upper bound on the eigenvalues is $b = 4/3$.

Lemma 1. *Let* $0 < a \leq 2$ *and* $b = 4/(4-a) > 1$. *If* $\gamma_i \in [0, a]$ *and* $0 \preceq P_i \preceq bI$ *then* $0 \preceq P_{i+1} \preceq bI$.

Proof. Since P_{i+1} is symmetric by construction it is remained to show that its eigenvalues are between zero and b. Rewriting Eq. (7) we get,

$$P_{i+1} = P_i + \gamma_i \left[\hat{X}_i - \frac{1}{2} \left(P_i \hat{X}_i + \hat{X}_i P_i \right) \right]$$

$$= \left(I - \frac{1}{2} \gamma_i \hat{X}_i \right) P_i \left(I - \frac{1}{2} \gamma_i \hat{X}_i \right) + \hat{X}_i \left(\gamma_i I - \frac{1}{4} \gamma_i^2 P_i \right) \hat{X}_i, \qquad (8)$$

where we used the equality $\hat{X} = \hat{X}\hat{X}$. Eq. (8) is a sum of two terms, the first term is PSD by definition and the second term is PSD as since $(1/4)\gamma_i^2 P_i \preceq (1/4) b a \gamma_i I \preceq a/(4-a)\gamma_i I \preceq \gamma_i I$. The last inequality holds since $a \leq 2$. Since PSD matrices are closed under addition we get that $0 \preceq P$. We show next that the eigenvalues of this matrix are always not greater than b and we do so by showing that for all vectors $\boldsymbol{v}$ we have that $\boldsymbol{v}^\top P_{i+1} \boldsymbol{v} \leq b \|\boldsymbol{v}\|^2$. Using Eq. (8) we get,

$$\boldsymbol{v}^\top P_{i+1} \boldsymbol{v} = \left[\boldsymbol{v}^\top \left(I - \frac{1}{2} \gamma_i \hat{X}_i \right) \right] P_i \left[\left(I - \frac{1}{2} \gamma_i \hat{X}_i \right) \boldsymbol{v} \right] + \boldsymbol{v}^\top \hat{X}_i \left(\gamma_i I - \frac{1}{4} \gamma_i^2 P_i \right) \hat{X}_i \boldsymbol{v}.$$

We first develop the left term by computing the norm of the vector multiplying P_i,

$$\left\| \left(I - \frac{1}{2} \gamma_i \hat{X}_i \right) \boldsymbol{v} \right\|^2 = \boldsymbol{v}^\top \left[I - \frac{1}{2} \gamma_i \hat{X}_i \right] \left[I - \frac{1}{2} \gamma_i \hat{X}_i \right] \boldsymbol{v} = \|\boldsymbol{v}\|^2 + \left(\frac{1}{4} \gamma_i^2 - \gamma_i \right) \langle \boldsymbol{v}, \hat{\boldsymbol{x}} \rangle^2.$$

Plugging into the last equation and using the assumption that the eigenvalues of P_i are not greater than b we get,

$$\boldsymbol{v}^\top P_{i+1} \boldsymbol{v} \leq b \|\boldsymbol{v}\|^2 + b \left(\frac{1}{4} \gamma_i^2 - \gamma_i \right) \langle \boldsymbol{v}, \hat{\boldsymbol{x}} \rangle^2 + \langle \boldsymbol{v}, \hat{\boldsymbol{x}} \rangle^2 \left(\gamma_i - \frac{1}{4} \gamma_i^2 \hat{\boldsymbol{x}}_i^\top P_i \hat{\boldsymbol{x}}_i \right)$$

$$\leq b \|\boldsymbol{v}\|^2 + \left(\frac{b}{4} \gamma_i^2 - (b-1)\gamma_i \right) \langle \boldsymbol{v}, \hat{\boldsymbol{x}} \rangle^2 \leq b \|\boldsymbol{v}\|^2,$$

where the last inequality holds because $\gamma_i \leq a$. ∎

We now turn and analyze the algorithm in the loss bound model. Concretely, we compare the performance of the algorithm to that of a *fixed* idempotent projection Q. The following lemma bounds the relative loss for an individual example. The proof generalizes similar bounds for vector adaptive filtering [4].

Lemma 2. *Let x_i be any vector with bounded norm $\|x_i\|^2 \leq R^2$. Let Q be any idempotent projection (symmetric matrix with eigenvalues either zero or one) and let the trade-off parameter be $\alpha = 1/R^2$ then,*

$$\frac{1}{2}\|P_i - Q\|^2 - \frac{1}{2}\|P_{i+1} - Q\|^2 \geq \frac{1}{2}\alpha\|P_i x_i - Qx_i\|^2 - \frac{1}{2}\alpha\|x_i - Qx_i\|^2 .$$

Before proving the lemma we like to comment that unlike relative-performance online bounds [12] for more standard problems such as classification and regression, the algorithm and the fixed projection are measured differently. The loss the algorithm suffers is measured compared to the uncorrupted point Qx_i and not to the input vector x_i. This is because we assume that the input data were generated using Q. Therefore, the loss of the idempotent projection Q is in fact the squared norm of the noise vector.

Proof. Tediously long algebraic manipulations give,

$$\frac{1}{2}\|P_i - Q\|^2 - \frac{1}{2}\|P_{i+1} - Q\|^2 = -\gamma_i\|\hat{x}_i - Q\hat{x}_i\|^2 + \gamma_i\hat{x}_i^\top \left[P_i - \frac{1}{2}(QP_i + P_iQ)\right]\hat{x}_i$$

$$-\frac{1}{4}\gamma_i^2\left[\|P_i\hat{x}_i - \hat{x}_i\|^2 + (1 - \hat{x}_i^\top P_i\hat{x}_i)^2\right] + \gamma_i\|\hat{x}_i - P_i\hat{x}_i\|^2 \quad (9)$$

Applying Cauchy-Schwartz inequality with the vectors $(I - P_i)\hat{x}_i$ and $\hat{x}_i$ we get

$$(1 - \hat{x}_i^\top P_i\hat{x}_i)^2 \leq \left\|\hat{x}_i^\top - P_i\hat{x}_i\right\|^2 . \quad (10)$$

Observing that the assumption $\alpha = 1/R^2$ implies $\gamma_i \leq 1$, which in turn yields $\gamma_i - \gamma_i^2/2 \geq \gamma_i/2$. We get,

$$\frac{1}{2}\|P_i - Q\|^2 - \frac{1}{2}\|P_{i+1} - Q\|^2 \geq \frac{1}{2}\alpha\|P_i x_i - x_i\|^2 - \alpha\|x_i - Qx_i\|^2$$

$$+\alpha x_i^\top\left[P_i - \frac{1}{2}(QP_i + P_iQ)\right]x_i , \quad (11)$$

We further derive the first term and use the fact that $x^\top Qx = x^\top QQx$ and get,

$$\|P_i x_i - x_i\|^2 = \|P_i x_i - Qx_i + Qx_i - x_i\|^2 \quad (12)$$

$$= \|P_i x_i - Qx_i\|^2 + \|Qx_i - x_i\|^2 - 2x_i^\top\left[P_i - \frac{1}{2}(QP_i + P_iQ)\right]x_i ,$$

Plugging Eq. (12) into Eq. (11) and rearranging the terms conclude the proof. ∎

We use the Lemma 2 to prove the main result of this section.

Parameters: $\alpha > 0$; $B > 0$
Initialize: Set $P_1 = 0$
Loop: For $i = 1, 2, \ldots, m$

- Get a new point $\boldsymbol{x}_i \in \mathbb{R}^n$
- Set $\gamma_i = \alpha \|\boldsymbol{x}_i\|^2$
- Update,

$$P'_{i+1} = P_i$$
$$+ \gamma_i \left[\hat{X}_i - \frac{1}{2} \left(P_i \hat{X}_i + \hat{X}_i P_i \right) \right]$$

- Set $P_{i+1} \leftarrow \texttt{Regularize}(P'_{i+1}, B)$

Output: PSD matrix $- P_{m+1}$

Fig. 1. The GST online algorithm

Parameters: $\epsilon > 0$; $B > 0$
Initialize: Set $P_1 = 0$
Loop: For $i = 1, 2, \ldots, m$

- Get a new point $\boldsymbol{x}_i \in \mathbb{R}^n$
- Find γ_i such that Eq. (16) holds.
- Update,

$$P'_{i+1} = P_i - \frac{\gamma_i}{2 - \gamma_i} (P_i \hat{X}_i + \hat{X}_i P_i)$$
$$+ \gamma_i \hat{X}_i + \frac{\gamma_i^2}{2 - \gamma_i} \hat{X}_i P_i \hat{X}_i$$

- Set $P_{i+1} \leftarrow \texttt{Regularize}(P'_{i+1}, B)$.

Output: PSD matrix $- P_{m+1}$

Fig. 2. The PST$_\epsilon$ online algorithm

Theorem 1. *Let $\boldsymbol{x}_1 \ldots \boldsymbol{x}_m \cdots$ be any input sequence for the PST algorithm (without the regularization). Denote by $R = \max_i \|\boldsymbol{x}_i\|^2$. Let Q be any idempotent projection and assume the tradeoff parameter is set to $\alpha = 1/R^2$. Then the loss the algorithm suffers is bounded as follows,*

$$\sum_i \|P_i \boldsymbol{x}_i - Q \boldsymbol{x}_i\|^2 \leq rank(Q)R^2 + \sum_i \|\boldsymbol{x}_i - Q \boldsymbol{x}_i\|^2 .$$

The theorem is proved by bounding $\sum_i \|P_i - Q\|^2 - \|P_{i+1} - Q\|^2$ from above and below. For the upper bound we note that it is a telescopic sum which is less than rank(Q). For the lower bound we bound each summand separately using Lemma 2. An important comment is in place. The form of the bound is identical to similar bounds for online algorithms for classification or regression [13], where the cumulative performance of the algorithm (P_i) compared to the target function (Q) is bounded by a property of the target (rank here; squared norm of a vector in classification or regression) plus the cumulative performance of a competitor compared to the target function (Q). Note that the second term in the bound is $\|I\boldsymbol{x}_i - Q\boldsymbol{x}_i\|^2$ and thus the competitor is the identity matrix I. However, there is one crucial difference. In classification and regression the target function is fixed (through the supervision) and we are free to choose any competitor. Here, the competitor is fixed (I) and we are free to choose any target (Q), which represents an arbitrary subspace underling the data.

Intuitively, the fixed term (rank) of the bound is related to a transient period of the algorithm when it shifts from its initial subspace toward the target subspace, and the cumulative performance of the competitor bounds the performance when eventually any new vector falls approximately in the span of the vectors already processed.

To exemplify the bound let us consider two extreme cases. First, assume that indeed all the points $\boldsymbol{x}_i$ lies exactly in a linear subspace of dimension $n \ll d$. So, there exists a projection Q such that $Q\boldsymbol{x}_i = \boldsymbol{x}_i$ and the second term of the bound thus vanishes. The algorithm suffers loss which is scaled linearly with the internal dimension n and is independent of d or the number of points m. Second, consider the case that there is no underlying linear subspace. We consider two options $Q = I$ or $Q = 0$. In the former case all the points are treated as data, again with no noise. The bound however scales like the true dimension d. In the latter case all the points are considered as noise around the origin, and the loss the algorithm suffers is bounded by the total variance.

3 Projection Based Algorithm

We now turn our attention to an alternative method for deriving online algorithms. We modify the squared loss function to ignore very small distances specified by a fixed insensitivity parameter ϵ,

$$\ell_\epsilon(\boldsymbol{x}, P\boldsymbol{x}) = \begin{cases} 0 & \|\boldsymbol{x} - P\boldsymbol{x}\| \leq \sqrt{2\epsilon} \\ \left(\|\boldsymbol{x} - P\boldsymbol{x}\| - \sqrt{2\epsilon}\right)^2 & \text{Otherwise} \end{cases}.$$

That is, if the squared loss is below some predefined tolerance level, then the value of the ϵ-insensitive loss is zero. Otherwise it is equal to a shift of the squared loss. The update rule for the new algorithm sets the new matrix P_{i+1} to be the solution to the following projection problem [13],

$$\min_P \frac{1}{2} \|P - P_i\|^2 \qquad \text{s.t.} \qquad \ell_\epsilon(\boldsymbol{x}_i, P\boldsymbol{x}_i) = 0\,, P = P^T\,, P \succeq 0\,.$$

The solution of the optimization problem is the projection of P onto the intersection of the positive semidefinite cone and the second order body of matrices P that satisfy $\|\boldsymbol{x}_i - P\boldsymbol{x}_i\| \leq \epsilon$ and are centered at the identity matrix I. Clearly the subset of matrices defined by the intersection is not empty as it contains the identity matrix. We refer to this algorithm as the PST$_\epsilon$ algorithm, for Projection based algorithm for Subspace Tracking with insensitivity level ϵ.

As with the GST algorithm, we derive an update rule by computing the corresponding Lagrangian. As before we omit for now the constraint of being positive semidefinite. We show below that the PSD constraint is indeed satisfied by the optimal solution.

$$\mathcal{L}(P; \alpha_i) = \frac{1}{2} \|P - P_i\|^2 + \alpha_i \left[\frac{1}{2} \|\boldsymbol{x}_i - P\boldsymbol{x}_i\|^2 - \epsilon\right] - \text{Tr}\left[Z(P - P^T)\right], \quad (13)$$

where $\alpha_i \geq 0$ is the Lagrange multiplier. To solve the problem we first differentiate $\mathcal{L}$ with respect to P and set the result to zero, $P_{i+1}(I + \alpha_i X_i) = P_i + \alpha_i X_i + \tilde{Z}$, where $\tilde{Z} = Z^T - Z$ is an anti-symmetric matrix. We solve the last equation by first computing the inverse of the matrix $I + \alpha_i X_i$ and then solving for $\tilde{Z}$. The details are omitted for lack of space. As before we define additional notation γ_i,

$$\gamma_i = \frac{\alpha_i \|\boldsymbol{x}_i\|^2}{1 + \alpha_i \|\boldsymbol{x}_i\|^2} \qquad , \qquad \alpha_i = \frac{1}{\|\boldsymbol{x}_i\|^2} \frac{\gamma_i}{1 - \gamma_i} \qquad (14)$$

which we use to write the update rule of this algorithm,

$$P_{i+1} = P_i + \gamma_i \hat{X}_i - \frac{\gamma_i}{2 - \gamma_i}(P_i \hat{X}_i + \hat{X}_i P_i) + \frac{\gamma_i^2}{2 - \gamma_i} \hat{X}_i P_i \hat{X}_i\,. \qquad (15)$$

Note that by definition $\gamma_i \in [0, 1]$. The update rule still depends on the unknown α_i (or γ_i). To find the value of γ_i we use the KKT conditions. Whenever γ_i is positive the inequality constraint $\frac{1}{2}\|x_i - P_i x_i\|^2 \le \epsilon$ is satisfied as equality. Long algebraic manipulations yield that the left side of this equality constraint is given by the function,

$$f(\gamma) = \frac{(1-\gamma)^2}{2(2-\gamma)^2} \|x_i\|^2 \left[4\|\hat{x}_i - P_i\hat{x}_i\|^2 + (-4\gamma + \gamma^2)\left(1 - \hat{x}_i^\top P_i \hat{x}_i\right)^2 \right]. \quad (16)$$

Theoretically, we can solve analytically the equation $f(\gamma_i) = \epsilon$ since it is a degree four polynomial. In practice, we use the following lemma, which states that the function $f(\gamma)$ is monotone. By definition $\gamma_i \in [0, 1]$ and thus we can find a value of γ which is far of the exact solution by at most δ in time complexity of $-\log_2(\delta)$.

Lemma 3. *The function $f(\gamma)$ defined in Eq. (16) is monotone decreasing in γ.*

The proof is omitted due to lack of space. To summarize the description of the algorithm: after receiving x_i the algorithm checks whether the Euclidean distance between x_i and $P_i x_i$ is below the predefined threshold, $\frac{1}{2}\|x_i - P_i x_i\|^2 \le \epsilon$. If so, it does nothing. Otherwise, it performs binary search in the range $[0, 1]$ and finds a value γ_i that solve the function $f(\gamma_i) = \epsilon$. We initialize $P_1 = 0$. A sketch of the algorithm is shown in Fig. 2. To conclude, we note that the PST algorithm may be extended with Mercer kernels. The proof and construction are similar to the those of the GST algorithm.

3.1 Analysis

As in the GST algorithm, in each iteration we set P_{i+1} to be a sum of the previous matrix P_i and another matrix, as given in Eq. (15). As before, this matrix is either of degree one or two, and in the latter case one of its eigenvalues is negative.

In the following we derive the analogous of Lemma. 1, which state that the eigenvalues of each of the transformations derived along the run of the algorithm $P_1 \ldots P_{m+1}$ falls in the interval $[0, 1]$, so P_i are close to be idempotent projections. This situation is simpler than for the GST algorithm, in which for all allowed learning rates the upper bound on the eigenvalues b was strictly greater than one. The proof is similar to the proof of Lemma. 1.

Lemma 4. *Throughout the running of the algorithm $0 \preceq P_i \preceq I$.*

We turn to analyze the algorithm in the loss bound model. For this algorithm we change slightly both the assumptions and the bound. Here we compare the performance of the algorithm to an idempotent projection Q with point-wise bounded noise, that is $(1/2)\|x_i - Qx_i\|^2 \le \epsilon$. The corresponding loss which we bound is the epsilon insensitive version of the Euclidean loss function. Before proving the theorem we prove the following auxiliary lemma, which provides a lower bound and an upper on the optimal value of γ_i.

Lemma 5. *Let γ_i be the solution of the equality $f(\gamma_i) = \epsilon$. If $\ell_\epsilon(x_i, P_i x_i) > 0$ then,*

$$1 - \frac{\sqrt{2\epsilon}}{\|x_i - P_i x_i\|} \le \gamma_i \le 1 - \frac{1}{2}\frac{\sqrt{2\epsilon}}{\|x_i - P_i x_i\|}.$$

Proof. If $\ell_\epsilon(\boldsymbol{x}_i, P_i \boldsymbol{x}_i) > 0$ we know that γ_i is defined to be the solution of the equation $f(\gamma_i) = \epsilon$. We start with the left hand-side of the desired inequality and lower bound the second term in Eq. (16). Since $\gamma_i \in [0,1]$ we have that $-4\gamma_i + \gamma_i^2 \leq 0$. Substituting Eq. (10) we get,

$$\epsilon \geq \frac{(1-\gamma_i)^2}{2(2-\gamma_i)^2} \|\boldsymbol{x}_i\|^2 \left[4 \|\hat{\boldsymbol{x}}_i - P_i \hat{\boldsymbol{x}}_i\|^2 + (-4\gamma_i + \gamma_i^2) \|\hat{\boldsymbol{x}}_i - P_i \hat{\boldsymbol{x}}_i\|^2 \right]$$

$$= (1-\gamma_i)^2 \frac{1}{2} \|\boldsymbol{x}_i - P_i \boldsymbol{x}_i\|^2 .$$

Solving for γ_i leads to the desired bound. For the right hand-side of the inequality we return to Eq. (16) and upper bound the right term by zero. We get,

$$\epsilon \leq \frac{(1-\gamma_i)^2}{2(2-\gamma_i)^2} \|\boldsymbol{x}_i\|^2 \left[4 \|\hat{\boldsymbol{x}}_i - P_i \hat{\boldsymbol{x}}_i\|^2 \right] \leq (1-\gamma_i)^2 4 \frac{1}{2} \|\boldsymbol{x}_i - P_i \boldsymbol{x}_i\|^2 .$$

Solving for γ_i leads to the desired bound. ∎

We are now ready to prove the main theorem of the section,

Theorem 2. *Let* $\boldsymbol{x}_1 \ldots \boldsymbol{x}_i \ldots$ *be a sequence of points. Assume that there exists an idempotent projection* Q *that suffers zero loss* $\ell_\epsilon(\boldsymbol{x}_i, Q\boldsymbol{x}_i) = 0$ *for all* i. *Denote by* $R = \max_i \|\boldsymbol{x}_i\|$. *Then the following bound holds for the PST algorithm (without the regularization),*

$$\sum_i \ell_{4\epsilon}(Q\boldsymbol{x}_i, P_i\boldsymbol{x}_i) \leq 2 \, rank\,(Q)R^2 .$$

Proof. Let P_i be the projection matrix before receiving the ith vector $\boldsymbol{x}_i$. Define $\Delta_i = \|P_i - Q\|^2 - \|P_{i+1} - Q\|^2$. We prove the theorem by bounding $\sum_{i=1}^m \Delta_i$ from above and below. First note that $\sum_{i=1}^m \Delta_i$ is a telescopic sum and therefore,

$$\sum_{i=1}^m \Delta_i = \sum_i \|P_i - Q\|^2 - \|P_{i+1} - Q\|^2 \leq \|Q\|^2 = \text{rank}\,(Q) . \qquad (17)$$

This provides an upper bound on $\sum_i \Delta_i$. To provide a lower bound on Δ_i we apply Thm. 2.4.1 in [14] and get that $\Delta_i = \|P_i - Q\|^2 - \|P_{i+1} - Q\|^2 \geq \|P_i - P_{i+1}\|^2$. We consider two cases. If $\|Q\boldsymbol{x}_i - P_i\boldsymbol{x}_i\| \leq 2\sqrt{2\epsilon}$ we use the trivial bound $\|P_i - P_{i+1}\|^2 \geq 0 = \ell_{2\epsilon}(Q\boldsymbol{x}_i, P_i\boldsymbol{x}_i)$. Otherwise, we assume that $\|Q\boldsymbol{x}_i - P_i\boldsymbol{x}_i\| \geq 2\sqrt{2\epsilon}$. Algebraic manipulations show that,

$$\Delta_i \geq \|P_i - P_{i+1}\|^2 \geq \frac{1}{2}\gamma_i^2 \|\hat{\boldsymbol{x}}_i - P_i\hat{\boldsymbol{x}}_i\|^2 . \qquad (18)$$

Substituting the lower bound of Lemma 5 we get, $\Delta_i \geq \frac{1}{2} \left(\|\boldsymbol{x}_i - P_i\boldsymbol{x}_i\| - \sqrt{2\epsilon} \right)^2 \frac{1}{\|\boldsymbol{x}_i\|^2}$. Using the triangle inequality we get, $\|\boldsymbol{x}_i - P_i\boldsymbol{x}_i\| \geq \|Q\boldsymbol{x}_i - P_i\boldsymbol{x}_i\| - \|Q\boldsymbol{x}_i - \boldsymbol{x}_i\| \geq \|Q\boldsymbol{x}_i - P_i\boldsymbol{x}_i\| - \sqrt{2\epsilon}$, where the last inequality holds since $\|Q\boldsymbol{x}_i - \boldsymbol{x}_i\| \leq \sqrt{2\epsilon}$. Substituting back in the last equation we get, $\Delta_i \geq \frac{1}{2} \left(\|Q\boldsymbol{x}_i - P_i\boldsymbol{x}_i\| - 2\sqrt{2\epsilon} \right)^2 \frac{1}{\|\boldsymbol{x}_i\|^2} \geq \frac{1}{2}\ell_{4\epsilon}(Q\boldsymbol{x}_i, P_i\boldsymbol{x}_i)/R^2$. Combining Eq. (17) together with the last equation concludes the proof. ∎

The theorem tells us that if the squared norm of the noise $(1/2) \|x_i - Qx_i\|^2$ is bounded by ϵ, then the cumulative 4ϵ-insensitive loss the algorithm suffer is bounded. To conclude, we derived two online algorithms which reconstruct corrupted input points x_i by tracking linear subspaces. The performance of both algorithms is compared to the performance of arbitrary idempotent projections Q. The learning algorithms do not know the identity of Q nor they have any feedback from Q. In this aspect the learning task is harder than typical regression or classification learning problems, as there is no supervision during the learning process.

4   Regularization

In our two algorithms, overfitting arises when the eigenvalues of the linear operator P_i have large components orthogonal to the target subspace. As a consequence, the *filtered* output $P_i x_i$ will include noise components as well as the true signal. Both algorithms may suffer from this problem since in our setting there is no feedback. Therefore, our algorithms approximate the true feedback Qx_i using x_i, which contains also noise components. Furthermore, the only goal of the update rule of both algorithms is to reduce the loss related to x_i, ignoring any other issue such as the rank or trace of the transformation P_i. Therefore, as we shall see next, both algorithms favor an increase in the trace of the transformations since, in general, that reduces the loss suffered.

We exemplify our claim for the GST algorithm, similar results hold for the PST algorithm. We compute the change in the trace by using Eq. (7) and get,

$$\mathrm{Tr}\,[P_{i+1}] = \mathrm{Tr}\left[P_i + \gamma_i \left[\hat{X}_i - \frac{1}{2}\left(P_i\hat{X}_i + \hat{X}_iP_i\right)\right]\right] = \mathrm{Tr}\,[P_i] + \gamma_i\hat{x}_i^\top (I - P_i)\,\hat{x}_i\,.$$

Examining the change in trace we observe that the single fixed point of the update is $P_i = I$, the identity matrix. Otherwise, if some of the eigenvalues of P_i are below one, the trace will increase. (Using our analogy, one-class algorithms are designed to capture the input data in a ball, a goal which favors increasing the radius of the ball.) We remind the reader that according to Lemma 1 the eigenvalues are not bounded from above by one, only by $4/3$. In this case, according to Eq. (19), the trace may slightly decrease to compensate this high value of the eigenvalues. The phenomenon is indeed observed in the simulations we performed and are shown in Sec. 5. Nevertheless, this will not stop the algorithm from overfitting, since when some of the eigenvalues are small, the update operation will increase the trace.

Following [4] we add a second step to the update rule, after the primary update of Eq. (7) (for the GST algorithm) or Eq. (15) (for the PST algorithm). Due to lack of space we focus in the GST algorithm. The algorithm employs an additional parameter $B > 0$, which is used to bound the norm of the eigenvalues after the update. We consider two versions for this update, which correspond to ℓ_1-norm regularization and ℓ_2-norm regularization. Intuitively, the parameter B specifies a continuous requirement that replaces a standard rank requirement. Specifically the update rule is defined as follows : we first perform the gradient step of Eq. (7) and define, $P'_{i+1} = P_i + \gamma_i\left[\hat{X}_i - \frac{1}{2}\left(P_i\hat{X}_i + \hat{X}_iP_i\right)\right]$. Then we set P_{i+1} to be the solution of the following optimization problem,

$$P_{i+1} = \arg\min_P \frac{1}{2}\left\|P - P'_{i+1}\right\|^2 \quad \text{s.t.} \quad P = P^T, \ P \succeq 0 \qquad (19)$$

$$L = 1 \ (\textbf{version 1}) \quad ; \ L = 2 \ (\textbf{version 2}) \qquad \text{Tr}\left(P^L\right) \le B \qquad (20)$$

For the first version we set $L = 1$ and bound the ℓ_1 norm of the eigenvalues of P. For the second version we set $L = 2$ and bound the ℓ_2 norm of the eigenvalues of P. We now describe in detail how to solve in practice these optimization problems. Note that in both cases if the norm condition (Eq. (20)) is satisfied for P'_{i+1} then $P_{i+1} = P'_{i+1}$. We thus assume this is not the case.

Version 1 – ℓ_1 norm: We omit the derivation of the solution due to lack of space and proceed with a formal description of it. To solve the optimization problem one needs to compute the eigenvectors v_j of P'_{i+1} and the corresponding eigenvalues $\lambda'_j \ge 0$. To be more concrete we write $P'_{i+1} = \sum_{j=1}^d \lambda'_j v_j v_j^T$. Then the optimal solution is given by $P_{i+1} = \sum_{j=1}^d \lambda_j v_j v_j^T$, where $\lambda_j = \max\{\lambda'_j - \eta, 0\}$ and η is chosen such that $\text{Tr}(P_{i+1}) = \sum_j \lambda_j = B$. Finding the value of η given the set of eigenvalues λ'_j can be computed using [15, Fig. 3] in $O(d \log d)$ time. To conclude, since it takes $O(d)$ time to compute the trace of a matrix and another $O(d^3)$ time to perform eigenvector decomposition, the time required to verify if an update is needed in $O(d)$ time and the total runtime of the update step is $O(d^3)$.

Version 2 – ℓ_2 norm: By writing the Lagrangian of the corresponding optimization problem, and taking the

---

Input: PSD matrix P'; Bound $B > 0$

Version 1:

If $\text{Tr}\,[P'] > B$ then

- Compute the eigen-decomposition of P',
  $$P' = \sum_{j=1}^d \lambda'_j v_j v_j^T$$
- Find η such that $\sum_j \max\{\lambda'_j - \eta, 0\} = B$.
- Set $P = \sum_{j=1}^d \max\{\lambda'_j - \eta, 0\} v_j v_j^T$

Else : $P = P'$.

Version 2:

- If $\text{Tr}\,[P'^2] > B$ then set $P = P' \dfrac{\sqrt{B}}{\|P'\|}$

  Else : $P = P'$.

Return: PSD matrix – P

Fig. 3. The `Regularize` Procedure

---

derivative with respect to P we get that the solution P_{i+1} is proportional to P'_{i+1}. Using KKT conditions we can compute the constants and get the update rule for this version: if $\left\|P'_{i+1}\right\|^2 > B$ then set $P_{i+1} = P'_{i+1}\sqrt{B}/\|P'_{i+1}\|$. Otherwise, $P_{i+1} = P'_{i+1}$. To conclude, since it takes $O(d^3)$ time to multiply matrices, then it takes $O(d^3)$ time to compute $\left\|P'_{i+1}\right\|^2 = \text{Tr}\left(P'_{i+1}P'_{i+1}\right)$ and verify if an update should be performed. If so, the update step takes $O(d^2)$ time since it involves a scaling of each element of P'_{i+1}.

The following theorem bounds the loss the modified GST algorithm suffers. As we shall see, although we consider a restricted set of projections P_i with a bounded trace or bounded trace squared, the performance of the algorithm does not deteriorate assuming it is compared to an idempotent projection Q under the same restriction. In other words, the loss bound for both versions has the same form. The only difference is the touchstone idempotent projection we use. Originally there were no restrictions over both the projection P_i and the reference projection Q. However, the modified algorithm restricts the projection P_i the algorithm maintains, and the corresponding analysis assumes similar restriction over the reference idempotent projection Q.

Restricting the set of possible projections to have eigenvalues with bounded norm has an additional benefit. It allows the algorithm (and the analysis) to perform well even if the sequence of input vectors is *not stationary*. Specifically, we no longer compare the algorithm to the performance of a *single* fixed idempotent projection Q, which corresponds to a fixed subspace. We allow more complicated comparisons in which different segments of the input points may be best filtered with a unique own idempotent projection.

Theorem 3. *Let $x_1 \ldots x_m \cdots$ be any input for the algorithm. Denote by $R = \max_i \|x_i\|^2$. Let Q_i (for $i = 1 \ldots m$) be any sequence of idempotent projections $Q_i^2 = Q_i$ with bounded trace $\mathrm{Tr}\,[Q_i] \leq B$. Assume the tradeoff parameter is set to $\alpha = 1/R^2$. Then,*

$$\sum_i \|P_i x_i - Q_i x_i\|^2 \leq R^2 B + \sum_i \|x_i - Q_i x_i\|^2 + A \qquad , \text{where},$$

$$A = \sum_i B \|Q_i - Q_{i+1}\|_\infty \text{ (\textbf{ver 1})} \qquad A = \sum_i \sqrt{B} \|Q_i - Q_{i+1}\|_2 \text{ (\textbf{ver 2})}$$

As Theorem 1, the bound includes a fixed penalty term and the cumulative loss suffered by a series of projection functions. For the case of non-stationary data it contains an additional penalty term for deviation of these projections. The skeleton of the proof is similar to the proof of analogous theorem in [4], but it is more involved since we are dealing with PSD matrices and not vectors.

5   Simulations

The theory developed so far can be nicely illustrated via some simple simulations. We briefly describe two such experiments. In the first experiment we generated $3,000$ points in $\mathbb{R}^2$. All the points lie in a linear subspace of degree 1 and in the unit ball around the origin. We added random uniform noise with maximal value of 0.1. We ran the GST algorithm with no regularization, using ℓ_1 regularization and using ℓ_2 regularization. In the latter cases we set $B = 1$ - the true dimension. The plot in the top-leftmost panel of Fig. 4 shows the cumulative squared error relative to the clean data. That is, the value at location j is $\sum_i^j \|P_i x_i - Q x_i\|^2$. Empirically, without regularization the performance is about four time worse than using regularization. Furthermore, the ℓ_1 regularization performs better than the ℓ_2 regularization. An explanation of these results appear in the top second-left panel. For each of the three algorithms we applied the projection obtained in the end of the training process P_{3001} on the unit circle and generating an ellipsoid. The axes of the ellipsoid correspond to the directions of the eigenvectors, and their relative length correspond to the eigenvalues. The plot also shows the same transformation of the unit circle using the competitor Q, which is represented as a black-solid line. (This is because it is of rank 1.) From the plot we observe that without regularization, the matrix P_{3001} is essentially the identity matrix, and no filtering is performed. The second eigenvalue of the matrix P_{3001} when using the ℓ_1 regularization is much smaller than the second eigenvalue when using the ℓ_2 regularization. This is reflected in the fact that one ellipsoid is more skewed than the other. Note that although the rank of the

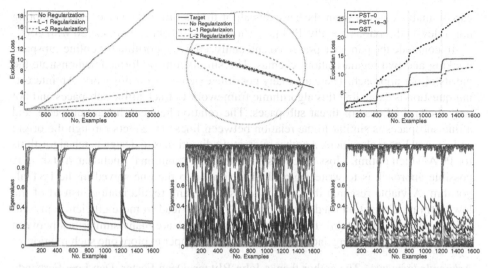

Fig. 4. Top, left to right: cumulative sum of ℓ_2 discrepancy evaluated with clean data for the first simulation and illustration of projection matrices obtained after training. Top-right : cumulative sum of ℓ_2 discrepancy for the second simulation. Bottom, left to right: top 20 eigenvalues of the projection matrix P for GST , PST_0 and PST_{1e-3} .

ℓ_1 matrix P_{3001} is closer to be one, the major subspace (which corresponds to the larger eigenvalue) is similar, but not identical, to the true subspace. This relationship between ℓ_1 and ℓ_2 regularization (where the former generates sparser solutions) appears in other contexts in machine learning. Our case is unique since the here the ℓ_1 regularization generates a matrix with sparse eigen-spectrum and not a sparse matrix.

In the second experiment we repeated the following process four times. We picked at random 400 points in $\mathbb{R}^{80}$. All the points lie in a linear subspace of degree 4 and in the unit ball around the origin. We added random uniform noise with maximal value of 0.1. Finally, we concatenated the four sequences into a single sequence of length 1, 600. We run three algorithms: GST , PST_0 and PST_{1e-3} . We ran all algorithms with ℓ_2 regularization and set $B = 5$, the actual dimension. The top-right panel of Fig. 4 shows the cumulative squared error relative to the clean data. The PST_0 algorithm performs worst, the GST algorithm second, and the PST_{1e-3} algorithm is the best. One possible explanation is that for $\epsilon = 0$ the PST tracks the noise since by definition $P_{i+1}\boldsymbol{x}_i = \boldsymbol{x}_i$. The two other algorithms cope with noise in different way, either by using a sensible learning rate or using the predefined tolerance ϵ. Interestingly, as indicated by the "stair-shaped" graph, the GST algorithm is more sensitive to the shift between chunks compared to being inside chunks, and vice versa for the PST algorithm. In other words, if we know that the subspaces will not be shifted or switched frequently, then GST is better, while PST is better to track non-stationary subspaces.

The three plots in the bottom of Fig. 4 show the top 20 eigenvalues of P_i for GST , PST_0 and PST_{1e-3} (left to right) at each time step. The eigenvalues of GST are smooth as a function of time. Note, as suggested by Lemma. 1, some eigenvalues of P_i are indeed larger than unit. For PST_0 , although the level of eigenvalues corresponding to the true subspace is constantly higher than the eigenvalues level for the noise, the gap is small. Again, it seems because this algorithm is fitting the noise and is adopting non-relevant directions. Finally, PST_{1e-3} shows noisier behavior compared with GST .

To conclude the paper we presented and analyzed two algorithm for online subspace tracking and two regularization schemas. The simulations performed demonstrate the merits of our approach. There are many possible extensions for this work. An interesting question is extending this algorithmic framework to track affine subspaces and not only the special case of linear subspaces. The relation between linear subspaces and affine subspaces is similar to the relation between linear classifiers through the origin and general linear classifiers. Another interesting direction is to design batch algorithms for PCA which optimize loss functions other than the traditional Euclidean distance. A possible approach is to write a global SDP similar to the one solved in the PST algorithm. A viable research direction is to use low-rank regularization instead of the low-norm regularization used in this paper. This may lead to more efficient representation and faster algorithms. Finally, it seems that there are many similarities between adaptive signal processing and online learning. This paper explore one such relation.

Acknowledgements. The author thanks John Blitzer, Dean Foster, Dan Lee, Fernando Pereira, Lawrence Saul and Abraham Weiner for many fruitful discussions.

References

1. J.P. Delmas and J.F. Cardoso. Performance analysis of an adaptive algorithm for tracking dominant subspaces. *IEEE Transactions on Signal Processing*, 46:3054–3057, 1998.
2. R. Kumaresanand D.W.Tufts. Estimating the angles of arrival of multiple plane waves. *IEEE Transactions on Aerospace and Electronic Systems*, 19:134–139, 1983.
3. A. M. Haimovich and Y. Bar-Ness. An eigenanalysis interference canceler. *IEEE Transactions on Signal Processing*, 39:76–84, 1991.
4. J. Kivinen, M. K. Warmuth, and B. Hassibi. The p-norm generalization of the lms algorithm for adaptive filtering. In *Proc. 13th IFAC Symposium on System Identification*, 2003.
5. A.H. Sayed. *Fundementals of Adaptive Filtering*. Wiley-Interscience, 2003.
6. D.M.J. Tax. *One-class classification; Concept-learning in the absence of counter-examples*. PhD thesis, Delft University of Technology, 2001.
7. H. Zou, T. Hastie, and R. Tibshirani. Sparse principal component analysis, 2004.
8. K. Q. Weinberger, John C. Blitzer, and L. K. Saul. Distance metric learning for large margin nearest neighbor classification. In *NIPS 18*, 2005.
9. S. Shalev-Shwartz, Y. Singer, and A. Y. Ng. Online and batch learning of pseudo-metrics. In *Proc. of the 21st international conf. on Machine learning*, page 94. ACM Press, 2004.
10. k. Tsuda, G. Rätsch, and M.K. Warmuth. Matrix exponentiated gradient updates for on-line learning and bregman projection. *Jornal of Machine Learning Research*, 6:995–1018, 2005.
11. G.H. Golub and C.F. Van Loan. *Matrix computations*. John Hopkins University Press, 1989.
12. J. Kivinen, D.P Helmbold, and M. Warmuth. Relative loss bounds for single neurons. *IEEE Transactions on Neural Networks*, 10(6):1291–1304, 1999.
13. K. Crammer, O. Dekel, S. Shalev-Shwartz, and Y. Singer. Online passive aggressive algorithms. In *Advances in Neural Information Processing Systems 16*, 2003.
14. Y. Censor and S.A. Zenios. *Parallel Optimization: Theory, Algorithms, and Applications*. Oxford University Press, New York, NY, USA, 1997.
15. K. Crammer and Y. Singer. On the learnability and design of output codes for multiclass problems. *Machine Learning*, 47, 2002.

Online Multitask Learning

Ofer Dekel[1], Philip M. Long[2], and Yoram Singer[1,2]

[1] School of Computer Science and Engineering, The Hebrew University,
Jerusalem 91904, Israel
[2] Google, 1600 Amphitheater Parkway, Mountain View, CA 94043, USA
{oferd, singer}@cs.huji.ac.il, plong@google.com

Abstract. We study the problem of online learning of multiple tasks in parallel. On each online round, the algorithm receives an instance and makes a prediction for each one of the parallel tasks. We consider the case where these tasks all contribute toward a common goal. We capture the relationship between the tasks by using a single global loss function to evaluate the quality of the multiple predictions made on each round. Specifically, each individual prediction is associated with its own individual loss, and then these loss values are combined using a global loss function. We present several families of online algorithms which can use any absolute norm as a global loss function. We prove worst-case relative loss bounds for all of our algorithms.

1 Introduction

Multitask learning is the problem of learning several related problems in parallel. In this paper, we discuss the multitask learning problem in the online learning context. We focus on the possibility that the learning tasks contribute toward a common goal. Our hope is that we can benefit by taking account of this to learn the tasks jointly, as opposed to learning each task independently.

For concreteness, we focus on the task of binary classification, and note that our algorithms and analysis can be adapted to regression problems using ideas in [1]. In the online multitask classification setting, we are faced with k separate online binary classification problems, in parallel. The online learning process takes place in a sequence of rounds. At the beginning of round t, the algorithm observes a set of k instances, one for each of the binary classification problems. The algorithm predicts the binary label of each of the instances it has observed, and then receives the correct label of each instance. At this point, each of the algorithm's predictions is associated with a non-negative loss, and we use $\boldsymbol{\ell}_t = (\ell_{t,1}, \ldots, \ell_{t,k})$ to denote the k-coordinate vector whose elements are the individual loss values of the respective tasks. Assume that we selected, ahead of time, a *global loss* function $\mathcal{L} : \mathbb{R}^k \to \mathbb{R}_+$, which is used to combine these individual loss values into a single number, and define the global loss attained on round t to be $\mathcal{L}(\boldsymbol{\ell}_t)$. At the end of the online round, the algorithm may use the k new labeled examples it has obtained to improve its prediction mechanism for the rounds to come. The goal of the learning algorithm is to suffer the smallest possible cumulative loss over the course of T rounds, $\sum_{t=1}^{T} \mathcal{L}(\boldsymbol{\ell}_t)$.

G. Lugosi and H.U. Simon (Eds.): COLT 2006, LNAI 4005, pp. 453–467, 2006.

O. Dekel, P.M. Long, and Y. Singer

The choice of the global loss function captures the overall consequences of the individual prediction errors, and therefore how the algorithm prioritizes correcting errors. For example, if $\mathcal{L}(\boldsymbol{\ell}_t)$ is defined to be $\sum_{j=1}^{k} \ell_{t,j}$ then the online algorithm is penalized equally for errors on any of the tasks; this results in effectively treating the tasks independently. On the other hand, if $\mathcal{L}(\boldsymbol{\ell}_t) = \max_j \ell_{t,j}$ then the algorithm is only interested in the worst mistake made on every round. We do not assume that the datasets of the various tasks are similar or otherwise related. Moreover, the examples presented to the algorithm for each task may come from different domains and may possess different characteristics. The multiple tasks are tied together by the way we define the objective of our algorithm.

In this paper, we focus on the case where the global loss function is an *absolute norm*. A norm $\| \cdot \|$ is a function such that $\|\mathbf{v}\| > 0$ for all $\mathbf{v} \neq 0$, $\|0\| = 0$, $\|\lambda\mathbf{v}\| = |\lambda|\|\mathbf{v}\|$ for all $\mathbf{v}$ and all $\lambda \in \mathbb{R}$, and which satisfies the triangle inequality. A norm is said to be absolute if $\|\mathbf{v}\| = \||\mathbf{v}|\|$ for all $\mathbf{v}$, where $|\mathbf{v}|$ is obtained by replacing each component of $\mathbf{v}$ with its absolute value. The most well-known family of absolute norms is the family of p-norms (also called L_p norms), defined for all $p \geq 1$ by $\|\mathbf{v}\|_p = (\sum_{j=1}^{n} |v_j|^p)^{1/p}$. A special member of this family is the L_∞ norm, which is defined to be the limit of the above when p tends to infinity, and can be shown to equal $\max_j |v_j|$. A less popular family of absolute norms is the family of r-max norms. For any integer r between 1 and k, the r-max norm of $\mathbf{v} \in \mathbb{R}^k$ is the sum of the absolute values of the r absolutely largest components of $\mathbf{v}$. Formally,

$$\|\mathbf{v}\|_{r\text{-max}} = \sum_{j=1}^{r} |v_{\pi(j)}| \quad \text{where} \quad |v_{\pi(1)}| \geq |v_{\pi(2)}| \geq \ldots \geq |v_{\pi(k)}| \ .$$

Note that both the L_1 norm and L_∞ norm are special cases of the r-max norm, as well as being p-norms.

On each online round, we balance a trade-off between retaining the information acquired on previous rounds and modifying our hypotheses based on the new examples obtained on this round. Instead of balancing this trade-off individually for each of the learning tasks, as would be done naively, we balance it for all of the tasks jointly. By doing so, we allow ourselves to make bigger modifications to some of the hypotheses at the expense of the others. To motivate our approach, we present a handful of concrete examples.

Multiclass Classification using the L_∞ Norm. Assume that we are faced with a multiclass classification problem, where the size of the label set is k. One way of solving this problem is by learning k binary classifiers, where each classifier is trained to distinguish between one of the classes and the rest of the classes, the *one-vs-rest* method. If all of the binary classifiers make correct predictions, we can correctly predict the multiclass label. Otherwise, a single binary mistake is as bad as many binary mistakes. Therefore, we only care about the worst binary prediction on round t, and we do so by setting the global loss to be $\|\boldsymbol{\ell}_t\|_\infty$.

Vector-Valued Regression using the L_2 Norm. Let us deviate momentarily from the binary classification setting, and assume that we are faced with multiple regression problems. Specifically, assume that our task is to predict the three-dimensional position of an object. Each of the three coordinates is predicted using an individual regressor, and the regression loss for each task is simply the absolute difference between the true and the predicted value on the respective axis. In this case, the most appropriate global loss function is the L_2 norm, which maps the vector of individual losses to the Euclidean distance between the true and predicted 3-D targets. (Note that we take the actual Euclidean distance and not the squared Euclidean distance often minimized in regression settings).

Error Correcting Output Codes and the r-max Norm. Error Correcting Output Codes is a technique for reducing a multiclass classification problem to multiple binary classification problems [2]. The power of this technique lies in the fact that a correct multiclass prediction can be made even when a few of the binary predictions are wrong. The reduction is represented by a code matrix $M \in \{-1, +1\}^{s,k}$, where s is the number of multiclass labels and k is the number of binary problems used to encode the original multiclass problem. Each row in M represents one of the s multiclass labels, and each column induces one of the k binary classification problems. Given a multiclass training set $\{(\mathbf{x}_i, y_i)\}_{i=1}^m$, with labels $y_i \in \{1, \ldots, s\}$, the binary problem induced by column j is to distinguish between the positive examples $\{(\mathbf{x}_i, y_i : M_{y_i,j} = +1\}$ and negative examples $\{(\mathbf{x}_i, y_i : M_{y_i,j} = -1\}$. When a new instance is observed, applying the k binary classifiers to it gives a vector of binary predictions, $\hat{\mathbf{y}} = (\hat{y}_1, \ldots, \hat{y}_k) \in \{-1, +1\}^k$. We then predict the multiclass label of this instance to be the index of the row in M which is closest to $\hat{\mathbf{y}}$ in Hamming distance. Define the *code distance* of M, denoted by $d(M)$, to be the minimal Hamming distance between any two rows in M. It is straightforward to show that a correct multiclass prediction can be guaranteed as long as the number of binary mistakes made on this instance is less than $d(M)/2$. In other words, making $d(M)/2$ binary mistakes is as bad as making more binary mistakes. Let $r = d(M)/2$. If the binary classifiers are trained in the online multitask setting, we should only be interested in whether the r'th largest loss is less than 1, which would imply that a correct multiclass prediction can be guaranteed. Regretfully, taking the r'th largest element of a vector (in absolute value) does not constitute a norm and thus does not fit in our setting. However, the r-max norm defined above can serve as a proxy.

In this paper, we present three families of online multitask algorithms. Each family includes algorithms for all the absolute norms. All of the algorithms presented in this paper follow the general skeleton outlined in Fig. 1. Specifically, all of our algorithms use an additive update rule, which enables us to transform them into kernel methods. For each algorithm we prove a relative loss bound, namely, we show that the cumulative global loss attained by the algorithm is not much greater than the cumulative loss attained by any fixed set of k linear hypotheses, even one defined in hindsight.

Much previous work on theoretical and applied multitask learning has concerned how to take advantage of cases in which a number of learning problems are related [3, 4, 5, 6, 7, 8]; in contrast, we do not assume that the tasks are related and instead we consider how to take account of common consequences of

---

input: norm $\| \cdot \|$

initialize: $\mathbf{w}_{1,1} = \ldots = \mathbf{w}_{1,k} = (0, \ldots, 0)$

for $t = 1, 2, \ldots$

- receive $\mathbf{x}_{t,1}, \ldots, \mathbf{x}_{t,k}$
- predict $\text{sign}(\mathbf{w}_{t,j} \cdot \mathbf{x}_{t,j})$ $\hspace{3cm}$ $[1 \leq j \leq k]$
- receive $y_{t,1}, \ldots, y_{t,k}$
- calculate $\ell_{t,j} = \left[1 - y_{t,j} \mathbf{w}_{t,j} \cdot \mathbf{x}_{t,j}\right]_+$ $\hspace{2cm}$ $[1 \leq j \leq k]$
- suffer loss $\ell_t = \|(\ell_{t,1}, \ldots, \ell_{t,n})\|$
- update $\mathbf{w}_{t+1,j} = \mathbf{w}_{t,j} + \tau_{t,j} y_{t,j} \mathbf{x}_{t,j}$ $\hspace{2cm}$ $[1 \leq j \leq k]$

Fig. 1. A general skeleton for an online multitask classification algorithm. A concrete algorithm is obtained by specifying the values of $\tau_{t,j}$.

errors. Kivinen and Warmuth [9] generalized the notion of matching loss [10] to multi-dimensional outputs; this enables analysis of algorithms that perform multi-dimensional regression by composing linear functions with a variety of transfer functions. It is not obvious how to directly use their work to address the problem of linear classification with dependent losses addressed in this paper. An analysis of the L_∞ norm of prediction errors is implicit in some past work of Crammer and Singer [11, 12]; the present paper extends this work to a broader framework, and tightens the analysis. When k, the number of multiple tasks, is set to 1, two of the algorithms presented in this paper reduce to the PA-I algorithm [1].

This paper is organized as follows. In Sec. 2 we present our problem more formally and prove a key lemma which facilitates the analysis of our algorithms. In Sec. 3 we present our first family of algorithms, which works in the finite horizon online setting. In Sec. 4 we extend the first family of algorithms to the infinite horizon setting. Finally, in Sec. 5, we present our third family of algorithms for the multitask setting, and show that it shares the analyses of both previous algorithms. The third family of algorithms requires solving a small optimization problem on each online round. Finally, in Sec. 6, we discuss some efficient techniques for solving this optimization problem.

2   Online Multitask Learning with Additive Updates

We begin by presenting the online multitask setting more formally. We are faced with k online binary classification problems in parallel. The instances of each problem are drawn from separate instance domains, and for concreteness, we assume that the instances of problem j are all vectors in $\mathbb{R}^{n_j}$. As stated in the previous section, online learning is performed in a sequence of rounds. On round t, the algorithm observes k instances, $(\mathbf{x}_{t,1}, \ldots, \mathbf{x}_{t,k}) \in \mathbb{R}^{n_1} \times \ldots \times \mathbb{R}^{n_k}$. The algorithm maintains k separate classifiers in its internal memory, one for each of the multiple tasks, and updates them from round to round. Each of these classifiers is a margin-based linear predictor, defined by a weight vector. Let $\mathbf{w}_{t,j} \in \mathbb{R}^{n_j}$ denote the weight vector used to define the j'th linear classifier on round t. The algorithm uses its classifiers to predict the binary labels $\hat{y}_{t,1}, \ldots, \hat{y}_{t,k}$, where $\hat{y}_{t,j} = \text{sign}(\mathbf{w}_{t,j} \cdot \mathbf{x}_{t,j})$. Then, the correct labels of the respective problems, $y_{t,1}, \ldots, y_{t,k}$, are revealed and each one of the predictions is evaluated. We use the hinge-loss function to penalize incorrect predictions, namely, the loss associated with the j'th problem is defined to be

$$\ell_{t,j} = \left[1 - y_{t,j} \mathbf{w}_{t,j} \cdot \mathbf{x}_{t,j}\right]_+ ,$$

where $[a]_+ = \max\{0, a\}$. As previously stated, the global loss is then defined to be $\|\boldsymbol{\ell}_t\|$, where $\|\cdot\|$ is a predefined absolute norm. Finally, the algorithm applies an update to each of the online hypotheses, and defines the vectors $\mathbf{w}_{t+1,1}, \ldots, \mathbf{w}_{t+1,k}$. All of the algorithms presented in this paper use an additive update rule, and define $\mathbf{w}_{t+1,j}$ to be $\mathbf{w}_{t,j} + \tau_{t,j} y_{t,j} \mathbf{x}_{t,j}$, where $\tau_{t,j}$ is a non-negative scalar. The algorithms only differ from one another in the way they set $\tau_{t,j}$. The general skeleton followed by all of our online algorithms is given in Fig. 1.

A concept of key importance in this paper is the notion of the *dual norm* [13]. Any norm $\|\cdot\|$ defined on $\mathbb{R}^n$ has a dual norm, also defined on $\mathbb{R}^n$, denoted by $\|\cdot\|^*$ and given by

$$\|\mathbf{u}\|^* = \max_{\mathbf{v} \in \mathbb{R}^n} \frac{\mathbf{u} \cdot \mathbf{v}}{\|\mathbf{v}\|} = \max_{\mathbf{v} \in \mathbb{R}^n \,:\, \|\mathbf{v}\|=1} \mathbf{u} \cdot \mathbf{v} . \tag{1}$$

The dual of a p-norm is itself a p-norm, and specifically, the dual of $\|\cdot\|_p$ is $\|\cdot\|_q$, where $\frac{1}{q} + \frac{1}{p} = 1$. The dual of $\|\cdot\|_\infty$ is $\|\cdot\|_1$ and vice versa. It can also be shown that the dual of $\|\mathbf{v}\|_{r\text{-max}}$ is

$$\|\mathbf{u}\|^*_{r\text{-max}} = \max\left\{\|\mathbf{u}\|_\infty, \frac{\|\mathbf{u}\|_1}{r}\right\} . \tag{2}$$

An important property of dual norms, which is an immediate consequence of Eq. (1), is that for any $\mathbf{u}, \mathbf{v} \in \mathbb{R}^n$ it holds that

$$\mathbf{u} \cdot \mathbf{v} \leq \|\mathbf{u}\|^* \|\mathbf{v}\| . \tag{3}$$

If $\|\cdot\|$ is a p-norm then the above is known as Hölder's inequality, and specifically if $p = 2$ then it is called the Cauchy-Schwartz inequality. Two additional properties which we rely on are that the dual of the dual norm is the original norm (see for instance [13]), and that the dual of an absolute norm is also an absolute norm. As previously mentioned, to obtain concrete online algorithms, all that remains is to define the update weights $\tau_{t,j}$. The different ways of setting $\tau_{t,j}$ discussed in this paper all share the following properties:

- *boundedness:* $\forall\, 1 \leq t \leq T \quad \|\boldsymbol{\tau}_t\|^* \leq C$ for some predefined parameter C
- *non-negativity:* $\forall\, 1 \leq t \leq T, \, 1 \leq j \leq k \quad \tau_{t,j} \geq 0$
- *conservativeness:* $\forall\, 1 \leq t \leq T, \, 1 \leq j \leq k \quad (\ell_{t,j} = 0) \Rightarrow (\tau_{t,j} = 0)$

Even before specifying the exact value of $\tau_{t,j}$, we can state and prove a powerful lemma which is the crux of our analysis. This lemma will motivate and justify our specific choices of $\tau_{t,j}$ throughout this paper.

Lemma 1. *Let* $\{(\mathbf{x}_{t,j}, y_{t,j})\}_{1 \le t \le T}^{1 \le j \le k}$ *be a sequence of* T *k-tuples of examples, where each* $\mathbf{x}_{t,j} \in \mathbb{R}^{n_j}$, $\|\mathbf{x}_{t,j}\|_2 \le R$ *and each* $y_{t,j} \in \{-1, +1\}$. *Let* $\mathbf{w}_1^\star, \ldots, \mathbf{w}_k^\star$ *be arbitrary vectors where* $\mathbf{w}_j^\star \in \mathbb{R}^{n_j}$, *and define the hinge loss attained by* $\mathbf{w}_j^\star$ *on example* $(\mathbf{x}_{t,j}, y_{t,j})$ *to be* $\ell_{t,j}^\star = \left[1 - y_{t,j} \mathbf{w}_j^\star \cdot \mathbf{x}_{t,j}\right]_+$. *Let* $\|\cdot\|$ *be a norm and let* $\|\cdot\|^\star$ *denote its dual. Assume we apply an algorithm of the form outlined in Fig. 1 to this sequence, where the update satisfies the boundedness property with* $C > 0$, *as well as the non-negativity and conservativeness properties. Then*

$$\sum_{t=1}^{T} \sum_{j=1}^{k} \left(2\tau_{t,j}\ell_{t,j} - \tau_{t,j}^2 \|\mathbf{x}_{t,j}\|_2^2\right) \le \sum_{j=1}^{k} \|\mathbf{w}_j^\star\|_2^2 + 2C \sum_{t=1}^{T} \|\boldsymbol{\ell}_t^\star\| .$$

Proof. Define $\Delta_{t,j} = \|\mathbf{w}_{t,j} - \mathbf{w}_j^\star\|_2^2 - \|\mathbf{w}_{t+1,j} - \mathbf{w}_j^\star\|_2^2$. We prove the lemma by bounding $\sum_{t=1}^{T} \sum_{j=1}^{k} \Delta_{t,j}$ from above and from below. Beginning with the upper bound, we note that for each $1 \le j \le k$, $\sum_{t=1}^{T} \Delta_{t,j}$ is a telescopic sum which collapses to

$$\sum_{t=1}^{T} \Delta_{t,j} = \|\mathbf{w}_{1,j} - \mathbf{w}^\star\|_2^2 - \|\mathbf{w}_{T+1,j} - \mathbf{w}^\star\|_2^2 .$$

Using the facts that $\mathbf{w}_{1,j} = (0, \ldots, 0)$ and $\|\mathbf{w}_{T+1,j} - \mathbf{w}^\star\|_2^2 \ge 0$ for all $1 \le j \le k$, we conclude that

$$\sum_{t=1}^{T} \sum_{j=1}^{k} \Delta_{t,j} \le \sum_{j=1}^{k} \|\mathbf{w}_j^\star\|_2^2 . \tag{4}$$

Turning to the lower bound, we note that we can consider only non-zero summands which actually contribute to the sum, namely $\Delta_{t,j} \ne 0$. Plugging the definition of $\mathbf{w}_{t+1,j}$ into $\Delta_{t,j}$, we get

$$\Delta_{t,j} = \|\mathbf{w}_{t,j} - \mathbf{w}_j^\star\|_2^2 - \|\mathbf{w}_{t,j} + \tau_{t,j} y_{t,j} \mathbf{x}_{t,j} - \mathbf{w}_j^\star\|_2^2$$

$$= \tau_{t,j} \left(-2 y_{t,j} \mathbf{w}_{t,j} \cdot \mathbf{x}_{t,j} - \tau_{t,j} \|\mathbf{x}_{t,j}\|_2^2 + 2 y_{t,j} \mathbf{w}_j^\star \cdot \mathbf{x}_{t,j}\right)$$

$$= \tau_{t,j} \left(2(1 - y_{t,j} \mathbf{w}_{t,j} \cdot \mathbf{x}_{t,j}) - \tau_{t,j} \|\mathbf{x}_{t,j}\|_2^2 - 2(1 - y_{t,j} \mathbf{w}_j^\star \cdot \mathbf{x}_{t,j})\right) . \tag{5}$$

Since our update is conservative, $\Delta_{t,j} \ne 0$ implies that $\ell_{t,j} = 1 - y_{t,j} \mathbf{w}_{t,j} \cdot \mathbf{x}_{t,j}$. By definition, it also holds that $\ell_{t,j}^\star \ge 1 - y_{t,j} \mathbf{w}_j^\star \cdot \mathbf{x}_{t,j}$. Using these two facts in Eq. (5) and using the fact that $\tau_{t,j} \ge 0$ gives $\Delta_{t,j} \ge \tau_{t,j}(2\ell_{t,j} - \tau_{t,j} \|\mathbf{x}_{t,j}\|_2^2 - 2\ell_{t,j}^\star)$. Summing this inequality over $1 \le j \le k$ gives

$$\sum_{j=1}^{k} \Delta_{t,j} \ge \sum_{j=1}^{k} \left(2\tau_{t,j}\ell_{t,j} - \tau_{t,j}^2 \|\mathbf{x}_{t,j}\|_2^2\right) - 2 \sum_{j=1}^{k} \tau_{t,j} \ell_{t,j}^\star . \tag{6}$$

Using Eq. (3) we know that $\sum_{j=1}^{k} \tau_{t,j} \ell_{t,j}^\star \le \|\boldsymbol{\tau}_t\|^\star \|\boldsymbol{\ell}_t^\star\|$. Using our assumption that $\|\boldsymbol{\tau}_t\|^\star \le C$, we have that $\sum_{j=1}^{k} \tau_{t,j} \ell_{t,j}^\star \le C \|\boldsymbol{\ell}_t^\star\|$. Plugging this inequality into Eq. (6) gives

$$\sum_{j=1}^{k} \Delta_{t,j} \geq \sum_{j=1}^{k} \left(2\tau_{t,j}\ell_{t,j} - \tau_{t,j}^2 \|\mathbf{x}_{t,j}\|_2^2\right) - 2C\|\boldsymbol{\ell}_t^\star\| .$$

We conclude the proof by summing the above over $1 \leq t \leq T$ and comparing the result to the upper bound in Eq. (4). $\qquad\square$

Under the assumptions of this lemma, our algorithm competes with a set of fixed margin classifiers, $\mathbf{w}_1^\star, \ldots, \mathbf{w}_k^\star$, which may even be defined in hindsight, after observing all of the inputs and their labels. The right-hand side of the bound is the sum of two terms, a complexity term $\sum_{j=1}^{k} \|\mathbf{w}_j^\star\|_2^2$ and a term which is proportional to the cumulative loss of our competitor, $\sum_{t=1}^{T} \|\boldsymbol{\ell}_t^\star\|$. The left hand side of the bound is the term

$$\sum_{t=1}^{T} \sum_{j=1}^{k} \left(2\tau_{t,j}\ell_{t,j} - \tau_{t,j}^2 \|\mathbf{x}_{t,j}\|_2^2\right) . \qquad (7)$$

This term plays a key role in the derivation of all three families of algorithms. As Lemma 1 provides an upper bound on Eq. (7), we prove matching lower bounds for each of our algorithms. Comparing each of these lower bounds to Lemma 1 yields a loss bound for the respective algorithm.

3   The Finite-Horizon Multitask Perceptron

Our first family of online multitask classification algorithms is called the *finite-horizon multitask Perceptron* family. This family includes algorithms for any global loss function defined by an absolute norm. These algorithms are finite-horizon online algorithms, meaning that the number of online rounds, T, is known in advance and is given as a parameter to the algorithm. An analogous family of infinite-horizon algorithms is the topic of the next section. Given an absolute norm $\|\cdot\|$ and its dual $\|\cdot\|^\star$, the multitask Perceptron sets $\tau_{t,j}$ to be

$$\boldsymbol{\tau}_t = \operatorname*{argmax}_{\boldsymbol{\tau}:\,\|\boldsymbol{\tau}\|^\star \leq C} \boldsymbol{\tau} \cdot \boldsymbol{\ell}_t , \qquad (8)$$

where $C > 0$ is specified later on. Using Eq. (1), we obtain the dual of $\|\cdot\|^\star$:

$$\|\boldsymbol{\ell}\|^{\star\star} = \max_{\boldsymbol{\tau}:\,\|\boldsymbol{\tau}\|^\star \leq 1} \boldsymbol{\tau} \cdot \boldsymbol{\ell} .$$

Since $\|\cdot\|^{\star\star}$ and $\|\cdot\|$ are equivalent [13] and since $\|\boldsymbol{\tau}/C\|^\star = \|\boldsymbol{\tau}\|^\star/C$, we conclude that $\boldsymbol{\tau}_t$ from Eq. (8) satisfies

$$\boldsymbol{\tau}_t \cdot \boldsymbol{\ell}_t = C\|\boldsymbol{\ell}_t\| . \qquad (9)$$

If the global loss is a p-norm, then Eq. (8) reduces to $\tau_{t,j} = C\ell_{t,j}^{p-1}/\|\boldsymbol{\ell}_t\|_p^{p-1}$. If the global loss is an r-max norm and π is a permutation such that $\ell_{t,\pi(1)} \geq \cdots \geq \ell_{t,\pi(k)}$, then Eq. (8) reduces to

$$\tau_{t,j} = \begin{cases} C & \text{if } j \in \{\pi(1), \ldots, \pi(r)\} \\ 0 & \text{otherwise} \end{cases} .$$

The correctness of both definitions of $\tau_{t,j}$ given above can be easily verified by observing that $\|\boldsymbol{\tau}_t\|^\star = C$ and that $\boldsymbol{\tau}_t \cdot \boldsymbol{\ell}_t = C\|\boldsymbol{\ell}_t\|$ in both cases.

An important component in our analysis is the *remoteness* of a norm $\|\cdot\|$, defined to be

$$\rho(\|\cdot\|, k) = \max_{\mathbf{u}\in\mathbb{R}^k} \frac{\|\mathbf{u}\|_2}{\|\mathbf{u}\|} .$$

Geometrically, the remoteness of $\|\cdot\|$ is simply the Euclidean length of the longest vector (again, in the Euclidean sense) which is contained in the unit ball of $\|\cdot\|$. For example, for any p-norm with $p \geq 2$, $\rho(\|\cdot\|_p, k) = k^{1/2-1/p}$. In this paper, we take a specific interest in the remoteness of the dual norm $\|\cdot\|^\star$, and we abbreviate $\rho(\|\cdot\|^\star, k)$ by ρ when $\|\cdot\|^\star$ and k are obvious from the context. With this definition handy, we are ready to prove a loss bound for the multitask Perceptron.

Theorem 1. *Let $\{(\mathbf{x}_{t,j}, y_{t,j})\}_{1\leq t\leq T}^{1\leq j\leq k}$ be a sequence of T k-tuples of examples, where each $\mathbf{x}_{t,j} \in \mathbb{R}^{n_j}$, $\|\mathbf{x}_{t,j}\|_2 \leq R$ and each $y_{t,j} \in \{-1,+1\}$. Let $\|\cdot\|$ be an absolute norm and let ρ denote the remoteness of its dual. Let $\mathbf{w}_1^\star,\ldots,\mathbf{w}_k^\star$ be arbitrary vectors where $\mathbf{w}_j^\star \in \mathbb{R}^{n_j}$, and define the hinge loss attained by $\mathbf{w}_j^\star$ on example $(\mathbf{x}_{t,j}, y_{t,j})$ to be $\ell_{t,j}^\star = \left[1 - y_{t,j}\mathbf{w}_j^\star \cdot \mathbf{x}_{t,j}\right]_+$. If we present this sequence to the finite-horizon multitask Perceptron with the norm $\|\cdot\|$ and the parameter C, then*

$$\sum_{t=1}^{T} \|\boldsymbol{\ell}_t\| \leq \frac{1}{2C} \sum_{j=1}^{k} \|\mathbf{w}_j^\star\|_2^2 + \sum_{t=1}^{T} \|\boldsymbol{\ell}_t^\star\| + \frac{TR^2 C \rho^2(\|\cdot\|^\star, k)}{2} .$$

Proof. The starting point of our analysis is Lemma 1. The choice of $\tau_{t,j}$ in Eq. (8) is clearly bounded by $\|\boldsymbol{\tau}_t\|^\star \leq C$ and conservative. It is also non-negative, due to the fact that $\|\cdot\|^\star$ is an absolute norm and that $\ell_{t,j} \geq 0$. Therefore, the definition of $\tau_{t,j}$ in Eq. (8) meets the requirements of the lemma, and we have

$$\sum_{t=1}^{T}\sum_{j=1}^{k}\left(2\tau_{t,j}\ell_{t,j} - \tau_{t,j}^2\|\mathbf{x}_{t,j}\|_2^2\right) \leq \sum_{j=1}^{k}\|\mathbf{w}_j^\star\|_2^2 + 2C\sum_{t=1}^{T}\|\boldsymbol{\ell}_t^\star\| .$$

Using Eq. (9), we rewrite the left-hand side of the above as

$$2C\sum_{t=1}^{T}\|\boldsymbol{\ell}_t\| - \sum_{t=1}^{T}\sum_{j=1}^{k}\tau_{t,j}^2\|\mathbf{x}_{t,j}\|_2^2 . \tag{10}$$

Using our assumption that $\|\mathbf{x}_{t,j}\|_2^2 \leq R^2$, we know that $\sum_{j=1}^{k}\tau_{t,j}^2\|\mathbf{x}_{t,j}\|_2^2 \leq R^2\|\boldsymbol{\tau}_t\|_2^2$. Using the definition of remoteness, we can upper bound this term by $R^2(\|\boldsymbol{\tau}_t\|^\star)^2\rho^2$. Finally, using our upper bound on $\|\boldsymbol{\tau}_t\|^\star$ we can further bound this term by $R^2 C^2\rho^2$. Plugging this bound back into Eq. (10) gives

$$2C\sum_{t=1}^{T}\|\boldsymbol{\ell}_t\| - TR^2 C^2\rho^2 .$$

Overall, we have shown that

$$2C \sum_{t=1}^{T} \|\boldsymbol{\ell}_t\| - TR^2C^2\rho^2 \leq \sum_{j=1}^{k} \|\mathbf{w}_j^\star\|_2^2 + 2C \sum_{t=1}^{T} \|\boldsymbol{\ell}_t^\star\| .$$

Dividing both sides of the above by $2C$ and rearranging terms gives the desired bound. □

Corollary 1. *Under the assumptions of Thm. 1, if $C = 1/(\sqrt{T}R\rho)$, then*

$$\sum_{t=1}^{T} \|\boldsymbol{\ell}_t\| \leq \sum_{t=1}^{T} \|\boldsymbol{\ell}_t^\star\| + \frac{\sqrt{T}R\rho}{2} \left(\sum_{j=1}^{k} \|\mathbf{w}_j^\star\|_2^2 + 1 \right) .$$

Since our algorithm uses C in its update procedure, and C is a function of $\sqrt{T}$, then this algorithm is a finite horizon algorithm.

4   An Extension to the Infinite Horizon Setting

We would like to devise an algorithm which does not require prior knowledge of the sequence length T. Moreover, we would like a bound which holds simultaneously for every prefix of the input sequence. In this section, we adapt the multitask Perceptron to the infinite horizon setting. This generalization comes at a price; our analysis only bounds a function similar to the cumulative global loss, but not the global loss per se (see Corollary 2 below).

To motivate the infinite-horizon multitask Perceptron, we take a closer look at the analysis of the finite-horizon Perceptron, from the previous section. In the proof of Thm. 1, we lower-bounded the term $\sum_{j=1}^{k} 2\tau_{t,j}\ell_{t,j} - \tau_{t,j}^2\|\mathbf{x}_{t,j}\|_2^2$ by $2C\|\boldsymbol{\ell}_t\| - R^2C^2\rho^2$. The first term in this lower bound is proportional to the global loss, and the second term is a constant. When $\|\boldsymbol{\ell}_t\|$ is small, the difference between these two terms may be negative, which implies that our update step-size may have been too large on that round, and that our update may have even increased our distance to the target. Here, we derive an update for which $\sum_{j=1}^{k} 2\tau_{t,j}\ell_{t,j} - \tau_{t,j}^2\|\mathbf{x}_{t,j}\|_2^2$ is always positive. The vector $\boldsymbol{\tau}_t$ remains in the same direction as before, but by limiting its dual norm we enforce an update step-size which is never excessively large. We replace the definition of τ_t in Eq. (8) by

$$\boldsymbol{\tau}_t = \operatorname*{argmax}_{\boldsymbol{\tau}:\, \|\boldsymbol{\tau}\|^\star \leq \min\left\{ C, \frac{\|\boldsymbol{\ell}_t\|}{R^2\rho^2} \right\}} \boldsymbol{\tau} \cdot \boldsymbol{\ell}_t , \tag{11}$$

where $C > 0$ is a user defined parameter, $R > 0$ is an upper bound on $\|\mathbf{x}_{t,j}\|_2$ for all $1 \leq t \leq T$ and $1 \leq j \leq k$, and $\rho = \rho(\|\cdot\|^\star, k)$. If the global loss function is a p-norm, then the above reduces to

$$\tau_{t,j} = \begin{cases} \dfrac{\ell_{t,j}^{p-1}}{R^2\rho^2\|\boldsymbol{\ell}_t\|_p^{p-2}} & \text{if } \|\boldsymbol{\ell}_t\|_p \leq R^2C\rho^2 \\[2ex] \dfrac{C\ell_{t,j}^{p-1}}{\|\boldsymbol{\ell}_t\|_p^{p-1}} & \text{otherwise} \end{cases} .$$

If the global loss function is an r-max norm and π is a permutation such that $\ell_{t,\pi(1)} \geq \cdots \geq \ell_{t,\pi(k)}$, then Eq. (11) becomes

$$
\tau_{t,j} = \begin{cases} \frac{\|\ell_t\|_{r\text{-max}}}{rR^2} & \text{if } \|\ell_t\|_{r\text{-max}} \leq R^2 C\rho^2 \text{ and } j \in \{\pi(1),\ldots,\pi(r)\} \\ C & \text{if } \|\ell_t\|_{r\text{-max}} > R^2 C\rho^2 \text{ and } j \in \{\pi(1),\ldots,\pi(r)\} \\ 0 & \text{otherwise} \end{cases} \quad .
$$

We now turn to proving a cumulative loss bound.

Theorem 2. *Let $\{(\mathbf{x}_{t,j}, y_{t,j})\}_{t=1,2,\ldots}^{1 \leq j \leq k}$ be a sequence of k-tuples of examples, where each $\mathbf{x}_{t,j} \in \mathbb{R}^{n_j}$, $\|\mathbf{x}_{t,j}\|_2 \leq R$ and each $y_{t,j} \in \{-1,+1\}$. Let $\|\cdot\|$ be an absolute norm and let ρ denote the remoteness of its dual. Let $\mathbf{w}_1^\star,\ldots,\mathbf{w}_k^\star$ be arbitrary vectors where $\mathbf{w}_j^\star \in \mathbb{R}^{n_j}$, and define the hinge loss attained by $\mathbf{w}_j^\star$ on example $(\mathbf{x}_{t,j}, y_{t,j})$ to be $\ell_{t,j}^\star = \left[1 - y_{t,j}\mathbf{w}_j^\star \cdot \mathbf{x}_{t,j}\right]_+$. If we present this sequence to the infinite-horizon multitask Perceptron with the norm $\|\cdot\|$ and the parameter C, then, for every T,*

$$
1/(R^2\rho^2) \sum_{t \leq T: \|\ell_t\| \leq R^2 C\rho^2} \|\ell_t\|^2 + C \sum_{t \leq T: \|\ell_t\| > R^2 C\rho^2} \|\ell_t\| \leq 2C \sum_{t=1}^{T} \|\ell_t^\star\| + \sum_{j=1}^{k} \|\mathbf{w}_j^\star\|_2^2 \quad .
$$

Proof. The starting point of our analysis is again Lemma 1. The choice of $\tau_{t,j}$ in Eq. (11) is clearly bounded by $\|\tau_t\|^\star \leq C$ and conservative. It is also non-negative, due to the fact that $\|\cdot\|^\star$ is absolute and that $\ell_{t,j} \geq 0$. Therefore, $\tau_{t,j}$ meets the requirements of Lemma 1, and we have

$$
\sum_{t=1}^{T} \sum_{j=1}^{k} \left(2\tau_{t,j}\ell_{t,j} - \tau_{t,j}^2 \|\mathbf{x}_{t,j}\|_2^2\right) \leq \sum_{j=1}^{k} \|\mathbf{w}_j^\star\|_2^2 + 2C \sum_{t=1}^{T} \|\ell_t^\star\| \quad . \tag{12}
$$

We now prove our theorem by lower-bounding the left hand side of the above. We analyze two different cases: if $\|\ell_t\| \leq R^2 C\rho^2$ then $\min\{C, \|\ell_t\|/(R^2\rho^2)\} = \|\ell_t\|/(R^2\rho^2)$. Again using the fact that the dual of the dual norm is the original norm, together with the definition of τ_t in Eq. (11), we get that

$$
2 \sum_{j=1}^{k} \tau_{t,j}\ell_{t,j} = 2\|\tau_t\|^\star \|\ell_t\| = 2\frac{\|\ell_t\|^2}{R^2\rho^2} \quad . \tag{13}
$$

On the other hand, $\sum_{j=1}^{k} \tau_{t,j}^2 \|\mathbf{x}_{t,j}\|_2^2$ can be bounded by $R^2 \|\tau_t\|_2^2$. Using the definition of remoteness, we bound this term by $R^2(\|\tau_t\|^\star)^2\rho^2$. Using the fact that, $\|\tau_t\|^\star \leq \|\ell_t\|/(R^2\rho^2)$, we bound this term by $\|\ell_t\|^2/(R^2\rho^2)$. Overall, we have shown that $\sum_{j=1}^{k} \tau_{t,j}^2 \|\mathbf{x}_{t,j}\|_2^2 \leq \frac{\|\ell_t\|^2}{R^2\rho^2}$. Subtracting both sides of this inequality from the respective sides of Eq. (13) gives

$$
\frac{\|\ell_t\|^2}{R^2\rho^2} \leq \sum_{j=1}^{k} \left(2\tau_{t,j}\ell_{t,j} - \tau_{t,j}^2 \|\mathbf{x}_{t,j}\|_2^2\right) \quad . \tag{14}
$$

input: aggressiveness parameter $C > 0$, norm $\|\cdot\|$

initialize $\mathbf{w}_{1,1} = \ldots = \mathbf{w}_{1,k} = (0, \ldots, 0)$

for $t = 1, 2, \ldots$

- receive $\mathbf{x}_{t,1}, \ldots, \mathbf{x}_{t,k}$

- predict $\text{sign}(\mathbf{w}_{t,j} \cdot \mathbf{x}_{t,j})$ $[1 \le j \le k]$

- receive $y_{t,1}, \ldots, y_{t,k}$

- suffer loss $\ell_{t,j} = \left[1 - y_{t,j} \mathbf{w}_{t,j} \cdot \mathbf{x}_{t,j} \right]_+$ $[1 \le j \le k]$

- update:

$$\{\mathbf{w}_{t+1,1}, \ldots, \mathbf{w}_{t+1,k}\} = \underset{\mathbf{w}_1, \ldots, \mathbf{w}_k, \boldsymbol{\xi}}{\operatorname{argmin}} \ \ \tfrac{1}{2} \sum_{j=1}^{k} \|\mathbf{w}_j - \mathbf{w}_{t,j}\|_2^2 + C\|\boldsymbol{\xi}\|$$

$$\text{s.t.} \ \ \forall j \ \ \mathbf{w}_j \cdot \mathbf{x}_{t,j} \ge 1 - \xi_j \ \ \text{and} \ \ \xi_j \ge 0$$

Fig. 2. The implicit update algorithm

Moving on to the second case, if $\|\boldsymbol{\ell}_t\| > R^2 C \rho^2$ then $\min\{C, \|\boldsymbol{\ell}_t\|/(R^2\rho^2)\} = C$. As in Eq. (9), we have that

$$2 \sum_{j=1}^{k} \tau_{t,j} \ell_{t,j} = 2\|\boldsymbol{\tau}_t\|^\star \|\boldsymbol{\ell}_t\| = 2C\|\boldsymbol{\ell}_t\| \ . \tag{15}$$

As before, we can upper bound $\sum_{j=1}^{k} \tau_{t,j}^2 \|\mathbf{x}_{t,j}\|_2^2$ by $R^2(\|\boldsymbol{\tau}_t\|^\star)^2 \rho^2$. Using the fact that $\|\boldsymbol{\tau}_t\|^\star \le C$, we bound this term by $R^2 C^2 \rho^2$. Finally, using our assumption that $\|\boldsymbol{\ell}_t\| > R^2 C \rho^2$, we conclude that $\sum_{j=1}^{k} \tau_{t,j}^2 \|\mathbf{x}_{t,j}\|_2^2 < C\|\boldsymbol{\ell}_t\|$. Subtracting both sides of this inequality from the respective sides of Eq. (15) gives

$$C\|\boldsymbol{\ell}_t\| \le \sum_{j=1}^{k} \left(2\tau_{t,j} \ell_{t,j} - \tau_{t,j}^2 \|\mathbf{x}_{t,j}\|_2^2 \right) \ . \tag{16}$$

Comparing the upper bound in Eq. (12) with the lower bounds in Eq. (14) and Eq. (16) proves the theorem.   □

Corollary 2. *Under the assumptions of Thm. 2, if C is set to be $1/(R^2\rho^2)$ then, for every T, it holds that*

$$\sum_{t=1}^{T} \min\left\{ \|\boldsymbol{\ell}_t\|^2, \|\boldsymbol{\ell}_t\| \right\} \le 2 \sum_{t=1}^{T} \|\boldsymbol{\ell}_t^\star\| + R^2\rho^2 \sum_{j=1}^{k} \|\mathbf{w}_j^\star\|_2^2 \ .$$

5   The Implicit Online Multitask Update

We now discuss a third family of online multitask algorithms, which leads to the strongest loss bounds of the three families of algorithms presented in this paper. In contrast to the closed form updates of the previous algorithms, the algorithms in this family require solving an optimization problem on every round, and are therefore called *implicit* update algorithms. This optimization problem captures the fundamental tradeoff inherent to online learning. On one hand, the algorithm wants its next set of hypotheses to remain close to the current set of hypotheses, so as to maintain the information learned so far. On the other hand, the algorithm wants to make progress using the new examples obtained on this round, where progress is measured using the global loss function. The pseudo-code of the implicit update algorithm is presented in Fig. 2.

Next, we find the dual of the optimization problem given in Fig. 2. By doing so, we show that the family of implicit update algorithms follows the skeleton outlined in Fig. 1 and satisfies the requirements of Lemma 1.

Lemma 2. *Let $\|\cdot\|$ be a norm and let $\|\cdot\|^\star$ be its dual. Then the online update defined in Fig. 2 is conservative and equivalent to setting $\mathbf{w}_{t+1,j} = \mathbf{w}_{t,j} + \tau_{t,j} y_{t,j} \mathbf{x}_{t,j}$ for all $1 \leq j \leq k$, where*

$$\boldsymbol{\tau}_t = \underset{\boldsymbol{\tau}}{\operatorname{argmax}} \sum_{j=1}^{k} \left(2\tau_j \ell_{t,j} - \tau_j^2 \|\mathbf{x}_{t,j}\|_2^2 \right) \quad \text{s.t.} \quad \|\boldsymbol{\tau}\|^\star \leq C \text{ and } \forall j \ \tau_j \geq 0 .$$

Proof Sketch. The update step in Fig. 2 sets the vectors $\mathbf{w}_{t+1,1}, \ldots, \mathbf{w}_{t+1,k}$ to be the solution to the following constrained minimization problem:

$$\min_{\mathbf{w}_1,\ldots,\mathbf{w}_k, \boldsymbol{\xi} \geq 0} \frac{1}{2} \sum_{j=1}^{k} \|\mathbf{w}_j - \mathbf{w}_{t,j}\|_2^2 + C\|\boldsymbol{\xi}\| \quad \text{s.t.} \quad \forall j \ y_{t,j} \mathbf{w}_j \cdot \mathbf{x}_{t,j} \geq 1 - \xi_j .$$

We use the notion of strong duality to restate this optimization problem in an equivalent form. The objective function above is convex and the constraints are both linear and feasible, therefore Slater's condition [14] holds, and the above problem is equivalent to

$$\max_{\boldsymbol{\tau} \geq 0} \min_{\mathbf{w}_1,\ldots,\mathbf{w}_k, \boldsymbol{\xi} \geq 0} \frac{1}{2} \sum_{j=1}^{k} \|\mathbf{w}_j - \mathbf{w}_{t,j}\|_2^2 + C\|\boldsymbol{\xi}\| + \sum_{j=1}^{k} \tau_j \left(1 - y_{t,j} \mathbf{w}_j \cdot \mathbf{x}_{t,j} - \xi_j \right) .$$

We can write the objective function above as the sum of two separate terms,

$$\underbrace{\frac{1}{2} \sum_{j=1}^{k} \|\mathbf{w}_j - \mathbf{w}_{t,j}\|_2^2 + \sum_{j=1}^{k} \tau_j (1 - y_{t,j} \mathbf{w}_j \cdot \mathbf{x}_{t,j})}_{\mathcal{L}_1(\boldsymbol{\tau}, \mathbf{w}_1, \ldots, \mathbf{w}_k)} + \underbrace{C\|\boldsymbol{\xi}\| - \sum_{j=1}^{k} \tau_j \xi_j}_{\mathcal{L}_2(\boldsymbol{\tau}, \boldsymbol{\xi})} .$$

Using the notation defined above, our optimization problem becomes,

$$\max_{\boldsymbol{\tau} \geq 0} \left(\min_{\mathbf{w}_1,\ldots,\mathbf{w}_k} \mathcal{L}_1(\boldsymbol{\tau}, \mathbf{w}_1, \ldots, \mathbf{w}_k) + \min_{\boldsymbol{\xi} \geq 0} \mathcal{L}_2(\boldsymbol{\tau}, \boldsymbol{\xi}) \right) .$$

For any choice of $\boldsymbol{\tau}$, $\mathcal{L}_1$ is a convex function and we can find $\mathbf{w}_1, \ldots, \mathbf{w}_k$ which minimize it by setting all of its partial derivatives with respect to the elements of $\mathbf{w}_1, \ldots, \mathbf{w}_k$ to zero. By doing so, we conclude that, $\mathbf{w}_j = \mathbf{w}_{t,j} + \tau_j y_{t,j} \mathbf{x}_{t,j}$ for all $1 \leq j \leq k$.

The update is conservative since if $\ell_{t,j} = 0$ then setting $\mathbf{w}_j = \mathbf{w}_{t,j}$ satisfies the constraints and minimizes $\|\mathbf{w}_t - \mathbf{w}_{t,j}\|_2^2$, without restricting our choice of any other variable. Plugging our expression for $\mathbf{w}_j$ into $\mathcal{L}_1$, we have that

$$\min_{\mathbf{w}_1, \ldots, \mathbf{w}_k} \mathcal{L}_1(\boldsymbol{\tau}, \mathbf{w}_1, \ldots, \mathbf{w}_k) = \sum_{j=1}^{k} \tau_j(1 - y_{t,j} \mathbf{w}_{t,j} \cdot \mathbf{x}_{t,j}) - \frac{1}{2} \sum_{j=1}^{k} \tau_j^2 \|\mathbf{x}_{t,j}\| .$$

Since the update is conservative, it holds that $\tau_j(1 - y_{t,j}\mathbf{w}_{t,j} \cdot \mathbf{x}_{t,j}) = \tau_t \ell_{t,j}$. Overall, we have reduced our optimization problem to

$$\boldsymbol{\tau}_t = \underset{\boldsymbol{\tau} \geq 0}{\operatorname{argmax}} \left(\sum_{j=1}^{k} \left(\tau_j \ell_{t,j} - \frac{1}{2} \tau_j^2 \|\mathbf{x}_{t,j}\| \right) + \min_{\boldsymbol{\xi} \geq 0} \mathcal{L}_2(\boldsymbol{\tau}, \boldsymbol{\xi}) \right) . \qquad (17)$$

We turn our attention to $\mathcal{L}_2$ and abbreviate $B(\boldsymbol{\tau}) = \min_{\boldsymbol{\xi} \geq 0} \mathcal{L}_2(\boldsymbol{\tau}, \boldsymbol{\xi})$. It can now be shown that B is a barrier function for the constraint $\|\boldsymbol{\tau}\|^* \leq C$, namely $B(\boldsymbol{\tau}) = 0$ if $\|\boldsymbol{\tau}\|^* \leq C$ and $B(\boldsymbol{\tau}) = -\infty$ if $\|\boldsymbol{\tau}\|^* > C$. Therefore, we replace $B(\boldsymbol{\tau})$ in Eq. (17) with the explicit constraint $\|\boldsymbol{\tau}\|^* \leq C$, and conclude the proof. □

Turning to the analysis, we now show that all of the loss bounds proven in this paper also apply to the implicit update family of algorithms. We formally prove that the bound in Thm. 1 (and specifically in Corollary 1) holds for this family. The proof that the bound in Thm. 2 (and specifically in Corollary 2) also holds for this family is identical and is therefore omitted.

Theorem 3. *The bound in Thm. 1 also holds for the algorithm in Fig. 2.*

Proof. Let $\tau'_{t,j}$ denote the weights defined by the multitask Perceptron in Eq. (8) and let $\tau_{t,j}$ denote the weights assigned by the implicit update in Fig. 2. In the proof of Thm. 1, we showed that,

$$2C\|\boldsymbol{\ell}_t\| - R^2 C^2 \rho^2 \leq \sum_{j=1}^{k} \left(2\tau'_{t,j} \ell_{t,j} - \tau'^2_{t,j} \|\mathbf{x}_{t,j}\|_2^2 \right) . \qquad (18)$$

According to Lemma 2, the weights $\tau_{t,j}$ maximize $\sum_{j=1}^{k}(2\tau_{t,j}\ell_{t,j} - \tau_{t,j}^2\|\mathbf{x}_{t,j}\|_2^2)$, subject to the constraints $\|\boldsymbol{\tau}_t\|^* \leq C$ and $\tau_{t,j} \geq 0$. Since the weights $\tau'_{t,j}$ also satisfy these constraints, it holds that $\sum_{j=1}^{k}(2\tau'_{t,j}\ell_{t,j} - \tau'^2_{t,j}\|\mathbf{x}_{t,j}\|_2^2)$ is necessarily upper-bounded by $\sum_{j=1}^{k}(2\tau_{t,j}\ell_{t,j} - \tau_{t,j}^2\|\mathbf{x}_{t,j}\|_2^2)$. Combining this fact with Eq. (18), we conclude that

$$2C\|\boldsymbol{\ell}_t\| - R^2 C^2 \rho^2 \leq \sum_{j=1}^{k} \left(2\tau_{t,j} \ell_{t,j} - \tau_{t,j}^2 \|\mathbf{x}_{t,j}\|_2^2 \right) . \qquad (19)$$

Since $\tau_{t,j}$ is bounded, non-negative, and conservative (due to Lemma 2), the right-hand side of the above inequality is upper-bounded by Lemma 1. Comparing the bound in Eq. (19) to the bound in Lemma 1 proves the theorem. □

6 Algorithms for the Implicit Online Multitask Update

In this section, we briefly describe efficient algorithms for calculating the update in Fig. 2. Due to space constraints we omit all proofs. If the global loss function is the L_2 norm, it can be shown that the solution to the optimization problem in Fig. 2 takes the form $\tau_{t,j} = \ell_{t,j}/(\|\mathbf{x}_{t,j}\|_2^2 + \theta_t)$, where θ_t is the solution to the equation $\sum_{j=1}^k (\frac{\ell_{t,j}}{\|\mathbf{x}_{t,j}\|_2^2 + \theta_t})^2 = C^2$. The exact value of θ_t can be found using binary search.

Similarly, in the case where the global loss function is the r-max norm, it can be shown that there exists some $\theta_t \geq 0$ such that

$$\tau_{t,j} = \begin{cases} 0 & \text{if } \ell_{t,j} - \theta_t < 0 \\ \frac{\ell_{t,j} - \theta_t}{\|\mathbf{x}_{t,j}\|_2^2} & \text{if } 0 \leq \ell_{t,j} - \theta_t \leq C\|\mathbf{x}_{t,j}\|_2^2 \\ C & \text{if } C\|\mathbf{x}_{t,j}\|_2^2 < \ell_{t,j} - \theta_t \end{cases} \tag{20}$$

That is, if the loss of task j is very small then the j'th predictor is left intact. If this loss is moderate then the size of the update step for the j'th predictor is proportional to the loss suffered by the j'th task, and inversely proportional to the squared norm of $\mathbf{x}_{t,j}$. In any case, the size of the update step does not exceed the fixed upper limit C. By plugging Eq. (20) back into the objective function of our optimization problem, we can see that the objective function is monotonically decreasing in θ_t. We conclude that θ_t should be the smallest non-negative value for which the resulting update vector $\boldsymbol{\tau}_t$ satisfies the constraint $\|\boldsymbol{\tau}_t\|_{r\text{-max}}^\star \leq C$.

First, we check whether the constraint $\|\boldsymbol{\tau}_t\|_{r\text{-max}}^\star \leq C$ holds when $\theta_t = 0$. If the answer is positive, we are done. If the answer is negative, the definition of $\|\cdot\|_{r\text{-max}}^\star$ in Eq. (2) and the KKT conditions of optimality yield that $\|\boldsymbol{\tau}_t\|_1 = rC$. This equality enables us to narrow the search for θ_t to a handful of candidate values. To see this, assume for a moment that we have some way of obtaining the sets $\Psi = \{1 \leq j \leq k : 0 < \ell_{t,j} - \theta_t\}$ and $\Phi = \{1 \leq j \leq k : C\|\mathbf{x}_{t,j}\|_2^2 < \ell_{t,j} - \theta_t\}$. The semantics of Ψ and Φ are readily available from Eq. (20): the set Ψ consists of all indices j for which $\tau_{t,j} > 0$, while Φ consists of all indices j for which $\tau_{t,j}$ is capped at C. Given these two sets and the fact that $\sum_{j=1}^k \tau_j = rC$ yields that

$$\sum_{j \in \Psi \setminus \Phi} \frac{\ell_{t,j} - \theta_t}{\|\mathbf{x}_{t,j}\|_2^2} + \sum_{j \in \Phi} C = rC .$$

Solving the above equation for θ_t gives

$$\theta_t = \frac{\sum_{j \in \Psi \setminus \Phi} \frac{\ell_{t,j}}{\|\mathbf{x}_{t,j}\|_2^2} - rC + \sum_{j \in \Phi} C}{\sum_{j \in \Psi \setminus \Phi} \frac{1}{\|\mathbf{x}_{t,j}\|_2^2}} . \tag{21}$$

Therefore, our problem has reduced to the problem of finding the sets Ψ and Φ.

Let $q_1, \ldots, q_{2k}$ denote the sequence of numbers obtained by sorting the union of the sets $\{\ell_{t,j}\}_{j=1}^k$ and $\{(\ell_{t,j} - C\|\mathbf{x}_{t,j}\|_2^2)\}_{j=1}^k$ in ascending order. For every $1 \leq s \leq 2k$, we define the sets $\Psi_s = \{1 \leq j \leq k : 0 < \ell_{t,j} - q_s\}$ and $\Phi_s =$

$\{1 \leq j \leq k : C\|\mathbf{x}_{t,j}\|_2^2 < \ell_{t,j} - q_s\}$. It is not difficult to see that if $\theta_t \in [q_s, q_{s+1})$ then $\Psi = \Psi_s$ and $\Phi = \Phi_s$. Essentially, we have narrowed the search for θ_t to $2k$ candidates defined by the sets Ψ_s and Φ_s for $1 \leq s \leq 2k$, and by Eq. (21). Of these candidates we choose the smallest one which results in an update that satisfies our constraints. When performing this process with careful bookkeeping, calculating the update takes only $O(k \log(k))$ operations.

References

1. Crammer, K., Dekel, O., Keshet, J., Shalev-Shwartz, S., Singer, Y.: Online passive aggressive algorithms. Journal of Machine Learning Research **7** (2006)
2. Dietterich, T.G., Bakiri, G.: Solving multiclass learning problems via error-correcting output codes. JAIR **2** (1995) 263–286
3. Caruana, R.: Multitask learning. Machine Learning **28** (1997) 41–75
4. Heskes, T.: Solving a huge number of silmilar tasks: A combination of multitask learning and a hierarchical bayesian approach. In: ICML 15. (1998) 233–241
5. Evgeniou, T., C.Micchelli, Pontil, M.: Learning multiple tasks with kernel methods. Journal of Machine Learning Research **6** (2005) 615–637
6. Baxter, J.: A model of inductive bias learning. Journal of Artificial Intelligence Research **12** (2000) 149–198
7. Ben-David, S., Schuller, R.: Exploiting task relatedness for multiple task learning. In: COLT 16. (2003)
8. Tsochantaridis, I., Hofmann, T., Joachims, T., Altun, Y.: Support vector machine learning for interdependent and structured output spaces. In: Proceedings of the Twenty-First International Conference on Machine Learning. (2004)
9. Kivinen, J., Warmuth, M.: Relative loss bounds for multidimensional regression problems. Journal of Machine Learning **45** (2001) 301–329
10. Helmbold, D., Kivinen, J., Warmuth, M.: Relative loss bounds for single neurons. IEEE Transactions on Neural Networks **10** (1999) 1291–1304
11. Crammer, K., Singer, Y.: On the algorithmic implementation of multiclass kernel-based vector machines. Jornal of Machine Learning Research **2** (2001) 265–292
12. Crammer, K., Singer, Y.: Ultraconservative online algorithms for multiclass problems. Jornal of Machine Learning Research **3** (2003) 951–991
13. Horn, R.A., Johnson, C.R.: Matrix Analysis. Cambridge Univ. Press (1985)
14. Boyd, S., Vandenberghe, L.: Convex Optimization. Cambridge Univ. Press (2004)

The Shortest Path Problem Under Partial Monitoring*

András György[1], Tamás Linder[1,2], and György Ottucsák[3]

[1] Informatics Laboratory, Computer and Automation Research Institute
of the Hungarian Academy of Sciences,
Lágymányosi u. 11, Budapest, Hungary, H-1111
gya@szit.bme.hu
[2] Department of Mathematics and Statistics,
Queen's University, Kingston, Ontario, Canada K7L 3N6
linder@mast.queensu.ca
[3] Department of Computer Science and Information Theory,
Budapest University of Technology and Economics,
Magyar Tudósok Körútja 2., Budapest, Hungary, H-1117
oti@szit.bme.hu

Abstract. The on-line shortest path problem is considered under partial monitoring scenarios. At each round, a decision maker has to choose a path between two distinguished vertices of a weighted directed acyclic graph whose edge weights can change in an arbitrary (adversarial) way such that the loss of the chosen path (defined as the sum of the weights of its composing edges) be small. In the multi-armed bandit setting, after choosing a path, the decision maker learns only the weights of those edges that belong to the chosen path. For this scenario, an algorithm is given whose average cumulative loss in n rounds exceeds that of the best path, matched off-line to the entire sequence of the edge weights, by a quantity that is proportional to $1/\sqrt{n}$ and depends only polynomially on the number of edges of the graph. The algorithm can be implemented with linear complexity in the number of rounds n and in the number of edges. This result improves earlier bandit-algorithms which have performance bounds that either depend exponentially on the number of edges or converge to zero at a slower rate than $O(1/\sqrt{n})$. An extension to the so-called label efficient setting is also given, where the decision maker is informed about the weight of the chosen path only with probability $\epsilon < 1$. Applications to routing in packet switched networks along with simulation results are also presented.

1 Introduction

In a typical sequential decision problem, a decision maker has to perform a sequence of actions. After each action the decision maker suffers some loss,

---

* This research was supported in part by the János Bolyai Research Scholarship of the Hungarian Academy of Sciences, the Mobile Innovation Center of Hungary, by the Natural Sciences and Engineering Research Council (NSERC) of Canada, and by the Hungarian Inter-University Center for Telecommunications and Informatics (ETIK).

G. Lugosi and H.U. Simon (Eds.): COLT 2006, LNAI 4005, pp. 468–482, 2006.

depending on the response (or state) of the environment, and its goal is to minimize its cumulative loss over a sufficiently long period of time. In the adversarial setting no probabilistic assumption is made on how the losses corresponding to different actions are generated. In particular, the losses may depend on the previous actions of the decision maker, whose goal is to perform well relative to a set of experts for any possible behavior of the environment. More precisely, the aim of the decision maker is to achieve asymptotically the same average loss (per round) as the best expert.

The basic theoretical results in this topic were pioneered by Blackwell [4] and Hannan [17], and brought to the attention of the machine learning community in the 1990's by Vovk [25], Littlestone and Warmuth [21], and Cesa-Bianchi *et al.* [6]. These results show that for any bounded loss function, if the decision maker has access to the past losses of all experts, then it is possible to construct on-line algorithms that perform, for any possible behavior of the environment, almost as well as the best of N experts. Namely, for these algorithms the per round cumulative loss of the decision maker is at most as large as that of the best expert plus a quantity proportional to $\sqrt{\ln N / n}$ for any bounded loss function, where n is the number of rounds in the decision game. The logarithmic dependence on the number of experts makes it possible to obtain meaningful bounds even if the pool of experts is very large. However, the basic prediction algorithms, such as weighted average forecasters, have a computational complexity that is proportional to the number of experts, and they are therefore practically infeasible when the number of experts is very large.

In certain situations the decision maker has only limited knowledge about the losses of all possible actions. For example, it is often natural to assume that the decision maker gets to know only the loss corresponding to the action it has made, and has no information about the loss it would have suffered had it made a different decision. This setup is referred to as the *multi-armed bandit problem*, and was solved by Auer *et al.* [1] and Cesa-Bianchi and Lugosi [7], who gave an algorithm whose average loss exceeds that of the best expert at most by an amount proportional to $\sqrt{N \ln N / n}$. Note that, compared to the *full information case* described above where the losses of all possible actions are revealed to the decision maker, there is an extra $\sqrt{N}$ term in the performance bound, which seriously limits the usefulness of the algorithm if the number of experts is large.

Another interesting example for the limited information case is the so-called *label efficient decision problem*, in which it is too costly to observe the state of the environment, and so the decision maker can query the losses of all possible actions for only a limited number of times. A recent result of Cesa-Bianchi, Lugosi, and Stoltz [8] shows that in this case, if the decision maker can query the losses m times during a period of length n, then it can achieve $O(\sqrt{\ln N / m})$ average excess loss relative to the best expert.

In many applications the set of experts has a certain structure that may be exploited to construct efficient on-line decision algorithms. The construction of such algorithms has been of great interest in computational learning theory. A partial list of works dealing with this problem includes Herbster and Warmuth [19], Vovk [26], Bousquet and Warmuth [5], Helmbold and Schapire [18], Takimoto and Warmuth [24], Kalai and Vempala [20], György, Linder, and Lugosi [12, 13, 14]. For a more complete survey, see Cesa-Bianchi and Lugosi [7, Chapter 5].

In this paper we discuss the on-line shortest path problem, a representative example of structured expert classes that has received attention in the literature for its many applications, including, among others, routing in communication networks, see, e.g., Takimoto and Warmuth [24], Awerbuch *et al.* [2], or György and Ottucsák [16], and adaptive quantizer design in zero-delay lossy source coding, see, György, Linder, and Lugosi [12, 13, 15]. In this problem, given is a weighted directed (acyclic) graph whose edge weights can change in an arbitrary manner, and the decision maker has to pick in each round a path between two given vertices, such that the weight of this path (the sum of the weights of its composing edges) be as small as possible.

Efficient solutions, with time and space complexity proportional to the number of edges rather than to the number of paths (the latter typically being exponential in the number of edges), have been given in the full information case, where in each round the weights of all the edges are revealed after a path has been chosen, see, e.g., Mohri [23], Takimoto and Warmuth [24], Kalai and Vempala [20], and György, Linder, and Lugosi [14].

In the bandit setting, where only the weights of the edges composing the chosen path are revealed to the decision maker, if one applies the general bandit algorithm of Auer *et al.* [1], then the resulting bound will be too large to be of practical use because of its square-root-type dependence on the number of paths N. On the other hand, utilizing the special graph structure in the problem, Awerbuch and Kleinberg [3] and McMahan and Blum [22] managed to get rid of the exponential dependence on the number of edges in the performance bound by extending black box predictors, and specifically the follow-the-perturbed-leader algorithm of Hannan [17] and the exponentially weighted average predictor [21], to the multi-armed bandit setting. However, their bounds do not have the right $O(1/\sqrt{n})$ dependence on the number of rounds.

In this paper we provide an extension of the bandit algorithm of Auer *et al.* [1] unifying the advantages of the above approaches, with performance bound that is only polynomial in the number of edges, and converges to zero at the right $O(1/\sqrt{n})$ rate as the number of rounds increases.

In the following, first we define formally the on-line shortest path problem in Section 2, then extend it to the multi-armed bandit setting in Section 3. Our new algorithm for the shortest path problem in the bandit setting is given in Section 4 together with its performance analysis. The algorithm is extended to solve the shortest path problem in a combined label efficient multi-armed bandit setting in Section 5. Simulation results are presented in Section 6. Finally, conclusions are drawn in Section 7.

2   The Shortest Path Problem

Consider a network represented by a set of nodes connected by edges, and assume that we have to send a stream of packets from a source node to a destination node. At each time slot a packet is sent along a chosen route connecting source and destination. Depending on the traffic, each edge in the network may have a different delay, and the total delay the packet suffers on the chosen route is the sum of delays of the edges composing the route. The delays may change from one time slot to the next one in an arbitrary way, and our goal is to find a way of choosing the route in each time slot such that the sum of the total delays over time is not significantly more than that of the best fixed route in the network. This adversarial version of the routing problem is most useful when the delays on the edges can change very dynamically, even depending on our previous routing decisions. This is the situation in the case of mobile ad-hoc networks, where the network topology can change rapidly, or in certain secure networks, where the algorithm has to be prepared to handle denial of service attacks, that is, situations where willingly malfunctioning nodes and links increase the delay, see, e.g., Awerbuch *et al.* [2].

This problem can be naturally cast as a sequential decision problem in which each possible route is represented by an action. However, the number of routes is typically exponentially large in the number of edges, and therefore computationally efficient algorithms are called for. Two solutions of very different flavors have been proposed. One of them is based on a follow-the-perturbed-leader forecaster, see Kalai and Vempala [20], while the other is based on an efficient computation of the exponentially weighted average forecaster, see, for example, Takimoto and Warmuth [24]. Both solutions have different advantages and may be generalized in different directions.

To formalize the problem, consider a (finite) directed acyclic graph with a set of edges $E = \{e_1, \ldots, e_{|E|}\}$ and a set of vertices V. Thus, each edge $e \in E$ is an ordered pair of vertices (v_1, v_2). Let u and v be two distinguished vertices in V. A *path* from u to v is a sequence of edges $e^{(1)}, \ldots, e^{(k)}$ such that $e^{(1)} = (u, v_1)$, $e^{(j)} = (v_{j-1}, v_j)$ for all $j = 2, \ldots, k-1$, and $e^{(k)} = (v_{k-1}, v)$, and let $\mathcal{R} = \{i_1, \ldots, i_N\}$ denote the set of all such paths. For simplicity, we assume that every edge in E is on some path from u to v and every vertex in V is an endpoint of an edge.

In each round $t = 1, \ldots, n$ of the decision game, the decision maker chooses a path I_t among all paths from u to v. Then a loss $\ell_{e,t} \in [0,1]$ is assigned to each edge $e \in E$. We write $e \in i$ if the edge $e \in E$ belongs to the path $i \in \mathcal{R}$, and with a slight abuse of notation the loss of a path i at time slot t is also represented by $\ell_{i,t}$ (however, the meaning of the subscript of ℓ will always be clear from the context). Then $\ell_{i,t}$ is given as

$$\ell_{i,t} = \sum_{e \in i} \ell_{e,t}$$

and therefore the cumulative loss of each path i takes the additive form

$$\sum_{s=1}^{t} \ell_{i,s} = \sum_{e \in i} \sum_{s=1}^{t} \ell_{e,s}$$

where the inner sum on the right hand side is the loss accumulated by edge e during the first t rounds of the game.

It is well known that for a general loss sequence, the decision maker must be allowed to use randomization to be able to achieve the performance of the best expert, see, e.g., Cesa-Bianchi and Lugosi [7]. Therefore, the path I_t is chosen according to some distribution p_t over all paths from u to v. We study the normalized regret

$$\frac{1}{n}\left(\sum_{t=1}^{n}\ell_{I_t,t} - \min_{i\in\mathcal{R}}\sum_{t=1}^{n}\ell_{i,t}\right)$$

where the minimum is taken over all paths i from u to v.

For example, the exponentially weighted average forecaster [21], calculated over all possible paths, yields regret bound of the form

$$\frac{1}{n}\left(\sum_{t=1}^{n}\ell_{I_t,t} - \min_{i\in\mathcal{R}}\sum_{t=1}^{n}\ell_{i,t}\right) \leq K\left(\sqrt{\frac{\ln N}{2n}} + \sqrt{\frac{\ln(1/\delta)}{2n}}\right)$$

with probability at least $1 - \delta$, where N is the total number of paths from u to v in the graph and K is the length of the longest path.

3   The Multi-armed Bandit Setting

In this section we discuss the "bandit" version of the shortest path problem. In this, in many applications more realistic problem, the decision maker has only access to the losses of those edges that are on the path it has chosen. That is, after choosing a path I_t at time t, the value of the loss $\ell_{e,t}$ is revealed to the forecaster if and only if $e \in I_t$. For example, in the routing problem it means that information is available on the delay of the route the packet is sent on, and not on other routes in the network.

Formally, the on-line shortest path problem in the multi-armed bandit setting is given as follows: at each time slot $t = 1, \ldots, n$, the decision maker picks a path $I_t \in \mathcal{R}$ form u to v. Then the environment assigns loss $\ell_{e,t} \in [0,1]$ to each edge $e \in E$, and the decision maker suffers loss $\ell_{I_t,t} = \sum_{e\in I_t}\ell_{e,t}$, and the losses $\ell_{e,t}$ are revealed for all $e \in I_t$. Note that $\ell_{e,t}$ may depend on $I_1, \ldots, I_{t-1}$, the earlier choices of the decision maker.

For the general multi-armed bandit problem, Auer et $al.$ [1] gave an algorithm, based on exponential weighting with a biased estimate of the gains defined, in our case, as $g_{i,t} = K - \ell_{i,t}$, combined with uniform exploration. Applying an improved version of this algorithm due to Cesa-Bianchi and Lugosi [7] to the on-line shortest path problem in the bandit setting results in a performance that can be bounded with probability at least $1 - \delta$ for any $0 < \delta < 1$ and fixed time horizon n as

$$\frac{1}{n}\left(\sum_{t=1}^{n}\ell_{I_t,t} - \min_{i\in\mathcal{R}}\sum_{t=1}^{n}\ell_{i,t}\right) \leq \frac{11K}{2}\sqrt{\frac{N\ln(N/\delta)}{n}} + \frac{K\ln N}{2n}\ .$$

However, this bound is unacceptable in our scenario because, unlike in the full information case when a simple usage of the exponentially weighted average forecaster yielded a good performance bound, here the dependence on the number of all paths N is not merely logarithmic. In order to achieve a bound that does not grow exponentially with the number of edges of the graph, it is imperative to make use of the dependence structure of the losses of the different actions (i.e., paths). Awerbuch and Kleinberg [3] and McMahan and Blum [22] attempted to do this by extending low complexity predictors, such as the follow-the-perturbed-leader forecaster [17], [20] to the bandit setting. However, the obtained bounds do not have the right $O(1/\sqrt{n})$ decay in terms of the number of rounds.

4   A Bandit Algorithm for Shortest Paths

In the following we describe a carefully defined variant of the bandit algorithm of [1] that achieves the desired performance for the shortest path problem in the bandit setting. The new algorithm utilizes the fact that when the losses of the edges of the chosen path are revealed, then this also provides some information about the loss of each path sharing common edges with the chosen path.

For each edge $e \in E$, introduce *gains* $g_{e,t} = 1 - \ell_{e,t}$, and for each path $i \in \mathcal{R}$, similarly to the losses, let the gain be the sum of the gains of the edges of the path, that is, let $g_{i,t} = \sum_{e \in i} g_{e,t}$. The conversion from losses to gains is done in order to facilitate the subsequent performance analysis, see, e.g. [7]. To simplify the conversion, we assume that each path $i \in \mathcal{R}$ is of the same length K for some $K > 0$. Note that although this assumption may seem to be restrictive at the first glance, from each acyclic directed graph (V, E) one can construct a new graph with adding at most $(K-2)(|V|-2)+1$ vertices and edges (with constant weight zero) to the graph without modifying the weights of the paths such that each path from u to v will be of length K, where K denotes the length of the longest path of the original graph. As typically $|E| = O(|V|^2)$, the size of the graph is usually not increased substantially.

A main feature of the algorithm below is that the gains are estimated for each edge and not for each path. This modification results in an improved upper bound on the performance with the number of edges in place of the number of paths. Moreover, using dynamic programming as in Takimoto and Warmuth [24], the algorithm can be computed efficiently. Another important ingredient of the algorithm is that one needs to make sure that every edge is sampled sufficiently often. To this end, we introduce a set $\mathcal{C}$ of *covering paths* with the property that for each edge $e \in E$ there is a path $i \in \mathcal{C}$ such that $e \in \mathcal{C}$. Observe that one can always find such a covering set of cardinality $|\mathcal{C}| \leq |E|$.

Note that the algorithm of [1] is a special case of the algorithm below: For any multi-armed bandit problem with N experts, one can define a graph with two vertices u and v, and N directed edges from u to v with weights corresponding to the losses of the experts. The solution of the shortest path problem in this case is equivalent to that of the original bandit problem, with choosing expert

i if the corresponding edge is chosen. For this graph, our algorithm reduces to the original algorithm of [1].

A BANDIT ALGORITHM FOR SHORTEST PATHS

Parameters: real numbers $\beta > 0$, $\eta > 0$, $0 < \gamma < 1$.
Initialization: Set $w_{e,0} = 1$ for each $e \in E$, $\boldsymbol{w}_{i,0} = 1$ for each $i \in \mathcal{R}$, and $\overline{W}_0 = |\mathcal{R}|$. For each round $t = 1, 2, \ldots$

(a) Choose a path $\boldsymbol{I}_t$ according to the distribution $\boldsymbol{p}_t$ on $\mathcal{R}$, defined by

$$p_{i,t} = \begin{cases} (1-\gamma)\frac{w_{i,t-1}}{\overline{W}_{t-1}} + \frac{\gamma}{|\mathcal{C}|} & \text{if } i \in \mathcal{C} \\ (1-\gamma)\frac{w_{i,t-1}}{\overline{W}_{t-1}} & \text{if } i \notin \mathcal{C}. \end{cases}$$

(b) Compute the probability of choosing each edge e as

$$q_{e,t} = \sum_{i:e\in i} p_{i,t} = (1-\gamma)\frac{\sum_{i:e\in i} w_{i,t-1}}{\overline{W}_{t-1}} + \gamma\frac{|\{i \in \mathcal{C} : e \in i\}|}{|\mathcal{C}|}.$$

(c) Calculate the estimated gains

$$g'_{e,t} = \begin{cases} \frac{g_{e,t}+\beta}{q_{e,t}} & \text{if } e \in \boldsymbol{I}_t \\ \frac{\beta}{q_{e,t}} & \text{otherwise.} \end{cases}$$

(d) Compute the updated weights

$$w_{e,t} = w_{e,t-1}e^{\eta g'_{e,t}}$$
$$\boldsymbol{w}_{i,t} = \prod_{e\in i} w_{e,t} = w_{i,t-1}e^{\eta g'_{i,t}}$$

where $g'_{i,t} = \sum_{e\in i} g'_{e,t}$, and the sum of the total weights of the paths

$$\overline{W}_t = \sum_{i\in\mathcal{R}} w_{i,t}.$$

The analysis of the algorithm is based on that of the original algorithm of [1] with necessary modifications required to transform parts of the argument for edges from paths, and to utilize the connection between the gains of paths sharing common edges.

Theorem 1. *For any $\delta \in (0,1)$ and parameters $0 < \gamma < 1/2$, $0 < \beta \leq 1$, and $\eta > 0$ satisfying $2\eta K|\mathcal{C}| \leq \gamma$, the performance of the algorithm defined above can be bounded with probability at least $1 - \delta$ as*

$$\frac{1}{n}\left(\sum_{t=1}^{n}\ell_{I_t,t} - \min_{i\in\mathcal{R}}\sum_{t=1}^{n}\ell_{i,t}\right) \le K\gamma + 2\eta K^2|\mathcal{C}| + \frac{K}{n\beta}\ln\frac{|E|}{\delta} + \frac{\ln N}{n\eta} + |E|\beta.$$

In particular, choosing $\beta = \sqrt{\frac{K}{n|E|}\ln\frac{|E|}{\delta}}$, $\gamma = 2\eta K|\mathcal{C}|$, and $\eta = \sqrt{\frac{\ln N}{4nK^2|\mathcal{C}|}}$ yields for all $n \ge \max\left\{\frac{K}{|E|}\ln\frac{|E|}{\delta}, 4|\mathcal{C}|\ln N\right\}$,

$$\frac{1}{n}\left(\sum_{t=1}^{n}\ell_{I_t,t} - \min_{i\in\mathcal{R}}\sum_{t=1}^{n}\ell_{i,t}\right) \le 2\sqrt{\frac{K}{n}}\left(\sqrt{4K|\mathcal{C}|\ln N} + \sqrt{|E|\ln\frac{|E|}{\delta}}\right).$$

Sketch of the proof. The proof of the theorem follows the main ideas of [1]. As usual, we start with bounding the quantity $\ln\frac{W_n}{W_0}$. The lower bound is obtained as

$$\ln\frac{W_n}{W_0} = \ln\sum_{i\in\mathcal{R}}e^{\eta\sum_{t=1}^{n}g'_{i,t}} - \ln N \ge \eta\max_{i\in\mathcal{R}}\sum_{t=1}^{n}g'_{i,t} - \ln N \qquad (1)$$

where we used the fact that $w_{i,n} = e^{\eta\sum_{t=1}^{n}g'_{i,t}}$.

On the other hand, from the conditions of the theorem it follows that $\eta g'_{i,t} \le 1$ for all i and t, and so using the inequalities $\ln(x+1) \le x$ for all $x > -1$ and $e^x < 1 + x + x^2$ for all $x \le 1$, one can show for all $t \ge 1$ that

$$\ln\frac{W_t}{W_{t-1}} \le \frac{\eta}{1-\gamma}\sum_{i\in\mathcal{R}}p_{i,t}g'_{i,t} + \frac{\eta^2}{1-\gamma}\sum_{i\in\mathcal{R}}p_{i,t}g'^2_{i,t}. \qquad (2)$$

The sums on the right hand side can be bounded as

$$\sum_{i\in\mathcal{R}}p_{i,t}g'_{i,t} = g_{I_t,t} + |E|\beta \quad \text{and} \quad \sum_{i\in\mathcal{R}}p_{i,t}g'^2_{i,t} \le K(1+\beta)\sum_{e\in E}g'_{e,t}. \qquad (3)$$

Summing (2) for $t = 1, \ldots, n$, and combining it with (1) and (3), it follows that

$$\sum_{t=1}^{n}g_{I_t,t} \ge (1 - \gamma - \eta K(1+\beta)|\mathcal{C}|)\max_{i\in\mathcal{R}}\sum_{t=1}^{n}g'_{i,t} - \frac{1-\gamma}{\eta}\ln N - n|E|\beta. \qquad (4)$$

Now one can show based on [7, Lemma 6.7] that for any $\delta \in (0,1)$, $0 < \beta \le 1$, and for all $e \in E$ we have

$$\mathbb{P}\left(\sum_{t=1}^{n}g_{e,t} > \sum_{t=1}^{n}g'_{e,t} + \frac{1}{\beta}\ln\frac{|E|}{\delta}\right) \le \frac{\delta}{|E|}. \qquad (5)$$

Then, applying the union bound, one can replace $\sum_{t=1}^{n}g'_{i,t}$ in (4) with $\sum_{t=1}^{n}g_{i,t}$ as

$$\sum_{t=1}^{n}g_{I_t,t} \ge (1-\gamma-\eta K(1+\beta)|\mathcal{C}|)\left(\max_{i\in\mathcal{R}}\sum_{t=1}^{n}g_{i,t} - \frac{K}{\beta}\ln\frac{|E|}{\delta}\right) - \frac{1-\gamma}{\eta}\ln N - n|E|\beta$$

which holds with probability at least $1 - \delta$. Then, applying the conversions

$$\sum_{t=1}^{n} \ell_{\mathbf{I}_t,t} = Kn - \sum_{t=1}^{n} g_{\mathbf{I}_t,t} \quad \text{and} \quad \sum_{t=1}^{n} \ell_{i,t} = Kn - \sum_{t=1}^{n} g_{i,t},$$

after some algebra one obtains the first statement of the theorem. The second statement follows by substituting the optimized parameters given in the theorem. $\square$

The algorithm can be implemented efficiently with time complexity $O(n|E|)$ and space complexity $O(|E|)$. The two complex steps of the algorithm are steps (a) and (b), both of which can be computed, similarly to Takimoto and Warmuth [24], using dynamic programming. To be able to perform these steps efficiently, first we have to order the vertices of the graph. Since we have an acyclic directed graph, its nodes can be labeled (in $O(|E|)$ time) from 1 to $|V|$ such that if $(v_1, v_2) \in E$ then $v_1 < v_2$, and $u = 1$ and $v = |V|$. For any pair of vertices $u_1 < v_1$ let $\mathcal{R}_{u_1,v_1}$ denote the set of paths from u_1 to v_1, and for any vertex $s \in V$, let

$$H_t(s) = \sum_{i \in \mathcal{R}_{s,v}} \prod_{e \in i} w_{e,t}$$

and

$$\widehat{H}_t(s) = \sum_{i \in \mathcal{R}_{u,s}} \prod_{e \in i} w_{e,t}.$$

Given the edge weights $\{w_{e,t}\}$, $H_t(s)$ can be computed recursively for $s = |V| - 1, \ldots, 1$, and $\widehat{H}_t(s)$ can be computed recursively for $s = 2, \ldots, |V|$ in $O(|E|)$ time (letting $H_t(v) = \widehat{H}_t(u) = 1$ by definition). In step (a), first one has to decide with probability γ whether $\mathbf{I}_t$ is generated according to the graph weights, or it is chosen uniformly from $\mathcal{C}$. If $\mathbf{I}_t$ is to be drawn according to the graph weights, it can be shown that its vertices can be chosen one by one such that if the first k vertices of $\mathbf{I}_t$ are $v_0 = u, v_1, \ldots, v_{k-1}$, then the next vertex of $\mathbf{I}_t$ can be chosen to be any $v_k > v_{k-1}$, satisfying $(v_{k-1}, v_k) \in E$, with probability $w_{(v_{k-1},v_k),t-1} H_{t-1}(v_k)/H_{t-1}(v_{k-1})$. The other computationally demanding step, namely step (b), can be performed easily by noting that for any edge (v_1, v_2),

$$q_{(v_1,v_2),t} = (1 - \gamma) \frac{\widehat{H}_{t-1}(v_1) w_{(v_1,v_2),t-1} H_{t-1}(v_2)}{H_{t-1}(u)} + \gamma \frac{|\{i \in \mathcal{C} : (v_1, v_2) \in i\}|}{|\mathcal{C}|}.$$

5   The Shortest Path Problem for a Combination of the Label Efficient and the Bandit Settings

In this section we investigate a combination of the multi-armed bandit and the label efficient setting problems, where the gain of the chosen path is available only on request. Just as in the previous section, it is assumed that each path of the graph is of the same length K.

In the general label efficient decision problem, after taking the action, the decision maker has the option to query the losses of all possible actions (in the original problem formulation, the decision maker can query the response of the environment, referred to as "label", and can compute all losses from this information). To query the losses, the decision maker uses an i.i.d. sequence $S_1, S_2, \ldots, S_n$ of Bernoulli random variables with $\mathbb{P}(S_t = 1) = \epsilon$ and asks for the losses if $S_t = 1$. For this problem, Cesa-Bianchi et $al.$ [8] proved an upper bound on the normalized regret of order $O(K\sqrt{\ln(4N/\delta)/(n\epsilon)})$ with probability at least $1 - \delta$.

We study a combined algorithm which, at each time slot t, queries the loss of the chosen path with probability ϵ (as in the label efficient case), and similarly to the multi-armed bandit case, computes biased estimates $g'_{i,t}$ of the true gains $g_{i,t}$. This combination is motivated by some realistic applications, where the information is costly in some sense, i.e., the request is allowed only for a limited number of times.

The model of label-efficient decisions is well suited to a particular packet switched network model, called the cognitive packet network, which was introduced by Gelenbe et $al.$ [10, 11]. In these networks, capabilities for routing and flow control are concentrated in packets. In particular, one type of packets, called smart packets, do not transport any useful data, but are used to explore the network (e.g. the delay of the chosen path). The other type of packets are data packets, which do not collect information about their paths, but transport useful data. In this model the task of the decision maker is to send packets from the source to the destination over routes with minimum average transmission delay (or packet loss). In this scenario, smart packets are used to query the delay of the chosen path. However, as these packets do not transport information, there is a tradeoff between the number of queries and the utilization of the network. If data packets are α times larger than smart packets on the average (note that typically $\alpha \gg 1$), then $\epsilon/(\epsilon + \alpha(1 - \epsilon))$ is the proportion of the bandwidth sacrificed for well informed routing decisions.

The algorithm differs from our bandit algorithm of the previous section only in step (c), which is modified in the spirit of [8]. The modified step is given below:

MODIFIED STEP FOR THE LABEL EFFICIENT BANDIT ALGORITHM FOR SHORTEST PATHS

(c') Draw a Bernoulli random variable S_t with $\mathbb{P}(S_t = 1) = \epsilon$, and compute the estimated gains

$$g'_{e,t} = \begin{cases} \frac{g_{e,t}+\beta}{q_{e,t}\epsilon} & \text{if } e \in I_t \text{ and } S_t = 1 \\ \frac{\beta}{q_{e,t}\epsilon} & \text{if } e \notin I_t \text{ and } S_t = 1 \\ 0 & \text{otherwise.} \end{cases}$$

The performance of the algorithm is analyzed in the next theorem, which can be viewed as a combination of Theorem 1 in the preceding section and Theorem 2 of [8].

Theorem 2. *For any* $\delta \in (0,1)$, $\epsilon \in (0,1]$ *and parameters* $\eta = \sqrt{\frac{\epsilon \ln N}{4nK^2|\mathcal{C}|}}$,
$\gamma = \frac{2\eta K|\mathcal{C}|}{\epsilon} \leq 1/2$ *and* $\beta = \sqrt{\frac{K}{n|E|\epsilon} \ln \frac{2|E|}{\delta}} \leq 1$ *and for all*

$$n \geq \frac{1}{\epsilon} \max \left\{ \frac{K^2 \ln^2(2|E|/\delta)}{|E| \ln N}, \frac{|E| \ln(2|E|/\delta)}{K}, 4|\mathcal{C}| \ln N \right\}$$

the performance of the algorithm defined above can be bounded, with probability at least $1 - \delta$ *as*

$$\frac{1}{n} \left(\sum_{t=1}^{n} \ell_{I_t,t} - \min_{i \in \mathcal{R}} \sum_{t=1}^{n} \ell_{i,t} \right)$$

$$\leq \sqrt{\frac{K}{n\epsilon}} \left(4\sqrt{K|\mathcal{C}| \ln N} + 5\sqrt{|E| \ln \frac{2|E|}{\delta}} + \sqrt{8K \ln \frac{2}{\delta}} \right) + \frac{4K}{3n\epsilon} \ln \frac{2}{\delta}$$

$$\leq \frac{27K}{2} \sqrt{\frac{|E| \ln \frac{2N}{\delta}}{n\epsilon}}.$$

Sketch of the proof. The proof of the theorem is a generalization of the proof of Theorem 1, and follows the same lines with some extra technicalities to handle the effects of the modified step (c'). Therefore, in the following we emphasize only the differences. First note that (1) and (2) also hold in this case. Now, instead of (3), one obtains

$$\sum_{i \in \mathcal{R}} p_{i,t} g'_{i,t} = \frac{S_t}{\epsilon} (g_{I_t,t} + |E|\beta) \quad \text{and} \quad \sum_{i \in \mathcal{R}} p_{i,t} g'^2_{i,t} \leq \frac{1}{\epsilon} K(1+\beta) \sum_{e \in E} g'_{e,t}$$

which imply, together with (1) and (2),

$$\sum_{t=1}^{n} \frac{S_t}{\epsilon} (g_{I_t,t} + |E|\beta) \geq \left(1 - \gamma - \frac{\eta K(1+\beta)|\mathcal{C}|}{\epsilon} \right) \max_{i \in \mathcal{R}} \sum_{t=1}^{n} g'_{i,t} - \frac{1-\gamma}{\eta} \ln N. \quad (6)$$

To relate the left hand side of the above inequality to the real gain $\sum_{t=1}^{n} g_{I_t,t}$, notice that

$$X_t = \frac{S_t}{\epsilon} (g_{I_t,t} + |E|\beta) - (g_{I_t,t} + |E|\beta)$$

is a martingale difference sequence. Then, it can be shown by applying Bernstein's inequality (see, e.g., [9]) that

$$\mathbb{P} \left(\sum_{t=1}^{n} X_t > \sqrt{\frac{8K^2 n}{\epsilon} \ln \frac{2}{\delta}} + \frac{4K}{3\epsilon} \ln \frac{2}{\delta} \right) \leq \frac{\delta}{2}. \quad (7)$$

Furthermore, similarly to (5) it can be proved that

$$\mathbb{P} \left(\sum_{t=1}^{n} g_{e,t} > \sum_{t=1}^{n} g'_{e,t} + \frac{4\beta n|E|}{K} \right) \leq \frac{\delta}{2|E|}. \quad (8)$$

An application of the union bound for (7) and (8) combined with (6) yields, with probability at least $1 - \delta$,

$$\sum_{t=1}^{n} g_{I_t,t} \geq \left(1 - \gamma - \frac{\eta K(1+\beta)|\mathcal{C}|}{\epsilon}\right) \left(\max_{i \in \mathcal{R}} \sum_{t=1}^{n} g_{i,t} - 4\beta n|E|\right)$$
$$- \frac{1-\gamma}{\eta} \ln N - \beta n|E| - \sqrt{\frac{8K^2 n}{\epsilon} \ln \frac{2}{\delta}} - \frac{4K}{3\epsilon} \ln \frac{2}{\delta}.$$

Using $\sum_{t=1}^{n} g_{I_t,t} = Kn - \sum_{t=1}^{n} \ell_{I_t,t}$ and $\sum_{t=1}^{n} g_{i,t} = Kn - \sum_{t=1}^{n} \ell_{i,t}$, and substituting the values of η, β, and γ yield, after some algebra, the statement of the theorem. $\qquad\square$

6 Simulations

To further investigate our new algorithms, simulations were conducted. We tested our bandit algorithm for shortest paths in a simple communication network shown in Figure 1. The simulation consisted of sending 10000 packets, from source node $u = 1$ to destination node $v = 6$, and our goal was to pick a route for each packet with small delay. We assumed the infinitesimal user scenario, that is, our choice for a path does not affect the delay on the links of the network.

Each link has a fixed propagation delay which is 0.1ms. To generate additional delays (so called traffic delays), three major flows were considered, with periodically changing dynamics with period length 1000 time slots. The flow is a path between two determined nodes (not necessarily u and v), which is loaded by traffic for a limited time period. The first flow, shown by a thick line in Figure 1, has a constant load, resulting in a constant 20ms traffic delay on all of its edges. The second flow, denoted by a dashed line, starts sending packets at time slot 200 of each period, and the traffic delays on its edges increase to 20ms by time slot 400, and stay there until time slot 700, when the flow is stopped, and the corresponding traffic delays drop back to 0. The third flow, denoted by a dotted line, has similar characteristics as the second flow, but it starts at time slot 500, the corresponding delay reaches 20ms at time slot 700, and remains there until the end of the period. Finally, the two thin lines in the graph denote links which are not used by the major flows.

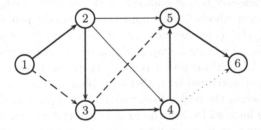

Fig. 1. Topology of the network

The difficulty in this configuration is that the best fixed path switches 3 times during a period. From time 0 to time slot 200 there are three paths with the same performance: path $(1,3,5,6)$, path $(1,3,4,6)$, and path $(1,2,4,6)$. From time slot 201 to time slot 700, path (1,2,4,6) has the smallest delay, and in the remainder of the period, path $(1,3,5,6)$ is the best. In the long run these are the three best fixed paths, with $(1,2,4,6)$ being the best, $(1,3,4,6)$ the second best, and $(1,3,5,6)$ the third.

In the simulations we ran the bandit algorithm for shortest paths with parameters optimized for $n = 10000$. We also ran an infinite horizon version of the algorithm, in which at each time instant t, the parameters η, β, and γ are set so that they are optimized for the finite horizon $n = t$. In this version $w_{e,t} = w_{e,t-1} \exp(\eta_t g'_{e,t})$, where η_t is decreasing in t and therefore this algorithm uses "reverse-discounted gains". Although we have not investigated the theoretical performance of this discounted style version, it can be observed that the modification substantially improves the performance of the algorithm in this example, and the modified version outperformed the second best route in the network. The reason for the good performance is that in the simulation the best fixed path in the long run does not change because of the periodicity of the flows and therefore a discounted algorithm can learn faster the best path than a non-discounted algorithm. We also compared our methods to that of Awerbuch and Kleinberg [3], and achieved better performance in all situations. The simulation results are summarized in Figure 2 that shows the normalized regret of the above algorithms (averaged over 30 runs), as well as the regrets of all fixed paths from node 1 to node 6 (the periodical small jumps on the curves correspond to the starting and ending times of the other flows). Note that in Figure 2, there are only 8 paths instead of 9, because of path (1,2,3,5,6) and path (1,3,4,5,6) have the same performance, and the curve for the best path $(1, 2, 4, 6)$ coincides with the x-axis.

7   Conclusions

Efficient algorithms have been provided for the on-line shortest path problem in the multi-armed bandit setting and in a combined label efficient multi-armed bandit setting. The regrets of the algorithms, compared to the performance of the best fixed path, converge to zero at an $O(1/\sqrt{n})$ rate as the time horizon n grows to infinity, and increases only polynomially in the number of edges (and vertices) of the graph. Earlier methods for the multi-armed bandit problem either do not have the right $O(1/\sqrt{n})$ convergence rate, or their regret increase exponentially in the number of edges for typical graphs. Simulation results showed the expected performance of the algorithms under realistic traffic scenarios.

Both problems are motivated by realistic problems, such as routing in communication networks, where the nodes do not have all the information about the state of the network. We have addressed the problem in the adversarial setting where the edge weights may vary in an arbitrary way, in particular, they may depend on previous routing decisions of the algorithm. Although this assumption may seem to be very strong in many network scenarios, it has applications in mobile ad-hoc

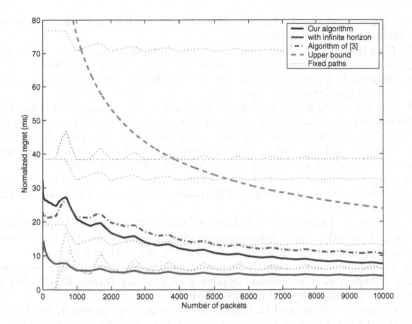

Fig. 2. Normalized regret of our bandit algorithm for shortest paths and that of the shortest path algorithm of [3]

networks, where the network topology changes dynamically in time, and also in certain secure networks that has to be able to handle denial of service attacks.

Acknowledgements

The authors would like to thank Gábor Lugosi and László Györfi for useful discussions.

References

1. P. Auer, N. Cesa-Bianchi, Y. Freund, and R. Schapire. The non-stochastic multi-armed bandit problem. *SIAM Journal on Computing*, 32(1):48–77, 2002.
2. B. Awerbuch, D. Holmer, H. Rubens, and R. Kleinberg. Provably competitive adaptive routing. In *Proceedings of IEEE INFOCOM 2005*, volume 1, pages 631–641, March 2005.
3. B. Awerbuch and R. D. Kleinberg. Adaptive routing with end-to-end feedback: distributed learning and geometric approaches. In *Proceedings of the 36th Annual ACM Symposium on the Theory of Computing, STOC 2004*, pages 45–53, Chicago, IL, USA, Jun. 2004. ACM Press.
4. D. Blackwell. An analog of the minimax theorem for vector payoffs. *Pacific Journal of Mathematics*, 6:1–8, 1956.
5. O. Bousquet and M. K. Warmuth. Tracking a small set of experts by mixing past posteriors. *Journal of Machine Learning Research*, 3:363–396, Nov. 2002.
6. N. Cesa-Bianchi, Y. Freund, D. P. Helmbold, D. Haussler, R. Schapire, and M. K. Warmuth. How to use expert advice. *Journal of the ACM*, 44(3):427–485, 1997.

7. N. Cesa-Bianchi and G. Lugosi. *Prediction, Learning, and Games*. Cambridge University Press, Cambridge, 2006.
8. N. Cesa-Bianchi, G. Lugosi, and G. Stoltz. Minimizing regret with label efficient prediction. *IEEE Trans. Inform. Theory*, IT-51:2152–2162, June 2005.
9. L. Devroye, L. Györfi, and G. Lugosi. *A Probabilistic Theory of Pattern Recognition*. Springer-Verlag, New York, 1996.
10. E. Gelenbe, M. Gellman, R. Lent, P. Liu, and P. Su. Autonomous smart routing for network QoS. In *Proceedings of First International Conference on Autonomic Computing*, pages 232–239, New York, May 2004. IEEE Computer Society.
11. E. Gelenbe, R. Lent, and Z. Xhu. Measurement and performance of a cognitive packet network. *Journal of Computer Networks*, 37:691–701, 2001.
12. A. György, T. Linder, and G. Lugosi. Efficient algorithms and minimax bounds for zero-delay lossy source coding. *IEEE Transactions on Signal Processing*, 52:2337–2347, Aug. 2004.
13. A. György, T. Linder, and G. Lugosi. A "follow the perturbed leader"-type algorithm for zero-delay quantization of individual sequences. In *Proc. Data Compression Conference*, pages 342–351, Snowbird, UT, USA, Mar. 2004.
14. A. György, T. Linder, and G. Lugosi. Tracking the best of many experts. In *Proceedings of the 18th Annual Conference on Learning Theory, COLT 2005*, pages 204–216, Bertinoro, Italy, Jun. 2005. Springer.
15. A. György, T. Linder, and G. Lugosi. Tracking the best quantizer. In *Proceedings of the IEEE International Symposium on Information Theory*, pages 1163–1167, Adelaide, Australia, June-July 2005.
16. A. György and Gy. Ottucsák. Adaptive routing using expert advice. *The Computer Journal*, 49(2):180–189, 2006.
17. J. Hannan. Approximation to bayes risk in repeated plays. In M. Dresher, A. Tucker, and P. Wolfe, editors, *Contributions to the Theory of Games*, volume 3, pages 97–139. Princeton University Press, 1957.
18. D. P. Helmbold and R. E. Schapire. Predicting nearly as well as the best pruning of a decision tree. *Machine Learning*, 27:51–68, 1997.
19. M. Herbster and M. K. Warmuth. Tracking the best expert. *Machine Learning*, 32(2):151–178, 1998.
20. A. Kalai and S Vempala. Efficient algorithms for the online decision problem. In B. Schölkopf and M. Warmuth, editors, *Proceedings of the 16th Annual Conference on Learning Theory and the 7th Kernel Workshop, COLT-Kernel 2003*, pages 26–40, New York, USA, Aug. 2003. Springer.
21. N. Littlestone and M. K. Warmuth. The weighted majority algorithm. *Information and Computation*, 108:212–261, 1994.
22. H. B. McMahan and A. Blum. Online geometric optimization in the bandit setting against an adaptive adversary. In *Proceedings of the 17th Annual Conference on Learning Theory, COLT 2004*, pages 109–123, Banff, Canada, Jul. 2004. Springer.
23. M. Mohri. General algebraic frameworks and algorithms for shortest distance problems. Technical Report 981219-10TM, AT&T Labs Research, 1998.
24. E. Takimoto and M. K. Warmuth. Path kernels and multiplicative updates. *Journal of Machine Learning Research*, 4:773–818, 2003.
25. V. Vovk. Aggregating strategies. In *Proceedings of the Third Annual Workshop on Computational Learning Theory*, pages 372–383, Rochester, NY, Aug. 1990. Morgan Kaufmann.
26. V. Vovk. Derandomizing stochastic prediction strategies. *Machine Learning*, 35(3):247–282, Jun. 1999.

Tracking the Best Hyperplane
with a Simple Budget Perceptron

Nicolò Cesa-Bianchi[1] and Claudio Gentile[2]

[1] Dipartimento di Scienze dell'Informazione
Università degli Studi di Milano, Italy
cesa-bianchi@dsi.unimi.it
[2] Dipartimento di Informatica e Comunicazione
Università dell'Insubria, Varese, Italy
claudio.gentile@uninsubria.it

Abstract. Shifting bounds for on-line classification algorithms ensure good performance on any sequence of examples that is well predicted by a sequence of smoothly changing classifiers. When proving shifting bounds for kernel-based classifiers, one also faces the problem of storing a number of support vectors that can grow unboundedly, unless an eviction policy is used to keep this number under control. In this paper, we show that shifting and on-line learning on a budget can be combined surprisingly well. First, we introduce and analyze a shifting Perceptron algorithm achieving the best known shifting bounds while using an unlimited budget. Second, we show that by applying to the Perceptron algorithm the simplest possible eviction policy, which discards a random support vector each time a new one comes in, we achieve a shifting bound close to the one we obtained with no budget restrictions. More importantly, we show that our randomized algorithm strikes the optimal trade-off $U = \Theta(\sqrt{B})$ between budget B and norm U of the largest classifier in the comparison sequence.

1   Introduction

On-line or incremental learning is a powerful technique for building kernel-based classifiers. On-line algorithms, like the kernel Perceptron algorithm and its many variants, are typically easy to implement, efficient to run, and have strong performance guarantees. In this paper, we study two important aspects related to incremental learning: tracking ability and memory boundedness. The need for tracking abilities arises from the fact that on-line algorithms are often designed to perform well with respect to the best fixed classifier in hindsight within a given comparison class. However, this is a weak guarantee: in many real-world tasks, such as categorization of text generated by a newsfeed, it is not plausible to assume that a fixed classifier could perform consistently well on a long sequence of newsitems generated by the feed. For this reason, a "shifting" performance model has been introduced (e.g., [19, 13, 2, 14, 15], and references therein) where the on-line algorithm is evaluated against an arbitrary sequence of *comparison classifiers*. In this shifting model, which is strictly harder than the traditional

G. Lugosi and H.U. Simon (Eds.): COLT 2006, LNAI 4005, pp. 483–498, 2006.
© Springer-Verlag Berlin Heidelberg 2006

nonshifting performance model, the tracking ability refers to the fact that the performance of the algorithm is good to the extent that the data sequence is well predicted by a sequence of classifiers whose coefficients change gradually with time. If the algorithm is kernel-based, then we face the additional issue of the time and space needed to compute the classifier. In fact, kernel-based learners typically use a subset of previously observed data to encode a classifier (borrowing the Support Vector Machine [22, 21] terminology, we call these data "support vectors"). The problem is that nearly all on-line algorithms need to store a new support vector after each prediction mistake. Thus, the number of supports grows unboundedly unless the data sequence is linearly separable in the RKHS induced by the kernel under consideration. To address this specific issue, variants of the Perceptron algorithm have been proposed [6, 23] and analyzed [7] that work using a fixed *budget* of support vectors. These algorithms use a rule that, once the number of stored supports has reached the budget, evicts a support from the storage each time a new vector comes in. Our eviction rule, at the basis of the Randomized Budget Perceptron algorithm, is surprisingly simple: On a mistaken trial, the algorithm adds in the new support vector after an old one has been chosen *at random* from the storage and discarded.

Since the tracking ability is naturally connected to a weakened dependence on the past, memory boundedness could be viewed as a way to obtain a good shifting performance. In fact, we will show that our Randomized Budget Perceptron algorithm has a strong performance guarantee in the shifting model. In addition, and more importantly, this algorithm strikes the optimal trade-off $U = \Theta(\sqrt{B})$ between the largest norm U of a classifier in the comparison sequence and the required budget B. This improves on $U = O(\sqrt{B/(\ln B)})$ obtained in [7], via a more complicated algorithm.

The paper is organized as follows. In the rest of this section we introduce our main notation, along with preliminary definitions. Section 2 introduces the Shifting Perceptron algorithm, a simple variant of the Perceptron algorithm achieving the best known shifting bound without budget restriction. This result will be used as a yardstick for the results of Section 3, where our simple Randomized Budget Perceptron algorithm is described and analyzed. Finally, Section 4 is devoted to conclusions and open problems.

All of our algorithms are kernel-based. For notational simplicity, we define and analyze them without using kernels.

Basic definitions, preliminaries and notation

An *example* is a pair $(\boldsymbol{x}, y)$, where $\boldsymbol{x} \in \mathbb{R}^d$ is an *instance* vector and $y \in \{-1, +1\}$ is the associated binary label. We consider the standard on-line learning model [1, 17] in which learning proceeds in a sequence of *trials*. In the generic trial t the algorithm observes instance $\boldsymbol{x}_t$ and outputs a prediction $\widehat{y}_t \in \{-1, +1\}$ for the label y_t associated with $\boldsymbol{x}_t$. We say that the algorithm has made a *prediction mistake* if $\widehat{y}_t \neq y_t$.

In this paper we consider variants of the standard Perceptron algorithm [3, 20]. At each trial $t = 1, 2, \dots$ this algorithm predicts y_t through the linear-threshold function $\widehat{y}_t = \text{SGN}(\boldsymbol{w}^\top \boldsymbol{x}_t)$, where $\boldsymbol{w} \in \mathbb{R}^d$ is a weight vector that is initially set to the zero vector $\mathbf{0}$. If a mistake is made at trial t, the algorithm updates $\mathbf{w}$ by performing the assignment $\mathbf{w} \leftarrow \mathbf{w} + y_t \mathbf{x}_t$.

When the Perceptron algorithm is run in a RKHS the current hypothesis is represented as a linear combination of (kernel) dot-products with all past mistaken ("support") vectors $\mathbf{x}_t$. Since in any given trial the running time required to make a prediction scales linearly with the number of mistakes made so far, the overall running time needed by the kernel Perceptron algorithm is *quadratic* in the total number m of mistakes made. A memory bounded Perceptron algorithm tries to overcome this drawback by maintaining only a prearranged number of past support vectors, thereby turning the quadratic dependence on m into a linear one.

We measure the performance of our linear-threshold algorithms by the total number of mistakes they make on an arbitrary sequence of examples. In the standard performance model, the goal is to bound this total number of mistakes in terms of the performance of the best *fixed* linear classifier $\mathbf{u} \in \mathbb{R}^d$ in hindsight (note that we identify an arbitrary linear-threshold classifier with its coefficient vector $\mathbf{u}$). Since the general problem of finding $\mathbf{u} \in \mathbb{R}^d$ that minimizes the number of mistakes on a known sequence is a computationally hard problem, the performance of the best predictor in hindsight is often measured using the cumulative *hinge loss* [8, 11]. The hinge loss of a linear classifier $\mathbf{u}$ on example $(\mathbf{x}, y)$ is defined by $d(\mathbf{u}; (\mathbf{x}, y)) = \max\{0, 1 - y\mathbf{u}^\top \mathbf{x}\}$. Note that d is a convex function of the margin $y\mathbf{u}^\top \mathbf{x}$, and is also an upper bound on the indicator function of $\text{SGN}(\mathbf{u}^\top \mathbf{x}) \neq y$.

In the *shifting* or *tracking* performance model the learning algorithm faces the harder goal of bounding its total number of mistakes in terms of the cumulative hinge loss achieved by an arbitrary sequence $\mathbf{u}_0, \mathbf{u}_1 \dots, \mathbf{u}_{n-1} \in \mathbb{R}^d$ of linear classifiers (also called *comparison vectors*). To make this goal feasible, the bound is allowed to scale also with the maximum norm $U = \max_t \|\mathbf{u}_t\|$ of the classifiers in the sequence and with the *total shift*

$$S_{\text{tot}} = \sum_{t=1}^{n-1} \|\mathbf{u}_{t-1} - \mathbf{u}_t\| \tag{1}$$

of the classifier sequence. We assume for simplicity that all instances $\mathbf{x}_t$ are normalized, that is, $\|\mathbf{x}_t\| = 1$ for all $t \geq 1$. Finally, throughout this paper, we will use $\{\phi\}$ to denote the indicator function of the event defined by a predicate ϕ.

2   The Shifting Perceptron Algorithm

Our learning algorithm for shifting hyperplanes (Shifting Perceptron Algorithm, SPA) is described in Figure 1. SPA has a positive input parameter λ which determines the rate of weight decay. The algorithm maintains a weight vector $\mathbf{w}$ (initially set to zero) and two more variables: a mistake counter k (initialized to zero) and a time-changing decaying factor λ_k (initialized to 1). When a mistake is made on some example $(\mathbf{x}_t, y_t)$ the signed instance vector $y_t \mathbf{x}_t$ is added to the old weight vector, just like in the Perceptron update rule. However, unlike the Perceptron rule, before adding $y_t \boldsymbol{x}_t$ SPA scales down the old weight, so as to diminish the importance of early update stages. The important thing to observe here is that the scaling factor $(1 - \lambda_k)$ changes with time, since $\lambda_k \to 0$ as more mistakes are made. Note that subscript t runs over all trials, while subscript k runs over mistaken trials only, thus k serves as an index for quantities ($\boldsymbol{w}_k$ and λ_k) which get updated only in those trials. In particular, at the *end* of each trial, k is equal to the number of mistakes made so far.

Algorithm: Shifting Perceptron.
Parameters: $\lambda > 0$;
Initialization: $\boldsymbol{w}_0 = \boldsymbol{0}$, $\lambda_0 = 1$, $k = 0$.
For $t = 1, 2, \ldots$

1. Get instance vector $\boldsymbol{x}_t \in \mathbb{R}^d$, $\|\boldsymbol{x}_t\| = 1$;
2. Predict with $\widehat{y}_t = \mathrm{SGN}(\boldsymbol{w}_k^\top \boldsymbol{x}_t) \in \{-1, +1\}$;
3. Get label $y_t \in \{-1, +1\}$;
4. **If** $\widehat{y}_t \neq y_t$ **then**

$$\boldsymbol{w}_{k+1} = (1 - \lambda_k)\boldsymbol{w}_k + y_t \boldsymbol{x}_t , \qquad k \leftarrow k + 1 , \qquad \lambda_k = \frac{\lambda}{\lambda + k} .$$

Fig. 1. The shifting Perceptron algorithm

It is worth observing what the algorithm really does by unwrapping the recurrence $\boldsymbol{w}_{k+1} = (1 - \lambda_k)\boldsymbol{w}_k + y_t \boldsymbol{x}_t$. Assume at the end of trial t the algorithm has made $k + 1$ mistakes, and denote the mistaken trials by $t_0, t_1, \ldots, t_k$. We have $\boldsymbol{w}_{k+1} = \alpha_0\, y_{t_0} \boldsymbol{x}_{t_0} + \alpha_1\, y_{t_1} \boldsymbol{x}_{t_1} + \cdots + \alpha_k\, y_{t_k} \boldsymbol{x}_{t_k}$ with[1]

$$\alpha_i = \prod_{j=i+1}^{k} (1 - \lambda_j) = \exp\Big(\sum_{j=i+1}^{k} \log(1 - \lambda_j) \Big) \approx \exp\Big(-\sum_{j=i+1}^{k} \lambda_j \Big)$$

$$= \exp\Big(-\sum_{j=i+1}^{k} \frac{\lambda}{\lambda + j} \Big) \approx \Big(\frac{\lambda + i + 1}{\lambda + k + 1} \Big)^\lambda \approx c_k\, (i + 1)^\lambda,$$

c_k being a positive constant independent of i. Thus SPA is basically following a (degree-λ) polynomial vector decaying scheme, where the most recent "support vector" $\boldsymbol{x}_{t_k}$ is roughly worth $(k+1)^\lambda$ times the least recent one (i.e., $\boldsymbol{x}_{t_0}$). Clearly enough, if $\lambda = 0$ all support vectors are equally important and we recover the classical Perceptron algorithm.

Now, since we are facing a shifting target problem, it is reasonable to expect that the optimal degree λ depends on how fast the underlying target is drifting with time. As we will see in a moment, the above polynomial weighting scheme gives SPA a desirable robustness to parameter tuning, beyond making the analysis fairly simple.

---

[1] See the appendix for more precise approximations.

2.1 Analysis

The analysis is a standard potential-based analysis for mistake-driven on-line algorithms [3, 17, 20].

The following simple lemma is central to our analysis. The lemma bounds the growth rate of the norm of the algorithm's weight vector. The key point to remark is that, unlike previous algorithms and analyses (e.g., [7, 14, 15]), we do not force the weight vector w_k to live in a ball of bounded radius. Instead, we allow the weight vector to grow unboundedly, at a pace controlled in a rather precise way by the input parameter λ. The proof is given in the appendix.

Lemma 1. *With the notation introduced in Figure 1, we have*

$$\|w_{k+1}\| \le e\sqrt{\frac{\lambda + k + 2}{2\lambda + 1}}$$

for any $k = 0, 1, 2 \dots$, where e is the base of natural logarithms.

The following theorem contains our mistake bounds for SPA. The theorem delivers shifting bounds for any constant value of parameter λ. For instance, $\lambda = 0$ gives a shifting bound for the classical (non-shifting) Perceptron algorithm.[2] For any sequence $(u_0, u_1, \dots)$ of comparison vectors, the bound is expressed in terms of the cumulative hinge loss D, the shift S, and the maximum norm U of the sequence. These quantities are defined as follows:

$$D = \sum_{k=0}^{m-1} d(u_k; (x_{t_k}, y_{t_k})), \quad S = \sum_{k=1}^{m-1} \|u_k - u_{k-1}\|, \quad U = \max_{t=0,\dots,n-1} \|u_t\| . \quad (2)$$

We recall that t_k is the trial at the end of which w_k gets updated and u_k is the comparison vector in trial t_k. Note that D and S are only summed over mistaken trials. Larger, but more interpretable bounds, can be obtained if these sums are replaced by sums running over all trials t. In particular, S may be replaced by S_{tot} defined in (1).

As expected, the optimal tuning of λ grows with S and, in turn, yields a mistake bound which scales linearly with S. We emphasize that, unlike previous investigations (such as [15]) our shifting algorithm is independent of scaling parameters (like the margin of the comparison classifiers $\langle u_t \rangle$). In fact, our "optimal" tuning of λ turns out to be scale-free.

Theorem 1. *For any $n \in \mathbb{N}$, any sequence of examples $(x_1, y_1), \dots, (x_n, y_n) \in \mathbb{R}^d \times \{-1, +1\}$ such that $\|x_t\| = 1$ for each t, and any sequence of comparison vectors $u_0, \dots, u_{n-1} \in \mathbb{R}^d$, the algorithm in Figure 1 makes a number m of mistakes bounded by*

$$m \le D + K^2 + K\sqrt{D + \lambda + 1} , \quad (3)$$

---

[2] Thus, even in a shifting framework the Perceptron algorithm, with no modifications, achieves a (suboptimal) shifting bound.

where $K = \dfrac{e}{\sqrt{2\lambda+1}}\,(S+(4\lambda+1)\,U)$. Moreover, if we set $\lambda = \dfrac{S}{4U}$, then we have $K \le e\,\sqrt{8SU+U^2}$ and

$$m \le D + e\,\sqrt{(8SU+U^2)\,D} + e^2\,(8SU+U^2) + e\,(2S+3U) . \qquad (4)$$

Proof. Consider how the potential $\boldsymbol{u}_k^\top \boldsymbol{w}_{k+1}$ evolves over mistaken trials. We can write

$$
\begin{aligned}
\boldsymbol{u}_k^\top \boldsymbol{w}_{k+1} &= \boldsymbol{u}_k^\top ((1-\lambda_k)\boldsymbol{w}_k + y_{t_k}\boldsymbol{x}_{t_k}) \\
&= (1-\lambda_k)\,(\boldsymbol{u}_k^\top \boldsymbol{w}_k - \boldsymbol{u}_{k-1}^\top \boldsymbol{w}_k + \boldsymbol{u}_{k-1}^\top \boldsymbol{w}_k) + y_{t_k}\boldsymbol{u}_k^\top \boldsymbol{x}_{t_k} \\
&= (1-\lambda_k)(\boldsymbol{u}_k - \boldsymbol{u}_{k-1})^\top \boldsymbol{w}_k + (1-\lambda_k)\boldsymbol{u}_{k-1}^\top \boldsymbol{w}_k + y_{t_k}\boldsymbol{u}_k^\top \boldsymbol{x}_{t_k} \\
&\ge -(1-\lambda_k)\,\|\boldsymbol{u}_k - \boldsymbol{u}_{k-1}\|\,\|\boldsymbol{w}_k\| - \lambda_k\,\|\boldsymbol{u}_{k-1}\|\,\|\boldsymbol{w}_k\| + \boldsymbol{u}_{k-1}^\top \boldsymbol{w}_k + y_{t_k}\boldsymbol{u}_k^\top \boldsymbol{x}_{t_k} \\
&\ge -(1-\lambda_k)\,\|\boldsymbol{u}_k - \boldsymbol{u}_{k-1}\|\,\|\boldsymbol{w}_k\| - \lambda_k\,\|\boldsymbol{u}_{k-1}\|\,\|\boldsymbol{w}_k\| + \boldsymbol{u}_{k-1}^\top \boldsymbol{w}_k \\
&\quad + 1 - d(\boldsymbol{u}_k; (\boldsymbol{x}_{t_k}, y_{t_k}))
\end{aligned}
$$

the last inequality following from the very definition of $d(\boldsymbol{u}_k; (\boldsymbol{x}_{t_k}, y_{t_k}))$. Rearranging yields

$$
\begin{aligned}
\boldsymbol{u}_k^\top \boldsymbol{w}_{k+1} &- \boldsymbol{u}_{k-1}^\top \boldsymbol{w}_k \\
&\ge -(1-\lambda_k)\,\|\boldsymbol{u}_k - \boldsymbol{u}_{k-1}\|\,\|\boldsymbol{w}_k\| - \lambda_k\,\|\boldsymbol{u}_{k-1}\|\,\|\boldsymbol{w}_k\| + 1 - d(\boldsymbol{u}_k; (\boldsymbol{x}_{t_k}, y_{t_k})) .
\end{aligned}
$$

Recalling that $\boldsymbol{w}_0 = \boldsymbol{0}$, we sum the above inequality over[3] $k = 0, 1, \ldots, m-1$, then we rearrange and overapproximate. This results in

$$
m \le D
$$
$$
+ \underbrace{\sum_{k=1}^{m-1}(1-\lambda_k)\|\boldsymbol{u}_k - \boldsymbol{u}_{k-1}\|\,\|\boldsymbol{w}_k\|}_{(I)} + \underbrace{\sum_{k=1}^{m-1}\lambda_k\|\boldsymbol{u}_{k-1}\|\,\|\boldsymbol{w}_k\|}_{(II)} + \underbrace{\|\boldsymbol{u}_{m-1}\|\,\|\boldsymbol{w}_m\|}_{(III)} .
$$

We now use Lemma 1 to bound from above the three terms (I), (II), and (III):

$$
\begin{aligned}
(I) &\le S \max_{k=1,\ldots,m-1}\left((1-\lambda_k)\,\|\boldsymbol{w}_k\|\right) \\
&\le S\,\frac{e\,(m-1)}{\lambda+m-1}\sqrt{\frac{\lambda+m}{2\lambda+1}} \qquad \text{(from Lemma 1 and the definition of } \lambda_k) \\
&\le e\,S\,\sqrt{\frac{\lambda+m}{2\lambda+1}} . \qquad\qquad\qquad\qquad\qquad (5)
\end{aligned}
$$

Moreover, from Lemma 1 and the inequality $\frac{\sqrt{x+1}}{x} \le 4(\sqrt{x+1} - \sqrt{x}),\ \forall x \ge 1$, applied with $x = \lambda + k$, we have

---

[3] For definiteness, we set $\boldsymbol{u}_{-1} = \boldsymbol{0}$, though $\boldsymbol{w}_0 = \boldsymbol{0}$ makes this setting immaterial.

$$(\text{II}) \le U \sum_{k=1}^{m-1} \lambda_k \, \|\boldsymbol{w}_k\|$$

$$\le U \sum_{k=1}^{m-1} \frac{e\lambda}{\lambda+k} \sqrt{\frac{\lambda+k+1}{2\lambda+1}}$$

$$\le U \frac{4e\lambda}{\sqrt{2\lambda+1}} \sum_{k=1}^{m-1} \left(\sqrt{\lambda+k+1} - \sqrt{\lambda+k} \right)$$

$$= U \frac{4e\lambda}{\sqrt{2\lambda+1}} \left(\sqrt{\lambda+m} - \sqrt{\lambda+1} \right). \tag{6}$$

Finally, again from Lemma 1, we derive

$$(\text{III}) \le e \, \|\boldsymbol{u}_{m-1}\| \sqrt{\frac{\lambda+m+1}{2\lambda+1}}. \tag{7}$$

At this point, in order to ease the subsequent calculations, we compute upper bounds on (5), (6) and (7) so as to obtain expressions having a similar dependence[4] on the relevant quantities around. We can write

$$(5) \le e\, S \sqrt{\frac{\lambda+m+1}{2\lambda+1}}, \quad (6) \le 4e\lambda U \sqrt{\frac{\lambda+m+1}{2\lambda+1}}, \quad (7) \le e\, U \sqrt{\frac{\lambda+m+1}{2\lambda+1}}.$$

Putting together gives

$$m \le D + e\, (S + (4\lambda+1)\, U) \sqrt{\frac{\lambda+m+1}{2\lambda+1}}.$$

Solving for m and overapproximating once again gets

$$m \le D + K^2 + K \sqrt{D+\lambda+1},$$

where $K = K(\lambda) = \dfrac{e}{\sqrt{2\lambda+1}} \, (S + (4\lambda+1)\, U)$. This is the claimed bound (3).

We now turn to the choice of λ. Choosing λ minimizing the above bound would require, among other things, prior knowledge of D. In order to strike a good balance between optimality and simplicity (and to rely on as little information as possible) we come to minimizing (an upper bound on) $K(\lambda)$. Set $\lambda = cS/U$, where c is some positive constant to be determined. This yields

$$K(\lambda) = e\, U \, \frac{(4c+1)\, S/U + 1}{\sqrt{2cS/U+1}} \le e \sqrt{\frac{(4c+1)^2}{2c} SU + U^2}, \tag{8}$$

where we used $\dfrac{\alpha\, r+1}{\sqrt{\beta\, r+1}} \le \sqrt{\dfrac{\alpha^2}{\beta} r + 1}$, $\alpha, r \ge 0$, $\beta > 0$, with $\alpha = 4c+1$, $\beta = 2c$, and $r = S/U$. We minimize (8) w.r.t. c by selecting $c = 1/4$. Plugging back into (3) and overapproximating once more gives (4). $\qquad\square$

---

[4] This seems to be a reasonable trade-off between simplicity and tightness.

3   A Randomized Perceptron with Budget

Consider the update $w_{k+1} = (1-\lambda_k)w_k + y_t x_t$ used by the algorithm in Figure 1. In the special case $\lambda_k = \lambda$ for all $k \geq 1$, this corresponds to associating with each support vector x_t a coefficient decreasing exponentially with the number of additional mistakes made. This exponential decay is at the core of many algorithms in the on-line learning literature, and has the immediate consequence of keeping bounded the norm of weight vectors. This same idea is used by the Forgetron [7], a recently proposed variant of the Perceptron algorithm that learns using a fixed budget of support vectors. In fact, it is not hard to show that the Forgetron analysis can be extended to the shifting model. In this section, we turn our attention to a way of combining shifting and budgeted algorithms by means of randomization, with no explicit weighting on the support vectors. As we show, this alternative approach yields a simple algorithm and a crisp analysis.

Consider a generic Perceptron algorithm with bounded memory. The algorithm has at its disposal a fixed number B of "support vectors", in the sense that, at any given trial, the weight vector w maintained by the algorithm is a linear combination of $y_{i_1} x_{i_1}, y_{i_2} x_{i_2}, \ldots, y_{i_B} x_{i_B}$ where $i_1, \ldots, i_B$ is a subset of past trials where a mistake was made. Following [6, 7, 23], we call B the algorithm's *budget*. As in the standard Perceptron algorithm, each example on which the algorithm makes a mistake becomes a support vector. However, in order not to exceed the budget, before adding a new support the algorithm has to discard an old one.

The analysis of the Forgetron is based on discarding the oldest support. The exponential coefficients $(1 - \lambda)^k$ assigned to supports guarantee that, when λ is properly chosen as a function of B, the norm of the discarded vector is at most $1/\sqrt{B}$. In addition, it can be proven that the norm of w_k is at most $\sqrt{B/(\ln B)}$ for all $k \geq B$. These facts can be used to prove a mistake bound in terms of the hinge loss of the best linear classifier u in hindsight, as long as $\|u\| = O(\sqrt{B/(\ln B)})$. In this section we show that a completely random policy of discarding support vectors achieves a mistake bound without imposing on $\|u\|$ any constraint stronger than $\|u\| = O(\sqrt{B})$, which must be provably obeyed by any algorithm using budget B.

More precisely, suppose w_k makes a mistake on example (x_t, y_t). If the current number of support vectors is less than B, then our algorithm performs the usual additive update $w_{k+1} = w_k + y_t x_t$ (with no exponential scaling). Otherwise the algorithm chooses a random support vector Q_k, where $\mathbb{P}(Q_k = y_{i_j} x_{i_j}) = 1/B$ for $j = 1, \ldots, B$, and performs the update $w_{k+1} = w_k + y_t x_t - Q_k$. Note that Q_k satisfies $\mathbb{E}_k Q_k = w_k/B$ where $\mathbb{E}_k[\cdot]$ denotes the conditional expectation $\mathbb{E}[\cdot \mid w_0, \ldots, w_k]$. The resulting algorithm, called Randomized Budget Perceptron (RBP), is summarized in Figure 2.

The main idea behind this algorithm is the following: by removing a random support we guarantee that, in expectation, the squared norm of the weight w_{k+1} increases by at most $2 - (2/B)\|w_k\|^2$ each time we make an update (Lemma 2). This in turn implies that, at any *fixed* point in time, the expected norm of the

Algorithm: Randomized Budget Perceptron.
Parameters: Budget $B \in \mathbb{N}$, $B \geq 2$;
Initialization: $\boldsymbol{w}_0 = \boldsymbol{0}$, $s = 0$, $k = 0$.
For $t = 1, 2, \ldots$

1. Get instance vector $\boldsymbol{x}_t \in \mathbb{R}^d$, $\|\boldsymbol{x}_t\| = 1$;
2. Predict with $\widehat{y}_t = \text{SGN}(\boldsymbol{w}_k^\top \boldsymbol{x}_t) \in \{-1, +1\}$;
3. Get label $y_t \in \{-1, +1\}$;
4. **If** $\widehat{y}_t \neq y_t$ **then**
   (a) **If** $s < B$ **then**

$$\boldsymbol{w}_{k+1} = \boldsymbol{w}_k + y_t \boldsymbol{x}_t, \qquad k \leftarrow k+1, \qquad s \leftarrow s+1$$

   (b) **else** let Q_k be a random support vector of $\boldsymbol{w}_k$ and perform the assignment

$$\boldsymbol{w}_{k+1} = \boldsymbol{w}_k + y_t \boldsymbol{x}_t - Q_k, \qquad k \leftarrow k+1 \ .$$

Fig. 2. The randomized Budget Perceptron algorithm

current weight is $O(\sqrt{B})$. The hard part of the proof (Lemma 3) is showing that the sum of the norms of all distinct weights generated during a run has expected value $O(\sqrt{B}) \, \mathbb{E} \, M + O(B^{3/2} \ln B)$, where M is the random number of mistakes.

3.1 Analysis

Similarly to Section 2.1, we state a simple lemma (whose proof is deferred to the appendix) that bounds in a suitable way the norm of the algorithm's weight vector. Unlike Lemma 1, here we do not solve the recurrence involved. We rather stop earlier at a bound expressed in terms of conditional expectations, to be exploited in the proof of Lemma 3 below.

Lemma 2. *With the notation introduced in this section, we have*

$$\mathbb{E}_k \left\| \boldsymbol{w}_{k+1} \right\|^2 \leq \begin{cases} k+1 & \text{for } k = 0, \ldots, B-1 \\ \left(1 - \frac{2}{B}\right) \left\| \boldsymbol{w}_k \right\|^2 + 2 & \text{for } k \geq B. \end{cases}$$

Moreover, using Jensen's inequality,

$$\mathbb{E}_k \left\| \boldsymbol{w}_{k+1} \right\| \leq \begin{cases} \sqrt{k+1} & \text{for } k = 0, \ldots, B-1 \\ \sqrt{\left(1 - \frac{2}{B}\right) \left\| \boldsymbol{w}_k \right\|^2 + 2} & \text{for } k \geq B. \end{cases}$$

The main result of this section bounds the expected number of mistakes, $\mathbb{E} \, M$, made by RBP in the shifting case. For any sequence $(\boldsymbol{u}_0, \boldsymbol{u}_1, \ldots, \boldsymbol{u}_{n-1})$ of comparison vectors, this bound is expressed in terms of the expectations of the cumulative hinge loss D, the shift S, and the maximal norm U of the sequence, defined in (2). (All expectations are understood with respect to the algorithm's randomization.) Following the notation of previous sections, t_k denotes the (random) trial where w_k is updated and u_k is the comparison vector in trial t_k. Moreover, in what follows, we assume the underlying sequence of examples and the sequence $u_0, u_1, \ldots$ of linear classifiers are fixed and arbitrary. This implies that the value of the random variable $\{M = k\}$ is determined given $w_0, \ldots, w_{k-1}$ (i.e., the event $\{M = k\}$ is measurable w.r.t. the σ-algebra generated by $w_0, \ldots, w_{k-1}$).

The next lemma is our key tool for proving expectation bounds. It may be viewed as a simple extension of Wald's equation to certain dependent processes.

Lemma 3. *With the notation and the assumptions introduced so far, we have, for any constant $\varepsilon > 0$,*

$$\mathbb{E}\left[\sum_{k=B}^{M} \|w_k\|\right] \leq \frac{B^{3/2}}{2} \ln \frac{B^2}{2\varepsilon} + (1+\varepsilon)\sqrt{B}\, \mathbb{E}[\max\{0, M - B\}] .$$

Proof. Set for brevity $\rho = 1 - B/2$. We can write

$$\mathbb{E}\left[\sum_{k=B}^{M} \|w_k\|\right] = \mathbb{E}\left[\sum_{k=B}^{\infty} \{M \geq k\} \|w_k\|\right]$$

$$= \mathbb{E}\left[\sum_{k=B}^{\infty} \mathbb{E}_{k-1}\Big[\{M \geq k\} \|w_k\|\Big]\right]$$

$$= \mathbb{E}\left[\sum_{k=B}^{\infty} \{M \geq k\}\mathbb{E}_{k-1} \|w_k\|\right]$$

(since $\{M \geq k\}$ is determined by $w_0, \ldots, w_{k-1}$)

$$\leq \mathbb{E}\left[\sum_{k=B}^{\infty} \{M \geq k\}\sqrt{\rho \|w_{k-1}\|^2 + 2}\right] \qquad \text{(from Lemma 2)}$$

$$\leq \mathbb{E}\left[\sum_{k=B}^{\infty} \{M \geq k - 1\}\sqrt{\rho \|w_{k-1}\|^2 + 2}\right]$$

$$= \mathbb{E}\left[\sum_{k=B-1}^{\infty} \{M \geq k\}\sqrt{\rho \|w_k\|^2 + 2}\right]$$

$$\leq \sqrt{\rho B + 2} + \mathbb{E}\left[\sum_{k=B}^{\infty} \{M \geq k\}\sqrt{\rho \|w_k\|^2 + 2}\right] \qquad (9)$$

the last inequality following from Lemma 2, which implies $\|w_{B-1}\|^2 \leq B$.

Now, (9) can be treated in a similar fashion. We have

$$(9) = \sqrt{\rho B + 2} + \mathbb{E}\left[\sum_{k=B}^{\infty} \{M \geq k\} \mathbb{E}_{k-1}\left[\sqrt{\rho \|\boldsymbol{w}_k\|^2 + 2}\right]\right]$$

(since, as before, $\{M \geq k\}$ is determined by $\boldsymbol{w}_0, \ldots, \boldsymbol{w}_{k-1}$)

$$\leq \sqrt{\rho B + 2} + \mathbb{E}\left[\sum_{k=B}^{\infty} \{M \geq k\}\sqrt{\rho\left(\rho \|\boldsymbol{w}_{k-1}\|^2 + 2\right) + 2}\right]$$

(from Jensen's inequality and Lemma 2)

$$\leq \sqrt{\rho B + 2} + \mathbb{E}\left[\sum_{k=B}^{\infty} \{M \geq k-1\}\sqrt{\rho\left(\rho \|\boldsymbol{w}_{k-1}\|^2 + 2\right) + 2}\right]$$

$$= \sqrt{\rho B + 2} + \mathbb{E}\left[\sum_{k=B-1}^{\infty} \{M \geq k\}\sqrt{\rho\left(\rho \|\boldsymbol{w}_k\|^2 + 2\right) + 2}\right]$$

$$\leq \sqrt{\rho B + 2} + \sqrt{\rho(\rho B + 2) + 2} + \mathbb{E}\left[\sum_{k=B}^{\infty} \{M \geq k\}\sqrt{\rho\left(\rho \|\boldsymbol{w}_k\|^2 + 2\right) + 2}\right]$$

the last inequality following again from $\|\boldsymbol{w}_{B-1}\|^2 \leq B$. Iterating for a total of i times we obtain that (9) is at most

$$\sum_{j=0}^{i-1}\sqrt{\rho^{j+1}B + 2\sum_{\ell=0}^{j}\rho^\ell} + \mathbb{E}\left[\sum_{k=B}^{\infty} \{M \geq k\}\sqrt{\rho^i \|\boldsymbol{w}_k\|^2 + 2\sum_{j=0}^{i-1}\rho^j}\right]$$

$$\leq \sum_{j=0}^{i-1}\sqrt{\rho^{j+1}B + B - \rho^{j+1}B} + \sqrt{\rho^i B^2 + B}\ \mathbb{E}\left[\sum_{k=B}^{\infty} \{M \geq k\}\right],$$

where for the first term we used $\sum_{\ell=0}^{j}\rho^\ell = \frac{1-\rho^{j+1}}{1-\rho} = B(1 - \rho^{j+1})/2$, and for the second term we used the trivial upper bound $\|\boldsymbol{w}_k\|^2 \leq B^2$ for all $k \geq 1$ and $\sum_{\ell=0}^{j}\rho^\ell \leq \frac{1}{1-\rho} = B/2$. We thus obtain

$$\mathbb{E}\left[\sum_{k=B}^{\infty} \{M \geq k\} \|\boldsymbol{w}_k\|\right] \leq i\sqrt{B} + \sqrt{\rho^i B^2 + B}\ \mathbb{E}\left[\sum_{k=B}^{\infty} \{M \geq k\}\right].$$

We are free to choose the number i of iterations. We set i in a way that the factor $\sqrt{\rho^i B^2 + B}$ gets as small as $(1+\varepsilon)\sqrt{B}$. Since $\rho^i \leq e^{-2i/B}$ and $\sqrt{1+x} \leq 1+x/2$ for any $x \geq 0$, it suffices to pick $i \geq \frac{B}{2}\ln\frac{B^2}{2\varepsilon}$, yielding the claimed inequality. $\square$

Theorem 2. *Given any $\varepsilon \in (0,1)$, any $n \in \mathbb{N}$, any sequence of examples $(\boldsymbol{x}_1, y_1), \ldots, (\boldsymbol{x}_n, y_n) \in \mathbb{R}^d \times \{-1, +1\}$ such that $\|\boldsymbol{x}_t\| = 1$ for each t, the algorithm in Figure 2 makes a number M of mistakes whose expectation is bounded as*

$$\mathbb{E}\,M \leq \frac{1}{\varepsilon}\,\mathbb{E}\,D + \frac{S_{\text{tot}}\sqrt{B}}{\varepsilon} + \frac{U B}{\varepsilon} + \frac{U \sqrt{B}}{2\varepsilon}\ln\frac{B^2}{2\varepsilon}$$

for any sequence of comparison vectors $\boldsymbol{u}_0, \ldots, \boldsymbol{u}_{n-1} \in \mathbb{R}^d$, *with expected hinge loss* $\mathbb{E}\, D$, *total shift* S_{tot}, *and such that* $\max_t \|\boldsymbol{u}_t\| = U \leq \frac{1-\varepsilon}{1+\varepsilon}\sqrt{B}$.

Remark 1. Note the role played by the free parameter $\varepsilon \in (0,1)$. If ε is close to 0, then the comparison vectors $\boldsymbol{u}_0, \ldots, \boldsymbol{u}_{n-1}$ are chosen from a large class, but the bound is loose. On the other hand, if ε is close to 1, our bound gets sharper but applies to a smaller comparison class. We can rewrite the above bound in terms of $U = \frac{1-\varepsilon}{1+\varepsilon}\sqrt{B}$. For instance, setting $\varepsilon = 1/2$ results in

$$\mathbb{E}\, M \leq 2\, \mathbb{E}\, D + 18\, U\left(S_{\text{tot}} + U^2\right) + 12\, U^2 \ln(3\, U) \ .$$

The dependence on S_{tot} is linear as in (4), which is the best bound we could prove on Perceptron-like algorithms without imposing a budget.

Remark 2. In the nonshifting case our bound reduces to

$$\mathbb{E}\, M \leq \frac{1}{\varepsilon}\, \mathbb{E}\, D + \frac{U\, B}{\varepsilon} + \frac{U\,\sqrt{B}}{2\varepsilon} \ln \frac{B^2}{2\varepsilon} \ .$$

This is similar to the (deterministic) Forgetron bound shown in [7], though we have a better dependence on D and a worse dependence on U and B. However, and more importantly, whereas the Forgetron bound can be proven only for $\|\boldsymbol{u}\| = O\big(\sqrt{B/(\ln B)}\big)$, our result just requires $\|\boldsymbol{u}\| = O\big(\sqrt{B}\big)$. This is basically optimal, since it was shown in [7] that the condition $\|\boldsymbol{u}\| < \sqrt{B+1}$ is necessary for any on-line algorithm working on a budget B.

Remark 3. From a computational standpoint, our simple randomized policy compares favourably with other eviction strategies that need to check the properties of *all* support vectors in the currect storage, such as those in [6, 23]. Thus, in this context, randomization exhibits a clear computational advantage.

Proof (of Theorem 2). We proceed as in the proof of Theorem 1 and adopt the same notation used there. Note, however, that the weights $\boldsymbol{w}_0, \boldsymbol{w}_1, \ldots$ are now the realization of a random process on $\mathbb{R}^d$ and that the number M of mistakes on a given sequence of example is a random variable. Without loss of generality, in what follows we assume $\boldsymbol{w}_k = \boldsymbol{w}_M$ for all $k > M$. We can write

$$\boldsymbol{u}_k^\top \boldsymbol{w}_{k+1} = \boldsymbol{u}_k^\top \left(\boldsymbol{w}_k + y_{t_k} \boldsymbol{x}_{t_k} - \{k \geq B\}\, Q_k \right)$$
$$= (\boldsymbol{u}_k - \boldsymbol{u}_{k-1})^\top \boldsymbol{w}_k + \boldsymbol{u}_{k-1}^\top \boldsymbol{w}_k + y_{t_k} \boldsymbol{u}_k^\top \boldsymbol{x}_{t_k} - \{k \geq B\}\, \boldsymbol{u}_k^\top Q_k$$
$$\geq (\boldsymbol{u}_k - \boldsymbol{u}_{k-1})^\top \boldsymbol{w}_k + \boldsymbol{u}_{k-1}^\top \boldsymbol{w}_k + 1 - d(\boldsymbol{u}_k; (\boldsymbol{x}_{t_k}, y_{t_k})) - \{k \geq B\}\, \boldsymbol{u}_k^\top Q_k \ .$$

We rearrange, sum over $k = 0, \ldots, M-1$, recall that $\boldsymbol{w}_0 = \boldsymbol{0}$, and take expectations on both sides of the resulting inequality,

$$\mathbb{E}\, M \leq \mathbb{E}\left[\sum_{k=0}^{M-1} d(\boldsymbol{u}_k; (\boldsymbol{x}_{t_k}, y_{t_k})) \right]$$

$$+ \underbrace{\mathbb{E}\left[\boldsymbol{u}_{M-1}^\top \boldsymbol{w}_M \right]}_{\text{(I)}} + \underbrace{\mathbb{E}\left[\sum_{k=B}^{M-1} \boldsymbol{u}_k^\top Q_k \right]}_{\text{(II)}} + \underbrace{\mathbb{E}\left[\sum_{k=1}^{M-1} (\boldsymbol{u}_{k-1} - \boldsymbol{u}_k)^\top \boldsymbol{w}_k \right]}_{\text{(III)}} \ .$$

The first term in the right-hand side equals $\mathbb{E}\, D$. Thus we need to find suitable upper bounds on (I), (II), and (III). Recalling that $U = \max_t \|\boldsymbol{u}_t\|$, and noting that $\|\boldsymbol{w}_k\| \leq B$ for all k, we have (I) $\leq U\,B$. To bound (II), we write

$$(\text{II}) = \mathbb{E}\left[\sum_{k=B}^{\infty} \{M \geq k+1\}\, \boldsymbol{u}_k^{\top} Q_k\right]$$

$$= \mathbb{E}\left[\sum_{k=B}^{\infty} \mathbb{E}_k\left[\{M \geq k+1\}\, \boldsymbol{u}_k^{\top} Q_k\right]\right]$$

$$= \mathbb{E}\left[\sum_{k=B}^{\infty} \{M \geq k+1\}\boldsymbol{u}_k^{\top} \mathbb{E}_k\, Q_k\right]$$

(since $\{M \geq k+1\}$ and $\boldsymbol{u}_k$ are determined given $\boldsymbol{w}_0, \ldots, \boldsymbol{w}_k$)

$$= \mathbb{E}\left[\sum_{k=B}^{\infty} \{M \geq k+1\}\frac{\boldsymbol{u}_k^{\top}\boldsymbol{w}_k}{B}\right] \qquad (\text{since } \mathbb{E}_k\, Q_k = \boldsymbol{w}_k/B)\,.$$

Hence

$$(\text{II}) \leq \frac{U}{B}\,\mathbb{E}\left[\sum_{k=B}^{\infty} \{M \geq k+1\}\,\|\boldsymbol{w}_k\|\right] \leq \frac{U}{B}\,\mathbb{E}\left[\sum_{k=B}^{M}\|\boldsymbol{w}_k\|\right]$$

$$\leq \frac{U\sqrt{B}}{2}\,\ln\frac{B^2}{2\varepsilon} + (1+\varepsilon)\frac{U}{\sqrt{B}}\,\mathbb{E}\, M \qquad (\text{from Lemma 3}).$$

Next, we bound (III) as follows

$$\mathbb{E}\left[\sum_{k=1}^{M-1}(\boldsymbol{u}_{k-1} - \boldsymbol{u}_k)^{\top}\boldsymbol{w}_k\right] = \mathbb{E}\left[\sum_{k=1}^{M-1}\sum_{t=t_{k-1}+1}^{t_k}(\boldsymbol{u}_{t-1} - \boldsymbol{u}_t)^{\top}\boldsymbol{w}_k\right]$$

$$\leq \mathbb{E}\left[\sum_{k=1}^{M-1}\sum_{t=t_{k-1}+1}^{t_k}\|\boldsymbol{u}_{t-1} - \boldsymbol{u}_t\|\,\|\boldsymbol{w}_k\|\right]$$

$$\leq \mathbb{E}\left[\sum_{t=1}^{n-1}\|\boldsymbol{u}_{t-1} - \boldsymbol{u}_t\|\,\|\boldsymbol{w}_t\|\right]$$

where $\boldsymbol{w}_t$ is the random weight used by the algorithm at time t. A simple adaptation of Lemma 2 and an easy induction argument together imply that $\mathbb{E}\,\|\boldsymbol{w}_t\| \leq \sqrt{B}$ for all t. Thus we have

$$\mathbb{E}\left[\sum_{t=1}^{n-1}\|\boldsymbol{u}_{t-1} - \boldsymbol{u}_t\|\,\|\boldsymbol{w}_t\|\right] = \sum_{t=1}^{n-1}\|\boldsymbol{u}_{t-1} - \boldsymbol{u}_t\|\,\mathbb{E}\,\|\boldsymbol{w}_t\| \leq S_{\text{tot}}\sqrt{B}\,.$$

Piecing together gives

$$\mathbb{E}\, M \leq \mathbb{E}\, D + (1+\varepsilon)\frac{U}{\sqrt{B}}\,\mathbb{E}\, M + S_{\text{tot}}\sqrt{B} + U\,B + \frac{U\sqrt{B}}{2}\,\ln\frac{B^2}{2\varepsilon}\,.$$

The condition $U \leq \frac{1-\varepsilon}{1+\varepsilon}\sqrt{B}$ implies the desired result.   □

4 Conclusions and Ongoing Research

In this paper we have shown that simple changes to the standard (kernel) Perceptron algorithm suffice to obtain efficient shifting and memory bounded algorithms. Our elaborations deliver robust on-line procedures which we expect to be of practical relevance in many real-world data-intensive learning settings.

From the theoretical point of view, we have shown that these simple algorithms compare favourably with the existing kernel-based algorithms working in the on-line shifting framework. Many of the results we have proven here can easily be extended to the family of p-norm algorithms [12, 10], to large margin on-line algorithms (e.g., [16, 9]) and to other Perceptron-like algorithms, such as the second-order Perceptron algorithm [5].

A few issues we are currently working on are the following. The bound exhibited in Theorem 2 shows an unsatisfactory dependence on U. This is due to the technical difficulty of finding a more sophisticated argument than the crude upper bound we use to handle expression (I) occurring in the proof. In fact, we believe this argument is within reach. Finally, we are trying to see whether our statement also holds with high probability, rather than just in expectation.

This paper introduces new on-line learning technologies which, as we said, can be combined with several existing techniques. We are planning to make experiments to give evidence of the theoretical behavior of algorithms resulting from such combinations.

References

1. D. ANGLUIN. Queries and concept learning. *Machine Learning*, 2(4):319–342, 1988.
2. P. AUER AND M. WARMUTH. Tracking the best disjunction. *Machine Learning*, 3:127–150, 1998.
3. H.D. BLOCK. The Perceptron: A model for brain functioning. *Reviews of Modern Physics*, 34:123–135, 1962.
4. A. BORDES, S. ERTEKIN, J. WESTON, AND L. BOTTOU. Fast kernel classifiers with online and active learning. *JMLR*, 6:1579–1619, 2005.
5. N. CESA-BIANCHI, A. CONCONI, AND C. GENTILE. A second-order Perceptron algorithm. *SIAM Journal of Computing*, 34(3):640–668, 2005.
6. K. CRAMMER, J. KANDOLA, AND Y. SINGER. Online classification on a budget. In *Proc. 16th NIPS*, 2003.
7. O. DEKEL, S. SHALEV-SHWARTZ, Y. SINGER, The Forgetron: a kernel-based Perceptron on a fixed budget. In Proc. 19th NIPS, 2005.
8. Y. FREUND, AND R. SCHAPIRE. Large margin classification using the Perceptron algorithm. *Journal of Machine Learning*, 37(3)277–296, 1999.
9. C. GENTILE. A new approximate maximal margin classification algorithm. *Journal of Machine Learning Research*, 2:213–242, 2001.
10. C. GENTILE. The robustness of the p-norm algorithms. *Machine Learning*, 53:265–299, 2003.
11. C. GENTILE AND M. WARMUTH. Linear hinge loss and average margin. In *Advances in Neural Information Processing Systems 10*, MIT Press, pp. 225–231, 1999.
12. A. J. GROVE, N. LITTLESTONE AND D. SCHUURMANS. General convergence results for linear discriminant updates. *Journal of Machine Learning*, 43(3):173–210.

13. M. HERBSTER AND M. WARMUTH. Tracking the best expert. *Machine Learning*, 32:151–178, 1998.

14. M. HERBSTER AND M. WARMUTH. Tracking the best linear predictor. *Journal of Machine Learning Research*, 1:281–309, 2001.

15. J. KIVINEN, A.J. SMOLA, AND R.C. WILLIAMSON. Online learning with kernels. *IEEE Transactions on Signal Processing*, 52(8):2165–2176, 2004.

16. Y. LI, AND P. LONG. The relaxed online maximum margin algorithm. *Journal of Machine Learning*, 46(1):361–387, 2002.

17. N. LITTLESTONE. Learning quickly when irrelevant attributes abound: A new linear-threshold algorithm. *Machine Learning*, 2:285–318, 1988.

18. N. LITTLESTONE. *Mistake Bounds and Logarithmic Linear-threshold Learning Algorithms*. PhD thesis, University of California Santa Cruz, 1989.

19. N. LITTLESTONE AND M. K. WARMUTH. The weighted majority algorithm. *Information and Computation*, 108(2):212–261, 1994.

20. A.B.J. NOVIKOV. On convergence proofs on Perceptrons. In *Proc. of the Symposium on the Mathematical Theory of Automata, vol. XII*, pages 615–622, 1962.

21. B. SCHÖLKOPF AND A. SMOLA, *Learning with kernels*, MIT Press, 2002.

22. V. VAPNIK. *Statistical learning theory*. J. Wiley & Sons, New York, 1998.

23. J. WESTON, A. BORDES, AND L. BOTTOU. Online (and offline) on an even tighter budget. In *Proc. 10th AIStat*, pp. 413-420, 2005.

A   Proof of Lemma 1

Let $t = t_k$ be the trial at the end of which $\boldsymbol{w}_k$ is updated. The update rule of Figure 1 along with the condition $y_t \boldsymbol{w}_k^\top \boldsymbol{x}_t \leq 0$ allow us to write for each $k \geq 0$

$$
\begin{aligned}
\|\boldsymbol{w}_{k+1}\|^2 &= (1 - \lambda_k)^2 \|\boldsymbol{w}_k\|^2 + 2(1 - \lambda_k)y_t \boldsymbol{w}_k^\top \boldsymbol{x}_t + \|\boldsymbol{x}_t\|^2 \\
&\leq (1 - \lambda_k)^2 \|\boldsymbol{w}_k\|^2 + 1 .
\end{aligned}
$$

Unwrapping the recurrence yields $\|\boldsymbol{w}_{k+1}\|^2 \leq \sum_{i=0}^{k} \prod_{j=i+1}^{k} (1 - \lambda_j)^2$, where the product is meant to be 1 if $i + 1 > k$. The above, in turn, can be bounded as follows.

$$
\begin{aligned}
\sum_{i=0}^{k} \prod_{j=i+1}^{k} (1 - \lambda_j)^2 &\leq \sum_{i=0}^{k} \exp\left(-2 \sum_{j=i+1}^{k} \lambda_j \right) \\
&= \sum_{i=0}^{k} \exp\left(-2\lambda \sum_{j=i+1}^{k} \frac{1}{\lambda + j} \right) \\
&\leq \sum_{i=0}^{k} \exp\left(-2\lambda \int_{i+1}^{k+1} \frac{dx}{\lambda + x} \right) \\
&= \sum_{i=0}^{k} \left(\frac{\lambda + i + 1}{\lambda + k + 1} \right)^{2\lambda}
\end{aligned}
$$

$$\leq \frac{1}{(\lambda + k + 1)^{2\lambda}} \int_{\lambda+1}^{\lambda+k+2} x^{2\lambda} dx$$

$$\leq \frac{1}{2\lambda + 1} \frac{(\lambda + k + 2)^{2\lambda+1}}{(\lambda + k + 1)^{2\lambda}}$$

$$= \left(\frac{\lambda + k + 2}{2\lambda + 1}\right) \left[\left(1 + \frac{1}{\lambda + k + 1}\right)^{\lambda+k+1}\right]^{\frac{2\lambda}{\lambda+k+1}}$$

$$\leq \left(\frac{\lambda + k + 2}{2\lambda + 1}\right) e^2 ,$$

where the last inequality uses $(1 + 1/x)^x \leq e$ for all $x > 0$, and $\frac{2\lambda}{\lambda+k+1} \leq 2$. Taking the square root completes the proof. □

B   Proof of Lemma 2

Let $t = t_k$ be the trial where w_k gets updated. We distinguish the two cases $k < B$ and $k \geq B$. In the first case no randomization is involved, and we have the standard (e.g., [3, 20]) Perceptron weight bound $\|w_k\| \leq \sqrt{k}$, $k = 1, \ldots, B$. In the case $k \geq B$ the update rule in Figure 2 allows us to write

$$\|w_{k+1}\|^2 = \|w_k + y_t x_t - Q_k\|^2$$

$$= \|w_k\|^2 + \|x_t\|^2 + \|Q_k\|^2 - 2w_k^\top Q_k + 2y_t(w_k - Q_k)^\top x_t$$

$$\leq \|w_k\|^2 + 2 - 2w_k^\top Q_k + 2y_t(w_k - Q_k)^\top x_t .$$

Recalling $\mathbb{E}_k Q_k = w_k/B$, we take conditional expectation $\mathbb{E}_k$ on both sides:

$$\mathbb{E}_k \|w_{k+1}\|^2 \leq \|w_k\|^2 + 2 - 2\frac{w_k^\top w_k}{B} + 2\left(1 - \frac{1}{B}\right) y_t\, w_k^\top x_t$$

$$\leq \left(1 - \frac{2}{B}\right) \|w_k\|^2 + 2$$

the last step following from $y_t\, w_k^\top x_t \leq 0$. This gives the desired bound on $\mathbb{E}_k \|w_{k+1}\|^2$. The bound on $\mathbb{E}_k \|w_{k+1}\|$ is a direct consequence of Jensen's inequality. □

Logarithmic Regret Algorithms for Online Convex Optimization

Elad Hazan[1,*], Adam Kalai[2], Satyen Kale[1,*], and Amit Agarwal[1]

[1] Princeton University
{ehazan, satyen, aagarwal}@princeton.edu
[2] TTI-Chicago
kalai@tti-c.org

Abstract. In an online convex optimization problem a decision-maker makes a sequence of decisions, i.e., chooses a sequence of points in Euclidean space, from a fixed feasible set. After each point is chosen, it encounters a sequence of (possibly unrelated) convex cost functions. Zinkevich [Zin03] introduced this framework, which models many natural repeated decision-making problems and generalizes many existing problems such as Prediction from Expert Advice and Cover's Universal Portfolios. Zinkevich showed that a simple online gradient descent algorithm achieves additive *regret* $O(\sqrt{T})$, for an arbitrary sequence of T convex cost functions (of bounded gradients), with respect to the best single decision in hindsight.

In this paper, we give algorithms that achieve regret $O(\log(T))$ for an arbitrary sequence of strictly convex functions (with bounded first and second derivatives). This mirrors what has been done for the special cases of prediction from expert advice by Kivinen and Warmuth [KW99], and Universal Portfolios by Cover [Cov91]. We propose several algorithms achieving logarithmic regret, which besides being more general are also much more efficient to implement.

The main new ideas give rise to an efficient algorithm based on the Newton method for optimization, a new tool in the field. Our analysis shows a surprising connection to follow-the-leader method, and builds on the recent work of Agarwal and Hazan [AH05]. We also analyze other algorithms, which tie together several different previous approaches including follow-the-leader, exponential weighting, Cover's algorithm and gradient descent.

1   Introduction

In the problem of *online convex optimization* [Zin03], there is a fixed convex compact feasible set $K \subset \mathbb{R}^n$ and an *arbitrary, unknown* sequence of convex cost functions $f_1, f_2, \ldots : K \to \mathbb{R}$. The decision maker must make a sequence of decisions, where the tth decision is a selection of a point $x_t \in K$ and there is a cost of $f_t(x_t)$ on period t. However, x_t is chosen with only the knowledge of

---

* Supported by Sanjeev Arora's NSF grants MSPA-MCS 0528414, CCF 0514993, ITR 0205594.

G. Lugosi and H.U. Simon (Eds.): COLT 2006, LNAI 4005, pp. 499–513, 2006.

the set K, previous points $x_1, \ldots, x_{t-1}$, and the previous functions $f_1, \ldots, f_{t-1}$. Examples include many repeated decision-problems:

Example 1: Production. Consider a company deciding how much of n different products to produce. In this case, their profit may be assumed to be a concave function of their production (the goal is maximize profit rather than minimize cost). This decision is made repeatedly, and the model allows the profit functions to be changing arbitrary concave functions, which may depend on various factors such as the economy.

Example 2: Linear prediction with a convex loss function. In this setting, there is a sequence of examples $(p_1, q_1), \ldots, (p_T, q_T) \in \mathbb{R}^n \times [0, 1]$. For each $t = 1, 2, \ldots, T$, the decision-maker makes a *linear* prediction of $q_t \in [0, 1]$ which is $x_t^\top p_t$, for some $x_t \in \mathbb{R}^n$, and suffers some loss $\mathcal{L}(q_t, x_t^\top p_t)$, where $\mathcal{L} : \mathbb{R} \times \mathbb{R} \to \mathbb{R}$ is some fixed, known convex loss function, such as quadratic $\mathcal{L}(q, q') = (q - q')^2$. The online convex optimization framework permits this example, because the function $f_t(x) = \mathcal{L}(q_t, x^\top p_t)$ is a convex function of $x \in \mathbb{R}^n$. This problem of linear prediction with a convex loss function has been well studied (e.g., [CBL06]), and hence one would prefer to use the near-optimal algorithms that have been developed especially for that problem. We mention this application only to point out the generality of the online convex optimization framework.

Example 3: Portfolio management. In this setting, for each $t = 1, \ldots, T$ an online investor chooses a distribution x_t over n stocks in the market. The market outcome at iteration t is captured by a price relatives vector c_t, such that the loss to the investor is $-\log(x_t^\top c_t)$ (see Cover [Cov91] for motivation and more detail regarding the model). Again, the online convex optimization framework permits this example, because the function $f_t(x) = -\log(x^\top c)$ is a convex function of $x \in \mathbb{R}^n$.

This paper shows how three seemingly different approaches can be used to achieve logarithmic regret in the case of some higher-order derivative assumptions on the functions. The algorithms are relatively easy to state. In some cases, the analysis is simple, and in others it relies on a carefully constructed potential function due to Agarwal and Hazan [AH05]. Lastly, our gradient descent results relate to previous analyses of stochastic gradient descent [Spa03], which is known to converge at a rate of $1/T$ for T steps of gradient descent under various assumptions on the distribution over functions. Our results imply a $\log(T)/T$ convergence rate for the same problems, though as common in the online setting, the assumptions and guarantees are simpler and stronger than their stochastic counterparts.

1.1   Our Results

The *regret* of the decision maker at time T is defined to be its total cost minus the cost of the best single decision, where the best is chosen with the benefit of hindsight.

$$\text{regret}_T = \text{regret} = \sum_{t=1}^T f_t(x_t) - \min_{x \in K} \sum_{t=1}^T f_t(x).$$

A standard goal in machine learning and game theory is to achieve algorithms with guaranteed low regret (this goal is also motivated by psychology). Zinkevich showed that one can guarantee $O(\sqrt{T})$ regret for an *arbitrary* sequence of differentiable convex functions of bounded gradient, which is tight up to constant factors. In fact, $\Omega(\sqrt{T})$ regret is unavoidable even when the functions come from a fixed distribution rather than being chosen adversarially. [1]

Variable	Meaning
$K \subseteq \mathbb{R}^n$	the convex compact feasible set
$D \geq 0$	the diameter of K, $D = \sup_{x,y \in K} \|x - y\|$
$f_1, \ldots, f_T$	Sequence of T twice-differentiable convex functions $f_t : \mathbb{R}^n \to \mathbb{R}$.
$G \geq 0$	$\|\nabla f_t(x)\| \leq G$ for all $x \in K, t \leq T$ (in one dimension, $|f_t'(x)| \leq G$.)
$H \geq 0$	$\nabla^2 f_t(x) \succeq H I_n$ for all $x \in K, t \leq T$ (in one dimension, $f_t''(x) \geq H$).
$\alpha \geq 0$	Such that $\exp(-\alpha f_t(x))$ is a concave function of $x \in K$, for $t \leq T$.

Fig. 1. Notation in the paper. Arbitrary convex functions are allowed for $G = \infty, H = 0, \alpha = 0$. $\|\cdot\|$ is the ℓ_2 (Euclidean) norm.

Algorithm	Regret bound
Online gradient descent	$\frac{G^2}{2H}(1 + \log T)$
Online Newton step	$3(\frac{1}{\alpha} + 4GD)n \log T$
Exponentially weighted online opt.	$\frac{n}{\alpha}(1 + \log(1 + T))$

Fig. 2. Results from this paper. Zinkevich achieves $GD\sqrt{T}$, even for $H = \alpha = 0$.

Our notation and results are summarized in Figures 1 and 2. Throughout the paper we denote by $\|\cdot\|$ the ℓ_2 (Euclidean) norm. We show $O(\log T)$ regret under relatively weak assumptions on the functions $f_1, f_2, \ldots$. Natural assumptions to consider might be that the gradients of each function are of bounded magnitude G, i.e., $\|\nabla f_t(x)\| \leq G$ for all $x \in K$, and that each function in the sequence is *strongly-concave*, meaning that the second derivative is bounded away from 0. In one dimension, these assumptions correspond simply to $|f_t'(x)| \leq G$ and $f_t''(x) \geq H$ for some $G, H > 0$. In higher dimensions, one may require these properties to hold on the functions in *every direction* (i.e., for the 1-dimensional function of θ, $f_t(\theta u)$, for any unit vector $u \in \mathbb{R}^n$), which can be equivalently written in the following similar form: $\|\nabla f_t(x)\| \leq G$ and $\nabla^2 f_t(x) \succeq H I_n$, where I_n is the $n \times n$ identity matrix and we write $A \succeq B$ if the matrix $A - B$ is positive semi-definite (symmetric with non-negative eigenvalues).

Intuitively, it is easier to minimize functions that are "very concave," and the above assumptions may seem innocuous enough. However, they rule out several interesting types of functions. For example, consider the function $f(x) =$

---

[1] This can be seen by a simple randomized example. Consider $K = [-1, 1]$ and linear functions $f_t(x) = r_t x$, where $r_t = \pm 1$ are chosen in advance, independently with equal probability. $\mathbf{E}_{r_t}[f_t(x_t)] = 0$ for any t and x_t chosen online, by independence of x_t and r_t. However, $\mathbf{E}_{r_1, \ldots, r_T}[\min_{x \in K} \sum_1^T f_t(x)] = \mathbf{E}[-|\sum_1^T r_t|] = -\Omega(\sqrt{T})$.

$(x^\top w)^2$, for some vector $w \in \mathbb{R}^n$. This is strongly convex in the direction w, but is constant in directions orthogonal to w. A simpler example is the constant function $f(x) = c$ which is not strongly convex, yet is easily (and unavoidably) minimized.

Some of our algorithms also work without explicitly requiring $H > 0$, i.e., when $G = \infty, H = 0$. In these cases we require that there exists some $\alpha > 0$ such that $h_t(x) = \exp(-\alpha f_t(x))$ is a concave function of $x \in K$, for all t. A similar *exp-concave* assumption has been utilized for the prediction for expert-advice problem [CBL06]. It turns out that given the bounds G and H, the exp-concavity assumption holds with $\alpha = G^2/H$. To see this in one dimension, one can easily verify the assumption on one-dimensional functions $f_t : \mathbb{R} \to \mathbb{R}$ by taking two derivatives,

$$h_t''(x) = ((\alpha f_t'(x))^2 - \alpha f_t''(x)) \exp(-\alpha f_t(x)) \leq 0 \iff \alpha \leq \frac{f_t''(x)}{(f_t'(x))^2}.$$

All of our conditions hold in n-dimensions if they hold in every direction. Hence we have that the exp-concave assumption is a *weaker* assumption than those of G, H, for $\alpha = G^2/H$. This enables us to compare the three regret bounds of Figure 2. In these terms, ONLINE GRADIENT DESCENT requires the strongest assumptions, whereas EXPONENTIALLY WEIGHTED ONLINE OPTIMIZATION requires only exp-concavity (and not even a bound on the gradient). Perhaps most interesting is ONLINE NEWTON STEP which requires relatively weak assumptions and yet, as we shall see, is very efficient to implement (and whose analysis is the most technical).

2   The Algorithms

The algorithms are presented in Figure 3. The intuition behind most of our algorithms stem from new observations regarding the well studied *follow-the-leader* method (see [Han57, KV05, AH05]).

The basic method, which by itself fails to provide sub-linear regret let alone logarithmic regret, simply chooses on period t the single fixed decision that would have been the best to use on the previous $t - 1$ periods. This corresponds to choosing $x_t = \arg\min_{x \in K} \sum_{\tau=1}^{t-1} f_\tau(x)$. The standard approach to analyze such algorithms proceeds by inductively showing,

$$\text{regret}_T = \sum_{t=1}^{T} f_t(x_t) - \min_{x \in K} \sum_{t=1}^{T} f_t(x) \leq \sum_{t=1}^{T} f_t(x_t) - f_t(x_{t+1}) \quad (1)$$

The standard analysis proceeds by showing that the leader doesn't change too much, i.e. $x_t \approx x_{t+1}$, which in turn implies low regret.

One of the significant deviations from this standard analysis is in the variant of follow-the-leader called ONLINE NEWTON STEP. The analysis does not follow this paradigm directly, but rather shows *average stability* (i.e. that $x_t \approx x_{t+1}$

ONLINE GRADIENT DESCENT. (Zinkevich's online version of Stochastic Gradient Descent)

Inputs: convex set $K \subset \mathbb{R}^n$, step sizes $\eta_1, \eta_2, \ldots \geq 0$.

- On period 1, play an arbitrary $x_1 \in K$.
- On period $t > 1$: play

$$x_t = \Pi_K(x_{t-1} - \eta_t \nabla f_{t-1}(x_{t-1}))$$

Here, Π_K denotes the *projection* onto nearest point in K, $\Pi_K(y) = \arg\min_{x \in K} \|x - y\|$.

ONLINE NEWTON STEP.

Inputs: convex set $K \subset \mathbb{R}^n$, and the parameter β.

- On period 1, play an arbitrary $x_1 \in K$.
- On period $t > 1$: play the point x_t given by the following equations:

$$\nabla_{t-1} = \nabla f_{t-1}(x_{t-1})$$

$$A_{t-1} = \sum_{\tau=1}^{t-1} \nabla_\tau \nabla_\tau^\top$$

$$b_{t-1} = \sum_{\tau=1}^{t-1} \nabla_\tau \nabla_\tau^\top x_\tau - \frac{1}{\beta} \nabla_\tau$$

$$x_t = \Pi_K^{A_{t-1}} \left(A_{t-1}^{-1} b_{t-1} \right)$$

Here, $\Pi_K^{A_{t-1}}$ is the projection in the norm induced by A_{t-1}:

$$\Pi_K^{A_{t-1}}(y) = \arg\min_{x \in K} (x - y)^\top A_{t-1}(x - y)$$

A_{t-1}^{-1} denotes the Moore-Penrose pseudoinverse of A_{t-1}.

EXPONENTIALLY WEIGHTED ONLINE OPTIMIZATION.

Inputs: convex set $K \subset \mathbb{R}^n$, and the parameter α.

- Define weights $w_t(x) = \exp(-\alpha \sum_{\tau=1}^{t-1} f_\tau(x))$.
- On period t play $x_t = \frac{\int_K x w_t(x) dx}{\int_K w_t(x) dx}$.
  (*Remark:* choosing x_t at random with density proportional to $w_t(x)$ also gives our bounds.)

Fig. 3. Online optimization algorithms

on the "average", rather than always) using an extension of the Agarwal-Hazan potential function.

Another building block, due to Zinkevich [Zin03], is that if we have another set of functions $\tilde{f}_t$ for which $\tilde{f}_t(x_t) = f_t(x_t)$ and $\tilde{f}_t$ is a lower-bound on f_t, so $\tilde{f}_t(x) \leq f_t(x)$ for all $x \in K$, then it suffices to bound the regret with respect to $\tilde{f}_t$, because,

$$\text{regret}_T = \sum_{t=1}^{T} f_t(x_t) - \min_{x \in K} \sum_{t=1}^{T} f_t(x) \leq \sum_{t=1}^{T} \tilde{f}_t(x_t) - \min_{x \in K} \sum_{t=1}^{T} \tilde{f}_t(x) \quad (2)$$

He uses this observation in conjunction with the fact that a convex function is lower-bounded by its tangent hyperplanes, to argue that it suffices to analyze online gradient descent for the case of linear functions.

We observe[2] that online gradient descent can be viewed as running follow-the-leader on the sequence of functions $\tilde{f}_0(x) = (x - x_1)^2/\eta$ and $\tilde{f}_t(x) = f_t(x_t) + \nabla f_t(x_t)^\top (x - x_t)$. To do this, one need only calculate the minimum of $\sum_{\tau=0}^{t-1} \tilde{f}_\tau(x)$.

As explained before, any algorithm for the online convex optimization problem with linear functions has $\Omega(\sqrt{T})$ regret, and thus to achieve logarithmic regret one necessarily needs to use the curvature of functions. When we consider strongly concave functions where $H > 0$, we can lower-bound the function f_t by a paraboloid,

$$f_t(x) \geq f_t(x_t) + \nabla f_t(x_t)^\top (x - x_t) + \frac{H}{2}(x - x_t)^2,$$

rather than a linear function. The follow-the-leader calculation, however, remains similar. The only difference is that the step-size $\eta_t = 1/(Ht)$ decreases linearly rather than as $O(1/\sqrt{t})$.

For functions which permit $\alpha > 0$ such that $\exp(-\alpha f_t(x))$ is concave, it turns out that they can be lower-bounded by a paraboloid $\tilde{f}_t(x) = a + (w^\top x - b)^2$ where $w \in \mathbb{R}^n$ is proportional to $\nabla f_t(x_t)$ and $a, b \in \mathbb{R}$. Hence, one can do a similar follow-the-leader calculation, and this gives the FOLLOW THE APPROXIMATE LEADER algorithm in Figure 4. Formally, the ONLINE NEWTON STEP algorithm is an efficient implementation to the follow-the-leader variant FOLLOW THE APPROXIMATE LEADER (see Lemma 3), and clearly demonstrates its close connection to the Newton method from classical optimization theory. Interestingly, the derived ONLINE NEWTON STEP algorithm does not directly use the Hessians of the observed functions, but only a lower-bound on the Hessians, which can be calculated from the $\alpha > 0$ bound.

Finally, our EXPONENTIALLY WEIGHTED ONLINE OPTIMIZATION algorithm does not seem to be directly related to follow-the-leader. It is more related to similar algorithms which are used in the problem of prediction from expert advice[3] and to Cover's algorithm for universal portfolio management.

2.1   Implementation and Running Time

Perhaps the main contribution of this paper is the introduction of a general logarithmic regret algorithms that are efficient and relatively easy to implement. The algorithms in Figure 3 are described in their mathematically simplest forms, but

---

[2] Kakade has made a similar observation [Kak05].

[3] The standard weighted majority algorithm can be viewed as picking an expert of minimal cost when an additional random cost of $-\frac{1}{\eta} \ln \ln r_i$ is added to each expert, where r_i is chosen independently from $[0, 1]$.

FOLLOW THE APPROXIMATE LEADER.
Inputs: convex set $K \subset \mathbb{R}^n$, and the parameter β.

- On period 1, play an arbitrary $x_1 \in K$.
- On period t, play the leader x_t defined as

$$x_t \triangleq \arg \min_{x \in K} \sum_{\tau=1}^{t-1} \tilde{f}_\tau(x)$$

Where for $\tau = 1, \ldots, t - 1$, define $\nabla_\tau = \nabla f_\tau(x_\tau)$ and

$$\tilde{f}_\tau(x) \triangleq f_\tau(x_\tau) + \nabla_\tau^\top (x - x_\tau) + \frac{\beta}{2}(x - x_\tau)^\top \nabla_\tau \nabla_\tau^\top (x - x_\tau)$$

Fig. 4. The FOLLOW THE APPROXIMATE LEADER algorithm, which is equivalent to ONLINE NEWTON STEP

implementation has been disregarded. In this section, we discuss implementation issues and compare the running time of the different algorithms.

The ONLINE GRADIENT DESCENT algorithm is straightforward to implement, and updates take time $O(n)$ given the gradient. However, there is a projection step which may take longer. For many convex sets such as a ball, cube, or simplex, computing Π_K is fast and straightforward. For convex polytopes, the projection oracle can be implemented efficiently using interior point methods. In general, K can be specified by a membership oracle ($\chi_K(x) = 1$ if $x \in K$ and 0 if $x \notin K$), along with a point $x_0 \in K$ as well as radii $R \geq r > 0$ such that the balls of radii R and r around x_0 contain and are contained in K, respectively. In this case Π_K can be computed (to ε accuracy) in time $\tilde{O}(n^4 \log(\frac{R}{r}))$ [4] using the Vaidya's algorithm [Vai96].

The ONLINE NEWTON STEP algorithm requires $O(n^2)$ space to store the matrix A_t. Every iteration requires the computation of the matrix A_t^{-1}, the current gradient, a matrix-vector product and possibly a projection onto K.

A naïve implementation would require computing the Moore-Penrose pseudoinverse of the matrix A_t every iteration. However, in case A_t is invertible, the matrix inversion lemma [Bro05] states that for invertible matrix A and vector x

$$(A + xx^\top)^{-1} = A^{-1} - \frac{A^{-1} xx^\top A^{-1}}{1 + x^\top A^{-1} x}$$

Thus, given A_{t-1}^{-1} and ∇_t one can compute A_t^{-1} in time $O(n^2)$. A generalized matrix inversion lemma [Rie91] allows for iterative update of the pseudoinverse also in time $O(n^2)$, details will appear in the full version.

The ONLINE NEWTON STEP algorithm also needs to make projections onto K, but of a slightly different nature than ONLINE GRADIENT DESCENT. The required projection, denoted by $\Pi_K^{A_t}$, is in the vector norm induced by the matrix A_t, viz. $\|x\|_{A_t} = \sqrt{x^\top A_t x}$. It is equivalent to finding the point $x \in K$ which

---

[4] The $\tilde{O}$ notation hides poly-logarithmic factors, in this case $\log(nT/\varepsilon)$.

minimizes $(x - y)^\top A_t(x - y)$ where y is the point we are projecting. We assume the existence of an oracle which implements such a projection given y and A_t. The runtime is similar to that of the projection step of ONLINE GRADIENT DESCENT.

Modulo calls to the projections oracle, the ONLINE NEWTON STEP algorithm can be implemented in time and space $O(n^2)$, requiring only the gradient at each step.

The EXPONENTIALLY WEIGHTED ONLINE OPTIMIZATION algorithm can be approximated by sampling points according to the distribution with density proportional to w_t and then taking their mean. In fact, as far as an expected guarantee is concerned, our analysis actually shows that the algorithm which chooses a single random point x_t with density proportional to $w_t(x)$ achieves the stated regret bound, in expectation. Using recent random walk analyses of Lovász and Vempala [LV03a, LV03b], m samples from such a distribution can be computed in time $\tilde{O}((n^4 + mn^3) \log \frac{R}{r})$. A similar application of random walks was used previously for an efficient implementation of Cover's Universal Portfolio algorithm [KV03].

3 Analysis

3.1 ONLINE GRADIENT DESCENT

Theorem 1. *Assume that the functions f_t have bounded gradient, $\|\nabla f_t(x)\| \leq G$, and Hessian, $\nabla^2 f_t(x) \succeq H I_n$, for all $x \in K$.*

The ONLINE GRADIENT DESCENT *algorithm of Figure 3, with $\eta_t = (Ht)^{-1}$ achieves the following guarantee, for all $T \geq 1$.*

$$\sum_{t=1}^{T} f_t(x_t) - \min_{x \in K} \sum_{t=1}^{T} f_t(x) \leq \frac{G^2}{2H}(1 + \log T)$$

Proof. Let $x^* \in \arg\min_{x \in K} \sum_{t=1}^{T} f_t(x)$. Define $\nabla_t \triangleq \nabla f_t(x_t)$. By H-strong convexity, we have,

$$f_t(x^*) \geq f_t(x_t) + \nabla_t^\top (x^* - x_t) + \frac{H}{2} \|x^* - x_t\|^2$$

$$2(f_t(x_t) - f_t(x^*)) \leq 2\nabla_t^\top (x_t - x^*) - H \|x^* - x_t\|^2 \qquad (3)$$

Following Zinkevich's analysis, we upper-bound $\nabla_t^\top (x_t - x^*)$. Using the update rule for x_{t+1}, we get

$$\|x_{t+1} - x^*\|^2 = \|\Pi(x_t - \eta_{t+1} \nabla_t) - x^*\|^2 \leq \|x_t - \eta_{t+1} \nabla_t - x^*\|^2.$$

The inequality above follows from the properties of projection onto convex sets. Hence,

$$\|x_{t+1} - x^*\|^2 \leq \|x_t - x^*\|^2 + \eta_{t+1}^2 \|\nabla_t\|^2 - 2\eta_{t+1} \nabla_t^\top (x_t - x^*)$$

$$2\nabla_t^\top (x_t - x^*) \leq \frac{\|x_t - x^*\|^2 - \|x_{t+1} - x^*\|^2}{\eta_{t+1}} + \eta_{t+1} G^2 \qquad (4)$$

Sum up (4) from $t = 1$ to T. Set $\eta_{t+1} = 1/(Ht)$, and using (3), we have:

$$2\sum_{t=1}^{T} f_t(x_t) - f_t(x^*) \leq \sum_{t=1}^{T} \|x_t - x^*\|^2 \left(\frac{1}{\eta_{t+1}} - \frac{1}{\eta_t} - H \right) + G^2 \sum_{t=1}^{T} \eta_{t+1}$$

$$= 0 + G^2 \sum_{t=1}^{T} \frac{1}{Ht} \leq \frac{G^2}{H}(1 + \log T)$$

∎

3.2 Online Newton Step

Before analyzing the algorithm, we need a couple of lemmas.

Lemma 2. *If a function $f : K \to \mathbb{R}$ is such that $\exp(-\alpha f(x))$ is concave, and has gradient bounded by $\|\nabla f\| \leq G$, then for $\beta = \frac{1}{2}\min\{\frac{1}{4GD}, \alpha\}$ the following holds:*

$$\forall x, y \in K : \ f(x) \geq f(y) + \nabla f(y)^\top (x - y) + \frac{\beta}{2}(x - y)\nabla f(y)\nabla f(y)^\top (x - y)$$

Proof. First, by computing derivatives, one can check that since $\exp(-\alpha f(x))$ is concave and $2\beta \leq \alpha$, the function $h(x) = \exp(-2\beta f(x))$ is also concave. Then by the concavity of $h(x)$, we have

$$h(x) \ \leq \ h(y) + \nabla h(y)^\top (x - y).$$

Plugging in $\nabla h(y) = -2\beta \exp(-2\beta f(y))\nabla f(y)$ gives,

$$\exp(-2\beta f(x)) \ \leq \ \exp(-2\beta f(y))[1 - 2\beta \nabla f(y)^\top (x - y)].$$

Simplifying

$$f(x) \geq f(y) - \frac{1}{2\beta} \log[1 - 2\beta \nabla f(y)^\top (x - y)].$$

Next, note that $|2\beta \nabla f(y)^\top (x - y)| \ \leq \ 2\beta GD \leq \frac{1}{4}$ and that for $|z| \leq \frac{1}{4}$, $-\log(1 - z) \geq z + \frac{1}{4}z^2$. Applying the inequality for $z = 2\beta \nabla f(y)^\top (x - y)$ implies the lemma. ∎

Lemma 3. *The* Online Newton Step *algorithm is equivalent to the* Follow The Approximate Leader *algorithm.*

Proof. In the Follow The Approximate Leader algorithm, one needs to perform the following optimization at period t:

$$x_t \triangleq \arg\min_{x \in K} \sum_{\tau=1}^{t-1} \tilde{f}_\tau(x)$$

By expanding out the expressions for $\tilde{f}_\tau(x)$, multiplying by $\frac{2}{\beta}$ and getting rid of constants, the problem reduces to minimizing the following function over $x \in K$:

$$\sum_{\tau=1}^{t-1} x^\top \nabla_\tau \nabla_\tau^\top x - 2(x_\tau^\top \nabla_\tau \nabla_\tau^\top - \frac{1}{\beta} \nabla_\tau^\top) x$$

$$= x^\top A_{t-1} x - 2b_{t-1}^\top x = (x - A_{t-1}^{-1} b_{t-1})^\top A_{t-1} (x - A_{t-1}^{-1} b_{t-1}) - b_{t-1}^\top A_{t-1}^{-1} b_{t-1}$$

The solution of this minimization is exactly the projection $\Pi_K^{A_{t-1}}(A_{t-1}^{-1} b_{t-1})$ as specified by ONLINE NEWTON STEP. ∎

Theorem 4. *Assume that the functions f_t are such that $\exp(-\alpha f_t(x))$ is concave and have gradients bounded by $\|\nabla f_t(x)\| \leq G$. Then the* ONLINE NEWTON STEP *algorithm with parameter $\beta = \frac{1}{2} \min\{\frac{1}{4GD}, \alpha\}$ achieves the following guarantee, for all $T \geq 1$.*

$$\sum_{t=1}^{T} f_t(x_t) - \min_{x \in K} \sum_{t=1}^{T} f_t(x) \leq 3 \left[\frac{1}{\alpha} + 4GD \right] n \log T$$

Proof. The theorem relies on the observation that by Lemma 2, the function $\tilde{f}_t(x)$ defined by the FOLLOW THE APPROXIMATE LEADER algorithm satisfies $\tilde{f}_t(x_t) = f_t(x_t)$ and $\tilde{f}_t(x) \leq f_t(x)$ for all $x \in K$. Then the inequality (2) implies that it suffices to show a regret bound for the follow-the-leader algorithm run on the $\tilde{f}_t$ functions. The inequality (1) implies that it suffices to bound $\sum_{t=1}^{T} \left[\tilde{f}_t(x_t) - \tilde{f}_t(x_{t+1}) \right]$, which is done in Lemma 5 below. ∎

Lemma 5.

$$\sum_{t=1}^{T} \left[\tilde{f}_t(x_t) - \tilde{f}_t(x_{t+1}) \right] \leq 3 \left[\frac{1}{\alpha} + 4GD \right] n \log T$$

Proof (Lemma 5). For the sake of readability, we introduce some notation. Define the function $F_t \triangleq \sum_{\tau=1}^{t-1} \tilde{f}_\tau$. Note that $\nabla f_t(x_t) = \nabla \tilde{f}_t(x_t)$ by the definition of $\tilde{f}_t$, so we will use the same notation ∇_t to refer to both. Finally, let Δ be the forward difference operator, for example, $\Delta x_t = (x_{t+1} - x_t)$ and $\Delta \nabla F_t(x_t) = (\nabla F_{t+1}(x_{t+1}) - \nabla F_t(x_t))$.

We use the gradient bound, which follows from the convexity of $\tilde{f}_t$:

$$\tilde{f}_t(x_t) - \tilde{f}_t(x_{t+1}) \leq -\nabla \tilde{f}_t(x_t)^\top (x_{t+1} - x_t) = -\nabla_t^\top \Delta x_t \qquad (5)$$

The gradient of F_{t+1} can be written as:

$$\nabla F_{t+1}(x) = \sum_{\tau=1}^{t} \nabla f_\tau(x_\tau) + \beta \nabla f_\tau(x_\tau) \nabla f_\tau(x_\tau)^\top (x - x_\tau) \qquad (6)$$

Therefore,

$$\nabla F_{t+1}(x_{t+1}) - \nabla F_{t+1}(x_t) = \beta \sum_{\tau=1}^{t} \nabla f_\tau(x_\tau) \nabla f_\tau(x_\tau)^\top \Delta x_t = \beta A_t \Delta x_t \qquad (7)$$

The LHS of (7) is

$$\nabla F_{t+1}(x_{t+1}) - \nabla F_{t+1}(x_t) \;=\; \Delta\nabla F_t(x_t) - \nabla_t \tag{8}$$

Putting (7) and (8) together, and adding $\varepsilon\beta\Delta x_t$ we get

$$\beta(A_t + \varepsilon I_n)\Delta x_t = \Delta\nabla F_t(x_t) - \nabla_t + \varepsilon\beta\Delta x_t \tag{9}$$

Pre-multiplying by $-\frac{1}{\beta}\nabla_t^\top (A_t + \varepsilon I_n)^{-1}$, we get an expression for the gradient bound (5):

$$
\begin{aligned}
-\nabla_t^\top \Delta x_t \;&=\; -\frac{1}{\beta}\nabla_t^\top (A_t + \varepsilon I_n)^{-1}[\Delta\nabla F_t(x_t) - \nabla_t + \varepsilon\beta\Delta x_t] \\
&=\; -\frac{1}{\beta}\nabla_t^\top (A_t + \varepsilon I_n)^{-1}[\Delta\nabla F_t(x_t) + \varepsilon\beta\Delta x_t] + \frac{1}{\beta}\nabla_t^\top (A_t + \varepsilon I_n)^{-1}\nabla_t
\end{aligned}
\tag{10}
$$

Claim. The first term of (10) can be bounded as follows:

$$-\frac{1}{\beta}\nabla_t^\top (A_t + \varepsilon I_n)^{-1}[\Delta\nabla F_t(x_t) + \varepsilon\beta\Delta x_t] \;\le\; \varepsilon\beta D^2$$

Proof. Since x_τ minimizes F_τ over K, we have

$$\nabla F_\tau(x_\tau)^\top (x - x_\tau) \;\ge\; 0 \tag{11}$$

for any point $x \in K$. Using (11) for $\tau = t$ and $\tau = t+1$, we get

$$0 \;\le\; \nabla F_{t+1}(x_{t+1})^\top (x_t - x_{t+1}) + \nabla F_t(x_t)^\top (x_{t+1} - x_t) \;=\; -[\Delta\nabla F_t(x_t)]^\top \Delta x_t$$

Reversing the inequality and adding $\varepsilon\beta\|\Delta x_t\|^2 = \varepsilon\beta\Delta x_t^\top \Delta x_t$, we get

$$
\begin{aligned}
\varepsilon\beta\|\Delta x_t\|^2 \;&\ge\; [\Delta\nabla F_t(x_t) + \varepsilon\beta\Delta x_t]^\top \Delta x_t \\
&=\; \frac{1}{\beta}[\Delta\nabla F_t(x_t) + \varepsilon\beta\Delta x_t]^\top (A_t + \varepsilon I_n)^{-1}[\Delta\nabla F_t(x_t) + \varepsilon\beta\Delta x_t - \nabla_t]
\end{aligned}
$$

$$\text{(by solving for } \Delta x_t \text{ in (9))}$$

$$
\begin{aligned}
&=\; \frac{1}{\beta}[\Delta\nabla F_t(x_t) + \varepsilon\beta\Delta x_t]^\top (A_t + \varepsilon I_n)^{-1}(\Delta\nabla F_t(x_t) + \varepsilon\beta\Delta x_t) \\
&\quad -\frac{1}{\beta}[\Delta\nabla F_t(x_t) + \varepsilon\Delta x_t]^\top (A_t + \varepsilon I_n)^{-1}\nabla_t \\
&\ge\; -\frac{1}{\beta}[\Delta\nabla F_t(x_t) + \varepsilon\beta\Delta x_t]^\top (A_t + \varepsilon I_n)^{-1}\nabla_t
\end{aligned}
$$

$$\text{(since } (A_t + \varepsilon I_n)^{-1} \succeq 0 \Rightarrow \forall x: \; x^\top (A_t + \varepsilon I_n)^{-1}x \ge 0\text{)}$$

Finally, since the diameter of K is D, we have $\varepsilon\beta\|\Delta x_t\|^2 \le \varepsilon\beta D^2$. ∎

Now we bound the second term of (10). Sum up from $t = 1$ to T, and apply Lemma 6 below with $A_0 = \varepsilon I_n$ and $v_t = \nabla_t$. Set $\varepsilon = \frac{1}{\beta^2 D^2 T}$.

$$\frac{1}{\beta} \sum_{t=1}^{T} \nabla_t^\top (A_t + \varepsilon I_n)^{-1} \nabla_t \ \leq\ \frac{1}{\beta} \log \left[\frac{|A_T + \varepsilon I_n|}{|\varepsilon I_n|} \right]$$

$$\leq\ \frac{1}{\beta} n \log(\beta^2 G^2 D^2 T^2 + 1) \ \leq\ \frac{2}{\beta} n \log T$$

The second inequality follows since $A_T = \sum_{t=1}^{T} \nabla_t \nabla_t^\top$ and $\|\nabla_t\| \leq G$, we have $|A_T + \varepsilon I_n| \leq (G^2 T + \varepsilon)^n$.

Combining this inequality with the bound of the claim above, we get

$$\sum_{t=1}^{T} \left[\tilde{f}_t(x_t) - f_t(x_{t+1}) \right] \ \leq\ \frac{2}{\beta} n \log T + \varepsilon \beta D^2 T \ \leq\ 3 \left[\frac{1}{\alpha} + 4GD \right] n \log T$$

as required.   ∎

Lemma 6. *Let A_0 be a positive definite matrix, and for $t \geq 1$, let $A_t = \sum_{\tau=1}^{t} v_t v_t^\top$ for some vectors $v_1, v_2, \dots, v_t$. Then the following inequality holds:*

$$\sum_{t=1}^{T} v_t^\top (A_t + A_0)^{-1} v_t \ \leq\ \log \left[\frac{|A_T + A_0|}{|A_0|} \right]$$

To prove this Lemma, we first require the following claim.

Claim. Let A be a positive definite matrix and x a vector such that $A - xx^\top \succ 0$. Then

$$x^\top A^{-1} x \ \leq\ \log \left[\frac{|A|}{|A - xx^\top|} \right]$$

Proof. Let $B = A - xx^\top$. For any positive definite matrix C, let $\lambda_1(C), \lambda_2(C), \dots, \lambda_n(C)$ be its (positive) eigenvalues.

$$
\begin{aligned}
x^\top A^{-1} x &= \mathbf{Tr}(A^{-1} xx^\top) \\
&= \mathbf{Tr}(A^{-1}(A - B)) \\
&= \mathbf{Tr}(A^{-1/2}(A - B)A^{-1/2}) \\
&= \mathbf{Tr}(I - A^{-1/2} B A^{-1/2}) \\
&= \sum_{i=1}^{n} \left[1 - \lambda_i(A^{-1/2} B A^{-1/2}) \right] && \because \mathbf{Tr}(C) = \sum_{i=1}^{n} \lambda_i(C) \\
&\leq \sum_{i=1}^{n} \log \left[\lambda_i(A^{-1/2} B A^{-1/2}) \right] && \because 1 - x \leq -\log(x) \\
&= -\log \left[\prod_{i=1}^{n} \lambda_i(A^{-1/2} B A^{-1/2}) \right] \\
&= -\log |A^{-1/2} B A^{-1/2}| = \log \left[\frac{|A|}{|B|} \right] && \because \prod_{i=1}^{n} \lambda_i(C) = |C|
\end{aligned}
$$

■

Lemma 6 now follows as a corollary:

Proof (Lemma 6). By the previous claim, we have

$$\sum_{t=1}^{T} v_t^\top (A_t + A_0)^{-1} v_t \leq \sum_{t=1}^{T} \log \left[\frac{|A_t + A_0|}{|A_t + A_0 - v_t v_t^\top|} \right]$$

$$= \sum_{t=2}^{T} \log \left[\frac{|A_t + A_0|}{|A_{t-1} + A_0|} \right] + \log \left[\frac{|A_1 + A_0|}{|A_0|} \right] = \log \left[\frac{|A_t + A_0|}{|A_0|} \right]$$

∎

3.3 EXPONENTIALLY WEIGHTED ONLINE OPTIMIZATION

Theorem 7. *Assume that the functions f_t are such that $\exp(-\alpha f_t(x))$ is concave. Then the* EXPONENTIALLY WEIGHTED ONLINE OPTIMIZATION *algorithm achieves the following guarantee, for all $T \geq 1$.*

$$\sum_{t=1}^{T} f_t(x_t) - \min_{x \in K} \sum_{t=1}^{T} f_t(x) \leq \frac{1}{\alpha} n(1 + \log(1 + T)).$$

Proof. Let $h_t(x) = e^{-\alpha f_t(x)}$. The algorithm can be viewed as taking a weighted average over points $x \in K$. Hence, by concavity of h_t,

$$h_t(x_t) \geq \frac{\int_K h_t(x) \prod_{\tau=1}^{t-1} h_\tau(x)\, dx}{\int_K \prod_{\tau=1}^{t-1} h_\tau(x)\, dx}.$$

Hence, we have by telescoping product,

$$\prod_{\tau=1}^{t} h_\tau(x_\tau) \geq \frac{\int_K \prod_{\tau=1}^{t} h_\tau(x)\, dx}{\int_K 1\, dx} = \frac{\int_K \prod_{\tau=1}^{t} h_\tau(x)\, dx}{\text{vol}(K)} \tag{12}$$

Let $x^* = \arg\min_{x \in K} \sum_{t=1}^{T} f_t(x) = \arg\max_{x \in K} \prod_{t=1}^{T} h_t(x)$. Following [BK97], define nearby points $S \subset K$ by,

$$S = \{x \in S | x = \frac{T}{T+1} x^* + \frac{1}{T+1} y, y \in K\}.$$

By concavity of h_t and the fact that h_t is non-negative, we have that,

$$\forall x \in S \quad h_t(x) \geq \frac{T}{T+1} h_t(x^*).$$

Hence,

$$\forall x \in S \quad \prod_{\tau=1}^{T} h_\tau(x) \geq \left(\frac{T}{T+1} \right)^T \prod_{\tau=1}^{T} h_\tau(x^*) \geq \frac{1}{e} \prod_{\tau=1}^{T} h_\tau(x^*)$$

512   E. Hazan et al.

Finally, since $S = x^* + \frac{1}{T+1} K$ is simply a rescaling of K by a factor of $1/(T+1)$ (followed by a translation), and we are in n dimensions, $\text{vol}(S) = \text{vol}(K)/(T+1)^n$. Putting this together with equation (12), we have

$$\prod_{\tau=1}^{T} h_\tau(x_\tau) \geq \frac{\text{vol}(S)}{\text{vol}(K)} \frac{1}{e} \prod_{\tau=1}^{T} h_\tau(x^*) \geq \frac{1}{e(T+1)^n} \prod_{\tau=1}^{T} h_\tau(x^*).$$

This implies the theorem.   ∎

4 Conclusions and Future Work

In this work, we presented efficient algorithms which guarantee logarithmic regret when the loss functions satisfy a mildly restrictive convexity condition. Our algorithms use the very natural follow-the-leader methodology which has been quite useful in other settings, and the efficient implementation of the algorithm shows the connection with the Newton method from offline optimization theory.

Future work involves adapting these algorithms to work in the *bandit* setting, where only the cost of the chosen point is revealed at every point (and no other information). The techniques of Flaxman, Kalai and McMahan [FKM05] seem to be promising for this.

Another direction for future work relies on the observation that the original algorithm of Agarwal and Hazan worked for functions which could be written as a one-dimensional convex function applied to an inner product. However, the analysis requires a stronger condition than the exp-concavity condition we have here. It seems that the original analysis can be made to work just with exp-concavity assumptions, more detail to appear in the full version of this paper.

Acknowledgements

The Princeton authors would like to thank Sanjeev Arora and Rob Schapire for helpful comments.

References

[AH05]   Amit Agarwal and Elad Hazan. Efficient algorithms for online game playing and universal portfolio management. *ECCC, TR06-033*, 2005.
[BK97]   Avrim Blum and Adam Kalai. Universal portfolios with and without transaction costs. In *COLT '97: Proceedings of the tenth annual conference on Computational learning theory*, pages 309–313, New York, NY, USA, 1997. ACM Press.
[Bro05]   M. Brookes. The matrix reference manual. *[online]* http://www.ee.ic.ac.uk/hp/staff/dmb/matrix/intro.html, 2005.
[CBL06]   N. Cesa-Bianchi and G. Lugosi. *Prediction, Learning, and Games*. Cambridge University Press, Cambridge, 2006.
[Cov91]   T. Cover. Universal portfolios. *Math. Finance*, 1:1–19, 1991.

[FKM05]   Abraham Flaxman, Adam Tauman Kalai, and H. Brendan McMahan. On-line convex optimization in the bandit setting: gradient descent without a gradient. In *Proceedings of 16th SODA*, pages 385–394, 2005.

[Han57]   James Hannan. Approximation to bayes risk in repeated play. *In M. Dresher, A. W. Tucker, and P. Wolfe, editors, Contributions to the Theory of Games, volume III*, pages 97–139, 1957.

[Kak05]   S. Kakade. Personal communication, 2005.

[KV03]   Adam Kalai and Santosh Vempala. Efficient algorithms for universal portfolios. *J. Mach. Learn. Res.*, 3:423–440, 2003.

[KV05]   Adam Kalai and Santosh Vempala. Efficient algorithms for on-line optimization. *Journal of Computer and System Sciences*, 71(3):291–307, 2005.

[KW99]   J. Kivinen and M. K. Warmuth. Averaging expert predictions. In *Computational Learning Theory: 4th European Conference (EuroCOLT '99)*, pages 153–167, Berlin, 1999. Springer.

[LV03a]   László Lovász and Santosh Vempala. The geometry of logconcave functions and an $o^*(n^3)$ sampling algorithm. Technical Report MSR-TR-2003-04, Microsoft Research, 2003.

[LV03b]   László Lovász and Santosh Vempala. Simulated annealing in convex bodies and an $0^*(n^4)$ volume algorithm. In *Proceedings of the 44th Symposium on Foundations of Computer Science (FOCS)*, pages 650–659, 2003.

[Rie91]   Kurt Riedel. A sherman-morrison-woodbury identity for rank augmenting matrices with application to centering. *SIAM J. Mat. Anal.*, 12(1):80–95, January 1991.

[Spa03]   J. Spall. *Introduction to Stochastic Search and Optimization*. John Wiley & Sons, Inc, New York, NY, 2003.

[Vai96]   Pravin M. Vaidya. A new algorithm for minimizing convex functions over convex sets. *Math. Program.*, 73(3):291–341, 1996.

[Zin03]   Martin Zinkevich. Online convex programming and generalized infinitesimal gradient ascent. In *Proceedings of the Twentieth International Conference (ICML)*, pages 928–936, 2003.

Online Variance Minimization*

Manfred K. Warmuth and Dima Kuzmin

Computer Science Department
University of California, Santa Cruz
{manfred, dima}@cse.ucsc.edu

Abstract. We design algorithms for two online variance minimization problems. Specifically, in every trial t our algorithms get a covariance matrix $\mathcal{C}_t$ and try to select a parameter vector $\boldsymbol{w}_t$ such that the total variance over a sequence of trials $\sum_t \boldsymbol{w}_t^\top \mathcal{C}_t \boldsymbol{w}_t$ is not much larger than the total variance of the best parameter vector $\boldsymbol{u}$ chosen in hindsight. Two parameter spaces are considered - the probability simplex and the unit sphere. The first space is associated with the problem of minimizing risk in stock portfolios and the second space leads to an online calculation of the eigenvector with minimum eigenvalue. For the first parameter space we apply the Exponentiated Gradient algorithm which is motivated with a relative entropy. In the second case the algorithm maintains a mixture of unit vectors which is represented as a density matrix. The motivating divergence for density matrices is the quantum version of the relative entropy and the resulting algorithm is a special case of the Matrix Exponentiated Gradient algorithm. In each case we prove bounds on the additional total variance incurred by the online algorithm over the best offline parameter.

1 Introduction

In one of the simplest settings of learning with expert advice [FS97], the learner has to commit to a probability vector $\boldsymbol{w}$ over the experts at the beginning of each trial. It then receives a loss vector $\boldsymbol{l}$ and incurs loss $\boldsymbol{w} \cdot \boldsymbol{l} = \sum_i w_i l_i$. The goal is to design online algorithms whose total loss over a sequence of trials is close to loss of the best expert in all trials, i.e. the total loss of the online algorithm $\sum_t \boldsymbol{w}_t \cdot \boldsymbol{l}_t$ should be close to the total loss of the best expert chosen in hindsight, which is $\inf_i \sum_t l_{t,i}$, where t is the trial index.

In this paper we investigate online algorithms for minimizing the total variance over a sequence of trials. Instead of receiving a loss vector $\boldsymbol{l}$ in each trial, we now receive a covariance matrix $\mathcal{C}$ of a random loss vector $\boldsymbol{l}$, where $\mathcal{C}(i,j)$ is the covariance between l_i and l_j at the current trial. Intuitively the loss vector provides first-order information (means), whereas covariance matrices give second order information. The variance/risk of the loss for probability vector $\boldsymbol{w}$ when the covariance matrix is $\mathcal{C}$ can be expressed as $\boldsymbol{w}^\top \mathcal{C} \boldsymbol{w} = \mathbf{Var}(\boldsymbol{w} \cdot \boldsymbol{l})$. Our goal

---

* Supported by NSF grant CCR 9821087. Some of this work was done while visiting National ICT Australia in Canberra.

is to minimize the total variance over a sequence of trials: $\sum_t \boldsymbol{w}_t^\top \boldsymbol{C}_t \boldsymbol{w}_t$. More precisely, we want algorithms whose total variance is close to the total variance of the best probability vector $\boldsymbol{u}$ chosen in hindsight, i.e. the total variance of the algorithm should be close to $\inf_{\boldsymbol{u}} \boldsymbol{u}^\top (\sum_t \boldsymbol{C}_t) \boldsymbol{u}$ (where the minimization is over the probability simplex).

In a more general setting one actually might want to optimize trade-offs between first-order and second order terms: $\boldsymbol{w} \cdot \boldsymbol{l} + \gamma \boldsymbol{w}^\top \boldsymbol{C} \boldsymbol{w}$, where $\gamma \geq 0$ is a risk-aversion parameter. Such problems arise in Markowitz portfolio optimization (See e.g. discussion in [BV04], Section 4.4). For the sake of simplicity, in this paper we focus on minimizing the variance by itself.

We develop an algorithm for the above online variance minimization problem. The parameter space is the probability simplex. We use the Exponentiated Gradient algorithm for solving this problem since it maintains a probability vector. The latter algorithm is motivated and analyzed using the relative entropy between probability vectors [KW97]. The bounds we obtain are similar to the bounds of the Exponentiated Gradient algorithm when applied to linear regression.

In the second part of the paper we focus on the same online variance minimization problem, but now the parameter space that we compare against is the unit sphere of direction vectors instead of the probability simplex and the total loss of the algorithm is to be close to $\inf_{\boldsymbol{u}} \boldsymbol{u}^\top (\sum_t \boldsymbol{C}_t) \boldsymbol{u}$, where the minimization is over unit vectors. The solution of the offline problem is an eigenvector that corresponds to a minimum eigenvalue of the total covariance $\sum_t \boldsymbol{C}_t$.

Note that the variance $\boldsymbol{u}^\top \boldsymbol{C} \boldsymbol{u}$ can be rewritten using the trace operator: $\boldsymbol{u}^\top \boldsymbol{C} \boldsymbol{u} = \text{tr}(\boldsymbol{u}^\top \boldsymbol{C} \boldsymbol{u}) = \text{tr}(\boldsymbol{u} \boldsymbol{u}^\top \boldsymbol{C})$. The outer product $\boldsymbol{u} \boldsymbol{u}^\top$ for unit $\boldsymbol{u}$ is called a *dyad* and the offline problem can be reformulated as minimizing trace of a product of a dyad with the total covariance matrix: $\inf_{\boldsymbol{u}} \text{tr}(\boldsymbol{u} \boldsymbol{u}^\top (\sum_t \boldsymbol{C}_t))$ (where $\boldsymbol{u}$ is unit length).[1]

In the original experts setting, the offline problem involved a minimum over experts. Now its a minimum over dyads and the best dyad corresponds to an eigenvector with minimum eigenvalue. The algorithm for the original expert setting maintains its uncertainty over which expert is best as a probability vector $\boldsymbol{w}$, i.e. w_i is the current belief that expert i is best. This algorithm is the Continuous Weighted Majority (WMC) [LW94] (which was reformulated as the Hedge algorithm in [FS97]). It uses exponentially decaying weights $w_{t,i} = \dfrac{e^{-\eta \sum_{q=1}^{t-1} l_{q,i}}}{Z_t}$, where Z_t is a normalization factor.

In the generalized setting we need to maintain uncertainty over dyads. The natural parameter space is therefore mixtures of dyads which are called density matrices in statistical physics (symmetric positive definite matrices of trace one). Note that the vector of eigenvalues of such matrices is a probability vector. Using the methodology of [TRW05, War05] we develop a matrix version of the Weighted Majority algorithm for solving our second online variance minimization problem.

---

[1] In this paper we upper bound the total variance of our algorithm, whereas the generalized Bayes rule of [War05, WK06] is an algorithm for which the sum of the negative logs of the variances is upper bounded.

Now the density matrix parameter has the form $\mathcal{W}_t = \dfrac{\exp(-\eta \sum_{q=1}^{t-1} \mathcal{C}_q)}{Z_t}$, where
exp is the matrix exponential and Z_t normalizes the trace of the parameter matrix to one. When the covariance matrices $\mathcal{C}_q$ are the diagonal matrices $\mathrm{diag}(l_q)$ then the matrix update becomes the original expert update. In other words the original update may be seen as a special case of the new matrix update when the eigenvectors are fixed to the standard basis vectors and are not updated.

The original weighted majority type update may be seen as a softmin calculation, because as $\eta \to \infty$, the parameter vector $\boldsymbol{w}_t$ puts all of its weight on $\arg\min_i \sum_{q=1}^{t-1} l_{q,i}$. Similarly, the generalized update is a soft eigenvector calculation for the eigenvectors with the minimum eigenvalue.

What replaces the loss $\boldsymbol{w} \cdot \boldsymbol{l}$ of the algorithm in the more general context? The dot product for matrices is a trace and we use the generalized loss $\mathrm{tr}(\mathcal{W}\mathcal{C})$. If the eigendecomposition of the parameter matrix $\mathcal{W}$ consists of the eigenvectors $\boldsymbol{w}_i$ and associated eigenvalues ω_i then this loss can be rewritten as

$$\mathrm{tr}(\mathcal{W}\mathcal{C}) = \mathrm{tr}\left(\left(\sum \omega_i \boldsymbol{w}_i \boldsymbol{w}_i^\top\right)\mathcal{C}\right) = \sum_i \omega_i\, \boldsymbol{w}_i^\top \mathcal{C} \boldsymbol{w}_i$$

In other words it may be seen as an expected variance along the eigenvectors $\boldsymbol{w}_i$ that is weighted by the eigenvalues ω_i. Curiously enough, this trace is also a quantum measurement, where $\mathcal{W}$ represents a mixture state of a particle and $\mathcal{C}$ the instrument (See [War05, WK06] for additional discussion). Again the dot product $\boldsymbol{w} \cdot \boldsymbol{l}$ is the special case when the eigenvectors are the standard basis vectors, i.e.

$$\mathrm{tr}(\mathrm{diag}(\boldsymbol{w})\,\mathrm{diag}(\boldsymbol{l})) = \mathrm{tr}\left(\left(\sum w_i e_i e_i^\top\right)\mathrm{diag}(\boldsymbol{l})\right) = \sum_i w_i\, e_i^\top \mathrm{diag}(\boldsymbol{l})e_i = \sum_i w_i l_i.$$

The new update is motivated and analyzed using the quantum relative entropy (due to Umegaki, see e.g. [NC00]) instead of the standard relative entropy (also called Kullback-Leibler divergence). The analysis is a fancier version of the original online loss bound for WMC that uses the Golden-Thompson inequality and some lemmas developed in [TRW05].

2   Variance Minimization over the Probability Simplex

2.1   Definitions

In this paper we only consider symmetric matrices. Such matrices always have an eigendecomposition of the form $\mathcal{W} = \boldsymbol{W}\omega\boldsymbol{W}^\top$, where $\boldsymbol{W}$ is an orthogonal matrix of eigenvectors and ω is a diagonal matrix of the corresponding eigenvalues. Alternatively, the decomposition can be written as $\mathcal{W} = \sum_i \omega_i \boldsymbol{w}_i \boldsymbol{w}_i^\top$, with the ω_i being the eigenvalues and the $\boldsymbol{w}_i$ the eigenvectors. Note that the dyads $\boldsymbol{w}_i \boldsymbol{w}_i^\top$ are square matrices of rank one.

Matrix $\mathcal{M}$ is called *positive semidefinite* if for all vectors $\boldsymbol{w}$ we have $\boldsymbol{w}^\top \mathcal{M} \boldsymbol{w} \geq 0$. This is also written as a generalized inequality $\mathcal{M} \succeq \boldsymbol{0}$. In eigenvalue terms this

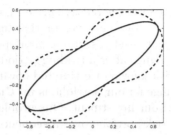

Fig. 1. An ellipse $\mathcal{C}$ in $\mathbb{R}^2$: The eigenvectors are the directions of the axes and the eigenvalues their lengths from the origin. Ellipses are weighted combinations of the one-dimensional degenerate ellipses (dyads) corresponding to the axes. (For unit $\boldsymbol{w}$, the dyad $\boldsymbol{ww}^\top$ is a degenerate one-dimensional ellipse which is a line between $-\boldsymbol{w}$ and $\boldsymbol{w}$). The solid curve of the ellipse is a plot of direction vector $\mathcal{C}\boldsymbol{w}$ and the outer dashed figure eight is direction $\boldsymbol{w}$ times the variance $\boldsymbol{w}^\top\mathcal{C}\boldsymbol{w}$. At the eigenvectors, this variance equals the eigenvalues and the figure eight touches the ellipse.

means that all eigenvalues of matrix are ≥ 0. A matrix is *strictly positive definite* if all eigenvalues are > 0. In what follows we will drop the semi- prefix and call any matrix $\mathcal{M} \succeq \boldsymbol{0}$ simply positive definite.

Let l be a random vector, then $\mathcal{C} = \boldsymbol{E}\left((\boldsymbol{l} - \boldsymbol{E}(\boldsymbol{l}))(\boldsymbol{l} - \boldsymbol{E}(\boldsymbol{l}))^\top\right)$ is its *covariance matrix*. It is symmetric and positive definite. For any other vector $\boldsymbol{w}$ we can compute the variance of the dot product $\boldsymbol{l}^\top\boldsymbol{w}$ as follows:

$$
\begin{aligned}
\mathbf{Var}(\boldsymbol{l}^\top\boldsymbol{w}) &= \boldsymbol{E}\left((\boldsymbol{l}^\top\boldsymbol{w} - \boldsymbol{E}(\boldsymbol{l}^\top\boldsymbol{w}))^2\right) \\
&= \boldsymbol{E}\left(((\boldsymbol{l}^\top - \boldsymbol{E}(\boldsymbol{l}^\top))\boldsymbol{w})^\top((\boldsymbol{l}^\top - \boldsymbol{E}(\boldsymbol{l}^\top))\boldsymbol{w})\right) \\
&= \boldsymbol{E}\left(\boldsymbol{w}^\top(\boldsymbol{l} - \boldsymbol{E}(\boldsymbol{l}))(\boldsymbol{l} - \boldsymbol{E}(\boldsymbol{l}))^\top)\boldsymbol{w}\right) \\
&= \boldsymbol{w}^\top\mathcal{C}\boldsymbol{w}.
\end{aligned}
$$

A covariance matrix can be depicted as an ellipse $\{\mathcal{C}\boldsymbol{w} : \|\boldsymbol{w}\|_2 = 1\}$ centered at the origin. The eigenvectors of $\mathcal{C}$ form the axes of the ellipse and eigenvalues are the lengths of the axes from the origin (See Figure 1 taken from [War05]).

For two probability vectors $\boldsymbol{u}$ and $\boldsymbol{w}$ (e.g. vectors whose entries are nonnegative and sum to one) their relative entropy (or Kullback-Leibler divergence) is given by:

$$
d(\boldsymbol{u}, \boldsymbol{w}) = \sum_{i=1}^n u_i \log \frac{u_i}{w_i}.
$$

We call this a divergence (and not a distance) since its not symmetric and does not satisfy the triangle inequality. It is however nonnegative and convex in both arguments.

2.2   Risk Minimization

The problem of minimizing the variance when the direction $\boldsymbol{w}$ lies in the probability simplex is connected to risk minimization in stock portfolios. In Markowitz portfolio theory, vector p denotes the relative price change of all assets in a given trading period. Let w be a probability vector that specifies the proportion of our capital invested into each asset (assuming short positions are not allowed). Then the relative capital change after a trading period is the dot product $w \cdot p$. If p is a random vector with known or estimated covariance matrix C, then the variance of the capital change for our portfolio is $w^\top C w$. This variance is clearly associated with the risk of our investment. Our problem is then to "track" the performance of minimum risk portfolio over a sequence of trading periods.

2.3 Algorithm and Motivation

Let us reiterate the setup and the goal for our algorithm. On every trial t it must produce a probability vector w_t. It then gets a covariance matrix C_t and incurs a loss equal to the variance $w_t^\top C_t w_t$. Thus for a sequence of T trials the total loss of the algorithm will be $L_{\text{alg}} = \sum_{t=1}^{T} w_t^\top C_t w_t$. We want this loss to be comparable to the total variance of the best probability vector u chosen in hindsight, i.e. $L_u = \min_u u^\top \left(\sum_{t=1}^{T} C_t \right) u$, where u lies in the probability simplex. This offline problem is a quadratic optimization problem with non-negativity constraints which does not have a closed form solution. However we can still prove bounds for the online algorithm.

The natural choice for an online algorithm for this problem is the Exponentiated Gradient algorithm of [KW97] since it maintains a probability vector as its parameter. Recall that for a general loss function $L_t(w_t)$, the probability vector of Exponentiated Gradient algorithm is updated as

$$w_{t+1,i} = \frac{w_{t,i} e^{-\eta(\nabla L_t(w_t))_i}}{\sum_i w_{t,i} e^{-\eta(\nabla L_t(w_t))_i}}.$$

This update is motivated by considering the tradeoff between the relative entropy divergence to the old probability vector and the current loss, where $\eta > 0$ is the tradeoff parameter:

$$w_{t+1} \approx \underset{w \text{ prob.vec.}}{\arg\min}\ \mathrm{d}(w, w_t) + \eta L_t(w),$$

where $\approx$ comes from the fact that the gradient at w_{t+1} that should appear in the exponent is approximated by the gradient at w_t (See [KW97] for more discussion). In our application, $L_t(w_t) = \frac{1}{2} w_t^\top C_t w_t$ and $\nabla L_t(w_t) = C_t w_t$, leading to the following update:

$$w_{t+1,i} = \frac{w_{t,i} e^{-\eta(C_t w_t)_i}}{\sum_{i=1}^{n} w_{t,i} e^{-\eta(C_t w_t)_i}}.$$

2.4 Proof of Relative Loss Bounds

We now use the divergence $\mathrm{d}(u, w)$ that motivated the update as a measure of progress in the analysis.

Lemma 1. *Let $\boldsymbol{w}_t$ be the weight vector of the algorithm before trial t and let $\boldsymbol{u}$ be an arbitrary comparison probability vector. Also, let r be the bound on the range of elements in covariance matrix $\boldsymbol{C}_t$, specifically let $\max_{i,j} |\boldsymbol{C}_t(i,j)| \leq \frac{r}{2}$. For any constants a and b such that $0 < a \leq \frac{b}{1+rb}$ and a learning rate $\eta = \frac{2b}{1+rb}$ we have:*

$$a\, \boldsymbol{w}_t^\top \boldsymbol{C}_t \boldsymbol{w}_t - b\, \boldsymbol{u}^\top \boldsymbol{C}_t \boldsymbol{u} \leq \mathrm{d}(\boldsymbol{u}, \boldsymbol{w}_t) - \mathrm{d}(\boldsymbol{u}, \boldsymbol{w}_{t+1}).$$

Proof. The proof given in Appendix A follows the same outline as Lemma 5.8 of [KW97] which gives an inequality for the Exponentiated Gradient algorithm when applied to linear regression. □

Lemma 2. *Let $\max_{i,j} |\boldsymbol{C}_t(i,j)| \leq \frac{r}{2}$ as before. Then for arbitrary positive c and learning rate $\eta = \frac{2c}{r(c+1)}$, the following bound holds:*

$$L_{alg} \leq (1+c)\, L_{\boldsymbol{u}} + \left(1 + \frac{1}{c}\right) r\, \mathrm{d}(\boldsymbol{u}, \boldsymbol{w}_1).$$

Proof. Let $b = \frac{c}{r}$, then for $a = \frac{b}{rb+1} = \frac{c}{r(c+1)}$ and $\eta = 2a = \frac{2c}{r(c+1)}$, we can use the inequality of Lemma 1 and obtain:

$$\frac{c}{c+1} \boldsymbol{w}_t^\top \boldsymbol{C}_t \boldsymbol{w}_t - c\, \boldsymbol{u}^\top \boldsymbol{C}_t \boldsymbol{u} \leq r(\mathrm{d}(\boldsymbol{u}, \boldsymbol{w}_t) - \mathrm{d}(\boldsymbol{u}, \boldsymbol{w}_{t+1})).$$

Summing over the trials t results in:

$$\frac{c}{c+1} L_{alg} - c L_{\boldsymbol{u}} \leq r(\mathrm{d}(\boldsymbol{u}, \boldsymbol{w}_1) - \mathrm{d}(\boldsymbol{u}, \boldsymbol{w}_{t+1})) \leq r\, \mathrm{d}(\boldsymbol{u}, \boldsymbol{w}_1).$$

Now the statement of the lemma immediately follows. □

The following theorem describes how to choose the learning rate for the purpose of minimizing the upper bound:

Theorem 1. *Let $\boldsymbol{C}_1, \ldots, \boldsymbol{C}_T$ be an arbitrary sequence of covariance matrices such that $\max_{i,j} |\boldsymbol{C}_t(i,j)| \leq \frac{r}{2}$ and assume that $\boldsymbol{u}^\top \sum_{t=1}^T \boldsymbol{C}_t \boldsymbol{u} \leq L$. Then running our algorithm with uniform start vector $\boldsymbol{w}_1 = (\frac{1}{n}, \ldots, \frac{1}{n})$ and learning rate $\eta = \frac{2\sqrt{L \log n}}{r\sqrt{\log n} + \sqrt{rL}}$ leads to the following bound:*

$$L_{alg} \leq L_{\boldsymbol{u}} + 2\sqrt{rL \log n} + r \log n.$$

Proof. By Lemma 2 and since $\mathrm{d}(\boldsymbol{u}, \boldsymbol{w}_1) \leq \log n$:

$$L_{alg} \leq L_{\boldsymbol{u}} + cL + \frac{r \log n}{c} + r \log n.$$

By differentiating we see that $c = \sqrt{\frac{r \log n}{L}}$ minimizes the r.h.s. and substituting this choice of c gives the bound of the theorem. □

3   Variance Minimization over the Unit Sphere

3.1   Definitions

The *trace* $\mathrm{tr}(\mathcal{A})$ of a square matrix $\mathcal{A}$ is the sum of its diagonal elements. It is invariant under a change of basis transformation and thus it is also equal to the sum of eigenvalues of the matrix. The trace generalizes the normal dot product between vectors to the space of matrices, i.e. $\mathrm{tr}(\mathcal{A}\mathcal{B}) = \mathrm{tr}(\mathcal{B}\mathcal{A}) = \sum_{i,j} \mathcal{A}(i,j)\mathcal{B}(i,j)$. The trace is also a linear operator, that is $\mathrm{tr}(a\mathcal{A} + b\mathcal{B}) = a\,\mathrm{tr}(\mathcal{A}) + b\,\mathrm{tr}(\mathcal{B})$. Another useful property of the trace is its cycling invariance, i.e. $\mathrm{tr}(\mathcal{A}\mathcal{B}\mathcal{C}) = \mathrm{tr}(\mathcal{B}\mathcal{C}\mathcal{A}) = \mathrm{tr}(\mathcal{C}\mathcal{A}\mathcal{B})$. A particular instance of this is the following manipulation: $\boldsymbol{u}^\top \mathcal{A}\boldsymbol{u} = \mathrm{tr}(\boldsymbol{u}^\top \mathcal{A}\boldsymbol{u}) = \mathrm{tr}(\mathcal{A}\boldsymbol{u}\boldsymbol{u}^\top)$.

Dyads have trace one because $\mathrm{tr}(\boldsymbol{u}\boldsymbol{u}^\top) = \boldsymbol{u}^\top \boldsymbol{u} = 1$. We generalize mixtures or probability vectors to *density matrices*. Such matrices are mixtures of any number of dyads, i.e. $\mathcal{W} = \sum_i \alpha_i \boldsymbol{u}_i \boldsymbol{u}_i^\top$ where $\alpha_j \geq 0$ and $\sum_i \alpha_i = 1$. Equivalently, density matrices are arbitrary symmetric positive definite matrices of trace one. Any density matrix $\mathcal{W}$ can be decomposed into a sum of exactly n dyads corresponding to the orthogonal set of its eigenvectors $\boldsymbol{w}_i$, i.e. $\mathcal{W} = \sum_{i=1}^{n} \omega_i \boldsymbol{w}_i \boldsymbol{w}_i^\top$ where the vector $\boldsymbol{\omega}$ of the n eigenvalues must be a probability vector. In quantum physics density matrices over the field of complex numbers represent the mixed state of a physical system.

We also need the matrix generalizations of the exponential and logarithm operations. Given the decomposition of a symmetric matrix $\mathcal{A} = \sum_i \alpha_i\,\boldsymbol{a}_i \boldsymbol{a}_i^\top$, the matrix exponential and logarithm denoted as **exp** and **log** are computed as follows:

$$\mathbf{exp}(\mathcal{A}) = \sum_i e^{\alpha_i}\,\boldsymbol{a}_i \boldsymbol{a}_i^\top, \quad \mathbf{log}(\mathcal{A}) = \sum_i \log \alpha_i\,\boldsymbol{a}_i \boldsymbol{a}_i^\top$$

In other words, the exponential and the logarithm are applied to the eigenvalues and the eigenvectors remain unchanged. Obviously, the matrix logarithm is only defined when the matrix is strictly positive definite. In analogy with the exponential for numbers, one would expect the following equality to hold: $\mathbf{exp}(\mathcal{A} + \mathcal{B}) = \mathbf{exp}(\mathcal{A})\,\mathbf{exp}(\mathcal{B})$. However this is only true when the symmetric matrices $\mathcal{A}$ and $\mathcal{B}$ commute, i.e. $\mathcal{A}\mathcal{B} = \mathcal{B}\mathcal{A}$, which occurs iff both matrices share the same eigensystem. On the other hand, the following trace inequality, called the Golden-Thompson inequality, holds for arbitrary symmetric matrices:

$$\mathrm{tr}(\mathbf{exp}(\mathcal{A} + \mathcal{B})) \leq \mathrm{tr}(\mathbf{exp}(\mathcal{A})\,\mathbf{exp}(\mathcal{B})).$$

The following quantum relative entropy is a generalization of the classical relative entropy to density matrices due to Umegaki (see e.g. [NC00]):

$$\Delta(\mathcal{U}, \mathcal{W}) = \mathrm{tr}(\mathcal{U}(\log \mathcal{U} - \log \mathcal{W})).$$

We will also use generalized inequalities for the cone of positive definite matrices: $\mathcal{A} \preceq \mathcal{B}$ if $\mathcal{B} - \mathcal{A}$ positive definite.

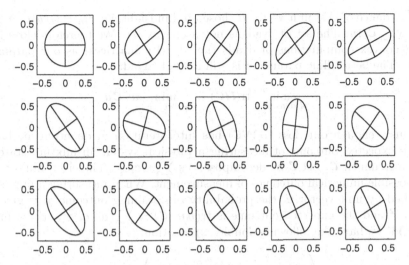

Fig. 2. The figure depicts a sequence of updates for the density matrix algorithm when the dimension is 2. All 2-by-2 matrices are represented as ellipses. The top row shows the density matrices $\mathcal{W}_t$ chosen by the algorithm. The middle row shows the covariance matrix $\mathcal{C}_t$ received in that trial. Finally, the bottom row is the average $\mathcal{C}_{\leq t} = \frac{\sum_{q=1}^{t} \mathcal{C}_t}{t}$ of all covariance matrices so far. By the update (1), $\mathcal{W}_{t+1} = \frac{\exp(-\eta t \mathcal{C}_{\leq t})}{Z_t}$, where Z_t is a normalization. Therefore, $\mathcal{C}_{\leq t}$ in the third row has the same eigensystem as the density matrix $\mathcal{W}_{t+1}$ in the next column of the first row. Note the tendency of the algorithm to try to place more weight on the minimal eigenvalue of the covariance average. Since the algorithm is not sure about the future, it does not place the full weight onto that eigenvalue but hedges its bets instead and places some weight onto the other eigenvalues as well.

3.2 Applications

We develop online algorithms that perform as well as the eigenvector associated with a minimum (or maximum) eigenvalue. It seems that online versions of principal component analysis and other spectral methods can also be developed using the methodology of this paper. For instance, spectral clustering methods of [CSTK01] use a similar form of loss.

3.3 Algorithm and Motivation

As before we briefly review our setup. On each trial t our algorithm chooses a density matrix $\mathcal{W}_t$ described as a mixture $\sum_i \omega_{t,i} \, \boldsymbol{w}_{t,i} \boldsymbol{w}_{t,i}^{\top}$. It then receives a covariance matrix $\mathcal{C}_t$ and incurs a loss equal to the expected variance of its mixture:

$$\text{tr}(\mathcal{W}_t \mathcal{C}_t) = \text{tr}((\sum_i \omega_{t,i} \, \boldsymbol{w}_{t,i} \boldsymbol{w}_{t,i}^{\top}) \mathcal{C}_t) = \sum_i \omega_{t,i} \, \boldsymbol{w}_{t,i}^{\top} \mathcal{C}_t \boldsymbol{w}_{t,i}.$$

On a sequence of T trials the total loss of the algorithm will be $L_{\text{alg}} = \sum_{t=1}^{T} \text{tr}(\mathcal{W}_t \mathcal{C}_t)$. We want this loss to be not too much larger than the total variance of best unit vector u chosen in hindsight, i.e. $L_u = \mathrm{tr}(uu^\top \sum_t C_t)$ $= u^\top (\sum_t C_t) u$. The set of dyads is not a convex set. We therefore close it by using convex combinations of dyads (i.e. density matrices) as our parameter space. The best offline parameter is still a single dyad:

$$\min_{\mathcal{U} \text{ dens.mat.}} \mathrm{tr}(\mathcal{U}\mathcal{C}) = \min_{u \,:\, \|u\|_2 = 1} u^\top \mathcal{C} u$$

Curiously enough our, loss $\mathrm{tr}(\mathcal{W}\mathcal{C})$ has interpretation in quantum mechanics as the expected outcome of measuring a physical system in mixture state $\mathcal{W}$ with instrument $\mathcal{C}$. Let $\mathcal{C}$ be decomposed as $\sum_i \gamma_i c_i c_i^\top$. The eigenvalues γ_i are the possible numerical outcomes of measurement. When measuring a pure state specified by unit vector u, the probability of obtaining outcome γ_i is given as $(u \cdot c_i)^2$ and the expected outcome is $\mathrm{tr}(uu^\top \mathcal{C}) = \sum_i (u \cdot c_i)^2 \gamma_i$. For a mixed state $\mathcal{W}$ we have the following double expectation:

$$\mathrm{tr}(\mathcal{W}\mathcal{C}) = \mathrm{tr}\left((\sum_i \omega_i w_i w_i^\top)(\sum_j \gamma_j c_j c_j^\top) \right) = \sum_{i,j} (w_i \cdot c_j)^2 \gamma_i \omega_j,$$

where the matrix of measurement probabilities $(w_i \cdot c_j)^2$ is a doubly stochastic matrix. Note also, that for the measurement interpretation the matrix $\mathcal{C}$ does not have to be positive definite, but only symmetric. The algorithm and the proof of bounds in fact work fine for this case, but the meaning of the algorithm when $\mathcal{C}$ is not a covariance matrix is less clear, since despite all these connections our algorithm does not seem to have the obvious quantum-mechanical interpretation. Our update clearly is not a unitary evolution of the mixture state and a measurement does not cause a collapse of the state as is the case in quantum physics. The question of whether this type of algorithm is still doing something quantum-mechanically meaningful remains intriguing. See also [War05, WK06] for additional discussion.

To derive our algorithm we use the trace expression for expected variance as our loss and replace the relative entropy with its matrix generalization. The following optimization problem produces the update:

$$\mathcal{W}_{t+1} = \underset{\mathcal{W} \text{ dens.mat.}}{\arg\min} \; \Delta(\mathcal{W}, \mathcal{W}_t) + \eta \, \mathrm{tr}(\mathcal{W}\mathcal{C}_t)$$

Using a Lagrangian that enforces the trace constraint [TRW05], it is easy to solve this constrained minimization problem:

$$\mathcal{W}_{t+1} = \frac{\exp(\log \mathcal{W}_t - \eta \mathcal{C}_t)}{\mathrm{tr}(\exp(\log \mathcal{W}_t - \eta \mathcal{C}_t))} = \frac{\exp(-\eta \sum_{q=1}^{t} \mathcal{C}_q)}{\mathrm{tr}(\exp(-\eta \sum_{q=1}^{t} \mathcal{C}_q))}. \tag{1}$$

Note that for the second equation we assumed that $\mathcal{W}_1 = \frac{1}{n} I$. The update is a special case of the Matrix Exponentiated Gradient update with the linear loss $\mathrm{tr}(\mathcal{W}\mathcal{C}_t)$.

3.4   Proof Methodology

For the sake of clarity, we begin by recalling the proof of the worst-case loss bound for the Continuous Weighted Majority (WMC)/Hedge algorithm in the expert advice setting [LW94]. In doing so we clarify the dependence of the algorithm on the range of the losses. The update of that algorithm is given by:

$$w_{t+1,i} = \frac{w_{t,i}e^{-\eta l_{t,i}}}{\sum_i w_{t,i}e^{-\eta l_{t,i}}} \tag{2}$$

The proof always starts by considering the progress made during the update towards any comparison vector/parameter $\boldsymbol{u}$ in terms of the motivating divergence for the algorithm, which in this case is the relative entropy:

$$\mathrm{d}(\boldsymbol{u}, \boldsymbol{w}_t) - \mathrm{d}(\boldsymbol{u}, \boldsymbol{w}_{t+1}) = \sum_i u_i \log \frac{w_{t+1,i}}{w_{t,i}} = -\eta\,\boldsymbol{u} \cdot \boldsymbol{l}_t - \log \sum_i w_{t,i}e^{-\eta l_{t,i}}.$$

We assume that $l_{t,i} \in [0, r]$, for $r > 0$, and use the inequality $\beta^x \le 1 - (1 - \beta^r)\frac{x}{r}$, for $x \in [0, r]$, with $\beta = e^{-\eta}$:

$$\mathrm{d}(\boldsymbol{u}, \boldsymbol{w}_t) - \mathrm{d}(\boldsymbol{u}, \boldsymbol{w}_{t+1}) \ge -\eta\,\boldsymbol{u} \cdot \boldsymbol{l}_t - \log(1 - \frac{\boldsymbol{w}_t \cdot \boldsymbol{l}_t}{r}(1 - e^{-\eta r})),$$

We now apply $\log(1 - x) \le -x$:

$$\mathrm{d}(\boldsymbol{u}, \boldsymbol{w}_t) - \mathrm{d}(\boldsymbol{u}, \boldsymbol{w}_{t+1}) \ge -\eta\,\boldsymbol{u} \cdot \boldsymbol{l}_t + \frac{\boldsymbol{w}_t \cdot \boldsymbol{l}}{r}(1 - e^{-\eta r}),$$

and rewrite the above to

$$\boldsymbol{w}_t \cdot \boldsymbol{l}_t \le \frac{r(\mathrm{d}(\boldsymbol{u}, \boldsymbol{w}_t) - \mathrm{d}(\boldsymbol{u}, \boldsymbol{w}_{t+1})) + \eta r\,\boldsymbol{u} \cdot \boldsymbol{l}_t}{1 - e^{-\eta r}}$$

Here $\boldsymbol{w}_t \cdot \boldsymbol{l}_t$ is the loss of the algorithm at trial t and $\boldsymbol{u} \cdot \boldsymbol{l}_t$ is the loss of the probability vector $\boldsymbol{u}$ which serves as a comparator.

So far we assumed that $l_{t,i} \in [0, r]$. However, it suffices to assume that $\max_i l_{t,i} - \min_i l_{t,i} \le r$. In other words, the individual losses can be positive or negative, as long as their range is bounded by r. For further discussion pertaining to the issues with losses having different signs see [CBMS05]. As we shall observe below, the requirement on the range of losses will become a requirement on the range of eigenvalues of the covariance matrices.

Define $\tilde{l}_{t,i} := l_{t,i} - \min_i l_{t,i}$. The update remains unchanged when the shifted losses $\tilde{l}_{t,i}$ are used in place of the original losses $l_{t,i}$ and we immediately get the inequality

$$\boldsymbol{w}_t \cdot \tilde{\boldsymbol{l}}_t \le \frac{r(\mathrm{d}(\boldsymbol{u}, \boldsymbol{w}_t) - \mathrm{d}(\boldsymbol{u}, \boldsymbol{w}_{t+1})) + \eta r\,\boldsymbol{u} \cdot \tilde{\boldsymbol{l}}_t}{1 - e^{-\eta r}}.$$

Summing over t and dropping the $\mathrm{d}(\boldsymbol{u}, \boldsymbol{w}_{t+1}) \ge 0$ term results in a bound that holds for any $\boldsymbol{u}$ and thus for the best $\boldsymbol{u}$ as well:

$$\sum_t \boldsymbol{w}_t \cdot \tilde{\boldsymbol{l}}_t \le \frac{r\mathrm{d}(\boldsymbol{u}, \boldsymbol{w}_t) + \eta r \sum_t \boldsymbol{u} \cdot \tilde{\boldsymbol{l}}_t}{1 - e^{-\eta r}}.$$

We can now tune the learning rate following [FS97]: if $\sum_t \boldsymbol{u} \cdot \tilde{\boldsymbol{l}}_t \leq \tilde{L}$ and $\mathrm{d}(\boldsymbol{u}, \boldsymbol{w}_1) \leq D \leq \ln n$, then with $\eta = \frac{\log(1+\sqrt{2D/\tilde{L}})}{r}$ we get the bound

$$\sum_t \boldsymbol{w}_t \cdot \tilde{\boldsymbol{l}}_t \leq \sum_t \boldsymbol{u} \cdot \tilde{\boldsymbol{l}}_t + \sqrt{2r\tilde{L}D} + r\mathrm{d}(\boldsymbol{u}, \boldsymbol{w}_1),$$

which is equivalent to

$$\underbrace{\sum_t \boldsymbol{w}_t \cdot \boldsymbol{l}_t}_{L_{\mathrm{alg}}} \leq \underbrace{\sum_t \boldsymbol{u} \cdot \boldsymbol{l}_t}_{L_u} + \sqrt{2r\tilde{L}D} + r\mathrm{d}(\boldsymbol{u}, \boldsymbol{w}_1).$$

Note that $\tilde{L}$ is defined wrt the tilde versions of the losses and the update as well as the above bound is invariant under shifting the loss vectors l_t by arbitrary constants. If the loss vectors $\boldsymbol{l}_t$ are replaced by gain vectors, then the minus sign in the exponent of the update becomes a plus sign. In this case the inequality above is reversed and the last two terms are subtracted instead of added.

3.5   Proof of Relative Loss Bounds

In addition to the Golden-Thompson inequality we will need lemmas 2.1 and 2.2 from [TRW05]:

Lemma 3. *For any symmetric $\boldsymbol{A}$, such that $0 \preceq \boldsymbol{A} \preceq \boldsymbol{I}$ and any $\rho_1, \rho_2 \in \mathbb{R}$ the following holds:*

$$\exp(\boldsymbol{A}\rho_1 + (\boldsymbol{I} - \boldsymbol{A})\rho_2) \preceq \boldsymbol{A}e^{\rho_1} + (\boldsymbol{I} - \boldsymbol{A})e^{\rho_2}.$$

Lemma 4. *For any positive semidefinite $\boldsymbol{A}$ and any symmetric $\boldsymbol{B}, \boldsymbol{C}$, $\boldsymbol{B} \preceq \boldsymbol{C}$ implies $\mathrm{tr}(\boldsymbol{AB}) \leq \mathrm{tr}(\boldsymbol{AC})$.*

We are now ready to generalize the WMC bound to matrices:

Theorem 2. *For any sequence of covariance matrices $\boldsymbol{C}_1, \ldots, \boldsymbol{C}_T$ such that $0 \preceq \boldsymbol{C}_t \preceq r\boldsymbol{I}$ and for any learning rate η, the following bound holds for arbitrary density matrix $\boldsymbol{\mathcal{U}}$:*

$$\mathrm{tr}(\boldsymbol{W}_t\boldsymbol{C}_t) \leq \frac{r(\Delta(\boldsymbol{\mathcal{U}}, \boldsymbol{W}_t) - \Delta(\boldsymbol{\mathcal{U}}, \boldsymbol{W}_{t+1})) + \eta r\,\mathrm{tr}(\boldsymbol{\mathcal{U}}\boldsymbol{C}_t)}{1 - e^{-r\eta}}.$$

Proof. We start by analyzing the progress made towards the comparison matrix $\boldsymbol{\mathcal{U}}$ in terms of quantum relative entropy:

$$\begin{aligned}
\Delta(\boldsymbol{\mathcal{U}}, \boldsymbol{W}_t) - \Delta(\boldsymbol{\mathcal{U}}, \boldsymbol{W}_{t+1}) &= \mathrm{tr}(\boldsymbol{\mathcal{U}}(\log\boldsymbol{\mathcal{U}} - \log\boldsymbol{W}_t)) - \mathrm{tr}(\boldsymbol{\mathcal{U}}(\log\boldsymbol{\mathcal{U}} - \log\boldsymbol{W}_{t+1})) \\
&= -\mathrm{tr}\left(\boldsymbol{\mathcal{U}}\left(\log\boldsymbol{W}_t + \log\frac{\exp(\log\boldsymbol{W}_t - \eta\boldsymbol{C}_t)}{\mathrm{tr}(\exp(\log\boldsymbol{W}_t - \eta\boldsymbol{C}_t))}\right)\right) \\
&= -\eta\,\mathrm{tr}(\boldsymbol{\mathcal{U}}\boldsymbol{C}_t) - \log(\mathrm{tr}(\exp(\log\boldsymbol{W}_t - \eta\boldsymbol{C}_t))).
\end{aligned}$$

$$\text{(3)}$$

We will now bound the log of trace term. First, the following holds via the Golden-Thompson inequality:

$$\mathrm{tr}(\exp(\log \boldsymbol{W}_t - \eta \boldsymbol{C}_t)) \leq \mathrm{tr}(\boldsymbol{W}_t \exp(-\eta \boldsymbol{C}_t)). \tag{4}$$

Since $\boldsymbol{0} \preceq \frac{\boldsymbol{C}_t}{r} \preceq \boldsymbol{I}$, we can use Lemma 3 with $\rho_1 = -\eta r$, $\rho_2 = 0$:

$$\exp(-\eta \boldsymbol{C}_t) \preceq \boldsymbol{I} - \frac{\boldsymbol{C}_t}{r}(1 - e^{-\eta r}).$$

Now multiply both sides on the left with $\boldsymbol{W}_t$ and take a trace. The inequality is preserved according to Lemma 4:

$$\mathrm{tr}(\boldsymbol{W}_t \exp(-\eta \boldsymbol{C}_t)) \leq \left(1 - \frac{\mathrm{tr}(\boldsymbol{W}_t \boldsymbol{C}_t)}{r}(1 - e^{-r\eta})\right).$$

Taking logs of both sides we have:

$$\log(\mathrm{tr}(\boldsymbol{W}_t \exp(-\eta \boldsymbol{C}_t))) \leq \log\left(1 - \frac{\mathrm{tr}(\boldsymbol{W}_t \boldsymbol{C}_t)}{r}(1 - e^{-\eta r})\right). \tag{5}$$

To bound the log expression on the right we use inequality $\log(1-x) \leq -x$:

$$\log\left(1 - \frac{\mathrm{tr}(\boldsymbol{W}_t \boldsymbol{C}_t)}{r}(1 - e^{-r\eta})\right) \leq -\frac{\mathrm{tr}(\boldsymbol{W}_t \boldsymbol{C}_t)}{r}(1 - e^{-r\eta}). \tag{6}$$

By combining inequalities (4-6), we obtain the following bound on the log trace term:

$$-\log(\mathrm{tr}(\exp(\log \boldsymbol{W}_t - \eta \boldsymbol{C}_t))) \geq \frac{\mathrm{tr}(\boldsymbol{W}_t \boldsymbol{C}_t)}{r}(1 - e^{-r\eta}).$$

Plugging this into equation (3) we obtain

$$r(\Delta(\boldsymbol{U}, \boldsymbol{W}_t) - \Delta(\boldsymbol{U}, \boldsymbol{W}_{t+1})) + \eta r\, \mathrm{tr}(\boldsymbol{U} \boldsymbol{C}_t) \geq \mathrm{tr}(\boldsymbol{W}_t \boldsymbol{C}_t)(1 - e^{-r\eta}),$$

which is the inequality of the theorem.   □

Note the our density matrix update (1) is invariant wrt the variable change $\widetilde{\boldsymbol{C}}_t = \boldsymbol{C}_t - \lambda_{\min}(\boldsymbol{C}_t)\boldsymbol{I}$. Therefore by the above theorem, the following inequality holds whenever $\lambda_{\max}(\boldsymbol{C}_t) - \lambda_{\min}(\boldsymbol{C}_t) \leq r$:

$$\mathrm{tr}(\boldsymbol{W}_t \widetilde{\boldsymbol{C}}_t) \leq \frac{r(\Delta(\boldsymbol{U}, \boldsymbol{W}_t) - \Delta(\boldsymbol{U}, \boldsymbol{W}_{t+1})) + \eta r\, \mathrm{tr}(\boldsymbol{U} \widetilde{\boldsymbol{C}}_t)}{1 - e^{-r\eta}}.$$

We can now sum over trials and tune the learning rate as done at the end of Section 3.4. If $\sum_t \mathrm{tr}(\boldsymbol{U}\widetilde{\boldsymbol{C}}_t) \leq \tilde{L}$ and $\Delta(\boldsymbol{U}, \boldsymbol{W}_1) \leq D$, with $\eta = \frac{\log(1 + \sqrt{\frac{2D}{\tilde{L}}})}{r}$ we get the bound:

$$\underbrace{\sum_t \mathrm{tr}(\boldsymbol{W}_t \boldsymbol{C}_t)}_{L_{\mathrm{alg}}} \leq \underbrace{\sum_t \mathrm{tr}(\boldsymbol{U} \boldsymbol{C}_t)}_{L_{\boldsymbol{U}}} + \sqrt{2r\tilde{L}D} + r\Delta(\boldsymbol{U}, \boldsymbol{W}_1).$$

4   Conclusions

We presented two algorithms for online variance minimization problems. For the first problem, the variance was measured along a probability vector. It would be interesting to combine this work with the online algorithms considered in [HSSW98, Cov91] that maximize the return of the portfolio. It should be possible to design online algorithms that minimize a trade off between the return of the portfolio (first order information) and the variance/risk. Note that it is easy to extend the portfolio vector to maintain short positions: Simply keep two weights w_i^+ and w_i^- per component as is done in the $EG^{\pm}$ algorithm of [KW97].

In our second problem the variance was measured along an arbitrary direction. We gave a natural generalization of the WMC/Hedge algorithm to the case when the parameters are density matrices. Note that in this paper we upper bounded the sum of the expected variances over trials, whereas in [War05, WK06] a Bayes rule for density matrices was given for which a lower bound was provided on the product of the expected variances over trials.[2]

Much work has been done on exponential weight updates for the experts. In particular, algorithms have been developed for shifting experts by combining the exponential updates with an additive "sharing update"[HW98]. In preliminary work we showed that these techniques easily carry over to the density matrix setting. This includes the more recent work on the "sharing to the past average" update, which introduces a long-term memory [BW02].

Appendix A

Proof of Lemma 1

Begin by analyzing the progress towards the comparison vector $\boldsymbol{u}$:

$$
\begin{aligned}
d(\boldsymbol{u}, \boldsymbol{w}_t) - d(\boldsymbol{u}, \boldsymbol{w}_{t+1}) &= \sum u_i \log \frac{u_i}{w_{t,i}} - \sum u_i \log \frac{u_i}{w_{t+1,i}} \\
&= \sum u_i \log w_{t+1,i} - \sum u_i \log w_{t,i} \\
&= \sum u_i \log \frac{w_{t,i} e^{-\eta(\boldsymbol{C}_t \boldsymbol{w}_t)_i}}{\sum w_{t,i} e^{-\eta(\boldsymbol{C}_t \boldsymbol{w}_t)_i}} - \sum u_i \log w_{t,i} \\
&= \sum u_i \log w_{t,i} - \eta \sum u_i (\boldsymbol{C}_t \boldsymbol{w}_t)_i - \\
&\quad - \log \left(\sum w_{t,i} e^{-\eta(\boldsymbol{C}_t \boldsymbol{w}_t)_i} \right) - \sum u_i \log w_{t,i} \\
&= -\eta \sum u_i (\boldsymbol{C}_t \boldsymbol{w}_t)_i - \log \left(\sum w_{t,i} e^{-\eta(\boldsymbol{C}_t \boldsymbol{w}_t)_i} \right)
\end{aligned}
$$

Thus, our bound is equivalent to showing $F \leq 0$ with F given as:

$$
F = a \boldsymbol{w}_t^\top \boldsymbol{C}_t \boldsymbol{w}_t - b \boldsymbol{u}^\top \boldsymbol{C} \boldsymbol{u} + \eta \boldsymbol{u}^\top \boldsymbol{C} \boldsymbol{w}_t + \log \left(\sum w_{t,i} e^{-\eta(\boldsymbol{C}_t \boldsymbol{w}_t)_i} \right)
$$

---

[2] This amounts to an upper bound on the sum of the negative logarithms of the expected variances.

We proceed by bounding the log term. The assumption on the range of elements of C_t and the fact that w_t is a probability vector allows us to conclude that $\max_i(C_t w_t)_i - \min_i(C_t w_t)_i \leq r$, since $(C_t w_t)_i = \sum_j C_t(i,j) w_t(j)$. Now, assume that l is a lower bound for $(C_t w_t)_i$, then we have that $l \leq (C_t w_t)_i \leq l + r$, or $0 \leq \frac{(C_t w_t)_i - l}{r} \leq 1$. This allows us to use the inequality $a^x \leq 1 - x(1 - a)$ for $a \geq 0$ and $0 \leq x \leq 1$. Let $a = e^{-\eta r}$:

$$e^{-\eta(C_t w_t)_i} = e^{-\eta l}(e^{-\eta r})^{\frac{(C_t w_t)_i - l}{r}} \leq e^{-\eta b}\left(1 - \frac{(C_t w_t)_i - l}{r}(1 - e^{-\eta r})\right)$$

Using this inequality we obtain:

$$\log\left(\sum w_{t,i} e^{-\eta(C_t w_t)_i}\right) \leq -\eta l + \log\left(1 - \frac{w_t^\top C_t w_t - l}{r}(1 - e^{-\eta r})\right)$$

This gives us $F \leq G$, with G given as:

$$G = a w_t^\top C_t w_t - b u^\top C_t u + \eta u^\top C w_t - \eta l + \log\left(1 - \frac{w_t^\top C_t w_t - l}{r}(1 - e^{-\eta r})\right)$$

It is sufficient to show that $G \leq 0$. Let $z = \sqrt{C_t} u$. Then $G(z)$ becomes:

$$G(z) = -b z^\top z + \eta z^\top \sqrt{C_t} w_t + \text{constant}.$$

The function $G(z)$ is concave quadratic and is maximized at:

$$\frac{\partial G}{\partial z} = -2bz + \eta \sqrt{C_t} w_t = 0, \quad z = \frac{\eta}{2b}\sqrt{C_t} w_t$$

We substitute this value of z into G and get $G \leq H$, where H is given by:

$$H = a w_t^\top C_t w_t + \frac{\eta^2}{4b} w_t^\top C_t w_t - \eta l + \log\left(1 - \frac{w_t^\top C_t w_t - l}{r}(1 - e^{-\eta r})\right).$$

Since $l \leq (C_t w_t)_i \leq l + r$, then obviously so is $w_t^\top C_t w_t$, since weighted average stays within the bounds. Now we can use the inequality $\log(1 - p(1 - e^q)) \leq pq + \frac{q^2}{8}$, for $0 \leq p \leq 1$ and $q \in \mathbb{R}$:

$$\log\left(1 - \frac{w_t^\top C_t w_t - l}{r}(1 - e^{-\eta r})\right) \leq -\eta w_t^\top C_t w_t + \eta l + \frac{\eta^2 r^2}{8}.$$

We get $H \leq S$, where S is given as:

$$S = a w_t^\top C_t w_t + \frac{\eta^2}{4b} w_t^\top C_t w_t - \eta w_t^\top C_t w_t + \frac{\eta^2 r^2}{8}$$

$$= \frac{w_t^\top C_t w_t}{4b}(4ab + \eta^2 - 4b\eta) + \frac{\eta^2 r^2}{8}.$$

By our assumptions $w_t^\top C_t w_t \leq \frac{r}{2}$, and therefore:

$$S \leq Q = \eta^2\left(\frac{r^2}{8} + \frac{r}{8b}\right) - \frac{\eta r}{2} + \frac{ar}{2}$$

We want to make this expression as small as possible, so that it stays below zero. To do so we minimize it over η:

$$2\eta(\frac{r^2}{8} + \frac{r}{8b}) - \frac{r}{2} = 0, \quad \eta = \frac{2b}{rb+1}$$

Finally we substitute this value of η into Q and obtain conditions on a, so that $Q \leq 0$ holds:

$$a \leq \frac{b}{rb+1}$$

This concludes the proof.   □

References

[BV04]   Stephen Boyd and Lieven Vandenberghe. *Convex Optimization*. Cambridge University Press, 2004.
[BW02]   O. Bousquet and M. K. Warmuth. Tracking a small set of experts by mixing past posteriors. *J. of Machine Learning Research*, 3(Nov):363–396, 2002.
[CBMS05]   Nicolo Cesa-Bianchi, Yishay Mansour, and Gilles Stoltz. Improved second-order bounds for prediction with expert advice. In *Proceedings of the 18th Annual Conference on Learning Theory (COLT 05)*, pages 217–232. Springer, June 2005.
[Cov91]   T. M. Cover. Universal portfolios. *Mathematical Finance*, 1(1):1–29, 1991.
[CSTK01]   Nello Cristianini, John Shawe-Taylor, and Jaz Kandola. Spectral kernel methods for clustering. In *Advances in Neural Information Processing Systems 14*, pages 649–655. MIT Press, December 2001.
[FS97]   Yoav Freund and Robert E. Schapire. A decision-theoretic generalization of on-line learning and an application to boosting. *Journal of Computer and System Sciences*, 55(1):119–139, August 1997.
[HSSW98]   D. Helmbold, R. E. Schapire, Y. Singer, and M. K. Warmuth. On-line portfolio selection using multiplicative updates. *Mathematical Finance*, 8(4):325–347, 1998.
[HW98]   M. Herbster and M. K. Warmuth. Tracking the best expert. *Journal of Machine Learning*, 32(2):151–178, August 1998.
[KW97]   J. Kivinen and M. K. Warmuth. Additive versus exponentiated gradient updates for linear prediction. *Information and Computation*, 132(1):1–64, January 1997.
[LW94]   N. Littlestone and M. K. Warmuth. The weighted majority algorithm. *Information and Computation*, 108(2):212–261, 1994.
[NC00]   M.A. Nielsen and I.L. Chuang. *Quantum Computation and Quantum Information*. Cambridge University Press, 2000.
[TRW05]   K. Tsuda, G. Rätsch, and M. K. Warmuth. Matrix exponentiated gradient updates for on-line learning and Bregman projections. *Journal of Machine Learning Research*, 6:995–1018, June 2005.
[War05]   Manred K. Warmuth. Bayes rule for density matrices. In *Advances in Neural Information Processing Systems 18 (NIPS 05)*. MIT Press, December 2005.
[WK06]   Manfred K. Warmuth and Dima Kuzmin. A Bayesian probability calculus for density matrices. Unpublished manuscript, March 2006.

Online Learning with Constraints

Shie Mannor[1] and John N. Tsitsiklis[2]

[1] Department of Electrical and Computer Engingeering
McGill University, Québec H3A-2A7
shie@ece.mcgill.ca
[2] Laboratory for Information and Decision Systems
Massachusetts Institute of Technology, Cambridge, MA 02139
jnt@mit.edu

Abstract. We study online learning where the objective of the decision maker is to maximize her average long-term reward given that some average constraints are satisfied along the sample path. We define the reward-in-hindsight as the highest reward the decision maker could have achieved, while satisfying the constraints, had she known Nature's choices in advance. We show that in general the reward-in-hindsight is *not* attainable. The convex hull of the reward-in-hindsight function is, however, attainable. For the important case of a single constraint the convex hull turns out to be the highest attainable function. We further provide an explicit strategy that attains this convex hull using a calibrated forecasting rule.

1 Introduction

We consider a repeated game from the viewpoint of a specific decision maker (player P1), who plays against Nature (player P2). The opponent (Nature) is "arbitrary" in the sense that player P1 has no prediction, statistical or strategic, regarding the opponent's choice of actions. This setting was considered by Hannan [1], in the context of repeated matrix games. Hannan introduced the Bayes utility against the current empirical distribution of the opponent's actions, as a performance goal for adaptive play. This quantity is the highest average reward that player P1 could achieve, in hindsight, by playing some fixed action against the observed action sequence of player P2. Player P1's *regret* is defined as the difference between the highest average reward-in-hindsight that player P1 could have hypothetically achieved, and the actual average reward obtained by player P1. It was established in [1] that there exist strategies whose regret converges to zero as the number of stages increases, even in the absence of any prior knowledge on the strategy of player P2.

In this paper we consider regret minimization under sample-path constraints. That is, in addition to maximizing the reward, or more precisely, minimizing the regret, the decision maker has some side constraints that need to be satisfied on the average. In particular, for every joint action of the players, there is an additional penalty vector that is accumulated by the decision maker. The decision maker has a predefined set in the space of penalty vectors, which represents the acceptable tradeoffs between the different components of the penalty

G. Lugosi and H.U. Simon (Eds.): COLT 2006, LNAI 4005, pp. 529–543, 2006.

vector. An important special case arises when the decision maker wishes to keep some constrained resource below a certain threshold. Consider, for example, a wireless communication system where the decision maker can adjust the transmission power to improve the probability that a message is received successfully. Of course, the decision maker does not know a priori how much power will be needed (this depends on the behavior of other users, the weather, etc.). The decision maker may be interested in the rate of successful transmissions, while minimizing the average power consumption. In an often considered variation of this problem, the decision maker wishes to maximize the transmission rate, while keeping the average power consumption below some predefined threshold. We refer the reader to [2] and references therein for a discussion on constrained average cost stochastic games and to [3] for constrained Markov decision problems.

The paper is organized as follows. In Section 2, we present formally the basic model, and provide a result that relates attainability and the value of the game. In Section 3, we provide an example where the reward-in-hindsight cannot be attained. In light of this negative result, in Section 4 we define the closed convex hull of the reward-in-hindsight, and show that it is attainable. Furthermore, in Section 5, we show that when there is a single constraint, this is the maximal attainable objective. Finally, in Section 6, we provide a simple strategy, based on calibrated forecasting, that attains the convex hull.

2   Problem Definition

We consider a repeated game against Nature, in which a decision maker tries to maximize her reward, while satisfying some constraints on certain time-averages. The stage game is a game with two players: P1 (the decision maker of interest) and P2 (who represents Nature and is assumed arbitrary). In this context, we only need to define rewards and constraints for P1.

A constrained game with respect to a set T is defined by a tuple (A, B, R, C, T) where:

1. A is the set of actions of P1; we will assume $A = \{1, 2, \ldots, |A|\}$.
2. B is the set of actions of P2; we will assume $B = \{1, 2, \ldots, |B|\}$.
3. R is an $|A| \times |B|$ matrix where the entry $R(a, b)$ denotes the expected reward obtained by P1, when P1 plays action $a \in A$ and P2 action $b \in B$. The actual rewards obtained at each play of actions a and b are assumed to be IID random variables, with finite second moments, distributed according to a probability law $\Pr_R(\cdot \mid a, b)$. Furthermore, the reward streams for different pairs (a, b) are statistically independent.
4. C is an $|A| \times |B|$ matrix, where the entry $C(a, b)$ denotes the expected d-dimensional penalty vector accumulated by P1, when P1 plays action $a \in A$ and P2 action $b \in B$. The actual penalty vectors obtained at each play of actions a and b are assumed to be IID random variables, with finite second moments, distributed according to a probability law $\Pr_C(\cdot \mid a, b)$. Furthermore, the penalty vector streams for different pairs (a, b) are statistically independent.

5. T is a set in $\mathbb{R}^d$ within which we wish the average of the penalty vectors to lie. We shall assume that T is convex and closed. Since C is bounded, we will also assume, without loss of generality that T is bounded.

The game is played in stages. At each stage t, P1 and P2 simultaneously choose actions $a_t \in A$ and $b_t \in B$, respectively. Player P1 obtains a reward r_t, distributed according to $\Pr_R(\cdot \mid a_t, b_t)$, and a penalty c_t, distributed according to $\Pr_C(\cdot \mid a_t, b_t)$. We define P1's average reward by time t to be

$$\hat{r}_t = \frac{1}{t}\sum_{\tau=1}^{t} r_\tau, \qquad (2.1)$$

and P1's average penalty vector by time t to be

$$\hat{c}_t = \frac{1}{t}\sum_{\tau=1}^{t} c_\tau. \qquad (2.2)$$

A strategy for P1 (resp. P2) is a mapping from the set of all possible past histories to the set of mixed actions on A (resp. B), which prescribes the (mixed) action of that player at each time t, as a function of the history in the first $t-1$ stages. Loosely, P1's goal is to maximize the average reward while keeping the average penalty vector in T, pathwise:

$$\text{for every } \epsilon > 0, \quad \Pr(\text{dist}(\hat{c}_t, T) > \epsilon \text{ infinitely often}) = 0, \qquad (2.3)$$

where $\text{dist}(\cdot)$ is the point-to-set Euclidean distance, i.e., $\text{dist}(x, T) = \inf_{y \in T} \|y - x\|_2$, and the probability measure is the one induced by the policy of P1, the policy of P2, and the randomness in the rewards and penalties.

We will often consider the important special case of $T = \{c \in \mathbb{R}^d : c \leq c_0\}$. We simply call such a game a constrained game with respect to (a vector) c_0. For that special case, the requirement (2.3) is equivalent to:

$$\limsup_{t \to \infty} \hat{c}_t \leq c_0, \quad \text{a.s.},$$

where the inequality is interpreted componentwise.

For a set D, we will use the notation $\Delta(D)$ to denote the set of all probability measures on D. If D is finite, we will identify $\Delta(D)$ with the set of probability vectors of the same size as D. (If D is a subset of Euclidean space, we will assume that it is endowed with the Borel σ-field.)

2.1 Reward-in-Hindsight

We define $\hat{q}_t \in \Delta(B)$ as the empirical distribution of P2's actions by time t, that is,

$$\hat{q}_t(b) = \frac{1}{t}\sum_{\tau=1}^{t} 1_{\{b_t=b\}}, \quad b \in B. \qquad (2.4)$$

If P1 knew in advance that $\hat{q}_t$ will equal q, and if P1 were restricted to using a fixed action, then P1 would pick an optimal response (generally a mixed action) to the mixed action q, subject to the constraints specified by T. In particular, P1 would solve the convex program[1]

$$\max_{p \in \Delta(A)} \sum_{a,b} p(a)q(b)R(a,b), \tag{2.5}$$

$$\text{s.t.} \sum_{a,b} p(a)q(b)C(a,b) \in T.$$

By playing a p that solves this convex program, P1 would meet the constraints (up to small fluctuations that are a result of the randomness and the finiteness of t), and would obtain the maximal average reward. We are thus led to define P1's reward-in-hindsight, which we denote by $r^* : \Delta(B) \mapsto \mathbb{R}$, as the optimal objective value in the program (2.5).

In case of a constrained game with respect to a vector c_0, the convex constraint $\sum_{a,b} p(a)q(b)C(a,b) \in T$ is replaced by $\sum_{a,b} p(a)q(b)C(a,b) \le c_0$ (the inequality is to be interpreted componentwise).

2.2   The Objective

Formally, our goal is to attain a function r in the sense of the following definition. Naturally, the higher the function r, the better.

Definition 1. *A function* $r : \Delta(B) \mapsto \mathbb{R}$ *is* attainable *by P1 in a constrained game with respect to a set* T *if there exists a strategy* σ *of P1 such that for every strategy* ρ *of P2:*

(i) $\liminf_{t \to \infty}(\hat{r}_t - r(\hat{q}_t)) \ge 0$,   *a.s., and*
(ii) $\limsup_{t \to \infty} \text{dist}(\hat{c}_t, T) \to 0$,   *a.s.,*

where the almost sure convergence is with respect to the probability measure induced by σ *and* ρ.

In constrained games with respect to a vector c_0 we can replace (ii) in the definition with

$$\limsup_{t \to \infty} \hat{c}_t \le c_0, \quad \text{a.s.}$$

2.3   The Value of the Game

In this section, we consider the attainability of a function $r : \Delta(B) \mapsto \mathbb{R}$, which is constant, $r(q) = \alpha$, for all q. We will establish that attainability is equivalent to having $\alpha \le v$, where v is a naturally defined "value of the constrained game."

We first introduce that assumption that P1 is always able to satisfy the constraint.

---

[1] If T is a polyhedron (specified by finitely many linear inequalities), then the optimization problem is a linear program.

Assumption 1. *For every mixed action $q \in \Delta(B)$ of P2, there exists a mixed action $p \in \Delta(A)$ of P1, such that:*

$$\sum_{a,b} p(a)q(b)C(a,b) \in T. \tag{2.6}$$

For constrained games with respect to a vector c_0, the condition (2.6) reduces to the inequality $\sum_{a,b} p(a)q(b)C(a,b) \leq c_0$.

If Assumption 1 is not satisfied, then P2 can choose a q such that for every (mixed) action of P1, the constraint is violated in expectation. By repeatedly playing this q, P1's average penalty vector is outside T.

The following result deals with the attainability of the value, v, of an average reward repeated constrained game, defined by

$$v = \inf_{q \in \Delta(B)} \sup_{p \in \Delta(A), \sum_{a,b} p(a)q(b)C(a,b) \in T} \sum_{a,b} p(a)q(b)R(a,b). \tag{2.7}$$

The existence of a strategy for P1 that attains the value was proven in [4] in the broader context of stochastic games.

Proposition 1. *Suppose that Assumption 1 holds. Then,*

(i) *P1 has a strategy that guarantees that the constant function $r(q) \equiv v$ is attained with respect to T.*

(ii) *For every number $v' > v$ there exists $\delta > 0$ such that P2 has a strategy that guarantees that either $\liminf_{t \to \infty} \hat{r}_t < v'$ or $\limsup_{t \to \infty} \text{dist}(\hat{c}_t, T) > \delta$, almost surely. (In particular, the constant function v' is not attainable.)*

Proof. The proof relies on Blackwell's approachability theory (see [5]). We construct a nested sequence of convex sets in $\mathbb{R}^{d+1}$ denoted by $S_\alpha = \{(r, c) \in \mathbb{R} \times \mathbb{R}^d : r \geq \alpha, c \in T\}$. Obviously, $S_\alpha \subset S_\beta$ for $\alpha > \beta$. Consider the vector-valued game in $\mathbb{R}^{d+1}$ associated with the constrained game. In this game P1's payoff at time t is the $d + 1$ dimensional vector $m_t = (r_t, c_t)$ and P1's average vector-valued payoff is $\hat{m}_t = (\hat{r}_t, \hat{c}_t)$. Since S_α is convex, it follows from approachability theory for convex sets [5] that every S_α is either approachable or excludable. If S_α is approachable, then S_β is approachable for every $\beta < \alpha$. We define $v_0 = \sup\{\beta \mid S_\beta \text{ is approachable}\}$. It follows that S_{v_0} is approachable (as the limit of approachable sets; see [6]). By Blackwell's theorem, for every $q \in \Delta(B)$, an approachable convex set must intersect the set of feasible payoff vectors when P2 plays q. Using this fact, it is easily shown that v_0 equals v, as defined by Eq. (2.7), and part (i) follows. Part (ii) follows because a convex set which is not approachable is excludable. $\qquad\square$

Note that part (ii) of the proposition implies that, essentially, v is the highest average reward P1 can attain while satisfying the constraints, if P2 plays an adversarial strategy. By comparing Eq. (2.7) with Eq. (2.5), we see that $v = \inf_q r^*(q)$.

Remark 1. We note in order to attain the value of the game, P1 may have to use a non-stationary strategy. This is in contrast to standard (non-constrained) games, in which P1 always has an optimal stationary strategy that attains the value of the game.

Remark 2. In general, the infimum and supremum in (2.7) *cannot* be interchanged. This is because the set of feasible p in the inner maximization depends on the value of q. Moreover, it can be shown that the set of (p, q) pairs that satisfy the constraint $\sum_{a,b} p(a)q(b)C(a, b) \in T$ is not necessarily convex.

3   Reward-in-Hindsight Is Not Attainable

As it turns out the reward-in-hindsight cannot be attained in general. This is demonstrated by the following simple 2×2 matrix game, with just a single constraint.

Consider a 2×2 constrained game specified by:

$$
\begin{pmatrix}
(1, -1) & (1, 1) \\
(0, -1) & (-1, -1)
\end{pmatrix},
$$

where each entry (pair) corresponds to $(R(a, b), C(a, b))$ for a pair of actions a and b. At a typical stage, P1 chooses a row, and P2 chooses a column. We set $c_0 = 0$. Let q denote the frequency with which P2 chooses the second column. The reward of the first row dominates the reward of the second one, so if the constraint can be satisfied, P1 would prefer to choose the first row. This can be done as long as $0 \leq q \leq 1/2$, in which case $r^*(q) = 1$. For $1/2 \leq q \leq 1$, player P1 needs to optimize the reward subject to the constraint. Given a specific q, P1 will try to choose a mixed action that satisfies the constraint while maximizing the reward. If we let α denote the frequency of choosing the first row, we see that the reward and penalty are:

$$
r(\alpha) = \alpha - (1 - \alpha)q \; ; \quad c(\alpha) = 2\alpha q - 1.
$$

We observe that for every q, $r(\alpha)$ and $c(\alpha)$ are monotonically increasing functions of α. As a result, P1 will choose the maximal α that satisfies $c(\alpha) \leq 0$, which is $\alpha(q) = 1/2q$, and the optimal reward is $1/2 + 1/2q - q$. We conclude that the reward-in-hindsight is:

$$
r^*(q) = \begin{cases}
1, & \text{if } 0 \leq q \leq 1/2, \\
\dfrac{1}{2} + \dfrac{1}{2q} - q, & \text{if } 1/2 \leq q \leq 1.
\end{cases}
$$

The graph of $r^*(q)$ is the thick line in Figure 1.

We now claim that P2 can make sure that P1 does not attain $r^*(q)$.

Proposition 2. *If $c_0 = 0$, then there exists a strategy for P2 such that $r^*(q)$ cannot be attained.*

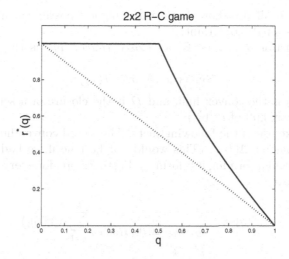

Fig. 1. The reward-in-hindsight of the constrained game. Here, $r^*(q)$ is the bold thick line, and the dotted line connects the two extreme values, for $q = 0$ and $q = 1$.

Proof. (Outline) Suppose that P2 starts by playing the second column for some long time τ. At time τ, P2's empirical frequency of choosing the second column is $\hat{q}_\tau = 1$. As computed before, $r^*(\hat{q}_\tau) = 0$. Since P1 tries to satisfy $\hat{c}_\tau \leq 0$, and also have the average reward by time τ as high as $r^*(\hat{q}_\tau)$, P1 must choose both rows with equal probability and obtain a reward of $\hat{r}_\tau = 0$, which equals $r^*(\hat{q}_\tau)$. This is essentially the best that can be achieved (neglecting negligible effects of order $1/\tau$). In the next τ time stages, P2 plays the first column. The empirical frequency of P2 at time 2τ is $\hat{q}_{2\tau} = 1/2$. During these last τ periods, P1 can choose the first row and achieve a reward of 1 (which is the best possible), and also satisfy the constraint. In that case, $\hat{r}_{2\tau} \leq 1/2$, while $r^*(\hat{q}_{2\tau}) = 1$. Player P2 can then repeat the same strategy, but replacing τ with some τ' which is much bigger than τ (so that the first 2τ stages are negligible). $\qquad\square$

Using the strategy that was described above, P2 essentially forces P1 to traverse the dotted line in Fig. 1. It so happens that $r^*(q)$ is not convex, and the dotted line is below $r^*(q)$ which precludes P1 from attaining $r^*(q)$. We note that the choice of c_0 is critical in this example. With other choices of c_0 (for example, $c_0 = -1$), the reward-in-hindsight may be attainable.

4   Attainability of the Convex Hull

Since the reward-in-hindsight is not attainable in general, we have to look for a more modest objective. More specifically, we look for functions $f : \Delta(B) \to \mathbb{R}$ that are attainable with respect to a given constraint set T. As a target we suggest the closed convex hull of the reward-in-hindsight, r^*. After defining it, we prove that it is indeed attainable with respect to the constraint set. In the next section, we will also show that it is the highest possible attainable function, when there is a single constraint.

Given a function $f : X \mapsto \mathbb{R}$, its *closed convex hull* is the function whose epigraph is

$$\overline{\mathrm{conv}}(\{(x,r) : r \geq f(x)\}),$$

where $\mathrm{conv}(D)$ is the convex hull, and $\overline{D}$ is the closure of a set D. We denote the closed convex hull of r^* by r^c.

We will make use of the following facts. The closed convex hull is guaranteed to be continuous on $\Delta(B)$. (This would not be true if we had considered the convex hull, without forming its closure.) Furthermore, for every q in the interior of $\Delta(B)$, we have

$$r^c(q) = \inf_{q_1, q_2, \ldots, q_k \in \Delta(B), \alpha_1, \ldots, \alpha_k} \sum_{i=1}^{k} \alpha_i r^*(q_i) \tag{4.8}$$

$$\text{s.t.} \quad \sum_{i=1}^{k} \alpha_i q_i(b) = q(b), \quad b \in B,$$

$$\alpha_i \geq 0, \quad i = 1, 2, \ldots, k,$$

$$\sum_{i=1}^{k} \alpha_i = 1,$$

where k can be taken equal to $|B| + 2$ by Caratheodory's Theorem.

The following result is proved using Blackwell's approachability theory. The technique is similar to that used in other no-regret proofs (e.g., [7,8]), and is based on the convexity of a target set that resides in an appropriately defined space.

Theorem 1. *Let Assumption 1 hold with respect to some convex set $T \subset \mathbb{R}^d$. Then r^c is attainable with respect to T.*

Proof. Define the following game with vector-valued payoffs, where the payoffs belong to $\mathbb{R} \times \mathbb{R}^d \times \Delta(B)$ (a $|B| + d + 1$ dimensional space which we denote by $\mathcal{M}$). Suppose that P1 plays a_t, P2 plays b_t, P1 obtains an immediate reward of r_t and an immediate penalty vector of c_t. Then, the vector-valued payoff obtained by P1 is

$$m_t = (r_t, c_t, e(b_t)),$$

where $e(b)$ is a vector of zeroes, except for a 1 in the bth location. It follows that the average vector-valued reward at time t, which we denote by $\hat{m}_t = \frac{1}{t} \sum_{\tau=1}^{t} m_\tau$, satisfies: $\hat{m}_t = (\hat{r}_t, \hat{c}_t, \hat{q}_t)$ (where $\hat{r}_t$, $\hat{c}_t$, and $\hat{q}_t$ were defined in Eqs. (2.1), (2.2), and (2.4), respectively). Consider the sets:

$$\mathcal{B}_1 = \{(r, c, q) \in \mathcal{M} : r \geq r^c(q)\}, \qquad \mathcal{B}_2 = \{(r, c, q) \in \mathcal{M} : c \in T\},$$

and let $\mathcal{B} = \mathcal{B}_1 \cap \mathcal{B}_2$. Note that $\mathcal{B}$ is a convex set. We claim that $\mathcal{B}$ is approachable. Let $m : \Delta(A) \times \Delta(B) \to \mathcal{M}$ describe the expected payoff in a one shot game, when P1 and P2 choose actions p and q, respectively. That is,

$$m(p,q) = \left(\sum_{a,b} p(a)q(b)R(a,b), \ \sum_{a,b} p(a)q(b)C(a,b), \ q \right).$$

Using the sufficient condition for approachability of convex sets ([5]), it suffices to show that for every q there exists a p such that $m(p,q) \in \mathcal{B}$. Fix $q \in \Delta(B)$. By Assumption 1, the constraint $\sum_{a,b} p(a)q(b)C(a,b) \in T$ is feasible, which implies that the program (2.5) has an optimal solution p^*. It follows that $m(p^*,q) \in \mathcal{B}$. We now claim that a strategy that approaches $\mathcal{B}$ also attains r^c in the sense of Definition 1. Indeed, since $\mathcal{B} \subseteq \mathcal{B}_2$ we have that $\Pr(d(c_t, T) > \epsilon$ infinitely often$) = 0$ for every $\epsilon > 0$. Since $\mathcal{B} \subseteq \mathcal{B}_1$ and using the continuity of r^c, we obtain $\liminf (\hat{r}_t - r^c(\hat{q}_t)) \geq 0$. □

Remark 3. Convergence rate results also follow from general approachability theory, and are generally of the order of $t^{-1/3}$; see [9]. It may be possible, perhaps, to improve upon this rate (and obtain $t^{-1/2}$ as in the non-constrained case), but this is beyond the scope of this paper.

Remark 4. For every $q \in \Delta(B)$, we have $r^*(q) \geq \mathrm{v}$, which implies that $r^c(q) \geq \mathrm{v}$. Thus, attaining r^c guarantees an average reward at least as high as the value of the game.

4.1 Degenerate Cases

In this section we consider the degenerate cases where the penalty vector is affected by only one of the players. We start with the case where P1 alone affects the penalty vector, and then discuss the case where P2 alone affects the penalty vector.

If P1 alone affects the penalty vector, that is, if $C(a,b) = C(a,b')$ for all $a \in A$ and $b, b' \in B$, then $r^*(q)$ is convex. Indeed, in this case Eq. (2.5) becomes (writing $C(a)$ for $C(a,b)$)

$$r^*(q) = \max_{p \in \Delta(A): \sum_a p(a)C(a) \in T} \sum_{a,b} p(a)q(b)R(a,b),$$

which is the maximum of a collection of linear functions of q (one function for each feasible p), and is therefore convex.

If P2 alone affects the penalty vector, then Assumption 1 implies that the constraint is always satisfied. Therefore,

$$r^*(q) = \max_{p \in \Delta(A)} \sum_{a,b} p(a)q(b)R(a,b),$$

which is again a maximum of linear functions, hence convex.

We observe that in both degenerate cases, if Assumption 1 holds, then the reward-in-hindsight is attainable.

5   Tightness of the Convex Hull

We now show that r^c is the maximal attainable function, for the case of a single constraint.

Theorem 2. *Suppose that $d = 1$, T is of the form $T = \{c \mid c \leq c_0\}$, where c_0 is a given scalar, and that Assumption 1 is satisfied. Let $\tilde{r}(q) : \Delta(B) \mapsto \mathbb{R}$ be an attainable continuous function with respect to the scalar c_0. Then, $r^c(q) \geq \tilde{r}(q)$ for all $q \in \Delta(B)$.*

Proof. The proof is constructive, as it provides a concrete strategy for P2, which prevents P1 from attaining $\tilde{r}$, unless $r^c(q) \geq \tilde{r}(q)$ for every q. Assume, in order to derive a contradiction, that there exists some $\tilde{r}$ that violates the theorem. Since $\tilde{r}$ and r^c are continuous, there exists some $q^0 \in \Delta(B)$ and some $\epsilon > 0$ such that $\tilde{r}(q) > r^c(q) + \epsilon$ for all q in an open neighborhood of q^0. In particular, q^0 can be taken to lie in the interior of $\Delta(B)$. Using Eq. (4.8), it follows that there exist $q^1, \ldots, q^k \in \Delta(B)$ and $\alpha_1, \ldots, \alpha_k$ (with $k \leq |B| + 2$) such that

$$\sum_{i=1}^{k} \alpha_i r^*(q^i) \leq r^c(q^0) + \frac{\epsilon}{2} < \tilde{r}(q^0) - \frac{\epsilon}{2};$$

$$\sum_{i=1}^{k} \alpha_i q^i(b) = q^0(b), \quad \forall\, b \in B; \qquad \sum_{i=1}^{k} \alpha_i = 1; \qquad \alpha_i \geq 0, \ \forall\, i.$$

Let τ be a large number (τ is to be chosen large enough to ensure that the events of interest occur with high probability, etc.). We will show that if P2 plays each q^i for $\alpha_i \tau$ time steps, in an appropriate order, then either P1 does not satisfy the constraint along the way or $\hat{r}_\tau \leq \tilde{r}(\hat{q}_\tau) - \epsilon/2$.

For $i = 1, \ldots, k$, we define a function $f_i : \mathbb{R}^d \to \mathbb{R} \cup \{-\infty\}$, by letting $f_i(c)$ be the maximum of

$$\sum_{a,b} p(a) q^i(b) R(a, b),$$

subject to

$$p \in \Delta(A), \qquad \text{and} \qquad \sum_{a,b} p(a) q^i(b) C(a, b) \leq c,$$

where the maximum over an empty set is defined to equal $-\infty$. We note that $f_i(c)$ is piecewise linear, concave, and nondecreasing in c. Furthermore, $f_i(c_0) = r^*(q^i)$. Let f_i^+ be the right directional derivative of f_i at $c = c_0$. From now on, we assume that the q^i have been ordered so that the sequence f_i^+ is non-increasing.

Suppose that P1 knows the sequence $q^1, \ldots, q^k$ (ordered as above) in advance, and that P2 will be following the strategy described earlier. We assume that τ is large enough so that we can ignore the effects of dealing with a finite sample, or of $\alpha_i \tau$ not being an integer. We allow P1 to choose any sequence of $p^1, \ldots, p^k$, and introduce the constraints

$$\sum_{i=1}^{\ell} \alpha_i \sum_{a,b} p^i(a) q^i(b) C(a, b) \leq c_0 \sum_{i=1}^{\ell} \alpha_i, \quad \ell = 1, 2, \ldots, k.$$

These constraints are required in order to guarantee that $\hat{c}_t$ has negligible probability of substantially exceeding c_0, at the "switching" times from one mixed action to another. If P1 exploits the knowledge of P2's strategy to maximize her average reward at time τ, the resulting expected average reward at time τ will be the optimal value of the objective function in the following linear programming problem:

$$\max_{p^1, p^2, \ldots, p^k} \sum_{i=1}^{k} \alpha_i \sum_{a,b} p^i(a) q^i(b) R(a,b)$$

$$\text{s.t.} \sum_{i=1}^{\ell} \alpha_i \sum_{a,b} p^i(a) q^i(b) C(a,b) \leq c_0 \sum_{i=1}^{\ell} \alpha_i, \quad \ell = 1, 2, \ldots, k, \qquad (5.9)$$

$$p^\ell \in \Delta(A), \quad \ell = 1, 2, \ldots, k.$$

Of course, given the value of $\sum_{a,b} p^i(a) q^i(b) C(a,b)$, to be denoted by c_i, player P1 should choose a p^i that maximizes rewards, resulting in $\sum_{a,b} p^i(a) q^i(b) R(a,b) = f_i(c_i)$. Thus, the above problem can be rewritten as

$$\max_{c_1, \ldots, c_k} \sum \alpha_i f_i(c_i)$$

$$\text{s.t.} \sum_{i=1}^{\ell} \alpha_i c_i \leq c_0 \sum_{i=1}^{\ell} \alpha_i, \quad \ell = 1, 2, \ldots, k. \qquad (5.10)$$

We claim that letting $c_i = c_0$, for all i, is an optimal solution to the problem (5.10). This will then imply that the optimal value of the objective function for the problem (5.9) is $\sum_{i=1}^{k} \alpha_i f_i(c_0)$, which equals $\sum_{i=1}^{k} \alpha_i r^*(q^i)$, which in turn, is bounded above by $\tilde{r}(q^0) - \epsilon/2$. Thus, $\hat{r}_\tau < \tilde{r}(q^0) - \epsilon/2 + \delta(\tau)$, where the term $\delta(\tau)$ incorporates the effects due to the randomness in the process. By repeating this argument with ever increasing values of τ (so that the stochastic term $\delta(\tau)$ is averaged out and becomes negligible), we obtain that the event $\hat{r}_t < \tilde{r}(q^0) - \epsilon/2$ will occur infinitely often, and therefore $\tilde{r}$ is not attainable.

It remains to establish the claimed optimality of $(c_0, \ldots, c_0)$. Suppose that $(\bar{c}_1, \ldots, \bar{c}_k) \neq (c_0, \ldots, c_0)$ is an optimal solution of the problem (5.10). If $\bar{c}_i \leq c_0$ for all i, the monotonicity of the f_i implies that $(c_0, \ldots, c_0)$ is also an optimal solution. Let us therefore assume that there exists some j for which $\bar{c}_j > c_0$. In order for the constraint (5.10) to be satisfied, there must exist some index $s < j$ such that $\bar{c}_s < c_0$. Let us perturb this solution by setting $\delta = \min\{\alpha_s(c_0 - \bar{c}_s), \alpha_j(\bar{c}_j - c_0)\}$, increasing $\bar{c}_s$ to $\tilde{c}_s = \bar{c}_s + \delta/\alpha_s$, and decreasing $\bar{c}_j$ to $\tilde{c}_j = \bar{c}_j - \delta/\alpha_j$. This new solution is clearly feasible. Let $f_s^- = \lim_{\epsilon \downarrow 0} (f_s(c_0) - f_s(c_0 - \epsilon))$, which is the left derivative of f_s at c_0. Using concavity, and the earlier introduced ordering, we have $f_s^- \geq f_s^+ \geq f_j^+$, from which it follows easily (the detailed argument is omitted) that $f_s(\tilde{c}_s) + f_j(\tilde{c}_j) \geq f_s(\bar{c}_s) + f_j(\bar{c}_j)$. Therefore, the new solution must also be optimal, but has fewer components that differ from c_0. By repeating this process, we eventually conclude that $(c_0, \ldots, c_0)$ is optimal. $\square$

To the best of our knowledge, this is the first tightness result for a performance envelope (the reward-in-hindsight) different than the Bayes envelope, for standard repeated decision problems.

6   Attaining the Convex Hull Using Calibrated Forecasts

In this section we consider a specific strategy that attains the convex hull, thus strengthening Theorem 1. The strategy is based on forecasting P2's action, and playing a best response (in the sense of Eq. (2.5)) against the forecast. The quality of the resulting strategy depends, of course, on the quality of the forecast; it is well known that using *calibrated* forecasts leads to no-regret strategies in standard repeated matrix games. See [10, 11] for a discussion of calibration and its implications in learning in games. In this section we consider the consequences of calibrated play for repeated games with constraints.

We start with a formal definition of calibrated forecasts and calibrated play, and then show that calibrated play attains r^c in the sense of Definition 1.

A forecasting scheme specifies at each stage k a probabilistic forecast $q_k \in \Delta(B)$ of P2's action b_k. More precisely a (randomized) forecasting scheme is a sequence of maps that associate with each possible history h_{k-1} during the first $k-1$ stages a probability measure μ_k over $\Delta(B)$. The forecast $q_k \in \Delta(B)$ is then selected at random according to the distribution μ_k. Let us clarify that for the purposes of this section, the history is defined to include the realized past forecasts.

We shall use the following definition of calibrated forecasts.

Definition 2 (Calibrated forecasts). *A forecasting scheme is* calibrated *if for every (Borel measurable) set $Q \subset \Delta(B)$ and every strategy of P2,*

$$\lim_{t \to \infty} \frac{1}{t} \sum_{\tau=1}^{t} 1\{q_\tau \in Q\}(e(b_\tau) - q_\tau) = 0 \quad a.s., \tag{6.11}$$

where $e(b)$ is a vector of zeroes, except for a 1 in the bth location.

Calibrated forecasts, as defined above, have been introduced into game theory in [10], and several algorithms have been devised to achieve them (see [11] and references therein). These algorithms typically start with predictions that are restricted to a finite grid, and gradually increase the number of grid points.

The proposed strategy is to let P1 play a best response against P2's forecasted play while still satisfying the constraints (in expectation for the one-shot game). Formally, we let:

$$p^*(q) = \arg \max_{p \in \Delta(A)} \sum_{a,b} p(a)q(b)R(a,b) \tag{6.12}$$

$$\text{s.t.} \sum_{a,b} p(a)q(b)C(a,b) \in T,$$

where in the case of a non-unique maximum we assume that $p^*(q)$ is uniquely determined by some tie-breaking rule; this is easily done, while keeping $p^*(\cdot)$ a measurable function. The strategy is to play $p_t = p^*(q_t)$, where q_t is a calibrated forecast of P2's actions[2]. We call such a strategy a *calibrated strategy*.

The following theorem states that a calibrated strategy attains the convex hull.

Theorem 3. *Let Assumption 1 hold, and suppose that P1 uses a calibrated strategy. Then r^c is attainable with respect to T.*

Proof. (Outline) Fix $\epsilon > 0$. We need to show that by playing the calibrated strategy, P1 obtains $\liminf \hat{r}_t - r^c(\hat{q}_t) \geq -\epsilon$ and $\limsup \operatorname{dist}(\hat{c}_t, T) \leq \epsilon$ almost surely. Due to lack of space, we only provide an outline of the proof.

Consider a partition of the simplex $\Delta(B)$ to finitely many measurable sets $Q_1, Q_2, \ldots, Q_\ell$ such that $q, q' \in Q_i$ implies that $\|q - q'\| \leq \epsilon/K$ and $\|p^*(q) - p^*(q')\| \leq \epsilon/K$, where K is a large constant. (Such a partition exists by the compactness of $\Delta(B)$ and $\Delta(A)$. The measurability of the sets Q_i can be guaranteed because the mapping $p^*(\cdot)$ is measurable.) For each i, let us fix a representative element $q^i \in Q_i$, and let $p^i = p^*(q^i)$.

Since we have a calibrated forecast, Eq. (6.11) holds for every Q_i, $1 \leq i \leq \ell$. Define $\Gamma_t(i) = \sum_{\tau=1}^{t} 1\{q_\tau \in Q_i\}$ and assume without loss of generality that $\Gamma_t(i) > 0$ for large t (otherwise, eliminate those i for which $\Gamma_t(i) = 0$ for all t and renumber the Q_i). To simplify the presentation, we assume that for every i, and for large enough t, we will have $\Gamma_t(i) \geq \epsilon t/K$. (If for some i, and t this condition is violated, the contribution of such an i in the expressions that follow will be $O(\epsilon)$.) In the sequel the approximate equality sign "$\approx$" will indicate the presence of an approximation error term, e_t, that satisfies $\limsup_{t\to\infty} e_t \leq L\epsilon$, almost surely, where L is a constant.

We have

$$\hat{c}_t \approx \frac{1}{t} \sum_{\tau=1}^{t} C(a_\tau, b_\tau)$$

$$= \sum_i \frac{\Gamma_t(i)}{t} \sum_{a,b} C(a,b) \frac{1}{\Gamma_t(i)} \sum_{\tau=1}^{t} 1\{q_\tau \in Q_i\} 1\{a_\tau = a\} 1\{b_\tau = b\}$$

$$\approx \sum_i \frac{\Gamma_t(i)}{t} \sum_{a,b} C(a,b) p^i(a) \frac{1}{\Gamma_t(i)} \sum_{\tau=1}^{t} 1\{q_\tau \in Q_i\} 1\{b_\tau = b\}$$

$$\approx \sum_i \frac{\Gamma_t(i)}{t} \sum_{a,b} C(a,b) p^i(a) q^i(b). \tag{6.13}$$

The first approximate equality follows from laws of large numbers. The second approximate equality holds because whenever $q_\tau \in Q_i$, p_τ is approximately equal to $p^*(q_i) = p^i$, and by laws of large numbers, the frequency with which a will be selected will be approximately $p^i(a)$. The last approximate equality holds by virtue of the calibration property (6.11) with $Q = Q_i$, and the fact that whenever $q_\tau \in Q_i$, we have $q_\tau \approx q^i$.

---

[2] When the forecast μ_t is mixed, q_t is the realization of the mixed rule.

Note that the right-hand side expression (6.13) is a convex combination (because the $\Gamma_t(i)/t$ sum to 1) of elements of T (because of the definition of p^i), and is therefore an element of T (because T is convex). This establishes that the constraint is asymptotically satisfied within ϵ. Note that in this argument, whenever $\Gamma_t(i)/t < \epsilon/K$, the summand corresponding to i is indeed of order $O(\epsilon)$ and can be safely ignored, as stated earlier.

Regarding the average reward, a similar argument yields

$$\hat{r}_t \approx \sum_i \frac{\Gamma_t(i)}{t} \sum_{a,b} R(a,b) p^i(a) q^i(b)$$

$$= \sum_i \frac{\Gamma_t(i)}{t} r^*(q^i)$$

$$\geq r^c \left(\sum_i \frac{\Gamma_t(i)}{t} q^i \right)$$

$$\approx r^c(\hat{q}_t).$$

The first approximate equality is obtained similar to (6.13), with $C(a,b)$ replaced by $R(a,b)$. The equality that follows is a consequence of the definition of p^i. The inequality that follows is obtained because of the definition of r^c as the closed convex hull of r^*. The last approximate equality relies on the continuity of r^c, and the fact

$$\hat{q}_t \approx \frac{1}{t} \sum_{\tau=1}^t q_\tau \approx \sum_i \frac{\Gamma_t(i)}{t} q^i.$$

To justify the latter fact, the first approximate equality follows from the calibration property (6.11), with $Q = \Delta(B)$, and the second because q_t is approximately equal to q^i for a fraction $\Gamma_t(i)/t$ of the time.

The above outlined argument involves a fixed ϵ, and a fixed number ℓ of sets Q_i, and lets t increase to infinity. As such, it establishes that for any $\epsilon > 0$ the function $r^c - \epsilon$ is attainable with respect to the set T^ϵ defined by $T^\epsilon = \{x \mid \text{dist}(x,T) \leq \epsilon\}$. Since this is true for every $\epsilon > 0$, we conclude that the calibrated strategy attains r^c as claimed. ☐

Acknowledgements. This research was partially supported by the National Science Foundation under contract ECS-0312921, by the Natural Sciences and Engineering Research Council of Canada, and by the Canada Research Chairs Program.

References

1. J. Hannan. *Approximation to Bayes Risk in Repeated Play*, volume III of *Contribution to The Theory of Games*, pages 97–139. Princeton University Press, 1957.
2. S. Mannor and N. Shimkin. A geometric approach to multi-criterion reinforcement learning. *Journal of Machine Learning Research*, 5:325–360, 2004.
3. E. Altman. *Constrained Markov Decision Processes*. Chapman and Hall, 1999.

4. N. Shimkin. Stochastic games with average cost constraints. In T. Basar and A. Haurie, editors, *Advances in Dynamic Games and Applications*, pages 219–230. Birkhauser, 1994.
5. D. Blackwell. An analog of the minimax theorem for vector payoffs. *Pacific J. Math.*, 6(1):1–8, 1956.
6. X. Spinat. A necessary and sufficient condition for approachability. *Mathematics of Operations Research*, 27(1):31–44, 2002.
7. D. Blackwell. Controlled random walks. In *Proc. Int. Congress of Mathematicians 1954*, volume 3, pages 336–338. North Holland, Amsterdam, 1956.
8. S. Mannor and N. Shimkin. The empirical Bayes envelope and regret minimization in competitive Markov decision processes. *Mathematics of Operations Research*, 28(2):327–345, 2003.
9. J. F. Mertens, S. Sorin, and S. Zamir. Repeated games. CORE Reprint Dps 9420, 9421 and 9422, Center for Operation Research and Econometrics, Universite Catholique De Louvain, Belgium, 1994.
10. D. P. Foster and R. V. Vohra. Calibrated learning and correlated equilibrium. *Games and Economic Behavior*, 21:40–55, 1997.
11. N. Cesa-Bianchi and G. Lugosi. *Prediction, Learning, and Games*. Cambridge University Press, New York, 2006.

Continuous Experts and the Binning Algorithm

Jacob Abernethy[1], John Langford[1], and Manfred K. Warmuth[2,3]

[1] Toyota Technological Institute, Chicago
[2] University of California at Santa Cruz
[3] Supported by NSF grant CCR CCR 9821087
{jabernethy, jl}@tti-c.org, manfred@cse.ucsc.edu

Abstract. We consider the design of online master algorithms for combining the predictions from a set of experts where the absolute loss of the master is to be close to the absolute loss of the best expert. For the case when the master must produce binary predictions, the Binomial Weighting algorithm is known to be optimal when the number of experts is large. It has remained an open problem how to design master algorithms based on binomial weights when the predictions of the master are allowed to be real valued. In this paper we provide such an algorithm and call it the Binning algorithm because it maintains experts in an array of bins. We show that this algorithm is optimal in a relaxed setting in which we consider experts as continuous quantities. The algorithm is efficient and near-optimal in the standard experts setting.

1 Introduction

A large number of on-line learning algorithms have been developed for the so-called *expert setting* [LW94, Vov90, CBFH+97, CBFHW96, HKW98]: learning proceeds in trials; at each trial the master algorithm combines the predictions from the experts to form its own prediction; finally a label is received and both the experts and master incur a loss that quantifies the discrepancy between the predictions and the label. The goal of the master is to predict as well as the best expert. In this paper we focus on the absolute loss when the predictions of the experts and the labels are binary in $\{0, 1\}$, but the prediction of the master can be continuous in the range $[0, 1]$.[1]

Perhaps the simplest expert algorithm is the Halving algorithm: the master predicts with the majority of experts and, whenever the majority is wrong, the incorrect experts are eliminated. If there is at least one expert that never errs then this algorithm makes at most $\log_2 n$ mistakes, where n is the number of experts.

Master algorithms often maintain a weight for each expert that represent the "belief" that the expert is best. In the Halving algorithm the weights of all consistent experts are uniform and the weights of inconsistent experts immediately drop to zero. When there is no consistent expert for the sequence of trials, then a more gradual decay of the weights is needed. Most expert algorithms (such as the

---

[1] The loss $|\hat{y} - y|$ (for prediction $\hat{y} \in [0, 1]$ and label $y \in \{0, 1\}$) equals $\mathbb{E}(|Z - y|)$ for a binary valued prediction random variable Z for which $\mathbb{E}(Z) = \hat{y}$.

G. Lugosi and H.U. Simon (Eds.): COLT 2006, LNAI 4005, pp. 544–558, 2006.

Weighted Majority (WM) algorithm [LW94] and Vovk's Aggregate algorithms [Vov90]) use exponentially decaying weights, i.e. the weights are proportional to $\exp(-\eta L_i)$, where L_i is the total loss of expert i and η a non-negative learning rate. If we assume that there is an expert that makes at most k mistakes, then large k (high noise) requires small η and small k (low noise) high η. In the Halving algorithm $k = 0$ and $\eta = \infty$.

A superior algorithm, Binomial Weighting (BW), uses binomial weights for the experts [CBFHW96]. These weights are motivated by a version space argument: if an expert has $k' \le k$ mistakes left, then it is expanded into $\binom{q^*+1}{\le k'}$ experts[2], where q^* is a bound on the number of remaining mistakes of the master. In each of the expansions, at most k' of the q^* trials are chosen in which the expanded expert negates its prediction. We now can run the Halving algorithm on the set of all expanded experts. However this argument requires that the number of mistakes q^* of the master is bounded. This is easily achieved when the master makes binary predictions and incurs units of loss. In that case, all trials in which the master predicts correctly can be ignored and in trials when the master makes a mistake, at least half of the expanded experts are eliminated and there can't be too many such trials.

Restricting the master to use binary predictions is a significant handicap as it does not allow the algorithm to hedge effectively when the experts produce a relatively even vote. In this case, the master prefers to predict .5 instead of predicting[3] 0 or 1. The main open problem posed in [CBFHW96] is the question of how the fancier binomial weights can be used in the case when the master's predictions lie in $[0, 1]$. In that case there are no good bounds on the number of trials because now all trials in which the master incurs any loss need to be counted.

In this paper we provide such a prediction strategy, called Binning, and we show that this strategy is essentially optimal. We generalize the standard experts setting to consider experts as continuous quantities: we allow each expert to split itself into parts r and $1-r$, where part r of the expert predicts 1 and part $1-r$ predicts 0. Intuitively, the relaxation to continuous quantities of experts removes the discretization effects that make the computation of the optimal strategy difficult.

In our approach we consider an associated game where the master plays against an adversary who controls the predictions of the experts and the outcomes of every round to maximize the master's total loss. We show that for this relaxed setting the adversary can always play optimally by splitting all remaining experts in half.

Binning is very similar to the Binomial Weighting algorithm (BW) in that it implicitly uses binomial weights. In the case of exponential weights, the bound for the algorithm with predictions in $[0, 1]$ (i.e. Vovks aggregating algorithm for the absolute loss) is half of the bound for the algorithm with binary predictions

---

[2] This number of expansions is the current binomial weight of the expert. Exponential weights always change by a fixed factor $exp(-\eta)$ in case of a mistake. However the update factors to the binomial weights "cool down" in subtle ways as k' gets close to k and q^* decreases.

[3] As discussed before predicting .5 is equivalent to predicting randomly.

(i.e. the WM algorithm). Essentially the same happens for binomial weights. The bound we prove for the new Binning algorithm (predictions in $[0,1]$) is a constant plus half of the bound of the BW algorithm (predictions in $\{0,1\}$) and the additive constant is well behaved. It is already known that for large n, BW is optimal when the prediction of the master must be binary. Since no algorithm with predictions in $[0,1]$ can be better that half of the best binary prediction algorithm, our new Binning algorithm is essentially optimal.

Summary of paper: We begin in Section 2 by introducing our notation and formulating the optimal prediction strategy of the expert's game when the master uses predictions in $[0,1]$. In Section 3 we define the continuous game in which we allow continuous quantities of experts. We show the following is always an optimal split in each trial of the continuous game: all experts split themselves in half (resulting in experts of size $\frac{1}{2^t}$). We also relate the optimal algorithm for this game (i.e. the new Binning algorithm) to the BW algorithm. In Section 4 we give some experimental results showing Binning's performance and its worst case bound on real world datasets. Finally, in Section 5 we discuss various open problems as well as high level goals that might be attainable with our new continuous-experts technique.

2   The Optimal Prediction Strategy

We have n experts that make binary predictions and we are to design a master algorithm that combines the predictions of the experts with the goal of performing well compared to the best expert. Our on-line learning model can be viewed as a game that proceeds in trials. At each trial the following occurs: first, each expert i produces a prediction $x_i \in \{0,1\}$; then the master produces a prediction $\hat{y} \in [0,1]$ and finally, the true label $y \in \{0,1\}$ is received and both the experts and the master incur a loss: expert i incurs loss $|x_i - y|$ and the master loss $|\hat{y} - y|$. Recall that the experts' predictions and the labels are binary, but the prediction of the master lies in $[0,1]$. (Generalizations are discussed in the conclusion).

The two parties of the game are nature and the master: nature provides the predictions of the experts, the master gives a prediction in each trial, and finally nature provides the true label. We must restrict the adversary, since an unrestricted adversary can continue to inflict loss at least $\frac{1}{2}$ in each round. A common restriction is the following: the true labels and the choices of the experts' predictions have to be such that at least one expert has total loss at most k. We call this restriction the k-*mistake rule*. It is assumed that k is known to both the master and the adversary before the game starts.

Notice that, with the addition of the k-mistake rule, the game is essentially finite. If, after many rounds, all but one expert has made more than k mistakes, and the last expert has made exactly k, then this expert is required to predict correctly from this point on. In this case, the master can simply mimic the prediction of this expert, and the adversary cannot allow this expert to err. Since this simple strategy of the master assures that the master incurs no future loss, the game has ended.

Observe that, after a number of trials, the only relevant information about the past is the number of experts that made $0, 1, \ldots, k$ mistakes. The experts can then be partitioned into $k+1$ bins and the past can therefore be summarized by the state vector $\mathbf{s} = (s_0, \ldots, s_k)$, where s_i is the number of experts that has made i mistakes. We also use the notation $|\mathbf{s}| := |\mathbf{s}|_1 = \sum_{i=0}^{k} s_i$ for the total number of experts. It is possible that $|\mathbf{s}| \leq n$, as some experts might have incurred already more than k mistakes and therefore will be ignored. Our state space is therefore the set $\mathcal{S} = \{\mathbf{s} \in \{0, 1, \ldots, n\}^k : |\mathbf{s}| \leq n\}$.

By choosing binary predictions for the experts, the adversary splits the state vector $\mathbf{s}$ into $\mathbf{r}$ and $\mathbf{s} - \mathbf{r}$ such that $\mathbf{r} \leq \mathbf{s}$ and $\mathbf{r} \in \mathcal{S}$. The vector $\mathbf{r}$ represents the experts that predict one and the vector $\mathbf{s} - \mathbf{r}$ the experts that predict zero. After the adversary provides the binary label y, the experts that predict wrongly advance by one bin. For any state vector $\mathbf{z} \in \mathcal{S}$, we use $\mathbf{z}^+$ to denote the shifted vector $(0, z_0, z_1, \ldots, z_{k-1})$. When $y = 0$, then $\mathbf{r}$ advances, and when $y = 1$, then $\mathbf{s} - \mathbf{r}$ does, and the successor state is

$$\mathbf{s}^{\mathbf{r}, y} = \begin{cases} \mathbf{r}^+ + (\mathbf{s} - \mathbf{r}) & \text{if } y = 0 \\ \mathbf{r} + (\mathbf{s} - \mathbf{r})^+ & \text{if } y = 1. \end{cases}$$

Let's give an example of one round of our game. Assume the mistake bound k is 2 and the number of experts n is 6. Initially, our state vector is $(6, 0, 0)$. However, after several rounds, 2 experts have made no mistakes, 1 expert has made 2 mistakes, and 3 experts have made more than 2 mistakes. Our state vector is now $(2, 0, 1)$. On the next round we receive predictions from the experts, and we find that the only expert to predict 1 was one of the experts with no mistakes. In this case, the split of the state vector is

$$\mathbf{s} + (2, 0, 1) = \overbrace{(1, 0, 0)}^{\mathbf{r}} + \overbrace{(1, 0, 1)}^{\mathbf{s}-\mathbf{r}},$$

and the two resulting possible states would be

$$\mathbf{s}^{\mathbf{r}, 0} = \overbrace{(0, 1, 0)}^{\mathbf{r}^+} + \overbrace{(1, 0, 1)}^{\mathbf{s}-\mathbf{r}} = (1, 1, 1)$$

$$\mathbf{s}^{\mathbf{r}, 1} = \underbrace{(1, 0, 0)}_{\mathbf{r}} + \underbrace{(0, 1, 0)}_{(\mathbf{s}-\mathbf{r})^+} = (1, 1, 0).$$

2.1 The Value of the Game

We define the value of our game at a state $\mathbf{s}$ as the total loss the adversary can force the master to incur if its choices satisfy the k-mistake rule. With the above notation we can express the value of the game as:

$$\ell(\mathbf{s}) := \begin{cases} -\infty & \text{if } \mathbf{s} = \mathbf{0} \\ 0 & \text{if } \mathbf{s} = (0, \ldots, 0, 1) \\ \max_{\mathbf{r} \leq \mathbf{s}, \mathbf{r} \in \mathcal{S}} \min_{\hat{y} \in [0,1]} \max_{y \in \{0,1\}} \left(|\hat{y} - y| + \ell(\mathbf{s}^{\mathbf{r}, y}) \right) & \mathbf{s} \in \text{ rest of } \mathcal{S}. \end{cases} \quad (1)$$

At various points in the paper we induct on the *mistake budget* $B(\mathbf{s})$ of a state, which we define as the total number of mistakes that can be made by all of the experts before arriving in the final state $\mathbf{b}_k = (0, ..., 0, 1)$. Explicitly, $B(\mathbf{s}) := -1 + \sum_{i=0}^{k}(k-i+1)s_i$. Notice, $B(\mathbf{0}) = -1$ and if $B(\mathbf{s}) = 0$ then $\mathbf{s}$ must be the final state $\mathbf{b}_k$.

Some care needs to be taken to assure that the above game is well defined because of the possibility that all of the experts make the same prediction. If a split is *unanimous*, i.e. all experts predict $u = 1$ and $\mathbf{r} = \mathbf{s}$, or all experts predict $u = 0$ and $\mathbf{r} = \mathbf{0}$, then the master must choose $\hat{y}$ as the unanimous label u. If the master chose $\hat{y} \neq u$, the adversary would simply choose $y = u$, inflicting positive loss $|\hat{y} - u|$ on the master while the experts incur no mistakes. Therefore whenever all experts predict with some unanimous label u, the optimal choice of the master is $\hat{y} = u$ also.

How should the adversary choose its label y when all experts predict with some unanimous label u and $\hat{y} = u$? If $y = u$ then the current trial is vacuous because $\mathbf{s}^{\mathbf{r},y} = \mathbf{s}$ and none of the parties incur any loss. We need to make the mild assumption that such vacuous trials are disallowed. Therefore $y \neq u$ in unanimous trials and in this case the successor state is $\mathbf{s}^{\mathbf{r},y} = \mathbf{s}^{+}$. In summary,

$$\mathbf{r} \in \{\mathbf{0}, \mathbf{s}\} \implies \min_{\hat{y} \in [0,1]} \max_{y \in \{0,1\}} (|\hat{y} - y| + \ell(\mathbf{s}^{\mathbf{r},y})) = 1 + \ell(\mathbf{s}^{+}).$$

We now expand the recurrence slightly by rewriting (1) as follows. As before, $\ell(\mathbf{0}) = -\infty$ and $\ell(\mathbf{b}_k) = 0$, and for every other state $\mathbf{s} \in \mathcal{S}$,

$$\ell(\mathbf{s}) = \max_{\substack{\mathbf{r} \leq \mathbf{s} \\ \mathbf{r} \in \mathcal{S}}} \begin{cases} 1 + \ell(\mathbf{s}^{+}) & \text{if } \mathbf{r} \in \{\mathbf{0}, \mathbf{s}\} \\ \max\{\ell(\mathbf{s}^{\mathbf{r},0}), \ell(\mathbf{s}^{\mathbf{r},1})\} & \text{if } \mathbf{r} \notin \{\mathbf{0}, \mathbf{s}\}, |\ell(\mathbf{s}^{\mathbf{r},1}) - \ell(\mathbf{s}^{\mathbf{r},0})| > 1 \\ \frac{\ell(\mathbf{s}^{\mathbf{r},1}) + \ell(\mathbf{s}^{\mathbf{r},0}) + 1}{2} & \text{if } \mathbf{r} \notin \{\mathbf{0}, \mathbf{s}\}, |\ell(\mathbf{s}^{\mathbf{r},1}) - \ell(\mathbf{s}^{\mathbf{r},0})| \leq 1 \end{cases} \quad (2)$$

The unanimous case (i.e. when $\mathbf{r} = \mathbf{0}, \mathbf{s}$) follows from the above discussion. The remaining two cases arise when we consider how the game is played once $\mathbf{r}$ has been chosen. The master algorithm wants to choose $\hat{y}$, while knowing that the adversary can simply choose the larger of $|\hat{y} - y| + \ell(\mathbf{s}^{\mathbf{r},y})$ for $y \in \{0,1\}$. Thus it would like to minimize $L(\mathbf{r}, \hat{y}) := \max\{\hat{y} + \ell(\mathbf{s}^{\mathbf{r},0}), 1 - \hat{y} + \ell(\mathbf{s}^{\mathbf{r},1})\}$. It can accomplish this by making these two quantities as close as possible. When $|\ell(\mathbf{s}^{\mathbf{r},0}) - \ell(\mathbf{s}^{\mathbf{r},1})| \leq 1$, it can make them exactly equal by setting $\hat{y} = \frac{\ell(\mathbf{s}^{\mathbf{r},1}) - \ell(\mathbf{s}^{\mathbf{r},0}) + 1}{2}$. However, when $\ell(\mathbf{s}^{\mathbf{r},1}) > \ell(\mathbf{s}^{\mathbf{r},0}) + 1$, the master should choose $\hat{y} = 1$ and $L(\mathbf{r}, \hat{y}) = \ell(\mathbf{s}^{\mathbf{r},1})$. Similarly when $\ell(\mathbf{s}^{\mathbf{r},0}) > \ell(\mathbf{s}^{\mathbf{r},1}) + 1$ then $\hat{y} = 0$ and $L(\mathbf{r}, \hat{y}) = \ell(\mathbf{s}^{\mathbf{r},0})$. The latter two cases are summarized in line 2 of above recursion, completing the argument that the above recursion is equivalent to (1).

A further and more subtle simplification of the above recurrence is provided by the following lemma which rules out the first two lines of (2). In particular, it implies two useful facts: (a) unanimous splits only occur when there is a single expert and (b) when $|\mathbf{s}| > 1$, the adversary will never choose $\mathbf{r}$ so that $|\ell(\mathbf{s}^{\mathbf{r},1}) - \ell(\mathbf{s}^{\mathbf{r},0})| > 1$.

Algorithm 1. OptPredict$_k$

At round t, the number of past mistakes of the experts are tallied in the state vector $\mathbf{s}$ and the experts that predict 1 (respectively 0) are tallied in the split vector $\mathbf{r}$ (respectively $\mathbf{s} - \mathbf{r}$). The master algorithm OptPredict$_k$ outputs prediction:

$$\hat{y} = clip\left(\frac{\ell(\mathbf{s^{r,1}}) - \ell(\mathbf{s^{r,0}}) + 1}{2}\right), \tag{4}$$

where $clip(x)$ is the point in $[0, 1]$ closest to x.

Note that when there is exactly one expert left which has made $i \leq k$ mistakes, i.e. $\mathbf{s}$ is the standard basis vector $\mathbf{b}_i$, then all splits must be unanimous and $\ell(\mathbf{b}_i) = k - i$.

Lemma 1. *For any state* $\mathbf{s} \in \mathcal{S}$ *s.t.* $|\mathbf{s}| > 1$,

$$\ell(\mathbf{s}) = \max_{0 < r < s} \left\{\frac{\ell(\mathbf{s^{r,0}}) + \ell(\mathbf{s^{r,1}}) + 1}{2}\right\}. \tag{3}$$

The proof requires a rather technical induction and is given in the appendix.

We now have a very simple recursion for computing ℓ, and we can easily define the optimal prediction strategy OptPredict$_k$, as in (4), with oracle access to this function. Unfortunately, ℓ is still too expensive to compute: it requires the solution of a dynamic programming problem over $O(|\mathcal{S}|) = O((n + 1)^k)$ states.

3   The Continuous Game

Computing the value function ℓ using (3) is too difficult: at every round we must consider all possible splits $\mathbf{r}$. However, empirical observations have suggested that splits $\mathbf{r}$ close to $\frac{\mathbf{s}}{2}$ are optimal for the adversary. In particular, we have observed that, whenever $\mathbf{s}$ has only even entries, the split $\mathbf{r} = \frac{\mathbf{s}}{2}$ is always optimal. This evidence leads one to believe that an optimal adversarial strategy is to evenly divide the experts, thus balancing the loss value of the two successor states as much as possible. Unfortunately, this is not always possible when the experts come in discrete units.

We therefore develop a continuous game that always allows for such "even splits" and show that the value of this continuous game is easy to compute and tightly upper bounds the value function of the original game. The continuous game follows the same on-line protocol given in the first paragraph of Section 2, however now each expert has a mass in $[0, 1]$ and at each trial each expert is allowed to split itself into two parts which predict with opposite labels. The total mass of the two parts must equal the original mass.

3.1   The Continuous Experts Setting

As in the discrete game, the state of the new game is again summarized by a vector, i.e. it is not necessary to keep track of the identities of the individual experts of mass in $[0, 1]$. The state space of the new game is $\widetilde{\mathcal{S}} = \{\mathbf{s} \in [0, n]^{k+1} : |\mathbf{s}| \leq n\}$. The initial state vector is again $(n, 0, \ldots, 0)$, but the split $\mathbf{r}$ may have non-negative real valued components.

We now define a new value function $\widetilde{\ell}$ on $\widetilde{\mathcal{S}}$. We would like the definition of $\widetilde{\ell}$ to mimic the recursive definition of ℓ in (3), yet we must be careful to define the "base case" of this recursion. In particular, how do we redefine the k-mistake rule within this "continuous experts" setting? We require the following constraints on $\widetilde{\ell}$: when $|\mathbf{s}| < 1$, which we call an *infeasible* state, we define $\widetilde{\ell}(\mathbf{s}) := -\infty$; when $|\mathbf{s}| \geq 1$, i.e. a total of one unit of experts remains, then $\widetilde{\ell}(\mathbf{s})$ should be non-negative.

These two requirements are not sufficient: we must consider the case when we are at a feasible state $\mathbf{s}$ in which, given any split $\mathbf{r}$ that the adversary chooses, at least one of the successor states is infeasible. This would be a state where the game has effectively ended, and we will therefore consider it a base case of our recursion. That is, the recursive definition in (3) would not be appropriate on such a state, for $\widetilde{\ell}(\mathbf{s}^{\mathbf{r},0})$ or $\widetilde{\ell}(\mathbf{s}^{\mathbf{r},1})$ is $-\infty$ (for any $\mathbf{r}$), and we must therefore fix the value $\widetilde{\ell}(\mathbf{s})$. We let S_0 denote the set of such base-case states:

$$
\begin{aligned}
S_0 &= \left\{ \mathbf{s} : |\mathbf{s}| \geq 1 \text{ and } \forall 0 < \mathbf{r} < \mathbf{s} : |\mathbf{s}^{\mathbf{r},0}| < 1 \text{ or } |\mathbf{s}^{\mathbf{r},1}| < 1 \right\} \\
&= \left\{ \mathbf{s} : |\mathbf{s}| \geq 1 \text{ and } \forall 0 < \mathbf{r} < \mathbf{s} : |\mathbf{s}| - r_k < 1 \text{ or } |\mathbf{s}| - s_k + r_k < 1 \right\} \\
&= \left\{ \mathbf{s} : |\mathbf{s}| \geq 1 \text{ and } |\mathbf{s}| - \frac{s_k}{2} < 1 \right\} \\
&= \text{convex-hull}\{\mathbf{b}_0, \ldots, \mathbf{b}_k, 2\mathbf{b}_k\} \setminus \left\{ \mathbf{s} : |\mathbf{s}| - \frac{s_k}{2} = 1 \right\}
\end{aligned}
$$

We obtain the convex hull representation because S_0 is described by $k + 3$ linear constraints: $s_0 \geq 0, \ldots, s_k \geq 0, \sum s_i \geq 1$ and $\frac{s_k}{2} + \sum_{i<k} s_i < 1$. The subsequent polytop has corners $\mathbf{b}_0, \ldots, \mathbf{b}_k$ and $2\mathbf{b}_k$. The region is not exactly the convex hull since the last constraint is a strict inequality, and thus we must subtract one face. Notice that, while $\mathbf{b}_k$ lies within S_0, the remaining states $\mathbf{b}_0, \ldots, \mathbf{b}_{k-1}$, and $2\mathbf{b}_k$ all lie on the subtracted face.

3.2   The Value of the Continuous Game

We are now in position to define our recursion for $\widetilde{\ell}$. For any state $\mathbf{s} \in \widetilde{\mathcal{S}}$,

$$
\widetilde{\ell}(\mathbf{s}) := \begin{cases} \widetilde{\ell}_0(\mathbf{s}) & \text{if } \mathbf{s} \in S_0 \\ \displaystyle\max_{\substack{\mathbf{r} \leq \mathbf{s}, \mathbf{r} \in \widetilde{\mathcal{S}} \\ \frac{1}{2} \leq |\mathbf{r}| \leq |\mathbf{s}| - \frac{1}{2}}} \frac{\widetilde{\ell}(\mathbf{s}^{\mathbf{r},0}) + \widetilde{\ell}(\mathbf{s}^{\mathbf{r},1}) + 1}{2} & \mathbf{s} \in \text{ rest of } \widetilde{\mathcal{S}}. \end{cases} \tag{5}
$$

Note that it is crucial that in the above recurrence for $\widetilde{\ell}$ we bound[4] the split $\mathbf{r}$ away from $\mathbf{0}$ and $\mathbf{s}$. Thus whenever we recurse, at least a total of half a unit of experts is advanced and the depth of the recurrence is bounded by $2n(k+1)$.

---

[4] $\widetilde{\ell}$ does not change if we use instead the constraint $\epsilon \leq |\mathbf{r}| \leq |\mathbf{s}| - \epsilon$ for any ϵ with $0 < \epsilon \leq \frac{1}{2}$.

We still need a natural definition of $\widetilde{\ell}_0(\mathbf{s})$ for states $\mathbf{s} \in S_0$. The simplest definition would be to define $\widetilde{\ell}_0$ as zero. However, this would cause the value function $\widetilde{\ell}$ to be discontinuous at the corners of the base region S_0. Intuitively, we want $\widetilde{\ell}$ to mimic ℓ as much as possible. Thus, the two properties that we require of $\widetilde{\ell}_0$ is (a) that it agrees with ℓ on the discrete corners of S_0, and (b) that it is continuous on the "in between" states. We therefore define $\widetilde{\ell}_0$ on the interior of S_0 as the linear interpolation of ℓ on the corner states $\{\mathbf{b}_0, \ldots, \mathbf{b}_k, 2\mathbf{b}_k\}$. We can explicitly define $\widetilde{\ell}_0(\mathbf{s})$ as follows: write $\mathbf{s} = \alpha_0 \mathbf{b}_0 + \ldots + \alpha_k \mathbf{b}_k + \alpha_{k+1}(2\mathbf{b}_k)$, where $\alpha_i \in [0,1]$ and $\sum \alpha_i = 1$. Let

$$\widetilde{\ell}_0(\mathbf{s}) := \left(\sum_{i=0}^{k} \alpha_i \ell(\mathbf{b}_i) \right) + \alpha_{k+1} \ell(2\mathbf{b}_k) = \left(\sum_{i=0}^{k} \alpha_i (k-i) \right) + \frac{\alpha_{k+1}}{2}$$

$$= \sum_{i=0}^{k-1} s_i (k-i) + \frac{|\mathbf{s}| - 1}{2}.$$

We chose S_0 and $\widetilde{\ell}_0(\mathbf{s})$ so that the following lemma holds:

Lemma 2. *For all* $\mathbf{s} \in S$, $\widetilde{\ell}(\mathbf{s}) \geq \ell(\mathbf{s})$.

Proof. The continuous game is identical to the discrete game, except that we have given the adversary a larger space to choose a split $\mathbf{r}$. Essentially, increasing the number of strategies for the adversary can only increase the loss of the game.   □

3.3   An Optimal Adversarial Strategy

We now show that for the value function $\widetilde{\ell}$ of the continuous game, $\mathbf{r} = \mathbf{s} - \mathbf{r} = \mathbf{s}/2$ is always an optimal split for the adversary. In this case the successor state is $h(\mathbf{s}) := \frac{\mathbf{s} + \mathbf{s}^+}{2}$ no matter how $y \in \{0, 1\}$ is chosen.

Define a function $\mathcal{L}$ as follows:

$$\mathcal{L}(\mathbf{s}) := \begin{cases} -\infty & \text{if } |\mathbf{s}| < 1 \\ \widetilde{\ell}_0(\mathbf{s}) & \text{if } \mathbf{s} \in S_0 \\ \frac{1}{2} + \mathcal{L}(h(\mathbf{s})) & \text{if } \mathbf{s} \text{ rest of } \widetilde{S}. \end{cases} \tag{6}$$

We prove $\widetilde{\ell} = \mathcal{L}$ in two steps. The first is the following crucial lemma.

Lemma 3. $\mathcal{L}$ *is concave.*

Proof. We have defined our base region S_0 above. Notice that we can rewrite S_0 as $\{\mathbf{s} \in \widetilde{S} : |\mathbf{s}| \geq 1, |h(\mathbf{s})| < 1\}$. Now define S_n for $n \geq 2$ as $\{\mathbf{s} : \mathbf{s} \notin S_{n-1} \text{ and } h(\mathbf{s}) \in S_{n-1}\} = \{\mathbf{s} : |h^n(\mathbf{s})| > 1, |h^{n+1}(\mathbf{s})| < 1\}$. We will show that we can effectively reduce the concavity of $\mathcal{L}$ to the concavity of $\mathcal{L}$ on the region $S_0 \cup S_1$.

It suffices to show that $\mathcal{L}$ is concave on a set of convex open neighbors which cover $\widetilde{S}$ since the concavity property always fails locally. Let $R_0 := S_0$, and for $n > 0$, define R_n as the interior of $S_{n-1} \cup S_n$, i.e. $\{\mathbf{s} \in \widetilde{S} : |h^{n-1}(\mathbf{s})| > 1, |h^{n+1}(\mathbf{s})| < 1\}$. Let $h^0(\mathbf{s}) := \mathbf{s}$ by convention. Notice that $\cup R_n = \widetilde{S}$ and each R_n is open and convex.

Let $\mathcal{L}$ restricted to R_n be denoted $\mathcal{L}|_{R_n}$. We show that $\mathcal{L}|_{R_n}$ is concave for every n. $\mathcal{L}|_{R_0}$ is certainly concave, for $\mathcal{L}$ is defined linearly on $R_0 = S_0$.

We show that $\mathcal{L}|_{R_1}$ is concave by first noting that

$$\mathcal{L}|_{R_1} = \begin{cases} \widetilde{\ell}_0(\mathbf{s}) = \sum s_i \, (k - i) + \frac{|\mathbf{s}| - 1}{2} & \text{if } \mathbf{s} \in S_0 \\ \widetilde{\ell}_1(\mathbf{s}) = \widetilde{\ell}_0(h(\mathbf{s})) + \frac{1}{2} = \sum s_i \, (k - i) + \frac{s_k}{4} & \text{if } \mathbf{s} \in S_1. \end{cases} \tag{7}$$

These two linear functions are equal when $\frac{|\mathbf{s}| - 1}{2} = \frac{s_k}{4} \implies |\mathbf{s}| - \frac{s_k}{2} = 1$, which is exactly the border between S_0 and S_1. Since S_0 is defined by the constraint $|\mathbf{s}| - s_k/2 < 1$, we see that $\widetilde{\ell}_0(\mathbf{s}) < \widetilde{\ell}_1(\mathbf{s})$ when $\mathbf{s} \in S_0$. These last two statements imply that $\mathcal{L}|_{R_1}(\mathbf{s}) = \min\{\widetilde{\ell}_0(\mathbf{s}), \widetilde{\ell}_1(\mathbf{s})\}$ and the minimum of two linear functions is always concave.

Assume $n > 1$. Notice, $\mathbf{s} \in R_n$ implies that $h(\mathbf{s}) \in R_{n-1}$. Thus $\mathcal{L}|_{R_n} = \mathcal{L}|_{R_{n-1}} \circ h + \frac{1}{2}$. Note that: (a) h is an orientation-preserving linear function $(\det(h) > 0)$, (b) addition by a constant preserves concavity, and (c) $\mathcal{L}|_{R_{n-1}}$ is concave by induction. Therefore, $\mathcal{L}|_{R_n}$ is concave as well. □

We are now in position to prove the following theorem.

Theorem 1. *For all* $\mathbf{s} \in \widetilde{S}$,

$$\widetilde{\ell}(\mathbf{s}) := \begin{cases} -\infty & \text{if } |\mathbf{s}| < 1 \\ \widetilde{\ell}_0(\mathbf{s}) & \text{if } \mathbf{s} \in S_0 \\ \frac{1}{2} + \widetilde{\ell}(h(\mathbf{s})) & \text{if } \mathbf{s} \text{ rest of } \widetilde{S}. \end{cases} \tag{8}$$

Proof. We show that, for all $\mathbf{s} \in \widetilde{S}$, $\widetilde{\ell}(\mathbf{s}) = \mathcal{L}(\mathbf{s})$. We induct on the mistake budget $B(\mathbf{s})$. When $B(\mathbf{s}) < \frac{1}{2}$, then $\mathbf{s} \in S_0$, and $\widetilde{\ell}$ and $\mathcal{L}$ are defined identically on S_0. Now assume that $\frac{p}{2} \le B(\mathbf{s}) < \frac{p+1}{2}$ for some positive integer p. It is possible that $\mathbf{s} \in S_0$, in which case certainly $\widetilde{\ell}(\mathbf{s}) = \mathcal{L}(\mathbf{s})$. Otherwise,

$$\widetilde{\ell}(\mathbf{s}) = \max_{\substack{\mathbf{r} \le \mathbf{s}, \mathbf{r} \in \widetilde{S} \\ \frac{1}{2} \le |\mathbf{r}| \le |\mathbf{s}| - \frac{1}{2}}} \frac{\widetilde{\ell}(\mathbf{s}^{\mathbf{r},0}) + \widetilde{\ell}(\mathbf{s}^{\mathbf{r},1}) + 1}{2}. \tag{9}$$

However, since we may only choose $\mathbf{r}$ such that $\frac{1}{2} \le |\mathbf{r}| \le |\mathbf{s}| - \frac{1}{2}$, it must be that $B(\mathbf{s}^{\mathbf{r},1}) < \frac{p}{2}$ and $B(\mathbf{s}^{\mathbf{r},0}) < \frac{p}{2}$. By induction, $\widetilde{\ell}(\mathbf{s}^{\mathbf{r},0}) = \mathcal{L}(\mathbf{s}^{\mathbf{r},0})$ and $\widetilde{\ell}(\mathbf{s}^{\mathbf{r},1}) = \mathcal{L}(\mathbf{s}^{\mathbf{r},1})$. However, by the concavity of $\mathcal{L}$, we see that for any $\mathbf{r}$,

$$\frac{\widetilde{\ell}(\mathbf{s}^{\mathbf{r},0}) + \widetilde{\ell}(\mathbf{s}^{\mathbf{r},1}) + 1}{2} = \frac{\mathcal{L}(\mathbf{s}^{\mathbf{r},0}) + \mathcal{L}(\mathbf{s}^{\mathbf{r},1}) + 1}{2} \le \mathcal{L}\left(\frac{\mathbf{s}^{\mathbf{r},0} + \mathbf{s}^{\mathbf{r},1}}{2}\right) + \frac{1}{2}$$

$$= \mathcal{L}\left(\frac{(\mathbf{s} - \mathbf{r}) + (\mathbf{r})^+ + \mathbf{r} + (\mathbf{s} - \mathbf{r})^+}{2}\right) + \frac{1}{2}$$

$$= \mathcal{L}\left(\frac{\mathbf{s} + \mathbf{s}^+}{2}\right) + \frac{1}{2} = \mathcal{L}(h(\mathbf{s})) + \frac{1}{2} = \mathcal{L}(\mathbf{s})$$

and thus $\mathcal{L}$ is an upper bound on $\widetilde{\ell}$. On the other hand, notice also that $B(h(\mathbf{s})) < \frac{p}{2}$ so $\widetilde{\ell}(h(\mathbf{s})) = \mathcal{L}(h(\mathbf{s}))$. Thus, for the choice $\mathbf{r} = \frac{\mathbf{s}}{2}$, we see that

$$\widetilde{\ell}(\mathbf{s}) \geq \frac{\widetilde{\ell}(\mathbf{s}^{\mathbf{r},0}) + \widetilde{\ell}(\mathbf{s}^{\mathbf{r},1}) + 1}{2} = \frac{\widetilde{\ell}(h(\mathbf{s})) + \widetilde{\ell}(h(\mathbf{s})) + 1}{2} = \mathcal{L}(h(\mathbf{s})) + \frac{1}{2} = \mathcal{L}(\mathbf{s}),$$

and thus $\mathcal{L}$ is also a lower bound on $\widetilde{\ell}$. Therefore, $\widetilde{\ell}(\mathbf{s}) = \mathcal{L}(\mathbf{s})$ and we are done. $\square$

Corollary 1. *The split* $\mathbf{r} = \frac{\mathbf{s}}{2}$ *is always an[5] optimal choice for the adversary in the continuous game.*

3.4   The Binning Algorithm

We can now define our new algorithm Binning_k by simply replacing ℓ in equation (4) with the new function $\widetilde{\ell}$. We will reason below that $\widetilde{\ell}$ can be computed efficiently.

Theorem 1 tells us that, to get the value of $\widetilde{\ell}(\mathbf{s})$, we apply the function h to $\mathbf{s}$ several times until we are in the base region S_0. Let

$$q^{\mathbf{s}} := \min\{q : h^q(\mathbf{s}) \in S_0\} = \max\{q : |h^q(\mathbf{s})| \geq 1\}. \tag{10}$$

This allows us to write $\widetilde{\ell}(\mathbf{s}) = \frac{q^{\mathbf{s}}}{2} + \widetilde{\ell}_0(h^{q^{\mathbf{s}}}(\mathbf{s}))$. The function h is linear on the state space $\widetilde{S}$ and can be represented as a square matrix of dimension $k+1$ (The matrix for $k = 3$ is given below). Thus h^n corresponds to an n-fold power of this matrix and leads to binomial coefficients:

$$h = \begin{bmatrix} 1/2 & 0 & 0 & 0 \\ 1/2 & 1/2 & 0 & 0 \\ 0 & 1/2 & 1/2 & 0 \\ 0 & 0 & 1/2 & 1/2 \end{bmatrix} \qquad h^n = \frac{1}{2^n}\left[\binom{n}{i-j}\right]_{i,j}.$$

From this observation, we see that, for any state $\mathbf{s}$,

$$|h^n(\mathbf{s})| = \frac{1}{2^n} \sum_{i=0}^{k} \binom{n}{\leq (k-i)} s_i,$$

where we define $\binom{a}{\leq b} := \sum_{0 \leq b' \leq b} \binom{a}{b'}$. This notation allows us to rewrite (10) as (11) and concisely define Binning_k.

The naive complexity of solving (11) at every round is $O(kq^{\mathbf{s}}) = O(k^2 + k \log |\mathbf{s}|)$, and for computing $\widetilde{\ell}_0 \circ h^q$ in (12) is $O(kq^{\mathbf{s}})$. The overall computation for one round requires therefore $O(k^2 + k \log |\mathbf{s}| + n)$, where n is the initial number of experts. Using bookkeeping one can reduce the per-round complexity to $O(n)$ by maintaining binomials $\binom{q}{k-i}$, binomial tails $\binom{q}{\leq k-i}$, and the function $\widetilde{\ell}_0 \circ h^q(\mathbf{b}_i)$ for an expert with i mistakes. These values can be updated in constant time using recurrences.

---

[5] In general, there are multiple optimal splits.

Algorithm 2. Binning$_k$

Summarize the expert performance with **s**, and current predictions with **r**. For both $y \in \{0,1\}$, compute

$$q_y = q^{\mathbf{s}^{\mathbf{r},y}} = \max\left\{ q : \frac{1}{2^q}\sum_{i=0}^{k}\binom{q}{\leq (k-i)}(\mathbf{s}^{\mathbf{r},y})_i \geq 1 \right\}. \tag{11}$$

Using the functions $clip(\cdot)$ defined in equation (4) and $\widetilde{\ell}_0(\cdot)$ defined in (6), output prediction

$$\hat{y} = clip\left(\frac{q_1 - q_0}{4} + \frac{\widetilde{\ell}_0(h^{q_1}(\mathbf{s}^{\mathbf{r},1})) - \widetilde{\ell}_0(h^{q_0}(\mathbf{s}^{\mathbf{r},0})) + 1}{2} \right) \tag{12}$$

3.5 Binning and Binomial Weighting

In the introduction we discussed the algorithm Binomial Weighting which makes deterministic predictions ($\hat{y} \in \{0,1\}$) when a mistake bound k is given. BW finds a bound, q^*, on the number of times the master errs, and considers a set of virtual experts of size $\sum_j \binom{q^*+1}{\leq k-m_j}$ where the sum is taken over all experts j, and m_j denotes the number of mistakes of expert j. In some sense, q^* is computed in hindsight: we make q^* big enough so that we produce "enough" virtual experts, i.e. so that we don't halve the set of virtual experts too many times. It is chosen as

$$q^* = \max\left\{ q : q \leq \log_2 \sum_j \binom{q}{\leq k - m_j} \right\}. \tag{13}$$

Recall that, if we summarize the past performance of our experts with a state vector **s**, then s_i is the number of experts e that have made i mistakes and therefore $\sum_j \binom{q^*}{k-m_j} = \sum_{i=0}^{k}\binom{q^*}{k-i}s_i$. Interestingly, if we exponentiate the above equation and divide by 2^{q^*} we arrive at equation (11) and thus $q^{\mathbf{s}} = q^*$.

The loss bound on Binning$_k$ is $\frac{q^{\mathbf{s}}}{2} + \widetilde{\ell}_0(h^{q^{\mathbf{s}}}(\mathbf{s}))$. Notice, the binomial nature of $h^{q^{\mathbf{s}}}$ forces the majority of the weight in **s** to be collected in s_k, yet this term has coefficient $\frac{1}{2}$ in the function $\widetilde{\ell}_0$. However, the term $\widetilde{\ell}_0(h^{q^{\mathbf{s}}}(\mathbf{s}))$ quickly drops to a constant c independent of k as the number of experts goes to ∞. Thus, the loss $\widetilde{\ell}(\mathbf{s}) \leq \frac{q^{\mathbf{s}}}{2} + c$ for large enough n. (The exact bound on $\widetilde{\ell}_0(h^{q^{\mathbf{s}}}(\mathbf{s}))$ requires some computation and is discussed in the full version of this paper.)

The factor of $\frac{1}{2}$ is to be expected: the deterministic algorithm BW suffers loss 1 at every round in the worst case, while Binning$_k$ will be forced to predict $\hat{y} = \frac{1}{2}$ against an optimal adversary, thus suffering loss $\frac{1}{2}$.

4 Experiments

We ran experiments with several real-world datasets (see table 1) obtained from the UCI Machine Learning Repository. We chose rather simple experts: real valued features were replaced with an "above or below median" expert. Categorical features were replaced with a set of experts, one for each category value. When category value v was encountered, expert v would be set to 1 and all others would be set to 0. We also included the constant expert and for every expert, the complement expert. The original ordering of the datasets was preserved.

data	echo	bupa	hep	wpbc	dia	bcw	Aust	ion	beast	wdbc	kr-kp	cat	a-l
rounds	131	345	155	198	768	699	690	351	286	569	3196	873	8124
experts	28	14	70	72	18	20	30	70	100	64	220	1234	280
mistakes	39	145	32	47	237	65	184	122	79	83	1012	3	920

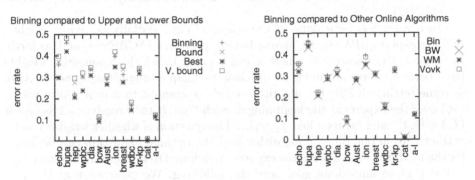

Fig. 1. In the table above we give the number of rounds, the number of experts, and the number of mistakes of the best expert. The datasets are ordered above by byte size. In the graph on the lower left we show how the performance of Binning compares to the upper Bound on Binning performance, the Best single expert, and the bound on Vovk's algorithm. The right graph shows how the performance of Binning compares to Binomial Weighting (BW) (2 entries missing), Weighted Majority (WM), and Vovk's algorithm.

All of the algorithms require the value k (the mistake bound) for tuning. Since we want to compare the algorithms when they are optimally tuned we precomputed this value and provided it to each algorithm. The results are graphed in Figure 1. The left graph shows that the Binning bound is tighter than the bound for Vovk's algorithm and often quite close to the actual Binning performance. The right graph is surprising: the performance appears to worsen with the tighter bound. In fact, BW and WM, both deterministic algorithms, performed better than the best expert on 2 datasets. Perhaps a tighter bound has an associated cost when, in actuality, we are not in an adversarial setting.

5 Conclusion

We discovered a new technique that replaces exponential weights by an optimal algorithm for a continuous game. The key idea is to allow partial experts. Our method uses binomial weights which are more refined then exponentially decaying weights. Note that the latter weights can be derived using a relative entropy as a divergence [KW97, KW99]. This reminds us of the application of entropies in statistical mechanics where the entropy is used to approximate exact counts that are based on binomial tails. In on-line learning we first discovered the entropy based algorithms which use approximate counting by approximating the binomial tails with exponentials. More recently refined algorithms are emerging that are based on binomial counting (See also [Fre95, FO02] for related work on Boosting).

The algorithms based on exponential weights are clearly simpler, but they also require knowledge of k for tuning the learning rate η well. The algorithms that use binomial weights always make use of k. If no tight upper bound of the true k is not known, then simple doubling tricks can be employed (see e.g. Section 4.6 of [CBFH+97]).

Much work has been done in the realm of exponentially decaying weights: shifting experts [HW98], multi-arm bandit problems [ACBFS95] and so forth. In general, the question is whether other cases in which exponential weights have been used are amenable to our new technique of splitting experts. Also, in some settings [FS97] the algorithm needs to commit to a probability vector (w_i) over the experts at the beginning of each trial. It then receives a loss vector $(L_i) \in [0,1]^n$ and incurs a loss $\sum_i w_i L_i$. The question is whether weights can be extracted from our Binning algorithm and the optimal algorithm can be found for the modified setting when the experts are allowed to be continuous quantities.

For a more immediate goal note the following. We assumed that the predictions of the experts and the labels were binary. However in the realm of exponentially decaying weights, Vovk's aggregating algorithm for the absolute loss [Vov90, CBFH+97] can handle expert's predictions in $[0,1]$ and the Vee algorithm of [HKW98] can in addition handle labels in $[0,1]$. We believe that with some additional effort our methods will generalize to handle these cases as well.

References

[ACBFS95] Peter Auer, Nicolò Cesa-Bianchi, Yoav Freund, and Robert E. Schapire. Gambling in a rigged casino: the adversarial multi-armed bandit problem. In *Proceedings of the 36th Annual Symposium on Foundations of Computer Science*, pages 322–331. IEEE Computer Society Press, Los Alamitos, CA, 1995.

[CBFH+97] N. Cesa-Bianchi, Y. Freund, D. Haussler, D. P. Helmbold, R. E. Schapire, and M. K. Warmuth. How to use expert advice. *Journal of the ACM*, 44(3):427–485, 1997.

[CBFHW96] Nicolo Cesa-Bianchi, Yoav Freund, David P. Helmbold, and Manfred K. Warmuth. On-line prediction and conversion strategies. *Machine Learning*, 25:71–110, 1996.

[FO02] Y. Freund and M. Opper. Drifting games and Brownian motion. *Journal of Computer and System Sciences*, 64:113–132, 2002.

[Fre95] Y. Freund. Boosting a weak learning algorithm by majority. *Information and Computation*, 121(2):256–285, September 1995.

[FS97] Yoav Freund and Robert E. Schapire. A decision-theoretic generalization of on-line learning and an application to boosting. *Journal of Computer and System Sciences*, 55(1):119–139, August 1997.

[HKW98]   D. Haussler, J. Kivinen, and M. K. Warmuth. Sequential prediction of individual sequences under general loss functions. *IEEE Transactions on Information Theory*, 44(2):1906–1925, September 1998.

[HW98]   M. Herbster and M. K. Warmuth. Tracking the best expert. *Journal of Machine Learning*, 32(2):151–178, August 1998.

[KW97]   J. Kivinen and M. K. Warmuth. Additive versus exponentiated gradient updates for linear prediction. *Information and Computation*, 132(1):1–64, January 1997.

[KW99]   J. Kivinen and M. K. Warmuth. Averaging expert predictions. In Paul Fischer and Hans Ulrich Simon, editors, *Computational Learning Theory: 4th European Conference (EuroCOLT '99)*, pages 153–167, Berlin, March 1999. Springer.

[LW94]   N. Littlestone and M. K. Warmuth. The weighted majority algorithm. *Information and Computation*, 108(2):212–261, 1994. An early version appeared in FOCS 89.

[Vov90]   V. Vovk. Aggregating strategies. In *Proc. 3rd Annu. Workshop on Comput. Learning Theory*, pages 371–383. Morgan Kaufmann, 1990.

A   Proof of Lemma 1

To prove the lemma it suffices to prove the following statements:

(a) For all splits $0 < \mathbf{r} < \mathbf{s}$ and $y \in \{0,1\}$, $\ell(\mathbf{s}) > \ell(\mathbf{s}^{\mathbf{r},y})$.

(b) For all $|\mathbf{s}| > 1$, $\ell(\mathbf{s}) > 1 + \ell(\mathbf{s}^+)$ and unanimous splits are not optimal.

Notice that (a) implies that $\ell(\mathbf{s}) > \max\{\ell(\mathbf{s}^{\mathbf{r},0}), \ell(\mathbf{s}^{\mathbf{r},1})\}$, which rules out line 2 of the recursion (2). Also, statement (b) rules out line 1 and together, they imply the lemma.

We prove the above two statements by induction on the mistake budget $B(\mathbf{s})$. Statements (a) and (b) trivially hold for the base case $\mathbf{s} = \mathbf{0}$, i.e. when $B(\mathbf{s}) = -1$. Assume that (a) and (b) holds for all states $\mathbf{s}'$ where $B(\mathbf{s}') < B(\mathbf{s})$. We now show that the statements holds for state $\mathbf{s}$.

For (a), let $\mathbf{r}$ be any non-unanimous split of $\mathbf{s}$ and let $\mathbf{z} := \mathbf{s}^{\mathbf{r},0}$. Consider two cases depending on the value of $|\mathbf{z}|$.

Assume $|\mathbf{z}| = 1$, then $\mathbf{z} = \mathbf{b}_i$. This implies that $\mathbf{s} = \mathbf{b}_i + m\mathbf{b}_k$ and $\mathbf{r} = m\mathbf{b}_k$ for some $m > 0$. Then $\mathbf{s}^{\mathbf{r},0} = \mathbf{b}_i$ and $\mathbf{s}^{\mathbf{r},1} = \mathbf{b}_{i+1} + m\mathbf{b}_k$, and by (2), we see that

$$\ell(\mathbf{s}) \geq \frac{\ell(\mathbf{b}_i) + \ell(\mathbf{b}_{i+1} + m\mathbf{b}_k) + 1}{2} = \frac{k - i + \ell(\mathbf{b}_{i+1} + m\mathbf{b}_k) + 1}{2}.$$

We now show that $\ell(\mathbf{b}_{i+1} + m\mathbf{b}_k) > k - i - 1$ which implies that $\ell(\mathbf{s}) > k - i = \ell(\mathbf{z})$. If $i = k$ then $\mathbf{b}_{i+1} = \mathbf{0}$ and $\mathbf{b}_{i+1} + m\mathbf{b}_k = m\mathbf{b}_k$. Therefore, we can see by induction that $\ell(m\mathbf{b}_k) \geq \ell(\mathbf{b}_k) = 0 > -1$. Also if $i < k$ then by a similar induction, $\ell(\mathbf{b}_{i+1} + m\mathbf{b}_k) > \ell(\mathbf{b}_{i+1}) = k - i - 1$. This implies that $\ell(\mathbf{s}) > k - i$ as desired.

Assume $|\mathbf{z}| \geq 2$. Since $B(\mathbf{z}) < B(\mathbf{s})$, it follows by induction that there is some non-unanimous split $\mathbf{q}$ of $\mathbf{z}$ s.t.

$$\ell(\mathbf{z}) = \frac{\ell(\mathbf{z}^{\mathbf{q},1}) + \ell(\mathbf{z}^{\mathbf{q},0}) + 1}{2} = \frac{\ell((\mathbf{s}^{\mathbf{r},0})^{\mathbf{q},1}) + \ell((\mathbf{s}^{\mathbf{r},0})^{\mathbf{q},0}) + 1}{2}.$$

Since $\mathbf{r}$ is non-unanimous it follows by induction that the above is less than $\frac{\ell(\mathbf{s}^{\mathbf{q},1})+\ell(\mathbf{s}^{\mathbf{q},0})+1}{2} \leq \ell(\mathbf{s})$.

For the proof of (b), let $\mathbf{z} := \mathbf{s}^+$. We consider two cases depending on the value of $|\mathbf{z}|$.

Assume $|\mathbf{z}| = 1$. Then $\mathbf{z} = \mathbf{b}_{i+1}$ for some i, and thus $\mathbf{s} = \mathbf{b}_i + m\mathbf{b}_k$ for some $m \geq 1$. Notice, we already proved above that, when $\mathbf{s}$ is of this form, that $\ell(\mathbf{s}) > k - i = \ell(\mathbf{s}^+) + 1$ as desired.

Assume $|\mathbf{z}| \geq 2$. We prove the statement by induction on the mistake budget $B(\mathbf{s})$. For the base case $B(\mathbf{s}) = 1$, we must be in state $(0,\ldots,0,2) = 2\mathbf{b}_k$ and therefore $\mathbf{z} = \mathbf{0}$, so the statement is true. We now proceed to the induction step. Notice that $B(\mathbf{z}) < B(\mathbf{s})$ and $|\mathbf{z}| \geq 2$. By induction, we can therefore find a non-unanimous split $\mathbf{q}'$ of $\mathbf{z}$ where $\ell(\mathbf{z}) = \frac{\ell(\mathbf{z}^{\mathbf{q}',1})+\ell(\mathbf{z}^{\mathbf{q}',0})+1}{2}$. We now choose $\mathbf{q}$ so that $\mathbf{q}^+ = \mathbf{q}'$. Observe that $(\mathbf{s}^{\mathbf{q},y})^+ = \mathbf{z}^{\mathbf{q}',y}$ for $y = 0,1$. Also, $B(\mathbf{s}^{\mathbf{q},y}) < B(\mathbf{s})$, and thus by induction we can apply (b), giving us that $\ell(\mathbf{s}^{\mathbf{q},y}) > \ell((\mathbf{s}^{\mathbf{q},y})^+)+1 = \ell(\mathbf{z}^{\mathbf{q}',y}) + 1$. Combining these statements, we see that

$$\ell(\mathbf{s}) \geq \frac{\ell(\mathbf{s}^{\mathbf{q},0}) + \ell(\mathbf{s}^{\mathbf{q},1}) + 1}{2} > \frac{\ell(\mathbf{z}^{\mathbf{q}',0}) + \ell(\mathbf{z}^{\mathbf{q}',1}) + 3}{2} = \ell(\mathbf{z}) + 1 = \ell(\mathbf{s}^+) + 1,$$

as desired. This completes the proof of the lemma.

Competing with Wild Prediction Rules

Vladimir Vovk

Computer Learning Research Centre, Department of Computer Science
Royal Holloway, University of London, Egham, Surrey TW20 0EX, UK
vovk@cs.rhul.ac.uk

Abstract. We consider the problem of on-line prediction competitive with a benchmark class of continuous but highly irregular prediction rules. It is known that if the benchmark class is a reproducing kernel Hilbert space, there exists a prediction algorithm whose average loss over the first N examples does not exceed the average loss of any prediction rule in the class plus a "regret term" of $O(N^{-1/2})$. The elements of some natural benchmark classes, however, are so irregular that these classes are not Hilbert spaces. In this paper we develop Banach-space methods to construct a prediction algorithm with a regret term of $O(N^{-1/p})$, where $p \in [2, \infty)$ and $p - 2$ reflects the degree to which the benchmark class fails to be a Hilbert space.

1   Introduction

For simplicity, in this introductory section we only discuss the problem of predicting real-valued labels y_n of objects $x_n \in [0, 1]$ (this will remain our main example throughout the paper). In this paper we are mainly interested in extending the class of the prediction rules our algorithms are competitive with; in other respects, our assumptions are rather restrictive. For example, we always assume that the labels y_n are bounded in absolute value by a known positive constant Y and only consider the problem of square-loss regression.

Standard methods allow one to construct a "universally consistent" on-line prediction algorithm, i.e., an on-line prediction algorithm whose average loss over the first N examples does not exceed the average loss of any continuous prediction rule plus $o(1)$. (Such methods were developed in, e.g., [5], [10], and, especially, [3], §3.2; for an explicit statement see [21].) More specifically, for any reproducing kernel Hilbert space (RKHS) on $[0, 1]$ one can construct an on-line prediction algorithm whose average loss does not exceed that of any prediction rule in the RKHS plus $O(N^{-1/2})$; choosing a universal RKHS ([19], Definition 4) gives universal consistency. In this paper we are interested in extending the latter result, which is much more specific than the $o(1)$ provided by universal consistency, to wider benchmark classes of prediction rules. First we discuss limitations of RKHS as benchmark classes.

The regularity of a prediction rule D can be measured by its "Hölder exponent" h, which is informally defined by the condition that $|D(x + dx) - D(x)|$ scale as $|dx|^h$ for small $|dx|$. The most regular continuous functions are those of classical analysis: say, piecewise differentiable with bounded derivatives. For

G. Lugosi and H.U. Simon (Eds.): COLT 2006, LNAI 4005, pp. 559–573, 2006.

such functions the Hölder exponent is 1. Functions much less regular than those of classical analysis are ubiquitous in probability theory: for example, typical trajectories of the Brownian motion (more generally, of non-degenerate diffusion processes) have Hölder exponent $1/2$. Functions with other Hölder exponents $h \in (0,1)$ can be obtained as typical trajectories of the fractional Brownian motion. Three examples with different values of h are shown in Figure 1.

The intuition behind the informal notion of a function with Hölder exponent h will be captured using function spaces known as Sobolev spaces. Roughly, the Sobolev spaces $W^{s,p}([0,1])$ (defined formally in the next section), where $p \in (1,\infty]$, $s \in (0,1)$, and $s > 1/p$, can be regarded as different ways of formalizing the notion of a function on $[0,1]$ with Hölder exponent h above the threshold s.

The most familiar Sobolev spaces are the Hölder spaces $W^{s,\infty}([0,1])$, consisting of the functions f satisfying $|f(x) - f(y)| = O\left(|x-y|^s\right)$. The Hölder spaces are nested, $W^{s,\infty}([0,1]) \subset W^{s',\infty}([0,1])$ when $s' < s$. As we will see in a moment, the standard Hilbert-space methods only work for $W^{s,\infty}([0,1])$ with $s > 1/2$ as benchmark classes; our goal is to develop methods that would work for smaller s as well.

The spaces $W^{s,\infty}([0,1])$ are rather awkward analytically and even poorly reflect the intuitive notion of Hölder exponent: they are defined in terms of $\sup_{x,y}|f(x) - f(y)|/|x-y|^s$, and f's behavior in the neighborhood of a single point can too easily disqualify it from being a member of $W^{s,\infty}([0,1])$. Replacing sup with the mean (in the sense of L^p) w.r. to a natural "almost finite" measure gives the Sobolev spaces $W^{s,p}([0,1])$ for $p < \infty$. Results for the case $p < \infty$ immediately carry over to $p = \infty$ since, as we will see in the next section, $W^{s,\infty}([0,1]) \subseteq W^{s',p}([0,1])$ whenever $s' < s$; s' can be arbitrarily close to s.

All Sobolev spaces (including the Hölder spaces) are Banach spaces, but $W^{s,2}([0,1])$ are also Hilbert spaces and, for $s > 1/2$, even RKHS. Therefore, they are amenable to the standard methods (see the papers mentioned above; the exposition of [21] is especially close to that of this paper, although we wrote H^s instead of $W^{s,2}$ in [21]).

The condition $s > 1/p$ appears indispensable in the development of the theory (cf. the reference to the Sobolev imbedding theorem in the next section). Since this paper concentrates on the irregular end of the Sobolev spectrum, $s < 1/2$, instead of the Hilbert spaces $W^{s,2}([0,1])$ we now have to deal with the Banach

$h = 0.2$　　　　　　$h = 0.5$　　　　　　$h = 0.8$

Fig. 1. Functions with Hölder exponent h for three different values of h

spaces $W^{s,p}([0,1])$ with $p \in (2, \infty)$, which are not Hilbert spaces. The necessary tools are developed in §§4–5.

The methods of [21] relied on the perfect shape of the unit ball in a Hilbert space. If p is not very far from 2, the unit ball in $W^{s,p}$ is not longer perfectly round but still convex enough to allow us to obtain similar results by similar methods. In principle, the condition $s > 1/p$ is not longer an obstacle to coping with any $s > 0$: by taking a large enough p we can reach arbitrarily small s. However, the quality of prediction (at least as judged by our bound) will deteriorate: as we will see (Theorem 1 in the next section), the average loss of our prediction algorithm does not exceed that of any prediction rule in $W^{s,p}([0,1])$ plus $O(N^{-1/p})$. (This gives a regret term of $O(N^{-s+\epsilon})$ for the prediction rules in $W^{s,\infty}([0,1])$, where $s < 1/2$ and $\epsilon > 0$.)

In this conference version of the paper some proofs are omitted; for complete proofs, see [20].

2   Main Result

We consider the following perfect-information prediction protocol:

FOR $n = 1, 2, \dots$:
    Reality announces $x_n \in \mathbf{X}$.
    Predictor announces $\mu_n \in \mathbb{R}$.
    Reality announces $y_n \in [-Y, Y]$.
END FOR.

At the beginning of each round n Predictor is given an object x_n whose label is to be predicted. The set of a priori possible objects, the object space, is denoted $\mathbf{X}$; we always assume $\mathbf{X} \neq \emptyset$. After Predictor announces his prediction μ_n for the object's label he is shown the actual label $y_n \in [-Y, Y]$. We consider the problem of regression, $y_n \in \mathbb{R}$, assuming an upper bound Y on $|y_n|$. The pairs (x_n, y_n) are called examples.

Predictor's loss on round n is measured by $(y_n - \mu_n)^2$, and so his average loss after N rounds of the game is $\frac{1}{N} \sum_{n=1}^{N} (y_n - \mu_n)^2$. His goal is to have

$$\frac{1}{N} \sum_{n=1}^{N} (y_n - \mu_n)^2 \lesssim \frac{1}{N} \sum_{n=1}^{N} (y_n - D(x_n))^2$$

($\lesssim$ meaning "is less than or approximately equal to") for each prediction rule $D : \mathbf{X} \to \mathbb{R}$ that is not "too wild".

Main theorem
Our main theorem will be fairly general and applicable to a wide range of Banach function spaces. Its implications for Sobolev spaces will be explained after its statement.

Let U be a Banach space and $S_U := \{u \in U \,|\, \|u\|_U = 1\}$ be the unit sphere in U. Our methods are applicable only to Banach spaces whose unit spheres do not have very flat areas; a convenient measure of rotundity of S_U is Clarkson's [6] modulus of convexity

$$\delta_U(\epsilon) := \inf_{\substack{u,v \in S_U \\ \|u-v\|_U = \epsilon}} \left(1 - \left\|\frac{u+v}{2}\right\|_U\right), \quad \epsilon \in (0,2] \tag{1}$$

(we will be mostly interested in the small values of ϵ).

Let us say that a Banach space $\mathcal{F}$ of real-valued functions f on $\mathbf{X}$ (with the standard pointwise operations of addition and of multiplication by scalar) is a *proper Banach functional space* (PBFS) on $\mathbf{X}$ if, for each $x \in \mathbf{X}$, the evaluation functional $\mathbf{k}_x : f \in \mathcal{F} \mapsto f(x)$ is continuous. We will assume that

$$\mathbf{c}_\mathcal{F} := \sup_{x \in \mathbf{X}} \|\mathbf{k}_x\|_{\mathcal{F}^*} < \infty, \tag{2}$$

where $\mathcal{F}^*$ is the dual Banach space (see, e.g., [16], Chapter 4).

The proof of the following theorem will be sketched in §§4–5.

Theorem 1. *Let $\mathcal{F}$ be a proper Banach functional space such that*

$$\forall \epsilon \in (0,2] : \delta_\mathcal{F}(\epsilon) \geq (\epsilon/2)^p / p \tag{3}$$

for some $p \in [2, \infty)$. There exists a prediction algorithm producing $\mu_n \in [-Y, Y]$ that are guaranteed to satisfy

$$\frac{1}{N} \sum_{n=1}^{N} (y_n - \mu_n)^2 \leq \frac{1}{N} \sum_{n=1}^{N} (y_n - D(x_n))^2 + 40Y\sqrt{\mathbf{c}_\mathcal{F}^2 + 1}\,(\|D\|_\mathcal{F} + Y)\, N^{-1/p}$$

$$\tag{4}$$

for all $N = 1, 2, \ldots$ and all $D \in \mathcal{F}$.

Conditions (2) and (3) are satisfied for the Sobolev spaces $W^{s,p}(\mathbf{X})$, which we will now define.

Sobolev spaces

Suppose $\mathbf{X}$ is an open or closed set in $\mathbb{R}^m$. (The standard theory assumes that $\mathbf{X}$ is open, but the results we need easily extend to many closed $\mathbf{X}$.) We only define the Sobolev spaces $W^{s,p}(\mathbf{X})$ for the cases $s \in (0,1)$ and $p > m/s$; for a more general definition see, e.g., [14] (pp. 57, 61).

Let $s \in (0,1)$ and $p > m/s$. For a function $f \in L^p(\mathbf{X})$ define

$$\|f\|_{s,p} := \left(\int_\mathbf{X} |f(x)|^p \, dx + \int_\mathbf{X} \int_\mathbf{X} \left|\frac{f(x) - f(y)}{|x-y|^s}\right|^p \frac{dx\,dy}{|x-y|^m}\right)^{1/p} \tag{5}$$

(we use $|\cdot|$ to denote the Euclidean norm). The Sobolev space $W^{s,p}(\mathbf{X})$ is defined to be the set of all f such that $\|f\|_{s,p} < \infty$. The Sobolev imbedding theorem says that, for a wide range of $\mathbf{X}$ (definitely including our main example

$\mathbf{X} = [0,1] \subseteq \mathbb{R}$), the functions in $W^{s,p}(\mathbf{X})$ can be made continuous by a change on a set of measure zero; we will always assume that this is true for our object space $\mathbf{X}$ and consider the elements of $W^{s,p}(\mathbf{X})$ to be continuous functions. Let $C(\mathbf{X})$ be the Banach space of continuous functions $f : \mathbf{X} \to \mathbb{R}$ with finite norm $\|f\|_{C(\mathbf{X})} := \sup_{x \in \mathbf{X}} |f(x)|$. The Sobolev imbedding theorem also says that the imbedding $W^{s,p}(\mathbf{X}) \hookrightarrow C(\mathbf{X})$ (i.e., the function that maps each $f \in W^{s,p}(\mathbf{X})$ to the same function but considered as an element of $C(\mathbf{X})$) is continuous, i.e., that

$$\mathbf{c}_{s,p} := \mathbf{c}_{W^{s,p}(\mathbf{X})} < \infty :$$

notice that $\mathbf{c}_{s,p}$ is just the norm of the imbedding $W^{s,p}(\mathbf{X}) \hookrightarrow C(\mathbf{X})$. These conclusions depend on the condition $p > m/s$ (there are other parts of the Sobolev imbedding theorem, dealing with the case where this condition is not satisfied). For a proof in the case $\mathbf{X} = \mathbb{R}^m$, see, e.g., [1], Theorems 7.34(c) and 7.47(a,c); this implies the analogous statement for $\mathbf{X}$ with smooth boundary since for such $\mathbf{X}$ every $f \in W^{s,p}(\mathbf{X})$ can be extended to an element of $W^{s,p}(\mathbb{R}^m)$ without increasing the norm more than a constant times (see, e.g., [14], p. 81). We will say "domain" to mean a subset of $\mathbb{R}^n$ which satisfies the conditions of regularity mentioned in this paragraph.

The norm (5) (sometimes called the Sobolev–Slobodetsky norm) is only one of the standard norms giving rise to the same topological vector space, and the term "Sobolev space" is usually used to refer to the topology rather than a specific norm; in this paper we will not consider any other norms. The restriction $s \in (0,1)$ is not essential for the results in this paper, but the definition of $\|\cdot\|_{s,p}$ becomes slightly more complicated when $s \geq 1$ (cf. [14]); [1] gives a different but equivalent norm.

We can now deduce the following corollary from Theorem 1. It is known that (3) is satisfied for the Sobolev spaces $W^{s,p}(\mathbf{X})$ (see (24)). Let $p \in [2, \infty)$ and $s \in (m/p, 1)$. There exists a constant $C_{s,p} > 0$ and a prediction algorithm producing $\mu_n \in [-Y, Y]$ that are guaranteed to satisfy

$$\frac{1}{N} \sum_{n=1}^{N} (y_n - \mu_n)^2 \leq \frac{1}{N} \sum_{n=1}^{N} (y_n - D(x_n))^2 + Y C_{s,p} \left(\|D\|_{s,p} + Y \right) N^{-1/p} \quad (6)$$

for all $N = 1, 2, \ldots$ and all $D \in W^{s,p}(\mathbf{X})$.

According to (4), we can take

$$C_{s,p} = 40 \sqrt{\mathbf{c}_{s,p}^2 + 1},$$

but in fact

$$C_{s,p} = 4 \times 8.68^{1-1/p} \sqrt{\mathbf{c}_{s,p}^2 + 1} \quad (7)$$

will suffice (see (30) below). In the special case $p = 2$ one can use Hilbert-space methods to improve (7), which now becomes, approximately,

$$11.78 \sqrt{\mathbf{c}_{s,2}^2 + 1}, \quad (8)$$

to

$$2\sqrt{\mathbf{c}_{s,2}^2 + 1} \tag{9}$$

([21], Theorem 1); using Banach-space methods we have lost a factor of 5.89.

Application to the Hölder continuous functions
An important limiting case of the norm (5) is

$$\|f\|_{s,\infty} := \max\left(\sup_{x\in\mathbf{X}}|f(x)|, \sup_{x,y\in\mathbf{X}:x\neq y}\left|\frac{f(x)-f(y)}{|x-y|^s}\right|\right),$$

where $f : \mathbf{X} \to \mathbb{R}$ is, as usual, assumed continuous. The space $W^{s,\infty}(\mathbf{X})$ consists of the functions f with $\|f\|_{s,\infty} < \infty$, and its elements are called *Hölder continuous of order s*.

The Hölder continuous functions of order s are perhaps the simplest formalization of the functions with Hölder exponent $h \geq s$. Let us see what Theorem 1 gives for them.

Suppose that $\mathbf{X}$ is a bounded domain in $\mathbb{R}^m$, $p \in (1,\infty)$, and $s,s' \in (0,1)$ are such that $s' < s$. If $f \in W^{s,\infty}(\mathbf{X})$, a routine calculation shows that

$$\|f\|_{s',p} \leq \|f\|_{s,\infty}\left(1 + m\frac{\pi^{m/2}}{\Gamma(m/2+1)}|\mathbf{X}|\frac{(\operatorname{diam}\mathbf{X})^{(s-s')p}}{(s-s')p}\right)^{1/p}, \tag{10}$$

where $|\mathbf{X}|$ stands for the volume (Lebesgue measure) of $\mathbf{X}$ and diam $\mathbf{X}$ stands for the diameter of $\mathbf{X}$. Inequality (10) gives an explicit bound for the norm of the continuous imbedding $W^{s,\infty}(\mathbf{X}) \hookrightarrow W^{s',p}(\mathbf{X})$.

Fix an arbitrarily small $\epsilon > 0$. Applying (6) to $W^{s',p}(\mathbf{X})$ with $p > m/s$ sufficiently close to m/s and to $s' \in (m/p, s)$, we can see from (10) that there exists a constant $C_{s,\epsilon} > 0$ such that

$$\frac{1}{N}\sum_{n=1}^{N}(y_n - \mu_n)^2 \leq \frac{1}{N}\sum_{n=1}^{N}(y_n - D(x_n))^2 + YC_{s,\epsilon}\left(\|D\|_{s,\infty} + Y\right)N^{-s/m+\epsilon} \tag{11}$$

holds for all $N = 1, 2, \ldots$ and all $D \in W^{s,\infty}(\mathbf{X})$.

3   Implications for a Stochastic Reality

In this section we discuss implications of Theorem 1 for statistical learning theory and filtering of random processes. Surprisingly, even when Reality follows a specific stochastic strategy, competitive on-line results do not trivialize but provide new meaningful information.

Statistical learning theory
In this subsection we apply the method of [4] to derive a corollary of Theorem 1 for the statistical learning framework, where (x_n, y_n) are assumed to be drawn independently from the same probability distribution on $\mathbf{X} \times [-Y, Y]$.

The *risk* of a prediction rule (formally, a measurable function) $D : \mathbf{X} \to \mathbb{R}$ with respect to a probability distribution P on $\mathbf{X} \times [-Y, Y]$ is defined as

$$\mathrm{risk}_P(D) := \int_{\mathbf{X} \times [-Y,Y]} (y - D(x))^2 P(dx, dy).$$

Our current goal is to construct, from a given sample, a prediction rule whose risk is competitive with the risk of small-norm prediction rules in $W^{s,p}(\mathbf{X})$.

Fix an on-line prediction algorithm and a sequence $(x_1, y_1), (x_2, y_2), \ldots$ of examples. For each $n = 1, 2, \ldots$ and each $x \in \mathbf{X}$, define $H_n(x)$ to be the prediction $\mu_n \in \mathbb{R}$ output by the algorithm when fed with $(x_1, y_1), \ldots, (x_{n-1}, y_{n-1}), x$. We will assume that the functions H_n are always measurable (they are for our algorithm). The prediction rule

$$\overline{H}_N(x) := \frac{1}{N} \sum_{n=1}^{N} H_n(x)$$

will be said to be *obtained by averaging* from the prediction algorithm.

The following result is an easy application of the method of [4] to (6); we refrain from stating the analogous result based on (11).

Corollary 1. *Let $\mathbf{X}$ be a domain in $\mathbb{R}^m$, $p \geq 2$, $s \in (m/p, 1)$, and let $\overline{H}_N$, $N = 1, 2, \ldots$, be the prediction rule obtained by averaging from some prediction algorithm guaranteeing (6). For any $D \in W^{s,p}(\mathbf{X})$, any probability distribution P on $\mathbf{X} \times [-Y, Y]$, any $N = 1, 2, \ldots$, and any $\delta > 0$,*

$$\mathrm{risk}_P(\overline{H}_N) \leq \mathrm{risk}_P(D) + Y C_{s,p} \left(\|D\|_{s,p} + Y \right) N^{-1/p} + 4Y^2 \sqrt{2 \ln \frac{2}{\delta}} N^{-1/2} \quad (12)$$

with probability at least $1 - \delta$.

Filtering of random processes
Suppose we are interested in the value of a "signal" $\Theta : [0, 1] \to \mathbb{R}$ sequentially observed at moments $t_n := n/N$, $n = 1, \ldots, N$, where N is a large positive integer; let $\theta_n := \Theta(t_n)$. The problem is that our observations of θ_n are imperfect, and in fact we see $y_n = \theta_n + \xi_n$, where each noise random variable ξ_n has zero expectation given the past. We assume that Θ belongs to $W^{s,p}([0, 1])$ (but do not make any assumptions about the mechanism, deterministic, stochastic, or other, that generated it) and that $\theta_n, y_n \in [-Y, Y]$ for a known positive constant Y. Let us use the μ_n from Theorem 1 as estimates of the true values θ_n. The elementary equality

$$a^2 = (a - b)^2 - b^2 + 2ab \quad (13)$$

implies

$$\sum_{n=1}^{N} (\mu_n - \theta_n)^2 = \sum_{n=1}^{N} (y_n - \mu_n)^2 - \sum_{n=1}^{N} (y_n - \theta_n)^2 + 2 \sum_{n=1}^{N} (y_n - \theta_n)(\mu_n - \theta_n). \quad (14)$$

Hoeffding's inequality in the martingale form shows that, for any $C > 0$,

$$\mathbb{P}\left\{2\sum_{n=1}^{N}(y_n - \theta_n)(\mu_n - \theta_n) \geq C\right\} \leq \exp\left(-\frac{C^2}{128Y^4N}\right).$$

Substituting this (with C expressed via the right-hand side, denoted δ) and (6) into (14), we obtain the following corollary, which we state somewhat informally.

Corollary 2. *Let $p \geq 2$, $s \in (1/p, 1)$, and $\delta > 0$. Suppose that $\Theta \in W^{s,p}([0,1])$ and $y_n = \theta_n + \xi_n \in [-Y, Y]$, where $\theta_n := \Theta(n/N) \in [-Y, Y]$ and ξ_n are random variables whose expectation given the past (including θ_n) is zero. With probability at least $1 - \delta$ the μ_n of (6) satisfy*

$$\frac{1}{N}\sum_{n=1}^{N}(\mu_n - \theta_n)^2 \leq YC_{s,p}\left(\|\Theta\|_{s,p} + Y\right)N^{-1/p} + 8Y^2\sqrt{2\ln\frac{1}{\delta}}N^{-1/2}. \quad (15)$$

The constant $C_{s,p}$ in (15) is the one in (7). From (11), we can also see that, if we assume $\Theta \in W^{s,\infty}([0,1])$,

$$\frac{1}{N}\sum_{n=1}^{N}(\mu_n - \theta_n)^2 \leq YC_{s,\epsilon}\left(\|\Theta\|_{s,\infty} + Y\right)N^{-s+\epsilon} + 8Y^2\sqrt{2\ln\frac{1}{\delta}}N^{-1/2} \quad (16)$$

will hold with probability at least $1 - \delta$.

It is important that the function Θ in (15) and (16) does not have to be chosen in advance: it can be constructed "step-wise", with $\Theta(t)$ for $t \in (n/N, (n+1)/N]$ chosen at will after observing ξ_n and taking into account all other information that becomes available before and including time n/N. A clean formalization of this intuitive picture seems to require the game-theoretic probability of [17] (although we can get the picture "almost right" using the standard measure-theoretic probability).

In the case where Θ is generated from a diffusion process, it will almost surely belong to $W^{(1-\epsilon)/2,\infty}([0,1])$ (this follows from standard results about the Brownian motion, such as Lévy's modulus theorem: see, e.g., [9], Theorem 9.25), and so, by (15) or (16), $\frac{1}{N}\sum_{n=1}^{N}(\mu_n - \theta_n)^2$ can be made $O(N^{-1/2+\epsilon})$, for an arbitrarily small $\epsilon > 0$. The Kalman filter, which is stochastically optimal, gives a somewhat better bound, $O(N^{-1/2})$. Corollary 2, however, does not depend on the very specific assumptions of the Kalman filter: we do not require the linearity, Gaussianity, or even stochasticity of the model; the assumption about the noise ξ_n is minimal (zero expectation given the past). Instead, we have the assumption that all θ_n and y_n are chosen from $[-Y, Y]$. It appears that in practice the interval to which the θ_n and y_n are assumed to belong should change slowly as new data are processed. This is analogous to the situation with the Kalman filter, which, despite assuming linear systems, has found its greatest application to non-linear systems [18]; what is usually used in practice is the "extended Kalman filter", which relies on a slowly changing linearization of the non-linear system.

4   More Geometry of Banach Spaces

The standard modulus of smoothness of a Banach space U was proposed by
Lindenstrauss [12]:

$$\rho_U(\tau) := \sup_{u,v \in S_U} \left(\frac{\|u + \tau v\|_U + \|u - \tau v\|_U}{2} - 1 \right), \quad \tau > 0. \tag{17}$$

Lindenstrauss also established a simple but very useful relation of conjugacy (cf.
[15], §12, although δ is not always convex [13]) between δ and ρ:

$$\rho_{U^*}(\tau) = \sup_{\epsilon \in (0,2]} \left(\frac{\epsilon \tau}{2} - \delta_U(\epsilon) \right); \tag{18}$$

we can see that $2\rho_{U^*}$ is the Fenchel transform of $2\delta_U$.

The following inequality will be the basis of the proof of Theorem 1 sketched
in the next section. Suppose a PBFS $\mathcal{F}$ satisfies the condition (3) of Theorem 1.
By (18) we obtain for the dual space $\mathcal{F}^*$ to $\mathcal{F}$, assuming $\tau \in (0,1]$:

$$\rho_{\mathcal{F}^*}(\tau) \le \sup_{\epsilon \in (0,2]} \left(\frac{\epsilon \tau}{2} - (\epsilon/2)^p/p \right) = \tau^q/q, \tag{19}$$

where $q := p/(p-1)$ (the supremum in (19) is attained at $\epsilon = 2\tau^{1/(p-1)}$).

If V is a Hilbert space, the "parallelogram identity"

$$\|u + v\|_V^2 + \|u - v\|_V^2 = 2\|u\|_V^2 + 2\|v\|_V^2 \tag{20}$$

immediately gives

$$\delta_V(\epsilon) = 1 - \sqrt{1 - (\epsilon/2)^2} \ge \epsilon^2/8$$

and

$$\rho_V(\tau) = \sqrt{1 + \tau^2} - 1 \le \tau^2/2. \tag{21}$$

If U_1 and U_2 are two Banach spaces, their *weighted direct sum* $U_1 \oplus U_2$ is
defined to be the Cartesian product $U_1 \times U_2$ with the operations of addition and
multiplication by scalar defined by

$$(u_1, u_2) + (u_1', u_2') := (u_1 + u_1', u_2 + u_2'), \quad c(u_1, u_2) := (cu_1, cu_2);$$

we will equip it with the norm

$$\|(u_1, u_2)\|_{U_1 \oplus U_2} := \sqrt{a_1 \|u_1\|_{U_1}^2 + a_2 \|u_2\|_{U_2}^2}, \tag{22}$$

where a_1 and a_2 are positive constants (to simplify formulas, we do not mention
them explicitly in our notation for $U_1 \oplus U_2$). The operation of weighted direct sum
provides a means of merging different Banach spaces, which plays an important
role in our proof technique (cf. [21], Corollary 4). The "Euclidean" definition
(22) of the norm in the direct sum suggests that the sum will be as smooth as

the components; this intuition is formalized in the following lemma (essentially a special case of Proposition 17 in [7], p. 132).

Lemma 1. *If U_1 and U_2 are Banach spaces and $f : (0,1] \to \mathbb{R}$,*

$$(\forall \tau \in (0,1] : \rho_{U_1}(\tau) \leq f(\tau) \ \& \ \rho_{U_2}(\tau) \leq f(\tau))$$
$$\implies (\forall \tau \in (0,1] : \rho_{U_1 \oplus U_2}(\tau) \leq 4.34 f(\tau)).$$

It was shown by Clarkson ([6], §3) that, for $p \in [2, \infty)$,

$$\delta_{L^p}(\epsilon) \geq 1 - (1 - (\epsilon/2)^p)^{1/p}.$$

(And this bound was shown to be optimal in [8].) A quick inspection of the standard proofs (see, e.g., [1], 2.34–2.40) shows that the underlying measurable space Ω and measure μ of $L^p = L^p(\Omega, \mu)$ can be essentially arbitrary (only the degenerate case where $\dim L^p < 2$ should be excluded), although this generality is usually not emphasized.

It is easy to see (cf. [1], 3.5–3.6) that the modulus of convexity of each Sobolev space $W^{s,p}(\mathbf{X})$, $s \in (0,1)$ and $p \in [2, \infty)$, also satisfies

$$\delta_{W^{s,p}(\mathbf{X})}(\epsilon) \geq 1 - (1 - (\epsilon/2)^p)^{1/p}. \tag{23}$$

Since, for $t \in [0,1]$ and $p \geq 1$, $(1-t)^{1/p} \leq 1 - t/p$ (the left-hand side is a concave function of t, and the values and derivatives of the two sides match when $t = 0$), we have

$$\delta_{W^{s,p}(\mathbf{X})}(\epsilon) \geq (\epsilon/2)^p / p. \tag{24}$$

Therefore, as we said in §2, the Sobolev spaces indeed satisfy the condition (3) of Theorem 1.

5 Proof Sketch of Theorem 1

In this section we partly follow the proof of Theorem 1 in [21] (§6).

The BBK29 algorithm

Let U be a Banach space. We say that a function $\Phi : [-Y, Y] \times \mathbf{X} \to U$ is *forecast-continuous* if $\Phi(\mu, x)$ is continuous in $\mu \in [-Y, Y]$ for every fixed $x \in \mathbf{X}$. For such a Φ the function

$$f_n(y, \mu) := \left\| \sum_{i=1}^{n-1} (y_i - \mu_i)\Phi(\mu_i, x_i) + (y - \mu)\Phi(\mu, x_n) \right\|_U$$
$$- \left\| \sum_{i=1}^{n-1} (y_i - \mu_i)\Phi(\mu_i, x_i) \right\|_U \tag{25}$$

is continuous in $\mu \in [-Y, Y]$.

BANACH-SPACE BALANCED K29 ALGORITHM (BBK29)
Parameter: forecast-continuous $\Phi : [-Y,Y] \times \mathbf{X} \to U$, with U a Banach space
FOR $n = 1, 2, \ldots$:
    Read $x_n \in \mathbf{X}$.
    Define $f_n : [-Y,Y]^2 \to \mathbb{R}$ by (25).
    Output any root $\mu \in [-Y,Y]$ of $f_n(-Y,\mu) = f_n(Y,\mu)$ as μ_n;
        if there are no such roots, output $\mu_n \in \{-Y,Y\}$
        such that $\sup_{y\in[-Y,Y]} f_n(y,\mu_n) \le 0$.
    Read $y_n \in [-Y,Y]$.
END FOR.

The validity of this description depends on the existence of $\mu \in \{-Y,Y\}$ satisfying $\sup_{y\in[-Y,Y]} f_n(y,\mu) \le 0$ when the equation $f_n(-Y,\mu) = f_n(Y,\mu)$ does not have roots $\mu \in [-Y,Y]$. The existence of such a μ is easy to check: if $f_n(-Y,\mu) < f_n(Y,\mu)$ for all $\mu \in [-Y,Y]$, take $\mu := Y$ to obtain

$$f_n(-Y,\mu) < f_n(Y,\mu) = 0$$

and, hence, $\sup_{y\in[-Y,Y]} f_n(y,\mu) \le 0$ by the convexity of (25) in y; if $f_n(Y,\mu) > f_n(Y,\mu)$ for all $\mu \in [-Y,Y]$, setting $\mu := -Y$ leads to

$$f_n(Y,\mu) < f_n(-Y,\mu) = 0$$

and, hence, $\sup_{y\in[-Y,Y]} f_n(y,\mu) \le 0$. The parameter Φ of the BBK29 algorithm will sometimes be called the *feature mapping*. The proof of the following result can be found in [20].

Theorem 2. *Let Φ be a forecast-continuous mapping from $[-Y,Y] \times \mathbf{X}$ to a Banach space U and set $\mathbf{c}_\Phi := \sup_{\mu\in[-Y,Y],x\in\mathbf{X}} \|\Phi(\mu,x)\|_U$. Suppose $\rho_U(\tau) \le a\tau^q$, $\forall \tau \in (0,1]$, for some constants $q \ge 1$ and $a \ge 1/q$. The BBK29 algorithm with parameter Φ outputs $\mu_n \in [-Y,Y]$ such that*

$$\left\| \sum_{n=1}^{N} (y_n - \mu_n)\Phi(\mu_n, x_n) \right\|_U \le 2Y\mathbf{c}_\Phi (2aqN)^{1/q} \tag{26}$$

always holds for all $N = 1, 2, \ldots$.

The feature mapping for the proof of Theorem 1
In the proof of Theorem 1 we need two feature mappings from $[-Y,Y] \times \mathbf{X}$ to different Banach spaces: first, $\Phi_1(\mu,x) := \mu$ (mapping to the Banach space $\mathbb{R}$), and second, $\Phi_2 : [-Y,Y] \times \mathbf{X} \to \mathcal{F}^*$ such that $\Phi_2(\mu,x)$ is the evaluation functional $\mathbf{k}_x : f \mapsto f(x)$, $f \in \mathcal{F}$. We combine them into one feature mapping

$$\Phi(\mu,x) := \big(\Phi_1(\mu,x), \Phi_2(\mu,x)\big) \tag{27}$$

to the weighted direct sum $U := \mathbb{R} \oplus \mathcal{F}^*$, with the weights a_1 and a_2 to be chosen later. By Lemma 1, (19), and (21), $\rho_U(\tau) \le a\tau^q$, where $a := 4.34/q$. With the help of Theorem 2, we obtain for the BBK29 algorithm with parameter Φ:

$$\left|\sum_{n=1}^{N}(y_n - \mu_n)\mu_n\right| = \left\|\sum_{n=1}^{N}(y_n - \mu_n)\Phi_1(\mu_n, x_n)\right\|_{\mathbb{R}}$$

$$\leq \frac{1}{\sqrt{a_1}}\left\|\sum_{n=1}^{N}(y_n - \mu_n)\Phi(\mu_n, x_n)\right\|_{U} \leq \frac{1}{\sqrt{a_1}}2Y\mathbf{c}_\Phi\,(2aqN)^{1/q} \quad (28)$$

and

$$\left|\sum_{n=1}^{N}(y_n - \mu_n)D(x_n)\right| = \left|\sum_{n=1}^{N}(y_n - \mu_n)\mathbf{k}_{x_n}(D)\right| = \left|\left(\sum_{n=1}^{N}(y_n - \mu_n)\mathbf{k}_{x_n}\right)(D)\right|$$

$$\leq \left\|\sum_{n=1}^{N}(y_n - \mu_n)\mathbf{k}_{x_n}\right\|_{\mathcal{F}^*}\|D\|_{\mathcal{F}} = \left\|\sum_{n=1}^{N}(y_n - \mu_n)\Phi_2(\mu_n, x_n)\right\|_{\mathcal{F}^*}\|D\|_{\mathcal{F}}$$

$$\leq \frac{1}{\sqrt{a_2}}\left\|\sum_{n=1}^{N}(y_n - \mu_n)\Phi(\mu_n, x_n)\right\|_{U}\|D\|_{\mathcal{F}} \leq \frac{1}{\sqrt{a_2}}2Y\mathbf{c}_\Phi\,(2aqN)^{1/q}\|D\|_{\mathcal{F}} \quad (29)$$

for each function $D \in \mathcal{F}$.

Proof proper
The proof is based on the inequality

$$\sum_{n=1}^{N}(y_n - \mu_n)^2$$

$$= \sum_{n=1}^{N}(y_n - D(x_n))^2 + 2\sum_{n=1}^{N}(D(x_n) - \mu_n)(y_n - \mu_n) - \sum_{n=1}^{N}(D(x_n) - \mu_n)^2$$

$$\leq \sum_{n=1}^{N}(y_n - D(x_n))^2 + 2\sum_{n=1}^{N}(D(x_n) - \mu_n)(y_n - \mu_n)$$

(immediately following from (13)). Using this inequality and (28)–(29) with $a_1 := Y^{-2}$ and $a_2 := 1$, we obtain for the $\mu_n \in [-Y, Y]$ output by the BBK29 algorithm with Φ as parameter:

$$\sum_{n=1}^{N}(y_n - \mu_n)^2$$

$$\leq \sum_{n=1}^{N}(y_n - D(x_n))^2 + 2\left|\sum_{n=1}^{N}\mu_n(y_n - \mu_n)\right| + 2\left|\sum_{n=1}^{N}D(x_n)(y_n - \mu_n)\right|$$

$$\leq \sum_{n=1}^{N}(y_n - D(x_n))^2 + 4Y\mathbf{c}_\Phi\,(2aqN)^{1/q}\left(\|D\|_{\mathcal{F}} + Y\right).$$

Since

$$\mathbf{c}_\Phi \leq \sqrt{a_1 Y^2 + a_2 \mathbf{c}_{\mathcal{F}}^2} = \sqrt{\mathbf{c}_{\mathcal{F}}^2 + 1},$$

we can see that (4) holds with

$$4(2aq)^{1/q} = 4 \times 8.68^{1/q} \tag{30}$$

in place of 40.

6   Banach Kernels

An RKHS can be defined as a PBFS in which the norm is expressed via an inner product as $\|f\| = \sqrt{\langle f, f \rangle}$. It is well known that all information about an RKHS $\mathcal{F}$ on a set Z is contained in its "reproducing kernel", which is a symmetric positive definite function on Z^2 ([2], §§I.1–I.2). The reproducing kernel can be regarded as the constructive representation of its RKHS, and it is the reproducing kernel rather than the RKHS itself that serves as a parameter of various machine-learning algorithms. In this section we will introduce a similar constructive representation for PBFS.

A *Banach kernel* B on a set Z is a function that maps each finite non-empty sequence $z_1, \ldots, z_n$ of distinct elements of Z to a seminorm $\|\cdot\|_{B(z_1, \ldots, z_n)}$ on $\mathbb{R}^n$ and satisfies the following conditions (familiar from Kolmogorov's existence theorem [11], §III.4):

- for each $n = 1, 2, \ldots$, each sequence $z_1, \ldots, z_n$ of distinct elements of Z, each sequence $(t_1, \ldots, t_n) \in \mathbb{R}^n$, and each permutation $\left(\begin{smallmatrix} 1 & 2 & \cdots & n \\ i_1 & i_2 & \cdots & i_n \end{smallmatrix} \right)$,

$$\|(t_{i_1}, \ldots, t_{i_n})\|_{B(z_{i_1}, \ldots, z_{i_n})} = \|(t_1, \ldots, t_n)\|_{B(z_1, \ldots, z_n)};$$

- for each $n = 1, 2, \ldots$, each $k = 1, \ldots, n$, each sequence $z_1, \ldots, z_n$ of distinct elements of Z, and each sequence $(t_1, \ldots, t_k) \in \mathbb{R}^k$,

$$\|(t_1, \ldots, t_k)\|_{B(z_1, \ldots, z_k)} = \|(t_1, \ldots, t_k, 0, \ldots, 0)\|_{B(z_1, \ldots, z_n)}.$$

The *Banach kernel of a PBFS* $\mathcal{F}$ on Z is the Banach kernel B defined by

$$\|(t_1, \ldots, t_n)\|_{B(z_1, \ldots, z_n)} := \|t_1 \mathbf{k}_{z_1} + \cdots + t_n \mathbf{k}_{z_n}\|_{\mathcal{F}^*},$$

where $\mathbf{k}_z : \mathcal{F} \to \mathbb{R}$, $z \in Z$, is the evaluation functional $f \in \mathcal{F} \mapsto f(z)$.

Proposition 1. *For each Banach kernel B on Z there exists a proper Banach functional space $\mathcal{F}$ on Z such that B is the Banach kernel of $\mathcal{F}$.*

Now we can state more explicitly the prediction algorithm described above and guaranteeing (4). Let B be the Banach kernel of the benchmark class $\mathcal{F}$ in (4).

Following (25) (with Φ defined by (27)), define

$$
f_n(y,\mu) := \left(\frac{1}{Y^2} \left(\sum_{i=1}^{n-1} (y_i - \mu_i)\mu_i + (y - \mu)\mu \right)^2 \right.
$$

$$
\left. + \|(y_1 - \mu_1, \ldots, y_{n-1} - \mu_{n-1}, y - \mu)\|^2_{B(x_1,\ldots,x_{n-1},x_n)} \right)^{1/2}
$$

$$
- \left(\frac{1}{Y^2} \left(\sum_{i=1}^{n-1} (y_i - \mu_i)\mu_i \right)^2 \right.
$$

$$
\left. + \|(y_1 - \mu_1, \ldots, y_{n-1} - \mu_{n-1})\|^2_{B(x_1,\ldots,x_{n-1})} \right)^{1/2}. \quad (31)
$$

This allows us to give the kernel representation of BBK29 with Φ defined by (27); its parameter is a Banach kernel on the object space $\mathbf{X}$.

ALGORITHM GUARANTEEING (4)
Parameter: Banach kernel B of $\mathcal{F}$
    FOR $n = 1, 2, \ldots$:
        Read $x_n \in \mathbf{X}$.
        Define $f_n : [-Y, Y]^2 \to \mathbb{R}$ by (31).
        Output any root $\mu \in [-Y, Y]$ of $f_n(-Y, \mu) = f_n(Y, \mu)$ as μ_n;
          if there are no such roots, output $\mu_n \in \{-Y, Y\}$
          such that $\sup_{y \in [-Y,Y]} f_n(y, \mu_n) \leq 0$.
        Read $y_n \in [-Y, Y]$.
    END FOR.

Acknowledgements

I am grateful to Glenn Shafer for a series of useful discussions. This work was partially supported by MRC (grant S505/65) and the Royal Society.

References

1. Robert A. Adams and John J. F. Fournier. *Sobolev Spaces*, volume 140 of *Pure and Applied Mathematics*. Academic Press, Amsterdam, second edition, 2003.
2. Nachman Aronszajn. Theory of reproducing kernels. *Transactions of the American Mathematical Society*, 68:337–404, 1950.
3. Peter Auer, Nicolò Cesa-Bianchi, and Claudio Gentile. Adaptive and self-confident on-line learning algorithms. *Journal of Computer and System Sciences*, 64:48–75, 2002.
4. Nicolò Cesa-Bianchi, Alex Conconi, and Claudio Gentile. On the generalization ability of on-line learning algorithms. *IEEE Transactions on Information Theory*, 50:2050–2057, 2004.

5. Nicolò Cesa-Bianchi, Philip M. Long, and Manfred K. Warmuth. Worst-case quadratic loss bounds for on-line prediction of linear functions by gradient descent. *IEEE Transactions on Neural Networks*, 7:604–619, 1996.

6. James A. Clarkson. Uniformly convex spaces. *Transactions of the American Mathematical Society*, 40:396–414, 1936.

7. T. Figiel. On the moduli of convexity and smoothness. *Studia Mathematica*, 56:121–155, 1976. Available free of charge at http://matwbn.icm.edu.pl.

8. Olof Hanner. On the uniform convexity of L^p and l^p. *Arkiv för Matematik*, 3:239–244, 1956.

9. Ioannis Karatzas and Steven E. Shreve. *Brownian Motion and Stochastic Calculus*. Springer, New York, second edition, 1991.

10. Jyrki Kivinen and Manfred K. Warmuth. Exponential Gradient versus Gradient Descent for linear predictors. *Information and Computation*, 132:1–63, 1997.

11. Andrei N. Kolmogorov. *Grundbegriffe der Wahrscheinlichkeitsrechnung*. Springer, Berlin, 1933. English translation: *Foundations of the theory of probability*. Chelsea, New York, 1950.

12. Joram Lindenstrauss. On the modulus of smoothness and divergent series in Banach spaces. *Michigan Mathematical Journal*, 10:241–252, 1963.

13. V. I. Liokumovich. The existence of B-spaces with non-convex modulus of convexity (in Russian). Известия высших учебных заведений. Математика, 12:43–50, 1973.

14. Sergei M. Nikolsky. On imbedding, continuation and approximation theorems for differentiable functions of several variables. *Russian Mathematical Surveys*, 16(5):55–104, 1961. Russian original in: Успехи математических наук, 16(5):63–114, 1961.

15. R. Tyrrell Rockafellar. *Convex Analysis*. Princeton University Press, Princeton, NJ, 1970.

16. Walter Rudin. *Functional Analysis*. McGraw-Hill, Boston, second edition, 1991.

17. Glenn Shafer and Vladimir Vovk. *Probability and Finance: It's Only a Game!* Wiley, New York, 2001.

18. H. W. Sorenson. Least-squares estimation: from Gauss to Kalman. *IEEE Spectrum*, 7:63–68, 1970.

19. Ingo Steinwart. On the influence of the kernel on the consistency of support vector machines. *Journal of Machine Learning Research*, 2:67–93, 2001.

20. Vladimir Vovk. Competing with wild prediction rules. Technical Report arXiv: cs.LG/0512059, arXiv.org e-Print archive, January 2006.

21. Vladimir Vovk. On-line regression competitive with reproducing kernel Hilbert spaces. In Jin-Yi Cai, S. Barry Cooper, and Angsheng Li, editors, *Theory and Applications of Models of Computation. Proceedings of the Third Annual Conference on Computation and Logic*, volume 3959 of *Lecture Notes in Computer Science*, pages 452–463, Berlin, 2006. Springer. Full version: Technical Report arXiv: cs.LG/0511058, arXiv.org e-Print archive, January 2006.

Learning Near-Optimal Policies with Bellman-Residual Minimization Based Fitted Policy Iteration and a Single Sample Path

András Antos[1], Csaba Szepesvári[1], and Rémi Munos[2]

[1] Computer and Automation Research Inst.
of the Hungarian Academy of Sciences
Kende u. 13-17, Budapest 1111, Hungary
{antos, szcsaba}@sztaki.hu
[2] Centre de Mathématiques Appliquées
Ecole Polytechnique
91128 Palaiseau Cedex, France
remi.munos@polytechnique.fr

Abstract. We consider batch reinforcement learning problems in continuous space, expected total discounted-reward Markovian Decision Problems. As opposed to previous theoretical work, we consider the case when the training data consists of a single sample path (trajectory) of some behaviour policy. In particular, we do not assume access to a generative model of the environment. The algorithm studied is policy iteration where in successive iterations the Q-functions of the intermediate policies are obtained by means of minimizing a novel Bellman-residual type error. PAC-style polynomial bounds are derived on the number of samples needed to guarantee near-optimal performance where the bound depends on the mixing rate of the trajectory, the smoothness properties of the underlying Markovian Decision Problem, the approximation power and capacity of the function set used.

1 Introduction

Consider the problem of optimizing a controller for an industrial environment. In many cases the data is collected on the field by running a fixed controller and then taken to the laboratory for optimization. The goal is to derive an optimized controller that improves upon the performance of the controller generating the data.

In this paper we are interested in the performance improvement that can be guaranteed given a finite amount of data. In particular, we are interested in how performance scales as a function of the amount of data available. We study Bellman-residual minimization based policy iteration assuming that the environment is stochastic and the state is observable and continuous valued. The algorithm considered is an iterative procedure where each iteration involves solving a least-squares problem, similar to the Least-Squares Policy Iteration algorithm of Lagoudakis and Parr [1]. However, whilst Lagoudakis and Parr considered the so-called least-squares fixed-point approximation to avoid problems with Bellman-residual minimization in the case of correlated samples, we

G. Lugosi and H.U. Simon (Eds.): COLT 2006, LNAI 4005, pp. 574–588, 2006.

modify the original Bellman-residual objective. In a forthcoming paper we study policy iteration with approximate iterative policy evaluation [2].

The main conditions of our results can be grouped into three parts: Conditions on the system, conditions on the trajectory (and the behaviour policy used to generate the trajectory) and conditions on the algorithm. The most important conditions on the system are that the state space should be compact, the action space should be finite and the dynamics should be smooth in a sense to be defined later. The major condition on the trajectory is that it should be rapidly mixing. This mixing property plays a crucial role in deriving a PAC-bound on the probability of obtaining suboptimal solutions in the proposed Bellman-residual minimization subroutine. The major conditions on the algorithm are that an appropriate number of iterations should be used and the function space used should have a finite capacity and be sufficiently rich at the same time. It follows that these conditions, as usual, require a good balance between the power of the approximation architecture (we want large power to get good approximation of the action-value functions of the policies encountered during the algorithm) and the number of samples: If the power of the approximation architecture is increased the algorithm will suffer from overfitting, as it also happens in supervised learning. Although the presence of the tradeoff between generalization error and model complexity should be of no surprise, this tradeoff is somewhat underrepresented in the reinforcement literature, presumably because most results where function approximators are involved are asymptotic.

The organization of the paper is as follows: In the next section (Section 2) we introduce the necessary symbols and notation. The algorithm is given in Section 3. The main results are presented in Section 4. This section, just like the proof, is broken into three parts: In Section 4.1 we prove our basic PAC-style lemma that relates the complexity of the function space, the mixing rate of the trajectory and the number of samples. In Section 4.2 we prove a bound on the propagation of errors during the course of the procedure. Here the smoothness properties of the MDP are used to bound the 'final' approximation error as a function of the individual errors. The proof of the main result is finished Section 4.3. In Section 5 some related work is discussed. Our conclusions are drawn in Section 6.

2   Notation

For a measurable space with domain S we let $M(S)$ denote the set of all probability measures over S. For $\nu \in M(S)$ and $f : S \to \mathbb{R}$ measurable we let $\|f\|_\nu$ denote the $L^2(\nu)$-norm of f: $\|f\|_\nu^2 = \int f^2(s)\nu(ds)$. We denote the space of bounded measurable functions with domain $\mathcal{X}$ by $B(\mathcal{X})$, the space of measurable functions bounded by $0 < K < \infty$ by $B(\mathcal{X}; K)$. We let $\|f\|_\infty$ denote the supremum norm: $\|f\|_\infty = \sup_{x \in \mathcal{X}} |f(x)|$. $\mathbb{I}_E$ denotes the indicator function of event E, whilst $\mathbf{1}$ denotes the function that takes on the constant value 1 everywhere over the domain of interest.

A discounted Markovian Decision Problem (MDP) is defined by a quintuple $(\mathcal{X}, \mathcal{A}, P, S, \gamma)$, where $\mathcal{X}$ is the (possible infinite) *state space*, $\mathcal{A} = \{a_1, a_2, \ldots, a_L\}$ is the set of *actions*, $P : \mathcal{X} \times \mathcal{A} \to M(\mathcal{X})$ is the *transition probability kernel*, $P(\cdot|x, a)$ defining the next-state distribution upon taking action a from state x, $S(\cdot|x, a)$ gives the corresponding distribution of *immediate rewards*, and $\gamma \in (0, 1)$ is the discount factor.

We make the following assumptions on the MDP:

Assumption 1 (MDP Regularity). $\mathcal{X}$ *is a compact subspace of the s-dimensional Euclidean space. We assume that the random immediate rewards are bounded by* $\hat{R}_{\max}$*, the conditional expectations* $r(x, a) = \int r S(dr|x, a)$ *and conditional variances* $v(x, a) = \int (r - r(x, a))^2 S(dr|x, a)$ *of the immediate rewards are both uniformly bounded as functions of* $(x, a) \in \mathcal{X} \times \mathcal{A}$. *We let* $R_{\max}$ *denote the bound on the expected immediate rewards:* $\|r\|_\infty \leq R_{\max}$.

A policy is defined as a mapping from past observations to a distribution over the set of actions. A policy is deterministic if the probability distribution concentrates on a single action for all histories. A policy is called stationary if the distribution depends only on the last state of the observation sequence.

The value of a policy π when it is started from a state x is defined as the total expected discounted reward that is encountered while the policy is executed: $V^\pi(x) = \mathbb{E}_\pi \left[\sum_{t=0}^\infty \gamma^t R_t | X_0 = x \right]$. Here R_t is the reward received at time step t, $R_t \sim S(\cdot|X_t, A_t)$, X_t evolves according to $X_{t+1} \sim P(\cdot|X_t, A_t)$ where A_t is sampled from the distribution assigned to the past observations by π. We introduce $Q^\pi : \mathcal{X} \times \mathcal{A} \to \mathbb{R}$, the action-value function, or simply the Q-function of policy π: $Q^\pi(x, a) = \mathbb{E}_\pi \left[\sum_{t=0}^\infty \gamma^t R_t | X_0 = x, A_0 = a \right]$.

The goal is to find a policy that attains the best possible values, $V^*(x) = \sup_\pi V^\pi(x)$ for all states $x \in \mathcal{X}$. V^* is called the optimal value function. A policy is called optimal if it attains the optimal values $V^*(x)$ for *any* state $x \in \mathcal{X}$, i.e., if $V_\pi(x) = V^*(x)$ for all $x \in \mathcal{X}$. The function $Q^*(x, a)$ is defined analogously: $Q^*(x, a) = \sup_\pi Q^\pi(x, a)$. It is known that for any policy π, V^π, Q^π are bounded by $R_{\max}/(1 - \gamma)$, just like Q^* and V^*. We say that a (deterministic stationary) policy π is *greedy* w.r.t. an action-value function $Q \in B(\mathcal{X} \times \mathcal{A})$ if, for all $x \in \mathcal{X}, a \in \mathcal{A}$, $\pi(x) \in \text{argmax}_{a \in \mathcal{A}} Q(x, a)$. Since $\mathcal{A}$ is finite, such a greedy policy always exist. It is known that under mild conditions the greedy policy w.r.t. Q^* is optimal [3]. For a deterministic stationary policy π define the operator $T^\pi : B(\mathcal{X} \times \mathcal{A}) \to B(\mathcal{X} \times \mathcal{A})$ by $(T^\pi Q)(x, a) = r(x, a) + \gamma \int Q(y, \pi(y)) P(dy|x, a)$.

For any deterministic stationary policy $\pi : \mathcal{X} \to \mathcal{A}$ let the operator $E^\pi : B(\mathcal{X} \times \mathcal{A}) \to B(\mathcal{X})$ be defined by $(E^\pi Q)(x) = Q(x, \pi(x))$; $Q \in B(\mathcal{X} \times \mathcal{A})$. We define two operators corresponding to the transition probability kernel P as follows: A right-linear operator is defined by $P \cdot : B(\mathcal{X}) \to B(\mathcal{X} \times \mathcal{A})$ and $(PV)(x, a) = \int V(y) P(dy|x, a)$, whilst a left-linear operator is defined by $\cdot P : M(\mathcal{X} \times \mathcal{A}) \to M(\mathcal{X})$ with $(\rho P)(dy) = \int P(dy|x, a)\rho(dx, da)$. This operator is also extended to act on measures over $\mathcal{X}$ via $(\rho P)(dy) = \frac{1}{L} \sum_{a \in \mathcal{A}} \int P(dy|x, a)\rho(dx)$.

FittedPolicyQ(D,K,Q_0,PEval)
// D: samples (e.g. trajectory)
// K: number of iterations
// Q_0: Initial Q-function
// PEval: Policy evaluation routine
$Q \leftarrow Q_0$ // Initialization
for $k = 0$ to $K - 1$ **do**
   $Q' \leftarrow Q$
   $Q \leftarrow$ PEval($\hat{\pi}(\cdot; Q'), D$)
end for
return Q // or $\hat{\pi}(\cdot; Q)$, the greedy policy w.r.t. Q

Fig. 1. Model-free Policy Iteration

By composing P and E^π, we define $P^\pi = PE^\pi$. Note that this equation defines two operators: a right- and a left-linear one.

Throughout the paper $\mathcal{F} \subset \{f : \mathcal{X} \to \mathbb{R}\}$ will denote some subset of real-valued functions. For convenience, we will treat elements of $\mathcal{F}^L$ as real-valued functions f defined over $\mathcal{X} \times \mathcal{A}$ with the obvious identification $f \equiv (f_1, \ldots, f_L)$, $f(x, a_j) = f_j(x)$, $j = 1, \ldots, L$. For $\nu \in M(\mathcal{X})$, we extend $\|\cdot\|_\nu$ to $\mathcal{F}^L$ by $\|f\|_\nu = \left(\frac{1}{L} \sum_{j=1}^L \|f_j\|_\nu^2\right)^{1/2}$.

3 Algorithm

Assume that we are given a finite but long trajectory $\{(X_t, A_t, R_t)\}_{1 \leq t \leq N}$ generated by some stochastic stationary policy π: $A_t \sim \pi(\cdot|X_t)$, $X_{t+1} \sim P(\cdot|X_t, A_t)$, $R_t \sim S(\cdot|X_t, A_t)$. We shall assume that π is 'persistently exciting' in the sense that $\{(X_t, A_t, R_t)\}$ mixes fast (this will be made precise in the next section).

The algorithm studied in this paper is shown in Figure 1. It is an instance of policy iteration, where policies are only implicitly represented via action-value functions. In the figure D denotes the sample $\{(X_t, A_t, R_t)\}_{1 \leq t \leq N}$, K is the number of iterations, Q_0 is the initial action-value function. $PEval$ is a procedure that takes data in the form of a long trajectory and a policy $\hat{\pi} = \hat{\pi}(\cdot; Q')$, the greedy policy with respect to Q'. Based on $\hat{\pi}$, $PEval$ should return an estimate of the action-value function $Q^{\hat{\pi}}$. There are many possibilities to approximate $Q^{\hat{\pi}}$. In this paper we consider Bellman-residual minimization (BRM). The basic idea of BRM is that $Q^{\hat{\pi}}$ is the fixed point of the operator $T^{\hat{\pi}}$: $Q^{\hat{\pi}} - T^{\hat{\pi}} Q^{\hat{\pi}} = 0$. Hence, given some function class $\mathcal{F}^L$, functions $Q \in \mathcal{F}^L$ with small Bellman-residual $L(Q; \hat{\pi}) = \|Q - T^{\hat{\pi}} Q\|^2$ (with some norm $\|\cdot\|$) should be close to $Q^{\hat{\pi}}$, provided that $\mathcal{F}$ is sufficiently rich (more precisely, the hope is that the performance of the greedy policy w.r.t. the obtained function will be close to the performance of the policy greedy w.r.t. $Q^{\hat{\pi}}$). The most widely used norm is the L^2-norm, so let $L(Q; \hat{\pi}) = \|Q - T^{\hat{\pi}} Q\|_\nu^2$. We chase $Q = \operatorname{argmin}_{f \in \mathcal{F}^L} L(f; \hat{\pi})$. In the sample based version the minimization of the norm $L(f; \hat{\pi})$ is replaced by minimizing a sample based approximation to it: If we let

$$\hat{L}_N(f;\hat{\pi}) = \frac{1}{NL} \sum_{t=1}^{N} \sum_{j=1}^{L} \frac{\mathbb{I}_{\{A_t=a_j\}}}{\pi(a_j|X_t)} \left(f(X_t,a_j) - R_t - \gamma f(X_{t+1},\hat{\pi}(X_{t+1}))\right)^2$$

then the most straightforward way to compute an approximation to $Q^{\hat{\pi}}$ seems to use $Q = \mathrm{argmin}_{f \in \mathcal{F}^L} \hat{L}_N(f;\hat{\pi})$. At a first sight, the choice of $\hat{L}_N$ seems to be logical as for any given X_t, A_t and f, $R_t + \gamma f(X_{t+1},\hat{\pi}(X_{t+1}))$ is an unbiased estimate of $(T^{\hat{\pi}}f)(X_t,A_t)$. However, as it is well known (see e.g. [4][pp. 220], [5,1]), $\hat{L}_N$ is not a "proper" approximation to the corresponding L^2 Bellman-error: $\mathbb{E}\left[\hat{L}_N(f;\hat{\pi})\right] \neq L(f;\hat{\pi})$. In fact, an elementary calculus shows that for $Y \sim P(\cdot|x,a)$, $R \sim S(\cdot|x,a)$,

$$\mathbb{E}\left[(f(x,a) - R - \gamma f(Y,\hat{\pi}(Y)))^2\right] = (f(x,a) - (T^{\hat{\pi}}f)(x,a))^2$$
$$+ \mathrm{Var}\left[R + \gamma f(Y,\hat{\pi}(Y))\right].$$

It follows that minimizing $\hat{L}_N(f;\hat{\pi})$ involves minimizing the term $\mathrm{Var}\left[f(Y,\hat{\pi}(Y))\right]$ in addition to minimizing the 'desired term' $L(f;\hat{\pi})$. The unwanted term acts like a penalty factor, favouring smooth solutions (if f is constant then $\mathrm{Var}\left[f(Y,\hat{\pi}(Y))\right] = 0$). Although in some cases smooth functions are preferable, in general it is better to control smoothness penalties in a direct way.

The common suggestion to overcome this problem is to use "double" (uncorrelated) samples. In our setup, however, this is not an option. Another possibility is to reuse samples that are close in space (e.g., use nearest neighbours). The difficulty with that approach is that it requires a definition of what it means for samples being close. Here, we pursue an alternative approach based on the introduction of an auxiliary function that is used to cancel the variance penalty. The idea is to select h to 'match' $(T^{\hat{\pi}}f)(x,a) = \mathbb{E}\left[R + \gamma f(Y,\hat{\pi}(Y))\right]$ and use it to cancel the unwanted term. Define $L(f,h;\hat{\pi}) = L(f;\hat{\pi}) - \|h - T^{\hat{\pi}}f\|_\nu^2$ and

$$\hat{L}_N(f,h;\hat{\pi}) = \frac{1}{NL} \sum_{t=1}^{N} \sum_{j=1}^{L} \frac{\mathbb{I}_{\{A_t=a_j\}}}{\pi(a_j|X_t)} \Big((f(X_t,a_j) - R_t - \gamma f(X_{t+1},\hat{\pi}(X_{t+1})))^2$$

$$- (h(X_t,a_j) - R_t - \gamma f(X_{t+1},\hat{\pi}(X_{t+1})))^2 \Big). \qquad (1)$$

Then, $\mathbb{E}\left[\hat{L}_N(f,h;\hat{\pi})\right] = L(f,h;\hat{\pi})$ and $L(f,T^{\hat{\pi}}f;\hat{\pi}) = L(f;\hat{\pi})$. Hence we let *PEval* solve for $Q = \mathrm{argmin}_{f \in \mathcal{F}^L} \sup_{h \in \mathcal{F}^L} \hat{L}_N(f,h;\hat{\pi})$. Note that for linearly parameterized function classes the solution can be obtained in a closed form. In general, one may expect that the number of parameters doubles as a result of the introduction of the auxiliary function. Although this may represent a considerable additional computational burden on the algorithm, given the merits of the Bellman-residual minimization approach over the least-squares fixed point approach [5] we think that the potential gain in the performance of the final policy might well worth the extra effort. However, the verification of this claim is left for future work.

Our main result can be formulated as follows: Let $\epsilon, \delta > 0$ be given and choose some target distribution ρ that will be used to measure performance. Regarding the function set $\mathcal{F}$ we need the following essential assumptions: $\mathcal{F}$ has finite pseudo-dimension (similarly to the VC-dimension, the pseudo-dimension of a function class also describes the 'complexity' of the class) and the set of 0 level-sets of the differences of pairs of functions from $\mathcal{F}$ should be a VC-class. Further, we assume that the set $\mathcal{F}^L$ is $\varepsilon/2$-invariant under operators from $\mathcal{T} = \{T^{\hat{\pi}(\cdot;Q)} : Q \in \mathcal{F}^L\}$ with respect to the $\|\cdot\|_\nu$ norm (cf. Definition 3) and that $\mathcal{F}^L$ approximates the fixed-points of the operators of $\mathcal{T}$ well (cf. Definition 4). The MDP has to be regular (satisfying Assumption 1), the dynamics has to satisfy some smoothness properties and the sample path has to be fast mixing. Then for large enough values of N, K the value-function V^{π_K} of the policy π_K returned by fitted policy iteration with the modified BRM criterion will satisfy

$$\|V^{\pi_K} - V^*\|_\rho \le \epsilon$$

with probability larger than $1 - \delta$. In particular, if the rate of mixing of the trajectory is exponential with parameters (b, κ), then $N, K \sim \mathrm{poly}(L, \hat{R}_{\max}/(1 - \gamma), 1/b, V, 1/\varepsilon, \log(1/\delta))$, where V is a VC-dimension like quantity characterizing the complexity of the function class $\mathcal{F}$ and the degree of the polynomial is $1 + 1/\kappa$.

The main steps of the proof are the followings:

1. *PAC-Bounds for BRM:* Starting from a (random) policy that is derived from a random action-value function, we show that BRM is "PAC-consistent", i.e., one can guarantee small Bellman-error with high confidence provided that the number of samples N is large enough.
2. *Error propagation:* If for approximate policy iteration the Bellman-error is small for K steps, then the final error will be small, too (this requires the smoothness conditions).
3. *Final steps:* The error of the whole procedure is small with high probability provided that the Bellman-error is small throughout all the steps with high probability.

4   Main Result

Before describing the main result we need some definitions.

We start with a mixing-property of stochastic processes. Informally, a process is mixing if future depends only weakly on the past, in a sense that we now make precise:

Definition 1. *Let $\{Z_t\}_{t=1,2,\ldots}$ be a stochastic process. Denote by $Z^{1:n}$ the collection $(Z_1, \ldots, Z_n)$, where we allow $n = \infty$. Let $\sigma(Z^{i:j})$ denote the sigma-algebra generated by $Z^{i:j}$ ($i \le j$). The m-th β-mixing coefficient of $\{Z_t\}$, β_m, is defined by*

$$\beta_m = \sup_{t \ge 1} \mathbb{E}\left[\sup_{B \in \sigma(Z^{t+m:\infty})} |P(B|Z^{1:t}) - P(B)| \right].$$

A stochastic process is said to be β-mixing if $\beta_m \to 0$ as $m \to \infty$.

Note that there exist many other definitions of mixing. The weakest among those most commonly used is called α-mixing. Another commonly used one is ϕ-mixing which is stronger than β-mixing (see [6]). A β-mixing process is said to mix at an *exponential* rate with parameters $b, \kappa > 0$ if $\beta_m = O(\exp(-bm^\kappa))$.

Assumption 2 (Sample Path Properties). *Assume that $\{(X_t, A_t, R_t)\}_{t=1,\ldots,N}$ is the sample path of π, X_t is strictly stationary, and $X_t \sim \nu \in M(\mathcal{X})$. Further, we assume that $\{(X_t, A_t, R_t, X_{t+1})\}$ is β-mixing with exponential-rate (b, κ). We further assume that the sampling policy π satisfies $\pi_0 \stackrel{\text{def}}{=} \min_{a \in \mathcal{A}} \inf_{x \in \mathcal{X}} \pi(a|x) > 0$.*

The β-mixing property will be used to establish tail inequalities for certain empirical processes.

Let us now define some smoothness constants $C(\nu)$ and $C(\rho, \nu)$, that depend on the MDP. Remember that ν is the stationary distribution of the samples X_t and ρ is the distribution that is used to evaluate the performance of the algorithm.

Definition 2. *We call $C(\nu) \in \mathbb{R}^+ \cup \{+\infty\}$ the **transition probabilities smoothness constant**, defined as the smallest constant such that for $x \in \mathcal{X}$, $B \subset \mathcal{X}$ measurable, $a \in \mathcal{A}$,*

$$P(B|x, a) \leq C(\nu)\nu(B),$$

(if no such constant exists, we set $C(\nu) = \infty$). Now, for all integer $m \geq 1$, we define $c(m) \in \mathbb{R}^+ \cup \{+\infty\}$ to be the smallest constant such that, for any m stationary policies $\pi_1, \pi_2, \ldots, \pi_m$,

$$\rho P^{\pi_1} P^{\pi_2} \ldots P^{\pi_m} \leq c(m)\nu, \tag{2}$$

and write $c(0) = 1$.[1] Note that these constants depend on ρ and ν.

*We let $C(\rho, \nu)$, the **second order discounted future state distribution smoothness constant**, be defined by the equation*

$$C(\rho, \nu) = (1 - \gamma)^2 \sum_{m \geq 1} m\gamma^{m-1}c(m). \tag{3}$$

One of the major restriction on the MDP's dynamics will be that $C(\rho, \nu) < \infty$ is finite. In fact, one can show that if $C(\nu) < \infty$ then $C(\rho, \nu) < \infty$ holds for any distribution ρ. Hence, the condition $C(\rho, \nu) < \infty$ is less restrictive than $C(\nu) < \infty$. $C(\nu) < \infty$ is satisfied whenever the transition density kernel is absolute continuous w.r.t. ν.[2]

During the course of the proof, we will need several capacity concepts of function sets. Here we assume that the reader is familiar with the concept of VC-dimension (see, e.g. [7]), but we introduce covering numbers because slightly different definitions of it exist in the literature:

For a semi-metric space $(\mathcal{M}, d)$ and for each $\varepsilon > 0$, define the covering number $\mathcal{N}(\varepsilon, \mathcal{M}, d)$ as the smallest value of m for which there exist $g_1, g_2, \ldots, g_m \in \mathcal{M}$

---

[1] Again, if there exists no such constants, we simply set $c(m) = \infty$. Note that in (2) $\leq$ is used to compare two operators. The meaning of $\leq$ in comparing operators H, G is the usual: $H \leq G$ iff $Hf \leq Gf$ holds for all $f \in \text{Dom}(H)$. Here ν is viewed as an operator acting on $B(\mathcal{X} \times \mathcal{A})$.

[2] Further discussion of this condition can be found in the forthcoming paper [2] where these smoothness constants are related to the top-Lyapunov exponent of the system's dynamics.

such that for every $f \in \mathcal{M}$, $\min_j d(f, g_j) < \varepsilon$. If no such finite m exists then $\mathcal{N}(\varepsilon, \mathcal{M}, d) = \infty$. In particular, for a class $\mathcal{F}$ of $\mathcal{X} \to \mathbb{R}$ functions and points $x^{1:N} = (x_1, x_2, \ldots, x_N)$ in $\mathcal{X}$, we use the empirical covering numbers, i.e., the covering number of $\mathcal{F}$ with respect to the empirical L_1 distance

$$l_{x^{1:N}}(f, g) = \frac{1}{N} \sum_{t=1}^{N} |f(x_t) - g(x_t)|.$$

In this case $\mathcal{N}(\varepsilon, \mathcal{F}, l_{x^{1:N}})$ shall be denoted by $\mathcal{N}_1(\varepsilon, \mathcal{F}, x^{1:N})$.

Assumption 3 (Capacity Assumptions on the Function Set). *Assume that $\mathcal{F} \subset B(\mathcal{X}; Q_{\max})$ and that the pseudo-dimension (VC-subgraph dimension) $V_{\mathcal{F}+}$ of $\mathcal{F}$ is finite.[3] Let $C_2 = \{\{x \in \mathcal{X} : f_1(x) \geq f_2(x)\} : f_1, f_2 \in \mathcal{F}\}$. Assume also that the VC-dimension, V_{C_2}, of C_2 is finite.*

We shall also need that $\mathcal{F}^L$ is almost-invariant with respect to (certain) policy-evaluation operators:

Definition 3. *$\mathcal{F}$, a subset of a normed function-space is said to be ϵ-invariant with respect to the set of operators $\mathcal{T}$ acting on the function-space if $\inf_{g \in \mathcal{F}} \|g - Tf\| \leq \epsilon$ holds for any $T \in \mathcal{T}$ and $f \in \mathcal{F}$.*

Similarly, we need that $\mathcal{F}^L$ contains ϵ-fixed points of (certain) policy-evaluation operators:

Definition 4. *f is an ϵ-fixed point of T w.r.t. the norm $\|\cdot\|$ if $\|Tf - f\| \leq \epsilon$.*

Our main result is the following:

Theorem 1. *Choose $\rho \in M(\mathcal{X})$ and let $\epsilon, \delta > 0$ be fixed. Let Assumption 1 and 2 hold and let $Q_{\max} \geq R_{\max}/(1 - \gamma)$. Fix $\mathcal{F} \subset B(\mathcal{X}; Q_{\max})$. Let $\mathcal{T}$ be the set of policy evaluation operators $\{T^{\hat{\pi}(\cdot; Q)} : Q \in \mathcal{F}^L\}$. Assume that $\mathcal{F}^L$ is $\epsilon/2$-invariant with respect to $\|\cdot\|_\nu$ and $\mathcal{T}$ and contains the $\epsilon/2$-fixed points of $\mathcal{T}$. Further, assume that $\mathcal{F}$ satisfies Assumption 3. Then there exists integers N, K that are polynomials in L, $Q_{\max}$, $1/b$, $1/\pi_0$, $V_{\mathcal{F}+}$, V_{C_2}, $1/\epsilon$, $\log(1/\delta)$, $1/(1 - \gamma)$ and $C(\nu)$ such that $\mathbb{P}(\|V^* - V^{\pi_K}\|_\infty > \epsilon) \leq \delta$.*

Similarly, there exists integers N, K that are polynomials of the same quantities except that $C(\nu)$ is replaced by $C(\rho, \nu)$ such that $\mathbb{P}\left(\|V^* - V^{\pi_K}\|_\rho > \epsilon\right) \leq \delta$.

4.1   Bounds on the Error of the Fitting Procedure

We first introduce some auxiliary results required for the proof of the main result of this section. For simplicity assume that $N = 2m_N k_N$ for appropriate positive integers m_N, k_N. We start with the following lemmata:

---

[3] The VC-subgraph dimension of $\mathcal{F}$ is defined as the VC-dimension of the subgraphs of functions in $\mathcal{F}$.

Lemma 2. *Suppose that $Z_0, \ldots, Z_N \in \mathcal{Z}$ is a stationary β-mixing process with mixing coefficients $\{\beta_m\}$, $Z'_t \in \mathcal{Z}$ ($t \in H$) are the block-independent "ghost" samples as in [8], and $H = \{2ik_N + j : 0 \le i < m_N, 0 \le j < k_N\}$, and that $\mathcal{F}$ is a permissible class of $\mathcal{Z} \to [-K, K]$ functions. Then*

$$\mathbb{P}\left(\sup_{f \in \mathcal{F}} \left| \frac{1}{N} \sum_{t=1}^{N} f(Z_t) - \mathbb{E}\left[f(Z_0)\right] \right| > \varepsilon\right) \le 16\mathbb{E}\left[\mathcal{N}_1(\varepsilon/8, \mathcal{F}, (Z'_t; t \in H))\right] e^{-\frac{m_N \varepsilon^2}{128 K^2}}$$

$$+ 2m_N \beta_{k_N}.$$

Note that this lemma is based on the following form of a lemma due to Yu [8]:

Lemma 3 (Yu [8] 4.2 Lemma). *Suppose that $\{Z_t\}$, $\{Z'_t\}$, and H are as in Lemma 2 and that $\mathcal{F}$ is a permissible class of bounded $\mathcal{Z} \to \mathbb{R}$ functions. Then*

$$\mathbb{P}\left(\sup_{f \in \mathcal{F}} \left| \frac{1}{N} \sum_{t=1}^{N} f(Z_t) \right| > \varepsilon\right) \le 2\mathbb{P}\left(\sup_{f \in \mathcal{F}} \left| \frac{1}{N} \sum_{i=1}^{m_N} \sum_{t \in H_i} f(Z'_t) \right| > \frac{\varepsilon}{2}\right) + 2m_N \beta_{k_N}.$$

Let Π be a family of partitions of $\mathcal{X}$. Define the *cell count* $m(\Pi) = \max_{\pi \in \Pi} |\{A \in \pi : A \neq \emptyset\}|$. For $x^{1:N} \in \mathcal{X}^N$, let $\Delta(x^{1:N}, \Pi)$ be the number of distinct partitions (regardless the order) of $x^{1:N}$ that are induced by the elements of Π. The *partitioning number* (generalization of shatter-coefficient) $\Delta^*_N(\Pi)$ equals to $\max\{\Delta(x^{1:N}, \Pi) : x^{1:N} \in \mathcal{X}^N\}$.

Given a class $\mathcal{G}$ of functions on $\mathcal{X}$ and a partition family Π, define

$$\mathcal{G} \circ \Pi = \left\{ f = \sum_{A_j \in \pi} g_j \mathbb{I}_{\{A_j\}} : \pi = \{A_j\} \in \Pi, g_j \in \mathcal{G} \right\}.$$

We quote here a result of Nobel (with any domain $\mathcal{X}$ instead of $\mathbb{R}^s$ and with minimised premise):

Proposition 4 (Nobel [9] Proposition 1). *Let Π be any partition family with $m(\Pi) < \infty$, $\mathcal{G}$ be a class of functions on $\mathcal{X}$, $x^{1:N} \in \mathcal{X}^N$. Let $\phi_N(\cdot)$ be such that for any $\varepsilon > 0$, the empirical ε-covering numbers of G on all subsets of the multiset $[x_1, \ldots, X_N]$ are majorized by $\phi_N(\varepsilon)$. Then, for any $\varepsilon > 0$,*

$$\mathcal{N}_1(\varepsilon, \mathcal{G} \circ \Pi, x^{1:N}) \le \Delta(x^{1:N}, \Pi) \phi_N(\varepsilon)^{m(\Pi)} \le \Delta^*_N(\Pi) \phi_N(\varepsilon)^{m(\Pi)}.$$

We extend this result to a refined bound in terms of the covering number of the partition family instead of its partitioning number:

Lemma 5. *Let Π, G, $x^{1:N}$, ϕ_N be as in Lemma 4. For $\pi = \{A_j\}$, $\pi' = \{A'_j\} \in \Pi$, introduce the metric $d(\pi, \pi') = d_{x^{1:N}}(\pi, \pi') = \mu_N(\pi \triangle \pi')$, where*

$$\pi \triangle \pi' = \{x \in \mathcal{X} : \exists j \neq j'; x \in A_j \cap A'_{j'}\} = \bigcup_{j=1}^{m(\Pi)} A_j \triangle A'_j,$$

and μ_N is the empirical measure corresponding to $x^{1:N}$ defined by $\mu_N(A) = \frac{1}{N}\sum_{i=1}^{N}\mathbb{I}_{\{x_i \in A\}}$ (here A is any measurable subset of $\mathcal{X}$). For every $\varepsilon > 0, \alpha \in (0,1)$

$$\mathcal{N}_1(\varepsilon, \mathcal{G} \circ \Pi, x^{1:N}) \leq \mathcal{N}\left(\frac{\alpha\varepsilon}{2K}, \Pi, d_{x^{1:N}}\right)\phi_N((1-\alpha)\varepsilon)^{m(\Pi)}.$$

Lemma 5 is used by the following lemma:

Lemma 6. *Let $\mathcal{F}$ be a class of uniformly bounded functions on $\mathcal{X}$ ($\forall f \in \mathcal{F} : |f| \leq K$), $x^{1:N} \in \mathcal{X}^N$, ϕ_N be such that the ε-empirical covering numbers of $\mathcal{F}$ on all subsets of the multiset $[x_1, \ldots, x_N]$ are majorized by $\phi_N(\varepsilon)$. Let $\mathcal{G}_2^1$ denote the class of indicator functions $\mathbb{I}_{\{f_1(x) \geq f_2(x)\}} : \mathcal{X} \to \{0,1\}$ for any $f_1, f_2 \in \mathcal{F}$. Then for every $\varepsilon > 0$,*

$$\mathcal{N}(\varepsilon, \mathcal{F}^L \times \mathcal{F}^L, x^{1:N}) \leq \mathcal{N}_1\left(\frac{\varepsilon}{2L(L-1)K}, \mathcal{G}_2^1, x^{1:N}\right)^{L(L-1)}\phi_N(\varepsilon/2)^L,$$

where the distance of (f, Q') and $(g, \tilde{Q}') \in \mathcal{F}^L \times \mathcal{F}^L$ in the left-hand-side covering number is defined in the unusual way

$$l_{x^{1:N}}((f, Q'), (g, \tilde{Q}')) = \frac{1}{N}\sum_{t=1}^{N}|f(x_t, \hat{\pi}(x_t; Q')) - g(x_t, \hat{\pi}(x_t; \tilde{Q}'))|.$$

Finally, see Haussler [10] (and Anthony and Bartlett [7, Theorem 18.4]) for

Proposition 7 (Haussler [10] Corollary 3). *For any set $\mathcal{X}$, any points $x^{1:N} \in \mathcal{X}^N$, any class $\mathcal{F}$ of functions on $\mathcal{X}$ taking values in $[0, K]$ with pseudo-dimension $V_{\mathcal{F}+} < \infty$, and any $\varepsilon > 0$, $\mathcal{N}_1(\varepsilon, \mathcal{F}, x^{1:N}) \leq e(V_{\mathcal{F}+} + 1)\left(\frac{2eK}{\varepsilon}\right)^{V_{\mathcal{F}+}}$.*

The following is the main result of this section:

Lemma 8. *Let Assumption 1,2, and 3 hold and let $Q_{\max} \geq \hat{R}_{\max}/(1-\gamma)$. Let Q' be a real-valued random function over $\mathcal{X} \times \mathcal{A}$, $Q'(\omega) \in \mathcal{F}^L$ (possibly not independent from the sample path). Let $\hat{\pi} = \hat{\pi}(\cdot; Q')$ be a policy that is greedy w.r.t. to Q'. Let f' be defined by $f' = \operatorname{argmin}_{f \in \mathcal{F}^L} \sup_{h \in \mathcal{F}^L} \hat{L}_N(f, h; \hat{\pi})$. Fix $\varepsilon, \delta > 0$ and assume that $\mathcal{F}^L$ $\varepsilon/2$-approximates the fixed point of $T^{\hat{\pi}(\cdot; Q')}$:*

$$\tilde{E}(\mathcal{F}) \overset{\text{def}}{=} \sup_{Q' \in \mathcal{F}^L} \inf_{f \in \mathcal{F}^L} \left\|f - T^{\hat{\pi}(\cdot; Q')}f\right\|_{\nu} \leq \varepsilon/2 \qquad (4)$$

and that $\mathcal{F}^L$ is $\varepsilon/2$-invariant w.r.t. T:

$$E(\mathcal{F}) \overset{\text{def}}{=} \sup_{f, Q' \in \mathcal{F}^L} \inf_{h \in \mathcal{F}^L} \left\|h - T^{\hat{\pi}(\cdot; Q')}f\right\|_{\nu} \leq \varepsilon/2. \qquad (5)$$

If $N = \operatorname{poly}(L, Q_{\max}, 1/b, 1/\pi_0, V_{\mathcal{F}+}, V_{C_2}, 1/\varepsilon, \log(1/\delta))$, where the degree of the polynomial is $O(1 + 1/\kappa)$, then $\mathbb{P}\left(\left\|f' - T^{\hat{\pi}}f'\right\|_{\nu} > \varepsilon\right) \leq \delta$.

Proof. (Sketch) We have to show that f' is close to the corresponding $T^{\hat{\pi}(\cdot;Q')}f'$ with high probability, noting that Q' may not be independent from the sample path. By (4), it suffices to show that $L(f';Q') \stackrel{\text{def}}{=} \left\|f' - T^{\hat{\pi}(\cdot;Q')}f'\right\|_\nu^2$ is close to $\inf_{f\in\mathcal{F}^L} L(f;Q')$. Denote the difference of these two quantities by $\Delta(f',Q')$. Note that $\Delta(f',Q')$ is increased by taking its supremum over Q'. By (5), $L(f;Q')$ and $\bar{L}(f;Q') \stackrel{\text{def}}{=} \sup_{h\in\mathcal{F}^L} L(f,h;\hat{\pi}(\cdot;Q'))$, as functions of f and Q', are uniformly close to each other. This reduces the problem to bounding $\sup_{Q'}(\bar{L}(f';Q') - \inf_{f\in\mathcal{F}^L} \bar{L}(f;Q'))$. Since $\mathbb{E}\left[\hat{L}_N(f,h;\hat{\pi})\right] = L(f,h;\hat{\pi})$ holds for any $f,h \in \mathcal{F}^L$ and policy $\hat{\pi}$, by defining a suitable error criterion $l_{f,h,Q'}(x,a,r,y)$ in accordance with (1), the problem can be reduced to a usual uniform deviation problem over $\mathcal{L}_\mathcal{F} = \{l_{f,h,Q'} : f,h,Q' \in \mathcal{F}^L\}$. Since the samples are correlated, Pollard's tail inequality cannot be used directly. Instead, we use the method of Yu [8]: We split the samples into m_N pairs of blocks $\{(H_i, T_i)|i = 1,\ldots,m_N\}$, each block compromised of k_N samples (for simplicity we assume $N = 2m_N k_N$) and then use Lemma 2 with $\mathcal{Z} = \mathcal{X} \times \mathcal{A} \times \mathbb{R} \times \mathcal{X}, \mathcal{F} = \mathcal{L}_\mathcal{F}$. The covering numbers of $\mathcal{L}_\mathcal{F}$ can be bounded by those of $\mathcal{F}^L$ and $\mathcal{F}^L \times \mathcal{F}^L$, where in the latter the distance is defined as in Lemma 6. Next we apply Lemma 6 and then Proposition 7 to bound the resulting three covering numbers in terms of $V_{\mathcal{F}^+}$ and $V_{\mathcal{C}_2}$ (note that the pseudo-dimension of $\mathcal{F}^L$ cannot exceed $LV_{\mathcal{F}^+}$). Defining $k_N = N^{\frac{1}{1+\kappa}}+1, m_N = N/(2k_N)$ and substituting $\beta_m \leq e^{-bm^\kappa}$, we get the desired polynomial bound on the number of samples after some tedious calculations. □

4.2 Propagation of Errors

Let Q_k denote the kth iterate of (some) approximate policy iteration algorithm where the next iterates are computed by means of some Bellman-residual minimization procedure. Let π_k be the kth policy. Our aim here is to relate the performance of the policy π_K to the magnitude of the Bellman-residuals $\varepsilon_k \stackrel{\text{def}}{=} Q_k - T^{\pi_k}Q_k, 0 \leq k < K$.

Lemma 9. *Let $p \geq 1$. For any $\eta > 0$, there exists K that is linear in $\log(1/\eta)$ and $\log R_{\max}$ such that, if the $L_{p,\nu}$ norm of the Bellman-residuals are bounded by some constant ϵ, i.e. $\|\varepsilon_k\|_{p,\nu} \leq \epsilon$ for all $0 \leq k < K$, then*

$$\|Q^* - Q^{\pi_K}\|_\infty \leq \frac{2\gamma}{(1-\gamma)^2}[C(\nu)]^{1/p}\epsilon + \eta \qquad (6)$$

and

$$\|Q^* - Q^{\pi_K}\|_{p,\rho} \leq \frac{2\gamma}{(1-\gamma)^2}[C(\rho,\nu)]^{1/p}\epsilon + \eta. \qquad (7)$$

Proof. We have $C(\nu) \geq C(\rho,\nu)$ for any ρ. Thus, if the bound (7) holds for any ρ, choosing ρ to be a Dirac at each state implies that (6) also holds. Therefore, we only need to prove (7).

Let $E_k = P^{\pi_{k+1}}(I - \gamma P^{\pi_{k+1}})^{-1} - P^{\pi^*}(I - \gamma P^{\pi_k})^{-1}$. Closely following the proof of [5][Lemma 4], we get $Q^* - Q^{\pi_{k+1}} \leq \gamma P^{\pi^*}(Q^* - Q^{\pi_k}) + \gamma E_k \varepsilon_k$. Thus, by induction, $Q^* - Q^{\pi_K} \leq \gamma \sum_{k=0}^{K-1} (\gamma P^{\pi^*})^{K-k-1} E_k \epsilon_k + \eta_K$ with $\eta_K = (\gamma P^{\pi^*})^K (Q^* - Q^{\pi_0})$. Hence, $\|\eta_K\|_\infty \leq 2Q_{\max} \gamma^K$.

Now, let $F_k = P^{\pi_{k+1}} (I - \gamma P^{\pi_{k+1}})^{-1} + P^{\pi^*} (I - \gamma P^{\pi_k})^{-1}$. By taking the absolute value pointwise in the above bound on $Q^* - Q^{\pi_K}$ we get $Q^* - Q^{\pi_K} \leq \gamma \sum_{k=0}^{K-1} (\gamma P^{\pi^*})^{K-k-1} F_k |\varepsilon_k| + (\gamma P^{\pi^*})^K |Q^* - Q^{\pi_0}|$. From this, using the fact that $Q^* - Q^{\pi_0} \leq \frac{2}{1-\gamma} R_{\max} \mathbf{1}$, we arrive at

$$|Q^* - Q^{\pi_K}| \leq \frac{2\gamma(1-\gamma^{K+1})}{(1-\gamma)^2} \left[\sum_{k=0}^{K-1} \alpha_k A_k |\varepsilon_k| + \alpha_K A_K R_{\max} \mathbf{1} \right].$$

Here we introduced the positive coefficients $\alpha_k = \frac{(1-\gamma)\gamma^{K-k-1}}{1-\gamma^{K+1}}$, for $0 \leq k < K$, and $\alpha_K = \frac{(1-\gamma)\gamma^K}{1-\gamma^{K+1}}$, and the operators $A_k = \frac{1-\gamma}{2} (P^{\pi^*})^{K-k-1} F_k$, for $0 \leq k < K$, $A_K = (P^{\pi^*})^K$. Note that $\sum_{k=0}^K \alpha_k = 1$ and the operators A_k are stochastic when considered as a right-linear operators: for any $(x,a) \in \mathcal{X} \times \mathcal{A}$, $\lambda_{(x,a)}^{(k)}(B) = (A_k \chi_B)(x,a)$ is a probability measure and $(A_k Q)(x,a) = \int \lambda_{(x,a)}^{(k)}(dy) Q(y, \pi(y))$. Here $\chi_B : B(\mathcal{X} \times \mathcal{A}) \to [0,1]$ is defined by $\chi_B(x,a) = \mathbb{I}_{\{x \in B\}}$.

Let $\lambda_K = \left[\frac{2\gamma(1-\gamma^{K+1})}{(1-\gamma)^2} \right]^p$. Now, by using two times Jensen's inequality we get

$$\|Q^* - Q^{\pi_K}\|_{p,\rho}^p = \frac{1}{L} \sum_{a \in \mathcal{A}} \int \rho(dx) |Q^*(x,a) - Q^{\pi_K}(x,a)|^p$$

$$\leq \lambda_K \rho \left[\sum_{k=0}^{K-1} \alpha_k A_k |\varepsilon_k|^p + \alpha_K A_K (R_{\max})^p \mathbf{1} \right].$$

From the definition of the coefficients $c(m)$, $\rho A_k \leq (1-\gamma) \sum_{m \geq 0} \gamma^m c(m+K-k)\nu$ and we deduce

$$\|Q^* - Q^{\pi_K}\|_{p,\rho}^p \leq \lambda_K \left[(1-\gamma) \sum_{k=0}^{K-1} \alpha_k \sum_{m \geq 0} \gamma^m c(m+K-k) \|\varepsilon_k\|_{p,\nu}^p + \alpha_K (R_{\max})^p \right].$$

Replace α_k by their values, and from the definition of $C(\rho, \nu)$, and since $\|\varepsilon_k\|_{p,\nu} \leq \epsilon$, we have

$$\|Q^* - Q^{\pi_K}\|_{p,\rho}^p \leq \lambda_K \left[\frac{1}{1-\gamma^{K+1}} C(\rho, \nu) \epsilon^p + \frac{(1-\gamma)\gamma^K}{1-\gamma^{K+1}} (R_{\max})^p \right].$$

Thus there is K linear in $\log(1/\eta)$ and $\log R_{\max}$, e.g. such that $\gamma^K < \left[\frac{(1-\gamma)^2}{2\gamma R_{\max}} \eta \right]^p$ so that the second term is bounded by η^p. Thus, $\|Q^* - Q^{\pi_K}\|_{p,\rho}^p \leq \left[\frac{2\gamma}{(1-\gamma)^2} \right]^p C(\rho, \nu) \epsilon^p + \eta^p$ and hence $\|Q^* - Q^{\pi_K}\|_{p,\rho} \leq \frac{2\gamma}{(1-\gamma)^2} [C(\rho, \nu)]^{1/p} \epsilon + \eta$, finishing the proof. $\square$

4.3 Proof of the Main Result

Proof. Consider the kth iteration of the algorithm. Let $\varepsilon_k = Q_k - T^{\pi_k} Q_k$. By the reasoning used in the proof of Lemma 9, we only need to prove the second part of the result. Since $0 < \gamma < 1$, there exists K that is linear in $\log(1/\epsilon)$ and $\log R_{\max}$ such that $\gamma^K < \left[\frac{(1-\gamma)^2}{2\gamma R_{\max}} \frac{\epsilon}{2} \right]^p$. Now, from Lemma 8, there exists N that is poly$(L, Q_{\max}, 1/b, 1/\pi_0, V_{\mathcal{F}^+}, V_{\mathcal{C}_2}, 1/\varepsilon, \log(1/\delta))$, such that, for each $0 \le k < K$, $\mathbb{P}\left(\|\varepsilon_k\|_{p,\nu} > \frac{(1-\gamma)^2}{2C^{1/p}} \frac{\epsilon}{2} \right) < \delta/K$. Thus, $\mathbb{P}\left(\|\varepsilon_k\|_{p,\nu} > \frac{(1-\gamma)^2}{2C^{1/p}} \frac{\epsilon}{2}, \text{ for all } 0 \le k < K \right) < \delta$. Applying Lemma 9 with $\eta = \epsilon/2$ ends the proof.   □

5 Discussion and Related Work

The idea of using value function approximation goes back to the early days of dynamic programming [11, 12]. With the recent growth of interest in reinforcement learning, work on value function approximation methods flourished [13, 14]. Recent theoretical results mostly concern supremum-norm approximation errors [15, 16], where the main condition on the way intermediate iterates are mapped (projected) to the function space is that the corresponding operator, Π, must be a non-expansion. Practical examples when Π satisfies the said property include certain kernel-based methods, see e.g. [15, 16, 17, 18]. However, the growth-restriction imposed on Π rules out many popular algorithms, such as regression-based approaches that were found, however, to behave well in practice (e.g. [19, 20, 1]). The need for analysing the behaviour of such algorithms provided the basic motivation for this work.

One of the main novelties of our paper is that we introduced a modified Bellman-residual that guarantees asymptotic consistency even with a single sample path.

The closest to the present work is the paper of Szepesvári and Munos [21]. However, as opposed to paper [21], here we dealt with a fitted policy iteration algorithm and unlike previously, we worked with dependent samples. The technique used to deal with dependent samples was to introduce (strong) mixing conditions on the trajectory and extending Pollard's inequality along the lines of Meir [22].

Also, the bounds developed in Section 4.2 are closely related to those developed in [5]. However, there only the case $C(\nu) < \infty$ was considered, whilst in this paper the analysis was extended to the significantly weaker condition $C(\nu, \rho) < \infty$. Although in [21] the authors considered a similar condition, there the propagation of the approximation errors was considered only in a value iteration context. Note that approximate value iteration *per se* is not suitable for learning from a single trajectory since approximate value iteration requires at least one successor state sample per action per sampled state.

That we had to work with fitted policy iteration significantly added to the complexity of the analysis, as the policy to be evaluated at stage k became dependent on the whole set of samples, introducing non-trivial correlations between successive approximants. In order to show that these correlations do not spoil convergence, we had to introduce problem-specific capacity conditions on the function class involved. Although these constraints are satisfied by many popular function classes (e.g., regression trees, neural networks, etc.), when violated unstable behaviour may arise (i.e., increasing the sample size does not improves the performance).

Note that the conditions that dictate that $\mathcal{F}$ should be rich (namely, that $\mathcal{F}$ should be "almost invariant" under the family of operators $\mathcal{T} = \{T^{\hat{\pi}(\cdot;Q)} : Q \in \mathcal{F}\}$ and that $\mathcal{F}$ should be close to the set of fixed points of $\mathcal{T}$) are non-trivial to guarantee. One possibility is to put smoothness constraints on the transition dynamics and the immediate rewards. It is important to note, however, that both conditions are defined with respect to weighted L^2-norm. This is much less restrictive than if supremum-norm were used here. This observation suggests that one should probably look at frequency domain representations of systems in order to guarantee these properties. However, this is well out of the scope of the present work.

6 Conclusions

We have considered fitted policy iteration with Bellman-residual minimization. We modified the objective function to allow the procedure to work with a single (but long) trajectory. Our results show that the number of samples needed to achieve a small approximation error depend polynomially on the pseudo-dimension of the function class used in the empirical loss minimization step and the smoothness of the dynamics of the system. Future work should concern the evaluation of the proposed procedure in practice. The theoretical results can be extended in many directions: Continuous actions spaces will require substantial additional work as the present analysis relies crucially on the finiteness of the action set. The exploration of interplay between the MDPs dynamics and the approximability of the fixed points and the invariance of function sets with respect to policy evaluation operators also requires substantial further work.

Acknowledgements

We would like to acknowledge support for this project from the Hungarian National Science Foundation (OTKA), Grant No. T047193 (Cs. Szepesvári) and from the Hungarian Academy of Sciences (Cs. Szepesvári, Bolyai Fellowship).

References

1. M. Lagoudakis and R. Parr. Least-squares policy iteration. *Journal of Machine Learning Research*, 4:1107–1149, 2003.
2. A. Antos, Cs. Szepesvári, and R. Munos. Learning near-optimal policies with fitted policy iteration and a single sample path: approximate iterative policy evaluation. (submitted to ICML'2006, 2006.
3. D. P. Bertsekas and S.E. Shreve. *Stochastic Optimal Control (The Discrete Time Case)*. Academic Press, New York, 1978.
4. R.S. Sutton and A.G. Barto. Toward a modern theory of adaptive networks: Expectation and prediction. In *Proc. of the Ninth Annual Conference of Cognitive Science Society*. Erlbaum, Hillsdale, NJ, USA, 1987.

5. R. Munos. Error bounds for approximate policy iteration. *19th International Conference on Machine Learning*, pages 560–567, 2003.
6. S.P. Meyn and R. Tweedie. *Markov Chains and Stochastic Stability*. Springer-Verlag, New York, 1993.
7. M. Anthony and P. L. Bartlett. *Neural Network Learning: Theoretical Foundations*. Cambridge University Press, 1999.
8. B. Yu. Rates of convergence for empirical processes of stationary mixing sequences. *The Annals of Probability*, 22(1):94–116, January 1994.
9. A. Nobel. Histogram regression estimation using data-dependent partitions. *Annals of Statistics*, 24(3):1084–1105, 1996.
10. D. Haussler. Sphere packing numbers for subsets of the boolean n-cube with bounded Vapnik-Chervonenkis dimension. *Journal of Combinatorial Theory Series A*, 69:217–232, 1995.
11. A.L. Samuel. Some studies in machine learning using the game of checkers. *IBM Journal on Research and Development*, pages 210–229, 1959. Reprinted in *Computers and Thought*, E.A. Feigenbaum and J. Feldman, editors, McGraw-Hill, New York, 1963.
12. R.E. Bellman and S.E. Dreyfus. Functional approximation and dynamic programming. *Math. Tables and other Aids Comp.*, 13:247–251, 1959.
13. Dimitri P. Bertsekas and J. Tsitsiklis. *Neuro-Dynamic Programming*. Athena Scientific, 1996.
14. Richard S. Sutton and Andrew G. Barto. Reinforcement learning: An introduction. *Bradford Book*, 1998.
15. Geoffrey J. Gordon. Stable function approximation in dynamic programming. In Armand Prieditis and Stuart Russell, editors, *Proceedings of the Twelfth International Conference on Machine Learning*, pages 261–268, San Francisco, CA, 1995. Morgan Kaufmann.
16. J. N. Tsitsiklis and B. Van Roy. Feature-based methods for large scale dynamic programming. *Machine Learning*, 22:59–94, 1996.
17. Carlos Guestrin, Daphne Koller, and Ronald Parr. Max-norm projections for factored mdps. *Proceedings of the International Joint Conference on Artificial Intelligence*, 2001.
18. D. Ernst, P. Geurts, and L. Wehenkel. Tree-based batch mode reinforcement learning. *Journal of Machine Learning Research*, 6:503–556, 2005.
19. X. Wang and T.G. Dietterich. Efficient value function approximation using regression trees. In *Proceedings of the IJCAI Workshop on Statistical Machine Learning for Large-Scale Optimization*, Stockholm, Sweden, 1999.
20. T. G. Dietterich and X. Wang. Batch value function approximation via support vectors. In T. G. Dietterich, S. Becker, and Z. Ghahramani, editors, *Advances in Neural Information Processing Systems 14*, Cambridge, MA, 2002. MIT Press.
21. Cs. Szepesvári and R. Munos. Finite time bounds for sampling based fitted value iteration. In *ICML'2005*, 2005.
22. R. Meir. Nonparametric time series prediction through adaptive model selection. *Machine Learning*, 39(1):5–34, April 2000.

Ranking with a P-Norm Push

Cynthia Rudin

Center for Neural Science and Courant Institute of Mathematical Sciences
New York University / Howard Hughes Medical Institute
4 Washington Place, Room 809, New York, NY 10003-6603
rudin@nyu.edu

Abstract. We are interested in supervised ranking with the following twist: our goal is to design algorithms that perform especially well near the top of the ranked list, and are only required to perform sufficiently well on the rest of the list. Towards this goal, we provide a general form of convex objective that gives high-scoring examples more importance. This "push" near the top of the list can be chosen to be arbitrarily large or small. We choose ℓ_p-norms to provide a specific type of push; as p becomes large, the algorithm concentrates harder near the top of the list. We derive a generalization bound based on the p-norm objective. We then derive a corresponding boosting-style algorithm, and illustrate the usefulness of the algorithm through experiments on UCI data. We prove that the minimizer of the objective is unique in a specific sense.

1 Introduction

The problem of supervised ranking is useful in many application domains, e.g., document processing, customer service routing, and drug discovery. Many of these domains require the construction of a ranked list, yet often, only the top portion of the list is used in practice. For instance, in the setting of supervised movie ranking, the learning algorithm provides the user (an avid movie-goer) with a ranked list of movies based on preference data. We expect the user to examine the top portion of the list as a recommendation. It is possible that she never looks at the rest of the list, or examines it only briefly. Thus, we wish to make sure that the top portion of the list is correctly constructed. This is the problem on which we concentrate.

Naturally, the design of these rankings requires a tradeoff. Given the option, we would correct a misrank towards the top of the list at the expense of possibly making a new misrank towards the bottom. This type of sacrifice will have to be made; assuming a learning machine with finite capacity, the best total ranking will not often correspond to the best ranking near the top of the list. The trick is to design an algorithm that knows when a misrank occurs at the top and forces us to pay a high price for it, relative to other misranks.

We have developed a somewhat general and fairly flexible technique for solving these types of problems. In our framework, a specific price is assigned for each misrank; the misranks at the top are given higher prices, and the ones towards

G. Lugosi and H.U. Simon (Eds.): COLT 2006, LNAI 4005, pp. 589–604, 2006.

the bottom are less expensive. Thus, the choice of these prices determines how much emphasis (or "push") is placed closer to the top. We may only desire to incorporate a small push; it is possible, for example, that our movie-goer has seen all of the movies near the top of the list and needs to look farther down in order to find a movie she has not seen. It is important that the rest of the list be sufficiently well-constructed in this case. The desired size of the push might be anywhere between very large and very small depending on the application. There is simply a tradeoff between the size of the push and the sacrifice made farther down the list. As mentioned, some sacrifice must always be made since, as usual, we take our algorithm to have limited capacity in order to enable generalization ability. Using the form of ranking objective introduced in Section 2, one can make the prices very high for misranking near the top (a big push), moderately high (a little push), or somewhere in between.

The algorithms we develop are motivated in the usual setting of supervised bipartite ranking. In this setting, each training instance has a label of +1 or -1, i.e., each movie is either a good movie or a bad movie. Here, we want to push the bad movies away from the top of the list where the good movies are desired. The quality of the ranking can be determined by examining the Receiver Operator Characteristic (ROC) curve. In the setting where all misranks are equally priced (no push), the AUC (Area Under the ROC Curve) is precisely a constant times one minus the total standard misranking error (see [4]). However, the quantity we measure in our problem is different. We care mostly about the leftmost portion of the ROC curve for this problem, corresponding to the top of the ranked list. This is precisely the sacrifice we must make; in order make the leftmost portion of the curve higher, we must sacrifice on the total area underneath the curve.

This problem is highly asymmetric with respect to the positive and negative classes. It is interesting to consider generalization bounds for such an asymmetric problem; we should not rely on a symmetrization step which requires natural symmetry. The generalization bound presented here holds even under such asymmetric conditions. The measure of complexity is the L_∞ covering number.

Recently, there has been a large amount of interest in the supervised ranking problem, and especially in the bipartite problem. Freund et al. have developed the RankBoost algorithm for the general setting [8]. We inherit the setup of RankBoost, since our algorithms will also be boosting-style algorithms. Oddly, there is a recent theoretical proof that Freund and Schapire's classification algorithm called AdaBoost [9] performs just as well for bipartite ranking as Rank-Boost; i.e., both algorithms achieve equally good values of the AUC [13, 14]. There are a number of algorithms designed to maximize variations of the AUC, for instance Mozer et al. [11] aim to manipulate specific points of the ROC curve in order to study "churn" in the telecommunications industry. Perhaps the closest algorithm to ours is the one proposed by Dekel et al. [6], who have used a similar form of objective with different specifics for the score to achieve a different goal, namely to rank labels. The work of Yan et al. [17] contains a brief mention of a method that optimizes the lower left corner of the ROC curve with a multi-layer perceptron approach that is highly non-convex. There is much recent work on generalization bounds for supervised ranking [8, 2, 1, 16, 13], though only the covering number bounds [13] can be naturally adapted to this setting due to the asymmetry of the problem.

In Section 2, we present a general form of objective function, allowing us to incorporate a push near the top of the ranked list. One must choose a loss function ℓ and a convex price function g to specify the objective function. If the price function is steep (e.g., the power law $g(r) = r^p$), then the push near the top is very strong. In Section 3, we provide a generalization bound for the objective function, for the "0-1" loss and the power law price function. In Section 4, we derive the "P-Norm Push" Algorithm, which is a coordinate descent algorithm based on the objective function. In Section 5, we prove that the minimizer of the algorithm's objective function is unique in a specific sense. This result is based on conjugate duality and the theory of Bregman distances [7], and is analogous to the result of Collins et al. [3] for AdaBoost. In Section 6, we demonstrate the P-Norm Push algorithm on UCI data. In Section 7, we use the generalization bound of Section 3 to indicate the limit of the algorithm's problem domain; we aim to find when the algorithm should (and should not) be used.

2 A General Objective for Ranking with a Push

The set of instances with positive labels is $\{\mathbf{x}_i\}_{i=1,\ldots,I}$, where $\mathbf{x}_i \in \mathcal{X}$. The negative instances are $\{\tilde{\mathbf{x}}_k\}_{k=1,\ldots,K}$, where $\tilde{\mathbf{x}}_k \in \mathcal{X}$. We always use i for the index over positive instances and k over negative instances. Our goal is to construct a ranking function $f : \mathcal{X} \to \mathcal{R}$, $f \in \mathcal{F}$ that gives a score to each instance in $\mathcal{X}$. Unlike in classification, we do not care about the exact values of each instance, only the relative values; for positive-negative pair $\mathbf{x}_i, \tilde{\mathbf{x}}_k$, we do not care if $f(\mathbf{x}_i) = .4$ and $f(\tilde{\mathbf{x}}_k) = .1$, but we do care that $f(\mathbf{x}_i) > f(\tilde{\mathbf{x}}_k)$, or that $f(\mathbf{x}_i) - f(\tilde{\mathbf{x}}_k) = .3$.

Let us now derive the general form of objective function as promised in the introduction. For a particular negative example, we wish to reduce its *Height*, i.e., the number of positive examples that are ranked beneath it. That is, for each k, we wish to make Height(k) small, where:

$$\text{Height}(k) := \sum_{i=1}^{I} \mathbf{1}_{[f(\mathbf{x}_i) \leq f(\tilde{\mathbf{x}}_k)]}.$$

Let us now add the push. We want to concentrate harder on negative examples with large Height's; we want to push these examples down from the top. Thus, for convex, non-negative, monotonically increasing function $g : \mathcal{R}_+ \to \mathcal{R}_+$, we place the price $g(\text{Height}(k))$ on negative example k. If g is very steep, we pay an extremely large price for a high-ranked negative example. Examples of steep functions include $g(r) = \exp(r)$ and $g(r) = r^p$ for p large; the latter price function will be used for the P-Norm Push. Thus we have derived an objective to minimize:

$$R_{g,1}(f) := \sum_{k=1}^{K} g \left(\sum_{i=1}^{I} \mathbf{1}_{[f(\mathbf{x}_i) \leq f(\tilde{\mathbf{x}}_k)]} \right).$$

If $R_{g,1}(f)$ is small, then no negative example is ranked very highly; this is exactly our design. It is hard to minimize $R_{g,1}$ directly due to the 0-1 loss in the inner sum. Instead, we minimize an upper bound, $R_{g,\ell}$, which incorporates $\ell : \mathcal{R} \to \mathcal{R}_+$, a convex, non-negative, monotonically decreasing upper bound on the 0-1 loss. Popular loss functions include the exponential, logistic, and hinge losses. We can now define the general form of objective:

$$R_{g,\ell}(f) := \sum_{k=1}^{K} g \left(\sum_{i=1}^{I} \ell(f(\mathbf{x}_i) - f(\tilde{\mathbf{x}}_k)) \right).$$

To construct a specific version of this objective, one chooses the loss ℓ, the price function g, and an appropriate hypothesis space $\mathcal{F}$ over which to minimize $R_{g,\ell}$.

For the moment, assume we care only about the very top of the list, that is, we wish to push the most offending negative example as far down the list as possible. Equivalently, we wish to minimize $R_{\max}$, the number of positives below the highest ranked negative example: $R_{\max}(f) := \max_k \text{Height}(k)$. It is hard to minimize $R_{\max}(f)$ directly, but $R_{g,\ell}$ can give us some control over this quantity. Namely, the following relationships exist between $R_{g,\ell}$, $R_{g,1}$ and $R_{\max}$.

Theorem 1

$$Kg \left(\frac{1}{K} R_{\max}(f) \right) \leq R_{g,1}(f) \leq R_{g,\ell}(f) \quad and \quad R_{g,1}(f) \leq Kg(R_{\max}(f)).$$

The proof uses Jensen's inequality for convex function g, monotonicity of g, and the fact that ℓ is an upper bound on the 0-1 loss. Theorem 1 suggests that $R_{g,\ell}$ is a reasonable quantity to minimize in order to incorporate a push at the top, e.g., in order to diminish $R_{\max}$. If g is especially steep, e.g., $g(r) = r^p$ for p large, then $g^{-1}(\sum_{k=1}^{K} g(r_k)) \approx \max_k r_k$, i.e., $g^{-1}(R_{g,1}) \approx R_{\max}$. From now on, we specifically consider the power law (or "p-norm") objectives. Since the user controls p, the amount of push can be specified to match the application.

3   A Generalization Bound for the p-Norm Objective

This bound is an adaptation of previous work [14, 13] inspired by works of Koltchinskii and Panchenko [10] and Cucker and Smale [5]. Assume that the positive instances $\{\mathbf{x}_i \in \mathcal{X}\}_{i=1,\dots,I}$ are chosen independently and at random (iid) from a fixed but unknown probability distribution $\mathcal{D}_+$ on $\mathcal{X}$. The negative instances $\{\tilde{\mathbf{x}}_k \in \mathcal{X}\}_{k=1,\dots,K}$ are chosen iid from $\mathcal{D}_-$. The notation $\mathbf{x} \sim \mathcal{D}$ means $\mathbf{x}$ is chosen randomly according to $\mathcal{D}$. The notation $S_+ \sim \mathcal{D}_+^I$ means each of the I elements of the training set S_+ are chosen iid according to $\mathcal{D}_+$. Similarly for $S_- \sim \mathcal{D}_-^K$. We now define the "true" objective function for which our algorithm has been designed. Our goal is to make this quantity small:

$$R_{\mathcal{D}_+\mathcal{D}_-}^p \mathbf{1}_f := \left(\mathbb{E}_{\mathbf{x}_- \sim \mathcal{D}_-} \left(\mathbb{E}_{\mathbf{x}_+ \sim \mathcal{D}_+} \mathbf{1}_{[f(\mathbf{x}_+) - f(\mathbf{x}_-) \leq 0]} \right)^p \right)^{1/p}$$
$$= \| \mathbb{P}_{\mathbf{x}_+ \sim \mathcal{D}_+}(f(\mathbf{x}_+) - f(\mathbf{x}_-) \leq 0 | \mathbf{x}_-) \|_{L_p(\mathcal{X}, \mathcal{D}_-)} .$$

The empirical loss associated with $R^p_{\mathcal{D}_+\mathcal{D}_-}1_f$ is:

$$R^p_{S_+,S_-}1_f := \left(\frac{1}{K}\sum_{k=1}^{K}\left(\frac{1}{I}\sum_{i=1}^{I}1_{[f(\mathbf{x}_i)-f(\tilde{\mathbf{x}}_k)\leq 0]}\right)^p\right)^{1/p}.$$

Here, for a particular $\tilde{\mathbf{x}}_k$, $R^p_{S_+,S_-}1_f$ takes into account the average number of positive examples that have scores below $\tilde{\mathbf{x}}_k$. It is a monotonic function of $R_{g,1}$. To make this notion more general, consider the average number of positive examples that have scores *close to* or below $\tilde{\mathbf{x}}_k$, namely:

$$R^p_{S_+,S_-}1_f^\theta := \left(\frac{1}{K}\sum_{k=1}^{K}\left(\frac{1}{I}\sum_{i=1}^{I}1_{[f(\mathbf{x}_i)-f(\tilde{\mathbf{x}}_k)\leq\theta]}\right)^p\right)^{1/p}.$$

This terminology incorporates the "margin" value θ. Now we can state our generalization bound:

Theorem 2. *For all $\epsilon > 0, \theta > 0$, and $f \in \mathcal{F}$:*

$$\mathbb{P}_{S_+\sim\mathcal{D}_+^I,S_-\sim\mathcal{D}_-^K}\left[R^p_{\mathcal{D}_+\mathcal{D}_-}1_f \leq R^p_{S_+,S_-}1_f^\theta + \epsilon\right]$$

$$\geq 1 - 2\mathcal{N}\left(\mathcal{F},\frac{\epsilon\theta}{8}\right)\left[\exp\left[-2\left(\frac{\epsilon}{4}\right)^{2p}K\right] + \exp\left[-\frac{\epsilon^2}{8}I\right]\right].$$

Here $\mathcal{N}(\mathcal{F},\epsilon)$ is the L_∞ covering number for $\mathcal{F}$. The theorem says that if I and K are large, then with high probability, the true error $R^p_{\mathcal{D}_+\mathcal{D}_-}1_f$ is not too much more than the empirical error $R^p_{S_+,S_-}1_f^\theta$. The proof is in Appendix A.

As noted, this is a generalization bound for a compulsorily asymmetric problem. It is important to note the implications of this bound for scalability. Since we are concentrating on the negative examples near the top of the ranked list (corresponding to a small chunk of negative input space), we must require more negative examples to achieve high accuracy, as we discuss in Section 7.

Theorem 2 provides a theoretical justification for our choice of objective. Let us now write an algorithm for minimizing that objective.

4   A Boosting-Style Algorithm

We choose a specific form for $R_{g,\ell}$ by specifying ℓ as the exponential loss, $\ell(r) = \exp(-r)$. One could easily choose another loss; we chose the exponential loss in order to compare with RankBoost, which corresponds to the $p = 1$ case for our price function $g(r) = r^p$. Our family of objective functions is thus:

$$F_p(f) := \sum_{k=1}^{K}\left(\sum_{i=1}^{I}\exp[-f(\mathbf{x}_i)+f(\tilde{\mathbf{x}}_k)]\right)^p.$$

Note that F_p is not normalized to approximate $R^p_{\mathcal{D}_+\mathcal{D}_-}\mathbf{1}_f$, but this can easily be accomplished via $\frac{1}{I(K)^{1/p}}(F_p(f))^{1/p}$, which is monotonically related to $F_p(f)$.

Now we describe our boosting-style approach. The hypothesis space $\mathcal{F}$ is the class of linear combinations of "weak" rankers $\{h_j\}_{j=1,\ldots,n}$, where $h_j : \mathcal{X} \to [0,1]$. The function f is constructed as: $f = \sum_j \lambda_j h_j$, where $\boldsymbol{\lambda} \in \mathcal{R}^n$. At iteration t, the coefficient vector (denoted by $\boldsymbol{\lambda}_t$) is updated. To describe how each individual weak ranker j ranks each positive-negative pair i, k, we use a structure $\mathbf{M}$ defined element-wise by: $M_{ikj} := h_j(\mathbf{x}_i) - h_j(\tilde{\mathbf{x}}_k)$. Thus, $M_{ikj} \in [-1,1]$. To define right multiplication, we write the product element-wise as: $(\mathbf{M}\boldsymbol{\lambda})_{ik} := \sum_{j=1}^n M_{ikj}\lambda_j = \sum_{j=1}^n \lambda_j h_j(\mathbf{x}_i) - \lambda_j h_j(\tilde{\mathbf{x}}_k)$ for $\boldsymbol{\lambda} \in \mathcal{R}^n$. Thus, $\ell(f(\mathbf{x}_i) - f(\tilde{\mathbf{x}}_k))$ can now be written as $\exp(-\mathbf{M}\boldsymbol{\lambda})_{ik}$. By construction, F_p is convex in $\boldsymbol{\lambda}$ (but not strictly convex).

We now derive a boosting-style coordinate descent algorithm for minimizing F_p as a function of $\boldsymbol{\lambda}$, notating F_p now as $F_p(\boldsymbol{\lambda})$. We start with the objective at iteration t: $F_p(\boldsymbol{\lambda}_t) := \sum_{k=1}^K \left(\sum_{i=1}^I \exp[(-\mathbf{M}\boldsymbol{\lambda}_t)_{ik}]\right)^p$. We then compute the variational derivative along each "direction", and choose weak ranker j_t to have largest variational derivative. Define the vector $\mathbf{q}_t$ on pairs i, k as: $q_{t,ik} := \exp[(-\mathbf{M}\boldsymbol{\lambda}_t)_{ik}]$, and $\mathbf{d}_t$ as: $d_{t,ik} := q_{t,ik}/\sum_{ik} q_{t,ik}$. Let the vector $\mathbf{e}_j$ be 1 in position j and 0 elsewhere. Then j_t becomes:

$$j_t \in \operatorname*{argmax}_j \left[-\frac{dF_p(\boldsymbol{\lambda}_t + \alpha \mathbf{e}_j)}{d\alpha}\bigg|_{\alpha=0} \right] = \operatorname*{argmax}_j \left[\sum_{k=1}^K \left[\left(\sum_{i=1}^I d_{t,ik}\right)^{p-1} \sum_{i=1}^I d_{t,ik} M_{ikj} \right] \right].$$

To update the coefficient of weak ranker j_t, we now perform a linesearch for the minimum of F_p along the j_t^{th} direction. The distance to travel in the j_t^{th} direction, denoted α_t, solves $0 = \frac{dF_p(\boldsymbol{\lambda}_t + \alpha \mathbf{e}_{j_t})}{d\alpha}\bigg|_{\alpha_t}$, or incorporating normalization,

$$0 = \sum_{k=1}^K \left[\left(\sum_{i=1}^I d_{t,ik} \exp[-\alpha_t M_{ikj_t}]\right)^{p-1} \left(\sum_{i=1}^I M_{ikj_t} d_{t,ik} \exp[-\alpha_t M_{ikj_t}]\right) \right]. \quad (1)$$

The value of α_t can be computed analytically in special cases, but more generally, we use a linesearch to solve for α_t. The full algorithm is shown in Figure 1.

5   Uniqueness of the Minimizer

One might hope that a function $f = \sum_j \lambda_j h_j$ (or limit of functions) minimizing our objective is unique in some sense. Since $\mathbf{M}$ is not required to be invertible (and often is not), a minimizing $\boldsymbol{\lambda}$ may not be unique. Furthermore, elements of $\boldsymbol{\lambda}_t$ and $\mathbf{M}\boldsymbol{\lambda}_t$ may approach $\pm\infty$ or ∞ respectively, so it would seem difficult to prove (or even define) uniqueness. It is useful to consider the set $Q' := \{\mathbf{q}' \in \mathcal{R}^{IK}_+ | q'_{ik} = e^{-(\mathbf{M}\boldsymbol{\lambda})_{ik}}$ for some $\boldsymbol{\lambda} \in \mathcal{R}^n\}$; with the help of convex analysis, we show that our objective function yields a unique minimizer in the closure of Q'.

1. **Input:** $\{x_i\}_{i=1,...,I}$ positive examples, $\{\tilde{x}_k\}_{k=1,...,K}$ negative examples, $\{h_j\}_{j=1,...,n}$ weak classifiers, $t_{\max}$ number of iterations, p power.

2. **Initialize:** $\lambda_{1,j} = 0$ for $j = 1, ..., n$, $d_{1,ik} = 1/IK$ for $i = 1, ..., I$, $k = 1, ..., K$
   $M_{ikj} = h_j(x_i) - h_j(\tilde{x}_k)$ for all i, k, j

3. **Loop for** $t = 1, ..., t_{\max}$

   (a) $j_t \in \text{argmax}_j \left[\sum_{k=1}^{K} \left[\left(\sum_{i=1}^{I} d_{t,ik} \right)^{p-1} \sum_{i=1}^{I} d_{t,ik} M_{ikj} \right] \right]$.

   (b) Find a value α_t that solves (1). That is, perform a linesearch for α_t.

   (c) $\lambda_{t+1} = \lambda_t + \alpha_t e_{j_t}$, where e_{j_t} is 1 in position j_t and 0 elsewhere.

   (d) $z_t = \sum_{ik} d_{t,ik} \exp[-\alpha_t M_{ikj_t}]$

   (e) $d_{t+1,ik} = d_{t,ik} \exp[-\alpha_t M_{ikj_t}]/z_t$ for $i = 1, ..., I$, $k = 1, ..., K$

4. **Output:** $\lambda_{t_{\max}}$

Fig. 1. Pseudocode for the "P-Norm Push Algorithm"

Theorem 3. *Define* $Q' := \{q' \in \mathcal{R}_+^{IK} | q'_{ik} = e^{-(M\lambda)_{ik}}$ *for some* $\lambda \in \mathcal{R}^n\}$ *and define* closure(Q') *as the closure of* Q' *in* $\mathcal{R}^{IK}$. *Then,* $q'^* \in$ closure(Q') *is uniquely determined by:*

$$q'^* = \text{argmin}_{q' \in \text{closure}(Q')} \sum_k \left(\sum_i q'_{ik} \right)^p.$$

Our uniqueness proof (in Appendix B) depends mainly on the theory of convex duality for a class of Bregman distances, as defined by Della Pietra et al. [7]. This proof is inspired by Collins et al. [3] who have proved uniqueness of this type for AdaBoost. In the case of AdaBoost, the primal optimization problem corresponds to a minimization over relative entropy. In our case, the primal is not a common function.

6 Experiments

We will now show the effect of adding a push by examining the leftmost portion of the ROC curve. Our goal is to illustrate the effect of the price g on the quality of the solution; the choice of g as a power law allows us to explore this effect. We hope that $R_{\max}$, or more generally, the leftmost portion of the ROC curve, increases steadily with p. Our demonstration shows this firmly; $R_{\max}$ does often increase (fairly dramatically) with p, for both training and testing.

Data for these experiments were obtained from the UCI machine learning repository [15]. Settings chosen were: **pima-indians-diabetes** with threshold features (Figure 2), **wdbc - Wisconsin Breast Cancer** (Figure 3) and **housing** (Figure 4). The (normalized) features themselves were used as the weak rankers. Results from other datasets can be found in the longer version of this paper [12]. The linesearch for α_t was performed using matlab's 'fminunc' subroutine. The total number of iterations, $t_{\max}$, was fixed at 200. In agreement

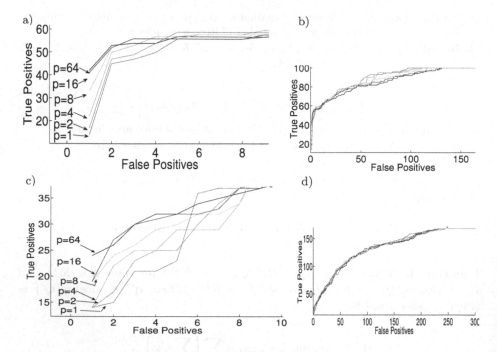

Fig. 2. pima-indians-diabetes with threshold features: 4 threshold features were obtained from each real valued feature, via $h_{\text{thresh}}(\mathbf{x}) = 1$ iff $h(\mathbf{x}) > \text{thresh}$, and $h_{\text{thresh}}(\mathbf{x}) = 0$ otherwise. Thresholds used were chosen so that no two threshold features would be equivalent with respect to the training data. Of 768 examples, 300 randomly chosen examples were used for training, and the rest for testing. (a) Leftmost portion of scaled ROC curve for training, up to and including the crossover point where the sacrifice begins. (b) Full scaled ROC training curve. (c) Leftmost portion of scaled ROC curve for testing. (d) Full scaled ROC testing curve.

with our algorithm's derivation, a larger push (p large) causes the algorithm to perform better near the top of the ranked list. As discussed, this ability to correct the top of the list is not without sacrifice; we do sacrifice the ranks of items farther down on the list, but we have made this choice on purpose. We believe it is important to show this sacrifice explicitly, thus full ROC curves have been included for all experiments. The **housing** setting yields the clearest view of the effect of the algorithm. The trend in $R_{\max}$ from $p = 1$ to $p = 64$ is clearly present and close to monotonic. There is a distinct crossover region, showing exactly what parts of the ROC curve are gained and what parts are sacrificed.

7   Limitations

We have included this section in order to more explicitly describe the problem domain for which the algorithm is useful. As no one algorithm is the best

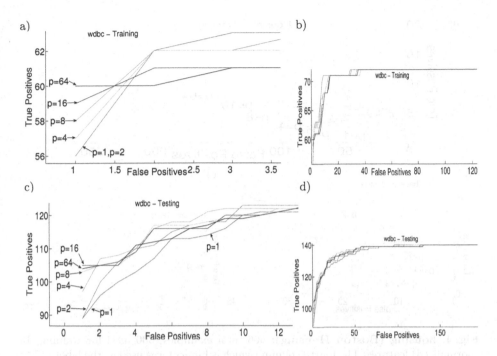

Fig. 3. wdbc (Wisconsin Breast Cancer): 569 total examples, 200 used for training. To ensure the algorithm would not achieve a separable solution, only the first six features (columns 3-8) were used. All features were normalized to $[0, 1]$. (a) Leftmost portion of scaled ROC curve for training (b) Full scaled ROC training curve. (c) Leftmost portion of scaled ROC curve for testing. (d) Full scaled ROC testing curve.

for every problem setting, we wish to make as clear as possible the settings in which our algorithm is meant to succeed, and in which domains it is not meant to be used. The most definitive boundary of the problem domain involves the sample size. The generalization bound of Theorem 2 indicates that for larger values of p, many more examples are needed in order to allow generalization ability; we are concentrating on a smaller region of the probability distribution, so this is natural. When the sample size is too small, the algorithm may still be able to generalize for smaller values of p, but for larger values, we cannot expect the training curve to represent the testing curve. For the settings shown in Section 6, we have used a few hundred examples per experiment, which is enough to allow the algorithm to generalize. In contrast, we now present a setting that compliments our theoretical prediction; the setting is the pima-indian-diabetes dataset with normalized real-valued features, but only 50 training examples. Above a certain p value, the performance degrades as p increases as shown in Figure 5. This shows (what we believe is) the main cautionary note to experimentalists when using this algorithm, and for that matter, when using any other algorithm that concentrates on a small part of the input space.

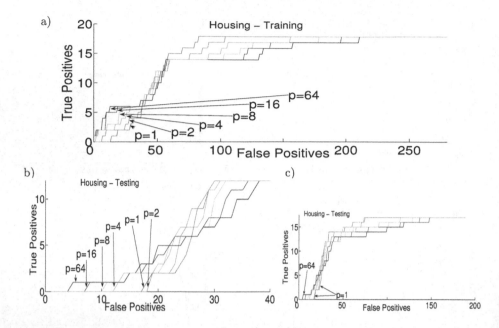

Fig. 4. housing (Boston Housing): 506 total examples, 300 used for training, 13 (normalized) features. The fourth column (which is binary) was used as the label y. The label specifies whether a tract bounds the Charles River. Since there is some correlation between the label and the features, it is reasonable for our learning algorithm to predict whether a tract bounds the river. This data set is skewed; there are significantly fewer positive examples than negative examples. (a) Full scaled ROC training curve. (b) Leftmost portion of scaled ROC curve for testing. (c) Full scaled ROC testing curve.

8 Discussion and Open Problems

In Section 6, we have shown that an increase in p tends to increase $R_{\max}$, but how severe is the sacrifice that we make farther down the ranked list? All of the full ROC training curves in Section 6 (with perhaps the exception of housing) do not show any significant sacrifice, even between the $p = 1$ and $p = 64$ curves. To explain this observation, recall that we are working with learning machines of very limited capacity. The number of real valued features has not exceeded 13, i.e., there is not too much flexibility in the set of solutions that yield good rankings; the algorithm chooses the best solution from this limited choice. A high capacity learning machine generally is able to produce a consistent (or nearly consistent) ranking, so it is a delicate matter to find a dataset and hypothesis space such that an increase in p causes a dramatic change in the full ROC curve. It is an open problem to find such a dataset and function space.

Another important direction for future research is the choice of loss function ℓ and price function g. The choice of loss function is a thoroughly-studied topic, however, the choice of price function adds a new dimension to this problem. One appealing possibility is to choose a non-monotonic function for g. The only

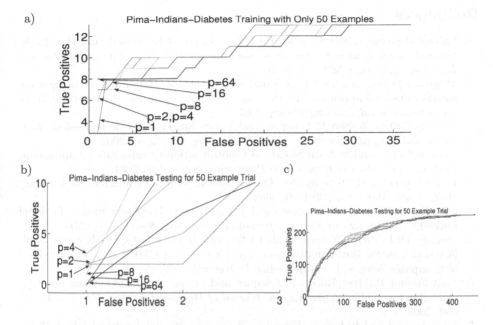

Fig. 5. The pima-indians-diabetes dataset with only 50 training examples. The algorithm is able to generalize for early values of p, but it does not generalize for large values of p. This underscores the need for a sufficiently large training set for large p values. (a) Full training ROC curve. (b) Leftmost portion of ROC testing curve. (c) Full ROC testing curve.

algorithmic requirement is that g be convex. Also, it is possible to use variations of our basic derivation in Section 2 to derive other specialized objectives. Of our experiments, the algorithm's most dramatic effect was arguably seen on the housing dataset, which is a very uneven dataset. It would be interesting to understand the algorithm's effect as a function of the unevenness of the data.

9   Conclusions

We have provided a method for constructing a ranked list where correctness at the top of the list is most important. Our main contribution is a general set of convex objective functions determined by a loss ℓ and price function g. A boosting-style algorithm based on a specific family of these objectives is derived. We have demonstrated the effect of a number of different price functions, and it is clear, both theoretically and empirically, that a steeper price function concentrates harder at the top of the list.

Acknowledgements. Thanks to Rob Schapire, Sinan Güntürk, and Eero Simoncelli. Funding for this research is provided by an NSF postdoctoral fellowship.

References

1. Shivani Agarwal, Thore Graepel, Ralf Herbich, Sariel Har-Peled, and Dan Roth. Generalization bounds for the area under the ROC curve. *Journal of Machine Learning Research*, 6:393–425, 2005.
2. Stéphan Clemençon, Gabor Lugosi, and Nicolas Vayatis. Ranking and scoring using empirical risk minimization. In *Proceedings of the Eighteenth Annual Conference on Computational Learning Theory*, 2005.
3. Michael Collins, Robert E. Schapire, and Yoram Singer. Logistic regression, Ada-Boost and Bregman distances. *Machine Learning*, 48(1/2/3), 2002.
4. Corinna Cortes and Mehryar Mohri. AUC optimization vs. error rate minimization. In *Advances in Neural Information Processing Systems 16*, 2004.
5. Felipe Cucker and Steve Smale. On the mathematical foundations of learning. *Bull. Amer. Math. Soc.*, 39:1–49, 2002.
6. Ofer Dekel, Christopher Manning, and Yoram Singer. Log-linear models for label ranking. In *Advances in Neural Information Processing Systems 16*, 2004.
7. Stephen Della Pietra, Vincent Della Pietra, and John Lafferty. Duality and auxiliary functions for Bregman distances. Technical Report CMU-CS-01-109R, School of Computer Science, Carnegie Mellon University, 2002.
8. Yoav Freund, Raj Iyer, Robert E. Schapire, and Yoram Singer. An efficient boosting algorithm for combining preferences. *Journal of Machine Learning Research*, 4:933–969, 2003.
9. Yoav Freund and Robert E. Schapire. A decision-theoretic generalization of on-line learning and an application to boosting. *Journal of Computer and System Sciences*, 55(1):119–139, August 1997.
10. Vladimir Koltchinskii and Dmitry Panchenko. Empirical margin distributions and bounding the generalization error of combined classifiers. *The Annals of Statistics*, 30(1), February 2002.
11. M. C. Mozer, R. Dodier, M. D. Colagrosso, C. Guerra-Salcedo, and R. Wolniewicz. Prodding the ROC curve: Constrained optimization of classifier performance. In *Advances in Neural Information Processing Systems 14*, pages 1409–1415, 2002.
12. Cynthia Rudin. Ranking with a p-norm push. Technical Report TR2005-874, New York University, 2005.
13. Cynthia Rudin, Corinna Cortes, Mehryar Mohri, and Robert E. Schapire. Margin-based ranking meets boosting in the middle. In *Proceedings of the Eighteenth Annual Conference on Computational Learning Theory*, 2005.
14. Cynthia Rudin and Robert E. Schapire. Margin-based ranking and why Adaboost is actually a ranking algorithm. in progress, 2006.
15. C.L. Blake S. Hettich and C.J. Merz. UCI repository of machine learning databases, 1998.
16. Nicolas Usunier, Massih-Reza Amini, and Patrick Gallinari. A data-dependent generalisation error bound for the AUC. In *Proceedings of the ICML 2005 Workshop on ROC Analysis in Machine Learning*, 2005.
17. Lian Yan, Robert H. Dodier, Michael Mozer, and Richard H. Wolniewicz. Optimizing classifier performance via an approximation to the Wilcoxon-Mann-Whitney statistic. In *Proc. ICML*, pages 848–855, 2003.

A   Proof of Theorem 2

We follow the outline of Rudin et al. [13]. Define a Lipschitz function ϕ : $\mathcal{R} \rightarrow \mathcal{R}$ (with Lipschitz constant $\mathrm{Lip}(\phi)$). Later we use a piecewise linear ϕ

(see [10]), but for now, take $0 \leq \phi(z) \leq 1 \; \forall z$ and $\phi(z) = 1$ for $z < 0$. Since $\phi(z) \geq 1_{[z \leq 0]}$, we have an upper bound on $R^p_{\mathcal{D}_+ \mathcal{D}_-} 1_f$, namely, $R^p_{\mathcal{D}_+ \mathcal{D}_-} \phi_f :=$ $\left(\mathbb{E}_{\mathbf{x}_- \sim \mathcal{D}_-} (\mathbb{E}_{\mathbf{x}_+ \sim \mathcal{D}_+} \phi(f(\mathbf{x}_+) - f(\mathbf{x}_-)))^p \right)^{1/p}$. The empirical error is thus:

$$R^p_{S_+,S_-} \phi_f := \left(\frac{1}{K} \sum_{k=1}^{K} \left(\frac{1}{I} \sum_{i=1}^{I} \phi(f(\mathbf{x}_i) - f(\tilde{\mathbf{x}}_k)) \right)^p \right)^{1/p}.$$

First, we upper bound $R^p_{\mathcal{D}_+ \mathcal{D}_-} \phi_f$ by two terms: the empirical error term $R^p_{S_+,S_-} \phi_f$, and a term characterizing the deviation of $R^p_{S_+,S_-} \phi_f$ from $R^p_{\mathcal{D}_+ \mathcal{D}_-} \phi_f$ uniformly:

$$R^p_{\mathcal{D}_+ \mathcal{D}_-} 1_f \leq R^p_{\mathcal{D}_+ \mathcal{D}_-} \phi_f \leq \sup_{\tilde{f} \in \mathcal{F}} (R^p_{\mathcal{D}_+ \mathcal{D}_-} \phi_{\tilde{f}} - R^p_{S_+,S_-} \phi_{\tilde{f}}) + R^p_{S_+,S_-} \phi_f.$$

The proof involves an upper bound on the first term. Let $L(f) := R^p_{\mathcal{D}_+ \mathcal{D}_-} \phi_f - R^p_{S_+,S_-} \phi_f$. The following lemma is true for every training set S:

Lemma 1. *For any two functions* $f_1, f_2 \in L_\infty(\mathcal{X})$, $L(f_1) - L(f_2) \leq 4\mathrm{Lip}(\phi)\|f_1 - f_2\|_\infty$.

The proof uses Minkowski's inequality twice and some algebraic manipulation. The following step is due to Cucker and Smale [5]. Let $\ell_\epsilon := \mathcal{N}\left(\mathcal{F}, \frac{\epsilon}{8\mathrm{Lip}(\phi)} \right)$, the covering number of $\mathcal{F}$ by L_∞ disks of radius $\frac{\epsilon}{8\mathrm{Lip}(\phi)}$. Define $f_1, f_2, ..., f_{\ell_\epsilon}$ to be the centers of such a cover, i.e., the collection of L_∞ disks B_r centered at f_r and with radius $\frac{\epsilon}{8\mathrm{Lip}(\phi)}$ is a cover for $\mathcal{F}$. The center of each disk will act as a representative for the whole disk. Now, the following lemma is not difficult to prove (see [5] or [13]).

Lemma 2. *For all* $\epsilon > 0$,

$$\mathbb{P}_{S_+ \sim \mathcal{D}_+^I, S_- \sim \mathcal{D}_-^K} \left\{ \sup_{f \in B_r} L(f) \geq \epsilon \right\} \leq \mathbb{P}_{S_+ \sim \mathcal{D}_+^I, S_- \sim \mathcal{D}_-^K} \left\{ L(f_r) \geq \frac{\epsilon}{2} \right\}.$$

Here is a small lemma from calculus that will be useful in the next proof.

Lemma 3. *For* $a, b \in \mathcal{R}_+$, *it is true that* $|a^{1/p} - b^{1/p}| \leq |a - b|^{1/p}$.

We now incorporate the fact that the training set is chosen randomly.

Lemma 4. *For all* $\epsilon_1 > 0$,

$$\mathbb{P}_{S_+ \sim \mathcal{D}_+^I, S_- \sim \mathcal{D}_-^K} (L(f) \geq \epsilon_1) \leq 2 \exp \left[-2 \left(\frac{\epsilon_1}{2} \right)^{2p} K \right] + 2 \exp \left[-\frac{\epsilon_1^2}{2} I \right].$$

Proof. Define $R^p_{S_+,\mathcal{D}_-} \phi_f := \left(\mathbb{E}_{\mathbf{x}_- \sim \mathcal{D}_-} \left(\frac{1}{I} \sum_{i=1}^{I} \phi(f(\mathbf{x}_i) - f(\mathbf{x}_-)) \right)^p \right)^{1/p}$. Now,

$$\mathbb{P}_{S_+ \sim \mathcal{D}_+^I, S_- \sim \mathcal{D}_-^K} (L(f) \geq \epsilon_1) \leq \mathbb{P}_{S_+ \sim \mathcal{D}_+^I} \left(R^p_{\mathcal{D}_+ \mathcal{D}_-} \phi_f - R^p_{S_+,\mathcal{D}_-} \phi_f \geq \frac{\epsilon_1}{2} \right)$$

$$+ \mathbb{P}_{S_+ \sim \mathcal{D}_+^I, S_- \sim \mathcal{D}_-^K} \left(R^p_{S_+,\mathcal{D}_-} \phi_f - R^p_{S_+,S_-} \phi_f \geq \frac{\epsilon_1}{2} \right)$$

$$=: \mathrm{term}_1 + \mathrm{term}_2. \tag{2}$$

Let us bound term$_2$. Since ϕ_f is bounded between 0 and 1, the largest possible change in $(R^p_{S_+,S_-}\phi_f)^p$ that one negative example can cause is $1/K$. Thus, McDiarmid's Inequality applied to the negative examples implies that for all $\epsilon_2 > 0$:

$$\mathbb{P}_{S_-\sim\mathcal{D}^K_-}\left[\left|\mathbb{E}_{\mathbf{x}_-\sim\mathcal{D}_-}\left(\frac{1}{I}\sum_{i=1}^{I}\phi(f(\mathbf{x}_i)-f(\mathbf{x}_-))\right)^p - \frac{1}{K}\sum_{k=1}^{K}\left(\frac{1}{I}\sum_{i=1}^{I}\phi(f(\mathbf{x}_i)-f(\tilde{\mathbf{x}}_k))\right)^p\right| \geq \epsilon_2\right]$$

$$\leq 2\exp\left[\frac{-2\epsilon_2^2}{K\frac{1}{K^2}}\right] = 2\exp\left[-2\epsilon_2^2 K\right]. \tag{3}$$

The following is true for any S_+, due to Lemma 3 above:

$$R^p_{S_+,\mathcal{D}_-}\phi_f - R^p_{S_+,S_-}\phi_f$$

$$\leq \left|\mathbb{E}_{\mathbf{x}_-\sim\mathcal{D}_-}\left(\frac{1}{I}\sum_{i=1}^{I}\phi(f(\mathbf{x}_i)-f(\mathbf{x}_-))\right)^p - \frac{1}{K}\sum_{k=1}^{K}\left(\frac{1}{I}\sum_{i=1}^{I}\phi(f(\mathbf{x}_i)-f(\tilde{\mathbf{x}}_k))\right)^p\right|^{1/p}. \tag{4}$$

Combining (3) and (4) yields a bound on term$_2$. Namely, for all $\epsilon_3 > 0$:

$$\mathbb{P}_{S_-\sim\mathcal{D}^K_-}\left(R^p_{S_+,\mathcal{D}_-}\phi_f - R^p_{S_+,S_-}\phi_f \geq \epsilon_3\right) \leq 2\exp\left[-2\epsilon_3^{2p}K\right]. \tag{5}$$

Letting $\epsilon_3 := \epsilon_1/2$ finishes our work on term$_2$. Now we consider term$_1$ of (2).

$$\mathbb{P}_{S_+\sim\mathcal{D}^I_+}\left(R^p_{\mathcal{D}_+,\mathcal{D}_-}\phi_f - R^p_{S_+,\mathcal{D}_-}\phi_f \geq \frac{\epsilon_1}{2}\right)$$

$$=\mathbb{P}_{S_+\sim\mathcal{D}^I_+}\left(\left\|\mathbb{E}_{\mathbf{x}_+\sim\mathcal{D}_+}\phi(f(\mathbf{x}_+)-f(\cdot))\right\|_{L_p(\mathcal{X},\mathcal{D}_-)} - \left\|\frac{1}{I}\sum_{i=1}^{I}\phi(f(\mathbf{x}_i)-f(\cdot))\right\|_{L_p(\mathcal{X},\mathcal{D}_-)} \geq \frac{\epsilon_1}{2}\right)$$

$$\leq \mathbb{P}_{S_+\sim\mathcal{D}^I_+}\left(\left\|\mathbb{E}_{\mathbf{x}_+\sim\mathcal{D}_+}\phi(f(\mathbf{x}_+)-f(\cdot)) - \frac{1}{I}\sum_{i=1}^{I}\phi(f(\mathbf{x}_i)-f(\cdot))\right\|_{L_\infty(\mathcal{X},\mathcal{D}_-)} \geq \frac{\epsilon_1}{2}\right).$$

We use McDiarmid's Inequality again to complete the proof. The largest possible change in $\frac{1}{I}\sum_{i=1}^{I}\phi(f(\mathbf{x}_i) - f(\mathbf{x}_-))$ due to the replacement of one positive example is $1/I$. Thus, for all $\mathbf{x}_-$,

$$\mathbb{P}_{S_+\sim\mathcal{D}^I_+}\left(\left|\mathbb{E}_{\mathbf{x}_+\sim\mathcal{D}_+}\phi(f(\mathbf{x}_+)-f(\mathbf{x}_-)) - \frac{1}{I}\sum_{i=1}^{I}\phi(f(\mathbf{x}_i)-f(\mathbf{x}_-))\right| \geq \frac{\epsilon_1}{2}\right) \leq 2\exp\left[-\frac{\epsilon_1^2 I}{2}\right].$$

Combining this result with (2) and (5) yields the statement of Lemma 4.   □

Proof. (Of Theorem 2) First applying the union bound over balls, then applying Lemma 2, and then Lemma 4 (as in [13]), we find:

$$\mathbb{P}_{S_+\sim\mathcal{D}^I, S_-\sim\mathcal{D}^K}\left\{\sup_{f\in\mathcal{F}} L(f) \geq \epsilon\right\} \leq \mathcal{N}\left(\mathcal{F}, \frac{\epsilon}{8\mathrm{Lip}(\phi)}\right)\left[2\exp\left[-2\left(\frac{\epsilon}{4}\right)^{2p}K\right] + 2\exp\left[-\frac{\epsilon^2}{8}I\right]\right].$$

Now we put everything together. With probability at least:

$$1 - \mathcal{N}\left(\mathcal{F}, \frac{\epsilon}{8\mathrm{Lip}(\phi)}\right)\left[2\exp\left[-2\left(\frac{\epsilon}{4}\right)^{2p}K\right] + 2\exp\left[-\frac{\epsilon^2}{8}I\right]\right], \quad \text{we have:}$$

$$R^p_{\mathcal{D}_+\mathcal{D}_-}\mathbf{1}_f \leq R^p_{S_+,S_-}\phi_f + \epsilon. \tag{6}$$

Let us choose $\phi(z) = 1$ for $z \leq 0$, $\phi(z) = 0$ for $z \geq \theta$, and linear in between, with slope $-1/\theta$. Thus, $\mathrm{Lip}(\phi) = 1/\theta$. Since $\phi(z) \leq 1$ for $z \leq \theta$, we have $R^p_{S_+,S_-}\phi_f \leq R^p_{S_+,S_-}\mathbf{1}^\theta_f$. Incorporating this into equation (6) finishes the proof of the theorem. $\qquad\Box$

B   Proof of Theorem 3

We will use a theorem of Della Pietra et al. [7], and follow their definitions leading to this theorem. Consider function $\phi : S \subset \mathcal{R}^{IK} \to [-\infty, \infty]$ which is *Legendre* (see [7]). The *effective domain* of ϕ, denoted Δ_ϕ, is the set of points where ϕ is finite. The *Bregman Distance* associated with ϕ is $B_\phi : \Delta_\phi \times \mathrm{int}(\Delta_\phi) \to [0, \infty]$ defined as:

$$B_\phi(\mathbf{p}, \mathbf{q}) := \phi(\mathbf{p}) - \phi(\mathbf{q}) - <\nabla\phi(\mathbf{q}), \mathbf{p} - \mathbf{q}>.$$

(Do not confuse the vector $\mathbf{p} \in \mathcal{R}^{ik}$ with the scalar power p.) The *Legendre-Bregman Conjugate* associated with ϕ is ℓ_ϕ defined as: $\ell_\phi(\mathbf{q}, \mathbf{v}) := \sup_{\mathbf{p}\in\Delta_\phi}(< \mathbf{v}, \mathbf{p} > -B_\phi(\mathbf{p}, \mathbf{q}))$. For fixed $\mathbf{q}$, the Legendre-Bregman conjugate is the convex conjugate of $B_\phi(\cdot, \mathbf{q})$. The *Legendre-Bregman Projection* is the argument of the sup whenever it is well-defined, $\mathcal{L}_\phi : \mathrm{int}(\Delta_\phi) \times \mathcal{R}^{IK} \to \Delta_\phi$, $\mathcal{L}_\phi(\mathbf{q}, \mathbf{v}) := \mathrm{argmax}_{\mathbf{p}\in\Delta_\phi}(< \mathbf{v}, \mathbf{p} > -B_\phi(\mathbf{p}, \mathbf{q}))$. Della Pietra et al. [7] showed that equivalently, $\mathcal{L}_\phi(\mathbf{q}, \mathbf{v}) = (\nabla\phi)^{-1}(\nabla\phi(\mathbf{q}) + \mathbf{v})$.

The domains of the primal and dual problems will be defined with respect to a matrix $\mathbf{M} \in \mathcal{R}^{IK \times n}$, and vectors $\mathbf{q}_0, \mathbf{p}_0 \in \Delta_\phi$. The domain of the primal problem is: $\mathcal{P} = \{\mathbf{p} \in \mathcal{R}^{IK} | \mathbf{p}^T\mathbf{M} = \mathbf{p}_0^T\mathbf{M}\}$. The domain of the dual problem is:

$$\mathcal{Q}(\mathbf{q}_0, \mathbf{M}) := \{\mathbf{q} \in \Delta_\phi | \mathbf{q} = \mathcal{L}_\phi(\mathbf{q}_0, -\mathbf{M}\boldsymbol{\lambda}) \text{ for some } \boldsymbol{\lambda} \in \mathcal{R}^n\}.$$

The following theorem will give us uniqueness within the closure of $\mathcal{Q}$.

Theorem 4. *(from Proposition 3.2 of [7]) Let ϕ satisfy the technical conditions A1.-A5. of [7] and suppose there is $\mathbf{p}_0$ and $\mathbf{q}_0 \in \Delta_\phi$ with $B_\phi(\mathbf{p}_0, \mathbf{q}_0) < \infty$. Then there exists a unique $\mathbf{q}^* \in \Delta_\phi$ satisfying:*

1. $\mathbf{q}^* = \mathrm{argmin}_{\mathbf{p}\in\mathcal{P}}B_\phi(\mathbf{p}, \mathbf{q}_0)$ *(primal problem)*
2. $\mathbf{q}^* = \mathrm{argmin}_{\mathbf{q}\in\mathrm{closure}(\mathcal{Q})}B_\phi(\mathbf{p}_0, \mathbf{q})$ *(dual problem)*

If we can prove that our objective function fits into this framework, this theorem will provide uniqueness in the closure of $\mathcal{Q}$, which is related to $\mathcal{Q}'$. Let us now do this. Consider function $\phi : \mathcal{R}_{>0}^{IK} \to [-\infty, \infty]$, which is Legendre (see [12] for details):

$$\phi(\mathbf{q}) := \sum_{ik} q_{ik} g(q_{ik}, \mathbf{q}), \quad \text{where } g(q_{ik}, \mathbf{q}) := \ln \left(\frac{q_{ik}}{p^{1/p}(\sum_{i'} q_{i'k})^{(p-1)/p}} \right).$$

Reducing carefully, one can show: $\mathcal{L}_\phi(\mathbf{q}, \mathbf{v})_{ik} = e^{v_{ik}} q_{ik} \left(\sum_{i'} e^{v_{i'k}} q_{i'k} \right)^{(p-1)}$ $\frac{1}{(\sum_{i'} q_{i'k})^{(p-1)}}$. Choosing $\mathbf{q}_0$ to be constant, $q_{0ik} = q_0$ for all i, k, we can now obtain $\mathcal{Q}$:

$$\mathcal{Q}(\mathbf{q}_0, \mathbf{M}) = \left\{ \mathbf{q} \in \Delta_\phi \Big| \mathbf{q} = e^{-(\mathbf{M}\boldsymbol{\lambda})_{ik}} \left(\sum_{i'} e^{-(\mathbf{M}\boldsymbol{\lambda})_{i'k}} \right)^{(p-1)} \frac{q_0}{I^{(p-1)}} \text{ for some } \boldsymbol{\lambda} \in \mathcal{R}^n \right\}.$$

In order to make the last fraction 1, let $q_0 = I^{(p-1)}$. The domain for the primal problem is fixed by choosing $\mathbf{p}_0 = \mathbf{0}$, namely $\mathcal{P} = \{\mathbf{p} \in \mathcal{R}^{IK} | \mathbf{p}^T \mathbf{M} = \mathbf{0}\}$. The dual objective is $B_\phi(\mathbf{0}, \mathbf{q})$. If $\mathbf{q} \in \mathcal{Q}$, i.e., $\mathbf{q}_{ik} = e^{-(\mathbf{M}\boldsymbol{\lambda})_{ik}} \left(\sum_{i'} e^{-(\mathbf{M}\boldsymbol{\lambda})_{i'k}} \right)^{(p-1)}$, then simplifying yields:

$$B_\phi(\mathbf{0}, \mathbf{q}) = (1/p) \, F_p(\boldsymbol{\lambda}).$$

Thus, we have arrived at exactly the objective function for our algorithm. That is, ϕ was carefully chosen so the dual objective would be exactly as we wished, modulo the constant $1/p$ which does not affect minimization. The technical conditions A1.-A5. are verified in [12]. Part (2) of Theorem 4 states that the objective function has a unique minimizer in closure($\mathcal{Q}$). It is not difficult to show that a vector in closure($\mathcal{Q}$) corresponds uniquely to a vector in closure($\mathcal{Q}'$). This finishes the proof. $\square$

It was unnecessary to state the primary objective $B_\phi(\mathbf{p}, \mathbf{q}_0)$ explicitly to prove the theorem, however, we state it (details omitted) in order to compare with the relative entropy case where $p = 1$.

$$B_\phi(\mathbf{p}, \mathbf{q}_0) = \sum_{ik} p_{ik} \ln \left[\frac{p_{ik}}{p^{1/p}(\sum_{i'} p_{i'k})^{(p-1)/p}} \right] - \frac{1}{p}(1 - \ln p) \sum_{ik} p_{ik} + \frac{1}{p} I^p K$$

By inspection, one can see that for $p = 1$ this reduces to the relative entropy case.

One interesting note is how to find a function ϕ to suit such a problem. We discovered the function ϕ again via convex duality. We knew the desired dual problem was precisely our objective F_p, thus, we were able to recover the primal problem and thus ϕ by convex conjugation.

Subset Ranking Using Regression

David Cossock[1] and Tong Zhang[2]

[1] Yahoo Inc., Santa Clara, CA, USA
dcossock@yahoo-inc.com
[2] Yahoo Inc., New York City, USA
tzhang@yahoo-inc.com

Abstract. We study the subset ranking problem, motivated by its important application in web-search. In this context, we consider the standard DCG criterion (discounted cumulated gain) that measures the quality of items near the top of the rank-list. Similar to error minimization for binary classification, the DCG criterion leads to a non-convex optimization problem that can be NP-hard. Therefore a computationally more tractable approach is needed. We present bounds that relate the approximate optimization of DCG to the approximate minimization of certain regression errors. These bounds justify the use of convex learning formulations for solving the subset ranking problem. The resulting estimation methods are not conventional, in that we focus on the estimation quality in the top-portion of the rank-list. We further investigate the generalization ability of these formulations. Under appropriate conditions, the consistency of the estimation schemes with respect to the DCG metric can be derived.

1 Introduction

We consider the general ranking problem, where a computer system is required to rank a set of items based on a given input. In such applications, the system often needs to present only a few top ranked items to the user. Therefore the quality of the system output is determined by the performance near the top of its rank-list.

Ranking is especially important in electronic commerce and internet, where personalization and information based decision making is critical to the success of such business. The decision making process can often be posed as a problem of selecting top candidates from a set of potential alternatives, leading to a conditional ranking problem. For example, in a recommender system, the computer is asked to choose a few items a user is most likely to buy based on the user's profile and buying history. The selected items will then be presented to the user as recommendations. Another important example that affects millions of people everyday is the internet search problem, where the user presents a query to the search engine, and the search engine then selects a few web-pages that are most relevant to the query from the whole web. The quality of a search engine is largely determined by the top-ranked results the search engine can display on the first page. Internet search is the main motivation of this theoretical study,

G. Lugosi and H.U. Simon (Eds.): COLT 2006, LNAI 4005, pp. 605–619, 2006.
© Springer-Verlag Berlin Heidelberg 2006

although the model presented here can be useful for many other applications. For example, another ranking problem is ad placement in a web-page (either search result, or some content page) according to revenue-generating potential.

Since for search and many other ranking problems, we are only interested in the quality of the top choices, the evaluation of the system output is different from many traditional error metrics such as classification error. In this setting, a useful figure of merit should focus on the top portion of the rank-list. To our knowledge, this particular characteristic of ranking problems has not been carefully explored in earlier studies. The purpose of this paper is to develop some theoretical results for converting a ranking problem into convex optimization problems that can be efficiently solved. The resulting formulation focuses on the quality of the top ranked results. The theory can be regarded as an extension of related theory for convex risk minimization formulations for classification, which has drawn much attention recently in the statistical learning literature[1, 2, 3, 4, 5, 6].

We organize the paper as follows. Section 2 introduces the subset ranking problem. We define two ranking metrics: one is the DCG measure which we focus on in this paper, and the other is a measure that counts the number of correctly ranked pairs. The latter has been studied recently by several authors. Section 3 contains the main theoretical results in this paper, where we show that the approximate minimization of certain regression errors lead to the approximate optimization of the ranking metrics defined earlier. This implies that asymptotically the non-convex ranking problem can be solved using regression methods that are convex. Section 4 presents the regression learning formulation derived from the theoretical results in Section 3. Similar methods are currently used to optimize Yahoo's production search engine. Section 5 studies the generalization ability of regression learning, where we focus on an L_1-boosting approach. Together with earlier theoretical results, we can establish the consistency of regression based ranking under appropriate conditions.

2   The Subset Ranking Problem

We first describe the abstract version of our subset ranking model, and then use web-search as a concrete example for this model.

2.1   Problem Definition

Let $\mathcal{X}$ be the space of observable features, and $\mathcal{Z}$ be the space of variables that are not necessarily directly used in the deployed system. Denote by $\mathcal{S}$ the set of all finite subsets of $\mathcal{X}$ that may possibly contain elements that are redundant. Let y be a non-negative real-valued variable that corresponds to the quality of $x \in \mathcal{X}$. Assume also that we are given a (measurable) feature-map F that takes each $z \in \mathcal{Z}$, and produces a finite subset $F(z) = S = \{x_1, \ldots, x_m\} \in \mathcal{S}$. Note that the order of the items in the set is of no importance; the numerical subscripts are for notational purpose only, so that permutations can be more conveniently defined.

In subset ranking, we randomly draw a variable $z \in \mathcal{Z}$ according to some underlying distribution on $\mathcal{Z}$. We then create a finite subset $F(z) = S = \{x_1, \ldots, x_m\} \in \mathcal{S}$ consisting of feature vectors x_j in $\mathcal{X}$, and at the same time, a set of grades $\{y_j\} = \{y_1, \ldots, y_m\}$ such that for each j, y_j corresponds to x_j. Whether the size of the set m should be a random variable has no importance in our analysis. In this paper we assume that it is fixed for simplicity.

Based on the observed subset $S = \{x_1, \ldots, x_m\}$, the system is required to output an ordering (ranking) of the items in the set. Using our notation, this ordering can be represented as a permutation $J = [j_1, \ldots, j_m]$ of $[1, \ldots, m]$. Our goal is to produce a permutation such that y_{j_i} is in decreasing order for $i = 1, \ldots, m$. Given the grades $y_j (j = 1, \ldots, m)$, the quality of the rank-list $J = [j_1, \ldots, j_m]$ is measured by the following weighted sum:

$$\mathbf{DCG}(J, [y_j]) = \sum_{i=1}^{m} c_i y_{j_i},$$

where $\{c_i\}$ is a pre-defined sequence of non-increasing non-negative discount factors that are independent of S. This metric, described in [7] as DCG (discounted cumulated gain), is one of the main metrics widely used in the evaluation of internet search systems, including the production system of Yahoo and that of Microsoft [8]. A typical choice of c_i is to set $c_i = 1/\log(1 + i)$ when $i \leq k$ and $c_i = 0$ when $i > k$ for some k. By choosing a decaying sequence of c_i, this measure focuses on the quality of the top portion of the rank-list.

Our goal is to train a ranking function r that can take a subset $S \in \mathcal{S}$ as input, and produce an output permutation $J = r(S)$ such that the expected DCG is as large as possible:

$$\mathbf{DCG}(r) = \mathbf{E}_S \mathbf{DCG}(r, S), \tag{1}$$

where

$$\mathbf{DCG}(r, S) = \sum_{i=1}^{m} c_i \mathbf{E}_{y_{j_i}|(x_{j_i}, S)} \, y_{j_i}. \tag{2}$$

An alternative ranking metric is the weighted total of correctly ranked pairs minus incorrectly ranked pairs:

$$\mathbf{T}(J, [y_j]) = \frac{2}{m(m-1)} \sum_{i=1}^{m-1} \sum_{i'=i+1}^{m} (y_{j_i} - y_{j_{i'}}).$$

If the output label y_i takes binary-values, and the subset $S = \mathcal{X}$ is global (we may assume that it is finite), then this metric is known to be equivalent to AUC (area under ROC) up to a scaling, and related to the Mann-Whitney-Wilcoxon statistics [9]. In the literature, theoretical analysis has focused mainly on global ranking (that is, the set S we observe is $\mathcal{X}$) and the $\mathbf{T}$-criterion (for example, see [10, 11, 12, 13]). However, such a model is inadequate for many practical ranking problems including web-search. Although we pay special attention to the DCG metric, we shall also include some analysis of the $\mathbf{T}$ criterion for completeness.

608   D. Cossock and T. Zhang

Similar to (1) and (2), we can define the following quantities:

$$\mathbf{T}(r) = \mathbf{E}_S\, \mathbf{T}(r, S), \tag{3}$$

where

$$\mathbf{T}(r, S) = \frac{2}{m(m-1)} \sum_{i=1}^{m-1} \sum_{i'=i+1}^{m} (\mathbf{E}_{y_{j_i}|(x_{j_i}, S)}\, y_{j_i} - \mathbf{E}_{y_{j_{i'}}|(x_{j_{i'}}, S)}\, y_{j_{i'}}). \tag{4}$$

Similar to the concept of Bayes classifier in classification, we can define the Bayes ranking function that optimizes the **DCG** and **T** measures. Based on the conditional formulations in (2) and (4), we have the following result:

Theorem 1. *Given a set $S \in \mathcal{S}$, for each $x_j \in S$, we define the Bayes-scoring function as*

$$f_B(x_j, S) = \mathbf{E}_{y_j|(x_j, S)}\, y_j$$

An optimal Bayes ranking function $r_B(S)$ that maximizes (4) returns a rank list $J = [j_1, \ldots, j_m]$ such that $f_B(x_{j_i}, S)$ is in descending order: $f_B(x_{j_1}, S) \geq f_B(x_{j_2}, S) \geq \cdots \geq f_B(x_{j_m}, S)$. An optimal Bayes ranking function $r_B(S)$ that maximizes (2) returns a rank list $J = [j_1, \ldots, j_m]$ such that $c_k > c_{k'}$ implies that $f_B(x_{j_k}, S) > f_B(x_{j_{k'}}, S)$.

Proof. Consider any $k, k' \in \{1, \ldots, m\}$. Define $J' = [j'_1, \ldots, j'_m]$, where $j'_i = j_i$ when $i \neq k, k'$, and $j'_k = j_{k'}$, and $j'_{k'} = j_k$.

We consider the **T**-criterion first, and let $k' = k + 1$. It is easy to check that $\mathbf{T}(J', S) - \mathbf{T}(J, S) = 4(f_B(x_{j_{k+1}}, S) - f_B(x_{j_k}, S))/m(m-1)$. Therefore $\mathbf{T}(J', S) \leq \mathbf{T}(J, S)$ implies that $f_B(x_{j_{k+1}}, S) \leq f_B(x_{j_k}, S)$.

Now consider the **DCG**-criterion. We have $\mathbf{DCG}(J', S) - \mathbf{DCG}(J, S) = (c_k - c_{k'})(f_B(x_{j_{k'}}, S) - f_B(x_{j_k}, S))$. Now $c_k > c_{k'}$ and $\mathbf{DCG}(J', S) \leq \mathbf{DCG}(J, S)$ implies $f_B(x_{j_k}, S) \geq f_B(x_{j_{k'}}, S)$. $\qquad \square$

2.2 Web-Search Example

The subset ranking model can be applied to the web-search problem, where the user submits a query q, and expects the search engine to return a rank-list of web-pages $\{p_j\}$ such that a more relevant page is placed before a less relevant page. In a typical internet search engine, the system takes a query and uses a simple ranking formula for the initial filtering, which limits the set of web-pages to an initial pool $\{p_j\}$ of size m (e.g., $m = 100000$).

After this initial ranking, the system go through a more complicated second stage ranking process, which reorders the pool. This critical stage is the focus of this paper. At this step, the system takes the query q, and possible information from additional resources, to generate a feature vector x_j for each page p_j in the initial pool. The feature vector can encode various types of information such as the length of query q, the position of p_j in the initial pool, the number of query terms that match the title of p_j, the number of query terms that match the body of p_j, etc. The set of all possible feature vectors x_j is $\mathcal{X}$. The ranking algorithm only observes a list of feature vectors $\{x_1, \ldots, x_m\}$ with each $x_j \in \mathcal{X}$. A human editor is presented with a pair (q, p_j) and assigns a score s_j on a scale, e.g., $1-5$ (least relevant to highly relevant). The corresponding target value y_j is defined as a transformation of y_j,[1] which maps the grade into the interval $[0, 1]$. Another possible choice of y_j is to normalize it by multiplying each y_j by a factor such that the optimal DCG is no more than one.

2.3 Set Dependent Features

Due to the dependency of conditional probability of y on S, and thus the optimal ranking function on S, subset ranking becomes a very difficult problem when m is large. In general, without further assumptions, the optimal Bayes ranking function rank the items using the Bayes scoring function $f_B(x, S)$ for each $x \in S$.

If the size m of S is small, then we may simply represent S as a feature vector $[x_1, \ldots, x_m]$ (although this may not be the best representation), so that we can learn a function of the form $f_B(x_j, S) = f([x_j, x_1, \ldots, x_m])$. In the general case when m is large, this approach is not practical. Instead of using the whole set S as a feature, we have to project S into a lower dimensional space using a feature map $g(\cdot)$, so that $f_B(x, g(S)) \approx f(x, g(S))$. Note that the information of $g(S)$ can be incorporated into x (this can be achieved by simply redefining x as $[x, g(S)]$), so that $f_B(x, S)$ can be approximated by a function of the form $f(x)$.

Definition 1. *If for every $S \in \mathcal{S}$ and $x, x' \in S$, we have*

$$f_B(x, S) > f_B(x', S) \quad \text{if and only if} \quad f(x) > f(x'),$$

then we say that f is an optimal rank preserving function.

An optimal rank preserving function may not exist for casual feature representations. As a simple example, we assume that $\mathcal{X} = \{a, b, c\}$ has three elements, with $m = 2$, $c_1 = 1$ and $c_2 = 0$ in the DCG definition. We observe $\{y_1 = 1, y_2 = 0\}$ for the set $\{x_1 = a, x_2 = b\}$, $\{y_1 = 1, y_2 = 0\}$ for the set $\{x_1 = b, x_2 = c\}$, $\{y_1 = 1, y_2 = 0\}$ for the set $\{x_1 = c, x_2 = a\}$. If an optimal rank preserving function f exists, then by definition we have: $f(a) > f(b)$, $f(b) > f(c)$, and $f(c) > f(a)$. This is impossible. The following result gives a sufficient condition for the existence of optimal rank preserving function.

Proposition 1. *Assume that for each x_j, we observe $y_j = n(S)y'_j$ where $n(S)$ is a normalization factor that may depend on S, and $\{y'_j\}$ is a set of random variables that satisfy:*

$$P(\{y'_j\}|S) = \mathbf{E}_\xi \prod_{j=1}^{m} P(y'_j|x_j, \xi),$$

where ξ is a hidden random variable independent of S. Then $\mathbf{E}_{y'_j|(x_j, S)} \, y'_j = \mathbf{E}_{y'_j|x_j} \, y'_j$. That is, the conditional expectation $f(x) = \mathbf{E}_{y'|x} \, y'$ is an optimal rank preserving function.

---

[1] For example, the formula $(2^{s_j} - 1)/(2^5 - 1)$ is used in [8]. Yahoo uses a different transformation based on empirical user surveys.

This result justifies using an appropriately defined feature function to remove set-dependency. If y'_j is a deterministic function of x_j and ξ, then the result always holds, which implies set-independent conditional expectation is optimal. We also note that the optimality of conditional expectation as the scoring function does not require that the grade y' to be independent of S.

In web-search, the model in Proposition 1 has a natural interpretation. Consider a pool of human editors indexed by ξ. For each query q, we randomly pick an editor ξ to grade the set of pages p_j to be ranked, and assume that the grade the editor gives to each page p_j depends only on the pair $x_j = (q, p_j)$.

In the literature, various methods for solving ranking problems have been proposed. The most relevant model in the statistics literature is ordinal regression, which was adapted to large margin methods in [14]. In machine learning, the focus was on pair-wise preference learning, where one learns a scoring function $f(x)$ so that pair-wise rank-orders are preserved. For example, this idea was adopted in the Microsoft system [8]. Proposition 1 (and discussion thereafter) suggests that regression based learning of the conditional expectation $\mathbf{E}_{y|x}\,y$ is asymptotically optimal under some assumptions that are reasonable. Moreover, as discussed earlier in this section, in the regression based approach, one may always introduce set-dependent features through a feature map $g(S)$. Due to these advantages, we shall focus on regression based methods in this paper.

2.4   Relationship to Multi-category Classification

The subset ranking problem is a generalization of multi-category classification. In this case, we observe an input x_0, and are interested in classifying it into one of the m classes. Let the output value be $k \in \{1, \ldots, m\}$. We encode the input x_0 into m feature vectors $\{x_1, \ldots, x_m\}$, where $x_i = [0, \ldots, 0, x_0, 0, \ldots, 0]$ with the i-th component being x_0, and the other components are zeros. We then encode the output k into m values $\{y_j\}$ such that $y_k = 1$ and $y_j = 0$ for $j \neq k$. In this setting, we try to find a scoring function f such that $f(x_k) > f(x_j)$ for $j \neq k$. Consider the DCG criterion with $c_1 = 1$ and $c_j = 0$ when $j > 1$. Then the classification error is given by the corresponding DCG.

Given any multi-category classification algorithm, one may use it to solve subset ranking as follows. Consider a sample S as input, and a set of outputs $\{y_j\}$. We randomly draw k from 1 to m according to the distribution $y_k / \sum_j y_j$. We form another sample with S as input, and $\{y'_j\}$ as output (where $y'_k = 1$, and $y'_j = 0$ when $j \neq k$). This changes the problem formulation into multi-category classification. Since this transformation does not change the order of conditional expectation $\mathbf{E}_{y_j|(x_j,S)}y_j$, it does not change the optimal Bayes ranking function. Therefore a multi-category classification solver that estimates conditional probability can be used to solve the subset ranking problem. The regression method we investigate in this paper is related to the one-versus-all approach.

3   Convex Surrogate Bounds

The subset ranking problem defined in Section 2 is combinatorial in nature, which is very difficult to solve. This section provides some theoretical results that relate the optimization of the ranking metrics defined in Section 2 to the minimization of some regression errors, which allow us to design appropriate convex learning formulations to solve the ranking problem efficiently.

A scoring function $f(x, S)$ maps each $x \in S$ to a real valued score. It induces a ranking function r_f, which ranks elements $\{x_j\}$ of S in descending order of $f(x_j)$. We are interested in bounding the DCG performance of r_f compared with that of f_B. This can be regarded as extensions of Theorem 1 that motivate regression based learning.

Theorem 2. *Let $f(x, S)$ be a real-valued scoring function, which induces a ranking function r_f. We have the following relationship for each $S = \{x_1, \ldots, x_m\}$:*

$$\mathbf{DCG}(r_B, S) - \mathbf{DCG}(r_f, S) \leq \left(2 \sum_{i=1}^{m} c_i^2\right)^{1/2} \left(\sum_{j=1}^{m} (f(x_j, S) - f_B(x_j, S))^2\right)^{1/2}.$$

Proof. Let $S = \{x_1, \ldots, x_m\}$. Let $r_f(S) = J = [j_1, \ldots, j_m]$, and let $J^{-1} = [\ell_1, \ldots, \ell_m]$ be its inverse permutation. Similarly, let $r_B(S) = J_B = [j_1^*, \ldots, j_m^*]$, and let $J_B^{-1} = [\ell_1^*, \ldots, \ell_m^*]$ be its inverse permutation. We have

$$\mathbf{DCG}(r_f, S) = \sum_{i=1}^{m} c_i f_B(x_{j_i}, S) = \sum_{i=1}^{m} c_{\ell_i} f_B(x_i, S)$$

$$= \sum_{i=1}^{m} c_{\ell_i} f(x_i, S) + \sum_{i=1}^{m} c_{\ell_i} (f_B(x_i, S) - f(x_i, S))$$

$$\geq \sum_{i=1}^{m} c_{\ell_i^*} f(x_i, S) + \sum_{i=1}^{m} c_{\ell_i} (f_B(x_i, S) - f(x_i, S))$$

$$= \sum_{i=1}^{m} c_{\ell_i^*} f_B(x_i, S) + \sum_{i=1}^{m} c_{\ell_i^*} (f(x_i, S) - f_B(x_i, S))$$

$$+ \sum_{i=1}^{m} c_{\ell_i} (f_B(x_i, S) - f(x_i, S))$$

$$\geq \mathbf{DCG}(r_B, S) - \sum_{i=1}^{m} c_{\ell_i} (f(x_i, S) - f_B(x_i, S))_+$$

$$- \sum_{i=1}^{m} c_{\ell_i^*} (f_B(x_i, S) - f(x_i, S))_+$$

$$\geq \mathbf{DCG}(r_B, S) - \left(2 \sum_{i=1}^{m} c_i^2\right)^{1/2} \left(\sum_{j=1}^{m} (f(x_j, S) - f_B(x_j, S))^2\right)^{1/2}.$$

where we used the notation $(z)_+ = \max(0, z)$. $\qquad\square$

The above theorem shows that the **DCG** criterion can be bounded through regression error. If regression error goes to zero, then the resulting ranking converges to the optimal DCG. Similarly, we can show the following result for the **T** criterion.

Theorem 3. *Let $f(x, S)$ be a real-valued scoring function, which induces a ranking function r_f. We have the following relationship for each $S = \{x_1, \ldots, x_m\}$:*

$$\mathbf{T}(r_B, S) - \mathbf{T}(r_f, S) \le \frac{4}{\sqrt{m}} \left(\sum_{j=1}^{m} (f(x_j, S) - f_B(x_j, S))^2 \right)^{1/2}.$$

Proof. Let $S = \{x_1, \ldots, x_m\}$. Let $r_f(S) = J = [j_1, \ldots, j_m]$, and let $r_B(S) = J_B = [j_1^*, \ldots, j_m^*]$. We have

$$\mathbf{T}(r_f, S)$$

$$= \frac{2}{m(m-1)} \sum_{i=1}^{m-1} \sum_{i'=i+1}^{m} (f_B(x_{j_i}, S) - f_B(x_{j_{i'}}, S))$$

$$\ge \frac{2}{m(m-1)} \sum_{i=1}^{m-1} \sum_{i'=i+1}^{m} (f(x_{j_i}, S) - f(x_{j_{i'}}, S)) - \frac{2}{m} \sum_{i=1}^{m} |f(x_{j_i}, S) - f_B(x_{j_i}, S)|$$

$$\ge \frac{2}{m(m-1)} \sum_{i=1}^{m-1} \sum_{i'=i+1}^{m} (f(x_{j_i^*}, S) - f(x_{j_{i'}^*}, S)) - \frac{2}{m} \sum_{i=1}^{m} |f(x_{j_i}, S) - f_B(x_{j_i}, S)|$$

$$\ge \frac{2}{m(m-1)} \sum_{i=1}^{m-1} \sum_{i'=i+1}^{m} (f_B(x_{j_i^*}, S) - f_B(x_{j_{i'}^*}, S)) - \frac{4}{m} \sum_{i=1}^{m} |f(x_{j_i}, S) - f_B(x_{j_i}, S)|$$

$$= \mathbf{T}(r_B, S) - \frac{4}{m} \sum_{i=1}^{m} |f(x_{j_i}, S) - f_B(x_{j_{i'}}, S)|$$

$$\ge \mathbf{T}(r_B, S) - \frac{4}{\sqrt{m}} \left(\sum_{i=1}^{m} (f(x_{j_i}, S) - f_B(x_{j_{i'}}, S))^2 \right)^{1/2}. \qquad \square$$

The above approximation bounds imply that least square regression can be used to learn the optimal ranking functions. The approximation error converges to zero when f converges to f_B in L_2. However, in general, requiring f to converge to f_B in L_2 is not necessary. More importantly, in real applications, we are often only interested in the top portion of the rank-list. Our bounds should reflect this practical consideration. In the following, we develop a more refined bound for the DCG metric, which will be used to motivate practical learning methods in the next section.

Theorem 4. *Let $f(x, S)$ be a real-valued scoring function, which induces a ranking function r_f. Given $S = \{x_1, \ldots, x_m\}$, let the optimal ranking order be $J_B = [j_1^*, \ldots, j_m^*]$, where $f_B(x_{j_i^*})$ is arranged in non-increasing order. Assume that $c_i = 0$ for all $i > k$. Then we have the following relationship for all $\gamma \in (0, 1)$, $u > 0$ and subset $K \subset \{1, \ldots, m\}$ that contains $j_1^*, \ldots, j_k^*$:*

$$\mathbf{DCG}(r_B, S) - \mathbf{DCG}(r_f, S)$$

$$\leq C(\gamma, u) \left(\sum_{j \in K} (f(x_j, S) - f_B(x_j, S))^2 + u \sup_{j \notin K} (f(x_j, S) - f'_B(x_j, S))^2_+ \right)^{1/2},$$

where $(z)_+ = \max(z, 0)$, *and*

$$C(\gamma, u) = \frac{1}{1 - \gamma} \sqrt{2 \sum_{i=1}^{k} c_i^2 + \frac{\left(\sum_{i=1}^{k} c_i \right)^2}{u}}, \quad f'_B(x_j) = f_B(x_j) + \gamma(f_B(x_{j_k^*}) - f_B(x_j))_+.$$

Proof. Let $S = \{x_1, \ldots, x_m\}$. Let $r_f(S) = J = [j_1, \ldots, j_m]$, and let $J^{-1} = [\ell_1, \ldots, \ell_m]$ be its inverse permutation. Similarly, let $J_B^{-1} = [\ell_1^*, \ldots, \ell_m^*]$ be the inverse permutation of $r_B(S) = J_B = [j_1^*, \ldots, j_m^*]$. Let $M = f_B(x_{j_k^*})$, we have

$$\mathbf{DCG}(r_B, S) - \mathbf{DCG}(r_f, S)$$

$$= \sum_{i=1}^{m} c_i((f_B(x_{j_i^*}, S) - M) - (f_B(x_{j_i}, S) - M))$$

$$= \sum_{i=1}^{m} c_i((f_B(x_{j_i^*}, S) - M) - (f_B(x_{j_i}, S) - M)_+) + \sum_{i=1}^{m} c_i(M - f_B(x_{j_i}, S))_+$$

$$\leq \frac{1}{1 - \gamma} \left[\sum_{i=1}^{m} c_i((f_B(x_{j_i^*}, S) - M) - (f'_B(x_{j_i}, S) - M)_+) + \sum_{i=1}^{m} c_i(M - f'_B(x_{j_i}, S))_+ \right]$$

$$= \frac{1}{1 - \gamma} \left(\sum_{i=1}^{m} c_i f_B(x_{j_i^*}, S) - \sum_{i=1}^{m} c_i f'_B(x_{j_i}, S) \right)$$

$$\leq \frac{1}{1 - \gamma} \left(\sum_{i=1}^{m} c_i(f_B(x_{j_i^*}, S) - f(x_{j_i^*}, S)) - \sum_{i=1}^{m} c_i(f'_B(x_{j_i}, S) - f(x_{j_i}, S)) \right)$$

$$\leq \frac{1}{1 - \gamma} \left(\sum_{i=1}^{m} c_i(f_B(x_{j_i^*}, S) - f(x_{j_i^*}, S))_+ + \sum_{i=1}^{m} c_i(f(x_{j_i}, S) - f'_B(x_{j_i}, S))_+ \right)$$

$$\leq \frac{1}{1 - \gamma} \left((\sum_{i=1}^{k} c_i^2)^{1/2} \left[(\sum_{j \in K} (f_B(x_j, S) - f(x_j, S))_+^2)^{1/2} + (\sum_{j \in K} (f(x_{j_i}, S) \right. \right.$$

$$\left. \left. - f'_B(x_{j_i}, S))_+^2)^{1/2} \right] + (\sum_{i=1}^{k} c_i) \sup_{j \notin K} (f(x_j, S) - f'_B(x_j, S))_+ \right)$$

$$\leq \frac{1}{1 - \gamma} \left(\sqrt{2 \sum_{i=1}^{k} c_i^2 \sum_{j \in K} (f_B(x_j, S) - f(x_j, S))^2} + \sum_{i=1}^{k} c_i \sup_{j \notin K} (f(x_j, S) - f'_B(x_j, S))_+ \right).$$

Note that in the above derivation, Cauchy-Schwartz inequality has been applied multiple times. From the last inequality, we can apply the Schwartz inequality (again) to obtain the desired bound. $\qquad \square$

Intuitively, the bound says the following: we should estimate the top ranked items using least squares. For the other items, we do not have to make very accurate estimation of their conditional expectations. The DCG score will not be affect as long as we do not over-estimate their conditional expectations to such a degree that some of these items are near the top of the rank-list.

4   Regression Based Learning

Motivated by the analysis in Section 3, we consider regression based training method to solve the DCG optimization problem. We shall not discuss the implementation details for modeling the function $f(x, S)$, which is beyond the scope of this paper. One simple model is to assume a form $f(x, S) = f(x)$. Section 2.3 discussed the validity of such models. For example, this model is reasonable if we assume that for each $x \in S$, and the corresponding y, we have: $\mathbf{E}_{y|(x,S)} y = \mathbf{E}_{y|x} y$ (see Proposition 1).

Let $\mathcal{F}$ be a function space that contains functions $\mathcal{X} \times \mathcal{S} \to R$. We draw n sets $S_1, \ldots, S_n$ randomly, where $S_i = \{x_{i,1}, \ldots, x_{i,m}\}$, with the corresponding grades $\{y_{i,j}\}_j = \{y_{i,1}, \ldots, y_{i,m}\}$. Based on Theorem 2, a simple regression based approach can be used to solve the ranking problem:

$$\hat{f} = \arg\min_{f \in \mathcal{F}} \frac{1}{n} \sum_{i=1}^{n} \left[\sum_{j=1}^{m} (f(x_{i,j}, S_i) - y_{i,j})^2 \right].$$

However, this direct regression method is not appropriate for large scale ranking problems such as web-search, for which there are many items to rank but only the top ranked pages are important. This is because the method pays equal attention to relevant and irrelevant pages. In reality, one should pay more attention to the top-ranked (relevant) pages. The grades of lower rank pages do not need to be estimated accurately, as long as we do not over-estimate them so that these pages appear in the top ranked positions.

The above mentioned intuition can be captured by Theorem 4, which motivates the following alternative training method:

$$\hat{f} = \arg\min_{f \in \mathcal{F}} \frac{1}{n} \sum_{i=1}^{n} L(f, S_i, \{y_{i,j}\}_j), \tag{5}$$

where for $S = \{x_1, \ldots, x_m\}$, with the corresponding $\{y_j\}_j$, we have

$$L(f, S, \{y_j\}_j)$$
$$= \sum_{j=1}^{m} w(x_j, S)(f(x_j, S) - y_j)^2 + u \sup_j w'(x_j, S)(f(x_j, S) - \delta(x_j, S))_+^2, \tag{6}$$

where u is a non-negative parameter. A variation of this method is used to optimize the production system of Yahoo's internet search engine. The detailed implementation and parameter choices are trade secrets of Yahoo, which we cannot completely disclose here[2]. It is also irrelevant for the purpose of this paper. However, in the following, we shall briefly explain the intuition behind (6) using Theorem 4, and some practical considerations.

The weight function $w(x_j, S)$ is chosen so that it focuses only on the most important examples (the weight is set to zero for pages that we know are irrelevant). This part of the formulation corresponds to the first part of the bound in Theorem 4 (in that case, we choose $w(x_j, S)$ to be one for the top part of the example with index set K, and zero otherwise). The specific choice of the weight function is not important for the purpose of this paper. In the second part of the formulation, we choose $w'(x_j, S)$ so that it focuses on the examples not covered by $w(x_j, S)$. In particular, it only covers those data points x_j that are low-ranked with high confidence. We choose $\delta(x_j, S)$ to be a small threshold that can be regarded as a lower bound of $f'_B(x_j)$ in Theorem 4, such as $\gamma f_B(x_k^*)$. An important observation is that although m is often very large, the number of points so that $w(x_j, S)$ is nonzero is often small. Moreover, $(f(x_j, S) - \delta(x_j, S))_+$ is not zero only when $f(x_j, S) \geq \delta(x_j, S)$. In practice the number of these points is usually small (that is, most irrelevant pages will be predicted as irrelevant). Therefore the formulation completely ignores those low-ranked data points such that $f(x_j, S) \leq \delta(x_j, S)$. This makes the algorithm computationally efficient even when m is large. The analogy here is support vector machines, where only the support vectors are useful in the learning formulation. One can completely ignore samples corresponding to non support vectors.

In the practical implementation of (6), we can use an iterative refinement scheme, where we start with a small number of samples to be included in the first part of (6), and then put the low-ranked points into the second part of (6) only when their ranking scores exceed $\delta(x_j, S)$. In fact, one may also put these points into the first part of (6), so that the second part always has zero values (which makes the implementation simpler). In this sense, the formulation in (6) suggests a selective sampling scheme, in which we pay special attention to important and highly ranked data points, while completely ignoring most of the low ranked data points. In this regard, with appropriately chosen $w(x, S)$, the second part of (6) can be completely ignored.

The empirical risk minimization method in (5) approximately minimizes the following criterion:

$$Q(f) = \mathbf{E}_S L(f, S), \tag{7}$$

where

$$L(f, S) = \mathbf{E}_{\{y_j\}_j | S} L(f, S, \{y_j\}_j)$$

$$= \sum_{j=1}^{m} w(x_j, S) \mathbf{E}_{y_j | (x_j, S)} (f(x_j, S) - y_j)^2 + u \sup_j w'(x_j, S)(f(x_j, S) - \delta(x_j, S))_+^2.$$

The following theorem shows that under appropriate assumptions, approximate minimization of (7) leads to the approximate optimization of DCG.

---

[2] Some aspects of the implementation were covered in [15].

Theorem 5. *Assume that $c_i = 0$ for all $i > k$. Assume the following conditions hold for each $S = \{x_1, \ldots, x_m\}$:*

- *Let the optimal ranking order be $J_B = [j_1^*, \ldots, j_m^*]$, where $f_B(x_{j_i^*})$ is arranged in non-increasing order.*
- *There exists $\gamma \in [0, 1)$ such that $\delta(x_j, S) \le \gamma f_B(x_{j_k^*}, S)$.*
- *For all $f_B(x_j, S) > \delta(x_j, S)$, we have $w(x_j, S) \ge 1$.*
- *Let $w'(x_j, S) = I(w(x_j, S) < 1)$.*

Then the following results hold:

- *A function f_* minimizes (7) if $f_*(x_j, S) = f_B(x_j, S)$ when $w(x_j, S) > 0$ and $f_*(x_j, S) \le \delta(x_j, S)$ otherwise.*
- *For all f, let r_f be the induced ranking function. Let r_B be the optimal Bayes ranking function, we have:*

$$\mathbf{DCG}(r_f) - \mathbf{DCG}(r_B) \le C(\gamma, u)(Q(f) - Q(f_*))^{1/2}.$$

Proof. Note that if $f_B(x_j, S) > \delta(x_j, S)$, then $w(x_j, S) \ge 1$ and $w'(x_j, S)$. Therefore the minimizer $f_*(x_j, S)$ should minimize $\mathbf{E}_{y_j|(x_j, S)}(f(x_j, S) - y_j)^2$, achieved at $f_*(x_j, S) = f_B(x_j, S)$. If $f_B(x_j, S) \le \delta(x_j, S)$, then there are two cases:

- $w(x_j, S) > 0$, $f_*(x_j, S)$ should minimize $\mathbf{E}_{y_j|(x_j, S)}(f(x_j, S) - y_j)^2$, achieved at $f_*(x_j, S) = f_B(x_j, S)$.
- $w(x_j, S) = 0$, $f_*(x_j, S)$ should minimize $\mathbf{E}_{y_j|(x_j, S)}(f(x_j, S) - \delta(x_j, S))_+^2$, achieved at $f_*(x_j, S) \le \delta(x_j, S)$.

This proves the first claim.

For each S, denote by K the set of x_j such that $w'(x_j, S) = 0$. The second claim follows from the following derivation:

$$Q(f) - Q(f_*)$$
$$= \mathbf{E}_S(L(f, S) - L(f_*, S))$$
$$= \mathbf{E}_S \left[\sum_{j=1}^{k} w(x_j, S)(f(x_j, S) - f_B(x_j, S))^2 + u \sup_j w'(x_j, S)(f(x_j, S) - \delta(x_j, S))_+^2 \right]$$
$$\ge \mathbf{E}_S \left[\sum_{j \in K} (f_B(x_j, S) - f(x_j, S))_+^2 + u \sup_{j \notin K} (f(x_j, S) - \delta(x_j, S))_+^2 \right]$$
$$\ge \mathbf{E}_S(\mathbf{DCG}(r_B, S) - \mathbf{DCG}(r_f, S))^2 C(\gamma, u)^{-2}$$
$$\ge (\mathbf{DCG}(r_B) - \mathbf{DCG}(r_f))^2 C(\gamma, u)^{-2}.$$

Note that the second inequality follows from Theorem 4.   □

5   Generalization Analysis

In this section, we analyze the generalization performance of an L_1-boosting method, similar to [16, 2, 17]. Yahoo's machine learning ranking system employs the closely related gradient boosting method in [18], which can be similarly analyzed.

Consider a class of so-called *weak learners* $\mathcal{H}$, consisting of binary functions $\mathcal{X} \times \mathcal{S} \rightarrow \{0, 1\}$, with a finite VC-dimension $\mathrm{VC}(\mathcal{H})$. We define for all $\beta \geq 0$: $\mathrm{co}_\beta(\mathcal{H}) = \{f : f(x) = \sum_{i=1}^{t} \alpha_i h_i(x), \sum_{i=1}^{t} |\alpha_i| \leq \beta, h_i \in \mathcal{H}\}$. We are interested in algorithms that select a hypothesis from $\mathrm{co}_\beta(\mathcal{H})$. Similar to Section 4, we use $(S_i, \{y_{i,j}\}_j)$ to indicate a sample point indexed by i. Note that for each sample i, we shall not assume that $y_{i,j}$ are independently generated for different j.

The following result is a simplified uniform convergence bound for the empirical risk minimization method in (5).

Theorem 6. *Assume that grades* $y \in [0, 1]$. *Consider* $\beta > 1$, *and let* $\hat{f}$ *be the estimator defined in (5), with* $\mathcal{F} = \mathrm{co}_\beta(\mathcal{H})$. *Then we have*

$$\mathbf{E}_{\{S_i, \{y_{i,j}\}_j\}_{i=1}^{n}} Q(\hat{f}) \leq \inf_{f \in \mathrm{CO}_\beta(\mathcal{H})} Q(f) + C\beta^2 \sqrt{\frac{W \cdot \mathrm{VC}(\mathcal{H})}{n}},$$

where C *is a universal constant and*

$$W = \mathbf{E}_S \left[\sum_{j=1}^{m} w(x_j, S) + u \sup_j w'(x_j, S) \right]^2.$$

Due to the limitation of space, we shall skip the proof, which is an adaptation of the standard Rademacher complexity analysis to our setting. Here we have paid special attention to the properties of (5). In particular, the quantity W is usually much smaller than m, which is large for web-search applications. The point we'd like to emphasize here is that even though the number m is large, the estimation complexity is only affected by the top-portion of the rank-list. If the estimation of the bottom ranked items is relatively easy (as is generally the case), then the learning complexity does not depend on the majority of items near the bottom of the rank-list.

We can combine Theorem 5 and Theorem 6, giving the following bound:

Theorem 7. *Suppose the conditions in Theorem 5 and Theorem 6 hold with* f_* *minimizing (7). We have*

$$\mathbf{E}_{\{S_i, \{y_{i,j}\}_j\}_{i=1}^{n}} \mathbf{DCG}(r_{\hat{f}})$$

$$\leq \mathbf{DCG}(r_B) + C(\gamma, u) \left[\inf_{f \in \mathrm{CO}_\beta(\mathcal{H})} Q(f) - Q(f_*) + C\beta^2 \sqrt{\frac{W \cdot \mathrm{VC}(\mathcal{H})}{n}} \right]^{1/2}.$$

Proof. From Theorem 5, we obtain

$$\mathbf{E}_{\{S_i, \{y_{i,j}\}_j\}_{i=1}^{n}} \mathbf{DCG}(r_{\hat{f}}) - \mathbf{DCG}(r_B)$$

$$\leq C(\gamma, u) \mathbf{E}_{\{S_i, \{y_{i,j}\}_j\}_{i=1}^{n}} (Q(\hat{f}) - Q(f_*))^{1/2}$$

$$\leq C(\gamma, u) (\mathbf{E}_{\{S_i, \{y_{i,j}\}_j\}_{i=1}^{n}} Q(\hat{f}) - Q(f_*))^{1/2}.$$

Now by applying Theorem 6, we obtain the desired bound.   □

618   D. Cossock and T. Zhang

The theorem implies that if $Q(f_*) = \lim_{\beta \to \infty} \inf_{f \in CO_\beta(\mathcal{H})} Q(f)$, then as $n \to \infty$, we can let $\beta \to \infty$ and $\beta^2/\sqrt{n} \to 0$ so that the second term on the right hand side vanishes in the large sample limit. Therefore asymptotically, we can achieve the optimal DCG score. This implies the consistency of regression based learning methods for the DCG criterion.

6   Conclusion

This paper considers the subset ranking problem, motivated by the web-search application. We investigated the DCG criterion that emphasizes the quality of the top-ranked items, and derived bounds that relate the optimization of DCG scores to the minimization of convex regression errors. These bounds can be used to motivate regression based methods that focus on the top-portion of the rank-list. In addition to conceptual advantages, these methods have significant computational advantages over standard regression methods because only a small number of items contribute to the solution. This means that they are computationally efficient to solve. As we have commented, the implementation of these methods can be achieved through appropriate selective sampling procedures. Moreover, we showed that the generalization performance of the system does not depend on m. Instead, it only depends on the estimation quality of the top ranked items. Again this is important for practical applications.

Results obtained here are closely related to the theoretical analysis for solving classification methods using convex optimization formulations. Our theoretical results show that the regression approach provides a solid basis for solving the subset ranking problem. The practical value of such methods is also significant. In Yahoo's case, substantial improvement of DCG has been achieved after the deployment of machine learning based ranking system. At the time of this writing, the system performance is already on par with the competitions, while further improvements are expected in the future.

Although the DCG criterion is difficult to optimize directly, it is a natural metric for ranking. The investigation of convex surrogate formulations provides a systematic approach to developing efficient machine learning methods for solving this difficult problem. We shall point out that the convex surrogate bounds proved in this paper are still quite loose. Therefore by deriving tighter bounds and developing better understanding of the ranking problem, we may obtain improved machine learning methods in the future.

References

1. Bartlett, P., Jordan, M., McAuliffe, J.: Convexity, classification, and risk bounds. Technical Report 638, Statistics Department, University of California, Berkeley (2003) to appear in JASA.
2. Lugosi, G., Vayatis, N.: On the Bayes-risk consistency of regularized boosting methods. The Annals of Statistics **32** (2004) 30–55 with discussion.
3. Zhang, T.: Statistical behavior and consistency of classification methods based on convex risk minimization. The Annals of Statistics **32** (2004) 56–85 with discussion.

4. Zhang, T.: Statistical analysis of some multi-category large margin classification methods. Journal of Machine Learning Research **5** (2004) 1225–1251
5. Steinwart, I.: Support vector machines are universally consistent. J. Complexity **18** (2002) 768–791
6. Tewari, A., Bartlett, P.: On the consistency of multiclass classification methods. In: COLT. (2005)
7. Jarvelin, K., Kekalainen, J.: IR evaluation methods for retrieving highly relevant documents. In: SIGIR'00. (2000) 41–48
8. Burges, C., Shaked, T., Renshaw, E., Lazier, A., Deeds, M., Hamilton, N., Hullender, G.: Learning to rank using gradient descent. In: ICML'05. (2005)
9. Hanley, J., McNeil, B.: The meaning and use of the Area under a Receiver Operating Characetristic (ROC) curve. Radiology (1982) 29–36
10. Agarwal, S., Graepel, T., Herbrich, R., Har-Peled, S., Roth, D.: Generalization bounds for the area under the ROC curve. Journal of Machine Learning Research **6** (2005) 393–425
11. Agarwal, S., Roth, D.: Learnability of bipartite ranking functions. In: Proceedings of the 18th Annual Conference on Learning Theory. (2005)
12. Clemencon, S., Lugosi, G., Vayatis, N.: Ranking and scoring using empirical risk minimization. In: COLT'05. (2005)
13. Rosset, S.: Model selection via the AUC. In: ICML'04. (2004)
14. Herbrich, R., Graepel, T., Obermayer, K.: Large margin rank boundaries for ordinal regression. In A. Smola, P. Bartlett, B.S., Schuurmans, D., eds.: Advances in Large Margin Classifiers. MIT Press (2000) 115–132
15. Cossock, D.: Method and apparatus for machine learning a document relevance function. US patent application, 20040215606 (2003)
16. Blanchard, G., Lugosi, G., Vayatis, N.: On the rate of convergence of regularized boosting classifiers. Journal of Machine Learning Research **4** (2003) 861–894
17. Mannor, S., Meir, R., Zhang, T.: Greedy algorithms for classification - consistency, convergence rates, and adaptivity. Journal of Machine Learning Research **4** (2003) 713–741
18. Friedman, J.: Greedy function approximation: A gradient boosting machine. The Annals of Statistics **29** (2001) 1189–1232

Active Sampling for Multiple Output
Identification

Shai Fine[1] and Yishay Mansour[2],[*]

[1] IBM Research Laboratory in Haifa, Israel
`shai@il.ibm.com`
[2] School of Computer Science, Tel Aviv University, Tel Aviv, Israel
`mansour@post.tau.ac.il`

Abstract. We study functions with multiple output values, and use active sampling to identify an example for each of the possible output values. Our results for this setting include: (1) Efficient active sampling algorithms for simple geometric concepts, such as intervals on a line and axis parallel boxes. (2) A characterization for the case of binary output value in a transductive setting. (3) An analysis of active sampling with uniform distribution in the plane. (4) An efficient algorithm for the Boolean hypercube when each output value is a monomial.

1 Introduction

Active sampling is much about "hitting" low probability events. In active learning the active sampling is used to guide the learning process to learn a high accuracy hypothesis while using a limited number or examples [16, 9, 8, 10, 6, 3, 1, 2]. While in many applications the goal of an accurate hypothesis is the most natural one, there are other applications which require only examples of those low probability events. Example of such application areas include hardware and software verification, fault tolerance, network security, data mining etc. The usage of such examples in each of the applications can be very different: in fault tolerance one would like to simulate the performance of the system in extreme conditions (e.g., very high load), in network security one would like to have examples of potential intruders, while in data mining one would like to find new interesting relationships, which are not explained by the existing ones. Our original motivation, though, stem from dynamic hardware verification and from software testing. In both domains, the main industrial vehicles are simulation-based methods which aimed at exciting (and impacting) the occurrence of events and scenarios of desired functional behaviors that need to be verified [19, 4]. Coverage [12] is an information collection mechanism that is often used to monitor the progress of the verification process, and point to areas in the design that have not been properly tested.

---

[*] This work was supported in part by the IST Programme of the European Community, under the PASCAL Network of Excellence, IST-2002-506778, by a grant no. 1079/04 from the Israel Science Foundation, by a grant from BSF and an IBM faculty award. This publication only reflects the authors' views.

G. Lugosi and H.U. Simon (Eds.): COLT 2006, LNAI 4005, pp. 620–634, 2006.

The analysis of coverage reports, and their translation to a set of directives that guides the implementation of the test plan, result in major manual bottlenecks in the otherwise highly automated verification process. A verification methodology called *coverage directed test generation* (CDG) aims to resolve this problem, either by utilizing a mechanism that can directly translate a verification task into a simulation test (CDG by Construction, cf. [17]), or by extracting useful information from the observed events, and use it to bias future simulation runs (CDG by Feedback, cf. [7] and ref. therein). However, too often, neither an accurate translation mechanism nor well structured coverage model can be provided, and we end up with the following naive, yet difficult, scenario: The verification team is given a list of events that should be covered, and the goal is to provide multiple sets of directives (inputs) that will tune the test generator to produce patterns that hit all items in the list. In these situations the common practice is "trial & error".

We abstracted the above motivation in the following learning model. There is an unknown target function f which maps every input in $\mathcal{X}$ to one of m output values. (For example, in the verification setting the output values would be desired scenarios for coverage.) The *output identification task* is to find m inputs, one for each output value.

The output identification algorithm is given some information about the target function. First, like much of the computational learning literature, it knows that the target function f is in a given function class $\mathcal{F}$. Second, it is given the number of output values, i.e., m (hence it knows when to terminate).

We assume that there is an unknown distribution D over the inputs. The algorithm has an access to an *induced distribution example oracle* which allows it to sample from sub-regions of the domain. (Namely, the algorithm specifies a subset $Y \subset \mathcal{X}$, and the oracle returns an example from Y, distributed according to the induced distribution of D over Y.) The goal of the output identification algorithm is to minimize the number of oracle samples it requires until a representative for each output value is found. The performance is measured as a function of the number of output values m and ϵ, a lower bound on the probability of each output value. (We remark that only for simplicity we assume that m and ϵ are known to the output identification algorithm, both of the requirements can be easily relaxed and similar results hold.)

We show efficient algorithms for many classes of functions. We start by showing efficient output identification algorithms for a few simple geometric classes. For the function class of m intervals on a line we show an expected active sample bound of $O(m \log 1/\epsilon)$. For m axis parallel boxes in $\mathbb{R}^d$ we give an expected active sample bound of $O(md \log 1/\epsilon)$. We also derive lower bounds that exhibit classes with a constant VC dimension, such as a linear separator in the plane, which require $\Omega(1/\epsilon)$ active samples.

Our main result is a characterization for the case of binary outputs, i.e., $m = 2$. We define a separation dimension and show that if the separation dimension is d then the function class can be output identified in $O(d^2 \log^2 s)$ queries in a transductive setting (where the output identification algorithm is given a set of

s unlabeled examples in advance). In addition, we show that for any function class with separation dimension d, there is an unlabeled sample for which no algorithm can output identify it in less than $\Omega(\min\{d, s\})$ queries.

The separation dimension is similar in flavor to the VC dimension[18]. It requires d points such that the function class induced on them has all the d singleton functions (rather than all 2^d possible functions in the VC dimension). We show that when a class has separation dimension d, then some input in the unlabeled sample can be queried and guarantee that either we terminate (finding a representative for each output value) or we reduce the space of consistent functions considerably. Using this property we derive an efficient output identification algorithm.

We also study the case of specific distributions, namely the uniform distribution in the plane. Using classical results from computational geometry we can show that many classes are efficiently learnable under the uniform distribution. Specifically, we show that the class of linear separators in the plane can be output identified with expected $O(m^2 \log^2 1/\epsilon)$ active samples with respect to the uniform distribution over the unit square.

We conclude with a concept class defined over the Boolean hypercube $\{0, 1\}^n$. We show that the class where each output value is represented by a monomial can be output identify in mn active samples.

Our model has obvious connections to active learning [16, 9, 8, 10, 6, 3, 1, 2]. In some sense the output identification task is much simpler than the usual learning task, since we do not need to find an accurate hypothesis, only to target one example for each output value. Still it seems that the techniques we present here and the active learning techniques share much in common. In both cases the goal is to reduce uncertainty, however since the tasks are different (learning vs. identification), so does the choice which of the samples to query – while an active learner will choose to query for the label of the sample which maximizes disagreement between the consistent hypotheses in the version space (cf. QBC [16, 8]), an output identifier will select to query for the label of the sample which maximize the probability of an unseen output value (ideally have the probability be almost one). Another major difference is that active learning is interested mainly in binary classification while the main motivation for output identification are cases with a large number of possible output values.

There are simple cases in which active learning fails to achieve a significant sample improvement, for example linear separator in the plane [1]. In such cases one should expect the output identification task to suffer from similar drawbacks (and indeed some of our lower bounds are much in that spirit).

A somewhat related question was discuss in [11] where efficient deterministic constructions for combinatorial hitting sets are given. A hitting set for a domain $\{1, \ldots, m\}^d$ guarantees to "hit" any combinatorial rectangle of volume at least ϵ, i.e., any combinatorial rectangle that includes at least ϵm^d points would intersect the hitting set in at least one point. The main contribution of [11] is to construct such a hitting set *deterministically* (i.e., without any randomization) and have its size and computation time be polynomial in m, d and $1/\epsilon$.

2   The Model

A function f is m-valued if f maps inputs from a domain $\mathcal{X}$ to an m valued range $\{1, \ldots, m\}$. An m-valued function class $\mathcal{F}$ is a set of m valued functions.

The *output identification task* for an m valued function class $\mathcal{F}$ is as follows. There is an unknown m valued *target function* $f \in \mathcal{F}$ and the goal of the output identification algorithm is to identify an input for each the m output values, i.e., find examples, $x^1, \ldots, x^m \in \mathcal{X}$ such that $f(x^i) = i$.

The output identification algorithm has access to examples of the target function as follows. There is some unknown distribution D over the domain $\mathcal{X}$. Given a subset of the domain $Y \subset \mathcal{X}$ let D_Y be the distribution D induces over Y. An *induced distribution example oracle* receives as an input a subset $Y \subset \mathcal{X}$ and returns a pair $< x, f(x) >$, where x is distributed according to D_Y and f is the target function. (We assume that Y has a non-empty intersection with the support of D, otherwise the oracle would generate an error.)

At each time step t, the output identification algorithm specifies a subset $Y_t \subset \mathcal{X}$ to the induced distribution example oracle and received an example $< x_t, f(x_t) >$. The process terminates when the algorithm has an example for each of the m output values. (I.e., $x^1, \ldots, x^m \in \mathcal{X}$ such that $f(x^i) = i$.)

In order to measure the complexity of an output identification algorithm we assume that each output value has a probability of at least ϵ under (the unknown) distribution D.

The *active sample complexity* of an output identification algorithm with respect to a distribution D and function $f \in \mathcal{F}$ is the number of examples it requests, i.e., the number of times it accesses the induced distribution example oracle. The active sample complexity of an output identification algorithm for a function class $\mathcal{F}$ is the worse case over all $f \in \mathcal{F}$ and distributions D of its active sample complexity. The active sample complexity of a function class $\mathcal{F}$ is the least active sample complexity of any output identification algorithm for $\mathcal{F}$.

3   Simple Geometric Concepts

In this section we consider simple geometric concepts where the domain is $\mathcal{X} = \mathbb{R}^d$. We start with the line $(d = 1)$ and consider the case where each of the m output values is represented by an interval. For this case we give an expected $O(m \log 1/\epsilon)$ active sample complexity output identification algorithm. We then extend our result to the case of axis parallel boxes and give an output identification algorithm whose expected active sample complexity is $O(dm \log 1/\epsilon)$. We end with a few simple lower bounds, showing examples of concept classes with a finite VC dimensions which require $\Omega(1/\epsilon)$ active sample complexity.

3.1   Generic Consistency Algorithm

We assume that the points mapped to a specific output value belong to some function class $\mathcal{A}$. (For intervals $A \in \mathcal{A}$ would be a single interval and for axis parallel boxes it would be a single axis parallel box.)

The *generic consistency algorithm* works as follows. Initially we have $C_0 = \emptyset$. At phase $t \geq 1$ we sample the induced distribution example oracle with the subset $\mathcal{X} - C_{t-1}$ and receive an example $< x_t, k_t >$. For each output value k let S_t^k be the set of examples sampled with output value k until time t. Let C_t^k be the *minimal concept* in A which is consistent with the examples in S_t^k (in our applications such a concept always exists). Let C_t be the union of all the C_t^k and proceed to phase $t+1$.

The generic consistency algorithm starts at phase $t = 1$ and terminate at the first phase where for every output value k we have $S_t^k \neq \emptyset$ (note that in such a case we have for each of the m output values at least one example).

To be more specific about the minimal consistent concept we define it for the case of intervals and axis parallel boxes. In the case that A is an interval then C_t^k is an interval $[\lambda_-^k, \lambda_+^k]$ such that $\lambda_-^k = \min\{x \in S_t^k\}$ and $\lambda_+^k = \max\{x \in S_t^k\}$. In the case that A is an axis parallel box then C_t^k is $([c_-^1, c_+^1], \ldots, [c_-^d, c_+^d])$ where $c_-^i = \min\{x_i : x \in S_t^k, x = x_1, \cdots x_d\}$ and $c_+^i = \max\{x_i : x \in S_t^k, x = x_1, \cdots x_d\}$.

The correctness of the generic consistency algorithm is obvious from its termination condition, the main interest in the analysis would be on the expected number of examples until termination, i.e., the expected active sample complexity.

3.2   Intervals on a Line

In this function class the domain is $\mathcal{X} = [0, 1]$, the examples corresponding to an output value k are in an interval A^k (which can be either open or closed interval), and the intervals are a partition of the domain $\mathcal{X} = [0, 1]$, i.e. $\cup_{k=1}^m A^k = [0, 1]$ and $A^i \cap A^j = \emptyset$ for $i \neq j$.

For the analysis of the generic consistency algorithm we introduce some additional notation. At time t, we have a set KN_t of output values which we have already sampled and UKN_t which are output values we have not been sampled. For each output $k \in KN_t$ let B_-^k and B_+^k be the points in A^k below and above C^k (respectively). I.e., if $C_t^k = [\lambda_-^k, \lambda_+^k]$ and $A^k = [\rho_-, \rho_+]$ then $B_-^k = [\rho_-, \lambda_-)$ and $B_+^k = (\lambda_+, \rho_+]$.

Given a distribution D over $[0, 1]$ let $D(I)$ be the probability of the interval I. At time t let $\beta_t = \sum_{k \in UKN_t} D(A^k)$ and let $\gamma_t = \sum_{k \in KN_t} D(B_-^k) + D(B_+^k)$. Let $\alpha_t = \beta_t + \gamma_t$, i.e., $\alpha_t = D(\mathcal{X} - C_t)$. Let $\mathcal{H}_t$ include all the history of the execution of the algorithm until and including time t.

Our analysis uses a potential function $\Phi_t = \alpha_t + \beta_t = \gamma_t + 2\beta_t$, and shows that Φ_t decreases by a certain factor each time step. Specifically we show that,

$$E[\Phi_t - \Phi_{t+1}|\mathcal{H}_t] = \frac{\beta_t}{\alpha_t} \sum_{k \in UKN_t} \frac{D(A^k)}{\beta_t} D(A^k) + \frac{\gamma_t}{\alpha_t} \sum_{k \in KN_t, b \in \{+, -\}} \frac{D(B_b^k)}{\gamma_t} \cdot \frac{D(B_b^k)}{2}$$

The first part follows from the fact that with probability $\frac{\beta_t}{\alpha_t}$ we sample an example with output value in UKN_t. Given that we sample such a point, the probability that the interval is A^k is $\frac{D(A^k)}{\beta_t}$. Given that we sample from A^k we reduce β_t by $2D(A^k)$ and increase γ_t by $D(A^k)$, so the net reduction in the potential is $D(A^k)$.

The second part follows from the fact that with probability $\frac{\gamma_t}{\alpha_t}$ we sample an example with output value in KN_t. Given that we sample such a point, the probability that it is in the interval B_b^k is $\frac{D(B_b^k)}{\gamma_t}$, where $b \in \{-, +\}$. Given that we sample from B_b^k the expected reduction is $D(B_b^k)/2$. Therefore,

$$E[\Phi_t - \Phi_{t+1}|\mathcal{H}_t] = \frac{1}{\alpha_t}[\sum_{k \in UKN_t} D(A^k)^2 + \sum_{k \in KN_t, b \in \{+,-\}} \frac{1}{2}D(B_b^k)^2]$$

Note that

$$\alpha_t = \beta_t + \gamma_t = \sum_{k \in UKN_t} D(A^k) + \sum_{k \in KN_t, b \in \{+,-\}} D(B_b^k).$$

Using the general inequality $\sum_{i=1}^n X_i^2 \geq (1/n)(\sum_{i=1}^n X_i)^2$, and since there are at most $2m$ elements in the summation (each output value appears only in one of the two summations), we have that

$$\sum_{k \in UKN} D(A^k)^2 + \sum_{k \in KN, b \in \{+,-\}} \frac{1}{2}D(B_b^k)^2 \geq \frac{1}{4m}\alpha_t^2$$

Since by definition $\beta_t \leq \alpha_t$, this implies that

$$E[\Phi_t - \Phi_{t+1}|\mathcal{H}_t] \geq \frac{1}{4m}\alpha_t \geq \frac{1}{8m}[\alpha_t + \beta_t] = \frac{1}{8m}\Phi_t$$

By averaging over $\mathcal{H}_t$ we have that

$$E[\Phi_{t+1}] \leq (1 - \frac{1}{8m})E[\Phi_t] \leq (1 - \frac{1}{8m})^t \Phi_1$$

Initially we have $\gamma_1 = 0$ and $\beta_1 = 1$, therefore the initial potential is $\Phi_1 = \gamma_1 + 2\beta_1 = 2$. After $t = O(m \log(1/\epsilon))$ samples, the expected value of the potential is less than $\epsilon/2$. This implies that with probability at least $1/2$ its value is less than ϵ. Once the value of the potential is less than ϵ we are guarantee to hit each output value (since each output value has probability at least ϵ). This establishes the following theorem.

Theorem 1. *The class of m intervals can be output identified in expected active sample complexity of $O(m \log 1/\epsilon)$.*

3.3 Axis Parallel Boxes

We extend the results from intervals to axis parallel boxes, where $\mathcal{X} = [0,1]^d$, each output value k is represented by an axis parallel box A^k, and the collection of A^k are a partition of $\mathcal{X}$. Again, we use the generic consistent algorithm.

The analysis is similar in spirit to that of the intervals on a line and it appears in the appendix, where we establish the following theorem:

Theorem 2. *The class of m axis parallel boxes can be output identified in expected active sample complexity of $O(dm \log 1/\epsilon)$.*

3.4   Lower Bounds

In this section we derive two simple lower bounds.

Example 1: Let $\mathcal{X} = [0,1]$ and U be the uniform distribution on $\mathcal{X}$. Consider the following function class $\mathcal{F}_{seg}^{\eta}$ that includes functions $f_z(x) = 1$ if $x \in [z, z+\eta]$ and otherwise $f_z(x) = 0$ (where $z \in [0, 1-\eta]$). Note that $\mathcal{F}_{seg}^{\eta}$ has a VC dimension equals to 2, and in addition, the points with output value 0 are not a convex set. We show the following lower bound.

Claim. Any output identification algorithm for $\mathcal{F}_{seg}^{\eta}$ with the uniform distribution U requires an expected active sample complexity of $\Omega(1/\epsilon)$, when $\epsilon = \eta$.

Example 2: Consider a linear separator in the plane (there are only two output values). Let $\mathcal{X} = [-1,1]^2$ and let $\mathcal{F}_{ls}$ include all linear separators. Namely, for each $f_{\alpha,\beta} \in \mathcal{F}$ we have $f_{\alpha,\beta}(x) = 1$ if $\alpha x_1 + \beta < x_2$ and otherwise $f_{\alpha,\beta}(x) = 0$ (where $\alpha, \beta \in \mathbb{R}$).

Following Dasgupta [1], we consider a distribution U_o whose support is the unit circle, e.g., $(x_1)^2 + (x_2)^2 = 1$ and it is uniform over it. Similar to the lower bound for active learning [1], we show the following lower bound for output identification.

Claim. Any output identification algorithm for $\mathcal{F}_{ls}$ with distribution U_o requires an expected active sample complexity of at least $\Omega(1/\epsilon)$.

4   Transductive Setting: Binary Output Values

In the transductive setting the algorithm is given in advance a set of unlabeled examples $S = \{x_1, \ldots x_s\}$. The goal of the output identification algorithm is to find a subset $S' \subset S$ of size at most m, such that each output value that appears in S has an example in S'. I.e., let $S^k = \{x \in S : f(x) = k\}$, we require that if $S^k \neq \emptyset$ then $S^k \cap S' \neq \emptyset$. The active sample complexity in the transductive setting is the number of queries the algorithm makes (i.e., the number of unlabeled examples from S for which it asks a label).

We give a characterization for the case of binary output values, i.e., $m = 2$. We first define the notion of a *separation dimension* of a function class $\mathcal{F}$. Then we show that if a function class $\mathcal{F}$ has separation dimension d then there is an algorithm that queries only $O(d^2 \log^2 s)$ examples. In addition we show that if a function class has separation dimension d then the expected number of examples queried is $\Omega(\min\{d, s\})$. This implies that the for the binary case we have a complete characterization when can a function class be output identified with a poly-logarithmic number of queries.

4.1   Separation Dimension: Definition

We start by defining the notion of separation dimension. Let the separation dimension of a function class $\mathcal{F}$ be the following. A function class $\mathcal{F}$ is said to

b-separate the set $\{x_1, \ldots x_d\} \subset \mathcal{X}$ if there are functions $f_1, \ldots f_d \in \mathcal{F}$ such that $f_i(x_i) = b$ and $f_i(x_j) = 1 - b$, for $j \neq i$, where $b \in \{0, 1\}$.

The b-separation dimension of $\mathcal{F}$ is the size of the largest set that $\mathcal{F}$ b-separates (or infinity, if it can b-separate sets of arbitrary size). The separation dimension of $\mathcal{F}$ is the maximum of the 0-separation dimension and the 1-separation dimension.

Separation Dimension - Examples: Let us start with a few examples of the separation dimension. Consider the function class $\mathcal{F}_{pre}$ over $[0, 1]$ such that $f_z(x) = 1$ if $z \leq x$ and $f_z(x) = 0$ otherwise (where $z \in [0, 1]$). The separation dimension of $\mathcal{F}_{pre}$ is 1 since for any two points $x_1 < x_2$ no function f_z can have $f_z(x_1) = 1$ and $f_z(x_2) = 0$.

A simple extension of $\mathcal{F}_{pre}$ is the function class $\mathcal{F}_{pre+suf}$ where $f_{z,b}(x) = b$ if $z \leq x$ and $f_z(x) = 1 - b$ otherwise (where $z \in [0, 1]$ and $b \in \{0, 1\}$). The separation dimension of $\mathcal{F}_{pre+suf}$ is 2. (Given, for example, $x_1 = 1/3$ and $x_2 = 2/3$, the functions $f_{1/2,1}$ and $f_{1/2,0}$ achieve a b-separation of $\{x_1, x_2\}$ for both $b = 1$ and $b = 0$. However, for any three points $x_1 < x_2 < x_3$ no function $f_{z,b}$ can have $f_{z,b}(x_2) = b$ and $f_{z,b}(x_1) = f_{z,b}(x_3) = 1 - b$, neither for $b = 1$ nor $b = 0$.)

Recall the function class $\mathcal{F}_{seg}^{\eta}$ that includes functions $f_z(x) = 1$ if $x \in [z, z+\eta]$ and otherwise $f_z(x) = 0$ (where $z \in [0, 1 - \eta]$). The function class $\mathcal{F}_{seg}^{\eta}$ has separation dimension of $\Theta(1/\eta)$.

An example of a function class with an infinite separation dimension is $\mathcal{F}_{ind}$, where for every $z \in \mathcal{X}$ we have an indicator function $f_z \in \mathcal{F}_{ind}$ (i.e., $f_z(x) = 1$ for $x = z$ and otherwise $f_z(x) = 0$), and $\mathcal{X}$ is infinite. Since for any set of s distinct points $x_1, \ldots, x_s \in \mathcal{X}$ the indicator functions $f_{x_1}, \ldots, f_{x_s}$ are a 1-separation, this implies that $\mathcal{F}_{ind}$ has an infinite separation dimension.

Separation Dimension - Number of Consistent Functions: Given a set of points $S = \{x_1, \ldots x_s\}$ let $\mathcal{F}^S$ be the function class $\mathcal{F}$ restricted to the set S. We would like to bound the number of consistent functions $\mathcal{F}^S$ as a function of $s = |S|$ and separation dimension of the function class $\mathcal{F}$.

It is obvious that if a function class $\mathcal{F}$ has a separation dimension of d then it has a VC dimension [18] of at most d. Therefore, using Sauer Lemma [15], we can bound $|\mathcal{F}^S|$. We can also show a function class for which this bound is almost tight also for separation dimension.

Lemma 1. *Let $\mathcal{F}$ be a function class with separation dimension d, then $|\mathcal{F}^S| \leq \sum_{i=0}^{d} \binom{|S|}{i}$. In addition, there is a function class $\mathcal{F}$ of separation dimension d such that $|\mathcal{F}^S| \geq (|S|/d)^d$.*

4.2   Separation Dimension: Lower Bound

In this section we give a lower bound based on the separation dimension.

Theorem 3. *Let $\mathcal{F}$ be a function class with separation dimension d, then its expected active sample complexity is $\Omega(\min\{d, s\})$. In addition, if $\mathcal{F}$ has an infinite separation dimension then its expected active sample complexity is $\Omega(s)$.*

Proof. Assume that $\mathcal{F}$ has 1-separation dimension of d (the other case is identical). Then there are $k = \min\{d, s\}$ inputs $x_1, \ldots x_k \in \mathcal{X}$ such that for any i there is an $f_i \in \mathcal{F}$ that $f_i(x_i) = 1$ and $f_i(x_j) = 0$, for $j \neq i$. (When $k < s$, we extend the set of k points to s points by duplicating point x_1 for $s - k$ times.)

Assume that we select the target function f to be f_i with probability $1/k$. Then any output identification algorithm would have to make at least $\Omega(k)$ queries before hitting the input which is labeled 1.

If $\mathcal{F}$ has an infinite separation dimension, then for every s, there are s inputs $x_1, \ldots x_s \in \mathcal{X}$ and functions $f_1, \ldots f_s \in \mathcal{F}$ such that $f_i(x_i) = 1$ and $f_i(x_j) = 0$, for $j \neq i$. Again, this implies that the expected number of queries is $\Omega(s)$.   □

4.3   Separation Dimension: Upper Bound

In this section we derive an upper bound on the sample complexity based of the separation dimension. Assume that the first point we sampled has label 0, and therefore the output identification task reduces to finding an input with label 1. (For this reason we will also concentrate on the 1-separation dimension.)

We start with a few notations. Let $\sup(f, S) = \{x_i \in S : f(x_i) = 1\}$, i.e., the set of points in S on which f is 1. Given a set of functions $\mathcal{F}$, let $\deg(x_i, \mathcal{F}^S) = \{f \in \mathcal{F}^S : f(x_i) = 1\}$, i.e., the set of functions which classify x_i as 1. We partition $\mathcal{F}^S$ according to the size of $\sup(f, S)$, and define $\mathcal{F}_k^S = \{f \in \mathcal{F}^S : k \leq |\sup(f, S)| < 2k\}$. Let $\ell = |\mathcal{F}|$ and $\ell_k = |\mathcal{F}_k^S|$.

Lemma 2. *Let $\mathcal{F}$ be a function class with 1-separation dimension d. Given an unlabeled sample S, for every $k \geq 1$, there exists an input $x_i \in S$ such that* $|\deg(x_i, \mathcal{F}_k^S)| \geq \lfloor \ell_k/8d \rfloor$.

Proof. For contradiction, assume that for some $k \geq 1$ no such $x_i \in S$ exists. We will show that the 1-separation dimension is at least $d + 1$, which would be a contradiction.

Since we assume that no such x_i exists for k, then for every $x_i \in S$ we have $|\deg(x_i, \mathcal{F}_k^S)| < \ell_k/8d$. By definition of $\mathcal{F}_k^S$, for every $f \in \mathcal{F}_k^S$ we have $|\sup(f, S)| \in [k, 2k)$. Consider the set of pairs Z that includes all the pairs (f, x) such that $x \in S$, $f \in \mathcal{F}_k^S$ and $f(x) = 1$. There are at least $k\ell_k$ such pairs in Z.

We would like to find a subset of pairs $(f_1, x_1) \ldots, (f_{d+1}, x_{d+1})$ in Z such that for any $i \neq j$ we have $f_j(x_i) = 0$. Recall that by the definition of the pairs in Z we have $f_i(x_i) = 1$. Therefore, such a subset would imply that the separation dimension of $\mathcal{F}$ is at least $d + 1$.

For the first pair we pick any (f, x) in Z. We would like to delete some of the pairs in Z such that any remaining pair (h, z) has the property that $f(z) = 0$ and $h(x) = 0$. This would guarantee that the subset that we select would have the required property.

Formally, we delete from Z both the set $\{(g, y) | g \in \mathcal{F}_k^S, y \in \sup(f, S)\}$ and the set $\{(g, y) | g \in \mathcal{F}_k^S, g \in \deg(x, \mathcal{F}_k^S)\}$. The deletion of the first set guarantees that any remaining pair (h, z) would have $f(z) = 0$ while the deletion of the second set guarantees that for any remaining pair (h, z) we have $h(x) = 0$. The size of the first set is at most $\sum_{y \in \sup(f, S)} \deg(y, \mathcal{F}_k^S) \leq k\ell_k/4d$ while the size of the second set is at most $\sum_{h \in \deg(x,\mathcal{F}_k^S)} \sup(h, S) \leq k\ell_k/4d$. This implies that we delete at most $k\ell_k/2d$ pairs.

By iteratively selecting a pair from Z and deleting from Z the two related sets, this implies that we can select $2d \geq d+1$ such pairs. This is a contradiction to the assumption that separation dimension is d. $\square$

We can now use Lemma 2 to derive an output identification algorithm in the transductive setting.

Theorem 4. *Let $\mathcal{F}$ be a function class of separation dimension d. For any unlabeled sample S, it can be output identified in active sample complexity of $O(d \log |S| \log |\mathcal{F}^S|)$.*

Proof. Initially we query an arbitrary point in S. W.l.o.g., assume that the first point has a label 0. This implies that we need to search for a point in S with a label of 1. Note that the 1-separation dimension of $\mathcal{F}$ is at most d.

We run the algorithm in rounds, where in each round we select at most $\log |S|$ inputs (one for to each $\mathcal{F}_{2^i}^S$, where $i \in [0, \log |S|]$). In each round for each $\mathcal{F}_{2^i}^S$ we select the input x which maximizes $\deg(x, \mathcal{F}_{2^i}^S)$. By Lemma 2, since $\mathcal{F}$ has 1-separation dimension of at most d, there exists an input x_i such that $|\deg(x, \mathcal{F}_{2^i}^S)| \geq \ell_k/8d$. Therefore, in each round, the number of possible target functions in each $\mathcal{F}_{2^i}^S$ shrink by a factor of $(1-1/8d)$. After at most $O(d \log |\mathcal{F}^S|)$ rounds we will either: (1) find an $x \in S$ with label 1, i..e, $f(x) = 1$, or, (2) the only remaining consistent function in $\mathcal{F}^S$ is the all zero function, i.e., there are no points in S with a label of 1. $\square$

Since, by Lemma 1, a d separation dimension implies that $|\mathcal{F}^S| = O(|S|^d)$, we have

Corollary 1. *If $\mathcal{F}$ has separation dimension d then any unlabeled sample S can be output identified with an active sample complexity of $O(d^2 \log^2 |S|)$.*

5   Uniform Distribution

In this section we discuss active sample complexity for specific distributions. We will concentrate on the case that the input distribution is uniform over the unit square, i.e., $\mathcal{X} = [0, 1]^2$. In this case we will be able to show that many natural geometric concepts, which for a general distribution they require $\Omega(1/\epsilon)$, are efficiently output identified with respect to the uniform distribution.

Generic Convex-Hull Algorithm: Our algorithm would be a generic consistency algorithm (Section 3.1) for the case where the domain of each output value is convex. Initially we have $S_0 = C_0 = \emptyset$. At time t we sample the induced distribution example oracle with $\mathcal{X} - C_t$ and receive an example $< x_t, k_t >$. For each output value k let S_t^k be the set of points sampled with output value k. Let C_t^k be the convex hull of the points in S_t^k, and let C_t be the union of all those sets. We terminate when for every output value k we have $S_t^k \neq \emptyset$.

Review from Computational Geometry: There are classical results in computational geometry regarding uniformly sampling from the plane. The results related the area of the convex-hull to the total area of the convex domain from which the points are sampled at uniform. For a set of points Z let $ConvexHull(Z)$ be their convex hull and for a body Y let $area(Y)$ be its area. The following theorem summarizes the related results (see, cf., [13]).

Theorem 5 ([14, 5]). *Let G be an r-gon in $[0,1]^2$, and S_n be a sample of size n sampled uniformly from G. Then, $E[area(G - ConvexHull(S_n))] = \Theta(\frac{r \ln n}{n})$.*

Triangles in the Plane: Let $\mathcal{X} = [0,1]^2$ be the unit square. Consider the case that there are m output values such that the domain of each output value is a triangle and their union is the unit square.

It would be more beneficial in this case to consider an alternative way of sampling. Assume that each time we access the induced distribution example oracle with $\mathcal{X} - C_t$, the oracle samples from $\mathcal{X}$ until it hits a point $x \notin C_t$. In our analysis let us consider also the extra points that oracle samples (but we will give them zero weight). Assume that in this process the total number of samples the oracle makes is T. (Recall that the generic convex hull algorithm terminates when each of the m output values is sampled at least once.) Let T_i be the number of times the oracle samples output value i (out of the T samples). Let X_j^i be a random variable which is 1 if the j-th point with output value i is outside the convex hull of the previous $j-1$ points, and 0 otherwise. This implies that the expected number of samples of the generic convex hull algorithm is $E_T E_{T_1 \ldots T_m}[\sum_{i=1}^m \sum_{j=1}^{T_i} X_j^i].$[1]

From Theorem 5, applied to triangles (i.e., $r = 3$), we can deduce that, $E[X_j^i] = O(\frac{\ln j}{j})$. Therefore, $\sum_{j=1}^{T_i} E[X_j^i] = \sum_{j=1}^{T_i} O(\frac{\ln j}{j}) \leq \alpha \log^2 T_i$, for some constant $\alpha > 0$. Summing over all possible output values we have

$$E_T E_{T_1,\ldots T_m} E[\sum_{i=1}^m \sum_{j=1}^{T_i} X_j^i] \leq E_T \left[\alpha \sum_{i=1}^m E_{T_i}[\log^2 T_i] \right]$$

$$\leq E_T[\alpha m \log^2 \frac{T}{m}] \leq \alpha m \log^2 \frac{1}{\epsilon}$$

where the second inequality follows since $\sum_{i=1}^m T_i = T$, and the last inequality uses the fact that $E[T] \leq m/\epsilon$ and the concavity of the logarithm function. This implies the following theorem,

Theorem 6. *Let $\mathcal{F}_\Delta$ be a function class such that every $f \in \mathcal{F}_\Delta$ partitions the unit square to m triangles each of area at least ϵ. Then for the uniform distribution U, the expected active sample complexity of the generic convex hull algorithm is $O(m \log^2 1/\epsilon)$.*

---

[1] This follows since an equivalent way of active sampling is to sample points from the distribution and request a label (and charge) only for points not in C_t.

Lines in the Plane: Consider the case where there are k lines in the plane that partition the unit square. Each of the m output values is one of the cells created by the intersection of the lines. We can perform a triangulation of the cells and have at most $O(k^2)$ triangles. (By performing a triangulation we are only increasing the running time of the generic convex hull algorithm, since each output value is de-composed to smaller convex hulls.) Since k lines in the plane create at least k cells, this implies that $m \geq k$. By using Theorem 6, we can show the following,

Theorem 7. *Let $\mathcal{F}_{k-line}$ be a function class such that every $f \in \mathcal{F}_{k-line}$ is represented by at most k lines in the plane. If each of the m cells has area at least ϵ then for the uniform distribution U the expected active sample complexity of the generic convex hull algorithm is $O(k^2 \log^2 1/\epsilon) = O(m^2 \log^2 1/\epsilon)$.*

Note that $\mathcal{F}_{ls}$, for which we showed a lower bound of $\Omega(1/\epsilon)$ with respect to an arbitrary distribution, is simply $\mathcal{F}_{1-line}$ and $m = 2$.

6   Monomials in a Hypercube

In this section we will concentrate on the Boolean cube and consider the case that each output value is a monomial. Formally, the domain $\mathcal{X}$ is $\{0,1\}^n$. The function class $\mathcal{F}_{mon}$ includes functions of the following type: For every output k there is a monomial M_k such that $f(x) = k$ iff $M_k(x) = 1$, where $f \in \mathcal{F}_{mon}$. (Note that the monomials M_i are a partition of the hypercube.)

For any i let x^i be the input $x \in \{0,1\}^n$ with the i-th bit flipped. Note that if $M_k(x) = 1$ then $M_k(x^i) = 0$ iff M_k depends on attribute x_i. This would be the basic property that will allow us to efficiently output identify $\mathcal{F}_{mon}$.

Monomial Output Identification Algorithm: The algorithm performs an exact identification using (essentially) membership queries. Let KN be the set of known output values and CH be a set of inputs we need to "check". Initially both $KN = \emptyset$ and $CH = \emptyset$. In the first phase, we sample any x, get its value $f(x) = k$ and add k to KN and x to CH. In every phase we take an input x from CH, and for every i such that $f(x) \neq f(x^i)$, if $f(x^i) \notin KN$ then we add the output value $f(x^i)$ to KN, add the input x^i to CH, and continue to the next input from CH. We terminate either when we have processed all the values in CH or have already recovered m output values (i.e., $|KN| = m$).

Theorem 8. *For any distribution which has non-zero probability for every example $\{0,1\}^n$, the class $\mathcal{F}_{mon}$ can be output identified with active sample complexity of mn.*

Note that the monomial output identification algorithm does not receive m as an input parameter. Also, note that it can output a complete model of the target function f in addition to the m output values.

References

1. S. Dasgupta. Analysis of a greedy active learning strategy. In *Advances in Neural Information Processing Systems (NIPS)*, 2004.
2. S. Dasgupta. Coarse sample complexity bounds for active learning. In *Advances in Neural Information Processing Systems (NIPS)*, 2005.
3. S. Dasgupta, A. Kalai, and C. Monteleoni. Analysis of perceptron-based active learning. In *Eighteenth Annual Conference on Learning Theory (COLT)*, 2005.
4. O. Edelstein, E. Farchi, Y. Nir G Ratzaby, and S Ur. Multithreaded java program test generation. *IBM Systems Journal*, 41(3):111–125, 2002.
5. B. Efron. The convex hull of a rndom set of points. *Biometrika*, 52:331–343, 1965.
6. S. Fine, R. Gilad-Bachrach, and E. Shamir. Query by committee, linear separation and random walks. *Theoretical Computer Science*, 284(1), 2002. (A preliminary version appeared in EuroColt 1999.).
7. S. Fine and A. Ziv. Coverage directed test generation for functional verification using Bayesian networks. In *Proceedings of the 40th Design Automation Conference*, pages 286–291, June 2003.
8. Y. Freund, H. Seung, E. Shamir, and N. Tishby. Selective sampling using the query by committee algorithm. *Machine Learning*, 28(2/3):133–168, 1997.
9. S. R. Kulkarni, S. K. Mitter, and J. N. Tsitsiklis. Active learning using arbitrary binary valued queries. *Machine Learning*, 11:23–35, 1993.
10. R. Liere and P. Tadepalli. Active learning with committees for text categorization. In *AAAI-97*, 1997.
11. N. Linial, M. Luby, M. Saks, and D. Zuckerman. Efficient construction of a small hitting set for combinatorial rectangles in high dimension. *Combinatorica*, 17(2):215–234, 1997. (A preliminary version appeard in STOC 1993).
12. Andrew Piziali. *Functional Verification Coverage Measurement and Analysis*. Springer, 2004.
13. F. P. Preparata and M. I Shamos. *Computational Geometry: An introduction*. Springer-Verlag, 1985.
14. A. Rényi and R. Sulamke. Uber die konvexe hulle von n zufallig gewahlten punkten. *Z. Wahrschein*, 2:75–84, 1963.
15. N. Sauer. On the density of family of sets. *J. of Combinatorial Theory*, Ser. A 13:145–147, 1972.
16. H. S. Seung, M. Opper, and H. Sompolinsky. Query by committe. In *Proceedings of the Fith Workshop on Computational Learning Theory*, pages 287–294. Morgan Kaufman, San Mateo, CA, 1992.
17. S. Ur and Y. Yadin. Micro-architecture coverage directed generation of test programs. In *Proceedings of the 36th Design Automation Conference*, pages 175–180, June 1999.
18. V. N. Vapnik and A. Ya. Chervonenkis. On the uniform convergence of relative frequencies of events to their probabilities. *Theory of Probability and its applications*, XVI(2):264–280, 1971.
19. B. Wile, J. C. Goss, and W. Roesner. *Comprehensive Functional Verification The Complete Industry Cycle*. Elsevier, 2005.

A   Axis Parallel Boxes: Analysis

The analysis of the axis parallel boxes would be similar to the analysis of intervals on a line. At time t, we have a set KN_t of output values which we have already sampled and UKN_t which are output values we have not sampled. For each output value $k \in KN_t$ we define $2d$ boxes which extend the current C_t^k to A^k, in each of the d dimensions both above and below. (Note that the boxes overlap unlike in the intervals case.)

Formally, let $C_t^k = ([c_-^1, c_+^1], \ldots, [c_-^d, c_+^d])$ and $A^k = ([a_-^1, a_+^1], \ldots, [a_-^d, a_+^d])$. Since $C_t^k \subset A^k$, then $a_-^i \leq c_-^i \leq c_+^i \leq a_+^i$. The $2d$ boxes are

$$B_-^{k,i} = [a_-^1, a_+^1], \ldots [a_-^{i-1}, a_+^{i-1}], [a_-^i, c_-^i), [a_-^{i+1}, a_+^{i+1}], \ldots, [a_-^d, a_+^d]).$$

and

$$B_+^{k,i} = [a_-^1, a_+^1], \ldots [a_-^{i-1}, a_+^{i-1}], (c_+^i, a_+^i], [a_-^{i+1}, a_+^{i+1}], \ldots, [a_-^d, a_+^d]).$$

Let, $\gamma_t = \sum_{k \in KN_t} \sum_{i=1}^d D(B_+^{k,i}) + D(B_-^{k,i})$, $\beta_t = \sum_{k \in UKN_t} D(A^k)$, and $\alpha_t = D(\mathcal{X} - C_t)$. The potential function would be $\Phi_t = \gamma_t + 2d\beta_t$. For intuition, note that when we sample an output value $k \in UNK_t$ for the first time, we decrease β_t by $D(A^k)$ and increase γ_t by at most $dD(A^k)$, so the net reduction in the potential is at least $dD(A^k)$. Let $\mathcal{H}_t$ include all the history of the execution of the algorithm until and including time t.

We will show that the potential Φ_t decreases by a certain factor each time step. Specifically we show that

$$E[\Phi_t - \Phi_{t+1}|\mathcal{H}_t] = \frac{\beta_t}{\alpha_t} \sum_{k \in UKN_t} \frac{D(A^k)}{\beta_t} dD(A^k) +$$

$$\frac{\alpha_t - \beta_t}{\alpha_t} \sum_{k \in KN_t, i \in [1,d], b \in \{+,-\}} \frac{D(B_b^{k,i})}{\alpha_t - \beta_t} \cdot \frac{D(B_b^{k,i})}{2}$$

The first part follows from the fact that with probability $\frac{\beta_t}{\alpha_t}$ we sample an example with output value in UKN_t. Given that we sample such an example, the probability that the output value is k is $\frac{D(A^k)}{\beta_t}$. Given that we sample from A^k we reduce β_t by $D(A^k)$ and increase γ_t by at most $dD(A^k)$, so the net reduction in the potential is at least $dD(A^k)$.

The second part follows from the fact that with probability $\frac{\alpha_t - \beta_t}{\alpha_t}$ we sample an example with output value in KN_t. Given that we sample such an example, the probability that the example is in box $B_b^{k,i}$ is $\frac{D(B_b^{k,i})}{\alpha_t - \beta_t}$. (Note that a point can be in more than one box. We used here the linearity of expectations, to be able to consider each box separately.) Given that we sample from $B_b^{k,i}$ the expected reduction is $D(B_b^{k,i})/2$. Therefore,

$$E[\Phi_t - \Phi_{t+1}|\mathcal{H}_t] = \frac{1}{\alpha_t}[\sum_{k \in UKN_t} dD(A^k)^2 + \sum_{k \in KN_t, i \in [1,d], b \in \{+,-\}} \frac{1}{2}D(B_b^{k,i})^2]$$

Again, we use the general inequality $\sum_{i=1}^n X_i^2 \geq (1/n)(\sum_{i=1}^n X_i)^2$, for each summation separately,

$$\sum_{k \in UKN_t} dD(A^k)^2 + \sum_{k \in KN_t, i \in [1,d]b \in \{+,-\}} \frac{1}{2}D(B_b^{k,i})^2 \geq \frac{1}{m}d\beta_t^2 + \frac{1}{4dm}\gamma_t^2$$

$$= \frac{1}{4dm}(4d^2\beta_t^2 + \gamma_t^2)$$

Therefore,

$$E[\Phi_t - \Phi_{t+1}|\mathcal{H}_t] \geq \frac{1}{4dm}\frac{4d^2\beta_t^2 + \gamma_t^2}{\alpha_t}$$

Since each point can be counted at most d times in γ_t, we have that,

$$\beta_t + \gamma_t \geq \alpha_t = D(\mathcal{X} - C_t) \geq \beta_t + \gamma_t/d$$

This implies that

$$E[\Phi_t - \Phi_{t+1}|\mathcal{H}_t] \geq \frac{1}{4dm}\frac{4d^2\beta_t^2 + \gamma_t^2}{\beta_t + \gamma_t} \geq \frac{1}{8dm}[2d\beta_t + \gamma_t] = \frac{1}{8dm}\Phi_t,$$

where in the second inequality we use that $X^2 + Y^2 \geq \frac{1}{2}(X+Y)^2$. By averaging over $\mathcal{H}_t$ we have that

$$E[\Phi_{t+1}] \leq (1 - \frac{1}{8dm})E[\Phi_t] \leq (1 - \frac{1}{8dm})^t \Phi_1$$

Initially we have $\gamma_1 = 0$ and $\beta_1 = 1$, therefore the initial potential is $\Phi_1 = 2d$. After $t = O(dm\log(1/\epsilon))$ samples the expected potential is less than $\epsilon/2$. Therefore with probability at least $1/2$ the potential is less than ϵ. If the potential is less than ϵ, this implies that we hit every output value (since we assume that each output value has probability of at least ϵ). Therefore we have establishes Theorem 2.

Improving Random Projections Using Marginal Information

Ping Li[1], Trevor J. Hastie[1], and Kenneth W. Church[2]

[1] Department of Statistics, Stanford University, Stanford CA 94305, USA
{pingli, hastie}@stat.stanford.edu
[2] Microsoft Research, One Microsoft Way, Redmond WA 98052, USA
church@microsoft.com

Abstract. We present an improved version of random projections that takes advantage of marginal norms. Using a maximum likelihood estimator (MLE), margin-constrained random projections can improve estimation accuracy considerably. Theoretical properties of this estimator are analyzed in detail.

1 Introduction

Random projections[1] have been used in machine learning [2, 3, 4, 5, 6] and many other applications in data mining and information retrieval, e.g., [7, 8, 9, 10, 11, 12].

One application of random projections is to compute the Gram matrix $\mathbf{AA}^\mathsf{T}$ efficiently, where $\mathbf{A} \in \mathbb{R}^{n \times D}$ is a collection of n data points $\in \mathbb{R}^D$. In modern applications, n and D can be very large hence computing $\mathbf{AA}^\mathsf{T}$ is prohibitive. The method of random projections multiplies $\mathbf{A}$ with a projection matrix $\mathbf{R} \in \mathbb{R}^{D \times k}$, which typically consists of i.i.d. $N(0,1)$ entries.[1] Let $\mathbf{B} = \frac{1}{\sqrt{k}}\mathbf{AR}$. Suppose u_i^T is the ith row of $\mathbf{A}$, and the corresponding i^{th} row in $\mathbf{B}$ is v_i^T, then as shown in Lemma 1.3 of [1]

$$\mathrm{E}\left(\|v_i - v_j\|^2\right) = \|u_i - u_j\|^2, \qquad \mathrm{Var}\left(\|v_i - v_j\|^2\right) = \frac{2}{k}\|u_i - u_j\|^4. \quad (1)$$

Therefore, one can compute pairwise distances in k dimensions, as opposed to D dimensions. When $k \ll \min(n, D)$, the savings from $O(n^2 D)$ to $O(n^2 k + nDk)$ is enormous.

Random projections generate a small sketch (i.e., $\mathbf{B}$) of the original data. $\mathbf{B}$ may be small enough to reside in the main memory. Operations such as query optimization or nearest neighbor searching can then be conducted on the much smaller space in the main memory, avoiding disk IO, which can be convenient for applications in databases, information retrieval, etc.

1.1 Our Results

We improve random projections by taking advantage of marginal norms, which we might as well compute, since they are useful and no harder to compute than the random

---

[1] The only necessary condition for preserving pairwise distance is that $\mathbf{R}$ consists of i.i.d. entries with zero mean[2]. The case of i.i.d. $N(0, 1)$ entries is the easiest to analyze.

G. Lugosi and H.U. Simon (Eds.): COLT 2006, LNAI 4005, pp. 635–649, 2006.

projections. Given an $n \times D$ matrix $\mathbf{A}$, it costs just $O(nD)$ time to compute the marginal norms, considerably less than the $O(nDk)$ time required for k random projections.

We will propose an estimator based on maximum likelihood. Some maximum likelihood estimators suffer from severe bias, slow rate of convergence toward normality, multiple roots, etc. These concerns will be addressed.

Some (approximate) tail bounds will also be presented, which can improve the current well-known tail bounds and consequently also improve some Johnson and Lindenstrauss (JL) embedding bounds in a practical sense.[2]

2   Random Projections Using Marginal Norms

Recall $u_i \in \mathbb{R}^D$ denotes data vectors in the original space and $v_i = \frac{1}{\sqrt{k}} \mathbf{R}^T u_i \in \mathbb{R}^k$ denotes vectors in the projection space, where the projection matrix $\mathbf{R} \in \mathbb{R}^{D \times k}$ consists of i.i.d $N(0,1)$ entries. We assume that the marginal norms, $\|u_i\|^2$, are known. As $\|u_1 - u_2\|^2 = \|u_1\|^2 + \|u_2\|^2 - 2u_1^T u_2$, we only need to estimate the dot product $u_1^T u_2$.

For convenience, we denote

$$a = u_1^T u_2, \quad m_1 = \|u_1\|^2, \quad m_2 = \|u_2\|^2, \quad d = \|u_1 - u_2\|^2 = m_1 + m_2 - 2a.$$

The following lemma is proved in Appendix A.

Lemma 1. *Given $u_1, u_2 \in \mathbb{R}^D$, and a random matrix $\mathbf{R} \in \mathbb{R}^{D \times k}$ consisting of i.i.d. standard normal $N(0,1)$ entries, if we let $v_1 = \frac{1}{\sqrt{k}} \mathbf{R}^T u_1$, and $v_2 = \frac{1}{\sqrt{k}} \mathbf{R}^T u_2$, then[3]*

$$E\left(v_1^T v_2\right) = a, \quad Var\left(v_1^T v_2\right) = \frac{1}{k}\left(m_1 m_2 + a^2\right), \quad E\left(v_1^T v_2 - a\right)^3 = \frac{2a}{k^2}\left(3 m_1 m_2 + a^2\right) \quad (2)$$

with the moment generating function

$$E\left(\exp(v_1^T v_2 t)\right) = \left(1 - \frac{2}{k}at - \frac{1}{k^2}\left(m_1 m_2 - a^2\right)t^2\right)^{-\frac{k}{2}}, \quad (3)$$

where $\frac{-k}{\sqrt{m_1 m_2} - a} \leq t \leq \frac{k}{\sqrt{m_1 m_2} + a}$.

The moment generating function may be useful for deriving tail bounds, from which one can hope to derive theorems similar to the JL-embedding bounds for $\|v_1 - v_2\|^2$ [13, 14, 15]. However, it is more difficult to derive practically useful tail bounds for $v_1^T v_2$ than for $\|v_1 - v_2\|^2$. One intuitive way to see this is via the coefficients of variations:

$$\frac{\sqrt{Var\left(\|v_1 - v_2\|^2\right)}}{\|u_1 - u_2\|^2} = \sqrt{\frac{2}{k}} \quad \text{(constant)}, \quad \frac{\sqrt{Var\left(v_1^T v_2\right)}}{u_1^T u_2} \geq \sqrt{\frac{2}{k}} \quad \text{(unbounded)}.$$

A straightforward unbiased estimator of the dot product $a = u_1^T u_2$ would be

$$\hat{a}_{MF} = v_1^T v_2, \quad Var\left(\hat{a}_{MF}\right) = \frac{1}{k}\left(m_1 m_2 + a^2\right), \quad (4)$$

where the subscript "MF" stands for "margin-free."

---

[2] The JL-embedding bound[13] was originally defined much more generally than for estimating the 2-norm distances, which is the only case we consider.

[3] A recent proof by [12, Lemma 5.4] verified that $Var\left(v_1^T v_2\right) \leq \frac{2}{k}\left(\|u_1\|^2 \|u_2\|^2\right) = \frac{2}{k} m_1 m_2$.

It is expected that if the marginal norms, $m_1 = \|u_1\|^2$ and $m_2 = \|u_2\|^2$, are given, one can do better. For example,

$$\hat{a}_{SM} = \frac{1}{2}\left(m_1 + m_2 - \|v_1 - v_2\|^2\right), \qquad Var\left(\hat{a}_{SM}\right) = \frac{1}{2k}\left(m_1 + m_2 - 2a\right)^2, \quad (5)$$

where the subscript "SM" stands for "simple margin (method)." Unfortunately $\hat{a}_{SM}$ is not always better than $\hat{a}_{MF}$. For example, when $a = 0$, $Var\left(\hat{a}_{SM}\right) = \frac{1}{2k}(m_1 + m_2)^2 \geq Var\left(\hat{a}_{MF}\right) = \frac{1}{k}(m_1 m_2)$. It is easy to show that

$$Var\left(\hat{a}_{SM}\right) \leq Var\left(\hat{a}_{MF}\right) \quad \text{only when } a \geq (m_1 + m_2) - \sqrt{\frac{1}{2}(m_1^2 + m_2^2) + 2m_1 m_2}.$$

We propose an estimator based on maximum likelihood in the following lemma, proved in Appendix B. This estimator has smaller variance than both $\hat{a}_{MF}$ and $\hat{a}_{SM}$.

Lemma 2. *Suppose the margins, $m_1 = \|u_1\|^2$ and $m_2 = \|u_2\|^2$, are known; a maximum likelihood estimator (MLE), denoted as $\hat{a}_{MLE}$, is the solution to a cubic equation:*

$$a^3 - a^2\left(v_1^T v_2\right) + a\left(-m_1 m_2 + m_1\|v_2\|^2 + m_2\|v_1\|^2\right) - m_1 m_2 v_1^T v_2 = 0. \quad (6)$$

The variance of $\hat{a}_{MLE}$ (asymptotic, up to $O(k^{-2})$ terms) is

$$Var\left(\hat{a}_{MLE}\right) = \frac{1}{k}\frac{\left(m_1 m_2 - a^2\right)^2}{m_1 m_2 + a^2} \leq \min\left(Var\left(\hat{a}_{MF}\right), Var\left(\hat{a}_{SM}\right)\right). \quad (7)$$

Figure 1 verifies the inequality in (7) by plotting $\frac{Var(\hat{a}_{MLE})}{Var(\hat{a}_{MF})}$ and $\frac{Var(\hat{a}_{MLE})}{Var(\hat{a}_{SM})}$. The improvement is quite substantial. For example, $\frac{Var(\hat{a}_{MLE})}{Var(\hat{a}_{MF})} = 0.2$ implies that in order to achieve the same mean square accuracy, the proposed MLE estimator needs only 20% of the samples required by the current margin-free (MF) estimator.

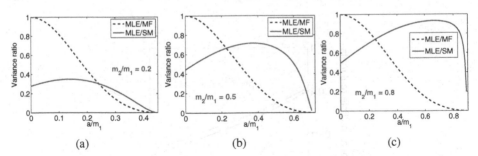

Fig. 1. The variance ratios, $\frac{Var(\hat{a}_{MLE})}{Var(\hat{a}_{MF})}$ and $\frac{Var(\hat{a}_{MLE})}{Var(\hat{a}_{SM})}$ verify that our proposed MLE has smaller variance than both the margin-free (MF) estimator and the simple margin (SM) method. $Var\left(\hat{a}_{MLE}\right)$, $Var\left(\hat{a}_{MF}\right)$, and $Var\left(\hat{a}_{SM}\right)$ are given in (7), (4), and (5), respectively. We consider $m_2 = 0.2m_1$, $m_2 = 0.5m_1$, and $m_2 = 0.8m_1$, in panels (a), (b), and (c), respectively.

Maximum likelihood estimators can be seriously biased in some cases, but usually the bias is on the order of $O(k^{-1})$, which may be corrected by [16] "Bartlett correction." In Lemma 3 (proved in Appendix C), we are able to show that the asymptotic bias of our $\hat{a}_{MLE}$ is only $O(k^{-2})$ and therefore there is no need for bias correction. Lemma 3 also derives the asymptotic third moment of $\hat{a}_{MLE}$ as well as a more accurate variance formula up to $O(k^{-3})$ terms. The third moment is needed if we would like to model the distribution of $\hat{a}_{MLE}$ more accurately. The more accurate variance formula may be useful for small k or in the region where the $O(k^{-2})$ term in the variance is quite large.

Lemma 3. *The bias, third moment, and the variance with $O(k^{-2})$ correction for the maximum likelihood estimator, $\hat{a}_{MLE}$, derived in Lemma 2, are given by*

$$E\left(\hat{a}_{MLE} - a\right) = O(k^{-2}), \tag{8}$$

$$E\left((\hat{a}_{MLE} - a)^3\right) = \frac{-2a(3m_1m_2 + a^2)(m_1m_2 - a^2)^3}{k^2(m_1m_2 + a^2)^3} + O(k^{-3}), \tag{9}$$

$$Var\left(\hat{a}_{MLE}\right)_2^c = \frac{1}{k}\frac{\left(m_1m_2 - a^2\right)^2}{m_1m_2 + a^2} + \frac{1}{k^2}\frac{4(m_1m_2 - a^2)^4}{(m_1m_2 + a^2)^4}m_1m_2 + O(k^{-3}). \tag{10}$$

Eq. (10) indicates that when $a = 0$, the $O(k^{-2})$ term of the asymptotic variance is $\frac{4}{k}$ of the $O(k^{-1})$ term. When $k \leq 10$ and a is very small, we might want to consider using (10) instead of (7) for $Var(\hat{a}_{MLE})$. However, as we will show next, for very small k, there is also a multiple root problem in solving the cubic MLE equation (6).

Lemma 4. *The cubic MLE equation (6) in Lemma 2 admits multiple real roots with a small probability, expressed as*

$$\mathbf{Pr}\left(multiple\ real\ roots\right) = \mathbf{Pr}\left(P^2(11 - Q^2/4 - 4Q + P^2) + (Q - 1)^3 \leq 0\right), \tag{11}$$

where $P = \frac{v_1^T v_2}{\sqrt{m_1m_2}}$, $Q = \frac{\|v_1\|^2}{m_1} + \frac{\|v_2\|^2}{m_2}$. This probability is (crudely) bounded by

$$\mathbf{Pr}\left(multiple\ real\ roots\right) \leq e^{-0.0085k} + e^{-0.0966k}. \tag{12}$$

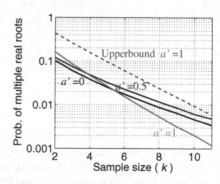

Fig. 2. Simulations show that $\mathbf{Pr}$ (multiple real roots) decreases exponentially fast with respect to increasing sample size k (notice the log scale in the vertical axis). After $k \geq 8$, the probability that the cubic MLE equation (6) admits multiple roots becomes so small ($\leq 1\%$) that it can be safely ignored in practice. Here $a' = \frac{a}{\sqrt{m_1m_2}}$. The curve for the upper bound is given by (13).

When $a = m_1 = m_2$, this probability can be (sharply) bounded by

$$\mathbf{Pr}\ (multiple\ real\ roots\ |\ a = m_1 = m_2) \le e^{-1.5328k} + e^{-0.4672k}. \tag{13}$$

Although the bound (12) is crude, the probability of admitting multiple real roots in (11) can be easily simulated. Figure 2 shows that this probability drops quickly to $< 1\%$ when $k \ge 8$.

To the best of our knowledge, there is no consensus on what is the best solution to multiple roots[17]. Because the probability of multiple roots is so small when $k \ge 8$ while in the large-scale applications we expect $k \gg 10$, we suggest not to worry about multiple roots. Also, we will only use the $O(k^{-1})$ term of $\mathrm{Var}(\hat{a}_{MLE})$, i.e, (7).

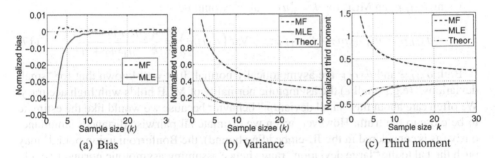

(a) Bias   (b) Variance   (c) Third moment

Fig. 3. Estimations of the dot products between two vectors "THIS" and "HAVE." (a): $\frac{\text{bias}}{a}$, (b): $\frac{\sqrt{\mathrm{Var}(\hat{a})}}{a}$, (c): $\frac{\sqrt[3]{\mathrm{E}(\hat{a}-a)^3}}{a}$. This experiment verifies that (A): Marginal information can improve the estimations considerably. (B): As soon as $k > 8$, $\hat{a}_{MLE}$ is essentially unbiased and the asymptotic variance and third moment match simulations remarkably well. (C): The margin-free estimator ($\hat{a}_{MF}$) is unbiased and the theoretical moments are indistinguishable from simulations.

Figure 3 presents some simulation results, using two words "THIS" and "HAVE," from some MSN Web crawl data. Here $u_{1,j}$ ($u_{2,j}$) is the number of occurrences of word "THIS" (word "HAVE") in the jth page, $j = 1$ to $D = 2^{16}$. As verified in Figure 3, due to the existence of multiple roots at small k, some small bias is observable, as well as some small discrepancies between the observed moments and the theoretical asymptotic moments. When $k \ge 8$, the asymptotic formulas for $\hat{a}_{MLE}$ are very accurate.

3 Some Tail Bounds

Tails bounds are necessary for deriving JL-type bounds for determining the number of projections (i.e., k) needed in order to achieve a certain specified level of accuracy.

Recall $u_i \in \mathbb{R}^D$ denotes data vectors in the original space and $v_i \in \mathbb{R}^k$ denotes vectors in the projection space. The usual estimator for $d = \|u_1 - u_2\|^2$ is

$$\hat{d}_{MF} = \|v_1 - v_2\|^2 = d, \qquad \frac{\hat{d}_{MF}}{d/k} \sim \chi_k^2, \qquad \mathrm{Var}\left(\hat{d}_{MF}\right) = \frac{2}{k}\|v_1 - v_2\|^4 = \frac{2d^2}{k}.$$

The well-known Chernoff chi-squared tail bound gives (for any $0 < \epsilon < 1$)[4]

$$\mathbf{Pr}\left(\left|\hat{d}_{MF} - d\right| \geq \epsilon d\right) \leq 2\exp\left(-\frac{k}{4}\epsilon^2 + \frac{k}{6}\epsilon^3\right), \tag{15}$$

from which a JL-embedding bound follows, using the Bonferroni union bound [15]:

$$\frac{n^2}{2}2\exp\left(-\frac{k}{4}\epsilon^2 + \frac{k}{6}\epsilon^3\right) \leq n^{-\gamma} \Rightarrow k \geq k_0 = \frac{4 + 2\gamma}{\epsilon^2/2 - \epsilon^3/3}\log n, \tag{16}$$

i.e., if $k \geq k_0$, then with probability at least $1 - n^{-\gamma}$, for any two rows u_i, u_j from the data matrix with n rows, we have $(1 - \epsilon)\|u_i - u_j\|^2 \leq \|v_i - v_j\|^2 \leq (1+\epsilon)\|u_i - u_j\|^2$.

As mentioned in [15], the above bounds are tight. We will show that, from a practical point of view, using the marginal information can actually improve the bounds.

Using $\hat{a}_{MLE}$, an MLE for $d = \|u_1 - u_2\|^2$, would be

$$\hat{d}_{MLE} = m_1 + m_2 - 2\hat{a}_{MLE}, \quad \mathrm{Var}\left(\hat{d}_{MLE}\right) = \frac{4}{k}\frac{(m_1 m_2 - a^2)^2}{m_1 m_2 + a^2}. \tag{17}$$

Both $\hat{a}_{MLE}$ and $\hat{d}_{MLE}$ are asymptotically normal. It is well-known that for "small deviations," (e.g., small ϵ) the asymptotic normality of MLE holds with high accuracy. We often care about the "small deviation" behavior because we would like the estimate to be close to the truth. However, when we estimate all pairwise distances simultaneously (as is considered in the JL-embedding bound), the Bonferroni union bound[5] may push the tail to the "large deviation" range hence assuming asymptotic normality could be a concern. On the other hand, the Bonferroni bound leads to larger k values; and larger k improves the accuracy of the asymptotic normality. Based on this (heuristic) argument, the asymptotic tail bounds of $\hat{a}_{MLE}$ may be still useful in practice.

3.1 Normal Approximation

Based on the asymptotic normality $\hat{a}_{MLE} \sim N(a, \mathrm{Var}(\hat{a}_{MLE}))$, we can obtain[6]

$$\mathbf{Pr}\left(|\hat{a}_{MLE} - a| \geq \epsilon a\right) \overset{\sim}{\leq} 2\exp\left(-\frac{k\epsilon^2}{2}\frac{a^2(m_1 m_2 + a^2)}{(m_1 m_2 - a^2)^2}\right), \tag{19}$$

where $\overset{\sim}{\leq}$ indicates that bound holds only asymptotically.

---

[4] Since we know the exact distribution in this case, we might as well compute k exactly by iteratively solving a nonlinear equation:

$$\frac{n^2}{2}\left(\mathbf{Pr}\left(\chi_k^2 \geq (1+\epsilon)k\right) + \mathbf{Pr}\left(\chi_k^2 \leq (1-\epsilon)k\right)\right) = \alpha \qquad (\text{e.g., } \alpha = 0.05), \tag{14}$$

which always outputs smaller k values than the JL-bound (e.g., by about 40% when $\epsilon = 0.5$).

[5] The Bonferroni bound is well-known for being too conservative, partly because it ignores the correlations. But the major problem is that the criterion is too stringent for large n (here we actually have $\frac{n^2}{2}$ tests). A reasonable alternative is to allow a certain fraction of tests to fail [18, Chapter 9]. For example, if we allow at most $1/p$ tests to fail, we can solve for k from

$$\left(\mathbf{Pr}\left(\chi_k^2 \geq (1+\epsilon)k\right) + \mathbf{Pr}\left(\chi_k^2 \leq (1-\epsilon)k\right)\right) = \alpha/p \qquad (\text{e.g., } \alpha = 0.05, p = 100) \tag{18}$$

[6] Of course, we can also use the exact normal tail probabilities instead of the upper bounds.

Similarly, the asymptotic normality $\hat{d}_{MLE} \sim N(d, \text{Var}(\hat{d}_{MLE}))$ yields

$$\mathbf{Pr}\left(\left|\hat{d}_{MLE} - d\right| \geq \epsilon d\right) \overset{\sim}{\leq} 2\exp\left(-\frac{k}{4}\epsilon^2 \frac{d^2}{2} \frac{m_1 m_2 + a^2}{(m_1 m_2 - a^2)^2}\right). \qquad (20)$$

Note that $\frac{d^2}{2}\frac{m_1 m_2 + a^2}{(m_1 m_2 - a^2)^2} = \frac{\text{Var}(\hat{a}_{SM})}{\text{Var}(\hat{a}_{MLE})} \geq 1$ (unbounded), with equality holds when $m_1 = m_2 = a$. Therefore, as expected, we can obtain better bounds using marginal information. In practice, we have to choose some reasonable values for m_1, m_2 and a based on prior knowledge of the data, or for the regions we are most interested in.

It would be interesting to see how normal approximation on $\hat{d}_{MF}$ affects its tail bound. Assuming normality, i.e., $\hat{d}_{MF} \sim N\left(d, \frac{2d^2}{k}\right)$, we obtain

$$\mathbf{Pr}\left(\left|\hat{d}_{MF} - d\right| \geq \epsilon d\right) \overset{\sim}{\leq} 2\exp\left(-\frac{k}{4}\epsilon^2\right), \qquad (21)$$

which agrees with the exact bound on the dominating ϵ^2 term.

When applying normal approximations, it is important to watch out for the third moments, which, to an extent, affect the rate of convergence:

$$\mathrm{E}\left(\hat{d}_{MF} - d\right)^3 = \frac{8d^3}{k^2}, \quad \mathrm{E}\left(\hat{d}_{MLE} - d\right)^3 = 8\frac{-2a(3m_1 m_2 + a^2)(m_1 m_2 - a^2)^3}{k^2(m_1 m_2 + a^2)^3}.$$

Some algebra can verify that

$$\left|\frac{\mathrm{E}\left(\hat{d}_{MLE} - d\right)^3}{\mathrm{E}\left(\hat{d}_{MF} - d\right)^3}\right| \leq \left(\frac{\text{Var}(\hat{a}_{MLE})}{\text{Var}(\hat{a}_{MF})}\right)^{\frac{3}{2}} \leq 1, \qquad (22)$$

which means the third moment of $\hat{d}_{MLE}$ (and $\hat{a}_{MLE}$) is well-behaved.

3.2 Generalized Gamma Approximation

The normal approximation matches the first two (asymptotic) moments. The accuracy can be further improved by matching the third moment. For example, [19] used a generalized gamma distribution to accurately approximate the finite-dimensional behavior of the random matrix eigenvalues arising in some wireless communication channels.

For convenience, we consider $a \geq 0$ (true in most applications). Assuming $-\hat{a}_{MLE} \sim G(\alpha, \beta, \xi)$, a generalized gamma distribution with three parameters (α, β, ξ), then

$$\mathrm{E}\left(-\hat{a}_{MLE}\right) = \alpha\beta, \quad \text{Var}\left(-\hat{a}_{MLE}\right) = \alpha\beta^2, \quad \mathrm{E}\left(-\hat{a}_{MLE} + a\right)^3 = (\xi + 1)\alpha\beta^3, \quad (23)$$

from which we can compute (α, β, ξ):

$$\alpha = \frac{ka^2(m_1 m_2 + a^2)}{(m_1 m_2 - a^2)^2} = ka', \quad \beta = \frac{-(m_1 m_2 - a^2)^2}{k(m_1 m_2 + a^2)a} = \frac{-1}{k}\beta',$$

$$\xi = \frac{2a^2(3m_1 m_2 + a^2)}{(m_1 m_2 + a^2)(m_1 m_2 - a^2)} - 1 \qquad (24)$$

The generalized gamma distribution does not have a closed-form density, but it does have closed-form moment generating functions [19, (69)(70)]:

$$
\mathrm{E}\left(\exp\left(-\hat{a}_{MLE}t\right)\right) =
\begin{cases}
\exp\left(\frac{\alpha}{\xi-1}\left(1-(1-\beta\xi t)^{\frac{\xi-1}{\xi}}\right)\right) & \text{when } \xi > 1 \\
\exp\left(\frac{\alpha}{1-\xi}\left(\left(\frac{1}{1-\beta\xi t}\right)^{\frac{1-\xi}{\xi}}-1\right)\right) & \text{when } \xi < 1 \\
(1-\beta t)^{-\alpha} & \text{when } \xi = 1
\end{cases}
$$

$\xi > 1$ happens when $\frac{a^2}{m_1 m_2} > \frac{\sqrt{17}-3}{4} = 0.2808$. Using the Chernoff inequality and assuming $\xi > 1$ (other cases are similar), we obtain

$$
\mathbf{Pr}\left(\hat{d}_{MLE} \geq (1+\epsilon)d\right) \stackrel{\sim}{\leq} \exp\left(-k\left(\left(\frac{2a}{2a-\epsilon d}\right)^{\xi-1}\left(\frac{\alpha'}{\xi-1}-\frac{a}{\beta'\xi}\right)-\frac{\alpha'}{\xi-1}+\frac{2a-\epsilon d}{2\beta'\xi}\right)\right),
$$

$$
\mathbf{Pr}\left(\hat{d}_{MLE} \leq (1-\epsilon)d\right) \stackrel{\sim}{\leq} \exp\left(-k\left(\left(\frac{2a}{2a+\epsilon d}\right)^{\xi-1}\left(\frac{\alpha'}{\xi-1}-\frac{a}{\beta'\xi}\right)-\frac{\alpha'}{\xi-1}+\frac{2a+\epsilon d}{2\beta'\xi}\right)\right).
$$

4 Sign Random Projections

We give a brief introduction to "sign random projections," (i.e., only storing the signs of the projected data), and compare sign random projections with regular random projections. For each data point, sign random projections store just one bit per projection. There are efficient algorithms for computing hamming distances [14, 10, 11].

We will show that when the data are roughly uncorrelated, the variance of sign random projections is only about $\frac{\pi^2}{4} \approx 2.47$ of the variance of regular random projections, which store real numbers. With highly correlated data, however, sign random projections can be quite inefficient compared to regular random projections.

Recall $u_i \in \mathbb{R}^D$ denotes data vectors in the original space and $v_i = \frac{1}{\sqrt{k}}\mathbf{R}^T u_i \in \mathbb{R}^k$ for vectors in the projection space. It is easy to show that[10]

$$
\mathbf{Pr}\left(\text{sign}(v_{1,j}) = \text{sign}(v_{2,j})\right) = 1 - \frac{\theta}{\pi}, \qquad j = 1, 2, ..., k, \tag{25}
$$

where $\theta = \cos^{-1}\left(\frac{u_1^T u_2}{\|u_1\|\|u_2\|}\right) = \cos^{-1}\left(\frac{a}{\sqrt{m_1 m_2}}\right)$ is the angle between u_1 and u_2.

We can estimate θ as a binomial probability, whose variance would be

$$
\text{Var}\left(\hat{\theta}\right) = \frac{\pi^2}{k}\left(1-\frac{\theta}{\pi}\right)\left(\frac{\theta}{\pi}\right) = \frac{\theta(\pi-\theta)}{k}. \tag{26}
$$

We can also estimate $a = u_1^T u_2$ from $\hat{\theta}$ if knowing the margins:

$$
\hat{a}_{Sign} = \cos(\hat{\theta})\sqrt{m_1 m_2}. \tag{27}
$$

By the Delta method, $\hat{a}_{Sign}$ is asymptotically unbiased with the asymptotic variance

$$
\text{Var}\left(\hat{a}_{Sign}\right) = \text{Var}(\hat{\theta})\sin^2(\theta)m_1 m_2 = \frac{\theta(\pi-\theta)}{k}\sin^2(\theta)m_1 m_2, \tag{28}
$$

provided $\sin(\theta)$ is nonzero, which is violated when $\theta = 0$ or π. In fact, when θ is close to 0 or π, due to the high nonlinearity, the asymptotic variance formula is not reliable.

Regular random projections store real numbers (32 or 64 bits). At the same number of projections (i.e., the same k) , obviously sign random projections will have larger variances. If the variance is inflated only by a factor of (e.g.,) 4, sign random projections would be preferable because we could increase k to (e.g.,) $4k$, to achieve the same accuracy while the storage cost will still be lower than regular random projections.

We compare the variance (Var ($\hat{a}_{Sign}$)) of sign random projections with the variance of regular random projections considering the margins (i.e., Var ($\hat{a}_{MLE}$)) by

$$V_{Sign} = \frac{\mathrm{Var}\,(\hat{a}_{Sign})}{\mathrm{Var}\,(\hat{a}_{MLE})} = \frac{\theta(\pi - \theta)\sin^2(\theta)m_1 m_2}{\frac{(m_1 m_2 - a^2)^2}{m_1 m_2 + a^2}} = \frac{\theta(\pi - \theta)(1 + \cos^2(\theta))}{\sin^2(\theta)}, \quad (29)$$

which is symmetric about $\theta = \frac{\pi}{2}$. It is easy to check (also shown in Figure 4) that V_{Sign} is monotonically decreasing in $(0, \frac{\pi}{2}]$ with minimum $\frac{\pi^2}{4} \approx 2.47$, attained at $\theta = \frac{\pi}{2}$.

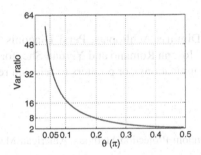

Fig. 4. The ratios of variance $V_{Sign} = \frac{\mathrm{Var}(\hat{a}_{Sign})}{\mathrm{Var}(\hat{a}_{MLE})}$ decreases monotonically in $(0, \frac{\pi}{2}]$, with minimum $= \frac{\pi^2}{4} \approx 2.47$ attained at $\theta = \frac{\pi}{2}$. Note that the horizontal axis is in π.

When the data points are nearly uncorrelated (θ close to $\frac{\pi}{2}$, in fact $\theta > \frac{\pi}{5}$ could be good enough), sign random projections should have good performance. However, some applications such as duplicate detections are interested in data points that are close to each other hence sign random projections may cause relatively large errors.

5   Some Recent Progress on Random Projections

There is considerable recent interest in *sparse random projections*, proposed by Achlioptas [15]. It replaces the $N(0, 1)$ entries in **R** with entries in $\sqrt{s} \times \{-1, 0, 1\}$ with probabilities $\{\frac{1}{2s}, 1 - \frac{1}{s}, \frac{1}{2s}\}$, $1 \leq s \leq 3$. With $s = 3$, one can get a threefold speedup.

We[20] recently proposed *very sparse random projections* by using $s = \sqrt{D}$, to obtain a $\sqrt{D}$-fold speedup. The analysis is based on the asymptotic properties of the projected data. For example, assuming bounded third moment on the original data, the projected data converge to normal at the rate of $O\left(\frac{1}{D^{1/4}}\right)$, which is sufficiently fast since D has to be large otherwise there would be no need of seeking approximate answers. The MLE proposed in this study is still useful in *very sparse random projections*.

The limitation of random projection is that it can not estimate multi-way distances nor can it estimate 1-norm distances. The authors' concurrent work[21] has proposed a new sketch-based sampling algorithm, which is capable of estimating two-way and multi-way distances in any norms. In particular, this algorithm provably outperforms random projections in boolean data and nearly independent data.

6 Conclusion

We propose a maximum likelihood estimator (MLE) for random projections, taking advantage of the marginal information, which can be easily computed at negligible incremental cost. This estimator has provably smaller variance than the current method; and therefore it can reduce the required number of projections.

Acknowledgement

We would like to thank Dimitris Achlioptas, Persi Diaconis, Bradley Efron, Jerome Friedman, Tze Leung Lai, Joseph Romano and Yiyuan She, for many very helpful conversations (or email communications), or pointers to relevant references.

References

1. Vempala, S.S.: The Random Projection Method. American Mathematical Society, Providence, RI (2004)
2. Arriaga, R., Vempala, S.: An algorithmic theory of learning: Robust concepts and random projection. In: Proc. of FOCS (Also to appear in Machine Learning), New York (1999) 616–623
3. Dasgupta, S.: Learning mixtures of gaussians. In: Proc. of FOCS, New York (1999) 634–644
4. Fradkin, D., Madigan, D.: Experiments with random projections for machine learning. In: Proc. of KDD, Washington, DC (2003) 517–522
5. Fern, X.Z., Brodley, C.E.: Random projection for high dimensional data clustering: A cluster ensemble approach. In: Proc. of ICML, Washington, DC (2003) 186–193
6. Balcan, M.F., Blum, A., Vempala, S.: On kernels, margins, and low-dimensional mappings. In: Proc. of ALT, Padova, Italy (2004) 194 – 205
7. Papadimitriou, C.H., Raghavan, P., Tamaki, H., Vempala, S.: Latent semantic indexing: A probabilistic analysis. In: Proc. of PODS, Seattle,WA (1998) 159–168
8. Achlioptas, D., McSherry, F., Schölkopf, B.: Sampling techniques for kernel methods. In: Proc. of NIPS, Vancouver, BC, Canada (2001) 335–342
9. Bingham, E., Mannila, H.: Random projection in dimensionality reduction: Applications to image and text data. In: Proc. of KDD, San Francisco, CA (2001) 245–250
10. Charikar, M.S.: Similarity estimation techniques from rounding algorithms. In: Proc. of STOC, Montreal, Quebec, Canada (2002) 380–388
11. Ravichandran, D., Pantel, P., Hovy, E.: Randomized algorithms and NLP: Using locality sensitive hash function for high speed noun clustering. In: Proc. of ACL, Ann Arbor, MI (2005) 622–629

12. Liu, K., Kargupta, H., Ryan, J.: Random projection-based multiplicative data perturbation for privacy preserving distributed data mining. IEEE Transactions on Knowledge and Data Engineering **18** (2006) 92–106
13. Johnson, W.B., Lindenstrauss, J.: Extensions of Lipschitz mapping into Hilbert space. Contemporary Mathematics **26** (1984) 189–206
14. Indyk, P., Motwani, R.: Approximate nearest neighbors: Towards removing the curse of dimensionality. In: Proc. of STOC, Dallas, TX (1998) 604–613
15. Achlioptas, D.: Database-friendly random projections: Johnson-Lindenstrauss with binary coins. Journal of Computer and System Sciences **66** (2003) 671–687
16. Bartlett, M.S.: Approximate confidence intervals, II. Biometrika **40** (1953) 306–317
17. Small, C.G., Wang, J., Yang, Z.: Eliminating multiple root problems in estimation. Statistical Science **15** (2000) 313–341
18. Lehmann, E.L., Romano, J.P.: Testing Statistical Hypothesis. Third edn. Springer, New York, NY (2005)
19. Li, P., Paul, D., Narasimhan, R., Cioffi, J.: On the distribution of SINR for the MMSE MIMO receiver and performance analysis. IEEE Trans. Inform. Theory **52** (2006) 271–286
20. Li, P., Hastie, T.J., Church, K.W.: Margin-constrained random projections and very sparse random projections. Technical report, Department of Statistics, Stanford University (2006)
21. Li, P., Church, K.W., Hastie, T.J.: A sketched-based sampling algorithm on sparse data. Technical report, Department of Statistics, Stanford University (2006)
22. Shenton, L.R., Bowman, K.: Higher moments of a maximum-likelihood estimate. Journal of Royal Statistical Society B **25** (1963) 305–317
23. Ferrari, S.L.P., Botter, D.A., Cordeiro, G.M., Cribari-Neto, F.: Second and third order bias reduction for one-parameter family models. Stat. and Prob. Letters **30** (1996) 339–345

A   Proof of Lemma 1

Recall $u_1, u_2 \in \mathbb{R}^D$, $v_1 = \frac{1}{\sqrt{k}}\mathbf{R}^{\mathsf{T}}u_1$, and $v_2 = \frac{1}{\sqrt{k}}\mathbf{R}^{\mathsf{T}}u_2$, where $\mathbf{R} \in \mathbb{R}^{D \times k}$ consists of i.i.d. $N(0, 1)$ entries. Note that $v_1^{\mathsf{T}}v_2 = \sum_{j=1}^{k} v_{1,j}v_{2,j} = \sum_{j=1}^{k} \frac{1}{k}u_1^{\mathsf{T}}\mathbf{R}_j\mathbf{R}_j^{\mathsf{T}}u_2$ is a sum of i.i.d. terms, where $\mathbf{R}_j$ is the jth column of $\mathbf{R}$.

It is easy to show that $(v_{1,j}, v_{2,j})$ are jointly normal with zero mean and covariance Σ (denoting $m_1 = \|u_1\|^2$, $m_2 = \|u_2\|^2$, and $a = u_1^{\mathsf{T}}u_2$)

$$\begin{bmatrix} v_{1,j} \\ v_{2,j} \end{bmatrix} \sim N\left(\begin{bmatrix} 0 \\ 0 \end{bmatrix}, \Sigma = \frac{1}{k}\begin{bmatrix} \|u_1\|^2 & u_1^{\mathsf{T}}u_2 \\ u_1^{\mathsf{T}}u_2 & \|u_2\|^2 \end{bmatrix} = \frac{1}{k}\begin{bmatrix} m_1 & a \\ a & m_2 \end{bmatrix} \right). \tag{30}$$

It is easier to work with the conditional probability:

$$v_{1,j}|v_{2,j} \sim N\left(\frac{a}{m_2}v_{2,j}, \frac{m_1m_2 - a^2}{km_2} \right), \tag{31}$$

from which we can get

$$E\left(v_{1,j}v_{2,j}\right)^2 = E\left(E\left(v_{1,j}^2 v_{2,j}^2 | v_{2,j}\right)\right) = E\left(v_{2,j}^2\left(\frac{m_1m_2 - a^2}{km_2} + \left(\frac{a}{m_2}v_{2,j} \right)^2 \right) \right)$$

$$= \frac{m_2}{k}\frac{m_1m_2 - a^2}{km_2} + \frac{3m_2^2}{k^2}\frac{a^2}{m_2^2} = \frac{1}{k^2}\left(m_1m_2 + 2a^2 \right). \tag{32}$$

Therefore,

$$\text{Var}\left(v_{1,j}v_{2,j}\right) = \frac{1}{k^2}\left(m_1 m_2 + a^2\right), \qquad \text{Var}\left(v_1^{\mathrm{T}} v_2\right) = \frac{1}{k}\left(m_1 m_2 + a^2\right). \tag{33}$$

The third moment can be proved similarly. In fact, one can compute any moments, using the moment generating function:

$$\mathrm{E}\left(\exp(v_{1,j}v_{2,j}t)\right) = \mathrm{E}\left(\mathrm{E}\left(\exp(v_{1,j}v_{2,j}t)\right)|v_{2,j}\right)$$

$$=\mathrm{E}\left(\exp\left(\left(\frac{a}{m_2}v_{2,j}\right)v_{2,j}t + \left(\frac{m_1 m_2 - a^2}{k m_2}\right)(v_{2,j}t)^2/2\right)\right)$$

$$=\mathrm{E}\left(\exp\left(v_{2,j}^2\frac{k}{m_2}\left(\frac{a}{k}t + \frac{1}{k^2}\left(m_1 m_2 - a^2\right)\frac{t^2}{2}\right)\right)\right)$$

$$=\left(1 - \frac{2a}{k}t - \frac{1}{k^2}\left(m_1 m_2 - a^2\right)t^2\right)^{-\frac{1}{2}}. \tag{34}$$

Here, we use the fact that $\frac{v_{2,j}^2}{m_2/k} \sim \chi_1^2$, a chi-squared random variable with one degree of freedom. Note that $\mathrm{E}\left(\exp(Yt)\right) = \exp\left(\mu t + \sigma^2 t^2/2\right)$ if $Y \sim N(\mu, \sigma^2)$; and $\mathrm{E}\left(\exp(Yt)\right) = (1 - 2t)^{-\frac{1}{2}}$ if $Y \sim \chi_1^2$. By independence, we have proved that

$$\mathrm{E}\left(\exp(v_1^{\mathrm{T}} v_2 t)\right) = \left(1 - \frac{2}{k}at - \frac{1}{k^2}\left(m_1 m_2 - a^2\right)t^2\right)^{-\frac{k}{2}}, \tag{35}$$

where $\frac{-k}{\sqrt{m_1 m_2} - a} \le t \le \frac{k}{\sqrt{m_1 m_2} + a}$. This completes the proof of Lemma 1.

B   Proof of Lemma 2

From Appendix A, we can write down the joint likelihood function for $\{v_{1,j}, v_{2,j}\}_{j=1}^k$:

$$\text{lik}\left(\{v_{1,j}, v_{2,j}\}_{j=1}^k\right) \propto |\Sigma|^{-\frac{k}{2}} \exp\left(-\frac{1}{2}\sum_{j=1}^k \begin{bmatrix} v_{1,j} & v_{2,j} \end{bmatrix} \Sigma^{-1} \begin{bmatrix} v_{1,j} \\ v_{2,j} \end{bmatrix}\right). \tag{36}$$

where (assuming $m_1 m_2 \ne a$ to avoid triviality)

$$|\Sigma| = \frac{1}{k^2}(m_1 m_2 - a^2), \qquad \Sigma^{-1} = \frac{k}{m_1 m_2 - a^2}\begin{bmatrix} m_2 & -a \\ -a & m_1 \end{bmatrix},$$

which allows us to express the log likelihood function, $l(a)$, to be

$$l(a) = -\frac{k}{2}\log\left(m_1 m_2 - a^2\right) - \frac{k}{2}\frac{1}{m_1 m_2 - a^2}\sum_{j=1}^k \left(v_{1,j}^2 m_2 - 2v_{1,j}v_{2,j}a + v_{2,j}^2 m_1\right).$$

Setting $l'(a)$ to zero, we obtain $\hat{a}_{MLE}$, which is the solution to the cubic equation:

$$a^3 - a^2\left(v_1^{\mathrm{T}} v_2\right) + a\left(-m_1 m_2 + m_1\|v_2\|^2 + m_2\|v_1\|^2\right) - m_1 m_2 v_1^{\mathrm{T}} v_2 = 0. \tag{37}$$

The well-known large sample theory says that $\hat{a}_{MLE}$ is asymptotically unbiased and converges weakly to a normal random variable $N\left(a, \text{Var}\left(\hat{a}_{MLE}\right) = \frac{1}{I(a)}\right)$, where $I(a)$, the expected Fisher Information, is $I(a) = -\text{E}\left(l''(a)\right)$. Recall $l(a)$ is the log likelihood function obtained in Appendix B. Some algebra will show that

$$I(a) = k\frac{m_1 m_2 + a^2}{(m_1 m_2 - a^2)^2}. \qquad \text{Var}\left(\hat{a}_{MLE}\right) = \frac{1}{k}\frac{(m_1 m_2 - a^2)^2}{m_1 m_2 + a^2}. \qquad (38)$$

Applying the Cauchy-Schwarz inequality a couple of times can prove

$$\text{Var}\left(\hat{a}_{MLE}\right) = \frac{1}{k}\frac{(m_1 m_2 - a^2)^2}{m_1 m_2 + a^2} \le \min\left(\text{Var}\left(\hat{a}_{MF}\right), \text{Var}\left(\hat{a}_{SM}\right)\right), \qquad (39)$$

where $\text{Var}\left(\hat{a}_{MF}\right) = \frac{1}{k}\left(m_1 m_2 + a^2\right)$, $\text{Var}\left(\hat{a}_{SM}\right) = \frac{1}{2k}\left(m_1 + m_2 - 2a\right)^2$.

C Proof of Lemma 3

We analyze the higher-order properties of $\hat{a}_{MLE}$ using stochastic Taylor expansions. We use some formulations appeared in [16, 22, 23]. The bias

$$\text{E}\left(\hat{a}_{MLE} - a\right) = -\frac{\text{E}\left(l'''(a)\right) + 2I'(a)}{2I(a)} + O(k^{-2}), \qquad (40)$$

which is often called the "Bartlett correction." Some algebra can show

$$I'(a) = \frac{2ka(3m_1 m_2 + a^2)}{(m_1 m_2 - a^2)^3}, \quad \text{E}\left(l'''(a)\right) = -2I'(a), \quad \text{E}\left(\hat{a}_{MLE} - a\right) = O(k^{-2}). \quad (41)$$

The third central moment

$$\text{E}\left(\hat{a}_{MLE} - a\right)^3 = \frac{-3I'(a) - \text{E}\left(l'''(a)\right)}{I^3(a)} + O(k^{-3})$$

$$= -\frac{2a(3m_1 m_2 + a^2)(m_1 m_2 - a^2)^3}{k^2(m_1 m_2 + a^2)^3} + O(k^{-3}). \qquad (42)$$

The $O(k^{-2})$ term of the variance, denoted by V_2^c, can be written as

$$V_2^c = \frac{1}{I^3(a)}\left(\text{E}\left(l''(a)\right)^2 - I^2(a) - \frac{\partial\left(\text{E}\left(l'''(a)\right) + 2I'(a)\right)}{\partial a}\right)$$

$$+ \frac{1}{2I^4(a)}\left(10\left(I'(a)\right)^2 - \text{E}\left(l'''(a)\right)\left(\text{E}\left(l''(a)\right) - 4I'(a)\right)\right)$$

$$= \frac{\text{E}\left((l''(a))^2\right) - I^2(a)}{I^3(a)} - \frac{(I'(a))^2}{I^4(a)}, \quad \text{(as } \text{E}\left(l'''(a)\right) + 2I'(a) = 0\text{)}. \qquad (43)$$

Computing $\mathrm{E}\left(\left(l''(a)\right)^2\right)$ requires some work. We can write

$$l''(a) = -\frac{k}{S^3}\left(T(4a^2 + S) - S(m_1m_2 + a^2) - 4aS(v_1^\mathrm{T}v_2)\right), \qquad (44)$$

where, for simplicity, we let $S = m_1m_2 - a^2$ and $T = \|v_1\|^2m_2 + \|v_2\|^2m_1 - 2v_1^\mathrm{T}v_2a$.
Expanding $\left(l''(a)\right)^2$ generates terms involving T, T^2, $Tv_1^\mathrm{T}v_2$. Rewrite

$$T = \frac{m_1m_2 - a^2}{k}\left(\sum_{j=1}^{k}\frac{km_2}{m_1m_2 - a^2}\left(v_{1,j} - \frac{a}{m_2}v_{2,j}\right)^2 + \sum_{j=1}^{k}v_{2,j}^2\frac{k}{m_2}\right)$$

$$= \frac{m_1m_2 - a^2}{k}\left(\eta + \zeta\right) \qquad (45)$$

Recall $v_{1,j}|v_{2,j} \sim N\left(\frac{a}{m_2}v_{2,j}, \frac{m_1m_2 - a^2}{km_2}\right)$, and $v_{2,j} \sim N\left(0, \frac{m_2}{k}\right)$. Then

$$\eta\,|\,\{v_{1,j}\}_{j=1}^{k} \sim \chi_k^2, \text{ (independent of } \{v_{1,j}\}_{j=1}^{k}), \quad \zeta = \sum_{j=1}^{k}v_{2,j}^2\frac{k}{m_2} \sim \chi_k^2, \quad (46)$$

implying that η and ζ are independent; and $\eta + \zeta \sim \chi_{2k}^2$. Thus,

$$\mathrm{E}(T) = 2(m_1m_2 - a^2) = 2S, \qquad \mathrm{E}(T^2) = 4S^2(1 + \frac{1}{k}). \qquad (47)$$

We also need to compute $\mathrm{E}\left(Tv_1^\mathrm{T}v_2\right)$. Rewrite

$$Tv_1^\mathrm{T}v_2 = (v_1^\mathrm{T}v_2)\|v_1\|^2m_2 + (v_1^\mathrm{T}v_2)\|v_2\|^2m_1 - 2\left(v_1^\mathrm{T}v_2\right)^2 a. \qquad (48)$$

Expand $(v_1^\mathrm{T}v_2)\|v_1\|^2$

$$(v_1^\mathrm{T}v_2)\|v_1\|^2 = \sum_{j=1}^{k}v_{1,j}v_{2,j}\sum_{j=1}^{k}v_{1,j}^2 = \sum_{j=1}^{k}v_{1,j}^3v_{2,j} + \sum_{i=1}^{k}\left(v_{1,i}^2\sum_{j\neq i}v_{1,j}v_{2,j}\right). \qquad (49)$$

Again, applying the conditional probability argument, we obtain $\mathrm{E}\left(v_{1,j}^3v_{2,j}\right) = \frac{3am_1}{k^2}$, from which it follows that

$$\mathrm{E}\left((v_1^\mathrm{T}v_2)\|v_1\|^2\right) = \sum_{j=1}^{k}\mathrm{E}\left(v_{1,j}^3v_{2,j}\right) + \sum_{i=1}^{k}\left(\mathrm{E}\left(v_{1,i}^2\right)\sum_{j\neq i}\mathrm{E}\left(v_{1,j}v_{2,j}\right)\right)$$

$$= \frac{3am_1}{k} + k\frac{m_1}{k}\sum_{j\neq i}\frac{a}{k} = am_1\left(1 + \frac{2}{k}\right). \qquad (50)$$

To this end, we have all the necessary components for computing $\mathrm{E}\left(\left(l''(a)\right)^2\right)$. After some algebra, we obtain

$$\mathrm{E}\left(\left(l''(a)\right)^2\right) = \frac{k^2}{S^4}\left((m_1m_2 + a^2)^2 + \frac{4}{k}\left(m_1^2m_2^2 + a^4 + 6a^2m_1m_2\right)\right), \qquad (51)$$

$$V_2^c = \frac{4}{k^2}\frac{(m_1m_2 - a^2)^4}{(m_1m_2 + a^2)^4}m_1m_2. \qquad (52)$$

We complete the proof of Lemma 3.

D   Proof of Lemma 4

The cubic MLE equation derived in Lemma 2 may admit multiple roots. (Recall a cubic equation always has at least one real root.) By the well-known Cardano condition,

$$\mathbf{Pr}\,(\text{multiple real roots}) = \mathbf{Pr}\left(P^2(11 - Q^2/4 - 4Q + P^2) + (Q - 1)^3 \leq 0\right), \quad (53)$$

where $P = \frac{v_1^T v_2}{\sqrt{m_1 m_2}}$, $Q = \frac{\|v_1\|^2}{m_1} + \frac{\|v_2\|^2}{m_2}$. We can obtain a crude upper bound using the fact that $\mathbf{Pr}(A + B \leq 0) \leq \mathbf{Pr}(A \leq 0) + \mathbf{Pr}(B \leq 0)$, i.e.,

$$\mathbf{Pr}\,(\text{multiple real roots}) \leq \mathbf{Pr}\left(11 - Q^2/4 - 4Q \leq 0\right) + \mathbf{Pr}\,(Q - 1 \leq 0). \quad (54)$$

We will soon prove the following moment generating function

$$\mathrm{E}\,(\exp(Qt)) = \left(1 - \frac{4t}{k} + \frac{4t^2}{k^2}\left(\frac{m_1 m_2 - a^2}{m_1 m_2}\right)\right)^{-\frac{k}{2}}, \quad (55)$$

which enables us to prove the following upper bounds:

$$\mathbf{Pr}\,(Q - 1 \leq 0) \leq e^{-0.0966k}, \quad \mathbf{Pr}\left(11 - Q^2/4 - 4Q \leq 0\right) \leq e^{-0.0085k}, \quad (56)$$

$$\mathbf{Pr}\,(\text{multiple real roots}) \leq e^{-0.0966k} + e^{-0.0085k}, \quad (57)$$

using the standard Chernoff inequality, e.g., $\mathbf{Pr}\,(Q > z) = \mathbf{Pr}\left(e^{Qt} > e^{zt}\right) \leq \mathrm{E}\left(e^{Qt}\right) e^{-zt}$, choosing t that minimizes the upper bound.

The upper bound (57) is very crude but nevertheless reveals that the probability of admitting multiple real roots decreases exponentially fast.

It turns out there is a simple exact solution for the special case of $a = m_1 = m_2$, i.e., $Q = 2P = \|v_1\|^2/m_1$, $kP = \frac{k\|v_1\|^2}{m_2} \sim \chi_k^2$, and a (sharp) upper bound:

$$\mathbf{Pr}\,(\text{multiple real roots}) = \mathbf{Pr}\left((P - 3)^2 \geq 8\right) \leq e^{-1.5328k} + e^{-0.4672k}. \quad (58)$$

To complete the proof of Lemma 4, we need to outline the proof for the moment generating function $\mathrm{E}\,(\exp(Qt))$. Using the conditional probability $v_{1,j}|v_{2,j}$, we know

$$\frac{km_2}{m_1 m_2 - a^2}v_{1,j}^2|v_{2,j} \sim \chi_{1,\lambda}^2, \quad \text{where } \lambda = \frac{ka^2}{m_2(m_1 m_2 - a^2)}v_{2,j}^2. \quad (59)$$

$\chi_{1,\lambda}^2$ denotes a non-central chi-squared random variable with one degree of freedom and non-centrality λ. If $Y \sim \chi_{1,\lambda}^2$, then $\mathrm{E}\,(\exp(Yt)) = \exp\left(\frac{\lambda t}{1-2t}\right)(1 - 2t)^{-\frac{1}{2}}$. Because

$$\mathrm{E}\,(\exp(Qt)) = \prod_{j=1}^{k} \mathrm{E}\left(\mathrm{E}\left(\exp\left(\frac{v_{1,j}^2}{m_1} + \frac{v_{2,j}^2}{m_2}\right)t\,\middle|\,v_{2,j}\right)\right), \quad (60)$$

we can obtain the moment generating function in (55) after some algebra.

Efficient Algorithms for General Active Learning

Claire Monteleoni

MIT
cmontel@csail.mit.edu

Selective sampling, a realistic active learning model, has received recent attention in the learning theory literature. While the analysis of selective sampling is still in its infancy, we focus here on one of the (seemingly) simplest problems that remain open. Given a pool of unlabeled examples, drawn i.i.d. from an arbitrary input distribution known to the learner, and oracle access to their labels, the objective is to achieve a target error-rate with minimum label-complexity, via an *efficient* algorithm. No prior distribution is assumed over the concept class, however the problem remains open even under the realizability assumption: there exists a target hypothesis in the concept class that perfectly classifies all examples, and the labeling oracle is noiseless.[1] As a precise variant of the problem, we consider the case of learning homogeneous half-spaces in the realizable setting: unlabeled examples, x_t, are drawn i.i.d. from a known distribution D over the surface of the unit ball in $\mathbb{R}^d$ and labels y_t are either -1 or $+1$. The target function is a half-space $u \cdot x \geq 0$ represented by a unit vector $u \in \mathbb{R}^d$ such that $y_t(u \cdot x_t) > 0$ for all t. We denote a hypothesis v's prediction as $v(x) = \mathtt{SGN}(v \cdot x)$.

Problem: Provide an algorithm for active learning of half-spaces, such that (with high probability with respect to D and any internal randomness):

1. After L label queries, algorithm's hypothesis v obeys $P_{x \sim D}[v(x) \neq u(x)] < \epsilon$.
2. L is at most the PAC sample complexity of the supervised problem, $\tilde{O}(\frac{d}{\epsilon} \log \frac{1}{\epsilon})$, and for a general class of input distributions, L is significantly lower.[2]
3. Total running time is at most $\mathrm{poly}(d, \frac{1}{\epsilon})$.

1 Motivation

In most machine learning applications, access to labeled data is much more limited or expensive than access to unlabeled samples from the same data-generating distribution. It is often realistic to model this scenario as active learning. Often the label-complexity, the number of labeled examples required to learn a concept via active learning, is significantly lower than the PAC sample complexity. While the query learning model has been well studied (see e.g. [1]), it is often unrealistic in practice, as it requires oracle access to the entire input space. In

---

[1] In the general setting, the target is the member of the concept class with minimal error-rate on the full input distribution, with respect to the (possibly noisy) oracle.

[2] Tilde notation suppresses terms in the high probability parameter, $\log d$ and $\log \log \frac{1}{\epsilon}$.

G. Lugosi and H.U. Simon (Eds.): COLT 2006, LNAI 4005, pp. 650–652, 2006.
© Springer-Verlag Berlin Heidelberg 2006

selective sampling (originally introduced by [4]) the learner receives unlabeled data and may request certain labels to be revealed, at a constant cost per label.

2   State of the Art

Recent work has provided several negative results. Standard perceptron was shown to require $\Omega(\frac{1}{\epsilon^2})$ labels under the uniform, using any active learning rule [6]. Dasgupta [5] provided a general lower bound for learning half-spaces of $\Omega(\frac{1}{\epsilon})$ labels, when the size of the unlabeled sample is bounded. Kääriäinen provided a lower bound of $\Omega(\frac{\eta^2}{\epsilon^2})$, where η is the noise rate in the fully agnostic case [9].

Several of the positive results to date have been based on intractable algorithms. Dasgupta [5] gave a general upper bound on labels for selective sampling to learn arbitrary concepts under arbitrary input distributions, which for half-spaces under distributions λ-similar to uniform is $\tilde{O}(d \log \lambda \log^2 \frac{1}{\epsilon})$. The algorithm achieving the bound is intractable: exponential storage and computation are required, as well as access to an exponential number of functions in the concept class (not just their predictions). Similarly, recent work by Balcan, Beygelzimer and Langford [2] provides an upper bound on label-complexity of $\tilde{O}(d^2 \log \frac{1}{\epsilon})$ for learning half-spaces under the uniform, in a certain agnostic scenario, via an intractable algorithm.

Several selective sampling algorithms have been shown to work in practice, e.g. [10]. Some lack performance guarantees, or have been analyzed in the regret framework, e.g. [3]. Under a Bayesian assumption, Freund et al. [7] gave a bound on label-complexity of $\tilde{O}(d \log \frac{1}{\epsilon})$ for learning half-spaces under the uniform, using Query By Committee [13], a computationally complex algorithm that has recently been simplified to yield encouraging empirical results [8]. This is the optimal label-complexity for the problem when the input distribution is uniform, in which case the PAC sample complexity is $\tilde{\Theta}(\frac{d}{\epsilon})$ [11, 12].

There have also been some positive results for efficient algorithms, however to date the analyses have only been performed with respect to input distributions that are uniform or near-uniform. Dasgupta, Kalai and Monteleoni [6] introduced an efficient and fully online algorithm yielding the optimal label-complexity for learning half-spaces under the uniform. An algorithm due to [4], which is tractable in the realizable case, was recently shown to require at most $\tilde{O}(d^2 \log \frac{1}{\epsilon})$ labels under the uniform [2].

3   Other Open Variants

Along with the simple version stated here, the following variants remain open:

1. D is unknown to the learner.
2. Agnostic setting, under low noise rates:[3] an efficient algorithm with a non-trivial label-complexity bound under the uniform, or arbitrary distributions.

---

[3] The fully agnostic setting faces the lower bound of [9].

3. Online constraint: storage and time complexity (of the online update) must not scale with the number of seen labels or mistakes.
4. Analagous goal for other concept classes, or for general concepts.

References

1. D. Angluin. Queries revisited. *In Proc. 12th Int. Conference on Algorithmic Learning Theory*, LNAI,2225:12–31, 2001.
2. M.-F. Balcan, A. Beygelzimer, and J. Langford. Agnostic active learning. In *International Conference on Machine Learning*, 2006.
3. N. Cesa-Bianchi, C. Gentile, and L. Zaniboni. Worst-case analysis of selective sampling for linear-threshold algorithms. In *Advances in Neural Information Processing Systems 17*, 2004.
4. D. A. Cohn, L. Atlas, and R. E. Ladner. Improving generalization with active learning. *Machine Learning*, 15(2):201–221, 1994.
5. S. Dasgupta. Coarse sample complexity bounds for active learning. In *Advances in Neural Information Processing Systems 18*, 2005.
6. S. Dasgupta, A. T. Kalai, and C. Monteleoni. Analysis of perceptron-based active learning. In *Proc. 18th Annual Conference on Learning Theory*, 2005.
7. Y. Freund, H. S. Seung, E. Shamir, and N. Tishby. Selective sampling using the query by committee algorithm. *Machine Learning*, 28(2-3):133–168, 1997.
8. R. Gilad-Bachrach, A. Navot, and N. Tishby. Query by committee made real. In *Advances in Neural Information Processing Systems 18*, 2005.
9. M. Kääriäinen. On active learning in the non-realizable case. In *Foundations of Active Learning Workshop at Neural Information Processing Systems Conference*, 2005.
10. D. D. Lewis and W. A. Gale. A sequential algorithm for training text classifiers. In *Proc. of SIGIR-94, 17th ACM International Conference on Research and Development in Information Retrieval*, 1994.
11. P. M. Long. On the sample complexity of PAC learning halfspaces against the uniform distribution. *IEEE Transactions on Neural Networks*, 6(6):1556–1559, 1995.
12. P. M. Long. An upper bound on the sample complexity of PAC learning halfspaces with respect to the uniform distribution. *Information Processing Letters*, 87(5):229–23, 2003.
13. H. S. Seung, M. Opper, and H. Sompolinsky. Query by committee. In *Proc. Fifth Annual ACM Conference on Computational Learning Theory*, 1992.

Can Entropic Regularization Be Replaced by Squared Euclidean Distance Plus Additional Linear Constraints

Manfred K. Warmuth

Univ. of Calif. at Santa Cruz

Abstract. There are two main families of on-line algorithms depending on whether a relative entropy or a squared Euclidean distance is used as a regularizer. The difference between the two families can be dramatic. The question is whether one can always achieve comparable performance by replacing the relative entropy regularization by the squared Euclidean distance plus additional linear constraints. We formulate a simple open problem along these lines for the case of learning disjunctions.

Assume the target concept is a k literal disjunction over n variables. The instances are bit vectors $\boldsymbol{x} \in \{0,1\}^n$ and the disjunction $V_{i_1} \vee V_{i_2} \vee \ldots V_{i_k}$ is true on instance $\boldsymbol{x}$ iff at least one bit in the positions $i_1, i_2, \ldots, i_k$ is one. We can represent the above disjunction as a weight vector $\boldsymbol{w}$: all relevant weights w_{i_j} are set to some threshold $\theta > 0$ and the remaining $n - k$ irrelevant weights are zero. Now the disjunction is a linear threshold function: the disjunction is true on $\boldsymbol{x}$ iff $\boldsymbol{w} \cdot \boldsymbol{x} \geq \theta$.

The following type of on-line algorithm makes at most $O(k \log n)$ mistakes on sequences of examples $(\boldsymbol{x}_1, y_1), (\boldsymbol{x}_2, y_2), \ldots$, when the labels y_t are consistent[1] with a k-literal monotone disjunction: The algorithm predicts true on instance $\boldsymbol{x}_t$ iff $\boldsymbol{w}_t \cdot \boldsymbol{x}_t \geq \theta$. The weight vector $\boldsymbol{w}_t$ for predicting at trial t is determined by minimizing the *relative entropy* to the initial weight vector $\boldsymbol{w}_1$ subject to some linear constraints implied by the examples. Here the relative entropy is defined as $\Delta(\boldsymbol{w}, \boldsymbol{w}_1) = \sum_i w_i \ln \frac{w_i}{w_{1,i}} + w_{1,i} - w_i$. More precisely, $\boldsymbol{w}_t := \min_{\boldsymbol{w}} \Delta(\boldsymbol{w}, \boldsymbol{w}_1)$ subject to the following *example constraints* (where $\theta, \alpha > 0$ are fixed):

- $\boldsymbol{w} \cdot \boldsymbol{x}_q = 0$, for all $1 \leq q < t$ and $y_t = false$,
- $\boldsymbol{w} \cdot \boldsymbol{x}_q \geq \alpha\theta$, for all $1 \leq q < t$ and $y_t = true$.

This algorithm is a variant of the Winnow algorithm [Lit88] which, for $\boldsymbol{w}_1 = (1, \ldots, 1)$, $\alpha = e$ and $\theta = \frac{n}{e}$, makes at most $e + ke \ln n$ mistakes on any sequence of examples that is consistent with a k out of n literal disjunction.[2]

The crucial fact is that the mistake bound of Winnow and its variants grows logarithmically in the number of variables, whereas the mistake bound of the Perceptron algorithm is $\Omega(kn)$ [KWA97]. The question is, what is responsible for this dramatic difference?

---

[1] For the sake of simplicity we only consider the noise-free case.

[2] An elegant proof of this bound was first given in [LW04] for the case when the additional constraint $\sum_i w_i = 1$ is enforced: for $\boldsymbol{w}_1 = (\frac{1}{n}, \ldots, \frac{1}{n})$, $\alpha = e$ and $\theta = \frac{1}{ek}$, this algorithm makes at most $ek \ln n$ mistakes.

G. Lugosi and H.U. Simon (Eds.): COLT 2006, LNAI 4005, pp. 653–654, 2006.
© Springer-Verlag Berlin Heidelberg 2006

The Perceptron type algorithm is motivated by minimizing a different divergence subject to threshold constraints defined by the positive and negative examples: the squared Euclidean distance $||\boldsymbol{w}||_2^2$. The algorithms in this family maintain a weight vector that is a linear combination of the past instances and all algorithms in this family require at least $\Omega(n + k)$ mistakes when learning k out of n literal disjunctions [KWA97].

The question is whether[3] minimizing $||w||_2^2$ subject to the example constraints **plus** some additional linear constraints can achieve the same feat as the relative entropy minimization and lead to the improved mistake bound of $O(k \log n)$. In our experiments on artificial data, two additional constraints do the trick: if $\sum_i w_i = 1$ and the n non-negativity constraints $w_i \geq 0$ are enforced in addition to the example constraints, then choosing $\theta = \frac{1}{2k}$ and $\alpha = 2$ seems to achieve the $O(k \log n)$ mistake bound. Dropping the $\sum_i w_i = 1$ constraint only slightly increases the number of mistakes. On the other hand, with only the example constraints, the mistake bound grows linearly with n. Adding the $\sum_i w_i = 1$ constraint helps only slightly and adding the $\sum_i |w_i| = 1$ constraint gives moderate improvements.

The advantage of the family that uses the squared Euclidean distance is that the algorithms can be kernelized. However, both the non-negativity constraints as well as the one-norm constraint destroy this property. See [KW97], Section 9.6, and [KRS01, SM05] for additional discussion in the context of regression.

Acknowledgements. Dima Kuzmin for providing experimental evidence.

References

[KRS01]   Roni Khardon, Dan Roth, and Rocco Servedio. Efficiency versus convergence of Boolean kernels for on-line learning algorithms. In *Advances in Neural Information Processing Systems 14*, pages 423–430. MIT Press, Cambridge, MA, 2001.

[KW97]   J. Kivinen and M. K. Warmuth. Additive versus exponentiated gradient updates for linear prediction. *Information and Computation*, 132(1):1–64, January 1997.

[KWA97]   J. Kivinen, M. K. Warmuth, and P. Auer. The perceptron algorithm vs. winnow: linear vs. logarithmic mistake bounds when few input variables are relevant. *Artificial Intelligence*, 97:325–343, December 1997.

[Lit88]   N. Littlestone. Learning when irrelevant attributes abound: A new linear-threshold algorithm. *Machine Learning*, 2:285–318, 1988.

[LW04]   P. M. Long and Xinyu Wu. Mistake bounds for maximum entropy discrimination. In *Advances in Neural Information Processing Systems 17*. MIT Press, Cambridge, MA, December 2004.

[SM05]   Vishwanathan S.V.N. and Warmuth M.K. Leaving the span. In *Proceedings of the 18th Annual Conference on Learning Theory (COLT 05)*, Bertinoro, Italy, June 2005. Springer. A longer journal version is in preperation.

---

[3] A slightly more general case is minimizing $||\boldsymbol{w} - \boldsymbol{w}_1||_2^2$ for some uniform start vector $\boldsymbol{w}_1$.

Author Index

Lecture Notes in Artificial Intelligence (LNAI)

Vol. 3802: Y. Hao, J. Liu, Y.-P. Wang, Y.-m. Cheung, H. Yin, L. Jiao, J. Ma, Y.-C. Jiao (Eds.), Computational Intelligence and Security, Part II. XLII, 1166 pages. 2005.

Vol. 3801: Y. Hao, J. Liu, Y.-P. Wang, Y.-m. Cheung, H. Yin, L. Jiao, J. Ma, Y.-C. Jiao (Eds.), Computational Intelligence and Security, Part I. XLI, 1122 pages. 2005.

Vol. 3789: A. Gelbukh, Á. de Albornoz, H. Terashima-Marín (Eds.), MICAI 2005: Advances in Artificial Intelligence. XXVI, 1198 pages. 2005.

Vol. 3782: K.-D. Althoff, A. Dengel, R. Bergmann, M. Nick, T.R. Roth-Berghofer (Eds.), Professional Knowledge Management. XXIII, 739 pages. 2005.

Vol. 3763: H. Hong, D. Wang (Eds.), Automated Deduction in Geometry. X, 213 pages. 2006.

Vol. 3755: G.J. Williams, S.J. Simoff (Eds.), Data Mining. XI, 331 pages. 2006.

Vol. 3735: A. Hoffmann, H. Motoda, T. Scheffer (Eds.), Discovery Science. XVI, 400 pages. 2005.

Vol. 3734: S. Jain, H.U. Simon, E. Tomita (Eds.), Algorithmic Learning Theory. XII, 490 pages. 2005.

Vol. 3721: A.M. Jorge, L. Torgo, P.B. Brazdil, R. Camacho, J. Gama (Eds.), Knowledge Discovery in Databases: PKDD 2005. XXIII, 719 pages. 2005.

Vol. 3720: J. Gama, R. Camacho, P.B. Brazdil, A.M. Jorge, L. Torgo (Eds.), Machine Learning: ECML 2005. XXIII, 769 pages. 2005.

Vol. 3717: B. Gramlich (Ed.), Frontiers of Combining Systems. X, 321 pages. 2005.

Vol. 3702: B. Beckert (Ed.), Automated Reasoning with Analytic Tableaux and Related Methods. XIII, 343 pages. 2005.

Vol. 3698: U. Furbach (Ed.), KI 2005: Advances in Artificial Intelligence. XIII, 409 pages. 2005.

Vol. 3690: M. Pěchouček, P. Petta, L.Z. Varga (Eds.), Multi-Agent Systems and Applications IV. XVII, 667 pages. 2005.

Vol. 3684: R. Khosla, R.J. Howlett, L.C. Jain (Eds.), Knowledge-Based Intelligent Information and Engineering Systems, Part IV. LXXIX, 933 pages. 2005.

Vol. 3683: R. Khosla, R.J. Howlett, L.C. Jain (Eds.), Knowledge-Based Intelligent Information and Engineering Systems, Part III. LXXX, 1397 pages. 2005.

Vol. 3682: R. Khosla, R.J. Howlett, L.C. Jain (Eds.), Knowledge-Based Intelligent Information and Engineering Systems, Part II. LXXIX, 1371 pages. 2005.

Vol. 3681: R. Khosla, R.J. Howlett, L.C. Jain (Eds.), Knowledge-Based Intelligent Information and Engineering Systems, Part I. LXXX, 1319 pages. 2005.

Vol. 3673: S. Bandini, S. Manzoni (Eds.), AI*IA 2005: Advances in Artificial Intelligence. XIV, 614 pages. 2005.

Vol. 3662: C. Baral, G. Greco, N. Leone, G. Terracina (Eds.), Logic Programming and Nonmonotonic Reasoning. XIII, 454 pages. 2005.

Vol. 3661: T. Panayiotopoulos, J. Gratch, R. Aylett, D. Ballin, P. Olivier, T. Rist (Eds.), Intelligent Virtual Agents. XIII, 506 pages. 2005.

Vol. 3658: V. Matoušek, P. Mautner, T. Pavelka (Eds.), Text, Speech and Dialogue. XV, 460 pages. 2005.

Vol. 3651: R. Dale, K.-F. Wong, J. Su, O.Y. Kwong (Eds.), Natural Language Processing – IJCNLP 2005. XXI, 1031 pages. 2005.

Vol. 3642: D. Ślęzak, J. Yao, J.F. Peters, W. Ziarko, X. Hu (Eds.), Rough Sets, Fuzzy Sets, Data Mining, and Granular Computing, Part II. XXIII, 738 pages. 2005.

Vol. 3641: D. Ślęzak, G. Wang, M. Szczuka, I. Düntsch, Y. Yao (Eds.), Rough Sets, Fuzzy Sets, Data Mining, and Granular Computing, Part I. XXIV, 742 pages. 2005.

Vol. 3635: J.R. Winkler, M. Niranjan, N.D. Lawrence (Eds.), Deterministic and Statistical Methods in Machine Learning. VIII, 341 pages. 2005.

Vol. 3632: R. Nieuwenhuis (Ed.), Automated Deduction – CADE-20. XIII, 459 pages. 2005.

Vol. 3630: M.S. Capcarrère, A.A. Freitas, P.J. Bentley, C.G. Johnson, J. Timmis (Eds.), Advances in Artificial Life. XIX, 949 pages. 2005.

Vol. 3626: B. Ganter, G. Stumme, R. Wille (Eds.), Formal Concept Analysis. X, 349 pages. 2005.

Vol. 3625: S. Kramer, B. Pfahringer (Eds.), Inductive Logic Programming. XIII, 427 pages. 2005.

Vol. 3620: H. Muñoz-Ávila, F. Ricci (Eds.), Case-Based Reasoning Research and Development. XV, 654 pages. 2005.

Vol. 3614: L. Wang, Y. Jin (Eds.), Fuzzy Systems and Knowledge Discovery, Part II. XLI, 1314 pages. 2005.

Vol. 3613: L. Wang, Y. Jin (Eds.), Fuzzy Systems and Knowledge Discovery, Part I. XLI, 1334 pages. 2005.

Vol. 3607: J.-D. Zucker, L. Saitta (Eds.), Abstraction, Reformulation and Approximation. XII, 376 pages. 2005.

Vol. 3601: G. Moro, S. Bergamaschi, K. Aberer (Eds.), Agents and Peer-to-Peer Computing. XII, 245 pages. 2005.

Vol. 3600: F. Wiedijk (Ed.), The Seventeen Provers of the World. XVI, 159 pages. 2006.

Vol. 3596: F. Dau, M.-L. Mugnier, G. Stumme (Eds.), Conceptual Structures: Common Semantics for Sharing Knowledge. XI, 467 pages. 2005.

Vol. 3593: V. Mařík, R. W. Brennan, M. Pěchouček (Eds.), Holonic and Multi-Agent Systems for Manufacturing. XI, 269 pages. 2005.

Vol. 3587: P. Perner, A. Imiya (Eds.), Machine Learning and Data Mining in Pattern Recognition. XVII, 695 pages. 2005.

Vol. 3584: X. Li, S. Wang, Z.Y. Dong (Eds.), Advanced Data Mining and Applications. XIX, 835 pages. 2005.

Vol. 3581: S. Miksch, J. Hunter, E.T. Keravnou (Eds.), Artificial Intelligence in Medicine. XVII, 547 pages. 2005.

Vol. 3577: R. Falcone, S. Barber, J. Sabater-Mir, M.P. Singh (Eds.), Trusting Agents for Trusting Electronic Societies. VIII, 235 pages. 2005.

Vol. 3575: S. Wermter, G. Palm, M. Elshaw (Eds.), Biomimetic Neural Learning for Intelligent Robots. IX, 383 pages. 2005.

Vol. 3571: L. Godo (Ed.), Symbolic and Quantitative Approaches to Reasoning with Uncertainty. XVI, 1028 pages. 2005.